CLINICAL HANDBOOK
OF PSYCHOLOGICAL DISORDERS

Clinical Handbook of Psychological Disorders

A Step-by-Step Treatment Manual

THIRD EDITION

Edited by
David H. Barlow

THE GUILFORD PRESS
New York   London

Library of Congress Cataloging-in-Publication Data

Clinical handbook of psychological disorders : a step-by-step treatment manual / edited
   by David H. Barlow — 3rd ed.
      p.   cm.
   Includes bibliographical references and index.
   ISBN 1-57230-611-4 (hardcover)
   1. Behavior therapy—Handbooks, manuals, etc.   I. Barlow, David H.
   [DNLM: 1. Mental Disorders—therapy.   2. Psychotherapy. WM 420 C6415 2001]
RC489.B4 C584 2001
616.89′1—dc21   00-067675

To Beverly: for love, loyalty, and perseverance

ABOUT THE EDITOR

David H. Barlow received his PhD from the University of Vermont in 1969 and has published over 400 articles and chapters and over 20 books, mostly in the areas of anxiety disorders, sexual problems, and clinical research methodology. His books include *Single Case Experimental Designs: Strategies for Studying Behavioral Change, 2nd Edition* (with M. Hersen; Pergamon Press, 1984); *Abnormal Psychology: An Integrative Approach, 2nd Edition* (with V. M. Durand; Brooks/Cole, 1999); and, most recently, *The Scientist Practitioner: Research and Accountability in the Age of Managed Care, 2nd Edition* (with S. C. Hayes and R. O. Nelson-Gray; Allyn & Bacon, 1999), and *Anxiety and Its Disorders: The Nature and Treatment of Anxiety and Panic, 2nd Edition* (Guilford Press, in press).

Dr. Barlow was formerly Professor of Psychiatry at the University of Mississippi Medical Center and Professor of Psychiatry and Psychology at Brown University. He founded clinical psychology internships in both settings. He was also Distinguished Professor in the Department of Psychology at the University at Albany, State University of New York, and Director of its Phobia and Anxiety Disorders Clinic. Currently, he is Professor of Psychology, Research Professor of Psychiatry, Director of Clinical Training Programs, and Director of the Center for Anxiety and Related Disorders at Boston University.

Dr. Barlow is the recipient of the 2000 American Psychological Association (APA) Distinguished Scientific Award for the Applications of Psychology. He is also the recipient of the First Annual Science Dissemination Award from the Society for a Science of Clinical Psychology of the APA, as well as the Distinguished Scientific Contribution Award from the Society of Clinical Psychology of the APA. He also received an award in appreciation of outstanding achievements from the General Hospital of the Chinese People's Liberation Army, Beijing, China, with an appointment as Honorary Visiting Professor of Clinical Psychology.

He is past president of the Division of Clinical Psychology of the APA, past president of the Association for Advancement of Behavior Therapy, past associate editor of the *Journal of Consulting and Clinical Psychology*, and past editor of the journals *Behavior Therapy* and *Journal of Applied Behavior Analysis*. Currently, he is editor of the journal *Clinical Psychology: Science and Practice*. He is also a Diplomate in Clinical Psychology of the American Board of Professional Psychology and maintains a private practice.

CONTRIBUTORS

AMY K. BACH, MA, Center for Anxiety and Related Disorders and Department of Psychology, Boston University, Boston, MA

DAVID H. BARLOW, PhD, Center for Anxiety and Related Disorders and Department of Psychology, Boston University, Boston, MA

AARON T. BECK, MD, School of Medicine, University of Pennsylvania, Philadelphia, PA, and Beck Institute for Cognitive Therapy and Research, Bala Cynwyd, PA

TIMOTHY A. BROWN, PsyD, Center for Anxiety and Related Disorders and Department of Psychology, Boston University, Boston, MA

ALAN J. BUDNEY, PhD, Departments of Psychiatry and Psychology, University of Vermont, Burlington, VT

KAREN S. CALHOUN, PhD, Department of Psychology, University of Georgia, Athens, GA

ANDREW CHRISTENSEN, PhD, Department of Psychology, University of California at Los Angeles, Los Angeles, CA

BRYAN N. COCHRAN, MS, Department of Psychology, University of Washington, Seattle, WA

MICHELLE G. CRASKE, PhD, Department of Psychology, University of California at Los Angeles, Los Angeles, CA

EDNA B. FOA, PhD, Department of Psychiatry, University of Pennsylvania School of Medicine, Philadelphia, PA

MARTIN E. FRANKLIN, PhD, Department of Psychiatry, University of Pennsylvania School of Medicine, Philadelphia, PA

LAURIE A. GILLIES, PhD, CPsych, Department of Psychiatry, University of Toronto, Toronto, Ontario, Canada

RICHARD G. HEIMBERG, PhD, Adult Anxiety Clinic and Department of Psychology, Temple University, Philadelphia, PA

STEPHEN T. HIGGINS, PhD, Departments of Psychiatry and Psychology, University of Vermont, Burlington, VT

DEBRA A. HOPE, PhD, Department of Psychology, University of Nebraska, Lincoln, NE

NEIL S. JACOBSON, PhD (deceased), Department of Psychology, University of Washington, Seattle, WA

CONSTANCE A. KEHRER, PhD, Department of Psychology, University of Washington, Seattle, WA

MARSHA M. LINEHAN, PhD, Department of Psychiatry and Behavioral Sciences, University of Washington, Seattle, WA

BARBARA S. MCCRADY, PhD, Center of Alcohol Studies and Graduate School of Applied and Professional Psychology, Rutgers University, Piscataway, NJ

DAVID J. MIKLOWITZ, PhD, Department of Psychology, University of Colorado, Boulder, CO

TRACY A. O'LEARY, PhD, Department of Psychiatry and Human Behavior, Brown University, Providence, RI

KATHLEEN M. PIKE, PhD, Department of Psychiatry, Columbia University, New York, NY

PATRICIA A. RESICK, PhD, Center for Trauma Recovery and Department of Psychology, University of Missouri–St. Louis, St. Louis, MO

STACEY C. SIGMON, MA, Departments of Psychiatry and Psychology, University of Vermont, Burlington, VT

CYNTHIA L. TURK, PhD, Adult Anxiety Clinic and Department of Psychology, Temple University, Philadelphia, PA

ARTHUR D. WEINBERGER, PhD, Cognitive Therapy Center of New York, New York, NY

JENNIFER G. WHEELER, MS, Department of Psychology, University of Washington, Seattle, WA

G. TERENCE WILSON, PhD, Graduate School of Applied and Professional Psychology, Rutgers University, Piscataway, NJ

JOHN P. WINCZE, PhD, Department of Psychiatry and Human Behavior and Department of Psychology, Brown University, Providence, RI

JEFFREY E. YOUNG, PhD, Department of Psychiatry, Columbia University, New York, NY, and Cognitive Therapy Centers of New York and Connecticut

PREFACE

The third edition of this book continues to represent a distinct departure from any number of similar books reviewing advances in the treatment of psychological disorders. Increasingly, during the decade of the 1990s and continuing into the new millennium, we have developed a technology of behavior change that necessarily differs from disorder to disorder. This technology consists of a variety of techniques or procedures with more or less proven effectiveness for a given disorder. Naturally, we have more evidence of the effectiveness of these treatments for some disorders than for others. It also has become more apparent since the first and second editions of this book that considerable clinical skill is required to apply this technology most effectively. Therefore, this book, in its third edition, is *not* another review of therapeutic procedures for a given problem with recommendations for further research. Rather, it is a detailed description of actual treatment protocols in which experienced clinicians implement the technology of behavior change in the context of the 14 most frequently encountered disorders.

In this edition, the originators of some of the best-known psychological treatment protocols have revised and updated their treatments to reflect the latest developments in an increasingly powerful array of psychological treatments. New to this edition of the book, and reflecting major developments in the past several years, are three original treatment protocols. Chapter 7, by Laurie Gillies, describes the application of interpersonal psychotherapy (IPT) to depression. Chapter 10, on cocaine dependence, by Stephen T. Higgins, Alan J. Budney, and Stacey C. Sigmon, illustrates exciting new psychological approaches

with increasing evidence of effectiveness for the very intransigent condition of drug abuse. Finally, Chapter 12, on bipolar disorder, by David J. Miklowitz, illustrates the power of psychological treatments targeting interpersonal systems of the patient. Every therapist and therapist-in-training will want to be familiar with these approaches, whether or not individuals with these problems are a major focus of their clinical activity.

As with the previous editions, this book was motivated by countless clinical psychology graduate students, psychiatric residents, and other mental health professionals, either in training or in practice, asking, "But how do I do it?" Realizing that there is no single source in which to find step-by-step treatment protocols for use as a guide to practice, this book attempts to fill the void. To accomplish this purpose, a number of specific topics are common to most chapters. Each chapter begins with a brief review of our knowledge of the specific disorder, followed by a description of the particular model or mini-theory that guides the technology utilized with the disorder in question. This model, or mini-theory, typically answers the question: What particular facets of the disorder should be assessed and treated? While clinical application always dilutes theoretical models, clinicians will recognize behavioral and systems approaches with some psychodynamic contributions as the predominant theoretical context.

This model is followed by a description of the typical setting in which the treatment is carried out. The setting varies from disorder to disorder, ranging from the more usual office setting to the home environment of the patient. Similar detailed descriptions of the social context of treatment (e.g., the importance of the involvement of family or friends) as well as therapist and client variables that are important within the context of the particular problem are discussed. For example, therapist variables that may be important in implementing techniques for treatment of agoraphobia or couple distress are described. In addition, the implications for treatment of client variables such as dependency and unassertiveness in individuals with panic disorder with agoraphobia are discussed.

A detailed description of the actual step-by-step process of assessment and treatment follows, liberally sprinkled in many chapters with transcripts of therapy sessions. Important components of this process are the specifics of the rationale given to the patient before treatment, as well as typical problems that arise during the implementation of the technology. Where data exist, information on clinical predictors of success or failure is provided.

In accomplishing the rather ambitious goals described above, I was very fortunate in this edition of the book, as in the last edition, to have leading clinicians and researchers document in some detail how they actually treat their patients. Once again, these authorities reported that the number of details they had to include in order to convey how they actually applied their treatment programs went far beyond their expectations. My hope is that practicing clinicians and clinical students everywhere will benefit from acquaintance with these details.

In closing, I would like to express my deep appreciation to Bette Selwyn, my administrative assistant, who virtually produced this third edition from beginning to end.

DAVID H. BARLOW
Boston and Nantucket Island

CONTENTS

CHAPTER 1
Panic Disorder and Agoraphobia   1
Michelle G. Craske and David H. Barlow

CHAPTER 2
Posttraumatic Stress Disorder   60
Patricia A. Resick and Karen S. Calhoun

CHAPTER 3
Social Anxiety Disorder   114
Cynthia L. Turk, Richard G. Heimberg, and Debra A. Hope

CHAPTER 4
Generalized Anxiety Disorder   154
Timothy A. Brown, Tracy A. O'Leary, and David H. Barlow

CHAPTER 5
Obsessive–Compulsive Disorder   209
Edna B. Foa and Martin E. Franklin

CHAPTER 6
Cognitive Therapy for Depression   264
Jeffrey E. Young, Arthur D. Weinberger, and Aaron T. Beck

CHAPTER 7
Interpersonal Psychotherapy for Depression and Other Disorders   309
Laurie A. Gillies

CHAPTER 8
Eating Disorders   332
G. Terence Wilson and Kathleen M. Pike

CHAPTER 9
Alcohol Use Disorders   376
Barbara S. McCrady

CHAPTER 10
Cocaine Dependence   434
Stephen T. Higgins, Alan J. Budney, and Stacey C. Sigmon

CHAPTER 11
Dialectical Behavior Therapy for Borderline Personality Disorder   470
Marsha M. Linehan, Bryan N. Cochran, and Constance A. Kehrer

CHAPTER 12
Bipolar Disorder   523
David J. Miklowitz

CHAPTER 13
Sexual Dysfunction   562
Amy K. Bach, John P. Wincze, and David H. Barlow

CHAPTER 14
Couple Distress   609
Jennifer G. Wheeler, Andrew Christensen, and Neil S. Jacobson

Author Index   631

Subject Index   651

Chapter 1

PANIC DISORDER AND AGORAPHOBIA

Michelle G. Craske
David H. Barlow

The treatment protocol described in this chapter represents one of the success stories in the development of empirically supported psychological treatments. Results from numerous studies indicate that this approach provides substantial advantages over placebo medication or alternative psychosocial approaches containing "common" factors, such as positive expectancies and helpful therapeutic alliances. In addition, this treatment has been cited by the National Institute of Mental Health Consensus Conference as having empirical support for panic disorder, and it forms an important part of every clinical practice guideline (from either public health or other sources) describing effective treatments for this disorder. Most recently, results from a large multicenter study evaluating this treatment protocol, both individually and in combination with leading pharmacological approaches, suggest that this approach compares favorably with pharmacological approaches and is more durable over the long term. But this treatment protocol has not stood still. In this chapter we present the latest version of this protocol, representing numerous changes and additions to the treatment since the second edition of this book.—D. H. B.

Advances continue in terms of cognitive-behavioral conceptualizations and treatments for panic disorder and agoraphobia. The conceptualization of panic disorder as an acquired fear of certain bodily sensations, and agoraphobia as a behavioral response to the anticipation of such bodily sensations or their crescendo into a full-blown panic attack, continues to be supported by experimental, clinical, and longitudinal research. Furthermore, the efficacy of cognitive-behavioral treatments that target fear of bodily sensations and associated agoraphobic situations is well established. In addition to presenting an up-to-date review of treatment outcome data, this chapter covers recent theoretical and empirical developments in reference to the role of comorbid diagnoses, the effect of treatment for panic on agoraphobia, ways to improve long-term outcome, and the effect of medica-

tion on cognitive-behavioral treatments. The chapter concludes with a detailed, session-by-session outline of a cognitive-behavioral treatment protocol for panic disorder with agoraphobia (PDA) or panic disorder without agoraphobia (PD; note that we also continue to use "panic disorder" as a general term). This protocol has been developed in our clinics and is hereafter referred to as "panic control treatment" (PCT). The full protocol is detailed in available treatment manuals (Barlow & Craske, 2000; Craske, Barlow, & Meadows, 2000).

NATURE OF PANIC AND AGORAPHOBIA

"Panic attacks" are discrete episodes of intense dread or fear, accompanied by physical and cognitive symptoms as listed in the panic attack checklist of the *Diagnostic and Statistical Manual of Mental Disorders*, fourth edition (DSM-IV; American Psychiatric Association, 1994). The panic attack is discrete by virtue of its sudden or abrupt onset and brief duration, as opposed to gradually building anxious arousal. Panic attacks in panic disorder often have an unexpected quality, meaning that from the client's perspective, they appear to happen without an obvious trigger or at times that were not expected.

As with all basic emotions (Izard, 1992), panic attacks are associated with strong action tendencies; most often these are urges to escape, and less often urges to fight. In other words, panic attacks are believed to represent activation of the fight–flight system. In accord, panic attacks usually involve elevated autonomic nervous system arousal needed to support such fight–flight reactivity. Furthermore, perceptions of imminent threat or danger, such as death, loss of control, or social ridicule, appear to drive such fight–flight reactivity. However, the features of urgency to escape, autonomic arousal, and perception of threat are not present in every self-reported occurrence of panic, and hence there is occasional discordance among the behavioral, verbal, and physiological response systems (see Lang, 1971; Rachman & Hodgson, 1974). For example, Margraf, Taylor, Ehlers, Roth, and Agras (1987) found that 40% of self-reported panic attacks were not associated with accelerated heart rate. Given that discordance between physiological and verbal response systems is more likely under mildly anxious conditions (Rachman & Hodgson, 1974), we believe that self-reported panic in the absence of actual autonomic activation reflects anticipatory anxiety as opposed to true panic (Barlow, Brown, & Craske, 1994). Moreover, in general, patients with panic disorder are more likely than nonanxious controls to report arrhythmic heart rate in the absence of actual arrhythmias (Barsky, Clearly, Sarnie, Ruskin, & Jeremy, 1994). Heightened attention to signs of autonomic arousal and threatening interpretations of such arousal may lead clients to perceive cardiac events when none exist (Barlow et al., 1994; Craske & Tsao, 1999). Another example of discordance occurs within the self-report response system, when perceptions of threat or danger are refuted despite the re-

port of intense fear. This has been called "noncognitive" panic (Rachman, Lopatka, & Levitt, 1988). Finally, the urgency to escape is sometimes weakened by situational demands for continued approach and endurance, such as masculine role expectations or job demands, thus creating discordance between behavioral responses on the one hand and verbal or physiological responses on the other hand.

Panic attacks are ubiquitous in a number of ways. First, panic attacks occur occasionally over the last 12 months in approximately 3%–5% of the general population who do not otherwise meet criteria for panic disorder (Norton, Cox, & Malan, 1992). Second, panic attacks occur across a variety of anxiety and mood disorders (Barlow et al., 1985), and are not limited to panic disorder. Consequently, the defining feature of panic disorder is not the presence of panic attacks per se; it involves additional anxiety about the recurrence of panic or its consequences, or a significant behavioral change because of the panic attacks. The additional anxiety about panic, combined with catastrophic cognitions in the face of panic, is what differentiates the person with panic disorder from the person with occasional nonclinical panic (see, e.g., Telch, Lucas, & Nelson, 1989) and from the person with other anxiety disorders who also happens to panic. The following exchange between a client (C) and therapist (T) exemplifies the latter point.

C: Sometimes I lay awake at night thinking about a million different possibilities—I think about what is going to happen to my daughter if I get sick, who will look after her, or what would happen if my husband died and we didn't have enough money to give my daughter a good education. Then I think about where we would live and how we would cope. Sometimes I can work myself up so much that my heart starts to race, my hands get sweaty, and I feel dizzy and scared. So I have to stop myself from thinking about all those things—I usually turn on TV—anything to get my mind off the worries.

T: Do the feelings of a racing heart, sweating, and dizziness scare you to the degree that you worry about those feelings happening again?

C: No. They're unpleasant, but they are the least of my concerns—I am more worried about my daughter and our future.

This scenario illustrates the experience of panic that is not the central focus of the person's anxiety. More likely, this woman is suffering from generalized anxiety disorder, and her uncontrollable worry leads her to panic on occasion. The next example is of someone with social phobia, who becomes very concerned about panicking in social situations, because the possibility of a panic attack elevates her concerns about being judged negatively by others.

C: I am terrified of panicking in meetings at work. I dread the thought of others noticing how anxious I am. They must be able to see my hands shaking, the sweat on my forehead, and worst of all, my face turning red.

T: What really worries you about others noticing your anxiety?

C: That they will think that I am weird or strange.

T: Would you be anxious in the meetings if the panic attacks were fully preventable?

C: I would still be worried about doing or saying the wrong thing. It is not just the panic attacks that worry me.

T: Are you worried about panic attacks in any other situations?

C: No, just formal social events and maybe when I meet someone for the first time.

"Agoraphobia" refers to avoidance or endurance with dread of situations from which escape might be difficult or help unavailable in the event of a panic attack, or in the event of developing symptoms that could be incapacitating and embarrassing, such as loss of bowel control or vomiting. Typical agoraphobic situations include shopping malls, waiting in line, being in movie theaters, traveling by car or bus, crowded restaurants, and being alone. Mild agoraphobia is exemplified by the person who hesitates about driving long distances alone but manages to drive to and from work, prefers to sit on the aisle at movie theaters but still goes to movies, and feels uncomfortable in crowded places. Moderate agoraphobia is exemplified by the person whose driving is limited to a 5-mile radius from home and only if accompanied, who shops at off-peak times and avoids large supermarkets, and who avoids flying or traveling by train. Severe agoraphobia refers to very limited mobility and sometimes even becoming housebound. The nature of the relationship between panic and agoraphobia is discussed in more detail below.

PRESENTING FEATURES

From 2% to 6% of the population are estimated to suffer from PD/PDA at some time in their lives (Kessler et al., 1994; Myers et al., 1984). Treatment for PD/PDA is usually sought at about the age of 34 years, even though the mean age of onset ranges from 23 to 29 (Breier, Charney, & Heninger, 1986; Craske, Miller, Rotunda, & Barlow, 1990; Noyes et al., 1986), and a significant number of adolescents report panic attacks (see, e.g., Hayward et al., 1992; King, Gullone, Tonge, & Ollendick, 1993). Most (approximately 72%; Craske et al., 1990) report identifiable stressors at about the time of their first panic attack. These include interpersonal stressors and stressors related to physical well-being, such as negative drug experiences, disease, or death in the family. However, the number of stressors does not differ from the number experienced prior to the onset of other types of anxiety disorders (Pollard, Pollard, & Corn, 1989; Rapee, Litwin, & Barlow, 1990; Roy-Byrne, Geraci, & Uhde, 1986). Approximately one-half report having experienced panicky feelings at some time before their first panic attack, suggesting that onset may be either insidious or acute (Craske et al., 1990).

Community-based epidemiological studies indicate higher rates for agoraphobia without a history of panic disorder than for PDA. In contrast, individuals with agoraphobia who seek treatment almost always report a history of panic that preceded their agoraphobia (Craske et al., 1990; Noyes et al., 1986; Pollard, Bronson, & Kenney, 1989). For example, only 6% of 562 patients with episodes of panic and/or agoraphobia met criteria for agoraphobia without history of panic disorder in a large naturalistic study (Goisman et al., 1994). There are at least two explanations for the contrast between population- and clinic-based data. First, population-based data may vastly overestimate the prevalence of agoraphobia due to misdiagnosis of specific phobias, generalized anxiety, or "normal" cautiousness about certain situations (e.g., walking in unsafe urban districts) as agoraphobia (Horwath, Lish, Johnson, Hornig, & Weissman, 1993). Second, individuals who panic are more likely to seek help (Boyd, 1986).

Rarely does the diagnosis of PD/PDA occur in isolation. Commonly occurring Axis I conditions include specific phobias, social phobia, and dysthymic disorder (Sanderson, Di Nardo, Rapee, & Barlow, 1990), generalized anxiety disorder, major depressive episode, and substance abuse (Goisman et al., 1994). Also, from 25% to 60% are estimated to meet criteria for a personality disorder. Most often these are avoidant and dependent personality disorders (Chambless & Renneberg, 1988; Mavissakalian & Hamman, 1986; Reich, Noyes, & Troughton, 1987). However, the nature of the relationship between PD/PDA and personality disorders remains unclear. For example, comorbidity rates are highly dependent on the method used to establish Axis II diagnosis, as well as the co-occurrence of depressed mood (Alnaes & Torgersen, 1990; Chambless & Renneberg, 1988). Moreover, the fact that abnormal personality traits improve and some "personality disorders" even remit after successful treatment of PD/PDA (Black, Monahan, Wesner, Gabel, & Bowers, 1996; Mavissakalian & Hamman, 1987; Noyes, Reich, Suelzer, & Christiansen, 1991) raises questions about the validity of Axis II diagnoses. The issue of comorbidity with personality disorders and its effect on treatment for PD/PDA is described in more detail in a later section.

HISTORY OF PSYCHOLOGICAL TREATMENT FOR PD/PDA

It was not until the publication of DSM-III (American Psychiatric Association, 1980) that PD/PDA was recognized as a distinct anxiety problem. Up until that time, panic attacks were viewed primarily as a form of free-floating anxiety. Consequently, psychological treatment approaches were relatively nonspecific. They included relaxation and cognitive restructuring about life events in general (see, e.g., Barlow, Cohen, et al., 1984). Many presumed that pharmacotherapy was neces-

sary for the control of panic. In contrast, the treatment of agoraphobia was quite specific from the 1970s onward, using primarily exposure-based approaches to target fear and avoidance of specific situations. However, relatively little consideration was given to panic attacks in either the conceptualization or treatment of agoraphobia. The development of PCT and similar treatments in the middle to late 1980s shifted interest away from agoraphobia. Only recently has interest in agoraphobia renewed, specifically in terms of whether the newer treatments are sufficient for the management of agoraphobia, and whether their combination with treatments that directly target agoraphobia is superior overall. We address these questions in more detail below, after describing the conceptualization that underlies PCT.

COGNITIVE-BEHAVIORAL CONCEPTUALIZATION OF PD/PDA

Several independent lines of research (Barlow, 1988; Clark, 1986; Ehlers & Margraf, 1989) converged in the 1980s on the same basic conceptualization of panic disorder as an acquired fear of bodily sensations, especially those elicited by autonomic arousal. Psychological and biological predispositions are believed to increase the likelihood of experiencing intense autonomic activation and to misinterpret signs of such activation in a catastrophic way.

Vulnerability Factors

Physiological vulnerabilities may be best summarized as elevated autonomic reactivity (see Bouton, Mineka, & Barlow, in press, or Barlow, in press, for a comprehensive review). A psychological vulnerability factor that has received some empirical support is the tendency to perceive anxiety as being harmful—known as "anxiety sensitivity" (Reiss, Peterson, Gursky, & NcNally, 1986). Scores on a measure of anxiety sensitivity predict panic attack history over and above more general indices of trait anxiety and negative affect (Lilienfeld, 1997). Also, several longitudinal studies find the predicted relationship. For example, Maller and Reiss (1992) found that three-fourths of individuals who experienced panic attacks for the first time between 1984 and 1987 scored high on the Anxiety Sensitivity Index in 1984. In a naturalistic, 1-year follow-up study, anxiety sensitivity predicted maintenance of panic disorder in a group with untreated panic disorder, and panic attacks in a group with nonclinical panic (Ehlers, 1995). Similarly, anxiety sensitivity predicted development of panic attacks 5 weeks after an acute military stressor (Schmidt, Lerew, & Jackson, 1997).

The tendency to view anxiety, and particularly bodily symptoms of anxiety, as being harmful probably derives from a lifetime of direct aversive experiences (such as personal history of significant illness or injury), vicarious observations (such as significant illnesses or death among family members, or family members who show distress over body sensations through hypochondriasis), and/or informational transmissions (such as parental warnings or overprotectiveness regarding physical well-being). In accord, Ehlers (1993) found that parents of patients with panic disorder were more likely to suffer from chronic illnesses that required treatment and physical symptoms typical of anxiety, in comparison to parents of patients with other anxiety disorders and parents of controls. In addition, patients with panic disorder observed sick role behavior related to panic symptoms in their parents more often than control participants. This was not true for non-panic-related sicknesses.

Associated with anxiety sensitivity is enhanced attentional selectivity or interoception for physical cues. Patients with panic disorder appear to have heightened awareness of, or ability to detect, bodily sensations of arousal (see, e.g., Ehlers & Breuer, 1992, 1996; Ehlers, Breuer, Dohn, & Feigenbaum, 1995), although discrepant findings exist, and whether they are more *accurate* in their detection is questionable (see, e.g., Antony et al., 1995; Rapee, 1994). Thus, along with vulnerability to experience bodily symptoms of autonomic arousal, and danger-laden appraisal of such symptoms, the ability to detect bodily symptoms may predispose an individual toward panic disorder.

Initial Panic Attacks

The large majority of initial panic attacks are recalled as occurring outside of the home—while driving, walking, at work or at school (Craske et al., 1990); in public in general (Lelliott, Marks, McNamee, & Tobena, 1989); or on a bus, plane, or subway, or in social evaluation situations (Shulman, Cox, Swinson, Kuch, & Reichman, 1994). We (Barlow, 1988; Craske & Rowe, 1997) believe that situations that set the scene for initial panic attacks are ones in which bodily sensations are perceived as particularly threatening due to impairment of functioning (e.g., driving), entrapment (e.g., air travel, elevators), negative social evaluation (e.g., job, formal social events), or distance from safety (e.g., unfamiliar locales). Entrapment concerns may be particularly salient for subsequent development of agoraphobia (Faravelli, Pallanti, Biondi, Paterniti, & Scarpato, 1992).

Many panic patients (48%) report similar but less intense or less frightening sensations prior to the first panic attack (Craske et al., 1990). Also, previous experiences of cardiac symptoms and shortness of breath predict later development of panic attacks and panic disorder (Keyl & Eaton, 1990). Perhaps such prior experiences reflect a state of autonomic reactivity, which develops into full-blown panic only when instances of autonomic arousal occur in threatening contexts or stressful conditions (i.e., when the sensations are more likely to be perceived as threatening).

Maintenance Factors

Acute "fear of fear," which develops after initial panic attacks, refers to fear of certain bodily sensations associated with panic attacks (e.g., racing heart, dizziness, parasthesias) (Barlow, 1988; Goldstein & Chambless, 1978). This fear is attributed to two factors. The first is "interoceptive conditioning," or conditioned fear of internal cues (such as elevated heart rate) because of their association with intense fear, pain, or distress (Bouton et al., in press; Razran, 1961). The notion of conditioning is consistent with the traumatic nature of panic attacks, as evidenced by the frequent attendance at emergency rooms, and the vivid recall that individuals have of their first panic attack as many as 20 years later. Interoceptive conditioning is relatively resistant to extinction and can be "unconscious." That is, interoceptively conditioned fear responses are not dependent on conscious awareness of triggering cues. Consequently, panic attacks that seem to occur from "out of the blue" may in fact be triggered by very subtle changes in physical state of which the person is not immediately aware (Barlow, in press; Bouton et al., in press). For example, a slight change in blood pressure may elicit fear, due to previous pairings of high blood pressure with the terror of panic. The second factor is misappraisals of bodily sensations (i.e., misinterpretation of sensations as signs of imminent death, loss of control, and so on), which can be viewed as a sensitization of tendencies to already view anxiety as being harmful. Like interoceptive conditioning, misappraisals are believed to operate at both conscious and subconscious levels of awareness, such that the individual may perceive bodily sensations in a catastrophic manner without being aware of so doing, and thus experience "out of the blue" panic attacks. The notion that fear conditioning and fearful appraisals are truly separable constructs has both proponents (e.g., LeDoux, 1996) and opponents (e.g., Rapee, 1991).

Nevertheless, the concept of "fear of fear" is well supported. Persons with panic disorder have strong beliefs and fears of physical or mental harm arising from bodily sensations that are associated with panic attacks (see, e.g., Chambless, Caputo, Bright, & Gallagher, 1984; McNally & Lorenz, 1987). They are more likely to interpret bodily sensations in a catastrophic fashion (Clark et al., 1988), and to allocate more attentional resources to words that represent physical threat (e.g., "disease" and "fatality"; Ehlers, Margraf, Davies, & Roth, 1988; Hope, Rapee, Heimberg, & Dombeck, 1990) and catastrophe words (e.g., "death" and "insane"; Maidenberg, Chen, Craske, Bohn, & Bystritsky, 1996; McNally, Riemann, Louro, Lukach, & Kim, 1992). Also, they are more likely to fear procedures that elicit bodily sensations similar to the ones experienced during panic attacks, including benign cardiovascular, respiratory, and audiovestibular exercises (Jacob, Furman, Clark, & Durrant, 1992; Zarate, Rapee, Craske, & Barlow, 1988), as well as more invasive procedures (e.g., carbon dioxide inhalation). Furthermore, they fear signals that ostensibly reflect heightened arousal, even in the absence of actual heightened arousal, as shown through paradigms involving false physiological feedback (Craske & Freed,

1995; Ehlers, Taylor, Margraf, Roth, & Birnbaumer, 1988). Not only is misappraisal associated with fearfulness, but reappraisal lessens fear. For example, persons with panic disorder and with nonclinical panic report significantly less fear and panic during laboratory-based panic provocation procedures, such as hyperventilation and carbon dioxide inhalation, when they perceive that the procedure is safe and/or controllable (see, e.g., Rapee, Mattick, & Murrell, 1986; Sanderson, Rapee, & Barlow, 1989), when accompanied by a safe person (Carter, Hollon, Carson, & Shelton, 1995), or after cognitive-behavioral treatment that reduces fears of bodily sensations (Schmidt, Trakowski, & Staab, 1997).

Several features distinguish fear of bodily sensations from fears of external stimuli. First, autonomic arousal generated by fear in turn intensifies the sensations that are feared, thus creating a reciprocating cycle of fear and sensations. (The cycle is sustained until autonomic arousal is exhausted or safety is perceived.) In contrast, fear of external stimuli does not intensify the object of fear. Second, as already stated, cues that trigger panic attacks (i.e., bodily sensations) are not always immediately obvious, thus generating the perception of unexpected or "out of the blue" panic attacks (Barlow, 1988). Furthermore, even when interoceptive cues are identifiable, they tend to be less predictable than external stimuli. Third, bodily sensations are more difficult to escape, on average, than external objects; that is, sensations are relatively uncontrollable. Unpredictability and uncontrollability elevate general anxiety about upcoming aversive events (see, e.g., Bouton et al., in press; DeCola & Rosellini, 1990; Maier, Laudenslager, & Ryan, 1985) and panic attacks (Craske, Glover, & DeCola, 1995). Consequently, the unpredictable and uncontrollable nature of panic is hypothesized to contribute to high levels of chronic anxious apprehension (Barlow, 1988), and to maintain anticipatory anxiety about the recurrence of panic (Rachman & Levitt, 1985). In turn, anxious apprehension increases the likelihood of panic, by directly increasing the availability of sensations that have become conditioned cues for panic and/or by increasing attentional vigilance for these bodily cues. Thus a maintaining cycle of panic and anxious apprehension develops. Also, subtle avoidance behaviors are believed to maintain negative beliefs about feared bodily sensations (Barlow & Craske, 1994; Clark & Ehlers, 1993). Examples include holding onto objects or persons for fears of fainting, sitting and remaining still for fears of heart attack, and moving slowly or searching for an escape for fears of acting foolish (Salkovskis, Clark, & Gelder, 1996). Finally, anxiety develops over specific contexts in which the occurrence of panic would be particularly troubling (i.e., situations associated with impairment, entrapment, negative social evaluation, and distance from safety). These anxieties contribute to agoraphobia, which in turn maintains fear of bodily sensations.

Agoraphobia

Not all persons who panic develop agoraphobia, and the extent of agoraphobia that emerges is highly variable (Craske & Barlow, 1988). Agoraphobia tends to increase as history of panic lengthens; however, a significant proportion experience panic attacks for many years without developing agoraphobic limitations. Nor is agoraphobia related to age of onset or frequency of panic (Cox, Endler, & Swinson, 1995; Craske & Barlow, 1988; Rapee & Murrell, 1988). Some studies report more intense physical symptoms during panic attacks when there is more agoraphobia (e.g., de Jong & Bouman, 1995; Goisman et al., 1994; Noyes, Clancy, Garvey, & Anderson, 1987; Telch, Brouillard, Telch, Agras, & Taylor, 1989). Others fail to find such differences (e.g., Cox et al., 1995; Craske et al., 1990). Although fears of dying, going crazy, or losing control do not relate to level of agoraphobia (Cox et al., 1995; Craske, Rapee, & Barlow, 1988), concerns about social consequences of panicking may be stronger when there is more agoraphobia (Amering et al., 1997; de Jong & Bouman, 1995; Rapee & Murrell, 1988; Telch et al., 1989). Also, anticipation of panic in specific situations predicts degree of avoidance of those situations (Cox et al., 1995; Craske et al., 1990). However, whether the social evaluation concerns and anticipation of panic attacks are precursors of or are secondary to agoraphobia remains to be determined.

Occupational status also predicts agoraphobia, accounting for 18% of the variance in one study: "the more one is forced to leave the house by means of employment, the less one is likely to suffer from agoraphobia" (de Jong & Bouman, 1995, p. 197). Perhaps the strongest predictor of agoraphobia is gender. The ratio of males to females shifts dramatically in the direction of female predominance as level of agoraphobia worsens (see, e.g., Thyer, Himle, Curtis, Cameron, & Nesse, 1985). Thus we believe that sex role expectations and demands contribute to agoraphobic behavior (Craske & Barlow, 1988).

The obvious targets for treatment that derive from this conceptualization are acute fear of bodily sensations, chronic anxiety about panic attacks and associated bodily sensations, and agoraphobic avoidance.

TREATMENT VARIABLES

Setting

There are several different settings for conducting cognitive-behavioral therapy for PD/PDA. The first is the outpatient clinic/office setting, which is suited to psychoeducation, cognitive restructuring, assignment and feedback regarding homework assignments, and role-play rehearsals. In addition, certain exposures can be conducted in the office setting, such as interoceptive exposure to feared bodily sensations described later. Recently, outpatient settings have extended from mental health care to primary care sites (see, e.g., Sharp, Power, Simpson, Swanson, & Anstee, 1997). This extension is particularly important because of the higher prevalence of PD/PDA in primary care settings. However, whether a mental health or a primary care office is being used, the built-in safety signals of an office setting may limit the generalizability of learning that takes place in that setting. For example, learning to be less afraid in the presence of the therapist, or in an office that is located near a medical center, may not necessarily generalize to conditions when the therapist is not present, or when the perceived safety of a medical center is not close by. It is for this reason that homework assignments to practice cognitive-behavioral skills in a variety of different settings are particularly important.

The second setting is the natural environment, where cognitive restructuring and other anxiety management skills are put into practice, and where feared situations are faced. The latter is called "*in vivo* exposure" and can be conducted with the aid of the therapist or alone. Therapist-directed exposure is particularly useful for clients who lack a social network to support *in vivo* exposure assignments, and is more valuable than self-directed exposure for more severe agoraphobia (Holden, O'Brien, Barlow, Stetson, & Infantino, 1983). For example, positive results from self-directed exposure guided by workbooks (e.g., Gould & Clum, 1995; Gould, Clum, & Shapiro, 1993; Lidren et al., 1994) and/or minimal therapist contact (Ghosh & Marks, 1987) do not seem to generalize to clients who are more severely affected (Holden et al., 1983), less motivated, less educated, or referred as opposed to recruited through advertisement (Hecker, Losee, Fritzler, & Fink, 1996). Furthermore, self-directed exposure alone is not considered to be an adequate treatment for PD/PDA (Murphy, Michelson, Marchione, Marchione, & Testa, 1998). Therapist-directed exposure is essential to "guided mastery exposure," in which the therapist gives corrective feedback about the way in which feared situations are faced in order to minimize unnecessary defensive behaviors. In fact, guided mastery exposure has been shown to be more effective than "stimulus exposure," where clients simply attempt to endure the situation alone until fear subsides, without the benefit of ongoing therapist feedback (Williams & Zane, 1989). On the other hand, self-directed exposure is very valuable also, especially to the degree that it encourages independence and generalization of the skills learned in treatment to conditions where the therapist is not present. Thus the most beneficial approach in the natural environment is to proceed from therapist-directed to self-directed exposure.

An interesting variation on use of the natural environment is telephone-guided treatment, in which therapists direct patients by phone to conduct *in vivo* exposure to agoraphobic situations (McNamee, O'Sullivan, Lelliott, & Marks, 1989; Swinson, Fergus, Cox, & Wickwire, 1995) or provide instruction in panic control skills (Cote, Gauthier, Laberge, Cormier, & Plamondon, 1994). Another variation is computer-guided treatment (see, e.g., Harcourt, Kirkby, Daniels, & Montgomery, 1998; Newman, Kenardy, Herman, & Taylor, 1997). For example, in the study by Newman and colleagues (1997), clients were prompted by a palmtop computerized program to alter their thinking and remain in the situation during *in vivo* exposure, practice breathing retraining, and engage in self-reinforcing statements following *in vivo* exposure.

A third setting is the inpatient facility. This setting is most appropriate when very intensive cognitive-behavioral therapy is being conducted (e.g., daily therapist contact), or when severely disabled persons can no longer function at home. In addition, certain medical or drug complications may warrant inpatient treatment. The greatest drawback to the inpatient setting is poor generalization to the home environment. Transition sessions and follow-up booster sessions in an outpatient clinic/office or in the client's own home can facilitate generalization.

Format

Treatment can be conducted in individual or group formats. Several of the clinical outcome studies have used group treatments (Cerny, Barlow, Craske, & Himadi, 1987; Craske, Street, & Barlow, 1989, Evans, Holt, & Oei, 1991; Feigenbaum, 1988; Hoffart, 1995; Lidren et al., 1994; Telch et al., 1993). The fact that their outcomes are generally consistent with the summary statistics obtained from individually formatted treatment suggests that group treatment is as effective as individual therapy. Only one study has directly compared the efficacy of group versus individual treatments with respect to panic disorder and agoraphobia. Neron, Lacroix, and Chaput (1995) compared 12 to 14 weekly sessions of individual or group cognitive-behavioral therapy ($n = 20$), although the group condition received two additional 1-hour individual sessions. The two conditions were equally effective for measures of panic and agoraphobia at posttreatment and 6-month follow-up. However, the individual format resulted in superior alleviation of generalized anxiety and depressive symptoms by the follow-up point. Another study (Lidren et al., 1994) found that group treatment and individually conducted self-help treatment were equally effective. Obviously, there is a need for more investigation of the efficacy of group treatments relative to individual therapy, but extant data suggest that group formats are generally effective for targeted symptoms of panic and agoraphobia. It is noteworthy, however, that groups are usually small in size, ranging from three to eight clients. Therapeutic efficacy may decrease with larger sizes.

Interpersonal Context

Interpersonal context variables have been researched in terms of the development, maintenance, and treatment of agoraphobia. The reason for this research interest is apparent from the following vignettes:

> "My husband really doesn't understand. He thinks it's all in my head. He gets angry at me for not being able to cope. He says I'm weak and irresponsible. He resents having to drive me around, and doing things for the kids that I used to do. We argue a lot because he comes home tired and frustrated from work, only to be frustrated more by the problems I'm having. But I can't do anything without him. I'm so afraid that I'll collapse into a helpless wreck without him, or that I'd be alone for the rest of my life. As cruel as he can be, I feel safe around him because he always has everything under control. He always knows what to do."

This vignette illustrates a dependency on the significant other for a sense of safety, despite a nonsympathetic response that may only serve to increase background stress for the client. The second vignette illustrates inadvertent reinforcement of fear and avoidance through attention from the significant other:

> "My boyfriend really tries hard to help me. He's always cautious of my feelings and doesn't push me to do things that I can't do. He phones me from work to check on me. He stays with me and holds my hand when I feel really scared. He never hesitates to leave and take me home if I'm having a bad time. Only last week we visited some of his friends, and we had to leave. I feel guilty because we don't do the things we used to enjoy doing together. We don't go to the movies any more. We used to love going to ball games, but now it's too much for me. I am so thankful for him. I don't know what I would do without him."

Perhaps some forms of agoraphobia represent a conflict between desire for autonomy and dependency in interpersonal relationships (Fry, 1962; Goldstein & Chambless, 1978); that is, the individual with agoraphobia is trapped in a domineering relationship without the skills needed to activate change. However, the concept of a distinct couple system that predisposes toward agoraphobia in particular lacks empirical evidence. That is not to say that couple or interpersonal systems are unimportant to agoraphobia. For example, interpersonal discord/dissatisfaction may represent one of several possible stressors that precipitate panic attacks. Also, interpersonal relations may be negatively affected by the development of agoraphobia (Buglass, Clarke, Henderson, & Presley, 1977), and in turn may contribute to its maintenance. Not unlike the first vignette above, consider a woman who has developed agoraphobia and now relies on her husband to do the shopping and other errands. These new demands upon the husband lead to resentment and marital discord. The marital distress adds to background stress, making progress and recovery even more difficult for the client.

Aside from whether interpersonal dysregulation contributes to the onset or maintenance of PD/PDA, some studies suggest that poor couple relations adversely affect exposure-based treatments (Bland & Hallam, 1981; Dewey & Hunsley, 1990; Milton & Hafner, 1979). However, other studies show no relationship between initial couple distress and outcome from cognitive-behavioral therapy (Arrindell & Emmelkamp, 1987; Emmelkamp, 1980; Himadi, Cerny, Barlow, Cohen, & O'Brien, 1986). Another line of research suggests that involving significant others in every aspect of treatment may override potential negative impacts of poor couple relations on phobic improvement (Barlow, O'Brien, & Last, 1984; Cerny et al., 1987). Furthermore, involvement of significant others resulted in better long-term outcomes from cognitive-behavioral therapy for agoraphobia (Cerny et al., 1987). Similarly, communications training with significant others as compared to relaxation training, after 4 weeks of *in vivo* exposure therapy, resulted in significantly greater reductions on measures of agoraphobia by posttreatment (Arnow, Taylor, Agras, & Telch, 1985). Also, the superiority was maintained over an 8-month follow-up

(Arnow et al., 1985). Together, these studies suggest the value of including significant others in the treatment for agoraphobia.

Yet another question is the degree to which treatment for PD/PDA influences couple/interpersonal relations. Some have noted that successful treatment can have deleterious effects (Hafner, 1984; Hand & Lamontagne, 1976). Others note that it has no effect or a positive effect on couple functioning (Barlow, O'Brien, Last, & Holden, 1983; Himadi et al., 1986). Barlow and colleagues (1983) suggest that negative effects may occur if exposure therapy is conducted intensively without the significant other's involvement, because of major role changes that the significant other perceives as being beyond his/her control. This again speaks to the value of involving significant others in the treatment process.

Therapist Variables

Therapist variables have been understudied with respect to cognitive-behavioral treatments. Williams and Chambless (1990) found that patients who rated their therapists as caring/involved, and as modeling self-confidence, achieved better outcomes on behavioral approach tests. However, an important confound in this study is that client ratings of therapist qualities may have depended on client responses to treatment. More recently, Keijsers, Schaap, Hoogduin, and Lammers (1995) reviewed findings regarding therapist relationship factors and behavioral outcome. They conclude that empathy, warmth, positive regard, and genuineness assessed early in treatment predict positive outcome. Second, patients who view their therapists as understanding and respectful improve the most. Also, patient perceptions of therapist expertness, self-confidence, and directiveness relate positively to outcome, although not consistently. In their own study of junior therapists who provided cognitive-behavioral treatment for PDA, Keijsers and colleagues (1995) found that therapists used more empathic statements and more questioning in Session 1 than later sessions. In Session 3, therapists became more active and offered more instructions and explanations. In Session 10, therapists employed more interpretations and confrontations than previously. In fact, directive statements and explanations in Session 1 predicted poorer outcome. Empathic listening in Session 1 related to better behavioral outcome, whereas empathic listening in Session 3 related to poorer behavioral outcome. Thus this study demonstrated the advantages of different interactional styles at different points in therapy.

Most clinicians assume that therapist training and experience improve the chances of successful outcome. Some believe this to be the case particularly with respect to the cognitive aspects of cognitive-behavioral therapy (e.g., Michelson et al., 1990). Extrapolation from comparing independent studies yields some supportive data. Specifically, cognitive-behavioral therapy conducted by "novice" therapists in a medical setting (Welkowitz et al.,1991) was somewhat less effective than the same therapy conducted by inexperienced but highly trained therapists in a psychological setting (Barlow, Craske, Cerny, & Klosko, 1989), or by experienced and highly trained therapists in a community mental health setting (Wade, Treat, & Stuart, 1998). These comparisons suggest that therapist training may be important, whereas therapist experience is not. Furthermore, there are strong reasons to suspect that clinical experience alone does not yield superior outcomes overall (Wilson, 1996). For example, clinical experience does not yield more accurate clinical judgment, given that experienced therapists are as vulnerable to cognitive distortions as are inexperienced therapists. Thus therapist training may be a more likely source of variance in outcome. Obviously, there is a need for more direct evaluation of the role of therapist experience and training in cognitive-behavioral therapy.

Client Variables

There has been a recent surge of interest in the effect of comorbid diagnoses, particularly personality traits and personality disorders, on PD/PDA treatment outcome. As mentioned above, there is a high rate of comorbidity between PD/PDA and avoidant, dependent, and histrionic personality disorders. Questions of diagnostic reliability and validity aside, several studies suggest that the presence of personality disorders worsens or slows the rate of response to cognitive-behavioral therapy for PD/PDA. For example, Hoffart and Martinsen (1993) found that avoidant personality disorder related negatively to degree of improvement from post-treatment to follow-up. Rathus, Sanderson, Miller, and Wetzler (1995) similarly found lower response rate with elevated scores on abnormal personality traits at pretreatment, with the exception of compulsive personality features, which correlated with superior treatment outcome. Marchand, Goyer, Dupuis, and Mainguy (1998) found that patients with any personality disorder improved less than did patients without a personality disorder. The one exception is a study by Dreessen, Arntz, Luttels, and Sallaerts (1994), in which patients with personality disorders responded equally well to cognitive-behavioral therapy for PD/PDA.

One might also expect initial depression to predict poorer response to cognitive-behavioral therapy for PD/PDA. Depression might be expected to lower motivation for homework practice or to result in negative self-diminution of treatment gains. However, in contrast to expectations and to pharmacology trials, there appear to be no detrimental effects of initial depression on the outcome of cognitive-behavioral therapy for PD/PDA. This is true whether depression is principal or primary (defined by severity or chronicity) versus secondary to PD/PDA (Brown, Antony, & Barlow, 1995; Laberge, Gauthier, Cote, Plamondon, & Cormier, 1993; McLean, Woody, Taylor, & Koch, 1998). Furthermore, McLean and colleagues (1998) failed to find the expected relationship between depression and poorer compliance with homework. Similarly, Murphy and colleagues (1998) found that depressed subjects with PD/PDA engaged in as many self-directed exposures as did non-depressed PD/PDA subjects, although they did experience more subjective anxiety during exposures.

There is a clear need to test the generalizability of findings to date with less selected samples. Most extant studies have excluded persons who suffer additional problems of substance abuse/dependence, bipolar disorders, or psychosis. In addition, the impact of other anxiety disorders, such as social phobia or generalized anxiety disorder, warrants further evaluation. For example, although comorbidity did not predict response to treatment overall in the study by Brown and colleagues (1995), the presence of social phobia was unexpectedly associated with superior

treatment outcome for panic disorder. Another source of comorbidity is medical conditions, such as arrhythmias or asthma, that may slow improvement rates, given the additional complications involved in discriminating anxiety symptomatology from disease symptomatology, increases in actual medical risk, and the stress of physical diseases.

Other client variables include socioeconomic status and general living conditions. In our recent multicenter trial, attrition from cognitive-behavioral and/or medication treatment for PD with minimal agoraphobia was predicted by lower education, which in turn was dependent on lower income (Grilo et al., 1998). This was interpreted to reflect less discretionary time to engage in activities such as weekly treatment. Consider a woman who is a mother of two and a full-time clerk, with a husband on disability due to back injury. Or consider the full-time student who works an extra 25 hours a week in order to pay his way through school. Under these conditions, treatment assignments of daily relaxation practices or *in vivo* exposure exercises are much less likely to be completed. Frustration with lack of treatment progress often results. Therapeutic success requires either a change in lifestyle that allows the cognitive-behavioral treatment to become a priority, or termination of therapy until a later time when life circumstances are less demanding. In fact, these kinds of life circumstance issues may explain the trend for African Americans to show less treatment benefit in terms of mobility, anxiety, and panic attacks than European Americans (Friedman & Paradis, 1991; Williams & Chambless, 1994). However, in contrast to these two studies, Friedman, Paradis, and Hatch (1994) found equivalent outcomes across the two racial groups. The influence of ethnic and cultural differences on treatment outcome and delivery is clearly in need of more evaluation.

Finally, clients' understanding of the nature of their problem may be important to the success of cognitive-behavioral treatments. Given the somatic nature of PD/PDA, many clients seek medical help first. Beyond that, however, differences in the way the problem is conceptualized could lead pharmacological treatment approaches or analytical treatment approaches to be perceived as more credible than cognitive-behavioral treatment approaches. For example, individuals who strongly believe that their condition is due to "a neurochemical inbalance" are more likely to seek medication and to refute psychological treatments. Similarly, individuals who attribute their condition to "something about my past—it must be unconscious influences" may resist cognitive-behavioral interpretations. Indeed, Grilo and colleagues (1998) found that PD/PDA patients who attributed their disorder to life stressors were more likely to drop out of treatment (perhaps because they saw cognitive-behavioral and pharmacological approaches as irrelevant), as were those assigned to a treatment condition toward which they had less favorable attitudes.

Concurrent Pharmacological Treatment

Many more patients receive medications than cognitive-behavioral therapy for PD/PDA, partly because primary care physicians usually constitute the first line of treatment. This is despite the fact that most patients express a preference for psychological treatment approaches when given a choice (see, e.g., Hofmann et al., 1998). Thus one-half or more of PD/PDA clients who attend clinics offering psychosocial approaches are already taking anxiolytic medications (selective serotonin reuptake inhibitors [SSRIs], high-potency benzodiazapines, or heterocyclic antidepressants being the most common). The obvious question, therefore, is this: To what extent do medications affect cognitive-behavioral therapy?

There are several reasons to believe that medications—particularly fast-acting and potent medications that cause a *noticeable* shift in state and are used on an as-needed basis (e.g., benzodiazepines, beta-blockers)—are detrimental relative to cognitive-behavioral therapy alone. For example, clients may attribute their therapeutic success to medications. The resultant lack of perceived self-control may increase relapse potential when medication is withdrawn, or may contribute to maintenance of a medication regimen under the assumption of its necessity in order to function. In support, attribution of therapeutic gains to alprazolam and lack of confidence in coping without alprazolam, even when given in conjunction with behavior therapy, was a major predictor of relapse in one study

(Basoglu, Marks, Kilic, Brewin, & Swinson, 1994). Second, medications may assume the role of "safety signals," or objects to which the person erroneously attributes safety from painful, aversive outcomes. Safety signals contribute to maintenance of fear and avoidance in the long term (Gray, 1987; Siddle & Bond, 1988), and may interfere with corrections of misappraisals of bodily symptoms. Third, medications may block physical symptoms of anxiety and panic, which are required for interoceptive exposure, and/or may block the capacity to experience fear, which, according to emotional processing theory (Foa & Kozak, 1986), is necessary initially in order to achieve final fear reduction. Fourth, medications may reduce the motivation to engage in practices of cognitive-behavioral skills, especially if they effectively reduce panic and anxiety. Finally, learning that takes place under the influence of medications may not necessarily generalize to the time when medications are removed, and thus contribute to relapse (Bouton & Swartzentruber, 1991). Some of these points are illustrated in the vignettes below:

> "I had been through a program of cognitive-behavioral therapy, but it was really the antidepressant that helped. Because I was feeling so much better, I considered tapering off the medication. At first I was very concerned about the idea. I had heard horror stories about what people go through when withdrawing. However, I thought it would be OK as long as I tapered slowly. So, I gradually weaned myself off. It really wasn't that bad. Well, I had been completely off the medication for about a month when the problem started all over again. I remember sitting in a restaurant, feeling really good because I was thinking about how much of a problem restaurants used to be for me before, and how easy it seemed now. Then, wammo. I became very dizzy and I immediately thought, 'Oh, no, here it comes.' I had a really bad panic attack. All I could think of was 'Why didn't I stay on the medication?'"

> "I started to lower my dose of Xanax [alprazolam]. I was OK for the first couple of days. . . . I felt really good. Then, when I woke up on Friday morning, I felt strange. My head felt really tight, and I worried about having the same old feelings all over

again. The last thing I want to do is to go through that again. So I took my usual dose of Xanax and, within a few minutes, I felt pretty good again. I need the medication— I can't manage without it right now."

Several studies have examined the combined effects of fast-acting medications (beta-blockers and benzodiazapines) with cognitive-behavioral (mostly behavioral) treatment for PD/PDA (mostly PDA). Results immediately after completion of cognitive-behavioral therapy, while medication continues to be administered, mostly show no differences in comparison to no medication (see, e.g., Chouinard, Annable, Fontaine, & Solyom, 1982—alprazolam; Marks et al., 1993—alprazolam), although one study showed superior outcomes without medications (Hafner & Milton, 1977—propranolol). Long-term results tend to show more relapse in groups treated with medication once the medication is discontinued (see, e.g., Hafner & Marks, 1977—waxing schedule of diazepam; Marks et al., 1993—alprazolam), and one study showed more relapse even when medications were not withdrawn (Otto, Pollack, & Sabatino, 1996—mostly benzodizepines). In contrast, Wardle and colleagues (1994) found no detrimental impact after low doses of diazepam were withdrawn. Also, detrimental effects are found consistently with chronic benzodiazapine regimens (see, e.g., van Balkom, de Beurs, Koele, Lange, & van Dyck, 1996). For example, Wardle and colleagues reported that benzodizapine users who averaged 11 years of use tended to drop out more often, achieved poorer outcomes from exposure therapy combined with either diazepam or placebo, and were more likely to resume taking diazepam after its discontinuation.

The results of combining cognitive-behavioral therapy and slower-acting medications for PD/PDA were reviewed by Telch and Lucas in 1994. Almost all of the psychological treatment was aimed at agoraphobia and thus consisted primarily of exposure-based treatments, while imipramine was the medication in 12 of the 13 studies reviewed. In terms of short-term efficacy, combined treatment produced a significant advantage across all domains relative to psychological treatments alone (pooled effect size = 0.45). Relative to medication treatments alone, the combined approach yielded a significant advantage across all domains except panic (pooled effect size = 0.39). From the very few studies that examined long-term efficacy, Telch and Lucas (1994) concluded that combination treatment was either no more effective or less effective than behavioral therapy alone in the long term.

MULTISITE COMPARATIVE STUDY FOR THE TREATMENT OF PANIC DISORDER

Results are now available from our Multisite Comparative Study for the Treatment of Panic Disorder, which compared single and combined effects of cognitive-behavioral treatment and imipramine for patients with PD with limited agoraphobia (Barlow, Gorman, Shear, & Woods, 2000). In this study, conducted between 1991 and 1998, 312 patients with PD were assigned to receive imipramine only, cognitive-behavioral therapy only (specifically, PCT, the protocol described in this chapter), placebo only, PCT plus imipramine, and PCT plus placebo. Patients were treated weekly for 3 months (acute phase). Patients who responded to treatment were then seen monthly for 6 months (maintenance phase); treatment was then discontinued; and patients were assessed again 6 months later (follow-up phase). This study has already had a significant impact on public health policy, since important and somewhat unexpected results were achieved. In addition, the study was conducted at two sites known principally for expertise in psychological treatments, and two sites well known for expertise in pharmacological approaches. Therefore, "allegiance" effects (in which treatments perform somewhat better in sites where therapists are adherents of a particular approach) were obviated, since no site differences were observed in the outcomes described below.

The results indicated that both imipramine and PCT were significantly superior to placebo after the acute phase of treatment, as were the two combined treatments. However, PCT plus imipramine was never better than PCT plus placebo; nor did the combined treatments confer any useful advantage over the individual treatments. One interesting finding was that among those patients who showed a good response to either individual treatment (responders), patients taking the drug showed a somewhat better-quality response, in that they were less depressed and generally felt a bit better.

After 6 months of maintenance treatment (9 months after the beginning of treatment), all treatments continued to be significantly more effective than placebo. The combined treatment showed somewhat more efficacy compared to the individual treatments, although very little, if any, advantage was observed for the combined treatment compared to PCT plus placebo. Six months after treatment discontinuation (follow-up), a substantial number of patients taking medication relapsed, particularly in the combined treatment group. Thus those patients who were treated with PCT without medication (PCT alone or PCT plus placebo) were doing significantly better than those who had taken medication, suggesting that PCT provides a more durable effect. In conclusion, each individual treatment worked well during the acute and maintenance phase, but patients treated with PCT retained their gains substantially better.

Current recommendations regarding pharmacological treatments consider SSRIs to be the first-line medications (American Psychiatric Association, 1998), due to a less adverse side effect profile. However, studies looking closely at comparisons between heterocyclic antidepressants and SSRIs do not consistently find higher efficacy for the SSRIs, even after considering rates of attrition from each drug due to intolerance of side effects. In fact, four randomized studies did not find significant differences at the end of the acute phase of the studies between the two drugs when attrition was taken into account (Bystritsky et al., 1994; Lecrubier, Bakker, Dunbar, & Judge, 1997; Nair et al., 1996; Wade, Lepola, Koponen, Pedersen, & Pedersen, 1997). Thus it seems likely that the efficacy of imipramine (the drug used in the multicenter study described above) and that of the SSRIs are roughly comparable.

In summary, the results suggest a greater risk of relapse when cognitive-behavioral therapy is combined with high-potency benzodiazepines, particularly after withdrawal and with chronic use of those drugs, relative to cognitive-behavioral therapy alone. Also, despite possible short-term advantages from combining cognitive-behavioral therapy with heterocyclics or SSRIs, there may be a long-term disadvantage from combination treatments with heterocyclics. Further evaluation is needed of the long-term effects of adding SSRIs to cognitive-behavioral therapy, and of the most effective ways to combine medications with cognitive-behavioral therapy in order to offset potential long-term relapse.

ASSESSMENT

Jane is a 33-year-old European American, the mother of two, who lives with her husband of 8 years. For the past 3 years she has been chronically anxious and panic-stricken. Her panic attacks are described as unbearable and increasing in frequency. The first time she felt panicky was just over 3 years ago, when she was rushing to her grandmother's house before her grandmother died. She was driving alone on the freeway. Jane remembers feeling as if everything was moving in slow motion, as if the cars were standing still, and as if things around her were unreal. She also recalls feeling short of breath and detached. However, it was so important to reach her destination that she did not dwell on how she felt until later. After the day was over, she reflected upon how lucky she was not to have had an accident. A few weeks later, the same type of feeling happened, again when she was driving on the freeway. This time it occurred without the pressure of getting to her dying grandmother. It scared her because she was unable to explain the feelings. She pulled off to the side of the road and called her husband, who came to meet her. She followed him home, feeling anxious all the way.

Now Jane has these feelings in many situations. She describes her panic attacks as feelings of unreality, detachment, shortness of breath, a racing heart, and a general fear of the unknown. It is the unreality that scares her the most. Consequently, Jane is sensitive to anything that produces "unreality" types of feelings, such as the semiconsciousness that occurs just before falling asleep, the period of the day when daylight changes to night, bright lights, concentrating on the same thing for long periods of time, alcohol or drugs, and being anxious in general. Even though she has a prescription of Klonopin (clonazepam—a high-potency benzodiazepine), she rarely if ever uses it because of her general fear of being under the influence of a drug, or of feeling an altered state of consciousness. She wants to be as alert as possible at all times, and keeps the Klonopin with her in the event that she has no other escape route. She is very sensitive to her body in general; she becomes scared of anything that feels a little different from usual. Even coffee, which she used to enjoy, is distressing to her now because of its agitating and racy effects. She was never a big exerciser, but to think of exerting herself now is also scary. She reports that she is constantly waiting for the next panic to occur. She avoids freeways, driving on familiar surface streets only. She limits herself to a 10-mile radius. She avoids crowds and large groups as well, partly because of the feeling of too much stimulation and partly because she is afraid to panic in front of others. In general, she prefers to be with her husband or her mother. However, she can do most things within her "safety" region alone.

Jane describes how different she is from the way she used to be—how weak and scared she is now. The only other incident with any similarity to her current panic attacks occurred in her early 20s. Jane recalls a negative drug (marijuana) experience, when she became very scared of the feeling of losing control and she feared that she would never return to reality. She has not taken illicit drugs since then. Otherwise, there is no history of serious medical conditions, nor has she had any previous psychological treatment. Jane was shy as a young child and throughout her teens. However, her social anxiety improved throughout her 20s to the point that, up until the onset of her panic attacks, she was mostly very comfortable around people. Since the onset of her panic attacks, she has become concerned that others will notice that she appears different or strange. However, her social anxiety is limited to panic attacks and does not reflect a broader social phobia.

In general, her appetite is good, but her sleep is restless. At least once a week she wakes abruptly in the middle of the night, feeling short of breath and scared. Her background anxiety is almost solely focused upon the possibility of having unreal feelings. She worries somewhat about other issues, such as her children and her parents. However, that worry is not excessive. She has some difficulty concentrating, but in general she functions well within her safety regions. For example, Jane works part-time as the manager of a business that she and her husband own. In that setting, she is more relaxed and successful. Nevertheless, she sometimes becomes depressed about her panic and the limitations on how far she can travel. She has occasional times of feeling hopeless about the future, doubting whether she will ever be able to get out of the anxiety.

A functional behavioral analysis involves several steps.

Interviews

An in-depth interview is the first step in establishing diagnostic and behavioral-cognitive profiles. Several semistructured and fully structured interviews exist. The Anxiety Disorders Interview Schedule for DSM-IV (ADIS-IV; Di Nardo, Brown, & Barlow, 1994) assesses anxiety disorders primarily, as well as mood disorders and somatoform disorders. Psychotic and drug conditions are also screened by this instrument. The value of structured interviews lies in their contribution to differential diagnosis and interrater reliability. Interrater agreement ranges from satisfactory to excellent for the various anxiety disorders on an earlier version of this instrument that was devised in accordance with DSM-III-R criteria, the ADIS-R (Di Nardo, Moras, Barlow, Rapee, & Brown, 1993). Similarly, the Schedule for Affective Disorders and Schizophrenia—Lifetime Version (Anxiety Modified) produced reliable diagnoses for most of the DSM-III-R anxiety disorders (generalized anxiety disorder and simple phobia being the exceptions) (Mannuzza et al., 1989). Another interview is the Structured Clinical Interview for DSM-IV, which covers a greater number of the mental disorders.

Differential diagnosis is sometimes difficult because, as described earlier, panic is a ubiquitous phenomenon (Barlow, 1988), occurring across a wide variety of emotional disorders. It is not uncommon for persons with specific phobias, generalized anxiety disorder, obsessive–compulsive disorder, or posttraumatic stress disorder to report panic attacks. For Jane, there was a differential diagnostic question regarding social phobia and PDA. Shown in Figure 1.1 are the ADIS-IV questions that addressed this differentiation (Jane's answers are in italics).

As you can see from Figure 1.1, Jane experiences panic attacks in social situations, and is concerned about negative evaluations if her anxiety is visibly apparent to others. How-

Parts of ADIS-IV Panic Disorder Section

Do you currently have times when you feel a sudden rush of intense fear or discomfort? *Yes.*

In what kinds of situations do you have those feelings? *Driving, especially on freeways . . . alone at home . . . at parties or in crowds of people.*

Did you ever have those feelings come "from out of the blue", for no apparent reason, or in situations where you did not expect them to occur? *Yes.*

How long does it usually take for the rush of fear/discomfort to reach its peak level? *It varies, sometimes a couple of seconds and at other times it seems to build more slowly.*

How long does the fear/discomfort usually last at its peak level? *Depends on where I am at the time. If it happens when I'm alone, sometimes it is over within a few minutes or even seconds. If I'm in a crowd, then it seems to last until I leave.*

In the last month, how much have you been worried about, or how fearful have you been about having another panic attack?

0	1	2	3	4	5	⑥	7	8
No worry/ no fear		Rarely worried/ mild fear		Occasionally worried/ moderate fear		Frequently worried/ severe fear		Constantly worried/ extreme fear

Parts of ADIS-IV Social Phobia Section

In social situations, where you might be observed or evaluated by others, or when meeting new people, do you feel fearful, anxious, or nervous? *Yes.*

Are you overly concerned that you might do and/or say something that might embarrass or humiliate yourself in front of others, or that others may think badly of you? *Yes.*

What are you concerned will happen in these situations? *That I will look anxious to others and they will think I'm weird . . . my face turns white and my eyes look strange when I'm panicky. That I'll flip out in front of them and they won't know what to do.*

Are you anxious about these situations because you are afraid that you will have an unexpected panic attack? *Yes (either a panic or that I'll feel unreal).*

Other than when you are exposed to these situations, have you experienced an unexpected rush of fear/anxiety? *Yes.*

FIGURE 1.1. Questions from the ADIS-IV Panic Disorder and Social Phobia sections. From Di Nardo, Brown, and Barlow (1994). Copyright 1994 by the Psychological Corporation. Reprinted by permission.

ever, despite her history of shyness, her current social discomfort is based primarily on the possibility of panicking. Because of this, and because she meets the other criteria for PDA (i.e., uncued/nonsocial panic attacks and pervasive apprehension about future panic attacks), the social distress is best subsumed under the domain of PDA. If Jane reported that she experienced panic attacks in social situations only, or that she worried about panic attacks in social situations only, then a diagnosis of social phobia would be more probable. A report of uncued panic attacks, as well as self-consciousness about things that she might do or say in social situations regardless of the occurrence of panic, would be consistent with a dual diagnosis of PDA and social phobia.

The same types of diagnostic questioning are useful for distinguishing between PDA and claustrophobia. Other differential diagnostic issues can arise with respect to somatoform disorders, real medical conditions, and avoidant or dependent personality disorder.

Medical Evaluation

A medical evaluation is generally recommended, because several medical conditions should be ruled out before assigning the diagnosis of PD/PDA. These include thyroid conditions, caffeine or amphetamine intoxication, drug withdrawal, or pheochromocytoma (a rare adrenal gland tumor). Furthermore, certain medical conditions can exacerbate PD/ PDA, although PD/PDA is likely to continue even when they are under medical control. Mitral valve prolapse, asthma, allergies, and hypoglycemia fall into this category. According to the model described earlier, these medical conditions exacerbate PD/PDA to the extent that they elicit the types of physical sensations that are feared. For example, mitral valve prolapse sometimes produces the sensation of a heart flutter, asthma produces shortness of breath, and hypoglycemia produces dizziness and weakness.

Self-Monitoring

Self-monitoring is a very important part of assessment and treatment for PD/PDA. Retrospective recall of past episodes of panic and anxiety, especially when made under anxious conditions, may inflate estimates of panic frequency and intensity (Margraf et al., 1987; Rapee, Craske, & Barlow, 1990). Moreover, such inflation may contribute to apprehension about future panic. Thus, to the degree that ongoing self-monitoring yields more accurate, less inflated estimates, then it is a therapeutic tool (see Craske & Tsao, 1999, for a comprehensive review of self-monitoring for panic and anxiety). Also, ongoing self-monitoring is believed to contribute to an objective self-awareness. Objective self-monitoring replaces

negative-affect-laden self-statements such as "I feel horrible—this is the worst it's ever been—my whole body is out of control" with "My anxiety level is 6—my symptoms include tremulousness, dizziness, unreal feelings, and shortness of breath—and this episode lasted 10 minutes." Objective self-awareness reduces negative affect. Finally, self-monitoring provides feedback for judging progress and useful material for in-session discussions.

Panic attacks are recorded on the Panic Attack Record, shown in Figure 1.2. This record is to be completed as soon as possible after a panic attack occurs, and therefore is carried on one's person (it is wallet-size). Daily levels of anxiety, depression, and worry about panic are monitored using the Daily Mood Record, shown in Figure 1.3. This record is completed at the end of each day. Finally, activities can be recorded by logging daily excursions in a diary, or by checking off completed activities on an agoraphobia checklist.

A common problem with self-monitoring is noncompliance. Sometimes noncompliance is due to misunderstanding or to lack of perceived credibility in self-monitoring. Most often, however, noncompliance is due to anticipation of more anxiety as a result of monitoring. This is particularly true for individuals whose preferred style of coping is to distract themselves as much as possible, and to avoid "quiet" times when thoughts of panic may become overwhelming: "Why should I

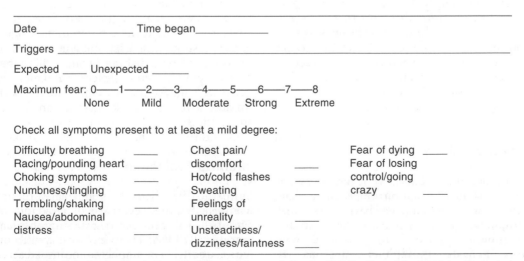

FIGURE 1.2. Panic Attack Record. From Barlow and Craske (2000). Copyright 2000 by Graywind Publications Inc. and the Psychological Corporation. Reprinted by permission.

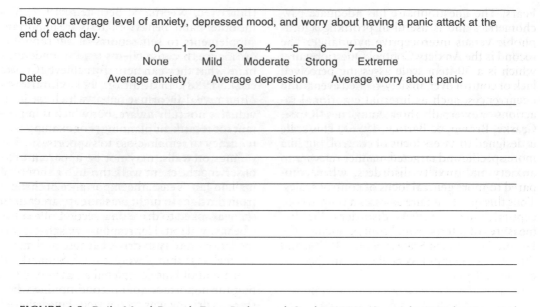

Rate your average level of anxiety, depressed mood, and worry about having a panic attack at the end of each day.

0——1——2——3——4——5——6——7——8
None   Mild   Moderate   Strong   Extreme

Date   Average anxiety   Average depression   Average worry about panic

FIGURE 1.3. Daily Mood Record. From Barlow and Craske (2000). Copyright 2000 by Graywind Publications Inc. and the Psychological Corporation. Reprinted by permission.

make myself worse by asking myself how bad I feel?" In Jane's case, the self-monitoring task proved to be particularly difficult, because explicit reminders of her anxiety elicited strong concerns about losing touch with reality. Prompting, reassurance that anxiety about self-monitoring would subside with perseverance at self-monitoring, and emphasis upon objective versus subjective self-monitoring were helpful for Jane. In addition, cognitive restructuring conducted in the first few sessions helped Jane to be less afraid of the feelings of unreality and therefore less afraid to be reminded of those feelings by self-monitoring. Finally, therapist attention to the self-monitored information and corrective feedback about the method of self-monitoring at the start of each treatment session reinforced Jane's self-monitoring.

Standardized Inventories

Several standardized self-report inventories provide useful information for treatment planning, as well as being sensitive markers of therapeutic change. The Mobility Inventory (Chambless, Caputo, Gracely, Jasin, & Williams, 1985) lists agoraphobic situations that are rated in terms of degree of avoidance, both when alone and when accompanied. This instrument is very useful for establishing *in vivo* exposure hierarchies. The Anxiety Sensitivity Index (Reiss et al., 1986) has received wide acceptance as a trait measure of threatening beliefs about bodily sensations. It has good psychometric properties and tends to discriminate PD/PDA from other types of anxiety disorders (see, e.g., Taylor, Koch, & McNally, 1992; Telch, Sherman, & Lucas, 1989). More specific information about which particular bodily sensations are feared the most, and what specific misappraisals occur most often, can be obtained from the Body Sensations Questionnaire and the Agoraphobia Cognitions Questionnaire (Chambless et al., 1984). Measures of trait anxiety include the State–Trait Anxiety Inventory (Spielberger, Gorsuch, Lushene, Vagg, & Jacobs, 1983) and the Beck Anxiety Inventory (Beck, Epstein, Brown, & Steer, 1988).

In addition, we have developed two standardized self-report inventories that are useful with PDA. The first is the Albany Panic and Phobia Questionnaire (Rapee, Craske, & Barlow, 1995). This 32-item questionnaire was designed to assess fear and avoidance of activities that produce frightening physical sensations, as well as more typical agoraphobic situations. Factor analysis confirmed three distinct factors, which have been labeled Agoraphobia, Social Phobia, and Interoceptive

Fears. The questionnaire has adequate psychometrics and is useful in profiling agoraphobic versus interoceptive avoidance. The second is the Anxiety Control Questionnaire, which is a 30-item scale assessing perceived lack of control over anxiety-related events and occurrences, such as internal emotional reactions or externally threatening cues (Rapee, Craske, Brown, & Barlow, 1996). This scale is designed to assess locus of control, but in a more specific and targeted manner relevant to anxiety and anxiety disorders, when compared to more general locus of control scales. Thus this questionnaire assesses a central conceptual issue in anxiety disorders. Finally, measures of interpersonal context include the Dyadic Adjustment Scale (Spanier, 1976), and the Marital Happiness Scale (Azrin, Naster, & Jones, 1973).

Behavioral Tests

The behavioral test is a useful measure of degree of avoidance of specific situations. Behavioral approach tests can be standardized or individually tailored. The standardized behavioral test for PD/PDA usually involves walking or driving a particular route, such as a 1-mile loop around the clinic setting. Anxiety levels are rated at regular intervals, and actual distance walked/driven is measured. The disadvantage is that the specific task may not be relevant to all clients. For some clients, a 1-mile walk may be only mildly anxiety-provoking. Hence it is generally preferable to use individually tailored tasks, which usually entail attempts at three to five individualized situations that the client has identified as being anywhere from somewhat to extremely difficult. These might include driving two exits on a freeway, waiting in a bank line, or shopping in a local supermarket for 15 minutes. Maximum levels of anxiety and degree of approach (i.e., refused task, attempted but escaped from task, or completed task) are measured for each situation. Individually tailored behavioral tests are more informative for clinical practice, although they confound between-subject comparisons for research purposes.

Standardized and individually tailored behavioral tests are both susceptible to demand biases for fear and avoidance prior to treatment, and for improvement after treatment (Borkovec, Weerts, & Bernstein, 1977). On the other hand, behavioral tests are important supplements to self-reports of agoraphobic avoidance, because clients tend to underestimate what they can actually achieve (Craske et al., 1988). In addition, behavioral tests often reveal information of which an individual is not fully aware, but which is important for treatment planning. For example, the tendency to remain close to supports, such as railings or walls, may not be apparent until observing the client walk through a shopping mall. In Jane's case, the importance of changes from daylight to night was not apparent until she was asked to drive on a section of road as a behavioral test. Her response was that it was too late in the day to drive, because dusk made her feel as if things were unreal. Similarly, it was not until Jane completed a behavioral test that the importance of air conditioning when she was driving was recognized. Jane believed that the cool air blowing on her face helped her to remain "in touch with reality." Finally, her physical position while driving was noticed as a factor that contributed to anxiety: Her shoulders were hunched, she leaned toward the steering wheel, and she held the steering wheel very tightly.

Psychophysiology

Physiological measures are not very practical tools for clinicians, but can provide important information (Hofmann & Barlow, 1996). In particular, the discrepancy described earlier between reports of symptoms and actual physiological arousal can serve as a therapeutic demonstration of the role of attention and cognition in symptom production. Similarly, actual recordings provide data to disconfirm misappraisals such as "My heart feels like it's going so fast that it will explode" or "I'm sure my blood pressure is so high that I could have a stroke at any minute." Finally, baseline levels of physiological arousal, which tend to be elevated in anxious individuals, may be sensitive measures of treatment outcome.

Functional Analysis

The various methods of assessment provide the material for a full functional analysis in the form shown below for Jane:

1. Panic attack topography
   - Sensations: Unreality, shortness of breath, palpitations
   - Frequency: Three per week on average
   - Duration: Few seconds to 5 minutes, if not in a crowd
   - Apprehension: On her mind 75% of the time
   - Types: Mostly expected, but some unexpected
2. Antecedents
   - Situational: Driving on freeways, crowds of people, being alone (especially at night), restaurants, dusk, reading and concentrating for long periods of time, aerobic activity
   - Internal: Heart rate fluctuations, lightheaded feelings, hunger feelings, weakness due to lack of food, thoughts of the "big one" happening, thoughts of not being able to cope with this for much longer, anger
3. Misappraisals
   - Physical: None
   - Mental: Never returning to normality, going crazy, losing control
   - Social: "Others will see I'm anxious and think I'm weird"
4. Behavioral reactions to panic attacks
   - Escape: Pull off to side of road, leave restaurants and other crowded places
   - Help seeking: Have called significant other on occasion, but rarely now
   - Protection: Cool air, checks for Klonopin although rarely uses
5. Behavioral reactions to anticipation of panic attacks
   - Avoidance: Driving long distances alone, unfamiliar roads and freeways, crowded areas, exercise, quiet time with nothing to do, doing one thing for a long period of time
   - Cognitive avoidance: Tries not to think about anxiety or unreality feelings
   - Safety signals: Carries medication, always knows location of husband
6. Consequences
   - Family: Husband is concerned and supportive; mother thinks she should pull herself together because "it's all in her head"
   - Work: Still works, but has cut back number of hours
   - Leisure: Travels much less
   - Social: Socializes much less
7. General mood
   - Some difficulty concentrating, sleep restlessness, headaches, muscular pains and aches
   - Occasionally tearful, sad, and hopeless

COMPONENTS OF COGNITIVE-BEHAVIORAL THERAPY

In this section, the components of our cognitive-behavioral treatment protocol, PCT, are described. They are integrated into a session-by-session treatment program later in the chapter.

Cognitive Restructuring

Initially, cognitive therapy did not directly target misappraisals of bodily sensations, but instead fostered coping self-statements in anxiety provoking situations (we call this "coping-oriented cognitive therapy"). Michelson, Mavissakalian, and Marchione (1985) published their first of a series of investigations comparing different behavioral treatments to various coping-oriented cognitive treatments for agoraphobia. They compared paradoxical intention, graduated exposure, and progressive deep muscle relaxation, although all participants conducted self-directed *in vivo* exposure between sessions. At posttreatment and 3 months later, paradoxical intention demonstrated equivalent rates of improvement, but significantly more remained symptomatic compared to graduated exposure and relaxation. Michelson, Mavissakalian, and Marchione (1988) replicated this design with almost twice as many participants. Contrary to the first study, few significant differences were detected between treatments. Lack of differences was replicated in a third study (Michelson et al., 1990). Thus coping-oriented cognitive treatments appeared to be as effective as behaviorally oriented treatments, although the cognitive treatments were all heavily contaminated by behavioral self-directed exposure. In a slightly different design, Murphy and colleagues (1998) compared three treatment conditions: cognitive therapy combined with therapist- and self-directed exposure; relaxation combined with therapist- and self-directed exposure; and just therapist- and self-directed exposure. Again, overall there were few significant differences, although the condition that included cognitive therapy yielded the most potent and stable changes. Without the self-directed exposure component, Emmelkamp and colleagues found that coping-oriented cognitive therapy (rational–emotive therapy and self-instruction training) was significantly less effective than prolonged *in vivo* exposure for agoraphobia, on an array of behavioral and self-report measures of anxiety and avoidance (Emmelkamp, Brilman, Kuipers, & Mersch, 1986; Emmelkamp, Kuipers, & Eggeraat, 1978; Emmelkamp & Mersch, 1982).

Newer cognitive therapies target misappraisals of bodily sensations and are clearly effective with samples with mild to moderate levels of agoraphobia, producing results that are either superior to (Arntz & van den Hout, 1996; Clark et al., 1994) or as effective as applied relaxation (Beck, Stanley, Baldwin, Deagle, & Averill, 1994; Öst & Westling, 1995), even though cognitive skills may take longer to lessen state anxiety (Stanley et al., 1996). The success may extend to more severe levels of agoraphobia as well. For example, cognitive therapy of this sort was more effective than guided mastery procedures for inpatients with moderate to severe agoraphobia who received 6 weeks of mostly intensive treatment (Hoffart, 1995), and equally effective for patients with varying levels of agoraphobia over the course of 8 weeks (Williams & Falbo, 1996). Bouchard and colleagues (1996), on the other hand, found that cognitive therapy was slightly less effective than *in vivo* exposure for patients with varying levels of agoraphobia. Behavioral exposure-based strategies are usually included as vehicles for obtaining data that disconfirm misappraisals. The importance of exposure-based strategies to the effectiveness of cognitive therapy is not known, although 2 weeks of focused cognitive therapy with antiexposure instructions reduced panic attacks in all but one of a series of seven cases in a single-case multiple-baseline design (Salkovskis, Clark, & Hackmann, 1991).

Breathing Retraining

Breathing retraining became a central component early in the development of PCT and similar treatments, because many patients with PD/PDA describe hyperventilatory symptoms as being very similar to their panic attack symptoms. It is noteworthy, however, that hyperventilation symptom report does not always accurately represent hyperventilation physiology: Only 50% of patients or fewer show actual reductions in end-tidal carbon dioxide values during panic attacks (Hibbert & Pilsbury, 1989; Holt & Andrews, 1989; Hornsveld, Garssen, Dop, & Van Spiegel, 1990).

Nevertheless, in the conception of panic attacks that emphasizes hyperventilation, panic attacks are viewed as stress-induced respiratory changes that either provoke fear because they are perceived as threatening, or augment fear already elicited by other phobic stimuli (Clark, Salkovskis, & Chalkley, 1985). Kraft and Hoogduin (1984) found that six biweekly sessions of breathing retraining and progressive relaxation reduced panic attacks from 10 to 4 per week. However, the treatment was no more effective than either repeated hyperventilation and control of symptoms by breathing into a bag, or identification of life stressors and problem solving. Two case reports described the successful application of breathing retraining in the context of cognitively based treatments, where patients are taught to reinterpret sensations as nonharmful (Rapee, 1985; Salkovskis, Warwick, Clark, & Wessels, 1986). Clark and colleagues (1985) reported a larger, although uncontrolled, study in which 18 patients with PD/PDA received two weekly sessions of respiratory control and cognitive reattribution training. Panic attacks were reduced markedly in that brief period of time, especially in subjects who did not have significant agoraphobia. Salkovskis and colleagues (1986) gave nine patients four weekly sessions of forced hyperventilation, corrective information, and breathing retraining, after which *in vivo* exposure to agoraphobic situations was provided if necessary. Panic attacks were reduced, on average, from seven to three per week after respiratory control training.

Although these studies demonstrate impressive results from brief therapeutic interventions, several questions arise. First, participants are usually selected for exhibiting hyperventilatory symptoms, and therefore generalizability to subjects who do not experience hyperventilatory symptoms is unclear.

On the other hand, this may be a moot point, because the mechanism of action may be independent of faulty breathing. That is, from their review of efficacy and mechanisms of action, Garssen, de Ruiter, and van Dyck (1992) concluded that breathing retraining probably affects change not through breathing per se, but through distraction and/or a sense of control. Second, it is unclear whether breathing retraining alone is therapeutic for agoraphobia, and several studies suggest that the addition of breathing retraining does not improve upon *in vivo* exposure alone (see, e.g., de Beurs, Lange, van Dyck, & Koele, 1995). Third, breathing retraining protocols typically include cognitive restructuring and interoceptive exposure. Therefore, it is difficult to attribute the results primarily to breathing retraining.

Applied Relaxation

A form of relaxation known as "applied relaxation" has shown promising results as a treatment for panic attacks. Applied relaxation entails training in progressive muscle relaxation (PMR) until patients are skilled in cue-control relaxation, at which point relaxation is used as a coping skill for practicing items from an hierarchy of anxiety-provoking tasks. A theoretical basis for relaxation for panic attacks has not been elaborated, beyond the provision of a somatic counterresponse to the muscular tension that is likely to occur during anxiety and panic. However, evidence does not lend support to this notion (Rupert, Dobbins, & Mathew, 1981). An alternative suggestion is that, as in breathing retraining, fear and anxiety are reduced to the extent that relaxation provides a sense of control or mastery (Bandura, 1977; Rice & Blanchard, 1982). The procedures and mechanisms accountable for therapeutic gains are further clouded in the case of applied forms of relaxation, given the involvement of exposure-based procedures as anxiety-provoking situations are faced.

Öst (1988) reported very favorable results with applied PMR: 100% of a group receiving applied PMR (*n* = 8) were panic-free after 14 sessions, in comparison to 71.7% of a group receiving nonapplied PMR (*n* = 8). Furthermore, the results of the first group were maintained at follow-up (approximately 19 months after treatment completion): All of the patients receiving applied PMR were classified as "high end-state" (i.e., nonsymptomatic) at follow-up, in comparison to 25% of the PMR group. Michelson and colleagues (1990) combined applied PMR with breathing retraining and cognitive training for 10 patients with panic. By treatment completion, all subjects were free of "spontaneous" panics, all but one were free of panic attacks altogether, and all met criteria for high end-state functioning. However, the specific contribution of applied PMR to these results is not known. Two subsequent studies by Öst and colleagues (Öst & Westling, 1995; Öst, Westling, & Hellstrom, 1993) indicate that applied relaxation is as effective as *in vivo* exposure and cognitive therapy. In contrast, we (Barlow et al., 1989) found that applied PMR was relatively ineffective for panic attacks, although we excluded all forms of interoceptive exposure from the hierarchy of tasks to which PMR was applied, whereas this was not necessarily the case in the studies by Öst. Clark and colleagues (1994) found that cognitive therapy was superior to applied PMR when conducted with equal amounts of *in vivo* exposure, whereas Beck and colleagues (1994) found very few differences between cognitive therapy and PMR when each was administered without exposure procedures.

Interoceptive Exposure

The purpose of interoceptive exposure is to lessen fear of specific bodily cues through repeated and systematic exposure to those cues. This is done through exercises that induce panic-type sensations reliably, such as cardiovascular exercise, inhalation of carbon dioxide, spinning in a chair, and hyperventilation. The exposure is conducted in a graduated format. A series of studies have reported on the effects of interoceptive exposure independent of other therapeutic strategies. In early work, Bonn, Harrison, and Rees (1971) and Haslam (1974) observed successful reduction in reactivity with repeated infusions of sodium lactate (a drug that produces panic-type bodily sensations). However, panic was not monitored in these investigations. Griez and van den Hout (1986) compared six sessions of graduated carbon dioxide inhalation to a treatment regimen of propranolol (a beta-blocker chosen because it suppresses the symptoms induced by carbon dioxide inhalation), both conducted over the course of 2 weeks. Carbon dioxide inhalation treatment resulted in a mean reduction from 12 to 4 panic attacks, which was superior to the results from propranolol. In addition, inhalation treatment resulted in significantly greater reductions in reported fear of sensations. A 6-month follow-up assessment suggested maintenance of treatment gains, although panic frequency was not reported. More recently, Beck, Shipherd, and Zebb (1997) replicated the finding that fear is reduced with repeated exposure to carbon dioxide inhalation. Furthermore, six sessions of inhalation decreased panic attacks and panic-related fears, although it had little effect on agoraphobia. Finally, a recent study of the effects of physical exercise may be seen as a version of interoceptive exposure. Broocks and colleagues (1998) tested the effects of exercise (with once-a-week supportive contact from a therapist) in comparison to clomipramine or a drug placebo over 10 weeks. The exercise group was trained to run 4 miles three times per week. Despite high attrition from this group (31%), exercise was more effective than the drug placebo condition. However, clomipramine was superior to exercise.

In the first comparison to other cognitive and behavioral treatments, we (Barlow et al., 1989) compared applied PMR, interoceptive exposure plus breathing retraining and cognitive restructuring, their combination with applied PMR, and a wait-list control, in patients who had PD with limited agoraphobia. Interoceptive exposure entailed repeated exposures to hyperventilation, spinning, and cardiovascular effort. The two conditions involving interoceptive exposure, breathing retraining, and cognitive restructuring were significantly superior to the applied PMR and wait-list conditions, in terms of panic frequency. Fully 87% of those two treatment groups were free of panic at posttreatment. The results were maintained 24 months following treatment completion for the group receiving interoceptive exposure, breathing retraining, and cognitive restructuring without PMR, whereas the combined group tended to deteriorate over the follow-up (Craske, Brown, & Barlow, 1991).

In an attempt to dismantle the different components (interoceptive exposure, breathing retraining, cognitive restructuring) in a group with varying levels of agoraphobia, we compared interoceptive exposure, cognitive therapy, and *in vivo* exposure to breathing retraining, cognitive therapy, and *in vivo* exposure. The condition that included interoceptive exposure was slightly superior to breathing retraining at posttreatment and 6 months later (Craske, Rowe, Lewin, & Noriega-Dimitri, 1997). Another dismantling study (Hecker, Fink, Vogeltanz, & Thorpe, 1998) found very few differences between four sessions of interoceptive exposure and four sessions of cognitive therapy in a crossover study, with a 1-month interval between each phase.

In Vivo Exposure

As noted earlier, "*in vivo* exposure" refers to repeated, systematic, real-life exposure—in this case, to agoraphobic situations. There are various ways in which *in vivo* exposure can be conducted: therapist-directed versus self-directed exposure (described in an earlier section), massed versus spaced exposure, graduated versus intense exposure, endurance versus controlled escape, and attention versus distraction.

Massed versus Spaced Exposure

At its most intensive, exposure therapy may be conducted 3–4 hours a day, 5 days a week. Long, continuous sessions are generally considered more effective than shorter or interrupted sessions (Chaplin & Levine, 1981; Marshall, 1985; Stern & Marks, 1973). The optimal rate for repeating exposure is unclear. Foa, Jameson, Turner, and Payne (1980) compared 10 weekly sessions with 10 daily sessions of *in vivo* exposure therapy for 11 patients with agoraphobia (counterbalanced crossover design). Short-term superior effects were apparent following massed treatment. Nevertheless, Barlow (1988) suggested that spaced exposure is preferred for the following reasons: Dropout rates are generally higher with massed exposures (Emmelkamp & Ultee, 1974; Emmelkamp & Wessels, 1975); relapse rates may be higher following massed exposure (Hafner, 1976; Jansson & Öst,

1982); and rapid changes are more stressful for the family. However, Chambless (1990) did not find these detrimental effects. In her study, 36 subjects (of whom approximately half had agoraphobia, and half had DSM-III-R simple phobias) were assigned to massed or spaced exposure. All subjects received 10 sessions of graduated *in vivo* exposure, as well as training in respiratory control, distraction techniques, and paradoxical intention. Spaced exposure was conducted weekly and massed exposure was conducted daily. The two conditions were equally effective in the short term and at the 6-month follow-up. There was no trend for a differential dropout rate, nor differential relapse rates over the 6-month follow-up period. However, some subjects were unwilling to accept massed exposure, creating a sample selection bias. In addition, Chambless pointed out that her results may lack generalizability, because spaced exposure is usually interspersed with homework assignments, which may increase outcome efficacy. Nevertheless, she concluded by suggesting that the choice of massed versus spaced exposure should be the decision of the therapist and client.

Unfortunately, none of the studies to date with PD/PDA have employed an expanding spaced schedule, which is predicted by the "new theory of disuse" (Bjork & Bjork, 1992) to be the most beneficial for long-term retention of learning. An "expanding schedule" refers to progressively longer intervals between trials of learning. We have tested this schedule with anxiety about public speaking (Tsao & Craske, in press), fears of heights (Lang & Craske, 2000), and fears of spiders (Rowe & Craske, 1998), to find least return of fear at follow-up after an expanding spaced schedule. Interestingly, superiority of expanding schedules at follow-up occurred despite higher heart rate throughout exposure treatment, and, in the spider study, despite higher anxiety, heart rate, and perceptions of danger at posttreatment. These findings directly contrast with emotional processing theory (Foa & Kozak, 1986), which posits that habituation during exposure is predictive of long-term fear reduction. Conversely, they are consistent with the notion that difficulty during learning bodes well for long-term retention (Schmidt & Bjork, 1992). Although our results are limited to analogue samples, they raise intriguing possibilities for the way in which exposure is spaced over time. A potentially important finding from the study of public speaking anxiety was a disproportionately high dropout rate after the first exposure session in the uniformly spaced group, especially in more anxious participants. This suggests the importance of closely spaced exposures initially, as if too much time before the second exposure generates high levels of anticipatory anxiety and decisions to discontinue.

Graduated versus Intense Exposure

In vivo exposure is typically conducted in a graduated format, progressing from least to most difficult hierarchy items. However, intense exposure is effective also. In a study by Feigenbaum (1988), treatment sessions were conducted in a massed format over the course of 6 to 10 consecutive days. One group received ungraded exposure ($n = 25$), beginning with the most feared items from avoidance hierarchies. Another group received graded exposure ($n = 23$), beginning with the least feared hierarchy items. The patients in the sample had severe agoraphobia; approximately one-third were housebound at initial assessment. At posttreatment and 8 months later, the conditions proved to be equally effective (although, intriguingly, the group receiving graded exposure reported the treatment to be more distressing). However, ungraded exposure was clearly superior at the 5-year follow-up assessment: 76% of the patients who received intense exposure, versus 35% of those who received graded exposure, reported themselves to be completely free of symptoms. When 104 subjects were added to the intense exposure format, the same results were obtained. Of the total of 129 subjects, 78% were reportedly completely symptom-free 5 years later. This dramatic set of results suggests that an intense approach can be very beneficial (at least when conducted in a massed format). The extent to which the outcome generalizes to spaced exposure formats, is unknown. We are in the process of testing brief intense exposure paradigms in Boston. In any case, these results raise the possibility that for those who do assent to intense exposure, the outcome is likely to be as effective as that of spaced or graduated exposure, if not more so.

Controlled Escape versus Endurance

Consistent with extinction models of fear reduction, a "golden rule" of *in vivo* exposure has been the continuation of an exposure trial until anxiety is reduced (Marks, 1978). Similarly, the emotional processing model, outlined by Foa and Kozak (1986), posits that long-term fear reduction is dependent upon activation of fearful arousal plus within-session fear reduction. In accord, Marshall (1985) observed substantial benefit from longer periods of exposure, in which time was allowed for complete anxiety reduction. In contrast, Emmelkamp (1982) demonstrated the value of instructing clients to terminate exposure when anxiety reaches "unduly high" levels. Agras, Leitenberg, and Barlow (1968) similarly reported successful results without endurance of high levels of anxiety in feared situations. DeSilva and Rachman (1984) and Rachman, Craske, Tallman, and Solyom (1986) obtained equally effective results, whether participants were allowed to escape exposure tasks when anxiety reached 70 on a 0–100 scale (as long as *escape was followed by immediate return to the situation*) or were instructed to remain in the situation until anxiety peaked and reduced by at least 50%. Interestingly, the escape group reported more perceived control and less fear during exposure than the no-escape group; this suggested that maximal fear elicitation was not essential for therapeutic benefit. These findings combined suggest that fear extinction is not the only pathway though which exposure therapy exerts its therapeutic effects.

The model of therapeutic change described by Bandura (1977, 1988) and Williams (1988) emphasizes performance accomplishment or "self-efficacy," as opposed to fear extinction or habituation. A "guided mastery" approach is taken, which emphasizes the way in which exposure is conducted versus mere approach to a stimulus. Unadaptive, defensive behaviors that inhibit the development of self-efficacy, and that result in performance attribution to protective behaviors instead of personal capabilities, are corrected. For example, clients are taught to drive in a relaxed position at the wheel and to walk across a bridge without holding the rail. This type of guided mastery has been shown to produce more effective results than "stimulus exposure" treatment (Williams, Turner, & Peer, 1985; Williams & Zane, 1989). Moreover, because mastery subjects tended to report the least anxiety during exposure, the results concur with other findings that high levels of fearful arousal are not a prerequisite for fear reduction from exposure.

The "safety signal perspective" (Rachman, 1984) similarly deemphasizes level of anxiety aroused during exposure. Rachman suggested that exposure treatment might be facilitated by incorporating safety signals. For example, instead of entering a supermarket while the therapist waits outside, clients might walk toward the therapist (i.e., the safety signal), who is waiting inside the supermarket. Sartory, Master, and Rachman (1989) compared safety signal exposure ($n = 9$) to standard exposure ($n = 10$) for the treatment of agoraphobia, over the course of four therapist-directed sessions and 2 weeks of self-directed practice. A small advantage was achieved in the safety signal condition, particularly during the self-directed practice phase. Although the results were preliminary, they concur with evidence outlined earlier suggesting that exposure can proceed effectively without eliciting and then habituating relatively high levels of fearful arousal. On the other hand, deliberate reliance on safety signals raises concerns about long-term relapse once those safety signals are removed. Safety signal exposure should be followed by exposure to the same situations without the presence of the safety signal.

Attention versus Distraction

Some believe that exposure is most functional when attention is directed fully toward the phobic object, and when internal and external sources of distraction are minimized (Borkovec, 1976; Foa & Kozak, 1986). Several studies have evaluated the role of distraction in exposure to specific fear objects, but only one study has addressed this issue with respect to PD/PDA. We (Craske et al., 1989) administered therapist-directed and self-directed exposure to patients with agoraphobia in small groups for 11 sessions. In one condition ($n = 16$), clients were instructed to monitor bodily sensations and thoughts objectively throughout *in vivo* exposure, and to use thought stopping and focusing self-statements to interrupt distraction. In a second condition ($n = 14$), clients were taught to use specific distraction tasks during *in vivo* exposures (e.g., word rhymes, spelling, etc.), and to use thought stopping and distracting self-statements to interrupt focusing of attention upon feared bodily sensations and images. The treatment groups did not differ at posttreatment or at follow-up assessment. However, consistent with previous findings for patients with obsessive–compulsive disorder (Grayson, Foa, & Steketee, 1982), the group receiving focused exposure improved significantly from posttreatment to follow-up, in contrast to a slight deterioration in the group receiving distracted exposure. All that being said, however, specifically structured exercises in distraction can be useful for demonstrating the importance of attention and cognition to ongoing levels of anxiety.

EFFICACY OF COGNITIVE-BEHAVIORAL THERAPY

Cognitive-behavioral treatment for panic disorder has proven highly effective. The following summary statistics are derived from all randomized controlled studies (most of which are reviewed above) that report percentages of freedom from panic and of "high end-state" outcome (i.e., no panic, and anxiety within normative ranges), and are based on outcomes from the most effective condition when variants of cognitive-behavioral treatments have been compared. In these studies, 76% of treatment completers are free of panic at posttreatment, as are 78% at follow-up (up to 2 years), after 11 treatment sessions, with a 10% attrition rate. However, outcome estimates based on panic-free status alone may be inflated. Fifty-two percent of patients are free of panic *and* excessive anxiety at posttreatment, as are 66% at follow-up. It is noteworthy that status is maintained or continues to improve over the follow-up interval, after active treatment is terminated. These treatments also significantly improve quality of life (Telch, Schmidt, Jaimez, Jacquin, & Harrington, 1995).

Despite these very promising results, close inspection reveals some caveats. First, the percentage of patients who no longer panic is usually less in samples with higher levels of agoraphobia (Williams & Falbo, 1996). Because most of the studies above have excluded patients with severe agoraphobia, they may overestimate the benefit of cognitive-behavioral therapy for patients with panic disorder as a whole, many of whom have substantial agoraphobia. Also, overall, the results from treatment for agoraphobia are less positive than treatment for PD (without agoraphobia). Controlled outcome studies for agoraphobia that have reported rates of improvement and high end state yield the following summary statistics: After 12 sessions and a 17% attrition rate, 50% show substantial improvement (defined as normative levels of functioning, or mild or less distress across a variety of measures) at posttreatment, as do 59% at follow-up.

Second, tracking the status of each individual patient over time in one study showed that cross-sectional data may misrepresent long-term outcomes. That is, Brown and Barlow (1995) reported that more than one-third of patients who were classified as panic-free 24 months after treatment had experienced a panic attack in the preceding year. Also, 27% of their sample had received additional treatment for panic over the follow-up interval. This suggests considerable return of fear and the value of strategies to minimize return of fear. On the other hand, more favorable results were reported using survival analyses for data from 2 to 9 years after noncognitive, *in vivo* exposure treatment: Only 18.5% of 81 patients who were panic-free after treatment experienced a relapse, defined as meeting criteria for PD/PDA (Fava, Zielezny, Savron, & Grandi, 1995). One possible explanation for this discrepancy is that Brown and Barlow (1995) used more stringent criteria (recurrence of panic attacks, or help seeking) than Fava and colleagues (1995). Nevertheless, this type of longitudinal analysis indicates the potential for a return of panic attacks and the value of relapse prevention plans for (1) minimizing the recurrence of panic, and (2) managing the recurrence of panic in order to minimize full relapse. Ways to minimize the recurrence of panic attacks may be guided by recent theorizing about the context-specific effects of fear extinction, which can be offset by conducting exposure in as many contexts as possible to enhance generalization of nonfearful learning to whatever context in which the stimulus is encountered once treatment is over (Bouton et al., in press; Bouton & Swartzentruber, 1991). Return of fear and panic is more likely if fear reduction is limited to a certain type of context, such as the presence of a therapist. Management of the recurrence of panic to prevent full relapse may be guided by stress inoculation models and decatastrophizing strategies.

Third, most of the outcome studies to date have been conducted in university or research settings, with carefully selected samples (although fewer exclusionary criteria are used in more recent studies). Consequently, of major concern is the degree to which these treatment methods and outcomes are transportable to nonresearch settings, with more severely impaired or otherwise different populations, and with less experienced or trained clinicians. One way to examine this issue is to identify predictors of treatment attrition from research studies. As mentioned previously, attrition from our multisite study of the single and combined effects of imipramine and cognitive-behavioral therapy for PD with relatively mild agoraphobia was predicted by attribution to life stressors and lower education level (as a function of household income) (Grilo et al., 1998). Thus one might expect more attrition from nonresearch than research sites because of lower education levels, and/or more life stressors to which to attribute PD/PDA. Interestingly, severity of illness and comorbidity did not predict attrition in that study. More direct evaluation obviously needs to test these treatments in nonresearch sites. This is exactly what was done by Wade and colleagues (1998), who used a benchmarking strategy to compare their results from a community mental health center with results from research sites. One hundred and ten individuals underwent cognitive-behavioral therapy for PD/PDA, concomitant with psychopharmacotherapy where appropriate. Therapists were trained extensively. As in the multisite study, treatment completion correlated positively with years of education; dropout rates, for reasons other than experimenter exclusion, were similar to those in the multisite study (21% and 26%). (Note that these rates are a little higher than is usually seen in cognitive-behavioral therapy studies, perhaps due to the involvement of medications.) Overall, the percentage of patients who were panic-free and the percentage achieving normative levels of functioning on a variety of measures were comparable to percentages obtained from research sites. The next question to be addressed is whether these treatment results can be obtained in other settings (such as primary care) and with less well-trained therapists.

Effect of Panic Treatment on Agoraphobia

Another very important treatment outcome question concerns the degree to which cognitive-behavioral therapy for panic influences agoraphobia. Does panic-focused treatment alone trickle down to influence agoraphobia, and does the addition of panic-focused treatment improve on the results obtained from *in vivo* exposure therapy? Results pertaining to the first question are limited, although van den Hout, Arntz, and Hoekstra (1994) showed no such benefits for agoraphobia from 4 weeks of cognitive panic-focused therapy. Clearly, however, 4 weeks may have been insufficient. de Ruiter, Rijken, Garssen, and Kraaimaat (1989) found that eight weekly sessions of breathing retraining and cognitive restructuring for panic-related misappraisals was as effective as eight weekly sessions of instruction in self-directed *in vivo* exposure, and as four sessions of each. The same results were obtained at follow-up as well (Rijken, Kraaimaat, de Ruiter, & Garssen, 1992). Furthermore, as mentioned previously, several studies indicate that cognitive therapy for panic misappraisals may be as effective as guided mastery exposure (Hoffart, 1995; Williams & Falbo, 1996) and *in vivo* exposure (Bouchard et al., 1996).

With respect to the second question, several studies find no added benefit for agoraphobia from the addition of cognitive treatments that target fears of bodily sensations (de Ruiter et al., 1989; Rijken et al., 1992; van den Hout et al., 1994; Williams & Falbo, 1996). For example, van den Hout and colleagues (1994) compared four sessions of cognitive therapy, followed by eight sessions of cognitive therapy plus *in vivo* exposure, to four sessions of associative therapy followed by eight sessions of *in vivo* exposure. Cognitive therapy did not potentiate exposure therapy. Also, breathing education, retraining, and repeated interoceptive exposure to hyperventilation did not increase benefits from *in vivo* exposure for agoraphobia (de Beurs, Lange, et al., 1995). On the other hand, Ito, Noshirvani, Basoglu, and Marks (1996) found a trend for those who added interoceptive exposure to their self-directed *in vivo* exposure and breathing retraining to be more likely to achieve at least a 50% improvement in phobic fear and avoidance.

Effect of Treatment for PD/PDA on Comorbid Diagnoses

Recent findings indicate that PD/PDA treatment influences comorbid conditions of anxiety and depression (Brown et al., 1995; Laberge et al., 1993; Tsao, Lewin, & Craske, 1998). In other words, co-occurring symptoms of depression and other anxiety disorders tend to improve after cognitive-behavioral therapy for PD/PDA. Furthermore, in a very exploratory single-case study, abuse of alcohol subsided in all three subjects who underwent cognitive-behavioral treatment for PD/PDA, although one patient later relapsed (Lehman, Brown, & Barlow, 1998). Similarly, for the most part, abnormal personality traits subside after cognitive-behavioral therapy for PD/PDA (see, e.g., Hoffart, 1997; Hoffart & Hedley, 1997; Rathus et al., 1995), and more so than following fluvoxamine treatment (Black et al., 1996).

On the other hand, the benefits for comorbid conditions may lessen over time once treatment is completed (Brown et al., 1995). That is, Brown and colleagues (1995) found that if remission of comorbid conditions was not complete, these conditions tended to return to pretreatment levels by follow-up. In addition, Woody, McLean, Taylor, and Koch (1999) found that reductions in co-occurring diagnoses of depression were no greater after PD/PDA treatment than after a wait-list period. Clearly, more research is needed on this important topic. Nevertheless, extant data suggest that treatment for comorbid conditions should be delayed until completion of PD/PDA treatment, in the event that those comorbid conditions are no longer problematic.

This interesting set of findings regarding comorbid conditions raises questions about mechanisms of action. For example, are all comorbid conditions secondary to panic, and therefore subside once panic is controlled? This seems to be the case for certain comorbid diagnoses, but it is unlikely to explain the entire set of findings. A second possibility is that treatment for PD/PDA teaches skills that are equally therapeutic and applicable to comorbid conditions. Certainly, patients in our treatments frequently comment on their use of cognitive skills for other sources of anxiety. Third, perhaps the treatment for PD/PDA influences core dimensions of psychopathology (such as perceived control or self-efficacy) that contribute to all disorders. Or perhaps all of these factors are operative.

Briefer Treatments for PD/PDA

Most study treatments are conducted individually, with a therapist, over the course of 10 to 20 treatment sessions. Given cost, unavailability of specialized treatment centers, and restrictions on travel, attempts have been made to increase treatment availability through group treatment, self-directed treatment, minimal-therapist-contact treatment, and brief treatment. The data concerning group treatment, minimal-therapist-contact treatment, and self-directed treatment have been described earlier in this chapter.

In terms of brief treatments, Evans and colleagues (1991) compared a 2-day group cognitive-behavioral treatment to a wait-list condition, although without random assignment. The 2-day program consisted of lectures (3 hours); teaching skills such as breathing, relaxation, and cognitive challenging (3 hours); *in vivo* exposure (9 hours); and group discussion, plus a support group of 2 hours for significant others. Eighty-five percent of treated patients were reported to be either symptom-free or symptomatically improved, and these results were maintained 1 year later. In contrast, the wait-list group did not demonstrate significant changes. In a randomized controlled study, we tested condensed cognitive-behavioral therapy for PD/PDA patients who were initially seeking medication treatment (Craske, Maidenberg, & Bystritsky, 1995). Before starting medication, patients were assigned to four weekly sessions of either cognitive-behavioral therapy or supportive nondirective therapy. Cognitive-behavioral therapy was more effective than supportive therapy, particularly with less severely impaired patients, although the results were not as good as those typically seen with more sessions. In contrast, in another uncontrolled study, Westling and Öst (1999) found that four sessions of cognitive-behavioral treatment for patients with PD and only mild or no agoraphobia yielded results comparable to those obtained with the more usual 10 to 15 treatment sessions. The fact that our sample included more agoraphobia may have accounted for the less dramatic results than those reported by Westling and Öst (1999). Finally, Clark and colleagues (1999) treated 43 patients with panic disorder, who were randomly allocated to either standard cognitive therapy, consisting of up to 12 sessions (1 hour each) in the first 3 months, or brief cognitive therapy, where patients were administered 5 sessions and afforded extensive use of between-session self-study modules. Treatments were equally effective, and both produced significantly better results than those from a wait-list control group.

TREATMENT DESCRIPTION: PROTOCOL

Overview

The basic aim of PCT, our treatment protocol for PD/PDA, is to influence directly the catastrophic misappraisal aspect of panic attacks and anxiety, hyperventilatory response, conditioned fear reactions to physical cues, and fear and avoidance of agoraphobic situations. This is done, first, through the provision of accurate information as to the nature of the fight–flight response. By provision of such information, clients are taught that they experience "sensations" and not "panics," and that these sensations are normal and harmless. Second, treatment aims at to identify and challenge aberrant, anxious beliefs. Next, specific information concerning the effects of hyperventilation and its role in panic attacks is provided, with extensive practice of breathing retraining. Then repeated exposure to feared internal cues is conducted to lessen fear and to practice cognitive and breathing strategies. *In vivo* exposure to feared and avoided situations is then included for any remaining agoraphobia. Notice that we have taken the approach of treating panic before agoraphobia, given the evidence described earlier.

Session 1

The goals of Session 1 are to describe anxiety, provide a treatment rationale and treatment description, and emphasize the importance of self-monitoring and homework practices between treatment sessions. Therapy begins with identifying anxiety patterns and the situations in which anxiety and panic attacks are likely to occur. Many clients have difficulty identifying specific antecedents, reporting that panic can occur at almost any time. Therapists help clients to identify internal triggers, specifically negative verbal cognitions, catastrophic imagery, and physical sensations. The following interchange took place between Jane (who represents a composite of actual interactions from several cases) and her therapist (J and T, respectively):

T: In what situations are you most likely to panic?

J: Crowded restaurants and when I'm driving on the freeway. But sometimes I am driving along, feeling OK, when all of a sudden it hits. And other times I can be sitting at home feeling quite relaxed and it just hits. That's when I really get scared, because I can't explain it.

T: So when you are driving on the freeway, what is the very first thing you notice that tells you you're about to panic?

J: Well, the other cars on the road look as if they are moving really slowly.

T: And what is the first thing you notice when you're at home?

J: An unreal feeling, like I'm floating.

T: So it sounds like the panic attacks that seem to occur for no reason are actually tied in with the sensations of unreality or when things look as if they are moving in slow motion.

J: I guess so. I always thought the physical feelings were the panic attack, but maybe they start the panic attack.

Next, the three-response system model for describing and understanding anxiety and panic is introduced. This model contributes to an objective self-awareness—to a client's becoming a personal scientist—and provides the groundwork for an alternative conceptual framework for explaining panic and anxiety to replace the client's own misassumptions. Clients are asked to describe cognitive, physiological, and behavioral aspects to their responding: to identify the things that they *feel*, *think*, and *do* when they are anxious and panicky. Differences between the response profiles of anxiety and panic are highlighted. For example, the cognitive component in general anxiety involves worrying about future events, whereas the cognitive component in panic involves worrying about immediate danger; the behavioral component in general anxiety consists of avoidance, caution, agitation and fidgeting, whereas the behavioral component in panic involves escape; the physiological component in general anxiety involves muscular tension, whereas the physiological component in panic involves palpitations and other symptoms of autonomic arousal. After a client has grasped the notion of three response systems that are partially independent, interactions among the response systems are described. The client is asked to describe the three response components in a recent panic attack and to identify ways in which they interacted to produce heightened distress, as in this example:

T: How would you describe the three components of the panic attack you had at home last week?

J: Well, physically, my head felt really light, and my hands were clammy. I thought that either I would pass out or that I would somehow dissolve into nothingness. My behavior was to lie down and call my husband, who was at work.

T: Now what was the very first thing you noticed?

J: When I stood up, my head started to feel really weird . . . as if it was spinning inside.

T: What was your very next reaction to that feeling?

J: I held onto the chair. I thought something was wrong . . . I thought it could get worse and that I'd collapse.

T: So it began with a physical sensation, and then you had some very specific thoughts about those sensations. What happened next?

J: I felt very anxious.

T: And what happened next?

J: Well, the dizziness seemed to be getting worse and worse. I became really concerned that it was different from any other experience I had ever had. I was convinced that this was "it."

T: So as you became more anxious, the physical feelings and the thoughts that something bad was going to happen intensified. What did you do next?

J: I called my husband and lay on the bed until he came home. It was horrible.

T: Can you see how one reaction fed off another, creating a cycle? That it began with a sensation, then some scary thoughts, then feeling anxious, then more sensations and more thoughts, and more fear, and so on? Now if we had interrupted the cycle earlier on by preventing the scary thoughts from coming into your mind, the anxiety and fear would not have developed.

Reasons why panic attacks first began are addressed briefly. Clients are informed that understanding the reasons why they began to panic is not necessary in order to benefit from the treatment, because the factors involved in onset are not necessarily the same as the factors involved in the maintenance of a problem. Nevertheless, the initial panic attack is described as a manifestation of anxiety/stress. The stressors surrounding the time of the first panic attack are explored with each client, particularly in terms of how they may have increased levels of physical arousal and primed certain danger-laden cognitive schemas.

The first session ends with a full treatment rationale and description. In response to this information, Jane became highly anxious about the possibility of becoming anxious. She felt unable to tolerate either the treatment procedures or her anticipation of them. She became very agitated in the office and reported feelings of unreality. She opened the office door to find her husband, who was waiting outside. The therapist then helped Jane understand how the cycle of panic had emerged in the current situation: (1) The trigger was the treatment description—eventually having to face feared sensations and situations; (2) this was anxiety-producing because Jane believed that she could not cope with the treatment demands, that the treatment would cause her so much anxiety that she would "flip out" and lose touch with reality permanently, or that she would never improve because she could not tolerate the treatment; (3) the current anxiety in the office elicited sensations of unreality and a racing heart; (4) Jane began to worry that she might panic and lose touch with reality permanently within the next few minutes; (5) the more anxious she felt, and the stronger her attempts to escape and find safety became, the stronger the physical sensations became; (5) she felt some relief upon finding her husband, because his presence reassured her that she would be safe. Jane was reassured that treatment would progress at a pace at which she was comfortable, but at the same time she was helped to understand that her acute distress over the notion of unreality was the exact target of this type of treatment and therefore attested to the relevance of this treatment for her. She was also calmed by preliminary cognitive restructuring of the probability of permanently losing touch with reality. After a lengthy discussion, Jane became more receptive to treatment. A team approach to treatment planning and progress was agreed upon, so that Jane did not feel that she would be forced to do things she did not think she could do.

The homework for this session entails self-monitoring, using the forms described earlier to enhance objective self-awareness. Clients are asked to monitor their fear and anxiety, keeping in mind the three-response system described in this session. As mentioned above, Jane became concerned that self-monitoring would only elevate her distress by reminding of the very thing she was afraid of (panic and unreality). The therapist clarified the difference between objective and subjective self-monitoring, and explained that distress would subside as Jane persevered with self-monitoring.

Session 2

The goals of this session are to describe the physiology underlying anxiety and panic and the concepts of hypervigilance and interoceptive conditioning. Basically, this session develops the first session's goals of an objective self-awareness and an alternative conceptual model. Clients are given a detailed handout (see Figure 1.4) to read after the session is over. The handout summarizes the didactic portion of the treatment.

The main concepts covered in this educational phase are (1) the survival value or protective function of anxiety and panic; (2) the physiological basis to the various sensations experienced during panic and anxiety, and the survival function of the underlying physiology; and (3) the role of specific learned and cognitively mediated fears of certain bodily sensations. The model of panic described earlier in this chapter is explained. In particular, the concepts of misappraisals and interoceptive conditioning are explained as accounting for panic attacks that seem to occur from "out of the blue"—that are triggered by very subtle internal cues or physical sensations that may occur at any time. Not only does this information reduce anxiety by decreasing uncertainty about panic attacks, but it enhances the credibility of the subsequent treatment procedures.

This session was very important for Jane, because the inability to explain her panic attacks was a very big source of distress. Here are some of the questions she asked in her attempt to understand more fully.

J: So if I understand you correctly, you're saying that my panic attacks are the same as the fear I experienced the time we found a burglar in our house. It doesn't feel the same at all.

T: Yes, those two emotional states—an unexpected panic attack and fear when confronted with a burglar—are essentially the same. However, in the case of the burglar, where were you focusing your attention—on the burglar or on the way you were feeling?

J: The burglar, of course, although I did notice my heart was going a mile a minute.

T: And when you have a panic attack, where are you focusing your attention—on the people around you or on the way you are feeling?

J: Well, mostly on the way I'm feeling, although it depends on where I am at the time.

T: Being most concerned about what's going on inside you can lead to a very different type of experience than being concerned about the burglar, even though basically the same physiological response is occurring. For example, remember our descrip-

Anxiety and panic are natural emotional states (reactions) that are experienced by everyone. They are part of the experience of being human. Anxiety is the reaction that all people have whenever they think that something bad or threatening could happen. These threatening things include physical threat, such as the possibility of illness, accident, or death; social threat, such as the possibility of embarrassment, rejection, or ridicule; or mental threat, such as the possibility of going crazy, losing control, or losing one's mental faculties.

Scientifically, immediate or short-term anxiety (i.e., panic attack) is named the *fight–flight response*. It is so named because all of its effects are aimed toward the organism's either fighting or fleeing from danger. Thus, the number one purpose of panic is to protect humans from danger. When humans' ancestors lived in caves, it was vital that when they were faced with danger, an automatic response took over, causing them to take immediate action (attack or run). Even in today's hectic world, this fight–flight response is a necessary mechanism. Just imagine if a person were crossing a street when a car suddenly sped toward him or her with its horn blasting. If the person experienced absolutely no anxiety, he or she would be killed. What actually happens is that the person's fight–flight response takes over and he or she runs out of the way. The moral of this story is a simple one—the purpose of panic is to protect humans, not to harm them. It is a human survival mechanism. To panic means to be fit for survival.

When the body detects danger, the brain sends messages to a section of the nerves called the autonomic nervous system. The autonomic nervous system has two subsections or branches called the sympathetic nervous system and the parasympathetic nervous system. These two branches of the nervous system are directly involved in controlling the body's energy levels and preparation for action. Very simply put, the sympathetic nervous system is the fight–flight system, which releases energy and readies the body for action (fighting or fleeing). The parasympathetic nervous system is the restoring system, which returns the body to a normal state. Activation of the sympathetic nervous system is believed to cause most panic attack symptoms.

An important point is that the sympathetic nervous system tends to be an all-or-none system. When it is activated, all of its parts respond. This characteristic may explain why most panic attacks involve many physical symptoms, not just one or two. In addition, the sympathetic nervous system responds immediately, as soon as danger is close at hand (e.g., think of the rush that you experience when you think another car on the freeway is about to hit you). This characteristic is the reason that the physical symptoms of panic attacks can occur almost instantaneously, within seconds.

The sympathetic nervous system releases two chemicals—adrenaline and noradrenaline from the adrenal glands attached to the kidneys. These chemicals, in turn, are used as messengers by the sympathetic nervous system to continue activity so that once activity begins, it often continues and increases for some time. However, it is very important to know that the activity of the sympathetic nervous system is stopped in two ways. First, other chemicals in the body eventually destroy the chemical messengers adrenaline and noradrenaline. Second, the parasympathetic nervous system (which generally has effects that oppose those of the sympathetic nervous system) becomes activated and restores a relaxed feeling. Eventually, the body will "have enough" of the fight–flight response and will activate the parasympathetic nervous system to restore a relaxed feeling. In other words, panic can neither continue forever nor spiral to ever-increasing and damaging levels. The parasympathetic nervous system is a built-in protector that prevents the sympathetic nervous system from getting "carried away."

Another important point is that the chemical messengers, adrenaline and noradrenaline, take some time to be fully destroyed. Thus, even after the sympathetic nervous system has stopped responding, the person is likely to feel keyed up or on edge for some time because the chemicals are still "floating" around in the person's system. This lingering excitement is perfectly natural and harmless. In fact, there is a purpose to this lingering effect—in the wilds, danger often returns. Thus, remaining in a keyed-up state helps the human quickly reactivate the fight–flight response if danger returns.

Activity in the sympathetic nervous system increases the heart rate and the strength of the heartbeat. These effects are vital to the body's preparation for action (to fight or flee) because they speed up the blood flow and thus improve delivery of oxygen to the tissues and removal of waste products from the tissues. Oxygen is needed by the muscle tissues as a source of energy for fighting or fleeing. Thus, a racing or pounding heart is typically experienced during periods of high anxiety or panic.

(cont.)

FIGURE 1.4. Handout describing the physiology and psychology of anxiety and panic (Session 2). From Barlow and Craske (2000). Copyright 2000 by Graywind Publications Inc. and the Psychological Corporation. Reprinted by permission.

Blood flow also changes. Basically, blood is taken away from the places where it is not needed (by a constriction, or tightening, of the blood vessels) and is directed toward the places where it is needed more (by an expansion of the blood vessels). For example, blood is taken away from the skin, fingers, and toes. This effect is useful. Consider, again, our human ancestors. The extremities were the most likely parts of the body to be attacked and injured. Having less blood flow to these parts reduced the possibility of bleeding to death. As a result of this effect, the skin looks pale and feels cold, especially around the hands and feet. Instead, the blood goes to the large muscles, such as the thighs, heart, and biceps, which need the oxygen for fighting or fleeing. That is, the big muscles are the most important for running or fighting.

The fight–flight response also affects the rate of breathing. Breathing becomes faster and deeper because the body needs more oxygen to be able to fight or flee. Oxygen is a source of energy for the muscle tissues. Sometimes, however, breathing can become unbalanced and cause harmless but unpleasant symptoms, such as breathlessness, choking or smothering feelings, and pains or tightness in the chest. Also, the blood supply to the head may be decreased. Although the amount of decrease is small and is not at all dangerous, it produces unpleasant (but harmless) symptoms, including dizziness, blurred vision, confusion, feeling of unreality (or feeling as if you are in a dream state), and hot flushes. Again, the protective physical changes produce physical symptoms that might be uncomfortable but that are not at all harmful or a sign that something is seriously wrong.

The fight–flight response increases sweating. Sweating cools the body to prevent it from overheating and thus allows the person to continue fighting or fleeing from danger without collapsing from heat. Excessive sweating also makes the skin slippery so that it is more difficult for a predator to grasp. Thus, perspiration is a common symptom of anxiety and panic.

The pupils (the black center of the eyes) widen (dilate) to let in more light. This effect helps the person to scan the environment for whatever is dangerous and to have more sensitive vision. Panic and anxiety are reactions to the perception of threat. Therefore, if something threatening or dangerous is expected, the body increases the person's field of vision so that the threat of danger can be seen. At the same time, the change in the pupils may cause other symptoms, such as blurred vision, "spots" in front of the eyes, or sensitivity to bright lights.

Another physical effect is a decrease in salivation, resulting in a dry mouth. In fact, the whole digestive system slows so that energy that would be required for food digestion can be redirected to the muscles that are needed to fight or flee. This effect often causes nausea and heavy feelings in the stomach. It sometimes also causes diarrhea so that material that might "weigh down" the body while the person is attempting to fight or flee is evacuated.

Also, many of the muscle groups tense in preparation for fight or flight. This effect results in feelings of tension and sometimes actual aches and pains as well as trembling and shaking. Another interesting effect is the release of natural analgesics (or painkillers) from the brain so that the body is less likely to feel pain when the person is afraid. Obviously, the purpose of this effect is to enable the person to continue fighting or fleeing from danger even when injured. That is, the pain does not stop the person from fleeing or fighting. Related to this effect is a release of coagulants and lymphocytes into the blood, which help in sealing wounds and in repairing damaged tissue. In addition, the spleen contracts so that more red blood cells are released to carry more oxygen, and the liver releases stored sugar so that the muscles have more sugar available as a source of energy.

Finally, because the fight–flight response produces a general activation of the whole body and because this activation takes a great amount of energy, the person generally feels tired, drained, and "washed out" afterward.

The fight–flight response is very understandable if a person is attacked, trapped in an elevator, scheduled for major surgery, or experiencing any other major stress. Why does the fight–flight response occur where there is nothing to fear, when there is no obvious danger? A panic attack is a normal bodily response to fear. The response is abnormal when it occurs at the wrong time, that is, when there is no real reason to be afraid.

As mentioned earlier, people who have panic attacks are apparently frightened by the physical symptoms of fear. In other words, panic attacks represent *fear of fear*. A panic attack follows a typical sequence. First, unexpected physical sensations are experienced (they are unexpected because they cannot be explained by any real, imminent danger). Second, those physical sensations themselves are feared.

Unexpected Physical Sensations + Fear of Physical Sensations = Panic

(*cont.*)

The second part of the sequence is easy to understand. As discussed earlier, the emergency, fight–flight response causes the brain to search for danger. Sometimes an obvious threat cannot be found, as is usually the case of panic attacks that seem to occur for no reason or from out of the blue. Most people, however, cannot accept having no explanation. When an explanation cannot be found, the search may be turned inward. In other words, "If there is nothing to explain my feelings of panic and anxiety, then there must be something wrong with me." Then, the brain invents an explanation such as "I must be dying, losing control, or going crazy." Nothing could be further from the truth, because the purpose of the fight–flight response is to protect the organism, not to harm it. Unfortunately, these types of scary thoughts about the physical symptoms of panic only contribute to a negative, snowballing cycle of more physical feelings, scary thougths, and behaviors of panic. This cycle is referred to as fear of fear.

Why does a person have the physical symptoms of the emergency, fight–flight response if he or she is not frightened? There are many reasons. One reason is stress. Stress from work pressures, rushing to appointments, relationships, or other life events can lead to an increase in the production of adrenaline and other chemicals. This response is the body's way of staying alert and prepared to deal with the stress. However, these stress effects can cause physical symptoms that are similar to the symptoms of panic.

A second reason is anxiety about panic. Anxious anticipation of anything contributes to higher levels of physical tension and, thus, to more physical symptoms of stress. Also, anxiety causes a person to focus attention on whatever he or she is anxious about. For example, anticipating a plane crash leads to an acute focus on the noises or vibrations in an airplane. In the case of panic, the attention becomes focused on physical sensations. The person scans the body for unusual physical sensations and detects physical symptoms that might not have been noticed otherwise. Thus, anxiety about having panic attacks causes more symptoms of panic and more attention to those symptoms. Consequently, anxiety about panic causes more of the very things that the person with panic disorder is afraid of and, therefore, more panic attacks.

A third reason is normal physical sensations that happen to everyone, all of the time. These are related to interoceptive conditioning [i.e., learning by negative association to become afraid of internal sensations], discussed previously. Conditioning follows a principle called *stimulus generalization*. According to this principle, stimuli that are similar to the primary stimulus can also cause a learned fear reaction. An example is a person's fear of closed-in situations that developed after being locked in a small attic as a child. Through stimulus generalization, the fear can generalize to similar situations, such as elevators, tunnels, restrooms, and small cars. Similarly, fears of the physical symptoms of the emergency, fight–flight response (e.g., racing heart) can generalize to other physical sensations (e.g., head pain). For example, people with panic disorder are commonly fearful of caffeine, exercise, hunger, hot or humid weather conditions, anger and excitement, fatigue, and so on. All of these activities and conditions produce physical symptoms that are similar to those experienced during panic.

In summary, panic is based on the emergency, fight–flight response, the primary purpose of which is to activate the organism and protect it from harm. Everyone is capable of this response when confronted with danger, whether real or perceived. Associated with this response are a number of physical sensations, thoughts, and behaviors. When physical symptoms occur in the absence of an obvious explanation, people often misinterpret the normal emergency symptoms as an indication of a serious physical or mental problem. In this case, the physical symptoms themselves can become threatening and can trigger the emergency response again.

Many people believe that the physical symptoms of fear or panic mean they are going crazy. They are most likely referring to the severe mental disorder known as schizophrenia. A brief description of schizophrenia reveals how unlikely this mistaken belief is. Schizophrenia is a major disorder characterized by severe symptoms such as disjointed thoughts and speech (e.g., rapid shifting from one topic to the next), sometimes extending to speech that does not make any sense; delusions or strange beliefs; and hallucinations. A person's believing that he or she receives messages from outer space is an example of a delusion. Hearing conversations when no one is around is an example of an hallucination.

Schizophrenia generally begins very gradually, not suddenly as does a panic attack. Also, because schizophrenia runs in families and has a strong genetic base, only a certain proportion of the population can become schizophrenic; in other people, no amount of stress will cause the disorder. A third important point is that people who become schizophrenic usually exhibit some mild symptoms

(cont.)

FIGURE 1.4. (*cont.*)

for most of their lives (such as unusual thoughts or little concern about personal hygiene). If these ongoing symptoms have not been noticed, then the chances are that the person will not become schizophrenic, especially if the person is over 25 years of age, because schizophrenia generally first appears in the late teens to early twenties. Finally, if a person has been through interviews with a psychologist or psychiatrist, the doctor would certainly have diagnosed schizophrenia if that were the case.

Some people believe they will lose control when they panic. They usually mean that they will become totally paralyzed and not able to move or that they will not know what they are doing and will run around wildly, hurting people, yelling obscenities, or embarrassing themselves. Others may not know what to expect but just experience an overwhelming feeling that something bad is going to happen.

From earlier discussions, you know the source of this feeling. During panic attacks, the entire body is ready for action and the person experiences an overwhelming desire to escape (called the fight–flight response). The fight–flight response, however, does not compel a person to hurt people who are not a threat and does not produce paralysis. Rather, the entire response is designed to get the person away from potential danger. There has never been a recorded case of someone going "wild" during a panic. Even though panic attacks can make a person feel somewhat confused and unreal, he or she is still able to think and function. In fact, most people are probably able to think faster and are actually physically stronger and have quicker reflexes. The same kinds of things happen when people are in real emergencies. For example, mothers and fathers have accomplished amazing things (such as lifting extremely heavy objects) and overcome their own intense fears in order to save their children.

Many people believe that their nerves might become exhausted and that they might collapse. As discussed earlier, panic is based on activity in the sympathetic nervous system, which is then counteracted by the parasympathetic nervous system. The parasympathetic nervous system is, in a sense, a safeguard to protect against the possibility that the sympathetic nervous system may become "worn out." Nerves are not like electrical wires, and anxiety cannot wear out, damage, or use up the nerves.

Many people mistake the symptoms of panic as signs of heart attack, probably because they lack knowledge about heart attacks. An examination of the symptoms of heart disease reveals their differences from those of panic attacks. The major symptoms of heart disease are breathlessness, chest pain, and occasional palpitations and fainting. The symptoms in heart disease are generally directly related to effort. That is, the harder one exercises, the more severe the symptoms become; the less one exercises, the less severe the symptoms become. The symptoms of heart disease usually go away fairly quickly with rest. This last characteristic is very different from the symptoms of panic attacks, which often occur at rest and seem to have a "mind of their own." Certainly, panic symptoms can occur and even intensify during exercise, but unlike the symptoms of a heart attack, panic symptoms occur equally often at rest. Of most importance, heart disease almost always produces major electrical changes in the heart, which are detected by an electrocardiogram (EKG) recording. In panic attacks, the only change that an EKG detects is an increase in heart rate. In an of itself, increased heart rate is not at all dangerous, unless it reaches extremely high rates (or more than 180 beats per minute). Thus, if a person has had an EKG and the doctor has given him or her the "all clear," he or she can safely assume that heart disease is not the cause of his or her symptoms.

---

tion of the way in which fear of sensations can intensify the sensations.

J: But what about the feelings of unreality? How can they be protective, or how can feeling unreal help me deal with a danger situation?

T: OK, remember that it's the physiological events that are protective—not the sensations—the sensations are just the end result of those events. Now feelings of unreality can be caused by changes in your blood flow to your brain (although not dangerously so), or by overbreathing, or by concentrating too intensely on what's going on inside you. So the unreality sensation may not be protective, but the changes in blood flow and overbreathing are.

J: I understand how I can create a panic attack by being afraid of my bodily feelings, like my heart racing or feeling unreal. But sometimes it happens so quickly that I don't have time to think.

T: Yes, these reactions can occur very quickly, at times automatically. But remember, we are tuned to react instantaneously to things (including our own bodies) that we think mean danger. Picture yourself walking through a jungle. Let's say that after about half an hour of relaxed walking, you are informed that a lion has been seen nearby. Now your attention shifts dramatically to anything that suggests the possibility of a lion, such as noises in the bushes, or branches moving. And when the noises are heard or the branches move, your reaction is extraordinarily fast. Well, the same thing happens with panic—but now it's the physical sensations that are the signals instead of the branches and noises in the jungle, and now it's the belief that you'll lose touch with reality permanently that is the danger instead of the lion.

The homework for this session is to continue the development of an alternative conceptual framework and an objective versus subjective self-awareness. This is achieved through self-monitoring of panics (keeping in mind the principles discussed to date) and rereading of the handout. In fact, we encourage patients to reread the handout several times, and to engage actively in the material by circling or marking the most personally relevant sections and so on. This is based on the notion that effort in learning enhances long-term retention of the material learned. Of course, for some patients, reading of the material draws their attention to things of which they are afraid (just as self-monitoring can do). Aside from providing an explanation for why that occurs, and assigning clients to read sections at a time rather than all at once, therapists reassure clients that anxiety will subside as they persist in reading the material.

Session 3

The primary goal of the third session is to begin breathing control. Clients are asked to hyperventilate voluntarily by standing and breathing fast and deep, as if blowing up a balloon, for 1½ minutes. With prompting and encouragement from the therapist, clients can often complete the full 1½ minutes, after which time they are asked to sit, close their eyes, and breathe very slowly, pausing at the end of each breath, until the symptoms have abated. The experience is then discussed in terms of the degree to which it produced symptoms similar to those that occur naturally during anxiety or panic. Approximately 50%–60% of clients report close similarity of the symptoms. Often, however, similarity of the symptoms is confused with similarity of the anxiety. Because the exercise is conducted in a safe environment, and the symptoms have an obvious cause, most clients rate the expe-

rience as less anxiety-provoking than if the same symptoms had occurred naturally. This distinction is important to make, because it demonstrates the significance of perceived safety for the degree of anxiety experienced. Jane rated the hyperventilation exercise as very anxiety-provoking (6 on a 0–8 scale), and rated the symptoms as being quite similar to her panic symptoms (5.5 on a 0–8 point scale). She terminated the task after approximately 40 seconds, in anticipation of experiencing a full-blown panic attack. This experience was discussed in terms of the three response systems and the role of misappraisals and interoceptive conditioning described in Session 2.

The next phase of breathing retraining is education about the physiological basis to hyperventilation. As before, the goal of the didactic presentation is to allay misinterpretations of the dangers of overbreathing, and to provide a factual information base upon which to draw when actively challenging misinterpretations. The educational content is shown in Figure 1.5 in protocol format, although it should be tailored to the client's own educational level.

The next step is to teach breathing control, which begins by learning to rely more on the diaphragm (abdomen) than on the chest muscles. In addition, clients are instructed to concentrate on their breathing, by counting on their inhalations, and thinking the word "relax" on exhalations. (Slow breathing is introduced in the next session.) Therapists model the suggested breathing patterns, and then provide corrective feedback to clients while they practice in the office setting.

Breathing control is a skill that requires considerable practice before it can be successfully applied to manage episodes of high anxiety or panic. In addition, initial reactions to the exercise can be negative for clients who are afraid of respiratory sensations, because the exercise directs their attention to breathing, or for clients who are chronic overbreathers and for whom any interruption of habitual breathing patterns initially increases respiratory symptomatology. In both cases, continued practice is advisable, with reassurance that sensations such as shortness of breath are not harmful. Finally, the integration of breathing control techniques and cognitive strategies is emphasized. On occasion, clients mistakenly view breathing control as

The body needs oxygen in order to survive. Whenever a person inhales, oxygen is taken into the lungs where it is picked up by the haemoglobin (the "oxygen-sticky" chemical in blood). The haemoglobin carries the oxygen around the body where it is released for use by the body's cells. The cells use the oxygen in their energy reactions, subsequently producing a by-product of carbon dioxide (CO_2) which is, in turn, released back to the blood, transported to the lungs, and exhaled.

Efficient control of the body's energy reactions depends on the maintenance of a specific balance between oxygen and CO_2. This balance can be maintained chiefly through an appropriate rate and depth of breathing. Obviously, breathing "too much" will have the effect of increasing levels of oxygen (in the blood only) and decreasing levels of CO_2, while breathing too little will have the effect of decreasing levels of oxygen and increasing levels of CO_2. The appropriate rate of breathing, at rest, is usually around 10–14 breaths per minute.

Hyperventilation is defined as a rate and depth of breathing which is too much for the body's needs at a particular point in time. Naturally, if the need for oxygen and the production of CO_2 both increase (such as during exercise), breathing should increase appropriately. Alternately, if the need for oxygen and the production of CO_2 both decrease (such as during relaxation), breathing should decrease appropriately.

While most of the body's mechanisms are controlled by "automatic" chemical and physical means (and breathing is no exception), breathing has an additional property of being able to be put under voluntary control. For example, it is quite easy for us to hold our breath (swimming under water) or speed up our breathing (blowing up a balloon). Therefore, a number of "non-automatic" factors such as emotion, stress, or habit can cause us to increase our breathing. These factors may be especially important in people who suffer panic attacks causing a tendency to breathe too much.

Interestingly, while most of us consider oxygen to be the determining factor in our breathing, the body actually uses CO_2 as its "marker" for appropriate breathing. The most important effect of hyperventilation, then, is to produce a marked drop in CO_2. This, in turn, produces a drop in the acid content of the blood leading to what is known as alkaline blood. It is these two effects—a decrease in blood CO_2 content and an increase in blood alkalinity—which are responsible for most of the physical changes that occur during hyperventilation.

One of the most important changes produced by hyperventilation is a constriction or narrowing of certain blood vessels around the body. In particular the blood going to the brain is somewhat decreased. Coupled together with this tightening of blood vessels is the fact that the haemoglobin increases its "stickiness" for oxygen. Thus, not only does less blood reach certain areas of the body, but the oxygen carried by this blood is less likely to be released to the tissues. Paradoxically, then, while overbreathing means more oxygen is taken in, less oxygen reaches certain areas of our brain and body. This effect results in two broad categories of symptoms: 1) centrally, some symptoms are produced by the slight reduction in oxygen to certain parts of the brain (including, dizziness, lightheadedness, confusion, breathlessness, blurred vision, and unreality); 2) peripherally, some symptoms are produced by the slight reduction in oxygen to certain parts of the body (including, an increase in heartbeat to pump more blood around, numbness and tingling in the extremities, cold clammy hands, and sometimes stiffness of muscles). It is important to remember that the reductions in oxygen are slight and are totally harmless. It is important, too, to note that hyperventilating (possibly through a reduction in oxygen to certain parts of the brain) can produce a feeling of breathlessness, sometimes extending to feelings of choking or smothering, so that it actually feels as if the person is not getting enough air.

Hyperventilation is also responsible for a number of overall effects. First the act of overbreathing is hard physical work. Hence, the individual may often feel hot, flushed and sweaty. In addition, because it is hard work to overbreathe, prolonged periods will often result in tiredness and exhaustion. Third, people who overbreathe often tend to breathe from their chest rather than their diaphragm. This means that their chest muscles tend to become tired and tense. Thus, they can experience symptoms of chest tightness or even severe chest pains. Finally, many people who overbreathe tend to engage in a habit of repeatedly sighing or yawning. These tics are actually forms of hyperventilation since whenever one yawns or sighs they are "dumping" a large quantity of CO_2 very quickly. Therefore, when combating the problem, it is important to become aware of habitual sighing and yawning and to try and suppress these habits.

One important point to be made about hyperventilation is that it need not necessarily be obvious to the observer. In many cases hyperventilation can be very subtle. This is especially true if the individual has been slightly overbreathing for a long period of time. In this case there can be marked

(cont.)

FIGURE 1.5. Handout describing the physiology of overbreathing (Session 3). From Barlow and Craske (2000). Copyright 2000 by Graywind Publications Inc. and the Psychological Corporation. Reprinted by permission.

drop in CO_2 but, due to compensation in the body, relatively little change in alkalinity. Thus, symptoms will not be produced. However, because CO_2 levels are kept low, the body loses its ability to cope with changes in CO_2 so that even a slight change in breathing (e.g., through a yawn) can be enough to suddenly trigger symptoms. This may account for the sudden nature of many panic attacks, as often occurs during sleep, and is one reason why many sufferers report "I don't feel as if I'm hyperventilating."

Probably the most important point to be made about hyperventilation is that it is not dangerous. Hyperventilation is an integral part of the fight/flight response and thus its purpose is to protect the body from danger, not to be dangerous. The changes associated with hyperventilation are those which prepare the body for action in order to escape potential harm. Thus, it is an automatic reaction for the brain to immediately expect danger and for the individual to feel the urge to escape. Consequently, it is perfectly understandable, if there is no obvious danger, for the sufferer to believe the danger must be internal. Nevertheless, this is not so. It is important to remember that far from being harmful, hyperventilation is part of a natural, biological response aimed at protecting the body from harm.

---

a way of relieving themselves of terrifying symptoms, thus falling into the trap of fearing dire consequences should they not succeed in correcting their breathing. This was what happened for Jane, as shown below.

J: So all I have to do is to slow down my breathing and then everything will be OK?

T: Certainly, slowing down your breathing will help to control the physical symptoms that you feel, but I am not sure what you mean when you ask whether everything will be OK.

J: That proper breathing will prevent me from losing touch with reality—that I won't disappear.

T: Remember, no matter whether you breathe slowly or quickly, from your chest or from your abdomen, you will not disappear. In other words, it is a misinterpretation to think that the sense of unreality means that you are permanently losing touch with reality or that you will disappear. Breathing control will help you to feel more relaxed and therefore be less likely to feel the sense of unreality, but the sense of unreality is not a sign of actual loss of touch with reality and disappearance.

The homework for this session consists of continued self-monitoring, and practice of abdominal breathing at least two times a day, at least 10 minutes each time.

Session 4

The goals of this session are to develop breathing control, and to begin active cognitive re-structuring. The therapist reviews the client's week of breathing control practice. Jane was disappointed with her attempts to control her breathing.

J: I just didn't seem to be able to do it the right way. Sometimes I would start off OK and then the more I tried, the more it felt like I was running out of air, and I'd have to take a big gulp between breaths. At other times, I felt dizzy and the unreal feelings would start, at which point I would stop the breathing and try to do "busy work" to keep my mind occupied.

T: It sounds like quite a few things were going on. First of all, remember that this is a skill, just like learning to ride a bike, and you cannot expect it to be easy from the get-go. Second, it sounds like you experienced some uncomfortable physical symptoms that worried you. You said it felt like you were running out of air. Based on what we talked about last week, what do you think might have caused that feeling?

J: Well, maybe I wasn't getting enough air into my lungs, because it's really hard for me to use my diaphragm muscle. I felt like I was suffocating myself.

T: Possibly it's just a matter of learning to use the diaphragm muscle, but were you really suffocating, or was it an interpretation that you might be suffocating?

J: I don't know . . . I've had the feeling of suffocating before, especially when I'm trapped in a crowded room.

T: So how do you know you were suffocating?

J: I don't know . . . it just felt that way.

T: So let's put all of the evidence together. You've had the feelings before and never suffocated. In fact, a lot of people have those feelings, and they do not actually suffocate. As we talked about last time, changing your breathing or becoming anxious can sometimes create a sensation of shortness of breath, even though you are getting plenty of air. Finally, the exercise was forcing you to concentrate on those feelings. On the basis of all of these facts, can you think of an alternative explanation?

J: Well, maybe I wasn't suffocating; maybe it just felt like that. I hope it doesn't always feel that way.

T: As you relax with the procedure, and realize that the sensations of dizziness or shortness of breath are not going to hurt you, and as you become more skilled at diaphragmatic and slow breathing, it will get easier.

Jane's complaints represent typical concerns that should be addressed. The next step is to slow the rate of breathing until the client can comfortably span a full inhalation and exhalation cycle over 6 seconds. Again, the therapist models and then provides corrective feedback as practice is conducted in the session. Clients are instructed to practice slow breathing in "safe" or relaxing environments. They are discouraged from applying slow breathing when anxious or panicking until they are fully skilled in its application.

Cognitive restructuring is introduced by explaining that errors in thinking can occur for anyone who is anxious, thus helping the client to expect his/her thinking to be distorted. This is because, like the physiological elements, the cognitive elements of fear and anxiety reflect adaptive and protective processes; chances of survival are greater if we perceive danger as probable and worthy of attention than if we minimize danger. Therefore, anxiety leads us to judge threatening events as being more likely and more threatening than they really are. However, the cognitive distortions are unnecessary, because there is no real threat in the case of panic disorder.

Then clients are taught to treat their thoughts as hypotheses or guesses rather than as facts. The notions of automatic thinking

and discrete predictions are explained also, to emphasize the need to become an astute observer of one's own habitual self-statements in each situation. This leads to a "downward arrow technique" to identify specific predictions made at any given moment, as shown with Jane.

T: What is it that scared you about feeling detached in the movie theater last night?

J: It is just such a horrible feeling.

T: What makes it so horrible?

J: I can't tolerate it.

T: What makes you think you cannot tolerate it? What is the feeling of detachment going to do to you that makes you think it is horrible and intolerable?

J: It might get to be so intense that it overwhelms me.

T: And if it overwhelms you, what would happen?

J: I could become so distressed that I lose touch with reality.

T: What would it mean if you lost touch with reality?

J: That I would be in a different mind state forever—I would never come back to reality. That I would be so crazy that I would have to be carted out of the movie theater to a mental hospital and locked away forever.

Overly general self-statements, such as "I feel terrible—something bad could happen," are insufficient and nontherapeutic; they may even serve to intensify anxiety by virtue of their global and nondirective nature. Instead, detail in thought content, such as "I am afraid that if I get too anxious while driving, then I'll lose control of the wheel and drive off the side of the road and die," allows for very constructive questioning to challenge misassumptions.

Analysis of anxious thought content yields two broad factors that are labeled as "risk" and "valence." These two main types of cognitive errors are described. Risk translates to overestimation, or jumping to conclusions by viewing negative events as being probable events when in fact they are unlikely to occur. The client is asked to identify overestimations from the anxiety and panic incidents over the past couple of weeks: "Can you think of events that you felt sure were going to happen when you were feeling anxious, only to find out in the end that they did not happen at all?" Usually clients can identify such events easily, but with protestations. Consider this example of Jane's:

J: Well, several times I thought that I really was going to lose it this time . . . that I would flip out and never return to reality. It never actually happened, *but* it could still happen.

T: Why do you think "it" could still happen?

J: Part of me feels like I've always managed to escape it just in time, by either removing myself from the situation, or by having my husband help me, or by holding on long enough for the feeling to pass. But what if next time I can't hold on?

T: Knowing what we know about our thoughts when we are anxious, can you classify any of the ideas you just expressed, of "just holding on" or "just escaping in time," as overestimations?

J: I suppose you're saying that I can hold on or I can always escape in time.

T: More that you feel the need to hold on and the need to escape because you are overestimating the likelihood of flipping out and never returning to reality.

J: But it really feels like I will.

T: The confusion between what you think will happen and what actually happens is the very problem that we are addressing in this session.

The reasons why overestimations persist despite repeated disconfirmation are explored. Typically, clients misattribute the absence of danger to external safety signals or safety behaviors (e.g., "I only made it because I managed to find help in time," "If I had not taken Xanax last week when I panicked in the store, I'm sure I would have passed out," or "I wouldn't have made it if I hadn't pull off the road in time"), or to "luck," instead of realizing the inaccuracy of the original prediction. Similarly, clients may assume that the only reason why they are still alive, sane, and safe is that the "big one" has not happened. In this case, clients err by assuming that intensity of panic attacks increase the risk of catastrophic outcomes, such as the risk of dying, losing control, or going crazy.

The method for countering overestimation errors is to question the evidence for probability judgments. The general format is to treat thoughts as hypotheses or guesses rather than facts and to examine the evidence for predictions, while considering alternative, more realistic predictions. This is best done in a Socratic style, so that clients can examine the content of their statements and arrive at alternative statements or predictions after they have considered all of the evidence. Questioning of the logic (e.g., "How does a racing heart lead to a heart attack?"), or of the bases from which judgments are made (e.g., misinformation from others, unusual sensations), is useful in this regard. To continue with the previous example from Jane, the questioning took the following course:

T: One of the specific self-statements you have identified is that you will flip out and never return to reality. What specifically leads you to think that that is likely to happen?

J: Well, I guess it really feels like that.

T: Be more specific. What feelings?

J: Well, I feel spacy and unreal, like things around me are different and that I'm not connected.

T: And why do you think those feelings mean that you have actually lost touch with reality?

J: I don't know—it feels as if I have.

T: So let's examine that assumption. What is your behavior like when you feel unreal? For example, do you respond if someone asks you a question during those episodes?

J: Well, I respond to you even though I feel that way sometimes in here.

T: OK, and can you walk or write or drive when you feel that way?

J: Yes, but it feels different.

T: But you do perform those functions despite feeling detached. So what does that tell you?

J: Well, maybe I haven't lost complete touch with reality. But what if I do?

T: How many times have you felt detached?

J: Hundreds and hundreds of times.

T: And how many times have you lost touch with reality permanently?

J: Never. But what if the feelings don't go away—maybe I'll lose it then?

T: So what else tells you that this is a possibility?

J: Well, what about my second cousin? He lost it when he was about 25, and now he's just a mess. He can hardly function at all, and he is constantly in and out of psychiatric hospitals. They have him on a bunch of heavy-duty drugs. I'll never forget the time I saw him totally out of it—he was talking to himself in jibberish.

T: So do you make a connection between him and yourself?

J: Yes.

T: What are the similarities between the two of you?

J: There are none really. It's just that he *is* what I think I will become.

T: Did he ever feel the way you feel now?

J: I don't know.

T: And if another one of your cousins had severe back problems, would you be concerned that you would end up with severe back problems?

J: No.

T: Why not?

J: Because it never crosses my mind—it is not something that I worry about.

T: So it sounds like you think you will end up like your cousin because you are afraid of ending up like him.

J: I suppose so.

T: So let's consider all of the evidence, and consider some alternatives. You have felt unreal hundreds of times, and you've never lost touch with reality because you've continued to function in the midst of those feelings, and they have never lasted forever. You are afraid of becoming like your cousin, but there are no data to show that he and you have the same problem. In fact, the data suggest otherwise, because you function and he does not. Also, you seem to be interpreting the feelings of detachment as the beginnings of becoming like your cousin. Let's keep

in mind our previous discussion of where feelings of unreality can come from. So what is the realistic probability that you will lose touch with reality permanently? Use a 0- to 100-point scale, where 0 means "no chance at all" and 100 means "definitely will happen."

J: Well, maybe it is lower than I thought. Maybe 20%.

T: So that would mean that you have actually lost touch with reality in a permanent way once every five times you have felt unreal?

J: When it's put like that, I guess not. Maybe it's a very small possibility.

T: Yes, so what is an alternative explanation?

J: Perhaps the feelings of unreality are caused by feeling anxious or overbreathing, and that having those feelings does not mean that I am actually losing touch with reality, and that I am not like my cousin at all.

The homework assignments for this session are to practice breathing control, to keep track of errors of overestimation, and to restructure these errors by questioning the odds and looking at the evidence.

Session 5

The goals of this session are application of breathing control, and extension of cognitive restructuring to the second type of cognitive error, which is catastrophizing. Clients are asked to practice breathing control in demanding environments, such as while sitting at a desk at work, or while waiting at a stop light in the car. They are encouraged to do "minipractices" often throughout the day.

The second cognitive error involves viewing an event as "dangerous," "unbearable," or "catastrophic," when in actuality it is not. Typical examples of catastrophic errors are "If I faint, people will think that I'm weak, and that would be unbearable," "Panic attacks are the worst thing I can imagine," and "The whole evening is ruined if I start to feel anxious." "Decatastrophizing" means to realize that the occurrences are not as catastrophic as stated, which is achieved by considering how negative events are managed versus how "bad" they are. For example, for the person who states that negative judgments from others are unbearable, it is important to discuss what he/she would do to cope should someone else make a direct negative judgment. Similarly, for the person who states that the physical symptoms of panic are intolerably embarrassing, the following type of questioning is helpful:

J: I am really worried that I might lose control and do something crazy, like yell and scream.

T: Aside from the very low likelihood of that happening (as we discussed before), let's face the worst and ask what is so bad about it. What would be so horrible about yelling and screaming?

J: I could never live it down.

T: Well, let's think it through. What are the various things you could do in the situation? You have just yelled and screamed—now what?

J: Well, I guess the yelling and screaming would eventually stop.

T: That's right—at the very least, you would eventually be exhausted. What else?

J: Well, maybe I would explain to the people around me that I was having a really bad day but that I would be OK. In other words, reassure them.

T: Good—what else?

J: Maybe I would just get away—find somewhere to calm down and reassure myself that the worst is over.

T: That's right. And there are other things you could do, too. You could ask someone to help you. Or you could do nothing.

J: But what if the police come and took me away, locked me up in a mental ward?

T: Again, let's face the worst. What if the police did come when you were yelling and screaming, and what if the police did take you away? As scary as that may sound to you, let's consider what actually would happen.

J: I have this image of myself not being able to tell them what is really going on—that I am so out of it that I don't have the ability to let them know that I am just anxious.

T: If you were so distraught that you could not clearly communicate, how long would that last?

J: You're right—I would eventually be exhausted, and then I could speak more clearly. But what if they didn't believe me?

T: What if they did not believe you at first? How long would it take before they would realize that you were not crazy?

J: I guess that after a while they would see that I was OK, and maybe I could call a friend or my doctor so that they could explain what was going on.

T: That's right. Now remember, all of this is about events that are extremely unlikely to happen. At the same time, however, it is helpful to face worst-case scenarios (even though unlikely) and realize that they are not as bad as you first thought.

The homework consists of applied breathing control, as well as identification and challenging of overestimations and catastrophic styles of thinking.

Session 6

The main goal of this session is to begin interoceptive exposure, after some initial time is spent reviewing cognitive restructuring, particularly in terms of the application of cognitive strategies to episodes of anxiety and panic over the preceding week. The therapist reviews the concept of interoceptive conditioning described in the second session. A rationale for interoceptive exposure emphasizes that natural tendencies to avoid feared sensations serve to maintain fear by preventing correction of misappraisals about the symptoms. Such avoidance may take the form of lying down, distracting oneself or seeking safety as soon as sensations are noticed, or avoiding activities or stimulants that induce sensations. Activities that are avoided because of the associated physical sensations may not be immediately obvious to the client. They may include physical exercise, emotional discussions, suspenseful movies, steamy rooms (e.g., a shower with doors and windows closed), certain foods, or stimulants. The purpose of interoceptive exposure is to repeatedly induce the sensations that are feared for long enough that the fear response weakens. Fear reduction is believed to occur through habituation and through learning that no actual danger results from the feared sensations. In addition, the repeated inductions allow practice in applying cognitive and breathing anxiety management strategies.

The procedure begins by assessing the client's response to a series of standardized exercises. The therapist models each exercise first. Then, after the client has completed the exercise, the therapist records the sensations, anxiety level (0–8), sensation intensity (0–8), and similarity to naturally occurring panic sensations (0–8). The exercises include shaking the head from side to side for 30 seconds; placing the head between the legs for 30 seconds and lifting the head to an upright position quickly; running in place or using steps for 1 minute; holding one's breath for as long as possible; maintaining complete body muscle tension for 1 minute or holding a pushup position for as long as possible; spinning in a swivel chair for 1 minute; hyperventilating for 1 minute; breathing through a narrow straw (with closed nasal passages) or breathing as slowly as possible for 2 minutes; and staring at a spot on the wall or at one's mirror image for 90 seconds. If none of these exercises produce sensations at least moderately similar to those that occur naturally, other individually tailored exercises can be generated. For example, tightness around the chest can be induced by a deep breath before hyperventilating; heat can be induced by wearing heavy clothing in a heated room; choking sensations can be induced by a tongue depressor, a high-collared sweater, or a necktie; and startle can be induced by an abrupt loud noise in the midst of relaxation.

Clients who report little or no fear because they feel safe in the presence of the therapist are asked to attempt each exercise alone while the therapist leaves the office, or at home. At the same time, the influence of perceived safety is discussed as a moderating factor in the amount of fear experienced, to reinforce the value of cognitive restructuring. For a minority of clients, the known cause and course of the sensations override the fear response; that is, because the sensations are predictably related to a clear cause (the interoceptive exercise), and because the sensations can be relatively easily controlled by simply terminating the interoceptive exercise, then fear is minimal. Under these conditions, discussion can productively center on the misassumptions that render naturally occurring sensations more frightening than the ones produced by the interoceptive exercises. Typically, these misassumptions are that naturally occurring sensations are always unpredictable; that unpredictable sensations are necessarily more harmful; and that naturally occurring sensations are uncontrollable and, if not controlled, pose a potential threat. The majority of clients fear at least several of the interoceptive exercises, despite knowing the cause of the sensations and their controllability.

Interoceptive exercises rated as producing at least somewhat similar sensations to naturally occurring panic (at least 3 on the 0–8 scale) are selected for repeated exposure in the next session. These selected exercises are ranked according to anxiety ratings. The homework is to continue breathing retraining, cognitive monitoring, and challenging.

Session 7

The primary goal of this session is to conduct repeated interoceptive exposure. But, first, breathing control is reviewed. Clients are encouraged to apply breathing control at times of anxiety or uncomfortable physical sensations from this point on. Also, hypothesis testing is introduced to facilitate cognitive restructuring. "Hypothesis testing" means designing experiments from which data can be gathered to disconfirm catastrophic predictions. For example, a client may be asked to stand away from a wall rather than lean on a wall when feeling dizzy, to test the hypothesis that he/she will fall. The likelihood of the prediction's coming true is rated in this session. For example, Jane predicted that it was 60% likely that someone at the business dinner she was attending during the week would comment on how weird she looked. It is important to note that Jane's hypothesis testing did not examine the likelihood of her having a panic attack at the business dinner, but rather the likelihood of the catastrophic event (i.e., "someone commenting on how weird I look"). At the next session, the client and therapist examine whether the evidence gathered from hypothesis testing supports or refutes the predictions that were made the week prior. In this manner, the client obtains more concrete evidence that few if any of his/her dire predictions come true. Hypothesis testing is particularly useful for catastrophic predictions about the effects of anxiety on ability to function.

A graduated approach is used for interoceptive exposure, beginning with the lowest item on the hierarchy established in Session 6. For each trial of exposure, the client is asked to begin the induction, indicate when the sensations are first experienced (such as by raising a hand), and continue the induction for at least 30 seconds longer in order to break the action tendency to avoid and resist the sensations. After terminating the induction, anxiety is rated, and the client is given time to apply cognitive and breathing management strategies. Finally, the therapist reviews the induction experience and the application of management strategies with the client. During this review, the therapist emphasizes the importance of experiencing the sensations fully during the induction, of concentrating objectively on the sensations as opposed to distracting from them, and the importance of identifying specific cognitions and challenging them by considering all of the evidence. In addition, the therapist asks key questions to help the client realize his/her safety (e.g., "What would have happened if you had continued spinning for another 60 seconds?"), and to generalize to naturally occurring experiences (e.g., "How is this different from when you feel dizzy at work?").

In other words, cognitive challenging extends the cognitive reprocessing already taking place implicitly as a result of repeated interoceptive exposure. Specific cognitions not previously recognized sometimes become apparent. For example, Jane became more aware of her assumption that she would lose control of her limbs if she felt "spacy" or lightheaded. This related to her concern about causing an accident when driving. During repeated hyperventilation exercises and with prompting of "what ifs" from the therapist, the fear of not being able to move her arms or legs in a controlled fashion was discovered. This assumption was then behaviorally challenged by having Jane overbreathe for longer periods of time, followed immediately by having her walk, pick up objects, and so on. The trials are repeated enough times until the anxiety

level for a given exercise is no greater than 2 (or mild). Then the procedure is repeated for the next exercise on the hierarchy.

As mentioned earlier, sometimes clients report that because the exercise-induced sensations are predictable and controllable, they are less fear-provoking than naturally occurring sensations. A cognitive approach, as in the following example, is helpful at these times.

J: After spinning and hyperventilating several times, I really do feel much less anxious. I was terrified at the start, but now I am mildly anxious only, if at all. But this is different from what happens to me when I'm on the freeway or at home.

T: How is it different?

J: I don't know when the feelings of dizziness and unreality are going to hit.

T: From our previous discussions, let's think of potential reasons why you might feel dizzy or unreal at a particular time.

J: I know . . . I have to keep remembering that it could be my breathing, or just feeling anxious, or tired, or a bunch of different things.

T: OK. Now, second, why is it so important to know when those feelings will occur?

J: Because I don't want them to be there at all.

T: And why not . . . what are you afraid of?

J: I guess it's the same old thing . . . that I'll lose it somehow.

T: So let's go back to the cognitive restructuring that you have been doing. What specifically are you afraid of? How likely is it to happen? What are the alternatives?

J: I understand.

T: So now you see that whether the sensations of dizziness or unreality are produced by anxiety, overbreathing, diet, or the exercises we do here, it's all the same—they are just uncomfortable physical sensations. The only reason they perturb you more when you are driving or at home is because of the meaning you still give to them in those situations.

Homework practice is very important, because safety signals present in the clinic setting or deriving from the therapist per se may again prevent generalizability to the natural setting. Clients are instructed to practice the interoceptive items conducted in session on a daily basis. If they express fear at doing the exercises alone, then further cognitive restructuring about the symptoms induced by the exercises is recommended. In addition, more graduation of homework may be necessary, such as practicing interoceptive exposure when someone else is close by at home before practicing when no one is around.

Session 8

The goals of this session are to continue the hypothesis testing and interoceptive exposure from Session 7. It is especially important to review daily practice of interoceptive exposure. The possibility of avoidance should be evaluated—either overt failure to practice, or covert avoidance by minimizing the intensity or duration of the sensations induced, or by limiting practices to the presence of a safety signal (such as a significant other) or to times when background anxiety is minimal. Reasons for avoidance may include continued misinterpretation of the dangers of bodily sensations (i.e., "I don't want to hyperventilate, because I'm afraid that I won't be able to stop overbreathing and no one will be there to help me"), or the belief that anxiety will not reduce with repetition of the task.

By this time in therapy, Jane was reporting very few panic attacks, and considerably fewer physical sensations overall. She practiced interoceptive exposure exercises about half of the days between sessions. However, she remained cautious for fear that the exercises would cause her to revert to her state of several weeks earlier. That is, she was concerned that the inductions would leave her in a persistent symptomatic state. Furthermore, she was particularly reluctant to practice interoceptive exposure at the end of the day, when she was more likely to feel "unreal," or on a day when an important social event was scheduled. Again, these avoidance patterns were related to fears that the symptoms would become too intense or would result in some type of mental or social catastrophe. All avoidance patterns must be addressed cognitively, using the principles described in previous sessions, as shown in the vignette below.

T: When did you practice deliberately spinning and hyperventilating?

J: Usually in the mornings. One day I left it until the end of the day, and that turned out to be a bad idea. I felt terrible.

T: Let's think about that a bit more. What made it terrible when you practiced at the end of the day?

J: Well, I was already feeling pretty unreal—I usually do around that time of the day. So I was much more anxious about the symptoms.

T: Being more anxious implies that you thought the symptoms were more harmful—is that what happened on the day that you practiced interoceptive exposure when you were already feeling unreal?

J: Yes. I felt that because I was already feeling unreal, I was on the edge, and that I might push myself over the edge if I tried to increase the feelings of unreality.

T: What do you mean by "pushing yourself over the edge"?

J: That I would make the feelings so intense that I really would lose it—go crazy.

T: So there is one of those hypotheses—to feel more intense unreality means to be closer to going crazy. Let's examine the evidence. Is it necessarily the case that more intense unreality means you are closer to craziness?

The homework from this session is to continue moving up the interoceptive exposure hierarchy, to continue with hypothesis testing, and to engage in cognitive restructuring when anxious or panicky.

Session 9

The primary goal of this session is to extend interoceptive exposure to natural activities. In addition, cognitive restructuring is continued through hypothesis testing and reinforcement of monitoring and challenging as anxiety arises.

"Naturalistic" interoceptive exposure refers to exposure to daily tasks or activities that have been avoided or endured with dread because of the associated sensations. Typical examples include engaging in aerobic exercise or vigorous physical activity, running up flights of stairs, eating foods that create a sensation of fullness or are associated with sensations of choking, standing quickly from a seated position, taking saunas or steamy showers, driving with the windows rolled up and the heater on, caffeine consumption, and so on. (Of course, these exercises may be modified in the event of actual medical complications, such as asthma or high blood pressure.) From a list of typically feared activities, and generation of items specific to the individual's own experience, a hierarchy is established. Each item is ranked in terms of anxiety ratings. Jane's hierarchy was as follows: looking out through venetian blinds (anxiety = 3); watching *One Flew over the Cuckoo's Nest* (4); playing tennis (anxiety = 4); scanning labels on a supermarket shelf (anxiety = 5); concentrating on needlework for an hour (anxiety = 6); driving with windows closed and heater on (anxiety = 6); a night club with strobe lights (anxiety = 7); and rides at Disneyland (anxiety = 8).

Clients are instructed to identify maladaptive cognitions and rehearse cognitive restructuring before beginning each activity. In-session rehearsal of the cognitive preparation allows therapists to provide corrective feedback. It is important to identify and remove (gradually, if necessary) safety signals or protective behaviors, such as portable phones, lucky charms, walking slowly, standing slowly, and staying in close proximity to medical facilities. These safety signals and behaviors reinforce catastrophic misappraisals about bodily sensations. Clients are asked to practice two items from their hierarchy at least three times each before the next treatment session.

Session 10

The primary goals of this session are to review the naturalistic exposure exercises the client has done over the past week, and to begin exposure to feared and avoided agoraphobic situations. As with earlier interoceptive exposure homework assignments, it is important to evaluate and correct tendencies to avoid naturalistic interoceptive exposure tasks, mainly by considering the underlying misassumptions that are leading to avoidance. Remember also that a form of avoidance is to rely on safety signals or safety behaviors, and so careful questioning of the way in which the naturalistic exposure was conducted, and under what conditions, may help to identify

inadvertent reliance on these unnecessary precautions. Two new items are selected for the coming week, with special attention to decreasing or eliminating the use of safety signals and safety behaviors. Cognitive restructuring is rehearsed in the session for each one.

In vivo exposure targets situations in which anxiety and panic are anticipated to occur and from which escape is difficult or help is unavailable. In contrast, naturalistic interoceptive exposure targets activities that produce sensations that are feared and avoided. *In vivo* exposure is introduced at this point because most clients have acquired sufficient control of their panic and anxiety to allow *in vivo* exposure to proceed relatively smoothly. However, *in vivo* exposure may be introduced earlier in certain cases. Examples are clients who report no fear of standard interoceptive exercises, and who are afraid of sensations only when they occur in the context of agoraphobic situations. Under these conditions, *in vivo* exposure can be initiated in Session 7. Other examples are clients who have controlled their fear of sensations very quickly, and who would thus benefit from earlier introduction of *in vivo* exposure.

The amount of time devoted to *in vivo* exposure is very dependent on the client's agoraphobic profile. Obviously, more time is needed for clients with more severe agoraphobia. Also, the benefit obtained from involving significant others in the treatment process may depend on the pervasiveness of agoraphobia, and the extent to which family roles and interactions have been affected by or contribute to the agoraphobic pattern. Another decision concerns the way in which *in vivo* exposure is conducted. A graduated, spaced (vs. intense, massed) approach is used most often. However, as reported earlier, choice of approach may be best decided upon with the client by describing the options and considering the client's preferred method.

The first step is to provide a rationale for conducting *in vivo* exposure. The rationale is very similar to that for interoceptive exposure: to learn through repeated and systematic exposure to feared situations that predicted catastrophic events are unlikely or are not really catastrophic, and that avoidance and escape contribute to ongoing fear and avoidance by preventing this type of corrective learning. Also as with interoceptive exposure, the fact that anxiety and fear reliably decrease when a situation is faced is repeatedly emphasized, in order to allay concerns that the situations will remain difficult. In addition, reasons why previous attempts at *in vivo* exposure may have failed are reviewed, again to allay patients' concerns that they will never learn to be less afraid of agoraphobic situations. Typical reasons for past failures at *in vivo* exposure include attempts that were too haphazard and/or brief, were spaced too far apart, or were conducted without a sense of mastery or while maintaining beliefs that catastrophe is very possible. Jane had certainly tried to face agoraphobic situations in the past, but each time she had escaped, feeling overwhelmed by panic and terrified of losing touch with reality permanently. The therapist helped Jane realize how to approach the agoraphobic situations differently in order to benefit from the exposure. Jane's typical safety signals were the presence of her husband (or at least knowing his whereabouts) and Klonopin (which was carried but rarely used). The therapist discussed the importance of Jane's eventually weaning herself from those safety signals.

Jane and her therapist selected a graduated, spaced approach with the aid of her husband, because he played a significant role in her agoraphobic patterns. Jane disliked the intense approach because she would not feel "in control." At this point in treatment, Jane had not had a panic attack for 4 weeks. Her sensitivity to bodily sensations, particularly feelings of unreality, had declined significantly. However, she retained a mild level of apprehension about "Is this going to last?" or "What if the panic attacks return?", which accounted for her resistance to intense *in vivo* exposure. Some of her agoraphobia had been reduced by the PCT. For example, Jane was now driving further distances on surface streets, although she still avoided the freeways. Also, Jane was spending more time alone than before, although she still preferred the presence of her husband or mother. She was eager to begin the *in vivo* exposure phase and become more independent. Jane's husband, Larry, was very willing to be involved in treatment. Although he could have been present from the beginning of treatment, Jane and the therapist chose to include Larry for the *in vivo* exposure component.

Over the next week, as part of Jane's homework, she and Larry generated a hierarchy of agoraphobic situations, ranked according to anxiety level. Each task on the hierarchy was worded very clearly, so that practices could be guided by the task itself rather than by the level of anxiety experienced in the task. For example, one task for Jane was to drive two exits on the freeway, as opposed to driving on the freeway until becoming anxious. Similarly, another task was to spend 2 hours alone during the day, as opposed to staying at home alone until becoming anxious. That way, accomplishment of each task would be more clearly determined, and behavioral accomplishment was emphasized independently of level of anxiety experienced during the task. Jane's final hierarchy consisted of the following situations: driving home from work, at dusk, alone; sitting in the middle row, on the aisle, of a crowded movie theater with her husband; sitting in the middle row, in the middle, of a crowded movie theater with her husband; spending 2 hours alone at home during the day; being alone at home as day turned to night; driving on surface streets to her brother's house (10 miles) alone; driving two exits on the freeway, with her husband in a car behind her; driving two exits on the freeway, alone; driving four exits on the freeway; and driving on the freeway to her brother's house alone. Then all of these tasks were to be repeated without Klonopin and without knowing the location of her husband.

Session 11

The primary goals of this session are to incorporate the significant other in treatment, and to assign the first *in vivo* exposure practice. Consequently, Jane's husband, Larry, attended this session and the remaining four sessions (four sessions were scheduled, given Jane's level of agoraphobic avoidance). A treatment conceptualization is provided to the significant other to reduce his/her frustration and/or negative attributions about the client's emotional functioning (e.g., "Oh, she's just making it up—there's nothing really wrong with her," or "He has been like this since before we were married and he'll never change"). The way in which the agoraphobic problem has disrupted daily routines and distribution of home responsibilities is explored and discussed also. Examples may include social activities, leisure activities, and household chores. It is explained that family activities may be structured around the agoraphobic fear and avoidance in order to help the client function without intense anxiety. At the same time, the reassignment of tasks that were previously performed by the client to the significant other may actually reinforce the agoraphobic pattern of behavior. Consequently, the importance of complying with homework *in vivo* exposure instructions, even though the client may initially experience some distress, is emphasized.

The significant other is encouraged to become an active participant by describing his/her perception of the client's behavior and fearfulness, as well as the impact on the home environment. Sometimes significant others provide information that the client is not fully aware of or does not report, particularly in relation to how the client's behavior affects the significant other's own daily functioning. Larry, for example, described how he felt restricted at home in the evenings; whereas before he occasionally played basketball with his friends at the local gym, now he stayed at home because he felt guilty if he left Jane alone.

The next step is to describe the role of the significant other regarding *in vivo* exposure tasks. The significant other is viewed as a coach, and the couple is encouraged to approach the tasks as a problem-solving team. This includes deciding exactly where and when to practice *in vivo* exposure. In preparation for practices, the client identifies his/her misappraisals about the task and generates cognitive alternatives. The significant other is encouraged to help the client question his/her own "anxious" thoughts. This questioning of the client by the significant other can be role-played in session, so that the therapist can provide corrective feedback to each partner. Throughout *in vivo* exposure, the significant other reminds the client to apply cognitive challenges and/or breathing control. Because the significant other is usually a safety signal, tasks are less anxiety-provoking. However, the client must be weaned from the safety signal eventually. Therefore, initial attempts at facing agoraphobic situations are conducted with the significant other, and later trials are conducted alone. Weaning from the significant other may be graduated, as in the case of (1) driving with the significant other in the car, (2) driving with the significant other in a car behind, (3) meeting the significant other at a destination point, and (4) driving alone.

Very important to the success of this collaboration is style of communication. The significant other is discouraged from magnifying the experience of panic and is encouraged to help the client apply coping statements when anxious. On the other hand, significant others are encouraged to be patient, given the fact that progress for the client may be erratic. The client and significant other are instructed to use a 0–8 rating scale to communicate with each other about the client's current level of anxiety or distress, as a way of diminishing the awkwardness associated with discussion of anxiety, especially in public situations. The client is warned about potential motivation to avoid discussing his/her feelings with the significant other, due to embarrassment or an attempt to avoid anxiety for fear that discussing it with the significant other and concentrating on anxiety may intensify his/her distress level. Avoidance of feelings is discouraged, because distraction is viewed as less beneficial in the long term than is objectively facing whatever it is that is distressing and learning that predicted catastrophes do not occur. The client is reassured that the initial discomfort and embarrassment are likely to decrease as the couple becomes more familiar with discussing anxiety levels and their management. Furthermore, clients' concerns about their significant others' being insensitive or too pushy are addressed. For example, a significant other may presume to know a client's level of anxiety and anxious thoughts without confirmation from the client, or the significant other may become angry toward the client for avoiding or escaping from situations or being fearful. All of these issues are described as relatively common and understandable patterns of communication, but nevertheless in need of correction. Role playing in the session of more adaptive communication styles during episodes of heightened anxiety is a useful learning technique. On occasion, more specific communication training may be beneficial, especially if the partners frequently argue in their attempts to generate items or methods for conducting *in vivo* exposure.

Jane and Larry rehearsed their approach to the *in vivo* exposure task (sitting in the middle row on the aisle of a crowded movie theater) in the session, while the therapist provided corrective feedback using the principles of communication and coping described above. They were instructed to practice this task at least three times over the next week. On at least one occasion, Jane was to practice the task alone.

Sessions 12–15

Each of the remaining sessions follows the same general procedure: a review of *in vivo* exposure practices over the past week; therapist feedback where appropriate about cognitive restructuring and the significant other's coaching; and rehearsal of new *in vivo* exposure tasks for the coming week. Issues commonly covered include specific danger cognitions that have not been identified previously. For example, Jane reported that during her practices at the movie theater, she became afraid of having to leave the theater and thereby disturb the audience's enjoyment of the movie. This cognition was identified as an overestimation and catastrophic thinking error. Other issues include controlling the urge to escape at times of heightened anxiety. Retreat from a situation (e.g., going to a restroom for relief from the crowded restaurant situation) is viewed as appropriate if it is used as a time out for cognitive restructuring and is followed by a return to the situation. In Session 13, Jane stated that she had "failed" because she had pulled off to the side of the road and waited for Larry to catch up to her. The therapist emphasized that difficulty in an exposure task does not represent failure, but rather shows that learning is often bumpy, with ups and downs; what was most important was to identify what had caused the escape behavior and how to manage that differently next time. The therapist rehearsed with Jane how to use time outs from a task to evaluate what had happened, engage in cognitive restructuring, and prepare for returning to the task. Finally, maintaining an objective awareness of the situational context and reactions is emphasized.

In addition, interoceptive exposure from earlier sessions is usually incorporated into the *in vivo* exposure. That is, clients are encouraged to deliberately induce bodily symptoms as they face agoraphobic situations. For example, wearing heavy clothing when in a restaurant helps clients to learn to be less afraid not only of the restaurant, but of feeling hot in a restaurant. Other examples include drinking coffee before any of the agoraphobic tasks, turning off the air conditioning or turning on the heater while driving, breathing very slowly in a crowded area, and so on. Any time clients express the concern that they might experience uncomfortable bodily symptoms as they face their agoraphobic situations, this is a sign that the clients need to deliberately face those symptoms, both cognitively and behaviorally.

In this protocol, the last few treatment sessions are scheduled biweekly in order to enhance generalization. The last treatment session reviews all of the principles and skills learned, and provides the client with a template of coping techniques for potential high-risk situations in the future. Jane finished the program after 15 sessions, by which time she had not panicked in 8 weeks, rarely experienced dizziness or feelings or unreality, and was driving longer distances. There were some situations still in need of exposure practices (such as very long distances away from home and freeway driving at dusk). However, she and Larry agreed to continue *in vivo* exposure practices over the next few months, in order to consolidate her learning and to continue her improvement.

CONCLUSION

As noted earlier in the chapter, cognitive-behavioral treatments for panic disorder and agoraphobia are highly effective, and represent one of the success stories of psychotherapeutic development. Between 80% and 100% of patients undergoing these treatments will be panic-free at the end of treatment, and these gains are maintained for follow-ups of at least 2 years. Recent controlled trials indicate that these results reflect substantially more durability than effective medications. Furthermore, between 50% and 80% of these patients are "cured," and many of the remainder have only residual symptomatology. Nevertheless, we should not be deluded into thinking that we have the answers for PD/PDA and can move on to some other problem. Several major difficulties remain.

First, the fact remains that these treatments are not foolproof. As noted above, as many as 50% of patients suffering from PD/PDA retain some substantial symptomatology despite initial improvement, particularly those with more severe agoraphobia. Further research must determine how treatments can be improved or better individualized to alleviate continued suffering. For example, one of us (D. H. B.) saw a client several years ago who had completed an initial course of treatment, but required continued periodic visits for over 4 years. This client was essentially better for approximately 9 months, but found himself relapsing during a particularly stressful time at work. A few booster sessions restored his functioning, but he was back in the office 6 months later with reemerging symptomatology. This pattern essentially continued for 4 years, and was characterized by symptom-free periods followed by (seemingly) stress-related relapses. Furthermore, the reemerging panic disorder would sometimes last from 3 to 6 months before disappearing again, perhaps with the help of the booster sessions.

Although this case was somewhat unusual in our experience, there was no easy explanation for this pattern of relapses and remissions. The client, who has a graduate degree, understood and accepted the treatment model, and fully implemented the treatment program. There was also no question that he fully comprehended the nature of anxiety and panic and the intricacies of the therapeutic strategies. While in the office, he could recite chapter and verse on the nature of these emotional states, as well as the detailed process of his own reaction while in these states. Nevertheless, while away from the office, the client found himself repeatedly hoping that he would not "go over the brink" during a panic, despite verbalizing very clearly the irrationality of this concept while in the office. In addition, he continued to attempt to reduce minor physiological symptoms associated with anxiety and panic, despite a full rational understanding of the nature of these symptoms (including the fact that they are the same symptoms that he experienced during a state of excitement, which he enjoyed). His limited tolerance of these physical sensations was also puzzling, in view of his tremendous capacity to endure pain.

Any number of factors might account for what seemed to be "overvalued ideation" or very strongly held irrational ideas during periods of anxiety, including the fact that the client has several relatives who have been repeatedly hospitalized for emotional disorders (seemingly mood disorders or schizoaffective disorder). Nevertheless, the fact remains that we do not know why this client did not respond as quickly as most people. Eventually the client made a full recovery, received several promotions at work, and considered treatment to be the turning point in his life. But it took 5 years.

Other clients, as noted above, seem uninterested in engaging in treatment, preferring to conceptualize their problems as chemical imbalances. Still others have difficulty grasping some of the cognitive strategies, and further attempts are necessary to make these treatments more "user-friendly."

It also may seem that this structured, protocol-driven treatment is applied in a very standard fashion across individuals. Nothing could be further from the truth. The clinical art involved in this, and all treatments described in this book, requires a careful adaptation of these treatment strategies to the individual case. Many of Jane's symptoms revolved around feelings of unreality (derealization and depersonalization). Emphasizing rational explanations for the production of such feelings, as well as adapting cognitive and exposure exercises so as to maximize these sensations, is an important part of this treatment program. Although standard interoceptive provocation exercises seemed sufficient to produce relevant symptomatology in Jane's case, we have had to develop new procedures to deal with people with more idiosyncratic symptoms and fears, particularly involving feelings of unreality or dissociation. Other innovations in both cognitive and behavioral procedures will be required by individual therapists as they apply these procedures.

Although these new treatments seem highly successful when applied by trained therapists, treatment is not readily available to individuals suffering from these disorders. In fact, these treatments, while brief and structured, are far more difficult to deliver than, for example, pharmacological treatments (which are also often misapplied). Furthermore, few people are currently skilled in the application of these treatments. What seems to be needed for these and other successful psychosocial treatments is a new method of disseminating them so that they reach the maximum number of clients. Modification of these treatment protocols into more user-friendly formats, as well as brief periods of training for qualified therapists to a point of certification, would seem important steps in successfully delivering these treatments. This may be difficult to accomplish.

Finally, it will be crucially important to continue to work out the relationship of these treatments to popular medication approaches. Here, client–treatment matching and investigations into the creative sequencing of these treatments, in view of the fact that many people with PD/PDA are initially placed on medications, will be important research agendas for the immediate future.

REFERENCES

Agras, W. S., Leitenberg, H., & Barlow, D. H. (1968). Social reinforcement in the modification of agoraphobia. *Archives of General Psychiatry, 19,* 423–427.

Alnaes, R., & Torgersen, S. (1990). DSM-III personality disorders among patients with major depression, anxiety disorders, and mixed conditions. *Journal of Nervous and Mental Disease, 178,* 693–698.

American Psychiatric Association. (1980). *Diagnostic and statistical manual of mental disorders* (3rd ed.). Washington, DC: Author.

American Psychiatric Association. (1994). *Diagnostic and statistical manual of mental disorders* (4th ed.). Washington, DC: Author.

American Psychiatric Association. (1998). Practice guideline for the treatment of patients with panic disorder. *American Journal of Psychiatry, 155*(Suppl. 5), 1–34.

Amering, M., Katschnig, H., Berger, P., Windhaber, J., Baischer, W., & Dantendorfer, K. (1997). Embarrassment about the first panic attack predicts agoraphobia in disorder patients. *Behaviour Research and Therapy, 35,* 517–521.

Antony, M., Brown, T. A., Craske, M. G., Barlow, D. H., Mitchell, W. B., & Meadows, E. A. (1995). Accuracy of heart beat perception in panic disorder, social phobia, and nonanxious subjects. *Journal of Anxiety Disorders, 9,* 355–371.

Arnow, B. A., Taylor, C. B., Agras, W. S., & Telch, M. J. (1985). Enchancing agoraphobia treatment outcome by changing couple communication patterns. *Behavior Therapy, 16,* 452–467.

Arntz, A., & van den Hout, M. (1996). Psychological treatments of panic disorder without agoraphobia: Cognitive therapy versus applied relaxation. *Behaviour Research and Therapy, 34,* 113–121.

Arrindell, W., & Emmelkamp, P. (1987). Psychological states and traits in female agoraphobics: A controlled study. *Journal of Psychopathology and Behavioral Assessment, 9,* 237–253.

Azrin, N., Naster, B., & Jones, R. (1973). Reciprocity counselling: A rapid learning-based procedure for marital counselling. *Behaviour Research and Therapy, 11,* 365–382.

Bandura, A. (1977). Self-efficacy: Toward a unifying theory of behavioral change. *Psychological Review, 84,* 191–215.

Bandura, A. (1988). Self-efficacy conception of anxiety. *Anxiety Research, 1,* 77–98.

Barlow, D. H. (1988). *Anxiety and its disorders: The nature and treatment of anxiety and panic.* New York: Guilford Press.

Barlow, D. H. (in press). *Anxiety and its disorders: The nature and treatment of anxiety and panic* (2nd ed.). New York: Guilford Press.

Barlow, D. H., Brown, T. A., & Craske, M. G. (1994). Definitions of panic attacks and panic disorder in the DSM-IV: Implications for research. *Journal of Abnormal Psychology, 103,* 553–564.

Barlow, D. H., Cohen, A., Waddell, M., Vermilyea, J., Klosko, J., Blanchard, E., & Di Nardo, P. (1984). Panic and generalized anxiety disorders: Nature and treatment. *Behavior Therapy, 15,* 431–449.

Barlow, D. H., & Craske, M. G. (1994). *Mastery of your anxiety and panic—II.* San Antonio, TX: Graywind/Psychological Corporation.

Barlow, D. H., & Craske, M. G. (2000). *Mastery of your anxiety and panic: Client workbook for anxiety and panic (MAP-3).* San Antonio, TX: Graywind/Psychological Corporation.

Barlow, D. H., Craske, M. G., Cerny, J. A., & Klosko, J. S. (1989). Behavioral treatment of panic disorder. *Behavior Therapy, 20,* 261–282.

Barlow, D. H., Gorman, J. M., Shear, M. K., & Woods, S. W. (2000). Cognitive-behavioral therapy, imipramine, or their combination for panic disorder: A randomized controlled trial. *Journal of the American Medical Association, 283,* 2529–2536.

Barlow, D. H., O'Brien, G. T., & Last, C. G. (1984). Couples treatment of agoraphobia. *Behavior Therapy, 15,* 41–58.

Barlow, D. H., O'Brien, G. T., Last, C. G., & Holden, A. (1983). Couples treatment of agoraphobia: Initial outcome. In K. D. Craig & R. J. McMahon (Eds.), *Advances in clinical behavior therapy.* New York: Brunner/Mazel.

Barlow, D. H., Vermilyea, J., Blanchard, E., Vermilyea, B., DiNardo, P., & Cerny, J. (1985). Phenomenon of panic. *Journal of Abnormal Psychology, 94,* 320–328.

Barsky, A. J., Cleary, P. D., Sarnie, M. K., & Ruskin, J. N. (1994). Panic disorder, palpitations, and the awareness of cardiac activity. *Journal of Nervous and Mental Disease, 182,* 63–71.

Basoglu, M., Marks, I. M., Kilic, C., Brewin, C. R., & Swinson, R. P. (1994). Alprazolam and exposure for panic disorder with agoraphobia: attribution of improvement to medication predicts subsequent relapse. *British Journal of Psychiatry, 164,* 652–659.

Beck, A. T., Epstein, N., Brown, G., & Steer, R. A. (1988). An inventory for measuring clinical anxiety: Psychometric properties. *Journal of Consulting and Clinical Psychology, 56,* 893–897.

Beck, J. G., Shipherd, J. C., & Zebb, B. J. (1997). How does interoceptive exposure for panic disorder work? An uncontrolled case study. *Journal of Anxiety Disorders, 11,* 541–556.

Beck, J. G., Stanley, M. A., Baldwin, L. E., Deagle, E. A., & Averill, P. M. (1994). Comparison of cognitive therapy and relaxation training for panic disorder. *Journal of Consulting and Clinical Psychology, 62,* 818–826.

Bjork, R. A., & Bjork, E. L. (1992). A new theory of disuse and an old theory of stimulus fluctuation.

In A. F. Healy & S. M. Kosslyn (Eds.), *Essays in honor of William K. Estes: Vol. 2. From learning processes to cognitive processes* (pp. 35–67). Hillsdale, NJ: Erlbaum.

Black, D. W., Monahan, P., Wesner, R., Gabel, J., & Bowers, W. (1996). The effect of fluvoamine, cognitive therapy, and placebo on abnormal personality traits in 44 patients with panic disorder. *Journal of Personality Disorders, 10,* 185–194.

Bland, K., & Hallam, R. (1981). Relationship between response to graded exposure and marital satisfaction in agoraphobics. *Behaviour Research and Therapy, 19,* 335–338.

Bonn, J. A., Harrison, J., & Rees, W. (1971). Lactate-induced anxiety: Therapeutic application. *British Journal of Psychiatry, 119,* 468–470.

Borkovec, T. (1976). Physiological and cognitive processes in the regulation of anxiety. In G. Schwartz & D. Shapiro (Eds.), *Consciousness and self-regulation: Advances in research* (Vol. 1, pp. 261–312). New York: Plenum Press.

Borkovec, T., Weerts, T., & Bernstein, D. (1977). Assessment of anxiety. In A. Ciminero, K. Calhoun, & H. Adams (Eds.), *Handbook of behavioral assessment* (pp. 367–428). New York: Wiley.

Bouchard, S., Gauthier, J., Laberge, B., French, D., Pelletier, M., & Godbout, D. (1996). Exposure versus cognitive restructuring in the treatment of panic disorder with agoraphobia. *Behaviour Research and Therapy, 34,* 213–224.

Bouton, M. E., Mineka, S., & Barlow, D. H. (in press). A modern learning-theory perspective on the etiology of panic disorder. *Psychological Review.*

Bouton, M., & Swartzentruber, D. (1991). Sources of relapse after extinction in Pavlovian conditioning and instrumental conditioning. *Behavioral Neuroscience, 104,* 44–55.

Boyd, J. H. (1986). Use of mental health services for the treatment of panic disorder. *American Journal of Psychiatry, 143,* 1569–1574.

Breier, A., Charney, D. S., & Heninger, G. R. (1986). Agoraphobia with panic attacks. *Archives of General Psychiatry, 43,* 1029–1036.

Broocks, A., Bandelow, B., Pekrun, G., George, A., Meyer, T., Bartmann, U., Hillmer-Vogel, U., & Ruther, E. (1998). Comparison of aerobic exercise, clomipramine, and placebo in the treatment of panic disorder. *American Journal of Psychiatry, 155,* 603–609.

Brown, T. A., Antony, M. M., & Barlow, D. H. (1995). Diagnostic comorbidity in panic disorder: Effect on treatment outcome and course of comorbid diagnoses following treatment. *Journal of Consulting and Clinical Psychology, 63,* 408–418.

Brown, T. A., & Barlow, D. H. (1995). Long-term outcome in cognitive-behavioral treatment of panic disorder: Clinical predictors and alternative strategies for assessment. *Journal of Consulting and Clinical Psychology, 63,* 754–765.

Buglass, P., Clarke, J., Henderson, A., & Presley, A. (1977). A study of agoraphobic housewives. *Psychological Medicine, 7,* 73–86.

Bystritsky, A., Rosen, R. M., Murphy, K. J., Bohn, P., Keys, S. A., & Vapnik, T. (1994). Double-blind pilot trial of desipramine versus fluoxetine in panic patients. *Anxiety, 1,* 287–290.

Carter, M. M., Hollon, S. D., Carson, R., & Shelton, R. C. (1995). Effects of a safe person on induced distress following a biological challenge in panic disorder with agoraphobia. *Journal of Abnormal Psychology, 104,* 156–163.

Cerny, J. A., Barlow, D. H., Craske, M. G., & Himadi, W. G. (1987). Couples treatment of agoraphobia: A two-year follow-up. *Behavior Therapy, 18,* 401–415.

Chambless, D. L. (1990). Spacing of exposure sessions in treatment of agoraphobia and simple phobia. *Behavior Therapy, 21,* 217–229.

Chambless, D. L., Caputo, G., Bright, P., & Gallagher, R. (1984). Assessment of fear in agoraphobics: The Body Sensations Questionnaire and the Agoraphobic Cognitions Questionnaire. *Journal of Consulting and Clinical Psychology, 52,* 1090–1097.

Chambless, D. L., Caputo, G., Gracely, S., Jasin, E., & Williams, C. (1985). The Mobility Inventory for agoraphobia. *Behaviour Research and Therapy, 23,* 35–44.

Chambless, D. L., & Renneberg, B. (1988, September). *Personality disorders of agoraphobics.* Paper presented at the World Congress of Behavior Therapy, Edinburgh, Scotland.

Chaplin, E. W., & Levine, B. A. (1981). The effects of total exposure duration and interrupted versus continued exposure in flooding therapy. *Behavior Therapy, 12,* 360–368.

Chouinard, G., Annable, L., Fontaine, R., & Solyom, L. (1982). Alprazolam in the treatment of generalized anxiety and panic disorders: A double-blind placebo-controlled study. *Psychopharmacology, 77,* 229–233.

Clark, D. M. (1986). A cognitive approach to panic. *Behaviour Research and Therapy, 24,* 461–470.

Clark, D. M., & Ehlers, A. (1993). An overview of the cognitive theory and treatment of panic disorder. *Applied and Preventive Psychology, 2,* 131–139.

Clark, D. M., Salkovskis, P., & Chalkley, A. (1985). Respiratory control as a treatment for panic attacks. *Journal of Behavior Therapy and Experimental Psychiatry, 16,* 23–30.

Clark, D. M., Salkovskis, P., Gelder, M., Koehler, C., Martin, M., Anastasiades, P., Hackmann, A., Middleton, H., & Jeavons, A. (1988). Tests of a cognitive theory of panic. In I. Hand & H. Wittchen (Eds.), *Panic and phobias II* (pp. 71–90). Berlin: Springer-Verlag.

Clark, D. M., Salkovskis, P. M., Hackmann, A., Middleton, H., Anastasiades, P., & Gelder, M. (1994). A comparison of cognitive therapy, applied relaxation and imipramine in the treatment of panic disorder. *British Journal of Psychiatry, 164,* 759–769.

Clark, D. M., Salkovskis, P. M., Hackmann, A., Wells, A., Ludgate, J., & Gelder, M. (1999). Brief cognitive therapy for panic disorder: A randomized controlled trial. *Journal of Consulting and Clinical Psychology, 67,* 583–589.

Cote, G., Gauthier, J. G., Laberge, B., Cormier, H. J., & Plamondon, J. (1994). Reduced therapist contact in the cognitive behavioral treatment of panic disorder. *Behavior Therapy, 25,* 123–145.

Cox, B. J., Endler, N. S., & Swinson, R. P. (1995). An examination of levels of agoraphobic severity in panic disorder. *Behaviour Research and Therapy, 33,* 57–62.

Craske, M. G., & Barlow, D. H. (1988). A review of the relationship between panic and avoidance. *Clinical Psychology Review, 8*, 667–685.

Craske, M. G., Barlow, D. H., & Meadows, E. A. (2000). *Mastery of your anxiety and panic: Therapist guide for anxiety, panics, and agoraphobia (MAP-3)*. San Antonio, TX: Graywind/Psychological Corporation.

Craske, M. G., Brown, T. A., & Barlow, D. H. (1991). Behavioral treatment of panic disorder: A two-year follow-up. *Behavior Therapy, 22*, 289–304.

Craske, M. G., & Freed, S. (1995). Expectations about arousal and nocturnal panic. *Journal of Abnormal Psychology, 104*, 567–575.

Craske, M. G., Glover, D., & DeCola, J. (1995). Predicted versus unpredicted panic attacks: Acute versus general distress. *Journal of Abnormal Psychology, 104*, 214–223.

Craske, M. G., Maidenberg, E., & Bystritsky, A. (1995). Brief cognitive-behavioral versus nondirective therapy for panic disorder. *Journal of Behavior Therapy and Experimental Psychiatry, 26*, 113–120.

Craske, M. G., Miller, P. P., Rotunda, R., & Barlow, D. H. (1990). A descriptive report of features of initial unexpected panic attacks in minimal and extensive avoiders. *Behaviour Research and Therapy, 28*, 395–400.

Craske, M. G., Rapee, R. M., & Barlow, D. H. (1988). The significance of panic-expectancy for individual patterns of avoidance. *Behavior Therapy, 19*, 577–592.

Craske, M. G., & Rowe, M. K. (1997). A comparison of behavioral and cognitive treatments of phobias. In G. C. L. Davey (Ed.), *Phobias: A handbook of theory, research and treatment* (pp. 247–280). Chichester, England: Wiley.

Craske, M. G., Rowe, M., Lewin, M., & Noriega-Dimitri, R. (1997). Interoceptive exposure versus breathing retraining within cognitive-behavioural therapy for panic disorder with agoraphobia. *British Journal of Clinical Psychology, 36*, 85–99.

Craske, M. G., Street, L., & Barlow, D. H. (1989). Instructions to focus upon or distract from internal cues during exposure treatment for agoraphobic avoidance. *Behaviour Research and Therapy, 27*, 663–672.

Craske, M. G., & Tsao, J. C. I. (1999). Self-monitoring with panic and anxiety disorders. *Psychological Assessment, 11*, 466–479.

de Beurs, E., Lange, A., van Dyck, R., & Koele, P. (1995). Respiratory training prior to exposure in vivo in the treatment of panic disorder with agoraphobia: Efficacy and predictors of outcome. *Australian and New Zealand Journal of Psychiatry, 29*, 104–113.

de Beurs, E., van Balkom, A. J. L. M., Lange, A., Koele, P., & van Dyck, R. (1995). Treatment of panic disorder with agoraphobia: Comparison of fluvoxamine, placebo, and psychological panic management combined with exposure and of exposure in vivo alone. *American Journal of Psychiatry, 152*, 683–691.

DeCola, J. P., & Rosellini, R. A. (1990). Unpredictable/uncontrollable stress proactively interferes with appetitive Pavlovian conditioning. *Learning and Motivation, 21*, 137–152.

de Jong, M. G., & Bouman, T. K. (1995). Panic disorder: A baseline period. Predictability of agoraphobic avoidance behavior. *Journal of Anxiety Disorders, 9*, 185–199.

deRuiter, C., Rijken, H., Garssen, B., & Kraaimaat, F. (1989). Breathing retraining, exposure and a combination of both, in the treatment of panic disorder with agoraphobia. *Behaviour Research and Therapy, 27*, 647–656.

DeSilva, P., & Rachman, S. J. (1984). Does escape behavior strengthen agoraphobic avoidance? A preliminary study. *Behaviour Research and Therapy, 22*, 87–91.

Dewey, D., & Hunsley, J. (1990). The effects of marital adjustment and spouse involvement on the behavioral treatment of agoraphobia: A meta-analytic review. *Anxiety Research, 2*, 69–83.

Di Nardo, P., Brown, T. A., & Barlow, D. H. (1994). *Anxiety Disorders Interview Schedule for DSM-IV (ADIS-IV)*. San Antonio, TX: Psychological Corporation.

Di Nardo, P. A., Moras, K., Barlow, D. H., Rapee, R. M., & Brown, T. A. (1993). Reliability of DSM-III-R anxiety disorder categories: Using the Anxiety Disorders Interview Schedule—Revised (ADIS-R). *Archives of General Psychiatry, 50*, 251–256.

Dreessen, L., Arntz, A., Luttels, C., & Sallaerts, S. (1994). Personality disorders do not influence the results of cognitive behavior therapies for anxiety disorders. *Comprehensive Psychiatry, 35*, 265–274.

Ehlers, A. (1993). Interoception and panic disorder. *Advances in Behaviour Research and Therapy, 15*, 3–21.

Ehlers, A. (1995). A 1-year prospective study of panic attacks: Clinical course and factors associated with maintenance. *Journal of Abnormal Psychology, 104*, 164–172.

Ehlers, A., & Breuer, P. (1992). Increased cardiac awareness in panic disorder. *Journal of Abnormal Psychology, 101*, 371–382.

Ehlers, A., & Breuer, P. (1996). How good are patients with panic disorder at perceiving their heartbeats? *Biological Psychology, 42*, 165–182.

Ehlers, A., Breuer, P., Dohn, D., & Feigenbaum, W. (1995). Heartbeat perception and panic disorder: Possible explanations for discrepant findings. *Behaviour Research and Therapy, 33*, 69–76.

Ehlers, A., & Margraf, J. (1989). The psychophysiological model of panic attacks. In P. M. G. Emmelkamp (Ed.), *Anxiety disorders: Annual series of European research in behavior therapy* (Vol. 4, pp. 1–29). Amsterdam: Swets & Zeitlinger.

Ehlers, A., Margraf, J., Davies, S., & Roth, W. T. (1988). Selective processing of threat cues in subjects with panic attacks. *Cognition and Emotion, 2*, 201–219.

Ehlers, A., Taylor, B., Margraf, J., Roth, W., & Birnbaumer, R. (1988). Anxiety induced by false heart rate feedback in patients with panic disorder. *Behaviour Research and Therapy, 26*, 2–11.

Emmelkamp, P. (1980). Agoraphobics' interpersonal problems. *Archives of General Psychiatry, 37*, 1303–1306.

Emmelkamp, P. (1982). *Phobic and obsessive–compulsive disorders: Theory, research, and practice*. New York: Plenum Press.

Emmelkamp, P. M., Brilman, E., Kuiper, H., & Mersch, P. (1986). The treatment of agoraphobia: A comparison of self-instructional training, rational emotive therapy, and exposure in vivo. *Behavior Modification, 10*, 37–53.

Emmelkamp, P. M., Kuipers, A. C., & Eggeraat, J. B. (1978) Cognitive modification versus prolonged exposure in vivo: A comparison with agoraphobics as subjects. *Behaviour Research and Therapy, 16*, 33–41.

Emmelkamp, P. M., & Mersch, P. P. (1982) Cognition and exposure in vivo in the treatment of agoraphobia: Short-term and delayed effects. *Cognitive Therapy and Research, 6*, 77–90.

Emmelkamp, P. M. G., & Ultee, K. A. (1974). A comparison of "successive approximation" and "self-observation" in the treatment of agoraphobia. *Behavior Therapy, 5*, 606–613.

Emmelkamp, P. M. G., & Wessels, H. (1975). Flooding in imagination vs. flooding in vivo: A comparison with agoraphobics. *Behaviour Research and Therapy, 13*, 7–15.

Evans, L., Holt, C., & Oei, T. P. S. (1991). Long term follow-up of agoraphobics treated by brief intensive group cognitive behaviour therapy. *Australian and New Zealand Journal of Psychiatry, 25*, 343–349.

Faravelli, C., Pallanti, S., Biondi, F., Paterniti, S., & Scarpato, M. A. (1992). Onset of panic disorder. *American Journal of Psychiatry, 149*, 827–828.

Fava, G. A., Zielezny, M., Savron, G., & Grandi, S. (1995). Long-term effects of behavioural treatment for panic disorder with agoraphobia. *British Journal of Psychiatry, 166*, 87–92.

Feigenbaum, W. (1988). Long-term efficacy of ungraded versus graded massed exposure in agoraphobics. In I. Hand & H. Wittchen (Eds.), *Panic and phobias: Treatments and variables affecting course and outcome* (pp. 149–158). Berlin: Springer-Verlag.

Foa, E. B., Jameson, J. S., Turner, R. M., & Payne, L. L. (1980). Massed vs. spaced exposure sessions in the treatment of agoraphobia. *Behaviour Research and Therapy, 18*, 333–338.

Foa, E. B., & Kozak, M. S. (1986). Emotional processing of fear: Exposure to corrective information. *Psychological Bulletin, 99*, 20–35.

Friedman, S., & Paradis, C. (1991). African-American patients with panic disorder and agoraphobia. *Journal of Anxiety Disorders, 5*, 35–41.

Friedman, S., Paradis, C. M., & Hatch, M. (1994). Characteristics of African-American and white patients with panic disorder and agoraphobia. *Hospital and Community Psychiatry, 45*, 798–803.

Fry, W. (1962). The marital context of an anxiety syndrome. *Family Process, 1*, 245–252.

Garssen, B., de Ruiter, C., & van Dyck, R. (1992). Breathing retraining: A rational placebo? *Clinical Psychology Review, 12*, 141–153.

Ghosh, A., & Marks, I. M. (1987). Self-directed exposure for agoraphobia: A controlled trial. *Behavior Therapy, 18*, 3–16.

Goisman, R. M., Warshaw, M. G., Peterson, L. G., Rogers, M. P., Cuneo, P., Hunt, M. F., Tomlin-Albanese, J. M., Kazim, A., Gollan, J. K., Epstein-Kaye, T., Reich, J. H., & Keller, M. B. (1994). Panic, agoraphobia, and panic disorder with agoraphobia: Data from a multicenter anxiety disorders study. *Journal of Nervous and Mental Disease, 182*, 72–79.

Goldstein, A., & Chambless, D. (1978). A reanalysis of agoraphobia. *Behavior Therapy, 9*, 47–59.

Gould, R. A., & Clum, G. A. (1995). Self-help plus minimal therapist contact in the treatment of panic disorder: A replication and extension. *Behavior Therapy, 26*, 533–546.

Gould, R. A., Clum, G. A., & Shapiro, D. (1993). The use of bibliotherapy in the treatment of panic: A preliminary investigation. *Behavior Therapy, 24*, 241–252.

Gray, J. A. (1987). *The psychology of fear and stress.* New York: Cambridge University Press.

Grayson, J. B., Foa, E. B., & Steketee, G. (1982). Habituation during exposure treatment: Distraction versus attention-focusing. *Behaviour Research and Therapy, 20*, 323–328.

Griez, E., & van den Hout, M. A. (1986). CO_2 inhalation in the treatment of panic attacks. *Behaviour Research and Therapy, 24*, 145–150.

Grilo, C. M., Money, R., Barlow, D. H., Goddard, A. W., Gorman, J. M., Hofmann, S. G., Papp, L. A., Shear, M. K., & Woods, S. W. (1998). Pretreatment patient factors predicting attrition from a multicenter randomized controlled treatment study for panic disorder. *Comprehensive Psychiatry, 39*, 323–332.

Hafner, R. J. (1976). Fresh symptom emergence after intensive behavior therapy. *British Journal of Psychiatry, 129*, 378–383.

Hafner, R. J. (1984). Predicting the effects on husbands of behavior therapy for agoraphobia. *Behaviour Research and Therapy, 22*, 217–226.

Hafner, J., & Marks, I. (1977). Exposure in vivo of agoraphobics: Contributions of diazepam, group exposure, and anxiety evocation. *Psychological Medicine, 6*, 71–88.

Hafner, J., & Milton, F. (1977). The influence of propranolol on the exposure in vivo of agoraphobics. *Psychological Medicine, 7*, 419–425.

Hand, I., & Lamontagne, Y. (1976). The exacerbation of interpersonal problems after rapid phobia removal. *Psychotherapy: Theory, Research and Practice, 13*, 405–411.

Harcourt, L., Kirkby, K., Daniels, B., & Montgomery, I. (1998). The differential effects of personality on computer-based treatment of agoraphobia. *Comprehensive Psychiatry, 39*, 303–307.

Haslam, M. T. (1974). The relationship between the effect of lactate infusion on anxiety states and their amelioration by carbon dioxide inhalation. *British Journal of Psychiatry, 125*, 88–90.

Hayward, C., Killen, J. D., Hammer, L. D., Litt, I. F., Wilson, D. M., Simmonds, B., & Taylor, C. B. (1992). Pubertal stage and panic attack history in sixth- and seventh-grade girls. *American Journal of Psychiatry, 149*, 1239–1243.

Hecker, J. E., Fink, C. M., Vogeltanz, N. D., & Thorpe, G. L. (1998). Cognitive restructuring and interoceptive exposure in the treatment of panic disorder: A crossover study. *Behavioural and Cognitive Psychotherapy, 26*, 115–131.

Hecker, J. E., Losee, M. C., Fritzler, B. K., & Fink, C. M. (1996). Self-directed versus therapist-directed cognitive behavioral treatment for panic disorder. *Journal of Anxiety Disorders, 10*, 253–265.

Hibbert, G., & Pilsbury, D. (1989). Hyperventilation: Is it a cause of panic attacks? *British Journal of Psychiatry, 155,* 805–809.

Himadi, W., Cerny, J., Barlow, D., Cohen, S., & O'Brien, G. (1986). The relationship of marital adjustment to agoraphobia treatment outcome. *Behaviour Research and Therapy, 24,* 107–115.

Hoffart, A. (1995). A comparison of cognitive and guided mastery therapy of agoraphobia. *Behaviour Research and Therapy, 33,* 423–434.

Hoffart, A. (1997). Interpersonal problems among patients suffering from panic disorder with agoraphobia before and after treatment. *British Journal of Medical Psychology, 70,* 149–157.

Hoffart, A., & Hedley, L. M. (1997). Personality traits among panic disorder with agoraphobia patients before and after symptom-focused treatment. *Journal of Anxiety Disorders, 11,* 77–87.

Hoffart, A., & Martinsen, E. W. (1993). The effect of personality disorders and anxious–depressive comorbidity on outcome in patients with unipolar depression and with panic disorder and agoraphobia. *Journal of Personality Disorders, 7,* 304–311.

Hofmann, S. G., & Barlow, D. H. (1996). Ambulatory psychophysiological monitoring: A potentially useful tool when treating panic relapse. *Cognitive and Behavioral Practice, 3,* 53–61.

Hofmann, S. G., Barlow, D. H., Papp, L. A., Detweiler, M. F., Ray, S. E., Shear, M. K., Woods, S. W., & Gorman, J. M. (1998). Pretreatment attrition in a comparative treatment outcome study on panic disorder. *American Journal of Psychiatry, 155,* 43–47.

Holden, A. E. O., O'Brien, G. T., Barlow, D. H., Stetson, D., & Infantino, A. (1983). Self-help manual for agoraphobia: A preliminary report of effectiveness. *Behavior Therapy, 14,* 545–556.

Holt, P., & Andrews, G. (1989). Hyperventilation and anxiety in panic disorder, agoraphobia, and generalized anxiety disorder. *Behaviour Research and Therapy, 27,* 453–460.

Hope, D. A., Rapee, R. M., Heimberg, R. G., & Dombeck, M. J. (1990). Representations of the self in social phobia: Vulnerability to social threat. *Cognitive Therapy and Research, 14,* 177–189.

Hornsveld, H., Garssen, B., Dop, M. F., & Van Spiegel, P. (1990). Symptom reporting during voluntary hyperventilation and mental load: Implications for diagnosing hyperventilation syndrome. *Journal of Psychosomatic Research, 34,* 687–697.

Horwath, E., Lish, J. D., Johnson, J., Hornig, C. D., & Weissman, M. M. (1993). Agoraphobia without panic: Clinical reappraisal of an epidemiologic finding. *American Journal of Psychiatry, 150,* 1496–1501.

Ito, L. M., Noshirvani, H., Basoglu, M., & Marks, I. M. (1996). Does exposure to internal cues enhance exposure to external exposure to external cues in agoraphobia with panic? *Psychotherapy and Psychosomatics, 65,* 24–28.

Izard, C. E. (1992). Basic emotions, relations among emotions, and emotion cognition relations. *Psychological Review, 99,* 561–565.

Jacob, R. G., Furman, J. M., Clark, D. B., & Durrant, J. D. (1992). Vestibular symptoms, panic, and phobia: Overlap and possible relationships. *Annals of Clinical Psychiatry, 4,* 163–174.

Jansson, L., & Ost, L.-G. (1982). Behavioral treatments for agoraphobia: An evaluative review. *Clinical Psychology Review, 2,* 311–336.

Keijsers, G. P. J., Schaap, C. P. D. R., Hoogduin, C. A. L., & Lammers, M. W. (1995) Patient–therapist interaction in the behavioral treatment of panic disorder with agoraphobia. *Behavior Modification, 19,* 491–517.

Kessler, R. C., McGonagle, K. A., Zhao, S., & Nelson, C. B., Hughes, M., Eshkeman, S., Wittchen, H. U., & Kendler, K. S. (1994). Lifetime and 12 month prevalence of DSM-III-R psychiatric disorders in the United States: Results from the National Comorbidity Study. *Archives of General Psychiatry, 51,* 8–19.

Keyl, P. M., & Eaton, W. W. (1990). Risk factors for the onset of panic disorder and other panic attacks in a prospective, population-based study. *American Journal of Epidemiology, 131,* 301–311.

King, N. J., Gullone, E., Tonge, B. J., & Ollendick, T. H. (1993) Self-reports of panic attacks and manifest anxiety in adolescents. *Behaviour Research and Therapy, 31,* 111–116.

Kraft, A. R., & Hoogduin, C. A. (1984). The hyperventiliation syndrome: A pilot study of the effectiveness of treatment. *British Journal of Psychiatry, 145,* 538–542.

Laberge, B., Gauthier, J. . G., Cote, G., Plamondon, J., & Cormier, H. J. (1993). Cognitive-behavioral therapy of panic disorder with secondary major depression: A preliminary investigation. *Journal of Consulting and Clinical Psychology, 61,* 1028–1037.

Lang, A. J., & Craske, M. G. (2000). Manipulations of exposure-based therapy to reduce return of fear: A replication. *Behaviour Research and Therapy, 38,* 1–12.

Lang, P. J. (1971). The application of psychophysiological methods to the study of psychotherapy and behavior modification. In A. E. Bergin & S. L. Garfield (Eds.), *Handbook of psychotherapy and behavior change: An empirical analysis* (pp. 75–125). New York: Wiley.

Lecrubier, Y., Bakker, A., Dunbar, G., & Judge, R. (1997). A comparison of paroxetine, clomipramine and placebo in the treatment of panic disorder. *Acta Psychiatrica Scandinavica, 95,* 145–152.

LeDoux, J. E. (1996). *The emotional brain: The mysterious underpinnings of emotional life.* New York: Simon & Schuster.

Lehman, C. L., Brown, T. A., & Barlow, D. H. (1998). Effects of cognitive-behavioral treatment for panic disorder with agoraphobia on concurrent alcohol abuse. *Behavior Therapy, 29,* 423–433.

Lelliott, P., Marks, I., McNamee, G., & Tobena, A. (1989). Onset of panic disorder with agoraphobia: Toward an integrated model. *Archives of General Psychiatry, 46,* 1000–1004.

Lidren, D. M., Watkins, P., Gould, R. A., Clum, G. A., Asterino, M., & Tulloch, H. L. (1994). A comparison of bibliotherapy and group therapy in the treatment of panic disorder. *Journal of Consulting and Clinical Psychology, 62,* 865–869.

Lilienfeld, S. O. (1997). The relation of anxiety sensitivity to higher and lower order personality dimensions: Implications for the etiology of panic attacks. *Journal of Abnormal Psychology, 106,* 539–544.

Maidenberg, E., Chen, E., Craske, M., Bohn, P., & Bystritsky, A. (1996). Specificity of attentional bias in panic disorder and social phobia. *Journal of Anxiety Disorders, 10,* 529–541.

Maier, S. F., Laudenslager, M. L., & Ryan, S. M. (1985). Stressor controllability, immune function and endogenous opiates. In F. R. Brush & J. B. Overmeier (Eds.), *Affect, conditioning and cognition: Essays on the determinants of behavior* (pp. 183–201). Hillsdale, NJ: Erlbaum.

Maller, R. G., & Reiss, S. (1992). Anxiety sensitivity in 1984 and panic attacks in 1987. *Journal of Anxiety Disorders, 6,* 241–247.

Mannuzza, S., Fyer, A. J., Martin, L. Y., Gallops, M. S., Endicott, J., Gorman, J. M., Liebowitz, M. R., & Klein, D. F. (1989). Reliability of anxiety assessment: I. Diagnostic agreement. *Archives of General Psychiatry, 46,* 1093–1101.

Marchand, A., Goyer, L. R., Dupuis, G., & Mainguy, N. (1998). Personality disorders and the outcome of cognitive-behavioural treatment of panic disorder with agoraphobia. *Canadian Journal of Behavioural Science, 30*(1), 14–23.

Margraf, J., Taylor, C. B., Ehlers, A., Roth, W. T., & Agras, W. S. (1987). Panic attacks in the natural environment. *Journal of Nervous and Mental Disease, 175,* 558–565.

Marks, I. M. (1978). *Living with fear.* New York: McGraw-Hill.

Marks, I. M., Swinson, R. P., Basoglu, M., Kuch, K., Noshirvani, H., O'Sullivan, G., Lelliott, P. T., Kirby, M., McNamee, G., Sengun, S., & Wickwire, K. (1993). Alprazolam and exposure alone and combined in panic disorder with agoraphobia: A controlled study in London and Toronto. *British Journal of Psychiatry, 162,* 776–787.

Marshall, W. L. (1985). The effects of variable exposure in flooding therapy. *Behavior Therapy, 16,* 117–135.

Mavissakalian, M., & Hamman, M. (1986). DSM-III personality disorder in agoraphobia. *Comprehensive Psychiatry, 27,* 471–479.

Mavissakalian, M., & Hamman, M. (1987). DSM-III personality disorder in agoraphobia: II. Changes with treatment. *Comprehensive Psychiatry, 28,* 356–361.

McLean, P. D., Woody, S., Taylor, S., & Koch, W. J. (1998). Comorbid panic disorder and major depression: Implications for cognitive-behavioral therapy. *Journal of Consulting and Clinical Psychology, 66,* 240–247.

McNally, R., & Lorenz, M. (1987). Anxiety sensitivity in agoraphobics. *Journal of Behavior Therapy and Experimental Psychiatry, 18,* 3–11.

McNally, R. J., Riemann, B. C., Louro, C. E., Lukach, B. M., & Kim, E. (1992). Cognitive processing of emotional information in panic disorder. *Behaviour Research and Therapy, 30,* 143–149.

McNamee, G., O'Sullivan, G., Lelliott, P., & Marks, I. M. (1989). Telephone-guided treatment for housebound agoraphobics with panic disorder: Exposure vs. relaxation. *Behavior Therapy, 20,* 491–497.

Michelson, L., Mavissakalian, M., & Marchione, K. (1985). Cognitive and behavioral treatments of agoraphobia: Clinical, behavioral, and psychophysiological outcomes. *Journal of Consulting and Clinical Psychology, 53,* 913–925.

Michelson, L., Mavissakalian, M., & Marchione, K. (1988). Cognitive, behavioral, and psychophysiological treatments of agoraphobia: A comparative outcome investigation. *Behavior Therapy, 19,* 97–120.

Michelson, L., Mavissakalian, M., Marchione, K., Ulrich, R., Marchione, N., & Testa, S. (1990). Psychophysiological outcome of cognitive, behavioral, and psychophysiologically-based treatments of agoraphobia. *Behaviour Research and Therapy, 28,* 127–139.

Milton, F., & Hafner, J. (1979). The outcome of behavior therapy for agoraphobia in relation to marital adjustment. *Archives of General Psychiatry, 36,* 807–811.

Murphy, M. T., Michelson, L. K., Marchione, K., Marchione, N., & Testa, S. (1998). The role of self-directed in vivo exposure in combination with cognitive therapy, relaxation training, or therapist-assisted exposure in the treatment of panic disorder with agoraphobia. *Behaviour Research and Therapy, 12,* 117–138.

Myers, J., Weissman, M., Tischler, C., Holzer, C., Orvaschel, H., Anthony, J., Boyd, J., Burke, J., Kramer, M., & Stoltzman, R. (1984). Six-month prevalence of psychiatric disorders in three communities. *Archives of General Psychiatry, 41,* 959–967.

Nair, N. P., Bakish, D., Saxena, B., Amin, M., Schwartz, G., & West, T. E. (1996). Comparison of fluvoxamine, imipramine, and placebo in the treatment of outpatients with panic disorder. *Anxiety, 2,* 192–198.

Neron, S., Lacroix, D., & Chaput, Y. (1995). Group vs individual cognitive behaviour therapy in panic disorder: An open clinical trial with a six month follow-up. *Canadian Journal of Behavioural Science, 27,* 379–392.

Newman, M. G., Kenardy, J., Herman, S., & Taylor, C. B. (1997). Comparison of palmtop-computer-assisted brief cognitive-behavioral treatment to cognitive-behavioral treatment for panic disorder. *Journal of Consulting and Clinical Psychology, 65,* 178–183.

Norton, G. R., Cox, B. J., & Malan, J. (1992). Nonclinical panickers: A critical review. *Clinical Psychology Review, 12,* 121–139.

Noyes, R., Clancy, J., Garvey, M. J., & Anderson, D. J. (1987). Is agoraphobia a variant of panic disorder or a separate illness? *Journal of Anxiety Disorders, 1,* 3–13.

Noyes, R., Crowe, R. R., Harris, E. L., Hamra, B. J., McChesney, C. M., & Chaudhry, D. R. (1986). Relationship between panic disorder and agoraphobia: A family study. *Archives of General Psychiatry, 43,* 227–232.

Noyes, R., Reich, J., Suelzer, M., & Christiansen, J. (1991). Personality traits associated with panic disorder: Change associated with treatment. *Comprehensive Psychiatry, 32,* 282–294.

Öst, L.-G. (1988). Applied relaxation vs. progressive relaxation in the treatment of panic disorder. *Behaviour Research and Therapy, 26,* 13–22.

Öst, L.-G., & Westling, B. E. (1995). Applied relaxation vs cognitive behavior therapy in the treatment of panic disorder. *Behaviour Research and Therapy, 33,* 145–158.

Öst, L.-G., Westling, B. E., & Hellstrom, K. (1993). Applied relaxation, exposure in vivo, and cognitive methods in the treatment of panic disorder with agoraphobia. *Behaviour Research and Therapy*, *31*, 383–394.

Otto, M. W., Pollack, M. H., & Sabatino, S. (1996). Maintenance of remission following cognitive behavior therapy for panic disorder: Possible deleterious effects of concurrent medication treatment. *Behavior Therapy*, *27*, 473–482.

Pollard, C. A., Bronson, S. S., & Kenney, M. R. (1989). Prevalence of agoraphobia without panic in clinical settings. *American Journal of Psychiatry*, *146*, 559.

Pollard, C. A., Pollard, H. J., & Corn, K. J. (1989). Panic onset and major events in the lives of agoraphobics: A test of contiguity. *Journal of Abnormal Psychology*, *98*, 318–321.

Rachman, S. J. (1984). Agoraphobia: A safety-signal perspective. *Behaviour Research and Therapy*, *22*, 59–70.

Rachman, S. J., Craske, M. G., Tallman, K., & Solyom, C. (1986). Does escape behavior strengthen agoraphobic avoidance?: A replication. *Behaviour Therapy*, *17*, 366–384.

Rachman, S. J., & Hodgson, R. S. (1974). Synchrony and desynchrony in fear and avoidance. *Behaviour Research and Therapy*, *12*, 311–318.

Rachman, S. J., & Levitt, K. (1985). Panics and their consequences. *Behaviour Research and Therapy*, *23*, 585–600.

Rachman, S. J., Lopatka, C., & Levitt, K. (1988). Experimental analyses of panic: II. panic patients. *Behaviour Research and Therapy*, *26*, 33–40.

Rapee, R. M. (1985). A case of panic disorder treated with breathing retraining. *Behavior Therapy and Experimental Psychiatry*, *16*, 63–65.

Rapee, R. M. (1991). Panic disorder. *International Review of Psychiatry*, *3*, 141–149.

Rapee, R. M. (1994). Detection of somatic sensations in panic disorder. *Behaviour Research and Therapy*, *32*, 825–831.

Rapee, R. M., Craske, M. G., & Barlow, D. H. (1990). Subject described features of panic attacks using a new self-monitoring form. *Journal of Anxiety Disorders*, *4*, 171–181.

Rapee, R. M., Craske, M. G., & Barlow, D. H. (1995). Assessment instrument for panic disorder that includes fear of sensation-producing activities: The Albany Panic and Phobia Questionnaire. *Anxiety*, *1*, 114–122.

Rapee, R. M., Craske, M. G., Brown, T. A., & Barlow, D. H. (1996). Measurement of perceived control over anxiety-related events. *Behavior Therapy*, *27*, 279–293.

Rapee, R. M., Litwin, E. M., & Barlow, D. H. (1990). Impact of life events on subjects with panic disorder and on comparison subjects. *American Journal of Psychiatry*, *147*, 640–644.

Rapee, R. M., Mattick, R., & Murrell, E. (1986). Cognitive mediation in the affective component of spontaneous panic attacks. *Journal of Behavior Therapy and Experimental Psychiatry*, *17*, 245–253.

Rapee, R. M., & Murrell, E. (1988) Predictors of agoraphobic avoidance. *Journal of Anxiety Disorders*, *2*, 203–217.

Rathus, J. H., Sanderson, W. C., Miller, A. L., & Wetzler, S. (1995). Impact of personality functioning on cognitive behavioral treatment of panic disorder: A preliminary report. *Journal of Personality Disorders*, *9*, 160–168.

Razran, G. (1961). The observable unconscious and the inferable conscious in current Soviet psychophysiology: Interoceptive conditioning, semantic conditioning, and the orienting reflex. *Psychological Review*, *68*, 81–147.

Reich, J., Noyes, R., & Troughton, E. (1987). Dependent personality disorder associated with phobic avoidance in patients with panic disorder. *American Journal of Psychiatry*, *144*, 323–326.

Reiss, S., Peterson, R., Gursky, D., & McNally, R. (1986). Anxiety sensitivity, anxiety frequency, and the prediction of fearfulness. *Behaviour Research and Therapy*, *24*, 1–8.

Rice, K. M., & Blanchard, E. B. (1982). Biofeedback in the treatment of anxiety disorders. *Clinical Psychology Review*, *2*, 557–577.

Rijken, H., Kraaimaat, F., de Ruiter, C., & Garssen, B. (1992). A follow-up study on short-term treatment of agoraphobia. *Behaviour Research and Therapy*, *30*, 63–66.

Rowe, M. K., & Craske, M. G. (1998). Effects of an expanding-spaced vs. massed exposure schedule on fear reduction and return of fear. *Behaviour Research and Therapy*, *36*, 701–717.

Roy-Byrne, P. P., Geraci, M., & Uhde, T. W. (1986). Life events and the onset of panic disorder. *American Journal of Psychiatry*, *143*, 1424–1427.

Rupert, P. A., Dobbins, K., & Mathew, R. J. (1981). EMG biofeedback and relaxation instructions in the treatment of chronic anxiety. *American Journal of Clinical Biofeedback*, *4*, 52–61.

Salkovskis, P. M., Clark, D. M., & Gelder, M. G. (1996). Cognition–behaviour links in the persistence of panic. *Behaviour Research and Therapy*, *34*, 453–458.

Salkovskis, P. M., Clark, D. M., & Hackmann, A. (1991). Treatment of panic attacks using cognitive therapy without exposure or breathing retraining. *Behaviour Research and Therapy*, *29*, 161–166.

Salkovskis, P. M., Warwick, H., Clark, D. M., & Wessels, D. (1986). A demonstration of acute hyperventilation during naturally occurring panic attacks. *Behaviour Research and Therapy*, *24*, 91–94.

Sanderson, W. C., DiNardo, P. A., Rapee, R. M., & Barlow, D. H. (1990). Syndrome comorbidity in patients diagnosed with a DSM-III-R anxiety disorder. *Journal of Abnormal Psychology*, *99*, 308–312.

Sanderson, W. S., Rapee, R. M., & Barlow, D. H. (1989). The influence of an illusion of control on panic attacks induced via inhalation of 5.5% carbon dioxide enriched air. *Archives of General Psychiatry*, *48*, 157–162.

Sartory, G., Master, D., & Rachman, S. J. (1989). Safety-signal therapy in agoraphobics: A preliminary test. *Behaviour Research and Therapy*, *27*, 205–209.

Schmidt, N. B., Lerew, D. R., & Jackson, R. J. (1997). The role of anxiety sensitivity in the pathogenesis of panic: Prospective evaluation of spontaneous panic attacks during acute stress. *Journal of Abnormal Psychology*, *106*, 355–364.

Schmidt, N. B., Trakowski, J. H., & Staab, J. P. (1997). Extinction of panicogenic effects of a 35% CO_2 challenge in patients with panic disorder. *Journal of Abnormal Psychology, 106,* 630–638.

Schmidt, R. A., & Bjork, R. A. (1992). New conceptualizations of practice: Common principles in three paradigms suggest new concepts for training. *Psychological Science, 3,* 207–217.

Sharp, D. M., Power, K. G., Simpson, R. J., Swanson, V., & Anstee, J. A. (1997). Global measures of outcome in a controlled comparison of pharmacological and psychological treatment of panic disorder and agoraphobia in primary care. *British Journal of General Practice, 47,* 150–155.

Shulman, I. D., Cox, B. J., Swinson, R. P., Kuch, K., & Reichman, J. T. (1994). Precipitating events, locations and reactions associated with initial unexpected panic attacks. *Behaviour Research and Therapy, 32,* 17–20.

Siddle, D. A., & Bond, N. W. (1988). Avoidance learning, Pavlovian conditioning, and the development of phobias. *Biological Psychology, 27,* 167–183.

Spanier, G. (1976). Measuring dyadic adjustment: New scales for assessing the quality of marriage and similar dyads. *Journal of Marriage and the Family, 38,* 15–38.

Spielberger, C., Gorsuch, R., Lushene, R., Vagg, P., & Jacobs, G. (1983). *Manual for the State–Trait Anxiety Inventory.* Palo Alto, CA: Consulting Psychologists Press.

Stanley, M. A., Beck, J. G., Averill, P. M., Baldwin, L. E., Deagle, E. A., & Stadler, J. G. (1996). Patterns of change during cognitive behavioral treatment for panic disorder. *Journal of Nervous and Mental Disease, 184,* 567–572.

Stern, R. S., & Marks, I. M. (1973). Brief and prolonged flooding: A comparison of agoraphobic patients. *Archives of General Psychiatry, 28,* 270–276.

Swinson, R. P., Fergus, K. D., Cox, B. J., & Wickwire, K. (1995). Efficacy of telephone-administered behavioral therapy for panic disorder with agoraphobia. *Behaviour Research and Therapy, 33,* 465–469.

Taylor, S., Koch, W. J., & McNally, R. J. (1992). How does anxiety sensitivity vary across the anxiety disorders? *Journal of Anxiety Disorders, 6,* 249–259.

Telch, M. J., Brouillard, M., Telch, C. F., Agras, W. S., & Taylor, C. B. (1989). Role of cognitive appraisal in panic-related avoidance. *Behaviour Research and Therapy, 27,* 373–383.

Telch, M. J., & Lucas, R. A. (1994). Combined pharmacological and psychological treatment of panic disorder: Current status and future directions. In B. E. Wolfe & J. D. Maser (Eds.), *Treatment of panic disorder: A consensus development conference* (pp. 177–197). Washington, DC: American Psychiatric Press.

Telch, M. J., Lucas, J. A., & Nelson, P. (1989). Nonclinical panic in college students: An investigation of prevalence and symptomatology. *Journal of Abnormal Psychology, 98,* 300–306.

Telch, M. J., Lucas, J. A., Schmidt, N. B., Hanna, H. H., Jaimez, T. L., & Lucas, R. A. (1993). Group cognitive-behavioral treatment of panic disorder. *Behaviour Research and Therapy, 31,* 279–287.

Telch, M. J., Schmidt, N. B., Jaimez, T. L., Jacquin, K. M., & Harrington, P. J. (1995) Impact of cognitive-behavioral treatment on quality of life in panic disorder patients. *Journal of Consulting and Clinical Psychology, 63,* 823–830.

Telch, M. J., Sherman, M., & Lucas, J. (1989). Anxiety sensitivity: Unitary personality trait or domain specific appraisals? *Journal of Anxiety Disorders, 3,* 25–32.

Thyer, B. A., Himle, J., Curtis, G. C., Cameron, O. G., & Nesse, R. M. (1985). A comparison of panic disorder and agoraphobia with panic attacks. *Comprehensive Psychiatry, 26,* 208–214.

Tsao, J. C. I., & Craske, M. G. (in press). Timing of treatment and return of fear: Effects of massed, uniform and expanding spaced exposure schedules. *Behavior Therapy.*

Tsao, J. C. I., Lewin, M. R., & Craske, M. G. (1998). The effects of cognitive-behavior therapy for panic disorder on comorbid conditions. *Journal of Anxiety Disorders, 12,* 357–371.

van Balkom, A. J. L. M., de Beurs, E., Koele, P., Lange, A., & van Dyck, R. (1996). Long-term benzodiazepine use is associated with smaller treatment gain in panic disorder with agoraphobia. *Journal of Nervous and Mental Disease, 184,* 133–135.

van den Hout, M., Arntz, A., & Hoekstra, R. (1994). Exposure reduced agoraphobia but not panic, and cognitive therapy reduced panic but not agoraphobia. *Behaviour Research and Therapy, 32,* 447–451.

Wade, A. G., Lepola, U., Koponen, H. J., Pedersen, V., & Pedersen, T. (1997). The effect of citalopram in panic disorder. *British Journal of Psychiatry, 170,* 549–553.

Wade, W. A., Treat, T. A., & Stuart, G. L. (1998). Transporting an empirically supported treatment for panic disorder to a service clinic setting: A benchmarking strategy. *Journal of Consulting and Clinical Psychology, 66,* 231–239.

Wardle, J., Hayward, P., Higgitt, A., Stabl, M., Blizard, R., & Gray, J. (1994). Effects of concurrent diazepam treatment on the outcome of exposure therapy in agoraphobia. *Behaviour Research and Therapy, 32,* 203–215.

Welkowitz, L., Papp, L., Cloitre, M., Liebowitz, M., Martin, L., & Gorman, J. (1991). Cognitive-behavior therapy for panic disorder delivered by psychopharmacologically oriented clinicians. *Journal of Nervous and Mental Disease, 179,* 473–477.

Westling, B. E., & Öst, L.-G. (1999). Brief cognitive behaviour therapy of panic disorder. *Scandinavian Journal of Behaviour Therapy, 28,* 49–57.

Williams, K. E., & Chambless, D. (1990). The relationship between therapist characteristics and outcome of in vivo exposure treatment for agoraphobia. *Behavior Therapy, 21,* 111–116.

Williams, K. E., & Chambless, D. L. (1994). The results of exposure-based treatment in agoraphobia. In S. Friedman (Ed.), *Anxiety disorders in African Americans* (pp. 111–116). New York: Springer.

Williams, S. L. (1988). Addressing misconceptions about phobia, anxiety, and self-efficacy: A reply to Marks. *Journal of Anxiety Disorders, 2,* 277–289.

Williams, S. L., & Falbo, J. (1996). Cognitive and performance-based treatments for panic attacks in people with varying degrees of agoraphobic disability. *Behaviour Research and Therapy, 34,* 253–264.

Williams, S. L, Turner, S. M., & Peer, D. F. (1985). Guided mastery and performance desensitization treatments for severe acrophobia. *Journal of Consulting and Clinical Psychology, 53,* 237–247.

Williams, S. L., & Zane, G. (1989). Guided mastery and stimulus exposure treatments for severe performance anxiety in agoraphobics. *Behaviour Research and Therapy, 27,* 237–245.

Wilson, T. (1996). Manual-based treatments: The clinical applications of research findings. *Behaviour Research and Therapy, 34,* 295–314.

Woody, S., McLean, P., Taylor, S., & Koch, W. J. (1999). Treatment of major depression in the context of panic disorder. *Journal of Affective Disorders, 53,* 163–174.

Zarate, R., Rapee, R. M., Craske, M. G., & Barlow, D. H. (1988). *Response norms for symptom induction procedures.* Poster presented at the 22nd Annual Convention of the Association for the Advancement of Behavior Therapy, New York.

Chapter 2

POSTTRAUMATIC STRESS DISORDER

Patricia A. Resick
Karen S. Calhoun

Thirdere are few, if any, more tragic examples of severe psychopathology than rape-induced posttraumatic stress disorder. The occurrence of rape is far more common than was previously thought, and the emotional consequences can be lifelong. In this chapter, the case of "Cindy" illustrates the psychopathology associated with posttraumatic stress disorder in all its nuances, and provides a very personal and lucid account of the impact of rape trauma. More important, the next generation of treatments for posttraumatic stress disorder, termed "cognitive processing therapy" by the authors, is sufficiently detailed to allow knowledgeable practitioners to incorporate this treatment program into their practice. This comprehensive treatment program takes advantage of the latest developments in our knowledge of the psychopathology of trauma impact by incorporating treatment strategies specifically tailored to overcome trauma-related psychopathology.—D. H. B.

DIAGNOSIS AND PREVALENCE

Posttraumatic stress disorder (PTSD) was first introduced in the third edition of the *Diagnostic and Statistical Manual of Mental Disorders* (DSM-III; American Psychiatric Association [APA], 1980). Previous editions had referred to stress reactions with terms like "gross stress reaction" and "transient situational disturbance," but without empirical support or specific criteria. Classified as a form of anxiety disorder (no longer a neurosis), the DSM-III description of PTSD was based on the existing empirical literature, most of it derived from studies of combat veterans. But it was recognized that exposure to other forms of trauma could lead to similar symptoms. This stimulated a convergence of disparate areas of research on different types of trauma, which is resulting in rapid developments in theory and treatment. It is now commonly accepted that the type of trauma experienced (although each has some unique features) is less impor-

tant than are trauma severity and individual reactions and vulnerabilities. In this chapter, we focus particularly on rape-related PTSD.

The criteria for PTSD in DSM-IV (APA, 1994) represent refinements over the DSM-III and DSM-III-R (APA, 1987) criteria, because the DSM-IV criteria are based on field trials. To qualify for a diagnosis of PTSD according to DSM-IV, the individual must have witnessed, experienced, or otherwise been confronted with an event that involved actual or possible death, grave injury, or threat to physical integrity. Second, the individual's response to the event must include severe helplessness, fear, or horror. Thus an event is defined as "traumatic" when it has involved death or serious injury or the threat of death or injury, and when the individual experiences strong negative affect in response to the event (Criterion A). In earlier versions of the DSM (APA, 1980, 1987), a "traumatic stressor" was defined as an event outside the range of usual human experience that almost anyone would find markedly distressing. Unfortunately, this technically eliminated relatively common traumatic experiences such as childhood abuse, domestic violence, and sexual assault, because of their high frequency across the population (although uncommon within an individual's life). The DSM-IV definition eliminates this problem and emphasizes that the direct or indirect threat to life or well-being and the individual's response to that threat are specifically what make a given event traumatic. This was derived from numerous research studies finding that the experience of life threat or subjective distress were significant predictors of PTSD development (Blank, 1993; Davidson & Smith, 1990; Girelli, Resick, Marhoefer-Dvorak, & Kotsis-Hutter, 1986; Kilpatrick & Resnick, 1993; March, 1993).

Symptom criteria fall into three broad categories. These include reexperiencing symptoms, avoidance and numbing symptoms, and physiological hyperarousal. According to Criterion B, the reexperiencing symptoms must be experienced in one of the following ways: Memories of the trauma may intrude into consciousness repetitively, without warning, seemingly "out of the blue," without triggers or reminders to elicit them. The person with PTSD may experience intensely vivid reenactment experiences, or "flashbacks." Intrusive memories may also occur during the sleeping state in the form of thematically related nightmares. In addition, when faced with cues associated with the traumatic event, whether actual or symbolic, the individual may exhibit intense psychological reactions (terror, disgust, depression, etc.) and/or physiological responses (increased heart rate, perspiration, and rapid breathing, etc.).

These reexperiencing symptoms are generally experienced as distressing and intrusive, because the individual has no control over when or how they occur and because they elicit strong negative emotions associated with the initial trauma (Janoff-Bulman, 1992; Resick & Schnicke, 1992). Fear stimuli (cues) are sometimes obvious, as in the case of a combat veteran who ducks in fear when a car backfires because it sounds like gunfire. However, sometimes the relationship between the trauma and the cue is not immediately clear. For example, one survivor of rape trauma was fearful of taking showers, even though the rape occurred away from her home. However, as she began to deal with the rape in treatment, she real-ized that every time she took a shower she felt very vulnerable because she was alone, naked, had no escape routes, and had diminished vision and hearing—all stimuli that reminded her of the rape.

The trauma survivor may also experience symptoms of increased physiological arousal (Criterion D). This suggests that the individual is in a constant state of "fight or flight," which is similar to how the individual's body responded during the actual traumatic event. In this state of alert, the individual is primed to react to new threats of danger in even relatively "safe" situations. During a crisis, this is adaptive because it facilitates survival. However, as a steady state, hyperarousal interferes with daily functioning and leads to exhaustion. In this state, the individual spends a great deal of energy scanning the environment for danger cues (hypervigilance). The individual is likely to experience sleep disturbance, decreased concentration, irritability, and an overreactivity to stimuli (extreme startle response). There is evidence to suggest that this constant state of tension has deleterious effects on overall physical health (Kulka et al., 1990). At least two of the Criterion D stressors must be present for a diagnosis of PTSD.

Avoidance and numbing symptoms (Criterion C) reflect the individual's attempt to gain psychological and emotional distance from the trauma. Some have suggested that avoidance symptoms are a response to reexperiencing symptoms (Creamer, Burgess, & Pattison, 1992). As traumatic memories intrude into consciousness, so do the painful negative emotions associated with the original trauma. Thus the individual may avoid thoughts and feelings about the trauma, may avoid situations and events reminiscent of the trauma, or may actually forget significant aspects of the trauma. Avoidance of the trauma memory leads to a temporary decrease in painful emotions, which increases avoidance behavior. Similarly, detachment or numbing symptoms are an attempt to cut off the aversive feelings associated with intrusive memories (Astin, Foy, Layne, & Camilleri, 1994; Resick & Schnicke, 1992). This may become generalized, resulting in detachment from most emotions, both positive and negative. Trauma survivors commonly state that they no longer have strong feelings, or that they feel numb. This sort of pervasive detachment may interfere profoundly with the individual's ability to relate to others, enjoy daily life, remain productive, and plan for the future. Trauma survivors have frequently reported highly constricted lifestyles after the traumatic experience, due to the need to avoid reminders of the traumatic memory and associated emotions. At least three types of avoidance behavior are required before a diagnosis of PTSD can be made.

These symptoms must be experienced concurrently for at least 1 month in order for an individual to receive a diagnosis of PTSD, and the symptoms must be distressing or cause functional impairment. A substantial proportion of trauma survivors exhibit full symptoms of PTSD immediately after the traumatic event. However, these rates drop almost by half within 3 months after the trauma, but then tend to stabilize. For example, rape survivors assessed at 2 weeks, 1 month, 3 months, 6 months, and 9 months exhibited PTSD rates of 94%, 65%, 47%, 42%, and 42%, respectively (Rothbaum & Foa, 1993). Thus, after 3 months, PTSD rates did not drop substantially. If symptoms do not remit within this time frame, PTSD tends to persist over time and may worsen without appropriate intervention. Delayed onset of PTSD is rare and may reflect earlier subthreshold symptoms (perhaps due to dissociation, amnesia, or extensive avoidance) or a change in the meaning of the event at a later time (e.g., the perpetrator kills a later victim, thereby changing the meaning of the event for a survivor).

Epidemiological studies have demonstrated high rates of trauma and PTSD in the population (Kessler, Sonnega, Bromet, Hughes, & Nelson, 1995; Kilpatrick, Saunders, Veronen, Best, & Von, 1987; Kulka et al., 1990). In a national (U.S.) random probability sample of 4,008 women, Resnick, Kilpatrick, Dansky, Saunders, and Best (1993) found a very high rate of trauma experiences (69%). When they extrapolated their results to the U.S. population based on census statistics for 1989, they estimated that 66 million women in the United States had experienced at least one major traumatic event. Of those who had experienced a Criterion A stressor, Resnick et al. found the following lifetime PTSD rates: completed rape, 32%; other sexual assault, 31%; physical assault, 39%; homicide of family or friend, 22%; any crime victimization, 26%; non-crime-related trauma (natural and human-made disasters, accidents, injuries, etc.), 9%.

In the largest civilian prevalence study of the psychological effects of trauma, Kessler and colleagues (1995) surveyed a representative U.S. national sample of 5,877 persons (2,812 men and 3,065 women). This study, which included both men and women, assessed 12 categories of traumatic stressor. They found that a majority of people had experienced at least one major traumatic event. They found that while 20.4% women and 8.2% of men were likely to develop PTSD following exposure to trauma, the rates for specific traumas were often much higher. For example, rape was identified as the trauma most likely to lead to PTSD among men as well as women, and 65% of men and 46% of women who identified rape as their worst trauma developed PTSD. Among men who identified other worst traumas, the probabilities of developing PTSD were 39% for those with combat exposure, 24% for those with childhood neglect, and 22% for those who experienced childhood physical abuse. Among women, aside from rape, PTSD was likely to be associated with physical abuse in childhood (49%), threat with a weapon (33%), sexual molestation (27%), and physical attack (21%). As in the Resnick and colleagues (1993) study, accidents and natural disasters were much less likely to precipitate PTSD among men or women. On the other hand, Norris (1992) has pointed out from her research that although motor vehicle accidents (MVAs) are less frequent than some traumas (e.g., tragic death or robbery), and less traumatic than some events (e.g., sexual and physical assault), MVAs may be the single most significant type of event when frequency and impact are considered together. The lifetime frequency of MVAs is 23% and the PTSD rate is 12%, which results in a rate of 28 seriously distressed people for every 1,000 adults in the United States, just from one type of event.

The largest study of combat veterans was the National Vietnam Veterans Readjustment Study (NVVRS), which was mandated by the U.S. Congress in 1983 (Kulka et al., 1990) to study PTSD and other psychological problems following the Vietnam war. During the years of the war, over 8 million people served in the U.S. military. Of those, 3.1 million served in Vietnam (theater veterans), and the remainder served in the United States or other areas abroad (era veterans). Of the 3.1 million serving in Vietnam, only 7,200 were women.

There were over 255,000 women who served elsewhere during the Vietnam era. This study conducted in-depth interviews and assessments with three groups—1,632 Vietnam theater veterans, 716 Vietnam era veterans, and 668 nonveterans/civilian counterparts—for a total of 3,016 interviews.

The main finding of the NVVRS was that the majority of Vietnam theater veterans made a successful readjustment to civilian life and did not suffer from PTSD or other problems. However, the researchers also found that 31% of male and 27% of female veterans had a full diagnosis of PTSD at some time during their lives. Furthermore, 15% of male and 9% of female veterans have PTSD currently. These rates translate to 479,000 Vietnam veterans with current PTSD. In addition, 11% of male and 8% of female veterans currently suffer from partial PTSD, which means that they have significant symptoms and distress but do not meet the full criteria for PTSD. This translates into an additional 350,000 men and women in the United States alone who are still suffering from the aftermath of the Vietnam war.

THEORETICAL MODELS OF PTSD

As researchers and behavioral therapists began to study and treat rape victims and Vietnam veterans in the 1970s, they began to draw upon learning theory as an explanation for the symptoms they were observing. Mowrer's (1947) two-factor theory of classical and operant conditioning was first proposed to account for posttrauma symptoms (Becker, Skinner, Abel, Axelrod, & Cichon, 1984; Holmes & St. Lawrence, 1983; Keane, Zimering, & Caddell, 1985; Kilpatrick, Veronen, & Best, 1985; Kilpatrick, Veronen, & Resick, 1982). Classical conditioning was used to explain the high levels of distress and fear that were observed in trauma survivors. Operant conditioning was believed to explain the development of PTSD avoidance symptoms and maintenance of fear over time, despite the fact that the unconditioned stimulus, the traumatic stressor, does not recur. Because the trauma memory and other cues (conditioned stimuli) elicit fear and anxiety (conditioned emotional responses), these cues are avoided (or escaped from), and the result is a reduction in fear and anxiety. In this manner,

avoidance of the conditioned stimuli are negatively reinforced; this prevents extinction of the link between the trauma cues and anxiety, which would normally be expected without repetition of the trauma itself.

Although learning theory accounts for much of the development and maintenance of the fear and avoidance in PTSD, it does not really explain intrusion symptoms—that is, the repetitive memories of the trauma that intrude into the survivors' thoughts in both conscious and unconscious states (nightmares). Based on Lang's (1977) concept of anxiety development in his emotional processing theory, Foa, Steketee, and Rothbaum (1989) suggested that PTSD emerges due to the development of a fear network in memory that elicits escape and avoidance behavior. Mental fear structures include stimuli, responses, and meaning elements. Anything associated with the trauma may elicit the fear structure or schema and subsequent avoidance behavior. The fear network in people with PTSD is thought to be stable and broadly generalized, so that it is easily accessed. Chemtob, Roitblat, Hamada, Carlson, and Twentyman (1988) proposed that these structures are always at least weakly activated in individuals with PTSD and guide their interpretation of events as potentially dangerous. When the fear network is activated by reminders of the trauma, the information in the network enters consciousness (intrusive symptoms). Attempts to avoid this activation result in the avoidance symptoms of PTSD. According to information-processing theory, repetitive exposure to the traumatic memory in a safe environment will result in habituation of the fear and subsequent change in the fear structure. As emotion decreases, clients with PTSD will begin to modify their meaning elements spontaneously, and will change their self-statements and reduce their generalization.

Social-cognitive theories of PTSD are also concerned with information processing, but they focus on the impact of the trauma on a person's belief system and the adjustment that is necessary to reconcile the traumatic event with prior beliefs and expectations. The first and most influential social-cognitive theorist was Horowitz, who moved from a more psychodynamic to a cognitive processing theory. Horowitz (1986) proposed that processing is driven by a "completion tendency"—the psychological need for new, incompatible information to be integrated with existing beliefs. The completion tendency keeps the trauma information in active memory until the processing is complete and the event is resolved. Horowitz also theorized that there is a basic conflict between the need to resolve and integrate the event into the person's history on the one hand, and the desire to avoid emotional pain on the other. When the images of the event (flashbacks, nightmares, intrusive recollections), thoughts about the meanings of the trauma, and emotions associated with the trauma become overwhelming, psychological defense mechanisms take over, and the person exhibits numbing or avoidance. Horowitz suggested that a person with PTSD oscillates between phases of intrusion and avoidance, and that if the trauma is successfully processed, the oscillations become less frequent and less intense. Chronic PTSD means that the event stays in active memory without becoming fully integrated and therefore is still able to stimulate intrusive and avoidant reactions.

Several other social-cognitive researchers and theorists have focused more on the actual content of the cognitions and propose that basic assumptions about the world and oneself are shattered. Constructivist theories are based on the idea that people actively create their own internal representations of the world (and themselves). New experiences are assigned meaning based on people's personal models of the world (Janoff-Bulman, 1985, 1992; Mahoney & Lyddon, 1988; McCann & Pearlman, 1990a). The task for recovery is to reconstruct fundamental beliefs and the establishment of equilibrium. Janoff-Bulman has suggested that this process is accomplished by reinterpreting the event to reduce the distance between the prior beliefs and the new beliefs. Other theorists have proposed that if preexisting beliefs were particularly positive or particularly negative, then greater PTSD symptoms should result (Foa, 1996; McCann & Pearlman, 1990a; Resick & Schnicke, 1992). Foa has focused particularly on beliefs regarding the predictability and controllability of the trauma, while McCann and Pearlman have proposed that several areas of cognition may be either disrupted or seemingly confirmed: beliefs regarding safety, trust, control/ power, esteem, and intimacy.

Resick and Schnicke (1992, 1993; Resick, 1995) have argued that posttrauma affect is not limited to fear; individuals with PTSD may be just as likely to experience a range of other strong emotions, including shame, anger, or sadness. Some emotions, such as fear, anger, or sadness, may emanate directly from the trauma ("primary" emotions) because the event is interpreted as dangerous and/or abusive, resulting in losses. It is possible that "secondary," or "manufactured," emotions can also result from faulty interpretations made by the survivor. For example, if someone is intentionally attacked by another person, the danger of the situation will lead to a fight–flight response, and the attending emotions may be anger or fear (primary). However, if in the aftermath the person blames himself/ herself for the attack, the person may experience shame or embarrassment. These manufactured emotions result from thoughts and interpretations about the event, rather than the event itself.

In a social-cognitive model, affective expression is needed not for habituation, but in order for the trauma memory to be processed fully. It is assumed that the natural affect, once accessed, will dissipate rather quickly, and that the work of accommodating the memory with beliefs can begin. Once faulty beliefs regarding the event (self-blame, guilt) and overgeneralized beliefs about oneself and the world (e.g., safety, trust, control, esteem, intimacy) are challenged, then the secondary emotions will also vanish along with the intrusive reminders.

In an attempt to reconcile the cognitive theories of PTSD, Brewin, Dalgleish, and Joseph (1996) have proposed a dual-representation theory that incorporates both the information-processing and social-cognitive theories. Brewin and colleagues have suggested that the concept of a single emotional memory is too narrow to describe the full range of memory that has been evident in research and clinical observations. Based on prior research, they propose that sensory input is subject to both conscious and nonconscious processing. The memories that are conscious can be deliberately retrieved and are termed "verbally accessible memories" (VAMs). These VAMs contain some sensory information, information about emotional and physical reactions, and information about the personal meaning of the event. Although VAMs may be reasonably detailed, they may also be very selective, because attention is narrowed under conditions of stress and short-term memory capacity may be decreased.

Memories of the other type are nonconscious and are called "situationally accessed memories" (SAMs). SAMs, which are probably much more extensive than the autobiographical memories of the event, cannot be deliberately accessed and are not as easily altered or edited as the more explicit VAMs. The SAMs are composed of sensory information (auditory, visual, tactile, etc.), physiological, and motoric information, which may be accessed automatically when a person is exposed to a stimulus situation that is similar in some fashion to the trauma or when he/she consciously thinks about the trauma. The SAMs are then experienced as intrusive sensory images or flashbacks accompanied by physiological arousal.

Dual-representation theory posits two types of emotional reactions. One type of emotional reaction is conditioned during the event (e.g., fear, anger), is recorded in the SAMs, and is activated along with reexperienced sensory and physiological information. The other emotions, secondary emotions, result from the consequences and implications (meaning) of the trauma. These secondary emotions may include fear and anger, but can also include guilt, shame, and sadness.

Brewin and colleagues (1996) have proposed that emotional processing of the trauma has two elements. One element of the processing is the activation of SAMs (as suggested by the information-processing theories), the purpose of which is to aid in cognitive readjustment by supplying the detailed sensory and physiological information concerning the trauma. The activation of SAMs may eventually diminish in frequency when they are blocked by the creation of new SAMs or when they are altered by the incorporation of new information. When the SAMs are brought into consciousness, they can be altered by being paired with different bodily states (e.g., relaxation or habituation) or different conscious thoughts. Eventually, if the SAMs are replaced or altered sufficiently, there will be a reduction in negative emotions and a subsequent reduction in attentional bias and accessibility of the memories.

The second element (as proposed by the social-cognitive theorists) is the conscious attempt to search for meaning, to ascribe cause or blame, and to resolve conflicts between the event and prior expectations and beliefs. The goal of this process is to reduce the negative emotions and to restore a sense of relative safety and control in one's environment. In order to obtain this second goal, the traumatized person may have to edit his/her autobiographical memories (VAMs) in order to reconcile conflicts between the event and the person's belief system. The traumatized person may alter the memory of the event in some way in order to reestablish the preexisting belief system, or he/she may alter their preexisting beliefs and expectations to accommodate this new information.

Brewin and colleagues (1996) have suggested that exposure therapy may be all that is needed in some cases (those in which the emotions are primary and are driven by SAMs). However, when secondary emotions are present—when clients are reporting self-blame, guilt, or shame and consequent depression—cognitive therapy may be needed. Although both exposure and cognitive therapies have been found to be effective in treating PTSD, there has been no research thus far that has matched types of therapy to client profiles. However, in a study comparing prolonged exposure (PE) with cognitive processing therapy (CPT), Resick, Nishith, Weaver, Astin, and Feuer (2000) found that rape survivors with comorbid depression and PTSD responded better to CPT than to PE. Survivors with only PTSD responded equally well to CPT and PE.

ASSESSMENT

The first essential step in assessment is to identify major traumas in the client's history. Many survivors of rape and child sexual abuse fail to disclose their trauma history without being specifically asked. This is consistent with their general pattern of avoidance of trauma-related reminders, and it may reflect shame and self-blame regarding the incidents. Even when seeking treatment, trauma survivors often fail to recognize that their psychological problems are associated with their assault. Kilpatrick (1983) suggested several other reasons why survivors may not be forthcoming with this information. They may fear a negative reaction to disclosure, especially if previous disclosure has resulted in disbelief or blame. In addition, many survivors do not recognize or label their experience as rape or abuse, especially if the assailant was an acquaintance or a relative. In actuality, the majority of interpersonal crimes are committed by someone known to the individual.

A behavioral, descriptive prompt, such as "Has anyone ever made you have unwanted sexual contact by physical force or threat of force?" (and then obtaining details about the contact), is a more detailed prompt than asking clients whether they have ever been raped. In the latter case, someone who is married (or dating) and who has been sexually assaulted may say "No," because "rape" may not be a term that is associated with forced sex by one's partner. The same problem may exist with child abuse. A client may indicate that he/she was not abused as a child, but will readily admit that a parent whipped him/her with a belt severely enough to raise welts. The therapist may want to begin with general questions about discipline and punishment in childhood, and then move to specific behaviorally anchored questions regarding injuries or sexual contact by family and others in childhood. Then the therapist can move to sexual assaults, domestic abuse, criminal victimization, and other significant traumas in adolescence and adulthood.

Weathers and Keane (1999) have observed that the assessment of trauma has lagged behind the assessment of PTSD among researchers. Unlike most other disorders, PTSD is only diagnosed in the aftermath of particular types of life events that meet the two specifications mentioned at the beginning of the chapter regarding seriousness and subjective response. Few studies actually assess whether these specifications are met, much less adequately assess the range and frequency of trauma in a person's life. Although many studies have attempted to assess traumatic events, there are few well-validated standardized measures of traumatic events (Weathers & Keane, 1999). Although clinicians should not rely on them exclusively, there are some checklists that can be used as a springboard for further inquiry. Among them are the Traumatic Stress Schedule (Norris, 1990) and the Traumatic Events Questionnaire (Vrana & Lauterbach, 1994). The Posttraumatic Stress Diagnostic Scale (PDS; Foa, 1995) has two sections prior to assessing symptoms. The first section assesses 13 potentially traumatic events, while the second section has questions to determine whether an event meets the definition of Criterion A. With regard to combat in particular, the Combat Exposure Scale

(Keane et al., 1989) has been used widely to assess the degree of combat exposure. Two interviews are recommended to assess traumas in more detail. The Potential Stressful Events Interview (Kilpatrick, Resnick, & Freedy, 1991) has behaviorally anchored questions that are particularly good for assessing interpersonal crimes as well as a range of other traumatic stressors. The DSM-IV version of the Clinician-Administered PTSD Scale (CAPS; Blake et al., 1995) includes a self-report screening scale (Life Events Checklist) followed by interviewer prompts to establish whether the traumas meet Criterion A.

There are two major aims in assessment: diagnosis and treatment planning. A third purpose is suggested by the high rates of comorbidity with PTSD. Depression and substance abuse are especially common comorbid disorders. Whether the primary purpose of assessment is diagnosis or treatment planning, a multidimensional, multiaxial approach is desirable. Because a cross-sectional view taken at a single point in time may fail to capture the full range and pattern of symptoms, a longitudinal approach to assessment has been advocated by Denny, Robinowitz, and Penk (1987) and Sutker, Uddo-Crane, and Allain (1991). Certainly for purposes of treatment, ongoing assessment of symptom patterns and treatment effectiveness is essential. Even when PTSD is measured cross-sectionally, it has been suggested that multiple measures be used, depending upon the purpose of the assessment (Keane, Wolfe, & Taylor, 1987; Kulka et al., 1991; Weathers & Keane, 1999). Please refer to Weathers and Keane (1999) for specific suggestions in a variety of assessment situations. Below, we review some of the most widely used assessment approaches for PTSD. For a more comprehensive discussion of issues and procedures in assessment of PTSD, the reader is referred to Wilson and Keane (1997).

A note of caution regarding assessment is in order: Suicide risk should always be carefully assessed and monitored. The National Women's Study (Kilpatrick, Edmunds, & Seymour, 1992) found that 13% of rape survivors had made a suicide attempt, compared to 1% of the participants who had not been raped. In addition, 33% of the rape survivors, compared to 8% of the other participants, stated that they had seriously considered suicide at some point.

Structured Diagnostic Interviews

For diagnostic purposes, the Structured Clinical Interview for DSM-III-R or DSM-IV (SCID) is one of the most widely used. The SCID (First, Spitzer, Gibbon, & Williams, 1996; Spitzer, Williams, & Gibbon, 1987) includes assessment of PTSD symptomatology and was developed for use by experienced clinicians. Resnick, Kilpatrick, and Lipovsky (1991) recommend modifications for use with rape survivors, because the PTSD module of the SCID was originally developed for use with combat veterans. These modifications include more sensitive screening questions for history of rape and other major traumatic events. In addition, assessment of exposure to multiple traumatic events is important for treatment planning purposes. The SCID results in diagnosis and a count of the number of positive symptoms. Because the interview does not assess for frequency or severity of symptoms, it may be less useful for research projects, for which continuous scores are desirable.

A second widely used structured interview is the Diagnostic Interview Schedule (DIS; Robins, Helzer, Croughan, & Ratcliff, 1981). It is a highly structured interview schedule that has the advantage of requiring less training and experience than does the SCID. Like the SCID, the DIS results in diagnosis but does not have continuous severity scores. The PTSD section assesses exposure to civilian trauma, but it uses the term "rape" without any further specification. Thus the modifications suggested by Resnick and colleagues (1991) are appropriate for this instrument as well when evaluators are assessing for interpersonal traumas. Resnick and colleagues (1993) have modified the DIS for better assessment of sexual assault. Kessler and colleagues (1995) have also modified the DIS for better diagnosis of PTSD in large studies with lay interviewers.

The PTSD Symptom Scale—Interview (Foa, Riggs, Dancu, & Rothbaum, 1993) has a particular advantage in its ease of administration and brevity, with 17 items and prompts. This interview can result in continuous scores reflecting frequency of symptoms as well as diagnosis. Another advantage is that scores on the interview version can be compared to scores on the self-report version without having to readminister the interview frequently. A disadvantage of the interview is that symp-toms are assessed only over a current 2-week period, instead of 1 month, so it is possible that some diagnoses could be incorrect. Lifetime diagnosis is also not assessed with this interview. The time frame should be modified if careful diagnosis is required.

The CAPS developed by Blake and colleagues (1995) has become perhaps the "gold standard" in assessment of PTSD (King, Leskin, King, & Weathers, 1998; Weathers, Ruscio, & Keane, 1999). The CAPS has several attractive features. It assesses both severity and frequency of symptoms, using specific criteria. In addition, it gives clear guidelines for assessing changes in behavior following exposure to trauma. Two forms are available. CAPS-1 (current and lifetime diagnostic version) assesses symptoms over a 1-month period. CAPS-2 (1-week status version) measures symptoms over the past week. The more recent DSM-IV version also includes assessment of traumas and Criterion A, as mentioned earlier, as well as assessment of dissociative symptoms, other associated features, and social and occupational impairment. The CAPS is the best and most thorough assessment of PTSD, but has the disadvantage of being a rather long interview.

Self-Report Instruments

At this point, a number of self-report scales of PTSD have good psychometric properties. Among them are the PTSD Symptom Scale—Self-Report (Falsetti, Resnick, Resick, & Kilpatrick, 1993; Foa et al., 1993); the Purdue PTSD Scale—Revised (Lauterbach & Vrana, 1996); the PTSD Checklist (Weathers, Litz, Herman, Huska, & Keane, 1993), and the PDS (Foa, 1995). The latter scale, the PDS, is especially noted for its assessment of Criterion A and for assessing social and occupational functioning as well as PTSD symptoms.

There are other scales that assess PTSD symptoms, but do not directly link to all of the PTSD symptoms, and therefore cannot be used for diagnosis per se. The Impact of Event Scale (IES; Horowitz, Wilner, & Alvarez, 1979; Weiss & Marmar, 1997) and the Mississippi Scale for Combat-Related PTSD (Keane, Caddell, & Taylor, 1988; Keane, Fairbank, Caddell, & Zimering, 1989) are the most widely known and used. The IES has been revised from its original version with intrusion and avoidance symptoms to include arousal symptoms as well (Weiss & Marmar, 1997), although it still does not include all of the PTSD symptoms. The Mississippi Scale has been revised from use only with combat veterans to a version that can be used with civilians as well.

Two measures of PTSD have been empirically derived from other scales. The *PK* scale of the Minnesota Multiphasic Personality Inventory (MMPI) and MMPI-2 has been used successfully to discriminate Vietnam combat veterans with and without PTSD (Keane, Malloy, & Fairbank, 1984; Weathers & Keane, 1999). The Symptom Checklist 90—Revised (SCL-90-R; Derogatis, 1983) has also been examined by Saunders, Arata, and Kilpatrick (1990) and by Weathers and colleagues (1999), who have developed PTSD subscales for female crime survivors and combat veterans, respectively.

Finally, it should be noted that only one trauma-related scale, the Trauma Symptom Inventory (TSI; Briere, 1995) includes scales to assess response bias. For forensic purposes, in which response bias may be of particular concern, the assessor may wish to include the TSI or administer the MMPI-2. Both of these scales include validity subscales. In addition to clinical scales, the TSI also includes subscales assessing tendencies to overendorse unusual or bizarre symptoms, to respond in an inconsistent or random manner, and to deny symptoms others commonly endorse.

Psychophysiological Assessment

The ideal assessment will include measurement in multiple response channels, including physiological. This may not be feasible in clinical settings, because the technology and expertise are not always available. However, research has demonstrated consistent group differences in physiological reactivity. Although generic stressors such as mental arithmetic do not prompt differential psychophysiological responding across groups with and without PTSD, combat-related stimuli, particularly individualized trauma scripts, consistently produce differences between groups with PTSD and various comparison groups. Vietnam veterans with PTSD were consistently more reactive to combat imagery than combat veterans without PTSD, even when the comparison samples had other anxiety disorders or other psychological problems (Keane et al., 1998; Pitman, Orr, Forgue, Altman, & deJong, 1990; Pitman, Orr, Forgue, deJong, & Claiborn, 1987). Similar results have been found with people suffering from PTSD as a result of motor vehicle accidents and child sexual abuse (Blanchard et al., 1996; Orr et al., 1998).

Although there have been overall group differences in psychophysiological studies of PTSD, that does not mean that every person in the group with PTSD exhibited such reactivity. In fact, Prins, Kaloupek, and Keane (1995) estimated that as many as 40% of subjects with PTSD do not exhibit the expected reactivity. Although they speculated that this nonreactivity could be due to methodological reasons or subject variables (use of caffeine or other nonreported medications), a recent study may have found an alternative explanation, at least for some nonresponders.

Griffin, Resick, and Mechanic (1997) studied psychophysiological reactivity in recent rape survivors, using a somewhat different methodology from that of prior studies. Rather than listening to scripts, participants were asked to talk for 5 minutes on a neutral recall topic or to describe their rapes. These neutral and trauma phases were interspersed with baseline conditions. Rather than looking at the group with PTSD as a whole, Griffin and colleagues examined skin conductance and heart rate with regard to "peritraumatic dissociation" (PD). PD is the extent to which someone dissociated during the traumatic event.

Griffin and colleagues (1997) found a small group of highly dissociative women who responded in a very different manner from other women with PTSD. Although the skin conductance and heart rate of those with low PD scores increased as expected while they were talking about the rape, those with high PD scores showed a decrease in the physiological measures. When they examined the participants' subjective distress during each of the phases, the group high in PD reported the same level of distress as the group low in PD. Therefore, although they were experiencing distress, their physiological responses were suppressed. Griffin et al. speculated that there may be a dissociative subtype of PTSD, which involves a very different physiological response from that seen in the more phobic type of PTSD. This might explain why some studies have found a proportion of nonresponders with PTSD.

TREATMENT

Stress Inoculation Training

The earliest comprehensive approach described specifically for use with rape survivors was stress inoculation training (SIT; Kilpatrick et al., 1982; Kilpatrick & Amick, 1985), based on Meichenbaum's (1985) approach. Its aim is to give clients a sense of mastery over their fears by teaching a variety of coping skills. The approach is tailored to the individual problems and needs of each client, so it is flexible and can be used in individual or group settings. SIT is approached in phases. The first phase is preparation for treatment and includes an educational element, to provide an explanatory or conceptual framework from which the client can understand the nature and origin of her/his fear and anxiety and make sense of the trauma and its aftermath. (Note that because the great majority of clients with rape-related PTSD are female, we use "her/his" rather than "his/her" in this discussion to refer to such a client.) In SIT, a social learning theory explanation is used. Along with this, fear and anxiety reactions are explained as occurring along three channels (Lang, 1968): (1) the physical or autonomic channel, (2) the behavioral or motoric channel, and (3) the cognitive channel. Specific examples are given for each, and the client identifies her/his own reactions within each channel. Interrelationships among the three channels are explained and discussed.

The second phase of SIT is the training of coping skills. At least two coping skills (a primary and a secondary, or backup, skill) are taught for each of the three channels. The client first selects three target fears she/he would like to reduce. The client is asked to complete an "emotion thermometer," rating her/his level of fear and level of happiness, three times a day. In addition, she/he keeps a daily record of the number of thoughts regarding each target fear during each morning, afternoon, and evening.

The general format for training of coping skills is the same for all six skills taught. It includes, in sequence, a definition of the cop-

ing skill; a rationale; an explanation of the mechanism by which the skill works; a demonstration of the skill; application by the client of the skill with a problem area that is unrelated to the target behaviors; a review of how well the skill worked; and, finally, application and practice of the skill with one of the target fears.

Muscle Relaxation

Skills taught most often for coping with fear in the physical channel are muscle relaxation and breathing control. To teach muscle relaxation, the Jacobsonian tension–relaxation contrast method is used most frequently. Total relaxation of all major muscle groups is included during the first training session. In addition, a tape of the relaxation session is provided for the client to take home and use in practice assignments. Training is continued until proficiency is reached. Clients are encouraged to practice their relaxation skills during everyday activities.

Breathing Control

Deep diaphragmatic breathing is taught via psychocybernetics exercises. This skill is practiced in session and at home between sessions.

Covert Modeling

For the behavioral channel, covert modeling and role playing are the coping skills usually taught. The client is taught to visualize a fear- or anxiety-provoking situation and to imagine herself/himself confronting it successfully. This skill is practiced until proficiency is obtained. Because people vary widely in their ability to visualize such situations, the time needed to master this skill is quite variable. The skill is useful in preparing for situations that a client knows are likely to produce fear and anxiety reactions.

Role Playing

The client and therapist act out successful coping in anxiety-producing scenes with which the client expects to be confronted. In group situations, other group members may be used in the role playing as well. The client may then be asked to role-play scenes with family members or friends.

Thought Stopping

For the cognitive channel, thought stopping may be useful in breaking into the ruminative thoughts that characterize many victims' reactions. The client is asked to begin generating thoughts about the feared stimuli, and then those thoughts are interrupted, initially by having the therapist yell "Stop!" while simultaneously clapping hands together loudly. Then the client is asked to use the word "Stop!" subvocally or to devise her/his own covert thought-stopping term or visualization. The client then learns to use thought stopping covertly and to substitute a relaxed state for the anxious state. (Note: Thought stopping should not be used to avoid thinking about the trauma at appropriate times and places. The event needs to be cognitively processed, so thought stopping should be used judiciously.)

Guided Self-Dialogue

The client is taught to focus on her/his internal dialogue and trained to label negative irrational and maladaptive self-statements. She/he is then taught to substitute more adaptive self-verbalizations. Self-dialogue is taught in four categories: preparation, confrontation and management, coping with feelings of being overwhelmed, and reinforcement. For each of these categories, a series of questions and/or statements is generated that will encourage the client to assess the actual probability of the negative event's happening; to manage the overwhelming fear and avoidance behavior; to control self-criticism and self-devaluation; to engage in the feared behavior; and, finally, to reinforce herself/himself for making the attempt and following the steps.

For each coping skill, practice assignments are given. Mild everyday stresses are confronted first. When the use of skills in these situations is mastered, the trauma-related target behaviors are confronted. The client confronts each of the target behaviors she/he has identified in sequence. Following successful coping with the first target behavior, treatment focuses on the second. During this phase, the client again completes the emotion ratings on a daily basis. This allows the therapist to check on progress and adjust the treatment as needed.

Effectiveness of SIT

Veronen and Kilpatrick (1980, 1983) and Kilpatrick and Amick (1985) reported that SIT was effective in reducing fear, anxiety, negative mood, and physiological reactivity in uncontrolled and case studies. Resick, Jordan, Girelli, Hutter, and Marhoefer-Dvorak (1988) compared SIT with assertion training and supportive therapy in a group format, conducted in 12 sessions lasting 2 hours each. All three approaches resulted in significant improvements that were maintained at a 6-month follow-up. Foa, Rothbaum, Riggs, and Murdock (1991) compared modified SIT to PE (see below), supportive counseling, and a wait-list control group, with clients being seen individually. Because they did not want overlapping techniques in their comparison, Foa and colleagues eliminated the *in vivo* exposure component, confronting feared cues. In this study, SIT was the most effective immediately after treatment in reducing PTSD symptoms, anxiety, and depression. However, at a 3½-month follow-up, there was a trend for the exposure approach to show the greatest efficacy.

Recently Foa and colleagues (1999) compared modified SIT, PE, and a combination of SIT and PE. They found that the combination did not improve the results over SIT or PE alone. However, it should be pointed out that because of the nature of the research, the participants only received half as much SIT or PE as the other participants, because they had sessions of the same length and had half SIT and half PE at each session. If some of the SIT skills had been taught first, followed by PE (or some other combination), the results might have been different.

Exposure Techniques

Beginning in the early 1980s, forms of exposure therapy were investigated as a treatment for PTSD. Although systematic desensitization has been demonstrated to be effective for treating PTSD in a number of case study reports and controlled studies, it has not been widely adopted as a preferred treatment (Bowen & Lambert, 1986; Brom, Kleber, & Defares, 1989; Frank et al., 1988; Frank & Stewart, 1983, 1984; Schindler, 1980; Shalev, Orr, & Pitman, 1992; Turner, 1979). Because people with PTSD may fear and avoid a wide range of trauma-related stimuli, systematic desensitization may require a number of hierarchies, which could be quite inefficient.

Extended exposure to feared cues or to the trauma memory itself is a more efficient treatment and has been employed more widely. Known variously as direct therapeutic exposure flooding, or prolonged exposure (PE), these exposure techniques require clients to confront feared situations *in vivo*, to imagine themselves in a fear-producing situation, or to recall their particular trauma for extended periods of time. Recently Rothbaum and colleagues (Rothbaum, 1998; Rothbaum et al., 1999) have even experimented with the use of virtual reality for treating Vietnam veterans. A veteran with PTSD can take a virtual helicopter trip in Vietnam, complete with gunfire and other stimuli that may evoke memories of traumatic events.

Foa, Rothbaum, and their colleagues (Foa et al., 1991; Rothbaum & Foa, 1992) were the first to focus extensively on the specific trauma memory, rather than fear-producing stimuli. PE is conducted individually in nine biweekly 90-minute sessions. The first two sessions are for information gathering, treatment planning, and explanation of treatment rationale. Clients are also taught breathing retraining. A hierarchical list is generated of major stimuli that are feared and avoided. Clients are instructed to confront feared cues for at least 45 minutes a day, starting with a moderate level on the hierarchy. Beginning with Session 3, the trauma scene is relived in imagination, and the client is asked to describe it aloud in the present tense. The level of detail is left to the client for the first two exposures, but thereafter she/he is encouraged to include more and more detail about external cues and internal cues (such as thoughts, physiological responses, and feared consequences). Descriptions are repeated several times each session (for 60 minutes) and tape-recorded. Clients are assigned homework: to listen to the tape and engage in *in vivo* tasks. Care is taken in sessions to ensure that anxiety decreases before the session is terminated, aided by the therapist if necessary (Foa & Rothbaum, 1998).

Marks, Lovell, Noshirvani, Livanou, and Thrasher (1998) have conducted exposure therapy somewhat differently. Their version of the therapy includes five sessions of imaginal exposure and then five sessions of live exposure. During the imaginal exposure sessions, clients are asked to relive the experience aloud—speaking in first person and present tense on audiotapes about the details of their experience—and then to imagine and describe critical aspects of the event (rewind and hold). Clients listen to their therapy tapes daily between sessions. During the live exposure portion of therapy, clients (most often therapist-accompanied) progress through a hierarchy of trauma-related stimuli that are feared, avoided, and disabling. They are asked to practice the live exposure for an hour a day between sessions.

As stated earlier, PE was found to be more effective than a wait-list control group (Foa et al., 1991), and there was a trend for PE to be more effective than SIT at a 3½-month follow-up. The form of SIT that was used did not include active behavioral exposure as originally developed, so it is possible that SIT might have been more effective if the exposure had been included. In a second study comparing PE, SIT, a combination of PE and SIT, and a wait-list control group, Foa and colleagues (1999) found that all three treatments were significantly better than no treatment, but in most respects did not differ from each other. The clients in the PE condition had more improvement on a measure of general anxiety.

Marks and colleagues (1998) compared four conditions: exposure therapy, cognitive restructuring, exposure combined with cognitive restructuring, and relaxation training. The participants were 87 men and women who had PTSD from a range of traumatic stressors. Seventy-seven participants completed treatment, and 52 completed the 36-week follow-up. The authors found that the cognitive, exposure, and combined treatments were more effective overall than relaxation, but that there were no major differences among any of the three treatments. The treatment gains were maintained through the 6-month follow-up.

Cognitive Processing Therapy/ Cognitive Therapy

Cognitive processing therapy (CPT) is a therapy model developed to treat the specific symptoms of PTSD in survivors of sexual assault (Resick, 1992; Resick & Schnicke, 1992, 1993). CPT is a 12-session structured therapy program based on an information-processing model of PTSD. A unique feature of CPT is that it combines the main ingredient of exposure-based therapies with the cognitive components found in most cognitively based therapies. Moreover, the content of the cognitive portion of the therapy challenges specific cognitions that are most likely to have been disrupted as a result of the trauma. Clients are given homework assignments at each session, so much of the therapeutic work is carried out between sessions. What follows is a brief description of CPT. A case illustrating the use of CPT is provided later in this chapter.

In their discussion of information-processing theory in PTSD, Foa and colleagues (1989) and Foa and Kozak (1986) described how established fear structures can be dismantled. They proposed that two conditions are necessary for the reduction of fear: (1) The fear memory must be activated, and (2) new information must be provided that is incompatible with the current fear structure in order for a new memory to be formed. They suggested that activation can occur through any of the three network elements—information about the stimuli, responses, or meaning. They recommend the use of some type of exposure-based therapy to achieve this goal.

Foa and colleagues (1989) proposed that systematic exposure to the traumatic memory in a safe environment serves to alter the feared memory, such that threat cues are reevaluated and habituated. However, while activation of the network, or schemas, in a safe environment may sufficiently alter perceptions of danger and hence fear, there may be no change in emotional reactions other than fear without direct confrontation of conflicts, misattributions, or expectations. Survivors may still blame themselves and feel shame, disgust, anger, or confusion, all of which can be sufficiently intense to facilitate intrusive memories, arousal, and avoidance reactions.

An approach that elicits memories of the event and then directly confronts conflicts and maladaptive beliefs may be more effective than exposure only. PE activates the memory structure but does not provide direct corrective information regarding misattributions or other maladaptive beliefs. CPT, specifically designed for treatment of PTSD, provides another means for activating the memory structure. This structure includes conflicting beliefs and

meanings attributed to the event and expectations regarding the future that may not be elicited by other forms of exposure therapy. Therefore, it appears more advantageous to implement a therapy that will activate the memories of the event and also provide corrective information for conflicts, faulty attributions, or expectations that interfere with complete processing or cause other symptoms (depression, low self-esteem, fear).

An underlying assumption of CPT is that the symptoms of PTSD are usually caused by conflict between this new information and prior schemas. These conflicts may be concerned with danger and safety ("I don't feel safe going out alone"), but they may reflect other conflicts on other themes, such as self-esteem, competence, and intimacy (McCann & Pearlman, 1990a). These cognitive conflicts may account for the intrusive, arousal, and avoidance symptoms observed in PTSD. Therefore, although CPT includes modules to introduce the concept of faulty thinking patterns or assumptions, most of its focus is on identifying and modifying "stuck points" (i.e., conflicts between prior schemas and this new information).

The exposure component of CPT is quite different from the type usually practiced with PE and similar therapies. In CPT, clients write about the event in detail, including sensory memories, thoughts, and feelings during the event. They are encouraged to write at a time and place where they can express their emotions, and they are instructed to read the account to themselves daily. During the session they read the account aloud, and the therapist helps them to label their feelings and identify stuck points. This component of the treatment lasts only two sessions. Although it could be argued that only two sessions do not constitute PE, the results obtained thus far do not indicate that more time is needed for single-incident traumas.

Findings regarding CPT are promising. In a first, quasi-experimental study, Resick and Schnicke (1992) compared 19 clients receiving CPT with 20 wait-list comparison subjects. They found that the wait-list group did not change over time, but the CPT group improved significantly on all PTSD and depression measures. Resick and Schnicke (1993) reported further findings on 45 women who had received either group or individual CPT. The findings reported for the first 19 subjects continued to hold. At posttreatment, 88% of the women who had initially met full criteria for PTSD no longer met the criteria. At the 6-month follow-up, this increased to 92%. At pretreatment, 60% of the women also met DSM-III-R criteria for depression. At posttreatment, 14% still met criteria for depression; 6 months later, 11% were depressed. At the current time, Resick and colleagues (2000) have completed a controlled trial comparing CPT, PE, and a minimal-attention waiting condition. The preliminary findings on 121 treatment completers indicate that both CPT and PE are highly effective in treating PTSD, but that CPT may be better for those with comorbid guilt cognitions.

As noted earlier, Marks and colleagues (1998) compared exposure, cognitive restructuring, a combination of both, and relaxation training. In this study, cognitive restructuring was more focused on here-and-now cognitions and somewhat less on cognitive processing of the trauma. The three more active treatments were equally likely to result in reduction of symptoms. Marks and colleagues, in responding to these findings, suggested a modification of theory. They suggested that emotions can be viewed as response syndromes consisting of loosely linked reactions of many physiological, behavioral, and cognitive components. The intensity of an emotion can be reduced by acting on any of several components. A change in one component can then affect others. Several components can be acted on at the same time by certain treatment combinations.

Eye Movement Desensitization and Reprocessing

Eye movement desensitization and reprocessing (EMDR) is a controversial therapy that evolved not from theory or application of effective techniques for other disorders, but from a personal observation. As originally developed by Shapiro (1989, 1995), EMDR was based on a chance observation that troubling thoughts were resolved when her eyes followed the waving of leaves during a walk in the park. Shapiro developed EMDR on the basis of this observation and argued that lateral eye movements facilitate cognitive processing of trauma. Subsequently, EMDR was conceptualized as a cognitive-behavioral treatment aimed at facilitating information processing of traumatic events and cognitive restructuring of negative trauma-related cognitions. In the early presentations of EMDR, it was touted as a one-session cure for a range of disorders. However, more recent studies are typically of trauma-related symptoms with a course of treatment more similar to the other trauma therapies. EMDR is now described as an eight-phase treatment that includes history taking, client preparation, target assessment, desensitization, installation, body scan, closure, and reevaluation of treatment effects. EMDR includes both exposure and cognitive components, as well as the lateral eye movements.

In the basic EMDR protocol, clients are asked to identify and focus on a traumatic image or memory (target assessment phase). Next, the therapist elicits negative cognitions or belief statements about the memory. Clients are asked to assign a rating to the memory and negative cognitions on an 11-point scale of distress, and to identify the physical location of the anxiety. The therapist helps clients generate positive cognitions that would be preferable to associate with the memory. These are rated on a 7-point scale of how much the clients believe the statement. Once the therapist has instructed the clients in the basic EMDR procedure, clients are asked to do four things simultaneously (desensitization phase): (1) visualize the memory; (2) rehearse the negative cognitions; (3) concentrate on the physical sensations of the anxiety; and (4) visually track the therapist's index finger. While a client does this, the therapist rapidly moves the index finger rapidly back and forth from right to left 30–35 cm from the client's face, with two back-and-forth movements per second. These are repeated 24 times. Then clients are asked to blank out the memory and take a deep breath. Subsequently, the clients bring back the memory and cognitions, and rate the level of distress. Sets of eye movements are repeated until the distress rating equals 0 or 1. At this point, clients are asked to indicate how they feel about the positive cognition and to give a rating for it (installation phase).

Although a number of case studies, noncontrolled studies, and anecdotal data have indicated improvement of PTSD symptoms with EMDR (Kleinknecht & Morgan, 1992; Lazgrove, Triffleman, Kite, McGlashan, &

Rounsaville, 1995; Lipke & Botkin, 1992; Marquis, 1991; McCann, 1992; Puk, 1991; Spector & Huthwaite, 1993; Wolpe & Abrams, 1991), empirical studies with adequate comparison groups have only recently begun to emerge in the literature. Several of these have found significant reductions in symptoms of PTSD and related symptomatology, such as depression or anxiety, in subjects who received EMDR when compared to nontreatment controls (Rothbaum, 1995; Wilson, Becker, & Tinker, 1995). Others have found significant improvements in subjects who received EMDR, but no outcome differences when compared to other treatments for PTSD (Boudewyns, Hyer, Peralme, Touze, & Kiel, 1995; Carlson, Chemtob, Rusnak, Hedlund, & Muraoka, 1995; Vaughan et al., 1994). Unfortunately, the majority of these studies have serious methodological shortcomings, such as inclusion of stressors that do not meet the Criterion A definition (Wilson et al., 1995); inclusion of substantial numbers of subjects who did not meet diagnostic criteria for PTSD (Vaughan et al., 1994; Wilson et al., 1995); and extremely small (fewer than 15 per cell) sample sizes (Carlson et al., 1995; Rothbaum, 1995; Vaughan et al., 1994).

However, in a sample of 61 combat veterans, all of whom met diagnostic criteria for PTSD, Boudewyns and colleagues (1995) found EMDR to be as effective as PE in reducing symptoms of PTSD, depression, anxiety, and heart rate. In this study, subjects were randomly assigned to one of three groups. All three groups received the standard treatment at their facility, which consisted of eight group therapy sessions and a few spontaneous individual sessions. One received only this form of treatment; the second and third groups also received either five to eight sessions of EMDR or five to eight sessions of PE. All three groups improved significantly on symptoms of PTSD. The group-therapy-only group did not improve on depression and showed increases in anxiety and heart rate, while the two other groups improved on all measures.

Two studies have found mixed or negative results for EMDR. Pitman and colleagues (1993), in a study of 17 combat veterans, compared 12 sessions of EMDR to an eyes-fixed procedure in which a therapist alternately tapped each leg of a subject. The group receiving EMDR reported significantly greater improvement on measures of subjective distress, self-report measures of PTSD intrusion and avoidance, and psychiatric symptoms. No effects were observed, however, on other standardized self-reports and structured interviews of PTSD. Jensen (1994) compared two sessions of EMDR with no treatment in 25 combat veterans and found no improvements in either group on standardized measures of PTSD. In both studies, concern was expressed about therapists' experience with EMDR.

Although Shapiro maintains that lateral eye movements are an essential therapeutic component of EMDR, studies that have examined this have found mixed results. Renfrey and Spates (1994) treated 23 survivors of heterogeneous traumas with standard EMDR, a variant in which lateral eye movements were engendered via a light-tracking task, or another variant in which no lateral eye movements were induced and subjects were instructed to fix their visual attention. All three groups improved significantly on measures of PTSD, depression, anxiety, heart rate, and SUDs scores at posttreatment and at a 1- to 3-month follow-up. No differences were found among treatments. In contrast, Wilson, Silver, Covi, and Foster (1996) studied 18 survivors of heterogeneous traumas and found significant improvements in subjects who received EMDR, but not in subjects who were instructed to fix their visual attention, or in subjects who alternated tapping right and left thumbs to a metronome. Physiological measures and subjective units of discomfort, but no standardized distress measures, were used to measure outcome. Pitman and colleagues (1993), as noted above, found mixed results.

Thus it is not clear whether lateral eye movements are an essential component of EMDR or not. EMDR forces clients to think about the trauma, to identify the negative cognitions associated with the trauma, and to work toward positive cognitions as they process the traumatic memory. Without the lateral eye movements, EMDR is quite similar to a form of CPT that facilitates the processing of the traumatic memory. Therefore, any efficacy demonstrated by EMDR may be more attributable to engagement of the traumatic memory and the facilitation of cognitive reassessment than to the eye movements. It remains to be seen how EMDR compares in efficacy to exposure or cognitive therapy.

Therapist, Client, and Setting Variables

Gender and Ethnicity

Women may be at greater risk for PTSD than men, due to biological differences and other factors, such as the types of trauma more likely to be experienced (see Saxe & Wolfe, 1999, for an excellent review of gender issues in PTSD). Women's traumas are more likely to be interpersonal in nature (sexual assault and molestation, intimate partner physical violence), while men are more likely to experience accidents, natural disasters, and combat. Treatment must be sensitive to gender issues, including in some cases therapist–client gender matching.

Because rape is a highly personal and intimate crime, because the vast majority of clients who have been raped are women, and because rape often leads to distrust of men, the issue of therapist gender is relevant. Frequently, female clients prefer or insist on a female therapist. The effectiveness of male therapists has not been studied specifically, but it is felt that they can be quite effective if well trained (Resick et al., 1988). Issues for male therapists are discussed by Silverman (1977) and Koss and Harvey (1991). They include the tendency for men to view rape as more of a sexual crime than a crime of violence (Burt, 1980), and therefore to focus too much on sexual aspects of the experience and its aftermath.

Whether the therapist is male or female, it is essential that the therapist be knowledgeable about rape and PTSD. This includes the literature on reactions to rape and mediating variables, as well as on rape myths and attitudes about rape. Therapists bring their culturally learned perceptions with them, as do clients, and these can interfere with their effectiveness if they follow any of the common misperceptions about rape (e.g., that rape is primarily about sex or that most rapists are strangers). Rape survivors are extremely sensitive to implications that they might have been to blame, for example, and many drop out of treatment when they sense that the therapist may harbor client-blaming attributions.

The role of ethnicity in cognitive-behavioral treatment for PTSD has received little attention in outcome research. Studies of prevalence rates among ethnic groups have shown mixed results, which may in part reflect differential rates of trauma exposure (Breslau, Davis, & Andreski, 1995; Norris, 1992). Two studies of treatment efficacy compared African American and European American male veterans with PTSD. Rosenheck, Fontana, and Cottrol (1995) found less improvement among African American veterans on some measures; however, Rosenheck and Fontana (1996) did not support this finding. Only one study to date has examined the effectiveness of cognitive-behavioral therapy with African American women with PTSD. Zoellner, Feeny, Fitzgibbons, and Foa (1999) compared African American and European American women who were survivors of either sexual or nonsexual assault. Treatment consisted of PE, SIT, or a combination of the two. There were no ethnic group differences in treatment efficacy. These results were achieved in spite of an inability to match clients and therapists on ethnicity. Although these results are encouraging, continued attention to ethnic and cultural issues in treatment is important (see McNair & Neville, 1996).

Vicarious Traumatization

Working with trauma survivors can have negative effects on therapists, similar to problems shown by their clients. These effects have been labeled "secondary" or "vicarious" traumatization. McCann and Pearlman (1990b) discussed this impact as disruption of the therapists' own cognitive schemas about self and the world. Hearing clients' traumatic experiences may be shocking and may lead to lasting alterations in assumptions and expectations, which in turn may affect therapists' feelings and relationships. Working with trauma survivors can challenge therapists' assumptions about personal invulnerability and safety, as well as beliefs that the world is a meaningful, orderly place filled with trustworthy people. According to the model presented by McCann and Pearlman (1990b), an individual therapist's reaction depends on the degree of discrepancy between the traumatic imagery and the therapist's cognitive schemas. For example, if the therapist's own complex experiences have led to the development of safety assumptions (schemas) as central to his/her well-being, working with crime victims can be distressing due to a heightened sense of vulnerability. In addition, the therapist's memory system may be altered to incorporate traumatic imagery that can become intrusive.

To counteract the effects of vicarious traumatization, therapists should be prepared to recognize and acknowledge these effects and take steps to deal with them. McCann and Pearlman (1990b) recommend avoiding isolation and using one's professional network as a source of support. Talking to other professionals who work with survivors is especially useful, because they can help recognize the effects of vicarious traumatization and normalize these reactions. Other coping strategies suggested by McCann and Pearlman include balancing survivor cases with other cases, engaging in other professional and personal activities, recognizing one's own limitations, working for social change, and focusing on the positive personal impact of this work and the ways it can enrich one's life.

"Resistance"

Clients with PTSD can be notoriously difficult, due to their ambivalence about therapy. They want help but fear confronting their memories, and they have difficulty trusting others (including therapists). Avoidance behaviors, including avoiding cognitions, are part of the criteria for PTSD. Therefore, no-shows are common at the first session, and both subtle and obvious avoidance may be seen throughout the beginning stages of therapy. If possible, treatment should start on the telephone prior to the first session. The no-show rate is likely to drop if a therapist expresses understanding of a client's hesitance to come in and encourages attendance. The therapist should describe avoidance as a symptom of PTSD and an ineffective means of coping. If this is seen only as "resistance," it interferes with therapist effectiveness. This and other challenges in working with rape survivors are discussed by Koss and Harvey (1991) and Kilpatrick and Veronen (1983). Shay and Munroe (1999) discuss the challenges of working with combat veterans with complex PTSD.

Multiple-Trauma Survivors

The treatment approaches presented have been shown to produce significant improvement in civilian trauma survivors within a brief time. It should be noted, however, that most of the research has been done with single-trauma survivors. More complicated cases, especially those with multiple-trauma histories, may take longer. Therapists should also be aware of recent evidence suggesting that PTSD in sexual assault survivors may play a role in repeat traumatization (see, e.g., Kilpatrick et al., 1987), although this relationship appears to be complex (Wilson, Calhoun, & Bernat, 1999). Cognitive-behavioral treatment approaches are flexible and readily adaptable to more complex cases. Survivors of child sexual abuse present additional challenges (Cloitre, 1998). Their traumatization often interferes with normal development. It usually involves a relative or trusted adult and represents a serious betrayal by someone on whom a child depends for basic safety and protection. The abuse often occurs in repeated incidents over time. Clients with this kind of history may need more time to process and integrate such an experience. They may need more help with skill development as well, especially interpersonal skills. In some cases, sexual dysfunctions must be addressed. This can be added to an individual treatment program, or referral to a sex therapy specialist may be made; in either case, however, this is recommended only after the treatment for other trauma-related problems is complete.

Group Treatment

The decision to use a group or an individual format for treatment is usually made on the basis of clinical judgment and practicality. There is little research comparing the two procedures. Most of the interventions that have been used with trauma survivors are adaptable for use in either format.

Group treatment may be a useful adjunct to individual therapy in many cases. Many rape crisis centers and other public service agencies offer self-help support groups for survivors. Many veterans' groups and Department of Veterans Affairs hospitals offer groups for combat veterans.

Group treatment has several advantages that make it popular among rape survivors as well as among professionals; Koss and Harvey (1991) have discussed a number of these. Group treatment reduces the sense of isolation felt by most survivors, who withdraw from interactions with others and believe that others cannot understand their feelings. It provides social support that is unambiguous and non-blaming. It helps to validate and normalize feelings and reactions to the trauma. Group treatment confirms the reality of the traumatic experience and allows sharing of coping strategies. It counteracts self-blame and promotes self-esteem. Because it is more egalitarian than individual therapy, group treatment can promote reempowerment and decrease dependency. It provides a safe environment for developing attachment and intimacy, and an opportunity for sharing grief and loss. Finally, group treatment can help survivors assign meaning to the event, promoting cognitive processing.

Group approaches have drawbacks as well, and care should be taken to screen clients to assess their readiness for joining a group. McCann and Pearlman (1990a) suggest that clients with severe PTSD should be in individual therapy simultaneously with group treatment, because a group may elicit strong affect and memories that can overwhelm an unprepared client. For similar reasons, Resick and Markaway (1991) warn against having group members share their rape experiences during the first few sessions. Although important for recovery, the sharing of "war stories" should be done later in the group process or in individual sessions, to avoid frightening other group members or sensitizing them to other vulnerable situations. Poor candidates for group treatment, as suggested by Koss and Harvey (1991) and McCann and Pearlman (1990a), are suicidal clients; those with severe substance abuse problems; self-mutilating or substance-abusing clients with a borderline personality disorder diagnosis; clients with very unstable, disorganized lives; and clients who have never before spoken about the trauma or whose memory of it is incomplete.

CASE STUDY

"Cindy" was a 26-year-old client who sought treatment for a rape that had occurred 10 years earlier. Because she was treated within an ongoing treatment study, she was assessed by a psychologist on staff, using standardized interviews and a battery of self-report questionnaires. She was then assigned to the first author (P. A. R.) for treatment, in which the standardized format for CPT was used.

Background

At the time of intake, Cindy was married, was the mother of two young children, and was not employed outside of the home, although she had just been hired for a freelance job that was scheduled to start during the course of her therapy. She had a 12th-grade education with some business school classes.

Cindy had become depressed during the fall of the year (3 months before the intake interview), following an affair she had had for 5 weeks. During the affair, she began to have flashbacks of events that had occurred a decade earlier. When she realized that this affair coincided with the exact time of year she had been raped, she broke it off and became increasingly depressed and agitated as more memories surfaced. It was only now, 10 years later, that she began to label what had previously occurred as rape. She had sought therapy before, three different times, each lasting only one session.

At the initial interview, Cindy reported that she had been raped repeatedly over a 5-week period by a close friend of the family who was her age and lived across the street. The boy came from an abusive family, and Cindy's family "adopted" him. He was best friends with her brother, so he spent a great deal of time in their home, and her parents were also quite fond of him. Cindy had always had a sibling-type relationship with "Mark." During the initial interview, Cindy gave only the sketchiest of accounts and had no eye contact with the interviewer. The interviewer did not press her for a detailed description of the events, but continued to ask standardized questions.

These interview questions revealed that Cindy had been a virgin prior to the rape and had trusted the assailant quite a bit before the assault. She was verbally threatened by him, although no weapons or physical injuries were involved. She was subjected to a range of sex acts, including oral, vaginal, and anal intercourse. During the assaults, her most prominent reactions were feeling detached and numb, guilty, and embarrassed. The incidents were never reported to the police, and she received no medical care. At the interview, Cindy reported receiving negative reactions to her disclosure about the rape from those who were closest to her, and she indicated that presently her social support was poor. She reported no child abuse or incest. During the initial interview, Cindy also stated that she smoked marijuana quite a bit. She was defensive about her use of it and said that she did not want to quit. She also stated that a prior therapist had made a big deal about it. When Cindy told the therapist that she felt she was using pot as a crutch, he informed her that the pot was the problem, not a symptom. She disagreed, told the interviewer that she did not want to make it the focus of the therapy, and quit therapy.

Cindy's scores on all of the initial assessment measures were very elevated and similar to those of other rape survivors entering treatment (Resick & Schnicke, 1992). She scored a total of 34 on the PTSD Symptom Scale, 35 on the IES Intrusion scale, and 30 on the IES Avoidance scale. She also scored a 36 on the Beck Depression Inventory. In addition to the self-report measures, she was given the PTSD and Depression modules from the SCID for DSM-III-R (Spitzer et al., 1987). Cindy was diagnosed as meeting criteria for PTSD and major depression.

Cindy was 45 minutes late for her first scheduled therapy session. The therapist labeled Cindy's behavior as avoidant and normalized it as a symptom of PTSD. The therapist then talked about how avoidance had prevented Cindy from recovering from the rape, and noted that Cindy was going to need to confront her fears head on in order to deal with them in therapy. Cindy admitted that she had been afraid to come to the session and that she could see the "storm" (emotions and memories) coming. The therapist reminded her that after a storm, the land dries up and the grass grows again. The flood waters don't last forever. Cindy expressed hopefulness about the future and made some positive statements about herself. The "session" lasted 10 minutes, and another session was scheduled.

Session 1

Cindy arrived on time for the next session, which became the first actual therapy session. She remained wrapped and huddled in her jacket the entire time. During the session, Cindy admitted that she had smoked marijuana before the session to calm her nerves. The therapist downplayed the marijuana use, but labeled it as another form of avoidance and requested that Cindy not use marijuana before sessions or while doing the homework, which would be assigned at every session. Later during the session, as the therapist was describing areas of functioning that are likely to be affected by rape, the marijuana use was described as an indicator of problems with self-intimacy—the ability to self-soothe without external substances. Cindy agreed to refrain from substance use while working on therapy issues.

The purposes of the first therapy session in CPT are to (1) describe the symptoms of PTSD; (2) give the client a framework for understanding why these symptoms developed and why they have not remitted; (3) present an overview of treatment to help the client understand why homework completion and therapy attendance are important, to elicit cooperation, and to explain the progressive nature of the therapy; (4) build rapport between the client and therapist; and (5) give the client an opportunity to talk about the rape or other issues.

Cindy's therapist began this session by going over the results of the assessment. At the time of assessment, Cindy was suffering from PTSD and major depression. The symptoms of PTSD and depression were described, and an information-processing explanation of these symptoms was offered. The therapist described how rape, for most people, is a schema-discrepant event: It does not fit prior beliefs about oneself, others, or the world. In order to incorporate this event into memory, the information becomes altered (assimilated), or beliefs are changed to accommodate the event. Examples of assimilation are distorting the event so that it is not labeled a rape or blaming oneself for its occurrence. Over-accommodation is changing one's beliefs too much as a result of the rape (e.g., no one can be trusted). Areas of beliefs often affected by rape are safety, trust, power, esteem, and intimacy. The therapist described how a person has beliefs in these areas regarding oneself and others, and that either locus can be affected. The therapist also pointed out that if one had a sheltered environment and positive beliefs prior to the rape, these beliefs are likely to be disrupted by the event. However, if one had negative beliefs prior to the rape on any of these topics, the rape would seemingly confirm these negative beliefs.

Cindy, at this point, described her childhood as a happy one. She described her house as the safe house in the neighborhood where all of the kids could come to play, and where some found refuge when there were problems in their own homes. She said that her father had been a Vietnam veteran and still had PTSD at this time. She described him as emotionally closed, but also spoke fondly of him. She described her mother as a self-help fanatic and said that their house was filled with self-help books. She also stated that she had a close and supportive relationship with her mother. Cindy has one older brother with whom she was close until the rape.

After describing her childhood before the rape, Cindy spent some time describing how drastically things changed after these incidents. Cindy said that she told her mother what had happened and that her mother stopped the abuse. However, upon further questioning by the therapist, what emerged was that Cindy told her mother that Mark had been "coming on" to her, that it had gotten out of control, and that she needed help getting out of the situation. She never told her mother that she had been raped. Therefore, her family did not understand why she changed. After the rape, Cindy withdrew from her normal high school activities and began to hang out with troubled kids. Over the next year, she lied a lot and began drinking. She described herself as floating in and out of reality. She and her mother fought a lot. A year later, a friend of hers was driving recklessly and crashed the car in which Cindy was a passenger. Cindy was out of school for 2 months and had a long recovery from a broken back. She became a "total rebel" and dated a "wild guy who was total bad news." She became pregnant by him and didn't know what to do. At that time Cindy let her father take over and arrange for an abortion. Although she might have come to the same decision, Cindy now regretted that she gave up the right to decide. Cindy did not have the confidence to go to college. Her mother talked her into going to a business school for secretarial training. Cindy had worked as an executive secretary until the current year. At the time she entered therapy, she had been unemployed for 6 months. She had been married for 5 years and had two children.

The therapist's comment after hearing this account was "When the rapes happened, it derailed you." Her response was "Yes, I've been lost." Fortunately, Cindy had "the good sense" to marry a fine man who had been very supportive of her and did not give up on her after the affair. He was very supportive of her efforts to receive therapy.

At this point in the session, the following sequence between Cindy (C) and the therapist (T) occurred:

C: (*Agitated*) It's so bad you don't want to think about it.

T: That's when the avoidance is a two-edged sword. On the one hand, it makes you more comfortable at the moment if you push it away, but it doesn't let you get better either.

C: No . . .

T: Our average length of time for someone to come into treatment with us is 8 years later.

C: (*Open-mouthed with surprise*) I was so embarrassed! I thought I was dredging up the bottom of the barrel.

T: No, you're typical. We get a few early on, but we've had women come in 30 years later.

C: I guess you reach a point where you start becoming in sync with your mind again— where you say this has to be dealt with.

T: It's not going to go away. You've got to get to the point where you say, "Whatever I'm doing, it's not working."

C: You say, "This was my life and it was . . . , and I'm . . . here today."

T: What we're going to be doing is very systematic. I'm going to be giving you homework assignments, and each thing will build upon the last. The first thing we're going to start with is a writing assignment. Next time we're going to talk about feelings and labeling them, and work on the connection between thoughts and feelings—what you say to yourself, your beliefs, and how you feel. And from there, you'll do some writing about the rape, and not just a police blotter version, but the real . . .

C: Rape.

T: (*Nods*) Yes, and that means feelings, and what you remember, and all the stuff you don't remember—the hard stuff that we'll get into in therapy. That's what you've got to do even if you don't want to.

C: (*Agitated*) Oh, God.

T: It'll get easier after that.

C: (*Covering face*) Oh, no.

T: That is to help you remember. We don't want any more closed doors in your mind. It's time to air out those rooms.

C: It's the hardest thing to open.

T: It is, and there are probably some points in there that are the hardest parts to remember, and that's what we'll have to get into. To get it out here and put it in black and white, talk about it, put it out here in front of you so you can accept it. The feelings get easier over time, and that's the one thing I can promise you. When you let yourself feel your feelings about something, it gets easier each time, and then eventually it doesn't bother you after that. On the other hand, if you have these strong feelings and you stuff them, then every time you think of it you feel the same feelings all over again. We've got to let all the feelings out and let them run their course.

C: It just scares the hell out of me.

T: I know. I know. And we're going to help you brace yourself for it. And my job is to sit here and keep you on track, and not let you avoid. And I'm going to be listening for all those little games that you play with yourself, and saying, "Now what are you skipping here?"

C: I do.

T: So that's what I'm going to be listening for—is there some little stuck point that you're skirting around? Is there some little fragment of a memory that you just can't get past? You know, the place where the record gets . . .

C&T: (*Simultaneously*) . . . stuck.

T: It's better if you're working with me than hiding from me. We need to work together.

The therapist explained that there would be three major goals for the therapy: to enable Cindy to remember and accept the rape; to allow her to feel her emotions and let them run their course (extinguish), so the memory could be put away without such strong feelings still attached; and to help her get beliefs that had been disrupted and distorted back in balance. After this description of the therapy, Cindy was given her first assignment—to write about the meaning of the event. This assignment is given to determine the client's interpretation of the rape and to begin to determine what assimilation, accommodation, and overaccommodation have occurred since the assault. "Stuck points"—places of conflict between the event and prior beliefs—are often identified with this first assignment. The assignment was given to Cindy as follows:

> Please write at least one page on what it means to you that you were raped. Please consider the effects the rape has had on your beliefs about yourself, your beliefs about others, and your beliefs about the world. Also consider the following topics while writing your answer: safety, trust, power/competence, esteem, and intimacy. Bring this with you to the next session.

Session 2

The purposes of the second session in CPT are to discuss the meaning of the event and to help the client begin to label emotions, recognize thoughts, and see the connection between self-statements and feelings. Cindy arrived at this session with obvious emotion and cried periodically throughout the session. She stated that she had been feeling quite angry all week. She said she was disgusted with society, and particularly politicians and people with money and power. She said they were all greedy and self-righteous. She expressed a great deal of anger over the William Kennedy Smith trial, which occurred just before she started therapy. It became evident to the therapist that Cindy had overgeneralized a great deal of anger and distrust from the rapist, who had gone on to a military academy and an illustrious career, to all people with money and power. She also felt anger at the people in her life who did not recognize what pain she was in.

C: I walked away from a lot of people. I didn't talk to none of them.

T: But you didn't tell them either.

C: No, but there were signs. I gave off signs, but they didn't choose to see or ask.

T: Have you been angry all along, or just this week?

C: All along. That's why I think I turned the bitterness inward.

The client went on to say that at the time, she didn't have the courage to tell her family. When asked, Cindy said that she thought her parents would have believed her and would not have blamed her (a perennial problem with teenage rape survivors), but that she did not want to break their hearts. They had taken Mark into their home and treated him like a son. They were quite proud of his accomplishments. The therapist attempted to reframe Cindy's decision to remain silent not as cowardly, but as protective of her parents and therefore courageous. Cindy then moved on to a topic that often emerges early in therapy.

C: Why did this have to happen? Why? Why?

T: Why did the rape have to happen?

C: Yeah. Why did he do that to me? Why should I have to feel this? I'm a product of my environment. I really feel like that.

T: We all are to a certain extent.

C: Yeah. We are.

T: What answer have you given yourself up to this point to that "why" question? Why did it have to happen? Why do you have to go through this?

C: Because, just, that's my life, that was my past. (*Laughs*) That is what happened.

T: But you still keep asking why.

C: I think my "why" question just stems from, you know, you stupid son of a bitch, you don't take that from people. (*Long pause*) You know, it's not why did he take it from me. One thing I get mad at myself is, (*crying*) why did I let him?

T: You didn't let him.

C: I know.

T: Did you? He just did it.

C: It happened. I was 15. I was so scared.

T: And confused.

C: Yeah, and alone. I think that's why I'm mad. Because I was so alone and I walked away from so many people. It kind of wiped away all the good memories.

T: It's a scary decision for a 15-year-old to try to reach out to people when she's feeling bad about herself. At times a person in that position is going to pull away, because she's so afraid of compounding the trauma by other people rejecting her. It seems almost better to walk away yourself than let other people reject you. So you were rejecting them first.

C: Well, for that year afterward I was really mixed up.

T: Um hmm.

C: I can see how I confused them, and that's why I say, you know, I was giving off signs.

T: But you didn't have a label for what happened to you. Did you? You weren't saying, "I have been raped," were you? So even if they had asked, you wouldn't have been able to put it into words to express what you had been through.

C: I didn't consider it rape. I didn't know what to consider it.

T: You knew it was awful, but you didn't have a word for it.

C: I was so ashamed of it.

T: When did you start to label it rape?

C: Two months ago.

T: That recently. Why not before that?

C: I just didn't remember. . . . I think a lot of years I've been angry.

At this point, the therapist asked Cindy to read her homework assignment aloud to the therapist. Clients in individual CPT are always asked to read their homework assignments aloud. If the therapist were to read them, the clients could dissociate or otherwise avoid their own reactions to their material. Cindy had written:

When Mark raped me he also raped and manipulated my mind. I no longer trusted anyone, not even myself. I was bitter and angry at the world. I was also very frightened. I didn't feel safe anywhere, unless I was in the woods. I hated my bedroom. It had always been my safest place. It was where I was raped every time. I've been angry at him for taking that from me. For raping me on my own bed. I had to sleep in the bed for two more years. I took nothing with me when I moved out. All of those years of good memories were shattered. I felt nothing was sacred or special. I walked away from childhood, junior high, high school, college, and work friends. I feel this relates to intimacy. It makes me sad that I turned and walked away from so many people.

The rape created a "hate" toward society, religion, politicians, and especially business people. After the rape I was very lost, hurt, bitter and alone. Society seemed so self-righteous and unbalanced. Before the rape I saw the world that way a little bit, but I had a lot of hope. The majority of people were good. I was going to make a difference. I had a lot of love and compassion to give.

After the rape and during, the world seemed distorted and grotesque. The majority of people are greedy, self-righteous scum. The Kennedy family really reinforces that. Every time I watch the news or read the newspaper it reinforces that idea.

I've turned some of this anger toward myself for letting the rape happen. This inward anger has created a war in my mind. This war took a lot of my self-confidence, esteem, and identity.

It is breaking my heart to look back and see how much was taken. The people, memories, and the feelings I feel for myself. It hurts that someone had the power and wanted to take this from someone else. Mark took this from me.

Her assignment and the first issues she brought into therapy made evident the first stuck points that would have to be challenged. Cindy was assimilating, in that she had difficulty labeling the events as rape and that she believed she had let them happen. She had also overaccommodated in her distrust of society and had a great deal of generalized anger. She had ambivalent feelings toward the rapist and felt unsupported by her family members, even though she had chosen not to tell them what happened. She also expressed self-esteem problems. Although safety did not appear to be a major content issue, trust, power, esteem, and intimacy were all disrupted.

After reading the composition, the therapist asked Cindy what her feelings were. Cindy said, "Lost, sad." From there the therapist described how important it would be for Cindy to be able to label emotions and to begin to identify what she was saying to herself. The therapist and client discussed how different interpretations (self-statements) of events could lead to very different emotional reactions. They generated several examples of how changes in self-statements would result in different reactions. The therapist also pointed out that some interpretations and reactions follow naturally from rape and do not need to be altered. For example, if Cindy

were to say that her rights had been violated and she felt angry, the therapist would not challenge that statement, but would encourage her to feel her anger and let it run its course. If she recognized that she had lost something, it would be perfectly natural to feel sad. At this point Cindy said, "My feelings scare me. What do I do with my anger?" The therapist gave her several options: "Feel it, write about it, cry, talk to someone. If you need to expend energy, do it in constructive ways: run, walk, or clean house. Don't do aggressive things." The therapist made sure that Cindy could discriminate anger from aggression, and stated that it was her own philosophy not to have clients practice aggression as a way of expressing anger (no pounding pillows or bataka bats). The therapist also reminded the client that she had observed that Cindy appeared to have many good coping skills.

Cindy was given some A-B-C sheets as homework to begin to identify what she was telling herself and what her emotions were. In the first column, Cindy was instructed to write down an event under A, "Something happens." Under the middle column, B, "I tell myself something," she was asked to record her thoughts about the event. Under column C, "I feel and/or do something," she was asked to write down her behavioral and emotional responses to the event. The therapist pointed out that if one says something to oneself a lot, it becomes automatic. After a while, one doesn't need to consciously think the thought, but can go straight to the feeling. It is important to stop and recognize automatic thoughts in order to decide whether they make sense or should be changed.

Session 3

Cindy handed the therapist her homework as soon as she arrived. The therapist went over the sheets with Cindy and pointed out that she had done a good job labeling her feelings and recognizing her thoughts. Some of the homework is shown in Figure 2.1.

Because the purpose of the exercise was to identify thoughts and feelings, not to challenge these heavily at this point, the therapist noted the self-blame that again emerged but did not argue with the client. The therapist just quietly restated that Cindy did not let

Activating Event	Belief	Consequence
	Date: _____ Client #: _____	
A ————————▶	B ————————▶	C
"Something happens"	"I tell myself something"	"I feel and do something"
I was raped.	I let it happen.	I feel ashamed.
My virginity is taken.	I told myself I'm used.	I feel a loss.
I feel the need to destroy Ted Kennedy.	I tell myself he's not worth it. God will deal with him.	I feel relieved and hopeful.
I'm told not all people are bad.	I know what I've seen. They are.	I feel bitter and misunderstood.
My husband is supportive.	I'm proud he's mine.	I feel good.

Does it make sense to tell yourself "B" above? _____

_____

What can you tell yourself on such occasions in the future? _____

_____

FIGURE 2.1. A-B-C sheet.

Mark rape her, and pointed out that "the alternative is scary—that you didn't let him but that he did it anyway."

The therapist asked Cindy why she focused on Ted Kennedy and not on William Kennedy Smith. Cindy said, "Ted Kennedy is even worse. He's in political power. He killed a girl and got away with it. He defended his nephew." With regard to the thought about mainstream society, the therapist said that she didn't understand how the self-statement led to the feelings Cindy had recorded. Cindy went on for many minutes about her belief that all people are bad. She said that there is violence and poverty, and people in power make too much money, while others are homeless. She was very agitated as she talked and was teary at times. The therapist asked whether the people who are trying to help the homeless are also bad. Cindy responded that it was not enough. The therapist decided to see how much Cindy would cling to the belief that all people are bad. She asked whether Cindy also included the homeless as "bad."

C: No.

T: You said *all*.

C: I don't include them in mainstream society. (*Pause*) I know I associate a lot of this in my mind because Mark went on and in society's mind is very successful.

T: And everyone who is in those positions is like Mark.

C: Yes, because they are probably the type to turn away and don't get involved, so they can keep what they have.

T: (*Trying to see if she would budge*) They might or they might not. There are some other kinds of people.

C: (*Pause*) I know they all aren't bad.

Although it might not be evident at first why Cindy kept coming back to her anger at society, it appeared to the therapist that it was probably more than overgeneralization from Mark to everyone who is successful or powerful. Focusing on her generalized anger helped deflect some of her feelings from the issue at hand—her rape. By being vague and general, she could avoid talking about the specifics of what happened to her. Because the goal in CPT is for clients to challenge and dismantle their own beliefs, the therapist probed but did not pursue the issue too far. And although Cindy did move away from her extreme stance a bit within the session, the therapist was not expecting any dramatic changes. She was focusing mostly on being supportive and building rapport to help the client get through the most difficult sessions, which were to come next. The therapist also remained quiet during most of Cindy's diatribe because she didn't want to reinforce avoidance by engaging in a major discussion of society and all its woes.

The therapist did praise the client for her ability to recognize and label thoughts and feelings, and said that she wanted Cindy to attend to both during the next assignment—writing about the rape. Cindy asked which rape to write about, because it was a series of assaults. The therapist asked which one was the most traumatic for Cindy, and she replied that the first one was. The therapist asked her to start with that one. Cindy was asked to write, for homework, a detailed account and to include as many sensory details as possible. She was also asked to include her thoughts and feelings during the rape. She was instructed to start as soon as possible, and to pick a time and place where she would have privacy and could express her emotions. If she was unable to complete the account in one sitting, she was asked to draw a line where she stopped. (The place where the client stops is often a place in the event where there is a stuck point, where the client gave up fighting, where something particularly heinous occurred, or the like.) Then, when she could continue, Cindy was to read what she had already written and then write more. She was told that if there were parts she didn't remember, she should draw a line and continue on at the point she remembered next. She was also instructed to read the account to herself every day until her next session.

Cindy was told that there were several purposes for the assignment: for her to get the full memory back, for her to feel her emotions about it, and for the therapist and client to begin to look for stuck points. Cindy was also reassured that although this might be a difficult week for her, it would not continue to be so intense, and she would soon be over the hardest part of the therapy.

Session 4

At the beginning of the session, the therapist asked Cindy to read her account. Before starting, Cindy asked the therapist to remind her of the benefit of reading. The therapist reminded Cindy of what they had talked about the previous session, and added that the act of reading aloud would help her to access the whole memory and her feelings about it. Cindy read what she had written quietly, crying most of the time.

We were in the front room dancing. We practiced all the time. It was a slow song. We weren't dancing nasty. We were practicing so we could win a contest and also because we both loved to dance. We were dance partners. As we were dancing he kissed me. We kept on dancing and I was enjoying it. He slid his hand on my breast and for a brief moment it felt really good, but I had a boyfriend. I pushed his hand away and gave him a dirty look but continued dancing. We never really stopped dancing. It was like it was part of the dance. When the song finished he was smiling at me. He had a hard-on. I felt very uncomfortable and confused. We never kissed when we danced. Inside I felt threatened. I'm standing there trying to comprehend the situation when he puts his arms around me and starts kissing my neck. I pushed him away but he tightened his arms around me. He whispers that he can tell I like it. This will feel good. Come on, he won't tell anyone, especially not my boyfriend. This angered me. It disgusted me. I tried to break free and I was talking hateful. I told him to leave me alone, let me go, and shut up. He tightened his grip more and wrestled me down the hall to my bedroom to the bed. He fell on me. I tried to wiggle free and I couldn't. I could not get away. He had me pinned. His hands were clenched around my wrists and he had his legs locked on top of mine. He put my right forearm under his right armpit and held my left wrist with his hand. With his other hand he pulled my shorts down and then his. He smiled at me while he gently stroked his dick like he was letting it know it was in for something good. I tried to break free again. He put both hands back on my wrists and then pried my legs apart with his legs. I screamed at the top of my lungs when he put himself in me. He shoved my own arm in my mouth. Then he started kissing me gently all over. I just laid there feeling hollow. I was crying but I felt very numb. The sheet was stuck to my cheek. It was all wet. I can feel myself laying there numb, tears rolling down my cheek, my head was turned completely to the side, and my eyes were squeezed shut. I thought about my parents, family, childhood, boyfriend, and friends, as if life was flashing before me. Then he kissed my cheek. He wasn't on me anymore. I opened my eyes and his shorts were up and he was walking out. I heard him go out the front door. It was over. I was laying on my bed in shock. I still didn't feel I could move. Then I felt the pain and the wetness between my legs. I knew what had happened. Crying, I got up. I noticed the cum on my belly and almost puked right then. I ripped the sheets off my bed, took off my shorts, and placed them on the sheets. I went into the bathroom and took a shower. I watched the water wash away the blood on my inner thighs. I scrubbed and scrubbed. Then I was too exhausted to stand. I sat all huddled in the shower sobbing uncontrollably. I was in there for about 30 minutes. Ten of those minutes were after the hot water ran out. It felt good though. It was almost icy. I finally got out and put on my pajamas. It was only 4:30 P.M. I went to bed in my parents' room. I didn't know what to think or feel. I didn't want to think about what had happened. I was so exhausted I just wanted to go to sleep. How would I even begin to explain. I wasn't quite sure myself. I knew the facts but it didn't make sense. I just wanted to go to sleep and forget. When my mom came home I told her I was sick. I laid in that dark room all night. I wasn't sleeping yet or dreaming, but I could feel my mind racing. It was as if my mind was thinking in more detail about the things I thought about when I was actually in the process of being raped. It was violent yet gentle. I loved him but hated him. I had been proud of him and now was disgusted. Oh my God, I'm not a virgin anymore. I didn't give it away, I let someone take it, or I lost it, or it was taken from me. I knew for sure though, I didn't give it away and that really hurt me. I wanted my first time to be special. I played around with my boyfriend. I knew it probably would feel good when I was ready, but it would be special with someone special. Hell I was only 15 years old. I really liked Bob my boyfriend. We had only been dating a month and really liked each other. He was two years older. He was a really good guy. We dated, kissed, and walked in the halls, but didn't even consider sex. I could feel myself transforming that night. I could feel myself changing my thoughts, fears, and wishes. It was on a totally subconscious level. Consciously, I was laying in my parents' bed curled up in blankets sleeping all night. I don't think I moved a muscle. Yet I could feel my subconscious working very hard. I knew I would never be the same. The change happened that night. I woke up a different person.

I chose not to tell to save a lot of people from being hurt. I would not be the messenger of that kind of hurt and pain. I knew they all had felt it before just as I did. That is what I chose as the best solution. I put the sheets and shorts in the washer and it was over.

I went to school as usual. I was quiet and distant. Mark passed me in the hall. I remember standing there at my locker glaring at him. Standing there in the hall around so many people, seeing him and remembering, I felt used and ashamed. For the rest of the day I avoided everyone and kept to myself. I stayed after school for softball. I got home around 6:00 P.M. and everyone was home at my house. I went to bed early again. The next day was a little better, but not much. I actually talked. That afternoon Mark said he wanted to talk to me when we got off the bus. I stared out the bus window the whole way home. It was always such a beautiful drive. I thought maybe he wanted to apologize. Even though it was violent, he had been gentle. I would rip him up with my words for what he did to me. Then I would forgive him, or at least try and handle it. But it didn't happen like that.

We sat on the couch and he started talking about what happened. He was sorry it happened like that. It could be a lot better if I wouldn't fight. He knew I liked it. I didn't scream until he stuck himself in me and I didn't tell anyone. I told him he was lying and that he was sick. I told him he violated me. He told me I was lying and that I did like it. I didn't scream or fight throughout the entire rape and didn't tell anyone. He starts talking about my boyfriend. What would he say if he knew? What would my parents think of me if they knew? If they all knew that I liked it. I didn't stop it from happening. He said I knew I was strong enough to stop it and I didn't. He took my hand and led me to the bedroom, pulled down my pants, and started kissing my body and neck. He told me how I was going to like it and that no one will know because I didn't want them to know I liked it. They'd be ashamed. It would be between he and I and we would both really enjoy it. I stood there dead. I can't let him tell anyone what happened two days before. He was going to tell them I wanted it. He was going to tell people what he did to me and that I liked it. I let him put me on the bed and have sex. It didn't matter anymore. I felt if anyone knew it would destroy me. People would look at me differently. They would treat me like a slut and here I lay with him on top of me. He manipulated me this way for three weeks. I hated myself. I hated him. I didn't care anymore. He would make me do things I knew I didn't like. One time he made me lie on my stomach and he put himself in my anus. I screamed out in pain and then cried, "No more!" He stopped then and left. A few days later he came over again. He was threatening. He will tell everything. The truth was even worse now. It has been four weeks. He became more violent and persistent. I went deeper into a black hole. I came home from school a few incidents later and called my mom. It had to stop, whatever the cost. As I told her I could see her heart breaking so I told her I let it happen but things were out of control and asked her to please make it stop. That next afternoon I went to my mom's work. I sat out back on the bluff. I remember singing "I'm on top of the world looking down on creation." I felt a lot of hope.

Then at school he started threatening me. Hanging it over my head. Whispering that I couldn't get away, even though my parents made arrangements for me to stay with a friend after school. The odd part was that my own home wasn't even safe. His sister told me not to cause any problems. After a while Mark went on and left me alone. He started becoming more involved with studies and sports. I kept it inside and blamed myself for all that happened. I probably was a slut. Nothing mattered anymore. A ten-year war had started in my mind. What he told me was true versus what I knew was true. He raped me. He manipulated me. He tortured and tormented me. He raped my mind and my body. Back then I didn't know what to believe or do so I started lying about who I was, like in a fantasy.

I was terrified at the thought that he might be right. That I wanted it. I couldn't believe it but why didn't I scream, fight, and tell. Maybe I did ask for it. Everyone became my enemy. The people close to me were pushed away so they wouldn't get hurt and everyone else was pushed away so I wouldn't get hurt.

After reading the account, Cindy turned it upside down and set it on the table in the therapy room. The therapist asked her what she was feeling.

C: (*Long pause, shakes head*) Bitter.

C: You have a right to that feeling. He black-mailed you.

C: I know.

T: And made you feel guilty.

C: That's why I've blamed myself for all these years and never considered it rape. After a while I just started believing it, seeing him go on to . . . (*drifts off*)

T: But it was rape.

C: I know.

T: And part of that rape was making you feel guilty—that somehow you should have responded differently.

C: And I didn't respond because I didn't want to hurt people, even him!

T: You know how most women respond? (*Cindy looks up*) They freeze. They go into emotional shock.

C: Yeah. You can't believe it. You're trying to take in what is happening. . . . And then other people all say, "You should have . . ."

At this point, a discussion ensued regarding how hurtful it is to hear other people's general comments about rape. Cindy described how much anger she had and how she turned her anger against society, especially when she heard people say unfair things. From there she went on to describe how difficult the week had been with her husband. They had gotten into several fights, and she was angry that her husband had stopped being supportive. The therapist talked about other people's reactions to rape, and noted that sometimes their strong feelings interfere with their ability to be supportive. The therapist offered to have another therapist meet with Cindy's husband to help him process his own reactions. Cindy also expressed disappointment in a friend's reaction. When she told this "friend" how difficult the week had been because of all the memories surfacing, the woman responded by saying, "Get over it." She continued making other unsupportive comments. Cindy said that they had been friends since high school, but that their relationship was rather one-sided. She supported her friend and listened to her problems but had never asked for support before. Later in the session, the therapist brought the discussion back to the rape and the assignment. She asked Cindy what stuck points she had identified. The following dialogue then occurred:

C: (*Crying*) Over the years, when I thought about it, I put all the blame back on myself. I could never remember what exactly happened the first time.

T: And now you do. Are any pieces missing? . . .

C: (*Interrupts, crying*) No . . .

T: Or is it the whole thing?

C: (*Very quietly sobbing*) I know. Oh. When I started remembering, I knew it was rape, without a doubt . . . then I started to get angry.

T: The fact that you didn't remember would have been a clue, if you'd known, that it was rape.

C: Yeah.

T: If it wasn't rape, you would have remembered.

C: I never could remember the first time.

T: Um hmm.

C: And then, that's why I told myself . . . maybe somehow, some way I started it.

T: In this case, you were just trying not to remember it. Because it clearly was.

C: (*Picks up writing assignment, puts it away, takes it out again*) Maybe I should look at that. (*Looks at assignment silently for a long time*) I don't know where to go from here.

T: You wrote in there about what he said and that you were at war between believing and not believing. Where are you in terms of that now?

C: I know what the truth is.

T: Do you have any self-blame at this point?

C: No, umm, other than that, I think I'll always have doubts . . . the fact that I didn't do anything and I'll always wish that . . .

T: There's a difference between wishing and blaming.

C: Yeah, that's true.

T: But I think we need to work on that, because I don't want you saying that you *always* will.

C: (*Interrupts*) I'll always blame myself.

T: Because there's no need for that.

C: And reading back to this, my God!

T: The ironic part to me is that you chose not to tell, not because you liked it, or because you were a coward, or anything else. You chose not to tell because you didn't want to hurt people.

C: (*Cries*)

T: You were doing what you considered the right and noble thing to do, and then he twisted it around.

C: He used it against me.

T: And he used it against you.

C: And then, after 4 weeks, then I'm really . . . you know . . . it's like . . . (*makes the sound of an explosion*) It's even worse

than the original, you know. Because it must be proof that . . . (*moans*) Oh, God. (*Looks up with a small smile*) Nobody ever found out.

The therapist's interpretation to Cindy was that Cindy had done the best she could in an impossible situation. The therapist then checked the client's emotional state to make sure she was calmer than she had been and was ready to close the session. She praised Cindy for doing a great job on the writing assignment and said it would be important not to quit now. Cindy's response was "I'm more determined than ever." The therapist then took the first account and gave the client the homework assignment to write the entire account again. The therapist asked Cindy to add any details she might have left out of the first account, as well as to record any thoughts and feelings she was having now in parentheses, along with her thoughts and feelings at the time.

Session 5

Cindy arrived at the next session looking quite animated and cheerful. She reported that she had felt a great deal of energy and had done a lot of housecleaning and 13 loads of laundry. The therapist asked how everything was going between her and her husband. Cindy said that they had talked, and he had apologized and had been extra sensitive, supportive, and loving. He didn't feel that he needed counseling at this time, and Cindy had been pleased by his responsiveness and her openness during their discussion. Cindy had also talked a lot with her mother during the week and had felt supported. She then went on to talk a bit about her long-time friend and began to realize more clearly that this woman was not a friend to her, but that she had stuck with her out of loyalty and perhaps for some self-destructive reasons. This woman confirmed Cindy's poor view of herself with her vitriolic attacks. Cindy began to suggest that perhaps, as a friend, she (Cindy) was like the battered wife who stays with a spouse who seems to need her, but is also abusive.

The therapist asked Cindy how the writing had gone the second time. Cindy responded that there were no tears. She was a little shaky but not as emotional. The first part of the account was very similar but a bit shorter. Cindy found herself writing more about the later events.

After Cindy had been reading for only a few minutes and had gotten to the part where she was being dragged down the hall, the therapist interrupted her with the following:

T: You don't have any thoughts and feelings in there that you had at the time. Were you having trouble bringing it to mind or . . .

C: No, I, umm, I, I felt numb. I mean I, I feel that way about it right now.

T: Numb or neutral?

C: Neutral.

T: OK. When I think of numb, I think of you holding something big back.

C: No, because I think I brought that out in the first one.

T: So you just feel like there's less feeling about it, then?

C: Yeah. I know that I experienced a lot of pain and there were a lot of emotions mixed in there and I brought those out, and I guess I did, because . . . it's just . . . that's what happened, (*laughs*) you know? I feel, I guess neutral is the right word.

T: Um hmm.

C: It doesn't seem like it took . . . I don't know. It doesn't seem as painful. It does, but it doesn't. When I was writing this it was, but when I read it back the first time it was a little bit.

T: But each time you do it, it gets a little less.

C: And then when I was out in the truck a little while ago, I read over it and it was like . . . (*laughs and makes determined gestures*)

T: It happened, didn't it? It happened, and there it is.

C: Yeah. You know, because it seems like for months I have been feeling all of the anger and the confusion, just remembering the pain, and here for a couple of weeks, kept dreaming about that person, and so I knew this was it. My mind wouldn't let me deny it, and I guess now it's, it's not as . . . it's better, you know.

T: Um hmm. OK.

C: I feel that way now.

T: Good. Well, let's just see. If you're not avoiding it, and you can think about it, and it doesn't cause you that much pain, then that probably is what you're looking for. If you have to avoid it, or if it's numb, holding back feelings, then you're not done—so you'll be able to tell the difference.

C: I mean it, it makes me feel uncomfortable. (*Laughs*)

T: Um hmm. Yeah, but it will get easier.

At this point Cindy went back to reading and read the remainder softly, quickly, with expression but not overt emotion. Totally new to this account was the following:

On my wedding night he showed up in his Academy uniform. He had apparently asked my brother if he could come. He said yes. He walked up to me with such sadness in his eyes. He asked me to dance. It was the first time we danced together since the rape. In my wedding dress, with everyone so cheerful and happy looking at the bride, I danced with him. It was a slow song. He told me I looked beautiful. The room seemed to be spinning. This white dress, his uniform, everyone smiling, we were dancing, it was my wedding night. Jim [Cindy's husband] drank too much at the reception and passed out at the hotel. I sat up all night. I was remembering bits and pieces. I was angry. I was sad. I had a lot of questions. Why did he want to go to my wedding, for forgiveness? That's not the time or place. Why dance with me? I hadn't seen him in a couple of years. Why now, tonight? Jim didn't know. He was over there talking to him, looking at him with admiration, and thanking him for coming. All the girls kept asking who that guy in the uniform was. Oh, he's so gorgeous, etc.

I kept it inside again. I had bad feelings about my wedding day for about two years. But I blamed it on my in-laws. I couldn't blame it on something that is not there. No one knew. I still wonder why he showed up on my wedding day. The more questions I answer, the more questions I have.

The therapist asked Cindy if the feelings this week were different or just less intense. Cindy responded that there were times when she was just tired of thinking about it. She said that there were moments that overwhelmed her, and she let them (the therapist told Cindy that was fine, to allow herself to have feelings), but that mostly she felt good. She was being more positive in her self-statements. The therapist helped Cindy recognize that she didn't have to be so afraid of her emotions any more, and that she was learning that she could tolerate her feelings, even big feelings. Cindy acknowledged that she had noticed that it was getting easier, and that when the feelings passed she felt normal again.

After discussing her reactions to her memories, Cindy talked some more about her reactions to other people. At this point she focused on her brother more and described how she had thought her brother had let her down because he didn't see the truth about Mark. She said she needed him to be her big brother. When asked whether she ever tried to talk to him about it, Cindy responded that it would be like talking to a brick wall. She was resistant to the possibility of discussing it with him now, because he was still friends with Mark and was wrapped up in his own life. After this discussion, the therapist turned to the first of a series of tools used in CPT to help challenge assumptions. She said:

T: You've moved through a lot already, but I think you're going to need to focus on any places you might have stuck points and start challenging them. So over the next few sessions we're going to work on skills to attack stuck points directly.

C: OK.

T: OK, because, remember, I said on some of this stuff you are going to have to feel your feelings. Some of those feelings are very legitimate. Now some examples of stuck points are if you blame yourself, if you say, "I let it happen," or if you say . . .

C: (*Laughs*) Those stuck points I'm bashing with a sledgehammer.

T: The time before that we were talking and you kind of generalized: Everybody who's got power, everybody who's got money is a bad guy. *Everybody.* So that's one we should chip away at.

C: I can't trust anyone.

T: Yeah. All those topics. I can't trust anyone or I can't trust myself. Safety, trust, power, esteem, intimacy. We're going to work on each of those themes. As a way of doing that we're going to go through a couple of different steps. I'm going to give you a more complicated worksheet to help you. Every time you have a stuck point, it helps you work right through it. So you can change what you're saying or at least challenge . . .

C: Kind of like that A-B-C thing . . .

T: Yeah, except it's a little bit more complicated because it actually takes you through the rest of the steps of how to analyze it, and if you want to change it, change it, and actually get to the point where it's changed.

C: OK.

T: This is the first step of this (*indicates Challenging Questions list*). [See Session 8 for the Challenging Questions list.] Let's go over these a little bit together. These are questions you can start asking yourself. So let's say you make a statement—"I let it happen," or "I let it happen for 5 weeks," or whatever. "So there's something wrong with me, I let it happen." The first question you ask yourself is "What's the evidence for or against this idea?"

C: That I let it happen.

T: That you let it happen. Did you let it happen or did it just happen?

C: Yeah.

T: What's the evidence that you let it happen?

C: I'd say, "I don't believe that any more." (*Laughs*)

T: OK. So, but if it's something that you're really stuck on . . . one of the ways I identify when people have a stuck point is that they'll say, "Well, I know it's this way, but I feel . . . the opposite." And I'll say, "No, you've got two sets of beliefs that are contradictory. It's possible to have two contradictory beliefs in your head at the same time."

C: Yeah. (*Nods understanding*)

T: So sometimes, when you're in the process of changing, you do have both in your head. You've got one you see as more logical and more fact-based, but then you have this gut feeling.

C: Emotional. Yeah, I know.

T: The other thought has all this feeling attached, and when the feeling is attached it seems more real.

C: Yeah.

T: Yeah, we'll be looking for those. Maybe we ought to pick one that you're still stuck on.

C: (*Thinks silently for a while*) Well, I don't know. I'm trying to think of something.

T: How about trust? How are you on this?

C: Thanks. That's a really hard one. Yeah, I think that would be a good one.

T: OK. What would the statement be that you would feel like . . . that you can't trust what?

C: But I don't want to trust too much, though.

T: We're looking for balance. Not that you need to trust everybody.

C: I just . . . it's almost like the *idea* of trust—I don't. I guess one of my really stuck points that I need to work on is the lack of confidence I have in my ability to judge who I can trust and who I can't trust.

T: OK.

C: And I think that's why I have problems with trust, because I don't know if my censoring devices are picking up . . . you know . . . is this a bad guy or . . .

T: So the statement you want to make is "I don't know if I can trust my own judgment."

C: Yeah, regarding trust.

T: So what we have here is a list of questions to start asking yourself. "What's the evidence for or against this?" What is the evidence that you have good judgment about who to trust and who not to trust? What's the evidence against that? How does that weigh out when you look at the facts and not just your feelings?

C: Yeah.

The rest of the session was spent going over the list of questions to make sure Cindy understood them. Although most of the questions focused on the issue of trust, at times other issues were brought in just to illustrate the meaning of the questions. For example, Cindy was asked, "Was the source reliable?" with reference to the rapist's insistence that she liked it (the rape). Cindy also engaged in a lively discussion with the therapist over the following questions: "Are you taking selected examples out of context?" "Are you focusing on irrelevant factors?" The therapist pointed out that perhaps the fact that Mark was popular and went on to the Academy was not relevant to the rape or to whether she could trust people. The more relevant context was that Mark was from a troubled, abusive home and that he was lashing out. Cindy began to accept that she had made a faulty connection between the person who raped her and went on to be successful and everyone else who is successful.

Session 6

Cindy started her new job and worked more than 40 hours in the first week. She was quite excited by the job and the people she was meeting. For the first time, Cindy came to a session without having her homework completed. She said that she had looked at it a few times. She then expressed concern about how much she was changing, and said that she wanted to figure out what things she didn't want to change. It seemed to the therapist that Cindy was still ambivalent about what it meant to be successful and was fearful that if she changed too much (i.e., became "successful"), she would become one of those people she had always despised. The therapist assured Cindy that it was not her intention to assist Cindy in becoming a person Cindy didn't like. Cindy expressed some dismay that the rape had affected her in so many ways. It was likely that she didn't complete her homework because the thoughts that were bothering her were still vague and unformed. The therapist helped her to pin them down.

T: You are certainly more than a rape victim. You always were. But the rape did affect some of your beliefs.

C: I am still very afraid to trust.

T: This isn't something that's going to change in a couple of sessions.

C: I wanted it to. (*Laughs*)

T: The purpose of the therapy is to give you the tools you need to empower you to decide what you want to change and not, and not to just react automatically to the rape, but to have choice . . .

C: . . . and control.

T: The whole idea is to give you different ways of viewing things so you're not stuck any more in your reactions. So that you're not always in that defensive posture, which is what that total lack of trust is, a defensive stance.

C: Yeah, because you don't let anybody in.

T: And then you can't choose who to trust or not trust, so you don't trust anybody. It's not a matter of exploring and deciding and having choice over it.

C: Even the people that you love dearly . . . that just hurts.

T: That wasn't something you intentionally did, but by not having a label for it, you didn't have an option either. For a long time you didn't have the option of recovering, because it wasn't labeled a rape; therefore you couldn't get the help that you needed to . . .

C: . . . get over it.

T: Yeah. In looking over the list, what comes to mind? You said you looked over it several times. In terms of some of the stuck points we talked about.

C: Trust was a big one. And identity was a big one. I just kept thinking about that.

T: When you looked at the list?

C: Yeah. I couldn't answer. It was like . . . am I?

T: Are you what?

C: Confusing habit with fact? Or am I somebody different, or am I the person I thought I was? I was raped, and that's affected some part of my life. But I look back and I see that all throughout that time it's always been on my mind, so is it habit or is it fact?

T: The other thing is that if there were certain things that preexisted the rape that you saw as being negative beliefs, those could have been seemingly confirmed by it . . . by that event. I mentioned that at the beginning of therapy, but we haven't talked about that much. If you were having identity issues or problems . . .

C: Well, I was 15.

T: So if you're feeling negative about yourself before it happens, which is pretty typical for . . .

C: Well, you don't know at that point.

T: So some of that stuff can get set off in another direction because of that event . . . because maybe you didn't have a good, solid sense of yourself, being a teenager.

C: Yeah, I was just starting into it.

T: But you described yourself when you read about the rape. You said, very clearly, "I changed that night." So that clearly means you changed from what you had been.

C: I did. (*Pauses*) I closed, I . . .

T: Then the idea of not being closed is a scary one for you.

C: Yeah.

T: What would it mean to change back again a bit, to find some balance point?

C: I think it would be so healthy. It's just habit.

T: There isn't anything you can label and say, "Here's the scary part, I'll get raped again"?

C: No.

T: Or "I'll be hurt by somebody"?

C: I guess it's "I'll be hurt by somebody." I just, it's just my security to stay closed up. Then nobody can hurt me. No one can take . . .

T: Can't they? Look at the sheet. What's the evidence that if you stay closed up, nobody can hurt you?

C: Because they don't know my inner core. They never reach that point.

T: But they still could hurt you in other ways.

C: Yeah.

T: But aren't you hurt when you're that closed up?

C: Yeah.

T: Seems like you're hurting yourself. You're not waiting for anyone else to do it.

C: Yeah, I, well . . . it's like paranoia, it really destroys you. Why should I be closed up? I want to be open, and I don't think people are out to hurt me.

T: Let's go through the list in terms of the stuck point: "I'm afraid to be open." What's the evidence that you're going to get hurt if you're open?

C: People are just . . . umm . . . there's no evidence. I don't think I was before.

T: It happened once?

C: Not just once, but a few times I did that. A few times I did kind of try to reach out. People, with human nature, reacted . . . *(leans back, makes a closed face)*

T: Could we change the word "will" to "might"? "I might get hurt," not "I will get hurt." It hasn't been uniform; 100% of the people haven't hurt you, have they?

C: No. And some of the time I was hurt because they didn't know how to help me.

T: Because in fact you weren't open.

C: Yeah. They did not know what was actually happening to help me.

T: OK. So, in fact, being closed didn't protect you in that sense.

C: No, it didn't.

T: OK. So there's some evidence that being closed doesn't necessarily keep you safe.

C: And that makes me feel alone.

T: Which then hurts. So there's some evidence right there, looking back. It's not necessarily that being open is going to get you hurt. Being closed can get you just as hurt, but in a different way.

C: Yeah. Inside me.

T: Because people don't understand. They don't know what you're going through.

C: What they see on the surface as opposed to what I see on the inside.

T: Um hmm.

C: And it protects me but yet it hurts me inside.

T: OK. So following up with this statement, "If I'm open, I'll get hurt," what's question number 2 on the list?

C: *(Reads)* "Are you confusing the habit with the fact?" It's a habit. I didn't know I chose it that night, but if I'm to carry this or whatever . . . I mean I'm alone. I'm going to walk alone and I'll be strong. Nobody will get inside. Nobody at all.

T: But now it's become a habit.

C: Yeah.

T: That you hadn't, at least until this point in time, questioned.

C: I see my father do it. That's the way he dealt with his problems and still does.

T: And has it worked for him?

C: No. *(Both laugh)* I think he's crazy.

T: Well.

C: It's one of those things they say, "You're just like your father." I say, "Don't say that," you know, but I am.

T: So you need to find a different way. If it didn't work for him and it's not working for you, then you've got to find a different path.

C: Well, I see why it doesn't work. It's just . . . people, they do want to help. It's very hard to convince people like me and him, because it's OK to hurt. Well, it's not OK to hurt, but in your mind you tell yourself it is, rather than having other . . .

T: You have control over it then.

C: Yeah. Rather than other people hurting you. You can't deal with that, but you can deal with . . .

C&T: *(Simultaneously)* . . . hurting yourself.

T: Probably for two reasons: One, you have some control over it, and, two, that it is more predictable and you know where it's coming from; you're doing it to yourself. On the other hand, look what you're missing: the opportunity for people to come through for you.

C: When you do need them.

T: Yeah.

C: And you want them.

T: Think how good you'd feel if you could open up and they could be there for you, if you'd give them the opportunity.

C: Yeah.

The therapist pointed out the example from the previous week where Cindy opened up with her husband and he responded by being supportive. Cindy agreed that it had worked well. The therapist and Cindy spent a considerable portion of the session going over the questions on the sheet with this particular stuck point in mind. At one point the therapist suggested that they might look at the statement "If I open up, I will get hurt" differently. The therapist asked, "Open up about what? The rape? Other things? Everything?" The therapist pointed out that some topics are probably lower-risk than others, like the weather. A place to start with people is with something that is less touchy. The therapist and client also talked about asking for support. The therapist reminded Cindy that people would often want to be supportive, but that they might not know what to do or what she wanted. The therapist and Cindy discussed how to tell people what Cindy wanted from them.

After this discussion, the therapist introduced the Faulty Thinking Patterns list (for a sample, see Session 8). The list includes seven types of faulty thinking patterns (e.g., oversimplifying, overgeneralizing, and emotional reasoning). The therapist described how one can move from very specific thoughts to examining more general patterns. The client and therapist went through the Faulty Thinking Patterns list and generated examples for each of the patterns. For example, for "Disregarding important aspects of a situation," the therapist pointed out something that Cindy had brought up several times during therapy: Cindy had said that she almost never watched the news, because it just showed how violent the world had become and how bad everyone was. The therapist said that what she was disregarding was that this was "news"—that events are announced because they are unusual, bad, and/or important. Broadcasters don't announce how many millions of people weren't traumatized by crimes or didn't do something illegal that day.

When they got to the item "Overgeneralizing from a single incident," Cindy said that she had noticed that she was beginning to change her thoughts. When she saw someone with a nice car or someone on television in a position of authority, she was beginning to say to herself, "Just because someone accomplishes something, that doesn't necessarily mean they walked over bodies to get there. Maybe they worked hard." The therapist added that people who work hard don't usually make the news. They are quietly getting on with their lives, working or studying or raising their families. Cindy was given the assignment to read over the list and note examples of times when she used some of these faulty thinking patterns.

Session 7

Cindy again started the session by talking about her new job. She was quite exhausted from working over 60 hours during the past week. The therapist asked whether she had been able to complete her homework assignment. She had not written on the form, but Cindy said she had looked at the Faulty Thinking Patterns list frequently and had found herself applying it to her friend. She recognized that she had used a number of faulty thinking patterns over the years in this friendship, and said that she also saw her friend using many of the same patterns. During the week, the friend called Cindy's house. Cindy's husband answered, and the woman said a number of insulting things about Cindy. Cindy's husband told the friend that Cindy was a wonderful woman and ordered her never to contact them again. Although it had been her husband who broke off the relationship, Cindy was glad he had and would have done so herself very soon. She expressed a sense of relief over finally being extricated from a destructive relationship.

The therapist spent some time going over the sheet while Cindy gave examples of faulty patterns she had experienced in the past. By this point in therapy, the therapist was sitting back and allowing Cindy to challenge her own cognitions. The therapist rarely needed to intervene any more, but just added information. At this point the therapist introduced the Challenging Beliefs worksheet (for examples, see Session 9):

T: Good. Good. Let's go over some of this new stuff I want to show you.

C: OK.

T: Now this you can't skip. You've got to do this.

C: OK.

T: We're going to add a new form. You know how you did the A-B-C sheets?

C: Yes.

T: (*Pointing to boxes on sheet*) This is A, B, and C. This is the new sheet, and this is to work on stuck points. And even if you feel some of them are resolved, just work through these to make sure you got it.

C: OK. I'm sure there are a few. I'm . . . you know.

T: Well, the issues about trust, who to trust and not trust, and intimacy.

C: Yeah, my own self-judgment, and even still a little bit of the confidence. I think self-esteem.

T: So I want you to pick a couple of the stuck points and start thinking about them. Now we're going to start talking about safety and see if you have any safety stuck points. And what you're talking about the news could be perceived as a safety stuck point, that the whole world is so violent that this is the norm. That was kind of a stuck point, because you were perceiving everything as being extreme rather than trying to . . .

C: Yeah, like the whole world was . . . just like the majority of it was rotten. Even the newscasters bringing it to me were rotten for bringing it to me. *(Both laugh)*

T: Yeah. This is A, B, and C, so here's the event, thought, or belief, and here's where you put your feelings. And here's your automatic thought, but this time we want you to actually rate your belief in it. In other words, how much do you believe this? Because you know when you're in transition, at the beginning you say, "Everybody's rotten. I believe that 100%." So as you're in transition, you might say, "Well, maybe. I think this mostly." So let's try to specify how much do you actually believe that. See if there are any chinks in the armor.

C: Yeah.

T: Then you put your feelings here. That's the C part. And again, we try to get you to rate them, because we're going to have you rate them at the end. When you get done with the sheet, you can see, "Have I changed?" I'll show you an example in a second. So you rate how strong is the emotion. Are you feeling 100% or 30% or 50%? And you can have more than one feeling. You might be sad, you might be angry, you might be scared, you might be happy.

C: I still do feel a little anger toward him.

T: Um hmm. So this is that part, then these are the questions you ask yourself. Here's the first question on the list: What's the evidence? So whatever your stuck point is, you go through your list and think about what's the evidence, and am I thinking in all-or-none terms? Is it taking this out of context, or whatever? And here are the faulty thinking patterns: Am I falling into these kinds of things? Am I exaggerating

the meaning of it? Am I disregarding the important?

C: Yeah.

T: Am I engaging in emotional reasoning?

C: Oversimplifying. That's as bad or good.

T: Yeah. So then, this is the important one: What else could I say? I mean, given that there's not as much evidence as I thought, or maybe I'm just kind of doing all-or-none stuff. What else could I say to myself? How else could I interpret it? What else could I say? How else could I interpret this event? OK?

C: Kind of pulling the opposite side that almost comes up.

T: Or the more balanced. Sometimes it's not moving something from one extreme to the other, but it's moving it *(gestures part way)*. "Well, OK, some people are bad. But that doesn't mean that I'm going to always get attacked, that I'll never be safe, or that there's nobody who can be trusted." Then you try to come up with something to say that's a little healthier to say to yourself.

C: Not everybody from the Academy is bad. *(Both laugh)*

T: OK? This little section's kind of fun to play with, because sometimes you get the idea if something happens it's totally catastrophic. What's the worst that could ever happen? If somebody betrays you, you could say, "Well, I'll give them another chance, or I'll find somebody else, or, I'll . . . you know. So you have to think about what's the worst that's going to happen, and if it did, how will I cope with it? What could I do about it? Because sometimes if you take that extreme view out here and bring it down a little bit, sometimes the catastrophe isn't so . . .

C: And address it too, it's not so overwhelming.

T: And address it directly. Then what you want to do when you get to the end of all this work, then you rerate your belief. Now, having gone through this, and asked yourself these questions, and looked at the pattern, and come up with the alternatives, how much do you really believe this any more? And what are you feeling now that you've finished the worksheet? So this is an active way of actually working through something on the spot.

C: Like the process your brain goes through, only it's visually . . .

T: We've been doing this all along. I've been giving you other ways of viewing things and saying, "Hold it a second."

C: Yeah.

T: So we've been doing this together and you've done a lot of it, and now, from here on out, you've got to take it over so you don't slide into some old patterns. The other point of this is that other things may happen in your life.

C: Well, that's what I thought.

T: This is going to give you some tools that you're going to have forever to deal with whatever comes up in your life.

C: I know these did (*indicating Challenging Questions and Faulty Thinking Patterns lists*), because when I had the problem with the friend, I sat down with that and it really made sense. I see a lot that I never . . .

T: Yeah. So I've got a lot of these for you to take home and work on.

C: OK.

T: The other thing I wanted to show you was an example of it. This is the one that another client did, and we just use it as an example because sometimes it's hard to see it on an empty sheet. OK, here's her stuck point: "I perceive myself to be damaged in some way, kind of ruined, because I was raped. There's something wrong with me now." OK. So she says to herself the thought that she had that was feeding that stuck point was "There's something wrong with me that he thought he could rape me in the first place." That sound familiar?

C: Yeah. (*Laughs*) Is this mine?

T: No.

The therapist and client went over the example sheet, and Cindy was able to follow it quite well. The therapist reminded Cindy that she might find that she wasn't using faulty patterns or statements, and in that case, no change in feelings would be expected. She was also cautioned that she shouldn't expect her beliefs and feelings to change completely in the process of doing the sheet. The old thought would need to be dismantled completely, and the new thought would need to become more habitual, for her to see a more permanent change. It was suggested that she read the sheets over to herself a number of times to facilitate the process.

The topic of safety was then introduced. Cindy was given the first of five modules (two-to three-page handouts on each of five topics: safety, trust, power, esteem, intimacy) to read, and some Challenging Beliefs worksheets to use. These modules discuss how beliefs about self and others can be shattered or seemingly confirmed after rape, depending on experiences prior to the rape. The modules describe the emotional and behavioral effects of faulty beliefs with each of the topics, and they suggest alternative self-statements (for the modules, see Resick & Schnicke, 1993).

Cindy reported that she had always felt safe before the rape and felt that she or her family could protect her. Since the rape, safety had not been as much of a problem as trust, but she did have some issues about it, as evidenced by her avoidance of television news. The therapist suggested that Cindy might want to complete a worksheet on this topic.

Session 8

Cindy arrived at the session with the two homework sheets that she had not completed previously: Challenging Questions and Faulty Thinking Patterns. She had not completed any worksheets on the safety module. On the Challenging Questions list (see Figure 2.2), Cindy decided to work on the statement "If I did come forth and get help when I was raped, I would have been the accused to some." The therapist noted that this statement already reflected some movement from previous statements that were more extreme. Cindy read off the answers shown in Figure 2.2.

After reading and discussing her answers, Cindy read three examples of faulty thinking patterns that she had noticed with regard to the rape. She left the remainder blank. The therapist and Cindy discussed the three items she did complete, as shown in Figure 2.3.

The therapist pointed out that sometimes the rape itself, the sex acts, is not as hard to remember as some other defining moments. Mark's dragging Cindy down the hall defined the event as a rape, so that was the part of the

Below are a list of questions to be used in helping you challenge your maladaptive or problematic beliefs. Not all questions will be appropriate for the belief you choose to challenge. Answer as many questions as you can for the belief you have chosen to challenge below.

Belief: *If I did come forth and get help when I was raped, I would have become the accused to some.*

1. What is the evidence for and against this idea?
   Although some people would believe, there were people who would think Mark wouldn't do that so I must have wanted it and now I'm trying to hurt him.

2. Are you confusing a habit with a fact?
   This is a fact.

3. Are your interpretations of the situation too far removed from reality to be accurate?
   Yes, I thought the majority of people viewed rape and abuse differently. The general population cares.

4. Are you thinking in all-or-none terms?
   I was. To sit by and let it happen makes you guilty. I believed they (general population) didn't want rape and abuse to happen and when it did they either don't want to get involved or, in some cases, the girl is told, even in court, she asked for it and liked it.

5. Are you using words or phrases that are extreme or exaggerated (i.e., always, forever, never, need, should, must, can't, and every time)?
   Yes.

6. Are you taking selected examples out of context?
   Yes, because I was raped repeatedly, I knew the hell of these other women and children. Keeping my own pain inside, I felt the anger and pain of each rape victim and sexually abused child that was broadcast on TV. My anger was built on the pain of a lot of others when I wouldn't think of my own pain.

7. Are you making excuses (e.g., I'm not afraid. I just don't want to go out; the other people expect me to be perfect; or I don't want to make the call because I don't have time)?
   No, other than they won't hurt me. If they try, I'll hurt them.

8. Is the source of information reliable?
   The TV was my source of information. The source was reliable. I was taking it out of context.

9. Are you thinking in terms of certainties instead of probabilities?
   I was certain if I told anyone it would ruin my life. Everyone would probably believe him.

10. Are you confusing a low probability with a high probability?
    Yes. I believe it would most likely work out for him and not me.

11. Are your judgments based on feelings rather than facts?
    Yes. It was based on feelings. I never gave fact a chance.

12. Are you focusing on irrelevant factors?
    Yes. Just because it did not work for some of the people that I had seen on TV, there were a lot of people that were being helped, but it wasn't a big media event.

FIGURE 2.2. Challenging questions.

event that was most schema-discrepant, and therefore most subject to distortion (or amnesia). The therapist asked Cindy whether she could now think of some examples of the items she had left blank: oversimplifying events as bad or good, emotional reasoning, and mind reading. Cindy responded by saying that she had been oversimplifying in many ways and rattled off a list: "These people are bad," "The judicial system is wrong," "I'm bad," "Because he went to the Academy, he's good." She gave several other examples of emotional reasoning, but remained a bit stuck on mind reading. The therapist gave the example of how she assumed people would react. Cindy responded, "I didn't give my parents a chance. I didn't give anyone a chance."

Even though she hadn't done the homework on safety, the therapist brought the session around to the topic of safety to explore

Below are listed several types of faulty thinking patterns that people use in different life situations. These patterns often become automatic, habitual thoughts that cause us to engage in self-defeating behavior.

Consider your own stuck points and find examples for each of the patterns. Write in the stuck point under the appropriate pattern and describe how it fits that pattern. Think about how that pattern affects you.

1. Drawing conclusions when evidence is lacking or even contradictory.
   I didn't tell anyone what happened to me but yet I was convinced I would be the accused. I would be shamed. I never came forth so I don't know how people would have reacted. For all I know they might have been supportive.

2. Exaggerating or minimizing the meaning of an event: blowing things way out of proportion or shrinking their importance inappropriately.
   I let it get out of control when I let him kiss me when we were dancing. When he kissed me then I was stimulated. Why didn't I fight more? Because I was in shock. A kiss is OK. Rape is not.

3. Disregarding important aspects of a situation.
   Rape is rape. Blocking out how he dragged me down the hallway.

4. Oversimplifying events or beliefs as good-bad, right-wrong.

5. Overgeneralizing from a single incident: viewing a negative event as a never-ending pattern of defeat, or applying an association of the rapist to a whole group.

6. Mind reading: assuming that people are thinking negatively of you when there is no definite evidence for this.

7. Emotional reasoning: reasoning from how you feel.

FIGURE 2.3. Faulty thinking patterns.

whether Cindy had any stuck points. Upon probing, Cindy responded that she didn't feel unsafe when alone with a man, she was vigilant when getting into her car, she frequently made game plans when she found herself in a potentially unsafe situation, and she didn't carry a gun. Generally she felt quite comfortable with her level of precautions and was not overly concerned about the dangerousness of others. She said she had realized when Mark raped her, that meant that anyone could. However, she felt she was now more able to protect herself, and she believed she would probably fight more if she were ever attacked

again. The therapist decided to leave the topic of safety, because Cindy's beliefs were not extreme and she did practice reasonable safety precautions.

They moved on to the topic of trust. Cindy pointed out that the people who were closest to her were the ones who scared her the most. However, she also readily admitted that her experiences prior to the rape were quite positive. The therapist and Cindy went over the trust module, and Cindy felt that all of the potential effects that were listed all pertained to her. She reported that she had really been trying to open up with her husband and was saying a lot more and was feeling more. They were communicating better, and she felt more relaxed and comfortable.

When the therapist asked her about other relationships, Cindy responded by saying that she didn't have any other close relationships except with her mother. She said that she had had that other friend, but that she couldn't trust her. She also added that at her new job, she was forcing herself to go up to people and be friendlier. The therapist asked Cindy whether there were any people on the horizon with whom she could develop friendships. Cindy said yes, there were lots. She also added thoughtfully that if she had met the people at work before therapy, she would have been suspicious and would have judged them to be fake. Now she recognized that they were not. They were sincere and nice. The therapist ended by reminding Cindy that trust does not work with an on–off switch. Trust moves through levels and takes time.

Session 9

Cindy canceled a session, due to another 60-hour work week compounded by a death in her husband's family. At the next session, however, she arrived with a number of completed Challenging Beliefs worksheets. Although she stated she did not currently feel as strongly as she once had, she had decided to complete several worksheets on her perceptions after the rape, because they had so strongly affected her level of trust in others. (Two of these sheets are shown in Figures 2.4 and 2.5.)

The therapist praised Cindy for completing the worksheets so well. She pointed out that on the first worksheet Cindy did not change her belief or feelings very much, but that there was a great deal of validity to the statement. She discussed the reality of coming forward with an acquaintance rape even now, let alone 10 years ago. And given how popular Mark was, it was likely that many people would not be able to comprehend that he could/would commit rape. The important thing to remember was that not everyone would disbelieve. Cindy readily agreed, and her second sheet evidenced the fact that she was moving away from her generalized distrust. The therapist and Cindy spent longer on the third sheet, shown in Figure 2.6.

T: Why do you want to forgive him?

C: Because I cared about him, and I don't want to go through life hating.

T: Do you have to go through life hating to not forgive him?

C: I don't know.

T: I mean forgiving is not the same thing . . .

T&C: (*Simultaneously*) . . . as hating.

T: You could let the angry feelings go at some point and still say, "I don't have to forgive him."

Column A	Column B	Column C	Column D	Column E	Column F
Situation	Automatic thoughts	Challenging your automatic thoughts	Faulty thinking patterns	Alternative thoughts	De-catastrophizing
Describe the event(s), thought(s), or belief(s) leading to the unpleasant emotion(s).	Write automatic thought(s) preceding emotion(s) in Column A. Rate belief in each automatic thought(s) below from 0–100%.	Use the Challenging Questions sheets to examine your automatic thought(s) from Column B.	Use the Faulty Thinking Patterns sheet to examine your automatic thought(s) from Column B.	What else can I say instead of Column B? How else can I interpret the event instead of Column B? Rate belief in alternative thought(s) from 0–100%.	What's the worst thought could ever *realistically* happen? *To become the accused.*
No one would believe me if I told them.	*I would have to prove I'm the victim. I did not have substantial proof.* *75%*	*The way I saw other rape victims that came forward. In most cases, they became the accused.*	*Assuming I would be the accused. Assuming no one would believe me. Drawing conclusions.*	*I did not tell so I can't assume no one would believe me.* *55%* *By not telling a lot of people were saved from a lot of pain. I cared for those people more than I cared about making Mark pay for his crime.* *90%*	Even if that happened, what could I do? *Fight for my honor. Not ever let them get inside of me.*
Emotion(s)					**Outcome**
Specify sad, angry, etc., and rate the degree you feel each emotion from 0–100%. *Angry: 85%* *Confused: 5%* *Sad: 10%*					Re-rate belief in automatic thought(s) in Column B from 0–100%. *65%* Specify and rate subsequent emotion(s) from 0–100%. *Angry: 60%* *Confused: 10%* *Sad: 30%*

FIGURE 2.4. Challenging Beliefs Worksheet 1.

Column A	Column B	Column C	Column D	Column E	Column F
Situation	**Automatic thoughts**	**Challenging your automatic thoughts**	**Faulty thinking patterns**	**Alternative thoughts**	**De-catastrophizing**
Describe the event(s), thought(s), or belief(s) leading to the unpleasant emotion(s).	Write automatic thought(s) preceding emotion(s) in Column A. Rate belief in each automatic thought(s) below from 0–100%.	Use the Challenging Questions sheets to examine your automatic thought(s) from Column B.	Use the Faulty Thinking Patterns sheet to examine your automatic thought(s) from Column B.	What else can I say instead of Column B? How else can I interpret the event instead of Column B? Rate belief in alternative thought(s) from 0–100%.	What's the worst thought could ever *realistically* happen? *Being hurt by someone*
Trustworthiness of people close to me. *—————————* **Emotion(s)** *—————————* Specify sad, angry, etc., and rate the degree you feel each emotion from 0–100%. *Sad: 80%* *Angry: 20%*	*Anyone can hurt me. I cannot trust anyone.* *100%*	*It is true anyone can hurt me and I may not be able to trust everyone, but that doesn't mean I have to stop trusting the people I used to trust.*	*Mind reading—I prejudged everyone.* *Exaggerating the meaning—I could not trust some people, but some I could have trusted.*	*It is easier to trust others once I started trusting myself and my judgment.* *I will always be a little skeptical of people in general, but there will be people I trust.*	Even if that happened, what could I do? *Stay focused. I cannot control other people. Hold my head up and stay proud of who I am.* *—————————* **Outcome** *—————————* Re-rate belief in automatic thought(s) in Column B from 0–100%. *0%* Specify and rate subsequent emotion(s) from 0–100%. *Sad: 20%* *Angry: 5%* *Happy: 75%*

FIGURE 2.5. Challenging Beliefs Worksheet 2.

C: But still, I want to know why. I want it explained, because we were very close.

T: How are you going to feel if you don't get the answer you want?

C: (*Long pause*) I don't know. I guess I'll just go on. In one sense, I feel I'll be just as determined with myself, but I don't want to be a mind reader. I want to hear it come out of his mouth.

T: What answer would be acceptable to you?

C: Anything other than just something manipulative and deceitful.

T: What could he say if he were honest enough . . .

C: "I'm sorry."

T: But that doesn't tell you why he did it. If he were going to be honest and say, "You're right. I did it," and then he'd say, "I was confused. I was young. I was angry. There was all this stuff going on at home. I wanted to get my needs

Column A	Column B	Column C	Column D	Column E	Column F
Situation	Automatic thoughts	Challenging your automatic thoughts	Faulty thinking patterns	Alternative thoughts	De-catastro-phizing
Describe the event(s), thought(s), or belief(s) leading to the unpleasant emotion(s).	Write automatic thought(s) preceding emotion(s) in Column A. Rate belief in each automatic thought(s) below from 0–100%.	Use the Challenging Questions sheets to examine your automatic thought(s) from Column B.	Use the Faulty Thinking Patterns sheet to examine your automatic thought(s) from Column B.	What else can I say instead of Column B? How else can I interpret the event instead of Column B? Rate belief in alternative thought(s) from 0–100%.	What's the worst thought could ever *realistically* happen? *It could be very disturbing.*
I want him to tell me why. Why did he do that to me?	*I deserve to know.* 100% *I want to forgive him.* 80% *I won't get completely over it until he and I talk about it.* 90%	*I just feel very strong about it. I want the truth to be told.*	*I don't want to mind read or draw conclusions. I want to know the truth from the only person who can give it.*	*I'm scared.* 25%	Even if that happened, what could I do? *Continue to know in my heart the truth. Hold my head up high and go on.*
Emotion(s)					
Specify sad, angry, etc., and rate the degree you feel each emotion from 0–100%. *Angry: 75%* *Sad: 20%* *Scared: 5%*					**Outcome**
					Re-rate belief in automatic thought(s) in Column B from 0–100%. 95% Specify and rate subsequent emotion(s) from 0–100%. *Angry: 75%* *Sad: 15%* *Scared: 10%*

FIGURE 2.6. Challenging Beliefs Worksheet 3.

met my way. I was wrong." Is that acceptable?

C: Yeah . . . I guess, more or less, I want to tell him, have him realize, how much it affected my life. How much pain it caused. How much I've had to work through . . . I guess more than anything, it's not that I want to ask him why, as much as I want to deliver a message.

T: That's different. That's why I was wondering how it would help to know why. That wouldn't excuse it.

Cindy responded that she still encountered him in social settings occasionally when he came home for visits, and that he was still friends with her brother. She reiterated her desire to confront him.

T: What would happen if he were in denial? "What are you talking about? I never did any such thing."

C: I'd remind him that I know the truth, and no matter what he says, I still know. That's all that matters to me. I'm not denying it to myself any more. He'd know that I know the truth and nothing could ever change that.

T: (*Nodding*) As long as you're not looking for him to confirm what happened.

C: No. I don't need him to confirm. I know. I'm almost proud of myself for knowing!

T: Good. That's what I wanted to hear from you. (*Both laugh*) Sometimes people have the idea of confronting someone to get them to acknowledge, to make it "real."

C: At the beginning, I did want him to.

T: Look at the need you had for 10 years to distort what happened and call it something else. Now if this is what the victim does, can you imagine how much the perpetrator distorts and does not remember?

The therapist asked whether she would feel more comfortable writing a letter than confronting him face to face. Cindy said she didn't want to write a letter because he might not read it. She wanted to look him right in the face.

T: What would that do to your relationship with your brother?

C: I don't think I'll tell him. . . . And I miss my brother. I haven't talked to him in a month.

T: Because of this? (*Waving her arm to indicate therapy*)

C: Yeah.

T: What are you going to do about that?

C: That's what my mother keeps asking me. Apparently he's upset and wishes I would call.

T: Do you realize you've stopped Mark from totally destroying your life? But he's still interfering with your relationship with your brother, and you haven't taken that back. Is it because you're afraid your brother will side with Mark?

C: No. It will hurt him.

T: So? He's still your brother, and it's hurting him that you're maintaining this distance. Maybe one way to do it is to say something like "There's something that happened a long time ago, and I never told you about it because I was afraid it would hurt you so badly. But on the other hand,

I can see what it's doing to our relationship to keep this giant secret between us. I need to know that you can be supportive of me so we can work this relationship out, so we can get close again. So I'm willing to take this risk, but I don't know if you can handle it." It might help him understand a lot of things, like why you changed and why you grew distant from him.

C: And a lot of people.

T: Sure. He is old enough to handle it now.

C: Part of me wants to talk to him, and part of me doesn't want to hurt him.

T: You're not allowing him the opportunity to grow closer to you. You're not allowing him the opportunity to provide you some support.

C: And I am hurting him, and myself, by not talking to him.

T: You're also protecting him and not allowing him to have his own reactions.

C: But I know he'll be upset.

T: That's for him to deal with.

C: Because it did happen. It did, to me, and that's something that can't be denied.

T: No. And it's OK to feel sad or hurt if something happened to his sister. Those are legitimate feelings that he should be allowed to have. But don't be surprised if he has a little anger at you because you haven't told him. Because sometimes when you wait a long time before you tell people, you have to preface it and explain why you never told them first. Otherwise, they get so caught up in "Why didn't you tell me?" that they kind of lose the message and forget to be supportive, because they're so busy being hurt themselves that you didn't trust them. So that's why you have to say, "I never told you because I knew you would be hurt. And I knew it would tear you in terms of your allegiances, and [whatever else you need to say]. Now I'm seeing it's done a lot of damage between us, and I don't want that to continue."

C: It has. I think that's why I just needed to stop talking to him. It just bothered me so.

T: Well, you can tell him you were working on it in therapy and before it was too painful to talk to him.

C: To talk, yeah. I'm sure once we'd sit down, we'd get it all out. Maybe it would even bring us closer.

T: That would be the purpose of doing it. It's also a way of taking back that relationship as one more area of your life that Mark messed up, and now you can take it back.

C: Because I was angry at him for a long time about it, you know.

T: Guilt by association?

C: Why couldn't I talk to him?

T: You could, but you couldn't.

C: I couldn't trust him, you know. I didn't know who he would side with. I wasn't sure he would side with me, because Mark was also someone very important in his life.

T: Well, and it's hard to tell. He'd have to struggle with that, but that's his struggle, not yours.

C: I need to talk to him.

The therapist then asked Cindy about her relationship with her father. In talking about it, it became apparent to the therapist that Cindy was still protecting her father, in this case because of his PTSD from Vietnam. The therapist suggested that rather than parenting him, it might be time to stop and allow him to parent her.

At this point, the therapist introduced the module on power/control. They went over the module, and the therapist speculated that Cindy had let go of control in the year after the rape. Cindy agreed that everything had seemed out of control then. They also talked about how she had attempted, and was still attempting, to control information as a way to protect people. As in every session, Cindy was given homework—this time, to complete Challenging Beliefs worksheets on power/control.

Session 10

Cindy began the session by announcing that she had written a letter to her brother that she thought she probably wouldn't send. She read the letter aloud, and in it she expressed her concerns that her brother would be hurt and might not believe what had happened. She

described the events generally and expressed her feelings about these events.

Cindy stated that she had read the power/control module over and over since the last session, and that she started to realize that she was not responsible for her brother's reactions. She said she felt some relief that she could let go of this burden. She stated that she had noticed a change in her whole outlook. She realized she had been using a lot of "should" words, like "I should have had control." The therapist and Cindy went over her latest worksheets, shown in Figures 2.7 and 2.8.

Cindy described how her belief in self-betrayal ("I had control, but didn't do anything") led to problems with self-esteem. The same was true of her belief that she was unable to make good decisions—the sense of helplessness that followed the rape. The natural flow in topics between feelings of helplessness and self-evaluation served as a perfect segue to the next topic—esteem. The therapist gave Cindy a list called Identifying Assumptions (see Table 2.1) and asked her to put a check mark by each statement that she believed to be true for her. Fortunately, she marked only a few of the items, in the areas of control and competence. Cindy admitted that the "accomplishment thing" became very large in her mind, because Mark went to the academy with a full 4-year scholarship while she only went on to business school.

After reviewing the esteem module, the therapist asked Cindy to complete Challenging Beliefs worksheets on any of the items from the Identifying Assumptions list on which she felt stuck, as well as any stuck points relating to esteem. She was also given two other assignments: She was to practice giving and receiving compliments every day, and she was to do one nice thing for herself everyday (noncontingently). These assignments were to help her with her self-esteem.

Session 11

Cindy completed a worksheet on self-esteem, but stated that it was how she used to feel about it, rather than how she felt now. She stated that she didn't feel stuck on esteem issues. The therapist and Cindy went over the items she had circled on the Identifying Assumptions list to make sure she was no longer

TABLE 2.1. Identifying Assumptions List

Listed below are beliefs that some people hold. Please circle the number next to the beliefs that are *true for you.*

A. Acceptance
  1. I have to be cared for by someone who loves me.
  2. I need to be understood.
  3. I can't be left alone.
  4. I'm nothing unless I'm loved.
  5. To be rejected is the worst thing in the world.
  6. I can't get others mad at me.
  7. I have to please others.
  8. I can't stand being separated from others.
  9. Criticism means personal rejection.
 10. I can't be alone.

B. Competence
  1. I am what I accomplish.
  2. I have to be somebody.
  3. Success is everything.
  4. There are winners and losers in life.
  5. If I'm not on top, I'm a flop.
  6. If I let up, I'll fail.
  7. I have to be the best at whatever I do.
  8. Others' successes take away from mine.
  9. If I make a mistake, I'll fail.
 10. Failure is the end of the world.

C. Control
  1. I have to be my own boss.
  2. I'm the only one who can solve my problems.
  3. I can't tolerate others telling me what to do.
  4. I can't ask for help.
  5. Others are always trying to control me.
  6. I have to be perfect to have control.
  7. I'm either completely in control or completely out of control.
  8. I can't tolerate being out of control.
  9. Rules and regulations imprison me.
 10. If I let someone get too close, that person will control me.

making extreme expectations for herself. Cindy stated that she really didn't feel stuck on any of them now. The therapist and Cindy spent some time talking about her previous assumption that people should be judged as bad if they had money or professional success. She was now able to see that people are much more than just their professional accomplishments. They also have other activities and relationships with their families, friends, and themselves.

The therapist asked about giving and receiving compliments. Cindy replied that it had gone fine. She had to make herself reach out and it felt awkward, but the results were good. She said she normally didn't talk to people out in public, but she made an effort to talk to people in the grocery store. The bagger was so pleased with her attention that in the parking lot, he ran over to her and told her about his comic book collection. She also found that she was able to disarm a usually critical in-law at a family gathering by complimenting her. The therapist asked Cindy whether she had received any compliments. She responded that she had from her husband. This time she didn't deflect them, but listened and thanked him for noticing.

The therapist told Cindy that she had asked her to do nice things for herself because women often take care of themselves only after everyone else has been cared for and only if they feel they deserve it, which many never do. She was instructed to do something nice for herself every day noncontingently. Cindy said she had complied with the assignment and had really enjoyed it. She found it relaxing and noticed that her mood improved. Cindy's list of compliments and activities is shown in Figure 2.9.

After discussing self-esteem, the therapist and client discussed esteem toward others. Cindy readily admitted that this had been a major problem for her prior to therapy. She had been overwhelmed with the belief that people are bad, malicious, or evil. She related a great deal to the content of the esteem module, but felt that it was in the past. She had worked on it so much in therapy that she had moved this belief a great deal. She realized how much stereotyping she had done, as well as judging based on first impressions. Because she felt fairly resolved on this issue, the therapist moved on to introduce the final module, on intimacy.

T: This, I think, is an interesting one. I mentioned it to you in the beginning because of the marijuana. Self-soothing is the ability to calm yourself when you're feeling strong emotions. It's the ability to regulate without having to do outside things. And that's something small children, babies, can't regulate. You know, you see them and one minute they're screaming and the next minute they're laughing and then they're crying again and their emotions are just . . .

C: Yeah, up and down.

T: And as they grow older, they're going to learn to contain their emotions a bit more

Column A	Column B	Column C	Column D	Column E	Column F
Situation	Automatic thoughts	Challenging your automatic thoughts	Faulty thinking patterns	Alternative thoughts	De-catastrophizing
Describe the event(s), thought(s), or beliefs (s) leading to the unpleasant emotion(s).	Write automatic thought(s) preceding emotion(s) in Column A. Rate belief in each automatic thought(s) below from 0–100%.	Use the Challenging Questions sheets to examine your automatic thought(s) from Column B.	Use the Faulty Thinking Patterns sheet to examine your automatic thought(s) from Column B.	What else can I say instead of Column B? How else can I interpret the event instead of Column B? Rate belief in alternative thought(s) from 0–100%.	What's the worst thought could ever *realistically* happen? *Feeling I betrayed myself.*
Feeling of self-betrayal for being raped.	*I should have had control. I should have gained control and not let it go on for five weeks.* *90%*	*I was not in control. Mark was in control of the rape. I was in control of who I told. I was not in total control of people knowing or not. Mark had the power to tell people and even lie about it.* *I cannot control all events outside of myself, but I do have some control over what happens to me and my reactions to events.*	*Drawing conclusions—I should have been in control.* *Disregarding important aspects—I do not have control over other people. I did have some control by not telling, but I was not in total control, I was in shock.*	*I did not betray myself. Mark betrayed me. I did not let him rape me. With what control I did have over the choices that were avaliable at that time, I did not betray myself. I chose a path that was very painful and lonely, but protected my inner self, perhaps out of a great sense of love for myself.* *95%*	Even if that happened what could I do? *Re-evaluate the situation. Get help, if needed. Remember who I am and where I came from. Read these sheets.*
Emotion(s) Specify sad, angry, etc., and rate the degree you feel each emotion from 0–100%. *Angry: 85%* *Sad: 15%*					**Outcome** Re-rate belief in automatic thought(s) in Column B from 0–100%. *5%* Specify and rate subsequent emotion(s) from 0–100%. *Angry: 3%* *Sad: 7%* *Determined: 90%*

FIGURE 2.7. Challenging Beliefs Worksheet 4.

and modulate them—to have some control over them, to express them or not to express them as the situation arises, and so forth. When emotions happen that are too strong and you don't know what to do with them, you may tend to go to outside things. Or sometimes people are taught to do outside things. You see this sometimes with overweight people. When they were babies, if every time they cried somebody stuck something in their mouth, they would learn that the way to soothe themselves is to stick something in their mouth. So when they get upset about something, they move their chair in front of the refrigerator and just stay there. Or it may be some other kind of external thing, like alcohol or going on spending binges. All those things end up being addictions, because it's not you that's controlling your own stuff; it's this outside thing that's bringing relief—and, of course, it doesn't last very long, so then you keep needing more and more.

Column A	Column B	Column C	Column D	Column E	Column F
Situation	**Automatic thoughts**	**Challenging your automatic thoughts**	**Faulty thinking patterns**	**Alternative thoughts**	**De-catastro-phizing**
Describe the event(s), thought(s), or belief(s) leading to the unpleasant emotion(s).	Write automatic thought(s) preceding emotion(s) in Column A. Rate belief in each automatic thought(s) below from 0–100%.	Use the Challenging Questions sheets to examine your automatic thought(s) from Column B.	Use the Faulty Thinking Patterns sheet to examine your automatic thought(s) from Column B.	What else can I say instead of Column B? How else can I interpret the event instead of Column B? Rate belief in alternative thought(s) from 0–100%.	What's the worst thought could ever *realistically* happen? *Make a bad decision or judgement.*
Inability to make decisions.	*Look at what I let happen to me in the past.* *85%*	*I made very wise decisions in the past. The outcome of all major decisions I've made have put me where I am today.*	*Disregarding important aspects of the situation— Even while being raped I was making decisions on how to handle the situation. My decisions in the past were well thought out even though I didn't know it at the time.*	*In re-evaluating the choices I've made, it makes me gain a stronger sense of respect for myself and a deep sense of respect in my ability to make sound decisions. This, in turn, makes me feel more secure with my judgments*	Even if that happened, what could I do? *Re-evaluate the situation and learn from it.*
Emotion(s) Specify sad, angry, etc., and rate the degree you feel each emotion from 0–100%. *Sad: 75%* *Angry: 25%*					**Outcome** Re-rate belief in automatic thought(s) in Column B from 0–100%. *2%* Specify and rate subsequent emotion(s) from 0–100%. *Sad: 0%* *Angry: 0%* *Happy: 75%* *Glad: 25%*

FIGURE 2.8. Challenging Beliefs Worksheet 5.

C: It can put you back, you know, even just . . .

T: Well, and it can cause a whole different set of problems. You can become addicted to alcohol. Now you just don't have an outside crutch, you have an alcohol addiction. So it ends up being a double whammy and a serious one. You end up in major debt if you go on spending binges. It's hard to make up for those outside crutches things. I got the impression you were using the marijuana initially that way to a certain extent. That you were needing . . .

C: Yeah, by myself.

T: And it wasn't because it was something you did to enjoy occasionally; it was because you were upset and were trying to calm yourself.

C: (*Nods*)

T: I also got the impression, we haven't talked about it much, that that's sort of dropped out.

C: Yeah. Yeah, it's really toned down. I don't want it in a pacifying sense. When I've got everything done and I'm sitting, relaxing

Use the worksheets to confront stuck points regarding self- and other-esteem. Make sure you examine the items you checked on the Identifying Assumptions List in order to identify stuck points regarding esteem and competence. Complete worksheets on some of the most troublesome beliefs.

In addition to the worksheets, practice giving and receiving compliments during the week and do at least one nice thing for yourself each day (without having to earn it). Write down on this sheet what you did for yourself and who you complimented.

	Activity	Compliment
Thursday	2 hr of reading	Lady in line at grocery store
Friday	Afternoon to myself	My mom bought lingerie
Saturday	Watched a movie	Jim [husband] on his helpfulness and charm
Sunday	_____	Jim, and cousin who's always very hateful and sarcastic
Monday	Watched a movie alone	Bag boy at grocery store

FIGURE 2.9. Homework Assignment 10.

. . . I mean, it's kind of like having a glass of wine, or drinking one of those little pony beers and it'll be real nice. But I think that it has toned itself down. I now feel myself wanting to give up cigarettes. You know, thinking about it, I think I wanted to smoke then because nobody else did and it was different, and "I'm not like you, I'm different from you."

T: Were you also using them as a way, when you're anxious, to calm yourself down?

C: Yeah. Oh, yeah.

T: So that may be one that you'll still want to focus on. And one of the things to notice is, when are you doing it? And is there something else you can do? So before you just automatically do it, is there some other way you can calm yourself, soothe yourself internally, before you do something external? And you are learning. That's what we've been doing here is learning ways to modulate.

C: I think so, yeah.

T: Because you can analyze what's going on. Then when you feel them, you know they're not going to just keep getting worse

and worse. But by feeling them, they do get less.

C: Usually by the time you reach that point, you've already peaked off.

T: You just kind of let it go. But the other part of this thing is how to look at things in a way and say, "OK, hold it a second. What's the evidence for this?"

C: Yeah. That's what I mean. You're at your peak going, "Wait a minute."

T: And then you can find out if it's based on something irrational. Other times the emotions are absolutely, perfectly legitimate. If you are hurt, it's perfectly legitimate to feel sad or angry. If somebody hurts you intentionally, it's OK to feel angry, and if it's a loss, to feel sad. You don't want to not feel those feelings, because that's part of what the experience is.

C: Yeah.

T: Umm. And I think sometimes that self-soothing stuff comes in when you feel like you're not supposed to feel those feelings. You've got so many bottled up that you start to feel that it's going to overwhelm you.

C: Yeah. Or it already does so I just want to get it out of my mind. I'm tired of thinking about it.

T: So hopefully, once we've finished here, you're going to kind of be back to a clean slate. So if you get an emotion, you can feel it and be done with it at the time, so that it doesn't pile up. So that you're not saying, "If I feel it, I'm just going to flood."

C: Yeah.

T: And so then you don't need the external stuff so much, because it's not something that's overwhelming and enormous. It's a . . .

C: I'm not as anxious.

T: Also, I think having known that you can get through this, that hopefully, when crises come up in the future you can say, "There is something I can do. I can get through this."

C: Well, I really believe that because I . . . this was something just really . . . It amazes me what an impact it had on my life and my thoughts. How much it really just impacted my life and, you know, I held it for a long time.

The therapist and client went on to discuss intimacy with others, a topic that had been introduced earlier in the context of trust. Although the client didn't feel stuck, the therapist stated that her goal for Cindy was for her to begin to open up and take chances with other people—at work, in the neighborhood, and through her children's school activities. The therapist pointed out that these last two modules are long-term, and that their purpose is to identify any remaining stuck points and to set out long-term goals. The homework assignments for the final session were to work on the intimacy module (with worksheets) and rewrite the "meaning of the event" assignment that Cindy had written at the first session.

Session 12

As usual, the therapist began by asking how the homework went. Cindy discussed her reactions to the module and how it related to her experience. She talked about attempting to fill empty feelings with "stuff." The therapist asked her whether she had any remaining stuck points, and Cindy replied that they were not stuck points but goals to work toward, and that she had a clearer idea where she was going now. With regard to intimacy with others, Cindy recognized that it was going to take some time. She observed that at the time she was raped, she had never yet experienced a real intimate relationship. She also added that she thought it was important that she was no longer ashamed that she had been raped.

The therapist talked generally about friendships and reminded Cindy that, because a friendship takes two people, it may not always work out. She may need to try again. She also reminded her that the quality of another person is no reflection on her.

The therapist then asked Cindy to read what she had written about the meaning of the event for her. It was as follows:

The rape deeply affected me. My views, opinions, thoughts, and feelings were affected. I cannot change this and don't want to. I now realize the need for balance and to put the rape

into perspective. It was once part of my life. I am who I am today because of that part of my life. I'm proud of who I am today. When Mark raped me I was shattered inside. It has taken me 10 years to pick up the pieces. The puzzle is almost done. The last few pieces are falling into place. It helps when you now know what the picture is. It's who I am and what I'm about and it's beautiful.

Because I was 15 years old and still developing at that time, I lost my sense of self. It almost feels as if until now I've never had a sense of who I am. I think that is why I was so sad and felt so alone inside. I feel very strong and have a very strong spirit. If I believe in myself, I can do anything. I still have a feeling that I will achieve a lot of my goals. In fact, it's even stronger. I'm being called. I don't know where, but I can feel it. My spiritual side is almost upsetting sometimes. It scares me. Since I've opened up inside my spirit has risen. My dreams always seem to have a point to them, symbolism is appearing everywhere. I have a great sense of well-being. A part of all of this is the girl who was raped, abused, and manipulated. I will never forget, but I will not let it destroy me. That girl survived and did a damn good job. I don't know if anything will ever be as traumatic as being raped was. I hope my view of life is different. The worst thing that could possibly happen is to lose my sense of self again. I don't think I could let that happen. I never want to go that deep into hell again.

I believe Mark raped me. I was not in control of the situation, Mark was. I was in shock. I did not let him rape me. I did not let him abuse me. I have nothing to feel ashamed about. He was responsible for raping me. I was not responsible for being raped. I have learned a lot through counseling. In the beginning, I knew it would help me. I knew a change needed to be made. I had to face the demon in my head. The rape emotionally continued for years. I hoped counseling would be cleansing. It has been. I hoped I would find those missing pieces and I did. To pull my deepest, darkest inner secret up has been very hard. It was poisoning me though. With genuine help, I pulled that secret demon out and faced him head on. Thank you. I couldn't do it alone. You helped me because you were let in. You were the first one I trusted. You helped me break the ice.

Cindy was a bit teary as she finished reading. The therapist asked Cindy whether she remembered what she wrote the first time. Cindy said no, so the therapist read to her her first assignment. Cindy laughed at the line that most people are greedy, self-righteous scum. The therapist pointed out that Cindy had come a long way, and she agreed. Cindy was also amazed to see her first A-B-C sheets. The therapist and Cindy reviewed the whole therapy process, what they had covered, and the stuck points that Cindy had challenged. Cindy offered that the faulty thinking patterns are really easy to pick out once you get the hang of it. She ended by talking about her goal of improving her relationship with her brother and father. She stated that the only things her father knew about her were secondhand through her mother. She recognized that she didn't communicate with him directly.

Follow-Up

The week after the therapy ended, Cindy met with another clinician for her posttherapy assessment, the results of which are given in Table 2.2. She no longer met criteria for PTSD or depression on the SCID, and she exhibited marked decreases in all of her scores. Cindy's assessment scores for the 3-month and 6-month follow-ups are also listed in Table 2.2.

Two weeks after completing treatment, she called the therapist with the news that she had told her brother about the rapes. As expected, he had difficulty hearing that his good friend had raped his sister. Because Cindy had distanced herself from him, he assumed that she blamed him in some way for the rape, or because he didn't know. He called back the next day, and they discussed it more. Cindy was pleased she had told her brother, so that he would understand why she had distanced from him. She also recognized that his conflict was his own and not hers. She did, however, ask that he not call Mark until she decided whether she wanted to talk with him. She said she was using worksheets to work through the decision whether to talk to Mark, what she was anticipating, and what the possible outcomes might be.

At 3 months after treatment, Cindy came in for a follow-up assessment. She was continuing to do well and continued to score low on all of the PTSD and depression measures. A few weeks after the assessment, the therapist asked her to come in for a follow-up interview for this chapter. Overall, she reported that she was doing very well and that she had a new outlook on life. She felt sad or hurt occasionally when she thought of Mark, and stated that it would probably take more time to let go of the feelings completely.

She reported that her relationship with her brother had become somewhat strained because he was pushing her to confront Mark, in the hope they (he?) could resolve it. She had not buckled under his pressure and was still debating whether to talk to Mark, but said

TABLE 2.2. Cindy's Scores before and after Treatment

Measure	Pretreatment	Posttreatment	3 mos.	6 mos.
PTSD Symptom Scale	34	2	5	3
Reexperiencing	6	1	2	1
Avoidance	14	1	2	2
Arousal	14	0	1	0
IES	65	16	18	17
Intrusion	35	13	10	13
Avoidance	30	3	8	4
Beck Depression Inventory	36	0	1	4
SCL-90-R				
Somatization	1.67	0.42	0.25	0.25
Obsessive–Compulsive	2.40	0.70	0.20	0.10
Interpersonal Sensitivity	3.11	0.11	0.22	0.11
Depression	2.31	0	0.23	0.31
Anxiety	2.40	0	0.10	0
Hostility	2.00	0	0.17	0
Phobic Anxiety	0.57	0	0	0
Paranoid Ideation	2.33	0.33	0.33	0.50
Psychoticism	2.00	0.30	0.10	0.20
PTSD	2.25	0.29	0.11	0.11

that it did not preoccupy her. She wanted to wait until she felt strong and confident enough to handle whatever reactions he had. Her job was still going well, and she and her husband and children were getting along very well.

Cindy reported that her relationship with her father was slowly improving. Although they didn't talk about the rape, they were spending more time together and talked about her work or other family news. Her friendships at work were also developing, and she had developed several close friends who went out together. She reported being cautious and that as yet she had not exposed much confidential material, but described her disclosures and efforts to trust as "dipping my toe in the water." However, she had been pleased with their reactions to her disclosures thus far and felt they were honest and positive. The ex-friend had also tried to reestablish contact, but Cindy had merely told her that they didn't have much to say to each other and asked her to please stay away from her. Cindy expressed relief at having such a negative influence out of her life and was pleased with her handling of the phone call when she didn't rise to baiting.

Finally, the therapist asked about her reactions to successful or powerful people she encountered or saw on the news. She responded that when she saw others who were greedy, she didn't take it so much to heart and just shrugged them off with "Boy, they're a real case."

REFERENCES

American Psychiatric Association (APA). (1980). *Diagnostic and statistical manual of mental disorders* (3rd ed.). Washington, DC: Author.

American Psychiatric Association (APA). (1987). *Diagnostic and statistical manual of mental disorders* (3rd ed., rev.). Washington, DC: Author.

American Psychiatric Association (APA). (1994). *Diagnostic and statistical manual of mental disorders* (4th ed.). Washington, DC: Author.

Astin, M. C., Foy, D. W., Layne, C. M., & Camilleri, A. J. (1994). Posttraumatic stress disorder in victimization-related traumata. In J. Briere (Ed.), *Assessing and treating victims of violence* (pp. 39–51). San Francisco: Jossey-Bass.

Becker, J. V., Skinner, L. J., Abel, G. G., Axelrod, R., & Cichon, J. (1984). Sexual problems of sexual assault survivors. *Women and Health, 9,* 5–20.

Blake, D. D., Weathers, F. W., Nagy, L. M., Kaloupek, D. G., Gusman, F. D., Charney, D. S., & Keane, T. M. (1995). The development of a Clinician-Administered PTSD Scale. *Journal of Traumatic Stress, 8,* 75–90.

Blanchard, E. B., Hickling, E. J., Buckley, T. C., Taylor, A. E., Vollmer, A., & Loos, W. R. (1996). Psychophysiology of posttraumatic stress disorder related to motor vehicle accidents: Replication and extension. *Journal of Consulting and Clinical Psychology, 64,* 742–751.

Blank, A. S. (1993). The longitudinal course of a posttraumatic stress disorder. In J. R. T. Davidson & E. B. Foa (Eds.), *Posttraumatic stress disorder: DSM-IV and beyond* (pp. 3–23). Washington, DC: American Psychiatric Press.

Boudewyns, P. A., Hyer, L. A., Peralme, L., Touze, J., & Kiel, A. (1995, August). *Eye movement desensitization and reprocessing (EMDR) and exposure therapy in the treatment of combat-related PTSD: An early look.* Paper presented at the annual meeting of the American Psychological Association, New York.

Bowen, G. R., & Lambert, J. A. (1986). Systematic desensitization therapy with post-traumatic stress disorder cases. In C. R. Figley (Ed.), *Trauma and its wake* (Vol. 2, pp. 280–291). New York: Brunner/Mazel.

Breslau, N., Davis, G. C., & Andreski, P. (1995). Risk factors for PTSD-related traumatic events: A prospective analysis. *American Journal of Psychiatry, 152*(4), 529–535.

Brewin, C. R., Dalgleish, T., & Joseph, S. (1996). A dual representation theory of posttraumatic stress disorder. *Psychological Review, 103,* 670–686.

Briere, J. (1995). *Trauma Symptom Inventory (TSI): Professional manual.* Odessa, FL: Psychological Assessment Resources.

Brom, D., Kleber, R. J., & Defares, P. B. (1989). Brief psychotherapy for posttraumatic stress disorders. *Journal of Consulting and Clinical Psychology, 57,* 607–612.

Burt, M. R. (1980). Cultural myths and supports for rape. *Journal of Personality and Social Psychology, 38,* 217–230.

Carlson, J. G., Chemtob, C. M., Rusnak, K., Hedlund, N. L., & Muraoka, M. Y. (1995, June). *Eye movement desensitization and reprocessing for combat-related posttraumatic stress disorder: A controlled study.* Paper presented at the 4th Annual Meeting of the European Conference on Traumatic Stress, Paris.

Chemtob, C., Roitblat, H., Hamada, R., Carlson, J., & Twentyman, C. (1988). A cognitive action theory of posttraumatic stress disorder. *Journal of Anxiety Disorders, 2,* 253–275.

Cloitre, M. (1998). Sexual revictimization: Risk factors and prevention. In V. M. Follette, J. I. Rusek, & F. R. Abueg (Eds.), *Cognitive behavioral therapies for trauma* (pp. 278–304). New York: Guilford Press.

Creamer, M., Burgess, P., & Pattison, P. (1992). Reaction to trauma: A cognitive processing model. *Journal of Abnormal Psychology, 101,* 453–459.

Davidson, J., & Smith, R. (1990). Traumatic experiences in psychiatric outpatients. *Journal of Traumatic Stress, 3,* 459–475.

Denny, N., Robinowitz, R., & Penk, W. (1987). Conducting applied research on Vietnam combat-related post-traumatic stress disorder. *Journal of Clinical Psychology, 43,* 56–66.

Derogatis, L. R. (1983). *SCL-90-R: Administration, scoring and procedures manual—II.* Towson, MD: Clinical Psychometric Research.

Falsetti, S., Resnick, H., Resick, P., & Kilpatrick, D. (1993). The Modified PTSD Symptom Scale: A brief self-report measure of posttraumatic stress disorder. *Behavior Therapist, 16,* 161–162.

First, M. B., Spitzer, R. L., Gibbon, M., & Williams, J. B. W. (1996). *Structured Clinical Interview for DSM-IV Axis I Disorders—Patient Edition* (SCID-I/P, Version 2.0). New York: Biometrics Research Department, New York State Psychiatric Institute.

Foa, E. B. (1995). *Posttraumatic Stress Diagnostic Scale (manual).* Minneapolis, MN: National Computer Systems.

Foa, E. B. (1996). Conceptualization of post-trauma psychopathology as failure in emotional processing. In P. A. Resick (Chair), *Information processing theories: Variations on a theme.* Symposium conducted at the 12th Annual Meeting of the International Society for Traumatic Stress Studies, San Francisco.

Foa, E. B., Dancu, C., Hembree, E., Jaycox, L., Meadows, E. A., & Street, G. P. (1999). A comparison of exposure therapy, stress inoculation training, and their combination for reducing posttraumatic stress disorder in female assault victims. *Journal of Consulting and Clinical Psychology, 67*(2), 194–200.

Foa, E. B., & Kozak, M. J. (1986). Emotional processing of fear: Exposure to corrective information. *Psychological Bulletin, 99,* 20–35.

Foa, E. B., Riggs, D. S., Dancu, C. V., & Rothbaum, B. O. (1993). Reliability and validity of a brief instrument for assessing post-traumatic stress disorder. *Journal of Traumatic Stress, 6,* 459–474.

Foa, E. B., & Rothbaum, B. O. (1998). *Treating the trauma of rape: Cognitive-behavioral therapy for PTSD.* New York: Guilford Press.

Foa, E. B., Rothbaum, B. O., Riggs, D. S., & Murdock, T. B. (1991). Treatment of posttraumatic stress disorder in rape victims: A comparison between cognitive-behavioral procedures and counseling. *Journal of Consulting and Clinical Psychology, 59*(5), 715–725.

Foa, E. B., Steketee, G. S., & Rothbaum, B. O. (1989). Behavioral/cognitive conceptualizations of posttraumatic stress disorder. *Behavior Therapy, 20,* 155–176.

Frank, E., Anderson, B., Stewart, B. D., Dancu, C., Hughes, C., & West, D. (1988). Efficacy of cognitive behavior therapy and systematic desensitization in the treatment of rape trauma. *Behavior Therapy, 19,* 403–420.

Frank, E., & Stewart, B. D. (1983). Treating depression in victims of rape. *Clinical Psychologist, 36,* 95–98.

Frank, E., & Stewart, B. D. (1984). Depressive symptoms in rape victims. *Journal of Affective Disorders, 1,* 269–277.

Girelli, S. A., Resick, P. A., Marhoefer-Dvorak, S., & Kotsis-Hutter, C. (1986). Subjective distress and violence during rape: Their effects on long-term fear. *Victims and Violence, 1,* 35–46.

Griffin, M. G., Resick, P. A., & Mechanic, M. B. (1997). Objective assessment of peritraumatic dissociation: Psychophysiological indicators. *American Journal of Psychiatry, 154*(8), 1081–1088.

Holmes, M. R., & St. Lawrence, J. S. (1983). Treatment of rape-induced trauma: Proposed behavioral conceptualization and review of the literature. *Clinical Psychology Review, 3,* 417–433.

Horowitz, M. (1986). *Stress response syndromes* (2nd ed.). New York: Aronson.

Horowitz, M., Wilner, N., & Alvarez, W. (1979). Impact of Event Scale: A measure of subjective stress. *Psychological Medicine, 4,* 209–218.

Janoff-Bulman, R. (1985). The aftermath of victimization: Rebuilding shattered assumptions. In C. R. Figley (Ed.), *Trauma and its wake: The study and treatment of post-traumatic stress disorder* (pp. 15–35). New York: Brunner/Mazel.

Janoff-Bulman, R. (1992). *Shattered assumptions: Towards a new psychology of trauma.* New York: Free Press.

Jensen, J. A. (1994). An investigation of eye movement desensitization and reprocessing (EMD/R) as a treatment for posttraumatic stress disorder (PTSD) symptoms of Vietnam combat veterans. *Behavior Therapy, 25,* 311–325.

Keane, T. M., Caddell, J. M., & Taylor, K. L. (1988). The Mississippi Scale for combat-related PTSD: Studies in reliability and validity. *Journal of Consulting and Clinical Psychology, 56,* 85–90.

Keane, T. M., Fairbank, J. A., Caddell, J. M., & Zimering, R. T. (1989). Implosive (flooding) therapy reduces symptoms of PTSD in Vietnam combat veterans. *Behavior Therapy, 20,* 245–260.

Keane, T. M., Fairbank, J. A., Caddell, J. M., Zimering, R. T., Taylor, K. L., & Mora, C. A. (1989). Clinical evaluation of a measure to assess combat exposure. *Psychological Assessment, 1,* 53–55.

Keane, T. M., Kolb, L. C., Kaloupek, D. G., Orr, S. P., Blanchard, E. B., Thomas, R. G., Hsieh, F. Y., & Lavori, P. W. (1998). Utility of psychophysiological measurement in the diagnosis of posttraumatic stress disorder: Results from a Department of Veterans Affairs cooperative study. *Journal of Consulting and Clinical Psychology, 66,* 914–923.

Keane, T. M., Malloy, P. F., & Fairbank, J. A. (1984). The empirical development of an MMPI-subscale for the assessment of combat-related post-traumatic stress disorders. *Journal of Consulting and Clinical Psychology, 52,* 888–891.

Keane, T. M., Wolfe, J., & Taylor, K. L. (1987). Posttraumatic stress disorder: Evidence for diagnostic validity and methods of psychological assessment. *Journal of Clinical Psychology, 43,* 32–43.

Keane, T. M., Zimering, R. T., & Caddell, J. M. (1985). A behavioral formulation of posttraumatic stress disorder in Vietnam veterans. *Behavior Therapist, 8,* 9–12.

Kessler, R., Sonnega, A., Bromet, E., Hughes, M., & Nelson, C. (1995). Post-traumatic stress disorder in the National Comorbidity Survey. *Archives of General Psychiatry, 52,* 1048–1060.

Kilpatrick, D. G. (1983). Rape victims: Detection, assessment and treatment. *Clinical Psychologist, 36,* 92–95.

Kilpatrick, D. G., & Amick, A. E. (1985). Rape trauma. In M. Hersen & C. Last (Eds.), *Behavior therapy casebook* (pp. 86–103). New York: Springer.

Kilpatrick, D. G., Edmunds, C. N., & Seymour, A. K. (1992). *Rape in America: A report to the nation.* Arlington, VA: National Victim Center.

Kilpatrick, D. G., & Resnick, H. S. (1993). Posttraumatic stress disorder associated with exposure to criminal victimization in clinical and community populations. In J. R. T. Davidson & E. B. Foa (Eds.), *Posttraumatic stress disorder: DSM-IV and beyond* (pp. 113–143). Washington, DC: American Psychiatric Press.

Kilpatrick, D. G., Resnick, H., & Freedy, J. (1991). *The potential Stressful Events Interview*. Unpublished manuscript, Medical University of South Carolina, Charleston.

Kilpatrick, D. G., Saunders, B. E., Veronen, L. J., Best, C. L., & Von, J. M. (1987). Criminal victimization: Lifetime prevalence, reporting to police, and psychological impact. *Crime and Delinquency, 33,* 479–489.

Kilpatrick, D. G., & Veronen, L. J. (1983). Treatment of rape-related problems: Crisis intervention is not enough. In L. H. Cohen, W. L. Claiborn, & G. A. Specter (Eds.), *Crisis intervention* (pp. 165–185). New York: Human Sciences Press.

Kilpatrick, D. G., Veronen, L. J., & Best, C. L. (1985). Factors predicting psychological distress among rape victims. In C. R. Figley (Ed.), *Trauma and its wake* (pp. 113–141). New York: Brunner/Mazel.

Kilpatrick, D. G., Veronen, L. J., & Resick, P. A. (1982). Psychological sequelae to rape. In D. M. Doleys, R. L. Meredith, & A. R. Ciminero (Eds.), *Behavioral medicine: Assessment and treatment strategies* (pp. 473–498). New York: Plenum Press.

King, D. W., Leskin, G. A., King, L. A., & Weathers, F. W. (1998). Confirmatory factor analysis of the Clinician-Administered PTSD Scale: Evidence for the dimensionality of posttraumatic stress disorder. *Journal of Traumatic Stress, 11,* 87–101.

Kleinknecht, R., & Morgan, M. P. (1992). Treatment of post-traumatic stress disorder with eye movement desensitization and reprocessing. *Journal of Behavior Therapy and Experimental Psychiatry, 23,* 43–49.

Koss, M. P., & Harvey, M. (1991). *The rape victim: Clinical and community approaches to treatment* (2nd ed.). Lexington, MA: Stephen Greene Press.

Kulka, R. A., Schlenger, W. E., Fairbank, J. A., Hough, R. L., Jordan, B. K., Marmar, C. R., & Weiss, D. S. (1990). *Trauma and the Vietnam war generation*. New York: Brunner/Mazel.

Kulka, R. A., Schlenger, W. E., Fairbank, J. A., Jordan, B. K., Hough, R. L., Marmar, C. R., & Weiss, D. S. (1991). Assessment of posttraumatic stress disorder in the community: Prospects and pitfalls from recent studies of Vietnam veterans. *Journal of Consulting and Clinical Psychology, 3,* 547–560.

Lang, P. J. (1968). Fear reduction and fear behavior: Problems in treating a construct. *Research in Psychotherapy, 3,* 9–102.

Lang, P. J. (1977). Imagery in therapy: An information processing analysis of fear. *Behavior Therapy, 8,* 862–886.

Lauterbach, D., & Vrana, S. (1996). Three studies on the reliability and validity of a self report measure of posttraumatic stress disorder. *Assessment, 3,* 17–25.

Lazrove, S., Triffleman, E., Kite, L., McGlashan, T., & Rounsaville, B. (1995, November). *The use of EMDR as treatment for chronic PTSD: Encouraging results of an open trial*. Paper presented at the annual meeting of the International Society for Traumatic Stress Studies, Boston.

Lipke, H., & Botkin, A. (1992). Brief case studies of eye movement desensitization and reprocessing with chronic post-traumatic stress disorder. *Psychotherapy, 29,* 591–595.

Mahoney, M., & Lyddon, W. (1988). Recent developments in cognitive approaches to counseling and psychotherapy. *Counseling Psychologist, 16,* 190–234.

March, J. S. (1993). The stressor criterion in DSM-IV posttraumatic stress disorder. In J. R. Davidson & E. B. Foa (Eds.), *Posttraumatic stress disorder: DSM-IV and beyond* (pp. 37–54). Washington, DC: American Psychiatric Press.

Marks, I., Lovell, K., Noshirvani, H., Livanou, M., & Thrasher, S. (1998). Treatment of post-traumatic stress disorder by exposure and/or cognitive restructuring: A controlled study. *Archives of General Psychiatry, 55,* 317–325.

Marquis, J. N. (1991). A report on seventy-eight cases treated by eye movement desensitization. *Journal of Behavior Therapy and Experimental Psychiatry, 22,* 187–192.

McCann, I. L. (1992). Post-traumatic stress disorder due to devastating burns overcome by a single session of eye movement desensitization. *Journal of Behavior Therapy and Experimental Psychiatry, 23,* 319–323.

McCann, I. L., & Pearlman, L. A. (1990a). *Psychological trauma and the adult survivor: Theory, therapy and transformation*. New York: Brunner/Mazel.

McCann, I. L., & Pearlman, L. A. (1990b). Vicarious traumatization: A framework for understanding the psychological effects of working with victims. *Journal of Traumatic Stress, 3*(l), 131–149.

McNair, L. D., & Neville, H. A. (1996). African American women survivors of sexual assault: The interaction of race and class. In M. Hill & E. Rothblum (Eds.), *Classism and feminist therapy: Counting costs* (pp. 107–118). New York: Harrington Park Press and Haworth Press.

Meichenbaum, D. H. (1985). *Stress inoculation training*. New York: Pergamon Press.

Mowrer, O. H. (1947). On the dual nature of learning: A re-interpretation of "conditioning" and "problemsolving." *Harvard Educational Review, 17,* 102–148.

Norris, F. H. (1990). Screening for traumatic stress: A scale for use in the general population. *Journal of Applied Social Psychology, 20,* 1704–1718.

Norris, F. H. (1992). Epidemiology of trauma: Frequency and impact of different potentially traumatic events on different demographic groups. *Journal of Consulting and Clinical Psychology, 60,* 409–418.

Orr, S. P., Lasko, N. B., Metzger, L. J., Berry, N. J., Ahern, C. E., & Pitman, R. K. (1998). Psychophysiologic assessment of women with posttraumatic stress disorder resulting from childhood sexual abuse. *Journal of Consulting and Clinical Psychology, 66,* 906–913.

Pitman, R. K., Orr, S. P., Altman, B., Longpre, R. E., Poire, R. E., & Lasko, N. B. (1993). *A controlled study of eye movement desensitization/reprocessing (EMDR) treatment for post traumatic stress disorder*. Poster presented at the annual meeting of the International Society for Traumatic Stress Studies, San Antonio, TX.

Pitman, R. K., Orr, S. P., Forgue, D. F., Altman, B., & de Jong, J. (1990). Psychophysiologic responses to combat imagery of Vietnam veterans with posttraumatic stress disorder versus other anxiety disorders. *Journal of Abnormal Psychology, 99*, 49–54.

Pitman, R. K., Orr, S. P., Forgue, D. F., de Jong, J., & Claiborn, J. M. (1987). Psychophysiological assessment of posttraumatic stress disorder imagery in Vietnam combat veterans. *Archives of General Psychiatry, 44*, 970–975.

Prins, A., Kaloupek, D. G., & Keane, T. M. (1995). Psychophysiological evidence for autonomic arousal and startle in traumatized adult populations. In M. J. Friedman, D. S. Charney, & A. Y. Deutch (Eds.), *Neurobiological and clinical consequences of stress: From normal adaptation to post-traumatic stress disorder* (pp. 291–314). Philadelphia: Lippincott/Raven.

Puk, G. (1991). Treating traumatic memories: A case report on the eye movement desensitization procedure. *Journal of Behavior Therapy and Experimental Psychiatry, 22*, 149–151.

Renfrey, G., & Spates, C. R. (1994). Eye movement desensitization: A partial dismantling study. *Journal of Behavior Therapy and Experimental Psychiatry, 25*, 231 239.

Resick, P. A. (1992). Cognitive treatment of crime-related post-traumatic stress disorder. In R. Peters, R. McMahon, & V. Quinsey (Eds.), *Aggression and violence throughout the life span* (pp. 171–191). Newbury Park, CA: Sage.

Resick, P. A., Jordan, C. G., Girelli, S. A., Hutter, C. H., & Marhoefer-Dvorak, S. (1988). A comparative outcome study of behavioral group therapy for sexual assault victims. *Behavior Therapy, 19*, 385–401.

Resick, P. A., & Markaway, B. E. G. (1991). Clinical treatment of adult female victims of sexual assault. In C. R. Hollin & K. Howells (Eds.), *Clinical approaches to sex offenders and their victims* (pp. 261–284). New York: Wiley.

Resick, P. A., Nishith, P., Weaver, T. L., Astin, M. C., & Feuer, C. A. (2000). *A comparison of cognitive processing therapy, prolonged exposure and a waiting condition for the treatment of posttraumatic stress disorder in female rape victims*. Manuscript submitted for publication.

Resick, P. A., & Schnicke, M. K. (1992). Cognitive processing therapy for sexual assault victims. *Journal of Consulting and Clinical Psychology, 60*, 748–756.

Resick, P. A., & Schnicke, M. K. (1993). *Cognitive processing therapy for rape victims: A treatment manual*. Newbury Park, CA: Sage.

Resnick, H. S., Kilpatrick, D. G., Dansky, B. S., Saunders, B. E., & Best, C. L. (1993). Prevalence of civilian trauma and posttraumatic stress disorder in a representative national sample of women. *Journal of Consulting and Clinical Psychology, 61*, 984–991.

Resnick, H. S., Kilpatrick, D. G., & Lipovsky, J. A. (1991). Assessment of rape-related posttraumatic stress disorder. Stressor and symptom dimensions. *Psychological Assessment, 3*, 561–572.

Robins, L. N., Helzer, J. D., Croughan, J., & Ratcliff, K. S. (1981). The National Institute of Mental Health Diagnostic Interview Schedule: Its history, characteristics, and validity. *Archives of General Psychiatry, 38*, 381–389.

Rosenheck, R., & Fontana, A. (1996). Race and outcome of treatment for veterans suffering from PTSD. *Journal of Traumatic Stress, 9*, 343–351.

Rosenheck, R., Fontana, A., & Cottrol, C. (1996). Effect of clinician–veteran racial pairing in the treatment of post-traumatic stress disorder. *American Journal of Psychiatry, 152*(4), 555–563.

Rothbaum, B. O. (1995, November). *A controlled study of EMDR for PTSD*. Poster presented at the 29th Annual Convention of the Association for Advancement of Behavior Therapy, Washington, DC.

Rothbaum, B. O. (1998, March). *Virtual reality exposure therapy for Vietnam veterans with PTSD: Preliminary results*. Paper presented at the Lake George Conference on Posttraumatic Stress Disorder, Bolton Landing, NY.

Rothbaum, B. O., & Foa, E. B. (1992). Exposure therapy for rape victims with post-traumatic stress disorder. *Behavior Therapist, 15*, 219–222.

Rothbaum, B. O., & Foa, E. B. (1993). Subtypes of posttraumatic stress disorder and duration of symptoms. In J. R. T. Davidson & E. B. Foa (Eds.), *Posttraumatic stress disorder: DSM-IV and beyond* (pp. 23–35). Washington, DC: American Psychiatric Press.

Rothbaum, B. O., Hodges, L., Alarcon, R., Ready, D., Shahar, F., Graap, K., Pair, J., Hebert, P., Gotz, D., Will, B., & Baltzell, D. (1999). Virtual reality exposure therapy for PTSD Vietnam veterans: A case study. *Journal of Traumatic Stress, 12*(2), 263–271.

Saunders, B., Arata, C., & Kilpatrick, D. (1990). Development of a crime-related posttraumatic stress disorder scale for women with the Symptom Checklist-90 Revised. *Journal of Traumatic Stress, 3*, 439–448.

Saxe, G., & Wolfe, J. (1999). Gender and posttraumatic stress disorder. In P. A. Saigh & J. D. Bremner (Eds.), *Posttraumatic stress disorder: A comprehensive text*. Boston: Allyn & Bacon.

Schindler, F. E. (1980). Treatment of systematic desensitization of a recurring nightmare of a real life trauma. *Journal of Behavior Therapy and Experimental Psychiatry, 11*, 53–54.

Shalev, A. Y., Orr, S. P., & Pitman, R. K. (1992). Psychophysiologic response during script-driven imagery as an outcome measure in posttraumatic stress disorder. *Journal of Clinical Psychiatry, 53*, 324–326.

Shapiro, F. (1989). Eye movement desensitization: A new treatment for post traumatic stress disorder. *Journal of Behavior Therapy and Experimental Psychiatry, 20*, 211–217.

Shapiro, F. (1995). *Eye movement desensitization and reprocessing: Basic principles, protocols, and procedures*. New York: Guilford Press.

Shay, J., & Munroe, J. (1999). Group and milieu therapy for veterans with complex PTSD. In P. A. Saigh & J. D. Bremner (Eds.), *Posttraumatic stress disorder: A comprehensive text* (pp. 391–413). Boston: Allyn & Bacon.

Silverman, D. (1977). First do no more harm: Female rape victims and the male counselor. *American Journal of Orthopsychiatry, 47*, 91–96.

Spector, J., & Huthwaite, M. (1993). Eye-movement desensitization to overcome post-traumatic stress disorder. *British Journal of Psychiatry, 163,* 106–108.

Spitzer, R. L., Williams, J. B., & Gibbon, M. (1987). *Structured Clinical Interview for DSM-III-R—Non-patient Version.* New York: New York State Psychiatric Institute.

Sutker, P. B., Uddo-Crane, M., & Allain, A. N. (1991). Clinical and research assessment of posttraumatic stress disorder: A conceptual overview. *Psychological Assessment, 3,* 520–530.

Turner, S. M. (1979, December). *Systematic desensitization of fears and anxiety in rape victims.* Paper presented at the 13th Annual Convention of the Association for Advancement of Behavior Therapy, San Francisco.

Vaughan, K., Armstrong, M. S., Gold, R., O'Connor, N., Jenneke, W., & Tarrier, N. (1994). A trial of eye movement desensitization compared to image habituation training, and applied muscle relaxation in posttraumatic stress disorder. *Journal of Behavior Therapy and Experimental Psychiatry, 25,* 283–291.

Veronen, L. J., & Kilpatrick, D. G. (1980). Self-reported fears of rape victims: A preliminary investigation. *Behavior Modification, 4,* 383–396.

Veronen, L. J., & Kilpatrick, D. G. (1983). Stress management for rape victims. In D. Meichenbaum & M. E. Jaremko (Eds.), *Stress reduction and prevention* (pp. 341–374). New York: Plenum Press.

Vrana, S., & Lauterbach, D. (1994). Prevalence of traumatic events and post-traumatic stress psychological symptoms in a nonclinical sample of college students. *Journal of Traumatic Stress, 7,* 289–302.

Weathers, F. W., & Keane, T. M. (1999). Psychological assessment of traumatized adults. In P. A. Saigh & J. D. Bremner (Eds.), *Posttraumatic stress disorder: A comprehensive text* (pp. 219–247). Boston: Allyn & Bacon.

Weathers, F. W., Litz, B. T., Herman, D. S., Huska, J. A., & Keane, T. M. (1993, October). *The PTSD Checklist (PCL): Reliability, validity, and diagnostic utility.* Paper presented at the annual meeting of the International Society for Traumatic Stress Studies, San Antonio, TX.

Weathers, F. W., Ruscio, A. M., & Keane, T. M. (1999). Psychometric properties of nine scoring rules for the Clinician-Administered Posttraumatic Stress Disorder Scale. *Psychological Assessment, 11*(2), 124–133.

Weiss, D. S., & Marmar, C. R. (1997). The Impact of Event Scale—Revised. In J. P. Wilson & T. M. Keane (Eds.), *Assessing psychological trauma and PTSD* (pp. 399–411). New York: Guilford Press.

Wilson, A. E., Calhoun, K. S., & Bernat, J. A. (1999). Risk recognition and trauma-related symptoms among sexually revictimized women. *Journal of Consulting and Clinical Psychology, 67,* 705–710.

Wilson, D., Silver, S. M., Covi, W., & Foster, S. (1996). Eye movement desensitization and reprocessing: Effectiveness and automatic correlates. *Journal of Behavior Therapy and Experimental Psychiatry, 27,* 219–229.

Wilson, J. P., & Keane, T. M. (Eds.). (1997). *Assessing psychological trauma and PTSD.* New York: Guilford Press.

Wilson, S. A., Becker, L. A., & Tinker, R. (1995). Eye movement desensitization and reprocessing (EMDR) treatment for psychologically traumatized individuals. *Journal of Consulting and Clinical Psychology, 63,* 928–937.

Wolpe, J., & Abrams, J. (1991). Post-traumatic stress disorder overcome by eye movement desensitization: A case report. *Journal of Behavior Therapy and Experimental Psychiatry, 22,* 39–43.

Zoellner, L. A., Feeny, N. C., Fitzgibbons, L. A., & Foa, E. B. (1999). Response of African American and Caucasian women to cognitive behavioral therapy for PTSD. *Behavior Therapy, 30,* 581–595.

Chapter 3

SOCIAL ANXIETY DISORDER

Cynthia L. Turk
Richard G. Heimberg
Debra A. Hope

Many people are very shy and somewhat inhibited. For this reason, the suffering associated with social anxiety disorder is often minimized as a trait common in the population that does not require the heavy artillery of formalized treatment interventions (either drugs or psychological treatments). Nothing could be further from the truth. For the very large segment of the population who suffer from debilitating social anxiety (over 10% and increasing), the seemingly simple process of interacting with people or forming relationships provokes overwhelming terror and is often avoided. The effects on career and quality of life can be devastating. This chapter examines the latest iteration of what is currently the most powerful psychological treatment for social anxiety disorder. As is increasingly true of our new generation of psychological interventions, cognitive-behavioral group therapy has proven to be significantly better than equally credible but less focused psychological interventions, and its effect is increasingly powerful over time. As such, this treatment is among the best of the new generation of psychological treatments characterized by power and specificity. The case of Brian, new to this edition, also illustrates the maturity and clinical sophistication of this remarkable approach to social anxiety.—D. H. B.

Our understanding of the nature and treatment of clinically significant social anxiety has expanded immensely since social phobia was included as a diagnostic category in the third edition of the *Diagnostic and Statistical Manual of Mental Disorders* (DSM-III; American Psychiatric Association [APA], 1980) over 20 years ago. At that time, social phobia was conceptualized as similar to specific (then termed simple) phobia, in that fears were thought to be limited to one or two social situations and unlikely to result in more than minimal disruption in role functioning. Research has since revealed that social phobia is a significant mental health problem that can be quite incapacitating. In fact, the DSM-IV (APA, 1994) Anxiety Disorders Work Group gave social phobia the parenthetical name of "social anxiety disorder," in order to commu-

nicate that this is a more pervasive and impairing disorder than implied by the label "social phobia" (Liebowitz, Heimberg, Fresco, Travers, & Stein, 2000). In keeping with our recommendation that "social anxiety disorder" become the primary name for this disorder in future editions of the DSM, we use this term throughout the chapter.

We begin this chapter with a brief overview of research on the epidemiology and psychopathology of social anxiety disorder. Studies examining the efficacy of combined exposure and cognitive restructuring treatments are then discussed. Next, we highlight our theoretical model of social anxiety disorder, as a general background to facilitate understanding of the treatment strategies discussed in the remainder of the chapter. The bulk of the chapter centers around a particular therapeutic approach, cognitive-behavioral group therapy (CBGT) for social anxiety disorder, and includes a detailed presentation of a treated case.

PSYCHOPATHOLOGY AND EPIDEMIOLOGY

According to DSM-IV (APA, 1994), individuals with social anxiety disorder fear a variety of social interaction and performance situations because they are concerned about being humiliated or embarrassed by performing inadequately or displaying visible anxiety symptoms in front of others. Persons with this disorder may fear one or two relatively specific social situations, such as public speaking or performing a complex motor behavior that would be visibly disrupted by a fine tremor or lack of concentration (e.g., eating, typing, writing, playing a musical instrument in front of others). More commonly, multiple social interaction situations (e.g., dating, being assertive) and performance situations (e.g., participating in meetings, job interviews) are feared (Holt, Heimberg, Hope, & Liebowitz, 1992; Turner, Beidel, Dancu, & Keys, 1986). A proportion of individuals with social anxiety disorder fear most social contact with others. Persons with broad-based fears of social contact are classified as having the "generalized" subtype. Feared social situations may be either avoided or endured despite intense anxiety.

Impairment

The fear and avoidance associated with social anxiety disorder often results in impaired occupational and social functioning. It is not unusual to find individuals with this disorder who are grossly underemployed. For example, when one former patient presented for treatment, he was employed as a night janitor despite having earned a college degree. He had recently refused a promotion and pay increase because he could not face the interpersonal demands of supervising two coworkers. It is also common for individuals with social anxiety disorder to suffer from extreme isolation and loneliness. One example is a 59-year-old retired man who recently presented for treatment at our clinic. He lived alone, and his

contact with others during a typical week consisted of a 1-hour session with his psychiatrist, brief interactions with store clerks, and one telephone conversation with his sister (who lived in another state). He reported having no friends and never having had a significant other, although he longed for relationships with other people. In fact, the vast majority of individuals with social anxiety disorder believe that their careers, academic lives, and/or general social functioning have been seriously impaired by their social fears (Liebowitz, Gorman, Fyer, & Klein, 1985; Schneier et al., 1994; Turner et al., 1986). In one study, despite a mean age in the early 30s, half of the individuals with social anxiety disorder had never married, compared to 36% of individuals with panic disorder and agoraphobia and 18% of those with generalized anxiety disorder (Sanderson, DiNardo, Rapee, & Barlow, 1990). Given the suffering that often accompanies social anxiety disorder, it is not surprising that individuals with this disorder rate their quality of life as very low (Safren, Heimberg, Brown, & Holle, 1997) and have increased rates of suicidal ideation relative to individuals with no psychiatric disorder (Schneier, Johnson, Hornig, Liebowitz, & Weissman, 1992).

Prevalence

The Epidemiologic Catchment Area (ECA) study reported the lifetime prevalence rate of social anxiety disorder to be 2.4% (Schneier et al., 1992). However, these findings were based on restrictive DSM-III criteria and on interviews that inquired about fear and impairment in only three situations relevant to social anxiety disorder. The more recent National Comorbidity Survey (NCS) utilized DSM-III-R (APA, 1987) criteria (which are quite similar to the current DSM-IV criteria) and inquired about fear and impairment in six social situations. The NCS revealed a lifetime prevalence rate of 13.3% for social anxiety disorder, making it the third most common psychiatric disorder, surpassed only by major depressive disorder and alcohol dependence (Kessler et al., 1994).

Recent analyses of data from the NCS suggest that the prevalence of social anxiety disorder is increasing. Magee, Eaton, Wittchen, McGonagle, and Kessler (1996) found higher lifetime prevalence rates of social anxiety disorder among younger cohorts (ages 15–24, 14.9%; ages 25–34, 13.8%) than older cohorts (ages 35–44, 12.1%; ages 45–54, 12.2%). In a more fine-grained analysis of these data, Heimberg, Stein, Hiripi, and Kessler (2000) discovered that the prevalence of social anxiety disorder limited exclusively to public speaking fears was similar across cohorts. An increased prevalence of broader social fears among younger respondents accounted for the findings of Magee and colleagues (1996). Thus, if these trends continue, social anxiety disorder may represent an even greater challenge to clinicians and public health officials in the future.

Social anxiety disorder appears to be more prevalent among women than men in the general population (Kessler et al., 1994; Schneier et al., 1992), although the sexes are more equally represented in treatment-seeking samples (Chapman, Mannuzza, & Fyer, 1995). The ECA data suggest a bimodal distribution for age of onset, with peaks at younger than age 5 and at 11–15 years old (Juster, Brown, & Heimberg, 1996; Schneier et al., 1992). The younger group was composed of persons who reported that they could not remember a time when they did not experience impairing social fear. Social anxiety disorder appears to be a chronic condition that does not remit for the majority of sufferers (Chartier, Hazen, & Stein, 1998; Reich, Goldenberg, Vasile, Goisman, & Keller, 1994).

Subtypes of Social Anxiety Disorder and Avoidant Personality Disorder

The heterogeneity of individuals suffering from social anxiety disorder has been the topic of much discussion and research. Numerous studies have attempted to subdivide samples of patients with social anxiety disorder, primarily on the basis of type of feared situation or pervasiveness of the fear. Currently, DSM-IV directs the diagnostician to specify the "generalized" subtype of social anxiety disorder if the person's fears include most social situations. Persons whose fears do not extend to most social situations are grouped together by many researchers into a "nongeneralized" subtype. Although DSM-IV does not define a "nongeneralized" subtype per se, it does describe those not meeting the definition of "generalized" as a diverse group that includes patients who fear one performance situation as well as patients who fear more than one, but not most, social situations (APA, 1994). Individuals with generalized social anxiety disorder tend to have an earlier age of onset and to be younger, less educated, more likely to be unemployed, and more often single than their counterparts with the nongeneralized subtype (Heimberg, Hope, Dodge, & Becker, 1990; Mannuzza et al., 1995). They experience more depression, social anxiety, avoidance, fear of negative evaluation, and functional impairment (see, e.g., Brown, Heimberg, & Juster, 1995; Herbert, Hope, & Bellack, 1992; Turner, Beidel, & Townsley, 1992). There is some evidence that patients with nongeneralized social anxiety disorder may experience more extreme heart rate reactivity when confronted with a feared social situation than patients with generalized social anxiety disorder (Boone et al., 1999; Heimberg, Hope, et al., 1990; Levin et al., 1993). Several studies have shown that patients with generalized social anxiety disorder improve as much as patients with the nongeneralized subtype in cognitive-behavioral treatment (Brown et al., 1995; Hope, Herbert, & White, 1995; Turner, Beidel, Wolff, Spaulding, & Jacob, 1996). However, because patients with the generalized subtype begin treatment with greater impairment, they remain relatively more impaired after treatment.

The inclusion of the generalized subtype in the DSM-III-R and DSM-IV has highlighted the confusion about the relationship between social anxiety disorder and avoidant personality disorder (APD). APD is characterized by a long-standing pattern of social reticence, feelings of inadequacy, and extreme sensitivity to disapproval or criticism (APA, 1994). In six recent studies (Brown et al., 1995; Herbert et al., 1992; Holt, Heimberg, & Hope, 1992; Schneier, Spitzer, Gibbon, Fyer, & Liebowitz, 1991; Tran & Chambless, 1995; Turner et al., 1992), the percentage of persons with social anxiety disorder who received an additional diagnosis of APD ranged from 22% to 70%. Each of these studies concluded that features of APD are common among persons with social anxiety disorder, particularly those with more generalized fears. In fact, the median percentage of patients with generalized social anxiety disorder who met criteria for APD was 57.6%, while the median percentage of patients with nongeneralized social anxiety disorder with APD was only 17.5% (Heimberg, 1996). However, the evidence is equivocal with respect to whether social anxiety disorder and APD should be classified as separate disorders. Perhaps individuals with APD are simply the most severely impaired persons with social anxiety disorder (Heimberg, Holt, Schneier, Spitzer, & Liebowitz, 1993). Furthermore, there is little empirical support for the notion that some individuals may meet the criteria for APD without also meeting the criteria for social anxiety disorder (Widiger, 1992). With regard to treatment outcome, some studies have found that patients with and without a comorbid diagnosis of APD make similar treatment gains (Brown et al., 1995; Hofmann, Newman, Becker, Taylor, & Roth, 1995; Hope, Herbert, & White, 1995), but others (Chambless, Tran, & Glass, 1997; Feske, Perry, Chambless, Renneberg, & Goldstein, 1996) suggest poorer treatment response among patients with comorbid APD.

Axis I Comorbidity

Social anxiety disorder commonly co-occurs with other disorders, and it typically predates the onset of the comorbid disorder (Davidson, Hughes, George, & Blazer, 1993; Magee et al., 1996; Schneier et al., 1992). In the ECA study, 69% of individuals with social anxiety disorder suffered from comorbid DSM-III disorders (Schneier et al., 1992). The most prevalent additional diagnoses were simple phobia (59%), agoraphobia (45%), alcohol abuse (19%), and major depression (17%). In the NCS, 81% of persons with social anxiety disorder were diagnosed with comorbid DSM-III-R conditions (Magee et al., 1996). In this study, the most common comorbidities were simple phobia (37.6%), major depression (37.2%), alcohol dependence (23.9%), and agoraphobia (23.3%). Compared to individuals with uncomplicated social anxiety disorder, persons with social anxiety disorder and another psychiatric disorder were at greater risk for a number of negative outcomes, including increased rates of suicide attempts and increased rates of medical and psychiatric outpatient treatment seeking (Schneier et al., 1992). Persons with social anxiety disorder and a comorbid diagnosis were also more likely to report significant role

impairment and medication use to control their social anxiety symptoms, relative to individuals with uncomplicated social anxiety disorder (Magee et al., 1996).

Consistent with the epidemiological data, research from clinical settings suggests that a significant percentage of individuals with social anxiety disorder abuse alcohol (Amies, Gelder, & Shaw, 1983; Schneier, Martin, Liebowitz, Gorman, & Fyer, 1989; Thyer et al., 1986). Elevated rates of social anxiety disorder have also been found among alcoholics (Chambless, Cherney, Caputo, & Rheinstein, 1987; Mullaney & Trippett, 1979; Smail, Stockwell, Canter, & Hodgson, 1984). These studies suggest that the majority of participants experienced symptoms of social anxiety prior to their difficulties with alcohol and may have been drinking to reduce their social anxiety. Little is known about the response of individuals with comorbid substance abuse and social anxiety disorder to treatment for either their social anxiety or their substance abuse. Individuals with substance abuse problems are typically excluded from most social anxiety disorder treatment outcome studies (see, e.g., Heimberg et al., 1998). Even outside research settings, individuals with social anxiety disorder may often be asked to address their substance abuse problems prior to being accepted for treatment for their social anxiety. Unfortunately, social anxiety disorder may interfere with treatment in many traditional chemical dependence programs and self-help organizations like Alcoholics Anonymous, given that interventions in these programs are typically administered in a group format. Social anxiety may also decrease compliance with aftercare programs or an individual's ability to follow through with many of the tasks often involved in establishing a sober lifestyle (e.g., obtaining employment, developing new relationships with individuals who do not drink or use substances). We are currently conducting a study examining whether treatment for social anxiety disorder decreases social anxiety symptoms and substance abuse relapse among veterans who have just completed a residential chemical dependence treatment program.

A recent study by our research group found that 51% of 141 patients with social anxiety disorder had a comorbid anxiety or mood disorder (Erwin, Heimberg, Juster, & Mindlin, in press). The most commonly assigned additional DSM-IV diagnoses were generalized anxiety disorder (23.4%), specific phobia (12.8%), and major depressive disorder (12.8%). In this study, a comorbid depressive disorder, but not a comorbid anxiety disorder, was generally associated with greater impairment before and after 12 weeks of CBGT. Nevertheless, comorbid diagnoses were not associated with differential rates of improvement with treatment, similar to the findings of other investigators (see, e.g., Turner et al., 1996; van Velzen, Emmelkamp, & Scholing, 1997).

EFFICACY OF COMBINED COGNITIVE AND EXPOSURE TREATMENT

Researchers have investigated the efficacy of a broad range of treatments for social anxiety disorder, including social skills training; cognitive therapy; various forms of relaxation; imaginal, *in vivo*, and role-played exposure; interpersonal psychotherapy; brief Morita therapy; dynamically oriented supportive psychotherapy; and various pharmacotherapies. This review only examines studies that have tested the efficacy of combined exposure and cognitive treatment, which is the focus of this chapter. (Readers interested in a more extensive discussion of the social anxiety disorder treatment outcome literature should consult reviews by Cohn & Hope, in press; Fresco, Erwin, Heimberg, & Turk, in press; Juster & Heimberg, 1998; and Turk, Coles, & Heimberg, in press.)

Combined cognitive and exposure treatments have been investigated more frequently than any other psychosocial treatments for social anxiety disorder. This is not surprising, since exposure treatments have been successful for many of the anxiety disorders. The addition of a cognitive component has not always added to the efficacy of exposure alone in the other anxiety disorders. Several researchers (e.g., Butler, 1989) have argued, however, that the fear of negative evaluation experienced by persons with social anxiety disorder is essentially a cognitive phenomenon, and that cognitive interventions may be particularly important in this group.

In an early study, Butler, Cullington, Munby, Amies, and Gelder (1984) compared *in vivo* exposure to *in vivo* exposure plus an anxiety management program consisting of distraction, relaxation, and rational self-talk, and to a waiting-list control. Although the anxiety management training was not a purely cognitive intervention, a post hoc analysis indicated that participants may have found the rational self-talk the most helpful aspect of the package. To control for time spent on the anxiety management program, the exposure-alone condition included a filler treatment that, unfortunately, was not entirely credible to participants. At posttest, both exposure treatments were more effective than the waiting-list control across a variety of measures, with few differences between the active treatments. However, at follow-up, participants who received exposure plus anxiety management training fared better than participants who received exposure alone.

Mattick and colleagues (Mattick & Peters, 1988; Mattick, Peters, & Clarke, 1989) conducted two studies examining the efficacy of a combined package of therapist-assisted and *in vivo* exposure and cognitive restructuring. In the first study (Mattick & Peters, 1988), the combined treatment was compared to exposure alone. Participants in both groups improved, with somewhat greater improvement in the combined condition, particularly at a 3-month follow-up. In the second study, the combined treatment was compared to each component alone and to a waiting-list control. All active treatments resulted in improvement relative to the control condition, but the type and pattern of change differed among the treatments. Participants in all three active treatments reduced phobic avoidance, but participants receiving cognitive restructuring alone or in combination with exposure also improved on measures of irrational beliefs and negative self-evaluation. Compared to the other treatments, the combined condition resulted in most improvement on behavioral measures. Cognitive-restructuring-alone participants were slowest to improve on the behavioral test, but made continued gains during the follow-up period, whereas the exposure-alone participants deteriorated somewhat. Although it appears that each of the components of the combined package was effective at reducing participants' social-evaluative fears, the combination of exposure and cognitive therapy may have been superior.

In a recent study, patients with social anxiety disorder were randomly assigned to eight

1½-hour individual sessions of either cognitive restructuring or the filler treatment used by Butler and colleagues (1984) (Taylor, Woody, Koch, et al., 1997). After these initial sessions, cognitive restructuring was superior to the control therapy, as reflected by greater reductions in global severity of social anxiety disorder, increased self-esteem, decreased worry about negative evaluation, decreased social avoidance, and fewer negative and more positive thoughts during a behavior test. Thereafter, all patients received eight 2-hour sessions of exposure in a group format. After this second phase of treatment, both groups of patients showed additional improvement in social anxiety severity and social avoidance. No differences were found between patients initially receiving cognitive restructuring and those initially receiving the control therapy. Exposure with and without prior cognitive restructuring produced similar improvement. Thus cognitive restructuring prior to exposure did not appear to facilitate its effectiveness in this study.

In the first of several studies evaluating CBGT (the treatment described in the case example later in this chapter), Heimberg, Becker, Goldfinger, and Vermilyea (1985) treated seven patients with social anxiety disorder—five with public speaking fears and two with heterosocial fears—in a multiple-baseline design. This early version of CBGT consisted of imaginal exposure, role-played exposure during group therapy sessions, cognitive restructuring, and homework for *in vivo* exposure. At the end of the 14-week treatment, all participants improved on a range of behavioral, physiological, and subjective measures. Gains were maintained at a 6-month follow-up for six of the seven participants.

Few studies in the social anxiety disorder treatment outcome literature have employed an attention placebo condition to control for the nonspecific effects of therapy. This is a more rigorous test than a comparison to a waiting-list condition, because participants are actively involved in a credible treatment but one that does not include the specific theoretically effective component(s). Using such a design, Heimberg, Dodge, and colleagues (1990) evaluated a version of CBGT that eliminated the imaginal exposure component and reduced treatment time to 12 weeks. The attention control treatment consisted of education about social anxiety disorder and nondirective supportive group therapy. As expected, participants in both treatments improved significantly on most measures. However, at both posttest and a 6-month follow-up, participants receiving CBGT were more improved on some key measures. In particular, these participants reported less anxiety during an individualized behavioral test and were more likely to be rated as improved by a clinical assessor. At the 6-month follow-up, the internal dialogue of participants receiving CBGT was characterized by a "positive dialogue"—a state associated with good mental health, according to Schwartz and Garamoni's (1989) "states of mind" model. The internal dialogue of attention control participants, in contrast, represented a "negative monologue"—the most pathological state of mind described in this model (Bruch, Heimberg, & Hope, 1991). A 5-year follow-up of a subset of participants from the original sample indicated that individuals who had received CBGT were more likely to maintain their gains and continued to be more improved than comparable participants who had received the attention control (Heimberg, Salzman, Holt, & Blendell, 1993).

Lucas and Telch (1993) compared the effectiveness of CBGT and an individual version of the CBGT protocol to the same attention control treatment used by Heimberg, Dodge, and colleagues (1990). CBGT and the individual format resulted in similar treatment gains, both superior to those of the attention control treatment. The group protocol, however, was more cost-effective than the individual treatment version.

In a component analysis of CBGT, Hope, Heimberg, and Bruch (1995) reported that CBGT and exposure alone were both more effective than a waiting-list control. At posttest, there was evidence that the exposure-alone condition was more effective than CBGT, but these differences disappeared at a 6-month follow-up. However, the authors noted that participants in both treatment conditions made less progress than anticipated, possibly due to attrition in some of the therapy groups.

CBGT has been compared to pharmacotherapy in a number of studies (Gelernter et al., 1991; Heimberg et al., 1998; Otto et al., 2000). In the largest of these studies, 133 patients were randomly assigned to CBGT, phenelzine, a pill placebo, or the attention control psychotherapy developed by Heimberg, Dodge, and colleagues (1990) (Heimberg et al., 1998). Of these 133 patients, 107 completed 12 weeks of treatment. At posttest, independent assessors classified 21 of 28 patients completing CBGT (75%) and 20 of 26 patients completing phenelzine treatment (77%) as "treatment responders." The response rates for patients receiving phenelzine and CBGT were significantly better than for patients receiving the pill placebo or the attention control psychotherapy. Although the phenelzine and CBGT groups did not differ significantly on independent assessor ratings of treatment response, the patients receiving phenelzine were more improved than the patients receiving CBGT on a subset of outcome measures.

In the second phase of this study, patients who responded to CBGT or phenelzine were continued through 6 additional months of maintenance treatment and then a 6-month treatment-free follow-up period (Liebowitz et al., 1999). Thereafter, 50% of patients previously responding to phenelzine relapsed, compared to only 17% of patients who had responded to CBGT. The difference in relapse between treatments was especially pronounced for patients with generalized social anxiety disorder. Thus CBGT appears to confer better protection against relapse than phenelzine alone. The combination of these two treatments has not yet been evaluated, although a study by our research group is currently addressing this question.

In summary, it appears that a combined package of exposure and cognitive restructuring such as CBGT represents an effective intervention for social anxiety disorder. Whether it is the most effective treatment, or more effective than exposure or cognitive therapy alone, is more difficult to determine, given the limited number of studies and mixed results. However, more important to practitioners is the mounting evidence that three of four patients with social anxiety disorder are likely to realize clinically significant change after a reasonably intensive trial of CBGT or a similar combination of exposure and cognitive restructuring.

AN INTEGRATED COGNITIVE-BEHAVIORAL MODEL

We now present the model of social anxiety disorder that provides the conceptual framework for the procedures used in CBGT. More detailed reviews of the theoretical and empirical foundations of this model can be found elsewhere (Rapee & Heimberg, 1997; Turk, Lerner, Heimberg, & Rapee, 2001). We begin by describing the beliefs and information-processing biases characteristic of individuals with social anxiety disorder. After laying this foundation, we walk through the process that occurs when individuals with social anxiety disorder confront a feared social situation.

Beliefs

Individuals with social anxiety disorder typically possess certain fundamental, negative beliefs about themselves and others. They are likely to view themselves as unacceptable to other people. Research suggests that persons with social anxiety disorder have an abundance of automatic thoughts, the majority of which are of a self-derogatory nature (Stopa & Clark, 1993). They expect to behave in an inept and unappealing manner in social situations, and research has shown that they rate their own social behavior more harshly than objective observers do (Rapee & Lim, 1992; Stopa & Clark, 1993). The evidence regarding whether socially anxious individuals actually exhibit objectively poor social behavior is mixed, with some studies suggesting deficiencies (Halford & Foddy, 1982; Stopa & Clark, 1993) and others not (Rapee & Lim, 1992). Furthermore, many persons with social anxiety are concerned about displaying symptoms of anxiety that will be visible to others, because they hold the belief that these symptoms must be indicative of mental illness (Roth, Antony, & Swinson, in press). Not surprisingly, although socially anxious individuals display more symptoms of anxiety than their nonanxious counterparts, they overestimate the visibility of their anxiety relative to ratings by objective observers (Alden & Wallace, 1995; Bruch, Gorsky, Collins, & Berger, 1989; McEwan & Devins, 1983).

Individuals with social anxiety disorder also hold negative beliefs relating to other people and social relationships. They view others as inherently critical and therefore likely to evaluate them negatively (Leary, Kowalski, & Campbell, 1988). They believe that others hold expectations that they are unlikely to be able to meet (see, e.g., Wallace & Alden, 1991). According to Trower and Gilbert's (1989) psychobiological/ethological theory of social anxiety, people with social anxiety disorder generally view social relationships as hierarchical and competitive in nature, and doubt their ability to compete for more dominant positions in the social group. In contrast, nonanxious individuals tend to view social relationships as cooperative and supportive. Consistent with this formulation, recent research has shown that persons with social anxiety disorder engage in fewer dominance behaviors (e.g., using commands or interrupting) during social interactions than do nonanxious controls (Walters & Hope, 1998).

Information Processing

Information-processing models propose that pathological fear is represented in memory in anxiety-specific cognitive structures (Foa & Kozak, 1986; Lang, 1977). These cognitive structures consist of integrated information about the characteristics of the feared stimulus; information about verbal, physiological, and behavioral responses to that stimulus; and information about the (dangerous) meaning of the stimulus and responses. This fear structure is activated when aspects of the present experience match features of the memory of the feared situation. Activation of the fear structures may facilitate the processing of threatening information (Dalgleish & Watts, 1990).

Individuals with social anxiety disorder appear to devote excessive attentional resources to the detection of potential social threat cues (see, e.g., Asmundson & Stein, 1994; Hope, Rapee, Heimberg, & Dombeck, 1990; Mattia, Heimberg, & Hope, 1993). As a consequence of this narrowing of attention to social threat cues, the importance of these cues may then be exaggerated, so that a barely noticeable stutter is equated with incoherence and a refused request for a date portends an isolated and solitary existence (Amir, Foa, & Coles, 1998; Stopa & Clark, 2000). These attentional and judgmental biases may interfere with the individuals' ability to process information contrary to their existing beliefs (e.g., frowns or yawns are more likely to be noticed than smiles or nods of approval, and more likely to be interpreted negatively when they are noticed). Enhanced attention to socially threatening information may occur at the ex-

pense of attending to, encoding, and remembering information relevant to the social task at hand, which could potentially result in impaired performance (e.g., making inappropriate remarks, having difficulty generating follow-up questions). Only a few studies have examined whether socially anxious individuals have poorer memory for aspects of the social environment. The results have been mixed, with some (Bond & Omar, 1990; Daly, Vangelisti, & Lawrence, 1989; Hope, Heimberg, & Klein, 1990; Kimble & Zehr, 1982) but not all (Stopa & Clark, 1993) studies suggesting disrupted memory.

The Model

The characteristic ways in which individuals with social anxiety disorder think about themselves and other people and process social information sets the stage for what happens when a social situation perceived as potentially dangerous is confronted (see Figure 3.1). Persons with social anxiety disorder construct a mental representation of how they appear to the people around them, using input from long-term memory, internal cues such as somatic sensations, and external cues such as others' facial expressions. This mental representation is likely to be distorted, with potential sources of negative evaluation being exaggerated. For example, a recent patient described being teased by her peers as a young teenager for being tall and skinny. Although she is now an attractive woman in her late 20s, she still describes her appearance as "gangly," "awkward," and "ugly." Similarly, we have had patients who describe themselves as becoming "beet-red" whenever they are the center of attention, and who explain this image of themselves as being based on past comments from other people about their blushing and on internal sensations of feeling warm. Recent research has demonstrated that individuals with social anxiety disorder do form images and memories of themselves in anxiety-provoking social situations that reflect excessive self-focused attention, in that these images and memories are more likely to be from an observer perspective (seeing oneself as if from an external point of view) than a field perspective (as if looking out through one's own eyes) (Coles, Turk, Heimberg, & Fresco,

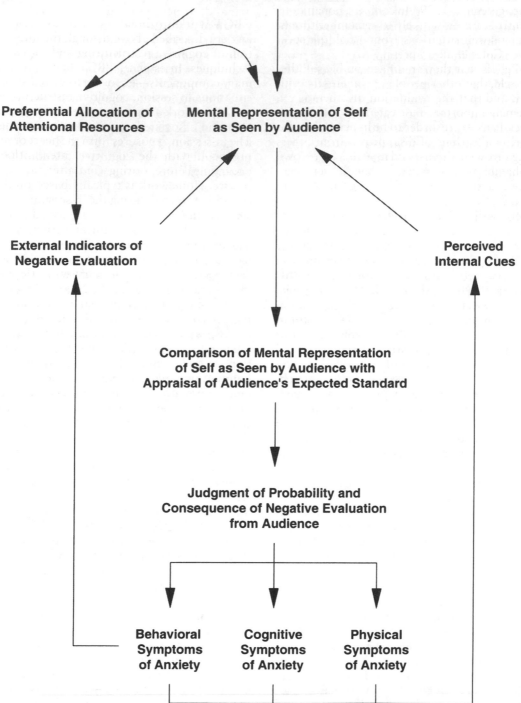

FIGURE 3.1. A model of the generation and maintenance of anxiety in social-evaluative situations. Reprinted from *Behaviour Research and Therapy*, 35, R. M. Rapee & R. G. Heimberg, A cognitive-behavioural model of anxiety in social phobia, page 743, copyright 1997, with permission from Elsevier Science.

1999; Hackmann, Surawy, & Clark, 1998; Wells, Clark, & Ahmad, 1998; Wells & Papageorgiou, 1999). In contrast, nonanxious controls are more likely to remember threatening social situations from a field perspective (Coles et al., in press).

Beliefs that they are unacceptable to other people, that other people are inherently critical, and that the evaluation of others is extremely important motivate individuals with social anxiety disorder to be hypervigilant for early indications of disapproval from others (e.g., frowns, yawns) and aspects of their own behavior or appearance that might elicit negative evaluation from others (e.g., making an inane comment, not being dressed appropriately, visible shaking). The division of attentional resources among external social threats, the (distorted) mental representation of the self, and the demands of the current social task *may* result in actual performance deficits (which may then elicit actual negative social feedback). In effect, persons with social anxiety disorder operate within the equivalent of a "multiple-task paradigm," which increases the probability of disrupted social performance (MacLeod & Mathews, 1991). Therefore, complex social tasks are more likely to result in poorer performance, due to limited processing resources, than are less complex tasks.

Persons with social anxiety disorder also attempt to predict the standards that the other person(s) (the "audience") will hold for them in the situation. Characteristics of the audience (e.g., importance, attractiveness) and features of the situation (e.g., whether the situation is formal or informal) influence the projected standards of the audience. Individuals with social anxiety disorder then attempt to judge to what extent their current mental representation of their appearance and behavior matches the predicted standards of the audience. Of course, given the negative bias present in their mental self-representation, they are likely to conclude that they are falling short of the audience's expectations and that painful outcomes such as loss of social status and rejection are likely to follow. Negative predictions result in cognitive, behavioral, and physiological symptoms of anxiety, which eventually feed back into the negatively biased mental representation of the self and perpetuate the cycle of anxiety.

How CBGT Operates within the Model

CBGT works to break the vicious cycle of anxiety described above through the integration of cognitive restructuring and exposure techniques. In essence, CBGT has three primary components—exposure to feared social situations in session, cognitive restructuring, and homework assignments for *in vivo* exposure and associated cognitive restructuring. The in-session exposures form the heart of the protocol, with the cognitive interventions occurring before, during, and after each exposure. Homework is typically based on the situation targeted during the in-session exposure. As in session, patients are asked to engage in cognitive restructuring activities before, during, and after each *in vivo* exposure.

Exposure serves to disrupt the spiral of social anxiety in three primary ways (Hope, Heimberg, Juster, & Turk, 2000). First, exposure short-circuits avoidance of anxiety-provoking social situations and allows a patient to experience the natural reduction in anxiety that comes with staying in the situation long enough on several occasions (i.e., habituation). Second, exposure allows a patient to practice the behavioral skills needed in situations that may have been long avoided (e.g., asking someone for a date, being assertive). Third, exposure gives the patient the opportunity to test the reality of his/her dysfunctional beliefs (e.g., "I won't be able to think of anything to say if I join my coworkers for lunch").

Cognitive restructuring also plays an important role in breaking the cycle of social anxiety (Hope et al., 2000). Cognitive restructuring challenges the patient's beliefs, assumptions, and expectations to see whether they really make sense or are helpful, and it provides more realistic ways of viewing the situation. Obviously, this technique is useful for the cognitive symptoms of anxiety. However, as the patient's assessment of the danger inherent in social situations becomes more realistic, physiological symptoms of anxiety often diminish as well. Furthermore, addressing the patient's cognitions often frees up additional attentional resources that can be used to increase focus on the social task at hand and potentially to improve performance. Lastly, changing dysfunctional beliefs helps decrease avoidance and increase the patient's ability to take credit for successes, which in turn gives the patient the opportunity to experience the naturally occurring positive reinforcement available from other people.

GENERAL CONSIDERATIONS IN CBGT

The Group Format

Exposure-based treatments require tremendous commitment and courage on the part of patients. After all, the purpose of exposure is to have individuals face the fears they may have avoided for many years. Although it may initially seem counterintuitive to treat socially anxious patients in a group format, the group provides a number of advantages. These advantages include vicarious learning, seeing others with similar problems, making a public commitment to change, the availability of multiple role-play partners, and a range of people to provide evidence to counter distorted thinking (Heimberg & Becker, 2001; Sank & Shaffer, 1984). Because of the nature of the disorder, many persons with social anxiety disorder have never discussed their fears with anyone, and consequently often believe that their problems are unique. The group provides a tremendous opportunity for members to discover that others have similar thoughts and feelings and to learn from each other's attempts to overcome their fears. As an illustration, here is an exchange between a group member (GM1) and a therapist (T1) in a recent CBGT session:

GM1: I was thinking all week about that rational response C. D. [another group member] was using last week.

T1: The rational response from the exposure we did of having a conversation with a next-door neighbor?

GM1: Yes. "I'm only responsible for 50% of the conversation" was what he said. When we were talking about that last week, it was like a light bulb went on. I realized that, just like C. D., I always feel a lot of pressure to keep the conversation going. When I tried thinking about only being responsible for 50% of the conversation, I felt a lot more comfortable. If it dies, it isn't necessarily my fault. The other person has to do their part, too.

This group member was able to accept the positive coping statement developed for another member and incorporate it into his own arsenal of strategies to combat anxiety.

One of the difficulties in treating social anxiety disorder is to create realistic, yet controllable, exposure situations (Butler, 1989). The group format greatly facilitates the design of exposures, because the other group members and two therapists are available to serve as role players or audience members as needed. Furthermore, group members can provide more credible feedback on the quality of an individual's performance in an exposure than is available from an individual therapist. During cognitive restructuring, group members often provide evidence to counter a fellow member's distorted thinking, as demonstrated below:

T1: So your automatic thought is "I don't know how to have a conversation," is that right?

GM1: Yeah, I always screw it up.

T1: All right, let's ask the rest of the group what they think about that. Who has had a conversation with [GM1] or noticed her talking with someone else?

GM2: Well, there is the role play she did last week when she talked to me.

T2: OK, how about something other than an exposure, something like chatting before group starts . . .

GM3: We walked out to our cars together last week and talked in the parking lot for a while.

[Several other group members list similar conversations.]

T1: So it sounds like you have had a number of conversations with the rest of the group.

GM1: I guess so.

T1: Group, how did she do? How did the conversations go?

GM2: It was fine. She was asking me about my car, because she has been looking for a new one, so we talked mostly about that.

[Other group members provide similar answers.]

T1: Well, [GM1], the rest of the group doesn't seem to agree that you don't know how to have conversations.

GM1: I guess I have always been so nervous that I never stopped to think that sometimes the conversations go OK.

Composition of Groups

Our experience in running groups ranging from four to seven members suggests that six is the ideal group size. With this number, each patient can get individual attention every other session. On the other hand, if one or two members are absent or drop out of treatment, there are still adequate numbers to constitute a workable group.

Ideally, the group should be balanced for gender, age, and severity of social anxiety disorder. If one group member differs dramatically from all the rest, he/she is likely to be uncomfortable and may drop out of the group. As a rule of thumb, each member should be matched to one other with whom he/she can identify (e.g., a second member over 45 years old, a second person who is reasonably high-functioning) if at all possible.

Several factors should be considered when recommending CBGT for a particular patient with social anxiety disorder. First, patients who are likely to be disruptive to the group process should be excluded. Typically, these include potential group members who have significant personality pathology (e.g., borderline personality disorder) or who are excessively hostile or demanding of attention. Occasionally a patient's social fears are of such intensity that he/she has developed an angry response to maintain distance from others. In such cases, the demands of the group may provoke this response. Not only is such a patient likely to derive little benefit, but he/she will be disruptive and impede others' progress as well. Second, a few patients with social anxiety disorder experience such severe anxiety in the group setting itself that they will not be able to tolerate it. Almost all potential group members experience some anxiety, particularly in the first few sessions. However, an occasional person will be too overwhelmed by anxiety to comprehend the concepts taught in the group and will attempt to reduce his/her anxiety by not participating in or avoiding sessions. It is unlikely that such an individual will benefit from CBGT. Third, social anxiety disorder should be the patient's primary problem. This determination requires a careful diagnostic assessment. In cases in which social anxiety disorder is comorbid with other disorders, the clinician and patient should reach a joint decision as to the primary problem. Furthermore, when the decision is made to invite a patient with significant comorbidity into a group, the clinician and patient must have a clear understanding that the group will focus specifically on social anxiety and that the patient's other problems will not be directly addressed in the context of the group.

Comorbid depression, in particular, should be carefully evaluated. Elevated depression is a predictor of negative outcome in CBGT (Chambless et al., 1997). Patients with social anxiety disorder and comorbid depression start treatment more severely impaired than nondepressed patients with social anxiety disorder and remain more impaired, despite similar rates of improvement, after 12 weeks of CBGT (Erwin et al., in press). The disruption in functioning caused by social fears results in some dysphoria for many individuals with social anxiety disorder. Such dysphoria is typically not problematic and typically decreases as improvement in the social anxiety disorder occurs. However, a more severely depressed patient with social anxiety disorder, particularly if he/she experiences significant lethargy, anhedonia, or hopelessness, may fare poorly in such a demanding treatment and may have an adverse impact on the group. The clinician should evaluate carefully whether treatment for depression should precede CBGT.

The Time and Setting

CBGT groups are designed to meet for 12 weekly 2½-hour sessions. When selecting the meeting time, the therapists should be aware of holidays or other activities that would disrupt the regularity of the meetings. An occasional skipped week is unavoidable, but more than that severely disrupts the momentum of the group.

The relatively long sessions require a comfortable setting. Living-room-style furniture is ideal, as long as group members do not have to sit too close to one another on a sofa. A portion of the furniture should be movable, as the role-played exposures frequently require the furniture to be rearranged.

The group room should be equipped with an audiocassette recorder and a newsprint easel or blackboard. Taping sessions allows the therapists to review the group activities with each other or with a supervisor between sessions. This allows continual feedback on their performance and frees them from note taking during sessions. A large newsprint easel or a blackboard is essential to record negative automatic thoughts and rational responses elicited during cognitive restructuring. It provides much-needed visual cues to group members, whose attention or recall may be limited by their heightened anxiety. The easel and pad are preferable to a blackboard, because they allow the group to refer back to previous material. In any case, the easel or blackboard should be portable, so that it can be set up for easier reference by the target patient during in-session exposures.

Therapists

On the surface, CBGT appears to be a straightforward series of structured but individualized activities. In reality, it is a complex process that requires experienced group therapists. Assuring that all group members are adequately involved, managing session time, and monitoring group members' emotional states while negotiating the intricacies of cognitive work and exposures are difficult for novice therapists. At a minimum, the therapists should be experienced with exposure treatments and cognitive therapy principles and procedures. They should also be intimately familiar with the cognitive-behavioral model of social anxiety disorder and with CBGT procedures. Ideally, they should have worked previously with patients with social anxiety disorder.

It is extremely difficult and fatiguing to conduct CBGT with only one therapist, and two are highly recommended. If necessary, one can be somewhat less experienced if he/she receives training, including role-playing the procedures, before the group meetings begin. Male–female therapist pairs are ideal. Not only do they bring different perspectives on the social interactions that the patients fear,

but this arrangement also provides maximum flexibility for therapists to serve as role-play partners. For example, in exposures for dating situations, the appropriate gender for the role player is crucial. Other patients may be too anxious or their reactions too unpredictable to have them participate in role plays, particularly early in treatment.

Potential Group Members Receiving Psychopharmacological Treatment

Many patients with social anxiety disorder will be taking one or more psychotropic medications when they present for treatment. Some will be taking medication to control their social anxiety, while others will be taking medications for depression or other comorbid conditions. Research has demonstrated that several pharmacological treatments are efficacious for social anxiety disorder (for a review, see Fresco et al., in press). Nevertheless, some patients experience little or only partial symptom relief from their medication, and pursue a psychological treatment with the hope of experiencing additional improvement. Other patients are satisfied with the symptom relief provided by their medication, but dislike being on a medication and hope that therapy will allow them to eventually discontinue pharmacotherapy.

Several consequences are possible when a psychosocial and pharmacological treatments for social anxiety disorder are combined: (1) The medication may interfere with the patient's ability to benefit from cognitive restructuring and exposure (e.g., insufficient anxiety is aroused during exposures); (2) the medication may enhance the effectiveness of cognitive-behavioral interventions (e.g., anxiety is reduced to a level that allows the patient to attend to and learn more from the exposure); or (3) no appreciable gains (or losses) are seen with the combination of psychotherapy and medication. Lack of research on this issue prevents us from drawing any definitive conclusions about the consequences of combining CBGT with an ongoing medication treatment. The possibility that different types of medication may interact with cognitive-behavioral therapy in different ways further complicates the matter.

We do not require patients to discontinue their medications prior to starting CBGT (unless doing so is dictated by a specific research protocol). However, we do ask patients to stabilize their dosage before starting treatment and to refrain from changing their dosage or trying any new medications during treatment. Clinically, we want patients to attribute positive changes in their symptoms to the work they are doing in therapy, rather than to changes in their medication regimen. Individuals who take medication on an "as-needed" basis are asked to refrain from taking it before group sessions or exposure homework assignments.

PRETREATMENT ASSESSMENT

Assessment should play a central role in informing and directing CBGT activities. Although administering all of the measures presented here will not be practical in most clinical settings, we highly recommend conducting a behavior test and administering a subset of the self-report and clinician-rated instruments described below (for a more thorough review of assessment issues in social anxiety disorder, see Hart, Jack, Turk, & Heimberg, 1999).

Initial Visit

Clinical Interview

As part of a series of ongoing studies evaluating the efficacy of CBGT, all patients presenting for treatment at the Adult Anxiety Clinic of Temple University are administered the Anxiety Disorders Interview Schedule for DSM-IV: Lifetime Version (ADIS-IV-L; DiNardo, Brown, & Barlow, 1994). The ADIS-IV-L assesses current and lifetime anxiety disorders, common comorbid conditions (e.g., mood disorders, substance abuse), and disorders that overlap with anxiety disorders either conceptually or in terms of presenting symptoms (e.g., hypochondriasis). Screening questions for other major disorders (e.g., psychotic disorders) are also included. In order to qualify for participation in one of our studies, a patient must receive a primary diagnosis of social anxiety disorder, with an ADIS-IV-L clinician severity rating of 4 or greater (on a scale of 0–8), operationally defined as meeting criteria for the diagnosis of social anxiety disorder. The ADIS-IV-L has demon-

strated adequate reliability (kappa = .64) for the diagnosis of social anxiety disorder (DiNardo, Brown, Lawton, & Barlow, 1995).

Semistructured interviews like the ADIS-IV-L have several advantages. They can be helpful in assisting with differential diagnosis and in providing systematic assessment for a broad range of comorbid conditions that may affect the course of treatment of social anxiety disorder. Nevertheless, diagnostic interviews can be costly and time-consuming. Regardless of whether a semistructured or unstructured clinical interview is conducted, devoting time to a thorough diagnostic evaluation minimizes the likelihood of problematic situations arising later. Realizing, several weeks into a group, that a patient's symptoms are better accounted for by another disorder or that a patient is too impaired by a secondary diagnosis to be well served by a group focusing on social anxiety has obvious negative implications for the patient and other group members.

Self-Report Instruments

At the conclusion of the ADIS-IV-L interview, our patients receive a packet of self-report measures to complete at home and mail back to the clinic. The responses to the ADIS-IV-L and self-report battery are used to determine whether the patient is appropriate for CBGT or other treatment programs available at the Adult Anxiety Clinic of Temple University.

Measures of Social Anxiety. A number of questionnaires are available to assess social anxiety and avoidance. The Social Interaction Anxiety Scale (SIAS) and Social Phobia Scale (SPS) are commonly used companion measures designed specifically for the assessment of social anxiety disorder (Mattick & Clarke, 1998). The SIAS assesses fear of interacting in dyads and groups, and the SPS assesses fear of being scrutinized or observed by others. The paper describing the development of these instruments was published fairly recently (Mattick & Clarke, 1998), although these measures have been in use for well over 10 years, with researchers relying upon unpublished materials in the interim. In most published studies, the SIAS and SPS contain 20 items each; however, the Mattick and Clarke (1998) version of the SIAS contains only 19 items. The 20-item version of the SIAS differs only by the inclusion of the reverse-scored item "I find it easy to make friends of my own age." No data are available regarding the correlation of the two versions, although one must suspect it is quite high, given that they differ by only a single item. For each instrument, respondents rate how characteristic each statement is of them on a 5-point Likert-type scale (0 = "not at all," 4 = "extremely"). Multiple studies suggest that the SIAS and SPS are reliable and valid measures and are sensitive to the effects of cognitive-behavioral treatments (see, e.g., Brown et al., 1997; Cox, Ross, Swinson, & Direnfeld, 1998; Heimberg, Mueller, Holt, Hope, & Liebowitz, 1992; Ries et al., 1998).

Another commonly used instrument specifically developed to assess social anxiety disorder is the Social Phobia and Anxiety Inventory (SPAI; Turner, Beidel, Dancu, & Stanley, 1989). The SPAI consists of a Social Phobia subscale, an Agoraphobia subscale, and a derived Difference (or Total) score (i.e., Social Phobia subscale – Agoraphobia subscale). The SPAI contains 45 items, 21 of which require multiple responses. For example, for the item that begins "I attempt to avoid social situations where there are . . . ," the patient separately rates how frequently situations involving "strangers," "authority figures," the "opposite sex," and "people in general" are avoided. In all, the patient makes a total of 109 responses, making the administration and scoring of the SPAI relatively time-consuming. Despite the disadvantages imposed by the length of the scale, the quantity and specificity of information that it elicits can be extremely helpful in case formulation and treatment planning. The Social Phobia subscale assesses somatic, cognitive, and behavioral responses to a variety of interaction, performance, and observation situations. The Agoraphobia subscale assesses anxiety in situations commonly feared by individuals with panic disorder with agoraphobia (e.g., waiting in line). The Difference score is intended to provide an index of social anxiety and avoidance distinct from the sometimes similar concerns of patients with agoraphobia. However, the very high correlation between the Difference score and the score of the Social Phobia subscale ($r = .91$; Ries et al., 1998) suggests that there is little benefit to this strategy. Respondents rate how frequently they feel anxious in each situation using a 7-point Likert-type scale (0 = "never," 6 = "always").

Multiple studies suggest that the SPAI is a reliable and valid instrument (see, e.g., Beidel, Turner, Stanley, & Dancu, 1989; Herbert, Bellack, & Hope, 1991; Turner et al., 1989) and sensitive to treatment-related change (see, e.g., Cox et al., 1998; Ries et al, 1998; Taylor, Woody, McLean, & Koch, 1997).

Although developed and validated with college students prior to the inclusion of social anxiety disorder in DSM-III, the original Fear of Negative Evaluation scale (FNE; Watson & Friend, 1969) and the brief version of the scale (BFNE; Leary, 1983) continue to be widely used because they target the core construct in social anxiety disorder. The FNE consists of 30 items and employs a true–false format. The BFNE contains 12 items, uses a 5-point Likert-type format (1 = "not at all characteristic of me," 5 = "extremely characteristic of me"), and correlates highly with the original scale ($r = .96$) (Leary, 1983). In treatment studies, changes on the FNE have been found to predict end-state functioning (Mattick & Peters, 1988; Mattick et al., 1989). After reviewing the literature, Heimberg (1994) concluded that the FNE appears to be sensitive to within-group change following treatment, although these changes are typically small in magnitude. The BFNE, with its 5-point Likert-type format, may ultimately prove to be a more sensitive measure.

Other Self-Report Measures. In addition to measures targeting social anxiety, we administer instruments assessing other constructs, such as depression and global impairment. We routinely administer the Beck Depression Inventory (BDI; Beck, Rush, Shaw, & Emery, 1979), which assesses symptoms of depression, including the affective, cognitive, behavioral, somatic, and motivational components as well as suicidal wishes. We also use the Liebowitz Self-Rated Disability Scale (Schneier et al., 1994) to broadly assess impairment across 11 domains (e.g., school, work, alcohol abuse), and the Quality of Life Inventory (Frisch, 1994) to assess the patient's overall sense of well-being and satisfaction with life.

Treatment Orientation Interview

After the patient has been deemed appropriate for CBGT, a treatment orientation interview is conducted. This interview has several purposes. First, the therapist reviews the assessment data with the patient, answers questions, and offers treatment recommendations. The therapist describes the nature of the treatment and then works with the patient to develop an explicit treatment contract. Next, the therapist teaches the patient how to use a subjective units of discomfort scale (SUDS; Wolpe & Lazarus, 1966), and helps the patient construct a fear and avoidance hierarchy. Lastly, preparations are made for remaining assessments. Each step of the treatment orientation interview is described below.

Review of Assessment Data

The therapist gives feedback to the patient regarding the information obtained during the ADIS-IV-L interview and from the self-report measures, and attempts to clarify any important discrepancies among the assessment instruments. Any questions the patient has about the diagnoses assigned or the assessment data are addressed.

Treatment Preview

CBGT requires a substantial time and energy commitment on the part of each patient; consequently, potential group members need to be apprised of what treatment will involve. The therapist should briefly outline the cognitive-behavioral model of social anxiety disorder in understandable terms, and should explain how confronting one's fears is essential to overcoming them. Furthermore, the role of cognitive interventions in helping group members benefit from exposure and cope with their anxiety should be emphasized. At this point, many individuals with social anxiety disorder will say they have tried exposure on their own without success. Typically, however, their attempts were not systematic, and their distorted cognitive processing prevented them from taking credit for any success they may have had. Many potential group members will also be alarmed at the prospect of *group* treatment. This can often be overcome by outlining the advantages of group treatment described above.

Although extensive "selling" of the group should be avoided, part of the therapist's job is to instill hope that the person will be able to make significant changes as a result of treatment. In fact, research has shown that posi-

tive expectancies are associated with more favorable CBGT outcomes (Chambless et al., 1997; Safren, Heimberg, & Juster, 1997). We typically share with patients that CBGT is an empirically supported treatment, and that studies have shown that approximately 75%–80% of individuals completing the 12 weeks of group therapy are rated by independent clinical interviewers as having experienced meaningful reductions in their social anxiety. We also emphasize that attending group regularly, doing homework, and being open to new ways of looking at the world, other people, and oneself are factors that we believe substantially influence whether or not someone becomes a "treatment responder"—and that these factors are largely under the patient's control.

Treatment Contract

Individuals with social anxiety disorder often fear and avoid a variety of situations, usually more than can be realistically addressed in the standard 12-week CBGT protocol. Therefore it is important to agree on the two or three classes of situations that will be the primary focus of treatment. The therapist should help pick reasonable goals, but ultimately the patient determines the targets of treatment. Fear and avoidance in other social situations are likely to improve also, particularly if the patient makes an effort to apply the skills learned in treatment to those situations.

Similarly, for patients with comorbid diagnoses, the therapist explains that the focus of the group is social anxiety and that other problems will not be addressed directly. Improvement may be seen in comorbid conditions, however, as symptoms of social anxiety become less prominent or as the skills learned during treatment are applied to other problems (e.g., depression). Lastly, patients are assured that the severity of their social anxiety symptoms and any comorbid conditions will be reassessed following treatment, and that, if necessary, additional treatment recommendations will be made at that time.

SUDS Training

SUDS ratings are used during the behavior test and throughout the course of treatment, so it is worthwhile to invest time and effort to maximize their validity and reliability. The therapist explains that the SUDS is a 0–100 scale, with higher numbers indicating greater anxiety. Anchor points are developed at 25 (mild anxiety, very alert with an "edge" of nervousness), 50 (moderate anxiety, beginning to have difficulty concentrating), 75 (high anxiety, thoughts of escaping), and 100 (worst anxiety experienced or can imagine experiencing in a social situation) by asking the patient to report specific social situations in which he/she experienced that level of anxiety. Later in treatment, if the patient's ratings seem to be drifting and/or the patient is using only a portion of the scale, the therapist can refer back to the original anchor points.

Fear and Avoidance Hierarchy

A completed hierarchy (see Table 3.7, later in the chapter, for an example) will include 10 rank-ordered situations rated for fear and avoidance. It is easiest to have the patient brainstorm potential hierarchy items, then rate and rank-order them. The hierarchy should contain representative situations that are important to the treatment contract and relevant to the patient's functioning. The hierarchy is utilized throughout treatment as therapists determine the nature and order of therapeutic exposures.

Preparation for Remaining Assessments

In our clinic, patients have one additional session during which clinician-administered measures are administered and a behavior test is completed. The clinician-administered instruments can be completed at any of the pretreatment assessment appointments. The behavior test, however, is an anxiety-provoking prospect for many patients, and spending time presenting a rationale regarding its value is an important part of the treatment orientation interview (see rationale below).

Final Pretreatment Assessment Session

Clinician-Administered Measures of Social Anxiety

The two most commonly used clinician-administered measures of social anxiety are the Liebowitz Social Anxiety Scale (LSAS; Liebowitz, 1987) and the Brief Social Phobia Scale (BSPS; Davidson et al., 1991, 1997). The LSAS separately evaluates fear and avoidance of 11 social interaction (e.g., talking to people in authority) and 13 performance (e.g., working while being observed) situations, using a 4-point Likert-type scale. The LSAS contains four subscales: Performance Anxiety, Performance Avoidance, Social Interaction Anxiety, and Social Interaction Avoidance. Total Fear and Total Avoidance subscale scores can also be calculated. Summing the Fear and Avoidance ratings for all 24 items yields an overall severity rating. The LSAS has been shown to have good reliability and validity (see, e.g., Cox et al., 1998; Heimberg at al., 1999). The LSAS has also demonstrated sensitivity to cognitive-behavioral and pharmacological treatment of social anxiety disorder (see, e.g., Heimberg et al., 1998).

The BSPS (Davidson et al., 1991, 1997) evaluates fear and avoidance of seven social situations and the severity of four physiological symptoms. All items are rated on a 0–4 Likert-type scale. Satisfactory test–retest reliability (Davidson et al., 1997) and excellent interrater reliability (Davidson et al., 1991) have been reported. With regard to validity, the scale has been shown to be positively correlated with patient- and clinician-rated measures of social anxiety (Davidson et al., 1991). The BSPS total score has demonstrated sensitivity to change following drug treatment (Davidson et al., 1993, 1997).

Behavioral Assessment

During behavioral tests, patients confront one or more fear-eliciting social situations, typically within the context of a role-play task. The clinician asks for anxiety ratings before, at several points during, and after the role play. Other assessments, such as asking patients to rate the quality of their performance or list the thoughts they had during the role play, are easily incorporated. Affordable ambulatory physiological equipment (particularly pulse monitors) is increasingly available and should be used if possible. Heart rate monitoring is of particular use with individuals with public speaking fears, who may demonstrate excessive cardiac reactivity (Heimberg, Hope, et al., 1990). The clinician can choose to test the limits of the patient's ability to perform when anxious by asking him/her to remain in the situation for a certain period of time (typically 4–5 minutes). On the other hand, the clinician may give the patient explicit permission to stop (see, e.g., Ries et al., 1998) when the anxiety is excessive, and latency to escape the situation becomes an additional measure of social avoidance.

Behavior tests may either be standardized or individualized. Standardized role plays allow for the observation of differences across patients for a particular task. Commonly used tasks include a conversation with a same-sex stranger (Turner, Beidel, Cooley, Woody, & Messer, 1994), a conversation with an opposite-sex stranger (see, e.g., Fydrich, Chambless, Perry, Buergner, & Beazley, 1998), a conversation with two or more people (see, e.g., Hope, Herbert, & White, 1995), and a speech to a small audience (see, e.g., Beidel, Turner, Jacob, & Cooley, 1989). In contrast, the advantage of individualized behavior tests is that they can be designed to target idiosyncratic fears more precisely. For example, an individual with a fear of displaying a hand tremor when eating in front of others may experience little anxiety during a one-on-one conversation. However, if the patient is asked to engage in a one-on-one conversation while eating a bowl of soup, that patient's anxiety is more likely to be activated. When we have utilized individualized behavior tests, the situation chosen has been selected from those rated higher than 75 on the patient's fear and avoidance hierarchy.

The information obtained during a behavior test is unique and important in several ways. As previously discussed, research and clinical experience suggest that individuals with social anxiety disorder are likely to describe their social behavior as inadequate (see, e.g., Rapee & Lim, 1992; Stopa & Clark, 1993) and their anxiety as highly visible to others (see, e.g., Alden & Wallace, 1995). Behavior tests can reveal whether such patient reports are largely accurate or essentially examples of thinking errors. Furthermore, level of anxiety and quality of performance exhibited by a patient during behavior tests can be used to calibrate the difficulty of the patient's first exposure and to increase the likelihood that the therapist will create an exposure that will provide both a challenge and a success experience for the patient. Information from behavior tests should also be factored into the decision regarding which group member will

be chosen for the very first exposure. Our preference is to choose a patient who will become moderately anxious during the exposure, but who is likely to perform well and serve as a good coping model for the more anxious members of the group.

OVERVIEW OF THE ACTIVITIES IN CBGT

Sessions 1 and 2

The first two sessions of CBGT are devoted to setting the stage for treatment and training patients in the fundamental skills of cognitive restructuring. This allows group members to become more comfortable in the group setting, develop a beginning sense of group cohesion, and gain an elementary understanding of cognitive restructuring skills before engaging in therapeutic exposure. CBGT procedures are described in more detail by Heimberg and Becker (2001). For a presentation of cognitive-behavioral procedures for social anxiety disorder adapted to an individual treatment format, see Hope and colleagues (2000) and Hope, Turk, and Heimberg (in press).

At the beginning of all sessions, patients are asked to complete the BFNE, with instructions rewritten to reflect the past week. This allows us to monitor group members' progress on the important construct of fear of negative evaluation. Other questionnaires, such as the BDI, may also be administered. After the first week (when the questionnaires are explained), they can be made available ahead of time, and group members can complete them while waiting for the session to begin. Therapists should review them briefly before starting each group session and discuss any notable changes, either during the session or individually afterward.

Session 1

Table 3.1 contains an outline of the tasks for the first session. After explaining and completing the questionnaires, the therapists and group members briefly introduce themselves, stating their names and one or two things about themselves. The therapists then take turns outlining basic issues related to the importance of attendance, participation, home-

TABLE 3.1. Outline of CBGT for Session 1

1. Complete BFNE and any other optional questionnaires.
2. Introductions.
3. Therapists review basic ground rules.
4. Each member shares about social fears and goals for treatment.
5. Therapists describe cognitive-behavioral model for social anxiety disorder and rationale for treatment.
6. Initial training in cognitive restructuring.
   a. Exercise 1: Therapist's personal situation.
   b. Exercise 2: Automatic thoughts regarding coming to group for the first time.
7. Assignment of homework.

Note. BFNE, Brief Fear of Negative Evaluation scale.

work completion, and confidentiality. Group members and therapists sign a contract asserting that each person promises to maintain confidentiality.

After these housekeeping details, group members are encouraged to speak briefly about their fears and goals for treatment. The therapists assist more reticent individuals to speak and draw out similarities between group members (similar feared situations or similar anxiety symptoms). This helps build cohesion as group members discover that others have similar concerns.

The next major portion of the first session is devoted to discussing a cognitive-behavioral model for social anxiety disorder. This will be a more extended version of what members have heard in the treatment orientation interview. The model offers a common understanding and language in which to discuss social anxiety disorder and promotes a rationale for the treatment. Social anxiety disorder is described as a learned response with interactive physiological, behavioral (avoidance and performance disruption), and cognitive components. The cognitive components emphasize the role of automatic thoughts in heightening and maintaining anxiety. The three primary components of treatment—role-played exposure in the group, cognitive restructuring, and homework for *in vivo* exposure and associated cognitive work—are described in the context of the model.

The final portion of the first session is devoted to training in cognitive restructuring. Two exercises center on the process of identifying automatic thoughts and a preview of strategies to confront them that will be taught in the second session. In the first exercise, one of the therapists utilizes a personal situation (often a professional presentation) and lists his/her automatic thoughts encountered in that situation on the newsprint easel. Group members are then asked to consider whether these thoughts might be irrational or problematic in some ways, and are instructed to ask specific questions that might help the therapist view the situation more realistically. The second therapist assists the group if problems are encountered in generating questions to challenge the automatic thoughts. After the challenging phase, the therapists work with the group members to summarize the discussion into a rational response of one or two sentences. This exercise allows the members to see how the cognitive techniques work without having to confront the idea that their own automatic thoughts may be irrational or problematic. In the second exercise, group members report the automatic thoughts they had about coming to the initial group session while one of the therapists records them on the easel. The session ends with the two therapists gently challenging these automatic thoughts.

Homework for Session 1 consists of recording two or three anxiety-provoking situations during the week and listing several automatic thoughts for each one. Group members are told that if they have not encountered an anxiety-provoking situation after 4 or 5 days, they should imagine one of the situations from their fear and avoidance hierarchy and record their automatic thoughts.

Session 2

Following completion of the questionnaires, the group reviews the previous week's homework (see Table 3.2). Two or three automatic thoughts from each group member are recorded on the easel for later exercises. Next therapists distribute a list of thinking errors. We are currently using an adaptation of the list of thinking errors outlined by Judith S. Beck in her 1995 book *Cognitive Therapy: Basics and Beyond* and based on the work of Aaron T. Beck (see Table 3.3). Each thinking error is described briefly by the therapists. The entire group then helps identify the thinking errors in each automatic thought recorded during the review of homework.

TABLE 3.2. Outline of CBGT for Session 2

1. Complete BFNE and any other optional questionnaires.
2. Review homework from previous week.
3. Continued training in cognitive restructuring.
   a. Therapists introduce concept of thinking errors.
   b. Exercise 3: Group identifies thinking errors in automatic thoughts from homework.
   c. Therapists introduce disputing questions and rational responses.
   d. Exercise 4: Hypothetical scenario
   e. Exercise 5: Group challenges automatic thoughts from homework and develops rational responses.
4. Assignment of homework.

Note. BFNE, Brief Fear of Negative Evaluation scale.

The next step in cognitive restructuring is to challenge the automatic thoughts and develop rational responses or rebuttals. This is done with the assistance of an adaptation of Sank and Shaffer's (1984) "disputing questions" (see Table 3.4). The disputing questions are generic questions that can be brought to bear on automatic thoughts. Before having the patients attempt to apply this procedure to their own thoughts, however, the therapists describe a scenario in which most people are likely to experience anxiety (the boss states that there is a problem with your work and asks to see you in his/her office in 5 minutes). Automatic thoughts generated by the imagined scenario are then listed on the easel. Together the group members identify the thinking errors in each automatic thought, question the automatic thoughts using the disputing questions, and answer the disputing questions to arrive at alternative, more realistic ways of viewing the situation. The answers to the disputing questions are then summarized into one or two statements that serve as rational responses. Once group members understand the basic procedure, the group returns to the automatic thoughts from the previous homework assignment and challenges them.

Homework for Session 2 involves recording automatic thoughts from anxiety-provoking situations as in the previous week, but also identifying the thinking errors, questioning the automatic thoughts, and developing rational responses. Thus group members enter Session 3 and their first in-session exposures with substantial practice in the logistics of the cognitive techniques.

TABLE 3.3. List of Thinking Errors

All-or-nothing thinking (also called *black-and-white*, *polarized*, or *dichotomous thinking*): You view a situation in only two categories instead of on a continuum.

Anticipating negative outcomes: You expect that something negative has happened or is going to happen. There are two types of thinking errors that fall into this category:

> *Fortune telling*: You predict that something negative is going to happen in the future, as if you were gazing into a crystal ball.

> *Catastrophizing*: You tell yourself the *very worst* is happening or is going to happen, without considering other possibilities that may be more likely and/or less negative.

Disqualifying or discounting the positive: You unreasonably tell yourself that positive experiences, deeds, or qualities do not count.

Emotional reasoning: You think something must be true because you "feel" (actually believe) it so strongly, ignoring or discounting evidence to the contrary.

Labeling: You put a fixed, global label on yourself or others without considering that the evidence might more reasonably lead to a less disastrous conclusion.

Mental filter (also called *selective abstraction*): You pay undue attention to one negative detail instead of seeing the whole picture.

Mind reading: You believe you know what others are thinking; you fail to consider other, more likely possibilities; and you make no effort to check it out.

Overgeneralization: You make a sweeping negative conclusion that goes far beyond the current situation.

"Should" and "must" statements (also called *imperatives*): You have a precise, fixed idea of how you or others should behave, and you overestimate how bad it is that these expectations are not met.

❊❊❊❊❊❊❊❊❊❊❊❊❊❊❊❊❊❊❊❊❊❊❊❊❊❊❊❊❊❊❊❊❊❊❊❊❊

Maladaptive thoughts: You have problematic thoughts that do not contain logical thinking errors. These thoughts may be true. However, dwelling on these thoughts make you feel more anxious and may interfere with your performance.

Note. From Beck (1995, p. 119). Copyright 1995 by The Guilford Press. Adapted by permission.

Sessions 3–11

Sessions 3–11 follow the same basic format (see Table 3.5). After completion of the questionnaires, homework from the previous week is reviewed. For the majority of the session, group members take turns completing role-played exposures. The therapists meet be-

TABLE 3.4. Disputing Questions

Use these questions to challenge your automatic thoughts. Be sure to *answer* each question you pose to yourself. You will find each question helpful for many different thoughts. Several examples are also presented to help you get started.

1. Do I know for certain that _____?

   Example: Do I know for certain that I won't have anything to say?

2. Am I 100% sure that _____?

   Example: Am I 100% sure that my anxiety will show?

3. What evidence do I have that _____? What evidence do I have that the opposite is true?

   Example: What evidence do I have that they *did not* understand my speech?

   What evidence do I have that they *did* understand my speech?

4. What is the worst that could happen? How bad is that? How can I cope with that?

5. Do I have a crystal ball?

6. Is there another explanation for _____?

   Example: Is there another explanation for his/her refusal to have coffee with me?

7. Does _____ have to lead to or equal _____?

   Example: Does "being nervous" have to lead to or equal "looking stupid"?

8. Is there another point of view?

9. What does _____ mean? Does _____ really mean that I am a(n) _____?

   Example: What does "looking like an idiot" mean? Does the fact that I stumbled over my words really mean that I look like an idiot?

Note. From Sank and Shaffer (1984, p. 223). Copyright 1984 by Plenum Press. Adapted by permission.

TABLE 3.5. Outline of CBGT for Sessions 3–11

1. Complete BFNE and any other optional questionnaires.
2. Review homework from previous week.
3. Complete three in-session exposures.
   a. Select target group member and briefly outline exposure situation.
   b. Elicit automatic thoughts.
   c. Pick one or two thoughts to pursue further.
   d. Label thinking errors in selected automatic thoughts.
   e. Challenge selected automatic thoughts using disputing questions (patients also answer the questions).
   f. Develop one or two rational responses.
   g. Develop details of the exposure situation.
   h. Set nonperfectionistic, behavioral goals.
   i. Complete role play.
   j. Debrief exposure.
      1. Review goal attainment.
      2. Other activities as appropriate.
4. Assignment of homework.

Note. BFNE, Brief Fear of Negative Evaluation scale.

Designing Exposures

The in-session exposures consist of role plays of anxiety-provoking situations. The therapists, other group members, and outside personnel serve as role-play partners. The exposure situations are individualized and range from having a conversation with an unfamiliar person to giving a formal presentation. The first exposure should be to a situation to which the patient assigns a SUDS rating of at least 50, with successive exposures moving up the hierarchy as quickly as the patient can tolerate. In selecting situations, it is important to consider that each group member will have approximately five in-session exposures over the course of treatment.

The exposures are made as realistic as possible by rearranging furniture, using props, and instructing role-play partners to behave in particular ways. A bit of effort in making the situation more realistic can make the difference between an exposure that elicits significant anxiety and one that is too artificial to be relevant. Commonly used props include food or drink for individuals with fears of eating, drinking, or serving food in front of others, and patient-prepared notes for presentations. Careful attention should be paid to aspects of the situation that make it more or less anxiety-provoking. For example, a patient with public speaking anxiety may be more

tween sessions to plan an exposure for each group member and the order in which the exposures should be completed. If specific members are unexpectedly absent, plans are in place for someone else. Typically, three exposures are completed each session, allowing an exposure every other session for every participant in a six-member group. Each session ends with homework assignments for the next week. These typically consist of *in vivo* exposure tasks and associated cognitive restructuring, and begin once a patient has completed his/her first in-session exposure. Until then, he/she continues the cognitive homework from the second session.

anxious when standing and speaking from notes with questions from the audience than when sitting and giving an unprepared talk to a silent audience.

Integrating Cognitive Restructuring and Exposure

The essence of CBGT is the coordination between the cognitive restructuring work and the exposure (see Table 3.5). After selecting a group member for the next exposure, one therapist sketches the proposed situation in three or four sentences. The patient has the opportunity to suggest modifications or alternatives to the proposed exposure. Once both the patient and therapist have agreed upon the nature of the exposure, the therapist then elicits automatic thoughts regarding the situation from the target group member while the second therapist records the thoughts on the easel. Once it seems that the most important thoughts have been identified, the therapist picks one or two thoughts for further attention. The selected automatic thought or thoughts should contain one or more obvious thinking errors, be important to the individual's experience of anxiety in the situation, and be reasonably challenged in the time available for discussion and exposure. The entire group helps label the thinking errors, challenge the thoughts with the disputing questions, and develop rational responses. Early in treatment, the therapists must take primary responsibility for this process, modeling a Socratic approach. However, as treatment progresses, the group members should increasingly be able to confront their own and others' automatic thoughts. Once a rational response is developed, it is written on a fresh sheet on the easel within view of the target patient during the exposure.

After the initial cognitive work is done, the details of the exposure are further discussed. The target patient assists by providing necessary details, such as the setting in which the activity would be likely to take place and the expected behavior of the other interactants. Next, behavioral goals for the exposure are set. This often requires some negotiation, as patients with social anxiety disorder tend to set unrealistic, perfectionistic goals (e.g., "I won't get anxious" or "I won't stumble over my words at all") or goals based on the re-

actions of other people and thus not under their control (e.g., make a good impression or make them feel comfortable). Therapists work to help the patients develop goals relating to what they want to accomplish in the situation (e.g., asking at least three questions to get to know the person better, stating an opinion, talking about three different points during a speech). The agreed-upon goals are then written on the easel below the rational responses, so that the patient can refer to them if necessary during the exposure.

During the exposure, one of the therapists requests SUDS ratings at 1-minute intervals and whenever anxiety appears to increase or decrease. At each SUDS prompt, the target member also reads his/her rational response (written on the easel) aloud. Patients quickly adjust to this disruption, particularly if the role player(s) help reorient them with a verbal cue (e.g., "You were talking about . . . "). The exposure should continue until anxiety has begun to decrease or plateau and the goal has been met, typically at about 10 minutes.

Debriefing the exposure includes a review of goal attainment, a discussion of the usefulness of the rational response, and identification of any unexpected automatic thoughts that should be addressed in the future. It is also useful to review the pattern of SUDS ratings given by the target patient (e.g., SUDS ratings increased when there was a pause, pattern of declining anxiety over time) and have group members give their impressions of the target patient's performance (e.g., to what extent anxiety symptoms were noticeable, whether the patient's voice projected adequately during a speech). One primary goal of the debriefing is to identify which thoughts make anxiety increase (irrational thoughts) and decrease (rational, coping thoughts). Finally, the patient is asked what he/she has learned from the exposure that can be applied to life outside the clinic. After this last step, the rest of the group congratulates the target member for his/her courage at facing the feared situation, and the procedure begins anew with the next person.

Session 12

The first half of the last session follows the format of the previous nine sessions, but only one or two exposures are completed rather than three. The second half is devoted to reviewing group members' progress, identifying important rational responses that they will want to continue to use, and setting goals for continued work on their own after treatment. The session concludes with a brief social time with refreshments, to allow members to say good-bye and close the group on a pleasant note.

CASE EXAMPLE

In order to illustrate more clearly how CBGT is implemented, a case example is presented. The patient presented received a standard 12-week trial of CBGT. This trial was followed by an additional 12 weeks of group treatment and then monthly maintenance sessions for 6 months. Previous research has shown that most patients receiving the standard 12 weeks of CBGT experience meaningful symptom reduction *after* the midpoint of treatment; therefore, the majority of change takes place between Sessions 6 and 12 (Heimberg et al., 1998). This finding raises the possibility that some patients may not have achieved their maximum possible benefit at the conclusion of 12 weeks of treatment. The patient presented in this case example participated in an ongoing study evaluating whether an extended period of intensive treatment beyond the standard 12 weeks leads to increased CBGT efficacy.

First, some background on the case is given, followed by data from the patient's pretreatment assessment. Then a description of the patient's progress through the first 12 therapy sessions (acute treatment phase) is provided. This account demonstrates the integration of cognitive restructuring with exposures in session and during homework assignments. For the intensive continuation phase (Weeks 13–24) and the maintenance phase (Weeks 25–52), we provide summary descriptions rather than session-by-session accounts of the patient's progress. We also review assessment data collected at Week 12 (after acute treatment), Week 24 (after intensive continuation), Week 52 (after maintenance), and a 6-month follow-up. Note that the patient's name and some identifying information have been changed to preserve anonymity.

Brian was a 22-year-old man who presented to our clinic with extreme anxiety concerning both social interaction and performance situations. Brian was studying photojournalism at a local college, working part-time jobs as a cashier and photographer, and living with two roommates. Brian was born in a small town on the west coast of Oregon, but had moved to the Philadelphia area several years ago to pursue his education. Brian was an only child and visited his parents once or twice each year.

Brian described himself as quiet around other people and said that he felt as if people never got to know him very well. Brian reported that he had opportunities to socialize with his coworkers and roommates, but often chose to stay at home because of his anxiety. Brian also expressed frustrations that his anxiety interfered with his ability to meet women and develop romantic relationships. When he did confront social situations like parties, Brian reported using alcohol to dampen his anxiety.

In addition to impairing his ability to have close social relationships, Brian's social anxiety had resulted in occupational and academic impairment. For example, a couple of years prior to treatment, Brian had been fired from a job as a waiter because he was not sociable and friendly enough with the customers. In class, Brian did not participate unless a question was specifically directed toward him, even when participation was required as part of grading procedures. Furthermore, Brian was required to do presentations of his photography several times each semester. Although he had never avoided any of these presentations, he worried about them for weeks in advance and then suffered through them with great anxiety. Brian anticipated that his social anxiety would cause him even greater impairment after graduation, when he would need to interact with and present his work to bosses, coworkers, and clients.

Pretreatment Assessment

During the ADIS-IV-L, Brian gave minimal responses to questions, spoke softly, engaged in very little eye contact, and appeared tense. His mood was mildly depressed, but he did not meet criteria for major depression or dysthymia. Nor did Brian's drinking meet criteria for alcohol abuse or dependence. Brian received a diagnosis of social anxiety disorder, generalized subtype, with an ADIS-IV-L clinician severity rating of 5, which indicates symptoms that are moderate to severe (see Table 3.6 for Brian's scores on all pretreatment self-report and clinician-rated measures).

With regard to measures of social anxiety, Brian's scores indicated significant fear in both social interaction and performance/observation situations. Heimberg and colleagues (1992) suggest cutoff scores of 34 for the SIAS (interaction fears) and 24 for the SPS (performance/observation fears) to differentiate between individuals with and without social anxiety disorder. Brian's scores exceeded both of these cutoffs. Similarly, on the LSAS, Brian reported fear and avoidance of both social interaction and performance situations, and his scores on each scale were similar to or slightly higher than the means reported for samples of individuals with social anxiety disorder (Heimberg et al., 1999).

Patients with similar levels of social anxiety may have very different levels of impairment; therefore, a measure of functionality like the Liebowitz Self-Rated Disability Scale may provide useful information beyond that provided by measures of social anxiety alone. The Liebowitz Self-Rated Disability Scale can be examined in terms of the total score, which reflects overall impairment, and in terms of individual items, which provide more specific information about the nature of the patient's impairment. Brian's score was elevated relative to the mean reported for patients with

social anxiety disorder ($M = 7.8$, $SD = 6.4$) and considerably higher than the mean observed for normal controls ($M = 0.2$, $SD = 0.6$) (Schneier et al., 1994). An examination of individual items revealed that Brian perceived himself as being limited by his social anxiety in terms of being able to drink alcohol in moderation, being in a good mood, being successful at school, working at a job to his highest ability, being comfortable interacting with family members, having a satisfying romantic relationship, having friends, and being able not to think about suicide.

Ideally, treatment should not only result in symptom reduction and improved functioning, but should also promote the patient's overall sense of well-being and life satisfaction. Safren, Heimberg, Brown, and Holle (1997) reported a mean score of 0.8 on the Quality of Life Inventory for patients with social anxiety disorder, which is significantly lower than the mean score of the nonclinical adult sample reported by Frisch (1994; $M = 2.6$, $SD = 1.3$). Thus Brian's quality of life could be described as very low, but similar to that of other individuals with social anxiety disorder.

The disruption in functioning caused by social anxiety and the associated poor quality of life frequently result in dysphoria. Brian's score of 15 on the BDI is typical of individuals in our treatment program (Elting, Hope, & Heimberg, 1997). Brian acknowledged having occasional thoughts of killing

TABLE 3.6. Brian's Self-Report and Clinician-Rated Assessment Measures at Pretreatment, Week 12 (after Acute Treatment), Week 24 (after Intensive Continuation Treatment), Week 52 (after Maintenance), and 6-Month Follow-Up

Measure	Pretest	Week 12	Week 24	Week 52	Follow-up
Self-report					
SIAS	64	27	22	17	28
SPS	29	9	6	5	15
BFNE	41	19	16	18	25
BDI	15	6	1	1	NA
Quality of Life Inventory	0.87	1.50	2.56	3.13	NA
Liebowitz Self-Report Disability Scale	15	2	1	2	NA
Clinician-rated					
ADIS-IV-L clinician severity rating	5	3	3	2	2
LSAS—Social Interaction Anxiety	23	5	6	5	7
LSAS—Social Interaction Avoidance	21	4	7	6	6
LSAS—Performance Anxiety	20	5	6	6	7
LSAS—Performance Avoidance	19	7	6	7	7

Note. SIAS, Social Interaction Anxiety Scale; SPS, Social Phobia Scale; BFNE, Brief Fear of Negative Evaluation Scale; BDI, Beck Depression Inventory; ADIS-IV-L, Anxiety Disorders Interview Schedule for DSM-IV: Lifetime Version; LSAS, Liebowitz Social Anxiety Scale; NA, not administered.

himself, but denied any plan or intention to act on these thoughts and had no history of past suicide attempts. Brian's dysphoric mood was judged to be secondary to his social anxiety and unlikely to have an adverse impact on his own treatment or that of other group members.

During the CBGT treatment orientation interview, Brian completed a fear and avoidance hierarchy with one of his group therapists (see Table 3.7). Situations were rank-ordered from the most difficult ("public speaking [large audience]") to least difficult ("introducing myself to a stranger"). After developing the hierarchy of situations, Brian rated each situation on two 0–100 scales (higher numbers indicate greater severity): (1) how fearful he became or would become in the situation, and (2) how likely he was to avoid the situation. During the interview, Brian and the therapist agreed that reducing his anxiety and avoidance relating to interacting with peers (especially women) would be his primary initial treatment goal.

Brian completed two standardized behavior tests. In our clinic, one behavior test consists of an impromptu speech to a small audience,

and the other consists of a one-on-two social interaction in a party situation. Each behavior test is preceded by a 2½-minute anticipatory phase during which patients prepare for the upcoming role play. The performance phase of the behavior test lasts 4 minutes. During each phase, patients are prompted for minute-by-minute SUDS ratings (see Figure 3.2 and Figure 3.3 for Brian's SUDS ratings).

For his speech, Brian chose the topic of photography. Brian's anxiety started at a relatively mild level during the anticipatory phase (SUDS = 30) and rapidly escalated to a very severe level as the performance phase approached (SUDS = 95). Brian's anxiety declined slightly at the beginning of the performance phase, but remained at a high level throughout the task. After speaking for about 2 minutes, Brian stated that he did not know what else to say and was able to continue only after being prompted by questions from the audience. For the interaction behavior test, Brian's anxiety started at a moderate level (SUDS = 65) and increased to a very high level (SUDS = 85) by the end of the anticipatory phase. During the performance phase, Brian's anxiety was initially high (SUDS = 75) but

TABLE 3.7. Brian's Fear and Avoidance Hierarchy at Pretreatment, Week 12 (after Acute Treatment), Week 24 (after Intensive Continuation Treatment), and Week 52 (after Maintenance)

Situation		Pretest	Week 12	Week 24	Week 52
1. Public speaking (large audience)	Fear	100	70	80	80
	Avoidance	100	80	80	90
2. Class presentation	Fear	90	60	10	20
	Avoidance	80	40	0	0
3. Introducing myself to a group	Fear	80	20	0	10
	Avoidance	70	10	0	0
4. Approaching a potential romantic interest	Fear	60	20	20	20
	Avoidance	70	20	50	40
5. Being called on in class	Fear	60	30	0	0
	Avoidance	60	30	0	0
6. Dancing in a night club	Fear	50	20	50	0
	Avoidance	70	20	50	0
7. Being the center of attention in a group	Fear	50	10	10	10
	Avoidance	60	10	20	0
8. Talking in a staff meeting	Fear	40	5	10	10
	Avoidance	50	10	10	10
9. Greeting a party of dinner guests	Fear	40	5	20	0
	Avoidance	40	4	0	0
10. Introducing myself to a stranger	Fear	30	0	0	0
	Avoidance	30	10	0	0

Note. Ratings are on 0–100, scales with higher numbers signifying greater fear and more avoidance.

decreased to a mild level after 3 minutes (SUDS = 30). His anxiety increased a bit at the end of the task following a pause in the conversation. Like many individuals with social anxiety disorder, Brian demonstrated adequate social skills during the interaction, but rated his performance as poor.

Acute Treatment (Weeks 1–12)

Sessions 1–2

As described above, the first two sessions of CBGT are devoted to laying the groundwork for the group, building group cohesion, educating members about the cognitive-behavioral model of social anxiety disorder, and beginning training on the cognitive restructuring skills. In these early sessions, Brian appeared visibly tense, made little eye contact, blushed when comments were directed toward him, and did not participate spontaneously. In his written homework, Brian repeatedly reported automatic thoughts relating to appearing anxious in front of other people (e.g., "I will blush"), to being unable to maintain a conversation (e.g., "I don't have anything to say"), and to being the center of attention (e.g., "People are looking at me"). Brian was able to label the thinking errors in his automatic thoughts, but had difficulty challenging them and arriving at a rational response. Like many patients, Brian would attempt to challenge his automatic thoughts (e.g., "Am I 100% certain that I will blush? No"), but then revert to offering evidence regarding why he believed the automatic thought (e.g., "But people have told me I am blushing many times in the past").

Session 3

In the third session, two of Brian's fellow group members completed their first exposure. Brian was not selected to be one of the first individuals to engage in an exposure. The therapists hoped an extra session would provide Brian with more time to habituate to the group setting, and thus enable him to begin his first exposure from a lower baseline anxiety level. His homework for Session 3 was to continue practicing his cognitive skills by analyzing the automatic thoughts generated by naturally occurring anxiety-provoking social situations during the upcoming week.

Session 4

Brian's first exposure occurred in Session 4. As with all first exposures, the therapists wanted to choose a situation that would seem relevant to his treatment goals, would elicit moderate anxiety, and would be one in which he was likely to perform reasonably well. For his first exposure, the therapists asked Brian to interact with a woman approximately his age who would be asking his professional opinion about some pictures she had taken in her photography class. This exposure was chosen for several reasons. First, it seemed relevant to his treatment goal of becoming more comfortable interacting with female peers. In addition, the exposure was structured around a topic that Brian knew well and found intrinsically interesting. The therapists hoped that structuring the exposure in this manner would decrease Brian's tendency to become self-focused by providing an activity to attend to during the conversation. Brian's role-play partner was a therapist who had not been involved in Brian's assessment or treatment. The following excerpts are from the cognitive restructuring prior to the exposure. (T1 and T2 are the two group therapists; B is Brian; GM1, GM2, etc., are other group members; and RP, who appears later, is the role-playing therapist.)

T2: Brian, we wanted to give you an opportunity to do an exposure tonight.

B: (*Nods and looks down*) OK.

T2: You have talked about how it is difficult for you to talk to unfamiliar people, especially women. So what we thought we would have you do tonight is practice having a conversation with a woman about your age. Does that sound like something that would be helpful for you?

B: Yes, it probably would be.

T2: OK, good. For this first exposure, we thought it would be best if the conversation were structured around a topic that both of you are interested in. Jane has brought in some pictures that she took for a photography class, and she is going to ask you for your opinion about them. Any advice or suggestions you might have about her work would be helpful. So, actually, this will also be a chance for you to practice sharing your opinion with other people. What do you think about doing something like that for your first exposure?

B: That's fine.

T2: Is it something that will cause you at least moderate anxiety?

B: Definitely.

T2: OK, then. Imagine yourself in that situation now. As you think about that situation, what thoughts come to mind?

B: I'll blush. I'll look nervous.

[T1 writes those thoughts on the easel.]

T2: That's good. What other automatic thoughts come into your mind as you imagine yourself in that situation?

B: I wonder what she will think about me.

T2: OK, so you are wondering about what she will think about you. What is the part of that thought that is making you anxious? For that thought to be causing you anxiety, I am guessing that you are not saying to yourself, "I wonder what she will think of me," and then thinking about all of the good things that she will be thinking about you.

B: Well, I suppose the thought actually is that she won't like me.

[T1 writes "She won't like me" on the easel.]

T2: OK, that's helpful. What other automatic thoughts can you identify?

B: She'll think I'm stupid.

[T1 adds that thought to the list.]

T2: Other thoughts?

B: No, I think that's it.

T2: All right. This is a good list for us to work with. What thinking errors do you see in these thoughts?

[Brian, with the assistance of the other group members, suggests several possible thinking errors, including fortune telling, mind reading, and labeling.]

T2: Now let's work on disputing some of these thoughts. Does everyone have the list of disputing questions? OK.

Brian, the thought "I'll blush" seems to come up for you quite a bit. It came up here, and we've seen it a lot on your homework. Let's start with that one. How might you challenge that thought?

B: Do I know for certain that I will blush?

T2: And what is the answer to that question?

B: No, I don't know for certain—but I usually do blush when I feel like I am the center of attention and people are looking at me.

T2: You are saying that you cannot be 100% certain that you will blush, even though you think that it is pretty likely. OK. Now, even though we cannot say for sure you will blush—because that would be fortune telling—let's work from the assumption that you will blush during this conversation. Tell us a little bit about why that would be bad for you. What would it mean if you were to blush during the conversation?

B: That I'll look stupid.

T2: I see. So the thought "I'll blush" actually leads you to this other thought on the easel: "She'll think I'm stupid." Would it be fair to say that you have the equation in your mind that blushing equals stupid?

B: Yeah, I suppose I do.

[T1 writes "blushing = stupid" on the easel.]

T2: Work on challenging that thought.

B: (Doubtful tone of voice) Does blushing have to lead to or equal looking stupid? Well, maybe not. I don't know. To me it does.

T2: Are there other ways of thinking about someone who blushes besides thinking that the person is stupid? Group, feel free to help Brian out on this.

GM1: Actually, Brian, I have noticed you blush a few times in group, but it is not something that's a big deal to me. I would never think that you were stupid or anything because of it. Whenever you talk, you seem very nice and have good things to say.

T2: Brian, what do you think about that?

B: (*Looking at GM1*) Thank you. It helps to hear you say that.

T1: Group, when you see someone blush, what are some other things that you think of?

GM2: I think it can be a compliment. Like the person really likes you or cares about what you think.

GM3: I might think that the person is shy like me, but I wouldn't think that the person was stupid.

T1: Or maybe the person just came in from outside, where it was really hot. Or the person just finished running up the stairs.

T2: So being flushed or blushing could mean a variety of things. Brian, can you take these things that we have been talking about and put them together into a rational response?

B: Just because I blush, it doesn't mean that everyone will think that I am stupid.

T2. Good. I like where you are going with the rational response. Let me suggest shortening it to something that will be easier to remember during the exposure. How about "blushing does not equal stupid"?

B: OK.

[T1 turns to the next page on the easel and writes the rational response at the top of the page.]

The therapists selected that particular automatic thought for cognitive restructuring because it had been a recurrent one for Brian in homework and seemed relevant to the upcoming exposure. The therapists also took Brian's suggestion for a rational response and phrased it in more positive terms. Also, the therapists made an effort to take Brian through the cognitive restructuring relatively quickly, because the longer the exposure was delayed, the more anxious he would get and the more difficult it would be for him to focus on the cognitive restructuring because of his anxiety. The next step was to set goals for the exposure.

T2: Before we start the exposure, we need to come up with some goals. What do you want to accomplish during the exposure?

B: I don't want to get anxious.

T2: Experiencing less anxiety is a good goal for the end of treatment. I'm not sure it is reasonable to expect yourself not to get anxious during your very first exposure. Also, it is better to put goals in terms of behaviors you can do instead of emotions or reactions that you want to avoid. You have much more control over your own behavior. What are some things you would like to do during this exposure?

B: Well, I should introduce myself, since I have never met her.

[On the page of the easel that has Brian's rational response at the top, T1 writes "Goals" in the middle of the page as a heading and writes "1. Introduce myself."]

T2: Good goal. What else?

B: Since she is asking my opinion, I could say something I like about her work, and also make a suggestion if I can think of one.

T2: Great. Let's add those to your list.

[T1 writes "2. Compliment one thing about her work" and "3. Offer one suggestion."]

Brian took a seat at a table. There was an empty chair beside him where the role player would be sitting. The easel was positioned so that Brian could see his rational response and goals. T1 arrived with the role player, who was carrying a portfolio containing photographs.

T1: Brian, what is your initial SUDS rating?

B: It's 80.

T1: OK, read and think about your rational response.

B: Blushing does not equal stupid.

Brian introduced himself to the role player, and they began to look at and talk about the different pictures in her portfolio. The therapists let the exposure continue for 10 minutes. At the prompting of the first therapist (T1), Brian gave SUDS ratings at 1-minute intervals and read his rational response aloud. After the exposure ended, the therapists asked the role player to remain in the room and began the postexposure processing.

T2: Did you meet your goals?

B: Let's see. I introduced myself. I definitely complimented several things about her work. I don't remember whether I offered any suggestions, though.

T1: I was keeping track of your goals. Like you said, you did introduce yourself. I counted six times that you complimented things about her work and four times that you offered suggestions. For example, one time you offered a suggestion about trying some different filters for her camera, remember?

B: That's right. I guess I did meet all of my goals.

T2: So how did you feel about how the exposure went in general?

B: Pretty good. It went a lot better than I expected it to, actually.

T2: What do you mean?

B: Well, by the end, I wasn't feeling that anxious, and it was actually kind of fun.

T2: That's important, Brian. Let's look at your pattern of anxiety over time. You went into the exposure with a SUDS rating of 80. Your anxiety was down to 60 by the end of the first minute, to 50 by the end of the second minute, and to 40 by the end of the seventh minute, where it stayed until the end. What does that tell you?

B: I think that I make things out to be worse in my mind beforehand than they actually end up being.

T2: That's how fortune telling seems to work, doesn't it? And also, as you stayed with the situation, it got easier for you. We will have to see if that is a pattern for you. How did your rational response work for you?

B: It helped. I know I was blushing at the beginning. I was still bothered by it but not as much as usual.

GM3: You thought you were blushing? I was watching for that, because I knew you were worried about it, but I didn't see it.

GM4: Me either.

GM2: I thought I noticed you getting a little bit red at first, but I don't think it is as bad as you think it is. I thought you did a really good job, by the way. I wish that I had been sitting up there with the two of you so that I could have seen the pictures that you were talking about. It was interesting.

GM5: I thought so too. (*Other group members nod*)

T1: (*To the role player*) Did you notice Brian blushing?

RP: Maybe a little bit at the beginning. (*To Brian*) I barely noticed and didn't even really care about that, because I was so involved in what we were talking about.

T2: (*To Brian*) Let's look at some of the other thoughts that you had going into the exposure: "She won't like me." "She'll think I'm stupid." Do you think that either of these things happened?

B: (*hesitantly*) Well, I don't think so . . .

T2: (*To the role player*) Did you dislike Brian? Or think that he was stupid?

RP: Of course not! (*To Brian*) You seem very nice to me. I enjoyed talking with you. You also seem very knowledgeable about photography. I'm going to take some of your suggestions.

T2: (*To Brian*) What can you take from this experience and what everyone has been saying that you can use in the future?

B: That, when I do blush, people won't necessarily take it to mean something negative about me. That my blushing might not always be as noticeable as I think it is. This experience also makes me feel a little more confidence about offering opinions and being able to carry on a conversation.

Brian's homework for Session 4 was to continue to do cognitive restructuring about blushing. Brian also agreed to offer an opinion at least twice during the upcoming week and to do cognitive restructuring relating to this homework assignment.

Session 5

The homework review revealed that Brian had completed his assignment. He seemed encouraged by the results of his efforts. He had asked for more money at one of his part-time jobs and was going to get a small raise as a result. He had also offered an opinion during a conversation at a party that he had attended with his roommates, and reported that other people seemed to react fine. Brian had been able to arrive at rational responses, including "Just because I blush, it doesn't mean I can't say what I have to say," and "I may blush but nobody cares." Brian received positive feedback from the therapist and the group on his efforts. Other group members were the targets of the exposures during this session. Brian served as an audience member for one public speaking exposure. For the first time, Brian contributed to the cognitive restructuring efforts of other group members without prompting. For homework, Brian agreed to offer an opinion twice (continuing to work on one of the themes of his first exposure) and to initiate one conversation.

Sessions 6 and 7

Brian did not attend these sessions, because he was visiting his family in Oregon.

Session 8

Brian reported that he had enjoyed his trip home. He stated that even during his trip, he tried to contribute more to conversations and to offer more opinions. For his exposure this session, the therapists decided to have Brian join two "coworkers" (one male, one female, each about his age) during lunch. It was anticipated that this exposure would be more difficult for Brian, because it required him to break into a conversation and the exposure was relatively unstructured. Brian reported the following automatic thoughts in anticipation of the exposure:

1. "I will appear nervous."
2. "I won't be coherent."
3. "They won't find what I have to say interesting."
4. "I'll look stupid."
5. "I won't be able to keep the conversation going."

As with the automatic thoughts in his first exposure, Brian was able to identify thinking errors, including fortune telling, mind reading, and labeling.

T1: Brian, which of these thoughts are most upsetting or anxiety-provoking for you?

B: "I won't be able to keep the conversation going." I am getting better at dealing with thoughts about blushing or looking nervous during conversations.

T1: OK. Let's do some work with that last thought. How might you challenge it? Look at your list of disputing questions if you need to.

B: Am I 100% sure that I won't be able to keep the conversation going? No, I'm not 100% sure, but I usually do run out of things to say.

T1: Brian, the way you are talking about this conversation, it sounds like you are viewing the whole thing as your responsibility. Is this another automatic thought that you have? "This conversation is my responsibility."

B: Right. I always feel like it is my fault if there are silences or if the conversation comes to a stop altogether.

T1: I see. What about the other two people? Do they have any responsibility for the conversation at all?

B: I suppose some of the conversation is their responsibility too. I never think about that.

T1: So, in a conversation with two other people, about how much of the conversation is your responsibility?

B: (*Smiling sheepishly*) About one-third.

T1: Right. Now, do you have any evidence that you will be able to say a few things to make a contribution to this conversation?

B: Yeah, I can probably come up with a few things to say. I have been practicing saying more in conversations and giving my opinion.

T1: Uh huh. And what about your last exposure? Did you contribute your share in that conversation?

B: There were just the two of us. I probably carried half of the conversation. Maybe more.

T1: OK, so what would be a good rational response for this exposure?

B: It is not only my responsibility to keep the conversation going.

Brian's goals were to say four things about himself and to ask two questions. Brian's SUDS ratings started out at 60 and decreased to 30 by the end of the fourth minute. His ratings remained in the 25–30 range for the last 6 minutes of the exposure. Brian's performance was objectively skilled, with little evidence of the behavioral manifestations of anxiety that he had exhibited during pretreatment assessments and early group sessions (e.g., poor eye contact, low voice volume, minimal responses). Brian received positive feedback from other group members and his role-play partners during the postexposure processing. Brian had easily met his goals and seemed pleased with how the exposure went. Brian's homework was to approach the new woman at work whom he found attractive and start a conversation.

Session 9

Brian was unable to complete his homework assignment because the woman had left the job. Nevertheless, he reported that he was continuing to make an effort to participate in conversations. Brian was not the focus of an exposure this session. Brian's homework was to introduce himself to someone new and say a few additional things. Brian was also to continue to work on contributing to conversations on a daily basis.

Session 10

During the homework review, Brian appeared anxious and depressed. He revealed that he had introduced himself to two different women at a party during the past weekend, and that neither of them had been interested in talking to him. Brian stated that he felt he should be over his problems with social anxiety by now; that he was no better off than when he started; and that, socially, things were never going to change for him. The therapists avoided getting into a debate with Brian regarding whether or not the interactions he described actually proceeded as poorly as he reported. Instead, they were empathic about what was obviously an upsetting experience for Brian, while at the same time gently challenging the distorted thinking apparent in the conclusions that he was drawing. The therapists acknowledged that, for all of us, there are realistically going to be times

when social interactions don't turn out how we would like them to, which doesn't feel good and can be disappointing. They then pointed out that although Brian did not obtain the results he wanted during these interactions, he did approach and talk to two attractive women—something he was almost never doing before treatment. Brian was also asked whether it would be overgeneralizing to assume that every attractive woman he ever introduced himself to would be uninterested in talking to him. Brian grudgingly admitted that since he started treatment, these were the only two women that he had approached for conversations, and that it was probably unfair to say that every single attractive woman his age would have the reaction that those two did. The therapists also asked Brian whether he might be disqualifying the positive things about his progress, and nudged him to recall some of the other things that he was doing that he was avoiding before treatment. After this cognitive restructuring, Brian appeared less tense and his affect brightened.

Brian had also been scheduled for an exposure this week. The therapists had planned an exposure in which Brian was to talk to a woman he had previously met and ask her to a social event. The female therapist from Brian's second exposure returned for this role play. This role play had been conceptualized by the therapists as a step toward Brian's initial treatment goals of becoming more comfortable with peers, especially women. Brian agreed that this exposure was very relevant to his current concerns and would make him very anxious. Brian reported the following automatic thoughts in anticipation of the exposure:

1. "She won't be interested in me."
2. "She won't be interested in what I have to say."
3. "People think that I am hard to talk to."
4. "I'm boring."

Brian was able to identify thinking errors, including all-or-nothing thinking, disqualifying the positive, overgeneralization, mind reading, and labeling. During the cognitive restructuring, Brian was encouraged to look at his success experiences in his two previous exposures as evidence that he has things to say that are of interest to other people. A couple of group members also told Brian that the conversations they had shared before and after group sessions were interesting and enjoyable. Lastly, the therapists pointed out that during the first one or two group sessions Brian had participated infrequently, but that now he was more openly sharing his thoughts and opinions. They asked the group members to share their reactions to this change. Brian received feedback that the rest of the group felt closer to him now that he was not holding back as much. With the help of the therapists and the rest of the group, Brian arrived at this rational response: "Many people will be interested in me if I make myself available to the conversation."

Brian's goals were to ask three questions, share three things about himself, and ask his role-play partner to join him for a social event. Brian's SUDS ratings started out at 40 and decreased to 20 by the end of the second minute. His ratings spiked up to 40 after he asked her out, but quickly declined to 10 after 2 more minutes and remained at that level throughout the rest of the exposure. Once again, Brian easily met his goals, and his performance was objectively skilled. Brian's homework was to continue contributing to conversations whenever possible and to initiate at least one conversation with a woman his age.

Session 11

During the homework review, Brian reported that he had gone to a party and spent a long time talking to a woman that he really liked. He asked her out that night and had since been on two dates with her. He described both dates in very positive terms. The group spent time sharing this success experience with Brian and contrasting how this experience was at odds with many of the automatic thoughts he was struggling with just a week ago. Brian was not the focus of an exposure this session, but contributed to the cognitive restructuring activities of other group members. Brian's homework was to continue initiating and contributing to conversations.

Session 12

Brian was not the focus of an exposure this week. Plans were finalized for each patient regarding when each would complete the Week 12 assessment, which included the majority of the pretreatment assessment measures. Each patient was also scheduled for an individual feedback session in which progress to date was discussed and goals for the 12-week intensive treatment continuation phase were established.

Week 12 Assessment (after Acute Treatment)

Brian was readministered the social anxiety disorder section of the ADIS-IV-L by an independent assessor who was unaware of his treatment condition. Brian received an ADIS-IV-L clinician severity rating of 3, which indicates symptoms that are mild to moderate in severity and below the operationally defined cutoff of 4 needed to meet criteria for a diagnosis of social anxiety disorder. In other words, Brian's social anxiety could be described as at the high end of the normal range. Brian also exhibited a substantial reduction in his self-rated fear of negative evaluation (BFNE), which is considered the core concept in social anxiety disorder. As discussed earlier, change in fear of negative evaluation has been found to be a potent predictor of functioning after treatment.

Although social interaction anxiety had been the focus of Brian's treatment to this point, Brian showed considerable improvements in both social interaction and performance/observation domains (see Table 3.6). Brian's self-reported interaction (SIAS) and performance/observation (SPS) fears were now below the clinical cutoff scores recommended by Heimberg and colleagues (1992). Similarly, on the LSAS, Brian's ratings of fear and avoidance of social and performance situations had dropped dramatically and were generally a standard deviation below the scores typically seen among individuals with social anxiety disorder prior to treatment (Heimberg et al., 1999). During the behavior tests, substantial improvements were observed for both the social interaction and public speaking tasks (see Figures 3.2 and 3.3). For the interaction task, Brian's anxiety climbed to a mild to moderate level (SUDS = 5, 40, 30, 30) during the anticipatory phase, but fell to a low level by the end of the performance phase (SUDS = 30, 40, 30, 20, 10). For the speech task, Brian's anxiety was at a mild to moderate level throughout both the anticipatory and performance phases. That Brian experienced improvement beyond the areas specifically dealt with in his exposures and homework is not atypical. Many of the basic concepts relevant to social interactions are applicable to performance/observation situations (e.g., it is OK to appear anxious), and some degree of generalization can be expected. In addition, participating in group discussions and completing role plays in front of the group essentially serve as informal exposures to performance/observation situations. Lastly, two of the members of Brian's group worked primarily on public speaking concerns during the first 12 weeks of treatment, and some amount of observational learning may have contributed to the reduction in his public speaking fears.

With regard to the measures targeting constructs other than social anxiety, Brian demonstrated significant improvement as well. Brian's self-reported depression (BDI) was well within the normal range. His overall self-rating of impairment due to his emotional difficulties (Liebowitz Self-Rated Disability Scale) had plummeted from a 15 to a 2. Importantly, Brian was no longer having any suicidal thoughts and denied any problems with being in a good mood, being successful at school, working at a job to his highest ability, being comfortable interacting with family members, and having friends. Brian reported mild problems having a satisfying romantic relationship and drinking alcohol in moderation. Brian indicated that his quality of life (Quality of Life Inventory) had improved substantially, although his score continued to be below the norm of nonclinical adult samples. Similarly, Safren, Heimberg, Brown, and Holle (1997) found significant changes in patient ratings of quality of life following 12 weeks of CBGT, but noted that these ratings remained lower than those found among normative samples. These authors speculated that 3 months might allow patients to begin to pursue many of their goals beyond symptom reduction (e.g., getting a better job, making new friends), but might be an insufficient length of time to realize them fully.

During the Week 12 assessment feedback session, Brian and the therapist agreed that the focus of the next 12 weeks of treatment would be on Brian's fear and avoidance of public speaking. Although Brian's public speaking fears were generally not as intense as they were prior to treatment, he still experienced marked fear and avoidance of some types of speeches.

Intensive Continuation Treatment (Weeks 12–24)

CBGT sessions during these additional 12 weeks of treatment followed the same format as the first 12 weeks. During the session prior to each of his exposures, the therapists and Brian agreed upon what his next in-session exposure would consist of and determined what materials Brian would need to bring to the group for that exposure (e.g., photojournalism projects, note cards).

Brian completed four in-session public speaking exposures during this phase. The first three exposures were constructed to be similar to the presentations that Brian was required to do several times each semester at school. For the first exposure, the audience consisted only of the therapists and other group members. The attitude of the audience was one of interest, and only nonthreatening questions were asked. Brian's anxiety started at a mild level (25), and, after 2 minutes, rapidly declined and remained at a low level (10) for the duration of the exposure.

For his second exposure, Brian presented a different project, and the situation was modified slightly in order to make it more anxiety-provoking. This time, two role players were added in order to increase the size of the audience and decrease Brian's familiarity with everyone in the audience. The role players and therapist took a moderately negative attitude toward his work in their comments and nonverbal behavior, and made an effort to ask challenging questions. Brian was informed of these changes prior to the exposure, so that cognitive restructuring could address any new automatic thoughts. Brian arrived at this rational response: "It is OK to say I don't know the answer to a question." Brian's anxiety started slightly higher than in his first exposure, but again rapidly decreased (40, 50, 40, 30, 30, 20, 20, 20, 20, 10, 10).

In his first two public-speaking exposures, Brian talked about his work for 2–3 minutes and then spent the rest of the time answering questions. For his third exposure, Brian was required to talk about the project that he was presenting until the therapists indicated that he could go to questions and answers. It was agreed that Brian would speak for 6–7 minutes. The audience again included additional role players and again took a moderately critical attitude. Brian's automatic thoughts included, among others, "My nervousness will affect my presentation negatively" and "I won't be able to express my ideas." In addition to challenging these thoughts in the usual manner using disputing questions, the therapists decided to implement a "silent SUDS" procedure during this exposure. In this procedure, when the therapist requests SUDS ratings, the patient writes down his/her anxiety rating rather than saying it aloud. At each SUDS prompt, all group members and role players write down how visibly anxious the patient appears. After his exposure, Brian reported the following SUDS ratings: 40, 30, 20, 10, 10, 20, 20, 30, 20, 10, 10. Then the group members, role players, and therapists reported the SUDS ratings that they made for Brian. In no case did anyone's ratings exceed Brian's ratings, and in most cases the ratings were substantially lower than those Brian made for himself. This information was also accompanied by subjective feedback about the quality of Brian's performance, and this feedback was almost entirely positive. Thus Brian was confronted with evidence from multiple sources that supported his rational response, which had been this: "I am capable of giving a good presentation even if I feel somewhat nervous."

Brian's last public speaking exposure was a presentation in the context of an interview involving a small group of potential bosses/coworkers. This exposure consisted only of role players enlisted from outside of the group. Brian experienced minimal anxiety during this exposure and once again received positive feedback about his performance.

As in the acute treatment phase, Brian agreed to weekly homework assignments that incorporated cognitive restructuring with *in vivo* exposures. Although Brian's in-session exposures focused on public speaking, Brian had weekly homework assignments addressing both social interaction and public speaking fears. Brian continued to work on issues such as initiating conversations, talking to unfamiliar people, stating his opinion, and so on. With regard to his public speaking fears, homework assignments included doing cognitive restructuring before and after class presentations, asking questions following other students' presentations, telling a story to a small group of two or three people, and asking a question or making a comment during work meetings. For patients with fewer public speaking opportunities than Brian, we often encourage them to join Toastmasters, an organization of members of the community who are working to overcome their public speaking fears and develop their skills as effective speakers.

Week 24 Assessment (after Intensive Continuation Treatment)

In terms of social anxiety symptom reduction, Brian maintained or improved upon his gains as measured by the SIAS, SPS, BFNE, LSAS, and ADIS-IV-L clinician severity rating. Brian experienced additional improvement in his mood (BDI) and continued to experience minimal disability associated with his symptoms. Notably, Brian reported further improvement in his quality of life. His score on the Quality of Life Inventory was now similar to that of normative samples (Frisch, 1994). (See Table 3.6.)

Although public speaking anxiety was the focus of Brian's second 12 weeks of treatment, Brian's social interaction behavior test showed further improvement: Brian's SUDS ratings never exceeded 20 (indicating mild anxiety) during the anticipatory and performance phases (see Figure 3.3). For the speech behavior test, Brian's SUDS ratings never exceeded 15 during either the anticipatory or performance phase (see Figure 3.2).

Maintenance Treatment (Weeks 25–52)

During the maintenance phase, exposures primarily occur outside of sessions. The time during each session focuses on assisting patients with cognitive restructuring regarding the social situations that they anticipate being the most problematic during the upcoming month. Difficulties with exposures and cognitive restructuring since the last session are also discussed.

During the maintenance phase, Brian's school schedule prohibited him from attending the group sessions. Therefore, his monthly maintenance sessions were conducted indi-

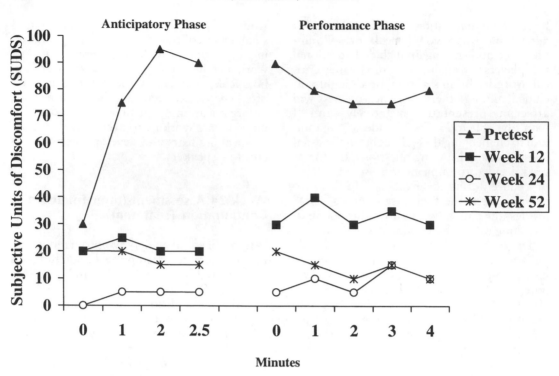

FIGURE 3.2. Subjective units of discomfort scale (SUDS) ratings for Brian during the anticipatory and performance phases of the speech behavior test at pretreatment, Week 12 (after acute treatment), Week 24 (after intensive continuation), and Week 52 (after maintenance).

vidually with one of the therapists. Throughout his maintenance treatment, Brian continued to work on the familiar themes of initiating conversations, stating his opinion, introducing himself to new people, and speaking in front of a group. With regard to his social relationships, Brian reported that he still did not feel as emotionally close to his friends and girlfriend as he would like to feel. Further discussion revealed that Brian experienced significant anxiety about disclosing personal information about himself and talking to others about issues that are important but painful to them. Over the course of the maintenance phase, Brian completed exposures that included discussing his feelings about his dating relationship with his roommate; discussing difficult aspects of his childhood with his girlfriend; and talking to and supporting one of his friends who was dealing with problems with his mother, who suffered from alcoholism. Through these behavioral experiments, Brian was able to test the automatic thoughts that he identified (e.g., "He will laugh at me,"

"He won't want to hang out with me," "She will think less of me"). Brian found that the people in his life in whom he chose to confide generally responded with warmth and support, and that he did feel closer to them the more he opened up to them. Brian also found that they opened up to him more in return, and that he was better able to handle talking to other people about emotionally laden issues than he had expected.

Week 52 Assessment (after Maintenance Treatment)

The independent assessor gave Brian an ADIS-IV-L clinician severity rating of 2, which indicates social anxiety disorder symptoms that are mild in severity and not really disabling. Brian maintained his gains on all self-report and clinician-administered measures of social anxiety. Brian's score on the Quality of Life Inventory reflected a high degree of satisfaction with his life (see Table 3.6). Brian's SUDS

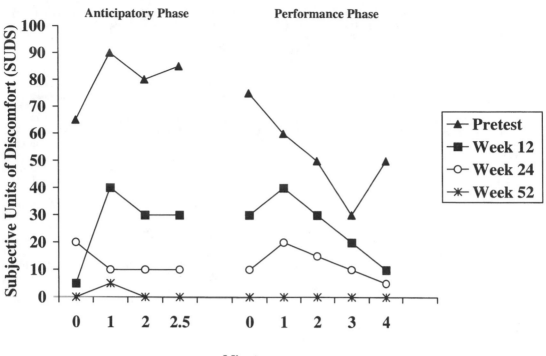

FIGURE 3.3. Subjective units of discomfort scale (SUDS) ratings for Brian during the anticipatory and performance phases of the social interaction behavior test at pretreatment, Week 12 (after acute treatment), Week 24 (after intensive continuation), and Week 52 (after maintenance).

ratings indicated that he was relaxed before and during the social interaction behavior test, and only mildly anxious before and during the public speaking behavior test (see Figures 3.2 and 3.3). In fact, Brian's SUDS ratings were lower than those of many of the controls without diagnosed social anxiety disorder who have participated in these behavior tests.

Six-Month Follow-Up Assessment

After 6 months with no treatment, Brian maintained his gains on all clinician-administered measures (see Table 3.6). Brian showed a slight increase in social anxiety since his Week 52 assessment, as measured by the self-report instruments. Nevertheless, his scores on these self-report measures of social anxiety remained substantially below his pretreatment scores and within the range of scores observed among controls. Measures of quality of life and functionality, behavior test measures, and hierarchy ratings are not collected at our 6-month follow-up assessment.

SUMMARY AND CONCLUSIONS

The primary purpose of this chapter has been to provide a step-by-step analysis of the conduct of CBGT, from initial screening of potential group members to following up on treatment response. Difficulties that may arise in the conduct of CBGT are discussed by Heimberg and Becker (2001) and Coles, Hart, and Heimberg (in press). Individuals like Brian who make dramatic improvements in their lives provide the impetus for continued research on the treatment of social anxiety disorder—a potentially debilitating disorder with an increasingly encouraging prognosis.

REFERENCES

Alden, L. E., & Wallace, S. T. (1995). Social phobia and social appraisal in successful and unsuccessful social interactions. *Behaviour Research and Therapy, 33,* 497–505.

American Psychiatric Association (APA). (1980). *Diagnostic and statistical manual of mental disorders* (3rd ed.). Washington, DC: Author.

American Psychiatric Association (APA). (1987). *Diagnostic and statistical manual of mental disorders* (3rd ed.—Revised). Washington, DC: Author.

American Psychiatric Association (APA). (1994). *Diagnostic and statistical manual of mental disorders* (4th ed.). Washington, DC: Author.

Amies, P. L., Gelder, M. G., & Shaw, P. M. (1983). Social phobia: A comparative clinical study. *British Journal of Psychiatry, 142,* 174–179.

Amir, N., Foa, E. B., & Coles, M. E. (1998). Negative interpretation bias in social phobia. *Behaviour Research and Therapy, 36,* 945–957.

Asmundson, G. J. G., & Stein, M. B. (1994). Selective attention for social threat in patients with generalized social phobia: Evaluation using a dot-probe paradigm. *Journal of Anxiety Disorders, 8,* 107–117.

Beck, A. T., Rush, A. J., Shaw, B. F., & Emery, G. (1979). *Cognitive therapy of depression.* New York: Guilford Press.

Beck, J. S. (1995). *Cognitive therapy: Basics and beyond.* New York: Guilford Press.

Beidel, D. C., Turner, S. M., Jacob, R. G., & Cooley, M. R. (1989). Assessment of social phobia: Reliability of an impromptu speech task. *Journal of Anxiety Disorders, 3,* 149–158.

Beidel, D. C., Turner, S. M., Stanley, M. A., & Dancu, C. V. (1989). The Social Phobia and Anxiety Inventory: Concurrent and external validity. *Behavior Therapy, 20,* 417–427.

Bond, C. F., Jr., & Omar, A. S. (1990). Social anxiety, state dependence, and the next-in-line effect. *Journal of Experimental Social Psychology, 26,* 185–198.

Boone, M. L., McNeil, D. W., Masia, C., Turk, C. L., Carter, L. E., Ries, B. J., & Lewin, M. R. (1999). Multimodal comprehensive assessment of social phobia subtypes. *Journal of Anxiety Disorders, 13,* 271–292.

Brown, E. J., Heimberg, R. G., & Juster, H. R. (1995). Social phobia subtype and avoidant personality disorder: Effect on severity of social phobia, impairment, and outcome of cognitive-behavioral treatment. *Behavior Therapy, 26,* 467–486.

Brown, E. J., Turovsky, J., Heimberg, R. G., Juster, H. R., Brown, T. A., & Barlow, D. H. (1997). Validation of the Social Interaction Anxiety Scale and the Social Phobia Scale across the anxiety disorders. *Psychological Assessment, 9,* 21–27.

Bruch, M. A., Gorsky, J. M., Collins, T. M., & Berger, P. (1989). Shyness and sociability reexamined: A multicomponent analysis. *Journal of Personality and Social Psychology, 57,* 904–915.

Bruch, M. A, Heimberg, R. G., & Hope, D. A. (1991). States of mind model and cognitive change in treated social phobics. *Cognitive Therapy and Research, 15,* 429–441.

Butler, G. (1989). Issues in the application of cognitive and behavioral strategies to the treatment of social phobia. *Clinical Psychology Review, 9,* 91–186.

Butler, G., Cullington, A., Munby, M., Amies, P., & Gelder, M. (1984). Exposure and anxiety management in the treatment of social phobia. *Journal of Consulting and Clinical Psychology, 52,* 642–650.

Chambless, D. L., Cherney, J., Caputo, G. C., & Rheinstein, B. J. G. (1987). Anxiety disorders and alcoholism: A study with inpatient alcoholics. *Journal of Anxiety Disorders, 1,* 29–40.

Chambless, D. L., Tran, G. Q., & Glass, C. R. (1997). Predictors of response to cognitive-behavioral group therapy for social phobia. *Journal of Anxiety Disorders 11,* 221–240.

Chapman, T. F., Mannuzza, S., & Fyer, A. J. (1995). Epidemiology and family studies of social phobia. In R. G. Heimberg, M. R. Liebowitz, D. A. Hope, & F. R. Schneier (Eds.), *Social phobia: Diagnosis, assessment, and treatment* (pp. 21–40). New York: Guilford Press.

Chartier, M. J., Hazen, A. L., & Stein, M. B. (1998). Lifetime patterns of social phobia: A retrospective study of the course of social phobia in a nonclinical population. *Depression and Anxiety, 7,* 113–121.

Cohn, L. G., & Hope, D. A. (2001). Treatment of social phobia: A treatment by dimensions review. In S. Hofmann & P. DiBartolo (Eds.), *From social anxiety to social phobia: Multiple perspectives* (pp. 354–378). Needham Heights, MA: Allyn & Bacon.

Coles, M. E., Hart, T. A., & Heimberg, R. G. (in press). Cognitive-behavioral group treatment for social phobia. In R. Crozier & L. E. Alden (Eds.), *International handbook of social anxiety.* Chichester, England: Wiley.

Coles, M. E., Turk, C. L., Heimberg, R. G., & Fresco, D. M. (in press). Effects of varying levels of anxiety within social situations: Relationship to memory perspective and attributions in social phobia. *Behaviour Research and Therapy.*

Cox, B. J., Ross, L., Swinson, R. P., & Direnfeld, D. M. (1998). A comparison of social phobia outcome measures in cognitive-behavioral group therapy. *Behavior Modification, 22,* 285–297.

Dalgleish, T., & Watts, F. N. (1990). Biases of attention and memory in disorders of anxiety and depression. *Clinical Psychology Review, 10,* 589–604.

Daly, J. A., Vangelisti, A. L., & Lawrence, S. G. (1989). Self-focused attention and public speaking anxiety. *Personality and Individual Differences, 10,* 903–913.

Davidson, J. R. T., Miner, C. M., De Veaugh-Geiss, J., Tupler, L. A., Colket, J. T., & Potts, N. L. S. (1997). The Brief Social Phobia Scale: A psychometric evaluation. *Psychological Medicine, 27,* 161–166.

Davidson, J. R. T., Hughes, D. L., George, L. K., & Blazer, D. G. (1993). The epidemiology of social phobia: Findings from the Duke Epidemiological Catchment Area Study. *Psychological Medicine, 23,* 709–718.

Davidson, J. R. T., Potts, N. L. S., Richichi, E. A., Krishnan, R. R., Ford, S. M., Smith, R. D., & Wilson, W. (1991). The Brief Social Phobia Scale. *Journal of Clinical Psychiatry, 52,* 48–51.

DiNardo, P. A., Brown, T. A., & Barlow, D. H. (1994). *Anxiety Disorders Interview Schedule for DSM-IV: Lifetime Version (ADIS-IV-L).* San Antonio, TX: Psychological Corporation.

DiNardo, P. A., Brown, T. A., Lawton, J. K., & Barlow, D. H. (1995, November). *The Anxiety Disorders Interview Schedule for DSM-IV Lifetime Version: Description and initial evidence for diagnostic reliability.* Paper presented at the 29th Annual Convention of the Association for Advancement of Behavior Therapy, Washington, DC.

Elting, D. T., Hope, D. A., & Heimberg, R. G. (1997). Inter-relationships among measures commonly used in research on social phobia. *Depression and Anxiety, 4,* 246–248.

Erwin, B. A., Heimberg, R. G., Juster, H. R., & Mindlin, M. (in press). Comorbid anxiety and mood disorders among persons with social anxiety disorder. *Behaviour Research and Therapy.*

Feske, U., Perry, K. J., Chambless, D. L., Renneberg, B., & Goldstein, A. J. (1996). Avoidant personality disorder as a predictor for severity and treatment outcome among generalized social phobics. *Journal of Personality Disorders, 10,* 174–184.

Foa, E. B., & Kozak, M. J. (1986). Emotional processing of fear: Exposure to corrective information. *Psychological Bulletin, 99,* 20–35.

Fresco, D. M., Erwin, B. A., Heimberg, R. G., & Turk, C. L. (in press). Social and specific phobias. In M. Gelder, N. Andreasen, & J. Lopez-Ibor (Eds.), *New Oxford textbook of psychiatry.* Oxford: Oxford University Press.

Frisch, M. B. (1994). *Manual and treatment guide for the Quality of Life Inventory.* Minneapolis, MN: National Computer Systems.

Fydrich, T., Chambless, D. L., Perry, K. J., Buergner, F., & Beazley, M. B. (1998). Behavioural assessment of social performance: A rating system for social phobia. *Behaviour Research and Therapy, 36,* 995–1010.

Gelernter, C. S., Uhde, T. W., Cimbolic, P., Arnkoff, D. B., Vittone, B. J., Tancer, M. E., & Bartko, J. J. (1991). Cognitive-behavioral and pharmacological treatment of social phobia. *Archives of General Psychiatry, 48,* 938–945.

Hackmann, A., Surawy, C., & Clark, D. M. (1998). Seeing yourself through others' eyes: A study of spontaneously occurring images in social phobia. *Behavioural and Cognitive Psychotherapy, 26,* 3–12.

Halford, K., & Foddy, M. (1982). Cognitive and social skills correlates of social anxiety. *British Journal of Clinical Psychology, 21,* 17–28.

Hart, T. A., Jack, M. S., Turk, C. L., & Heimberg, R. G. (1999). Issues for the measurement of social anxiety disorder (social phobia). In H. G. M. Westenberg & J. A. Den Boer (Eds.), *Focus on psychiatry: Social anxiety disorder* (pp. 133–155). Amsterdam: Syn-Thesis.

Heimberg, R. G. (1994). Cognitive assessment strategies and the measurement of outcome of treatment for social phobia. *Behaviour Research and Therapy, 32,* 269–280.

Heimberg, R. G. (1996). Social phobia, avoidant personality disorder, and the multiaxial conceptualization of interpersonal anxiety. In P. Salkovskis (Ed.), *Trends in cognitive and behavioural therapies* (Vol. 1, pp. 43–62). Chichester, England: Wiley.

Heimberg, R. G., & Becker, R. E. (2001). *Nature and treatment of social fears and phobias.* New York: Guilford Press.

Heimberg, R. G., Becker, R. E., Goldfinger, K., & Vermilyea, J. A. (1985). Treatment of social phobia by exposure, cognitive restructuring, and homework assignments. *Journal of Nervous and Mental Disease, 173,* 236–245.

Heimberg, R. G., Dodge, C. S., Hope, D. A., Kennedy, C. R., Zollo, L. J., & Becker, R. E. (1990). Cognitive-behavioral group treatment for social phobia: Comparison with a credible placebo control. *Cognitive Therapy and Research, 14,* 1–23.

Heimberg, R. G., Holt, C. S., Schneier, F. R., Spitzer, R. L., & Liebowitz, M. R. (1993). The issues of subtypes in the diagnosis of social phobia. *Journal of Anxiety Disorders, 7,* 249–269.

Heimberg, R. G., Hope, D. A., Dodge, C. S., & Becker, R. E. (1990). DSM-III-R subtypes of social phobia: Comparison of generalized social phobics and public speaking phobics. *Journal of Nervous and Mental Disease, 178,* 172–179.

Heimberg, R. G., Horner, K. J., Juster, H. R., Safren, S. A., Brown, E. J., Schneier, F. R., & Liebowitz, M. R. (1999). Psychometric properties of the Liebowitz Social Anxiety Scale. *Psychological Medicine, 29,* 199–212.

Heimberg, R. G., Liebowitz, M. R., Hope, D. A., Schneier, F. R., Holt, C. S., Welkowitz, L. A., Juster, H. R., Campeas, R., Bruch, M. A., Cloitre, M., Fallon, B., & Klein, D. F. (1998). Cognitive behavioral group therapy vs. phenelzine therapy for social phobia: 12-week outcome. *Archives of General Psychiatry, 55,* 1133–1141.

Heimberg, R. G., Mueller, G. P., Holt, C. S., Hope, D. A., & Liebowitz, M. R. (1992). Assessment of anxiety in social interaction and being observed by others: The Social Interaction Anxiety Scale and the Social Phobia Scale. *Behavior Therapy, 23,* 53–73.

Heimberg, R. G., Salzman, D. G., Holt, C. S., & Blendell, K. A. (1993). Cognitive-behavioral group treatment for social phobia: Effectiveness at five-year followup. *Cognitive Therapy and Research, 17,* 325–339.

Heimberg, R. G., Stein, M. B., Hiripi, E., & Kessler, R. C. (2000). Trends in the prevalence of social phobia in the United States: A synthetic cohort analysis of changes over four decades. *European Psychiatry, 15,* 29–37.

Herbert, J. D., Bellack, A. S., & Hope, D. A. (1991). Concurrent validity of the Social Phobia and Anxiety Inventory. *Journal of Psychopathology and Behavioral Assessment, 13,* 357–368.

Herbert, J. D., Hope, D. A., & Bellack, A. S. (1992). Validity of the distinction between generalized social phobia and avoidant personality disorder. *Journal of Abnormal Psychology, 101,* 332–339.

Hofmann, S. G., Newman, M. G., Becker, E., Taylor, C. B., & Roth, W. T. (1995). Social phobia with and without avoidant personality disorder: Preliminary behavior therapy outcome findings. *Journal of Anxiety Disorders, 9,* 427–438.

Holt, C. S., Heimberg, R. G., & Hope, D. A. (1992). Avoidant personality disorder and the generalized subtype in social phobia. *Journal of Abnormal Psychology, 101,* 318–325.

Holt, C. S., Heimberg, R. G., Hope, D. A., & Liebowitz, M. R. (1992). Situational domains of social phobia. *Journal of Anxiety Disorders, 6,* 63–77.

Hope, D. A., Heimberg, R. G., & Bruch, M. A. (1995). Dismantling cognitive-behavioral group therapy for social phobia. *Behaviour Research and Therapy, 33,* 637–650.

Hope, D. A., Heimberg, R. G., Juster, H., & Turk, C. L. (2000). *Managing social anxiety: A cognitive-behavioral therapy approach (client workbook).* San Antonio, TX: Psychological Corporation.

Hope, D. A., Heimberg, R. G., & Klein, J. R. (1990). Social anxiety and the recall of interpersonal information. *Journal of Cognitive Psychotherapy: An International Quarterly, 4,* 189–199.

Hope, D. A., Herbert, J. D., & White, C. (1995). Diagnostic subtype, avoidant personality disorder, and efficacy of cognitive behavioral group therapy for social phobia. *Cognitive Therapy and Research, 19,* 399–417.

Hope, D. A., Rapee, R. M., Heimberg, R. G., & Dombeck, M. (1990). Representation of the self in social phobia: Vulnerability to social threat. *Cognitive Therapy and Research, 14,* 177–189.

Hope, D. A., Turk, C. L., & Heimberg, R. G. (in press). *Managing social anxiety: A cognitive-behavioral therapy approach (therapist manual).* San Antonio, TX: The Psychological Corporation.

Juster, H. R., Brown, E. J., & Heimberg, R. G. (1996). Sozialphobie [Social phobia]. In J. Margraf (Ed.), *Lehrbuch der verhaltenstherapie [Textbook of behavior therapy]* (pp. 43–59). Berlin: Springer-Verlag.

Juster, H. R., & Heimberg, R. G. (1998). Social phobia. In A. S. Bellack & M. Hersen (Eds.), *Comprehensive clinical psychology* (Vol. 6, pp. 475–498). Oxford: Pergamon Press.

Kessler, R. C., McGonagle, K. A., Zhao, S., Nelson, C. B., Hughes, M., Eshleman, S., Wittchen, H.-U., & Kendler, K. S. (1994). Lifetime and 12-month prevalence of DSM-III-R psychiatric disorders in the United States: Results from the National Comorbidity Survey. *Archives of General Psychiatry, 51,* 8–19.

Kimble, C. E., & Zehr, H. D. (1982). Self-consciousness, information load, self-presentation, and memory in a social situation. *Journal of Social Psychology, 118,* 39–46.

Lang, P. J. (1977). Imagery in therapy: An information processing analysis of fear. *Behavior Therapy, 8,* 862–886.

Leary, M. R. (1983). A brief version of the Fear of Negative Evaluation Scale. *Personality and Social Psychology Bulletin, 9,* 371–375.

Leary, M. R., Kowalski, R. M., & Campbell, C. D. (1988). Self-presentational concerns and social anxiety: The role of generalized impression expectancies. *Journal of Research in Personality, 22,* 308–321.

Levin, A. P., Saoud, J. B., Strauman, T., Gorman, J. M., Fyer, A. J., Crawford, R., & Liebowitz, M. R. (1993). Responses of "generalized" and "discrete" social phobics during public speaking. *Journal of Anxiety Disorders, 7,* 207–221.

Liebowitz, M. R. (1987). Social phobia. *Modern Problems in Pharmacopsychiatry, 22,* 141–173.

Liebowitz, M. R., Gorman, J. M., Fyer, A. J., & Klein, D. F. (1985). Social phobia: Review of a neglected anxiety disorder. *Archives of General Psychiatry, 42,* 729–736.

Liebowitz, M. R., Heimberg, R. G., Fresco, D. M., Travers, J., & Stein, M. B. (2000). Social phobia or social anxiety disorder: What's in a name? *Archives of General Psychiatry, 57,* 191–192.

Liebowitz, M. R., Heimberg, R. G., Schneier, F. R., Hope, D. A., Davies, S., Holt, C. S., Goetz, D., Juster, H. R., Lin, S.-L., Bruch, M. A., Marshall, R., & Klein, D. F. (1999). Cognitive-behavioral group therapy versus phenelzine in social phobia: Long-term outcome. *Depression and Anxiety, 10,* 89–98.

Lucas, R. A., & Telch, M. J. (1993, November). *Group versus individual treatment of social phobia.* Paper presented at the 27th Annual Convention of the Association for Advancement of Behavior Therapy, Atlanta, GA.

MacLeod, C., & Mathews, A. (1991). Biased cognitive operations in anxiety: Accessibility of information or assignment of processing priorities? *Behaviour Research and Therapy, 29,* 599–610.

Magee, W. J., Eaton, W. W., Wittchen, H.-U., McGonagle, K. A., & Kessler, R. C. (1996). Agoraphobia, simple phobia, and social phobia in the National Comorbidity Survey. *Archives of General Psychiatry, 53,* 159–168.

Mannuzza, S., Schneier, F. R., Chapman, T. F., Liebowitz, M. R., Klein, D. F., & Fyer, A. J. (1995). Generalized social phobia: Reliability and validity. *Archives of General Psychiatry, 52,* 230–237.

Mattia, J. I., Heimberg, R. G., & Hope, D. A. (1993). The revised Stroop color-naming task in social phobics. *Behaviour Research and Therapy, 31,* 305–313.

Mattick, R. P., & Clarke, J. C. (1998). Development and validation of measures of social phobia scrutiny fear and social interaction anxiety. *Behaviour Research and Therapy, 36,* 455–470.

Mattick, R. P., & Peters, L. (1988). Treatment of severe social phobia: Effects of guided exposure with and without cognitive restructuring. *Journal of Consulting and Clinical Psychology, 56,* 251–260.

Mattick, R. P., Peters, L., & Clarke, J. C. (1989). Exposure and cognitive restructuring for social phobia: A controlled study. *Behavior Therapy, 20,* 3–23.

McEwan, K. L., & Devins, G. M. (1983). Is increased arousal in social anxiety noticed by others? *Journal of Abnormal Psychology, 92,* 417–421.

Mullaney, J. A., & Trippett, C. J. (1979). Alcohol dependence and phobias: Clinical description and relevance. *British Journal of Psychiatry, 135,* 565–573.

Otto, M. W., Pollack, M. H., Gould, R. A., Worthington, J. J., McArdle, E. T., Rosenbaum, J. F., & Heimberg, R. G. (2000). A comparison of the efficacy of clonazepam and cognitive-behavioral group therapy for the treatment of social phobia. *Journal of Anxiety Disorders, 14,* 345–358.

Rapee, R. M., & Heimberg, R. G. (1997). A cognitive-behavioural model of anxiety in social phobia. *Behaviour Research and Therapy, 35,* 741–756.

Rapee, R. M., & Lim, L. (1992). Discrepancy between self- and observer ratings of performance in social phobics. *Journal of Abnormal Psychology, 101,* 728–731.

Reich, J., Goldenberg, I., Vasile, R., Goisman, R., & Keller, M. (1994). A prospective follow-along study of the course of social phobia. *Psychiatry Research, 54,* 249–258.

Ries, B. J., McNeil, D. W., Boone, M. L., Turk, C. L., Carter, L. E., & Heimberg, R. G. (1998). Assessment of contemporary social phobia verbal report instruments. *Behaviour Research and Therapy, 36,* 983–994.

Roth, D., Antony, M. M., & Swinson, R. P. (in press). Interpretations for anxiety symptoms in social phobia. *Behaviour Research and Therapy.*

Safren, S. A., Heimberg, R. G., Brown, E. J., & Holle, C. (1997). Quality of life in social phobia. *Depression and Anxiety, 4,* 126–133.

Safren, S. A., Heimberg, R. G., & Juster, H. R. (1997). Client expectancies and their relationship to pretreatment symptomatology and outcome of cognitive-behavioral group treatment for social phobia. *Journal of Consulting and Clinical Psychology, 65,* 694–698.

Sanderson, W. C., DiNardo, P. A., Rapee, R. M., & Barlow, D. H. (1990). Syndrome comorbidity in patients diagnosed with a DSM-III-R anxiety disorder. *Journal of Abnormal Psychology, 99,* 308–312.

Sank, L. I., & Shaffer, C. S. (1984). *A therapist's manual for cognitive behavior therapy in groups.* New York: Plenum Press.

Schneier, F. R., Heckelman, L. R., Garfinkel, R., Campeas, R., Fallon, B. A., Gitow, A., Street, L., Del Bene, D., & Liebowitz, M. R. (1994). Functional impairment in social phobia. *Journal of Clinical Psychiatry, 55,* 322–331.

Schneier, F. R., Johnson, J., Hornig, C. D., Liebowitz, M. R., & Weissman, M. M. (1992). Social phobia: Comorbidity and morbidity in an epidemiologic sample. *Archives of General Psychiatry, 49,* 282–288.

Schneier, F. R., Martin, L. Y., Liebowitz, M. R., Gorman, J. M., & Fyer, A. J. (1989). Alcohol abuse in social phobia. *Journal of Anxiety Disorders, 3,* 15–23.

Schneier, F. R., Spitzer, R. L., Gibbon, M., Fyer, A. J., & Liebowitz, M. R. (1991). The relationship of social phobia subtypes and avoidant personality disorder. *Comprehensive Psychiatry, 32,* 1–5.

Schwartz, R. M., & Garamoni, G. L. (1989). Cognitive balance and psychopathology: Evaluation of an information processing model of positive and negative states of mind. *Clinical Psychology Review, 9,* 271–294.

Smail, P., Stockwell, T., Canter, S., & Hodgson, R. (1984). Alcohol dependence and phobic anxiety states: I. A prevalence study. *British Journal of Psychiatry, 144,* 53–57.

Stopa, L., & Clark, D. M. (1993). Cognitive processes in social phobia. *Behaviour Research and Therapy, 31,* 255–267.

Stopa, L., & Clark, D. M. (2000). Social phobia and interpretation of social events. *Behaviour Research and Therapy, 38,* 273–283.

Taylor, S., Woody, S., Koch, W., McLean, P., Paterson, R., & Anderson, K. W. (1997). Cognitive restructuring in the treatment of social phobia: Efficacy and mode of action. *Behavior Modification, 21,* 487–511.

Taylor, S., Woody, S., McLean, P. D., & Koch, W. J. (1997). Sensitivity of outcome measures for treatments of generalized social phobia. *Assessment, 4,* 181–191.

Thyer, B. A., Parrish, R. T., Himle, J., Cameron, O. G., Curtis, G. C., & Nesse, R. M. (1986). Alcohol abuse among clinically anxious patients. *Behaviour Research and Therapy, 24,* 357–359.

Tran, G. Q., & Chambless, D. L. (1995). Psychopathology of social phobia: Effects of subtype and avoidant personality disorder. *Journal of Anxiety Disorders, 9,* 489–501.

Trower, P., & Gilbert, P. (1989). New theoretical conceptions of social anxiety and social phobia. *Clinical Psychology Review, 9,* 19–35.

Turk, C. L., Coles, M., & Heimberg, R. G. (in press). Psychological treatment of social phobia: A literature review. In D. J. Stein & E. Hollander (Eds.), *Textbook of anxiety disorders.* Washington, DC: American Psychiatric Press.

Turk, C. L., Lerner, J., Heimberg, R. G., & Rapee, R. M. (2001). An integrated cognitive-behavioral model of social anxiety. In S. G. Hofmann & P. M. DiBartolo (Eds.), *From social anxiety to social phobia: Multiple perspectives* (pp. 281–303). Needham Heights, MA: Allyn & Bacon.

Turner, S. M., Beidel, D. C., Cooley, M. R., Woody, S. R., & Messer, S. C. (1994). A multicomponent behavioural treatment for social phobia: Social effectiveness therapy. *Behaviour Research and Therapy, 32,* 381–390.

Turner, S. M., Beidel, D. C., Dancu, C. V., & Keys, D. J. (1986). Psychopathology of social phobia and comparison to avoidant personality disorder. *Journal of Abnormal Psychology, 95,* 389–394.

Turner, S. M., Beidel, D. C., Dancu, C. V., & Stanley, M. A. (1989). An empirically derived inventory to measure social fears and anxiety: The Social Phobia and Anxiety Inventory. *Psychological Assessment, 1,* 35–40.

Turner, S. M., Beidel, D. C., & Townsley, R. M. (1992). Social phobia: A comparison of specific and generalized subtype and avoidant personality disorder. *Journal of Abnormal Psychology, 101,* 326–331.

Turner, S. M., Beidel, D. C., Wolff, P. L., Spaulding, S., & Jacob, R. G. (1996). Clinical features affecting treatment outcome in social phobia. *Behaviour Research and Therapy, 34,* 795–804.

van Velzen, C. M. J., Emmelkamp, P. M. G., & Scholing, A. (1997). The impact of personality disorders on behavioural treatment outcome for social phobia. *Behaviour Research and Therapy, 35,* 889–900.

Wallace, S. T., & Alden, L. E. (1991). A comparison of social standards and perceived ability in anxious and nonanxious men. *Cognitive Therapy and Research, 15,* 237–254.

Walters, K. S., & Hope, D. A. (1998). Analysis of social behavior in individuals with social phobia and nonanxious participants using a psychobiological model. *Behavior Therapy, 29,* 387–407.

Watson, D., & Friend, R. (1969). Measurement of social-evaluative anxiety. *Journal of Consulting and Clinical Psychology, 33,* 448–457.

Wells, A., Clark, D. M., & Ahmad, S. (1998). How do I look with my mind's eye?: Perspective taking in social phobic imagery. *Behaviour Research and Therapy, 36,* 631–634.

Wells, A., & Papageorgiou, C. (1999). The observer perspective: Biased imagery in social phobia, agoraphobia, and blood/injury phobia. *Behaviour Research and Therapy, 37,* 653–658.

Widiger, T. A. (1992). Generalized social phobia versus avoidant personality disorder: A commentary on three studies. *Journal of Abnormal Psychology, 101,* 340–343.

Wolpe, J., & Lazarus A. A. (1966). *Behavior therapy techniques.* New York: Pergamon Press.

Chapter 4

GENERALIZED ANXIETY DISORDER

Timothy A. Brown
Tracy A. O'Leary
David H. Barlow

Generalized anxiety disorder has been called the "basic" anxiety disorder, in the sense that generalized anxiety is, by definition, a component of other anxiety disorders. But only recently have we begun to delve into the nature of generalized anxiety disorder. Only recently have we begun to evaluate effective psychological treatments for this problem, and only in the past several years has evidence begun to appear that we can in fact treat this problem successfully. This is no small feat, since generalized anxiety disorder, although characterized by marked fluctuations, is chronic. Some have even considered that generalized anxiety disorder might be better conceptualized as a personality disorder, since many individuals with this problem cannot report a definitive age of onset; rather, they note that it has been with them all their lives. Drug treatments, although often tested, have also not produced robust results. For this reason, further study of new treatment protocols is all the more pressing.

The protocol presented in this chapter, developed in our Center, illustrates the procedures of "worry exposure" and "worry behavior prevention." These therapeutic procedures are derived from new theoretical conceptualizations of generalized anxiety disorder. In many ways, these procedures depart radically from more traditional treatment approaches to generalized anxiety.—D. H. B.

OVERVIEW: DEFINITION AND FEATURES

Since its inception as a diagnostic category in 1980, the definitional criteria for generalized anxiety disorder (GAD) have been revised substantially in each edition of the *Diagnostic and Statistical Manual of Mental Disorders* (DSM). In DSM-III (American Psychiatric Association, 1980), GAD was a residual category (i.e., diagnosis was permitted only if criteria were not met for any other Axis I disorder); it was defined as the presence of generalized, persistent anxiety (continuous for a period of at least 1 month) as manifested by symptoms from at least three of four categories: (1) motor tension (e.g., muscle aches, restlessness); (2) autonomic hyperactivity (e.g., sweating, dizziness, accelerated heart rate); (3) apprehensive expectation (e.g., anxiety, worry, fear); and (4) vigilance and scanning (e.g., concentration difficulties, irritability).

However, subsequent evidence (see Barlow & Di Nardo, 1991) indicated that a considerable proportion of patients presenting to anxiety clinics reported persistent symptoms of anxiety and tension emanating from worry and apprehension that were unrelated to other emotional disorders (e.g., worry about finances, job performance, minor details of everyday life). Accordingly, the diagnostic criteria for GAD were revised substantially in DSM-III-R (American Psychiatric Association, 1987). Major changes to GAD were as follows: (1) The criterion excessive and/or unrealistic worry in two or more areas unrelated to another Axis I disorder was established as the key definitional feature of the disorder; (2) the associated symptom criterion was revised to require the presence of at least 6 symptoms from a list of 18 forming the three clusters of motor tension, autonomic hyperactivity, and vigilance and scanning; (3) the duration criterion was extended from 1 to 6 months, in part to assist in the differentiation of GAD from transient reactions to negative life events (e.g., adjustment disorders; Breslau & Davis, 1985); and (4) GAD was no longer considered a residual category.

In DSM-IV (American Psychiatric Association, 1994), the criteria for GAD were revised further to make them more user-friendly and to emphasize the *process* of worry/apprehensive expectation (see Brown, Barlow, & Liebowitz, 1994). As shown in Table 4.1, DSM-IV GAD is defined by the key feature of excessive, uncontrollable worry about a number of life events/activities, accompanied by at least three of six associated symptoms of negative affect/tension. Thus the DSM-III-R requirement of two or more spheres of worry was eliminated and replaced by excessive worry about a number of life events/activities (i.e., intensity, duration, and frequency of the worry are out of proportion to the likelihood or impact of the feared event). Moreover, the DSM-IV definition specifies that the worry is perceived by the individual as *difficult to control*. This revision was based on evidence from comparisons of patients with GAD to persons with other or no mental disorders that although no appreciable differences are noted on the *content* of worry (e.g., both patients with GAD and nonanxious controls report worry about family matters, work, finances, etc.), considerable differentiation exists on measures reflecting the *controllability* of the worry process (e.g., percentage of the day worried, frequency of unprecipitated worry, self-perceptions of controllability of worry, number of worry spheres; see Borkovec, 1994; Borkovec, Shadick, & Hopkins, 1991; Craske, Rapee, Jackel, & Barlow, 1989). For example, in a study comparing patients with DSM-III-R GAD to nonanxious controls on various potential DSM-IV criteria, 100% of the patient

---

TABLE 4.1. Diagnostic Criteria for DSM-IV Generalized Anxiety Disorder

A. Excessive anxiety and worry (apprehensive expectation), occurring more days than not for at least 6 months, about a number of events or activities (such as work or school performance).

B. The person finds it difficult to control the worry.

C. The anxiety and worry are associated with three (or more) of the following six symptoms (with at least some symptoms present for more days than not for the past 6 months). **Note:** Only one item is required in children.

    (1) restlessness or feeling keyed up or on edge
    (2) being easily fatigued
    (3) difficulty concentrating or mind going blank
    (4) irritability
    (5) muscle tension
    (6) sleep disturbance (difficulty falling or staying asleep, or restless unsatisfying sleep)

D. The focus of the anxiety and worry is not confined to features of an Axis I disorder, e.g., the anxiety or worry is not about having a panic attack (as in Panic Disorder), being embarrassed in public (as in Social Phobia), being contaminated (as in Obsessive–Compulsive Disorder), being away from home or close relatives (as in Separation Anxiety Disorder), gaining weight (as in Anorexia Nervosa), having multiple physical complaints (as in Somatization Disorder), or having a serious illness (as in Hypochondriasis), and the anxiety and worry do not occur exclusively during Posttraumatic Stress Disorder.

E. The anxiety, worry, or physical symptoms cause clinically significant distress or impairment in social, occupational, or other important areas of functioning.

F. The disturbance is not due to the direct physiological effects of a substance (e.g., a drug of abuse, a medication) or a general medical condition (e.g., hyperthyroidism) and does not occur exclusively during a Mood Disorder, Psychotic Disorder, or a Pervasive Developmental Disorder.

Note. Reprinted with permission from the *Diagnostic and Statistical Manual of Mental Disorders.* Copyright 1994 American Psychiatric Association.

group reported difficulties controlling their worry, compared to only 5.6% of the comparison group (Abel & Borkovec, 1995). The distinguishability of the uncontrollable/excessive dimension of worry has also been upheld by findings that patients with GAD obtain significantly higher scores than patients with other anxiety disorders (including obsessive–compulsive disorder, or OCD) and non-anxious controls on the Penn State Worry Questionnaire (PSWQ), a psychometrically validated measure of the trait of worry (Brown, Antony, & Barlow, 1992; Brown, Moras, Zinbarg, & Barlow, 1993; Meyer, Miller, Metzger, & Borkovec, 1990).

In addition, the number of symptoms forming the associated symptom criterion in DSM-IV was reduced from 18 to 6, by retaining many of the symptoms that resided in the DSM-III-R motor tension and vigilance and scanning clusters and eliminating the symptoms from the DSM-III-R autonomic hyperactivity cluster (see Table 4.1). This change was based on converging evidence that GAD may be allied with a set of associated symptoms that fosters its distinction from the other anxiety disorders. For instance, studies using DSM-III-R criteria indicated that on structured interviews, patients with GAD endorsed symptoms from the autonomic hyperactivity cluster (e.g., accelerated heart rate, shortness of breath) less frequently than symptoms from the other two clusters (see, e.g., Brawman-Mintzer et al., 1994; Marten et al., 1993; Noyes et al., 1992). Indeed, the associated symptoms reported by patients with GAD at the highest frequency are irritability, restlessness/feeling keyed up, muscle tension, easy fatigability, sleep difficulties, and concentration difficulties (Marten et al., 1993). Additional research has indicated that although patients with GAD report autonomic symptoms with some frequency, these patients could be most strongly differentiated from patients with other anxiety disorders (panic disorder, social phobia, specific phobia, OCD) by the frequency and intensity of symptoms from the motor tension and vigilance and scanning clusters (Brown, Marten, & Barlow, 1995). In addition, these symptoms correlate more strongly with measures of worry and GAD severity than do symptoms of autonomic arousal (Brown, Chorpita, & Barlow, 1998; Brown, Marten, & Barlow, 1995).

These self-report-based findings are consistent with the results of several recent psychophysiological studies. For example, the one psychophysiological measure on which patients with GAD have been found to evidence *greater* responsiveness than nonanxious controls at baseline and in response to psychological challenge is muscle tension (as assessed via frontalis and gastrocnemius electromyograms; Hazlett, McLeod, & Hoehn-Saric, 1994; Hoehn-Saric, McLeod, & Zimmerli, 1989; see also Hoehn-Saric & McLeod, 1988). Conversely, initial studies failed to detect differences between worriers and nonworriers (or patients with GAD and normal controls) on cardiovascular indices collected while participants were at rest or were engaging in laboratory-induced worry challenges (see, e.g., Borkovec, Robinson, Pruzinsky, & DePree, 1983). Thus the collective findings of these investigations suggested that although patients with GAD and chronic worriers evidence elevated muscle tension (both while at rest and in response to laboratory challenges), they do not display a sympathetic activation response that is typically found in other anxiety disorders (see Hoehn-Saric & McLeod, 1988).

Subsequent research has indicated that GAD and worry are indeed associated with autonomic inflexibility (Borkovec & Hu, 1990; Borkovec, Lyonfields, Wiser, & Diehl, 1993; Hoehn-Saric et al., 1989). That is, relative to nonanxious controls, persons with GAD evidence a restricted range of autonomic activity (e.g., lowered heart rate variability) at baseline and in response to laboratory stressors (e.g., periods of worry or exposure to aversive imagery). Moreover, a significant reduction in cardiovascular variability has been observed in nonanxious controls from baseline to aversive imagery induction; however, this reduction in variability was most dramatic during a period of worrisome thinking (Lyonfields, Borkovec, & Thayer, 1995). Although findings of autonomic rigidity in GAD were initially attributed to an inhibition in sympathetic nervous system activity (Hoehn-Saric et al., 1989), more recent findings suggest that this phenomenon may be due to chronic reductions in parasympathetic (vagal) tone (see, e.g., Lyonfields et al., 1995). Regardless of the underlying mechanisms, these findings are consistent with the results of clinical assessment studies (see, e.g., Brown,

Marten, & Barlow, 1995) indicating that GAD is associated with a predominance of symptoms of negative affect/tension (e.g., muscle tension, irritability) and a relative infrequency of autonomic symptoms (e.g., accelerated heart rate). In addition to perhaps fostering the distinction between GAD and other anxiety disorders, these findings are emphasized in current conceptual models of GAD and pathological worry, discussed later in this chapter.

Finally, differential diagnosis guidelines for DSM-IV GAD specify that the disorder should not be assigned if its features are better accounted for by another mental or medical disorder (e.g., worry about future panic attacks in panic disorder should not be counted toward the diagnosis of GAD). In addition, the DSM-IV definition of GAD states that the disorder should not be assigned if its features occur exclusively during the course of a mood disorder, posttraumatic stress disorder, a psychotic disorder, or a pervasive developmental disorder. Thus, although GAD has not been a residual disorder since DSM-III, diagnostic hierarchy rules continue to exist for GAD in the context of some disorders. This is in part reflective of the continued controversy among researchers as to whether there is sufficient empirical justification for GAD as a distinct diagnostic category (Brown et al., 1994). The question of acceptable discriminant validity is particularly salient for mood disorders (major depression, dysthymia), in view of evidence of their high comorbidity and symptom overlap with GAD (see, e.g., Brown, Marten, & Barlow, 1995; Starcevic, 1995).

PREVALENCE, COURSE, AND COMORBIDITY

Prevalence

Studies of the lifetime prevalence for GAD in the general population have provided estimates ranging from 1.9% to 5.4%. The most recent prevalence data for GAD have come from the National Comorbidity Survey (NCS), where over 8,000 persons in the community (aged 15 to 54 years) were evaluated with structured interviews. This study obtained prevalence estimates of 1.6% and 5.1% for current and lifetime GAD, respectively, as defined by DSM-III-R criteria (Wittchen,

Zhao, Kessler, & Eaton, 1994). A consistent finding in these community surveys is a 2:1 female-to-male preponderance of GAD (see, e.g., Blazer, George, & Hughes, 1991; Wittchen et al., 1994). The prevalence of GAD in older populations awaits future research (see Beck, Stanley, & Zebb, 1996; Wisocki, 1994). However, there is some evidence suggesting that GAD may be one of the more common disorders in the elderly. For example, Himmelfarb and Murrell (1984) found that 17% of elderly men and 21.5% of elderly women had sufficiently severe anxiety symptoms to warrant treatment, although it is not clear how many of these individuals actually met criteria for GAD. Another indicator of the potential prevalence of GAD symptoms in the elderly comes from more recent evidence showing that the use of minor tranquilizers is very high (ranging from 17% to 50%) in this population (Salzman, 1991).

Onset and Course

Patients with GAD often present with a lifelong history of generalized anxiety. For example, several studies have found that a large proportion of patients with GAD cannot report a clear age of onset or report an onset dating back to childhood (see, e.g., Anderson, Noyes, & Crowe, 1984; Barlow, Blanchard, Vermilyea, Vermilyea, & Di Nardo, 1986; Butler, Fennell, Robson, & Gelder, 1991; Cameron, Thyer, Nesse, & Curtis, 1986; Noyes, Clarkson, Crowe, Yates, & McChesney, 1987; Noyes et al., 1992; Rapee, 1985; Sanderson & Barlow, 1990). Thus, whereas several other anxiety disorders (such as panic disorder) tend to have a later onset and more acute presentation characterized by exacerbations and remissions, initial evidence suggests that GAD has a more characterological presentation (although fluctuations in the course of GAD are often noted corresponding to the presence or absence of life stressors). These findings have contributed to Axis II conceptualizations of GAD (Sanderson & Wetzler, 1991).

However, GAD is not exclusively associated with an early age of onset. For instance, in the NCS, the lowest prevalence of GAD occurred in the 15- to 24-year age group (Wittchen et al., 1994). Yet, because prevalence estimates were based on the diagnostic level, they do not necessarily contradict the aforementioned findings indicating that many patients with GAD report symptoms dating back to childhood (i.e., the extent to which the features of GAD were present at subclinical levels was not examined in this study). Nevertheless, some people with GAD do report an onset in adulthood (Beck et al., 1996; Blazer et al., 1991; Blazer, Hughes, & George, 1987; Brown, O'Leary, Marten, & Barlow, 1993; Ganzini, McFarland, & Cutler, 1990; Hoehn-Saric, Hazlett, & McLeod, 1993). It has been suggested that compared to early-onset GAD, stressful life events may play a stronger role in onsets of GAD occurring later in life. This suggestion is bolstered by the findings of Blazer and colleagues (1987), who noted that the occurrence of one or more negative life events increased by threefold the risk of developing GAD in the following year. However, comparison of early- versus late-onset cases has revealed no consistent differences on variables such as GAD severity or comorbid symptoms or conditions (Beck et al., 1996; Brown et al., 1993; Hoehn-Saric et al., 1993).

Comorbidity

Although GAD was once thought to be a relatively minor problem that was not associated with a high degree of distress and impairment, recent data indicate that this is not the case. In the NCS, 82% of persons with GAD reported that their problem was associated with significant impairment, as indexed by past treatment-seeking behavior (either drugs or psychotherapy) or substantial lifestyle interference (Wittchen et al., 1994; see Massion, Warshaw, & Keller, 1993). In addition, research has routinely shown that GAD rarely presents in isolation. Community surveys indicate that 90% of persons with GAD have a history of some other mental disorder at some point in their lives (Wittchen et al., 1994); the NCS estimated that 65% of persons with current GAD had at least one other disorder at the time of their assessment. Studies of clinical samples have found that over 75% of patients with a current principal diagnosis of GAD have other co-occurring anxiety or mood disorders (Brawman-Mintzer et al., 1993; Brown & Barlow, 1992; Massion et al., 1993). The high comorbidity rates obtained

in patient samples may actually be *under*estimates, given that the presence of certain disorders (e.g., substance use disorders, disorders involving current suicidality) is an exclusion criterion in many investigations. Indeed, epidemiological data from the NCS suggest that substance use disorders are common (16%) in current GAD. In studies of patient samples, panic disorder, mood disorders (major depression, dysthymia), social phobia, and specific (formerly simple) phobia are typically found to be the most common additional diagnoses.

Some studies indicate that GAD is the most common comorbid diagnosis in patients seeking treatment for another anxiety or mood disorder (Brown & Barlow, 1992; Sanderson, Beck, & Beck, 1990). In addition, initial findings suggest that, relative to other anxiety and mood disorders, GAD may be the most commonly occurring disorder in persons presenting for treatment of physical conditions associated with stress (e.g., irritable bowel syndrome, chronic headaches; Blanchard, Scharff, Schwarz, Suls, & Barlow, 1990). The high comorbidity rate of GAD has also been construed in support of claims that it may not represent a distinct disorder, but rather a "prodrome" or symptoms better accounted for by other disorders such as major depression (see Brown et al., 1994). This concern is seemingly upheld by evidence that comorbid GAD often remits upon focused treatment of another anxiety disorder (Brown, Antony, & Barlow, 1995). This issue awaits empirical investigation (e.g., study of the temporal sequence of the emergence of GAD in relation to comorbid disorders).

CONCEPTUAL MODELS OF GAD

Although many of the findings discussed above may be taken as evidence of the questionable discriminant validity of GAD, conceptual models of the anxiety disorders have emerged that regard GAD as the "basic" anxiety disorder, because its core features may represent the fundamental processes of all emotional disorders (Barlow, 1988; Barlow, Chorpita, & Turovsky, 1996). Barlow (1988) has termed this fundamental process "anxious apprehension." Anxious apprehension refers to a future-oriented mood state in which one becomes ready or prepared to attempt to cope with upcoming negative events. This mood

state is associated with a state of high negative affect and chronic overarousal, a sense of
uncontrollability, and an attentional focus on
threat-related stimuli (e.g., high self-focused
attention, hypervigilance for threat cues).
Whereas the *process* of anxious apprehension
is present in all anxiety disorders, the *content*
(focus) of anxious apprehension varies from
disorder to disorder (e.g., anxiety over future
panic attacks in panic disorder, anxiety over
possible negative social evaluation in social
phobia). Nevertheless, the process of anxious
apprehension is viewed to be key in the progression of initial symptoms into a full-blown
disorder (e.g., isolated unexpected panic attacks are apt to develop into panic disorder
in the context of worry/anxious apprehension
over the possibility of having future panic
attacks).

Indeed, the features of GAD are considered
to be vulnerability dimensions in leading etiological models of emotional disorders (Clark,
Watson, & Mineka, 1994). For instance,
GAD is associated with high levels of negative affect (Brown et al., 1998), a construct
that is increasingly considered to be a higher-
order trait serving as a vulnerability dimension for anxiety and mood disorders (Clark
et al., 1994). In addition, in view of evidence
that GAD is most likely to have an early onset
and to precede the disorders with which it co-
occurs (see the "Prevalence, Course, and
Comorbidity" section), it has been posited
that the high comorbidity rate associated with
GAD may be due to the fact that its constituent features contribute to the predisposition
for the development of other anxiety and
mood disorders (Brown et al., 1994). Furthermore, studies have often found GAD to be
relatively less responsive to psychosocial and
pharmacological interventions—a result that
could be construed as consistent with a characterological or vulnerability conceptualization of this disorder (Sanderson & Wetzler,
1991).

As for the origins of GAD itself, the data
point to a confluence of genetic, biological,
and psychosocial factors, as with the other
emotional disorders. Although initial studies
failed to find a clear role of genetic factors in
GAD (see, e.g., Andrews, Stewart, Allen, &
Henderson, 1990; Torgersen, 1983), more recent findings have indicated otherwise (Kendler, Neale, Kessler, Heath, & Eaves, 1992a,
1992b; Kendler et al., 1995; Roy, Neale,

Pedersen, Mathé, & Kendler, 1995; Skre,
Onstad, Torgersen, Lygren, & Kringlen,
1993). For example, in a study of 1,033
female–female twin pairs assessed by evaluators unaware of the nature of the research,
Kendler and colleagues (1992a) concluded
that GAD is a moderately familial disorder,
with a heritability estimated at about 30%
(the remainder of variance in GAD liability
may result from environmental factors not
shared by the adult twins). Further research
in both all-female (Kendler et al., 1992b) and
mixed-sex (Roy et al., 1995) twin samples has
indicated that whereas a clear genetic influence exists in GAD, the genetic factors in
GAD are completely shared with major depression. However, although GAD and major
depression share the same genetic factors,
their environmental determinants appear to
be mostly distinct. These findings are consistent with the aforementioned conceptual
models of emotional disorders (Barlow et al.,
1996; Clark et al., 1994), which view the
anxiety and mood disorders as sharing common vulnerabilities, but differing on important dimensions (e.g., focus of attention, degree of psychosocial vulnerability arising from
environmental experiences) to the extent that
differentiation is warranted.

Relative to genetic/biological influences,
psychosocial factors have received less attention in the empirical study of the origins of
GAD. Current conceptual models suggest that
early experiences of uncontrollability represent a psychological vulnerability for the disorder (Barlow, 1988; Borkovec, 1994). For
instance, although the nature of these early
experiences may be multifold, Borkovec
(1994) has asserted that childhood histories
of psychosocial trauma (e.g., death of parent,
physical/sexual abuse) and insecure attachment to primary caregivers may be particularly salient to the origins of this psychological vulnerability.

Although the aforementioned models are
helpful to the understanding of the potential
causes of GAD and its relation to other emotional disorders, they are of limited value to
development of effective treatments for this
condition. Nonetheless, psychosocial models
of pathological worry have been devised that
have assisted greatly in this endeavor. The
most widely recognized model of this nature
has been provided by Borkovec (1994; Borkovec et al., 1991). Borkovec regards worry as

a predominantly conceptual, verbal/linguistic attempt to avoid future aversive events and aversive imagery (i.e., cognitive avoidance of threat); this process is experienced by the worrier as negative-affect-laden and uncontrollable. Pathological worry (GAD) is associated with diffuse perceptions that the world is threatening and that one may not be able to cope with or control future negative events (Barlow et al., 1996; Borkovec, 1994). A number of studies have confirmed the notion that worry is characterized by a predominance of thought activity and low levels of imagery (see, e.g., Borkovec & Inz, 1990; Borkovec & Lyonfields, 1993; see also East & Watts, 1994). Borkovec (1994) further postulates that worry is negatively reinforcing because it is associated with the avoidance of or escape from more threatening imagery and more distressing somatic activation. Support for the position that worry may prevent certain somatic experience comes from the host of studies reviewed earlier showing that worry suppresses autonomic activity (see, e.g., Lyonfields et al., 1995).

According to Borkovec's model, although the avoidant functions of worry provide short-term relief from more distressing levels of anxiety, the long-term consequences of worry include the inhibition of emotional processing and the maintenance of anxiety-producing cognitions (see Mathews, 1990). For example, whereas patients with GAD may regard worry as an effective problem-solving strategy that has other benefits (e.g., it prevents catastrophe or prepares one to cope with future negative events), it maintains clinical anxiety for a number of reasons. For example, if worry does indeed serve to foster the avoidance of imagery, then emotional processing of threatening material will be prevented because worry inhibits the complete activation of fear structures in memory—a process considered to be *necessary* for permanent anxiety reduction (Foa & Kozak, 1986). The failure to fully access these fear structures may also account for the autonomic inhibition associated with GAD. The avoidant nature of worry will hinder effective problem solving of true life circumstances (e.g., the content of worry often jumps from topic to another without resolution any particular concern). However, because pathological worry is perceived as uncontrollable and because it prevents emotional processing, the afflicted individual is prone to

experience heightened negative affect and cognitive intrusions in the future. For instance, research has shown that uncontrollability of negative thinking correlates with the intensity and frequency of such thoughts (see, e.g., Clark & DeSilva, 1985; Parkinson & Rachman, 1981). Moreover, although the underlying mechanisms are not clear (see Borkovec, 1994), evidence indicates that worry inductions prior to and/or following exposure to laboratory stressors (e.g., viewing aversive films, giving a speech) preclude emotional processing (anxiety reduction) and increase subsequent intrusive thinking about these stressors (Borkovec & Hu, 1990; Butler, Wells, & Dewick, 1995).

Summary of GAD Features: Targets of Treatment

On the basis of the evidence reviewed above, the two principal components that should form the targets of a treatment intervention for GAD are excessive, uncontrollable worry and its accompanying persistent overarousal (primarily tension-related, central nervous system symptoms). As the ensuing literature review will attest, these cognitive and somatic features have been most frequently addressed with cognitive therapy and some form of relaxation treatment, respectively. Moreover, following recent conceptualizations of the nature of pathological worry (see Borkovec, 1994), the utility of targeting GAD worry via an exposure-based paradigm has recently emerged as a potentially effective treatment component for GAD (see, e.g., Craske, Barlow, & O'Leary, 1992). For instance, as noted above, worry has been conceptualized as a negative reinforcer that serves to dampen physiological reactivity to emotional processing (Borkovec & Hu, 1990). In a sense, worry may serve to hinder complete processing of more disturbing thoughts or images. This is often evident during the process of decatastrophizing—a form of cognitive restructuring described later, where the patient is reluctant to elaborate on the worst possible outcome of a feared negative event. Instead, the patient may feel more comfortable ruminating over his/her anxious thoughts and then distracting from the catastrophic thought or image.

Perhaps due in part to the effects of some of the aforementioned characteristics of GAD (e.g., its "characterological" nature, the high rate of comorbidity), studies have noted only modest treatment gains following cognitive-behavioral or pharmacological interventions. This is particularly true in relation to the efficacy of these forms of treatments for other anxiety disorders (see Brown, Hertz, & Barlow, 1992). In addition, whereas most studies have found the treatments examined to be effective to some degree, comparative outcome studies have rarely observed differential efficacy among active treatment conditions. Another factor that may have contributed to these modest treatment gains and lack of differential efficacy concerns the types of treatments that have been examined thus far. Given that GAD did not possess a key diagnostic feature (i.e., excessive worry) until the publication of DSM-III-R, the majority of outcome studies conducted through the late 1980s examined the effectiveness of rather nonspecific interventions (e.g., relaxation training). By comparison, extant treatments for other anxiety disorders contain elements specifically tailored to address essential features of the disorder in question. For example, in panic control treatment for panic disorder, components of breathing retraining and interoceptive exposure address hyperventilation and fear of physical sensations, respectively (see Craske & Barlow, Chapter 1, this volume). However, as will be noted later in this chapter, new treatments have recently been developed that specifically target the key feature of excessive, uncontrollable worry. Prior to delineating these treatments, we provide an overview of the treatment literature on GAD.

OVERVIEW OF TREATMENT OUTCOME STUDIES

Early treatment studies for GAD typically entailed the examination of the efficacy of relaxation-based treatments or biofeedback. Whereas the majority of these earlier studies used analogue participants (e.g., mildly anxious college students), the few studies utilizing clinical samples observed quite modest treatment effects when using these forms of treatment in isolation from other procedures. For instance, LeBoeuf and Lodge (1980) reported that only 4 of 26 patients showed more than marginal improvement in response to relaxation alone.

Only within the past 15 years have studies emerged that examined the efficacy of treatments for GAD with rigorous methodology (e.g., use of structured interviews to establish diagnoses, inclusion of control or comparison groups, assessment of short- and long-term effects of treatment via multiple measures). The types of "active" treatments examined in these studies have typically included cognitive therapy, relaxation training, anxiety management training, or some combination of these procedures. Most often, these treatments have been compared to nondirective treatments and/or wait-list control conditions. With regard to the use of wait-list comparison groups, these active treatments have been shown to produce greater improvement than no treatment (see, e.g., Barlow et al., 1984; Barlow, Rapee, & Brown, 1992; Blowers, Cobb, & Mathews, 1987; Butler, Cullington, Hibbert, Klimes, & Gelder, 1987; Lindsay, Gamsu, McLaughlin, Hood, & Espie, 1987). Moreover, studies reporting long-term outcome data (i.e., clinical functioning 6 or more months after treatment) have generally shown a maintenance of treatment gains (see, e.g., Barlow et al., 1992; Borkovec & Costello, 1993; Borkovec & Mathews, 1988; Butler et al., 1987, 1991).

Another important finding observed in recent studies providing long-term outcome data is the substantial reduction in anxiolytic medication usage in treated subjects over the follow-up period (see, e.g., Barlow et al., 1992; Butler et al., 1991; White & Keenan, 1992). For instance, Barlow and colleagues (1992) noted that whereas many of their patients were using benzodiazepines at pretreatment (33%–55%), virtually all had discontinued medication usage by the 2-year follow-up. This finding is salient in light of the fact that benzodiazepines are particularly refractory to discontinuation (see Schweizer & Rickels, 1991), and it may indicate that psychosocial treatments of the nature examined in Barlow and colleagues (1992) may have utility as an approach to discontinuation of these types of medications.

However, as noted above, most studies have failed to observe clear evidence of differential efficacy when comparing two or more active treatments (see, e.g., Barlow et al., 1992; Borkovec & Mathews, 1988; Durham & Turvey, 1987; Lindsay et al., 1987), although there are a few exceptions to this general finding (see, e.g., Butler et al., 1991). Perhaps even more discouraging is the finding showing no differences between cognitive-behavioral treatments and credible nondirective treatments (Blowers et al., 1987; Borkovec & Mathews, 1988; White et al., 1991), although one study is a notable exception (Borkovec & Costello, 1993). Despite the lack of evidence for differential efficacy in most of these studies, both the "active" and nondirective treatments produced significant (relative to a wait-list control) and durable gains. Nevertheless, the collective findings indicating a lack of differential efficacy among active treatments or between active and nondirective treatments in most studies underscore the importance of continuing the search for effective mechanisms of action (see Butler & Booth, 1991).

Moreover, research on the development and effectiveness of psychosocial interventions for childhood and adolescent GAD is sorely needed. The virtual absence of research in this area is due mainly to the fact that GAD was not considered a childhood/adolescent disorder until publication of DSM-IV (replacing the category "overanxious disorder of childhood"). Currently, the most pertinent work in this area has focused on cognitive-behavioral and familial treatments targeting heterogeneous childhood anxiety samples (see, e.g., Barrett, Dadds, & Rapee, 1996; Kendall, 1994).

Prior to outlining the application of specific techniques pertaining to the assessment and treatment of GAD, we review, in greater detail, a few noteworthy treatment outcome studies (i.e., studies producing evidence for differential efficacy among active treatments and/or observing quite encouraging treatment gains). For example, in the first of a series of studies, Butler et al. (1987) evaluated an anxiety management package for GAD that was loosely based on the early important work on anxiety management by Suinn and Richardson (1971). Treatment consisted of teaching patients to cope with various aspects of their anxiety via such methods as self-administered relaxation procedures and distraction procedures to deal with cognitive aspects of anxiety. The subtle types of avoidance of both somatic and situational cues often found in patients with GAD were also addressed. Patients were encouraged to take control of their lives by scheduling more pleasurable activities and noting areas in their lives in which they

were functioning well. Patients receiving this treatment were compared to a wait-list control group. Relative to the wait-list controls ($n = 23$), patients receiving the anxiety management package ($n = 22$) evidenced greater improvement on all measures of anxiety (e.g., Hamilton rating scales, State–Trait Anxiety Inventory). At a 6-month follow-up, improvement on these measures was either maintained or increased further. For example, in the active treatment group, Hamilton Anxiety Scale scores showed an average 59% reduction immediately following treatment (from a mean of 16 to a mean of 6.6) and a 69% reduction by the 6-month follow-up (to a mean of 5.0). As we have noted elsewhere, the latter figure exceeds the greatest benefit reported in any study evaluating the short-term effects of benzodiazepines on generalized anxiety (Barlow, 1988; Brown et al., 1992). However, this observation should be tempered by the facts that direct comparisons to a medication group were not made and that the investigators only included patients who suffered substantial anxiety for 2 years or less, thereby eliminating any patients with "chronic" anxiety.

In their second study, Butler and colleagues (1991) compared a more extensive cognitive therapy based on the work of Beck, Emery, and Greenberg (1985) with a version of their anxiety management treatment stripped of any cognitive therapy. The investigators opted to evaluate cognitive therapy in this manner, because they hypothesized that this approach might have a more dramatic effect on the prominent symptom of worry in GAD. Treatment consisted of weekly sessions lasting up to 12 weeks. Booster sessions were also provided at 2, 4, and 6 weeks after treatment. At posttreatment, whereas both treatment groups evidenced significant improvement relative to a wait-list control group ($n = 19$), patients receiving cognitive therapy ($n = 19$) were significantly better on most measures than patients receiving the intervention without cognitive therapy ($n = 18$). At a 6-month follow-up, both treatment groups maintained their gains, with the cognitive therapy group continuing to show greater improvement than the behavior therapy group on most measures. Consistent with the findings of Barlow and colleagues (1992), treatment had a substantial impact on medication usage in this sample. Whereas 40% of patients in the two treatment groups were taking anxiolytic and/or hypnotic medication at pretreatment, only 24% were still taking medication at posttreatment. Six months later, this had fallen to 15%, with every patient reducing his/her usual dosage.

Butler and colleagues (1991) evaluated the clinical significance of treatment gains via the application of rather stringent criteria of end-state functioning (i.e., scoring within the "normal" range on three measures of anxiety: Hamilton Anxiety Scale, Beck Anxiety Inventory, Leeds Anxiety Scale). At posttreatment, the percentages of patients falling within the normal range on all three measures were 32% and 16% for the cognitive therapy and behavior therapy groups, respectively. At the 6-month follow-up, this percentage had risen in the cognitive therapy group (42%), but fallen markedly in the behavior therapy group (5%). These modest findings demonstrate once again that GAD can be a chronic and severe problem, and that there is much room for improvements in our treatments. Moreover, whereas the Butler and colleagues (1991) study represents one of the few providing evidence of differential efficacy among active treatment conditions, Borkovec and Costello (1993) noted that the behavior therapy condition in this study produced the lowest amount of change among the extant treatment studies on GAD. Thus, regardless of the reasons for the limited efficacy of this condition, the negligible gains produced by behavior therapy provided a liberal standard for detecting between-groups differences with another active treatment condition (e.g., only 5% of patients treated with behavior therapy met high end-state functioning criteria at 6-month follow-up).

The most recently published major psychosocial outcome study for GAD was authored by Borkovec and Costello (1993). In this investigation, the comparative efficacy of applied relaxation (AR), cognitive-behavioral therapy (CBT), and nondirective treatment (ND) was examined in a sample of 55 patients carefully diagnosed as having DSM-III-R GAD. AR consisted of teaching patients progressive muscle relaxation (PMR) with slow breathing. PMR initially entailed 16 muscle groups gradually reduced down to 4 groups, with the learning of cue-controlled relaxation and relaxation-by-recall to facilitate the deployment of relaxation procedures quickly and early in the process of anxiety activation. CBT included the elements of AR as well, but

also included the components of coping desensitization and cognitive therapy. Coping desensitization involved the generation of a hierarchy listing each patient's anxiety-provoking situations and his/her cognitive and somatic responses to these situations. After the patient was deeply relaxed, the therapist would present external and internal anxiety cues and instruct him/her to continue to imagine these cues while, at the same time, imagining himself/herself using relaxation skills in that situation. Each scene in the hierarchy was repeated until it no longer elicited anxiety. The cognitive therapy component of CBT was modeled after the procedures outlined in Beck and colleagues (1985), aimed at the generation of situation-specific cognitive coping responses.

Patients in the ND condition were told that the goals of treatment were to enhance self-understanding and to discover, through their own efforts, things that they could do differently to affect how they feel. Therapists did not provide specific information about GAD, nor did they provide direct advice or coping methods for dealing with anxiety; instead, their role was to provide a time of self-reflection while assisting patients to clarify or focus on their feelings.

Results indicated that despite the lack of differences among conditions in credibility, expectancy, and patient perception of the therapeutic relationship, the AR and CBT conditions were clearly superior to ND at posttreatment. This was evidenced by between-group comparisons, within-group change, and the proportion of patients meeting high end-state functioning criteria. Differences at posttreatment were particularly noteworthy because they indicated that elements of AR and CBT contained active ingredients independent of nonspecific factors. Whereas no clear evidence of differential efficacy was obtained for the AR and CBT conditions at posttreatment, 12-month follow-up results indicated that in addition to a maintenance of treatment gains across this follow-up period in both conditions, more patients treated with CBT met high end-state criteria (57.9%) than those in the AR condition (37.5%). Conversely, 12-month follow-up results indicated losses in treatment gains in the ND condition (percentage meeting high end-state criteria = 26.7%); in fact, a significantly greater number of patients (61.1%) treated in this condition requested further treatment at the end of the active treatment phase than subjects in the AR and CBT conditions (16.7% and 15.8%, respectively). Borkovec and Costello (1993) noted that the AR and CBT treatments in this study produced some of the largest treatment effect sizes noted in the GAD treatment literature to date; however, they acknowledged the fact that because only one-third and roughly one-half of patients in the AR and CBT groups, respectively, met high end-state functioning criteria at 12-month follow-up, the evolution of psychosocial treatments for GAD must continue.

Nevertheless, in a separate report based on this sample, Borkovec, Abel, and Newman (1995) observed that psychosocial treatment of GAD resulted in a significant decline in comorbid diagnoses (social phobia and specific phobia were the most commonly co-occurring conditions). Although treatment condition (AR, CBT, ND) was not found to have a differential impact on decline in comorbidity, a significantly higher drop in additional diagnoses was noted in patients who were classified as treatment successes. Specifically, whereas 45% of the treatment success group had at least one additional diagnosis at pretreatment, the comorbidity rate declined to 14%, 4%, and 4% at posttreatment, 6-month follow-up, and 12-month follow-up, respectively. In contrast, 83% of the treatment failure group had at least one additional diagnosis at pretreatment; this rate dropped to 67%, 40%, and 10% at posttreatment, 6-month follow-up, and 12-month follow-up, respectively.

We have developed a treatment for GAD that includes a component that addresses worry directly (i.e., worry exposure), taking advantage of the knowledge gained in the development of exposure-based treatments for panic disorder. In a pilot study (O'Leary, Brown, & Barlow, 1992), the efficacy of worry exposure in its pure form (i.e., without other elements such as relaxation training or cognitive therapy) was evaluated in three patients via a multiple-baseline across-subjects design. Worry exposure was completed in both intersession and intrasession exercises. Patients self-monitored daily levels of mood and worry; they also completed several questionnaires weekly, including the PSWQ (Meyer et al., 1990), the Depression Anxiety Stress Scales (DASS; Lovibond & Lovibond, 1995),

and an earlier version of the Anxiety Control Questionnaire (ACQ; Rapee, Craske, Brown, & Barlow, 1996).

Results indicated that two of the three patients evidenced clinically significant decreases in daily levels of anxiety and depression, along with dramatic declines in PSWQ scores. Although the third patient did not show as dramatic a decline in her levels of worry and anxiety, elevations in her ACQ scores over the course of treatment showed increased self-perceptions of control over worry and other emotional states. In addition, an examination of all patients' anxiety ratings after generating the worst possible feared outcome (peak anxiety) and then after having generated alternatives to that outcome (postanxiety) revealed habituation effects: Peak anxiety ratings were consistently higher than postanxiety ratings, suggesting that the intervention was indeed effective as a deconditioning strategy, as had been originally hypothesized. Over the past several years, our research has focused on a number of variables relevant to the process of worry (e.g., negative affect, attentional allocation, self-focused attention, autonomic arousability) and methods of effectively treating worry and related features of GAD (Brown, Marten, & Barlow, 1995; Brown et al., 1998; DiBartolo, Brown, & Barlow, 1997). At the same time, we have continued to administer our treatment protocol to patients with a principal diagnosis of GAD.

The remainder of this chapter is devoted to a description of this treatment and to our approach to the assessment of GAD. A combined treatment protocol for GAD is described that includes worry exposure, as well as cognitive therapy, relaxation training. and other strategies (e.g., worry behavior prevention, problem solving).

THE CONTEXT OF THERAPY

Setting

Assessment and treatment of patients with GAD occur within the Center for Anxiety and Related Disorders at Boston University. Presently at the center, we have close to 400 new admissions per year. GAD is roughly the fourth most frequent principal diagnosis in our center (behind panic disorder with agoraphobia, social phobia, and specific phobia, and occurring at about the same frequency as major depression), accounting for approximately 8% of our new admissions. "Principal" means that although a patient may have several comorbid diagnoses, GAD is the most severe. Patients requesting assessment and/or treatment at our center first undergo a brief screening (usually conducted over the telephone) to ascertain their eligibility (i.e., appropriateness) for an evaluation at our center. At this time, eligible patients are scheduled to undergo the standard intake evaluation. This evaluation entails the administration of one or two structured interviews, the Anxiety Disorders Interview Schedule for DSM-IV: Lifetime Version (ADIS-IV-L; Di Nardo, Brown, & Barlow, 1994), and a battery of questionnaires. Once a patient has completed the intake evaluation and has received a principal diagnosis (determined at a weekly staff meeting in which consensus diagnoses are established), he/she is contacted by the center staff member who conducted the initial ADIS-IV-L. At that time, the patient is provided the results of the evaluation and given a treatment referral. The majority of patients receiving a DSM-IV anxiety or mood disorder as their principal diagnosis are offered a referral to one of the ongoing treatment programs in our center. After acceptance in the program, patients typically complete additional assessments specific to the treatment program and their presenting, principal disorder (e.g., pretreatment self-monitoring of anxiety and worry; see below).

In the past, our treatment programs for GAD have been conducted in both individual and small-group (i.e., five to eight patients) formats. Whereas the GAD treatment protocol described in this chapter has been administered in both formats, at the present time we feel that it is best suited to be delivered in one-on-one hourly treatment sessions, given some of the practical difficulties of implementing the "worry exposure" component in a small-group format (see below). We have not found the integrity of the relaxation and cognitive restructuring components to be compromised substantially by the small-group format; in fact, in some cases this format may have certain advantages, depending on the composition of the group (e.g., group assistance in cognitive restructuring). Nevertheless, the extent to which the format of treatment is associated with treatment outcome is an area that awaits future investigation.

Patient Variables

The earlier section concerning the nature of GAD provides some indication of features of patients with GAD that may have an impact on the treatment process. Beyond the features constituting the DSM-IV criteria for the disorder, one characteristic that is particularly salient to the process of treatment is the high rate of comorbidity evident in patients with a principal diagnosis of GAD. Although this area has received little empirical attention as of yet (see Brown & Barlow, 1992), the existence of coexisting psychological disorders must be considered by the therapist in treatment planning. For example, given the close boundaries among generalized anxiety, worry, and depression (see Andrews & Borkovec, 1988; Zinbarg & Barlow, 1991), the extent to which the patient with GAD exhibits depression at either the symptom or syndrome level must be acknowledged, as depression has been associated with a poorer treatment response to cognitive-behavioral treatments for GAD (see, e.g., Barlow et al., 1992). Moreover, given that panic disorder and GAD often co-occur (see Brown & Barlow, 1992), the presence of comorbid panic disorder should be acknowledged, given its potential association with the problem of relaxation-induced anxiety.

Another characteristic that may be relevant to treatment outcome is the extent to which the patient's worry is "ego-syntonic." Adding some support for the conceptualization of GAD as a characterological disorder (see, e.g., Sanderson & Wetzler, 1991), we have observed that some patients with GAD evidence resistance in countering or attempting to reduce their worrying—either because they view their worry as adaptive (e.g., worry is perceived as reducing the likelihood of the occurrence of some negative event), or because they consider their worry as such an integral part of themselves that they express concern about how they will be when they no longer have anything to worry about. Often these patients present for treatment to receive help in reducing the somatic component of their disorder, and may not even see worry as related to their symptoms of persistent tension and hyperarousal. This has only been a clinical observation, and, to our knowledge, no evidence exists attesting to the prevalence and salience of this characteristic in predicting treatment outcome.

Therapist Variables

Given that research on the efficacy of cognitive-behavioral treatments for GAD is still in its infancy relative to research in conditions such as panic disorder, to date no data exist regarding therapist variables associated with treatment outcome. Although little can be said about the empirical basis of therapist qualities, we would certainly contend that therapists should possess a firm grounding in the use of cognitive-behavioral techniques, in addition to a thorough understanding of current models of worry and GAD. Moreover, because cognitive therapy is one of the core components of our treatment for GAD, therapists should possess the ability to deliver the active elements of this treatment (see Beck et al., 1985; Young, Weinberger, & Beck, Chapter 6, this volume)—for instance, the use of the Socratic method, collaborative empiricism, and ability to assist the patient in identifying and challenging automatic thoughts. Ideally, they should also possess the "nonspecific" qualities considered to be evident in the most effective cognitive therapists (e.g., ability to communicate trust, accurate empathy, and warmth; ability to reason logically themselves; ability to tailor the principles and techniques of cognitive therapy to the individual needs of the patient).

We find that among the various components of our treatment of GAD, patients have the most difficulty in learning and applying the cognitive techniques in a manner in which they are most effective. In addition, therapists who are training to learn our GAD treatment protocol are apt to require the most supervision and guidance in learning to deliver the cognitive therapy component. In the case of both the patients and the therapists-in-training, the most commonly occurring difficulty is that the methods of identifying and/or countering anxiogenic cognitions are not applied thoroughly (e.g., application of countering prior to identifying the most salient automatic thoughts; insufficient countering of automatic thoughts via the generation of incomplete or inappropriate counterarguments). We return to this issue in a later section.

As we also note later in this chapter, a solid background in cognitive-behavioral theory and therapy is an asset when applying the exposure-based treatment component of our GAD treatment package. This knowledge will help ensure that the parameters of effective therapeutic exposure are delivered with integrity (e.g., recognition and prevention of patients' distraction, provision of an ample exposure duration to promote habituation in patients' anxiety to images denoting their worry).

ASSESSMENT

Classification

Of the anxiety disorders, GAD remains among the diagnoses most difficult to establish with high reliability (see Di Nardo, Moras, Barlow, Rapee, & Brown, 1993). Whereas the revisions in diagnostic criteria of GAD introduced in DSM-III-R improved diagnostic agreement rates somewhat, in our study examining the reliability of the DSM-III-R anxiety disorders via the administration of two independent ADIS-R interviews, the kappa for GAD when assigned as a principal diagnosis was only fair (kappa = .57; Di Nardo et al., 1993). In our currently ongoing study involving DSM-IV anxiety and mood disorders evaluated with the ADIS-IV-L, reliability of the principal diagnosis of GAD has increased somewhat (kappa = .67; Brown, Di Nardo, Lehman, & Campbell, in press). Nevertheless, the consistent finding of lower diagnostic reliability of GAD relative to other anxiety disorders has led to the call by some investigators to mandate, as an inclusion criterion for studies examining patients with GAD, the confirmation of the GAD diagnosis via two independent diagnostic interviews (see Borkovec & Costello, 1993).

As we have articulated elsewhere (see, e.g., Brown et al., 1994; Di Nardo et al., 1993), many factors may be contributing to the lower rates of diagnostic agreement for GAD. For instance, some recent models noted earlier conceptualize GAD as the "basic" anxiety disorder because its defining features reflect fundamental processes of anxiety (see Barlow, 1988, 1991; Rapee, 1991). If these models are valid, one would expect that the distinctiveness of the diagnosis would be mitigated by the fact that its features are present to some extent in all of the anxiety and mood disorders. Moreover, GAD is defined solely by features involving internal processes (i.e., excessive worry, persistent symptoms of tension or arousal). Thus the lack of a clear "key feature" defining the disorder may also contribute to lower diagnostic reliability, in contrast to the high rates of diagnostic agreement for disorders in which these features are often, or necessarily, present (e.g., compulsions in OCD, phobic avoidance in specific phobia; see Di Nardo et al., 1993).

Other aspects of the diagnostic criteria for GAD should also be considered in the exploration of potential factors contributing to lower its diagnostic reliability. For example, DSM-IV specifies that GAD should not be assigned when the symptoms defining the disturbance occur only during the course of a mood disorder, psychotic disorder, or a pervasive developmental disorder (see Criterion F in Table 4.1). This diagnostic specification was incorporated in part to facilitate parsimony in the assignment of diagnoses (e.g., to prevent the assignment of both Diagnosis A and B when the features of Diagnosis B can be subsumed as associated features of Diagnosis A, the more debilitating disturbance of the two). However, particularly in the case of the mood disorders (e.g., major depression, dysthymia), many patients report a clinical history marked by a chronic course of alternating or overlapping episodes of depression and persistent anxiety (see Zinbarg & Barlow, 1991). Thus the clinician may often be in the somewhat difficult position of relying on the patient's retrospective report regarding the temporal sequence and duration of anxiety and depressive episodes to determine whether the diagnostic criteria for GAD have been met in the absence of a mood disorder.

In addition, DSM-IV criteria for GAD specify that "the focus of anxiety and worry is not confined to features of a single Axis I disorder" (see Criterion D in Table 4.1). In many cases, the determination of whether the patient's worries represent areas of apprehension relating to another disorder can be relatively straightforward (e.g., in a patient with comorbid panic disorder, excluding worry over experiencing a future unexpected panic as a potential GAD worry). Nevertheless, particularly in light of the evidence for the high rate of comorbidity between GAD and other anxiety and mood disorders (see, e.g., Brawman-Mintzer et al., 1993; Brown & Barlow, 1992; Sanderson et al., 1990), these distinctions can occasionally be quite difficult. For example, is persistent worry about being late for appointments a manifestation of fear of negative evaluation (characteristic of social phobia), or is it reflective of a general tendency to worry about a host of minor matters (often characteristic of GAD)? (See Chorpita, Brown, & Barlow, 1998.) In addition, careful interviewing may be needed to clarify whether an area of worry that appears ostensibly to be prototypical GAD worry is actually an area of worry that has arisen due to another disorder. For instance, has concern about job performance and finances been a long-standing, frequent worry for the patient, or did these concerns arise only after the onset of unexpected panic attacks and now the patient worries that the panics will occur at work, thereby interfering with job performance or attendance?

Under DSM-III-R, another potential source of diagnostic unreliability involved the requirement of the presence of two distinct spheres of worry. In an attempt to discern sources of unreliability of the GAD diagnosis, Di Nardo and colleagues (1993) noted that diagnosticians occasionally disagreed whether a topic of worry should be considered as a single sphere as opposed to two separate spheres (e.g., Interviewer A deems a patient's worry about the health of his wife and the health and safety of his children as a single sphere, "family concerns," whereas Interviewer B views these as two distinct spheres of worry). In DSM-IV, this issue may be less salient due to the fact that DSM-IV criteria do not require the presence of two separate spheres of worry (see Criterion A in Table 4.1). However, under DSM-IV, clinical judgment is still required to determine what constitutes excessive worry about "a *number* of events or activities" (Criterion A; our emphasis).

Finally, to achieve favorable diagnostic reliability of GAD, the criteria for the diagnosis should facilitate the distinction between "normal" and "pathological" worry. To aid in this distinction, the DSM-IV worry criteria state that the worry must be "excessive" and "occur more days than not for at least 6 months," and perceived by the worrier as "difficult to control" (see Criteria A and B, Table 4.1). As noted earlier, the 6-month duration criterion was specified in part to differentiate GAD from transient reactions to psychosocial stressors, which may be more aptly diagnosed as forms of adjustment disorder. We have previously reviewed evidence attesting to the ability to distinguish normal and pathological worry on such dimensions as amount of time spent worrying and perceived uncontrollability of the worry process (Borkovec et al., 1991; Craske, Rapee, et al., 1989; Di Nardo, 1991). Despite this evidence, Di Nardo and colleagues (1993) noted that confusion surrounding the excessive/unrealistic judgment requirements contributed to the occurrence of diagnostic disagreements in that study, which used DSM-III-R criteria. Whether or not this source of diagnostic confusion has been reduced by the changes to the worry criteria in DSM-IV (Criteria A and B) that emphasize and better operationalize the controllability and pervasiveness of worry reduce awaits empirical examination.

Collectively, the issues mentioned above suggest that the chances of reliably identifying GAD-related worries are slim. On the contrary, several studies have found that the content and presence of GAD-related worry can be reliably identified (Barlow & Di Nardo, 1991; Borkovec et al., 1991; Craske, Rapee, et al., 1989; Sanderson & Barlow, 1990). Moreover, in the process of revising diagnostic criteria for DSM-IV, researchers noted a possible boundary problem between GAD and OCD (see Turner, Beidel, & Stanley, 1992). This concern was raised following the observation that the features of OCD may have the most overlap with the features of GAD (e.g., pervasive worry vs. obsessions, characterological presentation). In addition, the findings of Craske, Rapee, and colleagues (1989) indicate that many GAD worries are associated with behavioral acts designed to reduce anxiety evoked by worry (e.g., checking the safety of one's child as he/she waits for the bus), thus introducing potential overlap with OCD compulsions. Nevertheless, results from Brown, Moras, and colleagues (1993) indicate that the lower diagnostic reliability of GAD is not due to a boundary problem with OCD. Support for this contention was obtained by contrasting 46 patients with GAD and 31 patients with OCD on the basis of interview (ADIS-R) and questionnaire responses. Of the 55% of patients who received two independent ADIS-Rs, in no case did one interviewer assign a principal diagnosis of GAD and the other OCD; this strongly suggested that GAD versus OCD was not a problematic differential diagnostic decision, More-

over, examination of comorbidity patterns indicated that GAD and OCD rarely co-occurred (OCD with additional GAD = 6.5%; GAD with additional OCD = 2%). As noted earlier, scores on the PSWQ, a 16-item measure of the trait of worry (Meyer et al., 1990), successfully discriminated patients with GAD from those with OCD in this study as well. However, despite evidence that various indices of worry can differentiate patients with GAD from patients with other anxiety disorders (see, e.g., Brown, Antony, & Barlow, 1992; Brown, Moras, et al., 1993; Di Nardo, 1991; Meyer et al., 1990; Sanderson & Barlow, 1990), initial evidence suggests that this may not be the case for major depression (Starcevic, 1995). Indeed, the mood disorders may pose a greater boundary problem for GAD than do the anxiety disorders.

In DSM-IV, the associated symptom criterion was revised considerably via the reduction in the number of symptoms in the list from 18 (in DSM-III-R) to 6 (of which the patient must endorse at least 3; see Criterion C in Table 4.1). Whereas initial evidence indicated difficulty in establishing the DSM-III-R symptom ratings reliably (see, e.g., Barlow & Di Nardo, 1991; Fyer et al., 1989), subsequent data indicated satisfactory reliability when interrater agreement was simply calculated on the presence or absence of a symptom (which was required in DSM-III-R), rather than examining interrater concordance on symptom severity ratings (Marten et al., 1993). However, as noted earlier, Marten et al. observed that the symptoms from the DSM-III-R associated symptom clusters of "vigilance and scanning" and "motor tension" were the most reliable and endorsed most frequently by patients with GAD. Accordingly, of the six symptoms retained in the DSM-IV associated symptom criterion, all were from these two clusters.

When a clinician is establishing these ratings, careful interviewing is required to ascertain whether a symptom reported by the patient is associated with excessive worry or is due to a coexisting condition (e.g., does the patient often experience concentration difficulties when worrying about finances, or does this symptom only occur during panic attacks?). Occasionally this is no small task, especially in light of the aforementioned evidence of high rates of comorbidity between GAD and the other anxiety and mood disorders (see, e.g., Brown & Barlow, 1992). Data from Marten and colleagues (1993) indicate that these distinctions may be easier for establishing ratings for the symptoms retained in the DSM-IV associated symptom criterion; indeed, these symptoms may also have discriminant validity, at least in comparison to other anxiety disorders (see Brown, Antony, & Barlow, 1992; Brown, Marten, & Barlow, 1995; Hoehn-Saric et al., 1989). However, initial data indicate that these symptoms do not discriminate GAD from the mood disorders (Brown, Marten, & Barlow, 1995).

The Clinical Interview

The section of the ADIS-IV-L (Di Nardo et al., 1994) that focuses on the clinical assessment of current GAD is presented in Figure 4.1. The preceding section has outlined several issues and potential difficulties that the clinician may encounter when attempting to decide whether to assign the GAD diagnosis. With regard to the worry criteria, these issues include the following: (1) Is the worry excessive? (2) Is the worry pervasive (i.e., worry about "a number of events or activities")? (3) Is the worry perceived by the individual as difficult to control? and (4) Is the focus of worry spheres unrelated to another Axis I condition? After initial screening questions on the possible presence of GAD (e.g., Items 1a and 2a under "Initial Inquiry"), the content of worry and the parameters of excessiveness, pervasiveness, and perceived controllability are assessed via Items 3a through 3j in the "Initial Inquiry" section. Note that all patients, regardless of whether or not GAD is suspected by the clinician, are administered the GAD section through Item 3j. In addition to assisting with assigning or ruling out the GAD diagnosis, this practice is guided by the philosophy that psychopathological phenomena are best regarded and assessed at the dimensional level (e.g., excessive, uncontrollable worry operates on a continuum, not in a dichotomous presence–absence fashion; see Brown et al., 1998).

If evidence of excessive, uncontrollable worry is noted in the "Initial Inquiry" section, the clinician proceeds to the "Current Episode" section for further and more direct assessment of the features bearing on the DSM-IV definition of GAD. This inquiry includes items on the duration and onset of the disor-

der (Items 1 and 8), excessiveness (Item 2), the associated symptom criterion (Item 4), interference and distress (Item 5), and items that provide information on whether the GAD features are better accounted for by other conditions (Items 3, 6, and 7). However, differential diagnosis cannot be accomplished reliably by administration of the GAD section alone. For instance, information obtained from the Major Depression, Dysthymia, and Bipolar Disorder sections of the ADIS-IV-L is needed to determine whether a GAD episode occurred during the course of a mood disorder, which would contraindicate the diagnosis.

Although the ADIS-IV-L provides suggested wording to assist the clinician in determining whether a worry area is excessive and uncontrollable, experience indicates that is often necessary to inquire further to make this determination. Although "prototypical" GAD patients may not require this prompting (e.g., they state that they worry about "everything" upon initial inquiry), some patients consider their worrying to be adaptive or productive, and thus not at all excessive, even though it is associated with considerable tension and arousal (e.g., excessive concern over finances is perceived as ensuring that money will always be available for paying bills or unexpected expenses). Potentially helpful follow-up questions of this nature include the following: (1) "Do you find it very difficult to stop worrying, or, if you need to focus on something else, are you able to successfully put the worry out of your mind?" (2) "Do you find that, if you are attempting to focus on something like reading, working, or watching TV, these worries often pop into your mind, making it difficult to concentrate on these tasks?" (3) "Do you worry about things that you recognize that other people do not worry about?" (4) "When things are going well, do you still find things to be worried and anxious about?" (5) "Does your worry rarely result in your reaching a solution for the problem that you are worrying about?"

Great care is often needed in distinguishing whether the worries identified by the patient represent areas that are independent of a coexisting condition or, in cases where no coexisting diagnosis is present, are more appropriately diagnosed as a disorder other than GAD. As mentioned earlier, some of the more common diagnostic decisions that arise involve distinguishing GAD worry from (1) ap-

GENERALIZED ANXIETY DISORDER

I. INITIAL INQUIRY

Ia. **Over the last several months, have you been continually worried or anxious about a number of events or activities in your daily life?**

YES __ NO __

If NO, skip to Ib.

What kinds of things do you worry about? _____

_____

Skip to 2a.

b. **Have you <u>ever</u> experienced an extended period when you were continually worried or anxious about a number of events or activities in your daily life?**

YES __ NO __

If NO, skip to 3.

What kinds of things did you worry about? _____

_____

When was the most recent time this occurred? _____

2a. **Besides this current/most recent period of time when you have been persistently worried about different areas of your life, have there been other, separate periods of time when you were continually worried about a number of life matters?**

YES __ NO __

If NO, skip to 3.

b. **So prior to this current/most recent period of time when you were worried about different areas of your life, there was a considerable period of time when you were not having these persistent worries?**

YES __ NO __

c. **How much time separated these periods?; When did this/these separate period(s) occur?**

_____

3. **Now I want to ask you a series of questions about worry over the following areas of life:**

If patient does not report current or past persistent worry (i.e., NO to 1a and 1b), inquire about CURRENT areas of worry only. If patient reports current or past persistent worry (i.e., YES to either 1a or 1b), inquire about both CURRENT and PAST areas of worry. Particularly if there is evidence of <u>separate</u> episodes, inquire for the presence of prior <u>discrete</u> episodes of disturbance (e.g., **"Since these worries began, have there been periods of time when you were not bothered by them?"**). Use the space below each general worry area to record the specific content of the patient's worry (including information obtained previously from items Ia and Ib). Further inquiry will often be necessary to determine whether areas of worry reported by patient are unrelated to a co-occurring Axis I disorder. If it is determined that an area of worry can be subsumed totally by another Axis I disorder, rate this area as "0." Use comment section to record clinically useful information (e.g., data pertaining to the discreteness of episodes, coexisting disorder with which the area of worry is related). For each area of worry, make separate ratings of excessiveness (i.e., frequency and intensity) and perceived uncontrollability, using the scales and suggested queries below.

EXCESSIVENESS:

0————1————2————3————4————5————6————7————8

| No worry/
No tension | | Rarely
worried/Mild
tension | | Occasionally
worried/Moderate
tension | | Frequently
worried/Severe
tension | | Constantly
worried/Extreme
tension |

(*cont.*)

FIGURE 4.1. Generalized Anxiety Disorder section of the Anxiety Disorders Interview Schedule for DSM-IV: Lifetime Version (ADIS-IV-L). From Di Nardo, Brown, and Barlow (1994). Copyright 1994 by the Psychological Corporation. Reprinted by permission.

CONTROLLABILITY:

0————1————2————3————4————5————6————7————8

Never/ No difficulty	Rarely/ Slight difficulty	Occasionally/ Moderate difficulty	Frequently/ Marked difficulty	Constantly/ Extreme difficulty

EXCESSIVENESS:

How often do/did you worry about _____?; If things are/were going well, do/did you still worry about _____?; How much tension and anxiety does/did the worry about _____ produce?

UNCONTROLLABILITY:

Do/did you find it hard to control the worry about _____ in that it is/was difficult to stop worrying about it?; Is/was the worry about _____ hard to control in that it will/would come into your mind when you are/were trying to focus on something else?

	CURRENT			PAST	
	EXCESS	CONTROL	COMMENTS	EXCESS	CONTROL
a. Minor matters (e.g., punctuality, small repairs)	___	___	_____	___	___
b. Work/school	___	___	_____	___	___
c. Family	___	___	_____	___	___
d. Finances	___	___	_____	___	___
e. Social/interpersonal	___	___	_____	___	___
f. Health (self)	___	___	_____	___	___
g. Health (significant others)	___	___	_____	___	___
h. Community/world affairs	___	___	_____	___	___
i. Other	___	___	_____	___	___
j. Other	___	___	_____	___	___

If no evidence of excessive/uncontrollable worry is obtained, skip to **OBSESSIVE–COMPULSIVE DISORDER**

II. CURRENT EPISODE

If evidence of a discrete past episode, preface inquiry in this section with: **Now I want to ask you a series of questions about this current period of worry over these areas that began roughly in _____ (specify** month/year).

List principal topics of worry: _____

1. During the past 6 months, have you been bothered by these worries more days than not?

YES __ NO __

(cont.)

2. **On an average day over the past month, what percentage of the day did you feel worried?**

_____%

3. **Specifically, what types of things do you worry might happen regarding** _____
   (inquire for each principal area of worry)**?**

_____

_____

_____

4. **During the past 6 months, have you often experienced** _____ **when you worried?; Has** _____
   been present more days than not over the past 6 months? (Do not record symptoms that are
   associated with other conditions such as panic, social anxiety, etc.)

   0————1————2————3————4————5————6————7————8
   None   Mild   Moderate   Severe   Very severe

	SEVERITY	MORE DAYS THAN NOT
a. Restlessness; feeling keyed up or on edge	____	Y N
b. Being easily fatigued	____	Y N
c. Difficulty concentrating or mind going blank	____	Y N
d. Irritability	____	Y N
e. Muscle tension	____	Y N
f. Difficulty falling/staying asleep; restless/unsatisfying sleep	____	Y N

5. **In what ways have these worries and the tension/anxiety associated with them interfered with your
   life (e.g., daily routine, job, social activities)?; How much are you bothered about having these
   worries?** _____

_____

Rate interference: _____ distress: _____

   0————1————2————3————4————5————6————7————8
   None   Mild   Moderate   Severe   Very severe

6. **Over this entire current period of time when you've been having these worries and ongoing feelings
   of tension/anxiety, have you been regularly taking any types of drugs** (e.g., drugs of abuse,
   medication)?

   YES __ NO __

   Specify (type; amount; dates of use): _____

_____

7. **During this current period of time when you've been having the worries and ongoing feelings of
   tension/anxiety, have you had any physical condition** (e.g., hyperthyroidism)?

   YES __ NO __

   Specify (type; date of onset/remission): _____

_____

8a. **For this current period of time, when did these worries and symptoms of tension/anxiety become a
   problem in that they occurred persistently, you were bothered by the worry or symptoms and found
   them hard to control, or they interfered with your life in some way?** (Note: If patient is vague in date of
   onset, attempt to ascertain more specific information, e.g., by linking onset to objective life events.)

_____

Date of onset: _____ Month _____ Year

b. **Can you recall anything that might have led to this problem?** _____

_____

_____

c. **Were you under any type of stress during this time?**

   YES __ NO __

   What was happening in your life at the time?

_____

_____

(*cont.*)

FIGURE 4.1. (*cont.*)

Were you experiencing any difficulties or changes in:

(1) **Family/relationships?** _____

(2) **Work/school?** _____

(3) **Finances?** _____

(4) **Legal matters?** _____

(5) **Health** (self/others)? _____

9. **Besides this current period of worry and tension/anxiety, have there been other, separate periods of time before this when you have had the same problems?**

YES __ NO __

If YES, go back and ask 2b and 2c from INITIAL INQUIRY.

If NO, skip to RESEARCH or OBSESSIVE–COMPULSIVE DISORDER.

---

prehension over future panic attacks or the feared consequences of panic, (2) OCD obsessions, and (3) apprehension over negative social evaluation. Differentiating excessive worry about one's health or contracting a physical illness from hypochondriacal concerns can at times be a difficult task. Follow-up questions beyond those suggested in the ADIS-IV-L are often required toward this end. Of course, the most important factor in correctly making these distinctions is the possession of a thorough knowledge of the diagnostic criteria for all disorders that may pose a boundary problem with GAD. Although it is sometimes difficult to establish this reliably (especially when patients report a long-standing history of two or more disorders), the temporal sequence of the onset of their symptoms can often be helpful in determining whether areas of worry (as well as associated somatic symptoms) have arisen in response to another disorder. As noted earlier, information pertaining to temporal sequence and duration is particularly important in the presence of signs of a coexisting mood disorder.

Item 4 of the "Current Episode" section assesses for the presence of the six associated symptoms. The patient must report that over the past 6 months, three or more of these symptoms have been present more days than not in association with the worry. The task of acquiring these ratings during the clinical interview is usually straightforward. However, care should be taken to ensure that the symptoms endorsed are ones that (1) have occurred often over the past 6 months (i.e., persistent symptoms); and (2) do not occur exclusively or predominantly as symptoms of another disorder (e.g., are not symptoms of a panic attack, generalized social anxiety, or substance use).

In many clinical settings, the administration of entire interview schedules such as the ADIS-IV-L is impractical. Nevertheless, the clinician should comprehensively screen for additional diagnoses (using, perhaps, portions of interview schedules such as the ADIS-IV-L), given (1) the need to determine whether the features of GAD are better accounted for by another disorder, and (2) the fact that patients with GAD rarely present with this as their sole diagnosis. In regard to the latter point, although data are sparse on this issue to date, the presence of comorbid conditions exerts a great influence on the patient's response to treatment (see Brown & Barlow, 1992). A brief medical history should be gathered as well, to determine whether current or past medical conditions (or medications) are contributing to, or even responsible for, symptoms constituting the patient's clinical presentation (e.g., hyperthyroidism, temporomandibular joint dysfunction). Often patients should be encouraged to schedule a physical examination if over 2 years have elapsed since their last medical workup. Moreover, patterns of alcohol and drug use should be evaluated, given that excessive use of or withdrawal from such substances may produce symptoms that are quite similar to those of GAD and other anxiety disorders (Chambless, Cherney, Caputo, & Rheinstein, 1987).

Questionnaires

The administration of a variety of self-report questionnaires is a useful part of the clinical process, both as an aid in the initial diagnostic process and for periodic assessment throughout the course of treatment to evaluate the extent of patients' progress. At our clinic, we routinely administer a battery of questionnaires as part of the intake evaluation; these measures were selected to assess the range of the key and associated features of the DSM-IV anxiety and mood disorders (e.g., anxiety sensitivity, social anxiety, obsessions, compulsions, worry, negative and positive affect, depression). Although this extensive intake battery is administered in part for research purposes at our clinic, a battery of questionnaires selected to assess several dimensions of the emotional disorders can be useful in purely clinical settings as well. For example, questionnaire results reflecting elevations in dimensions of anxiety or mood, in addition to dimensions constituting the patient's principal complaint, may have important ramifications in the delivery of treatment and the monitoring of treatment outcome. This is particularly true for GAD, which most often co-occurs with other disorders such as panic disorder and social phobia (Brown & Barlow, 1992).

Having noted that a comprehensive questionnaire battery can be an important component of the diagnostic and treatment armamentarium, we now discuss a few measures that we have found to be particularly useful in the assessment of GAD. We have previously mentioned the PSWQ (Meyer et al., 1990) as a measure that we have frequently used in our work with GAD. The PSWQ was developed by Borkovec and his colleagues at Penn State University to address the need for an easily administered, valid measure of the trait of worry. Indeed, at 16 items, the PSWQ can be administered to patients quite conveniently (range of possible scores = 16 to 80). In their initial study introducing this measure, these researchers found the PSWQ to possess high internal consistency and temporal stability, to have favorable convergent and discriminant validity, and to be uncorrelated with social desirability (Meyer et al., 1990). In a study we conducted using a large sample of patients with anxiety disorders (n = 436) and 32 nonanxious controls (Brown, Antony, & Barlow, 1992), we replicated the findings of Meyer and colleagues (1990) indicating the favorable psychometric properties of the PSWQ. Most encouraging was the finding in this study indicating that scores on the PSWQ distinguished patients with GAD (n = 50) from patients with each of the other anxiety disorders, including OCD. The mean PSWQ score for patients with GAD was 68.11 (SD = 9.59).

Means and standard deviations for selected other diagnoses were as follows: panic disorder with agoraphobia, M = 58.30, SD = 13.65; social phobia, M = 53.99, SD = 15.05; OCD, M = 60.84, SD = 14.55; no anxiety disorder, M = 34.90, SD = 10.98.

Although perhaps less well known than other measures of its kind, another measure (also mentioned earlier) that has proven quite valuable in our work with patients with GAD is the DASS (Lovibond & Lovibond, 1995). The DASS is a 42-item measure that yields three psychometrically distinct subscales reflective of current (i.e., past-week) symptoms. Among the three subscales, the Stress subscale has been particularly helpful in the assessment of GAD. For example, in the Brown, Antony, and Barlow (1992) study, the DASS Stress scale differentiated patients with GAD from those with all the other DSM-III-R anxiety disorders, with the exception of OCD. Of the variety of symptom measures (e.g., questionnaire and clinician ratings of anxiety, depression, stress/tension) in which correlations were calculated in this study, only DASS Stress was the most strongly correlated with the PSWQ (Brown, Marten, & Barlow, 1995).

Self-Monitoring

As will become evident later in the chapter, self-monitoring is an integral part of our treatment program for GAD. When a patient is trained in proper use and completion of the self-monitoring forms, the data obtained from this mode of assessment can be among the most valuable information that the clinician has in the formulation and evaluation of the treatment program. Among the reasons for the importance of self-monitoring are the following: (1) to gauge the patient's response to treatment by obtaining accurate information on relevant clinical variables (e.g., daily levels of anxiety, depression, positive affect, amount of time spent worrying); (2) to assist in acquiring a functional analysis of the patient's naturally occurring anxiety and worry episodes (e.g., situational factors or precipitants, nature of anxiogenic cognitions, methods or behaviors engaged in to reduce worry or anxiety); and (3) to assess integrity and compliance with between-session homework assignments. A filled-in example of a form that we often use in the treatment of GAD, the Weekly

Record of Anxiety and Depression, is shown in Figure 4.2.

Right from the start of therapy, self-monitoring is presented to the patient as an important part of the treatment process. In the spirit of collaborative empiricism (see Young et al., Chapter 6, this volume), the patient is told that both he/she and the therapist will be working together to first try to get a better understanding of the factors contributing to the patient's naturally occurring anxiety, tension, and worry. Accordingly, self-monitoring is introduced as one of the best ways for obtaining the most accurate information about these processes, because if the patient and therapist were to rely solely on retrospective recall of the patient's symptoms, much important information could be lost or distorted.

These forms are introduced to the patient by first defining the type of information that we are attempting to collect (e.g., helping the patient to distinguish anxiety from depres-

sion). Once the form has been explained thoroughly, we will often assist the patient in generating a sample entry on the form (using the current day or a recent episode of anxiety/worry, depending on the type of form being introduced). This is to increase the probability that the patient will use the forms properly between sessions. Whereas this step is critical when first introducing the self-monitoring forms, it is also helpful to repeat this step periodically throughout treatment to prevent drift.

OVERVIEW OF TREATMENT

Our treatment protocol for GAD typically averages 12–15 hourly sessions, held weekly except for the last two sessions (which are held biweekly). For reasons noted earlier, although treatments for GAD have been delivered efficaciously in a small-group format (see

Name: *Claire T.*

Each evening before you go to bed, please make the following ratings, using the scale below:
1. Your AVERAGE level of anxiety (taking all things into consideration);
2. Your MAXIMUM level of anxiety which you experienced that day;
3. Your AVERAGE level of depression;
4. Your AVERAGE level of pleasantness;
5. The percentage of the day that you felt worried, using a 0–100% scale where 0 means no worry at all and 100 means worrried all the waking day.

Level of Anxiety/Depression/Pleasantness feelings

0	1	2	3	4	5	6	7	8
None		Slight		Moderate		A lot		As much as you can imagine

Date	Average anxiety	Maximum anxiety	Average depression	Average pleasantness	Percentage of day worried
9/17	4	6	4	2	60%
9/18	5	5	4	3	60%
9/19	4	5	3	3	65%
9/20	6	6	4	2	75%
9/21	6	8	5	1	80%
9/22	7	8	5	1	90%
9/23	5	7	4	2	75%

FIGURE 4.2. Weekly Record of Anxiety and Depression.

our review of treatment studies above), at this stage in the development of our GAD treatment protocol we prefer a one-on-one format.

As it currently stands (see Craske et al., 1992), our GAD protocol has components that address each of the three systems of anxiety: (1) physiological (PMR training), (2) cognitive (cognitive restructuring), and (3) behavioral (worry behavior prevention, problem solving, time management). At the heart of our new treatment protocol for GAD is the element of worry exposure, in which the patient is directed to spend a specified period of time daily (usually an hour) processing his/her worry content.

Whereas some evidence points to the possibility that multicomponent treatments may in fact result in lower efficacy, due perhaps to dilution of the constituent treatment elements (see Barlow et al., 1992), we have retained a multicomponent protocol for a variety of reasons (e.g., early evidence reflecting the limited success of single-component treatments; the DSM-IV conceptualization of GAD as a multidimensional disorder). Moreover, whereas a dilution effect may certainly account for the few findings noting diminished efficacy of multicomponent treatments, this factor may be of less concern when combined protocols are delivered in the clinical setting without the time and methodological constraints inherent in controlled treatment outcome studies.

PROCESS OF TREATMENT

Initial Sessions

Table 4.2 provides a general outline of our combined GAD treatment program. The initial sessions are most important, because these are where the groundwork and rationale for what is to follow are delineated. Included in the first two sessions are the following elements: (1) delineation of patient and therapist expectations; (2) description of the three components of anxiety (i.e., physiological, cognitive, behavioral) and application of the three-system model to the patient's symptoms (e.g., discussion of the patient's somatic symptoms of anxiety, content of worry, and worry behaviors); (3) discussion of the nature of anxiety (e.g., the nature of adaptive and maladaptive anxiety, "normalizing" the patient's symp-

toms); (4) rationale and description of the treatment components; and (5) instruction in the use of self-monitoring forms.

The importance of regular session attendance and completion of homework assignments is emphasized to each patient as crucial to treatment. Patients are provided a general idea of what to expect in terms of their response to treatment over the coming weeks (e.g., improvement that is not immediate; possibility of experiencing initial increases in their anxiety due to the nature of therapy, and the reasons for this).

Cognitive Therapy

Cognitive therapy is an integral component of our treatment for GAD. The cognitive component of our treatment protocol is consistent in many ways with the procedures outlined by Beck and colleagues (1985). Early in the process of treatment, the patient is provided with an overview of the nature of anxiogenic cognitions (e.g., the concept of automatic thoughts, the situation-specific nature of anxious predictions, reasons why the inaccurate cognitions responsible for anxiety persist unchallenged over time). As part of this introduction to the tenets behind cognitive therapy, considerable care is taken to help the patient understand that in the case of inappropriate anxiety, a person's interpretations of situations rather than the situations themselves are responsible for the negative affect experienced in response to the situations. Thus, through examples offered by the therapist, as well as patient-generated examples solicited by the therapist, a most important first step in cognitive therapy is to assist patients in realizing that they must be able to identify the specific interpretations/predictions they are making in order to be in a position to challenge these cognitions effectively.

Like Beck and colleagues (1985), we approach the task of automatic thought identification via a variety of techniques. Within a treatment session, these may include any or all of the following: therapist questioning (e.g., "What did you picture happening in that situation that made you tense up?"); imagery (asking the patient to imagine the situation in detail, as a means of providing additional cues for retrieving automatic thoughts occurring in

TABLE 4.2. Outline of GAD Treatment Protocol

Session 1
   Patient's description of anxiety and worry
   Introduction to nature of anxiety and worry
   Three-system model of anxiety
   Overview of treatment (e.g., importance of self-monitoring, homework, regular attendance)
   Provision of treatment rationale
   Homework: Self-monitoring
Session 2
   Review of self-monitoring
   Review of nature of anxiety, three-system model
   Discussion of the physiology of anxiety
   Discussion of maintaining factors in GAD
   Homework: Self-monitoring
Session 3
   Review of self-monitoring forms
   Rationale for 16-muscle-group progressive muscle relaxation (PMR)
   In-session PMR with audiotaping for home practices
   Homework: Self-monitoring, PMR
Session 4
   Review of self-monitoring forms, PMR practice
   In-session 16-muscle-group PMR with discrimination training
   Introduction to role of cognitions in persistent anxiety (e.g., nature of automatic thoughts, solicitation of examples from patient)
   Description and countering of probability overestimation cognitions
   Introduction to Cognitive Self-Monitoring Form
   Homework: Self-monitoring (anxiety, cognitive monitoring and countering), PMR
Session 5
   Review of self-monitoring, PMR, probability overestimation countering
   In-session 8-muscle-group PMR with discrimination training
   Description and countering of catastrophic cognitions
   Homework: Self-monitoring (anxiety, cognitive monitoring and countering), PMR
Session 6
   Review of self-monitoring, PMR, cognitive countering (probability overestimation, decatastrophizing)
   In-session 8-muscle-group PMR with discrimination training; introduction of generalization practice
   Review of types of anxiogenic cognitions and methods of countering
   Homework: Self-monitoring (anxiety, cognitive monitoring and countering), PMR
Session 7
   Review of self-monitoring, PMR, cognitive countering
   In-session 4-muscle-group PMR
   Introduction to worry exposure (e.g., imagery training, hierarchy of worry spheres, in-session worry exposure)
   Homework: Self-monitoring (anxiety, cognitive monitoring and countering), PMR, daily worry exposure

Session 8
   Review of self-monitoring, PMR, cognitive countering, worry exposure practices
   Introduction of relaxation-by-recall
   Review of rationale for worry exposure
   In-session worry exposure
   Homework: Self-monitoring (anxiety, cognitive monitoring and countering), worry exposure, relaxation-by-recall
Session 9
   Review of self-monitoring, cognitive countering, worry exposure, relaxation-by-recall
   Practice relaxation-by-recall
   Introduction of worry behavior prevention (e.g., rationale, generation of list of worry behaviors, development of behavior prevention practices)
   Homework: Self-monitoring (anxiety, cognitive monitoring and countering), worry exposure, worry behavior prevention, relaxation-by-recall
Session 10
   Review of self-monitoring, cognitive countering, worry exposure, worry behavior prevention, relaxation-by-recall
   Introduction to cue-controlled relaxation
   Homework: Self-monitoring (anxiety, cognitive monitoring and countering), worry exposure, worry behavior prevention, cue-controlled relaxation
Session 11
   Review of self-monitoring, cognitive countering, worry exposure, worry behavior prevention, cue-controlled relaxation
   Practice cue-controlled relaxation
   Introduction to time management or problem solving
   Homework: Self-monitoring (anxiety, cognitive monitoring and countering), worry exposure, worry behavior prevention, cue-controlled relaxation
Session 12
   Review of self-monitoring, cognitive countering, worry exposure, worry behavior prevention, cue-controlled relaxation
   Generalization of relaxation techniques
   Time management or problem-solving practice
   Homework: Self-monitoring (anxiety, cognitive monitoring and countering), worry exposure, worry behavior prevention, cue-controlled relaxation, time management/problem-solving practice
Session 13
   Review of self-monitoring, cognitive countering, worry exposure, worry behavior prevention, cue-controlled relaxation, time management/problem-solving practice
   Practice of cue-controlled relaxation
   Review of skills and techniques
   Discussion of methods of continuing to apply techniques covered in treatment

that situation); and role playing. Beginning with the first session of cognitive therapy, patients are trained to use the Cognitive Self-Monitoring Form (see Figure 4.3 for a completed example) to prospectively self-monitor and record their thoughts associated with anxiety. As noted earlier, a common problem with both patients and therapists-in-training is that the process of eliciting anxiogenic cognitions is carried out in an incomplete or superficial manner (e.g., discontinuing the process of questioning to uncover anxiogenic cognitions prematurely, prior to identifying the thought[s] principally responsible for the negative affect).

In addition to the problem of incomplete self-monitoring, the therapist may often need to assist patients in identifying the appropriate times to make entries on the Cognitive Self-Monitoring Form. For instance, one suggestion that we offer to patients is to use any increase in their anxiety level as a cue to self-monitor—for instance, "My anxiety level just went from a 2 to a 6. What was I thinking just then that may have contributed to this?" (Shifts in the patient's affect noted by the therapist in session are also good opportunities to assist the patient in eliciting automatic thoughts.)

With regard to the problem of identifying the specific thought(s) that are chiefly responsible for a given episode of anxiety, we encourage patients to determine whether the thoughts they have identified would satisfy the criterion of producing the same emotion in anyone if they were to make the same interpretation of the situation. This is also an important guideline for therapists to adhere to when assisting a patient to identify automatic thoughts in the session.

After providing an overview of the nature of anxiogenic cognitions and methods of identifying them, the therapist defines two types of cognitive distortions involved in excessive anxiety: (1) "probability overestimation," and (2) "catastrophic thinking." Cognitions involving probability overestimation are defined as those in which a person overestimates the likelihood of the occurrence of a negative event (which is actually unlikely to occur). For example, a patient who is apprehensive over the possibility of job termination, despite a very good job record, would be committing this type of cognitive error in overpredicting the likelihood of losing his/her job. After de-

fining and providing examples of probability overestimation thoughts, the therapist describes some reasons why these types of thoughts may persist over time, even despite repeated disconfirmation (e.g., the belief in having been "lucky" thus far; the belief that worry or its associated "worry behaviors" have prevented the negative outcome from occurring; the tendency to focus habitually on negative outcomes without examining other alternatives).

Catastrophic thinking is defined as the tendency to view an event as "intolerable," "unmanageable," and beyond one's ability to cope with successfully, when in actuality it is less "catastrophic" than it may appear on the face of it. In addition to catastrophic thoughts associated with perceptions of being unable to cope with negative events, regardless of their actual likelihood of occurrence (see the dialogue below between a therapist [T] and a patient called "Chloe" [C]), we would also put under the category of catastrophic thinking thoughts that involve drawing extreme conclusions or ascribing dire consequences to minor or unimportant events (e.g., "If my child fails an exam, it must mean that I have failed as a parent"). Cognitions reflecting a strong need for perfection or personal responsibility (and of drawing extreme negative conclusions of the consequences of not being perfect or responsible) would be apt to fall under this category as well.

Often patients will have some difficulty in making the distinction between probability overestimation thoughts and catastrophic thinking. The therapist should provide examples emphasizing their distinction of the basis of the dimension of likelihood (probability overestimation) and on the dimension of perceived inability to cope or tendency to ascribe overly dire consequences to minor events (catastrophic thinking). Moreover, the therapist should note that the two types of thoughts are often associated with one another in the patient's chain of worry.

T: You mentioned that two nights ago it was particularly difficult for you to get to sleep.

C: Well, it is always difficult, but that night I didn't fall asleep until 3:30.

T: Do you have an idea why that night was particularly difficult?

Name: *Claire T.*

Trigger/ Event	Automatic thought	Anxiety (0–8)	Prob. (0–100%)	Countering (Alternatives, evidence)	Realistic prob. (0–100%)	Anxiety (0–8)
Son's football game today	*He'll get hurt or paralyzed.*	*6*	*75%*	*Only had sprained ankle. Never anything major. Might not get hurt. He's tough and a good player, like his dad. Maybe a minor injury*	*10%*	*3*

FIGURE 4.3. Cognitive Self-Monitoring Form (worry record).

C: The phone rang at, I'd say, around 11:30, and as you know by now, the damn phone is always a source of my anxiety. But at that hour, I was worried that something was wrong. As it turned out, it was a wrong number, but by then . . .

T: What did you think the call might be about?

C: Well, you know, bad news of some sort, someone dying or something like that. After my visit home this summer, I have often worried that my father is getting up there in years. He turned 55 in July, and, well, since I moved to Boston I haven't seen my folks nearly as much as I would have liked to.

T: So when the phone rang, were you worried that something may have happened with your father?

C: I don't think just then, because I picked up the phone real fast, but the phone ringing kind of startled me. But after I hung up, I wondered why I was so anxious, and I realized that I must have thought that something happened to him. Once I realized that, I was worried about him the rest of the night.

T: If I recall from what you said before, he's in pretty good health, isn't he?

C: Yeah. He had a mole removed a while ago. Since he's worked outside all of his life, I worry that all that sun will have caused him to get skin cancer some day.

T: What do you picture happening if your dad did pass away?

C: What do you mean? Do you mean what would I do? We shouldn't even talk about this unless you want to see me in a real state . . . you know, being an only child and all . . .

T: Thinking about that really upsets you.

C: Well, I'm already anxious enough already. Something like that would really set me over the edge. I mean, the fact that I'm this anxious as it is shows that I can't cope well with situations. I imagine that if my dad died, I would really shut down and not be able to cope with anything. And not want to!

Although the therapist in this case example should go further to elucidate the nature of the patient's catastrophic predictions associated with the loss of a parent, he/she would also be making a good point to clarify the distinction between probability overestimation (e.g., overestimating the likelihood of the passing of a parent who is in good health; overestimating the risk associated with sun exposure) and catastrophic thinking (e.g., predicting that the parent's death would result in a permanent breakdown in one's emotions and ability to cope), and to indicate how these two types of thoughts are interconnected in the patient's "worry chain."

Whereas it would be appropriate at this point to provide an overview of the most common examples of probability overestimation and catastrophic thoughts reported by patients with GAD, it should be noted that the few studies that have examined the nature of

GAD worries (see, e.g., Borkovec et al., 1991; Craske, Rapee, et al., 1989; Sanderson & Barlow, 1990) have found that the content of worries obtained using a structured interview (i.e., the ADIS-R or ADIS-IV-L) has not fallen neatly into the a priori categories that have been used thus far (e.g., illness/health, family matters, work/school). Indeed, in each of the studies cited in the prior sentence, the category "miscellaneous" was among the top one or two most commonly categorized sphere of worry. Thus, unlike what has been found regarding the nature of the anxiogenic cognitions reported by patients with panic disorder (see Craske & Barlow, Chapter 1, this volume)—that is, the content of the majority of these patients' cognitions falls within relatively finite categories (e.g., fear of dying, going crazy, losing control)—no such evidence has been obtained pertaining to the content of GAD worries thus far. Nevertheless, to reiterate findings reviewed earlier, the extant data bearing on this issue suggest that the nature of GAD worry reflects an excess of the same process (and content) found in nonclinical individuals; the parameter of uncontrollability of the worry process is the principal feature differentiating pathological and nonpathological worry (see Barlow, 1991; Borkovec et al., 1991).

As with the case of identifying anxiogenic cognitions, the therapist cannot underscore enough the importance of being *thorough* and *systematic* in the countering of these thoughts. The therapist introduces countering not to replace negative thoughts with positive thoughts (e.g., "There is nothing to worry about, everything will be fine"). Instead, it is introduced as part of the process of examining the validity of the interpretations/predictions the patient is making, and in order to help the patient replace inaccurate cognitions with realistic, evidence-based ones. The importance of repeated, systematic countering is emphasized by noting that whereas the thoughts responsible for excessive anxiety can be habit-like and hard to break, they indeed can be unlearned and replaced with more accurate cognitions via practice and repeated application of the techniques of countering.

In addition, the patient is instructed that countering of anxiogenic cognitions involves the following guidelines: (1) considering thoughts as hypotheses (rather than facts) that can be either supported or negated by available evidence; (2) utilizing all available evidence, past and present, to examine the validity of the beliefs; and (3) exploring and generating all possible alternative predictions or interpretations of an event or situation. In the case of countering probability overestimation thoughts, these guidelines are utilized to evaluate the realistic likelihood (i.e., real odds) of the future occurrence of the negative event.

To counter catastrophic thoughts, the therapist asks the patient to imagine the worst possible feared outcome's actually happening, and then to critically evaluate the severity of the impact of the event. This entails giving an estimation of the patient's perceived ability to cope with the event, if it were to occur. Also, in countering catastrophic thinking, it is extremely useful to have the patient generate as many alternatives to the worst feared possible outcome as possible. The therapist may note difficulty on the patient's part in generating alternatives, as patients with GAD typically manifest a negative attentional bias. The therapist should emphasize that decatastrophizing does not entail trying to get the patient to view a negative event as positive or even neutral (e.g., "It would indeed be upsetting for most people if a parent passes on"); rather, via critically evaluating the actual impact of the negative event, the patient may come to view that its effects would be time-limited and manageable.

Worry Exposure

Guided by new conceptualizations of the nature of pathological worry reviewed earlier (see Borkovec & Hu, 1990; Rapee & Barlow, 1991), worry exposure (see Craske et al., 1992) entails the following procedures: (1) identification and recording of the patient's two or three principal spheres of worry (ordered hierarchically, beginning with the least distressing or anxiety-provoking worry); (2) imagery training via the practice of imagining pleasant scenes; (3) practice in vividly evoking the first worry sphere on the hierarchy by having the patient concentrate on his/her anxious thoughts while trying to imagine the worst possible feared outcome of that sphere of worry (e.g., for a patient who worries when her husband is late from work, this might entail imagining her husband unconscious and slumped over the steering wheel of the car);

(4) once the patient is able to evoke these images vividly, introducing the crux of the worry exposure technique, which entails reevoking these images and holding them clearly in mind for at least 25–30 minutes; and (5) after 25–30 minutes have elapsed, having the patient generate as many alternatives as he/she can to the worst possible outcome (e.g., "If my husband is late, he may have gotten tied up at work, gotten caught in traffic, stopped at the store, etc."). As indicated on the Daily Record of Worry Exposure (a completed example of this form is presented in Figure 4.4), at the end of the "alternative-generating" phase of the exposure practice, patients record their levels of anxiety and imagery vividness for various points in the exposure (e.g., maximum anxiety during the 25–30 minutes of worry exposure; anxiety levels after generating alternatives to the worst outcome).

After 30 minutes or more have been spent processing the first sphere of worry according to the preceding procedures, patients are often instructed to repeat these steps for the second worry on the hierarchy. After the therapist is assured that the patient is carrying out the worry exposure technique properly in sessions, the exercise is assigned as daily home practice. Patients are instructed that when the exposure exercise no longer evokes more than a mild level of anxiety (i.e., 2 or less on the 0–8 anxiety scale) despite several attempts of vividly imagining that worry, they should

---

Name: *Claire T.*   **Date:** *11/15*
Time began: *3* am/pm
Time ended: *5* am/pm

Anxiety/Imagery (circle)	0	1	2	3	4	5	6	7	8
	None		Slight		Moderate		A lot		Extreme

Symptoms during exposure:

Trembling/shaky	_____	Nausea/abdominal distress	✓
Muscle tension	✓	Hot flashes/chills	_____
Restlessness	_____	Frequent urination	_____
Fatigue	✓	Trouble swallowing	_____
Shortness of breath	_____	Keyed up/on edge	✓
Pounding/racing heart	✓	Easily startled/jumpy	_____
Sweating/clammy hands	_____	Difficulty concentrating	_____
Dry mouth	_____	Trouble sleeping	_____
Dizzy/lightheaded	_____	Irritability	✓

Worry 1: Content *Friend dropping by later—she'll see my messy house and be shocked. She'll laugh and think less of me.*

Worst possible feared outcome: *She'll call our friends to tell tell them—they'll also laugh, and not respect me.*

Anxiety (0–8): *7*   **Imagery (0–8):** *7*

Possible alternatives: *She won't even care—she's there to see me, not my house. She might not notice the floors. Even if she does, she might not think it so interesting to call everyone about it. She might be glad not to see me cleaning for a change.*

Anxiety (0–8): *2*   **Imagery (0–8):** *2*

FIGURE 4.4. Daily Record of Worry Exposure.

move on to the next sphere of worry on the hierarchy.

Of course, an important initial step in the application of the worry exposure technique is to prepare the patient adequately by providing a thorough description of the rationale and purposes of the exercise. This should involve, at some level, a discussion of the concept of habituation and the reasons why habituation has not occurred naturally despite repeated exposures to these worries over time (e.g., the natural tendency to shift rapidly from one worry to the next in the worry chain). In addition, worry exposure should be introduced as providing additional opportunities to apply strategies learned thus far in the treatment protocol (i.e., cognitive restructuring and perhaps applied relaxation). Indeed, the therapist may wish to note that repeated exposure to the same worry thought or image may make it easier for the patient to develop a more objective perspective on the worry, thus enhancing the patient's facility in applying cognitive countering techniques.

Several possible difficulties may arise during the application of worry exposure. Theoretically (see Foa & Kozak, 1986), therapeutic exposure to feared thoughts, images, or situations should generally be reflected by the following patterns: (1) Initial exposures elicit at least moderate anxiety levels; (2) protracted in-session exposure to fear cues results in the reduction of the high levels of anxiety elicited at the onset of the exposure (i.e., within-session habituation); (3) across several separate exposure trials, maximum anxiety levels evoked by exposure will decrease until the fear cues no longer elicit considerable anxiety (i.e., between-sessions habituation).

A potential problem is that the worry exposure may fail to elicit more than minimal anxiety during the *initial* exposures. Various reasons may contribute to this phenomenon, including the following: (1) The imagery is insufficiently vivid; (2) the images are too general, thereby hindering the patient's focus on the worst outcome; (3) the images are not salient to the patient's sphere of worry, or the sphere itself does not contribute appreciably to the patient's GAD symptoms; (4) the patient is applying coping techniques (e.g., cognitive restructuring, cue-controlled relaxation) during the 25–30 minutes of worry exposure; or (5) the patient is covertly avoiding the processing of the most salient worry

cues, perhaps via distraction to neutral thoughts or images.

Another difficulty that may arise is that the patient evidences negligible within- or between-sessions habituation of anxiety to the worry exposure cues, despite repeated exposure trials. Again, there may be several reasons accounting for this problem, including (1) covert avoidance when high levels of anxiety are beginning to be experienced; (2) a failure to maintain exactly the same image throughout the exposure (e.g., a tendency to shift continually from one distressing image to another), thereby mitigating habituation to the image; or (3) insufficient exposure time (e.g., the patient maintains the worry image for less than 25 minutes, or, in some cases, 25–30 minutes do not provide ample exposure time for particularly distressing images).

As noted in the discussion of therapist variables that may contribute to treatment outcome, it is important that the therapist possess a thorough understanding of the theoretical parameters of therapeutic exposure. Accordingly, this underscores the importance of the systematic collection of patients' anxiety ratings during the worry exposures (both in sessions and during home practice), as these ratings will be useful indices of progress and potential problems.

Occasionally patients evidence difficulties in generating alternatives to the worst feared outcome. This difficulty may be reflective of a patient's limited facility in applying cognitive countering techniques (covered prior to worry exposure in our GAD protocol), or it may indicate a relatively strong belief conviction associated with the sphere of worry in question. Related to this problem, therapists will sometimes observe that patients' anxiety ratings do not subside after alternatives to the worst feared outcome have been generated. When problems of this nature are noted, a therapist should question a patient for his/her hypotheses about why anxiety reduction did not occur. In accordance with the common pitfalls of cognitive therapy (e.g., failure to challenge anxiogenic predictions thoroughly with evidence-based counterarguments), initially the therapist may need to assist the patient in the generation of alternatives. In our experience, anxiety reduction will begin to occur with this feedback, in tandem with continued worry exposure (e.g., habituation to imaginal cues associated with the worst feared outcome may enhance the patient's objectivity concerning the sphere of worry in question, thereby facilitating cognitive restructuring).

As noted above, distraction is an issue that should be routinely addressed in GAD treatment. Specifically, a patient may try not to think of the worst possible feared outcome, or may allow his/her thoughts to wander during the procedure. The therapist needs to point out that, although distraction from anxious thoughts or feelings may relieve anxiety in the short term, it is essentially an ineffective long-term strategy for anxiety management. In fact, distraction may reinforce the patient's view that certain thoughts and images are to be avoided, and it has proven detrimental to positive treatment outcome in other anxiety disorders (Craske, Street, & Barlow, 1989). Moreover, distraction will not allow for a proper appraisal of the patient's anxiogenic cognitions and prohibits the rise in anxiety level necessary for adequate emotional processing of worry (see Foa & Kozak, 1986). Therefore, the therapist must be especially watchful for instances of patient distraction, pointing these instances out to the patient and offering reasons why this behavior is not beneficial to long-term anxiety reduction.

Relaxation Training

Relaxation training in our current combined treatment protocol for GAD does not differ appreciably from the manner in which we have administered this treatment component in the past (see, e.g., Barlow, Craske, Cerny, & Klosko, 1989; Barlow et al., 1992). Our relaxation component is based on the procedures outlined by Bernstein and Borkovec (1973). The procedures begin with PMR (16 muscle groups) with discrimination training. Discrimination training entails teaching the patient to discriminate sensations of tension and relaxation in each muscle group during the PMR exercise. The ultimate goal of discrimination training is to increase the patient's ability to detect sources and early signs of muscle tension, and thereby to facilitate the rapid deployment of relaxation techniques to those areas (see below). After the patient has worked through each of the 16 muscle groups, relaxation-deepening techniques are employed during the induction, including slow breathing (i.e., slow diaphragmatic breathing, repeating the word "Relax" on the exhale).

Patients are given the rationale that relaxation is aimed at alleviating the symptoms associated with the physiological component of anxiety, partly via the interruption of the learned association between autonomic overarousal and worry. The 16-muscle-group PMR exercise averages 30 minutes in duration. Usually, we have the therapist conduct in-session PMR while simultaneously audiotaping the procedure, so that the patient may practice PMR twice daily at home using the tape. In addition to the practice of audiotaping, we adhere to all the typical guidelines of PMR administration (e.g., directives to the patient to initially practice PMR in quiet, comfortable locations, but not immediately before going to bed).

After the patient has had considerable practice with the 16-muscle-group exercise (typically over a span of 2 weeks), the number of muscle groups is gradually reduced from 16 to 8 and then to 4 (e.g., stomach, chest, shoulders, forehead). During the course of muscle group reduction, the therapist should nonetheless be attuned to the specific body areas that the patient reports to be problematic, consequently adapting the 4-group exercise to target those problem areas.

Of course, the rationale behind muscle group reduction (i.e., 16 to 8 to 4) is to make the relaxation techniques more "portable," such that the patient can rapidly deploy the technique at any time, when needed. Thus, after the patient has practiced the 4-muscle group exercise, "relaxation-by-recall" is introduced. Relaxation-by-recall consists of concentrating on each of the four muscle groups that have been targeted up to this point, and releasing tension in each muscle area in turn, via the recall of the feelings of relaxation achieved in past practices. It therefore does not involve tensing the muscles as in the prior methods, but simply recalling the experience of relaxing the muscles (e.g., "As you concentrate on your stomach, think of your stomach muscles letting go, and feel the warmth of relaxation as your stomach relaxes"). As with the full PMR exercise, patients are instructed to maintain a pattern of slow, regular breathing, covertly repeating the word "Relax" with every exhalation. At this phase, patients are instructed to continue practicing the relaxation exercises daily in nondistracting environments, but are also encouraged to begin trying "minipractices" in other situations (e.g., at the workplace).

After the patient has mastered relaxation-by-recall, "cue-controlled relaxation" is introduced. This essentially entails the steps of taking a few slow breaths (about four or five) and repeating the word "Relax" on the exhale. With the exhale, the patient is instructed to release all of the tension in his/her body, concentrating on the feelings of relaxation. Thus cue-controlled relaxation is the most "portable" of the relaxation strategies covered in the protocol, and the patient is directed to employ the technique in a variety of situations, particularly those in which anxiety or tension is frequently experienced (e.g., work, home, waiting in line, talking on the phone, driving). In addition, we encourage patients to continue to go periodically through the full 16-muscle-group PMR exercise, for a variety of reasons (e.g., rehearsing discrimination training, strengthening the association of the cue "Relax" to feelings of relaxation).

Patients will vary in the time it takes them to work through the various phases of relaxation training. When implemented in the clinical setting (i.e., without the confines of protocol treatment in controlled, outcome studies), the therapist should not guide the patient through the phases of the relaxation training too quickly (e.g., reduce from 16 to 8 to 4 muscle groups too rapidly) as the patient's success with implementing subsequent techniques (e.g., relaxation-by-recall, cue-controlled relaxation) may depend largely on his/her mastery of earlier strategies (e.g., discrimination training during 16-muscle-group PMR).

In addition to several practical difficulties that may be associated with patients' relaxation training (e.g., noncompliance with homework due to not finding sufficient time to practice, problems in maintaining a sufficient attentional focus during practice), one problem noted in the research literature associated with these techniques has been referred to as "relaxation-induced anxiety" (RIA). Anxiety induced by the relaxation procedure itself appears to be associated with a heightened sensitivity to internal somatic cues (e.g., feelings of floating, subjective feelings of loss of control; see Borkovec et al., 1987; Heide & Borkovec, 1984). Attesting to the potential relevance of this phenomenon to clinical outcome, Borkovec and colleagues (1987), in a

study comparing cognitive to nondirective therapy in patients who all received PMR as part of the treatment package, found RIA to be significantly and negatively associated with change on the Hamilton Anxiety and Depression Scales.

Thus the therapist should be watchful for signs of RIA, particularly in patients with comorbid panic disorder (see Cohen, Barlow, & Blanchard, 1985), a commonly occurring additional diagnosis in patients with a principal diagnosis of GAD (Brown & Barlow, 1992). When RIA is observed, the therapist should reassure the patient that it is most likely a temporary automatic response to a learned pattern of autonomic overarousal, and that these feelings usually abate with repeated practice.

Worry Behavior Prevention

As noted earlier in the chapter, Craske, Rapee, and colleagues (1989) found that over half of GAD worries recorded in self-monitoring were associated with carrying through some corrective, preventative, or ritualistic behavior. Thus, as is the case with compulsions in OCD, these "worry behaviors" are negatively reinforcing to patients, as they usually result in temporary anxiety reduction (see Brown, Moras, et al., 1993). Examples of worry behaviors include frequent telephone calls to loved ones at work or at home, refusal to read obituaries or other negative events in the newspaper, and cleaning one's house daily in the event that someone drops by. As in the treatment of OCD (see Foa & Franklin, Chapter 5, this volume), a potentially useful intervention in the treatment of GAD is the systematic prevention of responses that are functionally related to worry.

Because patients may not see the contribution of these behaviors to the maintenance of their anxiety, it is useful for the therapist to approach this area as an opportunity to test out patients' beliefs that these behaviors actually prevent dire consequences from occurring (i.e., prediction testing). The procedure begins with the therapist's assisting a patient to generate a list of the patient's common worry behaviors. Once these behaviors have been identified, the therapist will often have the patient self-monitor and record the frequency with which each behavior occurs during the week. The next step is to instruct the patient to refrain from engaging in the worry behavior, perhaps engaging in a competing response in its place (e.g., keeping the car radio on a news station during the entire commute home, instead of turning it off to avoid hearing about reports of traffic accidents). Prior to performing the worry behavior prevention exercise, the therapist records the patient's predictions concerning the consequences of response prevention. After the worry behavior prevention exercise has been completed, the therapist assists the patient in comparing the outcome of the exercise to the patient's predictions (e.g., the frequency of engaging in worry behaviors is not correlated with the likelihood of the occurrence of future negative events). As is the case with the treatment of panic disorder (see Craske & Barlow, Chapter 1, this volume), prediction testing can be a very useful adjunct to cognitive restructuring. An example of a completed Worry Behavior Prevention Form is presented in Figure 4.5.

Time Management

Many patients with GAD report feeling overwhelmed by obligations and deadlines, in addition to everyday hassles and stressors. Because of the nature of GAD (e.g., anxious apprehension), these patients are apt to magnify these daily hassles, augmenting the impact of these minor stressors. Accordingly, basic skills in time management and goal-setting are highly useful adjuncts to the treatment of GAD, partly because these techniques

may assist patients to focus their efforts on the tasks at hand rather than worrying about accomplishing future tasks.

Our time management strategies involve three basic components: delegating responsibility, assertiveness (e.g., saying "no"), and adhering to agendas. With regard to responsibility delegation, we often note to our patients that perfectionistic tendencies may prevent them from allowing others to take on the tasks that they typically assume themselves. Moreover, persons with GAD may be reluctant to refuse unexpected or unrealistic demands placed on them by others, preventing them from completing planned activities (this is particularly likely in patients with comorbid social phobia, a commonly occurring additional diagnosis). Usually we target issues pertaining to responsibility delegation and assertiveness via the utilization of worry behavior prevention and prediction-testing exercises, outlined above. For example, this might entail asking the patient to delegate small tasks to coworkers to test the patient's predictions associated with this activity (e.g., "The quality of work will suffer," "It will take longer to explain it to someone than do it myself," "I'll be perceived by other as shirking my responsibilities").

Agenda adherence should first begin with the examination of the patient's daily activities (generated by at least a week of self-monitoring). Next, the therapist can assist the patient in establishing an organized strategy for sticking to agendas and structuring daily activities, so that the patient's most important activities are accomplished. This objective can be facilitated via the generation of a "goal-

Name: *Claire T.*

Date	Practice task	Anxiety before task (0–8)	Anxiety after task (0–8)
11/27	*Ask husband to call only when leaving from work, not earlier*	4	3
11/28	" "	3	3
11/29	" "	3	2
11/30	" "	3	1
12/1	" "	2	2
12/2	" "	2	0
12/3	" "	1	0

FIGURE 4.5. Worry Behavior Prevention Form.

setting list" in which the activities planned for the day are categorized as follows: "A tasks," extremely important activities that need to be done that same day; "B tasks," very important tasks that must get done soon, but not necessarily on that same day; and "C tasks," important tasks that need to be done, but not very soon. Next, the therapist assists the patient in allotting sufficient time to complete each activity (perhaps by allotting up to twice the amount of time expected to complete the task, if the patient evidences a tendency to rush through tasks or has unrealistic expectations regarding the length of time necessary to get things done).

After time estimates have been established for each task, the patient is instructed to place the A, B, and C tasks into time slots on his/her daily schedule. If a patient's day is so erratic that this strategy is infeasible, the patient is instructed to make a three-header list of A, B, and C tasks and cross each task off upon completion. Although these time management strategies have not been evaluated in controlled treatment trials to date, our clinical experience suggests that they can be quite helpful in reducing patients' daily levels of stress while increasing their sense of mastery and control over their day-to-day lives.

Problem Solving

A final component of our combined GAD treatment protocol is problem solving. As Meichenbaum recommends (see, e.g., Meichenbaum & Jaremko, 1983), we present the technique to patients by noting that individuals often encounter two types of difficulties when problem solving: (1) viewing the problem in general, vague, and catastrophic ways; and (2) failing to generate any possible solutions. The first difficulty is addressed by teaching the patients how to conceptualize problems in specific terms and to break the problem into smaller, more manageable segments (which will have already been addressed to some degree during cognitive therapy).

The second difficulty is addressed by teaching patients to brainstorm their way through the problem. For instance, a patient may report trouble with incurring costly repairs to his/her car. The therapist can assist the patient in generating as many possible solutions to the dilemma as possible, no matter how unreason-

able they may sound at first (e.g., buying a used car, buying a new car, going to a different mechanic, deliberately totaling the car and collecting the insurance money). After a host of potential solutions have been generated, each one is evaluated to determine which are the most practical, with the end goal of selecting and acting on the best possible solution (which may have not been realized prior to brainstorming). Patients are informed that, with practice, brainstorming can be accomplished more efficiently (i.e., it requires less time and effort).

In addition to facilitating reaching a solution for the given problem, another potential benefit of this technique is that it fosters patients' ability to think differently about situations in their lives and to focus on the realistic rather than the catastrophic. In this sense, this benefit of problem solving is similar to the mechanism of action presumed to be partly responsible for the efficacy of worry exposure.

TREATMENT TRANSCRIPTS

The dialogues that follow between a therapist (T) and a patient called "Claire" (C) are representative of our combined treatment protocol for GAD, covering a span of 13 individual hourly sessions. Because both patient and novice therapists may have the most difficulty applying the cognitive strategies, we have highlighted these techniques in the transcripts.

Session 1

As noted in Table 4.2, the first session serves as an introduction of the patient to the therapist, as well as an overview of the treatment program.

T: This treatment program is geared toward helping you learn about generalized anxiety and develop skills that will help you cope with high anxiety. Because the program involves learning and applying skills, there will be some exercises that I will ask you to do both in our sessions and at home. We'll arrange to have 13 sessions, each usually lasting about one hour. In addition, we'll meet periodically through the next 12 months to monitor your progress. First, Claire, I'd like to get a sense from you about the kinds of problems you're experiencing that have brought you to the clinic.

C: I just feel anxious and tense all the time. It all started in high school. I was a straight-A student, and I worried constantly about my grades, whether the other kids and the teachers liked me, being prompt for classes—things like that. There was a lot of pressure from my parents to do well in school and to be a good role model for my younger sisters. I guess I just caved in to all that pressure, because my stomach problems began in my sophomore year of high school. Since that time, I've had to be really careful about drinking caffeine and eating spicy meals. I notice that when I'm feeling worried or tense my stomach will flare up, and because I'm usually worried about something, I'm always nauseous. My husband thinks I'm neurotic. For example, I vacuum four times a week and clean the bathrooms every day. There have even been times when I've backed out of going out to dinner with my husband because the house needed to be cleaned. Generally, my husband is supportive, but it has caused a strain on our marriage. I get so upset and irritated over minor things, and it'll blow up into an argument. I'm here because I'd like to live like normal people do, without all of this unending tension and anxiety.

T: You've mentioned, Claire, that you suffer from a number of physical symptoms, such as irritability, stomach problems, tension, and the like. In high school, you worried about your grades, whether others liked you, being on time, etc. What sorts of things do you worry excessively about now?

C: Oh, everything, really. I still worry about being on time to church and to appointments. Now I find I worry a lot about my husband. He's been doing a tremendous amount of traveling for his job, some of it by car, but most of it by plane. Because he works on the northeastern seaboard, and because he frequently has to travel in the winter, I worry that he'll be stuck in bad weather and get into an accident or, God forbid, a plane crash. It's just so scary. Oh, and I worry about my son. He

just started playing on the varsity football team, so he's bound to get an injury some time. It's so nerve-wracking to watch him play that I've stopped going to his games with my husband. I'm sure my son must be disappointed that I'm not watching him play, but it's simply too much for me to take.

T: Earlier you said that minor things get you upset. Give me some examples of those minor things.

C: When my son leaves his room a mess, or when my husband tracks dirt into the house, that annoys me so much! I pride myself on a neat and clean house, with floors so spotless that you could eat off them. It irritates me when they're not neat, and I let them know about it.

T: What you've been saying is quite typical of individuals who have generalized anxiety disorder. Let me first give you an overview of the nature of anxiety. Anxiety is one of the basic emotions that all species have, and thus it is a natural and necessary part of life. We as human beings experience anxiety in situations that might be dangerous, threatening, or challenging in some way. For instance, if you were walking in a jungle and heard a twig snap behind you, what would you think?

C: I suppose I'd imagine that a lion or tiger were behind me. I'd try to be still and listen.

T: Right. Physically, you'd probably feel your heart race, your breath get shorter and deeper, and some perspiration. Your body is in the process of preparing for fighting or fleeing the potential danger. Your heart races and pounds so that more blood will rapidly go toward your major muscle groups, like your upper thighs and arms. Your breath adjusts in the event that you'll need to exert yourself by running or fighting. Sweating helps you in that a predator will have a harder time grasping onto something slippery. That's where the term "fight-or-flight response" originates. By imagining the worst, you're in a better position to prepare for danger. How do you think you'd respond if, instead of thinking that the snapped twig was due to a tiger or lion, [you were] thinking that it was due to a fallen branch?

C: I wouldn't be afraid at all.

T: So you can see how important your thoughts are in determining your level of anxiety. Anxiety can be a productive and driving force in situations that are less dramatic. For instance, when you were in high school, how did you prepare for an exam?

C: I'd study like a madwoman the week beforehand, and review my notes over and over again until it was imprinted on my mind.

T: Why?

C: Fear of failure, I guess. Or more like fear of getting less than an A.

T: How do you think you would have studied if you didn't have that anxiety?

C: Like most of my friends, who were perfectly content to study the night before and settle for a B or C.

T: That's a good example of how anxiety can really help you to achieve goals and accomplish tasks. When anxiety is maladaptive or excessive is when it interferes with your ability to relax when you want to, when it's too intense or too frequent for the situation at hand, or when there's no danger present. In this treatment, we'll focus on removing that excessive anxiety—the anxiety that fuels your worries and those physical symptoms that you have.

We view anxiety as a reaction to a trigger that might be internal or external. Examples of triggers include your thoughts, physical sensations, certain events or situations, and so on. Because anxiety is a reaction, you can learn to control it through skills and exercises designed to help you manage your high anxiety episodes. Along with viewing anxiety as a reaction, we also break it apart into three distinct components: physical, cognitive, and behavioral. Before I explain each component, let me ask you if anyone's ever told you to just relax and stop worrying as a remedy for your anxiety.

C: Oh, yeah! That's my husband's favorite line.

T: Do you find it helpful for you?

C: Not at all. It doesn't tell me how to relax, or how to stop worrying.

T: Exactly. By looking at anxiety in a global way, it can be difficult to see how to control it. That's where examining your anxiety with the three-component model is useful, as we can break up your anxiety into specific parts and target each individually. The physical component of your anxiety is manifested in the bodily sensations that occur during anxiety and worry. In your case, it might be upset stomach, tension, irritability, etc. The second component, called the cognitive component, is shown in the thoughts you have during anxiety or worry. Finally, the behavioral component is manifested in the specific behaviors that occur during or as a consequence of anxiety. Some examples of these behaviors include leaving very early for appointments, pacing, foot or finger tapping, perfectionism, procrastination, cleaning, safety checks, and so on. As we continue in the sessions, it will be easier to identify some of those behaviors. These behaviors tend to reduce anxiety in the short run, but may actually be maintaining your anxiety over the longer term. In many ways, those behaviors are similar to your anxious thoughts. Through time and repeated practice, they've become second nature or automatic for you.

Worry is a very interesting phenomenon. We as human beings worry so that we can prepare for future danger or threat. It helps us to problem-solve, in a sense, the things that we're afraid might happen in the future. By thinking things completely through, we can come up with a variety of solutions and occasionally alternatives to what we might be predicting in a situation. It's when we don't allow ourselves to think things through and to imagine our worst possible fears coming true that worry can spiral into increased worry and anxiety. You stated earlier, Claire, that you worried about being on time for classes in high school. Why was that?

C: The teachers were very strict, and would take points off each time you walked in the door late.

T: What was so bad about that?

C: It would come off your grade point average for that class. I didn't want to be late so that I could avoid those points taken off, to preserve my 4.0 average.

T: What if you had arrived to class late a few times?

C: I wouldn't have graduated with a perfect GPA, and my parents would have been very disappointed in me.

T: And then what?

C: I'm not sure. Maybe they wouldn't have paid my college tuition bill or something. I couldn't have afforded college on my own, and would have missed the opportunity to go. That would have been terrible. I would never have met my husband, or gotten my present job, or been able to pay my bills.

T: I can see how being late was anxiety-provoking for you, given those concerns. But do you really think that your parents would not have paid for college if you hadn't graduated with a 4.0 GPA?

C: Looking back, probably not. My sisters just partied through school, and my parents footed the bill for them.

T: By *not* allowing yourself to think through the worst and *not* asking yourself the likelihood of the worst happening, you in effect reinforced your worry over being late to classes. As we continue with the sessions, we'll be examining your worries in a similar fashion and have you systematically experience your worry so that you can overcome this approach–avoidance mode for handling worries. You'll also learn to identify and challenge your anxious thoughts, learn how to physically relax your entire body, and learn to change some of your anxiety- and worry-related behaviors to ones that are more effective in the long run in decreasing your anxiety. Is that clear?

C: Yes, pretty much.

T: Good. Another important element in this program is self-monitoring and homework. Self-monitoring of your levels of anxiety and worry will allow you to be a more accurate observer of your experiences. Sometimes our patients tell us that they feel anxious continuously, but when they begin to self-monitor, we discover that some days of the week are better or worse than others. Another advantage of self-monitoring is its ability to give you a more objective understanding of your anxiety. You'll feel less like a victim and more like a scientist, trying to figure out

and examine your anxiety. By monitoring your progress, we can evaluate the effectiveness of this treatment program for you and make any necessary adjustments along the way. Finally, because there will be regular homework assignments, you will learn the strategies much more rapidly if you consistently self-monitor. You may find a temporary increase in your anxiety when you first begin to self-monitor and attempt the homework, which is perfectly normal. This may happen because you're facing your anxiety, perhaps for the first time. It's a good sign that we're on the right track in identifying and targeting your anxiety.

[Claire is then instructed in the use of the Weekly Record of Anxiety and Depression and the Cognitive Self-Monitoring Form.]

Session 2

In this session, the therapist begins with a brief review of the week's self-monitoring and reiterates the treatment rationale provided in Session 1.

T: Let's start off today by reviewing your forms. It looks as though you had quite a bit of anxiety on the 20th through the 22nd; you gave average anxiety ratings of 6's and a 7 on those days [see Figure 4.2].

C: Yes, those were tough days. My husband went away on business for a couple of days, and I was pretty worried about him while he was gone. You know, the same old thing of whether he's OK—if he's run into bad weather or has gotten into an accident. He came home in one piece, of course, but it's tough for me to see him go. I had him call when he arrived at the hotel and every night before he went to bed, so that made me feel somewhat better.

T: I'm glad that you mentioned that you had your husband call you several times during his trip. Does he call you from work regularly?

C: Yes, he does, because he knows it makes me feel better. But I think sometimes it annoys him to have to keep "checking in" with me, as if I were his mother or something.

T: That's useful information to note, for we'll be on the lookout for those kinds of behaviors that you might do to relieve your anxiety in the short run.

To review items from our last session, we mentioned that the program will last a year. The first 13 sessions will take place over the next 15 weeks, with Sessions 12 and 13 occurring biweekly. It's vital that you regularly practice the strategies covered over the next several meetings in order to make them almost second nature, so that they'll eventually replace the anxious thoughts and behaviors that are fueling your high anxiety and worry. When you get a good checkup from the dentist, you wouldn't stop brushing, right? We use the same principle here: that complete consolidation of these skills takes time and daily practice.

As I mentioned last week, anxiety and worry are normal responses to danger or threat. As such, anxiety's main function is to protect and prepare the body for survival by initiating the fight-or-flight response. The physical component of anxiety is responsible for automatically activating certain sensations to prepare the body for action. This fight-or-flight response is part of the autonomic nervous system, composed of two distinct parts: the sympathetic nervous system and the parasympathetic nervous system. The sympathetic nervous system is activated in the face of danger and is responsible for sending impulses to the adrenal gland. The adrenal gland then releases the neurochemicals adrenaline and noradrenaline, which send impulses to other parts of the body to signal the need to prepare for action. The parasympathetic nervous system, on the other hand, is the restoring branch of the autonomic nervous system and serves to return the body to its natural resting state. When you are anxious, the autonomic nervous system will propel various body systems, such as the cardiovascular, respiratory, and digestive systems. Your heart might race and pound; you might feel slightly short of breath; and your digestion might be disrupted, which results in feelings of nausea and upset.

The second component of the model of anxiety is the cognitive component. This refers to your specific thoughts and predictions occurring when the fight-or-flight response is initiated. Worrying is an attempt to problem-solve possible future danger or threat. If you are worried or anxious, your attentional focus will be diverted to those possible sources of threat, and it therefore will be difficult to concentrate on other things going on around you that do not pose an imminent threat. Because your concentration is affected, you might experience forgetfulness or a poor memory. This does not mean that you're losing your mind or your faculties. Rather, it indicates that your anxiety and worry are interfering with your ability to attend to sources of incoming information other than threat or danger. This inability to focus attention onto tasks is protective in the sense that when faced with real threat or danger, you need full attention onto what is going on around you.

Behaviorally, when you are anxious, you may engage in certain behaviors designed to reduce or alleviate your anxiety. Moving around a lot by pacing, foot tapping, cleaning, etc., releases extra energy produced by anxiety and aids in distracting you from your thoughts at hand. Similarly, procrastinating on tasks is a common way people attempt to avoid feeling anxious about getting something completed. This can stem from a fear of failure or a fear of not doing something perfectly. You've mentioned before that you often feel irritable. This is another common behavioral manifestation of anxiety. Additionally, when we're anxious we might do other things to help reduce our anxiety and worry. For you, that might be having your husband phone you from work several times a day to make sure he's safe. Another example that you mentioned before, Claire, was that you've stopped going to your son's football games because of your anxiety while watching him play. Although you may feel temporarily better by not watching his games, you simultaneously are reinforcing your anxious belief that something dangerous will happen to your son on the football field.

C: You're right, but I couldn't bear seeing my son hurt or injured. It would really upset me, so it's much easier to avoid going to the games so that if he does get hurt, I won't have to see it.

T: You seem fairly convinced that your son will be seriously injured while playing football, but in fact the odds of his getting seriously injured are quite low. By not going to the games, you're really telling yourself that the odds of him getting hurt are much higher than they really are. Also, you seem to be predicting that you wouldn't be able to bear seeing him hurt. Has there ever been a time in your life when you did see someone injured?

C: Umm, yes. My husband collided with another fielder during a softball game and had to get stitches in his forehead.

T: Were you able to tolerate seeing that?

C: Barely! I managed to get him to the hospital, but I was pretty shaky while I drove there.

T: The point is that although you were anxious in that situation, you did in fact cope with your husband's injury. We'll return to some of these concepts in a later session. I'd now like to describe how excessive worry and anxiety can develop.

C: That should be fairly easy to do in my case. Both of my parents were big worry warts who were always 5 minutes ahead in their thinking. I had to call home any time I went out; I had to keep my room immaculate; and I sometimes told white lies because I knew how little things would set them off, like the time I was pulled over for going 10 miles over the speed limit when I first got my license. Even though I didn't get a ticket from the officer, I knew that if I told them that I got pulled over, my parents would be too worried and upset to ever let me drive on my own again. So I said I went to the library to drop off some books. It's funny, but to this day I never go over the speed limit, and I get this little rush of anxiety if I see a patrol car while I'm driving.

T: It sounds as though you grew up with parents who modeled anxious behaviors around you. In actuality, having anxious parents does not necessarily guarantee that an individual will be anxious as an adult. Several contributing factors interact to produce excessive anxiety and worry. These factors include a physical responsivity, or generalized overarousal to all kinds of events (both positive and negative). Are you moved to tears easily when watching a sad movie or being at a wedding?

C: Definitely.

T: We refer to that tendency as "overarousal" or "being emotional." It appears that part of that overarousal may be inherited, while part of it may be learned from your environment. Other factors that may be responsible for excessive anxiety and worry are a tendency to view the world as a dangerous and threatening place, along with a tendency to feel a need to control things happening in your life.

Along with these factors, life experiences and stressors may trigger excessive anxiety and worry. In your case, Claire, the experiences of being in high school and stressors of grades and friends may have initially triggered your excessive worry. Of course, because those triggers are no longer in the picture, we will begin to identify current triggers and maintaining factors to your anxiety and worry.

There are several factors that maintain excessive worry. One is the tendency to try to resist worrying or to try to distract yourself from worrying without feeling as though you've resolved anything in your mind. Do you ever find yourself trying to think about something else when you start worrying?

C: Sure, all the time. I also try to keep busy, which sometimes helps me take my mind off what's bothering me.

T: Another factor is due to the interference in the ability to effectively problem-solve due to high emotional arousal. Because you're in a relatively frequent state of high anxiety and overarousal, you may be focusing exclusively on all the possible negative things, while not giving more realistic, less threat-laden alternatives proper attention. Also, worry can serve a superstitious function, in that some individuals who worry excessively believe that worrying can avert negative outcomes, or that worrying is a sign of a conscientious person.

In the treatment program, we'll target the three components of anxiety, using strategies specifically designed for each. First, you'll learn a technique called "progressive muscle relaxation," involving tensing and releasing your muscles to reduce your physical anxiety. Next, you'll learn methods designed to counteract your negative predictions and to develop more realistic thoughts while anxious. You'll also learn to break the learned and automatic association between high arousal and specific images or thoughts fueling your worry. This will be accomplished by having you systematically experience your worry in a very controlled way. Finally, you'll develop the ability to engage in certain behaviors or activities that you may be avoiding, and changing the behaviors that reinforce your anxiety, so that you can test out some of your negative predictions if you do or don't carry the behaviors out.

For this week, it will be important to pay special attention to the kinds of thoughts you experience when anxious or worried, and the specific physical sensations and behaviors that accompany those anxious or worrisome thoughts.

Session 3

T: Today we'll cover progressive muscle relaxation. First, tell me about your anxiety and worry this past week.

C: It was fairly high. A boy on my son's football team broke his leg in a scrimmage before the game. His leg was broken in two different places, and he'll be out for the rest of the season. That just threw me for a loop. My son was right next to the boy when this all happened. Then, to top it all off, my in-laws dropped by unexpectedly for the weekend, and I was a basket case trying to prepare good meals and make them feel welcome. Naturally, my husband was laid back about both events, saying that I got myself worked up for nothing. I was really worried for a good 3 days in a row—probably for about 75% of each day, as I wrote down on the Weekly Record. You know, I was a bit leery about self-monitoring, because it would take time out of my schedule. But it's not so bad, and I do feel a little bit more in control of my anxiety. It's just sort of pathetic that I wasted my weekend worrying about stupid things like getting dinner on the table and whether my in-laws were comfortable in the guest room, like I wrote on the cognitions form.

T: It's great that you've been monitoring regularly. The amount of time that you invest in monitoring and practicing the skills is directly correlated with the amount of benefit you will gain from the treatment program.

Recall that general tension and overarousal contributes to high anxiety and worry, and may result from excessive worry. By learning how to physically relax your body, you can stop your anxiety to spiral and can help yourself to feel better physically. Progressive muscle relaxation involves tensing and releasing your muscles, with fewer muscle groups being targeted as your skill in the technique increases. We'll first start with 16 muscle groups, then follow with 8 groups, and then down to 4. When you first begin this procedure, it will take about 30 minutes. Gradually, you will require less time to feel fully relaxed. Remember that because relaxation is a skill, it takes time and practice to become an expert in it. However, you should feel some effects almost immediately.

C: I know that I have to set aside time for homework, but 30 minutes sounds like a lot to me.

T: It may be that sense of time pressure that adds to your anxiety. Put it to yourself this way: By completing the relaxation every day, you're doing something that will help you physically and emotionally. All the other things that are going on in your life that "have to get done by such-and-such time" can wait. If you try to fit the relaxation in between several things on your daily agenda, you will most likely feel pressured to get it done and over with. So you won't feel relaxed at all! Make sure that you do the relaxation exercise at a time when you won't feel rushed or pressured by other responsibilities.

The procedure entails tensing and then releasing or relaxing your muscles. By tensing, you can accentuate the feeling of release, as well as discriminate when you might be unconsciously tensing your muscles during the day. Tensing your muscles shouldn't produce pain, but rather a sensation of tightness or pressure. You'll progress in sequence by tensing and releasing your lower and upper arms, lower and upper legs, abdomen, chest, shoulders, neck, face, eyes, and lower and upper forehead.

Be certain to practice in the beginning in quiet, nondistracting places. Concentration is a key element in learning how to relax, so you'll need to be in an environment where you can focus you attention completely on the sensations of tensing and releasing your muscles. This means no phone, TV, radio, or kids around during the exercise. It may help to lie on your bed during the exercise, but be sure not to fall asleep. Loosen or remove tight clothing, eyeglasses, contact lenses, shoes, belts, and the like. This exercise should be practiced twice a day, 30 minutes each time, for the following week.

Now I'll turn on the audiotape and record the relaxation procedure that I'll have you do to my voice in the session. You can use the audiotape at home for your practices. [The therapist then begins the 16-muscle-group relaxation procedure and gives the tape to Claire at the end of the session.]

T: (*After relaxation has been conducted*) How was that?

C: Wow. Great. I don't want to get up. At one point, I felt as though I were floating. It was a little scary, so I opened my eyes, and it went away.

T: That can happen when you first try relaxation. Sometimes people find the procedure frightening due to the feeling that they're not in control of their feelings, like floating or heaviness. The more you do the relaxation, the less that will occur. [Claire is then given a form called the Relaxation Record, to self-monitor practices and to note any problems with concentration or relaxation.]

Session 4

Following a review of the patient's week and his/her relaxation homework exercises, the 16-muscle-group relaxation is refined to involve discrimination training. After the therapist and patient have rehearsed this technique, the cognitive component of the treatment protocol is introduced.

T: I'd like to turn now to the cognitive component of anxiety. Remember that your thoughts are instrumental in determining emotions, like anxiety. Concerning excessive worry and anxious thoughts, the key question to ask yourself is whether your judgment of risk or danger is valid—that is, if it can be supported by existing and available evidence. In many cases, worry over the worst possible feared outcome is out of proportion. To challenge your worries and anxious thoughts, keep in mind several basic principles. First, challenging your thoughts does not mean positive thinking. Instead, when you challenge your anxious cognitions, you'll be thinking more realistically about situations. Second, because thinking is often an automatic process, it may be difficult at first to identify these thoughts when you're anxious. Think back to the very first time you learned how to drive. Was it easy?

C: Sort of. I enjoyed it, but I had to focus on my turning and braking when I first started to drive.

T: Do you think about those things now when you drive?

C: Not at all. I don't focus any attention on my driving. I'm usually thinking about how much time I have to get somewhere, and the shortest way to arrive at my destination.

T: That's because driving has become automatic for you. You are still thinking when you drive, but because you've driven so many times, your thoughts are more rapid and automatic when you're behind the wheel. The same idea applies to your anxious thoughts. Because you've lived with high anxiety for so long, you may have certain automatic thoughts associated with anxiety. A large part of the treatment will center on identifying and challenging these anxious thoughts in order to reduce your worry and anxiety. It is important to be as specific as possible from now on about the thoughts you have when you're anxious or worried. Try to envision what it is that's making you anxious or nervous.

On one of your cognitive monitoring forms for this week, Claire, you wrote that you were afraid about your son playing in his football game. What specifically were you worried about?

C: That he'd get seriously hurt. His team was playing last year's state champions, so you know that those boys are big and strong. My son is good, but he hasn't been playing for years and years.

T: How specifically do you imagine your son getting hurt?

C: Getting a broken back or neck. Something that will result in paralysis or death. It happened to two NFL players this past year, remember?

T: What happened to your son when he played in the game?

C: Nothing, really. He came home that afternoon with a sore thumb, but that went away after a while. He said he scored a touchdown and had an interception. I guess he played really well.

T: So what you're saying is that you had predicted that he would be injured during the game, but that didn't happen. When we're anxious, we tend to commit a common cognitive error, called "probability overestimation." In other words, we overestimate the likelihood of an unlikely event. While you were feeling anxious and worried, what was the probability in your mind that your son would be hurt, from 0 to 100%?

C: About 75%.

T: And now what would you rate the probability of your son getting hurt in a future game?

C: Well, if you put it that way, I suppose around a 50% chance of him getting injured.

T: So that means that for every two times that your son plays football, he gets hurt once. Is that correct?

C: Umm, no, I don't think it's that high. Maybe about 30%.

T: That would be one out of every three times that your son gets hurt. To counter the tendency to overestimate the probability of negative future events, it's helpful to ask yourself what evidence from the past supports your anxious belief. What evidence can you provide from your son's playing history to account for your belief that he'll get hurt in one out of every three games?

C: Well, none. He had a sprained ankle during summer training, but that's it.

T: So what you're saying is that you don't have very much evidence at all to prove that your son has a 30% chance of getting hurt in a game.

C: Gee, I never thought of it that way.

T: What are some alternatives to your son getting seriously hurt in a football game?

C: He might not get hurt at all. But I know he must have some pain, with all those bruises covering his arms and legs. He's a real stoic, just like his father.

T: What other alternatives can you think of instead of your son getting seriously hurt?

C: He could get a minor injury, like a sprained ankle or something of that nature.

T: Right. And what would be the probability of your son getting a minor versus a major injury?

C: Probably higher, like 60% or 70%.

T: To go back to your original worry, what would you rate the probability of your son getting seriously injured during a football game?

C: Low, about 10%.

T: So 1 out of every 10 times your son will get seriously hurt playing football. How many times has your son played football?

C: He just started varsity this year, and he's a junior. But he's been playing since he got to high school, about 3 years. All in all, about 25 games.

T: And how many times in those 3 years has he been seriously injured?

C: Not once. I see what you're doing. It's so foolish for me to think these irrational thoughts.

T: Well, it's understandable that your predictions about the future are biased toward negative possibilities. When we're in a state of high anxiety, we naturally focus on the more negative possibilities, in order to prepare for them should they come true. Because you worry excessively, your thoughts will be more negative regarding future events. That's why it's essential that you regularly counter these probability overestimations every time you have a worry. On your Cognitive Self-Monitoring Form, you indicated that your anxiety was a 6 on the 0–8 scale while thinking about your son getting hurt. What would you rate your anxiety now, after having had gone through the countering?

C: Much lower. Around a 3 or so. But it could still happen to him, getting paralyzed. And by worrying over that possibility, no matter how small, I can somehow prepare myself emotionally if it were to really happen.

T: There's always that possibility, however minute. However, every time you tell yourself that "it could still happen," you're effectively throwing out all the evidence disconfirming that belief. You're also saying to yourself that your son's personal chances of paralysis from a football injury are much higher than everyone else's. To counter this tendency, remember that his chances of a serious injury remain the same as that of the rest of the team, every day.

Additionally, worrying about a future event does nothing to change its probability of occurring. What worrying will do, however, is make you feel even more anxious and distressed, along with giving you a false sense of control over the future.

Starting this week, record the countering of your worries on the Cognitive Self-Monitoring Form [see Figure 4.3]. As before, you'll jot down every time you feel moderately anxious or worried about something. In the first column, identify the trigger or event that started the worry or anxiety. Then write down your specific automatic thought, and rate your anxiety from 0 to 8. In the next column, rate (from 0 to 100%) the probability of that automatic thought occurring. However, from now on, counter that thought by asking yourself, "What's the evidence for my belief or prediction? Are there other alternative possibilities that I can think of?" After countering the thought, rerate the probability of your automatic thought and then rate your anxiety. Ask yourself, "What's the worst possible consequence of that automatic thought?" and write it down. If you are still moderately anxious (4 or above on the 0–8 scale), go back to the first column and repeat the procedure, using the worst possible feared consequence that you wrote down in the column headed "Trigger or event." Continue this until your anxiety is 3 or less [see Figure 4.3]. Next time, we'll talk about an-

other cognitive strategy to target your worry and anxiety.

Session 5

Following a review of the patient's week and the relaxation homework exercises, the eight-muscle-group relaxation is introduced in order to begin to make the relaxation strategies more readily applicable in naturalistic settings. When reducing the number of muscle areas, the therapist should instruct the patient to continue to involve areas that are particularly salient (e.g., if the patient reports considerable jaw tension or teeth clenching, the therapist should instruct the patient to spend extra time focusing on the jaw and mouth when doing the exercise). After this exercise is rehearsed, probability overestimation is reviewed and decatastrophizing is introduced.

T: Last week, we went over the concept of probability overestimation. Tell me in your own words what is meant by probability overestimation.

C: If I remember correctly, it means that when I'm overly anxious, I will predict some future negative event as more likely than it really is.

T: That's exactly right. Did you monitor any instances this week when you overestimated the probability of a negative event?

C: Of course. My husband had to take an unexpected overnight business trip because his coworker caught the flu. It was raining when he drove off, and naturally I assumed the worst, that he'd get into a car accident.

T: How did you rate the probability of that event?

C: I gave that an 80%, because it was coming down like cats and dogs. And other drivers aren't necessarily defensive drivers like my husband and I are.

T: Were you able to come up with any past evidence contrary to your belief that he'd get in an accident?

C: As a matter of fact, I realized that my husband has never been in a car accident before in his life. He's a great driver, very safe like I am, and he also never speeds. I remembered from a driver's ed. class back in high school that most accidents are caused by speeding and drunk driving. That made me feel much better.

T: Could you think of any alternatives to your husband getting in an accident, Claire?

C: I wrote that maybe if he did get in an accident, it would be a little fender-bender, like most accidents usually are. Or he'd arrive at the hotel without any incident whatsoever. Or, if it were really dangerous to drive, he'd pull over until the storm passed. My husband has a good head on his shoulders. This exercise made me realize that I don't give him enough credit.

T: Given what you've just provided in the way of evidence and alternatives, what probability would you assign to your husband getting involved in an accident while driving?

C: Very low. I'd still give a slightly higher rating, like 10%, because of inclement weather. But really low.

T: What is your anxiety when you think about it that way?

C: Practically nothing, a 1 or 2.

T: Great. Along with probability overestimations, another common cognitive error associated with anxiety is called "catastrophizing." This refers to the tendency to blow things out of proportion, or to "make mountains out of molehills." Using adjectives such as "intolerable," "awful," "terrible," "unbearable," and "horrible" to describe future negative events is one way to catastrophize. Another way to catastrophize is to jump to an extreme conclusion from an unimportant or irrelevant event. For instance, what do you think the nurse at the doctor's office thought of you when you were late a few weeks ago?

C: She probably thought I wasn't punctual or conscientious. I was a little concerned that she'd think I was irresponsible, and maybe because of that she wouldn't accept a personal check as a form of payment from me. I wouldn't be dependable in her eyes.

T: In order to *decatastrophize*, you must first imagine the worst possible outcome of what you're worried or anxious about, and then judge its realistic severity. Very often, when people are chronically anxious, they underestimate their ability to cope with future negative events. They also tend to believe that the event might continue forever—for example, that everyone would begin to think of you as undependable. It helps to keep in mind that events cannot continue forever. Even if a very negative event were to happen, like losing a loved one or facing a serious illness, we would still be able to cope with it, despite feeling like we couldn't. How you feel and what you do are two very different things. You might feel in your heart that you wouldn't be able to cope with a negative event, but the fact is that the hallmark of being a human being is having an extraordinary ability to adapt to our surroundings.

C: Sure, but how do I convince myself of that? I really don't believe that I could cope with losing my son or husband. It scares me so much that I dislike even talking about this.

T: Which is why we should probably discuss your fears, being that a majority of your worry centers on the safety of your husband and son. What would happen if you lost your son?

C: I'd be devastated. It really would be terrible. I'd never get over it. Maybe I'd have a breakdown and be placed in the psychiatric ward or something. I don't know, but it would be bad.

T: How do you know that it would be bad? What evidence can you provide to support your belief that you'd never get over your son's death?

C: Well, none, but children shouldn't die before their parents. I'm such a nervous wreck already that it would put me over the edge.

T: Again, you're using your anxious feelings as proof of your belief. We refer to that as "emotional reasoning." Tell me some alternatives to having a breakdown or being placed in a hospital.

C: I would cope, I guess, but I really can't fathom how I'd do that.

T: Has anyone in your life died?

C: Sure. When I was 17, my boyfriend was killed in a motorcycle accident. It was really hard on me. On a certain level, I never really got over it. Sometimes I dream about him. He was a great guy, and his poor mother went through hell when he passed away. I never want to experience what she went through.

T: It must have been a very difficult time for you. An experience like that is unusual for a 17-year-old to have. It's pretty natural to have dreams about loved ones who have died, especially when the death was of a violent nature. Tell me some of the emotions you went through at the time.

C: I went through a whole range of feelings: anger, disbelief, anxiety, loneliness, pain. It was a tough time for me. He died the summer we graduated from high school, and we were supposed to go to college together.

T: Do you still feel those emotions?

C: Not at the same intensity. I sometimes feel anger when I see motorcycles on the road, and of course I get pretty anxious. But now, when I think of Todd, I try to think of the happy memories. He was a wonderful guy, and I was lucky to have known him for the time that I did. He's in heaven right now, I'm sure of it, and looking out for me, like he said he would before he died. I met my husband several months after Todd's death while I was in college, and felt like I met someone who could have been Todd's twin brother. Without Jim, I don't know how I would have ever gotten over Todd's death.

T: Despite having experienced the unexpected death of Todd, Claire, you did cope with your loss. You experienced the full range of emotions the people go through when they lose someone close, and you were still able to function. Is that right?

C: Yes, but it was a struggle to get up in the morning for a while there. I cried almost every day for a month or two.

T: What do you think would happen if you lost your husband or son?

C: Probably the same thing, maybe even more intense. But you're right. I would be able to cope. It would be a job and a half, but I would have to. Luckily, I have a very supportive and close-knit family who's always there for me.

T: Let's turn to another example of decatastrophizing. You mentioned that by com-

ing in late, the nurse would think of you as being undependable, and that she wouldn't accept your personal check to pay for the visit. What would happen then?

C: I'd have to incur a balance, and I would pay it later.

T: Anything else?

C: No, other than embarrassment.

T: Why would that be bad?

C: I hate being embarrassed like that. People would think badly of me, and I'd lose the respect of others.

T: Then what?

C: Then I would lose friends and be lonely.

T: Then what?

C: Then I would feel sad and miserable, and lead a miserable little existence.

T: Tell me how able you would be to cope with that possibility, from 0 to 100%, where 0 equals "completely unable to cope."

C: 5%.

T: Now try to think of some ways that you could cope with that possibility.

C: First of all, a true friend wouldn't lose respect for me because of something as mundane as not having a personal check accepted. And if I did lose friends over that, then what kinds of friends are they? Also, I could use a credit card, or go get a cash withdrawal from the bank if the doctor didn't accept credit cards.

T: Do you think you'd be miserable and sad for the rest of your life?

C: Oh, not at all. I'd feel bad for a little while, but it would eventually go away.

T: And how likely is it that all your friends would remember a minor event like that for years to come?

C: Not very likely at all.

T: Have you ever been embarrassed before?

C: Too many times to count!

T: How long, on average, does the embarrassment last?

C: A few minutes at the most. A day in rare instances, but usually not longer.

T: So, Claire, you see how these catastrophic images can add to your anxiety. To counter your catastrophic thoughts, write your anxious thoughts and worries down on the Cognitive Self-Monitoring Form as you've been doing for probability overestimations. Then ask yourself, "What's the worst possible consequence that could happen? If it happens, so what? Why would it be bad? How likely would it be to occur? How could I cope with it if it were to occur?" You should notice a substantial decline in your anxiety levels when you use your cognitive strategies regularly for each and every worry and anxious thought.

Session 6

Prior to the review of the types of anxiogenic cognitions (i.e., probability overestimation, catastrophic thinking) and corresponding methods of countering, eight-muscle-group relaxation is reviewed and refined to incorporate discrimination training. In addition, generalization practices are assigned.

T: By doing the relaxation as frequently as possible, you will enhance your skill in the technique and find it more and more helpful in dampening tension when it arises. So, now I'd like you to begin applying the relaxation procedure in more distracting and challenging situations. In this way, you'll be making the relaxation more portable. You can start applying the relaxation while you're in traffic, waiting in line, at home watching TV, and in the grocery store. OK, why don't we review some of your records on the Cognitive Self-Monitoring Form? You wrote down that you hadn't yet finished doing the laundry at 10:00 P.M. as one of your triggers, and that your automatic thought was that you'll have to stay up late to finish it all. You then rated your anxiety as a 6. Why was that so anxiety-provoking for you?

C: I really need about 9 hours of sleep every night. If I don't get that amount, I feel dragged out and exhausted the next day, and find it difficult to get anything done at all because of my low energy level.

T: And what will happen if that takes place?

C: Well, I'll get behind in all the other things that need to be done in the house, and I won't be able to catch up on it all.

T: And then what?

C: It'll just pile up, and my family will be living in a pigsty. It's disgusting to think about it.

T: Then what will happen?

C: Then my husband will be embarrassed to bring people over to the house, and get angry with me.

T: And then?

C: And maybe he'd want to leave me. Occasionally, we do some entertaining at our home, and so it is important that my husband and I make a good impression. If I can't have the house in presentable condition, then his colleagues and supervisors will think less of him and demote him, all because of my inability to do my job as a homemaker right.

T: Do you see how you chain these anxious thoughts together so that the end result is really quite negative? That's fairly typical of individuals who have generalized anxiety. It becomes crucial to identify these thoughts specifically so that you can target each one in your chain of worry and anxiety. Let's then begin with the first automatic thought—namely, that you would have to stay up later and lose some sleep, which would make it difficult to get things accomplished the next day. What is the probability of that happening, from 0 to 100%?

C: Oh, I suppose about 75%.

T: What evidence can you provide in support of your belief that there's a 75% chance that you won't get things accomplished the next day if you don't get 9 hours of sleep?

C: Once I had to stay up until 4 in the morning because one of the cakes I was making for our dinner party the following day was burned accidentally. I was so wiped out that I had to ask my husband to take care of setting the table and arranging to pick up the flowers from the florist that next day.

T: Does that necessarily translate into your not being able to do those things?

C: Well, no, but I felt I needed to take a nap if I wanted to be alert for the dinner conversation.

T: So you could have gone to the florist and set the table if you had wanted to. Is that correct?

C: Yes.

T: How many times in the past have you had to stay up until 4 A.M.?

C: Really only that one time.

T: And how many times have you thrown dinner parties?

C: Oh, about 20 times so far.

T: That means that once out of 20 times have you not done something in preparation for a dinner party, and that due to your own choice. Correct?

C: If you put it that way, yes.

T: Now, back to the example at hand, how much later did you have to stay up to get your laundry done?

C: Until midnight.

T: And what happened the next day?

C: Nothing much. I felt a little sleepy, but I did manage to get up in time for my 9 A.M. hair appointment.

T: Did you fall behind on your other household responsibilities?

C: Not at all. In fact, yesterday I managed to have a very productive day. I was even able to fit in going to a movie in the evening with my husband, and write a letter to my mother later that evening.

T: So things didn't pile up. Do you think that your husband would be demoted if things did pile up?

C: You never know with his company! Oh, I just remembered something when we first got married. We were moving into our new apartment, and things still needed to be unpacked. We had some boxes in the corner, and I remember that we had some friends over at the time for the Super Bowl. Instead of commenting on the boxes, they said that they couldn't believe how quickly we settled into our new home. Wow, I really do focus on the negative, don't I?

T: Tell me some alternatives to your prediction that if things did in fact pile up in your house and his colleagues were over for a dinner party, that your husband would be demoted because of that.

C: Hmmm. Maybe they wouldn't notice, like our friends hadn't noticed in our first home. Or maybe they'd compliment us on the house, which is what they always do anyway. Or maybe they're just interested in having a good meal and a fun time and don't care either way. Perhaps they'd rib my husband a little bit at work about our house if it were messy, because they know how neat and clean we keep it, but that would be it. I guess it wouldn't be as bad as I think it would be.

T: And your final prediction, that your husband would leave you if he were demoted. Are there alternatives to that consequence?

C: That he wouldn't leave; that he loves me no matter what; that he would take an early retirement or find another job in a different field, because he's been considering a job change; that he might actually be relieved that I wasn't spending tons of time cleaning the house.

T: Based on all the evidence and the alternatives that you've just generated, what would you rate the likelihood that if you don't get the laundry done and you have to stay up later in the night, that you wouldn't get things accomplished the next day and that all of these other consequences would follow? Recall that you originally assigned a probability of 75%.

C: Looking at it in the way you went through it, around 2%.

T: I think you can see the importance of being highly specific about your anxious thoughts, because more often than not, they are chained together in a larger sphere of worry. By breaking up that chain into its individual components (those thoughts and negative predictions), you can counter your worries more efficiently and effectively. How would you rate your anxiety now about not getting enough sleep?

C: Really low, a 2 or 1. I don't like feeling sleepy, because it makes me feel that I'm not on top of things in my life if I'm having to go to bed late, but I know that it's my anxiety and overly high standards that make me think that way.

T: Right. Sometimes it's helpful to consider the pros and cons of holding such high expectations and standards for yourself. It might be useful to write down the advantages and disadvantages of that belief, and then to ask yourself if you're being harder on yourself than other people are. To put it another way, would you think badly of a friend who didn't get everything done that she had wanted to do in a day, or who went to bed a little later one night and was tired the next day?

C: Oh, no, it's just in regard to myself. I have these standards that have been ingrained in me since childhood, so it's hard to break them, if you know what I mean. I would love to learn how to be less hard on myself.

T: Great. In a later session we'll discuss some exercises, called "worry behavior prevention exercises," designed specifically for challenging some of your assumptions about your standards and what will or won't happen if you don't always abide by them.

Session 7

The main emphasis in Session 7 is on the introduction and rehearsal of worry exposure. However, this material is preceded by four-muscle-group relaxation (stomach, chest, shoulders, forehead). With this relaxation exercise, the therapist should remind the patient that this refinement is to make the relaxation more "portable," but that the patient should continue to include any muscle groups that represent particular problem areas.

T: Today we will cover one of the most essential parts of the treatment program: systematic exposure to your worries. Recall that worrying is usually an attempt to problem-solve future threatening or dangerous situations. Often excessive worry gets in the way of effective problem solving, and the individual focuses not on realistic solutions, but rather on anxiety-laden, negative predictions that only serve to increase anxiety. The method that I'll teach you will help you gain a sense of control over these worries, and will also help you to manage them a bit more productively than you might be doing. The reason that these worries persist is because you might not be thinking about them completely, or may not be processing what you're thinking about completely. You might be trying to distract yourself when you experience these thoughts by saying things like "Oh, I can't think about this now," or by doing some busy work to turn your attention away from the thoughts. You might also be saying, "I can't think about this at all," because the thoughts are so anxiety-provoking. It's natural that you don't want to think about something that makes you upset. At the same time, though, if someone tells you not to think of pink elephants, probably the first thing you think about is pink elephants! That's why it's very difficult to successfully avoid the worries, because you're not allowing yourself to think about what it is that's frightening or scaring you. This technique is designed to help you overcome what we refer to as an "approach–avoidance" pattern. You'll learn to think about your fears and worries in a different manner than the way you currently think about them. I'm going to ask you to think about a worry that we identify for at least 30 minutes a day. You'll do nothing but concentrate on worrying and thinking about this area of worry for 30 minutes. In this way, we're actually reducing the amount of time that you're worrying from 100% of the day, like you had first reported at the interview, to worrying for around 30 minutes a day. Generate the most feared possible outcomes to your worry that you can imagine, and then generate as many alternatives to that worst outcome that you can think of [see Figure 4.4].

Let's use an example from your Cognitive Self-Monitoring Form to illustrate the process of worry exposure. Here you have that your friend called to say that she was dropping by in half an hour without having given you advance notice. What is the very worst image that you can envision when your friend comes over?

C: She'll have a look of shock on her face when she sees my dirty floors and unvacuumed rugs. She'll laugh at me and she'll go home and tell everyone that I'm not a good housekeeper or mother. I'll lose everyone's respect, and everyone will be laughing at me.

T: How vivid or clear is that image in your mind, from 0 to 8?

C: About a 5.

T: I want you to imagine that you're watching yourself in a movie. You can see very clearly the shock and then the hidden laughter on your friend's face as she comes into your apartment. You also see her dial the phone number of another mutual friend and tell that person in great detail how awful your house looked, and you see and hear her cruel laughter. How vivid is that image?

C: Very clear. About a 7.

T: Good. Now hold onto that image for at least another 5 or 10 minutes. Concentrate on what you're seeing and hearing in the situation. It is as though you can feel and touch what is happening around you. What is your anxiety level?

C: Umm, around a 7.

T: Continue to hold the image. [Therapist waits until 5–10 minutes have elapsed.] What is your anxiety level now?

C: Still a 7.

T: Now continue to hold that image for a bit longer. [Therapist waits another 5 minutes or so.] How is your anxiety?

C: Approximately a 5.

T: Very good. Now, Claire, I want you to begin to use your cognitive strategies to counter that catastrophic image in your mind. What are some alternatives to that image, first of all?

C: My friend won't care about the condition of my house. She's there to see me. Maybe she won't even notice that I haven't vacuumed the rugs or mopped the kitchen floor. She might notice, but not care and not think it so interesting to tell everyone we know that I keep a messy house. My house really isn't messy, according to other people's standards. Compared to her place, my house is a temple anyway. She probably thinks that I'm too preoccupied with keeping the house neat and clean. Maybe she'd be glad or relieved to see that I wasn't cleaning for a change.

T: Great. How is your anxiety level now?

C: Wow, it went down to about a 2 or 1. But it feels uncomfortable to do this worry exposure. My stomach was doing little butterflies when you asked me to imagine

the worst. I don't know if I can do this at home.

T: It is to be expected that you'll feel some emotional and physical discomfort, perhaps, while implementing the worry exposure. What you're doing in essence is facing and confronting the very thoughts that you avoid because of those same feelings and emotions that they evoke in you. Like anything else, becoming skilled in this procedure will take time and practice. If you're too anxious to continue the exposure while imagining the worst image, still try as best as you can to stick with the image. Your anxiety will come down, as you saw today. It is absolutely crucial that you allow 25–30 minutes at the very least for focusing on and envisioning the worst possible image of your worry. By giving yourself that much time, you're permitting the process of habituation to occur. Your anxiety will reach a peak and then decline to lower levels, once you acclimate to the image. Remember to use the cognitive strategies *after* you've imagined the worst. Additionally, you can use the relaxation after imagining the worst, if physically you're reactive to this procedure. Just make certain that during the exposure itself, you don't allow any sort of distraction from imagining the worst.

Session 8

In Session 8, worry exposure is reviewed and rehearsed, and relaxation-by-recall is introduced.

T: You've been doing a tremendous job with the homework, especially with the worry exposure every day. It can be a lot of work, but keep in mind that it will all pay off in the long run, the more investment you make in the program.

C: Yes, I can see that. My anxiety has really dropped to lower levels, compared to when I first came to the clinic. I feel more relaxed, and although I still worry a lot, it doesn't bother me as much as it used to.

T: Your efforts are to be commended. This is an intensive program that requires a good deal of motivation and desire to change your negative thought patterns and worry-related behaviors. How has the relaxation been going?

C: Very well. I do it every day, all through the day. Sometimes I'll do it in the shower, or when I'm driving, and I try to make a point of relaxing before I get up out of bed in the morning. I still have this scared feeling when I wake up, anticipating the day, I guess. But it's been getting less and less noticeable.

T: That's good to hear. Because you've seemed to master the relaxation exercise, I think you're ready now to start "relaxation-by-recall." This procedure entails recalling the feelings of relaxation. Instead of tensing the muscles before releasing them, you'll simply relax your muscles through the power of concentration and recall. You can concentrate on each of the four groups that you've been doing, and concentrate on releasing all the tension and pressure as you think back to how it feels to be relaxed in each part of your body. Maintain a regular pattern of fluid, smooth breathing with relaxation-by-recall, as you've been doing for the other forms of progressive muscle relaxation. Try to do this procedure in distracting, noisy, even stressful situations, so that the relaxation becomes a truly portable skill that can be used anywhere you are, in whatever circumstances that may be.

Session 9

In addition to a review of skills introduced in the last two sessions (e.g., worry exposure, relaxation-by-recall), worry behavior prevention is introduced.

T: As I've mentioned several times in our earlier meetings together, part of the treatment program involves identifying certain behaviors and activities that you may either be doing or avoiding that serve to relieve your anxiety in the short term. What happens, however, is that those behaviors actually reinforce your worry and anxiety in the long term, so that they are counterproductive. Today I'd like to generate a list of some of those behaviors that you might be doing, or activities that you may be avoiding, due to anxiety and worry. Some examples of such behaviors and activities include avoiding certain parts of the newspaper (like the health section or the obituaries), cleaning the house several times, being early for appointments, etc. Let's come up with some for you, Claire.

C: I think the most obvious behavior is my total avoidance of my son's football games. He's been begging me to go to the homecoming game, and I would really like to, because it's a big day for the team and there's a lot of pageantry about it. But it'll be tough to do, that I know for sure.

T: So that's one activity. What is your anxiety about going to the game, from 0 to 8?

C: Around a 7.

T: What other things can we put on the list? How about not cleaning for a few days?

C: Umm, that would also be around a 6 or 7.

T: How about not making your bed one morning?

C: Maybe a 4.

T: And cleaning the bathroom only once that day instead of your usual twice-a-day routine?

C: That would only be a 3. If I couldn't clean the bathroom at all one day, it would jump up to a 5.

T: And having your husband call you at work? What if he didn't call one day?

C: That might be a 6.

T: What if he didn't call until he left to come home?

C: Oh, so long as he calls at least once, it's not too bad. Maybe about a 2.

T: We have a few things that can comprise the list. Here it is: Going to the homecoming game, 7. Not cleaning for a few days, 6 to 7. Not having your husband call home at all, 6. Not cleaning the bathroom at all one day, 5. Not making the bed one morning, 4. Cleaning the bathroom only once one day, 3. Your husband calls only before leaving, 2.

For this week, you can begin the last item on the hierarchy—namely, having your husband call only when leaving work. Rate your anxiety during the day each week when you know he's not going to call until later, and then rate your anxiety after he calls. Let me know how this goes. If you find yourself worrying about him during the day, be sure to implement your cognitive strategies and the relaxation-by-recall to help you to control your worry and anxiety [see Figure 4.5].

Session 10

In Session 10, the therapist should concentrate on reviewing the worry exposure and cognitive countering, relaxation-by-recall, and the worry behavior prevention exercises. He/she should then assign the next higher item(s) on the worry behavior hierarchy that has been composed in Session 9, depending on how well the patient has mastered the exercise and whether any problems are noted. In addition, cue-controlled relaxation is discussed.

Sessions 11 and 12

These sessions should be devoted to a review of all material thus covered, along with an inclusion of time management and problem-solving principles and strategies. Because these techniques often overlap with some of the cognitive strategies previously covered, they are not covered in this section.

For example, if the patient finds it difficult to fit everything in the day or has problems with meeting deadlines, the therapist should investigate overly high, unrealistic self-standards about performance and the perceived consequences of not getting everything done. Cognitive countering is usually the best intervention, along with teaching the patient how to stick to a daily schedule and allocate ample time for tasks. Similarly, if the patient reports difficulty making decisions due to fear of not making the right decision or choice, the therapist may wish to target the fear of making mistakes and the perceived consequences through decatastrophizing and probability estimations. Of course, introducing the concept of brainstorming, or generating as many alternatives as possible for a given problem situation, is very useful and should have already been fostered by regular practice of worry exposure exercises and use of the Cognitive Self-Monitoring Form.

Session 13

In addition to reviewing the skills covered over the prior 12 sessions and progress that the patient has made, a major objective of Session 13 is to provide an agenda for the patient's continued application and consolidation of the treatment techniques.

T: Claire, we've covered a great deal of information about generalized anxiety and coping skills for it. As this is our last treatment session together before you go on your own for a while, it would be ideal for us to go over some of the skills you've been faithfully practicing and to talk about the future.

C: That's reassuring to hear, because I've been feeling a little nervous about stopping therapy.

T: Why is that?

C: Well, I'm afraid that if I don't come regularly, I'll lose all the gains that I've made and I'll be right back where I started: a nervous wreck who is miserable and unhappy with life. I don't want to go back to being that way.

T: Tell me some reasons why that might happen.

C: I won't be seeing you regularly, and maybe I'll forget the exercises and not know how to control my thoughts and feelings.

T: How can you be sure of that?

C: I can't. It's just a fear that I have. I guess I'm doing that "emotional reasoning" that you're always pointing out to me. I've been feeling so much better lately that I don't want it to end.

T: OK, but how have you accomplished that?

C: By doing the exercises and trying to change myself, which I think I've done to a big extent.

T: And where have you done most of the changing?

C: At home, and by myself! I see where you're getting. I'm not giving myself credit for the work I've done.

T: And you're discounting the fact that you are responsible for the change that you see. When we meet, our sessions are intended to introduce material and to review your homework, much like a teacher–student relationship. Except in our case, there's no grade given, just feedback on how you're doing and areas on which you could focus more attention. If you were to experience a resurgence in high anxiety and worry, Claire, what would you do? If you could write a letter to yourself in the future if that were to happen, what would you say?

C: I would say that I shouldn't let one minor setback color my whole view of myself, that I can always start doing the full hour of worry exposures and relaxation, and take out some of the Cognitive Self-Monitoring Forms, now that I know how to do them like the back of my hand. And I would tell myself, like you've told me, that it's OK and normal to feel anxious sometimes, that it doesn't necessarily mean that there's something wrong with me. It's so easy when I talk to you, but I struggle sometimes when I'm home trying to do these exercises and manage my worry. I am getting better, without a doubt, but it's been hard.

T: And that is to be expected, because what we're doing in essence is changing some ways of thinking, feeling, and acting when you're anxious that have been automatic reactions for you for some time. As you continue using the strategies, you've seen some changes in how you think about and act in anxiety-provoking situations. Is there any evidence you can provide to show that you won't see further changes so long as you regularly use these techniques?

C: No, of course not. It's just my fear getting the better of me. I know I can do it on my own.

T: Let's discuss briefly some of the strategies. First, you learned about the nature of anxiety and worry, and how it is maintained over time. Then we went over relaxation, and now you're managing to relax your body in some highly stressful and distracting situations, like driving and while shopping. We spent a lot of time challenging your negative, anxious thoughts by identifying and countering probability overestimations and decatastrophizing. Next, we went over worry exposure—the daily hour of exposing yourself systematically to your worries and allowing yourself to fully visualize your anxious images and thoughts and then countering those. We followed this with worry behavior prevention exercises, when you gradually accomplished doing tasks that made you nervous or worried due to your negative predictions. You were even able to go to your son's homecoming game last week, right?

C: Yes! It wasn't bad at all. He played well, had some major running gains, and really impressed the coach, who complimented him in front of the team after the game. I was so proud of myself. My anxiety was pretty high at first—about a 6—but it went down eventually, and I was doing the relaxation and the cognitive strategies all the while. It was actually a lot of fun for both my husband and I to go, because we sat with some close friends whose son is also on the team.

T: That's great. Then we talked about time management and problem solving, with which you didn't have too many difficulties.

We'll be meeting again a month from now to monitor your progress and to troubleshoot any problems or difficulties you're experiencing. Then we'll meet again several months later to discuss your progress to date. Certainly, if you're having any serious difficulties, you can give me a call. For now, concentrate on trying to use the techniques on your own. You've made tremendous progress, Claire, and there's no evidence to indicate that won't continue.

Claire's Progress

As is customary for patients who complete a treatment program at our clinic (whether it is a research protocol or not), Claire underwent posttreatment and follow-up assessments, each of which entailed administration of the ADIS-IV-L and some self-report questionnaires. At posttreatment and across the follow-up period, Claire continued to experience decreasing levels of general anxiety and worry. When asked what components of the treatment she found especially useful for coping with her anxiety, Claire replied that the daily worry exposure and cognitive monitoring/restructuring were particularly helpful and were strategies that she employed regularly. In addition, Claire reported that most of her once-debilitating stomach problems had ceased to occur, and that she felt more in control of her worry and anxiety, both cognitively as well as physically. Claire maintained that although she still experienced some worry during the day, she felt more in control of it. Moreover, she stated that she noticed herself engaging in problem solving when she did worry, instead of distracting herself as she had for many years.

In comparison to her initial DSM-IV diagnosis of GAD, with an ADIS-IV-L clinical severity rating of 6, Claire received a post-treatment diagnosis of "GAD in partial remission," with a severity rating of 2, from an independent interviewer who was unaware of her original diagnosis. At 1-year follow-up, Claire was assigned a DSM-IV diagnosis of "GAD in full remission."

A CONCLUDING NOTE

Typically we will see patients a few more times on roughly a monthly basis in order to refine the patients' application of treatment techniques or to assist in the handling of any setbacks. As noted in the review of the treatment literature, patients who have completed a psychosocial treatment program for GAD generally evidence a maintenance of their treatment gains. Moreover, in many instances medication usage (e.g., anxiolytics) is reduced or eliminated (see Barlow et al., 1992). Nevertheless, a substantial number of patients undergoing these program show no more than modest gains. This finding may in part be due to the fact that treatments have only recently been tailored to address specifically the core component of GAD—namely, excessive and uncontrollable worry. Research is continuing at our center and elsewhere to determine whether these highly specialized treatments provide more substantial and lasting improvements in individuals with GAD.

REFERENCES

Abel, J. L., & Borkovec, T. D. (1995). Generalizability of DSM-III-R generalized anxiety disorder to proposed DSM-IV criteria and cross-validation of proposed changes. *Journal of Anxiety Disorders, 9,* 303–315.

American Psychiatric Association. (1980). *Diagnostic and statistical manual of mental disorders* (3rd ed.). Washington, DC: Author.

American Psychiatric Association. (1987). *Diagnostic and statistical manual of mental disorders* (3rd ed., rev.). Washington, DC: Author.

American Psychiatric Association. (1994). *Diagnostic and statistical manual of mental disorders* (4th ed.). Washington, DC: Author.

Anderson, D. J., Noyes, R., & Crowe, R. R. (1984). A comparison of panic disorder and generalized anxiety disorder. *American Journal of Psychiatry, 141,* 572–575.

Andrews, G., Stewart, G., Allen, R., & Henderson, A. S. (1990). The genetics of six neurotic disorders: A twin study. *Journal of Affective Disorders, 19,* 23–29.

Andrews, V. H., & Borkovec, T. D. (1988). The differential effects of inductions of worry, somatic anxiety, and depression on emotional experience. *Journal of Behavior Therapy and Experimental Psychiatry, 19,* 21–26.

Barlow, D. H. (1988). *Anxiety and its disorders: The nature and treatment of anxiety and panic.* New York: Guilford Press.

Barlow, D. H. (1991). The nature of anxiety: Anxiety, depression, and emotional disorders. In R. M. Rapee & D. H. Barlow (Eds.), *Chronic anxiety: Generalized anxiety disorder and mixed anxiety–depression* (pp. 1–28). New York: Guilford Press.

Barlow, D. H., Blanchard, E. B., Vermilyea, J. A., Vermilyea, B. B., & Di Nardo, P. A. (1986). Generalized anxiety and generalized anxiety disorder: Description and reconceptualization. *American Journal of Psychiatry, 143,* 40–44.

Barlow, D. H., Chorpita, B. F., & Turovsky, J. (1996). Fear, panic, anxiety, and disorders of emotion. In D. A. Hope (Ed.), *Perspectives on anxiety, panic, and fear* (Vol. 43, pp. 251–328). Lincoln: University of Nebraska Press.

Barlow, D. H., Cohen, A. S., Waddell, M., Vermilyea, J. A., Klosko, J. S., Blanchard, E. B., & Di Nardo, P. A. (1984). Panic and generalized anxiety disorders: Nature and treatment. *Behavior Therapy, 15,* 431–449.

Barlow, D. H., Craske, M. G., Cerny, J. A., & Klosko, J. S. (1989). Behavioral treatment of panic disorder. *Behavior Therapy, 20,* 261–282.

Barlow, D. H., & Di Nardo, P. A. (1991). The diagnosis of generalized anxiety disorder: Development, current status, and future directions. In R. M. Rapee & D. H. Barlow (Eds.), *Chronic anxiety: Generalized anxiety disorder, and mixed anxiety–depression* (pp. 95–118). New York: Guilford Press.

Barlow, D. H., Rapee, R. M., & Brown, T. A. (1992). Behavioral treatment of generalized anxiety disorder. *Behavior Therapy, 23,* 551–570.

Barrett, P. M., Dadds, M. R., & Rapee, R. M. (1996). Family treatment of childhood anxiety: A controlled trial. *Journal of Consulting and Clinical Psychology, 64,* 333–342.

Beck, A. T., Emery, G., & Greenberg, R. (1985). *Anxiety disorders and phobias: A cognitive perspective.* New York: Basic Books.

Beck, J. G., Stanley, M. A., & Zebb, B. J. (1996). Characteristics of generalized anxiety disorder in older adults: A descriptive study. *Behaviour Research and Therapy, 34,* 225–234.

Bernstein, D. A., & Borkovec, T. D. (1973). *Progressive relaxation training*. Champaign, IL: Research Press.

Blanchard, E. B., Scharff, L., Schwarz, S. P., Suls, J. M., & Barlow, D. H. (1990). The role of anxiety and depression in the irritable bowel syndrome. *Behaviour Research and Therapy, 28,* 401–405.

Blazer, D. G., George, L. K., & Hughes, D. (1991). The epidemiology of anxiety disorders: An age comparison. In C. Salzman & B. D. Lebowitz (Eds.), *Anxiety disorders in the elderly* (pp. 180–203). New York: Free Press.

Blazer, D. G., Hughes, D., & George, L. K. (1987). Stressful life events and the onset of the generalized anxiety disorder syndrome. *American Journal of Psychiatry, 144,* 1178–1183.

Blowers, C., Cobb, J., & Mathews, A. (1987). Generalized anxiety: A controlled treatment study. *Behaviour Research and Therapy, 25,* 493–502.

Borkovec, T. D. (1994). The nature, functions, and origins of worry. In G. Davey & F. Tallis (Eds.), *Worrying: Perspectives on theory, assessment, and treatment* (pp. 5–33). New York: Wiley.

Borkovec, T. D., Abel, J. L., & Newman, H. (1995). Effects of psychotherapy on comorbid conditions in generalized anxiety disorder. *Journal of Consulting and Clinical Psychology, 63,* 479–483.

Borkovec, T. D., & Costello, E. (1993). Efficacy of applied relaxation and cognitive-behavioral therapy in the treatment of generalized anxiety disorder. *Journal of Consulting and Clinical Psychology, 61,* 611–619.

Borkovec, T. D., & Hu, S. (1990). The effect of worry on cardiovascular response to phobic imagery. *Behaviour Research and Therapy, 28,* 69–73.

Borkovec, T. D., & Inz, J. (1990). The nature of worry in generalized anxiety disorder: A predominance of thought activity. *Behaviour Research and Therapy, 28,* 153–158.

Borkovec, T. D., & Lyonfields, J. D. (1993). Worry: Thought suppression of emotional processing. In H. Krohne (Ed.), *Vigilance and avoidance* (pp. 101–118). Toronto: Hogrefe & Huber.

Borkovec, T. D., Lyonfields, J. D., Wiser, S. L., & Diehl, L. (1993). The role of worrisome thinking in the suppression of cardiovascular response to phobic imagery. *Behaviour Research and Therapy, 31,* 321–324.

Borkovec, T. D., & Mathews, A. M. (1988). Treatment of nonphobic anxiety disorders: A comparison of nondirective, cognitive, and coping desensitization therapy. *Journal of Consulting and Clinical Psychology, 56,* 877–884.

Borkovec, T. D., Mathews, A. M., Chambers, A., Ebrahimi, S., Lytle, R., & Nelson, R. (1987). The effects of relaxation training with cognitive therapy or nondirective therapy and the role of relaxation-induced anxiety in the treatment of generalized anxiety. *Journal of Consulting and Clinical Psychology, 55,* 883–888.

Borkovec, T. D., Robinson, E., Pruzinsky, T., & DePree, J. A. (1983). Preliminary exploration of worry: Some characteristics and processes. *Behaviour Research and Therapy, 21,* 9–16.

Borkovec, T. D., Shadick, R., & Hopkins, M. (1991). The nature of normal and pathological worry. In R. M. Rapee & D. H. Barlow (Eds.), *Chronic anxiety: Generalized anxiety disorder, and mixed anxiety–depression* (pp. 29–51). New York: Guilford Press.

Brawman-Mintzer, O., Lydiard, R. B., Crawford, M. M., Emmanuel, N., Payeur, R., Johnson, M., Knapp, R. G., & Ballenger, J. C. (1994). Somatic symptoms in generalized anxiety disorder with and without comorbid psychiatric disorders. *American Journal of Psychiatry, 151,* 930–932.

Brawman-Mintzer, O., Lydiard, R. B., Emmanuel, N., Payeur, R., Johnson, M., Roberts, J., Jarrell, M. P., & Ballenger, J. C. (1993). Psychiatric comorbidity in patients with generalized anxiety disorder. *American Journal of Psychiatry, 150,* 1216–1218.

Breslau, N., & Davis, G. C. (1985). DSM-III generalized anxiety disorder: An empirical investigation of more stringent criteria. *Psychiatry Research, 14,* 231–238.

Brown, T. A., Antony, M. M., & Barlow, D. H. (1992). Psychometric properties of the Penn State Worry Questionnaire in a clinical anxiety disorders sample. *Behaviour Research and Therapy, 30,* 33–37.

Brown, T. A., Antony, M. M., & Barlow, D. H. (1995). Diagnostic comorbidity in panic disorder: Effect on treatment outcome and course of comorbid diagnoses following treatment. *Journal of Consulting and Clinical Psychology, 63,* 408–418.

Brown, T. A., & Barlow, D. H. (1992). Comorbidity among anxiety disorders: Implications for treatment and DSM-IV. *Journal of Consulting and Clinical Psychology, 60,* 835–844.

Brown, T. A., Barlow, D. H., & Liebowitz, M. R. (1994). The empirical basis of generalized anxiety disorder. *American Journal of Psychiatry, 151,* 1272–1280.

Brown, T. A., Chorpita, B. F., & Barlow, D. H. (1998). Structural relationships among dimensions of the DSM-IV anxiety and mood disorders and dimensions of negative affect, positive affect, and autonomic arousal. *Journal of Abnormal Psychology, 107,* 179–192.

Brown, T. A., Di Nardo, P. A., Lehman, C. L., & Campbell, L. A. (in press). Reliability of DSM-IV anxiety and mood disorders: Implications for the classification of emotional disorders. *Journal of Abnormal Psychology.*

Brown, T. A., Hertz, R. M., & Barlow, D. H. (1992). New developments in cognitive-behavioral treatment of anxiety disorders. In A. Tasman (Ed.), *American Psychiatric Press review of psychiatry* (Vol. 11, pp. 285–306). Washington, DC: American Psychiatric Press.

Brown, T. A., Marten, P. A., & Barlow, D. H. (1995). Discriminant validity of the symptoms constituting the DSM-III-R and DSM-IV associated symptom criterion of generalized anxiety disorder. *Journal of Anxiety Disorders, 9,* 317–328.

Brown, T. A., Moras, K., Zinbarg, R. E., & Barlow, D. H. (1993). Diagnostic and symptom distinguishability of generalized anxiety disorder and obsessive–compulsive disorder. *Behavior Therapy, 24,* 227–240.

Brown, T. A., O'Leary, T. A., Marten, P. A., & Barlow, D. H. (1993, November). *Clinical features of generalized anxiety disorder with an early vs. late onset.* Paper presented at the meeting of the Association for Advancement of Behavior Therapy, Atlanta, GA.

Butler, G., & Booth, R. G. (1991). Developing psychological treatments for generalized anxiety disorder.

In R. M. Rapee & D. H. Barlow (Eds.), *Chronic anxiety: Generalized anxiety disorder, and mixed anxiety–depression* (pp. 187–209). New York: Guilford Press.

Butler, G., Cullington, A., Hibbert, G., Klimes, I., & Gelder, M. (1987). Anxiety management for persistent generalized anxiety. *British Journal of Psychiatry, 151,* 535–542.

Butler, G., Fennell, M., Robson, P., & Gelder, M. (1991). Comparison of behavior therapy and cognitive behavior therapy in the treatment of generalized anxiety disorder. *Journal of Consulting and Clinical Psychology, 59,* 167–175.

Butler, G., Wells, A., & Dewick, H. (1995). Differential effects of worry and imagery after exposure to a stressful stimulus: A pilot study. *Behavioural and Cognitive Psychotherapy, 23,* 44–55.

Cameron, O. G., Thyer, B. A., Nesse, R. M., & Curtis, G. C. (1986). Symptom profiles of patients with DSM-III anxiety disorders. *American Journal of Psychiatry, 143,* 1132–1137.

Chambless, D. L., Cherney, J., Caputo, G. C., & Rheinstein, B. J. G. (1987). Anxiety disorders and alcoholism: A study with inpatient alcoholics. *Journal of Anxiety Disorders, 1,* 29–40.

Chorpita, B. F., Brown, T. A., & Barlow, D. H. (1998). Diagnostic reliability of the DSM-III-R anxiety disorders: Mediating effects of patient and diagnostician characteristics. *Behavior Modification, 22,* 307–320.

Clark, D. A., & DeSilva, P. (1985). The nature of depressive and anxious intrusive thoughts: Distinct or uniform phenomena? *Behaviour Research and Therapy, 23,* 383–393.

Clark, L. A., Watson, D., & Mineka, S. (1994). Temperament, personality, and the mood and anxiety disorders. *Journal of Abnormal Psychology, 103,* 103–116.

Cohen, A. S., Barlow, D. H., & Blanchard, E. B. (1985). The psychophysiology of relaxation-associated panic attacks. *Journal of Abnormal Psychology, 94,* 96–101.

Craske, M. G., Barlow, D. H., & O'Leary, T. A. (1992). *Mastery of your anxiety and worry.* San Antonio, TX: Psychological Corporation.

Craske, M. G., Rapee, R. M., Jackel, L., & Barlow, D. H. (1989). Qualitative dimensions of worry in DSM-III-R generalized anxiety disorder subjects and nonanxious controls. *Behaviour Research and Therapy, 27,* 189–198.

Craske, M. G., Street, L., & Barlow, D. H. (1989). Instructions to focus upon or distract from internal cues during exposure treatment of agoraphobic avoidance. *Behaviour Research and Therapy, 27,* 663–672.

DiBartolo, P. M., Brown, T. A., & Barlow, D. H. (1997). Effects of anxiety on attentional allocation and task performance: An information processing analysis using nonanxious and generalized anxiety disorder subjects. *Behaviour Research and Therapy, 35,* 1101–1111.

Di Nardo, P. A. (1991). *MacArthur reanalysis of generalized anxiety disorder.* Unpublished manuscript.

Di Nardo, P. A., Brown, T. A., & Barlow, D. H. (1994). *Anxiety Disorders Interview Schedule for DSM-IV: Lifetime Version (ADIS-IV-L).* San Antonio, TX: Psychological Corporation.

Di Nardo, P. A., Moras, K., Barlow, D. H., Rapee, R. M., & Brown, T. A. (1993). Reliability of the DSM-III-R anxiety disorder categories using the Anxiety Disorders Interview Schedule—Revised (ADIS-R). *Archives of General Psychiatry, 50,* 251–256.

Durham, R. C., & Turvey, A. A. (1987). Cognitive therapy vs. behavior therapy in the treatment of chronic general anxiety. *Behaviour Research and Therapy, 25,* 229–234.

East, M. P., & Watts, F. N. (1994). Worry and the suppression of imagery. *Behaviour Research and Therapy, 32,* 851–855.

Foa, E. B., & Kozak, M. J. (1986). Emotional processing of fear: Exposure to corrective information. *Psychological Bulletin, 99,* 20–35.

Fyer, A. J., Mannuzza, S., Martin, L. Y., Gallops, M. S., Endicott, J., Schleyer, B., Gorman, J. M., Liebowitz, M. R., & Klein, D. F. (1989). Reliability of anxiety assessment: II. Symptom agreement. *Archives of General Psychiatry, 46,* 1102–1110.

Ganzini, L., McFarland, B. H., & Cutler, D. (1990). Prevalence of mental disorders after catastrophic financial loss. *Journal of Nervous and Mental Disease, 178,* 680–685.

Hazlett, R. L., McLeod, D. R., & Hoehn-Saric, R. (1994). Muscle tension in generalized anxiety disorder: Elevated muscle tonus or agitated movement? *Psychophysiology, 31,* 189–195.

Heide, F. J., & Borkovec, T. D. (1984). Relaxation-induced anxiety: Mechanisms and theoretical implications. *Behaviour Research and Therapy, 22,* 1–12.

Himmelfarb, S., & Murrell, S. A. (1984). The prevalence and correlation of anxiety symptoms in older adults. *Journal of Psychiatry, 116,* 159–167.

Hoehn-Saric, R., & McLeod, D. R. (1988). The peripheral sympathetic nervous system: Its role in normal and pathological anxiety. *Psychiatric Clinics of North America, 11,* 375–386.

Hoehn-Saric, R., Hazlett, R. L., & McLeod, D. R. (1993). Generalized anxiety disorder with early and late onset of anxiety symptoms. *Comprehensive Psychiatry, 34,* 291–298.

Hoehn-Saric, R., McLeod, D. R., & Zimmerli, W. D. (1989). Somatic manifestations in women with generalized anxiety disorder: Psychophysiological responses to psychological stress. *Archives of General Psychiatry, 46,* 1113–1119.

Kendall, P. C. (1994). Treating anxiety disorders in children: Results of a randomized clinical trial. *Journal of Consulting and Clinical Psychology, 62,* 100–110.

Kendler, K. S., Neale, M. C., Kessler, R. C., Heath, A. C., & Eaves, L. J. (1992a). Generalized anxiety disorder in women: A population-based twin study. *Archives of General Psychiatry, 49,* 267–272.

Kendler, K. S., Neale, M. C., Kessler, R. C., Heath, A. C., & Eaves, L. J. (1992b). Major depression and generalized anxiety disorder: Same genes, (partly) different environments? *Archives of General Psychiatry, 49,* 716–722.

Kendler, K. S., Walters, E. E., Neale, M. C., Kessler, R. C., Heath, A. C., & Eaves, L. J. (1995). The structure of the genetic and environmental risk factors for six major psychiatric disorders in women: Phobia, generalized anxiety disorder, panic disorder, bulimia, major depression, and alcoholism. *Archives of General Psychiatry, 52,* 374–383.

LeBoeuf, A., & Lodge, J. (1980). A comparison of frontalis EMG feedback training and progressive relaxation in the treatment of chronic anxiety. *British Journal of Psychiatry, 137,* 279–284.

Lindsay, W. R., Gamsu, C. V., McLaughlin, E., Hood, E. M., & Espie, C. A. (1987). A controlled trial of treatments for generalized anxiety. *British Journal of Clinical Psychology, 26,* 3–15.

Lovibond, P. F., & Lovibond, S. H. (1995). The structure of negative emotional states: Comparison of the Depression Anxiety Stress Scales (DASS) with the Beck Depression and Anxiety Inventories. *Behaviour Research and Therapy, 33,* 335–342.

Lyonfields, J. D., Borkovec, T. D., & Thayer, J. F. (1995). Vagal tone in generalized anxiety disorder and the effects of aversive imagery and worrisome thinking. *Behavior Therapy, 26,* 457–466.

Marten, P. A., Brown, T. A., Barlow, D. H., Borkovec, T. D., Shear, M. K., & Lydiard, R. B. (1993). Evaluation of the ratings comprising the associated symptom criterion of DSM-III-R generalized anxiety disorder. *Journal of Nervous and Mental Disease, 181,* 676–682.

Massion, A. O., Warshaw, M. G., & Keller, M. B. (1993). Quality of life and psychiatric morbidity in panic disorder and generalized anxiety disorder. *American Journal of Psychiatry, 150,* 600–607.

Mathews, A. (1990). Why worry?: The cognitive function of anxiety. *Behaviour Research and Therapy, 28,* 455–468.

Meichenbaum, D. S., & Jaremko, M. E. (Eds.). (1983). *Stress reduction and prevention.* New York: Plenum Press.

Meyer, T. J., Miller, M. L., Metzger, R. L., & Borkovec, T. D. (1990). Development and validation of the Penn State Worry Questionnaire. *Behaviour Research and Therapy, 28,* 487–495.

Noyes, R., Clarkson, C., Crowe, R. R., Yates, W. R., & McChesney, C. M. (1987). A family study of generalized anxiety disorder. *American Journal of Psychiatry, 144,* 1019–1024.

Noyes, R., Woodman, C., Garvey, M. J., Cook, B. L., Suelzer, M., Clancy, J., & Anderson, D. J. (1992). Generalized anxiety disorder vs. panic disorder: Distinguishing characteristics and patterns of comorbidity. *Journal of Nervous and Mental Disease, 180,* 369–379.

O'Leary, T. A., Brown, T. A., & Barlow, D. H. (1992, November). *The efficacy of worry control treatment in generalized anxiety disorder: A multiple baseline analysis.* Paper presented at the meeting of the Association for Advancement of Behavior Therapy, Boston.

Parkinson, L., & Rachman, S. (1981). The nature of intrusive thoughts. *Advances in Behaviour Research and Therapy, 3,* 101–110.

Rapee, R. M. (1985). The distinction between panic disorder and generalized anxiety disorder: Clinical presentation. *Australian and New Zealand Journal of Psychiatry, 19,* 227–232.

Rapee, R. M. (1991). Generalized anxiety disorder: A review of clinical features and theoretical concepts. *Clinical Psychology Review, 11,* 419–440.

Rapee, R. M., & Barlow, D. H. (Eds.). (1991). *Chronic anxiety: Generalized anxiety disorder, and mixed anxiety–depression.* New York: Guilford Press.

Rapee, R. M., Craske, M. G., Brown, T. A., & Barlow, D. H. (1996). Measurement of perceived control over anxiety-related events. *Behavior Therapy, 27,* 279–293.

Roy, M. A., Neale, M. C., Pedersen, N. L., Mathé, A. A., & Kendler, K. S. (1995). A twin study of generalized anxiety disorder and major depression. *Psychological Medicine, 25,* 1037–1040.

Salzman, C. (1991). Pharmacologic treatment of the anxious elderly patient. In C. Salzman & B. D. Lebowitz (Eds.), *Anxiety disorders in the elderly* (pp. 149–173). New York: Free Press.

Sanderson, W. C., & Barlow, D. H. (1990). A description of patients diagnosed with DSM-III-R generalized anxiety disorder. *Journal of Nervous and Mental Disease, 178,* 588–591.

Sanderson, W. C., Beck, A. T., & Beck, J. (1990). Syndrome comorbidity in patients with major depression or dysthymia: Prevalence and temporal relationships. *American Journal of Psychiatry, 147,* 1025–1028.

Sanderson, W. C., & Wetzler, S. (1991). Chronic anxiety and generalized anxiety disorder: Issues in comorbidity. In R. M. Rapee & D. H. Barlow (Eds.), *Chronic anxiety: Generalized anxiety disorder and mixed anxiety–depression* (pp. 119–135). New York: Guilford Press.

Schweizer, E., & Rickels, K. (1991). Pharmacotherapy of generalized anxiety disorder. In R. M. Rapee & D. H. Barlow (Eds.), *Chronic anxiety: Generalized anxiety disorder and mixed anxiety–depression* (pp. 172–186). New York: Guilford Press.

Skre, I., Onstad, S., Torgersen, S., Lygren, S., & Kringlen, E. (1993). A twin study of DSM-III-R anxiety disorders. *Acta Psychiatrica Scandinavica, 88,* 85–92.

Starcevic, V. (1995). Pathological worry in major depression: A preliminary report. *Behaviour Research and Therapy, 33,* 55–56.

Suinn, R. M., & Richardson, F. (1971). Anxiety management training: A nonspecific behavior therapy program for anxiety control. *Behavior Therapy, 2,* 498–511.

Torgersen, S. (1983). Genetic factors in anxiety disorders. *Archives of General Psychiatry, 40,* 1085–1089.

Turner, S. M., Beidel, D. C., & Stanley, M. A. (1992). Are obsessional thoughts and worry different cognitive phenomena? *Clinical Psychology Review, 12,* 257–270.

White, J., & Keenan, M. (1992). Stress control: A controlled comparative investigation of large group therapy for generalized anxiety disorder. *Behavioral Psychotherapy, 20,* 97–114.

Wisocki, P. A. (1994). The experience of worry in the elderly. In G. C. L. Davey & F. Tallis (Eds.), *Worrying: Perspectives on theory, assessment, and treatment* (pp. 247–261). Chichester, England: Wiley.

Wittchen, H. -U., Zhao, S., Kessler, R. C., & Eaves, W. W. (1994). DSM-III-R generalized anxiety disorder in the National Comorbidity Survey. *Archives of General Psychiatry, 51,* 355–364.

Zinbarg, R. E., & Barlow, D. H. (1991). Mixed anxiety–depression: A new diagnostic category? In R. M. Rapee & D. H. Barlow (Eds.), *Chronic anxiety: Generalized anxiety disorder and mixed anxiety–depression* (pp. 136–152). New York: Guilford Press.

Chapter 5

OBSESSIVE–COMPULSIVE DISORDER

Edna B. Foa
Martin E. Franklin

It will not take the reader long to see that successful therapy for obsessive–compulsive disorder is markedly different both in structure and in content from the usual therapeutic approaches. For this reason, regrettably, few therapists feel self-efficacious enough to undertake this therapy. And yet this approach is clearly the treatment of choice for the most beneficial short- and long-term effects in obsessive–compulsive disorder, according to recent clinical trials. The information provided in this detailed chapter should be sufficient for any reasonably well-trained mental health professional to undertake this treatment, particularly if few other options are available. For the suffering involved with obsessive–compulsive disorder can be extraordinary, and even imperfect attempts at therapy can relieve much of this suffering. This chapter describes the detailed conduct of intensive daily sessions involving both imaginal and direct *in vivo* practice. Also noticeable is the ingenuity required of therapists (e.g., where do you find dead animals?). The importance of involving significant others continues a theme first described by Craske and Barlow in Chapter 1 of this volume, where spouses/partners or other people close to the individual with the problem become an important and integral part of treatment. Finally, this chapter contains an up-to-date review of the current status of psychological and pharmacological approaches to obsessive–compulsive disorder.

Advances in cognitive-behavioral and pharmacological treatments in the last three decades have greatly improved the prognosis for patients with obsessive–compulsive disorder (OCD). In this chapter we first discuss diagnostic and theoretical issues of OCD and review the available treatments. We then describe assessment procedures and illustrate in detail how to implement intensive cognitive-behavioral treatment (CBT) involving exposure and ritual prevention (EX/RP) for OCD. Throughout the chapter, we use case material illustrating interactions between therapist and patient in order to demonstrate the process that occurs during treatment.

DEFINITION

According to the *Diagnostic and Statistical Manual of Mental Disorders*, fourth edition (DSM-IV; American Psychiatric Association, 1994), OCD is characterized by recurrent obsessions and/or compulsions that interfere substantially with daily functioning. Obsessions are anxiety-evoking and persistent ideas, thoughts, impulses, or images. Common obsessions are repeated thoughts about contamination, causing harm to others, and doubting whether one locked the front door. Compulsions are repetitive behaviors or mental acts to prevent or reduce anxiety or distress. Common compulsions in-clude handwashing, checking, and counting.

Compared to the previous definition of OCD in DSM-III-R (American Psychiatric Association, 1987), the DSM-IV definition includes several substantive changes. In DSM-IV, obsessions and compulsions are defined as functionally related: Obsessions are defined as mental phenomena that *cause* pronounced anxiety or distress, and compulsions are defined as overt (behavioral) or covert (mental) actions that are performed in an attempt to *reduce* the distress brought on by obsessions or rigid rules. This modification is supported by findings from the DSM-IV field study on OCD, in which over 90% of participants reported that their compulsions aimed either to prevent harm associated with their obsessions or to reduce obsessional distress (Foa et al., 1995).

Data from the DSM-IV field study also indicated that the vast majority (over 90%) of patients with OCD manifested both obsessions and behavioral rituals. When mental rituals were included, only 2% of the sample reported "pure" obsessions (Foa et al., 1995). Behavioral rituals (e.g., handwashing) are equivalent to mental rituals (e.g., silently repeating special prayers) in their functional relationship to obsessions: Both serve to reduce obsessional distress, prevent feared harm, or restore safety. Thus the traditional view that obsessions are mental events and compulsions are behavioral events no longer holds true; although all obsessions are indeed mental events, compulsions can be either mental or behavioral. Identification of mental rituals is an especially important aspect of treatment planning, as obsessions and compulsions are addressed via different techniques. For example, we once treated a patient who described himself as a "pure obsessional," who would experience intrusive and unwanted images of harm coming to his girlfriend from an animal attack. The patient would quickly and intentionally insert his own image into the scene to become the victim of the animal's mauling, thereby reducing his distress and, in his estimation, reducing the likelihood of future harm coming to his girlfriend. The substitution of his own image into the scene constituted a mental ritual, and the success of imaginal exposure exercises required that the patient refrain from this form of compulsion.

Another definitional shift in DSM-IV is the deemphasis on the requirement for insight in diagnosing OCD. It has been argued that a continuum of "insight" or "strength of belief" better represents the clinical picture of OCD than the previously prevailing view that *all* persons with OCD recognize the senselessness of their obsessions and compulsions (Kozak & Foa, 1994). The growing consensus about a continuum of insight (Foa et al., 1995; Insel & Akiskal, 1986; Lelliott, Noshirvani, Basoglu, Marks, & Monteiro, 1988) led to the inclusion of a subtype of OCD "with poor insight" to include individuals who indeed have obsessions and compulsions but fail to recognize their senselessness. Clinically, it is important to assess degree of insight prior to initiating treatment, because fixed belief about the consequences of refraining from compulsions and avoidance behaviors has been found to be associated with attenuated treatment outcome (see, e.g., Foa, Abramowitz, Franklin, & Kozak, 1999).

As in DSM-III-R, there continues to be a requirement that the obsessions or compulsions are severe enough to cause marked distress, are time-consuming, and interfere with daily functioning. If another Axis I disorder is present, the obsessions and compulsions cannot be restricted to the content of that disorder (e.g., preoccupation with food in the presence of eating disorders). There is much current discussion about the presence of an obsessive–compulsive spectrum that includes a wide variety of compulsive and impulsive disorders (e.g., pathological gambling, trichotillomania), but DSM-IV nosology specifies that these disorders should not be diagnosed as OCD.

CLINICAL PICTURE

"Debbie" is a 36-year-old married woman with no children. At the time of presentation, she reported a 15-year history of obsessive fears and rituals. In the past, she had fears of making mistakes, forgetting things, and hurting people physically or emotionally, resulting in her spending time checking and mentally reviewing her activities. Debbie's fears at the time she presented for treatment centered around becoming contaminated with unspecified "germs" and passing this contamination to others, who would become ill and die as a result, and she would be held responsible for their deaths. These fears developed while she was working as a surgical nurse. She became concerned that during an operation she would contaminate the surgical field, and that this would result in serious consequences to the patient. She was no longer able to work because of the OCD symptoms and spent a substantial portion of her day washing and cleaning objects around her home. She avoided contact with objects she thought might contain germs, including bathrooms, certain food products, and hospitals. In addition, she avoided most contact with other people, particularly children, for fear of contaminating them with germs.

PREVALENCE AND COURSE OF OCD

Once thought to be a rare disorder, OCD is now estimated to occur in about 2.5% of the adult population in the United States (Karno, Golding, Sorensen, & Burnam, 1988). Recent epidemiological studies with children and adolescents suggest similar lifetime prevalence rates in these samples (see, e.g., Flament et al., 1988; Valleni-Basile et al., 1994). Slightly more than half of the adults suffering from OCD are female (Rasmussen & Tsuang, 1986), whereas a 2:1 male-to-female ratio has been observed in several pediatric clinical samples (see, e.g., Hanna, 1995; Swedo, Rapoport, Leonard, Lenane, & Cheslow, 1989). Age of onset of the disorder typically ranges from early adolescence to young adulthood, with earlier onset in males; modal onset age in males is 13–15 years, and in females is 20–24 (Rasmussen & Eisen, 1990). However, cases of OCD have been documented in children as young as age 2 (Rapoport, Swedo, & Leonard, 1992).

Development of the disorder is usually gradual, but acute onset has been reported in some cases. Although chronic waxing and waning of symptoms is typical, episodic and deteriorating courses have been observed in about 10% of patients (Rasmussen & Eisen, 1989). OCD is frequently associated with impairments in general functioning, such as disruption of gainful employment (Leon, Portera, & Weissman, 1995), and with couple and other interpersonal relationship difficulties (Emmelkamp, de Haan, & Hoogduin, 1990;

Riggs, Hiss, & Foa, 1992). Adolescents identified as having OCD (Flament et al., 1988) reported in a subsequent follow-up study that they had withdrawn socially to prevent contamination and to conserve energy for obsessive–compulsive behaviors (Flament et al., 1990).

Many individuals with OCD suffer for years before seeking treatment. In one study, individuals first presented for psychiatric treatment over 7 years after the onset of significant symptoms (Rasmussen & Tsuang, 1986). The disorder may cause severe impairment in functioning, resulting in job loss and disruption of couple and other interpersonal relationships. Marital distress is reported by approximately 50% of married individuals seeking treatment for OCD (Emmelkamp et al., 1990; Riggs et al., 1992).

COMORBIDITY

OCD commonly co-occurs with other symptoms and complaints, such as depression, anxiety, phobic avoidance, and excessive worry (Tynes, White, & Steketee, 1990; Karno et al., 1988; Rasmussen & Tsuang, 1986). Epidemiological studies found that about 30% of individuals with OCD also met criteria for a major depressive episode (Karno et al., 1988); sleep disturbances have been found in approximately 40% of people with OCD. The presence of depression with OCD is important, in that some studies have suggested that severe depression may impede the efficacy of behavioral treatment of OCD (Foa, 1979; Foa, Grayson, & Steketee, 1982). Indeed, a recent study of CBT involving EX/RP in clinic outpatients with OCD indicated that patients with *severe* depressive symptoms experienced somewhat attenuated EX/RP outcomes compared to less depressed patients (Abramowitz, Franklin, Street, Kozak, & Foa, 2000).

The comorbidity of OCD with other anxiety disorders also appears to be substantial. Rasmussen and Tsuang (1986) reported that in a sample of patients with OCD, the lifetime incidence of DSM-III simple phobia was about 30%; for social phobia, 20%; and for panic disorder, 15%. A relationship of OCD with eating disorders has also been reported. About 10% of women with OCD had a history of anorexia nervosa (Kasvikis, Tsakiris,

Marks, Basoglu, & Noshirvani, 1986), and over 33% of patients with bulimia nervosa had a history of OCD (Hudson, Pope, Yurgelun-Todd, Jonas, & Frankenburg, 1987; Laessle, Kia, Fichter, Wittchen, & Pirke, 1987).

Disorders such as Tourette's syndrome and other tic disorders also appear to be related to OCD. Some 20% to 30% of individuals with OCD reported a current or past history of tics (Pauls, 1989). Estimates of the comorbidity of Tourette's and OCD range from 36% to 52% (Leckman & Chittenden, 1990; Pauls, Towbin, Leckman, Zahner, & Cohen, 1986). Also, 5% to 7% of OCD patients are thought to suffer from Tourette's syndrome (Rasmussen & Eisen, 1989).

DIFFERENTIAL DIAGNOSIS

The high comorbidity of OCD with other disorders noted above, as well as the similarity between the criteria for OCD and other DSM-IV disorders, can pose diagnostic quandaries. Below we review some of the more common diagnostic difficulties likely to confront clinicians, and we provide recommendations for making these difficult diagnostic judgments.

Obsessions versus Depressive Rumination

It is sometimes difficult to differentiate depressive ruminations from obsessions. The distinction rests primarily on thought content and on the patient's reported resistance to such thoughts. Unlike obsessions, ruminations are typically pessimistic ideas about the self or the world, and content frequently shifts in rumination. In addition, depressive ruminators tend not to make repeated attempts to suppress their ruminations, the way that individuals with OCD try to suppress obsessions. When depression and OCD co-occur, both phenomena may be present, but only obsessions should be targeted with exposure exercises. We have also found clinically that the generally pessimistic presentation of depressed patients can undermine hopefulness about improving during EX/RP, and thus these beliefs may require therapeutic intervention even though they are not obsessional.

Other Anxiety Disorders

OCD often co-occurs with other anxiety disorders, and diagnostic criteria are sometimes similar among anxiety disorders, but the symptoms associated with each diagnosis can usually be distinguished. For example, the excessive worries characteristic of generalized anxiety disorder (GAD) may appear similar to OCD, but, unlike obsessions, worries are excessive concerns about real-life circumstances and are experienced by the individual as appropriate (ego-syntonic). In contrast, obsessive thinking is more likely to be unrealistic or magical, and obsessions are usually experienced by the individual as inappropriate (ego-dystonic). There are, however, exceptions to this general rule: Individuals with either GAD or OCD may worry about everyday matters such as their children getting sick. However, if worried about their children catching cold, parents with GAD may focus their concern on the long-term consequences (e.g., falling behind in school, development of a lifelong pattern of debilitation), whereas parents with OCD may focus more on the contamination aspect of illness (e.g., their children being infested with "cold germs"). The problem of distinguishing obsessions from worries in a particular patient is most relevant when the patient exhibits no compulsions, but, as mentioned above, patients with "pure" obsessions constitute only about 2% of patients with OCD (Foa et al., 1995).

In the absence of rituals, the avoidance associated with specific phobias can also appear similar to OCD. For example, excessive fear of germs and specific phobia can both result in persistent avoidance of cats. However, unlike an individual with OCD, a person with a cat phobia can successfully avoid cats for the most part or reduce distress quickly by escaping cats when avoidance is impractical. In contrast, the individual with OCD who is obsessed with "cat germs" continues to feel contaminated even after the cat is gone, and sometimes the known presence of a cat in the vicinity several hours earlier can also produce obsessional distress even if there is no possibility that the cat will return. This distress often prompts subsequent avoidance behaviors (e.g., taking off clothing that might have been near the contaminating cat) not typically observed in specific phobias.

Hypochondriasis and Body Dysmorphic Disorder

The health concerns that characterize hypochondriasis and the preoccupation with imagined physical defects of body dysmorphic disorder are both formally similar to the obsessions of OCD. The best way to differentiate these disorders from OCD is to examine for content specificity of the fear-provoking thoughts. Most individuals with hypochondriasis or body dysmorphic disorder are singly obsessed, whereas most individuals with OCD have multiple obsessions. Moreover, patients with OCD typically obsess about contracting diseases or becoming ill in the future, whereas patients with hypochondriasis focus on physical and psychological symptoms that lead them to fear that they have already contracted diseases or illnesses.

Tourette's Syndrome and Other Tic Disorders

In order to differentiate the stereotyped motor behaviors that characterize Tourette's syndrome and other tic disorders from compulsions, the functional relationship between these behaviors and any obsessive thoughts must be examined. Motor tics are generally experienced as involuntary and are not aimed at neutralizing distress brought about by obsessions. There is no conventional way of differentiating them from "pure" compulsions, but OCD with "pure" compulsions is extremely rare (Foa et al., 1995). As noted above, there appears to be a high rate of comorbidity between OCD and tic disorders (e.g., Pauls et al., 1986); thus both disorders may be present simultaneously in a given patient. As is the case with ruminations and obsessions, differentiating among tics and compulsions in patients with both disorders is especially important, as response prevention would not be the intervention of choice for tics, whereas it would be for compulsions.

Delusional Disorder and Schizophrenia

Individuals with OCD may present with obsessions of delusional intensity (see Kozak & Foa, 1994, for a review). Approximately 5%
of patients with OCD report complete conviction that their obsessions and compulsions are realistic, with an additional 20% reporting strong but not fixed conviction. Therefore, it is important to consider the diagnosis of OCD "with poor insight" even if these beliefs are very strongly held. The differentiation of delusional disorder from OCD can depend on the presence of compulsions in OCD (Eisen et al., 1998). In OCD, obsessions of delusional intensity are usually accompanied by compulsions.

It is also important to recognize that the content of obsessions in OCD may be quite bizarre, as in the delusions of schizophrenia, but bizarreness in and of itself does not preclude a diagnosis of OCD. For example, one patient seen at our center was fearful that small bits of her "essence" would be forever lost if she passed too close to public trash cans. This patient did not report any other symptoms of formal thought disorder, such as loose associations, hallucinations, flat or grossly inappropriate affect, and thought insertion or projection. Following a course of EX/RP that focused on exercises designed to expose the patient to the loss of her "essence" (e.g., driving by the city dump), the patient's OCD symptoms were substantially reduced. On occasion patients do meet diagnostic criteria for both OCD and schizophrenia, and a dual diagnosis is appropriate under these circumstances. EX/RP should proceed with such patients only if treatment exercises do not cause exacerbations of their comorbid thought disorder symptoms.

THEORETICAL MODELS

Cognitive and Behavioral Models

Mowrer's (1939) two-stage theory for the acquisition and maintenance of fear and avoidance behavior has been commonly adopted to explain phobias and OCD. Further elaborated by Mowrer in 1960, this theory proposes that first a neutral event becomes associated with fear by being paired with a stimulus that by its nature provokes discomfort or anxiety. Through conditioning processes, objects as well as thoughts and images acquire the ability to produce discomfort. In the second stage of this process, escape or avoidance responses are developed to reduce the anxiety or discomfort evoked by the various conditioned stimuli and are maintained by their success in doing so. Dollard and Miller (1950) adopted Mowrer's two-stage theory to explain the development of phobias and OCD. As noted earlier, because of the intrusive nature of the obsessions, many of the situations that provoke obsessions cannot readily be avoided. Passive avoidance behaviors, such as those utilized by phobics, are also less effective in controlling obsessional distress. Active avoidance patterns in the form of ritualistic behaviors are then developed and maintained by their success in alleviating this distress.

Although empirical evidence in support of Mowrer's conceptualization of fear acquisition is lacking (see, e.g., Rachman & Wilson, 1980), there are data to support the hypothesized second stage of two-factor theory regarding the maintenance of ritualistic behavior. Studies have demonstrated that obsessions give rise to anxiety/discomfort and that compulsions reduce it. Obsessions were found to increase heart rate and deflect skin conductance more than did neutral thoughts (Boulougouris, Rabavilas, & Stefanis, 1977; Rabavilas & Boulougouris, 1974). Similarly, contact with contaminants resulted in increased heart rate and subjective anxiety (Hodgson & Rachman, 1972), as well as increased skin conductance level (Hornsveld, Kraaimaat, & van Dam-Baggen, 1979). A series of experiments with washers and checkers revealed that anxiety typically decreased following the performance of a ritual after deliberate provocation of an urge to ritualize (Hodgson & Rachman, 1972; Hornsveld et al., 1979; Roper & Rachman, 1976; Roper, Rachman, & Hodgson, 1973).

In light of the equivocal empirical support for two-factor theory, several cognitive explanations have been offered to account for the development and maintenance of OCD symptoms. Carr (1974) proposed that individuals with OCD have unusually high expectations of negative outcome; they overevaluate the negative consequences for a variety of actions. He noted that obsessional content typically includes exaggerations of the concerns of normal individuals—health, death, welfare of others, sex, religion, and the like. According to this theory, the sources of obsessive–compulsive concerns are identical to those of GAD, agoraphobia, and social phobia. In this way, Carr's explanation of OCD is similar to that offered by Beck (1976), who suggested that the content of obsessions is related to danger in the form of doubt or warning. However, neither account distinguishes between threat-related obsessions and threat-related thoughts in persons with phobias.

In an attempt to explain the specific psychopathology of OCD, McFall and Wollersheim (1979) suggested that individuals with OCD hold erroneous beliefs, such as that one must be completely competent in all endeavors to be worthwhile. Other erroneous ideas include the belief that failure to live up to perfectionistic ideals should be punished and that certain magical rituals can prevent catastrophes. Such mistaken beliefs, the authors suggested, lead to erroneous perceptions of threat, which in turn provoke anxiety. The tendency of a person with OCD to devalue his/her ability to cope successfully with such threats exacerbates the dysfunctional process. The resulting feelings of uncertainty, discomfort, and helplessness are reduced via magical rituals that the patient views as the only available method for coping with threat.

Salkovskis (1985) has offered an even more comprehensive cognitive analysis of OCD. He posits that intrusive obsessional thoughts are stimuli that may provoke certain types of negative automatic thoughts. Accordingly, an intrusive thought will lead to mood disturbances only if they trigger these negative automatic thoughts through interaction between the unacceptable intrusion and the individual's belief system (e.g., only bad people have sexual thoughts). According to Salkovskis, an exaggerated sense of responsibility and self-blame are the central themes in the belief system of a person with OCD. Neutralization, in the form of behavioral or cognitive compulsions, can be understood as an attempt to reduce this sense of responsibility and to prevent blame. In addition, frequently occurring thoughts regarding unacceptable actions may be perceived by the individual with OCD as equivalent to the actions themselves; for example, even if the person has not sinned, the thought of sinning is as bad as sinning itself.

Salkovskis (1985) has further proposed that five dysfunctional assumptions characterize persons with OCD and differentiate them from persons without OCD:

1) Having a thought about an action is like performing the action; 2) failing to prevent (or failing to try to prevent) harm to self or others is the same as having caused the harm in the first place; 3) responsibility is not attenuated by other factors (e.g., low probability of occurrence); 4) not neutralizing when an intrusion has occurred is similar or equivalent to seeking or wanting the harm involved in that intrusion to actually happen; 5) one should (and can) exercise control over one's thoughts. (p. 579)

Thus, while the obsession may be ego-dystonic, the automatic thought that it elicits will be ego-syntonic. By extension, this model suggests that treatment of OCD should largely focus on identifying the erroneous assumptions and modifying the automatic thoughts.

Salkovskis's theory sparked interest in examining the role of responsibility in the psychopathology of OCD (Ladouceur et al., 1995; Rachman, Throdarson, Shafran, & Woody, 1995; Rheaume et al., 1995). Most of these investigations were conducted on nonclinical samples of individuals with high scores on self-report measures of OCD. One study by Lopatka and Rachman (1995) utilized patients who met DSM-III-R criteria for OCD. In this study, the authors examined the hypothesis that a manipulation that increases responsibility would increase the urge to check, the amount of discomfort experienced, and the estimated probabilities of bad outcome, whereas deflating levels of responsibility would decrease scores on these variables. Whereas subjects in the "high-responsibility" condition did perceive a higher degree of responsibility compared to subjects in the "low-responsibility" condition, they did not differ in urges to perform checking rituals, discomfort, or in their estimates regarding the probability of anticipated harm. However, individuals in the "low-responsibility" condition experienced a decrease in urge to check, discomfort, and estimated probability of anticipated harm. Thus the hypothesis regarding the role of responsibility in OCD checking was only partially supported.

To further examine the role of responsibility in OCD, Foa and colleagues (in press) developed the Obsessive Compulsive Responsibility Scale (OCRS) that includes high-risk, low-risk, and OCD-relevant scenarios. For each scenario, patients with OCD, patients with generalized social phobia (GSP), and non-

anxious controls were asked to estimate the degree of urge to rectify the situation, distress upon leaving the situation unrectified, and personal responsibility for harm to others if the unrectified situation were to result in harm. Patients with OCD reported more urges, distress, and responsibility in low-risk and OCD-relevant situations; no group differences were detected on high-risk situations. Patients with GSP and controls differed only in their responsibility in OCD-relevant situations, where the patients with GSP reported higher responsibility than controls. These results seem to indicate that nonpatients and patients with GSP better differentiate situations that merit attention and corrective action from situations in which the risk is too low to merit concern. Although individuals with OCD can also make such discriminations, they tend to display inflated responsibility for low-risk situations.

The explanations above focus on the pathology in the content of OCD thoughts. In contrast, Reed (1985) has proposed that the disorder reflects impairment not in the content, but in the organization and integration of experiences (i.e., in the form rather than the content of the thinking). According to Reed, the individual with OCD tries to compensate for this impairment by overstructuring his/her life, imposing strict categorical limits and time markers. Although Reed (1985) has suggested that this style is used consistently by such an individual and affects all aspects of his/her life, he leaves open the possibility that the difficulties will be exacerbated when the task involves threatening content.

Foa and Kozak (1985) have conceptualized anxiety disorders in general as specific impairments in emotional memory networks. Following Lang (1979), they view fear as an information network existing in memory that includes representation about fear stimuli, fear responses, and their meaning. With regard to the fear content, Foa and Kozak (1985) have suggested that the fear networks of individuals with anxiety disorders are characterized by the presence of erroneous estimates of threat, unusually high negative valence for the feared event, and excessive response elements (e.g., physiological reactivity), and are resistant to modification. This persistence may reflect failure to access the fear network, either because of active avoidance or because the content of the fear network precludes spontaneous encounters with situations that evoke anxiety in everyday life. In addition, anxiety may persist because of some impairment in the mechanism of extinction. Cognitive defenses, excessive arousal with failure to habituate, faulty premises, and erroneous rules of inference are all impairments that would hinder the processing of information necessary for modifying the fear structure so as to reduce fear behavior.

Foa and Kozak (1985) have suggested that several forms of fear occur in persons with OCD. The patient who fears contracting venereal disease from public bathrooms and washes to prevent such harm has a fear structure that includes excessive associations between the stimuli (e.g., bathroom) and the anxiety/distress responses, as well as mistaken beliefs about the harm related to the stimulus. For other patients with OCD, fear responses are associated with mistaken meaning rather than with a particular stimulus. For example, some patients who are disturbed by perceived asymmetry and who reduce their distress by rearranging objects do not fear the objects themselves, nor do they anticipate disaster from the asymmetry. Rather, they are upset by their view that certain arrangements of stimuli are "improper."

Like Reed (1985), Foa and Kozak (1985) have proposed that in addition to the pathological content of the obsessions, OCD is distinguished from other disorders by pathology in the mechanisms underlying information processing. Specifically, they suggested that patients with OCD share an impairment in the interpretive rules for making inferences about harm. Such patients often conclude that a situation is dangerous based on the absence of evidence for safety, and they often fail to make inductive leaps about safety from information about the absence of danger. Consequently, rituals that are performed to reduce the likelihood of harm can never really provide safety and must be repeated.

In contrast to the more general theories of OCD described above, some theorists have posed more specific hypotheses to account for the pathology observed in certain OCD subtypes. For example, clinical observations have led some investigators to hypothesize that memory deficits for actions underlie compulsive checking (see, e.g., Sher, Frost, & Otto, 1983). However, the results of experimental

investigations of this hypothesis are equivocal. Some support for an action memory deficit was found in persons exhibiting nonclinical checking (see, e.g., Rubenstein, Peynirgioglu, Chambless, & Pigott, 1993; Sher et al., 1983). In contrast, a study using a clinical sample found that, compared to nonpatients, the patients with checking rituals *better* recalled their fear-relevant actions (e.g., plugging in an iron, unsheathing a knife), but not fear-irrelevant actions (e.g., putting paper clips in a box; Constans, Foa, Franklin, & Mathews, 1995). From these data, it appears that teaching mnemonic strategies to patients with OCD-related checking is probably not the optimal clinical strategy; rather, having patients repeatedly confront the low-risk situations that provoke obsessional distress while simultaneously refraining from checking behavior or mental reviewing of actions is preferred.

Neurochemical Factors

The prevailing biological account of OCD hypothesizes that abnormal serotonin metabolism is expressed in OCD symptoms. The efficacy of serotonin reuptake inhibitors (SRIs) for OCD as compared to nonserotonergic compounds and to pill placebo (PBO) has provided a compelling argument for this hypothesis (Zohar & Insel, 1987). Significant correlations between clomipramine (CMI) plasma levels and improvement in OCD have led researchers to suggest that serotonin function mediates obsessive–compulsive symptoms, thus lending further support to the serotonin hypothesis (Insel, Donnelly, Lalakea, Alterman, & Murphy, 1983; Stern, Marks, Wright, & Luscombe, 1980). However, the studies that have directly investigated serotonin functioning in persons with OCD are inconclusive (Joffe & Swinson, 1991). For example, serotonin platelet uptake studies have failed to differentiate individuals with OCD from controls (Insel, Mueller, Alterman, Linnoila, & Murphy, 1985; Weizman et al., 1985). The serotonin agonist metachlorophenylpoprazine (mCPP) has been administered to patients with OCD in order to directly test the role of serotonin in the pathology of OCD. In two studies, Zohar and his colleagues (Zohar & Insel, 1987; Zohar, Mueller, Insel, Zohar-Kadouch, & Murphy, 1987) found an increase in obsessive–compulsive symptoms following the oral administration of mCPP. Moreover, after treatment with CMI, the effect of mCPP was no longer observed. However, the administration of mCPP intravenously did not produce an increase in OCD symptoms (Charney et al., 1988). Why oral but not intravenous administration of mCPP exacerbates OCD symptoms is unclear. Also inconsistent with the serotonin hypothesis is the finding that CMI, a nonselective serotonergic medication, appears to produce greater OCD symptom reduction than selective SRIs such as fluoxetine, fluvoxamine, and sertraline (Greist, Jefferson, Kobak, Katzelnick, & Serlin, 1995).

Neuroanatomical Factors

Several studies suggest a neuroanatomical basis to OCD. Some studies have indicated that many individuals with OCD have some deficits in frontal lobe functioning (see, e.g., Behar et al., 1984; Cox, Fedio, & Rapoport, 1989; Head, Bolton, & Hymas, 1989), but other studies have failed to find such deficits (Insel et al., 1983). Further support for the role of the frontal lobe in OCD comes from the therapeutic efficacy of psychosurgical techniques such as capsulotomy and cingulotomy (Ballentine, Bouckoms, Thomas, & Giriunas, 1987). Additional evidence for neurobiological deficits in OCD comes from the relationship of this disorder to a variety of disorders with a known neurological basis in the basal ganglia. In particular, a high incidence of OCD has been noted following encephalitis lethargica (Schilder, 1938), Sydenham's chorea (Swedo, Rapoport, Cheslow, et al., 1989), and Tourette's syndrome (Rapoport & Wise, 1988). Finally, the results of four studies using positron emission tomography to assess metabolic activity in the brain suggested that patients with OCD show increased metabolic rates in the prefrontal cortex (Baxter et al., 1987; for a review, see Rapoport, 1991).

TREATMENTS

Exposure and Ritual Prevention

The prognostic picture for OCD has improved dramatically since Victor Meyer (1966) first reported on two patients who responded well to a treatment that included prolonged exposure to obsessional cues and strict prevention of rituals. This procedure, which became known at the time as "exposure and response prevention," was later found to be extremely successful in 10 of 15 cases and partly effective in the remainder. Patients treated with this regimen also appeared to maintain their treatment gains; at a 5-year follow-up, only 2 of 15 patients had relapsed (Meyer & Levy, 1973; Meyer, Levy, & Schnurer, 1974).

As was the case with Meyer's program, EX/RP treatments conducted today typically include both prolonged exposure to obsessional cues and procedures aimed at blocking rituals. Exposure exercises are often done in real-life settings (*in vivo*); for instance, the patient who fears accidentally causing a house fire by leaving the stove on is asked to leave the house without checking the burners. When patients report specific feared consequences from refraining from rituals, these fears can also be addressed via imaginal exposure. In fact, *in vivo* and imaginal exposure exercises are designed specifically to prompt obsessional distress. It is believed that repeated, prolonged exposure to feared thoughts and situations provides information that disconfirm mistaken associations and evaluations held by the patients and thereby promotes habituation (Foa & Kozak, 1986). Exposure is usually done gradually, with situations provoking moderate distress confronted before more upsetting ones. Exposure homeworks are routinely assigned between sessions, and patients are also asked to refrain from rituals.

Since Meyer's (1966) initial positive report of the efficacy of his program, many subsequent studies of EX/RP have indicated that most patients completing this treatment make and maintain clinically significant gains. Randomized controlled trials have indicated that EX/RP is superior to a variety of control treatments, including placebo medication (Marks, Stern, Mawson, Cobb, & McDonald, 1980), relaxation (Fals-Stewart, Marks, & Schafer, 1993), and anxiety management training (Lindsay, Crino, & Andrews, 1997). Foa and Kozak's (1996) review of 12 outcome studies (n = 330) that reported treatment responder rates indicated that 83% of patients completing EX/RP treatment were classified as responders at posttreatment. In 16 studies reporting long-term outcome (n = 376; mean follow-up interval of 29 months), 76% were responders. Moreover, a recent study conducted in our center indicated that these encouraging findings for EX/RP are not limited to highly selected samples in randomized controlled trials: 86% of clinic outpatients with OCD who completed intensive EX/RP on a fee-for-service basis were classified as meeting a conservative criterion for clinically significant improvement (Franklin, Abramowitz, Kozak, Levitt, & Foa, 2000).

In general, EX/RP has been found to be quite effective in ameliorating OCD symptoms and has produced great durability of gains following treatment discontinuation. In our review of the literature, it is also apparent that there are many variants of EX/RP treatment, some that are relevant for outcome and some that do not appear to be so. We review the literature on the relative efficacy of the ingredients that constitute EX/RP, in order to help clinicians decide which EX/RP components are most essential.

EX/RP Treatment Variables

Exposure versus Ritual Prevention versus EX/RP. To separate the effects of exposure and ritual prevention on OCD symptoms, Foa, Steketee, Grayson, Turner, and Latimer (1984) randomly assigned patients with washing rituals to treatment by exposure only, ritual prevention only, or their combination (EX/RP). Each treatment was conducted intensively (15 daily 2-hour sessions conducted over 3 weeks) and followed by a home visit. Patients in each condition were found to be improved at both posttreatment and follow-up, but EX/RP was superior to the single-component treatments on almost every symptom measure at both assessment points. When exposure only was compared to ritual prevention only, patients who received exposure reported lower anxiety when confronting feared contaminants, whereas those who received ritual prevention reported greater decreases in urge to ritualize. Thus it appears that exposure and ritual prevention affect different OCD symptoms. The findings from this study clearly suggest that the two components should be implemented concurrently; treatments that do not include both yield inferior outcome. It is important to convey this information to patients, especially when they are experiencing difficulty refraining from rituals or engaging effectively in exposure exercises during and between sessions.

Implementation of Ritual Prevention. Promoting abstinence from rituals during treatment is thought to be essential for successful treatment outcome, but the preferred method of ritual prevention has changed over the years. In Meyer's (1966) treatment program, the hospital staff physically prevented patients from performing rituals (e.g., turning off the water supply in patients' rooms). However, physical intervention by staff or family members to prevent patients from ritualizing is no longer typical nor recommended. It is believed that such prevention techniques are too coercive to be accepted practices today. Moreover, physical prevention by others may actually limit generalizability to nontherapy situations in which others are not present to intercede. Instead, instructions and encouragement to refrain from ritualizing and avoidance are now recommended. As noted above, although exposure can reduce obsessional distress, in itself it is not so effective in reducing compulsions. To maximize treatment effects, the patient needs to voluntarily refrain from ritualizing while engaging in systematic exposure exercises. The therapist should strongly emphasize the importance of refraining from rituals and should help the patient with this difficult task by providing support, encouragement, and suggestions about alternatives to ritualizing.

Use of Imaginal Exposure. Treatment involving imaginal exposure plus *in vivo* exposure and ritual prevention was found to be superior at follow-up to an *in vivo* EX/RP program that did not include imaginal exposure (Foa, Steketee, Turner, & Fischer, 1980; Steketee, Foa, & Grayson, 1982). However, a second study did not find that the addition of imaginal exposure enhanced long-term efficacy compared to *in vivo* exposure only (DeAraujo, Ito, Marks, & Deale, 1995). The treatment program in the former study differed from that of DeAraujo and colleagues on several parameters (e.g., 90-minute vs. 30-minute imaginal exposures, respectively), and thus the source of these studies' inconsistencies cannot be identified.

In our clinical work, we have found imaginal exposure to be helpful for patients who report that disastrous consequences will result if they refrain from rituals. Because many of these consequences cannot be readily translated into *in vivo* exposure exercises (e.g., burning in hell), imaginal exposure allows the patient an opportunity to confront these feared thoughts. Also, the addition of imagery to *in vivo* exposure may circumvent the cognitive avoidance strategies used by patients who try intentionally not to consider the consequences of exposure while confronting feared situations *in vivo*. In sum, although imaginal exposure does not appear essential for immediate outcome, it may enhance long-term maintenance and can be used as an adjunct to *in vivo* exercises for patients with disastrous consequences. For patients who only report extreme distress as a consequence of refraining from rituals and avoidance behaviors, imaginal exposure may not be needed.

Gradual versus Abrupt Exposures. No differences in OCD symptom reduction were detected in a study comparing patients who confronted the most distressing situations from the start of therapy to those who confronted less distressing situations first; however, patients preferred the more gradual approach (Hodgson, Rachman, & Marks, 1972). Because patient motivation and agreement with treatment goals are core elements of successful EX/RP, situations of moderate difficulty are usually confronted first, followed by several intermediate steps before the most distressing exposures are accomplished. Thus we emphasize that exposure will proceed at a pace that is acceptable to the patient, and that no exposure will ever be attempted without the patient's approval. At the same time, it is preferable to confront the highest item on the treatment hierarchy within the first week of intensive treatment (daily 2-hour sessions conducted over 3 weeks) to allow for sufficient time to repeat these difficult exposures over the latter 2 weeks.

Duration of Exposure. Duration of exposure is also thought to be important for outcome; prolonged continuous exposure is more effective than short interrupted exposure (Rabavilas, Boulougouris, & Stefanis, 1976). Indeed, reduction in anxiety (habituation) within the exposure session to the most distressing item and reduction in the peak anxiety across sessions were associated with improvement following EX/RP treatment (Kozak, Foa, & Steketee, 1988). Studies have indicated that continuous exposure of approximately 90 minutes' duration is needed for anxiety reduction (Foa & Chambless, 1978) and for a decrease in urges to ritualize (Rachman, DeSilva, & Roper, 1976). Although useful as a general guideline, exposure should sometimes be continued beyond 90 minutes if the patient has not experienced anxiety reduction within that time, or terminated if the patient reports substantial reduction in obsessional distress sooner.

Frequency of Exposure Sessions. Optimal frequency of exposure sessions has yet to be established. Intensive exposure therapy programs that have achieved excellent results (see Foa, Kozak, Steketee, & McCarthy, 1992) typically involve daily sessions over the course of approximately 1 month, but quite favorable outcomes have also been achieved with more widely spaced sessions (see, e.g., DeAraujo et al., 1995). Clinically, we have found that less frequent sessions may be sufficient for highly motivated patients with mild OCD symptoms who readily understand the importance of daily exposure homeworks. A study is underway in our center to examine the immediate and long-term efficacy of a twice-weekly EX/RP program identical to the intensive regimen except with respect to session frequency. Data from this investigation may help to clarify optimal session frequency. Clinically, patients with more severe symptoms or those who for various reasons cannot readily comply with EX/RP tasks are typically offered intensive treatment.

Therapist-Assisted Exposure versus Self-Exposure. Evaluations of the presence of a therapist during exposure have yielded inconsistent results. In one study, patients with OCD receiving therapist-assisted exposure were more improved immediately after treatment than those receiving CMI and self-exposure, but this difference was not evident at follow-up (Marks et al., 1988). However, these results are difficult to interpret in light of the study's complex design. A second study using patients with OCD also indicated that therapist-assisted treatment was not superior to self-exposure at posttreatment or at follow-up (Emmelkamp & van Kraanen, 1977), but the number of patients in each condition was too small to render these findings conclusive. In contrast to the negative findings of

Marks and colleagues (1988) and Emmel-kamp and van Kraanen (1977), therapist presence yielded superior outcome of a single 3-hour exposure session compared to self-exposure for persons with specific phobia (Öst, 1989). Since specific phobias are on the whole less disabling and easier to treat than OCD, one may surmise that therapist presence should also influence treatment outcome with OCD. Moreover, using meta-analytic procedures, Abramowitz (1996) found that therapist-controlled exposure was associated with greater improvement in OCD and general anxiety symptoms than were self-controlled procedures. In light of the inconsistent findings reported above, no clear answer is available on the role of therapist assistance with exposure tasks in OCD treatment.

EX/RP versus Other Treatment Approaches

In this section we review the literature on the efficacy of standard individual EX/RP treatment versus other therapeutic approaches, including group treatment, family-based EX/RP treatment, cognitive therapy, and pharmacotherapy.

Individual versus Group EX/RP. Intensive individual EX/RP, although effective, can pose practical obstacles (such as high cost of treatment and scheduling problems) for patient and therapist alike. In addition, because experts in EX/RP treatment are few and far between, patients may need to wait for long periods of time or travel substantial distances in order to be treated. Thus some researchers have begun to examine the efficacy of more affordable and efficient treatment modalities. One such treatment alternative is group treatment. Fals-Stewart and colleagues (1993) conducted a controlled study in which OCD patients were randomly assigned to individual EX/RP, group EX/RP, or a psychosocial control condition (relaxation). Each of the active treatments was 12 weeks long with sessions held twice weekly, and included daily exposure homework. Significant improvement in OCD symptoms was evidenced in both active treatments, with no differences detected between individual and group EX/RP either at posttreatment or at a 6-month follow-up. Profile analysis of OCD symptom ratings collected throughout treatment did indicate a faster reduction in symptoms for patients receiving individual treatment.

These results offer evidence for the efficacy of group treatment. However, because patients were excluded from this study if they were diagnosed with *any* personality disorder or with comorbid depression based on a Beck Depression Inventory (BDI; Beck, Ward, Mendelson, Mock, & Erbaugh, 1961) score greater than 22, it may be that the sample was somewhat atypical. In addition, none of the participants had received previous OCD treatment, which is also unusual for this population and suggestive of a sample with less severe impairment. Thus inferences about the broader population of patients with OCD merit caution until these results are replicated.

Family Involvement versus Standard EX/RP Treatment. Emmelkamp and colleagues (1990) examined whether family involvement in treatment would enhance the efficacy of EX/RP for OCD. Patients who were married or living with a romantic partner were randomly assigned to receive EX/RP either with or without partner involvement in treatment. Each treatment lasted 5 weeks and consisted of eight 45- to 60-minute sessions with the therapist; exposures were not practiced in sessions. Results indicated that OCD symptoms were significantly lowered following treatment for both groups. No differences between the treatment emerged, and initial couple distress did not predict outcome. However, the reduction in anxiety/distress reported for the sample as a whole was modest (33%), which could have resulted from the relatively short treatment sessions and absence of *in vivo* exposure exercises in treatment sessions.

Mehta (1990) also examined the effect of family involvement on EX/RP treatment outcome. In order to adapt the treatment to serve the large numbers of young unmarried people seeking OCD treatment and the "joint family system" prevalent in India, a family-based rather than partner-based treatment approach was utilized. Patients who did not respond to previous pharmacotherapy were randomly assigned to receive treatment by systematic desensitization and EX/RP either with or without family assistance. Sessions in both conditions were held twice per week for 12 weeks; response prevention was described as "gradual." In the family condition, a designated family member (parent, spouse, or adult child) assisted with homework assignments, supervised relaxation therapy, participated in response prevention, and was instructed to be supportive. On self-reported OCD symptoms, a greater improvement was found for the family-based intervention at posttreatment and a 6-month follow-up. Although this study had methodological problems that complicate interpretation of findings (e.g., use of self-report OCD measures only, unclear description of treatment procedures), it offers some preliminary evidence that family involvement may be helpful in OCD treatment. Clinically, we routinely enlist the support of family members in EX/RP; we provide psychoeducation about the illness and its consequences during the early stages of treatment planning, as well as advice and encouragement regarding how to manage the patient's request for assurances, avoidant behaviors, and violation of EX/RP rules between sessions. We also try to reduce family members' criticism of the patient and unconstructive arguing about OCD and related matters when these issues arise in the therapy.

EX/RP versus Cognitive Therapies. Increased interest in cognitive therapy (see, e.g., Beck, 1976; Ellis, 1962), coupled with dissatisfaction with formulations of treatment as mediated by processes such as extinction (Stampfl & Levis, 1967) or habituation (Watts, 1973), prompted examination of the efficacy of cognitive procedures for anxiety disorders in general and for OCD in particular. In the first of these studies, Emmelkamp and colleagues (1980) compared self-instructional training (SIT; Meichenbaum, 1974) plus EX/RP to EX/RP alone. Following two sessions of relaxation training for both groups, the SIT and EX/RP treatments were conducted twice weekly for 5 weeks; sessions were of 2-hour duration. Both groups improved on all outcome measures; on assessor-rated avoidance associated with main compulsion, a superiority of EX/RP alone emerged. Thus SIT may have slightly hindered, rather than enhanced, efficacy.

Emmelkamp, Visser, and Hoekstra (1988) then examined the efficacy of rational–emotive therapy (RET), a cognitive therapy program that focuses on irrational beliefs. Patients were randomly assigned to receive EX/RP or RET. Treatment consisted of 10 sessions (60 minutes each) conducted over 8 weeks. In the EX/RP condition, patients were assigned exposure exercises from their treatment hierarchy to perform at home twice per week for at least 90 minutes; no exposure within sessions was conducted. RET involved determining the irrational thoughts that mediated negative feelings, confronting these thoughts via cognitive techniques, and modifying them with the aim of reducing anxiety and thereby decreasing the need to ritualize. Irrational beliefs were challenged Socratically by the therapist during sessions; patients were instructed to challenge their irrational thinking between sessions. Patients receiving RET were not instructed to expose themselves to feared situations, nor were they explicitly instructed to refrain from such exposure. Results indicated that both groups were improved at posttreatment, with no between-group differences. Because a large percentage of the sample received additional treatment during the follow-up period, long-term comparisons were difficult to interpret.

Emmelkamp and Beens (1991) examined whether a combined package of cognitive therapy plus EX/RP would enhance the effects of EX/RP. They compared a program that included 6 sessions of RET alone followed by 6 sessions of RET plus self-controlled EX/RP to a program that included 12 sessions of self-controlled EX/RP. In both programs, the first 6 sessions were followed by 4 weeks of no treatment, after which the additional 6 sessions were delivered. As in Emmelkamp and colleagues' (1988) study, treatment sessions were conducted approximately once per week and lasted for 60 minutes each. EX/RP sessions did not include therapist-assisted exposure, and patients were assigned twice-weekly exposure homework exercises. The first 6 sessions of the RET program were equivalent to those employed in the Emmelkamp and colleagues (1988) study and did not include exposure homework or antiexposure instructions. When self-controlled EX/RP was introduced following the first 6 RET-only sessions, the latter was focused on irrational thoughts that emerged during exposure homeworks. Mean reduction of anxiety associated with the main OCD problem was 25% for RET and 23% for EX/RP following 6 sessions. Following 6 more sessions (RET + EX/RP in one condition and EX/RP only in the other), both groups continued to improve on most measures compared to pretreatment; no significant group differences emerged. About 30% of the sample dropped out during treatment, which is a relatively high rate and a limitation to the generalizability of the findings.

Van Oppen and colleagues (1995) compared self-controlled EX/RP to an OCD-specific cognitive intervention. Patients were randomly assigned to receive 6 sessions (45-minute duration) of cognitive therapy or EX/RP, followed by 10 sessions of treatment including components from both. In order to examine the effects of "purer" versions of cognitive therapy and EX/RP, behavioral experiments (exposures) were not introduced into the cognitive treatment until after Session 6. Conversely, in the first 6 EX/RP sessions, care was taken by the therapist to specifically avoid any discussion of disastrous consequences. Results indicated that cognitive therapy without behavioral experiments and EX/RP without discussion of disastrous consequences led to OCD symptom reductions of 20% and 23%, respectively. After the second phase (10 additional sessions), both groups continued to improve.

Hiss, Foa, and Kozak (1994) investigated whether formal relapse prevention techniques following intensive EX/RP enhanced maintenance of gains. All discussions about cognitive factors typically included during the core treatment (e.g., discussion of lapse vs. relapse, posttreatment exposure instructions, themes of guilt and personal responsibility, and feared consequences) were removed. Patients received this modified EX/RP, followed by either a relapse prevention treatment or a psychosocial control treatment (associative therapy). All patients in both conditions were classified as responders at posttreatment ("response" was defined as 50% or greater reduction in OCD symptoms), with treatment gains better maintained in the relapse prevention group than in the associative therapy condition at a 6-month follow-up. The percentages of responders at follow-up were 75% in the relapse prevention condition and 33% in associative therapy. Notably, the higher than usual relapse rate in the associative therapy may have resulted from the removal of cognitive techniques that are typically utilized during the core treatment, such as discussion of feared consequences.

Findings from studies that have examined the relative and combined efficacy of EX/RP and cognitive interventions have been mixed.

In general, the EX/RP treatments used in these studies involved shorter sessions, fewer sessions, and absence of therapist-assisted exposure. These factors may have attenuated outcome compared to programs using intensive regimens with therapist-assisted exposure in session (e.g., 80% reduction on assessors' ratings of rituals in Foa et al., 1992; 60% and 66% reduction in Hiss et al., 1994). Thus the issue of whether the cognitive therapies described above are comparable or preferable to intensive EX/RP including therapist-aided exposure has yet to be determined.

The question of whether or not cognitive therapy improves the efficacy of EX/RP is difficult to disentangle, since both exposure therapy and cognitive therapy intend to modify mistaken cognitions. Indeed, Foa and Kozak (1986) have argued that the disconfirmation of erroneous associations and beliefs is a crucial mechanism underlying the efficacy of exposure treatments. For example, a patient and therapist sitting on the bathroom floor in a public restroom conducting an exposure to contaminated surfaces routinely discuss risk assessment, probability overestimation, and the like, as the therapist helps the patient achieve the cognitive modification necessary for improvement. The practical issue of interest is how to maximize efficacy: Is informal discussion of cognitive distortions during the exposure exercises sufficient, or should the therapist engage in formal Socratic questioning of hypothesized distortions such as inflated responsibility? Investigations that compare amputated versions of exposure and cognitive therapy (see, e.g., van Oppen et al., 1995) cannot provide an answer to this question. Notably, a recent meta-analytic study indicated that cognitive therapies for OCD that included some form of exposure to feared stimuli were superior to those that did not, suggesting that exposure may be necessary to maximize outcomes (Abramowitz & Franklin, in press).

Serotonergic Medications

Effectiveness of Medications

The use of serotonergic medications in the treatment of OCD has received a great deal of attention in the last two decades. Of the tricyclic antidepressants, CMI has been studied most extensively. In controlled trials, CMI has been found consistently superior to PBO (see, e.g., Clomipramine Collaborative Study Group, 1991). Similar results have been obtained with the selective SRIs fluvoxamine (Greist, Jefferson, et al., 1995), fluoxetine (see, e.g., Tollefson et al., 1994), sertraline (see, e.g., Greist, Chouinard, et al., 1995), and paroxetine (see, e.g., Zohar, Judge, & OCD Paroxetine Study Investigators, 1996). Accordingly, each of these medications has been approved by the Food and Drug Administration as treatments for adult OCD. These serotonergic compounds have also demonstrated superior outcome in comparisons with tricyclic antidepressants (e.g., imipramine; Rauch & Jenike, 1998), with CMI showing the strongest and most consistent therapeutic effects (Pato et al., 1998).

On the whole, these studies suggest that up to 60% of patients show some response to treatment with SRIs. However, the average treatment gain achieved even by treatment responders is moderate at best (Greist, 1990). In addition, amelioration of OCD symptoms is maintained only as long as the drug is continued (Thoren, Asberg, Chronholm, Jornestedt, & Traskman, 1980). In a controlled double-blind discontinuation study, 90% of patients relapsed within a few weeks after being withdrawn from CMI (Pato, Zohar-Kadouch, Zohar, & Murphy, 1988). Thus it appears that maintenance treatment is necessary in order to sustain achievements attained with pharmacotherapy alone for OCD.

EX/RP versus Pharmacotherapy

Many controlled studies have indicated that serotonergic antidepressants are superior to placebo in ameliorating OCD symptoms (for a review, see Greist, Jefferson, et al., 1995). However, only a few controlled studies have examined the relative or combined efficacy of antidepressant medications and EX/RP. These studies are reviewed below.

Using a rather complex experimental design, Marks and colleagues (1980) randomly assigned 40 patients to initially receive either CMI or PBO for 4 weeks. Six weeks of inpatient psychological treatment (daily 45-minute sessions) followed for both groups. During the first 3 weeks of this phase, 10 patients from each medication condition received EX/RP, while the other 10 received relaxation. At Week 7, those patients who had received re-

laxation were switched to EX/RP and the remaining continued to receive EX/RP. At the end of the 6-week psychosocial treatment period, patients were discharged from the hospital but remained on medication until Week 36, when a 4-week taper period commenced. Patients were followed for another year upon drug discontinuation. Results suggested that, compared to PBO, CMI produced significant improvements in mood and rituals only in those patients who were initially depressed. Compared to relaxation at Week 7, EX/RP was associated with greater reductions in rituals, but not with improvements in mood.

Several methodological issues, including the overly complex experimental design, complicated interpretation of findings. In particular, the inpatient behavior therapy condition, consisting of 45-minute-long daily sessions for 3–6 weeks (depending on treatment condition), may have employed insufficiently strict response prevention instructions as patients were asked to refrain from rituals only for the rest of the session and for a specified time thereafter. Length of treatment session may also have been problematic, as is the lack of information regarding what patients did on the inpatient unit for 6 weeks when they were not in session. Weaknesses in the experimental design led to underestimation of changes attributable to the behavioral treatment at Week 7 (EX/RP vs. relaxation comparison), and the design did not allow for a direct comparison of CMI and exposure alone across the same time period. Moreover, the drug-only period was too short (4 weeks) to allow optimal assessment of the efficacy of CMI alone.

The efficacy of CMI and EX/RP was examined again by Marks and colleagues (1988). Forty-nine patients were randomly assigned to one of four treatment conditions, three of which included CMI for approximately 6 months and one a PBO. One of the groups receiving CMI received antiexposure instructions for 23 weeks; the second group had self-controlled exposure for 23 weeks; and the third group received self-controlled exposure for 8 weeks, followed by therapist-aided exposure from Week 8 until Week 23. The group receiving PBO also received self-controlled exposure for 8 weeks, followed by therapist-aided exposure from Week 8 until Week 23. Inspection of the means at the different treatment stages in the group receiving PBO indicated that therapist-aided exposure was superior to self-exposure: Mean reductions after 8 weeks of self-exposure were 20% for rituals and 23% for OCD-related discomfort, whereas mean reductions after an additional 9 sessions of therapist-aided exposure were 71% and 68%, respectively. However, in the absence of a PBO group that received therapist-aided exposure first, it remains possible that order effects mediated the superiority of therapist-aided exposure. Because of confounds introduced by the complicated design, it is not possible to compare the effects of CMI directly with those of EX/RP. An additional issue is that evaluators were able to guess accurately 90% of the time whether patients received CMI or PBO, indicating problems with the drug assignment procedure.

With the growing awareness of the severe side effects associated with CMI, Cottraux and colleagues (1990) compared the efficacy of a more serotonergically selective medication, fluvoxamine, to that of EX/RP. Patients were assigned to one of three conditions: fluvoxamine with antiexposure instructions, fluvoxamine + EX/RP, and PBO + EX/RP. In the antiexposure condition, patients were specifically instructed to avoid feared situations or stimuli. Treatment continued for 24 weeks, after which EX/RP was stopped and medication was tapered over 4 weeks. EX/RP treatment was provided in weekly sessions and consisted of two distinct treatment phases: self-controlled exposure between sessions and imaginal exposure during sessions for the first 8 weeks, followed by 16 weeks of therapist-guided EX/RP. Other psychosocial interventions (e.g., couple therapy, cognitive restructuring, assertiveness training) were also provided as deemed necessary. Assessment included ratings by evaluators who were unaware of treatment assignments as well as self-report measures. At posttreatment (Week 24), reductions in assessor-rated duration of rituals per day were as follows: fluvoxamine + antiexposure, 42%; fluvoxamine + EX/RP, 46%; and PBO + EX/RP, 25%. At 6-month follow-up, reductions in assessor-rated duration of rituals per day were as follows: fluvoxamine + antiexposure, 42%; fluvoxamine + EX/RP, 45%; and PBO + EX/RP, 35%. Although fluvoxamine + EX/RP produced slightly greater improvement in depression at posttreatment than did PBO + EX/RP, the superiority of the combined treatment for

depression was not evident at follow-up. Interestingly, the majority of the fluvoxamine + antiexposure patients reported engaging in exposure on their own, thus invalidating the comparison between exposure and antiexposure with fluvoxamine.

To examine whether antidepressant medication reduces OCD symptoms only via reduction of depression, Foa and colleagues (1992) divided patients with OCD into highly depressed (BDI > 21) and mildly depressed (BDI < 20) groups, and then randomly assigned patients in both groups to receive either 6 weeks of treatment by imipramine or PBO. Upon completion of the medication-only phase, all patients received 3-week (15-session) intensive EX/RP followed by 12 weekly supportive sessions. Contrary to the hypothesis, while imipramine reduced depression in the depressed patients, it did not significantly reduce OCD symptoms in either depressed or nondepressed patients at Week 6: Mean reductions in assessor-rated fear of 13% and 26% were observed in depressed and nondepressed patients receiving imipramine, respectively, as were reductions of 17% and 34% on assessor-rated compulsive behavior. Moreover, imipramine did not enhance immediate or long-term outcome of EX/RP: OCD and depressive symptoms were both significantly reduced in each of the four groups following EX/RP, even in the depressed patients who initially received placebo. Mean percentage reductions in assessor ratings of obsessions and compulsions at posttreatment (Week 10) were as follows: 58% and 82% for the depressed group receiving imipramine, 42% and 85% for the depressed group receiving PBO, 51% and 82% for the nondepressed group receiving imipramine, and 64% and 84% for the nondepressed group receiving PBO.

The relative and combined efficacy of CMI and intensive EX/RP is being examined in a study in progress at our center and at Columbia University. An EX/RP program that includes an intensive phase (15 sessions lasting 2 hours each, conducted over 3 weeks) and follow-up phase (6 brief sessions delivered over 8 weeks) is compared to CMI, EX/RP + CMI, and PBO. Preliminary findings with treatment completion data as well as intent-to-treat data suggest that the active treatments appear superior to PBO, EX/RP appears superior to CMI, and the combination of the two treatments does not appear superior to EX/RP alone (Kozak, Liebowitz, & Foa, 2000). However, the design used in the Penn–Columbia study may not optimally promote an additive effect of CMI, because the intensive portion of the EX/RP program was largely completed before patients reached their maximum dose of CMI.

In summary, although there is clear evidence that both pharmaceutical treatment with serotonergic medications and EX/RP treatments are effective for OCD, information about their relative and combined efficacy remains scarce, because most of the studies examining these issues have been methodologically limited. Nevertheless, no study has found clear long-term superiority for combined pharmacotherapy plus EX/RP over EX/RP alone. The absence of conclusive findings notwithstanding, many experts continue to advocate combined procedures as the treatment of choice for OCD (e.g., Greist, 1992). In clinical practice, it is common to see patients in EX/RP treatment who are taking SRIs concurrently. In a recent uncontrolled examination of EX/RP treatment outcome for clinic outpatients with OCD, no posttreatment differences in OCD symptom severity were detected between patients who received EX/RP alone, EX/RP in combination with an SRI, EX/RP with an anxiolytic (with or without an SRI), and EX/RP plus multiple medications including neuroleptics (Franklin, Abramowitz, Bux, Zoellner, & Feeny, 2000); statistically significant and clinically meaningful changes were observed in each of the four treated groups. From these data, we can surmise that concomitant pharmacotherapy is not required for every patient to benefit substantially from EX/RP, and that concomitant pharmacotherapy does not appear to inhibit EX/RP treatment response. More definitive conclusions about the effects of augmenting pharmacotherapy with EX/RP await a more carefully controlled examination, however.

ASSESSMENT

Following a diagnostic interview to ascertain the presence of OCD, it is advisable to quantify the severity of the OCD symptoms by using one or more of the instruments described below. Quantification of symptom severity will assist the therapist in evaluating how successful treatment was for a given patient. In our clinic, we use several assessment instruments. As in most OCD clinical research studies, however, the primary measure of OCD symptom severity used in our center is the Yale–Brown Obsessive Compulsive Scale (Y-BOCS).

Yale–Brown Obsessive Compulsive Scale

The Y-BOCS (Goodman, Price, Rasmussen, Mazure, Delgado, et al., 1989; Goodman, Price, Rasmussen, Mazure, Fleischmann, et al., 1989) is a standardized semistructured interview that takes approximately 30 minutes to complete. The Y-BOCS severity scale includes 10 items (5 assess obsessions and 5 compulsions), each of which is rated on a 5-point scale ranging from 0 (no symptoms) to 4 (severe symptoms). Assessors rate the time occupied by the obsessions and compulsions, the degree of interference with functioning, the level of distress, attempts to resist the symptoms, and level of control over the symptoms. Goodman and colleagues note that the Y-BOCS has shown adequate interrater agreement, internal consistency, and validity. The Y-BOCS has served as the primary measure of outcome in most of the published OCD pharmacotherapy and CBT treatment studies conducted during the 1990s.

Assessor Ratings

In assessor ratings, a patient is rated on 8-point Likert scales in each of three areas: anxiety/distress, avoidance, and rituals. Based on information gathered in an initial interview, the assessor identifies three primary problems in each of these areas and rates their severity. When rating the patient's anxiety/distress, the therapist should take into account how distressed the patient feels when confronted with the situation or object, how often he/she gets distressed, and how strongly he/she is convinced that the feared consequence will occur. For example, if a patient is concerned with contamination, the therapist should determine the three main contaminating stimuli (objects or situations) and rate each separately. Next, the therapist should assess the degree to which the patient avoids situations related to the stimuli identified as main distressing stimuli. For example, if the main contaminant is feces, the avoidance item selected for rating might be public restrooms. Third, the therapist should rate the severity of the three main compulsive rituals. The severity of rituals is based on both the frequency and the duration of the ritualistic behavior. For example, the severity rating of a ritual that occurs 75 times a day and lasts only 30 seconds each time would be based on the high frequency, whereas the severity of a ritual that occurs only twice a day and takes 90 minutes to complete would be determined by the time spent on the ritual.

Although researchers have used these and similar ratings in treatment outcome studies of OCD (see, e.g., Emmelkamp & Beens, 1991; Foa, Grayson, Steketee, Doppelt, et al., 1983; Foa et al., 1982; Marks et al., 1988; O'Sullivan, Noshirvani, Marks, Monteiro, & Lelliott, 1991), information about their psychometric properties is scarce. The scales appear to have adequate interrater agreement when completed by two independent assessors (Foa, Grayson, Steketee, Doppelt, et al., 1983), but there is less agreement between the ratings of therapists and patients (Foa, Steketee, Kozak, & Dugger, 1985). Support for the validity of these rating scales is derived mainly from their demonstrated sensitivity to therapeutic change.

Self-Report Measures

The Compulsive Activity Checklist (CAC), originally the Obsessive–Compulsive Interview Checklist (Philpott, 1975), was developed as an assessor-rated measure of the extent to which OCD symptoms interfere with daily functioning. Originally the CAC included 62 items, but a shorter version containing 37 items has been developed (Marks, Hallam, Connelly, & Philpott, 1977). The self-report version of the CAC, which includes 38 items, was developed by Freund, Steketee, and Foa (1985). This version was found to be reliable, valid, and sensitive to treatment change (for a review, see Freund, 1986).

A few other self-report instruments for assessing OCD symptoms, such as the Leyton Obsessional Inventory (Kazarian, Evans, & Lefave, 1977), and the Lynfield Obsessional Compulsive Questionnaire (Allen & Tune, 1975), are available. These instruments are limited in that they assess only certain forms of obsessive–compulsive behavior and/or they include items that are unrelated to OCD symptoms.

INITIAL INTERVIEW

After a diagnosis of OCD has been established, and before treatment actually begins, the therapist should schedule 4 to 6 hours of appointments with the patient. In these sessions, the therapist needs to accomplish three important tasks. First, the sessions are used to collect information necessary to develop a treatment plan. Specifically, the therapist must identify specific cues that cause the patient distress (threat cues), avoidance, rituals, and feared consequences. Second, the therapist should develop good rapport with the patient. Because during intensive EX/RP the patient will engage in exposure exercises designed to elicit anxiety and distress, the lack of a good relationship between the therapist and the patient may compromise outcome. Third, the therapist needs to explore the patient's beliefs about OCD and the perceived consequences of refraining from rituals and avoidance, as this information will be used to guide the informal discussions of cognitive processes that take place throughout EX/RP.

Threat cues may be either (1) tangible objects in the environment or (2) thoughts, images, or impulses that the person experiences (for lack of better terms, we have labeled them "external cues" and "internal cues," respectively). Passive avoidance and ritualistic behavior (sometimes called "active avoidance") both serve to reduce the distress associated with the threat cues. Rituals may be further divided into overt or covert (mental) forms. It is essential that patients understand the difference between obsessions and mental compulsions, because obsessions are treated with systematic exposure, and mental compulsions with ritual preventions. During treatment, the patient should be instructed to report any mental compulsions to the therapist, because the performing of such compulsions during exposure exercises attenuate the effects of these exercises in the same way that behavioral compulsions do.

External Fear Cues

Most patients with OCD experience fear in reaction to specific environmental cues (objects, persons, or situations), but each patient will have his/her own idiosyncratic threat cues. For example, individuals who fear contamination from toilets may differ as to whether all toilets are feared or only those open to the public. One patient may fear only the toilet itself, whereas another patient also fears bathroom floors, doorknobs, and faucets. Similarly, two individuals may experience distress at the prospect of a house fire, but one experiences the distress only when he/she is the last person to leave the house, whereas the other experiences distress before going to bed at night when his children are present.

The therapist needs to gather specific information about cues that elicit the patient's distress, in order to identify the basic sources of the fear. Identification of the basic source is important for planning the treatment program. Confronting the source of the fear is essential for successful behavioral treatment of OCD. Often, when such exposure does not take place during treatment, relapse will occur. For example, a patient who feared contamination by her hometown was treated with EX/RP 3,000 miles away from the town. Because of the distances involved, direct exposure to the town was impossible, so treatment consisted of exposure to objects contaminated directly or indirectly by contact with the town. Although the patient habituated to the objects used in the exposure sessions, she continued to fear her hometown. Within 1 year after treatment, she had developed fears to new objects related to her hometown. It was not until she engaged in repeated exposures to the town itself that she experienced lasting improvement.

It is important that the therapist conduct a thorough investigation of objects, situations, and places that evoke obsessional distress for the patient at the time of presentation and at onset. Such information will help identify the source of the distress. To facilitate communication with the patient about situations that evoke distress, a subjective units of discomfort scale (SUDS) ranging from 0 to 100 is introduced. Patients are asked to rate each situation with respect to the level of distress that they expect to experience upon exposure. The following dialogue between therapist (T) and patient (P) illustrates the process of gathering information about distressing situations.

T: When do you get the urge to wash your hands?

P: In a lot of places. There are so many places.

T: Are there any places where the urges are particularly strong?

P: Well, when I am sitting in my living room, particularly near the fireplace. Also in the laundry room, which I never go to. Also, when I walk in the park.

T: Let's talk about your living room. How upset are you when you are sitting next to your fireplace?

P: That's bad. I guess about a 90.

T: Can you tell me what makes you so upset in your living room?

P: Well, that is a long story . . . and I know it doesn't make sense.

T: Go on. It's important that we understand what makes you uncomfortable and fearful in your living room.

P: About 2 years ago, I got up in the morning and went into the living room, and I saw a dead squirrel in the fireplace. I guess he got in through the chimney. So I figured that if the squirrel was dead, he must have been sick. I know that a lot of squirrels have rabies, so I thought that if the squirrel died of rabies, then the germs are all over the chimney.

T: Have you tried to have the chimney and the fireplace cleaned?

P: Yes, we did have a company come in and clean the whole area, but I'm not sure that they can clean away the germs.

T: I understand. How about the laundry room? How upsetting is it to be in the laundry room?

P: That would be a 100. That's why I don't go in there.

T: How did the laundry room become dangerous?

P: Oh, that's another story. Until a year ago, my children used to keep their guinea pigs in the laundry room. One day we found the female guinea pig dead. So I thought that it probably died of rabies too.

T: Oh, I understand. So you are generally afraid that you will contract rabies if you come in contact with things that you think are contaminated with rabies germs. Is this true?

P: Exactly. That's why I don't like to walk in the woods or the park. You know those places have all kind of animals, and you can never tell where the germs might be.

It is clear from the conversation above that it was not living rooms, laundry rooms, or parks per se that the patient feared. Rather, any situation or object that, in her mind, had some probability of being infested with rabies germs would become a source of contamination. Some contamination-fearful patients, however, cannot specify the feared consequences of coming into contact with stimuli they perceive to be contaminated. For these patients, the primary fear is that they will not be able to tolerate the extreme emotional distress generated by being contaminated. With such patients, it is also important to probe further to discern whether the patients have fears about the long-term health consequences of experiencing high and unremitting anxiety in response to stimuli that prompt obsessions.

Internal Fear Cues

Anxiety and distress may also be generated by images, impulses, or abstract thoughts that the individual finds disturbing, shameful, or disgusting. Examples of such cues include impulses to stab one's child, thoughts of one's spouse or partner being injured in an accident, or images of religious figures engaged in sexual activity. Clearly, internal threat cues may be produced by external situations, such as the sight of a knife's triggering the impulse to stab one's child. Some patients may get distressed when experiencing certain bodily sensations, such as minor pains' triggering the fear of having cancer.

In many cases, patients may be reluctant to express their obsessive thoughts, either because they are ashamed of them or because they fear that expressing them will make the consequence more likely to occur. In these cases, the therapist needs to encourage the

expression of these thoughts through direct questioning and a matter-of-fact attitude. Sometimes it helps to tell the patient that many people with and without OCD (as many as 85% of nonanxious individuals) have unwanted thoughts (Rachman & DeSilva, 1978). It may also be helpful to remind the patient that talking about the obsessions will be a part of therapy, and that the evaluation session provides an opportunity to begin this process.

T: So tell me, when is it that you feel the urge to count?

P: It seems like I'm always counting something, but it's mostly when I think about certain things.

T: What kind of things?

P: I don't know. Bad things.

T: Can you give me some examples of bad thoughts that will make you want to count?

P: (Brief silence) I really prefer not to talk about them. It makes things worse.

T: You mean it makes the counting worse?

P: Yes.

T: All right, I know now that when you think or talk about certain bad things you have an urge to count, but I still don't know what those bad things are. How about you tell me so that I can help you with them?

P: I'd really rather not. Can't we talk about something else?

T: It is important that I know what the thoughts are in order to plan your treatment. I'll try to help you. Do the thoughts involve someone being hurt?

P: Yes.

T: Do the thoughts involve only certain people getting hurt, or could it be anyone?

P: Mostly my family.

T: OK, what else can you tell me about the thoughts?

P: I really don't want to say any more.

T: I know this is scary, but remember, facing your fears is what this treatment is all about.

P: OK. It's not always thoughts. Sometimes I see pictures in my mind where my brother or my mom and dad are killed. I'm afraid when I talk about these thoughts and pictures that they really will die.

T: A lot of people have thoughts that they don't like to have. Even people without OCD. Just because you have these thoughts, or talk about them, doesn't mean that bad things will actually happen or that you want them to come true.

It is important to reassure the patient that unpleasant thoughts occur often and to emphasize the distinction between thoughts and reality. Many patients with OCD have magical ideas in which the distinction between "thinking about things" and "making things happen" is blurred—a process labeled by Salkovskis (1985) as "thought–action fusion." It is important to point out to the patient that thoughts are different from actions. Also, many patients think that if negative thoughts enter their minds, it means that they wish the bad thing will happen. The therapist should assure the patient that thinking about bad things does not mean that one wants them to happen. These sorts of informal discussions of mistaken beliefs are an integral part of correct implementation of EX/RP. Such discussions should accompany the treatment-planning process, and should be reiterated as needed during exposure exercises. It is, however, important that such discussions accompany EX/RP exercises rather than replace them.

Feared Consequences

Many patients with OCD are afraid that something terrible will happen if they fail to perform their rituals. Those with washing rituals, for example, typically fear that they and/or someone else will become ill, become disabled, or die as a result of being contaminated. Many patients with checking rituals fear that, because of their negligence, certain catastrophes will happen, such as their homes' burning down or someone's being killed by their driving. Some patients have only a vague notion of what these negative consequences might be (e.g., "I don't know exactly what will happen, but I feel that if I don't count to 7, something bad will happen to my family"). Others do not fear catastrophes at all, but they cannot tolerate the emotional distress they experience if they do not perform rituals. Some

fear that unless they ritualize, anxiety will increase continually until they have a nervous breakdown. Data from the DSM-IV field trial indicated that approximately two-thirds of patients with OCD could clearly identify consequences that would follow from refraining from rituals other than emotional distress, whereas the remainder could report no such consequences (Foa et al., 1995).

It is important to identify the specific details of the patient's feared consequences in order to plan an effective exposure program. For example, the content of the imaginal exposure of a patient who checks while driving for fear of having hit a pedestrian and being sent to jail will differ from that of a patient who fears that hitting a pedestrian will result in being punished by God. Similarly, patients who ritualistically place objects in a specific order may differ with respect to their feared catastrophes. Some perform the ritual in order to prevent catastrophic consequences (e.g., death of parents), whereas others do so only to reduce the distress elicited by disordered objects. The former would benefit from treatment that includes both imaginal and *in vivo* exposure, whereas the latter is likely to profit from *in vivo* exposure alone.

Strength of Belief

Clinical observations led Foa (1979) to suggest that patients with OCD who are overvalued ideators do not respond well to EX/RP, although two later studies failed to find a linear relationship between strength of belief in feared catastrophes and improvement following EX/RP (Foa, Abramowitz, Franklin, & Kozak, 1999; Lelliott et al., 1988). Two issues need to be considered in evaluating these collective findings. First, the reliability and validity of the strength-of-belief measures used in previous studies are unknown. Second, the relationship between overvalued ideation and treatment outcome may not be linear. Clinical observation suggests that only patients who express extreme belief in their obsessional ideation show poor outcome. Indeed, Foa and colleagues (1999) found that only extremely strong belief (fixed belief) was associated with attenuated outcome. Such patients may appear delusional when discussing their feared catastrophes. We hypothesize that the effect of fixed belief on outcome may be mediated by treatment compliance: If a patient is convinced that feared disasters will ensue if he/she engages in prescribed exercises, the patient probably will not complete the tasks as assigned.

When a therapist is assessing the strength of belief, it is important to remember that a patient's insight into the senselessness of his/her belief often fluctuates. Some patients readily acknowledge that their obsessional beliefs are irrational, but they still cause marked distress. A few individuals firmly believe that their obsessions and compulsions are rational. In most patients, though, the strength of belief fluctuates across situations, making it difficult to ascertain the degree to which they believe the obsessions are irrational. The following is an example of an inquiry into the strength of a patient's belief in her obsessional fear of contracting acquired immune deficiency syndrome (AIDS).

T: How likely is it that you will contract AIDS from using a public restroom?

P: I'm really terrified that I will get AIDS if I use a bathroom in a restaurant.

T: I know that you are afraid of getting AIDS, but if you think logically, how likely do you think you are to get AIDS by sitting on a public toilet?

P: I think I will get AIDS if I use a public toilet.

T: So do you mean to say that there is a 100% chance of you getting AIDS if you sat on a public toilet once?

P: Well, I don't know about once, but if I did it again and again I would.

T: What about other people? Will they get AIDS if they use a public toilet?

P: I guess so. I'm not sure.

T: Since most people use public bathrooms, almost everyone should have AIDS by now. How do you explain the fact that there are a relatively small number of people with AIDS?

P: Maybe not everybody is as susceptible to AIDS as I am.

T: Do you think that you are more susceptible than other people?

P: I don't know for sure. Maybe the likelihood of my getting AIDS is only 50%.

Based on the interaction described above, the therapist concluded that the patient did not have an "overvalued ideation," and thus that the prognosis for this patient was brighter than if she had continued to strongly hold her original belief. Accordingly, the implementation of EX/RP for this patient followed the standard guidelines.

Avoidance and Rituals

In order to maximize treatment efficacy, all avoidance and ritualistic behaviors, even seemingly minor ones, should be prevented. Therefore, the therapist should gather complete information about all passive avoidance and rituals. When the therapist is in doubt as to whether a particular avoidance behavior is related to OCD, he/she may suggest an "experiment" in which the patient is exposed to the avoided situation. If the patient experiences anxiety or distress, the avoidance behavior should be prevented as part of treatment. Similarly, if it is unclear whether a given action constitutes a ritual, a ritual prevention "experiment" may be implemented. If refraining from performing the action evokes distress, the action can be identified as a ritual and should be addressed in therapy.

Patients with OCD, like those with phobias, often attempt to avoid anxiety-evoking situations. Most passive avoidance strategies are fairly obvious (e.g., not entering public restrooms, not preparing meals, and not taking out the trash). However, the therapist also needs to be attentive to subtle forms of avoidance, such as carrying money in one's pockets to avoid opening a wallet, wearing slip-on shoes to avoid touching laces, and using drinking straws to avoid contact with a glass or a can. Patients with checking rituals also engage in subtle avoidance behaviors that are important to explore, such as arranging their work schedules to ensure that they are rarely if ever the last person to leave the workplace (and thus that the responsibility for checking the safe will fall on a coworker).

Active rituals, like passive avoidance, may be explicit (e.g., prolonged washing, repeated checks of the door, and ordering of objects) and/or subtle (e.g., wiping hands on pant legs, blinking, and thinking "good" thoughts). It is important that the therapist identify both explicit and subtle rituals so that they all can be addressed during treatment.

Although compulsive rituals are intended to reduce the distress associated with obsessions, patients sometimes report that the performance of these rituals is aversive in itself. For example, Ms. S, who was obsessed with the orderliness of objects on her shelves, found reordering the shelves aversive because she was unable to find the "perfect" place for everything. Similarly, Mr. J, who felt contaminated by chemicals, found the act of decontaminating himself by repeated hand-washing aversive because he was unable to decide when his hands were sufficiently clean; therefore, he washed until his hands became raw. Another reason why rituals may become aversive is their intrusion into other aspects of the person's life. For example, Mr. J, who would take 2-hour-long showers in order to feel adequately clean, was reprimanded repeatedly by his supervisor for arriving late to work.

When certain compulsions become aversive, some patients decrease the time they spend performing the ritual by increasing avoidance behaviors or by substituting other, less time-consuming rituals. For example, Ms. E was obsessed with fears of contamination by funeral-related objects (e.g., cemeteries, people returning from a funeral), to which she responded with hours of showering and handwashing. She eventually retreated into her bedroom and avoided all contact with the outside world. Mr. J, described above, avoided taking a shower for days at a time, but in between showers he would wipe his hands compulsively and avoid touching his wife. In some cases, seemingly "new" rituals may develop during the course of treatment to fill the function of those previously identified and prevented. For example, Mr. F, who was concerned about his hands' becoming contaminated, was successful in resisting the urge to wash his hands, but soon after ritual prevention was implemented, he started to rub his hands together vigorously in order to "decontaminate" them. When such a substitute ritual is identified, it too needs to be addressed in treatment with ritual prevention. Therapists must remain alert to such shifts in ritualistic behaviors, and help patients to become alert to the possibility of such shifts as well.

History of Main Complaint and Treatment History

Many patients with OCD are unable to give a detailed account of the onset of their symptoms, because the symptoms began subtly many years ago. Nevertheless, attempts should be made to collect as much information as possible about the onset and course of the disorder. Such information may provide clues about aspects of the fear network and variables associated with the maintenance of symptoms, and may help anticipate difficulties that could arise during treatment (e.g., old obsessions or rituals that may resurface as more prominent ones diminish).

Many patients with OCD have an extensive history of psychological and pharmacological treatments, and it is important to make a detailed inquiry about the outcome of previous treatments. If a patient has been treated with EX/RP, the therapist should assess whether the treatment was implemented appropriately and whether the patient was compliant with treatment demands. Knowledge that a patient experienced difficulty complying with ritual prevention instructions, or that previous therapy failed to provide adequate exposure experiences or ritual prevention instructions, is important for designing the behavioral program. Other factors that may have prevented successful outcome or caused relapse, such as job stress, death in the family, or pregnancy, should be discussed. At the same time, a prior failed course of EX/RP should not necessarily be viewed as prognostic, especially if the patient recognizes why the therapy was less successful in the past. One of our patients who had failed multiple trials of less intensive EX/RP came to our center with the knowledge that his noncompliance with exposure exercises between weekly sessions had greatly reduced the effects of treatment. He also noted that that the slow progress he had observed in these previous therapies demoralized him and caused further disengagement from the treatment. When offered a choice of daily versus twice-weekly sessions, he opted for the daily treatment, noting that the more intensive approach might decrease the chance of similar lapses. He has now successfully completed the intensive regimen.

In our clinic we have observed that a substantial majority of our clinic outpatients have been treated, or are currently being treated, with serotonergic medications. Some seek EX/RP in order to augment the partial gains they have achieved with the medication. Others wish to discontinue the medication because it was ineffective, because of side effects, or because they do not want to continue taking medicine indefinitely. Assessing the patient's treatment goals is necessary for planning his/her treatment program.

Social Functioning

Obsessive–compulsive symptoms may severely disrupt the daily functioning of patients. Therapists should assess the impact of OCD symptoms on the various areas of functioning. Where appropriate, this information should be used to design suitable exposure exercises. For example, Ms. D experienced difficulties completing assignments at work because she repeatedly checked each task. Treatment included exposures to performing tasks at work without checking. Even if the client is not currently working, exposures simulating work situations may be necessary if symptoms created difficulties in previous jobs.

OCD clearly has a deleterious effect on the intimate relationships of many patients. About half of married individuals seeking treatment for OCD experience marital distress (Emmelkamp et al., 1990; Riggs et al., 1992). Other family and social relationships may also suffer as a result of the OCD symptoms. The impairment in social functioning may arise either because social contact is perceived as threatening (e.g., "I may spread germs to other people"), or because so much of the patient's time and energy is invested in performing rituals and planning ways to avoid distressing situations. Again, information about the relation of social dysfunction to OCD symptoms may lead the therapist to include specific exposures aimed at ameliorating these social difficulties.

The assessment of social functioning should also include an evaluation of what role, if any, other people play in the patient's compulsive rituals. If the patient relies on others for reassurance or compliance with rituals (e.g., family members must remove their shoes before entering the house), the therapist should instruct the family in how to respond appropriately when they are asked to participate in the

patient's rituals. A careful analysis of the relationship is called for before specific instructions are given to significant others. Moreover, if family members tend to criticize the patient when obsessional distress arises, it is important to address these negative exchanges in treatment. We have often dealt with this issue through a combination of empathic discussion of the frustration experienced by the family member and role playing of more effective responses.

Mood State

Although some patients with serious depression and OCD may benefit from behavioral therapy for OCD (Foa et al., 1992), research has suggested that severe depression may limit the extent to which the OCD symptoms are reduced and the maintenance of those gains (Abramowitz et al., 2000; Foa et al., 1982; Foa, Grayson, Steketee, & Doppelt, 1983; Marks, 1977; Rachman & Hodgson, 1980). Therefore, it is important to assess the mood state of the patient prior to beginning behavioral therapy. Patients with severe depression should be treated with antidepressant medication or cognitive therapy to reduce the depressive symptoms prior to implementing behavioral therapy for the OCD. Treatment with serotonergic antidepressants may reduce OCD symptoms as well as depression. Since the effects of such medications on OCD symptoms may not be evidenced until 3 months after treatment begins, the therapist needs to use his/her clinical judgment to decide whether to begin EX/RP when the depression decreases, or to wait until the effects of the medication on OCD symptoms can be assessed.

Choice of Treatment

How should a therapist determine what is the most suitable treatment for a given patient? As discussed earlier, EX/RP as well as serotonergic medications have demonstrated efficacy for OCD. The therapist and patient are faced with the choice of EX/RP, pharmacotherapy, or a combination of the two. Neither treatment is effective with all patients, and no predictors of who will benefit most from which treatment modality have been identified. Therefore, unless the patient has been particularly successful or unsuccessful with some previous course of treatment, the decision should be based on factors such as availability of treatment, amount of time the patient is able or willing to invest in treatment, his/her motivation, and the patient's willingness to tolerate side effects.

The intensive treatment requires a considerable investment of time over a period of several weeks. Many patients are unable or unwilling to devote 4 to 5 hours a day to treatment. These patients should be advised to try pharmacological treatment, because it does not require the same extensive time commitment. As noted earlier, we are currently investigating the effects of a twice-weekly EX/RP regimen in our center, in order to examine whether a program that requires less frequent visits to the clinic can yield satisfactory outcomes; results so far have been encouraging (Abramowitz et al., 2000). Some patients may be unwilling (sometimes expressed as "I can't do that") to experience the temporary discomfort caused by EX/RP. These patients, too, may be advised to try medications. The need to develop "readiness programs" to prepare such patients to accept EX/RP treatment has often been raised, in light of the relatively high refusal rate among patients offered EX/RP. Such programs may include testimonials from previously treated patients, cognitive strategies designed to help the patient calculate objective risks more accurately, psychoeducation about OCD and EX/RP, and a review of the outcome literature for various treatments. The manualizing of such programs, and the investigation of their effectiveness in increasing the acceptance rate for EX/RP and the efficacy of EX/RP for patients who enter such programs, await controlled studies.

Some patients are concerned about the potential (or already experienced) side effects of medications or their unknown long-term effects. These patients often prefer EX/RP. Other patients are concerned with the prospect of entering an "endless" treatment, since, according to present knowledge, relapse occurs when medication is withdrawn (Pato et al., 1988; Thoren et al., 1980). This concern is particularly relevant for women who plan to bear children in the future and will need to withdraw from the medication during pregnancy. EX/RP should be recommended to these patients, because its effects are more enduring.

As discussed above, the long-term effects of combining EX/RP and medication are unclear; therefore, it is premature to necessarily recommend treatment programs that combine the two therapies. However, some patients who present for treatment are already on antidepressant medication. Because these medications were not found to interfere with the effectiveness of EX/RP (Franklin et al., 2000), it is recommended that patients continue to take the medication if they have experienced some improvement in either obsessive–compulsive symptoms or depression. However, if a patient has not experienced improvement with medication, withdrawal of the medication before or during EX/RP should be considered. Special consideration should be given to patients with severe depression concurrent with their OCD. It is recommended that these patients be treated with antidepressants or with cognitive therapy for the depression prior to entering intensive EX/RP for the OCD, given the recent findings of somewhat attenuated outcome for severely depressed patients (Abramowitz et al., in press).

INTENSIVE TREATMENT PROGRAM

The intensive treatment program consists of four phases: (1) information gathering and treatment planning, (2) intensive EX/RP, (3) a home visit, and (4) a maintenance and relapse prevention phase.

Information Gathering and Treatment Planning

The first step in information gathering consists of a thorough diagnostic evaluation to determine that the patient's main psychopathology is OCD. The second step is to assess whether the patient is appropriate for EX/RP. We recommend that individuals who are abusing drugs or alcohol should be treated for the substance abuse prior to intensive treatment for OCD. Patients who have clear delusions and hallucinations are also poor candidates for intensive treatment. Individuals with severe major depressive disorder should be treated for depression before beginning treatment for OCD. Patients' motivation to comply with the demands of intensive treatment should be carefully evaluated. It is important to describe the treatment program in enough detail that the patient is not surprised when treatment begins. If the patient does not express strong motivation and commitment to treatment, it might be preferable to delay the implementation of intensive treatment or to offer alternative treatments such as medication. As noted earlier, a study of less intensive EX/RP for patients who appear otherwise motivated, yet cannot accommodate the daily regimen into their schedules, is underway at our center.

Once a patient is judged to be appropriate for intensive treatment, information gathering and treatment planning begin. This phase typically consists of 4 to 6 hours of contact with the patient, conducted over a period of 2 to 3 days. During this phase, the therapist collects information about the patient's obsessive–compulsive symptoms, general history, and the history of treatment for OCD as described above. During these sessions, the rationale for treatment is discussed, the program is described in detail, the patient is taught to monitor his/her rituals, and a treatment plan is developed.

First Information-Gathering Session

It is very important to discuss the rationale for treatment and to describe the treatment program in detail. The program requires that the patient abandon his/her OCD habits, and therefore temporarily experience substantial discomfort. If patients do not understand why they are asked to suffer this short-term distress or are not convinced that treatment will work, they will be unlikely to comply with treatment instructions. The treatment rationale is explained as follows:

"You have a set of habits that, as you know, are called 'obsessive–compulsive symptoms.' These are habits of thinking, feeling, and acting that are extremely unpleasant, wasteful, and difficult to get rid of on your own. Usually these habits involve thoughts, images, or impulses that habitually come to your mind even though you don't want them. Along with these thoughts, you have unwanted feelings of extreme distress or anxiety and strong urges to do something to reduce the distress. To try to get rid of the anxiety, people get into the habit of engaging in various special thoughts or actions, which we call 'rituals.'

"Unfortunately, as you know, the rituals do not work all that well, and the distress goes down for a short time only and comes back again. Eventually, you may find yourself doing more and more ritualizing to try to reduce anxiety, but even then, the relief is temporary and you have to do the ritual all over again. Gradually, you find yourself spending so much time and energy ritualizing—which does not work that well anyway—that other areas of your life get seriously disrupted.

"The treatment we are about to begin is called 'exposure and ritual prevention.' It is designed to break two types of associations. The first one is the association between sensations of anxiety and the objects, situations, or thoughts that produce this distress. [Use information you have collected as examples—for instance, 'Every time you touch anything associated with urine, you feel anxious, distressed, or contaminated.'] The second association we want to break is the one between carrying out ritualistic behavior and the feeling of less anxiety or less distress. In other words, after you carry out [specify the identified rituals], you temporarily feel less distress. Therefore, you continue to engage in this behavior frequently. The treatment we offer will break the automatic bond between the feelings of discomfort/anxiety/contamination of [specify the obsession] and your rituals. It will also train you not to ritualize when you are anxious."

After presenting the treatment rationale, the therapist should begin to collect information about the patient's OCD symptoms. The rationale for information gathering and a description of the treatment are presented as follows:

"In the next two sessions, I will ask you specific questions about the various situations and thoughts that generate discomfort or anxiety in you. We will order them according to the degree of distress they generate in you on a scale from 0 to 100, where 0 means 'no anxiety' and 100 means 'maximum anxiety or panic.' The exposure treatment program involves confronting you with situations and thoughts that you avoid because they generate anxiety and urges to carry out ritualistic behavior. Why do we want to expose you to places and objects that will make you uncomfortable—situations that you have attempted to avoid even at much cost? We know that when people are exposed to situations that they fear, anxiety gradually declines. Through exposure, then, the association between anxiety and [specify obsessions] will weaken because you will be repeatedly exposed to these situations so that the previously evoked anxiety decreases with time.

"For many people with OCD, the obsessions occur within their imagination and rarely take place in reality. This makes it impossible to practice exposure by actually confronting those situations for prolonged periods. For example, if a person fears that her home will burn down, we certainly do not wish to have her house catch on fire in order to practice exposure. Similarly, someone who fears that he has run over a person who is now lying in the road cannot be exposed in reality to such a situation.

"If confrontation with the feared situation is necessary to reduce obsessions, how can you improve without directly confronting the situation? You can confront these fears through imagery, in which you visualize the circumstances that you fear will happen. In imagery practice, you create in your mind detailed pictures of the terrible consequences that you are afraid will occur if you do not engage in their ritualistic behavior. During prolonged exposure to these images, the distress level associated with them gradually decreases.

"When people with OCD encounter their feared situations or their obsessional thoughts, they become anxious or distressed and feel compelled to perform the ritualistic behavior as a way to reduce their distress. Exposure practices can cause this same distress and urge to ritualize. Usually, performing rituals strengthens the pattern of distress and rituals. Therefore, in treatment, ritual prevention is practiced to break the habit of ritualizing. This requires that you stop ritualizing, even though you are still having urges to do so. By facing your fears without resorting to compulsions, you will gradually become less anxious. Behavior therapists call this process 'habituation.' Therefore, during the 3 weeks of intensive exposure, the association between relief from anxiety and carrying out [specify patient's rituals] will become weaker, be-

cause you will not be allowed to engage in such behaviors. Therefore, you will find out that anxiety decreases even without resorting to these activities."

The initial information-gathering session is also used to begin training the patient to accurately monitor his/her rituals. Accurate reports of the frequency and duration of ritualistic behavior are important for evaluating the progress of treatment and for demonstrating the reality of changes to the patient. In some cases, the monitoring also serves an active role in treatment. Patients begin to recognize that rituals do not truly occur "all day long," and the act of monitoring the rituals may decrease their frequency and duration.

"It is very important for the treatment program that we have an accurate picture of the extent to which you engage in obsessive thinking and compulsive behavior. Having a clear picture of how much of your time is taken up by your problem will help you and me to monitor your progress and adjust the treatment program accordingly. Therefore, during this week while I am still collecting information in order to form a treatment program, I would like you to record your symptoms every day. It is not easy to report accurately on how much you engage in your obsessive–compulsive behavior, and therefore we will spend some time now and in the next session going over some rules for how to record your symptoms. Here are some monitoring forms on which you will record your thoughts and rituals."

The therapist should specify which ritual(s) the patient is to record; go over the instructions carefully with the patient; and practice with the patient by filling out the form together, using an "imaginary day" of his/her life. The following rules can be helpful to the patient in monitoring rituals:

1. Use your watch to monitor the time you spend on your rituals.
2. Do not guess the time of ritualizing; be exact.
3. Write the time immediately on your monitoring form.
4. Do not save the recording until the end of the day or the beginning of the next day.
5. Write a short sentence to describe the trigger for ritualizing.

Prior to beginning treatment, the patient should identify an individual (e.g., parent, spouse/partner, or close friend) who can serve as a support person during the intensive treatment program. The patient is instructed to rely on this person for support during exposures, and the support person is asked to help monitor compliance with ritual prevention instructions. If the patient experiences difficulty resisting the urge to ritualize, the support person should be contacted to offer support. Because the support person will be involved in the therapy, the therapist should allocate time during the information-gathering phase to describe the treatment and discuss its rationale with the support person.

The therapist should make an effort to ensure that the support person and the patient find a mutually agreed-on way for the support person to offer constructive criticism and observations. In making these suggestions, the therapist should be sensitive to any difficulties that have arisen in the past. For example, Mr. B, who served as his wife's primary source of reassurance, also criticized her severely when he "caught" her performing her handwashing ritual. To prevent these responses from hampering treatment, the therapist spent time with the couple negotiating appropriate responses to requests for reassurance and a means for the husband to help supervise his wife's ritual prevention without being critical.

The support person should be in regular (at least twice-weekly) contact with the therapist, in order to be informed about the specific homework exposures that the patient has to accomplish and to relay his/her observations about the patient's behavior outside the therapy session. In addition, the support person should, with the consent of the patient, contact the therapist if major treatment violations occur (e.g., refusal to do homework or engaging in ritualistic behavior).

Second Information-Gathering Session

At the beginning of the second information-gathering session, the therapist should devote time to examining the patient's self-monitoring form. This includes examining the descriptions of situations that trigger ritualistic behavior and offering constructive comments when necessary. The patient should be reminded to use short phrases or sentences to describe the trigger situations. The therapist should assess the accuracy of the patient's time estimates and remind him/her of the need for accurate measurements.

Generating Treatment Plan. The bulk of the second information-gathering session is allotted to gathering detailed information about the patient's symptoms and, based on what is learned about the symptoms, developing a treatment with the patient. It is important to explain to the patient how the exposure exercises that are part of his/her treatment will reduce the OCD symptoms. For example, a patient with religious obsessions will be told that the imaginal exposure to his/her burning in hell in excruciating detail is designed to reduce his/her obsessional distress when a less elaborated image of burning in hell comes to mind. It is important for patients to understand the rationale underlying the central concept in EX/RP— that confronting obsession-evoking stimuli during treatment increases their suffering in the short run, but will reduce it in the long run. We often describe to patients that the difficulties they are likely to experience during the first week of exposure sessions are likely to diminish with proper implementation of EX/RP.

Describing Homework. At the end of the second information-gathering session, the therapist should describe the homework assignments that will be included in the treatment program. The homework usually requires 2 to 3 hours, in addition to the 2-hour treatment session. Homework consists of additional exposure exercises to be done between treatment sessions at the patient's home or elsewhere (e.g., shopping malls or a relative's home). We suggest that the patient monitor his/her SUDS Level every 10 minutes during the homework exposures. In some cases, it will be impossible for the patient to maintain an exposure for 45–60 minutes. In these cases, the therapist should work with the patient to develop a plan that will allow the exposure to be prolonged. For example, instead of asking the patient to spend 45 minutes sitting in the restroom of a local restaurant, the therapist may suggest that he/she contaminate a handkerchief on the toilet seat and carry this "contamination rag" in a pocket.

Treatment Period: Intensive EX/RP

The treatment program at our center typically consists of 15 treatment sessions lasting 2 hours each and conducted 5 days a week for 3 weeks. Clinical observations suggest that massed sessions produce better results than do sessions spread out over time; therefore, we recommend a minimum of three sessions per week. Each session begins with a 10- to 15-minute discussion of homework assignments and ritual monitoring of the previous day. The next 90 minutes are divided into 45 minutes of imaginal exposure and 45 minutes of *in vivo* exposure. The final 15 minutes are spent discussing the homework assignment for the following day. This format should be adjusted when necessary. For example, if an *in vivo* exposure requires that the therapist and patient travel to a local shopping mall to contaminate children's clothing, the entire session will be devoted to this activity. Some patients have difficulty engaging emotionally in imaginal exposures (i.e., the images fail to elicit distress). In these cases, treatment should focus exclusively on *in vivo* exercises.

At the beginning of the session, it is recommended that the therapist discuss the plan for that session with the patient. Barring any unusual circumstances (e.g., the patient's stated objection to proceeding with the planned exposure), it is important to limit these discussions to no more than 15 minutes. Patients with OCD are usually very fearful of engaging in exposure tasks, and elaborated discussion of the task at hand may serve as a form of avoidance from going ahead with the exposure. These preexposure discussions are also fertile ground for assurance seeking (i.e., the patient's asking the therapist whether the therapist is certain that the proposed exercise is safe). The therapist should answer such questions carefully, avoiding either extreme of providing compulsive reassurance or of conveying to the patient that the proposed exposure is objectively dangerous.

Imaginal exposure exercises are typically conducted prior to *in vivo* exercises in each session, often as a prelude to the scheduled *in vivo* exercises. During imaginal exposure, the patient is seated in a comfortable chair and is given the following instructions:

"Today you will be imagining [describe scene]. I'll ask you to close your eyes so that you won't be distracted. Please try to picture this scene as fully and vividly as possible—not like you're being told a story, but as if you were experiencing it now, right here. Every few minutes, I will ask you to rate your anxiety level on a scale from 0 to 100. Please answer quickly and try not to leave the image."

The imaginal exposure sessions are audiotaped, and the patient is asked to repeat the exposure by listening to the tape as part of that day's homework.

The situations that are included in *in vivo* exposure vary greatly from patient to patient (particularly with checkers). Below are some examples of instructions that might be offered to patients during *in vivo* exposure exercises.

For patients with washing rituals:

"Today you will be touching [specify item(s)]. This means that I will ask you to touch it with your whole hand, not just the fingers, and then to touch it to your face and hair and clothing—all over yourself, so you feel that no part of you has avoided contamination. Then I'll ask you to sit and hold it and repeatedly touch it to your face, hair, and clothes during the rest of the session. I know that this is likely to make you upset, but remember the anxiety will eventually decrease. I also want you to go ahead and let yourself worry about the harm you are afraid will happen—for example, disease—since you won't he washing or cleaning after this exposure. I am sorry that this treatment has to be difficult and cause so much discomfort, but I'm sure you can do it. You'll find it gets easier as time goes on. OK, here it is. Go ahead and touch it."

The therapist should give the patient the object to hold, then ask him/her to touch it and then ask the patient to touch the object or the "contaminated" hands directly to the face, hair, and clothing. Every 10 minutes the patient should be asked, "What is your level of anxiety or discomfort from 0 to 100 right now as you focus on what you're touching?" This can be shortened to "What is your SUDS level?" once the patient understands the question.

For patients with checking rituals:

"Now I'd like you to [e.g., write out your checks to pay your monthly bills without looking at them after you've finished; just put them in the envelope, and then we will mail them right away without checking even once after you've done it]. Then we will go on and do [e.g., drive on a bumpy road without looking in the rear-view mirror] in the same way. While doing this, I would like you to worry about what harm might happen because you aren't checking your actions, but don't let the thoughts interfere with actually doing those activities."

Patients should be reminded of the specific instructions for ritual prevention on the first day of treatment and periodically during treatment. We have found that giving patients a printed copy of the rules for ritual prevention (see Figure 5.1) can help them to understand and remember the rules. If the rules outlined for the patient do not adequately cover the type(s) of ritual(s) the patient exhibits, the therapist should provide him/her with a written set of instructions modeled after these forms.

During the last few sessions of treatment, the patient should be introduced to rules of "normal" washing, cleaning, or checking. Guidelines for such "normal" behavior are presented in Figure 5.2. Prevention requirements should be relaxed to enable the patient to return to what would be considered a normal routine.

Home Visit

It is important to ensure that the patient's gains from the treatment program generalize to the home environment. Usually homework assignments function to produce this generalization, but we have found that visits made by the therapist to the patient's home can be quite helpful, especially in cases where a patient is not able to return home daily during the intensive treatment phase (e.g., a patient from out of town or a hospitalized patient). The home visit also offers an opportunity for the therapist and patient to discuss guidelines for "normal" behavior. The therapist should discuss the plans for these visits with the patient and his/her family before the treatment ends. It is also important to note that in some cases the majority of the treatment sessions need to be conducted at the patient's home, such as when the patient's rituals involve hoarding. The frequency of home visiting during the core treatment should be determined by whether the patient's OCD symptoms are readily "transportable" to situations outside the home, or whether they are specific to home. For patients with washing rituals who have "safe" rooms and areas in their houses, contamination of these areas is imperative and also quite difficult; it is often advisable that the therapist assist directly with these home-based exposures when there is a question of whether such patients can contaminate these "sanctuaries" successfully on their own.

Typically, the home visit consists of 4-hour sessions held on each of 2 days at the end of the treatment program. The bulk of the time in these sessions is used for conducting additional exposures to obsessive stimuli in and around the patient's home or workplace. For example, the therapist may accompany the patient as he/she contaminates objects around the house or at the local grocery store. Similarly, the patient may be asked to turn the stove on and off without checking and leave the house with the therapist. Most patients, particularly those patients who were able to return home during treatment, will report little or no discomfort when doing these exposures because they represent repetition of homework assignments. In some cases, though, the therapist will discover some areas that a patient has not contaminated or some areas at home that continue to generate distress despite previous exposures. The home visit should focus on exposure to situations or objects that remain problematic.

Maintenance Period

In addition to prescribing continued self-exposure tasks to help the patient maintain therapy gains, the therapist may wish to schedule regular maintenance sessions. These sessions may be used to plan additional exposures, refine guidelines for normal behavior, and address issues that arise as the patient adjusts to life without OCD.

There is some evidence that patients benefit from continued contact with the therapist following the intensive therapy sessions. In one study, 12 weekly supportive therapy sessions (no exposure exercises) appeared to reduce the number of relapses in a sample of patients with OCD treated with 3 weeks of intensive EX/RP (Foa et al., 1992). In another

CLIENT INSTRUCTIONS FOR RITUAL PREVENTION: WASHING

- During the treatment period, you are not permitted to use water on your body. No handwashing, no rinsing, no wet towels, and no washcloths are permitted.
- The use of creams and other toiletry articles (bath powder, deodorant, etc.) is permitted unless you find that the use of these items reduces your feeling of contamination.
- Shave with an electric shaver.
- Use water for drinking or brushing your teeth, but take care not to get it on your face or hands.
- Supervised showers are permitted every 3 days for 10 minutes each, including hair washing. Ritualistic or repetitive washing on specific areas of the body (e.g., genitals, hair) during showers is prohibited. Showers should be timed by your support person, but he/she does not need to observe you directly.
- Exceptions to these rules may be made for unusual circumstances—for example, medical conditions necessitating cleaning. Check with your therapist.
- At home, if you have an urge to wash or clean that you are afraid you cannot resist, talk to your support person and ask him/her to remain with you until the urge decreases to a manageable level.
- Your support person should report observed violations of ritual prevention to your therapist. He/she should attempt to stop such violations through firm verbal insistence, but without using physical force or arguing. Faucets can be turned off by the support person if you give prior consent to such a plan.

Special Instructions _____

_____
_____
_____
_____

CLIENT INSTRUCTIONS FOR RITUAL PREVENTION: CHECKING

- Beginning with the first session of exposure and ritual prevention, you are not permitted to engage in any ritualistic behavior.
- Only "normal" checking is permitted for most items (such as one check of door locks).
- For items ordinarily not checked (e.g., empty envelopes to be discarded), all checking is prohibited.
- Exceptions may be made in unusual circumstances, but you must check with your therapist first.
- At home, if you have an urge to check that you are afraid you cannot resist, talk to your support person and ask him/her to remain with you until the urge decreases to a manageable level.
- Your support person should report violations of response prevention to your therapist. He/she should attempt to stop such violations through firm verbal insistence, but without using physical force or arguing.

Special Instructions _____

_____
_____
_____
_____

FIGURE 5.1. Ritual prevention guidelines for patients with washing and checking rituals.

study, following the intensive treatment with 1 week of daily cognitive-behavioral sessions followed by eight brief (10-minute) weekly telephone contacts resulted in better long-term outcome than following intensive treatment with 1 week of treatment with free association (Hiss et al., 1994).

Therapeutic Setting

It is advisable for patients to remain in their normal environments during intensive treatment. This is particularly important for patients whose fears are cued mainly by stimuli in their home environments. The hospital may be an artificially protected setting, particularly for patients with checking rituals, who may not feel responsible for their surroundings and hence will not experience their usual urges to check. If patients live too far away to commute for daily sessions, we recommend that they rent an apartment or hotel room near the clinic. When this is not possible, hospitalization should be considered. Hospitalization is recommended for patients deemed to be at risk for suicide or psychotic breakdown, and for those who need close supervision but lack a support system sufficient to aid them during treatment.

GUIDELINES FOR "NORMAL" BEHAVIOR: WASHING

- Do not exceed one 10-minute shower daily.
- Do not exceed five 30-second handwashings per day.
- Restrict handwashing to the following occasions:
    Before meals
    After using the bathroom
    After handling greasy or visibly dirty things
- Continue to expose yourself deliberately on a weekly basis to objects or situations that used to disturb you.
- If objects or situations are still somewhat disturbing, expose yourself twice weekly to them.
- Do not avoid situations that cause some discomfort. If you detect a tendency to avoid a situation, make it a point to confront it deliberately at lease twice a week.

Other Rules _____
_____
_____
_____
_____

GUIDELINES FOR "NORMAL" BEHAVIOR: CHECKING

- Do not repeat more than once any checking of objects or situations that used to trigger an urge to check.
- Do not check even once in situations that your therapist has advised you do not require checking.
- Do not avoid situations that trigger an urge to check. If you detect a tendency to avoid, confront these situations deliberately twice a week and exercise control by refraining from checking.
- Do not assign responsibility for checking to friends or family members in order to avoid checking.

Other Rules _____
_____
_____
_____
_____

FIGURE 5.2. Guidelines for "normal" washing and checking behavior.

If a patient is employed, and his/her OCD symptoms are work-related, the patient should be encouraged to continue working so that relevant exposures can be included in treatment. However, since treatment requires 5 to 6 hours per day, the patient may opt to work half days during the intensive treatment.

In cases where the patient's symptoms are unrelated to work, the patient may decide not to continue working during intensive treatment. Because of the time-consuming nature of the treatment, we often suggest that patients take some time off from work. If it is not possible for the patient to take 3 full weeks away from work, the therapist might suggest that the patient work half days or take time off from work during Weeks 1 and 2 of the treatment program.

Therapist Variables

Intensive treatment with exposure to feared situations and response prevention of ritual-istic behavior provokes considerable stress for patients. Their willingness to undergo such "torture" attests to their strong motivation to rid themselves of the OCD symptoms. The intensive treatment regimen requires that the therapist maintain a delicate balance between pressuring the patient to engage in the treatment and empathizing with his/her distress. Clinical observations and findings from a study by Rabavilas, Boulougouris, and Perissaki (1979) suggest that a respectful, understanding, encouraging, explicit, and challenging therapist will be more likely to achieve a successful outcome than a permissive, tolerant therapist.

During treatment, patients' behavior may range from being extremely cooperative and willing to participate in exposures to being blatantly manipulative and refusing to follow the therapist's instructions. An individual patient's behavior may fluctuate, depending on what exposure is conducted during a particular session. To a great extent, the "art" of conducting behavioral therapy for OCD involves knowing when to push, when to confront, and when to be more flexible. Such decisions require that the therapist carefully observe the patient's reactions and make a judgment based on his/her experience. As much as possible, the therapist should display an attitude that counteracts the harshness of the treatment program, while holding to the rules for therapy established at the beginning of the program. The therapist should assure the patient that he/she will not use force to implement exposure, and that no exposure will be planned without the patient's consent. If the patient cannot trust that the therapist will adhere to these essential guidelines, the treatment is likely to be compromised. We also assure patients that family members will be asked not to present unplanned exposures to the patients (e.g., taking out the garbage) without discussing it.

Patient Variables

A primary factor that influences a patient's potential for benefiting from intensive behavioral treatment is the level of his/her motivation. Because EX/RP treatment causes high distress, patients need to be highly motivated to undertake the treatment. Often the level of motivation is related to the severity of a patient's symptoms. When symptoms are sufficiently intolerable, patients are more likely to tolerate considerable discomfort for a short period in order to gain relief from their symptoms in the long run.

Sometimes individuals are pressured into entering therapy by their families, and they agree to participate in treatment only to appease a spouse/partner or a parent. These patients are unlikely to follow the therapist's instructions strictly, and therefore they are less likely to make lasting gains in therapy. In light of these observations, we do not recommend that patients enter into EX/RP if they are not committed to follow such instructions; alternative treatment strategies are typically recommended in such circumstances.

It is important that the therapist clearly explain to the patient that 1 month of therapy, albeit intensive, is unlikely to eliminate all OCD symptoms. Rather, patients should expect that their anxiety and the urges to ritualize will diminish and become more manageable. An expectation of becoming

symptom-free at the end of treatment may lead to disappointment and can potentiate relapse, because maintenance of treatment gains usually requires continued effort over time following the intensive treatment. Thus we tell patients in the initial interview that we do not have a "cure" for OCD, but rather a treatment that is likely to help them substantially reduce their symptoms in both the short and long run.

It is also important to explain to patients that EX/RP treatment is not a panacea for all of their psychological and interpersonal problems. This treatment is specifically aimed at reducing a patient's obsessions and urges to ritualize. Problems that existed prior to treatment (e.g., couple discord or depression) are likely to remain, although they may be somewhat alleviated after treatment.

As mentioned earlier, patients with severe depression and/or an extremely strong belief in the reality of the obsessive fear may not benefit from EX/RP. An additional factor that has been identified as a potential hindrance to the cognitive-behavioral and pharmacological treatment of OCD is concurrent schizotypal personality disorder (Jenike, Baer, Minichiello, Schwartz, & Carey, 1986; Minichiello, Baer, & Jenike, 1987). Although some questions have been raised about the method used to diagnose schizotypy (see Stanley, Turner, & Borden, 1990), therapists should be alerted to the probability that schizotypal patients may respond poorly to treatment for OCD.

CASE STUDY

In this section we demonstrate through verbatim material the process of gathering information relevant to treatment, planning the treatment program, and conducting exposure sessions.

Case Description

"June," a 26-year-old married woman who had just completed her bachelor's degree in nursing, sought treatment for a severe washing and cleaning problem. She was extremely agitated in the first interview and described herself as "crying a whole lot" during the previous 6 weeks. She arrived in the company of her husband of 6 months and her sister-in-law, whom she considered a good friend. Previous treatment by systematic desensitization, antidepressants, tranquilizers, and cognitive restructuring had proven ineffective. June had been unable to seek employment as a nurse due to her symptoms.

The information above was collected at June's initial evaluation for participation in treatment by EX/RP. After the evaluator ascertained the absence of psychosis, drug and alcohol abuse, and organic disorders, June was assigned a therapist.

Information Gathering

Current Symptoms

First, the therapist (T) sought information from June (J) about the obsessional content, including external and internal fear cues, beliefs about consequences, and information about passive avoidance patterns and types of rituals. Because rituals are the most concrete symptom, it is often convenient to begin the inquiry by asking for a description of this behavior.

T: I understand from Dr. F that you are having a lot of difficulty with washing and cleaning. Can you tell me more about the problem?

J: I can't seem to control it at all recently. I wash too much. My showers are taking a long time, and my husband is very upset with me. He and my sister-in-law are trying to help, but I can't stop it. I'm upset all the time, and I've been crying a whole lot lately (*on the verge of tears*). Nothing seems to help.

T: I see. You look upset right now. Please try to explain what your washing has been like in the past few days, so I can understand. How much washing have you been doing?

J: Much too much. My showers use up all the hot water. And I have to wash my hands, it seems like all the time. I never feel clean enough.

T: About how long does a shower take? How many minutes or hours would you say?

J: About 45 minutes, I guess. I try to get out sooner. Sometimes I ask Kenny to make me stop.

T: And how often do you take one?

J: Usually only twice, once in the morning and once at night before bed, but sometimes if I'm really upset about something I could take an extra one.

T: And what about washing your hands? How much time does that take?

J: You mean how many times do I wash?

T: How long does it take each time you wash your hands, and how often do you wash your hands in a day?

J: Umm, maybe 20 times a day. It probably takes me 5 minutes each time, maybe more sometimes. I always have the feeling they're not really clean, like maybe I touched them to the side of the sink after I rinsed and then I think they're dirty again.

The therapist now had some basic information about the most prominent rituals. Some further questioning clarified whether other compulsions were also in evidence.

T: Do you do anything else to make your self feel clean?

J: Yes, I alcohol things. I wipe with alcohol, like the car seat before I sit down.

T: Do you wipe yourself with alcohol?

J: No, only things that I think are dirty.

T: Can you tell me how much you do that?

J: I use about a bottle of alcohol a week.

Here the therapist had to choose whether to inquire about what objects June cleaned or to ask about possible additional rituals. The therapist chose to continue the inquiry about ritualistic actions, and to turn to the subject of "contaminants" as soon as the inquiry was completed.

T: OK, can you think of any other things that you do to clean yourself or other things around you that you feel are dirty?

J: That's all I can think of right now.

T: What about other kinds of what we call "compulsive" type of activities? Do you have to check or repeat things over and over?

J: No, except when I wash if I don't feel it's enough. Then I wash again.

T: No other repetitive actions besides washing?

Since this patient did not appear to have multiple types of ritualistic behaviors, the therapist turned to the obsessional content. External cues are usually solicited first.

T: What are the things that make you feel you want to wash? For instance, why do you wipe the car seat with alcohol?

J: I think that maybe I got "dog dirt" on it when I got in from before, or Kenny might have.

T: From your shoes?

J: Yes. I also worry about the hem of my dress touching the seat. I've been worrying that my shoe could kick my skirt hem, or when I step up a step like to go in a building, the dress could touch the step.

T: A dress like this? [June was wearing a dress that came to just below her knee. The likelihood that it could have touched a curb or sole of her shoe was very slim.]

J: Yes.

T: Has your skirt ever had dog dirt on it?

J: I don't think so, but in my mind I think that maybe it could have gotten some on it. I suppose it would be hard for that to happen, wouldn't it?

Thoughts that highly improbable events might have occurred are common in OCD. Such distortions may be the result of intense anxiety. Doubts about "safety" often lead to requests for reassurance or to rituals. Reassuring June that her dress was unlikely to be soiled would have been countertherapeutic, since it would have perpetuated the neurotic fears. Rather, the therapist proceeded to inquire further about the obsessional content.

T: Is dog dirt the most upsetting thing that you worry about?

J: Probably. Yes, I think so, but bathroom germs are pretty bad too.

T: What sort of germs?

J: From toilets. You know, when you go to the bathroom.

T: Urine and feces?

J: Yes, urine doesn't bother me as much as the other.

T: Why?

J: Because I learned in nursing school that it's almost sterile. I had a hard time in the course about microbiology, because it upset me to try to learn about bacteria and microorganisms. They make it sound like there are all kinds of germs everywhere that are real dangerous. I didn't learn it very well; I tried to avoid thinking about it.

June's concerns with both "dog dirt" and bathroom germs suggested that her fear structure included apprehension about potential illness. The therapist questioned her to better understand the nature of the feared consequences of contamination.

T: Are you afraid of diseases that could come from feces?

J: Yes, I guess so. The thing of it is, though, I know other people don't worry about it like I do. To them, you know, they just go to the bathroom and wash their hands and don't even think about it. But I can't get it out of my head that maybe I didn't get clean enough.

T: If you didn't wash enough, would you get sick, or would you cause someone else to get sick?

J: Mostly I worry that I'll get sick, but sometimes I worry about Kenny too.

T: Do you worry about a particular kind of disease?

J: I'm not sure. Some kind of illness.

It is not uncommon for patients who fear harm that may ensue from not ritualizing to be unable to identify a specific feared consequence. Patients with checking rituals often fear they will forget or throw out something important, but they do not always know exactly what this will be. Those with repeating rituals may fear that something bad will happen to a loved one, but often cannot specify what particular disaster will befall them. However, many patients with OCD do fear specific consequences (e.g., blindness or leukemia). At this point, the therapist may choose either to complete the inquiry about external threat cues or to pursue the investigation about the feared consequences and the belief that such harm is indeed likely to occur. The latter course was selected here.

T: Let's say that you did actually touch dog feces or human feces and you weren't aware of it, so you didn't wash to remove it. What is the likelihood that you or Kenny would really get seriously ill?

J: Well, I feel like it really could happen.

T: I understand that when it happens and you become very distressed, it feels like you will actually become sick, but if I ask you to judge objectively, right now how likely is it that you will get sick from touching feces and not washing? For example, if you were to touch feces 10 times, how many times would you get sick?

J: Oh, I know it's pretty unlikely, but sometimes it seems so real.

T: Can you put a number on it? What's the percent chance that if you touched a small amount of feces and didn't wash that you'd get sick?

J: I'd say low, less than 25%.

T: That means that one time in every four, you'd get sick.

J: No, that's not right. I guess it's really less than 1%.

From the dialogue above, it is clear that June did not strongly believe that her feared disasters would actually occur, although her initial estimate of the likelihood was high. A person with poor insight regarding the senselessness of his/her OCD symptoms would have assigned higher probabilities (usually over 80%) and would insist on the accuracy of his/her estimate even in the face of persistent questioning. Note also that this exchange is an example of the informal cognitive restructuring accompanying EX/RP that we have discussed earlier. The therapist might need to repeat this discussion during subsequent exposure sessions if June, highly anxious about confronting contaminants, readjusted her likelihood estimates. Strength of belief can change in a given patient; belief can become stronger when the patient perceives threat.

T: OK. Now, besides disease, what else could happen if you got feces on you?

J: I suppose I'm also afraid of what other people might think if I got dog feces on my shoe or on my dress. Somebody would see it or smell it and think it was really disgusting and I was a dirty person. I think I'm afraid they would think I'm not a good person.

The therapist then questioned June further about this feared consequence, inquiring about the possibility of others evaluating her character negatively because she had feces on her dress. The material regarding feared consequences was collected for later inclusion in the imaginal exposure scenes. To conclude the inquiry about the nature of the obsessions, the external feared stimuli were further elucidated.

T: Besides dog and human feces and toilets, what else can "contaminate" you? Is it OK if I use the word "contaminated" to describe how you feel if you handle these things?

J: Yes, it's like I can feel it on my skin, even if I can't see it. Umm, I also get upset if I see "bird doo" on my car.

T: Bird droppings? The whitish spots?

J: Yeah. I have to hold my skirt close to me so that I don't touch any of these spots with my clothes.

T: OK, bird doo, what else?

J: Dead animals, like on the roadside. I feel like the germs, or whatever it is, get on the tires from the pavement and get on the car. Even if I don't run over it. Like it's spread around the street near it.

T: What do you do if you see a dead animal?

J: I swerve wide around it. Once I parked the car and as I got out, I saw this dead cat right behind the car. I had to wash all my clothes and take a shower right away. It was really a mess that day.

T: It sounds like that was very difficult for you. Is there anything else besides dead animals that contaminates you?

J: I can't think of any. There are lots of places I avoid now, but that's because of what we just talked about.

The therapist questioned the patient further about other items that were likely to be contaminated because of their potential relationship to the ones she had already noted.

T: What about trash or garbage?

J: Yeah, that bothers me. And I also avoid gutters on the street.

T: What's in the gutter that upsets you?

J: Dead animals, I guess. And then the rain spreads the germs down the street. Also rotten garbage. It's really dirty. Sometimes the gutters are really disgusting.

T: Um hmm. Are you afraid you could get sick from dead animals and garbage?

J: Yes, it's like the toilets or dog dirt.

In order to prepare for an exposure program in which objects are presented hierarchically with respect to their ability to provoke discomfort, the patient was asked to rank her major contaminants. Here the patient also provided information about avoidance behaviors associated with her contaminants.

T: Now let's make a list of the main things that upset you. I'm going to ask you how distressed you would be on a 0–100 scale if you touched the thing I'll name. Zero indicates no distress at all, and 100 means you'd be extremely upset, the most you've ever felt.

J: OK.

T: What if you touched dog dirt?

J: And I could wash as much as I wanted?

T: No, let's say you couldn't wash for a while.

J: That would be 100.

T: A dead animal?

J: Also 100.

T: Bird doo on your car?

J: That depends on whether it is wet or dry.

T: Tell me for both.

J: It would be 100 wet and 95 dry.

T: Street gutter?

J: About 95.

T: Garbage in your sink at home?

J: Not too bad. Only 50. But the trash can outdoors would be 90.

T: Why the difference?

J: Because the inside of the trash can is dirty from lots of old garbage.

T: I see. What about a public toilet seat?

J: That's bad—95.

T: Car tires?

J: Usually 90. But if I just passed a dead animal, that'd be 99.

T: What about a doorknob to a public bathroom?

J: The outside knob is low, like 40. But the inside knob is 80, because people touch it right after they've used the bathroom, and I've seen that some don't wash their hands.

T: I understand. How about grass in a park where dogs are around?

J: If I did walk in the grass, it would be about 80 or 85, but I don't usually do it. I also have a lot of trouble on sidewalks. You know, the brown spots on the concrete. I guess most of it is just rust or other dirt, but I think maybe it could be dog dirt.

T: How much does that bother you?

J: To step on a brown spot? About 90. I always walk around them.

The therapist should continue in this manner until a list of 10 to 20 items is formed. More items may be necessary for patients with multiple obsessional fears or rituals. The items will be ordered from low to high in preparation for treatment by exposure. Items equivalent with regard to their disturbance are grouped together. Moreover, it is important to probe the reasons why one stimulus differs from another, as these provide further information about the patient's particular "OCD logic." This information is highly relevant for the construction of the exposure hierarchy and for the informal cognitive discussions about risk assessment, responsibility, and so forth.

Considerable information about avoidance patterns and rituals emerged from the interview with June about external threat cues. More details can be obtained by asking a patient to provide a step-by-step description of a typical day's activities from the time he/she awakens until he/she goes to sleep. Usually patients are not entirely accurate when describing their compulsive behaviors during the interview, because, as one patient told us, they have not "thought of their OCD in that way before." Thus the self-monitoring tasks assist the patients in raising their awareness about the OCD patterns, and they provide the therapist with more accurate data about rituals and avoidant behaviors.

For June, we were particularly concerned with bathroom routines, her shower, use of the toilet, handling of towels and dirty clothes, and dressing and putting on shoes. Additional information about avoidance patterns can be ascertained by inquiring about other routine activities, such as shopping, eating out, housecleaning, preparing meals, working, and so on. The following dialogue exemplifies the degree of detail desired.

T: June, in order for us to plan your treatment carefully, I need to know what you avoid in your daily routine. Why don't you start by describing what you do first when you wake up?

J: I go to use the bathroom first.

T: Nightgown on or off?

J: I take off my nightgown, because I don't want it to touch the toilet. That way it's clean at night after I shower.

T: Go on.

J: I go to the toilet. I suppose I use a lot of toilet paper because I don't want to get anything on my hand. Then I have to shower after a bowel movement.

T: How do you get ready to shower?

J: I have to put a new towel on the rod near the shower. I don't like it to touch anything before I use it. Oh, and I put my slippers facing the door, near the shower, so I can put them on without stepping on the bathroom floor when I get out of the shower. Then I get into the shower.

T: You said you shower for 45 minutes. Why does it take so long?

J: I have to wash myself in a special order, and I count how many times I wash each part. Like I wash my arm four times. That's why it takes so long.

T: What is the order you use?

J: First I wash my hands, then my face and hair, and then I go from the top down.

T: What about the genital and anal area? [This area should disturb this patient most, since she feels contamination from fecal "germs."]

J: Oh yes, those are last, after my feet.

Such a detailed description helps the therapist to anticipate possible avoidance by the patient during treatment and to plan specific exposure instructions. Supervision of normal washing behavior at the end of treatment

would address June's tendency to count and to order her washing. During the initial session of information gathering, June was instructed to self-monitor the frequency and duration of her compulsions.

T: Between now and our next session, I'd like you to record all the washing and cleaning that you do, including wiping things with alcohol. You can use this form (*hands patient a form for self-monitoring of rituals*). Please write down every time you wash, how long you washed, what made you wash, and how anxious you were before you washed. This kind of record will help us identify any sources of contamination you've forgotten to mention, and we can also use it to measure your progress during treatment.

J: Do you want me to write in each space for each half hour?

T: No, only when you wash or use alcohol.

J: OK.

History of Symptoms and Treatment History

After assessing June's current symptoms, the therapist sought information about the onset of the problem, with particular reference to the presence of specific stressors at the time and whether these stressors were still present.

T: How long have you been washing like this?

J: It started about 2 years ago in my first year of nursing school. It wasn't real bad right away. It started with the city. I had to go into the city to classes, and the city seemed real dirty.

T: Did nursing have something to do with it?

J: Maybe. I was under a lot of tension. I had to quit working as a secretary, and it was pretty hard without an income and a lot of school bills. My mother and dad weren't much help. And then we started to learn all the sterilizing techniques, and I already told you about the course in microbiology.

T: Did it gradually get worse?

J: Mostly, but I did notice that it was a lot worse after a rotation on surgery, where I was really worried about germs contaminating the instruments. That's when I started to wash more than usual.

T: Did you seek help at that time?

J: I was already seeing Dr. W at the university, and he tried to help.

T: You were already in treatment with him? For what reason?

J: He was helping me with an eating problem. I had anorexia. I'd been seeing him for about a year when the washing started.

T: Anorexia? Did treatment help?

J: Yes, I was down to 85 pounds, and I'm up around 105 now. He mostly asked me to increase my weight every week, and he did "cognitive therapy," I think it's called.

T: I see. What about the washing problem?

J: He tried the same type of therapy, but it didn't work for that. That's why I'm here. My sister-in-law heard about it, and Dr. W said I should come.

T: What about drugs? Were you ever given medication for this problem?

J: Yes, I tried Anafranil [CMI] for a while, it helped a little, but it made me dizzy and sleepy, so I decided to stop taking it. Also, I heard that you can't take the medication when you are pregnant, and Kenny and I want to have a baby soon. Before that, I took Xanax [alprazolam]. It calmed me down, but didn't stop the washing.

T: Have you tried any other treatments?

J: Only for the anorexia. I went to another counseling center at the university for about a year, but that didn't really help at all.

June's history was unusual only in the relatively recent onset of her symptoms. Typically, patients in our clinic present a much longer duration of symptoms, with the mean about 8 years. Other centers in England and Holland report similar figures. June's treatment history of trying various psychotherapeutic and pharmacological treatments prior to seeking EX/RP was quite typical. Since previous failure with nonbehavioral treatments has not been found to influence outcome with EX/RP, the clinician should not be discouraged by such a history. However, because of a possible skeptical attitude about the value of treatment, the therapist should provide the patient with a clear rationale for EX/RP treatment, along the lines discussed earlier and demonstrated below.

T: Before I continue to collect more information about your problem, let me tell you about our treatment.

J: Well, Dr. F told me something about it, but I'm still not sure what this treatment is going to be like.

T: The treatment is called "exposure and ritual prevention." I'll be asking you to confront situations and things that frighten you or make you feel contaminated. We will do this gradually, working up to the hardest things. For example, we may begin with the outside door handles of bathrooms and work our way up to toilet seats and bird doo. We'll do this together, and I'll be there to help you. The sessions will last an hour and a half or 2 hours, and we'll meet every weekday. In addition, I'll assign you homework to do similar things between the therapy sessions.

J: You mean I have to touch them, even dog dirt?

T: Yes, in order to get over these kind of fears, people must learn to confront what they're afraid of and stay with it until the discomfort decreases.

J: Even if I did, it would probably take me a year to get used to it.

T: Remember, you didn't always feel like this about dog dirt. When you were younger, did you ever step in dog dirt and just wipe it off on the grass and go on playing?

J: Yeah, I forget that. It seems such a long time ago. I used to not think twice about this stuff.

T: To get you back to how you used to feel, we need to expose you directly to what you're afraid of. Now there's a second part to treatment. I'm also going to ask you not to wash for 3 days at a stretch. No handwashing or showering for 3 days. Then you can take a shower, but you will have to limit it to 10 minutes. After the shower, you will have to contaminate yourself again and then wait another 3 days for your next shower.

J: I can't believe it! I'll never be able to do that. If I could, I wouldn't be here. How can I not wash? Every day I resolve to stop, but I always give in. You mean I wouldn't be able to wash after I use the bathroom or before I eat? Other people wash after they use the toilet. Why can't I just wash less, like normal people do?

T: Other people don't have OCD. Remember, for you, washing makes you feel less "contaminated" and less anxious. Right?

J: Yes.

T: If you wash, even briefly, whenever you feel "contaminated," you never get a chance to learn that the feeling of contamination would go away by itself without washing. If you are really very anxious, it might take a while, even several hours, before you feel better, but it will eventually happen. On the other hand, if you wash, even briefly, every few hours, it will reinforce your idea that you have to wash to feel better.

J: But why 3 days? Couldn't I shower once a day like other people?

T: For the same reason. You'd still feel relief even if you waited 24 hours between washings. And that would strengthen your belief that you need to "decontaminate" by washing yourself. You must learn to use soap and water to feel clean and fresh, but not to "decontaminate" yourself.

J: I think I understand. I know I shower now to get the things I'm afraid of off my body. I used to shower just to get sweat and dirt off and feel nice. I'm still not sure I could stand it, though—not washing for that long.

T: The treatment is very demanding. Before we start the treatment program, you will need to make a commitment to yourself that even though you will feel very uncomfortable and even quite upset at times, you won't wash. I'll try to help you as much as I can, by planning the treatment so you know what to expect each day and by supporting you whenever you need it. Someone will have to be available to help supervise and support you any time you need it. Between sessions, you can always call me here or at home if a problem comes up. I know the treatment won't be easy for you, but I'm sure you can do it if you make up your mind.

At this point, a firm commitment should not be requested. Rather, the patient should be made aware of what will be required of him/her, so that he/she can adjust to these expectations and plan activities during the treatment period accordingly. The patient should make the arrangements necessary for attending daily treatment sessions for 3 to 4 weeks. As we have discussed earlier, two to three sessions per week may be sufficient for patients with less severe symptoms. It is important that the therapist not minimize the difficulty of the treatment regimen, so the patient is prepared to struggle and enters treatment with a readiness to mobilize inner resources and emotional support from family and friends.

The history of the patient is usually taken in the first session. Since collecting the histories of patients with OCD does not differ from collecting the histories of other psychiatric patients, details are not provided here.

Treatment Planning

The therapist began the second session by briefly reviewing the patient's self-monitoring of rituals. The remainder of the session was devoted to developing a treatment plan.

T: OK, now. I want to discuss our plan for each day during the first week of therapy. We need to expose you both in imagination and in reality to the things that bother you, which we talked about in our first sessions. As I said already, we'll also limit your washing. The scenes you will imagine will focus on the harm that you fear will happen if you do not wash. The actual exposures will focus on confronting the things that contaminate you. Restricting your washing will teach you how to live without rituals. In imagination you will picture yourself touching something you're afraid of, like toilet seats, and not washing and then becoming ill. We can have you imagine going to a doctor who can't figure out what's wrong and can't fix it. That's the sort of fear that you have, right?

J: Yes, that and Kenny getting sick and it being my fault.

T: OK, so in some scenes you'll be sick and in others Kenny will get sick. Should I add that other people blame you for not being careful? Is this what you're afraid of?

J: Yes, especially my mother.

T: OK. We'll have her criticize you for not being careful enough. Can you think of anything else we should add to the image?

J: No, that's about it.

T: We can compose the scenes in detail after we plan the actual exposures. Let's review the list of things you avoid or are afraid to touch, to make sure that we have listed them in the right order. Then we'll decide what to work on each day. OK?

J: OK.

June reviewed the list, which included such items as trash cans, kitchen floor, bathroom floor, public hallway carpet, plant dirt, puddles, car tires, dried "dog dirt," and "bird doo." Changes were made as needed.

T: Good. Now let's plan the treatment. On the first day, we should start with things that you rated below a 60. That would include touching this carpet, doorknobs that are not inside bathrooms, books on my shelves, light switches, and stair railings. On the second day, we'll do the 60- to 70-level items, like faucets, bare floors, dirty laundry, and the things on Ken's desk. [The therapist continued to detail Sessions 3 to 5 as above, increasing the level of difficulty each day.] In the second week we will repeat the worse situations like gutters, tires, public toilets, bird doo, and dog dirt, and we'll also find a dead animal to walk near and touch the street next to it.

On rare occasions, direct confrontation with a feared object (e.g., pesticides or other chemicals) may have some actual likelihood of producing harm. In such cases, judgment should be exercised to find a middle ground between total avoidance and endangerment. With chemicals, for example, patients are exposed to small quantities that are objectively nonharmful. In June's case, the therapist decided that direct contact with a dead animal was not called for, and that stepping on the animal's fur with her shoe and then touching the shoe sole would constitute sufficient exposure. In general, the therapist must weigh the level of obsessional distress that will be evoked by a given exposure with the objective risks entailed in completing that exposure. Patients with OCD have difficulty assessing such risks realistically, and thus it is the responsibility of the therapist to evaluate whether exposure is warranted. For example, patients with fears of contracting AIDS would certainly be highly distressed if asked to handle a dirty hypodermic needle found in a city gutter, but exposure to such stimuli is objectively risky and therefore should not be included on the treatment hierarchy.

T: How does this plan sound?

J: The first week is OK, but I'm really scared about the second week. I'm not sure I'll be ready to do the bathrooms and dog dirt by then.

T: Many people feel this way at the beginning, but by the end of the first week, you won't be as frightened as you are now about touching tires or public toilets. Remember, I will be here to help you, because it will probably be difficult in the beginning.

J: Yes, I know it. I feel like I don't really have a choice anyhow. This washing is crazy, and I'm disgusted with myself. I suppose I'm as ready as I'll ever be.

T: Good. Now remember, I'll ask you to keep working on these things for 2 to 3 hours at home after each session, but you will already have done it with me, so I don't think it will be too hard. I take it that you talked to Kenny about assisting us with supervising, since I saw him out in the waiting room.

J: Yes, he said that that's fine. He wanted to know what he should do.

T: Let's call him in. Did you talk to your sister-in-law about being available when Kenny is at work during the day?

J: Yes, she was really good about it, but she couldn't come today because of the kids.

T: If it's difficult for her to come, I could talk to her on the phone. Why don't you go get Kenny now?

Treatment

June was seen for 15 treatment sessions, which were held every weekday for a period of 3 weeks. During Week 4, the therapist visited her twice for 4 hours each time at her home. During these visits June, under the therapist's supervision, contaminated her entire house and exposed herself to objects that provoked distress at home and in her neighborhood. Thereafter, once-weekly follow-up sessions were instituted to ensure maintenance of gains and to address any other issues of concern to her.

As discussed earlier, treatment begins with exposure to moderately difficult items on the hierarchy and progresses to the most disturbing ones by the beginning of Week 2. The most distressing items are repeated during the remainder of Week 2 and during Week 3. The following sequence, which occurred on Day 6 of treatment, exemplifies this process.

T: How was your weekend?

J: Not that great. I suppose it was as good as I could expect. I took my shower Sunday night, and I was so nervous about finishing in time I don't even know if I washed right.

T: Most people feel the same way. Remember, though, you aren't supposed to wash "right," just to wash. Did Ken time it?

J: Yes, he called out the minutes like you said, "5, 7, 9," and then "Stop."

T: You stopped when he said to.

J: Yes, but it still wasn't easy.

T: I know. I'm really pleased that you were careful to follow the rules.

J: I have pretty much decided that this is my chance to get better, so I'm trying my best.

T: Good. I am glad you feel so positive. How was the homework?

J: I touched the floor and the soles of my shoes and the cement. It is all written on the daily sheet there. On Saturday, I went to my sister's so I could play with the kids, like we said. They stepped on me when I lay on the floor, and I tried to touch their bottoms when I held them. On Sunday, Kenny and I went to the park. I didn't sit in the grass, but I did walk around and touched my shoes afterward.

T: The soles?

J: Yeah. We also went downtown, and I threw some things in the trash cans and pushed them down and tried to touch the sides. It's sort of hard, because I felt conspicuous, but I did it anyway.

T: That sounds really good. I'm glad to hear it. How about your doormat and going into the garden?

J: I did the doormat and I stood in the garden, but I couldn't touch the dirt. The neighbor's dog always runs all over. I know I should have touched it, but I just couldn't get up the courage.

T: Well, you did do many other things. Let's plan to go outside today and do it together so it will be easier for you to walk in the garden when you go home.

J: OK.

June was very compliant with the treatment regimen. Some patients occasionally lapse on ritual prevention, particularly during Week 1 of the treatment program. The therapist should reinforce the patient for partial compliance, but should emphasize the need to fully comply with treatment instructions. With regard to exposure homework, it is not uncommon that patients will neglect to complete some assignments. Again, they should be reinforced for what they have achieved and encouraged to complete all of the assignments.

T: How are you and Kenny doing?

J: He got mad on Sunday night after the shower, because I started to ask him how he showered and if I was clean enough. I think I nagged him too much, so he lost his temper. We just watched TV, and after a while we talked a bit and he sort of apologized for getting mad. But I understand; I ask too many questions. Otherwise, the rest of the weekend was OK.

T: Well, it's unfortunate that Ken got mad, but it's good that he didn't answer your questions. He's not supposed to reassure you about cleanliness.

J: I think he has a hard time knowing when to answer me and when not to. I am not real sure either, so if you could talk to him before Wednesday when I shower again . . .

T: That's a good idea. I'll call him after we're done with today's session. Now today we'll start with the scene about you driving your car to an appointment with me, and you get a flat tire and have to change it. The cars splash the puddle near you, and it lands on the car and on you. Then you notice a dead animal when you walk behind the car and it's right behind you. You really feel contaminated. You walk to the gas station nearby to see if they can fix the tire, and you have to urinate so badly that you have to use their restroom. They agree to fix the tire if you remove it and bring it to them, because otherwise they are too busy. Of course, that means you will have to handle the tire that is contaminated by the dead animal. We'll add some bird doo on the street and on the sidewalk too. Then later you start to feel sick, and you feel like it's from the dead animal. Sound awful enough?

J: Yeah. Ugh. That one is really bad. Do I have to? Never mind, I know the answer.

T: OK. I want you to close your eyes now and imagine that you are driving your car on West Avenue.

Note that the therapist checked the patient's assignment from the previous day to verify that she completed it and did not engage in avoidance and rituals. This provided an opportunity to reinforce efforts at self-exposure. It is important to keep track of completion of homework, since patients do not always volunteer information about omissions. They will admit failure to comply if directly asked, however, and are likely to carry out the next assignment if reinforced adequately.

With regard to the conflict between June and Kenny, it is our experience that, like Kenny, most family members are quite willing to help. However, difficulty may arise when they are unable to help without becoming upset, thereby increasing the patient's tension. Providing them with an opportunity to ventilate their frustration by contacting the therapist, who also may coach them in alternative reactions, may reduce familial tension.

That same session also included imaginal exposure to do a scenario that had been planned in advance. Since that scenario had already been discussed in detail with the patient, it posed no surprises for her. Such a scenario is presented for up to 1 hour, or until a substantial decrease in anxiety is evident. Next, the patient is confronted *in vivo* with situations like those included in the fantasized scene.

T: It's time to do the real thing now. I looked for a dead animal by the side of the road yesterday, and I found one about a mile away. I think we should go there.

J: Yuck, that's terrific. Just for me, you had to find it.

T: Today's our lucky day. You knew we were going to have to find one today anyhow. At least it's close.

J: Great.

Humor is encouraged and can be quite helpful if the patient is capable of responding to it. At the same time, it is important that the therapist not laugh *at* but rather *with* the patient. Patients and therapists often develop a shorthand lexicon for discussing OCD and its treatment that is specific to them and aimed at promoting compliance with treatment. For example, one patient–therapist pair began to discuss exposure homework as "swallowing the frog," based on a proverb that the patient introduced. When the therapist asked the patient if she had "swallowed the frog" that morning, it conveyed the difficulty of the exposure tasks that needed to be done between sessions. It is important for the therapist to observe the patient's interpersonal style, in order to determine whether such banter is likely to promote the therapeutic goals.

T: (*Outside the office*) There it is, behind the car. Let's go and touch the curb and street next to it. I don't think that you need to touch it directly because it's a bit smelly, but I want you to step next to it and touch the sole of your shoe.

J: Yuck! It's really dead. It's gross!

T: Yeah, it is a bit gross, but it's also just a dead cat if you think about it plainly. What harm can it cause?

J: I don't know. Suppose I got germs on my hand?

T: What sort of germs?

J: Dead cat germs.

T: What kind are they?

J: I don't know. Just germs.

T: Like the bathroom germs that we've already handled?

J: Sort of. People don't go around touching dead cats.

T: They also don't go running home to shower or alcohol the inside of their car. It's time to get over this. Now come on over and I'll do it first. (*Patient follows*) OK. Touch the curb and the street. Here's a stone you can carry with you and a piece of paper from under its tail. Go ahead, take it.

J: (*Looking quite uncomfortable*) Ugh!

T: We'll both hold them. Now touch it to your front and your skirt and your face and hair. Like this. That's good. What's your anxiety level?

J: Ugh! It's 99. I'd say 100, but it's just short of panic. If you weren't here, it'd be 100.

T: You know from past experience that this will be much easier in a while. Just stay with it and we'll wait here. You're doing fine.

J: (*A few minutes pass in which she looks very upset*) Would you do this if it wasn't for me?

T: Yes, if this were my car and I dropped my keys here, I'd just pick them up and go on.

J: You wouldn't have to wash them?

T: No. Dead animals aren't delightful, but they're part of the world we live in. What are the odds that we'll get ill from this?

J: Very small, I guess. I feel a little bit better than at first. It's about 90 now.

T: Good! Just stay with it now.

The session continued for another 45 minutes, until anxiety decreased substantially. During this period, conversation focused generally on the feared situations and the patient's reaction to them. The therapist inquired about June's anxiety level approximately every 10 minutes. It is important to note that a patient and therapist engage in conversation throughout the exposure task, discussing issues such as habituation, risk, responsibility, and long-term outcomes. At the same time it is imperative to refocus the patient on the exposure task at hand to ensure that he/she remains engaged with it. Asking for SUDS ratings thus serves two purposes: It provides data about fear reduction, and it refocuses the patient on the exposure. However, if the informal discussion serves as a distractor, helping the patient "not think about" what he/she is doing, the therapist should limit such conversations.

T: How do you feel now?

J: Well, it is easier, but I sure don't feel great.

T: Can you put a number on it?

J: About 55 or 60, I'd say.

T: You worked hard today. You must be tired. Let's stop now. I want you to take this stick and pebble with you, so that you continue to be contaminated. You can keep them in your pocket and touch them frequently during the day. I want you to contaminate your office at work and your apartment with them. Touch them to everything around, including everything in the kitchen, chairs, your bed, and the clothes in your dresser. Oh, also, I'd like you to drive your car past this spot on your way to and from work. Can you do that?

J: I suppose so. The trouble is going home with all of this dirt.

T: Why don't you call Ken and plan to get home after he does, so he can be around to help you? Remember, you can always call me if you have trouble.

J: Yeah. That's a good idea. I'll just leave work after he does. See you tomorrow.

This scenario illustrates the process of *in vivo* exposure. The therapist clearly answered the questions raised, without detouring from the essential purpose of the session—exposure to the feared contaminant. After the initial increase, the anxiety may begin to drop relatively quickly for some patients and may require longer for others. As noted previously, it is advisable to continue the exposure until the patient appears visibly more at ease and reports a substantial decrease in anxiety (40% or 50%).

After 10 to 15 sessions, the patient's reported anxiety level is expected to decrease considerably. At the 15th session, June reported a maximum SUDS rating of 70 (still somewhat high, although reduced from 99), which lasted for a few minutes. Her minimal SUDS rating was 35. Her average SUDS level during this session was 45. Ideally, by the end of treatment the highest SUDS level should not exceed 50, and it should drop below 20 at the end of the session. In June's case, more follow-up sessions were required because her anxiety was still quite high.

To facilitate a transition to normal washing and cleaning behavior, the therapist instituted a normal washing regimen during Week 3 of treatment. The patient was allowed one 10-minute shower daily and no more than five 30-second handwashings when there was visible dirt on her hands or when they were sticky.

When the therapist arrived for a home treatment session the next week, the following conversation ensued:

T: How did it go over the weekend?

J: Not too bad. But I got sort of upset Saturday. We went to a picnic and there were several piles of dog dirt around. I had on my flip-flops and I wanted to play volleyball. You can't in flip-flops, so I went barefoot.

T: That's great! I'm glad to hear it.

J: Yeah, but then I got really upset about going home and carrying it into the apartment. I did it—I walked all over, barefoot and with the flip-flops—but I worried about it for another whole day, till I talked to Kenny about my thoughts on Sunday around noon. I felt better when he said he wouldn't worry about it. It seems like I feel guilty or something, like the house isn't clean enough. But lately, if he says it is, I've been able to take his word for it.

T: Well, in time you'll be able to make this kind of judgment yourself. How about your washing and cleaning?

J: It was all right. I washed for half a minute before I ate, because I was dusty from playing volleyball. I deliberately didn't wash when I got home because I felt bad, and I knew if I did, it would be to "decontaminate" myself. I showered Saturday night and I did feel relieved, but I knew I should go and walk around barefoot and touch the floors I'd walked on. So I did that.

T: That's great! It sounds like you handled it fine. I'm really pleased. You avoided washing when it would mean reducing feelings of contamination, and you exposed yourself when you felt concerned about germs. That's excellent. Now let's go over the problem situations that still need work here at home. What things still disturb you?

J: The basement. I haven't done much with the kitty litter box and old shoes that I threw down there a year ago because they got contaminated. The closet still has some contaminated clothes. And I still worry about the backyard some. Also the porch. Pigeons have been perching on the roof, and there are droppings on the railing now, so I thought I'd wait until you came to do that.

T: OK. Let's start low and work up. Which is easiest?

J: The basement and closets.

T: Fine. Down we go.

Exposure to contaminants during the home visit is conducted in the same manner as during treatment sessions. Typically, home sessions last longer (from 2 to 4 hours), until all "dirty" items are touched and "clean" places are contaminated. These visits should be repeated if the patient expresses considerable concern about his/her ability to adopt a permanent regimen of nonavoidance.

Follow-Up Sessions

June was seen weekly for 3 months, until she experienced a setback following the development of a new obsession. She became concerned about hitting a pedestrian while driving. Thoughts that she "might have hit someone" intruded, particularly after turning a corner or glancing in the mirror to change lanes. Once evoked, they persisted for several hours. To overcome this new problem, the therapist directed her to increase her driving and refrain from retracing her path or looking in the mirror to check for casualties. June was told that she could stop her car only if she knew for certain that she hit someone. Thoughts that it "might" have occurred were to be ignored. To reduce June's anxiety about having obsessions (e.g., "Oh, my God, here it is again, this is terrible"), she was advised to expect occasional recurrences of obsessive thoughts. The frequency of obsessions about hitting someone decreased from several each day to once weekly after 3 weeks of self-exposure; the associated SUDS levels diminished from 95 to 50 or less.

Of June's germ-related obsessions, only that of dog feces partially recurred. Fears of public bathrooms and dead animals remained low. The therapist felt that the fear of dog feces had received insufficient attention during treatment. To address this return of fear, June was seen three times a week for 1-hour exposure sessions in which she touched brown spots on the sidewalk and walked near and eventually stepped on dog feces. Homework consisted of going to parks, walking on sidewalks without looking, stepping on dog feces, and stepping on the grass where she thought dogs had been. This treatment continued for 4 weeks and was reduced to twice a week for an additional 3 weeks. Thereafter, June came once weekly for another 6 weeks, during which self-exposure was assigned and everyday concerns were dealt with. News media coverage of herpes led to a brief concern about public toilets, but this dissipated within a few days.

In the dialogue below, the therapist reviewed with June her progress at a 9-month follow-up.

T: I'd like to know how you feel, compared to when you first came here 9 months ago.

J: I'm definitely a lot better. But I still have some bad days when I worry a lot about something, and I get down on myself. But when I remember how upset I was last summer and all that washing I did, it's really a whole lot better. Maybe about 80% better. I'm not ready to be a floor nurse yet, but the job I got after treatment is pretty good for now. Kenny and I are doing fine, except he's real sensitive if I bring up one of my fears. I wish he'd just listen and say "OK" or something instead of looking worried about me. It's like he's afraid I'm going to get upset again. It makes it hard to talk freely, but sometimes he does handle it fine. I really can't complain. He's been through a lot too, when I was really a mess last year and before that.

T: I'm glad to hear you feel so much better. You look a lot more at ease. You laugh more now. I don't know if you recall, but you never did in the beginning.

J: I remember.

T: What's left now—the other 20%?

J: Obsessions, I guess. I can still work on driving over someone. Mostly lasts less than 15 minutes, but now and then it hangs on through an evening.

T: How often?

J: Once every week or two, I think. And I still have an urge to avoid walking on the grass in parks. Like I'm hyperalert. I do it pretty often, but I'm self-conscious.

T: You mean you have to remind yourself not to avoid dog feces?

J: Yeah. And I tend to see things in black and white, all good or all bad. I catch myself feeling guilty for dumb things like eating dessert after a full meal. I can stop, but it's like I'm out to punish myself or think badly about what I did. I have to watch out for it. Still, the thoughts are nothing like they used to be. I can have fun now. And work is pretty absorbing, so I can go whole days without getting down on myself for something. Will I always do that?

T: Maybe to some extent. We know that you have a tendency to obsess. Most people who have had an obsessive–compulsive problem say that the rituals and urges to do them decrease more quickly than the obsessive ideas. You might have disturbing thoughts for a while, but you can expect them to become less frequent if you're careful not to attempt to control them through rituals or by avoiding things. Can you handle that?

J: I suppose so. They're not a lot of fun, but I feel like I'm living a normal life again. I suppose everyone has some problems to deal with.

Rarely do patients report complete remission of all obsessions. It is unrealistic to lead a patient to expect that 4 weeks of treatment will result in a total absence of obsessions and rituals. Patients should expect some continued struggle with obsessions and urges to ritualize. Strategies for coping with such occasional difficulties should be rehearsed.

COMPLICATIONS DURING EX/RP TREATMENT

Obviously, difficulties may arise during implementation of EX/RP treatment for OCD. Several of these are described below, and possible solutions are discussed.

Noncompliance with Ritual Prevention

Patients with OCD often report engaging in rituals despite the ritual prevention instructions. In most cases these represent brief "slips," and the therapist should address them by reiterating the rationale for the treatment regimen and the need to follow the ritual prevention instructions strictly. The therapist also may offer ways in which a ritual might be "undone" (e.g., recontaminating or turning the stove on and off again).

Sometimes the patient's support person will report violations of ritual prevention to the therapist. These should be discussed with the patient, and the fact that continued failure to comply with the ritual prevention instructions will result in treatment failure should be emphasized. The following is an example of how violations of ritual prevention can be presented to the patient.

"I understand from your father that on three occasions this weekend he saw you checking the front door lock five or six times before you left the house. As we agreed in the first session, he called to inform me about your checking. I am sure you remember that we had an agreement that you would check the doors only once, and that if you had a problem, you would discuss it with me or your father right away so we could help you overcome your urge to ritualize. Will you explain to me what happened?"

If the patient acknowledges the slip and responds with a renewed agreement to follow instructions, the therapist need not pursue the issue further. However, if a second significant infraction of the ritual prevention instructions occurs, the therapist should again remind the patient of the therapy rules and the rationale for these rules, and "troubleshoot" with the patient regarding how to successfully implement ritual prevention. If during the course of this discussion it becomes evident that the patient is unwilling to consider these recommendations and remains committed to rituals and avoidance as a means to reduce obsessional distress, the therapist may broach the subject of discontinuing treatment if the patient is not ready to comply.

"It seems that right now you aren't able to stop ritualizing. For treatment to be successful, it is essential that you *completely* stop your rituals. Every time that you relieve your discomfort by ritualizing, you prevent yourself from learning that anxiety would have declined eventually without rituals, and you don't permit your obsessional fears to be disconnected from distress and anxiety. Exposing you to feared situations without stopping your rituals won't be helpful. If you cannot follow the no-rituals rule quite strictly, then we ought to stop treatment now and wait until you are really prepared to follow through with all the requirements. It is very hard for people to resist the urge to ritualize, and it may be that you are just not ready yet and will feel more able to do so in the future. It is much better for us to stop treatment now than to continue under conditions where you are unlikely to benefit from treatment. That would only leave you feeling more hopeless about future prospects for improvement."

As discussed above, patients sometimes replace identified rituals with less obvious avoidance patterns. For example, a patient may use hand lotion to "decontaminate" the hands, instead of the excessive washing that was done originally. If this occurs, the therapist should immediately instruct the patient to stop the new ritual. Other examples of replacement washing rituals include brushing off one's hands or blowing off "germs"; extensive checks are often replaced with quick glances. Direct questioning of the patient to solicit such information should proceed as follows:

"Now that you've stopped your washing rituals, do you find yourself doing other things to relieve your anxiety? For example, some people start to wipe their hands with paper towels or tissues as a substitute for washing with soap and water. Are you doing anything like this?"

If the answer is positive, the therapist should identify these new behaviors as rituals and instruct the patient to resist engaging in these new behaviors in the same manner as he/she resists other compulsions.

Continued Passive Avoidance

Patients who continue to avoid situations likely to evoke obsessional distress are also likely to experience attentuated outcome in EX/RP. For example, a patient may put "contaminated" clothing back in the closet as instructed, but in doing so he/she may ensure that the contaminated clothes do not touch clean garments. Such avoidance reflects an ambivalent attitude toward treatment and hinders habituation of anxiety to feared situations. Because such processes may hinder outcome, the presence of continued and frequent avoidance behavior calls for the therapist (T) and patient (P) to reevaluate whether the patient should continue treatment.

T: Jim, let's make sure that you are doing your homework the right way. I know that you had a problem putting your dirty underwear in with your other dirty clothes. How are you doing with it now?

P: Well, I was afraid you might ask that. I still haven't mixed them up. I was too scared to do it.

T: We discussed this several days ago, and you were instructed to have done it that night. It would have been better had you told me the next day that you weren't able to. What I'd like you to do for tomorrow is to bring in some dirty clothes. Bring in the underwear and the other clothes in separate bags, and we will mix them here in the office. Are there any other things that you have been avoiding that you haven't told me about?

P: I don't think so.

T: I want you to pay careful attention to things that you are doing or not doing, and make a list of anything you are avoiding, particularly things that you are supposed to do for therapy. It is very important that you don't protect yourself by avoiding distressing situations, since if you don't face these situations, your obsessive–compulsive symptoms won't get better. Let's give it another try, but if you can't bring yourself to confront these problematic situations without these little avoidances, perhaps you would be better off delaying your treatment to a later time when you will be more ready to comply with the treatment program.

Arguments

Some individuals who carry out the required exposure without ritualizing may attempt to engage the therapist in arguments about the assignments. It is quite tempting to get involved in arguments with patients over what they will or will not do during treatment. In order to avoid this, it is important for the therapist and the patient to agree on some ground rules before the intensive program begins. Patients must agree to follow the treatment plan that they developed in conjunction with the therapist, and to expose themselves to the distressing situations without argument. If new feared situations are discovered, they should be discussed, and a new exposure program should be developed and agreed to before exposures to the new situations are carried out. If a patient balks at a planned exposure or attempts to alter the exposure, the therapist should acknowledge and empathize with the patient's the discomfort, inquire about the reasons for the hesitation, and encourage the patient to proceed in the following manner:

"I'm sorry to see that you are having so much trouble sitting on the floor. I know it's difficult and that you're frightened, but it won't do you any good if we delay the exposure for another day or let you skip it altogether. You really need to touch the floor, so let's go ahead and do it now. We have agreed that today is the 'floor' day, and I wouldn't be doing you a favor if I allowed you to avoid it. Remember, though, I am here to support you as much as I can when you become upset."

In some instances, difficulties can be overcome by first exposing the patient to similar items that generate a lower level of distress. For example, if a patient is refusing to touch a toilet seat, the therapist may ask him/her first to touch the bathroom floor or the door to the bathroom stall. Thereafter, the patient may touch the walls of the stall and the toilet handle before proceeding to the toilet seat itself.

Emotional Overload

Occasionally during treatment, a patient will become overwhelmed by fear or another emotion that is not directly related to his/her OCD symptoms. For example, a patient may be upset by a recent event (e.g., the death of a relative) or by fears of facing future plans (e.g., living on his/her own or getting a job). When the patient is extremely upset, implementing exposure exercises is inadvisable, because it is unlikely that the patient will adequately attend to the exposure stimulus; therefore, the anxiety is unlikely to habituate. Instead, the therapist should discuss the distressing situation with the patient and proceed with exposure only when the patient is calmer. On rare occasions, exposure may be postponed altogether until the next day's session. If this becomes a repetitive pattern, it may be advisable to interrupt treatment until the crisis is over.

Nonanxious Reactions to Exposures

Occasionally patients will respond to exposures with emotions other than anxiety or distress, such as anger or depression. Clinical observations suggest that anger often serves as a means for a patient to avoid the distress or anxiety that is the target of exposure. If this happens, the anger should be viewed as an avoidance. The therapist should refocus the patient on the anxiety-evoking aspects of the situation and point out to the patient that anger will only stand in the way of progress.

Sometimes, when patients are exposed during imaginal exposure to the feared consequences of their behaviors, they become depressed. Such depression and other emotional reactions may reduce the efficacy of treatment, and therapists need to help these patients focus on the anxiety-evoking cues. This may be done by directing the content of the imaginal exposure away from the feared consequences and toward the external threat cues. In some cases, such redirection does not resolve the problem, and the patients continue to display a depressive reaction to the exposure. When this happens, alternative scenarios that do not elicit depression should be developed.

Emergent Fears and Rituals

As mentioned earlier, sometimes patients develop "new" fears or rituals during treatment. Often the contents of these new symptoms are closely related to the original fears and may

be treated by extending to these fears the EX/RP instructions given earlier in treatment. For example, following the successful implementation of ritual prevention for his compulsive handwashing, Mr. F began to rub his hands together to decontaminate them. His therapist identified this as another ritual and instructed him to resist the urge to rub his hands together. Next, Mr. F began subtly to rub his fingers against the palms of his hands to cleanse his hands and reduce anxiety. He was asked to stop this ritual as he had the others and was again successful.

Some emergent fears may not be as clearly connected to the patient's original fears. For example, the fear that June developed of hitting someone while driving was not obviously related to her fears of contamination. Further assessment often results in the discovery of a conceptual link between the two reported fears. In June's case, her fear of being blamed for causing someone to become ill or die, and her concern about being thought of as a "bad person" because she killed someone or because she smelled of dog feces, may have been the connection between her two identified fears. In cases such as these, it is important for the therapist to develop exposures that include cues for this more general fear. June's therapist conducted imaginal exposures that included images of people criticizing her or blaming her for causing someone to die.

Negative Family Reactions

Because family members have typically experienced years of frustration with the patient's symptoms, it is not surprising that some are impatient, expecting treatment to progress smoothly and to result in total symptom remission. It is not uncommon for family members to become disappointed or angry when they perceive that the symptoms are not subsiding quickly enough. In such cases, the therapist should assure family members that occasional strong anxiety reactions are to be expected and do not reflect failure. The family should be encouraged to respond calmly and be supportive, should the patient experience a burst of anxiety.

Often families have developed patterns of behavior designed to reduce the patient's distress. Some family members may continue these patterns, either because they are trying to protect the patient from upsetting situations or because it is difficult to break habits established over years of accommodating the patient's requests. For example, Mr. P, who was accustomed to entering his home through the basement, immediately removing his clothes, and showering for his wife's sake, was instructed to enter through the front door and toss his overcoat on the couch. Similarly, family members may find themselves continuing to perform a variety of household activities that they have come to regard as their responsibility because of the patient's wishes to avoid the distress that the activity caused. For instance, Mr. P was responsible for preparing all the family meals, because his wife was distressed by the possibility that she might inadvertently contaminate the food. Because such familiar patterns may hinder progress in treatment, the therapist should question both the patient and family members about such habits, and should prescribe appropriate alternative behaviors that maximize the patient's exposure and minimize avoidance.

Functioning without Symptoms

At the end of treatment, many patients with OCD find themselves left with a considerable void in their daily routines. The fact that they no longer need to allocate a large portion of their day to performing rituals leaves them wondering what to do. The therapist should be sensitive to these issues and aid in planning new social or occupational goals to be achieved following therapy. If needed, the therapist should conduct additional sessions or refer a patient to another therapist who will focus on adjustment-related issues.

Because they have spent years performing their rituals, patients may be unsure about what constitutes "normal" behavior. The therapist should offer guidelines for what constitutes appropriate washing, checking, repeating, or ordering (see Figure 5.2). If rituals are still present, the therapist needs to give instructions to continue the ritual prevention of some behaviors, in order to help ensure maintenance of treatment gains. Patients may also develop a fear that the OCD symptoms will return. The therapist should reassure such a patient that a single washing of his/her hands does not signal the beginning of a relapse.

CONCLUSION

In this chapter we have reviewed the literature on OCD and its treatment, and have provided verbatim dialogue from patient–therapist interactions to demonstrate how EX/RP is implemented. Our review illustrates clearly that much is already known about CBT and pharmacotherapy for OCD. In our clinical practice with adults, we are guided by the empirical research summarized in this chapter, although not all of our clinical decisions are unequivocally supported by empirical studies. For example, no controlled, direct comparison study has indicated that intensive EX/RP yields superior outcome to less intensive treatment; yet we typically provide intensive treatment to our adult patients with at least moderately severe OCD. Although our clinical experience suggests that weekly sessions are probably insufficient to produce meaningful gains in most adult patients with OCD, it has yet to be established whether twice- or thrice-weekly sessions would yield results that are comparable to daily sessions both immediately after treatment and at follow-up. Future research should examine this important issue in order to establish a "dose–response" curve for EX/RP. Another important issue is how to best combine EX/RP with medication. Future research will allow us to identify the optimal treatment course for a particular patient.

Empirical results and clinical observations converge to indicate that psychosocial treatment for OCD must involve both exposure and ritual prevention instructions, and that failure to conduct exposures to the most anxiety-evoking situations is likely to compromise outcome. With respect to the therapist-assisted versus self-exposure issue, we routinely choose therapist-assisted exposure in our clinical practice. At present, eliminating therapist assistance with exposure exercises seems premature, because existing studies have methodological problems such as insufficient sample sizes. With respect to the role of cognitive interventions in the treatment of OCD, the EX/RP program described in this chapter is a "cognitive-behavioral" treatment in that it targets both cognitions and behaviors; however, we do not typically include formal cognitive restructuring. Future research needs to delineate which cognitive and behavioral procedures are most effective for correcting particular pathological emotions. Cognitive procedures may also be utilized in "readiness programs" designed to help patients who are highly ambivalent about EX/RP realize that the treatment is both tolerable and effective. Empirical research to date suggest that although antidepressant medications for OCD do not interfere with the efficacy of CBT, combination treatment is not necessarily more effective than EX/RP alone. However, the partial symptom reduction typically found in pharmacotherapy studies for OCD may render some patients more willing to tolerate the distress associated with EX/RP, and thus premedication may be helpful in promoting readiness in such cases.

What factors seem to enhance long-term efficacy of EX/RP for OCD? Our studies suggest that patients with OCD who show great improvement immediately after EX/RP are more likely to retain their gains at follow-up than those who make only moderate posttreatment gains. Thus an emphasis on procedures that are likely to lead to maximal short-term efficacy also serves to yield superior maintenance of gains. In our clinical experience, thorough understanding of the treatment rationale, active engagement in exposure exercises, strict adherence to ritual prevention instructions, willingness to design and implement exposure exercises between sessions, and willingness to confront even the most difficult points on the fear hierarchy are all factors associated with positive treatment outcome. Thus verbal reinforcement of patients when they accomplish these goals and reinstruction when they do not are important in promoting lasting improvement. In addition, relapse prevention techniques designed specifically for OCD have been found effective in promoting maintenance of gains at follow-up (Hiss et al., 1994). In clinical practice, we begin discussing relapse prevention procedures long before treatment is completed, and we focus on maintaining gains in the last few active treatment sessions. Some continuing contact with the treating clinician is also thought to be of benefit; thus brief follow-up sessions are held in the first few months after the active treatment is completed, with contacts as needed following the formal follow-up phase. As part of relapse prevention, we often ask our patients to plan EX/RP exercises for hypothetical obsessions they may encounter in the future (e.g., "If you became obsessed in 6 months that touching tree bark would result in your contracting a terrible illness, what exercises should you do?") to encourage patients to problem-solve OCD issues for themselves, rather than relying on the therapist's instruction. We also emphasize that the occasional occurrence of obsessions should not be a cause for great alarm, provided that the patients implement EX/RP to combat these recurring obsessions and urges to ritualize. The patients who accept this reality are often the ones most able to apply what they learned in treatment, and this process enables them to keep their OCD symptoms under control long after treatment has terminated.

REFERENCES

Abramowitz, J. S. (1996). Variants of exposure and response prevention in the treatment of obsessive compulsive disorder: A meta-analysis. *Behavior Therapy, 27,* 583–600.

Abramowitz, J. S., Foa, E. B., & Franklin, M. E. (in press). Empirical status of cognitive methods in the treatment of OCD. In M. H. Freestont & S. Taylor (Eds.), *Cognitive approaches to treating obsessions and compulsions: A clinical casebook*. Mahwah, NJ: Erlbaum.

Abramowitz, J. S., Franklin, M. E., Street, G. P., Kozak, M. J., & Foa, E. B. (2000). Effects of comorbid depression on response to treatment for obsessive compulsive disorder. *Behavior Therapy, 31,* 517–528.

Allen, J. J., & Tune, G. S. (1975). The Lynfield Obsessional/Compulsive Questionnaire. *Scottish Medical Journal, 20,* 21–24.

American Psychiatric Association. (1987). *Diagnostic and statistical manual of mental disorders* (3rd ed., rev.). Washington, DC: Author.

American Psychiatric Association. (1994). *Diagnostic and statistical manual of mental disorders* (4th ed.). Washington, DC: Author.

Ballentine, H. T., Bouckoms, H. A., Thomas, F. K., & Giriunas, L. L. (1987). Treatment of psychiatric illness by stereotactic singulotomy. *Biological Psychiatry, 22,* 807–809.

Baxter, L. R., Phelps, M. L., Maziotta, J. C., Guze, B. H., Schwartz, J. M., & Selin, C. L. (1987). Local cerebral glucose metabolic rates in obsessive and compulsive disorder: A comparison with rates in unipolar depression and normal controls. *Archives of General Psychiatry, 44,* 211–218.

Beck, A. T. (1976). *Cognitive therapy and the emotional disorders*. New York: International Universities Press.

Beck, A. T., Ward, C. H., Mendelson, M., Mock, J., & Erbaugh, J. (1961). An inventory for measuring depression. *Archives of General Psychiatry, 4,* 561–571.

Behar, D., Rapoport, J. L., Berg, C. J., Denckla, M., Mann, L., Cox, C., Fedio, P., Zahn, T., & Wolfman, H. (1984). Computerized tomography and neuropsychological test measures in adolescents with obsessive–compulsive disorder. *American Journal of Psychiatry, 141,* 363–369.

Boulougouris, J. C., Rabavilas, A. D., & Stefanis, C. (1977). Psycho-physiological responses in obsessive compulsive patients. *Behaviour Research and Therapy, 15,* 221–230.

Carr, A. T. (1974). Compulsive neurosis: A review of the literature. *Psychological Bulletin, 81,* 311–318.

Charney, D. S., Goodman, W. K., Price, L. H., Woods, S. W., Rasmussen, S. A., & Heninger, G. R. (1988). Serotonin function in obsessive–compulsive disorder: A comparison of the effects of tryptophan and m-chlorophenylpiperazine in patients and healthy subjects. *Archives of General Psychiatry, 45,* 177–185.

Constans, J. I., Foa, E. B., Franklin, M. E., & Mathews, A. (1995). Memory for actions in obsessive compulsives with checking rituals. *Behaviour Research and Therapy, 33,* 665–671.

Cottraux, J., Mollard, L., Bouvard, M., Marks, I., Sluys, M., Nury, A. M., Douge, R., & Ciadella, P. (1990). A controlled study of fluvoxamine and exposure in obsessive–compulsive disorder. *International Clinical Psychopharmacology, 5,* 17–30.

Cox, C. S., Fedio, P., & Rapoport, J. L. (1989). Neuropsychological testing of obsessive-compulsive adolescents. In J. L. Rapoport (Ed.), *Obsessive–compulsive disorder in children and adolescents* (pp. 73–86). Washington, DC: American Psychiatric Press.

DeAraujo, L. A., Ito, L. M., Marks, I. M., & Deale, A. (1995). Does imaginal exposure to the consequences of not ritualising enhance live exposure for OCD? A controlled study: I. Main outcome. *British Journal of Psychiatry, 167,* 65–70.

Dollard, J., & Miller, N. L. (1950). *Personality and psychotherapy: An analysis in terms of learning, thinking and culture.* New York: McGraw-Hill.

Eisen, J. L., Phillips, K. A., Baer, L., Beer, D. A., Atala, K. D., & Rasmussen, S. A. (1998). The Brown Assessment of Beliefs Scale: Reliability and validity. *American Journal of Psychiatry, 155,* 102–108.

Ellis, A. (1962). *Reason and emotion in psychotherapy.* New York: Lyle Stuart.

Emmelkamp, P. M. G., & Beens, H. (1991). Cognitive therapy with obsessive–compulsive disorder: A comparative evaluation. *Behaviour Research and Therapy, 29,* 293–300.

Emmelkamp, P. M. G., de Haan, E., & Hoogduin, C. A. L. (1990). Marital adjustment and obsessive–compulsive disorder. *British Journal of Psychiatry, 156,* 55–60.

Emmelkamp, P. M. G., Van der Helm, M., Van Zanten, B. L., & Plochg, I. (1980). Treatment of obsessive–compulsive patients: The contribution of self-instructional training to the effectiveness of exposure. *Behaviour Research and Therapy, 18,* 61–66.

Emmelkamp, P. M. G., & van Kraanen, J. (1977). Therapist-controlled exposure *in vivo*: A comparison with obsessive–compulsive patients. *Behaviour Research and Therapy, 15,* 491–495.

Emmelkamp, P. M. G., Visser, S., & Hoekstra, R. J. (1988). Cognitive therapy vs. exposure *in vivo* in the treatment of obsessive–compulsives. *Cognitive Therapy and Research, 12,* 103–114.

Fals-Stewart, W., Marks, A. P., & Schafer, J. (1993). A comparison of behavioral group therapy and individual behavior therapy in treating obsessive compulsive disorder. *Journal of Nervous and Mental Disease, 181,* 189–193.

Flament, M., Koby, E., Rapoport, J. L., Berg, C. J., Zahn, T., Cox, C., Denckla, M., & Lenane, M. (1990). Obsessive-compulsive disorder: A prospective follow-up study. *Journal of Child Psychology and Psychiatry, 31,* 363–380.

Flament, M., Whitaker, A., Rapoport, J. L., Davies, M., Berg, C. Z., Kalikow, K., Sceery, W., & Shaffer, D. (1988). Obsessive-compulsive disorder in adolescence: An epidemiological study. *Journal of the American Academy of Child and Adolescent Psychiatry, 27,* 764–771.

Foa, E. B. (1979). Failure in treating obsessive compulsives. *Behaviour Research and Therapy, 16,* 391–399.

Foa, E. B., Abramowitz, J. S., Franklin, M. E., & Kozak, M. J. (1999). Feared consequences, fixity of belief, and treatment outcome in patients with obsessive compulsive disorder. *Behavior Therapy, 30,* 717–724.

Foa, E. B., Amir, N., Bogert, K., Molnar, C., Przeworski, A. (in press). Inflated perception of responsibility for harm in obsessive compulsive disorder. *Journal of Anxiety Disorders.*

Foa, E. B., & Chambless, D. L. (1978). Habituation of subjective anxiety during flooding in imagery. *Behaviour Research and Therapy, 16,* 391–399.

Foa, E. B., Grayson, J. B., & Steketee, G. (1982). Depression, habituation and treatment outcome in obsessive–compulsives. In J. C. Boulougouris (Ed.), *Practical applications of learning theories in psychiatry* (pp. 129–142). New York: Wiley.

Foa, E. B., Grayson, J. B., Steketee, G. S., Doppelt, H. G., Turner, R. M., & Latimer, P. I. (1983). Success and failure in the behavioral treatment of obsessive–compulsives. *Journal of Consulting and Clinical Psychology, 51,* 287–297.

Foa, E. B., & Kozak, M. J. (1985). Treatment of anxiety disorders: Implications for psychopathology. In A. H. Tuma & J. D. Maser (Eds.), *Anxiety and the anxiety disorders* (pp. 421–452). Hillsdale, NJ: Erlbaum.

Foa, E. B., & Kozak, M. J. (1986). Emotional processing of fear: Exposure to corrective information. *Psychological Bulletin, 99,* 20–35.

Foa, E. B., & Kozak, M. J. (1996). Psychological treatments for obsessive compulsive disorder. In M. R. Mavissakalian & R. P. Prien (Eds.), *Long-term treatments of anxiety disorders* (pp. 285–309). Washington, DC: American Psychiatric Press.

Foa, E. B., Kozak, M. J., Goodman, W. K., Hollander, E., Jenike, M. A., & Rasmussen, S. (1995). DSM-IV field trial: Obsessive compulsive disorder. *American Journal of Psychiatry, 152,* 90–96.

Foa, E. B., Kozak, M. J., Steketee, G., & McCarthy, P. R. (1992). Treatment of depressive and obsessive-compulsive symptoms in OCD by imipramine and behavior therapy. *British Journal of Clinical Psychology, 31,* 279–292.

Foa, E. B., Steketee, G., Grayson, J. B., & Doppelt, H. C. (1983). Treatment of obsessive–compulsives: When do we fail? In E. B. Foa & P. M. G. Emmelkamp (Eds.), *Failures in behavior therapy* (pp. 10–34). New York: Wiley.

Foa, E. B., Steketee, G., Grayson, J. B., Turner, R. M., & Latimer, P. (1984). Deliberate exposure and blocking of obsessive–compulsive rituals: Immediate and long-term effects. *Behavior Therapy, 15*, 450–472.

Foa, E. B., Steketee, G. S., Kozak, M. J., & Dugger, D. (1985). *Effects of imipramine on depression and on obsessive–compulsive symptoms.* Paper presented at the European Association for Behavior Therapy, Munich, Federal Republic of Germany.

Foa, E. B., Steketee, G., Turner, R. M., & Fischer, S. C. (1980). Effects of imaginal exposure to feared disasters in obsessive–compulsive checkers. *Behaviour Research and Therapy, 18*, 449–455.

Franklin, M. E., Abramowitz, J. S., Bux, D. A., Zoellner, L. A., & Feeny, N. C. (2000). *Exposure and ritual prevention with and without concomitant pharmacotherapy in the treatment of OCD.* Manuscript submitted for publication.

Franklin, M. E., Abramowitz, J. S., Kozak, M. J., Levitt, J. T., & Foa, E. B. (2000). Effectiveness of exposure and ritual prevention for obsessive compulsive disorder: Randomized versus non-randomized samples. *Journal of Consulting and Clinical Psychology, 68*, 594–602.

Freund, B. (1986). *Comparison of measures of obsessive–compulsive symptomatalogy and standardized assessor- and self-rated.* Unpublished doctoral dissertation, Southern Illinois University.

Freund, B., Steketee, G., & Foa, E. B. (1985). *Comparison of obsessive–compulsive symptomatology measures: versus self-rated.* Unpublished manuscript.

Goodman, W. K., Price, L. H., Rasmussen, S. A., Mazure, C., Delgado, P., Heninger, G. R., & Charney, D. S. (1989). The Yale–Brown Obsessive–Compulsive Scale: II. Validity. *Archives of General Psychiatry, 46*, 1012–1016.

Goodman, W. K., Price, L. H., Rasmussen, S. A., Mazure, C., Fleischmann, R. L., Hill, C. L., Heninger, G. R., & Charney, D. S. (1989). The Yale–Brown Obsessive–Compulsive Scale: I. Development, use, and reliability. *Archives of General Psychiatry, 46*, 1006–1011.

Greist, J. H. (1990). Treatment of obsessive–compulsive disorder: Psychotherapies, drugs, and other somatic treatments. *Journal of Clinical Psychiatry, 51*, 44–50.

Greist, J. H. (1992). An integrated approach to treatment of obsessive compulsive disorder. *Journal of Clinical Psychiatry, 53*(Suppl.), 38–41.

Greist, J. H., Chouinard, G., DuBoff, E., Halaris, A., Kim, S., Koran, L., Liebowitz, M. Lydiard, R., Rasmussen, S., White, K., & Sikes, C. (1995). Double-blind parallel comparison of three dosages of sertraline and placebo in outpatients with obsessive–compulsive disorder. *Archives of General Psychiatry, 52*, 289–295.

Greist, J. H., Jefferson, J. W., Kobak, K. A., Katzelnick, D. J., & Serlin, R. C. (1995). Efficacy and tolerability of serotonin reuptake inhibitors in obsessive compulsive disorder: A meta-analysis. *Archives of General Psychiatry, 46*, 53–60.

Hanna, G. L. (1995). Demographic and clinical features of obsessive compulsive disorder in children and adolescents. *Journal of the American Academy of Child and Adolescent Psychiatry, 34*, 19–27.

Head, D., Bolton, D., & Hymas, N. (1989). Deficit in cognitive shifting in patients with obsessive–compulsive disorder. *Biological Psychiatry, 25*, 929–937.

Hiss, H., Foa, E. B., & Kozak, M. J. (1994). A relapse prevention program for treatment of obsessive compulsive disorder. *Journal of Consulting and Clinical Psychology, 62*, 801–808.

Hodgson, R. J., & Rachman, S. (1972). The effects of contamination and washing in obsessional patients. *Behaviour Research and Therapy, 10*, 111–117.

Hodgson, R. J., Rachman, S., & Marks, I. M. (1972). The treatment of chronic obsessive–compulsive neurosis: Follow-up and further findings. *Behaviour Research and Therapy, 10*, 181–189.

Hornsveld, R. H. J., Kraaimaat, F. W., & van Dam-Baggen, R. M. J. (1979). Anxiety discomfort and handwashing in obsessive–compulsive and psychiatric control patients. *Behaviour Research and Therapy, 17*, 223–228.

Hudson, J. I., Pope, H. G., Yurgelun-Todd, D., Jonas, J. M., & Frankenburg, F. L. (1987). A controlled study of anorexia nervosa and obsessive nervosa. *British Journal of Psychiatry, 27*, 57–60.

Insel, T. R., & Akiskal, H. (1986). Obsessive–compulsive disorder with psychotic features: A phenomenologic analysis. *American Journal of Psychiatry, 12*, 1527–1533.

Insel, T. R., Donnelly, L. F., Lalakea, M. L., Alterman, I. S., & Murphy, D. L. (1983). Neurological and neuropsychological studies of patients with obsessive–compulsive disorder. *Biological Psychiatry, 18*, 741–751.

Insel, T. R., Mueller, E. A., Alterman, I. S., Linnoila, M., & Murphy, D. L. (1985). Obsessive–compulsive disorder and serotonin: Is there a connection? *Biological Psychiatry, 20*, 1174–1188.

Jenike, M., Baer, L., Minichiello, W., Schwartz, C., & Carey, R. (1986). Concomitant obsessive-compulsive disorder and schizotypal personality disorder. *American Journal of Psychiatry, 143*, 530–532.

Joffe, R. T., & Swinson, R. P. (1991). *Biological aspects of obsessive–compulsive disorder.* Paper prepared for the DSM-IV Committee on Obsessive–Compulsive Disorder.

Karno, M. G., Golding, M., Sorensen, S. B., & Burnam, A. (1988). The epidemiology of OCD in five U.S. communities. *Archives of General Psychiatry, 45*, 1094–1099.

Kasvikis, Y. G., Tsakiris, F., Marks, I. M., Basoglu, M., & Noshirvani, H. F. (1986). Past history of anorexia nervosa in women with obsessive–compulsive disorder. *International Journal of Eating Disorders, 5*, 1069–1075.

Kazarian, S. S., Evans, D. L., & Lefave, K. (1977). Modification and factorial analysis of the Leyton Obsessional Inventory. *Journal of Clinical Psychology, 33*, 422–425.

Kozak, M. J., & Foa, E. B. (1994). Obsessions, over-valued ideas, and delusions in obsessive compulsive disorder. *Behaviour Research and Therapy, 32*, 343–353.

Kozak, M. J., Foa, E. B., & Steketee, G. (1988). Process and outcome of exposure treatment with obsessive–compulsives: Psychophysiological indicators of emotional processing. *Behavior Therapy, 19*, 157–169.

Kozak, M. J., Liebowitz, M. R., & Foa, E. B. (2000). Cognitive-behavior therapy and pharmacotherapy for OCD: The NIMH-sponsored collaborative study. In W. Goodman, M. Rudorfer, & J. Maser (Eds.), *Obsessive–compulsive disorder: Contemporary issues in treatment* (pp. 501–530). Mahwah, NJ: Erlbaum.

Ladouceur, R., Rheame, J., Freeston, M. H., Aublet, F., Jean, K., Lachance, S., Langlois, F., & dePolomandy-Morin, K. (1995). Experimental manipulations of responsibility: An analogue test for models of obsessive–compulsive disorder. *Behaviour Research and Therapy, 33,* 937–946.

Laessle, R. G., Kia, S., Fichter, M. M., Wittchen, H., & Pirke, K. M. (1987). Major affective disorder in anorexia nervosa and bulimia: A descriptive diagnostic study. *British Journal of Psychiatry, 151,* 785–789.

Lang, P. J. (1979). A bio-informational theory of emotional imagery. *Psychophysiology, 6,* 495–511.

Leckman, J. F., & Chittenden, E. H. (1990). Gilles de la Tourette's syndrome and some forms of obsessive–compulsive disorder may share a common genetic diathesis. *L'Encephale, 16,* 321–323.

Lelliott, P. T., Noshirvani, H. F., Basoglu, M., Marks, I. M., & Monteiro, W. O. (1988). Obsessive–compulsive beliefs and treatment outcome. *Medicine, 18,* 697–702.

Leon, A. C., Portera, L., & Weissman, M. M. (1995). The social costs of anxiety disorders. *British Journal of Psychiatry, 166*(Suppl.), 19–22.

Lindsay, M., Crino, R., & Andrews, G. (1997). Controlled trial of exposure and response prevention in obsessive–compulsive disorder. *British Journal of Psychiatry, 171,* 135–139.

Lopatka, C., & Rachman, S. (1995). Perceived responsibility and compulsive checking: An experimental analysis. *Behaviour Research and Therapy, 33*(6), 673–684.

Marks, I. M. (1977). Recent results of behavioral treatments of phobias and obsessions. *Journal of International Medical Research, 5,* 16–21.

Marks, I. M., Hallam, R. S., Connelly, J., & Philpott, R. (1977). *Nursing in behavioral psychotherapy.* London: Royal College of Nursing of the United Kingdom.

Marks, I. M., Lelliott, P., Basoglu, M., Noshirvami, H., Monteiro, W., Cohen, D., & Kasvikis, Y. (1988). Clomipramine self-exposure, and therapist-aided exposure for obsessive–compulsive rituals. *British Journal of Psychiatry, 152,* 522–534.

Marks, I. M., Stern, R. S., Mawson, D., Cobb, J., & McDonald, R. (1980). Clomipramine, and exposure for obsessive–compulsive rituals: I. *British Journal of Psychiatry, 136,* 1–25.

McFall, M. E., & Wollersheim, J. P. (1979). Obsessive–compulsive neurosis: A cognitive-behavioral formulation and approach to treatment. *Cognitive Therapy and Research, 3,* 333–348.

Mehta, M. (1990). A comparative study of family-based and patients-based behavioural management in obsessive–compulsive disorder. *British Journal of Psychiatry, 157,* 133–135.

Meichenbaum, D. (1974). Self-instructional methods. In F. H. Kanfer & A. P. Goldstein (Eds.), *Helping people change* (pp. 357–392). New York: Pergamon Press.

Meyer, V. (1966). Modification of expectations in cases with obsessional rituals. *Behaviour Research and Therapy, 4,* 273–280.

Meyer, V., & Levy, R. (1973). Modification of behavior in obsessive–compulsive disorders. In H. E. Adams & P. Unikel (Eds.), *Issues and trends in behavior therapy* (pp. 77–136). Springfield, IL: Charles C Thomas.

Meyer, V., Levy, R., & Schnurer, A. (1974). A behavioral treatment of obsessive-compulsive disorders. In H. R. Beech (Ed.), *Obsessional states* (pp. 233–258). London: Methuen.

Minichiello, W. E., Baer, L., & Jenike, M. A. (1987). Schizotypal personality disorder: A poor prognostic indicator for behavior therapy in the treatment of obsessive–compulsive disorder. *Journal of Anxiety Disorders, 1,* 273–276.

Mowrer, O. A. (1939). A stimulus–response analysis of anxiety and its role as a reinforcing agent. *Psychological Review, 46,* 553–565.

Mowrer, O. A. (1960). *Learning theory and behavior.* New York. Wiley.

O'Sullivan, G., Noshirvani, H., Marks, I., Monteiro, W., & Lelliott, P. (1991). Six-year follow-up after exposure and clomipramine therapy for obsessive–compulsive disorder. *Journal of Clinical Archives, 52,* 150–155.

Öst, L. G. (1989). One-session treatment for specific phobias. *Behaviour Research and Therapy, 27,* 1–7.

Pato, M. T., Pato, C. N., & Gunn, S. A. (1998). Biological treatments for obsessive–compulsive disorder: Clinical applications. In R. P. Swinson, M. M. Antony, S. Rachman, & M. A. Richter (Eds.), *Obsessive–compulsive disorder: Theory, research, and treatment* (pp. 327–348). New York: Guilford Press.

Pato, M. T., Zohar-Kadouch, R., Zohar, J., & Murphy, D. L. (1988). Return of symptoms after discontinuation of clomipramine in patients with obsessive–compulsive disorder. *American Journal of Psychiatry, 145,* 1521–1525.

Pauls, D. L. (1989). *The inheritance and expression of obsessive–compulsive behaviors.* Paper presented at the annual meeting of the American Psychiatric Association, San Francisco.

Pauls, D. L., Towbin, K. E., Leckman, J. F., Zahner, G. E., & Cohen, D. J. (1986). Gilles de la Tourette's syndrome and obsessive–compulsive disorder. *Archives of General Psychiatry, 43,* 1180–1182.

Philpott, R. (1975). Recent advances in the behavioral measurement of obsessional illness: Difficulties common to them and other instruments. *Scottish Medical Journal, 20,* 33–40.

Rabavilas, A. D., & Boulougouris, J. C. (1974). Physiological accompaniments of ruminations, flooding and thought–stopping in obsessive patients. *Behaviour Research and Therapy, 12,* 239–243.

Rabavilas, A. D., Boulougouris, J. C., & Perissaki, C. (1979). Therapist qualities related to outcome with exposure *in vivo* in neurotic patients. *Journal of Behavior Therapy and Experimental Psychiatry, 10,* 293–299.

Rabavilas, A. D., Boulougouris, J. C., & Stefanis, C. (1976). Duration of flooding sessions in the treatment of obsessive–compulsive patients. *Behaviour Research and Therapy, 14,* 349–355.

Rachman, S., & DeSilva, P. (1978). Abnormal and normal obsessions. *Behaviour Research and Therapy, 16,* 233–248.

Rachman, S., DeSilva, P., & Roper, G. (1976). The spontaneous decay of compulsive urges. *Behaviour Research and Therapy, 14,* 445–453.

Rachman, S., & Hodgson, R. (1980). *Obsessions and compulsions.* Englewood Cliffs, NJ: Prentice-Hall.

Rachman, S., Throdarson, D. S., Shafran, R., & Woody, S. R. (1995). Perceived responsibility: Structure and significance. *Behaviour Research and Therapy, 33*(7), 779–784.

Rachman, S., & Wilson, G. T. (1980). *The effects of psychological therapy.* Oxford: Pergamon Press.

Rapoport, J. L. (1991). Recent advances in obsessive–compulsive disorder. *Neuropsychopharmacology, 5*, 1–10.

Rapoport, J. L., Swedo, S. E., & Leonard, H. L. (1992). Childhood obsessive compulsive disorder. *Journal of Clinical Psychiatry, 53*(4, Suppl.), 11–16.

Rapoport, J. L., & Wise, S. P. (1988). Obsessive–compulsive disorder: Evidence for basal ganglia dysfunction. *Psychopharmacology Bulletin, 24*, 380–384.

Rasmussen, S. A., & Eisen, J. L. (1989). Clinical features and phenomenology of obsessive–compulsive disorder. *Psychiatric Annals, 19*, 67–73.

Rasmussen, S. A., & Eisen, J. L. (1990). Epidemiology of obsessive–compulsive disorder. *Journal of Clinical Psychiatry, 51*, 10–14.

Rasmussen, S. A., & Tsuang, M. T. (1986). Clinical characteristics and family history in DSM III obsessive–compulsive disorder. *American Journal of Psychiatry, 143*, 317–382.

Rauch, S. L., & Jenike, M. A. (1998). Pharmacological treatment of obsessive–compulsive disorder. In P. E. Nathan & J. M. Gorman (Eds.), *A guide to treatments that work* (pp. 358–376). New York: Oxford University Press.

Reed, G. E. (1985). *Obsessional experience and compulsive behavior: A cognitive structural approach.* Orlando, FL: Academic Press.

Rheaume, J., Ladouceur, R., Freesten, M. H., & LeTarte, H. (1995). Inflated responsibility in obsessive–compulsive disorder. *Behaviour Research and Therapy, 33*, 159–169.

Riggs, D. S., Hiss, H., & Foa, E. B. (1992). Marital distress and the treatment of obsessive–compulsive disorder. *Behavior Research and Therapy, 23*, 585–597.

Roper, G., & Rachman, S. (1976). Obsessional–compulsive checking: Experimental replication and development. *Behaviour Research and Therapy, 14*, 25–32.

Roper, G., Rachman, S., & Hodgson, R. (1973). An experiment on obsessional checking. *Behaviour Research and Therapy, 11*, 271–277.

Rubenstein, C. S., Peynirgioglu, Z. F., Chambless, D. L., & Pigott, T. A. (1993). Memory in sub-clinical obsessive-compulsive checkers. *Behaviour Research and Therapy, 31*(8), 759–765.

Salkovskis, P. M. (1985). Obsessional compulsive problems: A cognitive-behavioral analysis. *Behaviour Research and Therapy, 23*, 571–583.

Schilder, P. (1938). The organic background of obsessions and compulsions. *American Journal of Psychiatry, 94*, 1397.

Sher, K. J., Frost, R. O., & Otto, R. (1983). Cognitive deficits in compulsive checkers: An exploratory study. *Behaviour Research and Therapy, 21*, 357–364.

Stampfl, T. G., & Levis, D. J. (1967). Essentials of implosive therapy: A learning-based psychodynamic behavioral therapy. *Journal of Abnormal Psychology, 72*, 496–503.

Stanley, M. A., Turner, S. M., & Borden, J. W. (1990). Schizotypal features in obsessive–compulsive disorder. *Comprehensive Psychiatry, 31*, 511–518.

Steketee, G. S., Foa, E. B., & Grayson, J. B. (1982). Recent advances in the treatment of obsessive–compulsives. *Archives of General Psychiatry, 39*, 1365–1371.

Stern, R. S., Marks, I. M., Wright, J., & Luscombe, D. K. (1980). Clomipramine: Plasma levels, side effects and outcome in obsessive–compulsive neurosis. *Postgraduate Medical Journal, 56*, 134–139.

Swedo, S. E., Rapoport, J. L., Cheslow, D. L., Leonard, H. L., Ayoub, L. M., Hosier, D. M., & Wald, L. R. (1989). High prevalence of obsessive–compulsive symptoms in patients with Sydenham's chorea. *American Journal of Psychiatry, 146*, 246–249.

Swedo, S. E., Rapoport, J. L., Leonard, H. L., Lenane, M., & Cheslow, D. (1989). Obsessive compulsive disorder in children and adolescents: Clinical phenomenology of 70 consecutive cases. *Archives of General Psychiatry, 46*, 335–341.

Thoren, P., Asberg, M., Chronholm, B., Jornestedt, L., & Traskman, L. (1980). Clomipramine treatment of obsessive–compulsive disorder: I. A controlled clinical trial. *Archives of General Psychiatry, 37*, 1281–1285.

Tollefson, G. D., Rampey, A. H., Potvin, J. H., Jenike, M. A., Rush, A. J., Dominguez, R. A., Koran, L. M., Shear, M. K., Goodman, W., & Genduso, L. A. (1994). A multicenter investigation of fixed-dose fluoxetine in the treatment of obsessive–compulsive disorder. *Archives of General Psychiatry, 51*, 559–567.

Tynes, L. L., White, L., & Steketee, G. S. (1990). Toward a new nosology of obsessive–compulsive disorder. *Comprehensive Psychiatry, 31*, 465–480.

Valleni-Basile, L. A., Garrison, C. Z., Jackson, K. L., Waller, J. L., McKeown, R. E., Addy, C. L., & Cuffe, S. P. (1994). Frequency of obsessive compulsive disorder in a community sample of young adolescents. *Journal of the American Academy of Child and Adolescent Psychiatry, 33*, 782–791.

van Oppen, P., de Haan, E., van Balkom, A. J. L. M., Spinhoven, P., Hoogduin, K., & van Dyck, R. (1995). Cognitive therapy and exposure *in vivo* in the treatment of obsessive compulsive disorder. *Behaviour Research and Therapy, 33*, 379–390.

Watts, F. N. (1973). Desensitization as an habituation phenomenon: II: Studies of interstimulus interval length. *Psychological Reports, 33*, 715–718.

Weizman, A., Carmi, M., Hermesh, H., Shahar, A., Apter, A., Tyano, S., & Rehavi, M. (1985). *High-affinity imipramine binding and serotonin uptake platelets of adolescent and adult obsessive-compulsive patients.* Paper presented at the 4th International Congress of Biological Psychiatry, Philadelphia.

Zohar, J., & Insel, T. (1987). Obsessive–compulsive disorder: Psychobiological approach to diagnosis, treatment and pathophysiology. *Biological Psychiatry, 22*, 667–687.

Zohar, J., Judge, R., & OCD Paroxetine Study Investigators. (1996). Paroxetine versus clomipramine in the treatment of obsessive-compulsive disorder. *British Journal of Psychiatry, 169*, 468–474.

Zohar, J., Mueller, E. A., Insel, T. R., Zohar-Kadouch, I. L., & Murphy, D. L. (1987). Serotonergic responsivity in obsessive–compulsive disorder. Comparison of patients and healthy controls. *Archives of General Psychiatry, 44*, 946–951.

Chapter 6

COGNITIVE THERAPY FOR DEPRESSION

Jeffrey E. Young
Arthur D. Weinberger
Aaron T. Beck

One of the most important developments in psychosocial approaches to emotional problems has been the success of cognitive therapy for depression. Evidence for the powerful efficacy of this approach has increased since the second edition of this book, particularly in regard to successful long-term outcome. Employing a variety of well-specified cognitive and behavioral techniques, cognitive therapy is also distinguished by the detailed structure of each session with its specific agendas, and by the very deliberate and obviously effective therapeutic style of interacting with the patient through a series of questions. Moreover, the authors underscore very clearly the importance of the collaborative relationship between the therapist and the patient, and outline specific techniques to achieve this collaborative state so that the patient and therapist become an investigative team.

In this chapter, the authors present a second important phase of treatment that represents an interesting variation of cognitive therapy. This phase, called the "schema-focused" phase of treatment, concentrates on identifying and modifying early maladaptive or "core" schemas that developed during childhood. These schemas may make the patient vulnerable to relapse. Detailed explication of this second phase of treatment will be invaluable to experienced cognitive therapists, as well as to those becoming acquainted with cognitive therapy for depression for the first time.—D. H. B.

OVERVIEW AND RESEARCH

Depression and the Emergence of Cognitive Therapy

Depression is one of the most common disorders encountered by mental health professionals. Data provided by the National Institute of Mental Health (NIMH) indicate the following:

- More than 19 million adult Americans will experience some form of depression each year.
- Depression increases the risk of heart attacks and is a frequent and serious complicating factor in stroke, diabetes, and cancer.
- Depression is the leading cause of disability.
- The associated costs are more than $30 billion per year. (NIMH, 1999)

Further estimates suggest that by the year 2010, depression will be the second most costly of all illnesses worldwide—in 1990 it was ranked fourth (Keller & Boland, 1998). As these reports indicate, depression is widespread, debilitating, and costly.

Although there are many theories regarding the precipitants of depression,

Research dealing with the onset of particular episodes of adult depression has concluded that the majority are provoked by life events or on-going difficulties; the role of events has emerged as clearly the more important of the two.... Studies have suggested that about 66%–90% of depressed episodes have a severe event occurring within six months of onset.... The majority of these events involve some element of loss ... (Brown, 1996, pp. 151–154)

No amount of data can adequately capture or convey the personal pain and suffering experienced in depression. Yet most depressed people do not get professional help (Frank & Thase, 1999; Jarrett, 1995). The stigma still attached to people suffering from depression is no doubt one factor, but the obstacles encountered while looking for appropriate care can be another stumbling block in avoiding getting help. Obtaining the right type of help can be at once inhibiting and overwhelming, especially to those already impaired:

Americans who do seek treatment for depressive symptoms must decide where to seek which treatment and from what type of practitioner ... the clinician must select a somatic, psychological, or combination of treatment, at a given dose and/or schedule of appointments.... Throughout this procedure, the patient decides to what extent he/she will comply with the recommendations, for how long, against recognized and unrecognized economic, practical, physical, and emotional costs.... Sadly, the lack of information as well as the continued social stigma of psychiatric illness and treatment influence decision-making. Simultaneously, the decisions occur in an environment filled with social, political, and economic debate, and tension among policy makers, third-party payers, and clinicians, as well as among different types of practitioner guilds. (Jarrett, 1995, p. 435)

When care is provided, it is frequently inadequate, reflecting a public health crisis (Keller & Boland, 1998). The need for delivery of treatments with proven and rapid efficacy remains paramount.

One of the major developments in the treatment of depression has been the emergence of cognitive therapy. Developed by Aaron T. Beck over the past 30 years, his work and that of his colleagues (Beck, 1967, 1976; Beck, Rush, Shaw, & Emery, 1979) has led to a paradigm shift within psychotherapy (Salkovskis, 1996). Due in part to Beck's development of testable hypotheses and clinical protocols,

cognitive therapy has received an enormous amount of professional attention (Hollon, 1998; McGinn & Young, 1996; Rehm, 1990). Of all the cognitive-behavioral treatment (CBT) approaches to depression, Beck's paradigm (Beck, 1967; Beck et al., 1979) has received the greatest amount of empirical study, validation, and clinical application (Barlow & Hofmann, 1997; de Oliveira, 1998; Dobson & Pusch, 1993; Hollon, 1998; Rehm, 1990; Roberts & Hartlage, 1996; Scott, 1996a). There are also many excellent books for practitioners that teach cognitive therapy procedures (e.g., J. S. Beck, 1995).

Along with this attention, however, has come confusion about what is actually meant by the term "cognitive therapy":

... the actual cognitive therapeutic strategies employed in "cognitive" treatments may differ in many ways from one another and from those explicitly prescribed by Beck et al. (1979) in their manual for cognitive therapy of depression. Thus, the reader should be aware that common use of the term "cognitive therapy" does not necessarily imply uniformity in procedures. Also lending confusion to this area is use of the terms "cognitive therapy" and "cognitive-behavioral therapy." The therapy described by Beck et al. (1979) involves the use of both cognitive and behavioral techniques, and thus could be accurately labeled "cognitive-behavioral"; however, in the literature both terms have been applied in describing the Beck et al. (1979) procedures, with more recent articles utilizing the term "cognitive therapy." (Sacco & Beck, 1995, p. 345)

Research Findings on the Treatment of Depression at Termination

Outcome research has consistently found that cognitive therapy is at least as effective as tricyclic antidepressants (TCAs) in the treatment of outpatients with nonbipolar depression at the termination of treatment (Beck et al., 1979; Blackburn & Bishop, 1979, 1980; McLean & Hakstian, 1979; Rush, Beck, Kovacs, & Hollon, 1977). In one group of studies, the mean percentage changes in the level of depression for such outpatients immediately after treatment were as follows: 66% for those receiving cognitive therapy alone, 63% for those treated with TCAs alone, and 72% for patients receiving some combination of the two (Williams, 1997). Although there has been considerable variability in improvement rates from study to study (see Biggs & Rush, 1999), the improvement rate in all three conditions has rarely fallen below 50% at termination, and the differences at termination among the three conditions are not typically large enough to be meaningful. Several studies have failed to find the combination of CBT and drugs to be superior to either treatment alone (Biggs & Rush, 1999; Evans et al., 1992; Hollon, Shelton, & Loosen, 1991; Scott, 1996a; Shaw & Segal, 1999). Furthermore, despite a limited number of studies, beneficial results have also been found in treating depressed inpatients with cognitive therapy (Stuart & Bowers, 1995; Wright, 1996).

Some studies have found cognitive therapy to be superior to drug treatment for depression at termination, although this is not a consistent finding. There is also some debate over whether the cognitive components of the treatment are necessary in treating depression, with some researchers arguing that the behavioral aspects of cognitive therapy are primarily responsible for the improvement. For example, the results of a recent meta-analysis (Gloaguen, Cottraux, Cucherat, & Blackburn, 1998), based on clinical trials conducted between 1977 and 1996, found that cognitive therapy was superior to antidepressants and to a set of miscellaneous psychotherapies, while being equal to behavior therapy. The researchers concluded: "Although its therapeutic process may be shared with behavior therapy, cognitive therapy has been demonstrated effective with patients with mild or moderate depression and its effects exceed those of antidepressants" (p. 69). A study by Hautzinger and de Jong-Meyer (1996) found that "CBT is an efficient, short- and long-term alternative to the standard drug treatment of patients with a major depression or dysthymic disorder. . . . Drug treatment alone produced more drop-outs and less clinically significant responders than CBT alone or the combination treatment" (p. 339).

Research Controversy and Criticism

Despite the fact that cognitive therapy is the most empirically tested psychotherapy for depression currently available, it has not been unequivocally embraced. Some have questioned the validity of the findings on the basis of methodological flaws or insufficient data (Gelder, 1994; Klein, 1996; Scott, 1996a), while others have attempted to temper the results by attributing them to "experimental allegiance"—the preference by the researcher for one therapy over others (Gaffan, Tsaousis, & Kemp-Wheeler, 1995; Luborsky et al., 1999). Some behaviorists have tried to dismiss cognitive therapy altogether by claiming that it is based on "cognitivist oversell" and "self deception" (Wolpe, 1993, p. 143).

The most serious questions about the efficacy of cognitive therapy were raised by the NIMH Treatment of Depression Collaborative Research Program (TDCRP). The initial results (Elkin et al., 1989) suggested lower rates of improvement with cognitive therapy than did earlier studies. It also appeared that in some patient groups, interpersonal psychotherapy and antidepressant drugs might be superior to cognitive therapy. The high visibility and prestige of the NIMH TDCRP study generated a great deal of debate (Hollon, DeRubeis, & Evans, 1996; Wolpe, 1993), because it appeared that the benefits of cognitive therapy in the acute treatment phase might have been overestimated in previous studies.

After reanalysis of the data, however, using more powerful statistical procedures, these findings have been revised: ". . . an examination of final scores and percentages of patients improved suggests that the results for patients in CBT are in the same general range as those in most comparable studies" (Elkin, Gibbons, Shea, & Shaw, 1996, p. 99).

Research Findings on Relapse Rates in Treating Depression

Even though the vast majority of patients recover from an episode of depression, they nevertheless remain vulnerable to future depression.[1]

> Recurrence is a major problem for many individuals suffering from depression: at least 50% of individuals who suffer from one depressive episode will have another within 10 years. Those experiencing two episodes have a 90% chance of suffering a third, while individuals with three or more lifetime episodes have relapse rates of 40% within 15 weeks of recovery from an episode. (Kupfer, Frank, & Wamhoff, 1996, p. 293)

Other investigators have estimated that 85% of patients with unipolar depression are likely to experience recurrences (Keller & Boland, 1998, p. 350). As these numbers clearly show, there is an urgent need for treatments capable of minimizing and preventing relapse.

What we consider the most exciting finding in the treatment of depression with cognitive therapy is the consistent observation that patients treated with cognitive therapy alone, or with a combination of cognitive therapy and medication, fare far better in terms of relapse than do patients treated with medication alone (when both treatments are stopped at termination). Despite differences in sample characteristics and methodologies employed across studies, cognitive therapy appears to have important prophylactic properties. After a 1-year follow-up, reported relapse rates for patients treated with cognitive therapy are far lower than for patients treated with antidepressants: 12% versus 66% (Simons, Murphy, Levine, & Wetzel, 1986); 20% versus 80% (Bowers, 1990); and 9% versus 28% (Shea et al., 1992). The results of a meta-analysis revealed: "On average, only 29.5% of the patients treated with [cognitive therapy] relapsed versus 60% of those treated with antidepressants" (Gloaguen et al., 1998, p. 68). The prophylactic benefits of cognitive therapy are all the more significant, because "there is no evidence that pharmacotherapy confers any protection against the return of symptoms after treatment has been terminated.[2] Since the majority of depressed individuals will experience multiple episodes, the capacity of an intervention to prevent the return of symptoms after treatment may be at least as important as its ability to treat the current episode" (Evans et al., 1992, p. 802).

A related concern—and one of the most salient with psychotropic agents—is the presence of residual symptoms after treatment: ". . . treatment of depression by pharmacological means is likely to leave a substantial amount of residual symptoms in most patients" (Fava, Rafanelli, Grandi, Conti, & Belluardo, 1998, p. 820). Inevitably, patients who improve on antidepressants continue to manifest some of the symptoms of depression; and as numerous investigators have concluded, unless patients achieve full recovery, residual symptoms increase the risk of relapse (Evans et al., 1992; Fava, Rafanelli,

Grandi, Conti, & Belluardo, 1998; Keller & Boland, 1998).

One group of investigators, concerned about the risk of relapse associated with residual symptoms, looked at the lingering symptoms after treatment with fluoxetine (Prozac). They found that:

> . . . even among subjects who are considered full responders to fluoxetine 20 mg for 8 weeks, more than 80% had 1 or more residual DSM-III-R symptoms of major depressive disorder, more than 30% had 3 or more symptoms, and 10.2% met formal criteria for either minor or subsyndromal depression. . . . These findings imply that minimal depressive symptoms are prodromal and increase the risk of developing an initial full-blown episode of major depression. (Nierenberg et al., 1999, pp. 224–225).

Cognitive therapy has been found to be effective in reducing both residual symptoms and relapse, after the termination of medication: "Short-term CBT after successful antidepressant drug therapy had a substantial effect on relapse rate after discontinuation of antidepressant drugs. Patients who received CBT reported a substantially lower relapse rate (25%) during the 2-year follow-up than those assigned to [clinical management] (80%)" (Fava, Rafanelli, Grandi, Conti, & Belluardo, 1998, p. 818). The protective benefits of cognitive therapy were still noticeable in a 4-year follow-up study, although the benefits faded after a 6-year period (Fava, Rafanelli, Grandi, Canestrari, & Morphy, 1998). Another study found that only 5% of the "CBT treated and recovered" group sought additional treatment, compared with 39% of the antidepressant group (see Williams, 1997).

What is the optimum frequency and duration of sessions for cognitive therapy to be effective, both at termination and at long-term follow-up? According to Sacco and Beck (1995),

> General guidelines suggest 15 to 25 (50-minute) sessions at weekly intervals, with more seriously depressed clients usually requiring twice-weekly meetings for the initial 4–5 weeks. To avoid an abrupt termination, a "tapering-off" process is recommended, with the last few sessions occurring once every 2 weeks. After termination, some clients may also need a few "booster sessions" (four or five are common). (p. 332)

Some writers have noted that longer treatment may be necessary for a full and more lasting recovery (Elkin et al., 1996; Thase, 1992).

The latest trend among psychiatrists in dealing with the high relapse rates associated with antidepressant medication is "continuation medication"—long-term (and in many cases lifelong) maintenance treatment (Evans et al., 1992; Fava, Rafanelli, Grandi, Conti, & Belluardo, 1998; Thase, 1999)—usually at the same dosage provided during the acute phase of treatment. In light of the superiority of cognitive therapy over medication in terms of relapse rates, without the need for maintenance cognitive therapy, the data do not seem to support this practice. Some researchers have pointed out the tautological nature of this solution: "Drug treatment results in a higher relapse rate than cognitive-behavioral therapy; therefore patients should be maintained on drugs to prevent relapse" (Antonuccio, Danton, & DeNelsky, 1995, p. 578). We further address the reluctance of many psychiatrists to incorporate cognitive therapy into their treatment plans in the next section.

The Politics of Depression: Medication as the Treatment of Choice

Despite the findings cited above, drugs are still the initial and most frequently prescribed form of treatment for unipolar depression in the United States (Antonuccio et al., 1995). One government publication, for example, recommends that two trials of antidepressants, both unsuccessful, should be completed before recommending psychotherapy for depression (Depression Guideline Panel, 1993); the most recent White House Conference on Mental Health reveals a similar treatment bias (Saeman, 1999). Although psychotropic medications clearly provide enormous benefit and relief to a substantial portion of depressed patients, research does not support this unilateral bias toward medication. Research has shown that "a sizeable group of patients either chooses not to continue long-term pharmacotherapy in the absence of any depressive symptoms, cannot take medication due to a medical condition that precludes the use of antidepressants, or suffer from side effects that are intolerable to them" (Spanier, Frank, McEachran, Grochocinski, & Kupfer, 1999,

p. 250). In fact, one group of researchers concluded that "there is much evidence that antidepressant medications are not benign treatments. . . . Many antidepressants are cardiotoxic, have dangerous side effects, and are often used in suicide attempts. . . . [They also] result in relatively poorer compliance than psychotherapy, have a higher dropout rate, and result in as much as a 60% nonresponse rate with some patient populations" (Antonuccio et al., 1995, p. 581). Of course, psychotherapy may also have unintended and undesirable side effects (Mohr, 1995); but very little is known about any negative effects associated with cognitive therapy.

Another consideration in making treatment recommendations about depression should be the preference of patients, the "consumers." Research suggests that consumers seem to have a preference for psychotherapy over medication for depression: "The results of treatment acceptability studies show that, as treatments for depression in adults, psychotherapies are perceived by potential consumers as more acceptable than pharmacotherapy alone as well as combinations of psychotherapy and pharmacotherapy" (Hall & Robertson, 1998, p. 271). This is not surprising, given that most people attribute their depressions to negative life experiences, with stress and environmental factors playing major roles (Antonuccio et al., 1995; Brown, 1996; Eifert, Beach, & Wilson, 1998).

Research Findings on Severe Depression

Treatment protocols for severe depression, such as the one issued by the American Psychiatric Association (1993), often recommend antidepressants as the first and only avenue of treatment. However, a group of researchers who compared the efficacy of cognitive therapy to medication for severe depression (through a "mega-analysis" of randomized comparisons) found:

> Cognitive behavior therapy has fared as well as antidepressant medication with severely depressed outpatients in four major comparisons. . . . Until more data become available, we recommend that the field recognize, and treatment guidelines reflect, the findings obtained thus far in the major comparisons of antidepressant medication with cognitive behavior therapy:

that antidepressant medication and cognitive behavior therapy have not differed in acute efficacy in the treatment of severely depressed outpatients. (DeRubeis, Gelfand, Tang, & Simons, 1999, pp. 1007–1013)

Similar findings and conclusions have been reported elsewhere (Hautzinger & de Jong-Meyer, 1996).

Current Status and Future Research on Treating Depression

There is now a considerable body of research regarding antidepressant and cognitive treatments for depression. Certainly there are still enough inconsistencies in the literature to warrant continued debate and research regarding the relative merits of different treatments for depression (Agosti & Ocepek, 1997; Gortner, Gollan, Dobson, & Jacobson, 1998; Oei & Free, 1995; Robinson, Berman, & Neimeyer, 1990; Stewart, Garfinkel, Nunes, Donovan, & Klein, 1998; Thase et al., 1997). Nevertheless, the efficacy of cognitive therapy for depression is clearly a replicable and robust finding. Based on the available data, some researchers have even recommended that cognitive therapy be considered the treatment of first choice for many depressed patients—not only because it entails fewer medical risks, but because of its superior long-term benefits (Antonuccio et al., 1995; de Oliveira, 1998; Hollon, 1998).

Our own hope, however, is that we will see a movement away from the current "horse race" approach so prevalent in the research literature (Williams, 1997). There are many important, unanswered questions that make it impossible, in our opinion, for proponents of any one treatment to make firm recommendations favoring one treatment for depression over another. Regardless of the treatment modality studied, fully a third of patients in some studies do not respond to either treatment (Blackburn & Moore, 1997), while a much higher percentage do not achieve lasting improvements (Evans et al., 1992; Shaw & Segal, 1999). Through more sophisticated research studies, we hope that it will be possible to assess which types of depressed patients will benefit most from which type of treatment, or combination of treatments, and in what sequence.

The remainder of this chapter is devoted to detailing the basic characteristics of cognitive therapy, and to demonstrating the application of cognitive therapy to depression in clinical practice.

COGNITIVE MODEL OF DEPRESSION

The cognitive model assumes that cognition, behavior, and biochemistry are all important components of depressive disorders. We do not view them as competing theories of depression, but rather as different levels of analysis. Each treatment approach has its own "focus of convenience." The pharmacotherapist intervenes at the biochemical level; the cognitive therapist intervenes at the cognitive, affective, and behavioral levels. Our experience suggests that when we change depressive cognitions, we simultaneously change the characteristic mood, the behavior, and, as some evidence suggests (Free, Oei, & Appleton, 1998; Joffe, Segal, & Singer, 1996), the biochemistry of depression. Although the exact mechanism of change remains a target of considerable investigation, speculation, and debate (Barber & DeRubeis, 1989; Castonguay, Goldfried, Wiser, Raue, & Hayes, 1996; Crews & Harrison, 1995; DeRubeis et al., 1990; DeRubeis & Feeley, 1990; Hayes & Strauss, 1998; Oei & Free, 1995; Oei & Shuttlewood, 1996; Shea & Elkin, 1996; Sullivan & Conway, 1991; Whisman, 1993), "there are indications that cognitive therapy works by virtue of changing beliefs and information-processing proclivities and that different aspects of cognition play different roles in the process of change" (Hollon et al., 1996, p. 314).

Our focus in this chapter is on the cognitive disturbances in depression. Cognitive science research emphasizes the importance of information processing in depressive symptomatology (Ingram & Holle, 1992). According to these theories, negatively biased cognition is a core process in depression. This process is reflected in the "cognitive triad of depression": Depressed patients typically have a negative view of themselves, of their environment, and of the future. They view themselves as worthless, inadequate, unlovable, and deficient. Depressed patients view the environment as overwhelming, as presenting insuperable obstacles that cannot be overcome, and as continually resulting in failure or loss. Moreover, they view the future as hopeless; they believe their own efforts will be insufficient to change the unsatisfying course of their lives. This negative view of the future often leads to suicidal ideation and actual attempts.

Depressed patients consistently distort their interpretations of events so that they maintain negative views of themselves, the environment, and the future. These distortions represent deviations from the logical processes of thinking used typically by people. For example, a depressed woman whose husband comes home late one night may conclude that he is having an affair with another woman, even though there is no other evidence supporting this conclusion. This example illustrates an "arbitrary inference"—the patient has reached a conclusion that is not justified by the available evidence. Other distortions include all-or-nothing thinking, overgeneralization, selective abstraction, and magnification (Beck et al., 1979).

According to subsequent developments within the cognitive model, an important predisposing factor for many patients with depression is the presence of early schemas (Stein & Young, 1992; Young, 1999).[3] Beck (1976) has emphasized the importance of schemas in depression, and provided the following definition:

> A schema is a (cognitive) structure for screening, coding, and evaluating the stimuli that impinge on the organism. . . . On the basis of this matrix of schemas, the individual is able to orient himself in relation to time and space and to categorize and interpret experiences in a meaningful way. (p. 283)

Furthermore, Beck, Freeman, and Associates (1990) have noted:

> In the field of psychopathology, the term "schema" has been applied to structures with a highly personalized idiosyncratic content that are activated during disorders such as depression, anxiety, panic attacks, and obsessions, and become prepotent. . . . Thus, in clinical depression, for example, the negative schemas are in ascendancy, resulting in a systematic negative bias in the interpretation and recall of experiences as well as in short-term and long-term predictions, whereas the positive schemas become less accessible. It is easy for depressed patients to see the negative aspects of an event, but difficult to see the positive. They can recall negative events much more readily than positive ones. They weigh the probabilities of undesirable outcomes more heavily than positive outcomes. (p. 32)

It is also becoming increasingly recognized that "Focusing on core schemas is a key to effective short-term therapy" (Freeman & Davison, 1997, p. 8).

Through clinical observation, Young has identified a subset of schemas that he terms Early Maladaptive Schemas: "Early Maladaptive Schemas refer to extremely stable and enduring themes that develop during childhood and are elaborated upon throughout the individual's lifetime and that are dysfunctional to a significant degree" (Young, 1999, p. 9). Young has identified 18 Early Maladaptive Schemas in five hypothesized domains (Figure 6.1). Most of these schemas have been supported by subsequent research (Lee, Taylor, & Dunn, 1999; Schmidt, 1994; Schmidt, Joiner, Young, & Telch, 1995).

According to Young's schema approach, children learn to construct reality through early experiences with the environment, especially with significant others. Sometimes these early experiences lead children to accept attitudes and beliefs that will later prove maladaptive. For example, a child may develop the schema that no matter what he/she does, his/her performance will never be good enough. These schemas are usually out of awareness, and may remain dormant until a life event (such as being fired from a job) stimulates the schema. Once the schema is activated, the patient categorizes, selects, and encodes information in such a way that the failure schema is maintained. Early Maladaptive Schemas therefore predispose depressed patients to distort events in a characteristic fashion, leading to a negative view of themselves, the environment, and the future.

Early Maladaptive Schemas have several defining characteristics. They are experienced as (1) a priori truths about oneself and/or the environment; (2) self-perpetuating and resistant to change; (3) dysfunctional; (4) often triggered by some environmental change (e.g., loss of a job or mate); (5) tied to high levels of affect when activated; and (6) usually resulting from an interaction of the child's innate temperament with dysfunctional developmental experiences with family members or caretakers (Young, 1999).

DISCONNECTION AND REJECTION

(*Expectation that one's needs for security, safety, stability, nurturance, empathy, sharing of feelings, acceptance, and respect will not be met in a predictable manner. Typical family origin is detached, cold, rejecting, withholding, lonely, explosive, unpredictable, or abusive.*)

1. ABANDONMENT/INSTABILITY (AB)

The perceived *instability* or *unreliability* of those available for support and connection. Involves the sense that significant others will not be able to continue providing emotional support, connection, strength, or practical protection because they are emotionally unstable and unpredictable (e.g., angry outbursts), unreliable, or erratically present; because they will die imminently; or because they will abandon the patient in favor of someone better.

2. MISTRUST/ABUSE (MA)

The expectation that others will hurt, abuse, humiliate, cheat, lie, manipulate, or take advantage. Usually involves the perception that the harm is intentional or the result of unjustified and extreme negligence. May include the sense that one always ends up being cheated relative to others or "getting the short end of the stick."

3. EMOTIONAL DEPRIVATION (ED)

Expectation that one's desire for a normal degree of emotional support will not be adequately met by others. The three major forms of deprivation are:

A. *Deprivation of nurturance:* Absence of attention, affection, warmth, or companionship.

B. *Deprivation of empathy:* Absence of understanding, listening, self-disclosure, or mutual sharing of feelings from others.

C. *Deprivation of protection:* Absence of strength, direction, or guidance from others.

4. DEFECTIVENESS/SHAME (DS)

The feeling that one is defective, bad, unwanted, inferior, or invalid in important respects; or that one would be unlovable to significant others if exposed. May involve hypersensitivity to criticism, rejection, and blame; self-consciousness, comparisons, and insecurity around others; or a sense of shame regarding one's perceived flaws. These flaws may be *private* (e.g., selfishness, angry impulses, unacceptable sexual desires) or *public* (e.g., undesirable physical appearance, social awkwardness).

5. SOCIAL ISOLATION/ALIENATION (SI)

The feeling that one is isolated from the rest of the world, different from other people, and/or not part of any group or community.

IMPAIRED AUTONOMY AND PERFORMANCE

(*Expectations about oneself and the environment that interfere with one's perceived ability to separate, survive, function independently, or perform successfully. Typical family origin is enmeshed, undermining of child's confidence, overprotective, or failing to reinforce child for performing competently outside the family.*)

6. DEPENDENCE/INCOMPETENCE (DI)

Belief that one is unable to handle one's *everyday responsibilities* in a competent manner, without considerable help from others (e.g., take care of oneself, solve daily problems, exercise good judgment, tackle new tasks, make good decisions). Often presents as helplessness.

7. VULNERABILITY TO HARM OR ILLNESS (VH)

Exaggerated fear that *imminent* catastrophe will strike at any time and that one will be unable to prevent it. Fears focus on one or more of the following: (A) *medical catastrophes* (e.g., heart attacks, AIDS); (B) *emotional catastrophes* (e.g., going crazy); (C) *external catastrophes* (e.g., elevators collapsing, victimized by criminals, airplane crashes, earthquakes).

8. ENMESHMENT/UNDEVELOPED SELF (EM)

Excessive emotional involvement and closeness with one or more significant others (often parents), at the expense of full individuation or normal social development. Often involves the belief that at least one of the enmeshed individuals cannot survive or be happy without the constant support of the other. May also include feelings of being smothered by, or fused with, others OR insufficient individual identity. Often experienced as a feeling of emptiness and floundering, having no direction, or in extreme cases questioning one's existence.

(*cont.*)

FIGURE 6.1. Early maladaptive schemas with associated schema domains (revised November 1998). Copyright 1999 by Jeffrey E. Young, PhD. Reprinted with permission. Unauthorized reproduction without written consent of the author is prohibited. For more information, write Cognitive Therapy Center of New York, 120 East 56th Street, Suite 530, New York, NY 10022.

9. FAILURE (FA)

The belief that one has failed, will inevitably fail, or is fundamentally inadequate relative to one's peers, in areas of *achievement* (school, career, sports, etc.). Often involves beliefs that one is stupid, inept, untalented, ignorant, lower in status, less successful than others, etc.

IMPAIRED LIMITS

(Deficiency in internal limits, responsibility to others, or long-term goal orientation. Leads to difficulty respecting the rights of others, cooperating with others, making commitments, or setting and meeting realistic personal goals. Typical family origin is characterized by permissiveness, overindulgence, lack of direction, or a sense of superiority—rather than appropriate confrontation, discipline, and limits in relation to taking responsibility, cooperating in a reciprocal manner, and setting goals. In some cases, child may not have been pushed to tolerate normal levels of discomfort, or may not have been given adequate supervision, direction, or guidance.)

10. ENTITLEMENT/GRANDIOSITY (ET)

The belief that one is superior to other people; entitled to special rights and privileges; or not bound by the rules of reciprocity that guide normal social interaction. Often involves insistence that one should be able to do or have whatever one wants, regardless of what is realistic, what others consider reasonable, or the cost to others; OR an exaggerated focus on superiority (e.g., being among the most successful, famous, wealthy—in order to achieve *power* or *control* (not primarily for attention or approval). Sometimes includes excessive competitiveness toward, or domination of, others: asserting one's power, forcing one's point of view, or controlling the behavior of others in line with one's own desires—without empathy or concern for others' needs or feelings.

11. INSUFFICIENT SELF-CONTROL/SELF-DISCIPLINE (IS)

Pervasive difficulty or refusal to exercise sufficient self-control and frustration tolerance to achieve one's personal goals, or to restrain the excessive expression of one's emotions and impulses. In its milder form, patient presents with an exaggerated emphasis on *discomfort avoidance:* avoiding pain, conflict, confrontation, responsibility, or overexertion—at the expense of personal fulfillment, commitment, or integrity.

OTHER-DIRECTEDNESS

(An excessive focus on the desires, feelings, and responses of others, at the expense of one's own needs— in order to gain love and approval, maintain one's sense of connection, or avoid retaliation. Usually involves suppression and lack of awareness regarding one's own anger and natural inclinations. Typical family origin is based on conditional acceptance: Children must suppress important aspects of themselves in order to gain love, attention, and approval. In many such families, the parents' emotional needs and desires—or social acceptance and status—are valued more than the unique needs and feelings of each child.)

12. SUBJUGATION (SB)

Excessive surrendering of control to others because one feels *coerced*—usually to avoid anger, retaliation, or abandonment. The two major forms of subjugation are:

A. *Subjugation of needs:* Suppression of one's preferences, decisions, and desires.

B. *Subjugation of emotions:* Suppression of emotional expression, especially anger.

Usually involves the perception that one's own desires, opinions, and feelings are not valid or important to others. Frequently presents as excessive compliance, combined with hypersensitivity to feeling trapped. Generally leads to a buildup of anger, manifested in maladaptive symptoms (e.g., passive–aggressive behavior, uncontrolled outbursts of temper, psychosomatic symptoms, withdrawal of affection, "acting out," substance abuse).

13. SELF-SACRIFICE (SS)

Excessive focus on *voluntarily* meeting the needs of others in daily situations, at the expense of one's own gratification. The most common reasons are to prevent causing pain to others; to avoid guilt from feeling selfish; or to maintain the connection with others perceived as needy. Often results from an acute sensitivity to the pain of others. Sometimes leads to a sense that one's own needs are not being adequately met and to resentment of those who are taken care of. (Overlaps with concept of codependency.)

14. APPROVAL SEEKING/RECOGNITION SEEKING (AS)

Excessive emphasis on gaining approval, recognition, or attention from other people, or fitting in, at the expense of developing a secure and true sense of self. One's sense of esteem is dependent primarily on the reactions of others rather than on one's own natural inclinations. Sometimes includes an overemphasis on

(cont.)

FIGURE 6.1. *(cont.)*

status, appearance, social acceptance, money, or achievement—as means of gaining *approval, admiration*, or *attention* (not primarily for power or control). Frequently results in major life decisions that are inauthentic or unsatisfying, or in hypersensitivity to rejection.

OVERVIGILANCE AND INHIBITION

(Excessive emphasis on suppressing one's spontaneous feelings, impulses, and choices OR on meeting rigid, internalized rules and expectations about performance and ethical behavior—often at the expense of happiness, self-expression, relaxation, close relationships, or health. Typical family origin is grim, demanding, and sometimes punitive: Performance, duty, perfectionism, following rules, hiding emotions, and avoiding mistakes predominate over pleasure, joy, and relaxation. There is usually an undercurrent of pessimism and worry—that things could fall apart if one fails to be vigilant and careful at all times.)

15. NEGATIVITY/PESSIMISM (NP)

A pervasive, lifelong focus on the negative aspects of life (pain, death, loss, disappointment, conflict, guilt, resentment, unsolved problems, potential mistakes, betrayal, things that could go wrong, etc.) while minimizing or neglecting the positive or optimistic aspects. Usually includes an exaggerated expectation—in a wide range of work, financial, or interpersonal situations—that things will eventually go seriously wrong, or that aspects of one's life that seem to be going well will ultimately fall apart. Usually involves an inordinate fear of making mistakes that might lead to financial collapse, loss, humiliation, or being trapped in a bad situation. Because potential negative outcomes are exaggerated, these patients are frequently characterized by chronic worry, vigilance, complaining, or indecision.

16. EMOTIONAL INHIBITION (EI)

The excessive inhibition of spontaneous action, feeling, or communication—usually to avoid disapproval by others, feelings of shame, or losing control of one's impulses. The most common areas of inhibition involve (A) inhibition of *anger* and aggression; (B) inhibition of *positive impulses* (e.g., joy, affection, sexual excitement, play); (C) difficulty expressing *vulnerability* or *communicating* freely about one's feelings, needs, etc.; or (D) excessive emphasis on *rationality* while disregarding emotions.

17. UNRELENTING STANDARDS/HYPERCRITICALNESS (US)

The underlying belief that one must strive to meet very high *internalized standards* of behavior and performance, usually to avoid criticism. Typically results in feelings of pressure or difficulty slowing down; and in hypercriticalness toward oneself and others. Must involve significant impairment in pleasure, relaxation, health, self-esteem, sense of accomplishment, or satisfying relationships.

Unrelenting standards typically present as (A) *perfectionism*, inordinate attention to detail, or an underestimate of how good one's own performance is relative to the norm; (B) *rigid rules* and "shoulds" in many areas of life, including unrealistically high moral, ethical, cultural, or religious precepts; or (C) preoccupation with *time and efficiency*, so that more can be accomplished.

18. PUNITIVENESS (PU)

The belief that people should be harshly punished for making mistakes. Involves the tendency to be angry, intolerant, punitive, and impatient with those people (including oneself) who do not meet one's expectations or standards. Usually includes difficulty forgiving mistakes in oneself or others, because of a reluctance to consider extenuating circumstances, allow for human imperfection, or empathize with feelings.

The focus of cognitive therapy is on changing depressive thinking. These changes may be brought about in a variety of ways: through behavioral experiments, logical discourse, examination of evidence, problem solving, role playing, and imagery restructuring, to name just a few.

CHARACTERISTICS OF THERAPY

Cognitive therapy with adult depressed outpatients is usually undertaken in the therapist's office. It has most frequently been applied in a one-to-one setting. However, group cognitive therapy has also been shown to be successful with many depressed outpatients (Beutler et al., 1987; Jarrett & Nelson, 1987), although it may not be as effective as individual treatment (Wierzbicki & Bartlett, 1987). It is not unusual to involve spouses/partners, parents, and other family members during treatment. They may be used, for example, to provide information that will help patients test the validity of their thinking regarding how other family members view them. Moreover, couple therapy based on the cognitive model is often very effective in relieving depression related to chronic inter-personal problems (Beck, 1988; O'Leary & Beach, 1990).

In our clinical experience, a number of therapist characteristics contribute to effective cognitive therapy. First, cognitive therapists should ideally demonstrate the "nonspecific" therapy skills identified by other writers (see, e.g., Truax & Mitchell, 1971): They should be able to communicate warmth, genuineness, sincerity, and openness. Second, the most effective cognitive therapists seem to be especially skilled at seeing events from their patients' perspective (accurate empathy). They are able to suspend their own personal assumptions and biases while they are listening to depressed patients describe their reactions and interpretations. Third, skilled cognitive therapists can reason logically and plan strategies; they are not "fuzzy" thinkers. In this respect they resemble good trial lawyers, who can spot the sometimes subtle flaws in another individual's reasoning, and skillfully elicit a more convincing interpretation of the same events. Cognitive therapists plan strategies several steps ahead, anticipating the desired outcome. Fourth, the best practitioners of this approach are active. They have to be comfortable with taking the lead, providing structure and direction to the therapy process.

Although patient characteristics have received some empirical attention (Eifert et al., 1998; Padesky & Greenberger, 1995; Persons, Burns, & Perloff, 1988; Shea et al., 1990), we do not yet adequately know which patient characteristics are related to success in cognitive therapy. Our experience suggests that patients with major depressive disorder (single episode or recurrent)[4] and dysthymic disorder (with or without major depressive disorder) respond well to the cognitive therapy approach described in this chapter. The relapse prevention phase has proven particularly valuable in reducing the frequency of relapse with these patients. To the extent that the patient is diagnosed with Axis II personality disorders, the schema-focused phase of treatment may be significantly longer in duration and may become more crucial in obtaining a positive response to treatment.

Cognitive therapy can serve an important adjunctive role to pharmacotherapy with bipolar disorders (Basco & Rush, 1996; Colom, Vieta, Martinez, Jorquera, & Gasto, 1998;

Craighead, Miklowitz, Vajk, & Frank, 1998; Scott, 1996b), and is effective in treating patients with severe endogenous depression (Thase, Bowler, & Harden, 1991; Whisman, 1993).

It is advisable to assess patients' suitability for cognitive therapy (Padesky & Greenberger, 1995; Safran & Segal, 1990; Safran, Segal, Vallis, Shaw, & Samstag, 1993). In our experience, certain patient characteristics are predictive of a more rapid response. Patients who are appropriately introspective; can reason abstractly; are well organized and good planners; are conscientious about carrying out responsibilities; are employed; are not excessively angry, either at themselves or at other people; are less dogmatic and rigid in their thinking; can identify a clear precipitating event for the depressive episode; and have close relationships with others often show faster improvement in depressive symptoms through cognitive therapy. Age is not an obstacle, as both younger patients (Harrington, Wood, & Verduyn, 1998; Reinecke, Ryan, & DuBois, 1998) and older adults (Beutler et al., 1987; Gallagher-Thompson, Hanley-Peterson, & Thompson, 1990; Levendusky & Hufford, 1997; Koder, Brodaty, & Anstey, 1996) seem to benefit from cognitive therapy. A recent meta-analysis revealed that 63% of adolescents showed significant clinical improvement following CBT (Lewinsohn & Clarke, 1999). Studies of older patients show that "various forms of cognitive and behavioral psychotherapy can be as effective in treating geriatric depression as depressions occurring earlier in life" (Futterman, Thompson, Gallagher-Thompson, & Ferris, 1995, p. 511).

COLLABORATION

Basic to cognitive therapy is a collaborative relationship between patient and therapist. When the therapist and patient work together, the learning experience is enhanced for both, and a cooperative spirit is developed that contributes greatly to the therapeutic process. Equally important, the collaborative approach helps to ensure compatible goals for treatment and to prevent misunderstandings and misinterpretations between patient and therapist. Because of the importance of the collaborative relationship, we place great emphasis on the interpersonal skills of the therapist, the process of joint selection of problems to be worked on, regular feedback, and the investigative process we call "collaborative empiricism."

Interpersonal Qualities

Since collaboration requires that the patient trust the therapist, we emphasize those interpersonal qualities that contribute to trust. As noted above, warmth, accurate empathy, and genuineness are desirable personal qualities for the cognitive therapist, as for all psychotherapists. It is important that the cognitive therapist not seem to be playing the *role* of therapist. The therapist should be able to communicate, both verbally and nonverbally, that he/she is sincere, open, concerned, and direct. It is also important that the therapist not seem to be withholding impressions or information, or evading questions. The therapist should be careful not to seem critical or disapproving of the patient's perspective.

Rapport between patient and therapist is crucial in the treatment of depressed patients. When rapport is optimal, patients perceive the therapist as someone who is tuned in to their feelings and attitudes, someone who is sympathetic and understanding, and someone with whom they can communicate without having to articulate feelings in detail or qualify statements. When the rapport is good, both patient and therapist feel comfortable and secure.

A confident professional manner is also important in cognitive therapy. A therapist should convey relaxed confidence in his/her ability to help a depressed patient. Such confidence can help counteract the patient's initial hopelessness about the future. Since the cognitive therapist must sometimes be directive and impose structure, especially in the early stages of treatment, it is helpful to maintain a clear sense of professionalism.

Joint Determination
of Goals for Therapy

In the collaborative relationship, the patient and therapist work together to set therapeutic goals, determine priorities among them, and set an agenda for each session. Problems to be addressed over the course of therapy include specific depressive symptoms (e.g., hopelessness, crying, difficulty concentrating) and external problems (e.g., couple difficulties, career issues, child-rearing concerns). Priorities are then jointly determined in accordance with how much distress is generated by a particular problem and how amenable to change the particular problem is. During the agenda-setting portion of each therapy session (discussed in detail in the next section), therapist and patient together determine the items to be covered in that session. Through this collaborative process, target problems are selected on a weekly basis.

The process of problem selection often presents difficulties for the new cognitive therapist. These include failure to reach agreement on specific problems on which to focus, selection of peripheral concerns, and the tendency to move from problem to problem instead of persistently seeking a satisfactory solution to only one problem at a time. Because the problem selection process entails both structuring and collaboration on the part of the therapist, considerable skill is necessary.

Regular Feedback

Feedback is especially important in therapy with depressed patients; it is a crucial ingredient in developing and maintaining the collaborative therapeutic relationship. The cognitive therapist initiates the feedback component early in therapy by eliciting the patient's thoughts and feelings about many aspects of the therapy, such as the handling of a particular problem, the therapist's manner, and homework assignments. Since many patients misconstrue therapists' statements and questions, it is only through regular feedback that the therapist can ascertain whether he/she and the patient are on the same "wavelength." The therapist must also be alert for verbal and nonverbal clues to covert negative reactions.

As part of the regular feedback process, the cognitive therapist shares the rationale for each intervention mode. This helps to demystify the therapy process and facilitates the patient's questioning the validity of a particular approach. In addition, when the patients understand the connection between a technique or assignment the therapist uses and the solution of a problem, they are more likely to participate conscientiously.

The third element of the feedback process is for the therapist to check regularly to determine whether the patient understands his/her formulations. Patients sometimes agree with a formulation simply out of compliance, and depressed patients frequently exhibit both compliance and reluctance to "talk straight" with their therapists for fear of being rejected, criticized, or of making a mistake. The therapist must therefore make an extra effort to elicit feelings or wishes relevant to compliance (e.g., anxiety about rejection, wish to please) from the patient, and must be alert for verbal and nonverbal clues that the patient may not indeed understand the explanations.

As a regular part of the feedback process, at the close of each session the cognitive therapist provides a concise summary of what has taken place, and asks the patient to abstract and write down the main points from the session. The patient keeps this summary for review during the week. In practice, the therapist uses capsule summaries at least three times during a standard therapeutic interview: in preparing the agenda, in a midpoint recapitulation of the material covered up to that point, and in the final summary of the main points of the interview. Patients generally respond favorably to the elicitation of feedback and presentation of capsule summaries. We have observed that the development of empathy and rapport is facilitated by these techniques.

Collaborative Empiricism

When the collaborative therapeutic relationship has been successfully formed, the patient and therapist act as an investigative team. Though we elaborate on the investigative process later, it is appropriate to introduce it in the context of the collaborative relationship. As a team, patient and therapist approach the patient's automatic thoughts and schemas in the manner that scientists approach questions: Each thought or schema becomes a hypothesis to be tested, and evidence is gathered that supports or refutes the hypothesis. Events in the past, circumstances in the present, and possibilities in the future are the data that constitute evidence, and the conclusion to accept or reject the hypothesis is jointly reached by subjecting the evidence to logical analysis. Experiments may also be devised to

test the validity of particular cognitions. Cognitive therapists need not persuade patients of illogicality or inconsistency with reality, since patients "discover" their own inconsistencies. This guided discovery process is a widely accepted educational method and is one of the vital components of cognitive therapy.

THE PROCESS OF COGNITIVE THERAPY

We here attempt to convey a sense of how cognitive therapy sessions are structured and a sense of the course of treatment. Detailed discussion of particular techniques follows this section.

The Initial Sessions

A main therapeutic goal of the first interview is to produce some symptom relief. Relief of symptoms serves the patient's needs by reducing suffering, and also helps to increase rapport, collaboration, and confidence in the therapeutic process. Symptom relief should be based on more than rapport, sympathy, and implied promise of "cure," however, so the cognitive therapist seeks to provide a rational basis for reassurance by attempting to define a set of problems and demonstrating some strategies for dealing with them.

Problem definition continues to be a goal in the early stages of therapy. The therapist works with the patient to define specific problems to focus on during therapy sessions. The cognitive therapist does this by obtaining as complete a picture as possible of the patient's psychological and life situation difficulties. The therapist also seeks details concerning the depth of depression and particular symptomatology. Cognitive therapists are especially concerned with how patients see their problems.

Once the specific problems have been defined, the patient and the therapist establish priorities among them. Decisions are made on the basis of amenability to therapeutic change and centrality of the life problem or cognition to the patient's emotional distress. In order to help establish priorities effectively, the therapist must see the relationships among particular thoughts, particular life situations, and particular distressing emotions.

Another goal of the initial session is to illustrate the close relationship between cognition and emotion. When the therapist is able to observe the patient's mood change (e.g., crying), he/she points out the alteration in affect and asks for the patient's thoughts just before the mood shift. The therapist then labels the negative thought and points out its relationship to the change in mood. The therapist initially gears homework assignments toward helping the patient see the intimate connection between cognition and emotion.

A frequent requirement in the early stage of therapy is to socialize the patient to cognitive therapy. Particularly if they have previously undertaken analytically oriented or Rogerian therapies, many patients begin cognitive therapy expecting a more insight-oriented, nondirective therapeutic approach. The cognitive therapist can facilitate the transition to a more active and structured one by maintaining a problem-oriented stance, which often entails gently interrupting patients who tend to speculate about the sources of their problems and seek interpretations from the therapist.

Finally, the therapist must communicate the importance of self-help homework assignments during the initial session. The therapist can do this by stressing that doing the homework is actually more important than the therapy session itself. The therapist can also provide incentive by explaining that patients who complete assignments generally improve more quickly. The nature and implementation of self- help homework assignments are considered in further detail in a later section of this chapter.

The Progress of a
Typical Therapy Session

Each session begins with the establishment of an agenda for the session. This ensures optimal use of time in a relatively short-term, problem-solving therapeutic approach. The agenda generally begins with a short synopsis of the patient's experiences since the last session, including discussion of the homework assignment. The therapist then asks the patient what he/she wants to work on during the session, and often offers topics to be included.

When a short list of problems and topics has been completed, the patient and therapist determine the order in which to cover them and, if necessary, the time to be allotted to each topic. There are several issues to be considered in establishing priorities, including stage of therapy, severity of depression, likelihood of making progress in solving the problem, and potential pervasiveness of effect of a particular theme or topic. The cognitive therapist is sensitive to patients' occasional desires to talk about something that seems important to them at the moment, even if such discussion seems not to be productive in terms of other goals. This kind of flexibility characterizes the collaborative therapeutic relationship.

After these preliminary matters have been covered, the patient and therapist move on to the one or two problems to be considered during the session. The therapist begins the discussion of a problem by asking the patient a series of questions designed to clarify the nature of the patient's difficulty. In doing so, the therapist seeks to determine whether early maladaptive schemas, misinterpretations of events, or unrealistic expectations are involved. The therapist also seeks to discover whether the patient had unrealistic expectations, whether the patient's behavior was appropriate, and whether all possible solutions to the problem were considered. The patient's responses will suggest to the therapist a cognitive-behavioral conceptualization of why the patient is having difficulty in the area concerned. The therapist will now have discerned the one or two significant thoughts, schemas, images, or behaviors to be worked on. When this target problem has been selected, the therapist chooses the cognitive or behavioral techniques to apply and shares their rationale with the patient. The specific techniques used in cognitive therapy are explained in the following sections of this chapter.

At the close of the session, the therapist asks the patient for a summary, often in writing, of the major conclusions drawn during the session. The therapist asks for the patient's reactions to the session, in order to ascertain whether anything disturbing was said and in order to forestall any delayed negative reactions following the interview. Finally, the therapist gives a homework assignment designed to assist the patient in applying the particular skills and concepts from the session to the problem during the following week.

Progression of Session Content over Time

Although the structure of cognitive therapy sessions does not change during the course of treatment, the content often changes significantly. The first phase of treatment, symptom reduction, focuses on overcoming hopelessness, identifying problems, setting priorities, socializing the patient to cognitive therapy, establishing the collaborative relationship, demonstrating the relationship between cognition and emotion, labeling errors in thinking, and making rapid progress on a target problem. Therapy is initially centered on the patient's symptoms, with attention given to behavioral and motivational difficulties. Once the patient shows some significant changes in these areas, the emphasis shifts to the content and pattern of the patient's thinking.

In contrast to the first phase, the second, or schema-focused, phase emphasizes relapse prevention. Once the patient is feeling less depressed, the therapist and patient turn from specific thoughts about particular problems to core schemas about self and life, because they often underlie many of the patient's problems. Once identified, schemas reveal rules and formulas by which developing individuals learned to "make sense" of the world, and the schemas continue to determine how they organized perceptions into cognitions, set goals, evaluated and modified behavior, and understood events in their lives. Cognitive therapy aims at counteracting the effects of schemas and replacing dysfunctional techniques and methods with new approaches. If the schemas themselves can be changed, we believe that the patient will become less vulnerable to future depressions. Rehm (1990, p. 80) has noted:

> The negative schemata may be replaced in use by more realistic schemata under usual life circumstances, but they remain intact as "latent" schemata with the potential of reactivation under circumstances of loss. With time and the improvement of circumstances, these schemata may again become latent unless they are modified by some form of intervention.

In this second phase, the patient assumes increased responsibility for identifying problems, coming up with solutions, and implementing the solutions through homework assignments. The therapist increasingly assumes the role of advisor or consultant as the patient learns to implement therapeutic techniques without constant support. As the patient becomes a more effective problem solver, the frequency of sessions is reduced, and therapy is eventually discontinued.

The remainder of this chapter is devoted to a detailed description of these two phases of treatment.

PHASE 1: SYMPTOM REDUCTION

Cognitive Techniques

The specific cognitive techniques provide points of entry into the patient's cognitive organization. The cognitive therapist uses techniques for eliciting automatic thoughts, testing automatic thoughts, and identifying schemas to help both therapist and patient understand the patient's construction of reality. In applying specific cognitive techniques in therapy, it is important that the therapist work within the framework of the cognitive model of depression. Each set of techniques is discussed in turn.

Eliciting Automatic Thoughts

"Automatic thoughts" are those thoughts that intervene between outside events and the individual's emotional reactions to them. They often go unnoticed because they are part of a repetitive pattern of thinking and because they occur so often and so quickly. People rarely stop to assess their validity, because they are so believable, familiar, and habitual. The patient in cognitive therapy must learn to recognize these automatic thoughts for therapy to proceed effectively. The cognitive therapist and the patient make a joint effort to discover the particular thoughts that precede such emotions as anger, sadness, and anxiety. The therapist uses questioning, imagery, and role playing to elicit automatic thoughts.

The simplest method to uncover automatic thoughts is for therapists to ask patients what thoughts went through their minds in response to particular events. This questioning provides patients with a model for introspective exploration that they can use on their own when the therapist is not present and after completing of treatment.

Alternatively, when a patient is able to identify those external events and situations that evoke a particular emotional response, a therapist may use imagery by asking the patient to picture the situation in detail. The patient is often able to identify the automatic thoughts connected with actual situations when the image evoked is clear. In this technique, therapists ask patients to relax, close their eyes, and imagine themselves in the distressing situation. Patients describe in detail what is happening as they relive the event.

If a distressing event is an interpersonal one, cognitive therapists can utilize role playing. The therapist plays the role of the other person in the encounter, while patients play themselves. The automatic thoughts can usually be elicited when the patient becomes sufficiently engaged in the role play.

In attempting to elicit automatic thoughts, the therapist is careful to notice and point out any mood changes that occur during the session and to ask the patient's thoughts just before the shift in mood. Mood changes include any emotional reaction, such as tears or anger. This technique can be especially useful when the patient is first learning to identify automatic thoughts.

Once patients become familiar with the techniques for identifying automatic thoughts, they are asked to keep a Daily Record of Dysfunctional Thoughts (Beck et al., 1979; see Figure 6.2), in which they record the emotions and automatic thoughts that occur in upsetting situations between therapy sessions. In later sessions, they are taught to develop rational responses to their dysfunctional automatic thoughts and to record them in the appropriate column. The therapist and patient generally review the daily record from the preceding week near the beginning of the next therapy session.

Eliciting automatic thoughts should be distinguished from the interpretation process of other psychotherapies. In general, cognitive therapists work only with those automatic thoughts mentioned by patients. Suggesting thoughts to patients may undermine collaboration and may inhibit patients from learning to continue the process on their own. As a last resort, however, when nondirective strategies fail, a cognitive therapist may offer several possible automatic thoughts, asking a patient whether any of the choices fit.

Even when many efforts to elicit automatic thoughts have been made by the therapist,

SITUATION Describe: 1. Actual event leading to unpleasant emotion, or 2. Stream of thoughts, daydream, or recollection, leading to unpleasant emotion. DATE	EMOTION(S) 1. Specify sad/ anxious/ angry, etc. 2. Rate degree of emotion, 1-100.	AUTOMATIC THOUGHT(S) 1. Write automatic thought(s) that preceded emotion(s). 2. Rate belief in automatic thought(s), 0-100%.	RATIONAL RESPONSE 1. Write rational response to automatic thought(s). 2. Rate belief in rational response, 0-100%.	OUTCOME 1. Rerate belief in automatic thought(s), 0-100%. 2. Specify and rate subsequent emotions, 0-100.

Explanation: When you experience an unpleasant emotion, note the situation that seemed to stimulate the emotion. (If the emotion occurred while you were thinking, daydreaming, etc., please note this.) Then note the automatic thought associated with the emotion. Record the degree to which you believe this thought: 0% = not at all; 100% = completely. In rating degree of emotion: 1 = a trace; 100 = the most intense possible.

FIGURE 6.2. Daily record of dysfunctional thoughts.

sometimes the thought remains unavailable. When this is the case, the cognitive therapist tries to ascertain the particular meaning of the event that evoked the emotional reaction. For example, one patient began to cry whenever she had an argument with her roommate, who was a good friend. Efforts to elicit automatic thoughts proved unsuccessful. Only after the therapist asked a series of questions to determine the meaning of the event did it become clear that the patient connected having an argument or fight with the ending of the relationship. Through this process, the therapist and patient were able to see the meaning that triggered the crying.

Testing Automatic Thoughts

When the therapist and patient have managed to isolate a key automatic thought, they approach the thought as a testable hypothesis. This "scientific" approach is fundamental to cognitive therapy, where the patient learns to think in a way that resembles the investigative process. Through the procedures of gathering data, evaluating evidence, and drawing conclusions, the patient learns firsthand that one's view of reality can be quite different from what actually takes place. By designing experiments that subject their automatic thoughts to objective analysis, patients learn how to modify their thinking because they learn the *process* of rational thinking. Patients who learn to think this way during treatment will be better able to continue the empirical approach after the end of formal therapy.

The cognitive therapist approaches the testing of automatic thoughts by asking patients to list evidence from their experience for and against the hypothesis. Sometimes, after considering the evidence, patients will immediately reject the automatic thought, recognizing that it is either distorted or actually false.

When previous experience is not sufficient or appropriate to test a hypothesis, the therapist asks the patient to design an experiment for that purpose. The patient then makes a prediction and proceeds to gather data. When the data contradict the prediction, the patient can reject the automatic thought. The outcome of the experiment may, of course, confirm the patient's prediction. It is therefore very important for the therapist not to *assume* that the patient's automatic thought is distorted.

Some automatic thoughts do not lend themselves to hypothesis testing through the examination of evidence. In these cases, there are two options available: The therapist may produce evidence from his/her experience and offer it in the form of a question that reveals the contradiction; or the therapist can ask a question designed to uncover a logical error inherent in the patient's beliefs. The therapist might say, for example, to a male patient who is sure he cannot survive without a close personal relationship, "You were alone last year, and you got along fine; what makes you think you can't make it now?"

In testing automatic thoughts, it is sometimes necessary to refine the patient's use of a word. This is particularly true for global labels such as "bad," "stupid," or "selfish." What is needed in this case is an operational definition of the word. To illustrate, a patient at our clinic had the recurring automatic thought "I'm a failure in math." The therapist and patient had to narrow down the meaning of the word before they could test the thought. They operationalized "failure" in math as "being unable to achieve a grade of C after investing as much time studying as the average class member." Now they could examine past evidence and test the validity of the hypothesis. This process can help patients to see the all-inclusiveness of their negative self-assessments and the idiosyncratic nature of many automatic thoughts.

Reattribution is another useful technique for helping the patient to reject an inappropriate self-blaming thought. It is a common cognitive pattern in depression to ascribe blame or responsibility for adverse events to oneself. Reattribution can be used when the patient unrealistically attributes adverse occurrences to a personal deficiency, such as lack of ability or effort. The therapist and patient review the relevant events and apply logic to the available information to make a more realistic assignment of responsibility The aim of reattribution is not to absolve the patient of all responsibility, but to examine the many factors that help contribute to adverse events. Through this process, patients gain objectivity, relieve themselves of the burden of self-reproach, and can then search for ways to solve realistic problems or prevent their recurrence.

Another strategy involving reattribution is for therapists to demonstrate to patients that they use stricter criteria for assigning responsibility to their own unsatisfactory behavior than they use in evaluating the behavior of others. Cognitive therapists also use reattribution to show patients that some of their thinking or behavior problems can be symptoms of depression (e.g., loss of concentration) and not signs of physical decay.

When a patient is accurate in identifying a realistic life problem or skill deficit, the cognitive therapist can use the technique of generating alternatives, in which therapist and patient actively search for alternative solutions. Because a depressed person's reasoning often becomes restricted, an effort to reconceptualize the problem can result in the patient's seeing a viable solution that may previously have been rejected.

It should be noted that the cognitive techniques outlined above all entail the use of questions by the therapist. A common error we observe in new cognitive therapists is an exhortative style. We have found that therapists help patients to change their thinking more effectively by using carefully formed questions. If patients are prompted to work their own way through problems and reach their own conclusions, they will learn an effective problem-solving process. We elaborate on the use of questioning in cognitive therapy later in the chapter.

Behavioral Techniques

Behavioral techniques are used throughout the course of cognitive therapy, but are generally concentrated in the earlier stages of treatment. Behavioral techniques are especially necessary for those more severely depressed patients who are passive, anhedonic, socially withdrawn, and unable to concentrate for extended periods of time. By engaging such a patient's attention and interest, the cognitive therapist tries to induce the patient to counteract withdrawal and become more involved in constructive activity. From a variety of behavioral techniques, the therapist selects those that will help the patient cope more effectively with situational and interpersonal problems. Through homework assignments, the patient implements specific procedures for dealing with concrete situations or for using time more adaptively.

The cognitive therapist uses behavioral techniques with the goal of modifying automatic thoughts. For example, a patient who believes "I can't stay with anything any more" can modify this thought after completing a series of graded tasks designed to increase mastery. The severely depressed patient is caught in a vicious cycle in which a reduced activity level leads to a negative self-label, which in turn results in even further discouragement and consequent inactivity. Intervention with behavioral techniques can enter and change this self-destructive pattern.

The most commonly used behavioral techniques include scheduling activities that include both mastery and pleasure exercises, cognitive rehearsal, self-reliance training, role playing, and diversion techniques. The scheduling of activities is frequently used in the early stages of cognitive therapy to counteract loss of motivation, hopelessness, and excessive rumination. The therapist uses the Weekly Activity Schedule for planning activities hour by hour, day by day (see Figure 6.3). Patients maintain an hourly record of the activities that they engaged in. Activity scheduling also helps patients obtain more pleasure and a greater sense of accomplishment from activities on a daily basis. The patients rate each completed activity (using a 0–10 scale) for both mastery and pleasure. The ratings usually contradict patients' beliefs that they cannot accomplish or enjoy anything any more. In order to assist some patients in initiating mastery and pleasure activities, the therapist sometimes finds it necessary to subdivide an activity into segments ranging from the simplest to the most difficult and complex aspects of the activity. We call this the "graded task" approach. The subdivision enables depressed patients to undertake tasks that were initially impossible, and thus provides proof of success.

Cognitive rehearsal entails asking a patient to picture or imagine each step involved in the accomplishment of a particular task. This technique can be especially helpful with those patients who have difficulty carrying out a task that requires successive steps for its completion. Sometimes impairment in the ability to concentrate creates difficulties for the patient in focusing attention on the specific task. The imagery evoked by the cognitive rehearsal technique helps the patient to focus and helps the therapist to identify ob-

Note: Grade activities *M* for mastery and *P* for pleasure 0–10.							
		Mon.	Tues.	Wed.	Thurs.	Fri.	Sat..	Sun.
Morning	6–7							
	7–8							
	8–9							
	9–10							
	10–11							
	11–12							
Afternoon	12–1							
	1–2							
	2–3							
	3–4							
	4–5							
	5–6							
	6–7							
	7–8							
	8–9							
Evening	9–10							
	10–11							
	11–12							
	12–6							

FIGURE 6.3. Weekly activity schedule.

stacles that make the assignment difficult for the particular patient.

Some depressed patients rely on others to take care of most of their daily needs. With self-reliance training, patients learn to assume increased responsibility for routine activities such as showering, making their beds, cleaning the house, cooking their own meals, and shopping. Self-reliance involves gathering increased control over emotional reactions.

Role playing has many uses in cognitive therapy. It may be used to bring out automatic thoughts through the enactment of particular interpersonal situations, such as an encounter with a supervisor at work. Role playing may also be used, through homework assign-ments, to guide the patient in practicing and attending to new cognitive responses in problematic social encounters. A third use of role playing is to rehearse new behaviors. Thus role playing may be used as part of assertiveness training and is often accompanied by modeling and coaching.

Role reversal, a variation of role playing, can be very effective in helping patients test how other people might view their behavior. This is well illustrated by a patient who had a "humiliating experience" while buying some clothes in a store. After playing the role of the clerk, the patient had to conclude that she had insufficient data for her previous conclusion that she appeared clumsy and inept. Through role reversal, patients begin to view themselves less harshly as "self- sympathy" responses are elicited.

Finally, the therapist may introduce various diversion techniques to assist the patient in learning to reduce the intensity of painful affects. The patient learns to divert negative thinking through physical activity, social contact, work, play, and visual imagery. Practice with diversion techniques also helps the patient gain further control over emotional reactivity.

Questioning

As we have stressed throughout this chapter, questioning is a major therapeutic device in cognitive therapy. A majority of the therapist's comments during the therapy session are questions. Single questions can serve several purposes at one time, while carefully designed series of questions can help the patient consider a particular issue, decision, or opinion. The cognitive therapist seeks through questioning to elicit what patients are thinking, instead of telling patients what he/she believes they are thinking.

In the beginning of therapy, questions are employed to obtain a full and detailed picture of a patient's particular difficulties. They are used to obtain background and diagnostic data; to evaluate the patient's stress tolerance, capacity for introspection, coping methods, and so on; to obtain information about the patient's external situation and interpersonal context; and to modify vague complaints by working with the patient to arrive at specific target problems to work on.

As therapy progresses, the therapist uses questioning to explore approaches to problems, to help the patient to weigh advantages and disadvantages of possible solutions, to examine the consequences of staying with particular maladaptive behaviors, to elicit automatic thoughts, and to demonstrate early maladaptive schemas and their consequences. In short, the therapist uses questioning in most cognitive therapeutic techniques.

Although questioning is itself a powerful means of identifying and changing automatic thoughts and schemas, it is important that the questions be carefully and skillfully posed. If questions are used to "trap" patients into contradicting themselves, patients may come to feel that they are being attacked by the therapist or manipulated. Too many open-ended questions can leave patients wondering what the therapist expects of them. Therapists must carefully time and phrase questions to help patients recognize their thoughts and schemas and to weigh issues objectively.

Self-Help Homework Assignments

Rationale

Regular homework assignments are very important in cognitive therapy. When patients systematically apply what they have learned during therapy sessions to their outside lives, they are more likely to make significant progress in therapy and to be able to maintain their gains after termination of treatment. Homework assignments are often the means through which patients gather data, test hypotheses, and thus begin to modify their thoughts and schemas. In addition, the data provided through homework assignments help to shift the focus of therapy from the subjective and abstract to more concrete and objective concerns. When a patient and therapist review the previous week's activities during the agenda-setting portion of the interview, they may do so quickly, and the therapist can draw relationships between what takes place in the session and specific tasks, thereby avoiding tangents and side issues. Homework assignments further the patient's self-reliance and provide methods for the patient to continue working on problems after the end of treatment. Cognitive therapists emphasize the importance of homework by sharing with patients their rationale for assigning homework in therapy. They are also careful to explain the particular benefits to be derived from each individual assignment.

Assigning and Reviewing Homework

The cognitive therapist designs each assignment for the particular patient. The assignment should be directly related to the content of the therapy session, so that the patient understands its purpose and importance. Each task should be clearly articulated and very specific in nature. Near the end of each session, the assignment is written in duplicate, with one copy going to the therapist and one to the patient.

Some typical homework assignments include reading a book or article about a specific problem, practicing diversion or relaxation techniques, counting automatic thoughts on a wrist counter, rating activities for pleasure and mastery on the Weekly Activity Schedule, maintaining a Daily Record of Dysfunctional Thoughts, and listening to a tape of the therapy session.

During the therapy session, therapists ask for patients' reactions to homework assignments. They ask, for example, whether the assignment is clear and manageable. In order to determine potential impediments, the therapist may ask the patient to imagine taking the steps involved in the assignment. This technique can be especially helpful during the earlier stages of therapy. The patient assumes greater responsibility for developing homework assignments as therapy progresses through the middle and later stages.

It is essential that the patient and therapist review the previous week's homework during the therapy session itself. If they do not, the patient may conclude that the homework assignments are not important. During the first part of the therapy sessions, the therapist and patient discuss the last week's assignment, and the therapist summarizes the results.

Difficulties in Completing Homework

When a patient does not complete homework assignments, or does them without conviction, the cognitive therapist elicits automatic thoughts, schemas, or behavioral problems that may help both therapist and patient understand where the difficulty resides. The therapist does not presuppose that the patient is being "resistant" or "passive–aggressive." When the difficulties have been successfully identified, the therapist and patient work collaboratively to surmount them. It is, of course, common for patients to have difficulties in completing homework, and here we consider some of the typical problems and ways to counteract them.

When patients do not understand the assignment completely, the therapist should explain it more fully, specifying his/her expectations in detail. Sometimes using the behavioral technique of cognitive rehearsal (described above) can be helpful in such situations.

Some patients believe that they are naturally disorganized and cannot maintain records

and follow through on detailed assignments. The therapist can usually help invalidate such general beliefs by asking patients about other circumstances in which they make lists—for example, when planning a vacation or shopping trip. The therapist can also ask these patients whether they could complete the assignment if there were a substantial reward entailed. This kind of question helps such a patient recognize that self-control is not the problem; rather, the patient does not believe that the reward is great enough. When the patient comes to see that the problem is an attitudinal one, the therapist and patient can proceed to enumerate the advantages of completing the assignment.

More severely depressed patients may need assistance to structure their time so that homework becomes a regular activity. This can generally be accomplished by setting a specific time each day for the homework assignment. If necessary, a patient and therapist can set up a reward or punishment system to make sure the homework gets done. For example, patients can reward themselves for doing the assignment with a special purchase, or punish themselves for not doing it by not watching a favorite television program.

Some patients are afraid of failing the assignments or of doing them inadequately. In these cases, the therapist can explain that self-help assignments cannot be "failed": Doing an assignment partially is more helpful than not doing it at all, and mistakes provide valuable information about problems that still need to be worked on. In addition, since performance is not evaluated, patients cannot lose if they view the activity from a more adaptive perspective.

Sometimes patients believe their problems are too deeply embedded and complex to be resolved through homework assignments. The therapist can explain to these patients that even the most complex undertakings begin with and consist of small concrete steps. Some writers, for example, resolve their "writers' blocks" by taking the attitude "If I can't write a book, I can at least write a paragraph." When enough paragraphs have been written, the result is a book. A therapist and patient can consider the advantages and disadvantages of the patient's believing that problems cannot be solved by doing homework. Or the therapist can ask the patient to experiment before reaching such a conclusion. In those instances where a patient believes that he/she has not made enough progress, and therefore that the homework is not helpful, the therapist can detail the progress the patient has made or can help the patient see that it may take more time before substantial change can be perceived.

When patients seem to resent being given assignments, the therapist can encourage them to develop their own assignments. The therapist might also offer the patients alternative assignments from which to choose, making one of the alternatives noncompliance with homework assignments. If patients choose noncompliance, the therapist can help to examine the consequences of that choice. Still another strategy is to present patients with a consumer model of therapy: Patients have a certain goal (overcoming depression), and the therapist has a means of achievement to offer; patients are free to use or reject the tools, just as they are free to buy or not to buy in the marketplace.

When patients believe that improvement can be made just as readily without homework, therapists have two options. First, they can offer their own clinical experience that most patients who held that opinion were proven wrong and progressed more slowly in therapy. The other option is to set up an experiment for a given period of time, during which patients do not have to complete assignments. At the end of the predetermined period, therapists and patients can evaluate the patients' progress during that time interval. Once again, it is important for cognitive therapists to keep an open mind: Some patients do indeed effect significant change without formally completing homework assignments.

Special Problems

The novice cognitive therapist often makes the error of staying with the standard method outlined above even if it is not working very well. The cognitive therapist should be flexible enough to adapt to the needs of patients and to the several special problems that commonly arise in therapy. We have grouped these special problems into two categories: difficulties in the therapist–patient relationship, and problems in which the therapy itself seems not to be working.

Therapist–Patient Relationship Difficulties

The first set of problems concerns the therapist–patient relationship itself. When the therapist first perceives a patient to be dissatisfied, angry, or hostile, it is imperative that the therapist present the patient with these observations. The therapist can then ask about the accuracy of the observations, the patient's feelings, and thoughts the patient has about the therapist. It is essential for therapists to be aware that many interventions can be misinterpreted by depressed patients in a negative way.

With problems of misinterpretation, therapists approach the misinterpretations in the same way that they approach other thoughts: They work with the patients to gather data and search for alternative accounts of the evidence. Difficulties in the therapist–patient relationship can generally be resolved through dialogue. There are times when therapists may need to tailor behavior to the particular needs of individual patients. For instance, therapists may become freer with self-disclosure and personal reactions to meet the needs of patients who persist in seeing the therapists as impersonal. Similarly, therapists can make a point of checking formulations of the patients' thoughts more frequently to meet the needs of patients who continue to believe that the therapists do not understand them.

It is imperative in situations like these for the therapist not to assume that the patient is being stubbornly resistant or irrational. Cognitive therapists collaborate with patients to achieve a better understanding of the patients' responses. The reactions themselves often provide data regarding the kinds of distortions patients make in their other social and personal relationships. The patients' responses therefore give the therapists the opportunity to work with patients on their maladaptive interpretations in relationships.

Unsatisfactory Progress

A second set of problems occurs when the therapy appears not to be working, even when the patient conscientiously completes homework assignments and the collaborative relationship seems successful. Sometimes problems stem from inappropriate expectations on the part of the patient—or unrealistic expectations on the part of the therapist—regarding the rapidity and consistency of change. When therapy seem not to be progressing as quickly as it "should," both patient and therapist must remember that ups and downs are to be anticipated in the course of treatment. It is important for therapists to keep in mind that some patients simply progress more slowly than others. The therapist or patient, or both, may be minimizing small changes that have indeed been taking place. In this case the therapist can emphasize the small gains that have been made and remind the patient that large goals are attained through small steps toward them.

At times, patients' hopelessness can lead them to invalidate their gains. Therapists should seek to uncover the thoughts and maladaptive assumptions that contribute to the pervasive hopelessness. In these cases, therapists must work to correct mistaken notions about the process of change and about the nature of depression before further progress in therapy can occur.

In some cases in which therapy seems not to be working successfully, it may be that some of the therapeutic techniques have not been correctly used. Problems often arise when patients do not really believe the rational responses or are not able to remember them in times of emotional distress. It is important for a therapist to determine the amount of belief a patient has in the rational responses and help the patient use the new responses as closely as possible to the moment when the automatic thoughts occur. To the patient who does not fully believe a rational response, the therapist can suggest an experimental stance—taking the new belief and "trying it on for size." The patient who cannot think of answers because of emotional upset should be told that states of emotional distress make reasoning more difficult, and that thoughts such as "If this doesn't work, nothing will" can only aggravate the problem. Patients should be assured that they will be able to think of rational responses more readily with practice.

Another problem deriving from the misapplication of cognitive therapy techniques occurs when the therapist uses a particular technique inflexibly. It is often necessary for the therapist to try out several behavioral or cognitive techniques before finding an approach to which a patient responds well. The cognitive therapist must stay with a particular technique for a while to see whether it works, but he/she must also be willing to try an alternative technique when it becomes apparent that the patient is not improving. To give a specific example, behavioral homework assignments are sometimes more helpful with particular patients, even though the therapist has every reason to predict in advance that cognitive assignments will be more effective.

In some instances where it appears that little progress is being made in therapy, it turns out that the therapist has selected a tangential problem. The cognitive therapist should be alert to this possibility, especially during the early stages of therapy. When there appears to be little or no significant change in depression level, even when the patient seems to have made considerable progress in a problem area, the therapist should consider the possibility that the most distressing problem has not yet been uncovered. A typical example of this kind of difficulty is the patient who presents difficulty at work as the major problem when it turns out that couple problems are contributing significantly to the work difficulties. The real issue may be withheld by the patient because it seems too threatening.

Finally, cognitive therapy is not for everyone. If the therapist has tried all available approaches to the problem and has consulted with other cognitive therapists, it may be best to refer the patient to another therapist, with either the same or a different orientation.

Regardless of why therapy is not progressing satisfactorily, cognitive therapists should attend to their own cognitions. They must maintain a problem-solving stance and not allow themselves to be influenced by their patients' despair or to see themselves as incompetent. Hopelessness in patients or therapists is an obstacle to problem solving. If therapists can effectively counteract their own negative self-assessments and other dysfunctional thoughts, they will be better able to concentrate on helping patients find solutions to their problems.

Case Study of Irene: The Symptom Reduction Phase

In the case study that follows, we describe the course of treatment for a depressed woman seen at our clinic. Through the case study, we illustrate many of the concepts described earlier in this chapter, including the eliciting of automatic thoughts, the cognitive triad of depression, collaborative empiricism, structuring a session, and feedback.

Assessment and Presenting Problems

The patient, whom we will call "Irene," phoned the center for help because she had heard about cognitive therapy on a local radio show. Irene recognized that she was experiencing many of the symptoms of depression described on the program. She went through the typical assessment procedure at the center, which consists of 1½ hours of a standard clinical interview and an additional 1½ hours of paper-and-pencil testing.

The intake interviewer reported that Irene was a 29-year-old woman, living with her husband and two young children. She was a high school graduate who had stopped work after marrying. Irene described her major problems as depression (for the past few years), difficulty coping with her children, marital conflict, and a sense of "being kept back" by her husband. In terms of her marriage, Irene said she felt stigmatized because her husband had just been released from a drug abuse treatment center. Furthermore, her husband had just been laid off from work and was thus unemployed. He refused to participate in marital counseling with her.

Irene said she had been socially isolated since her marriage, although she reported having had normal friendships as a child and teenager. One factor that she felt made it difficult for her to socialize with other women in the neighborhood was her belief that they looked down on her because she had such poor control over her children and because of her husband's drug record.

The interviewer diagnosed the patient as having major depressive disorder, recurrent, on Axis I and dependent personality disorder on Axis II. Her test scores verified the diagnosis of depression. Irene's Beck Depression Inventory (BDI) score was 29, placing her in the moderate to severe range of depression. Her most prominent depressive symptoms included guilt, self-blame, loss of pleasure, irritability, social withdrawal, inability to make decisions, fatigue, difficulty motivating herself to perform daily functions, loneliness, and loss of libido.

Session 1

Irene was treated initially by one of us (A. T. B.). Since an intake interview had already been completed by another therapist, this therapist did not spend time reviewing symptoms in detail or taking a history. The session began with Irene's describing the "sad states" she was having. The therapist (T) almost immediately started to elicit the patient's (P) automatic thoughts during these periods.

T: What kind of thoughts were you having during these 4 days when you said your thoughts kept coming over and over again?

P: Well, they were just—mostly, "Why is this happening again?"—because, you know, this isn't the first time he's been out of work. You know, "What am I going to do?"—like I have all different thoughts. They are all in different things, like being mad at him, being mad at myself for being in this position all the time. Like I want to leave him, or if I could do anything to make him straighten out and not depend so much on him. There's a lot of thoughts in there.

T: Now can we go back a little bit to the sad states that you have? Do you still have that sad state?

P: Yeah.

T: You have it right now?

P: Yeah, sort of. They were sad thoughts about—I don't know—I get bad thoughts, like a lot of what I'm thinking is bad things. Like not—there is like, ah, it isn't going to get any better, it will stay that way. I don't know. Lots of things go wrong, you know, that's how I think.

T: So one of the thoughts is that it's not going to get any better?

P: Yeah.

T: And sometimes you believe that completely?

P: Yeah, I believe it, sometimes.

T: Right now do you believe it?

P: I believe—yeah, yeah.

T: Right now you believe that things are not going to get better?

P: Well, there is a glimmer of hope, but it's mostly . . .

T: What do you kind of look forward to in terms of your own life from here on?

P: Well, what I look forward to—I can tell you, but I don't want to tell you. (*Giggles*) Um, I don't see too much.

T: You don't want to tell me?

P: No, I'll tell you, but it's not sweet and great what I think. I just see me continuing on the way I am, the way I don't want to be, like not doing anything, just being there, like sort of with no use—that like my husband will still be there, and he will, you know, he'll go in and out of drugs or whatever he is going to do, and I'll just still be there, just in the same place.

By inquiring about Irene's automatic thoughts, the therapist began to understand her perspective—that she would go on forever, trapped, with her husband in and out of drug centers. This illustrates the hopelessness about the future that is characteristic of most depressed patients. A second advantage to this line of inquiry is that the therapist introduced Irene to the idea of looking at her own thoughts, which is central to cognitive therapy.

As the session continued, the therapist probed the patient's perspective regarding her marital problems. The therapist then made a decision not to focus on the marriage as the first therapeutic target, since it would probably require too much time before providing symptom relief. Instead, the therapist chose to focus on Irene's inactivity and withdrawal. This is frequently the first therapeutic goal in working with a severely depressed patient.

In the sequence that follows, the therapist guided Irene to examine the advantages and disadvantages of staying in bed all day.

P: Usually I don't want to get out of bed. I want to stay there and just keep the covers up to my head and stay there, you know. I don't want to do anything. I just want to be left alone and just keep everything out, keep everything away from me.

T: Now do you feel better when you get under the covers and try to shut everything out?

P: Yeah.

T: You do feel better?

P: Yeah, I feel better that way.

T: And so how much time do you spend doing that?

P: Now, lately? I don't get to do it too much, because I have two kids. I don't ever get to do it all that much. I would love to do it more. It would help. I mean, I feel safe, sort of secure, like they are over on the other side of the wall and they are not near me.

T: Now after you have spent some time in the covers, how do you feel about yourself?

P: If I'm laying there, I don't know.

T: Let's say afterwards?

P: Afterwards? I don't usually have any bad feeling about—oh, yeah. I do, I feel like, "Oh, Christ, you've been laying there doing nothing. You should have been doing this, you should have been doing that, you should have got up and done something"—whatever it is I was supposed to do. You know, even when I'm there, I'm not making any solutions to any problems. I'm just there.

T: On the one hand you seem to enjoy, and on the other hand afterwards you're a little bit critical of yourself?

Note that the therapist did not try to debate or exhort Irene to get out of bed. Rather, through questioning, he encouraged her to examine more closely her assumption that she was really better off in bed. This is the process we call "collaborative empiricism." By the second session, Irene had reexamined her hypothesis about remaining in bed.

P: About staying in bed versus getting up, I thought about that the other day. I thought when I told you—like I said something about like keeping the bad things away from me. Like when I was under the covers or just staying in bed, they weren't really kept away from me. Like I always felt like I was always beating them down, I always had to ward them off. I don't know. I thought I told you it made me feel better to stay there, but I don't know if it really did. I don't think it did, now that I am thinking about it.

T: It is funny then that when you talked about it, your recollection was that it actually was comforting, but that sometimes happens with people. It happens to me too. I think that something is really good that's not so hot when I actually check it out.

We now return to the first session. After some probing by the therapist, Irene mentioned that cognitive therapy "is like my last hope." The therapist used this as an opportunity to explore her hopelessness and suicidal thinking.

T: What was going through your mind when you said, "This is my last hope"? Did you have some kind of vision in your mind?

P: Yeah, that if it doesn't work out that I don't think that I could take living like this the rest of my life.

T: If it doesn't work out, then what?

P: Then I wouldn't really care what happened to me.

T: Did you have something more concrete in mind?

P: Well, right this minute I don't think I could commit suicide, but maybe if afterwards I thought there was nothing left, I could. I don't know, though—I thought about suicide before, but I have never been able to bring myself to do it. I've come close, but I've never been able to succeed. I know certain things stop me, like my kids. I don't think—even though I sometimes think I'm not as good a mother as I could be—I think they would be a lot worse off with my husband. I think it would destroy some other people, like my mother, if I did something like that, you know. That is what I think mainly stops me, my children and my mother. Just that they would—I guess I'm afraid that if I did something like that, maybe my mother would feel that she failed somewhere, which is not true, I don't think. And just about my kids—I couldn't trust my husband with my kids. I think it would really—even though I'm messed up—I think that he would mess them up more.

T: Now these are some of the reasons for not committing suicide. Now what are some of the reasons why you wanted to, do you think?

P: Because sometimes it is just hopeless, there are no solutions, there's no—it continues constantly the same way, all the time.

The therapist wanted the patient to feel as free as possible to discuss suicidal thoughts; thus he tried hard to understand both the reasons for her hopelessness and the deterrents to suicide. After determining that she had no imminent plans to make an attempt (although she had made an attempt a couple of years earlier), the therapist said that he would work with her to solve the problems in her life now, and also "work things out inside your own head." He then asked her to select a small problem that they could work on together.

T: Now are there any other smaller decisions that you could make that would affect your life right away?

P: I don't know. Well, I guess just trying—like for a long time I have been wanting to go out and do other things, like I don't know, join something, feel like I'm a part of something, you know, and I haven't been able to do it. I don't know if it's financial why I haven't been able to do it. I mean, that is the excuse I come up with, but I think sometimes it is not financial. Sometimes it's just I don't get up and do it.

T: Well, is there some specific group that you have in mind you could join?

P: I don't know. (*Giggles*) I guess that is another decision I can't make. I think, like, everything interests me and nothing interests me.

T: Why don't we make a list and see what happens—a mental list? What are some of the things you would be interested in doing?

P: Tennis, I have been wanting to do that for a long time.

T: Now does this involve joining a tennis team?

P: Yeah, well, that is what I would want to do.

T: Well, do you know people who belong to it?

P: No, I know other people, but they don't belong to it in Philadelphia. Well, they do, but I guess . . .

T: How would you go about finding out about a tennis team?

P: You would only have to go down to the nearest tennis court and that's it.

T: What would happen when you went down there?

P: I don't know. I have never been on one.

T: Well, what do you think you could do when you got there?

P: I guess you just—I don't know how many people are in one group. I don't know if you have to have a whole group go down with you and say, "OK, we want to be a team," but I guess there are some people who are short of the whole group and then you could get on that team. You know, I guess.

T: Well, how could you get that information?

P: I guess if I went down there.

T: Do you think you could get the information if you went down there?

P: Yeah.

T: You could find out then whether you join as individuals or groups of how many, if they need somebody to fill in?

P: Yeah, uh huh.

T: How do you feel about doing that?

P: Kind of stupid. (*Giggles*)

T: Does it seem so trivial?

P: Yeah, it seems like, well, why didn't I just do it before?

T: Well, you probably had good reasons for not doing it before. Probably you were just so caught up in the hopelessness.

P: Right, right.

T: When you are hopeless you tend to deny, as it were, or cut off possible solutions. Remember when your husband lost his job, you said that you refused to accept the fact that he would get compensation?

P: Right.

T: When you get caught up in hopelessness, then, there is nothing you can do—is that what you think?

P: Yeah.

T: So then, rather than be down on yourself because you haven't gone over before, why don't we carry you right through?

This excerpt illustrates the process of graded tasks that is so important in the early stages of therapy with a depressed patient.

The therapist asked the patient a series of questions to break down the process of joining a tennis league into smaller steps. Irene realized that she had known all along what to do, but, as the therapist pointed out, her hopelessness prevented her from seeing possible solutions.

P: First steps are really hard for me.

T: First steps are harder for everybody, but that's why there is an old expression: "A journey of a thousand miles starts with the first step."

P: That's very true.

T: Because that step—it's very important to take the first step, and second step, and third step, and so on. So all you have to do is take one, and you don't have to take giant steps.

P: Well, yeah, I can see that now. I don't think I'd seen it before. I think before I was thinking every step was just as hard as the first step, and maybe it's not that way at all. Maybe it's easier.

In the second session, Irene reported success.

P: I called about the tennis, and they said just to come in and give them your name. That's all you had to do, just come in and give them your name, which was really easy to do. It would have been a first step. I was surprised that it was so easy. I guess I thought it was going to be a lot harder, but it wasn't.

At the end of the first session, the therapist helped Irene fill out the Weekly Activity Schedule for the coming week. The activities were quite simple, such as taking the children out, visiting her mother, reading a book, going shopping, and checking out the tennis team. Finally, the therapist asked her for feedback about the session and about her hopelessness.

T: Do you have any reactions?

P: I know I went through stages from happy to sad to happy to sad to happy to sad.

T: Where are you at now?

P: Where am I at now? Half-decent.

T: Half-sad, half-happy?

P: No, a little more happier than I am sadder.

T: Now it may be that when you leave, you'd be thinking that we haven't really worked on the big problems, and you have to have a way to answer that.

P: I guess I'll just say it will take a little more time.

Session 2

In the second session, the therapist began by collaborating with Irene to set an agenda. Irene wanted to discuss an argument she had had with her husband and to deal with her feelings of inferiority; the therapist added the issue of activity versus inactivity to the agenda. They then reviewed the previous homework. Irene had carried out all the scheduled activities and had also listed some of her negative thoughts in between sessions. Her BDI score had dropped somewhat. (Patients routinely fill out the BDI before each session, so that both the patient and the therapist can monitor the progress of treatment.)

Irene then shared her list of negative thoughts with the therapist. One concern was that she had cried during the first session.

P: Well, I know you are a professional, but I felt like I was changed from one mood so easily to another. Like that sort of—when I interpreted it to myself, I felt like I could be manipulated, and that was like—I don't know, I don't want to be easily led.

T: Well, that's good. You had the thought then that I was manipulating you, that I was somehow pushing the buttons and turning the knobs?

P: Well, yeah.

The therapist offered Irene an alternative perspective:

T: I would say just that I wasn't intending to manipulate you, that you yourself are not so gullible that you were easily manipulated. It is just that the way we were going through the interview, we were hitting some points that were sensitive and other points that were not so sensitive. And when we talked about the negatives, you felt worse, and when we talked about some positive things, then you felt better or perhaps when you were able to work

through some particular problem, get on top of it, made you feel better. Then we go on to another problem, you feel worse. So it was just the nature of the interview, rather than having anything to do with you being weak and me being overpowering, manipulative. But that was very good, and going through this explanation again [may help] not only to give you the information, but to show you how to cope with the negative thoughts.

This is an illustration of how a cognitive therapist can utilize events during the session to teach patients to identify their automatic thoughts and to consider alternative interpretations.

Irene next discussed her argument with her husband, and specifically her thought that maybe she should leave him. She and the therapist agreed that it might be better to wait until her depression lifted a little before trying to make such a major decision. We often recommend that depressed patients postpone major decisions until they are able to regain a realistic perspective on their lives.

The therapist provided a summary of the two key themes he had identified from listening to Irene's automatic thoughts about her husband and about therapy. The first theme was her fear of being controlled by other people, including the therapist (subjugation schema); the second was that other people did not care about her (emotional deprivation schema). Cognitive therapists often identify and begin to correct early maladaptive schemas during the first phase of treatment. They work more intensively on changing these schemas during the second phase when the patient is less depressed, as we elaborate in the next section of this chapter. In the segment that follows, the therapist explained how he arrived at the conclusion that emotional deprivation was an important schema for Irene.

T: Like, for instance, when you say the way your husband treats you, it sounded as though you were really bothered about his lack of concern for your feelings and wishes.

P: Yeah, yeah.

T: I don't want to make too much out of this at the moment, but you also said that after your second baby was born, you had the feeling that nobody cared for you—namely, your family.

P: Well, I don't know what happened. I can't remember the circumstances of what happened.

T: But whatever it was, this was the upshot.

P: Yeah.

T: So one of the things that seizes you—can really grab hold and make you feel terrible—is this notion that nobody cares, and that you are so sensitive in that one area that you thought that we were just using you as a guinea pig here, and they were just interested in seeing how I work and not interested in you. The clinic wasn't interested in you, and I wasn't interested in you. So, again, it seems to be this notion of people who are important not caring. Is that correct?

P: Yeah. In most instances, yeah.

T: In all the instances I have mentioned?

P: Yeah.

T: Well, what this tells us is that you have to be alert to the sense that they don't care, because this can really make you feel bad. It may not even be correct. If you found out, for instance, that your mother does care, so that you are wrong in thinking that, but still the thought came through very strongly. And your current thought is that we don't care, or it was.

About halfway through the session, the therapist asked the patient for feedback thus far:

T: Now at this point, is there anything that we have discussed today that bothered you?

P: That bothered me?

T: Yeah.

P: Uh, I'm feeling stupider and stupider as we go along.

T: That is important, OK. Can you . . .

P: Well, I'm trying not to, but I don't know.

T: Well, if you are, you are. Why don't you just let yourself feel stupid and tell me about it?

P: Well, I just feel that I should be recognizing all these things, too.

This comment led to identification of a third theme, the incompetence schema. Irene

had been viewing herself as increasingly dumb for the past few years. By this point, however, the patient was beginning to catch on to the idea of answering her thoughts more rationally. After the therapist pointed out the negative thought in the excerpt above, the patient volunteered:

P: I know what to do with the thought "I'm stupid for not recognizing these things myself."

T: What are you going to do with it right this minute?

P: I am going to say, "Well, you are the professional. You are supposed to see these things."

T: Right, you'd fire me if I didn't see them. Right?

P: I didn't think of that, but (laughs) . . . no, I wouldn't fire you. I wouldn't fire anybody.

T: So what you are saying is that since I am professionally trained, I can see certain things. The other thing is that other people are objective and can often see things in us much more readily than we can in ourselves. It just happens to be a fact of human nature.

P: Yeah.

The same automatic thoughts arose again later in the session, when Irene felt stupid for not knowing the answer to one of the therapist's questions. In the extended excerpt below, the therapist helped her set up an experiment to test the thought "I look dumb."

T: OK, now let's just do an experiment and see if you yourself can respond to the automatic thought, and let's see what happens to your feeling. See if responding rationally makes you feel worse or makes you feel better.

P: OK.

T: OK, "Why didn't I answer that question right? I look dumb." What is the rational answer to that? A realistic answer?

P: Why didn't I answer that question? Because I thought for a second that was what I was supposed to say, and then when I heard the question over again, then I realized that was not what I heard. I didn't hear the question right; that's why I didn't answer it right.

T: OK, so that is the fact situation. And so is the fact situation that you look dumb, or you just didn't hear the question right?

P: I didn't hear the question right.

T: Or is it possible that I didn't say the question in such a way that it was clear?

P: Possible.

T: Very possible. I'm not perfect, so it's very possible that I didn't express the question properly.

P: But instead of saying you made a mistake, I would still say I made a mistake.

T: We'll have to watch the video and see. Whichever. Does it mean if I didn't express the question, if I made a mistake, does it make me dumb?

P: No.

T: And if you made the mistake, does it make you dumb?

P: No, not really.

T: But you felt dumb?

P: But I did, yeah.

T: Do you feel dumb still?

P: No.

The preceding exchange demonstrates the use of reattribution. At first, the patient interpreted her difficulty answering the therapist as evidence that she was stupid. As a result of the guided discovery approach, she reattributed the problem to one of two factors: Either she didn't hear the question right, or the therapist did not ask the question clearly enough. At the end of the experiment, Irene expressed satisfaction that she was finally recognizing this tendency to distort her appraisals.

P: Right now I feel glad. I'm feeling a little better that at least somebody is pointing all these things out to me, because I have never seen this before. I never knew that I thought that I was that dumb.

T: So you feel good that you have made this observation about yourself?

P: Right.

After summarizing the main points of the second session, the therapist assigned home-work for the coming week: to fill out the Daily Record of Dysfunctional Thoughts (see Figure 6.2) and the Weekly Activity Schedule (with mastery and pleasure ratings) (see Figure 6.3).

Session 3

By the beginning of the third session, Irene's mood had visibly improved. She had joined a tennis league with her sister, and had begun to respond more rationally to her automatic thoughts about being dumb. In fact, she was practicing her cognitive therapy skills by helping a friend with a similar problem of self-blame. The primary agenda item Irene chose to work on was "how I back away from other people," an aspect of her subjugation schema. She described an incident in which a neighbor was taking advantage of her, but she could not assert herself. In discussing her thoughts, Irene expressed the ambivalence that is characteristic of the subjugation schema, and that interfered with her behaving assertively.

P: I want to be a nice person. I don't want to cause a lot of trouble. I don't want to be fighting with everybody constantly. But I don't like myself when I give in too much, too.

T: Well, is it possible to be a nice person without giving in all the time?

P: I guess.

The therapist continued probing to understand why the patient believed that a nice person cannot get angry or be assertive. As the discussion progressed, it became obvious that in the abstract the patient could see that she was not necessarily bad because she got angry, but that in real-life situations Irene nevertheless felt she was wrong. The therapist's task next was to help the patient bring her rational thinking to bear on her distorted thinking *in the context of a concrete event*. At the therapist's request, Irene then described an argument in which she yelled at a neighbor with good justification, yet felt she was bad. The therapist helped her use logic to evaluate her maladaptive schema.

T: You had the thought "I was wrong to get mad at her, to yell at her." It seems likely that you believed that thought, and that [you believed] the thought was right and that you were wrong. And since you thought that thought was right, you then had the wish to withdraw behind your hat, as it were.

P: Right.

T: Now, let's look at it. Do you think that thought is correct?

P: No. I don't see how it could have been correct.

T: So, according to your own values, you don't think that it is wrong to stick up for your rights?

P: Right.

T: And do you think that you were sticking up for yourself when she called the cops for a car that is blocking her car?

P: Well, the car shouldn't have been blocking her car . . .

T: That wasn't—the question was, should she have called the cops?

P: No. I didn't call the cops when she put her car in the middle of both driveways.

T: Right. So do you think that it is natural for anybody to get mad at someone who calls the cops over something like that?

P: Wait. What was that?

T: Let me put it again. Do you think it was natural for you to get mad in that situation?

P: Yeah.

T: OK, so you don't see anything wrong in getting mad?

P: No.

T: No. And yet you have the thought right after that that it was wrong to get mad and yell at her?

P: Yeah, I did have that thought.

T: OK, now this is one of the problems. If you want to get over this sense of giving in all the time, one of the things that you can do is look for this thought—"I was wrong to do such and such a thing"—and refer back to this conversation that we are having now and decide for yourself whether, indeed, you were wrong. Now if every time you asserted yourself in that particular way, you think "I was wrong to do that," you are going to feel bad, and

then you are not going to want to assert yourself again. Is that clear?

P: Uh huh.

T: So we have to decide here and now. Do you indeed think that you were wrong to assert yourself with her?

P: No.

T: Now the next time you get the thought "I was wrong, I shouldn't have said that, I shouldn't have stood up for my rights," how are you going to answer that thought?

P: If I was wrong? I wasn't wrong, and I should stick up for my rights.

T: Now are you saying that because that is the answer, or because you really believe it?

P: No, I believe it. I did the right thing there, I think. I did the right thing there. I did the right thing.

The therapist followed this discussion with a technique called "point–counterpoint," to help Irene practice rational responses to her automatic thoughts even more intensively. In this excerpt, the therapist expressed the patient's own negative thinking, while she tried to defend herself more rationally.

T: Now I am going to be like the prosecuting attorney, and I'll say, "Now I understand you were yelling at your neighbor because she called the cops. Is that true?"

P: Yeah.

T: Now it seems to me that that was a very bad thing for you to do.

P: No, it wasn't.

T: You don't think it was?

P: No, I should have hit her.

T: Well, you can sit there and say you should have hit her. I thought you said before that you wanted to be a nice person.

P: I was a nice person when I didn't call the cops when she blocked the driveway.

T: I know, but now you are saying that you are going to go out and hit her.

P: No, I wouldn't hit her. I wouldn't hit her unless she hit me.

T: Well, but still you yelled at her.

P: I yelled at her, yeah.

T: It doesn't seem to me that nice people yell at other people.

P: Well, I am still a nice person, but she did something wrong, and I had to do something wrong.

T: Well, how can you still be a nice person if you yell at people?

P: How can you still be a nice person? You just are. You are a nice person. It is just that a nice person gets mad too.

T: You say a nice person gets mad too?

P: When somebody does something wrong to them.

T: Where did you ever get that idea—nice people get mad when they are wrong?

P: When the other person is wrong? Where did I get that idea? It's true.

T: You really believe that's true?

P: Yeah. Nice people are the same as everybody else.

T: So nice people can get mad?

P: Uh huh.

Finally, the therapist returned to the schema and asked the patient how much she believed the new perspective.

T: If you get mad, you are not a nice person. Now do you believe that?

P: No.

T: Do you believe it partially?

P: Ummm, no. Well, they don't get mad for nothing. They get mad when there is a reason.

T: OK, so right now would you say that you believe—now what about the belief—let's put it the other way, the belief that you can get mad and still be a nice person. How much do you believe that?

P: A hundred.

T: 100%?

P: Yeah.

T: You are sure 100%, not 90% or 80%?

P: No, I think 100%.

For the remainder of Session 3, Irene and the therapist reviewed other instances of nonassertiveness to reinforce the main point of the session: that nice people can behave assertively and sometimes even get mad. The session ended with a summary of the main issues raised in the first three sessions.

Summary of Initial Sessions

In the first three sessions, the therapist laid the groundwork for the remainder of treatment. He began immediately by teaching Irene to identify her negative automatic thoughts. By doing this, the therapist began to understand her feelings of hopelessness and to explore her suicidal ideation. By identifying her thoughts in a variety of specific situations, he was able to deduce several key schemas that later proved central to Irene's thinking: the belief that other people did not care about her, that she could be easily controlled by others, that she was dumb, and that she would not be a nice person if she asserted herself. The therapist made especially skillful use of the patient's thoughts during the second therapy session to help Irene see that she was distorting evidence about the therapeutic interaction and coming to the inaccurate conclusion that she was easily manipulated and dumb.

Beyond identifying thoughts and distortions, the therapist guided Irene to take concrete steps to overcome her inactivity and withdrawal: He asked her to weigh the advantages and disadvantages of staying in bed; he broke down the task of joining a tennis group into small, manageable steps; and he worked with her to develop an activity schedule to follow during the week.

Finally, the therapist employed a variety of strategies to demonstrate to Irene that she could test the validity of her thoughts, develop rational responses, and feel better. For example, during the course of the three sessions the therapist set up an experiment, used reattribution, offered alternative perspectives, and practiced the point–counterpoint technique.

One final point we want to emphasize is that the primary therapeutic mode was questioning. Most of the therapist's comments were in the form of questions. This helped Irene to evaluate her own thoughts outside of the session and prevented her from feeling attacked by the therapist.

By the end of these initial sessions, Irene reported being more optimistic that her life could change. She was then transferred to another cognitive therapist, Dr. Judith Eidelson, for the remainder of treatment. (This transfer had been explained to the patient before she saw the first therapist [A. T. B.].)

Later Sessions

The first issue that the second therapist dealt with was Irene's belief that she was stupid. The patient began to fill out the Daily Record of Dysfunctional Thoughts and gathered evidence that she was not as stupid as she believed. In fact, Irene brought up the possibility of taking a college course. There were several obstacles to this, however: (1) Her husband had never given her keys to either their car or their house; (2) she did not have enough money to take the course; and (3) she worried that her husband would try to punish her if she tried to become more independent.

The therapist set up several experiments with Irene to test a series of beliefs: that her husband would punish her; that she would fail at a job even if she could get one; and that she would fail a college-level course. Through graded tasks, Irene asked her husband about obtaining keys, joined the tennis league, and began socializing with friends. Although her husband felt rejected and accused her of being stupid, he never took any active steps to stop her, despite her predictions. Irene then got a job as a waitress; again, contrary to her expectations, she was very successful and received a great deal of positive feedback on the job. Soon after getting the job, Irene enrolled in a sociology course and received a grade of A. At each step in the sequence, Irene would identify her automatic thoughts and respond to them before taking the next step toward independence.

During the final sessions of therapy, the patient raised the issue of leaving her husband. The therapist worked with Irene to evaluate several thoughts: (1) "Somehow he'll change and the marriage will work," (2) "Marriage is a lifetime commitment," (3) "I can't manage on my own," and (4) "Leaving him would represent a failure to me." Irene eventually discarded each of these beliefs as invalid or unlikely, and decided to end the marriage. Shortly thereafter, Irene terminated therapy. She felt confident about herself and her decision, and her BDI score was in the normal range. The symptom reduction phase of treatment was successfully completed in 20 sessions.

The next section describes and illustrates the relapse prevention phase of cognitive therapy.

PHASE 2: SCHEMA-FOCUSED TREATMENT FOR RELAPSE PREVENTION

In order to ensure against relapse, an additional phase of treatment has been developed to deal with the deeper, predisposing psychological structures. This phase is termed the "schema-focused" phase of treatment, because of the emphasis on identifying and changing the patient's underlying schemas. Young (1999) has written extensively about this schema-focused approach, and Young and Klosko (1994) have published a self-help book for patients to guide them through this phase.

Beck and colleagues (1990) have noted that

> . . . schemas are difficult to alter. They are held firmly in place by behavioral, cognitive, and affective elements. The therapeutic approach must take a tripartite approach. To take a strictly cognitive approach and try to argue patients out of their distortions will not work. Having the patients abreact within the session to fantasies or recollections will not be successful by itself. A therapeutic program that addresses all three areas is essential. A patient's cognitive distortions serve as signposts that point to the schema. (p. 10)

As a result, the schema-focused phase of treatment is significantly different from the earlier phase: It places more emphasis on early developmental patterns and origins, long-term interpersonal difficulties, the patient–therapist relationship, and emotive or experiential exercises.

Case Study of Michelle: The Relapse Prevention Phase

The second case study[5] demonstrates the importance of treating schemas in depressive episodes by highlighting the schema-focused phase of treatment.

History and Presenting Problems

The patient, "Michelle," read about cognitive therapy in a number of magazines, thought it could help her, and called the center for an appointment. The intake interviewer reported that Michelle was a 30-year-old Jewish woman married for the past 6 years to Jim, a Catholic who worked on Wall Street in investment banking. Neither of them had been married before. She reported being "happily married until about 6 to 8 months ago." Up to that time, she had maintained a successful career selling real estate.

Her immediate impetus to enter treatment was her reaction to a visit to her gynecologist: Upon hearing that she was not pregnant, she broke out crying uncontrollably, and was prevailed upon to seek psychological assistance.

She scored 28 on the BDI, placing her in the moderate to severe range of depression. She also completed the Multimodal Life History Inventory (Lazarus & Lazarus, 1991), a 15-page assessment tool covering a wide range of issues dealing with feelings, thoughts, behaviors, and a variety of other psychotherapeutic issues. On her Multimodal Life History Inventory, she reported her main problems as depression, being unhappy with self, feeling unloved, and feeling unappreciated. She also listed the following behaviors as applicable to her: procrastination, withdrawal, concentration difficulties, sleep disturbance, crying, and outbursts of temper. She further indicated that she often felt angry, sad, depressed, conflicted, unhappy, hopeless, and lonely. She endorsed the following statements: "I am worthless," "Life is empty, a waste," and "There is nothing to look forward to."

At the time she came in for her first interview, Michelle was no longer working, hardly left the house except to go shopping, and spent most of her time in bed or watching TV. Based on all the intake data, the interviewer diagnosed the patient as having major depressive disorder, single episode. She was referred to one of us (A. D. W.) for treatment.

The therapist (T) followed the same general approach described earlier in this chapter for Irene: He identified and challenged dysfunctional thoughts, kept thought records, and constructed and followed agendas and activity schedules until the patient's (P) depression lifted. The schema-focused phase of treatment usually begins after patients start to feel better and resume more effective functioning. After 18 sessions Michelle's BDI score was 17, and the therapist then shifted into the schema-focused phase, with an explanation for the transition:

T: Well, what I thought we could work on now, Michelle—now that you're not so depressed, and you're able to get out of bed, and you're able to function during the day—is the issue that's going on with you and your husband.

P: Well, yes, I was afraid we were going to have to deal with that.

T: And when we start looking at relationship problems and these kinds of issues, we try to look at what we call "schemas." And schemas are like lifelong patterns, lifelong themes in our lives that we sort of repeat over and over again. They're like buttons that get pushed, and when they get pushed, we react very emotionally to them.

P: Well, I think he certainly knows how to push my buttons.

T: Yes, and what I think we could do now in this part of the therapy is try to find out exactly what those buttons are that he pushes in you and help you to learn how to work better with those buttons.

In this phase, the therapist focuses on longer-term patterns, problems, and themes that might predispose the patient to future episodes of depression. In Michelle's case, the therapist focused on the following life problems:

1. Her inability to express herself and ask for things, especially from her husband. She readily acknowledged that "I know I need to demand more, but just can't." Specifically, this included wanting a child, but believing that "it would spoil things for Jim."

2. Recurrent thoughts about her marriage dissolving, because "he always makes me feel as if he has one foot out the door."

3. Low self-esteem—specifically, feeling undesirable and unlovable, because "I'm 12–15 pounds overweight."

Assessment and Education Component

The schema-focused phase can be divided into two distinct components: an assessment and education component and a change component. The assessment and education component itself consists of four interrelated parts: (1) a focused review of the patient's history, linking past experiences to current problems;

(2) the use of schema inventories, which may include the Young Schema Questionnaire (Young & Brown, 1999), Young Parenting Inventory (Young, 1994b), Young Compensation Inventory (Young, 1994a), and the Young–Rygh Avoidance Inventory (Young & Rygh, 1994); (3) experiential work, including imagery, to activate, or trigger, schemas; and (4) patient education regarding schemas.

The therapist initiated the focused life review with Michelle by probing into the patient's childhood and the onset and course of her emotional difficulties. Part of this investigation entails the collection of ratings of childhood impression of parents through the Young Parenting Inventory (Young, 1994b), a 72-item instrument designed to identify the developmental origins of schemas. Michelle's recollection of her early family life was sketchy. She remembered her father as very bright and a good provider who was "hardly ever around." Her mother she recalled as gentle but seemingly passive. While growing up, she could not confide in either of them for fear of engendering anger, ridicule, or "worse," especially on the part of her father. A sister, 2 years her junior, was favored by her parents, and "she has remained their darling even up to now."

Michelle reported no "real" depressive episodes until she started dating and began experiencing feelings of "being terribly lonely and discarded" whenever her relationships suffered. Further questions about her past and her previous experience with psychotherapy revealed several minor episodes of depression and at least one major depressive episode. Perceived or actual fluctuations in her relationship with Jim, her husband, seemed to have triggered many of her depressive reactions, during their marriage as well as during their courtship. Her previous major depression was triggered by Jim's announcement, after months of dating, that he was breaking up with her. She became listless and unmotivated to continue her studies, and was on the verge of dropping out of school. Her family advised her to seek help, and she entered treatment with a counselor in college. Though therapy was "somewhat helpful," she recovered fully only after she and Jim were securely reunited and treatment was discontinued.

Based on this focused review of her history, which revealed themes of emotional isolation, an "absentee" father, fear of self-expression, and devaluation, the therapist hypothesized that Michelle's current difficulties—inability to express her needs to her husband and feelings of insecurity about her marriage—were linked to specific Early Maladaptive Schemas that fell into the domain of Disconnection and Rejection. According to the schema approach, disconnection themes revolve around the expectation that one's need for safe, stable, and secure relationships will not be met in a predictable way. Rejection refers to the belief that one will not be acceptable or lovable to others (see Figure 6.1).

To explore this hypothesis further, the therapist proceeded to the next step in the assessment process and asked Michelle to complete the YSQ as homework. The YSQ, consisting of 205 items, is used to assess most of the 18 underlying schemas listed in Figure 6.1. Patients are asked to rate each statement according to how accurately they feel it represents them. The therapist then reviews the responses in detail with the patient, asking for additional information or clarification during the process. Michelle scored highest on items tapping Abandonment/Instability (the perceived instability or unreliability of those available for support and connection), Defectiveness/Shame (the belief that one is fundamentally unlovable, defective, flawed, or invalid), and Subjugation (excessive surrendering of one's decisions and preferences to others, usually to avoid anger, retaliation, or abandonment) schemas. She strongly endorsed such items as "I find myself clinging to people I'm close to because I'm afraid they'll leave me," "No one I desire would want to stay close to me if he/she knew the real me," and "I let other people have their way because I fear the consequences." She also endorsed a number of items dealing with emotional deprivation, but to a lesser extent. The YSQ was a useful tool in hypothesis building with Michelle. With this additional information, the therapist was able to identify four different schemas, strengthening the hypothesis that part of Michelle's current problem was schema-driven.

Up to this point, the assessment is essentially historical and "rational." In the third component of the assessment, the therapist investigates and triggers schemas experientially in order to further test relevant assumptions, explore the schemas' origins, and find out how they may be related to the presenting problems. A clear indication that a schema has been triggered is the presence of a high degree of affect. As Beck and his colleagues (1990) have noted, "The arousal of a strong feeling suggests not only that a core schema has been exposed, but also that the dysfunctional thinking is more accessible to modification" (p. 82). An additional rationale for triggering schemas is to have the patient experience directly both the content and the intensity of the schema.

In the following excerpt, the therapist helped Michelle identify and reexperience the origins of her Abandonment schema.

T: Michelle, why don't you close your eyes now and see if you can get a visual image of anything that comes into your mind? Just tell me what you see.

P: Do I have to see it?

T: Yes, it's not thoughts but pictures that we want. It could be a picture of a person, of a place, anything at all—almost as if you were looking at a movie in your head.

P: What is the point of all this again?

T: Well, the point is to try to discover feelings and themes—buttons, if you like—that are getting pushed, but that you're not aware of right now. Like, right now you told me you're feeling butterflies but you don't know why. We often find that when people close their eyes, they get pictures that tell them why they're feeling those butterflies, why they're nervous. So it's a way of sort of getting to deeper issues without directly talking about them, but rather through picturing them.

P: Well, nothing's coming.

T: Just continue to relax, because sometimes it takes a while and you have to let it happen. So don't worry. Just keep your eyes closed, and eventually something will come.

P: What if nothing comes?

T: Well, that's all right. If nothing comes, we can always come back and try this again later.

P: I'm seeing something. I see my father leaving the house. He doesn't want to come in and be with me.

T: You're actually picturing him leaving the house?

P: Yeah, he's outside the house now leaving, and he knows I'm inside. He knows I want to be with him, but he just doesn't care to be with me (*cries*).

T: OK, he's leaving the house. Where is he going?

P: I don't know. He just wants to get away from me.

T: And does he know that you want to see him?

P: Yes, he knows. But he makes believe as if I don't exist, that I'm not worth being with. That's the way he always made me feel.

This emotive strategy poignantly revealed Michelle's unhealthy childhood experiences with her father, as it epitomized her feelings of abandonment and defectiveness. The therapist then guided the imagery to assess whether or not there was a link between these early childhood experiences with her father and her current problems with her husband.

T: Now, Michelle, please keep your eyes closed and see if you can get an image of Jim, and tell me what you see.

P: Well, as you said that, what I saw Jim doing was just walking out the door and just slamming the door. He had his suitcase packed and with him, and he just walked out the door, and there I was in the house all alone by myself.

T: Just like you were with your father—the same feeling that you had there?

P: Yeah, it feels exactly the same.

Based on these types of links, the therapist was able to conjecture that as a result of Michelle's painful experiences with her father, she was now struggling with similar feelings in her relationship with her husband. By continuing to view her marriage as unstable and worrying that she would be left alone once again, especially if she expressed her needs and feelings, she continued to reinforce her link with her past and her Abandonment schema. In the following session, the patient remembered through imagery that when she was 6 years old, she broke into tears in a supermarket when she couldn't find her father, thinking that he had left her. Taken together, the results of the first three elements of the assessment corroborated one another; they allowed the therapist to form a comprehensive conceptualization of the origins of the patient's schemas, how they interrelated, and how they were contributing to her present problems. The therapist completed the Schema Conceptualization Form (Young, 1992) to guide the conceptualization process.

In the final element of assessment and education, the therapist educates the patient about schemas. As part of this educational process with Michelle, the therapist shared his formulation with her and asked her for feedback.

T: Why don't we begin by summarizing where we are right now in terms of understanding some of the schemas that we've been discussing and how they are affecting your life? Through reviewing your early life history, the Young Schema Questionnaire, imagery, and the other work we did, the three schemas we have identified are Abandonment, Subjugation, and Defectiveness.

Subjugation, you may recall, is the belief that you can't express what you want for fear of retaliation, which in your case means somebody getting angry at you and ultimately leaving you. It means that you can't ask for what you want without Jim or your father getting annoyed at you, withdrawing, or actually leaving you.

Underneath your Subjugation is the Abandonment schema—the sense that people are going to leave you, that you can't count on them to stay. This is why you become so frightened and terrified, as a child with your father, and now in your life with Jim.

The explanation that you came up with to explain why you would be abandoned was that somehow you are defective—the sense that there is something bad about you; that you are worthless; that you could be discarded easily; that somehow, by asking for what you want, you're a nuisance or a bad person. This serves to explain, in your head, why Jim would want to leave you—why, when you disagree, you already see him as being out the door. And the way you've dealt with your fear of being abandoned up till now is through subjugating your needs.

Does this explanation feel as if we're on the right track? Does it sound right to

you? Are these the three buttons or schemas that are being triggered by the situation with Jim?

Michelle agreed with the therapist's formulation; yet she continued to insist, "If I ask for things, he *will* leave me. He's happy to stay with me as long as I ask for nothing."

In order to prepare Michelle for the change component of schema-focused treatment, the therapist explained to her about the nature of early schemas and the process of schema change. Although Michelle had been given considerable information about the significance of schemas after she completed the YSQ, the therapist now provided a more thorough description.

He then recommended that she read the chapters in *Reinventing Your Life* (Young & Klosko, 1994) that applied to her schemas. He also gave her a fuller description of how schemas originate, why they are such strong beliefs, and how they come to be supported by a lifetime of attitudes and behaviors. To prepare her further for the change phase, the therapist also advised her that she should expect a great deal of resistance on the part of her schemas, and that her fears of abandonment and defectiveness would be triggered whenever she would attempt to express herself and overcome her Subjugation schema.

Change Component

The interventions, strategies, and techniques used during the treatment or change component vary from patient to patient. The particular methods employed depend upon the nature of the specific schemas involved and how they interrelate (Bricker, Young, & Flanagan, 1993). We now illustrate how the four elements of schema change—cognitive, experiential, interpersonal, and behavioral—were applied in working with Michelle.

Though patients with abandonment issues have a tendency to select partners who re-trigger underlying schemas as a way of maintaining them, they often overestimate the extent to which their partners are indeed abandoning them. Consequently, the therapist began the change phase with a cognitive strategy: examining the evidence for Michelle's insecurity about her marriage, and her husband's willingness to leave her should she divulge her needs to him.

T: Is it possible, based on some of these schemas that we talked about—some of the feelings of being defective or that people will leave you—that you have tended to exaggerate how little Jim is attracted to you?

P: That would be wonderful if it were true, but I don't think so.

T: Well, let's look. What could you point to as evidence that he is attached and committed to you?

P: He says he loves me. Often he's happy to see me, to be around me. . . . He compliments me at times when we go out, so I know he's attracted to me. He buys me very nice gifts—rings, jewelry, pocketbooks—and he takes me out on weekends. He asks me where I want us to go on vacation. I guess he does think of me.

T: Is there any evidence about his leaving you? Has he ever left you or threatened to leave you?

P: When we dated, he left several times.

T: And since you've been married?

P: No, not since we've been married. He's never left.

T: Did he ever say anything about wanting to leave?

P: No.

Because the therapeutic effects of these cognitive interventions tend to dissipate over time when patients' beliefs are schema-driven, they have to be repeated again and again until the patients can challenge their schemas more consistently. A follow-up cognitive technique that we have found extremely effective is the use of the Schema Flashcard form (Young, Wattenmaker, & Wattenmaker, 1996). A Schema Flashcard is a simple index card containing a summary of the schema and a cognitive antidote or counter. The card that Michelle was instructed to read regularly was constructed, with her collaboration, so as to combat her schemas in a way that directly addressed her presenting problems as they related to subjugation, defectiveness, and abandonment:

Right now I believe that I must give up on the idea of a baby, or else Jim will certainly leave me. I feel this way, though, because of my Subjugation, Abandonment, and Defectiveness

schemas. I developed these beliefs as a result of my father's lack of attention, and his frustration with me whenever I wanted to be with him. The reality is that Jim has never threatened to leave me since we were married, and even when we were dating, he came back every time he actually left me. I have much evidence that Jim is very attached to me, loves me, and would not leave. The evidence is: He says he loves me; he's stayed with me for 10 years; he buys me expensive gifts; he takes me out on weekends; he never wants to take separate vacations; he worries about me if I go away; and his family approves of me. The one time that I really insisted on what I wanted regarding moving to the suburbs, he put up a fight but gave in and did not leave me. Therefore I can tell Jim what I want, and trust that he probably will not leave me.

The first part of this cognitive strategy revealed how Michelle misperceived her husband. She underestimated Jim's commitment and overestimated his willingness to leave her. She recognized the discrepancy between her feelings and expectations and her actual experiences with Jim; a review of the facts showed him to be responsive to her when she really asked for something. And even when he disagreed with her, he did not voice or demonstrate any inclination to leave her. The therapist explained to Michelle that by not expressing herself and by continuing to suppress her needs, she actually reinforced her schemas. The second part of the strategy, involving the use of the Schema Flashcard, provided her with an effective tool she could use to fight her schemas outside of sessions.

It is relevant to note here that, had Jim turned out to be truly uncaring and prone to abandoning Michelle, the therapist then would have pursued a different therapeutic route, including couple therapy or possibly leaving the marriage.

The therapist then went on to apply experiential exercises to help Michelle loosen her schemas still further. This entailed, in part, getting into a dialogue with her father and expressing her anger at him for making her feel abandoned and defective. She also needed to "feel" that her father's neglect of her was not her fault.

T: Can you now get an image of your father walking away from you and you asking him to come back to spend some time with you?

P: "Daddy, Daddy, Daddy, I want you to come back and play with me."

T: What does he say?

P: He pretends he doesn't hear me and continues to walk away.

T: And now see if you can say out loud what he's thinking.

P: (As father) "There she goes whining again, wanting me to be with her. She just expects too much. There must be something wrong with her to be so demanding."

T: And what do you want to tell your father, as an adult, now that you've overheard his thoughts?

P: (To father) "I'm very angry at you. How could you feel that way about me?"

T: Good. Continue to tell him how you feel right now and what you think.

P: OK. (To father) "I'm your daughter. I'm not a pest. I just want to be with you because I love you and I feel good being next to you. I'm your daughter; you're supposed to love me and want to be with me. You're a bad father for not feeling the same way."

The dialogue with her father allowed Michelle to ventilate her feelings toward her father in a constructive fashion, and thus to feel empowered to assert her needs and rights. The imagery work was then continued by accessing a related situation between Michelle and her husband.

Throughout the schema-focused phase of treatment, close attention is paid to schemas that are activated between patient and therapist within the sessions. This provides patients with additional knowledge about how they play out their schemas even in situations that are neutral or supportive. In the following vignette, the therapist helped Michelle see how her Defectiveness schema became activated during a session in which he explained the concept of schema maintenance.

T: The upsetting thing about schemas is that they perpetuate themselves, even though they make the person unhappy. It's like it's more comfortable to stay with a belief that's familiar, even if it's painful, than to change to a belief that's different, even though it would make the person happier.

P: I must be very stupid for doing that to myself, then. It just makes me feel so terrible to think that I would be doing this to myself.

T: "Terrible" meaning like you're blaming yourself, or "terrible" like it's sad that you're doing this?

P: Both. And that now you, too, see my stupidity.

T: Well, see if you could try to step out of yourself for a second and be more objective. If every patient who comes in to see me has schemas, and they all repeat patterns over and over again like you're doing, do you think I view them as stupid for having these problems?

P: No, I'm sure you don't. But I just feel so convinced that that's how you see me.

T: Well, I'm wondering then if you're not using this Defectiveness schema against yourself as proof that there is something wrong with you again. Is that what you're doing right now?

P: Yeah, yeah.

T: So here is another example of how here in the therapy, and in other situations, you can take what is really an expression of concern and empathy for what you're going through and interpret it as a put-down, or that somehow you are inadequate. And maybe we can keep trying to watch for situations here in the therapy and outside where you feel that you're stupid or that someone's thinking you're stupid, and keep getting yourself to question it and to say, "Wait. Maybe this is my schema operating. Maybe that's not really what Arthur means, or that's not really what Jim means."

As this exchange indicates, the therapy relationship itself can be a useful vehicle for identifying, discussing, and subsequently modifying schemas. By paying close attention to Michelle's moods, responses, and behaviors *in vivo*, the therapist demonstrated to her additional and very convincing instances of how she continued to misinterpret some of her experiences based on her schemas.

The therapist then targeted specific schemas for change within the therapeutic relationship. For Michelle, this included not subjugating herself—not even to the directions of her therapist. Otherwise, going along with the therapist's formulations, homework assignments, and suggestions when she genuinely opposed them could easily have prolonged the pattern of her schema maintenance or even sabotaged her progress. In order to prevent this, the therapist routinely asked her for feedback, as a way of ensuring that she was not merely "yes-ing" him to avoid triggering her schemas. An essential part of Michelle's therapy focused on her becoming increasingly aware of her own needs and expressing them, initially to her therapist and later on to her husband.

The next and final step to be illustrated is the changing of schema- driven behaviors. This entails getting patients to modify long-term behavior patterns that have been used to reinforce their schemas for the better part of a lifetime. To act against the dictates of these beliefs is no doubt the hardest and most difficult part of the therapeutic process. To achieve success, the therapist needs to push patients to act contrary to years of dysfunctional patterns of behavior. For Michelle, this meant expressing her needs to her husband and not feeling defective for it, or feeling that she would be abandoned as a result. Keeping in mind her Subjugation schema, the therapist asked Michelle to set her own agenda.

T: Is there something that you would like to do with or around Jim that you're avoiding, that you're fearful of pursuing?

P: I'm sure there are many things, but what I would really like is to make love more frequently. But I'm scared of asking him. I'm afraid of approaching him.

T: Can you think of a way that you could present it to him so that you'd be more likely to get a positive or at least a neutral answer, so that you wouldn't buy into your schemas the way you used to?

P: Yes, I could snuggle up to him and kiss him and not actually ask him for it outright, but indicate to him in a way that I do want to make love with him, that I want to be close. So I would try kissing him, stroking him, seducing him, you know.

T: Good. Then how would you feel about making that your homework assignment, to snuggle up to him and to initiate lovemaking?

P: Wonderful. I think that's the best homework assignment you've given me.

After the patient followed up on her homework and reported success, she was subsequently encouraged (through more Schema Flashcards and other techniques) to speak directly to her husband not only about her sexual needs, but also about her desire to have a baby and to raise a family. She soon was sufficiently improved, and felt confident enough, to stop treatment. At the present time, she has been out of treatment for several years. Through a patient she referred to us, we heard that Michelle had a baby, that her marriage seems much happier, and that she has not had any relapses of depression.

CONCLUSION

Evidence continues to mount demonstrating the efficacy of cognitive therapy in the treatment of unipolar and bipolar depression. Adolescents, adults, and geriatric patients have all been shown to benefit from cognitive therapy.

Cognitive therapy helps patients understand the relationship among their thoughts, behaviors, and feelings. Cognitions are "put to the test" by examining evidence, setting up *in vivo* experiments, weighing advantages and disadvantages, trying graded tasks, and employing other intervention strategies. Through this process, patients begin to view themselves and their problems more realistically, feel better, change their maladaptive behavior patterns, and take steps to solve real-life difficulties. These changes take place as a direct result of carefully planned, self-help homework assignments—one of the hallmarks of cognitive treatment. Cognitive therapy reduces symptoms by helping patients identify and modify automatic thoughts and the behaviors associated with them.

A second phase of treatment—the schema-focused phase—has been developed to deal with the deeper psychological structures that predispose patients to relapse. After utilizing interventions aimed at symptom reduction in the first phase, a great deal of subsequent attention and effort are directed toward identifying and modifying the underlying schemas that often predispose individuals to depression. Following a thorough assessment, an extensive change component is developed and implemented. During this relapse prevention phase of treatment, patients come to understand their own schemas; their developmental origins; and the ways they are triggered, reinforced, and maintained.

Throughout the treatment, cognitive therapists maintain a collaborative alliance with their patients. They are very active in structuring sessions, yet go to considerable lengths to help patients reach conclusions on their own. A therapist serves as a guide, helping a patient maneuver through a labyrinth of dysfunctional cognitions, including Early Maladaptive Schemas. As a result, patients attain the necessary psychological tools to become more proactive on their own behalf, and are able to make the necessary cognitive, affective, interpersonal, and behavioral changes necessary to minimize further episodes of depression.

NOTES

1. Researchers have found it useful to differentiate between "relapse" (the return of symptoms within 6 months after termination of treatment) and "recurrence" (a whole new episode of depression, occurring at least 12 months after treatment has ended (Gelder, 1994; see also Overholser, 1998). However, because this distinction has not been uniformly incorporated into the literature (and for clarity of presentation), we have elected to use the term "relapse" to indicate the return of symptoms, regardless of the time frame.

2. Reported relapse rates for patients treated with medication have varied, depending on the definition of relapse, the duration of the follow-up period, and the severity of depression within the patient population (Williams, 1997). Because of these differences, some of the estimates have ranged from 34% to 92% (Frank, 1996; Overholser, 1998; Versiani, 1999; Williams, 1997), though lower rates have also been reported (Keller & Boland, 1998).

3. The 1999 book by Young cited here and throughout the chapter, *Cognitive Therapy for Personality Disorders: A Schema-Focused Approach*, refers to the third edition. However, the ideas expressed were developed in 1990, for the original edition. Similarly, the Young Schema Questionnaire was developed in 1990, then reprinted in the 1999 third edition.

4. In this chapter, diagnoses are generally based on the *Diagnostic and Statistical Manual of Mental Disorders*, fourth edition (DSM-IV; American

Psychiatric Association, 1994). However, diagnoses for patients described in the case materials are based on DSM-III-R (American Psychiatric Association, 1987), the system in effect at the time of assessment.

5. At the time Irene was in treatment, the schema-focused phase of treatment had not yet been fully developed. She terminated once her symptoms were relieved, as many patients do. We are therefore using a different case, that of Michelle, to illustrate the second phase of therapy. The case presentation has been updated for this edition to reflect the latest revision in the listing of Early Maladaptive Schemas.

REFERENCES

Agosti, V., & Ocepek, W. K. (1997). The efficacy of imipramine and psychotherapy in early-onset chronic depression: A reanalysis of the National Institute of Mental Health Treatment of Depression Collaborative Research Program. *Journal of Affective Disorders, 43*(3), 181–186.

American Psychiatric Association. (1987). *Diagnostic and statistical manual of mental disorders* (3rd ed., rev.). Washington, DC: Author.

American Psychiatric Association. (1993). Practice guidelines for major depressive disorder in adults. *American Journal of Psychiatry, 150*(Suppl.), 1–26.

American Psychiatric Association. (1994). *Diagnostic and statistical manual of mental disorders* (4th ed.). Washington, DC: Author.

Antonuccio, D. O., Danton, W. G., & DeNelsky, G. Y. (1995). Psychotherapy versus medication for depression: Challenging the conventional wisdom with data. *Professional Psychology: Research and Practice, 26*(6), 574–585.

Barber, J. P., & DeRubeis, R. J. (1989). On second thought: Where the action is in cognitive therapy for depression. *Cognitive Therapy and Research, 13*(5), 441–457.

Barlow, D. H., & Hofmann, S. G. (1997). Efficacy and dissemination of psychological treatments. In D. M. Clark & C. G. Fairburn (Eds.), *Science and practice of cognitive behaviour therapy* (pp. 95–117). Oxford: Oxford University Press.

Basco, M. R., & Rush, A. J. (1996). *Cognitive-behavioral therapy for bipolar disorder*. New York: Guilford Press.

Beck, A. T. (1967). *Depression: Causes and treatment*. Philadelphia: University of Pennsylvania Press.

Beck, A. T. (1976). *Cognitive therapy and the emotional disorders*. New York: International Universities Press.

Beck, A. T. (1988). *Love is never enough*. New York: Harper & Row.

Beck, A. T., Freeman, A., & Associates. (1990). *Cognitive therapy of personality disorders*. New York: Guilford Press.

Beck, A. T., Rush, A. J., Shaw, B. F., & Emery, G. (1979). *Cognitive therapy of depression*. New York: Guilford Press.

Beck, J. S. (1995). *Cognitive therapy: Basics and beyond.* New York: Guilford Press.

Beutler, L. E., Scogin, F., Kirkish, P., Schretlen, D., Corbishley, A., Hamblin, D., Meredith, K., Potter, R., Bamford, C. R., & Levenson, A. I. (1987). Group cognitive therapy and alprazolam in the treatment of depression in older adults. *Journal of Consulting and Clinical Psychology, 55*(4), 550–556.

Biggs, M. M., & Rush, A. J. (1999). Cognitive and behavioral therapies alone or combined with antidepressant medication in the treatment of depression. In D. S. Janowsky (Ed.), *Psychotherapy indications and outcomes* (pp. 121–172). Washington, DC: American Psychiatric Press.

Blackburn, I. M., & Bishop, S. (1979, July). *A comparison of cognitive therapy, pharmacotherapy, and their combination in depressed outpatients.* Paper presented at the annual meeting of the Society for Psychotherapy Research, Oxford.

Blackburn, I. M., & Bishop, S. (1980, July). *Pharmacotherapy and cognitive therapy in the treatment of depression: Competitors or allies?* Paper presented at the First World Congress on Behavior Therapy, Jerusalem.

Blackburn, I. M., & Moore, R. G. (1997). Controlled acute and follow-up trial of cognitive therapy and pharmacotherapy in out-patients with recurrent depression. *British Journal of Psychiatry, 171,* 328–334.

Bowers, W. A. (1990). Treatment of depressed inpatients: Cognitive therapy plus medication, and medication alone. *British Journal of Psychiatry, 156,* 73–58.

Bricker, D. C., Young, J. E., & Flanagan, C. (1993). Schema-focused cognitive therapy: A comprehensive framework for characterological problems. In K. T. Kuehlwein & H. Rosen (Eds.), *Cognitive therapies in action* (pp. 88–125). San Francisco: Jossey-Bass.

Brown, G. W. (1996). Onset and course of depressive disorders: Summary of a research programme. In C. Mundt, M. J. Goldstein, K. Hahlweg, & P. Fiedler (Eds.), *Interpersonal factors in the origin and course of affective disorders* (pp. 151–167). London: Gaskell/Royal College of Psychiatrists.

Castonguay, L. G., Goldfried, M. R., Wiser, S., Raue, P. J., & Hayes, A. M. (1996). Predicting the effect of cognitive therapy for depression: A study of unique and common factors. *Journal of Consulting and Clinical Psychology, 64*(3), 497–504.

Colom, F., Vieta, E., Martinez, A., Jorquera, A., & Gasto, C. (1998). What is the role of psychotherapy in the treatment of bipolar disorder? *Psychotherapy and Psychosomatics, 67,* 3–9.

Craighead, W. E., Miklowitz, D. J., Vajk, F. C., & Frank, E. (1998). Psychological treatments for bipolar disorder. In P. E. Nathan & J. M. Gorman (Eds.), *A guide to treatments that work* (pp. 240–248). New York: Oxford University Press.

Crews, W. D., Jr., & Harrison, D. W. (1995). The neuropsychology of depression and its implications for cognitive therapy. *Neuropsychology Review, 5*(2), 81–123.

de Oliveira, I. R. (1998). The treatment of unipolar major depression: Pharmacotherapy, cognitive behaviour therapy or both? *Journal of Clinical Pharmacy and Therapeutics, 23,* 467–475.

Depression Guideline Panel. (1993). *Depression is a treatable illness: A patient's guide* (AHCPR Publication No. 93-0553). Rockville, MD: U.S. Department of Health and Human Services.

DeRubeis, R. J., & Feeley, M. (1990). Determinants of change in cognitive therapy for depression. *Cognitive Therapy and Research, 14*(5), 469–482.

DeRubeis, R. J., Gelfand, L. A., Tang, T. Z., & Simons, A. D. (1999). Medications versus cognitive behavior therapy for severely depressed outpatients: Mega-analysis of four randomized comparisons. *American Journal of Psychiatry, 156*(7), 1007–1013.

DeRubeis, R. J., Hollon, S. D., Grove, W. M., Evans, M. D., Garvey, M. J., & Tuason, V. B. (1990). How does cognitive therapy work?: Cognitive change and symptom change in cognitive therapy and pharmacotherapy for depression. *Journal of Consulting and Clinical Psychology, 58*(6), 862–869.

Dobson, K. S., & Pusch, D. (1993). Towards a definition of the conceptual and empirical boundaries of cognitive therapy. *Australian Psychologist, 28*(3), 137–144.

Eifert, G. H., Beach, B. K., & Wilson, P. H. (1998). Depression: Behavioral principles and implications for treatment and relapse prevention. In J. J. Plaud & G. H. Eifert (Eds.), *From behavior theory to behavior therapy* (pp. 68–97). Boston: Allyn & Bacon.

Elkin, I., Gibbons, R. D., Shea, M. T., & Shaw, B. F. (1996). Science is not a trial (but it can sometimes be a tribulation). *Journal of Consulting and Clinical Psychology, 64*(1), 92–103.

Elkin, I., Shea, M. T., Watkins, J. T., Imber, S. D., Sotsky, S. M., Collins, J. F., Glass, D. R., Pilkonis, P. A., Leber, W. R., Docherty, J. P., Fiester, S. J., & Parloff, M. B. (1989). National Institute of Mental Health Treatment of Depression Collaborative Research Program: General effectiveness of treatments. *Archives of General Psychiatry, 46,* 971–982.

Evans, M. D., Hollon, S. D., DeRubeis, R. J., Piaseki, J. M., Grove, W. M., Garvey, M. J., & Tuason, V. B. (1992). Differential relapse following cognitive therapy and pharmacotherapy for depression. In D. S. Janowsky (Ed.), *Psychotherapy indication and outcomes* (pp. 802–808). Washington, DC: American Psychiatric Press.

Fava, G. A., Rafanelli, C., Grandi, S., Canestrari, R., & Morphy, M. A. (1998). Six-year outcome for cognitive behavioral treatment of residual symptoms in major depression. *American Journal of Psychiatry, 155*(10), 1443–1445.

Fava, G. A., Rafanelli, C., Grandi, S., Conti, S., & Belluardo, P. (1998). Prevention of recurrent depression with cognitive behavioral therapy: Preliminary findings. *Archives of General Psychiatry, 55*(9), 816–820.

Frank, E. (1996). Long-term treatment of depression: Interpersonal psychotherapy with and without medication. In C. Mundt & M. J. Goldstein (Eds.), *Interpersonal factors in the origin and course of affective disorders* (pp. 303–315). London: Gaskell/Royal College of Psychiatrists.

Frank, E., & Thase, M. E. (1999). Natural history and preventative treatment of recurrent mood disorders. *Annual Review of Medicine, 50,* 453–468.

Free, M. L., Oei, T. P. S., & Appleton, C. (1998). Biological and psychological processes in recovery from depression during cognitive therapy. *Journal of Behavior Therapy and Experimental Psychiatry, 29,* 213–226.

Freeman, A., & Davison, M. R. (1997). Short-term therapy for the long-term patient. In L. Vandecreek, S. Knapp, & T. L. Jackson (Eds.), *Innovations in clinical practice: A source book* (pp. 5–24). Sarasota, FL: Professional Resource Press.

Futterman, A., Thompson, L., Gallagher-Thompson, D., & Ferris, R. (1995). Depression in later life: Epidemiology, assessment, etiology, and treatment. In E. E. Beckham & W. R. Leber (Eds.), *Handbook of depression* (2nd ed., pp. 494–525). New York: Guilford Press.

Gaffan, E. A., Tsaousis, J., & Kemp-Wheeler, S. M. (1995). Researcher allegiance and meta-analysis: The case of cognitive therapy for depression. *Journal of Consulting and Clinical Psychology, 63*(6), 966–980.

Gallagher-Thompson, D., Hanley-Peterson, P., & Thompson, L. W. (1990). Maintenance of gains versus relapse following brief psychotherapy for depression. *Journal of Consulting and Clinical Psychology, 58*(3), 371–374.

Gelder, M. G. (1994). Cognitive therapy for depression. In H. Hippius & C. N. Stefanis (Eds.), *Psychiatry in progress series: Vol. 1. Research in mood disorders: An update* (pp. 115–124). Goettingen, Germany: Hogrefe & Huber.

Gortner, E. T., Gollan, J. K., Dobson, K. S., & Jacobson, N. S. (1998). Cognitive-behavioral treatment for depression: Relapse prevention. *Journal of Consulting and Clinical Psychology, 2,* 377–384.

Gloaguen, V., Cottraux, J., Cucherat, M., & Blackburn, I. M. (1998). A meta-analysis of the effects of cognitive therapy in depressed patients. *Journal of Affective Disorders, 49,* 59–72.

Hall, L. H., & Robertson, M. H. (1998). Undergraduate ratings of the acceptability of single and combined treatments for depression: A comparative analysis. *Professional Psychology: Research and Practice, 3,* 269–272.

Harrington, R., Wood, A., & Verduyn, C. (1998). Clinically depressed adolescents. In P. J. Graham (Ed.), *Cognitive-behaviour therapy for children and families* (pp. 156–193). New York: Cambridge University Press.

Hautzinger, M., & de Jong-Meyer, R. (1996). Cognitive-behavioural therapy versus pharmacotherapy in depression. In C. Mundt, M. J. Goldstein, K. Hahlweg, & P. Fiedler (Eds.), *Interpersonal factors in the origin and course of affective disorders* (pp. 329–340). London: Gaskell/Royal College of Psychiatrists.

Hayes, A. M., & Strauss, J. L. (1998). Dynamic systems theory as a paradigm for the study of change in psychotherapy: An application to cognitive therapy for depression. *Journal of Consulting and Clinical Psychology, 66*(6), 939–947.

Hollon, S. D. (1998). What is cognitive behavioural therapy and does it work? *Current Opinion in Neurobiology, 8,* 289–292.

Hollon, S. D., DeRubeis, R. J., & Evans, M. D. (1996). Cognitive therapy in the treatment and prevention of depression. In P. M. Salkovskis (Ed.), *Frontiers of cognitive therapy* (pp. 293–317). New York: Guilford Press.

Hollon, S. D., Shelton, R. C., & Loosen, P. T. (1991). Cognitive therapy and pharmacotherapy for depression. *Journal of Consulting and Clinical Psychology, 59*(1), 88–99.

Ingram, R. E., & Holle, C. (1992). Cognitive science of depression. In D. J. Stein & J. E. Young (Eds.), *Cognitive science and clinical disorders* (pp. 187–209). San Diego, CA: Academic Press.

Jarrett, R. B. (1995). Comparing and combining short-term psychotherapy and pharmacotherapy for depression. In E. E. Beckham & W. R. Leber (Eds.), *Handbook of depression* (2nd ed., pp. 435–464). New York: Guilford Press.

Jarrett, R. B., & Nelson, R. O. (1987). Mechanisms of change in cognitive therapy of depression. *Behavior Therapy, 18,* 227–241.

Joffe, R., Segal, Z., & Singer, W. (1996). Change in thyroid hormone levels following response to cognitive therapy for major depression. *American Journal of Psychiatry, 153*(3), 411–413.

Keller, M. B., & Boland, R. J. (1998). Implications of failing to achieve successful long-term maintenance treatment of recurrent unipolar major depression. *Biological Psychiatry, 44*(5), 348–360.

Klein, D. F. (1996). Preventing hung juries about therapy studies. *Journal of Consulting and Clinical Psychology, 64,* 81–87.

Koder, D. A., Brodaty, H., & Anstey, K. J. (1996). Cognitive therapy for depression in elderly. *International Journal of Geriatric Psychiatry, 11*(2), 97–107.

Kupfer, D. J., Frank, E., & Wamhoff, J. (1996). Mood disorders: Update on prevention of recurrence. In C. Mundt, M. M. Goldstein, K. Hahlweg, & P. Fiedler (Eds.), *Interpersonal factors in the origin and course of affective disorders* (pp. 289–302). London: Gaskell/Royal College of Psychiatrists.

Lazarus, A. A., & Lazarus, C. N. (1991). *Multimodal Life History Inventory* (2nd ed.). Champaign, IL: Research Press.

Lee, C. W., Taylor, G., & Dunn, J. (1999). Factor structure of the Schema Questionnaire in a large clinical sample. *Cognitive Therapy and Research, 23*(4), 441–451.

Levendusky, P. G., & Hufford, M. R. (1997). The application of cognitive-behavior therapy to the treatment of depression and related disorders in the elderly. *Journal of Geriatric Psychiatry, 30*(2), 227–238.

Lewinsohn, P. M., & Clarke, G. N. (1999). Psychosocial treatments for adolescent depression. *Clinical Psychology Review, 19*(3), 329–342.

Luborsky, L., Diguer, L., Seligman, D. A., Rosenthal, R., Krause, E. D., Johnson, S., Halperin, G., Bishop, M., Berman, J. S., & Schweizer, E. (1999). The researcher's own therapy allegiances: A "wild child" in comparisons to treatment efficacy. *Clinical Psychology: Science and Practice, 6*(1), 95–106.

McGinn, L. K., & Young, J. E. (1996). Schema-focused therapy. In P. M. Salkovskis (Ed.), *Frontiers of cognitive therapy* (pp. 182–207). New York: Guilford Press.

McLean, P. D., & Hakstian, A. R. (1979). Clinical depression: Comparative efficacy of outpatient treatments. *Journal of Consulting and Clinical Psychology, 47,* 818–836.

Mohr, D. C. (1995). Negative outcome in psychotherapy: A critical review. *Clinical Psychology: Science and Practice, 2*, 1–27.

National Institute of Mental Health (NIMH). (1999). *The numbers count* (NIH Publication No. NIH 99-4584) [Online]. Available: http://www.NIMH.NIH.gov/publicat/numbers.CFM

Nierenberg, A. A., Alpert, J. E., Pava, J. A., Worthington, J. J. III, Rosenbaum, J. F., & Fava, M. (1999). Residual symptoms in depressed patients who respond accutely to fluoxetine. *Journal of Clinical Psychiatry, 60*(4), 221–225.

Oei, T. P. S., & Free, M. L. (1995). Do cognitive behaviour therapies validate cognitive models of mood disorders?: A review of the empirical evidence. *International Journal of Psychology, 30*(2), 145–180.

Oei, T. P. S., & Shuttlewood, G. J. (1996). Specific and nonspecific factors in psychotherapy: A case of cognitive therapy for depression. *Clinical Psychology Review, 16*(2), 83–103.

O'Leary, K. D., & Beach, S. R. H. (1990). Marital therapy: A viable treatment for depression and marital discord. *American Journal of Psychiatry, 147*(2), 183–186.

Overholser, J. C. (1998). Cognitive-behavioral treatment of depression: Part X. Reducing the risk of relapse. *Journal of Contemporary Psychotherapy, 28*(4), 381–396.

Padesky, C. A., & Greenberger, D. (1995). *Clinician's guide to mind over mood.* New York: Guilford Press.

Persons, J. B., Burns, D. D., & Perloff, J. M. (1988). Predictors of dropout and outcome in cognitive therapy for depression in a private practice setting. *Cognitive Therapy and Research, 12*(6), 557–575.

Rehm, L. P. (1990). Cognitive and behavioral theories. In B. B. Wolman & G. Stricker (Eds.). *Depressive disorders: Facts, theories, and treatment methods* (pp. 64–91). New York: Wiley.

Reinecke, M. A., Ryan, N. E., & DuBois, D. L. (1998). Cognitive-behavioral therapy of depression and depressive symptoms during adolescence: A review and meta-analysis. *Journal of the American Academy of Child and Adolescent Psychiatry, 37*(1), 26–34.

Roberts, J. E., & Hartlage, S. (1996). Cognitive rehabilitation interventions for depressed patients. In P. W. Corrigan & S. C. Yudofsky (Eds.), *Cognitive rehabilitation for neuropsychiatric disorders* (pp. 371–392). Washington, DC: American Psychiatric Press.

Robinson, L. A., Berman, J. S., & Neimeyer, R. A. (1990). Psychotherapy for the treatment of depression: A comprehensive review of controlled outcome research. *Psychological Bulletin, 108*, 30–49.

Rush, A. J., Beck, A. T., Kovacs, M., & Hollon, S. (1977). Comparative efficacy of cognitive therapy and imipramine in the treatment of depressed outpatients. *Cognitive Therapy and Research, 1*, 17–37.

Sacco, W. P., & Beck, A. T. (1995). Cognitive theory and therapy. In E. E. Beckham & W. R. Leber (Eds.), *Handbook of depression* (2nd ed., pp. 329–351). New York: Guilford Press.

Saeman, H. (1999). Psychotherapy gets short shrift at White House MH meeting. *The National Psychologist, 8*(4), 21.

Safran, J. D., & Segal, Z. V. (1990). *Interpersonal processes in cognitive therapy.* New York: Basic Books.

Safran, J. D., Segal, Z. V., Vallis, T. M., Shaw, B. F., & Samstag, L. W. (1993). Assessing patient suitability for short-term cognitive therapy with an interpersonal focus. *Cognitive Therapy and Research, 17*(1), 23–38.

Salkovskis, P. M. (Eds.). (1996). *Frontiers of cognitive therapy* . New York: The Guilford Press.

Schmidt, N. B. (1994). The Schema Questionnaire and the Schema Avoidance Questionnaire. *Behavior Therapist, 17*(4), 90–92.

Schmidt, N. B., Joiner, T. E., Young, J. E., & Telch, M. J. (1995). The Schema Questionnaire: Investigation of psychometric properties and the hierarchical structure of a measure of maladaptive schemata. *Cognitive Therapy and Research, 19*(3), 295–321.

Scott, J. (1996a). Cognitive therapy of affective disorders: A review. *Journal of Affective Disorders, 37*, 1–11.

Scott, J. (1996b). The role of cognitive behaviour therapy in bipolar disorders. *Behavioural and Cognitive Psychotherapy, 24*(3), 195–208.

Shaw, B. F., & Segal, Z. V. (1999). Efficacy, indications, and mechanisms of action of cognitive therapy of depression. In D. S. Janowsky (Ed.), *Psychotherapy indications and outcomes* (pp. 173–196). Washington, DC: American Psychiatric Press.

Shea, M. T., & Elkin, I. (1996). The NIMH Treatment of Depression Collaborative Research Program. In C. Mundt, M. J. Goldstein, K. Hahlweg, & P. Fiedler (Eds.), *Interpersonal factors in the origin and course of affective disorders* (pp. 316–328). London: Gaskell/Royal College of Psychiatrists.

Shea, M. T., Elkin, I., Imber, S. D., Sotsky, S. M., Watkins, J. T., Collins, J. F., Pilkonis, P. A., Beckham, E., Glass, D. R., Dolan, R. T., & Parloff, M. B. (1992). Course of depressive symptoms over follow-up: Findings from the National Institute of Mental Health Treatment of depression Collaborative Research Program. *Archives of General Psychiatry, 49*(10), 782–787.

Shea, M. T., Pilkonis, P. A., Beckham, E., Collins, J. F., Elkin, I., Sotsky, S. M., & Docherty, J. P. (1990). Personality disorders and treatment outcome in the NIMH Treatment of Depression Collaborative Research Program. *American Journal of Psychiatry, 147*(6), 711–718.

Simons, A. D., Murphy, G. D., Levine, J. L., & Wetzel, R. D. (1986). Cognitive therapy and pharmacotherapy for depression. Sustained improvement over 1 year. *Archives of General Psychiatry, 43*, 43–48.

Spanier, C. A., Frank, E., McEachran, A. B., Grochocinski, V. J., & Kupfer, D. J. (1999). Maintenance interpersonal psychotherapy for recurrent depression: Biological and clinical correlates and future directions. In D. S. Janowsky (Ed.), *Psychotherapy indications and outcomes* (pp. 249–273). Washington, DC: American Psychiatric Press.

Stein, D. J., & Young, J. E. (1992). Schema approach to personality disorders. In D. J. Stein & J. E. Young (Eds.), *Cognitive science and clinical disorders* (pp. 271–288). San Diego, CA: Academic Press.

Stewart, J. W., Garfinkel, R., Nunes, E. V., Donovan, S., & Klein, D. F. (1998). Atypical features and treatment response in the National Institute of Mental Health Treatment of Depression Collaborative Research Program. *Journal of Clinical Psychopharmacology, 18*(6), 429–434.

Stuart, S., & Bowers, W. A. (1995). Cognitive therapy with inpatients: Review and meta-analysis. *Journal of Cognitive Psychotherapy, 9*(2), 85–92.

Sullivan, M. J. L., & Conway, M. (1991). Dysphoria and valence of attributions for others' behavior. *Cognitive Therapy and Research, 15*(4), 273–282.

Thase, M. E. (1992). Long-term treatments of recurrent depressive disorders. *Journal of Clinical Psychiatry, 53*(Suppl. 9), 32–44.

Thase, M. E. (1999). How should efficacy be evaluated in randomized clinical trials of treatments for depression? *Journal of Clinical Psychiatry, 60*(Suppl. 4), 23–32.

Thase, M. E., Bowler, K., & Harden, T. (1991). Cognitive behavior therapy of endogenous depression: Part 2. Preliminary findings in 16 unmedicated inpatients. *Behavior Therapy, 22*, 469–477.

Thase, M. E., Greenhouse, J. B., Frank, E., Reynolds, C. F., III, Pilkonis, P. A., Hurley, K., Grochocinski, V., & Kupfer, D. J. (1997). Treatment of major depression with psychotherapy or psychotherapy–pharmacotherapy combinations. *Archives of General Psychiatry, 54*(11), 1009–1015.

Truax, C. B., & Mitchell, K. M. (1971). Research on certain therapist interpersonal skills in relation to process and outcome. In A. E. Bergin & S. L. Garfield (Eds.), *Handbook of psychotherapy and behavior change: An empirical analysis* (pp. 299–344). New York: Wiley.

Versiani, M. (1998). Pharmacotherapy of dysthymic and chronic depressive disorders: Overview with focus on moclobemide. *Journal of Affective Disorders, 51*(3), 323–332.

Whisman, M. A. (1993). Mediators and moderators of change in cognitive therapy of depression. *Psychological Bulletin, 114*, 248–265.

Wierzbicki, M., & Bartlett, T. S. (1987). The efficacy of group and individual cognitive therapy for mild depression. *Cognitive Therapy and Research, 11*(3), 337–342.

Williams, J. M. G. (1997). Depression. In D. M. Clark & C. G. Fairburn (Eds.), *Science and practice of cognitive behaviour therapy* (pp. 259–283). Oxford: Oxford University Press.

Wolpe, J. (1993). Commentary: The cognitivist oversell and comments on symposium contributions. *Journal of Behavior Therapy and Experimental Psychiatry, 24*(2), 141–147.

Wright, J. H. (1996). Inpatient cognitive therapy. In P. M. Salkovskis (Ed.), *Frontiers of cognitive therapy* (pp. 208–225). New York: Guilford Press.

Young, J. E. (1999). *Cognitive therapy for personality disorders: A schema-focused approach* (3rd ed.). Sarasota, FL: Professional Resource Press.

Young, J. E. (1992). *Schema Conceptualization Form.* New York: Cognitive Therapy Center of New York.

Young, J. E. (1994a). *Young Compensation Inventory.* New York: Cognitive Therapy Center of New York.

Young, J. E. (1994b). *Young Parenting Inventory.* New York: Cognitive Therapy Center of New York.

Young, J. E., & Brown, G. (1999). Young Schema Questionnaire (3rd ed.). In J. E. Young, *Cognitive therapy for personality disorders: A schema-focused approach* (Rev. ed., pp. 63–76). Sarasota, FL: Professional Resource Press.

Young, J. E., & Klosko, J. S. (1994). *Reinventing your life: How to break free of negative life patterns.* New York: Plume.

Young, J. E., & Rygh, J. (1994). *Young–Rygh Avoidance Inventory.* New York: Cognitive Therapy Center of New York.

Young, J. E., Wattenmaker, D. & Wattenmaker, R. (1996). *Schema Flashcard.* New York: Cognitive Therapy Center of New York.

Chapter 7

INTERPERSONAL PSYCHOTHERAPY FOR DEPRESSION AND OTHER DISORDERS

Laurie A. Gillies

In this edition, for the first time, a chapter on interpersonal psycho-therapy (IPT) appears in this clinical handbook. Much evidence that has emerged over the past decade supports the clinical effectiveness of this procedure for a variety of problems, particularly depression. A substantial advantage of IPT is the relative ease with which clinicians can learn to administer this protocol with integrity. In this chapter, the process of IPT is illustrated in some detail in the context of the treatment of "Fred," who was suffering from a major depressive episode. Notable is the fact that Fred's therapist—a nurse practitioner working under the close supervision of the author, Laurie Gillies, an international authority on training in IPT—was treating her first case. Although IPT is relatively easy to comprehend, the twists and turns encountered in the administration of IPT (or any therapeutic approach) are particularly evident in this chapter, when the therapist chose to focus on grief as opposed to the recent role transitions experienced by the patient. The clinical evidence that led the therapist to decide on a specific focus, which is one of the crucial elements in administering IPT, is nicely illustrated in this case. Also notable about IPT is the finding that the treatment is more successful when administered with fidelity to the goals of IPT and adherence to the protocol. The power of a therapist and patient working well together and staying on task provides some good evidence for the specific effects of an interpersonal focus to psychotherapy.

Interpersonal psychotherapy (IPT) is a brief individual treatment that is well established as an effective treatment for depression (Klerman, Weissman, Rounsaville, & Chevron, 1984; Weissman, Markowitz, & Klerman, 2000). A published manual has been used in research and treatment since 1984 (Klerman et al., 1984). The senior authors of this manual, Gerald Klerman and Myrna Weissman, were actively involved in depression research in the 1970s and early 1980s and saw a need for a brief treatment that would make treat-ment more readily accessible to those suffering from untreated depression. Since then, IPT has been developed and refined over a number of treatment trials and clinical adaptations. Although it was initially developed for the treatment of major depression, more recently it has been used to treat individuals with other diagnoses, including bulimia nervosa and dysthymic disorder. It has also been used to treat depression in medically ill persons, adolescents, and the elderly (Klerman & Weissman, 1993; Markowitz, 1998). There continue to be several emerging areas of research on new applications of IPT (see Weissman et al., 2000).

EVIDENCE OF IPT'S EFFICACY

IPT was first used in a controlled study by Weissman and her colleagues. In this study, 16 weeks of IPT combined with relatively low doses (by today's standards) of amitriptyline (100–200 mg/day), was found to be more effective for the treatment of depression than either treatment alone or a nonscheduled control treatment (as-needed 50-minute sessions, to a maximum of one per month) (Weissman et al., 1979). In addition, those patients treated with IPT showed significant improvement in social functioning 1 year after treatment; this was not the case for the control condition or for the amitriptyline-alone condition (Weissman et al., 1981).

The most carefully controlled study to date for the treatment of depression, the National Institute of Mental Health Treatment of Depression Collaborative Research Program (NIMH TDCRP; Elkin et al., 1989), was the largest multicenter comparative clinical treatment trial in psychotherapy ever conducted. The study compared IPT, cognitive-behavioral therapy (CBT), imipramine with clinical management (IMI-CM), and placebo with clinical management (PLA-CM). All treatments were standardized and manualized, and treatment adherence measures were carefully monitored to ensure that adequate standardization of the treatment was provided. The control condition (PLA-CM) was designed to help distinguish response to specific treatment from general treatment response or response to nonspecific treatment conditions.

There were no differences among treatments (including PLA-CM) in the less severely depressed patient group. For the more severely depressed patients, however, consistent differences emerged. For patients defined by the Global Assessment Scale (GAS; Endicott, Spitzer, Fleiss, & Cohen, 1976) as more severely depressed and functionally impaired, IPT resulted in better outcomes than PLA-CM did on both the Hamilton Depression Rating Scale (HDRS; Hamilton, 1967) mean scores and on recovery criteria (HDRS scores ≤ 6 and Beck Depression Inventory [BDI; Beck, Ward,

Mendelson, Mock, & Erbaugh, 1961] scores ≤ 9). IMI-CM was consistently superior to PLA-CM on a broader range of measures for this patient group. CBT did not demonstrate significant superiority to PLA-CM for severely depressed and functionally impaired patients. These are compelling findings, because they indicate support for the notion that a talk therapy (IPT) can be effective for severely depressed patients. Traditionally, talk therapies have been recommended for mild to moderately depressed patients.

Slotsky and colleagues (1991) examined patient predictors in the NIMH TDCRP trial and found six predictors that indicated overall prognosis across the treatments. These were social dysfunction, cognitive dysfunction, patient expectation of improvement, endogenous depression, double depression, and duration of current episode. There were *no* significant predictors of differential response among the three active treatments. The patients in the IPT group with better initial social adjustment had a higher rate of complete response than did the patients with high social dysfunction. Among patients with low cognitive dysfunction, those who received IMI-CM or CBT became significantly less depressed than those who received PLA-CM. Patients with high work dysfunction who received IMI-CM had a higher rate of complete response than those with low work dysfunction.

Slotsky and colleagues (1991) suggest that low social dysfunction is a good general predictor of favorable prognosis for outcome from depression, and they note evidence that low social dysfunction is associated with specific responsiveness to IPT. In the NIMH trial, patients with the least social dysfunction responded best to IPT, and patients with the least cognitive impairment responded well to CBT.

In further reanalyses of the data, Klein and Ross (1993) reported that at the conventional $p < .05$ level, IMI-CM was superior to PLA-CM on both the HDRS and the GAS. In the completer group (see below), they noted that IMI-CM was also superior to PLA-CM at a point slightly higher along the severity dimension. IMI-CM was superior to both IPT and CBT on the GAS.

Using Johnson–Neyman analyses, Klein and Ross (1993) found that CBT was superior to PLA-CM on the GAS. IPT was superior to

PLA-CM on the HDRS in the "endpoint" sample (all 239 patients who entered treatment) and on the GAS in the "completer" sample (204 patients who received 3½ weeks of treatment). IPT was superior to CBT on the BDI for both the endpoint and completer samples, while IMI-CM was superior to PLA-CM on the HDRS for the completer group. Klein and Ross (1993) pointed out that on BDI scores among completers, the finding that CBT was significantly inferior to IPT was surprising, noting that the BDI is "the standard instrument for evaluation of CBT effects" (p. 248). In further analyses, they indicated that CBT was relatively inferior to IPT for the moderately to severely depressed patients (i.e., those with a score > 30 on the BDI).

More recent research on IPT has included a number of new treatment populations (see Weissman et al., 2000), as well as two studies using neuroimaging. Martin and Martin (1999) used single-photon emission computed tomography to compare venlafaxine to IPT in 28 patients with major depression. Although both groups showed improvement, different areas of the brain appeared to be affected by the different treatments. Patients treated with venlafaxine showed changes in the angular gyrus and dorsolateral prefrontal cortical area; patients treated with IPT showed the same dorsolateral changes, but also had changes in the limbic central cingulate area.

In a study of posttreatment regional brain metabolic changes using positron emission tomography scan analysis, Brody and colleagues (in press) treated 24 patients with either paroxetine or IPT (based on patient preference). They found that both groups showed decreases in normalized prefrontal cortex and left anterior cingulate gyrus metabolism, as well as increased normalized left temporal lobe metabolism. It should be noted that the paroxetine-treated patients showed a greater mean decrease in HDRS scores (61.4%) than did the IPT-treated patients (38.0%).

The neuroimaging findings are fascinating, in that both studies show change in regional brain metabolic changes following psychotherapy (IPT) alone. Both studies had relatively small sample sizes, however, and so the results must be viewed with caution, in addition, the finding of changes in different areas of the brain when an antidepressant (venlafaxine) was compared with IPT in the Martin (1999) study, as opposed to the same areas of the brain showing change in the Brody and colleagues (in press) study regardless of method of treatment (IPT or paroxetine), suggests a need for further study.

IPT TREATMENT RECOMMENDATIONS

IPT is currently recommended as an acute treatment for symptom removal, prevention of relapse and recurrence, correction of causal psychological problems for secondary symptom resolution, and correction of secondary consequences of depression (Weissman & Markowitz, 1994). The report of the Task Force on Promotion and Dissemination of Psychological Procedures of the Division of Clinical Psychology of the American Psychological Association (American Psychological Association, 1995) has recommended IPT as an empirically validated, well-established treatment for depression as well as bulimia nervosa. Although there is a growing literature on IPT for eating disorders, and a number of clinical trials are currently underway, a complete discussion of the topic is beyond the scope of this chapter (see Weissman et al., 2000).

Other practice guidelines have been developed by the American Psychiatric Association (1993) and the American Medical Association (Depression Guideline Panel, 1993); these guidelines do not require efficacy data from controlled clinical trials as criteria for inclusion. Nonetheless, IPT is defined in both the psychiatric and medical association guidelines as an appropriate acute and maintenance treatment for depression, either alone or in combination with medication. In the continuation and maintenance phases of treatment, the guidelines state that medication alone may be sufficient to prevent relapse or recurrence and to maintain remission of recurrent depression. The guidelines state that IPT, cognitive therapy, and behavior therapy are effective treatments for mild to moderate depression. The primary care guide does not recommend psychotherapy as a sole treatment for patients with severe or psychotic depression. Treatments with established efficacy are recommended over less tested or untested interventions; presumably, "less tested" interventions would include the newer antidepressant medications.

RECENT ADAPTATIONS OF IPT WITH DEPRESSED PATIENTS

IPT and Postpartum Depression

Several authors have noted the need to study psychological treatments for women suffering depression during the childbearing years (Buist, Norman, & Dennerstein, 1990; Frank, Kupfer, Jacob, Blementhal, & Jarrett, 1987; O'Hara, 1994). Stuart and O'Hara (1995) note that the incidence of postpartum depression across all childbearing women is estimated to range from 7% to 16%. Women who experience postpartum depression are at higher than normal risk for recurrent episodes of depression. Specific factors relating to postpartum depression include social isolation, feelings of inadequacy as a parent, concern about the ability to care for a newborn, and sleep and appetite disturbances (Stuart & O'Hara, 1995).

Interpersonal functioning appears to be particularly vulnerable in postpartum depression. O'Hara (1994) has noted that depressed women report perceiving significantly less social support than they desire during the postpartum period. This perceived lack of social support is particularly pronounced in their couple relations.

Stuart, O'Hara, and Blehar (1998) treated 120 women in a comparison of IPT with a wait-list condition. The women were between 2 and 6 months postpartum (average 4.1 months postpartum) and met *Diagnostic and Statistical Manual of Mental Disorders*, third edition, revised (DSM-III-R; American Psychiatric Association, 1987) criteria for a major depressive episode. Patients were referred by their obstetricians or through community screening.

Preliminary results of this study (reported in Weissman et al., 2000) indicate that IPT is effective for the treatment of postpartum depression: 44% of the IPT group showed remission on the BDI, as compared to 14% of the wait-list group. IPT has also been used effectively for the treatment of postpartum depression with depressed adolescent mothers (Gillies, 2000), as well as in a group format (Stuart et al., 1998).

IPT and Depression in HIV-Seropositive Patients

Markowitz, Klerman, and Perry (1992) note that for a number of reasons, the IPT model may be a particularly helpful treatment for depressed patients who are HIV-seropositive. The psychoeducation about depression may enable these patients to understand that depressive symptomatology is not an inevitable sequela of HIV status. The framework of IPT places depression in the present-day interpersonal context; this can also help patients to develop a day-to-day sense of mastery.

Markowitz and colleagues (1992) conducted an open pilot study with 23 depressed HIV-positive patients. Subjects consisted of 18 male and 5 female patients (70% white, 22% black, and 8% other ethnicity). Fifty-seven percent of the patients were gay males, 17% were bisexual males, 13% used intravenous drugs, 9% had heterosexual partners, and 4% were blood transfusion recipients. All patients were aware of their HIV status, and only two met criteria for AIDS. There was no neurological impairment, and none of the patients were actively suicidal. The mean age was 37.3 (SD = 13.1, range = 17 to 61 years).

Outcome was measured according to therapists' global clinical impression, the patients' subjective assessment, and the HDRS. According to these measures, depression was considered resolved in 20 cases (87%). HDRS scores showed a significant improvement, with a baseline mean score of 25.8 (SD = 7.5) and an endpoint score of 6.8 (SD = 5.3) at termination (p < .01).

Markowitz and colleagues (1995) then carried out an NIMH-funded treatment trial comparing IPT to (1) CBT, (2) supportive psychotherapy (SP), and (3) imipramine plus SP (IMI-SP). Preliminary results showed IPT and IMI-SP to be superior to SP and CBT on the BDI (Markowitz, cited in Weissman et al., 2000).

IPT and Late-Life Depression

Blazer and Williams (1980) point out that depression in late life is a serious problem, with 10% to 15% of elderly community residents suffering from depression at any given point in time. They note that whereas those over 65 years of age account for only 11% of the U.S. population, they account for 25% of all suicides.

Frank and colleagues (1993) suggest that IPT is particularly suited to an aging population, given the many losses and role transitions the elderly frequently face. In adaptation of the IPT model to elderly patients, a number of modifications are appropriate. Some allowance is made with regard to length of sessions with older patients; physically frail or acutely depressed elderly patients may not be able to tolerate a 1-hour session. The IPT therapist working with the elderly may also need to coordinate treatment with caseworkers and medical staff. Frank and colleagues point out further that with role disputes, particularly of a long-standing nature in a patient with a diminished social network, the best that can be accomplished may be a tolerance for the dispute rather than an amelioration of it. Such disputes often have to do with long-standing social skills or interpersonal deficits, and these are unlikely to remit in brief treatment.

High activity level on the part of the therapist is essential to the engagement of the older patient. Long silences may be interpreted as lack of interest in the patient; it is better to terminate a session early than to fill the time with extended silences. Care must also be taken with the termination of treatment or the shift from the intensive phase to less frequent maintenance sessions. Given the number of losses the elderly have often tolerated, it is especially important to be sensitive to termination issues in the treatment and to begin working on the issue early.

IPT has been used as a treatment for late-life depression in a number of studies. Although none of the trials included a comparison with another psychotherapy, IPT was effective for the treatment of depression. Rothbloom and colleagues (1982) provided IPT with pharmacotherapy to 18 elderly patients; scores on the HDRS dropped from a mean of 20.9 to 7.2.

Reynolds and colleagues (1992) conducted a double-blind trial of IPT with 61 elderly patients. The study examined the efficacy of maintenance nortriptyline and IPT, both alone and in combination, in a randomized placebo-controlled trial. The trial examined maintenance of recovery over a 3-year period after an open-trial acute treatment phase aimed at an index episode of depression. Pa-

tients were eligible for the maintenance study if they achieved remission of the depressive episode in acute treatment and remained well for 16 weeks of continuation therapy (with both modalities). Seventy-nine percent of the patients achieved full remission of depression following acute treatment with IPT and nortriptyline.

IPT and Adolescent Depression

Brief treatment is particularly well suited to adolescents, given their reluctance to seek out or remain in treatment. Mufson, Morreau, Weissman, and Klerman (1993) point out that the IPT focus on the "here and now" may be particularly developmentally appropriate for teenagers. They conducted an open trial of a modification of IPT for adolescents (IPT-A) with 14 depressed adolescents and found that none of the patients met criteria for major depressive episode following 12 weeks of IPT; at 1 year after treatment, only one patient met criteria for depression.

Modifications of IPT for adolescents include flexibility in the timing and spacing of the sessions, and telephone contact once or twice a week to provide support for the development of a working alliance. Telephone calls can come from therapist to client or vice versa. Calling generally occurs in the first 4 weeks of treatment. A therapist may have to be more active outside of therapy with an adolescent client. This may involve advocating on behalf of the client with school or parent(s); it is not uncommon for IPT-A therapists to meet with parent(s) and school officials.

The IPT-A model has added a fifth area of focus to the four original foci (grief, interpersonal role disputes, interpersonal transitions, and interpersonal deficits—discussed in detail "in the IPT Model," below): single-parent families. This area was chosen since, for an adolescent, the interparental conflicts that frequently follow a separation or divorce can result in a prolonged depressed mood (Mechanic & Hansell, 1989).

IPT Maintenance Treatment

Maintenance IPT therapy has been developed in the hope of maintaining wellness in depressed patients or lengthening the time period between depressive episodes. This is an important goal, given the findings of Prien and colleagues (1984) that 50% of severely depressed patients had a recurrent depressive episode within 3 years of beginning treatment. Frank and colleagues (1993) found that groups receiving IPT maintenance treatment, either alone or with placebo, "survived" (i.e., did not have a recurrence of depression) nearly twice as long between depressive episodes as did the group of patients receiving medication clinic and placebo (*p* < .05).

Maintenance IPT usually occurs once a month for a 50-minute session. The patient continues to work with the therapist on the chosen focal area, and the therapist continues to use the techniques and strategies of IPT during this phase of treatment. Maintenance treatment tends to be open-ended and is most frequently used with patients who have had multiple depressive episodes and are clearly at risk for future episodes. Ideally, maintenance treatment should be offered in the early sessions of IPT, following the history taking when a number of depressive episodes have been identified.

Emerging Applications of IPT

IPT has been used in a number of new applications, in terms of both treatment populations and treatment methodologies. In terms of the latter, IPT has been used in group format, telephone treatment, and conjoint therapy (see Weissman et al., 2000). IPT has also been provided to patients with a diversity of medical illnesses and physical disabilities, including breast cancer, heart and lung transplants, multiple sclerosis, and myocardial infarctions (see Weissman et al., 2000).

In terms of psychological comorbidities, Weissman and colleagues (1979) found that when depressed patients with personality disorders were treated with IPT, their depression was as amenable to treatment as that of patients without personality disorders; however, depressed patients with personality disorders relapsed more quickly than those without Axis II diagnoses. I have adapted IPT for use with patients with borderline personality disorder (with or without comorbid depression) and found it to be a highly effective treatment with a low dropout rate in a small open trial (Angus & Gillies, 1994; Gillies, 1999).

THE IPT MODEL

IPT emphasizes current relationship issues, while recognizing the biopsychosocial factors that contribute to the individual's difficulties. One goal of IPT is to help the patient recognize and alter maladaptive interpersonal interactions. IPT includes the assessment of symptoms of depression, interpersonal functioning, and general psychiatric symptomatology. At the end of the early phase of the treatment, the therapist briefly summarizes for the patient what has been learned to date and describes how the ensuing sessions will use a central interpersonal issue as a framework or focus.

Middle sessions consist of applying specific IPT strategies to the interpersonal focus area, and final sessions provide an opportunity to consolidate gains and educate the patient about possible future episodes of depression. Treatment generally consists of 12 to 16 individual sessions.

The Setting

IPT is typically conducted face to face in 50-minute individual outpatient sessions. IPT is carried out in outpatient units in hospitals, community mental health settings, and private practitioners' offices. Novel approaches are beginning to emerge, however; for example, IPT has been successfully offered by telephone to patients with breast cancer who are suffering from depression (J. Donnelly, personal communication, December 1998). Group IPT and conjoint family work have also been successfully carried out, although IPT remains primarily an individual treatment (Weissman et al., 2000).

In some cases, house calls are carried out initially in order to help family members cope with the depressed patient, or to see a patient who is too depressed to leave his/her bed. This strategy can also be useful in aiding families in their understanding and acceptance of depression. Where possible, psychoeducation about depression can also help family and friends cope. Frank (personal communication, August 1994) found that a psychoeducational program, held on one Saturday afternoon for family and friends of patients, significantly increased medication and IPT treatment compliance, as well as significantly reducing dropout rates and improving outcomes when compared to a control group.

The Patient

IPT is not an appropriate treatment for patients with psychotic disorders or for most inpatients. In the few cases I have supervised with inpatients, the work was untenable because the patients' interpersonal networks were not available to them in the same way they were after hospitalization. Patients who are acutely suicidal or currently using substances are also not suitable candidates for IPT; however, ruling out such patients is sometimes easier said than done. Patients may lie, consciously or unconsciously, to themselves and their therapists about levels of substance use. Assessing the acuteness of suicidal impulses is a highly imperfect science, and most depressed patients I have encountered have at least thought about suicide. When such patients disclose suicidality and/or substance problems, the decision to continue IPT treatment must be made on a case-by-case basis, using clinical judgment. Consulting other IPT practitioners can often be helpful in these situations.

Comorbidity is another important patient variable. Many patients will have "double depression"—that is, a major depressive episode superimposed on dysthymic disorder. This does not appear to affect the efficacy of IPT, but in my experience and that of others, working with patients who have dysthymia presents special challenges for the IPT therapist. Such patients often cannot recall a good premorbid level of functioning and may believe that their dysthymia is simply inborn—as much a part of them as an arm or a leg. Therapists can themselves buy into this and become discouraged working with patients who have dysthymia or double depression. Supervision with peers or an IPT supervisor can be especially helpful with this issue.

The Therapist

The IPT therapist takes an active, supportive role in the treatment. The therapist needs to be well informed about depression, as well as comfortable providing psychoeducation and assuming an expert role with regard to depression. It is also critical for the IPT therapist to maintain optimism in the face of the patient's depression; this serves as a model for the patient and helps the therapist to remain positive about the treatment.

Given that IPT is a manual-based treatment, it is important for the IPT therapist to feel comfortable adhering to specified treatment strategies. It is also very helpful for the IPT therapist to be able to maintain the focus of treatment. Whereas most therapists identify themselves as "eclectic" in their approach to therapy, in IPT specificity appears to be an important factor in outcome. Frank, Kupfer, Wagner, McEachran, and Cornes (1991) found that the greater the adherence to the IPT model, the better the outcome for the patient.

Adhering to the model is a challenge for any therapist, and some therapists may feel unduly inhibited by the need to remain focused on IPT strategies. There is a dyadic element to this for any therapist doing IPT; that is, both patient and therapist contribute to the adherence to the model. Frank and colleagues (1991) found that even the therapists who were able to adhere most closely to the IPT model had great difficulty doing so with some patients. Some therapists experience the IPT approach as "too cookbook" or "too here and now"; for such therapists, IPT may not be suitable.

Therapists bring their previous training with them, and a capacity to unlearn the old and suspend judgment while learning to apply IPT is helpful. IPT trainers have discussed the differing backgrounds of supervisees; it is my sense that there is general agreement that CBT therapists may find the transition to IPT a challenge because of the emphasis on feeling states, whereas psychodynamic clinicians may find it difficult to keep from interpreting or being lured into material from their patients' past. Both CBT and psychodynamic therapists comment on the emphasis on the broad interpersonal network of the patient as novel, and it may be a challenge for therapists from both backgrounds to move from the intrapsychic to the interrelational.

The IPT therapist also needs to be comfortable with the medical model, to the point where he/she feels comfortable encouraging the patient to reduce responsibilities for a few weeks, as would be the case with any serious illness. Some therapists find it difficult to support patients in this way, perhaps because it evokes some of their own conflicts about depression. Therapists may also have philosophical differences with the conceptualization of depression as an illness. I can recall working with a psychologist who was opposed to using the word "illness" in relation to depression, but who felt quite comfortable conceptualizing depression as a "disorder." She was able to work with patients in this way by regarding the temporary reduction of responsibilities by the patients as a means of self-nurturing.

Both novice and highly experienced therapists seem to learn the IPT model quite readily. I have found IPT to be an especially suitable treatment for novice therapists to learn. Both psychiatric residents and psychology interns have commented on their relief in learning a straightforward, easy-to-follow treatment method. Psychiatric residents just out of their medical school training seem especially comfortable with the medical aspects of the model. A colleague and I (Gillies & Frey, 1996) compared a small sample of expert and novice therapists learning IPT. Interestingly, there were no significant differences in the development of the therapeutic alliance, as measured by the Working Alliance Inventory (Horvath & Greenberg, 1989). The patients did not differ significantly on pretreatment measures. All the patients improved, and there were no significant differences on outcome between novice and experienced therapists' patients' scores. These findings suggest that IPT is an easily generalizable and eminently teachable model. Further studies should be carried out, however, to assess differences between therapists who are not only highly experienced, but highly experienced in IPT, compared to novice IPT therapists.

For seasoned therapists, learning IPT means having to apply new treatment methods. "Changing horses in midstream" is a challenge for most of us; however, having trained senior psychoanalysts as well as very experienced CBT therapists, I have found many therapists able to make use of the model. In my experience, most therapists take to the model quite readily.

Another important consideration for the IPT therapist is his/her social support network. Working with depressed patients can be a taxing and demanding job at times, and having strong social support lessens the burden of the work at such times. Over the years,

I have had therapists call to say that working in the IPT model has influenced their own relationship patterns for the better. They report having more balanced work lives and maintaining stronger ties with colleagues. Doing therapy with patients who have experienced catastrophic losses can stir difficult feelings in anyone, and having a supportive network both within the workplace and outside it goes a long way in preventing burnout.

Lastly, IPT therapists must be satisfied with discrete gains. The goal of IPT is not a characterological makeover, but improved interpersonal functioning and the amelioration of depressive symptoms. It can be a challenging shift for anyone to move from a long-term to a short-term therapy mode. Therapists from a long-term therapy background may generally find it difficult to begin doing short-term treatment; this is not an issue specific to IPT.

Early Sessions

Building a Working Alliance

In the early phase of treatment (Sessions 1 through 4), the two major tasks are (1) the establishment of a collaborative working alliance with the patient, and (2) the identification of the interpersonal focus best representing the patient's reported interpersonal relationships. Alliance building in IPT has a particular cast that is influenced both by the structure of the IPT model and by the use of the medical model. The engenderment of hope is often accomplished during the first session, when the therapist notes that IPT is a highly successful treatment for depression. There is also some easing of the burden on the patient when the medical model is explored, and the patient is encouraged to regard the depression as an illness and begin to pull back temporarily from some of the tasks of day-to-day life. This alleviates some pressure on the patient in his/her daily life.

The focus or problem area is established by emphasizing the present history of the problem in terms of interpersonal episodes, followed by a discussion of how the individual experiences these episodes. At this stage the therapist should develop, though not necessarily articulate to the patient, potential hypotheses regarding the patient's interpersonal focus area. It is often useful to look at the past 6 months when choosing a focus, since the course of depression can vary tremendously over time. Initial precipitants of the episode may have very little to do with the patient's recent or current symptoms and difficulties; this is particularly the case when the patient has dysthymic disorder.

Educating the patient about depression can help him/her to feel more optimistic about battling it. For example, in order to help a patient and his/her social network understand the seriousness of depressive illnesses, I may talk about the high social, health, and economic costs of depression. Wells and colleagues (1989) found that individuals with double depression were more likely to lose more time from work than those with any number of serious health conditions, including diabetes, arthritis, back, lung, or gastrointestinal problems. Patients with depression also had significantly worse social functioning and spent more days in bed than patients in any of the aforementioned groups. Only patients with acute coronary artery disease lost more time from work or had worse social functioning than the depressed group. Interestingly, it now appears that depression is a high risk factor even among coronary patients. Frasure-Smith, Lesperance, and Talajic (1993) found that depressed patients with poor social support following myocardial infarctions were significantly more likely to die than were those with good social support.

The depressed patient may also feel isolated and alone with his/her depression. Letting the patient know how common depression is can help combat some of this sense of isolation. The stigma of mental illness remains high, and helping the patient to understand how common depression is can help reduce some of the stigma. I have given patients and their families brochures from the local mental health association that include figures on the incidence and prevalence of depression.

Three other tasks are addressed in the early sessions of IPT: reviewing depressive symptoms, taking the interpersonal inventory, and giving the patient the sick role. These tasks are described below, followed by a discussion of choosing an interpersonal focus for treatment.

Reviewing Depressive Symptoms

Symptom review serves a number of purposes in IPT: It helps the patient to learn about his/her symptom picture; it educates the patient about symptoms he/she may not recognize as part of depression; and it gives the therapist a benchmark to use for monitoring the depression. Patients are often unaware of the full range of depressive symptoms, and frequently target one or two symptoms as "the depression." I have found, for example, that many patients view memory and concentration problems as evidence of "craziness" or dementia, rather than as part of the picture of depression. They are often very relieved to learn that these functions will improve as their depression abates.

Another area of frequent concern for depressed patients is sexuality. Although loss of libido is a frequent symptom of depression, many patients and some clinicians are embarrassed to discuss it. It is especially important to determine a clear time line for the loss of libido, to ensure that it is not the result of medical illness or a side effect of antidepressant or other medications. Since loss of interest in sex can be a side effect for more than 60% of patients on selective serotonin reuptake inhibitors (SSRI) (Montejo-Gonzalez et al., 1997), it is important to establish whether changes in libido occurred following the introduction of an antidepressant rather than being symptomatic of depression. When such a change is associated with antidepressant use, changing medication may alleviate the symptom.

The Interpersonal Inventory

There are a number of ways for the IPT therapist to gather and assess the functioning of the patient's interpersonal inventory. The method used is a matter of personal preference; however, the goal is to have a clear sense of the important people (past and present) in the patient's life. Both the quality and quantity of the relationships need to be assessed. Some IPT therapists use genograms that include friends and family members. Others diagram using a "solar system" approach, with the patient as the sun and his/her closest relationships placed on orbits in concentric rings, moving from the closest to the most distant relations. For some patients beginning IPT treatment, articulating a social support network can feel like an overwhelming task. Poor concentration or a sense of social isolation may be symptomatic of the depression. For such patients, asking which people they saw yesterday or this week may be a useful starting point, and the patients can then work back in time. Some IPT therapists simply gather a thorough interpersonal inventory by carefully focusing on relationships while taking a patient's history.

Regardless of the method used to assess the interpersonal inventory, several types of relationships should be explored. The IPT therapist needs to listen for important omissions in the network; that is, the patient may not mention a key relationship, such as a spouse or parent. This may be because the patient has a conflictual relationship with the person or because there has been some other disturbance in the relationship. It is also important to listen for disruptions in the network: Has the patient moved or started a new job? Have any important figures in the network exited? Are there expected losses in the near future (e.g., the death of someone due to a lingering illness, or potential loss of a network due to a job layoff)? Have there been multiple losses? Are there interconnections among the various clusters on the network, or are members of the network isolated from one another?

The quality of relationships also needs to be assessed. I often ask my patients which persons they would take with them to a desert island and why. This has yielded some surprises over the years; one patient said she would take both the man she was having an affair with and her husband. Asking a final general question about anyone else who is important to the patient at the end of the inventory assessment may prevent such surprises. Both emotional support and instrumental aid should be examined. Does the patient have members of his/her network who supply both? Is there a preponderance of one type of support over the other? Does the patient have a negative network? The classic example of a negative network is the patient with a drinking problem whose network consists of other people who drink; if the patient decides to make changes in drinking behaviors, the majority of the network may be lost.

Another important area to assess in the interpersonal inventory is that of lost or distant relationships. Such relationships may be salvageable and can be especially useful when the patient's immediate circle of friends and family has become exhausted or burned out over the course of the patient's depression. E-mail and long-distance calling can make the strengthening of such ties relatively easy for many patients.

The Sick Role

The assumption of the sick role allows the individual a temporary respite from responsibilities. This is helpful in treating the fatigue and concentration difficulties that are often symptomatic of depression. Patients often feel a sense of shame about being depressed; they believe it to be a moral weakness or failing rather than an illness. It is not unusual for it to be quite difficult for a patient to assume the sick role, and the therapist may have to be quite active in encouraging the patient to take on the sick role. Using the analogy of another illness may help the patient to respect the seriousness of the depression. I have said to patients that no one would expect them to run a marathon with a broken leg, and then question why they expect themselves to be fully functional when they have a serious depressive illness. This generally leads to a discussion of the fears patients have about burdening others, and sometimes to their concerns that no one else can manage the tasks they have to perform. Perfectionism as part of the depressive picture is extremely destructive, and I point out to such patients that someone would carry out the tasks they face if they were so ill they had to be hospitalized. The sick role requires a patient to lean on others for a time; the experience of doing so can lead to a healthy diminishing of perfectionistic tendencies.

The depressed patient faces a difficult task in the acknowledgment of depression as an illness. "Depression" in popular parlance has become a word that can mean anything from "I got a B on my test" to a catastrophic mood state. One of the goals of IPT is to educate the depressed patient and his/her family and friends about the distinctions between the depressive disorders and "a case of the blues." I tell patients that most people will look depressed for a day or two over the course of a year; this is normal. The persistence and severity of symptoms over weeks, months, or years are what distinguish depressive illness from merely "feeling blue" for a day or two.

Choosing a Focus

The four areas defined by Klerman and colleagues (1984) as foci of treatment are grief, interpersonal disputes, role transitions, and interpersonal deficits. The therapist usually ends the first phase of therapy by defining with the patient what the primary interpersonal focus will be; this definition sets the stage for the middle and final phases of the treatment.

Choosing a focus helps the therapist and patient make full use of the limited treatment time. Beginning IPT therapists often feel a bit daunted about choosing a focus; however, a number of strategies can make the task easier. Often the patient will elucidate the focal area connected to the beginning or worsening of depressive symptoms during the initial sessions. It is important to assess when symptoms were at their worst in the immediate past, and to examine this in relation to the functioning of the patient's interpersonal relationships. Recent exacerbations of symptoms are often clues as to the appropriate focal area.

Many depressed patients globalize their symptoms and find it difficult to describe nuances in mood initially. Asking what were the best and worst parts of the past week is often helpful; if a patient has difficulty with this, it may help to ask about the day before the session. It is not uncommon for there to be a number of possibilities for the choice of focal area, but choosing one is important in terms of optimizing the treatment. Very occasionally, I have seen a therapist complete work on one focal area and move on to a second area toward the end of treatment.

It rarely happens that the "wrong" focus is chosen. More often, when the therapist thinks a change in focus may be necessary, there are problems in the therapeutic alliance. In supervising over 100 cases, I have only seen a truly wrong choice of focus a handful of times. In such cases, a key piece of information has often not been disclosed during the early sessions. When this happens, it may be helpful to add a limited number of sessions to the treatment. Sometimes the patient and the therapist may disagree as to the area of focus; in such cases, it is best to follow the patient's lead.

Some IPT therapists discuss all four foci with their patients, while others never discuss the foci per se and simply choose one of the four focal areas to work on. I have found that discussing four different foci with a depressed patient can be somewhat overwhelming for the patient, who often has difficulty with concentration as part of the symptom picture. I generally choose what I consider to be the two most appropriate foci based on the patient's initial presentation, and discuss with the patient which area he/she feels would be most productive to work on.

Summary of the Early Sessions

The early sessions require a concentrated effort to fulfill the various IPT tasks; however, the treatment is quite straightforward, because the tasks are so clear-cut. The sick role must be clearly assigned. This enables the patient to be temporarily excused from some social or work obligations; it also begins the process of activating the interpersonal inventory. A thorough examination of the interpersonal inventory aids in assessing the strengths and weaknesses of the patient's social network. This is a critical feature of IPT, and in turn aids in choosing the focal area for treatment. The IPT therapist chooses one focus from among four: grief, interpersonal role disputes, transitions, and interpersonal deficits. The IPT patient is educated about depression during the early sessions and is encouraged to educate family members and friends about symptoms. The symptoms of depression are reviewed during each session, and any change is noted. The need for medication is also assessed during the early sessions.

The Middle Phase

The middle sessions of IPT are characterized by working through the chosen focal area. In the middle phase (Sessions 4 through 12) dysfunctional aspects of the specific focus are explored, using specific strategies for each focal area. Therapist tasks during the middle phase of treatment include the provision of reassurance and support, the clarification of cognitive–affective markers that precede and often ignite interpersonal difficulties, and active problem solving in relation to interpersonal problems. The patient's symptoms are reviewed each week and tied to the focus area. A discussion of each focal area in turn follows.

Grief

In IPT, grief can only be chosen as the focus when there has been a death of an actual person. The loss of a relationship or employment is considered a transition, and appropriate mourning is facilitated within that focus. The IPT therapist working with a grief focus helps the patient to reactivate the mourning process; this is often a very painful process for the patient. The patient may fear that he/she will be overwhelmed by the grief and "go crazy." The IPT therapist provides reassurance that such fears are normal, but that working through the feelings will help resolve the depression. When this is complete, the focus of the therapy shifts to helping the patient establish interests and relationships that may act as a substitute for the lost relationship.

The initial strategy for grief work in IPT is to tie symptoms of depression to the death of the significant person. Other tasks include reconstructing the relationship, examining the sequence of events surrounding the death, and exploring related feelings. When this has been carried out, it is possible to begin the work of contemplating ways of becoming involved with others.

Role Disputes

Disputes can take a number of forms. They may consist of loud battles, or there may be silent disagreements with a great deal of grudge holding. When silent disputes are taking place, the initial presentation of the relationship may consist of an overidealized account; a balanced picture of a healthy relationship includes both positive and negative aspects. The goal of the IPT therapist in assessing disputes is to clarify the stage of the dispute and to help the patient identify and plan actions toward resolving the dispute.

There are three possible stages of dispute: renegotiation, impasse, and dissolution. The IPT therapist attempts to encourage renegotiation of the dispute unless the patient is clearly endangered, such as in cases of domestic violence. Often renegotiation involves "heating up" a cold or difficult relationship, and some patients may need to be warned that the dispute may get worse before it gets better. Patients often present in the impasse stage of a dispute. They are clearly stuck, and there may be little direct communication in the relationship. Communication analysis with such patients often reveals the use of silence as a weapon, unnecessarily indirect or nonverbal communications, and a lack of meaningful discussion about many aspects of the relationship. Dissolution is rarely a first step in IPT; however, if renegotiation fails, the therapist then helps the patient to grieve for the relationship and move on.

The goals of treatment when dispute is the area of focus consist of identifying the dispute, planning a course of action, and assessing communication styles. Specific strategies include relating symptoms of depression to the dispute, determining the stage of the dispute, and examining nonreciprocal role expectations. A lack of reciprocity in relationship is characterized by differences in expectations, values, and goals for the relationship. In some cases, differences may be irreconcilable. For example, I supervised a case where the patient did not want to have children, while his wife did. Eventually the marriage broke down, and part of the treatment consisted of helping the patient grieve for the loss of this relationship. Negotiating such differences involves examining the patient's options and alternatives. In this case, both parties were very committed to their views, and no viable alternatives to separation were found.

It is also important to examine patterns in disputes. The patient may present with a single dispute, or there may be issues that are similar across a number of relationships. The therapist can choose to work on a key relationship or on disputes across relationships. Lastly, it is important to examine how the dispute is perpetuated and whether or not there is any unconscious gain for the patient in continuing the dispute. It is also helpful to look at the assumptions that underlie the dispute; clarifying these assumptions may aid in improving the communication in the relationship.

Transitions

Transitions often involve role change resulting from life events—for example, moving from being single to married, or being a student to being an employee. Such changes can be wished for, dreaded, or neutral in valence, but most will require a new repertoire of behavior. The goals of treatment when transition is the focus are to help the patient mourn the loss of the old role and accept the new role. Most people experience a loss of self-esteem when they enter a new role. They frequently experience a diminished sense of competency, because it takes time to develop a sense of mastery in most new roles. For the depressed patient, such transitions can be especially painful.

IPT strategies when dealing with transitions consist of reviewing depressive symptoms and tying them to the transition. The therapist helps the patient come to terms with role changes. An examination of the positive and negative aspects of both the new and the old roles is a key IPT strategy when working with transitions. Another strategy is to encourage the patient to experience all of his/her feelings about both roles. Over the course of IPT, the patient should develop a sense of mastery in the new role; this frequently involves developing new relationships or expanding present ones to learn from those who have expertise in the functions associated with the new role. I remember working with a survivor of breast cancer who had gone to a self-help group prior to her therapy but had found it singularly unhelpful. She spoke disparagingly of the women in the group as "losers" and "ghosts waiting to die." Once she began IPT, however, and her depression began to remit, she spontaneously rejoined the group and was able to make considerable use of the expertise of the other survivors in dealing with her own cancer.

Transitions can be negative or positive, and while the difficulties associated with negative transitions (such as job demotion or being fired) may seem readily apparent, it is also important to consider positive transitions. I once had a workshop participant come up during a break and tell me that she now understood why her recent job promotion was less pleasurable than she had expected. She was in transition and was now the boss of her former peers; however, she had not yet developed relationships with other supervisors. Those experiencing wished-for transitions, such as promotions, may feel guilty about not enjoying their success more and may feel sheepish or ungrateful about discussing such feelings with others. This isolation can contribute to the development of a depression in vulnerable individuals.

Extremely negative transitions, such as developing a catastrophic illness, may seem to offer little in the way of opportunities for mastery or an improved quality of life. In working with patients who have cancer or AIDS, though, I have come to believe that it is possible to improve the patients' experience of the quality of life by effectively treating the depression. Gravely ill depressed patients have taught me that a sense of connectedness and emotional well-being are possible, even in the face of devastating illness. Such moments can provide a sense of meaning and value to a patient's life.

Interpersonal Deficits

The goals for treating interpersonal deficits are quite straightforward; they are to help the patient increase the quality and quantity of interpersonal relationships. "Deficits" is an unfortunate term and should never be used with patients; a more useful term is "loneliness." In IPT, depressive symptoms are reviewed and tied to the patient's sense of isolation. Past relationships may need to be reviewed, as there may be a paucity of present-day relationships. When a patient's social support network is very limited, the therapeutic relationship may become a focus in the treatment. This is the only focal area where the therapeutic relationship is examined. Unlike traditional psychodynamic approaches, IPT does not generally emphasize the nature of the transference, apart from in the focal area of deficits.

The exception is when transference issues jeopardize the therapeutic relationship. In such cases, the issues must be addressed, regardless of the area of focus. Should therapist and patient find themselves at an impasse due to difficulties between them, the therapist is encouraged to acknowledge and explore such difficulties openly, and to use this dispute as a model for the resolution of interpersonal problems. Klerman and colleagues (1984) report that with depressed patients, the therapy relationship often remains positive because of the supportive nature of the approach; this has also been my experience.

When the focus is on deficits, the patient's relationships need to be examined in terms of both their positive and negative aspects. Patterns and parallels in relationships are also examined. The gains made by these patients are generally modest, and it is especially important for the therapist working with this focus to have limited expectations. Given that the research shows patients with limited social networks do less well with IPT than those with strong social support, circumscribed gains should be expected from patients with interpersonal deficits. In my experience, patients with interpersonal deficits may not show marked change in the quantity of relationships until well after the treatment has ended.

The Final Phase

The last quarter of the treatment in IPT features an emphasis on termination of the therapy, although the focal area continues to be worked with actively. The end of therapy should never come as a surprise for the IPT patient; indeed, it should have been discussed from the first session. Nonetheless, it is important to acknowledge termination as a time of loss. For many patients working with grief as a focus, the end of the therapeutic relationship represents an important opportunity to rework an experience of loss, though clearly a less emotionally laden one than the death of a loved one. Many patients comment that they are surprised by the attachment they feel toward their therapists; they had not expected it, given the brevity of the treatment. For some, the treatment may be the first successful treatment they have had for depression, and they are understandably reluctant to break the tie. I believe the opportunity to master feelings about loss is especially important for patients with depression, and termination provides an opportunity for mastery. In addition, one of the basic tenets of most brief treatments is that the pressure of the looming termination helps the treatment to move forward; clearly, this is diluted when treatment is extended.

There are a number of tasks to be carried out during the termination phase. The patient needs to be reminded of his/her strengths and of the strategies he/she has learned to employ to treat the depression. It is also important for the patient to be able to identify "early warning systems" of depression; that is, the patient needs to be able to know when depressive symptoms are reaching a level that requires professional intervention. The patient has to develop a plan to access help when it is needed. A review of the interpersonal inven-

tory, and a discussion of the importance of increasing social attachments when symptoms of depression flare up, are critical for the patient who is completing IPT.

The final phase of treatment (Sessions 12 through 16) marks an integration of the major interpersonal themes discussed in the earlier sessions and focuses on identifying and maintaining new interpersonal coping strategies. The therapist should actively identify and concretize the advances and goals the patient has achieved throughout the therapy program. In addition, as noted above, the therapist reviews depressive symptomatology with the patient and discusses strategies for appropriate intervention should another depressive episode develop.

If maintenance treatment has been agreed upon, it is still important to mark the end of the intensive phase of the treatment and to carry out the final sessions' tasks. The therapist should highlight the work carried out in this phase of treatment and demarcate the transition to the maintenance phase of treatment.

IPT Treatment Failure

In the event that IPT has not been helpful, the patient must be helped to deal with the difficult feelings associated with a treatment failure. It should be no surprise to the therapist or the patient if there has been no improvement, since the weekly review of symptoms should make a lack of improvement readily apparent. Given the difficulties of arranging referrals in many health care systems, it is appropriate to discuss such referrals with the patient at the midpoint of treatment and to begin to set such referrals in place. It is also important to access the patient's feelings of anger, disappointment, and helplessness in the face of a failed treatment, and for the patient to be helped to understand that it is the treatment that has failed, not the patient.

Summary of the Final Sessions

The final sessions of IPT treatment emphasize the termination of the therapeutic relationship while work continues on the focal area. A review of the treatment is carried out. This includes revisiting the patient's depressive symptoms and coping strategies; in addition, a plan for help seeking in the event of future depressive episodes is developed. Where appropriate, the transition to maintenance treatment is reviewed and discussed. When IPT has failed to provide relief from the depression, feelings regarding the failure of the treatment and appropriate referrals are discussed.

CASE EXAMPLE: THE MAN WHO WAS FROZEN WITH GRIEF

Fred felt that his depression was "ruining his life." He was a 48-year-old married father of four. For the past 12 years he had worked in a meat-packing plant. Fred left work after a number of difficulties culminating in an incident where he felt an overwhelming wish to stab a fellow employee. He did not act on the impulse, but left work that day and did not feel he could return. He was referred for IPT by his general practitioner, following a 3-month absence from work due to "stress."

On initial presentation, Fred's symptoms included early-morning wakening, tearfulness, lethargy, poor motivation, and a weight gain of 30 pounds over the previous 4-month period. He was sleeping 14 hours a day and felt the future looked hopeless. He could not imagine returning to work and was increasingly isolated from family and friends. He experienced a great deal of shame about not functioning in the provider role and had passive suicidal thoughts.

A recurrent image for Fred, prior to his leaving work, had been taking off his "cold suit" and allowing himself to freeze to death in the refrigerator section where he worked. He did not believe he would actually kill himself, however, because of "what it would do to the family." He found it difficult to concentrate, and while he had been an avid reader in the past, he could no longer get through a newspaper or magazine article. Fred had also lost interest in sex, and he had not had sexual relations with his wife in several months.

Fred had enjoyed a good relationship with his wife, Doris, prior to the depressive episode. One of the precipitants to his depression appeared to be a resolution on Doris' part to live life to its fullest. Six months prior to his consultation, Doris had had her 45th birthday and resolved to go back to school and pursue a teaching degree. She also began spending time on weekend with friends in her new program.

Fred described his wife as a kind and loving woman, but he missed her, resented her absences, and felt guilty about his resentment. He "never got to see her any more," and there had been increasing estrangement between the spouses. Fred's two daughters were married and lived several hours away. His elder son, Fred Jr., had gone away to junior college the preceding year, and this had created a noticeable absence in Fred's life. He and Fred Jr. had been very close. They used to garden together and play guitar. His younger son, Ernest, was 16 years old and was beginning to make plans for college. Fred acknowledged wishing his children to have these opportunities, but also expressed some regret and sadness about the loss of connection with his sons. Ernest had recently become involved with his first serious girlfriend and was frequently absent from the house. Fred ruminated that perhaps his poor moods had driven Ernest away from home.

Depression is frequently associated with stressful life events. In Fred's case, he was off work; one son had recently left home and the other was preparing to leave; and his wife had become involved in college life. Although life events can be positive (such as a promotion or marriage) or negative (job loss or illness), most are associated in some way with loss or feared loss (Brown, Harris, & Copeland, 1977). Life events typically involve changes in relationships; for example, a job loss or promotion will generally involve developing some new relationships or redefining existing ones. Improving interpersonal relationships is critical for the depressed patient, because frequently such patients have either withdrawn from or burned out their social networks. Fred was fairly typical in this regard; he saw very few people outside his immediate family when he first began treatment.

The Setting

Fred saw his therapist in a free-standing community mental health clinic in rural Illinois. They met for 16 sessions, and the therapist had weekly 30-minute supervision sessions with me by telephone. She sent a tape of the session to me each week, having obtained signed written consent from the patient to do so. I reviewed each tape prior to our telephone supervision.

The Patient

Fred presented with a major depressive episode of 4 months' duration following a referral from his doctor. He was skeptical about psychotherapy and couldn't conceive of depression as a serious problem. He had initially presented to his family doctor with heart palpitations and shortness of breath. At that time he was convinced his heart was failing, and he was not happy about his subsequent referral to the mental health clinic. Beneath his fear of heart disease was a greater fear that he was going crazy, as this exchange between Fred (F) and his therapist, Beth (B), indicates.

F: . . . so my doctor said to come and see you because I'm stressed—whatever that means.

B: What does it mean for you?

F: I think the doc thinks I'm going nuts.

B: I don't think you're going nuts, and I don't think your doctor thinks you're going nuts, but you do have a serious clinical depression. You were sent to us because we specialize in treating depression. There's a lot of good research showing that interpersonal psychotherapy is an effective treatment for depression, and I hope it'll be helpful for you.

F: What if it's not?

B: Most people I see who are depressed don't think it'll help them. Hopelessness is a symptom of depression, you know. But most of the people I see do get better. If IPT doesn't help, there are other treatments we can refer you for.

The therapist was helping the patient to identify depressive symptoms, as well as relieving his very real fears of being ill with heart disease or psychosis. She was also giving the patient hope by pointing out the research on IPT's efficacy.

The Therapist

Fred's therapist was Beth, a nurse practitioner with 20 years of therapy experience. This was her first IPT case. Beth is a therapist of considerable personal warmth, and she very ably conveyed concern and compassion for Fred. She is herself a mother of five children and grandmother of two, and could talk easily with Fred about the challenges of parenting.

The Early Sessions

As noted above, Fred entered treatment feeling angry and upset about his referral to a mental health team. Anger and irritability are cardinal signs of depression, although in clinical practice they can be mistakenly assumed to be characterological. Beth took a careful history of Fred's angry outbursts and paid special attention to the people in his life with whom he was angry.

B: So has your temper always been like this?

F: No, I wouldn't say so. Work has really been getting me down for a while now, and I get pretty angry with the guys at work.

B: Which ones?

F: Well, mostly Bill and Emry, the boss and his sidekick. They were really rubbing me the wrong way before I left work.

B: When did they start getting to you?

Beth now has the names of two key players in Fred's social network. She has established that he was not globally angry at work, and she was working on establishing a time frame for the beginning of the depressive episode. Detailed descriptions of the patient's social network and a clear picture of when the depressive episode began are critical tasks in the early sessions of IPT. Having a time line for the depression helps to clarify the interpersonal events that were occurring at the time the episode began and their possible impact on the development of the depression.

The Sick Role

It is often quite difficult for the patient to assume the sick role. The therapist frequently has to be quite active, as Beth was in this case.

B: So, Fred, it's pretty clear to me that when we look at all the symptoms you describe —the irritability, fatigue, your weight gain, the suicidal thoughts you've been having, the loss of interest in sex—these are symptoms of a major depressive episode. You're really not well, and while you're beginning to recover in the next few weeks, it's important that you take it easy.

F: Take it easy? I've been off work for 3 months. You can't take it much easier than that.

B: Well, actually, Fred, you can and you should. I know you've been doing a lot of work around the yard and the house, and I'm wondering if you could ease up on that kind of thing for the next few weeks? If you had pneumonia, you wouldn't be out shoveling snow. We know that depression is a serious illness, and if we don't take it seriously and treat it seriously, you're not likely to get better. So for the next few weeks, I'd like you to take it a little easier on the chores, maybe ask someone to lend a hand. Could you try?

F: Well, I guess I could get my neighbor's kid to shovel snow for a couple of weeks. He came by yesterday looking for the work.

B: That's a great idea.

Taking the sick role requires that the patient have a social network capable of supporting and bestowing the sick role. With effort and Beth's active support, Fred was able to ask his neighbor to take on yard tasks that Fred had felt he should assume while at home. Beth was able to help Fred understand that the sick role was a temporary phase, and when it became clear to him that this was not to be a permanent condition, he was able to relax a bit and allow others to care for him in instrumental ways.

In encouraging the patient to take on the sick role, using the analogy of another illness may help the patient to respect the seriousness of the depression. Beth also cast herself as an expert about depression; this is important for the IPT therapist, since it helps the patient to feel confident about the treatment. Beth also took on a coaching role, offering suggestions and praising Fred when he began to take on the sick role.

An important secondary function of the sick role is that it often begins to activate a moribund social network. Even the simple task of Fred's speaking to the neighbor began the process of getting Fred out into the world and a little more connected to people. Assessing the individual's interpersonal network aids in understanding the patient's world, as well as determining potentially helpful or harmful relationships to focus on in treatment.

The Patient's Interpersonal Inventory

Fred and his wife had been married for 25 years at the time of his treatment. In addition to their four surviving children, there had been a daughter who had died of sudden infant death syndrome at 11 days of age. She was born 18 months after the birth of their younger son. Fred and his wife had decided to have the baby after a number of weeks of worrying about the financial and emotional strain of adding a fifth child to their young family. After deciding to have the baby, they had enjoyed the pregnancy and were wholeheartedly looking forward to the new baby. Doris had hemorrhaged during the birth and had spent 2 weeks in the hospital after the delivery.

Fred had enjoyed close relationships with all his children, though he found the adjustment to their increasing independence as young adults a difficult transition. In terms of other social support, Fred described a good, if somewhat distant, relationship with his parents. He also described a good relationship with his in-laws, who were frequent visitors in the family home. The family had lived on the same street for the past 22 years and enjoyed good relationships with a number of neighbors. Fred noted that he had seen less of his neighbors since leaving work. He felt ashamed and unable to look them in the eye, for fear that they would feel he was a "slacker."

Fred's relationships had become increasingly fractious at work prior to his leaving. He noted arguments with a number of colleagues and had been "put on warning" by his boss for comments he had made about the boss in front of coworkers. Fred was ashamed of his outbursts at work and globalized these outbursts to a rather pessimistic view of himself as an angry, difficult man. Prior to his depression, he had been friendly with a number of the men at work, frequently joining them for a drink at the end of their shift.

Choosing a Focus

Fred and his therapist had a number of possible foci to choose from. These included transition (his work situation, the recent changes in his marriage, and his "emptying nest"), disputes (with coworkers and possibly with his wife), and unresolved grief. The choice of grief was made for a number of reasons. The changes that had occurred in his marriage were a result of Fred's wife's resolution to try to end her own silent mourning for her lost daughter and live a richer, fuller life. The discord this precipitated in the marriage was directly connected to the unresolved grief Fred was experiencing. Similarly, the therapist understood Fred's reaction to his emptying nest as especially acute, because his unresolved grief due to the earlier loss of his infant daughter was reactivated by the growing distance as his children entered adulthood.

Another important factor in choosing a focus is to choose "the hot spot"—that is, the area with the greatest emotional resonance for the patient. Clearly, for Fred, this was the loss of his infant daughter:

B: How old was your daughter when she died?

F: (*Tears welling up*) Eleven days. My wife was still in the hospital. My mother-in-law was helping with the kids (*sobbing*). It was me that found her. (*He cries for a few minutes*) She's so little and so perfect, so healthy-looking.

As is frequently the case with patients who have unresolved grief, Fred spoke of his daughter in the present tense. The immediacy of the experience of her death belied the many years that had passed for Fred and was also indicative of unresolved mourning.

Fred expressed surprise when Beth recommended grief as the focal area for treatment:

F: But it was all so long ago. And I'm really worried about work right now.

B: Yes, but whenever we speak of your baby daughter, it feels like it all happened yesterday.

F: That's true.

B: And I know you have a lot of other things on your plate right now, but I think you'd be able to manage them better if you had a chance to work through the terrible loss of your daughter. I really think it could help you to have a chance to talk with me about that terrible time in your life.

F: OK. I'll try anything to feel better.

The Middle Sessions

Fred's case illustrates many of the key elements of working with grief as a focus in IPT. Beth tied Fred's symptoms to his feelings of loss. She worked hard with him to help him remember and discuss the actual facts of the death of his infant daughter. This was very painful for both of them. As is pointed out in the text *Interpersonal Psychotherapy of Depression* (Klerman et al., 1984), one of the key features of IPT is helping the patient to tolerate difficult feelings. Focusing on the actual death, as well as the events surrounding the death (including the baby's birth and the funeral), appeared to be instrumental in Fred's improvement.

B: Tell me about finding your daughter's body.

F: I did.

B: Can you tell me about it?

F: Why? What's it going to help?

B: I think it may help you. Have you ever talked to anyone about it?

F: No.

B: It seems to me that's a pretty heavy burden to bear alone, and I suspect it's affecting your mood.

F: (*Starting to cry*) It didn't seem fair to bother anyone with it. (*Long pause*) I had gotten up to give her a bottle. The sun was up, and usually she was awake by then. I remember thinking it was nice to get a little extra sleep. I can't believe I thought that now.

B: You didn't know.

F: I went into her room and she didn't look right; she looked bluish-gray. I felt myself starting to panic. Then it was like a bad dream. I went to the crib and touched her face; it was cold. (*Sobbing*) I picked her up and took her to the change table. I tried to do CPR—I put my mouth over her nose and mouth and breathed, but nothing happened. Then I called my mother-in-law. She came and called an ambulance. It's sort of a blur after that.

Fred had vivid memories of his daughter's death scene, but had never shared them with anyone. A few weeks after speaking of it in the therapy, Fred asked his wife whether she wanted to know what he had seen. She did, and in telling her Fred felt more relief. As is often the case, the family had wanted to know all that he knew, but had been afraid to ask him for fear of upsetting him. Fred and Doris later sat down with all their children and talked about what had happened. They grew closer as a family as a result of talking about their loss.

Beth had felt concerned about making Fred's mood worse by talking about the details of the death, and she spoke in supervision about feeling ghoulish when pressing Fred for information. This is a common fear for IPT therapists, and Beth was relieved to hear from Fred at the end of treatment that he had found it very helpful to talk about these extremely painful events.

Beth was able to actively maintain the focus on grief, and this appeared to be critical for Fred's recovery. She and Fred spent several very sad sessions recounting the death, the period leading up to it, and the weeks and months following the death. Fred had never spoken to anyone but Doris about his early ambivalence concerning the pregnancy, and found it very helpful to talk about his subsequent guilt and the irrational belief that if he had not been ambivalent his daughter would have lived. Beth reassured him that the belief that the death could somehow have been prevented is ubiquitous among survivors, but irrational nonetheless. This was very helpful to Fred; he had feared he was going crazy for holding such a belief, and thought he was the only one to hold the belief. As Fred talked with Doris between sessions, she confessed she thought the baby's death was somehow her fault and could have been prevented if she had been home rather than in the hospital. Fred and Doris were able to reassure each other, and this further strengthened their relationship.

Termination

As can be imagined, termination was difficult for Fred. Beth felt worried about abandoning Fred. As is frequently the case with novice IPT therapists, she also felt that there were a number of other areas (e.g., his transition at work and some of the marital discord) where productive work could continue to occur. In supervision, Beth was able to work through her feelings about termination. She was reminded that the goals of IPT are to restore the patient to the previous level of functioning (i.e., the level prior to the depressive episode) and to improve social functioning. By Session 8, Fred had lost all of his symptoms. By Session 12, he had joined a gymnasium and was losing some of the 30 pounds he had put on during his depressive episode. His sleep pattern had normalized, and he felt active and motivated. He was much more connected to his family and was once again involved in his community and neighborhood.

Termination brought a sense of loss, as is often the case with grief issues. Beth was able to normalize Fred's feelings at termination. She explained that many people who had benefited from treatment found it difficult to end the weekly sessions with their therapists. She followed standard IPT practice by pointing out the considerable gains Fred had made in therapy. She noted the decrease in his symptomatology and his considerable efforts in dealing with his loss. She tied the symptoms to his loss experience and noted that he might be vulnerable in the future to other losses. They worked together on strategizing how Fred might both identify and cope with a future depressive episode. He agreed to contact his family physician in the event that he noticed a return of symptomatology.

Beth acknowledged to Fred how much she had enjoyed working with him and how impressed she was by his efforts to come to terms with such a terrible loss. She told him directly that she thought he had dealt successfully with the death of his daughter, and that she felt confident that he now had many resources available to him to deal with future stress and strain. She counseled him to continue to stay in touch with close members of his network. Two years after the completion of treatment, Beth received a Christmas card from Fred, letting her know that he was happy and had no further symptoms of depression.

LIMITATIONS OF IPT TREATMENT

Although IPT is now being used in a number of purely clinical settings, it is important to remember that most of the research on the efficacy of the model has been carried out in universities and teaching hospitals. The practical applicability of IPT outside the controlled environment of research protocols must be considered. In research trials, therapists are usually highly experienced, and a great deal of time and effort goes into training them to deliver the treatment accurately. Patients are usually selected on the basis of discrete diagnoses and frequently lack the complicated multiple diagnoses encountered in many practitioners' offices. Although the issue is not distinct to IPT, the empirical question about the applicability of manual-based, research-driven treatments to general clinical practice remains unanswered.

Another consideration with regard to generalizability is dropout rate. Again, this is a problem for both drug treatments and psychotherapies in general; however, in the NIMH TDCRP, 32% of the 239 patients who entered treatment dropped out prior to completion of the study. Interestingly, there were no significant treatment × termination status interactions on the HDRS, although patients who terminated early across treatments were more severely depressed prior to treatment than were patients completing treatment (pretreatment HDRS scores, 20.6 vs. 19.0, respectively; $F(1, 231) = 6.32, p < .02$). Dropout rates consisting of a third of the sample need to be carefully considered when one is evaluating the efficacy of treatment modalities. This is particularly true when it is taken into account that the more severely depressed patients dropped out.

Another limitation of IPT is the lack of randomized clinical trials with regard to particular treatment populations. Apart from studies of patients with diagnoses of bulimia nervosa, major depression, and dysthymic disorder, there are few comparisons of IPT to other treatments in the literature. Extremely small samples are common for most other groups treated with IPT, and these findings should be reviewed with some caution. It is also important to consider the role of medication, given (1) that many patients in open trials of IPT are taking antidepressants during the studies and (2) that because the sample size is so small, medication is often not adequately controlled for in the data analyses.

Although IPT appears to be effective with a number of different treatment populations (notwithstanding the limitations of open treatment trials), it is important to note that it does not appear to be an effective treatment for substance use disorders. Rounsaville and Carroll (1993) studied patients with opioid addiction who were being maintained on methadone. Patients had to have had 6 weeks of treatment in a methadone program prior to IPT. Patients with schizophrenia and mania were excluded. As with many studies of substance use, there were high dropout rates: 38% of the patients in the IPT group and 54% of the low-contact group completed the full 24 weeks of treatment. IPT was not an effective treatment in this treatment trial. The findings on the treatment of substance use with IPT are particularly important and welcome, in that they provide some evidence that IPT has specificity with regard to treatment. It appears that for patients with severe, active substance abuse or dependence, IPT is not the treatment of choice. It is regrettable that there are not more publications of negative findings, as this would enhance understanding with regard to the efficacy of treatment.

Finally, it is important to note that purity of treatment effect is a compelling variable, because it begins to answer questions about specific suitability for specific treatments. Frank and colleagues (1991) point out that treatment quality is seldom studied and must relate to treatment outcome. In most well-controlled psychotherapy studies, therapists must demonstrate adequate levels of adherence to a model, but the impact beyond simple adherence is rarely measured. Very little is known about truly expert therapists in almost any model and how they differ from and are similar to novice therapists. Although meeting adherence in clinical trials has been a consistent problem in psychotherapy outcome research, it is also important to gather information on expert therapists, as they may have much to teach about training in specific models. This is offset, of course, by the need for a generalizable model that is useful and learnable.

In a cleverly designed study, Frank and colleagues (1991) looked at whether or not specificity of IPT treatment had an impact on the length of time until the next depressive episode. This research was based on earlier studies (Frank, Kupfer, & Perel, 1989; Frank et al., 1990) where patients with recurrent unipolar depression received a combination of IPT and pharmacotherapy (imipramine, 150–300 mg) for the treatment of an acute episode. In the Frank and colleagues (1993) study, patients who received the less specific IPT had a mean survival time between depressive episodes of 18.1 weeks, while patients who received the more specific (i.e., more model-adherent) IPT had a median survival time between episodes of 101.7 weeks. This finding was not moderated by baseline clinical levels of depression, by depression levels at the time of random assignment, or by differences among clinicians. It appears that the specificity of treatment is a stable feature that grows out of individual patient–therapist dyads. This is a compelling finding and warrants further research. Since all the therapists in the study had some patients with whom they were able to work most specifically within the model and others with whom they were unable to work specifically, more research about patient characteristics in these dyads would enable greater prediction in terms of which patient–therapist dyads would be most effective with IPT. In a subsample, those who received IPT maintenance therapy (on a monthly basis) following drug discontinuation remained well significantly longer than those who did not. These findings were maintained a full 3 years after the beginning of treatment ($p = .05$). Frank and colleagues (1991) are careful to point out that the results of the larger study indicate that antidepressant medication, when used at the dose equivalent to that used during the acute episode, has a substantial prophylactic value. The authors comment, however, that not all patients are willing to take antidepressant medication for prolonged periods of time. Furthermore, there are patients who may need to be withdrawn from medication or may not be suitable for medication for medical reasons (e.g., pregnancy, lactation, some heart diseases).

Frank and colleagues (1991) also point out that it is very important to understand more about how both to teach and to measure high-quality therapy. Simple adherence to a treatment manual clearly does not account for additional variance among therapists, and this aspect of psychotherapy research is sorely understudied. Given that the survival rate of the lower-quality therapy group in the Frank and colleagues (1990) study matched that of the general population (whereas patients in the higher-quality treatment had a survival rate to the next depressive episode that was more than four times greater than expected), there is a strong argument to be made for studying expert or high-quality treatment from a clinical point of view.

REFERENCES

American Psychiatric Association. (1980). *Diagnostic and statistical manual of mental disorders* (3rd ed.). Washington, DC: Author.

American Psychiatric Association. (1987). *Diagnostic and statistical manual of mental disorders* (3rd ed., rev.). Washington, DC: Author.

American Psychiatric Association. (1993). Practice guidelines for major depressive disorder in adults. *American Journal of Psychiatry, 150*(Suppl.), 1–26.

American Psychological Association. (1995). Training and dissemination of empirically-validated psychological treatments: Report and recommendations. *The Clinical Psychologist, 48*(1), 3–24.

Angus, L., & Gillies, L. A. (1994). Counseling the borderline client: An interpersonal approach. *Canadian Journal of Counseling, 28*, 69–82.

Beck, A. T., Ward, C. H., Mendelson, M., Mock, J., & Erbaugh, J. (1961). An inventory for measuring depression. *Archives of General Psychiatry, 4*, 561–571.

Blazer, D. G., & Williams, C. D. (1980). Epidemiology of dysphoria and depression in an elderly population. *American Journal of Psychiatry, 137*, 439–444.

Brody, A. L., Saxena, S., Stoessel, P., Gillies, L. A., Fairbanks, L. A., Alborzian, S., Phelps, M., Huang, S.-C., Wu, H.-M., Ho, M. L., Ho, M. K., Au, S. C., Maidment, K., & Baxter, L. R., Jr. (in press). Regional brain metabolic changes in patients with major depression treated with either paroxetine or interpersonal therapy: Preliminary findings. *Archives of General Psychiatry*.

Brown, G. W., Harris, T., & Copeland, J. R. (1977). Depression and loss. *British Journal of Psychiatry, 130*, 1–18.

Buist, A., Norman, T. R., & Dennerstein, L. (1990). Breast feeding and the use of psychotropic medication. *Journal of Affective Disorders, 178*, 197–206.

Depression Guideline Panel. (1993). *Clinical practice guideline: Depression in primary care: Treatment of major depression* (AHCPR Publication No. 93-0551). Rockville, MD: U.S. Department of Health and Human Services.

Elkin, I., Shea, M. T., Watkins, J. T., Imber, S. D., Sosky, S. N., Collins, J. F., Glass, D. R., Pilkonis, P. A., Leber, W. R., Docherty, J. P., Fiester, S. J., & Parloff, M. B. (1989). National Institute of Mental Health Treatment of Depression Collaborative Research Program: General effectiveness of treatments. *Archives of General Psychiatry, 46*, 971–982.

Endicott, J., Spitzer, R. L., Fleiss, J. L., & Cohen, J. (1976). The Global Assessment Scale: A procedure for measuring overall severity of psychiatric disturbance. *Archives of General Psychiatry, 33*, 766–771.

Frank, E., Frank, N., Cornes, C., Imber, F. D., Miller, M. D., Morris, F. M., Reynolds, C. F. (1993). Interpersonal psychotherapy and the treatment of late life depression. In G. L. Klerman & M. M. Weissman (Eds.), *New applications of interpersonal psychotherapy* (pp. 167–198). Washington, DC: American Psychiatric Press.

Frank, E., Kupfer, D. J., Jacob, M., Blementhal, S. J., & Jarrett, D. B. (1987). Pregnancy-related affective episodes among women with recurrent depression. *American Journal of Psychiatry, 144*(3), 288–293.

Frank, E., Kupfer, D. J., & Perel, J. M. (1989). Early recurrence in unipolar depression. *Archives of General Psychiatry, 40,* 771–775.

Frank, E., Kupfer, D. J., Perel, J. M., Cornes C., Jarrett, D. B., Mallinger, A. G., Thase, M. E., McEachran, A. B., & Grochocinski, V. J. (1990). Three-year outcomes for maintenance therapies in recurrent depression. *Archives of General Psychiatry, 47,* 1093–1099.

Frank, E., Kupfer, D. J., Wagner, E. F., McEachran, A. B., & Cornes, C. (1991). Efficacy of interpersonal psychotherapy as a maintenance treatment of recurrent depression: Contributing factors. *Archives of General Psychiatry, 48,* 1053–1059.

Frasure-Smith, N., Lesperance, F., & Talajic, J. (1993). Depression following myocardial infarction: Impact on six month survival. *Journal of the American Medical Association, 270,* 1819–1861.

Gillies, L. A. (1999, May). *Interpersonal psychotherapy with BPD.* Symposium: New Developments in Interpersonal Psychotherapy, American Psychiatric Association Annual Convention, Washington, DC.

Gillies, L. A. (2000). *Interpersonal psychotherapy with depressed adolescent mothers.* Unpublished manuscript, University of Toronto.

Hamilton, M. A. (1967). Development of a rating scale for primary depressive illness. *British Journal of Social and Clinical Psychology, 6,* 278–296.

Horvath, A. O., & Greenberg, L. S. (1989). Development and validation of the Working Alliance Inventory. *Journal of Counseling Psychology, 36,* 223–233.

Klein, D. K., & Ross, D. C. (1993). Reanalysis of the National Institute of Mental Health Treatment of Depression Collaborative Research Programme: General effectiveness report. *Neuropsychopharmacology, 8*(3), 241–251.

Klerman, G. L., & Weissman, M. M. (Eds.). (1993). *New applications of interpersonal psychotherapy.* Washington, DC: American Psychiatric Press.

Klerman, G. L., Weissman, M. M., Rounsaville, B. J., & Chevron, E. S. (1984). *Interpersonal psychotherapy of depression.* New York: Basic Books.

Markowitz, J. C. (1998). *Interpersonal psychotherapy.* Washington, DC: American Psychiatric Press.

Markowitz, J. C., Klerman, G. L., Clougherty, K. F., Spielman, L. A., Jacobsberg, L. B., Fishman, B., Frances, A. J., Kocsis, J. H., & Perry, S. W. (1995). Individual psychotherapies for depressed HIV-seropositive patients. *American Journal of Psychiatry, 152,* 1504–1509.

Markowitz, J. C., Klerman, G. L., & Perry, S. W. (1992). Interpersonal psychotherapy of depressed HIV-seropositive patients. *Hospital and Community Psychiatry, 43,* 885–890.

Martin, S. D. (1999). *SPECT changes with interpersonal psychotherapy versus venlafaxine for depression.* In M. M. Weissman (Chair), Symposium conducted at the annual meeting of the American Psychiatric Association, Washington, DC.

Mechanic, D., & Hansell, S. (1989). Divorce, family conflict, and adolescents' well-being. *Journal of Health and Social Behavior, 30,* 105–116.

Montejo-Gonzalez, A. L., Llorca, G., Izquierdo, J. A., Ledesma, M., Bousono, M., Calcedo, A., Carrasco, J. L., Ciudad, J., Daniel, F., De la Gandara, J., Derecho, J., Franco, M., Gomez, M. J., Macias, J. A., Martin, T., Perez, V., Sanchez, J. M., Sanchez, S., & Vicens, E. (1997). SSRI-induced sexual dysfunction: Fluoxetine (Prozac), paroxetine (Paxil), sertraline (Zoloft) and fluvoxamine (Luvox) in a prospective, multicenter, and descriptive clinical trial. *Journal of Sex and Marital Therapy, 23,* 176–194.

Mufson, L. H., Morreau, D., Weissman, M. M., Klerman, G. L. (1993). Interpersonal psychotherapy for adolescent depression. In G. L. Klerman & M. M. Weissman (Eds.), *New applications of interpersonal psychotherapy* (pp. 129–166). Washington, DC: American Psychiatric Press, Inc.

O'Hara, M. W. (1994). *Postpartum depression: Causes and consequences.* New York: Springer-Verlag.

Prien, R. F., Kupfer, D. J., Mansky, P. A., Small, J. G., Tualon, V. B., Voss, C. B., & Johnsen, W. E. (1984). Drug therapy in the prevention of recurrences in unipolar and bipolar affective disorders: A report of the National Institute of Mental Health Collaborative Study Group comparing lithium carbonate, imipramine and a lithium carbonate–imipramine combination. *Archives of General Psychiatry, 41,* 1096–1104.

Reynolds, C. F., Frank, E., Perel, J. M., Imber, F. D., Cornes, C., Morycz, R. K., Mazumdar, S., Miller, M. D., Pollock, B. G., Rifai, A. H., Stack, J. A., George, C. J., Houck, P. R., & Kupfer, D. J. (1992). Combined pharmacotherapy and psychotherapy in the acute and continuation treatment of elderly patients with recurrent major depression: A preliminary report. *American Journal of Psychiatry, 149*(12), 1687–1692.

Rothbloom, E., Sholomskas, A., Barry, C., & Prusoff, B. A. (1982). Issues in clinical trials with depressed elderly. *Journal of the American Geriatric Society, 30,* 694–699.

Rounsaville, B. J., & Carroll, K. (1993). Interpersonal psychotherapy for patients who abuse drugs. In G. L. Klerman & M. M. Weissman (Eds.), *New applications of interpersonal psychotherapy* (pp. 319–352). Washington, DC. American Psychiatric Press.

Slotsky, S. M., Glass, D. R., Shea, M. T., Pilkonis, P. A., Collins, J. F., Elkin, I., Watkins, J. T., Imber, S. D., Leber, W. R., Moyer, J., & Oliveri, M. E. (1991). Patient predictors of response to psychotherapy and pharmacotherapy: Findings in the NIMH Treatment of Depression Collaborative Research Program. *American Journal of Psychiatry 148,* 997–1008.

Stuart, S., & O'Hara, M. W. (1995). Treatment of postpartum depression with interpersonal psychotherapy. *Archives of General Psychiatry, 52,* 75–76.

Stuart, S., O'Hara, M. W., & Blehar, M. C. (1998). Mental disorders associated with childbearing: Report of the biennial meeting of the Marce Society. *Psychopharmacology Bulletin, 34,* 333–338.

Weissman, M. M., Klerman, G. L., Prusoff, B. A., et al. (1981). Depressed outpatients: Results of one year after treatment with drugs and/or interpersonal psychotherapy. *Archives of General Psychiatry, 38,* 51–55.

Weissman, M. M., & Markowitz, J. C. (1994). Interpersonal psychotherapy: Current status. *Archives of General Psychiatry, 51,* 599–605.

Weissman, M. M., Markowitz, J. C., & Klerman, G. L. (2000). *Comprehensive guide to interpersonal psychotherapy.* New York: Basic Books.

Weissman, M. M., Prusoff, B. A., DiMascio, A., Neu, C., Goklaney, M., & Klerman, G. L. (1979). The efficacy of drugs and psychotherapy in the treatment of acute depressive episodes. *American Journal of Psychiatry, 136,* 555–558.

Wells, K. B., Stewart, A., Hays, R. D., Burnham, M. A., Rogers, W., Daniels, M., Berry, S., Greenfield, S., & Ware, J. (1989). The functioning and well-being of depressed patients: Results from the Medical Outcomes Studies. *Journal of the American Medical Association, 262,* 914–919.

Chapter 8

EATING DISORDERS

G. Terence Wilson
Kathleen M. Pike

The fourth edition of the *Diagnostic and Statistical Manual of Mental Disorders* (DSM-IV) clearly defined and separated anorexia nervosa and bulimia nervosa, and described for the first time a new eating disorder termed "binge-eating disorder." This chapter is written by authors involved in the creation of the DSM-IV eating disorder categories, who are also among the originators of the most successful treatment yet devised for these disorders. In this chapter they describe their state-of-the-art treatment for bulimia nervosa, as well as the most recent evidence from large clinical trials supporting these efforts. Although concentrating on bulimia nervosa, the eating disorder we know the most about, the authors point out that the treatment protocol has wide applicability to anorexia nervosa and binge-eating disorder. In what may be a surprising departure to some readers, the authors note that the central problem requiring intervention is not necessarily bingeing or purging, but rather the culturally driven abnormal attitudes and beliefs regarding shape and weight. The recommendation for applying various treatment components in a "modular" fashion speaks to the art of administering this treatment. The detailed explication of cognitive-behavioral therapy as applied to eating disorders should be extraordinarily useful to clinicians working with these difficult problems.—D. H. B.

CLASSIFICATION AND DIAGNOSIS

The two most well-established eating disorders are anorexia nervosa (AN) and bulimia nervosa (BN). According to the *Diagnostic and Statistical Manual of Mental Disorders*, fourth edition (DSM-IV; American Psychiatric Association, 1994), three features define AN. The first is the presence of an abnormally low body weight (at least 15% below that expected). The second—in females, in whom the disorder predominantly occurs—is amenorrhea (i.e., the absence of three consecutive menstrual cycles). The third is disturbance in the way body weight or shape is experienced, such as the denial of the seriousness of abnormally low weight or the undue influence of body weight and shape on self-evaluation. Two subtypes of AN are distinguished in DSM-IV: (1) a restricting type, for individuals who neither binge nor purge; and (2) a binge-eating/purging type, for those who

regularly engage in either binge eating or purging (American Psychiatric Association, 1994). The prevalence of AN in young women is roughly 0.5% to 1%.

BN is also characterized by three major clinical features: (1) binge eating (i.e., the uncontrolled consumption of large amounts of food); (2) the regular resort to methods designed to influence weight and shape, such as purging (self-induced vomiting or laxative abuse), strict dieting or fasting, or vigorous exercise; and (3) self-evaluation that is excessively affected by body shape and weight. There are two subtypes; one is defined by the presence of purging (e.g., self-induced vomiting or laxative misuse), the other by the absence of purging.

The diagnosis of BN excludes patients who currently meet diagnostic criteria for AN. The vast majority of patients with BN are within the normal weight range. An important reason for allowing the diagnosis of AN to "trump" that of BN is the prognostic significance of the former. There is an urgent need for weight gain in these patients, whose dangerously low weight can be life-threatening. Furthermore, clinical experience has shown that patients with AN pose much greater problems for clinical management, because they actively resist attempts to change their eating behavior and weight. They typically fare far more poorly in treatment than patients with BN. The prevalence of BN among young women is estimated to be roughly 1% to 3%, but it rarely occurs in males (Hsu, 1990). BN is concentrated primarily among young adults, although it also occurs in adolescence and middle age. This eating disorder is frequently associated with other forms of psychopathology (e.g., major depression, anxiety disorders, substance abuse, and personality disorders), both in patients themselves and in their family members (Kassett et al., 1989). Among cases that present for treatment, BN is marked by a chronic, unremitting course (Fairburn et al., 1995).

A third category of eating disorder is included in DSM-IV as "eating disorder not otherwise specified" (EDNOS). This category embraces individuals who have an eating disorder of clinical severity but do not meet formal diagnostic criteria for either AN or BN. For example, there are individuals with all of the features of BN, except that the frequency of their binge eating is too low to meet diagnostic criteria. Although rarely the focus of research, patients in this category are well known to practitioners who treat the full range of eating disorders. An example of the EDNOS category, and one that has attracted intense recent interest, is identified in DSM-IV as "binge-eating disorder" (BED). Patients with this proposed diagnosis engage in recurrent binge eating, but do not show extreme compensatory behavior (such as purging), as in BN. They closely resemble patients with BN in terms of dysfunctional concerns with body shape and weight (Wilfley, Schwartz, Spurrell, & Fairburn, 2000), and similarly show high rates of comorbid psychopathology, especially depression (Wilfley, Friedman, Dounchis, Stein, & Welch, 2000; Yanovski, Nelson, Dubbert, & Spitzer, 1993). Yet patients with BED differ from patients with BN in several important ways that have implications for treatment. BED is characterized by significantly lower levels of dietary restraint than is

the case in either BN or AN (Wilfley, Schwartz, et al., 2000). Consistent with this difference, the majority of patients with BED seeking treatment are overweight or obese (Marcus, 1993). Finally, a significant minority of patients with BED are males.

In summary, research findings have suggested that bulimic eating disorders exist on a continuum of clinical severity. The most severe form is the purging subtype of BN. The nonpurging subtype of BN is of intermediate severity, and BED the least severe (Hay & Fairburn, 1998).

The present chapter focuses on the cognitive-behavioral treatment (CBT) of patients with BN, the most intensively researched of all the eating disorders. The therapeutic strategies described here are also relevant to the other disorders, however. There have been few controlled treatment studies of CBT for AN (Garner, Vitousek, & Pike, 1997; Serfaty, Turkington, Heap, Ledsham, & Jolley, 1999), although the clinical literature on applications to AN is growing (Fairburn, Shafran, & Cooper, 1999; Vitousek, Watson, & Wilson, 1998). The lack of treatment research on AN is due in large part to the difficulty of recruiting sufficient patients, given the low incidence of the disorder.

CBT, adapted from its use with BN, has been more widely applied to the treatment of BED, where it has proven highly effective (Agras, Telch, et al., 1994; Marcus, Wing, & Fairburn, 1995; Wilfley, 1999).

ETIOLOGY OF BN

One of the most striking features of both BN and AN is that they occur almost exclusively in women. (For this reason, we use feminine pronouns in this chapter to refer to a patient with either of these disorders.) Furthermore, BN was largely unknown prior to the late 1970s, strongly indicating the role of current cultural context in its genesis.

Psychosocial Influences

The current cultural milieu defines the ideal female body shape as slim and lithe, and women experience considerable pressure to conform to this physical ideal (Striegel-Moore, Silberstein, & Rodin, 1986). As a result, the majority of young women in the United States diet to influence their body weight and shape. It is no coincidence that BN is most common among that segment of the population—predominantly white women from the middle and upper middle socioeconomic classes—who diet most to meet cultural expectations. There is an overall correlation between cultural pressure to be thin and prevalence of eating disorders, both across and within different ethnic groups (Hsu, 1990).

Dieting

The desire to be thin leads to dieting. Dieting (rigid, unhealthy restriction of both the amount and range of food consumed) is a risk factor for BN. A consistent clinical finding is that patients report the onset of binge eating following a period of dieting. Prevalence studies reveal that eating disorders are most common in populations with high rates of dieting. Prospective research has verified the link between dieting and the development of eating disorders. In a representative sample of 15-year-old schoolgirls in London, Patton, Johnson-Sabine, Wood, Mann, and Wakeling (1990) found that compared with those who did not diet, those who did diet were significantly at risk for developing an eating disorder within 1 year. Girls who dieted were eight times more likely than girls who did not to develop an eating disorder. (Dieting may not be a risk factor for BED. As noted above, obese patients with BED show significantly less dieting than patients with BN. In contrast to individuals with BN, binge eating often precedes dieting in individuals with BED. (See Abbott et al., 1998.)

Although linked to eating disorders, dieting is neither necessary nor sufficient to cause BN. It cannot be a sufficient condition because a majority of adolescent and young adult women diet to influence shape and weight, but only a minority develop an eating disorder. For example, in the study of London schoolgirls, only one in five who were dieting at the beginning of the study were subsequently diagnosed as having an eating disorder (Patton et al., 1990). Some other factor or set of factors must interact with diet-induced mechanisms to cause the eating disorder. Research on risk factors for BN has shown that the eating disorder is most likely to develop in

dieters who are vulnerable to obesity and psychiatric disorder in general (Fairburn, Welch, Doll, Davies, & O'Connor, 1997).

Dieting is not necessary for the development of an eating disorder. Although it typically precedes the onset of binge eating in BN, there are cases in which dieting is not the first sign of the development of BN (Haiman & Devlin, 1999). In obese individuals who binge-eat, dieting is just as likely to follow the onset of binge eating as it is to precede it.

Why does dieting help contribute to BN? Individuals with BN tend to have unrealistically rigid standards for their control over food intake, which are often part of a broader picture of perfectionism. On a cognitive level, these standards leave them with feelings of deprivation. Under these strict conditions, dieters are vulnerable to loss of control if they break their diets. And dietary lapses lead to all-or-nothing cognitive reactions. According to this phenomenon—called the "abstinence violation effect"—individuals attribute their lapses to a complete inability to maintain control. Thus they abandon all attempts to regulate food intake and overeat.

Repeated unsuccessful dieting, which leads to chaotic everyday eating behavior, is thought to put a person at risk for an eating disorder as noted above. The explanation may be that this behavior helps undermine the conditioning processes that regulate normal eating. For example, terminating meals because of a self-imposed limit rather than true satiation, combined with variability in intake (skipping meals), can extinguish conditioned satiety responses. This can lead to binge eating.

Dieting also has biological consequences that may predispose individuals to eating disorders. Short-term dieting in subjects without psychiatric disorders can result in altered serotonin function in the brain (Walsh, Oldman, Franklin, Fairburn, & Cowen, 1995). Serotonin is an important neurotransmitter that is intimately involved in the regulation of mood and food intake. Reduced levels of serotonin have been linked to eating disorders. Particularly intriguing is the finding that dieting-induced changes in brain serotonin function are seen in women but not men. Females are much more likely than males to develop eating disorders. Dieting therefore represents a double danger for females: Not only do they diet more often than men because of societal pressures to be thin, but they are also more vulnerable to adverse biological effects of even moderate dieting.

Familial Factors

AN and BN run in families. Both AN and BN aggregate in the first-degree family members of probands with either BN or AN. Specifically, the incidence of BN is 3.7 times as high in the relatives of probands with BN than relatives of normal controls, and the rate of AN was 12 times as high in the relatives of probands with BN (Strober, Freeman, Lampert, Diamond, & Kaye, 2000). This cross-transmission of AN and BN within families suggests a shared familial diathesis.

Research on risk factors for BN has identified the role of specific parental problems, such as parental obesity and alcohol abuse. In addition, critical comments by family members about a girl's body weight or eating are associated with BN (Fairburn et al., 1997).

Genetic Influences

Evidence of familial transmission of BN does not allow us to distinguish between genetic and environmental influences. Twin studies are necessary to disentangle these interactive influences. However, existing twin studies have yielded inconsistent results, with estimates of heritability ranging from 30% to as much as 83% (Bulik, Sullivan, & Kendler, 1998). Fairburn, Cowen, and Harrison (1999) have detailed the many methodological limitations of these studies, including questionable definitions of the phenotype of BN, issues of diagnostic reliability, and small sample sizes. Fairburn, Cowen, and Harrison (1999) prudently recommend that we keep a broad view of the etiology of BN, "not least because an understanding of the environmental and neurobiological correlates of eating disorders will probably lead to clinically relevant applications more rapidly than, and independent of, their genetic component—however large the latter proves to be" (p. 356).

TREATMENTS FOR BN

Many different psychological therapies have been used to treat patients with BN, includ-ing CBT, behavior therapy, psychodynamic therapy, family therapy, experiential therapy, and a Twelve-Step approach based on an addiction model of the disorder (American Psychiatric Association, 2000; Garner & Garfinkel, 1997). In addition, various pharmacological treatments have been tested, the most widely used being antidepressant medication (Devlin & Walsh, 1995; Wilson & Fairburn, 1998).

Antidepressant Medication

The original rationale for treating BN with antidepressant drugs was that this eating disorder is a form of major depression (Pope, Hudson, Jonas, & Yurgelun-Todd, 1983). Although this view has been discredited, the evidence is consistent in showing that antidepressant drugs produce significantly greater reductions in binge eating and purging than treatment with placebo does. Numerous controlled studies have shown that different classes of antidepressant drugs, including tricyclics (e.g., imipramine and desipramine), monoamine oxidase inhibitors (e.g., phenelzine), and selective serotonin reuptake inhibitors (e.g., fluoxetine), are more effective than a pill placebo in reducing binge eating and purging at the end of treatment.

Some of the findings on antidepressant drugs for BN can be summarized as follows: First, different types of drugs seem to be equally effective. The data on fluoxetine (Fluoxetine Bulimia Nervosa Collaborative Study Group, 1992) are comparable to those on tricyclic antidepressants. At present, fluoxetine would appear to be the drug of choice, on account of its relative freedom from adverse side effects. Second, data from uncontrolled studies suggest that patients who fail to respond to an initial antidepressant drug may respond to another (Mitchell et al., 1989; Walsh, Hadigan, Devlin, Gladis, & Roose, 1991). Additional evidence for the sequencing of different drugs comes from a study in which treatment with desipramine (for 8 weeks) was followed by treatment with fluoxetine (60 mg/day for 8 weeks) if a patient's binge frequency had not declined by at least 75% or the patient experienced intolerable side effects (Walsh et al., 1997). This two-stage regimen was designed to approximate actual clinical practice more closely than conventional single-drug protocols do. Of the patients randomly assigned to active medication, two-thirds were sequentially administered the two drugs. Their average reduction in binge frequency was 69%, and 29% ceased binge eating. These figures compare with 47% and 13%, respectively, among patients treated with desipramine alone in an earlier placebo-controlled study conducted at the same center with a similar patient population (Walsh et al., 1991). Third, the mechanism or mechanisms whereby antidepressant medication exerts its effects are unknown. Its effects cannot be mediated by reductions in depression, since pretreatment levels of depression are unrelated to outcome. The apparent comparability of different classes of antidepressant drugs suggests some mechanism common to these agents. One possibility is that antidepressant medication attenuates hunger, thereby making it easier for patients with BN to maintain their strict dieting (McCann & Agras, 1990; Rossiter, Agras, Losch, & Telch, 1988). Fourth, the maintenance of drug-induced treatment effects has been largely ignored. What data exist are discouraging. Most patients relapse rapidly when antidepressant medication is withdrawn, and even those who continue on active medication during posttreatment maintenance phases relapse or drop out (Pyle et al., 1990; Walsh et al., 1991). The absence of evidence of longer-term effects, taken in conjunction with a relatively high dropout rate and a general reluctance on the part of patients to accept medication as the sole form of treatment (Wilson & Fairburn, 1998), underscores the importance of effective psychological treatment for this disorder.

Cognitive-Behavioral Treatment

Treatment Model and Rationale

The commonly used form of CBT for BN derives directly from Fairburn's first formulation of this approach in Oxford in a treatment manual in the early 1980s. A more recent, expanded version of this manual was published in 1993 (Fairburn, Marcus, & Wilson, 1993). Although there are differences in the ways in which CBT has been implemented across different clinical and research settings, all are derived at the core from the Oxford approach.

Therapy is based on a model that emphasizes the critical role of both cognitive and behavioral factors in the maintenance of the disorder (Fairburn, 1997a). Briefly, this model posits that sociocultural pressures on women to be thin and conform to the societal ideal of female beauty lead some to overvalue the importance of body weight and shape. This causes women to restrict their food intake in rigid and unrealistic ways—a process that leaves them physiologically and psychologically susceptible to periodic loss of control over eating (namely, binge eating). Purging and other extreme forms of weight control are attempts to compensate for the effects of binge eating. Purging helps maintain binge eating by reducing a patient's anxiety about potential weight gain and disrupting learned satiety that regulates food intake. In turn, binge eating and purging cause distress and lower self-esteem, thereby reciprocally fostering the conditions that will inevitably lead to more dietary restraint and binge eating. As this self-sustaining process develops, binge eating comes to function as a means of regulating negative affect by serving to blunt or distract from sources of personal distress. As such, binge eating provides negative reinforcement that can become a potent factor in its maintenance.

It follows from this model of the maintenance of BN that treatment must address more than the presenting behaviors of binge eating and purging. Treatment consists of cognitive and behavioral procedures for developing a regular pattern of eating that includes previously avoided foods; for developing more constructive skills for coping with high-risk situations for binge eating and purging; for modifying abnormal attitudes; and for preventing relapse at the conclusion of acute treatment (Fairburn et al., 1993). Treatment is time-limited, directive, and problem-oriented.

Treatment Efficacy

CBT for BN has been rigorously evaluated in numerous randomized controlled trials in North America and Europe. The treatment has been shown to be consistently superior to waiting-list control groups, which show no improvement across a range of measures (Wilson & Fairburn, 1998). On average, CBT eliminates binge eating and purging in roughly 50% of all patients. The percentage reduction in binge eating and purging across all patients treated with CBT is typically 80% or more. CBT has broadly beneficial effects on all aspects of the psychopathology of BN (Wilfley & Cohen, 1997; Wilson & Fairburn, 1998). Aside from binge eating and purging, dietary restraint is decreased, and the concerns about shape and weight are attenuated if not normalized. Associated with these changes are a decrease in the level of general psychiatric symptoms and an improvement in self-esteem and social functioning. CBT-induced improvement also appears to be durable. Available evidence suggests that therapeutic changes are well maintained at 1 year following treatment (Agras, Walsh, Fairburn, Wilson, & Kraemer, 2000). The longest follow-up of CBT (mean length of follow-up = 5.8 years) found that roughly two-thirds of patients had no eating disorder, the great majority of whom were functioning well (Fairburn et al., 1995).

A noteworthy feature of CBT for BN is its rapid onset of action. For example, Wilson and colleagues (1999) showed that 76% of total improvement in frequency of binge eating and 69% of frequency of vomiting was evident by Week 3 (i.e., Session 5) (Wilson, Vitousek, & Loeb, 2000). Rapid response to CBT for BN has been consistently documented in several other studies as well (Agras, Walsh, et al., 2000; Garner et al., 1993; Jones, Peveler, Hope, & Fairburn, 1993). This rapid treatment effect of CBT cannot be dismissed as a "nonspecific" response to receiving treatment, because CBT quickly becomes significantly more effective than equally credible alternative psychological therapies, including interpersonal psychotherapy (IPT) (Jones et al., 1993) and supportive psychotherapy (Wilson et al., 1999). Wilson (1999a) has speculated that behavioral homework assignments may explain the rapid effect of CBT. The systematic and focal nature of behavioral homework assignments, and their function as an integral feature of therapy, set CBT apart from other psychotherapies. They arguably enhance self-efficacy by fostering a sense of control over behavior previously experienced as out of control.

CBT versus Pharmacological Treatment

Aside from CBT, the most intensively researched treatment for BN has been antidepressant medication. Both tricyclics and fluoxetine have been shown to be significantly more effective than pill placebo (Devlin & Walsh, 1995), even though the longer-term effects of antidepressant medication remain to be tested in controlled studies (Wilson & Fairburn, 1998). Consequently, antidepressant medication provides a stringent standard of comparison for the effects of CBT.

Several studies have directly evaluated the relative and combined effectiveness of CBT and antidepressant drug treatment in controlled studies (Agras et al., 1992; Fichter et al., 1991; Leitenberg et al., 1994; Mitchell et al., 1990; Walsh et al., 1997). Collectively, these studies have been consistent in yielding the following findings:

1. CBT seems more acceptable to patients than antidepressant medication. Patients with BN appear reluctant to take antidepressant medication and seem to prefer psychological treatment.

2. The dropout rate is lower with CBT than with pharmacological treatments. For example, Agras and colleagues (1992) had only one patient receiving CBT drop out, a rate of 4.3%, compared with 17% for desipramine.

3. CBT seems to be superior to treatment with a single antidepressant drug (Agras et al., 1992; Leitenberg et al., 1994). It remains to be established whether or not CBT is superior to a two-stage drug intervention or to longer-duration pharmacotherapy than has typically been the case.

4. Combining CBT with antidepressant medication is significantly more effective than medication alone (Agras et al., 1992; Mitchell et al., 1990; Walsh et al., 1997).

5. Combining CBT and antidepressant medication produces few consistent benefits over CBT alone. However, the statistical power in these studies might have been insufficient to demonstrate a combined effect. For example, in the Walsh and colleagues (1997) study, although the difference was not statistically significant, medication plus CBT resulted in a higher remission rate for binge eating and vomiting (50%) than placebo plus CBT did (24%). An important design feature of this study was that patients received a two-stage pharmacological treatment. The first drug administered was desipramine. Patients who did not respond (a reduction of at least 75% in binge eating) or who could not tolerate this medication were switched to 60 mg

of fluoxetine. Uncontrolled research has suggested that superior effects may be obtained with the use of more than one medication (Mitchell et al., 1989).

6. The combination of CBT and antidepressant medication may be more effective than CBT alone in reducing anxiety and depressive symptoms (Mitchell et al., 1990; Walsh et al., 1997).

7. Longer-term maintenance of change appears to be better with CBT than with antidepressant drugs. A follow-up of the Mitchell and colleagues (1989) study showed poor maintenance of improvement in patients who had received medication, in contrast to those who had received psychological treatment (Pyle et al., 1990). Similarly, Agras, Rossiter, and colleagues (1994) found that 4 months of desipramine were followed by a high relapse rate, but one that was prevented when the drug was combined with CBT. It is possible that combining CBT with medication might prevent relapse associated with drug treatment, as in the treatment of panic disorder (Otto, Jones, Craske, & Barlow, 1996).

CBT versus Alternative Psychotherapies

CBT has proved superior to other psychological treatments with which it has been compared (Fairburn et al., 1993; Garner et al., 1993; Laessle et al., 1991; Walsh et al., 1997). An exception to this pattern is the outcome of two important studies comparing CBT with IPT. IPT was originally devised by Klerman, Weissman, Rounsaville, and Chevron (1984) as a short-term treatment for depression. IPT is a focal psychotherapy, the main emphasis of which is to help patients identify and modify current interpersonal problems. Unlike traditional psychodynamic therapies, the treatment is noninterpretive. It is also nondirective, following the initial identification of focal interpersonal problem areas that will be addressed in the remainder of treatment. The therapist does not directly instruct patients in what specific changes to make or how to go about making changes. Rather, patients are encouraged to initiate changes themselves. (For a fuller discussion, see Gillies, Chapter 7, this volume.)

Controlled studies have documented the efficacy of IPT as a treatment for depression (Spanier, Frank, McEachran, Grochocinski, & Kupfer, 1996). As adapted for BN (Fairburn, 1997b), IPT focuses exclusively on interpersonal issues, with little or no attention directed to symptom management—that is, to modification of binge eating, purging, disturbed eating, or dysfunctional concern with body shape and weight. Specific eating problems are viewed as a means of understanding the interpersonal context that is assumed to be their cause. As such, IPT is very different from CBT in nature.

Fairburn and colleagues (1991) compared CBT with both IPT and a narrowly behavioral treatment that was essentially a stripped-down version of CBT. At posttreatment, IPT was as effective as CBT at reducing the frequency of binge eating, but it was clearly inferior with respect to vomiting, dietary restraint, and attitudes toward body shape and weight. During the 1-year follow-up, however, patients who received IPT showed continuing improvement to the point where their outcome was comparable to that of those who received CBT. Forty-four percent of IPT patients were no longer binge-eating or purging. IPT was as effective as CBT on all measures by the 8- and 12-month follow-ups. Both CBT and IPT fared significantly better than the comparison behavior therapy condition over the course of follow-up: Patients in both conditions showed an impressive 95% reduction in binge eating, and a 91% reduction in vomiting (Fairburn et al., 1993). The patients were followed up once more after an average of almost 6 years. Those patients who had received CBT or IPT were doing equally well, with 63% and 72%, respectively, having no DSM-IV eating disorder compared with 14% among those who had received behavior therapy (Fairburn et al., 1995).

The results of this study by Fairburn and his colleagues in Oxford were significant on at least three counts. First, they indicated that there is an alternative evidence-based psychological treatment to CBT. Second, the differences between CBT and IPT in their temporal pattern of response suggests that although the treatments were equivalent in their longer-term outcome, each treatment had specific effects, arguably through the operation of different mechanisms rather than the presence of common mechanisms (Fairburn et al., 1993). And, third, the results raised questions about the nature of BN itself. If a psychological treatment—one that did not directly address disturbed eating or issues of body weight and shape—was effective in reducing binge eating and purging, theorists would have to broaden their view of the factors that maintained the eating disorder.

Accordingly, Agras, Walsh, and colleagues (2000) conducted a multisite study comparing exactly the same CBT with IPT, with a large sample size (n = 110 patients in each treatment). The findings largely replicated the previous Oxford study by Fairburn and his colleagues. At posttreatment, CBT was significantly superior to IPT in the number of patients who had ceased all binge eating and purging over the preceding 4 weeks. The proportions were 29% versus 6% in the intent-to-treat analysis, and 45% versus 8% in the analysis of only those patients who completed treatment. CBT was also significantly superior in reducing dietary restraint, but not in modifying another core clinical feature of BN—namely, dysfunctional concerns with body shape and weight. Nor were there any differences between the two treatments on measures of associated psychopathology, such as depression, self-esteem, or interpersonal functioning.

The follow-up findings showed a different picture, however. At the 8- to 12-month follow-up, there were no statistically significant differences between the two therapies in terms of remission from binge eating and purging over the preceding 4 weeks. The differential time course of the effects of CBT and IPT once again suggests that they operate via different mechanisms. A mediational analysis of treatment outcome showed that, consistent with the underlying theoretical model, the effects of CBT but not of IPT were partially mediated by treatment-induced changes in dietary restraint.

Although there is evidence that CBT and IPT operate via different theoretical mechanisms, the posttreatment course of patients in the two treatments was not dissimilar. For example, 66% of those who had recovered with CBT at the end of treatment remained recovered at follow-up, compared with 57% (4 of 7) of those treated with IPT. For those remitted at the end of CBT, 29% (6 of 21) recovered, compared with 33% (8 of 24) for the IPT group. Of the remaining participants,

7% (4 of 57) had recovered at follow-up in the CBT group, compared with 9% (7 of 79) in the IPT group. The percentages in each category at the end of treatment were similar for both treatments. These findings suggest that the absence of a statistically significant difference between CBT and IPT over follow-up may be more a function of their differential posttreatment status (a regression-toward-the-mean effect) than any delayed "catch-up" property of IPT.

The Agras, Walsh, and colleagues (2000) study had several distinctive methodological strengths. First, in contrast to virtually all previous controlled studies of the treatment of BN, it had sufficient statistical power to detect differences between the two therapies. Second, the quality of the two therapies was rigorously controlled by using manual-based treatment protocols. The study was conducted at two sites in the United States (Stanford and Columbia), where the therapists were closely monitored on a weekly basis throughout the study by two experienced supervisors. In addition, each treatment was independently and continually monitored by the investigator (Fairburn) who had originally developed each protocol and conducted the earlier study at Oxford. Third, assessment was detailed and comprehensive: The semistructured Eating Disorder Examination (EDE) interview, which is widely viewed as the "gold standard" for assessment of eating disorders (Wilson, 1993), was used.

Despite its strengths, the study was not without its limitations. Perhaps the key limitation is the absence of a third comparison treatment to control for factors such as the passage of time and nonspecific therapeutic influences. Indeed, given the absence of statistically significant differences at follow-up, conclusions about specific long-term effects cannot be drawn. Lacking this control for nonspecific therapeutic influences, it is also impossible to conclude definitively that IPT has any specific therapeutic effects. However, the results of the previous controlled study indicated that both IPT and CBT were significantly superior to an exclusively behavioral form of CBT, which was equivalent in therapist contact and in ratings of suitability and expectancy. These results suggest that IPT may have a specific mode of action in the treatment of BN.

THE CONTEXT OF THERAPY

Setting

CBT for BN is typically conducted on an out-patient basis. Individual treatment is probably the most common clinical practice, although several studies have administered CBT in a group setting. Only one study has directly compared individual versus group CBT (Chen et al., 1999). This controlled trial, in which the Fairburn and colleagues (1993) manual was adapted for use with closed groups of five to six patients, suggested that individual treatment was significantly more effective in reducing both binge eating and vomiting than its group adaptation. As Chen and colleagues (1999) point out, this finding challenges the frequently made assumption that group CBT should be as effective as individual CBT.

Treatment studies that have used group CBT have included relatively homogeneous samples of patients meeting formal diagnostic criteria for BN. More traditional group psychotherapy for more heterogeneous groups, which include patients with different eating disorders, is not uncommon in clinical practice. In our clinical experience, however, the often marked differences among patients with AN, BN, and BED in clinical management and response to treatment outweigh the commonalities, and create more problems than therapeutic opportunities in such mixed groups. Group CBT is more appropriately conducted with diagnostically homogeneous patients.

There are few reasons to hospitalize patients with BN. One exception is if a patient is too depressed to be treated as an outpatient, or if there is a risk of suicide. A second exception is the presence of a compelling medical problem, such as severe electrolyte disturbance. Such complications are relatively rare in normal-weight patients with BN, and can be managed as part of outpatient treatment. It is not unusual even for hospital-based treatment programs to forgo routine screening for electrolyte abnormalities. However, a more conservative view favors routine screening, which is our recommendation. The third reason to hospitalize a patient is if intensive outpatient treatment fails. A tightly supervised hospital setting can be useful in directly modifying refractory eating habits.

Patient Variables

Most patients with BN and AN are women, as we have noted earlier. Among patients with BED, women also appear to be in the majority; in contrast to BN and AN, however, there is a much higher proportion of men (Spitzer et al., 1992). Relatively little is known about the small number of male patients with BN. There appears to be a higher than expected prevalence of homosexuality among men with BN, which has been attributed to greater disturbances in psychosexual development than in their female counterparts (Fichter & Hoffman, 1990). Nevertheless, our clinical experience is consistent with the sparse literature on this subject in indicating that male and female patients with BN are more alike than dissimilar. They show the same core eating disorder psychopathology and response to treatment.

Rates of AN and BN are lower among African American women than among European American women in the United States (Hsu, 1990), possibly because the former report a more positive body image and experience less social pressure to be thin than the latter (Miller et al., 2000). In contrast, there are reports that the prevalence of recurrent binge eating is comparable across European Americans and African Americans in the United States (Striegel-Moore & Smolak, 1996). Clinical accounts from non-Western countries have documented the absence of dysfunctional body shape and weight concerns in otherwise typical cases of AN (Lee, Ho, & Hsu, 1993). Based on these reports, the American Psychiatric Association practice guideline for eating disorders calls for "Culturally flexible diagnostic criteria to allow for the identification and treatment of the many 'atypical' cases, which may represent a large number of eating disorders in non-Western societies" (American Psychiatric Association, 2000, p. 30).

Most patients with BN seek treatment in late adolescence or early adulthood (Hsu, 1990). Patients with AN are often younger, whereas those with BED are typically older. The average age of patients with BED in clinical samples is typically in the early 40s.

Therapist Variables

As in all CBT, it is imperative that the therapist and patient form an effective therapeutic relationship. The therapist must earn the patient's trust and respect. The success of CBT depends in large part on the willingness of the patient to play an active role in treatment and follow through on homework assignments. In CBT for BN, patients are asked to engage in activities that can be very threatening and run contrary to their deeply held beliefs about eating and regulation of body weight. For example, they are urged to resume eating three balanced meals a day, instead of skipping meals and severely restricting food intake. The majority of patients understandably fear that this will cause weight gain, the very outcome that they dread. Patients will not take what for them is the major psychological risk of altering their eating habits unless they have confidence in their therapists and are persuaded that the approach being advocated is credible.

Patients with eating disorders often feel ashamed about their behavior, and are very sensitive to cues of disapproval and rejection. Accordingly, therapists must convey an acceptance of the patients and an understanding of their problem. It is not uncommon to encounter patients with eating disorders who have previously received unsympathetic treatment from professionals—male and female alike—not experienced in the treatment of these disorders.

There is no evidence that the gender of the therapist affects treatment outcome. As in CBT of other disorders, whether the therapist is female or male is much less important than considerations of caring, interpersonal effectiveness, and technical competence. Therapists must be knowledgeable about the nature of eating disorders and have specific training in their treatment. The optimal combination from a CBT viewpoint is a therapist who has a strong background in CBT of clinical problems in general, with specific training in the application of these principles and procedures to eating disorders.

Therapists should ideally be specialists in the treatment of eating disorders, rather than generalists who adopt the same basic approach with virtually all patients, regardless of diagnosis. They must be informed about the biological disturbances associated with the disorder, so that they can intervene or make referrals where appropriate. They must also know about weight regulation and the processes governing dieting, binge eating, and purging. Finally, they must have sufficient clinical experience and acumen to identify—and, if necessary, treat—associated psychopathology, such as depression and psychoactive substance abuse. Clinical psychologists and psychiatrists with the requisite training are the professionals who are most likely to provide this level of expertise.

CBT for Nonspecialists

There are ways in which cognitive-behavioral principles of behavior change can be applied to eating disorders by professionals who are not experts in CBT, including dieticians and nutritionists (Wilson et al., 2000). One is the use of self-help strategies. Preliminary studies have suggested that at least a subset of patients with BN and BED can be effectively treated via brief and cost-effective intervention such as guided self-help (Fairburn & Carter, 1997). This approach is illustrated in a well-controlled study of the treatment of women with BED (Carter & Fairburn, 1998). Participants received 12 weeks of either guided use of the Fairburn (1995) manual, pure self-help with the book, or no treatment (a wait-list control condition). A primary aim of this study was to evaluate self-help as it would be used in primary care settings or in the general community. Thus the guided self-help treatment was conducted by nonspecialist therapists (labeled "facilitators") with no formal clinical qualifications. These facilitators had worked in primary care and received only a limited amount of training and supervision on how to conduct the treatment. As would happen in normal clinical practice, the facilitators were not required to adhere rigidly to the treatment manual. Wait-list control patients were randomly assigned at 12 weeks to one of the two treatment conditions, and were included in the longer-term comparisons of the two self-help groups. The two active interventions produced significant improvements in binge eating that were maintained at the 6-month follow-up. Both treatment conditions were superior to the control group, but similar to one another in reducing binge-eating frequency and general psychopathology over the 12 weeks. Binge eating results for the full sample across the 9 months of the study, however, favored guided self-help.

A second approach that allows the use of nonspecialists given appropriate training is psychoeducation. The goal of psychoeducation is the normalization of eating patterns and body shape/weight concerns through didactic instruction; the content comprises education and cognitive-behavioral change strategies. For example, Davis, Olmsted, and Rockert (1990) developed a psychoeducation program comprising five 90-minute group sessions that produced significantly greater improvement than a wait-list control. Compared with a longer course of 19 sessions of individual CBT, the program was less effective overall. But for the subset of patients with less severe specific eating disorder symptoms and associated psychopathology, the group psychoeducational program was comparably effective (Olmsted et al., 1991).

A third approach involves simplifying manual-based CBT. Illustrating such an approach, Waller and colleagues (1996) devised an abbreviated version of manual-based CBT, consisting of eight 20-minute sessions, that could be administered in primary care settings by nonspecialist therapists. Components of CBT that require more specialist training (e.g., cognitive restructuring) were omitted. This scaled-down treatment proved effective with some patients. Nonresponders, who in the Waller and colleagues (1996) example suffered from other psychiatric problems, could be referred for more intensive treatment delivered by specialists.

ASSESSMENT

The Clinical Interview

Some sort of clinical interview has been among the most widely used means of assessing binge eating in patients. These interviews vary widely in how structured they are, and in whether they are respondent- or investigator-based. The best known clinical interview for assessing the specific psychopathology of eating disorders is the EDE, mentioned earlier (Fairburn & Cooper, 1993). The EDE is widely used in clinical and epidemiological research in North America, Europe, and Australia, and has been translated into several different languages.

The EDE offers the practitioner several advantages (see Rosen, Vara, Wendt, & Leitenberg, 1990, and Wilson, 1993, for further details). First, it has excellent reliability and validity. Second, it directly assesses the diagnostic criteria of all eating disorders. Third, it provides both depth and breadth of assessment of the core features of BN and other eating disorders that no other interview or questionnaire equals.

Recurrent "binge eating" is a diagnostic criterion not only for BN but also for AN, binge-eating/purging subtype, and BED (American Psychiatric Association, 1994). The EDE has the most detailed and comprehensive scheme for classifying different forms of overeating. The EDE defines four different forms of overeating, depending on whether or not the amount of food consumed is genuinely large (objective overeating), and whether or not the person experiences a sense of loss of control (bulimic episodes). These different patterns of actual and perceived overeating are not mutually exclusive, and the data indicate that both patients with BN and obese patients with BED engage in both objective and subjective bulimic episodes.

In contrast to most self-report questionnaires, the EDE defines binge eating and ensures that therapist and patient share the same meaning of key concepts. A "large amount" is defined by the interviewer as what other people would regard as an unusually large amount under the specific circumstances. The interviewer asks a number of probe questions to make this judgment. "Loss of control" is defined as the inability to resist an episode of overeating, or to stop eating once started. Uncontrolled consumption of an objectively large amount of food defines binge eating in DSM-IV.

Self-induced vomiting and laxative abuse are relatively unambiguous and straightforward to assess. Severe dieting, however, is difficult to assess. Although DSM-IV, unlike DSM-III-R, no longer includes dieting as an inappropriate compensatory behavior for binge eating, it is important to assess in order to obtain a full clinical picture of the patient's eating and her attitudes regarding it. This is of particular clinical relevance in CBT, given the importance attributed to dieting in the cognitive-behavioral model of BN. The EDE provides a detailed analysis of dietary restraint, including skipping meals, avoidance of particular foods, adherence to caloric limits, reactions to breaking self-imposed dietary rules, and preoccupation with food and its caloric content. The effect of mood on eating is also probed.

Attitudinal disturbance about body weight and shape is one of the diagnostic criteria for BN and AN. Yet it is rarely defined or assessed systematically. The EDE provides detailed information on attitudes about weight and shape. A Weight Concern subscale consists of five items (importance of weight, reaction to prescribed weighing, preoccupation with shape or weight, dissatisfaction with weight, pursuit of weight loss); a Shape Concern subscale consists of eight items (importance of shape, preoccupation with shape or weight, dissatisfaction with shape, fear of fatness, discomfort seeing body, avoidance of exposure, feelings of fatness, desire for a flat stomach). Figure 8.1 describes the EDE item "importance of shape."

The major disadvantage of the EDE is that it requires specific training in its administration and can take an hour or more to administer. Nevertheless, the rich detail it provides, coupled with the intensive interaction with the patient that it entails, can greatly help the therapist in understanding the patient and details of her eating disorder.

Self-Report Questionnaires

A number of different questionnaires can be used to assess the overall psychopathology of patients with eating disorders. Two of the more commonly used instruments are the Eating Disorders Inventory—2 (EDI-2; Garner, 1991) and the Binge Eating Scale (BES; Gormally, Black, Daston, & Rardin, 1982). The EDI-2 provides a psychometrically sound, broad-gauge assessment of the psychopathology of AN and BN. The BES has been widely used to assess binge eating in obese patients (Marcus, 1993). These questionnaires provide a general gauge of the overall severity of the symptoms of an eating disorder; however, they do not provide a direct measure of the frequency of adequately defined binge eating, which is needed for diagnosis, for planning therapeutic interventions, and for monitoring treatment progress and outcome (Wilson, 1993). Research has shown that the BES correlates poorly with the "gold standard" method of assessment—namely, the EDE—because of the high false-positive rate on the BES (Greeno, Marcus, & Wing, 1995).

---

*Over the past four weeks has your shape been important in influencing how you feel about (judge, think, evaluate) yourself as a person? . . .

*If you imagine the things which influence how you feel about (judge, think, evaluate) yourself—such as your performance at work, being a parent, your marriage, how you get on with other people—and put these things in order of importance, where does your shape fit in?

If, over the past four weeks, your shape had changed in any way, would this have affected how you feel about yourself?

Is it important to you that your shape does *not* change?

(Rate the degree of importance the subject has placed on body shape and its position in his or her scheme for *self-evaluation*. To make this rating, comparisons need to be made with other aspects of the subject's life which are of importance in his or her scheme for self-evaluation, e.g., quality of relationships, being a parent, performance at work or in leisure activities. Do not prompt with the terms "some," "moderate," or "supreme." If the subject has regarded both shape and weight as being of equivalent "supreme" importance, rate 6 on this item and on "Importance of weight.")

0—No importance
1—
2—Some importance (definitely an aspect of self-evaluation)
3—
4—Moderate importance (definitely one of the main aspects of self-evaluation)
5—
6—Supreme importance (nothing is more important in the subject's scheme for evaluating himself or herself)

FIGURE 8.1. Standardized assessment of the personal importance attached to shape and weight: The "importance of shape" item from the Eating Disorder Examination (EDE), 12th edition. Questions with an asterisk *must* be asked. From Fairburn and Cooper (1993). Copyright 1993 by The Guilford Press. Reprinted by permission.

A more useful questionnaire is the Eating Disorder Examination Questionnaire (EDE-Q), a self-report version of the EDE (Fairburn & Beglin, 1994). In general, studies comparing the EDE and EDE-Q show good agreement, although the questionnaire form tends to yield higher estimates of eating disorder psychopathology. The EDE-Q is acceptable for assessing clinical progress and outcome in patients with either BN or BED (Fairburn & Beglin, 1994; Grilo, Masheb, & Wilson, in press).

A widely used questionnaire in studies of BED has been the Stunkard and Messick (1985) Three-Factor Eating Questionnaire, a 51-item questionnaire that has three subscales derived from factor analysis of the scale as a whole: Cognitive Restraint, Disinhibition of Eating, and Perceived Hunger. The Disinhibition of Eating subscale, which measures eating in response to emotional stimuli, reliably differentiates obese patients who binge-eat from those who do not.

Self-Monitoring

Self-monitoring is an indispensable assessment method in CBT in general, and is invaluable in CBT of eating disorders. It typically consists of patients' recording in eating diaries or on special monitoring forms their entire daily food and liquid intake, usually over the period of a week. Figure 8.2 shows an example of a self-monitoring form. Patients should also be asked to record food intake as soon as possible after eating, to maximize accuracy. Patients need to be given an explanation of self-monitoring's purpose and its importance to assessment and treatment. Potential obstacles to completing self-monitoring should be anticipated and suggestions made for overcoming them.

Self-monitoring provides the therapist with an ongoing, daily account of binge eating and purging, and the circumstances under which they occur. The proximal antecedents or triggers of binge eating are identified primarily by asking a patient to record the circumstances in which episodes occurred. Self-monitoring provides the information that allows the therapist to determine when and where each episode took place; what the patient was thinking, feeling, and doing at the time; and the nature of the interpersonal context. This information is essential in CBT for selecting and implementing cognitive and behavioral change strategies. (See Wilson & Vitousek, 1999, for a more detailed analysis of the use of self-monitoring as an assessment tool).

Self-monitoring, which is usually introduced during the first session of CBT, is more than merely a method of assessing patients' eating problems. It is a prototypical homework assignment in CBT that may help contribute to the rapid onset of action. Its reactivity is well documented, and it serves as a catalyst for change. By prompting increased awareness of the connections between the problem behavior and variables that influence the behavior, self-monitoring is fundamental to the self-evaluative reactions that are part of improved self-regulation (Wilson & Vitousek, 1999).

THE PROCESS OF TREATMENT

The now widespread use of CBT in North America, Europe, and Australia for the treatment of BN derives directly from Fairburn's first formulation of this approach in the early 1980s. The publication of a detailed treatment manual greatly facilitated the dissemination of CBT and controlled research on its effectiveness (Fairburn, 1985).

As described by Fairburn (1985), CBT consists of 19 sessions of individual treatment spanning roughly 20 weeks. Treatment is problem-oriented and focused primarily on the present and future. The treatment has three stages. The first stage involves education about BN and orientation to its treatment with CBT. The cognitive view of the maintenance and modification of the disorder is explained, and its relevance to the patient's current problems is made clear. The structure and goals of treatment are discussed. Information about nutrition and weight regulation, and about how these are critical to eliminating eating disorders, is detailed. Core behavioral techniques are introduced. Self-monitoring is initiated for tracking eating habits and for assessing situations that trigger binge eating and purging. Other self-regulatory strategies for reducing the frequency of binge eating and normalizing eating patterns, such as stimulus control, are also used. The goal at

DAILY FOOD RECORD

Name _____ Day _____ Date _____

Time	Food and Liquid Consumed	Place	Meal (M) Snack (S) Binge (B) Purge (V, L)	Circumstances
10:00 A.M.	2 cups coffee with skim milk & Equal Half a bagel	On way to class	M	Rushing, but feel OK—in control
1:00 P.M.	1 pear	Room	S	
7:30 P.M.	Large bag potato chips Large blueberry muffin Bag M&Ms Salad 4 slices bread 2 cereal bars Peanut butter & jelly sandwich	Room	B V	Just got in from class; hungry and anxious; feeling depressed and hopeless— why do I keep doing this to myself? I had tried so hard to be good about eating
11:00 P.M.	3 slices bread 15 graham crackers Raisins ¼ jar peanut butter	Room	B V	Automatic—time of day Already binged & purged earlier—still depressed; out of control
1:00 A.M.	15 pretzels 6 oz. orange juice	Room	S	Reading; felt empty after purges

FIGURE 8.2. Illustrative self-monitoring form.

345

this stage is to return the patient to eating three meals a day with the provision for healthy snacks.

Although the emphasis during this early stage tends to be on behavioral change, the therapist repeatedly relates the cognitive view of BN to the patient's particular problems. For example, "if an episode of overeating was precipitated by the breaking of a dietary rule, this may be used to make the important point that the patient's attempts to follow rigid dietary rules result in her being prone to binge eat. The aim is to help the patient gain an understanding of the mechanisms that perpetuate the eating problem and to appreciate the need for both behavior and cognitive change" (Fairburn et al., 1993, p. 375).

The second stage has an increasingly cognitive focus. The techniques from Stage 1 are supplemented with a variety of procedures for reducing dietary restraint and developing cognitive and behavioral coping skills for resisting binge eating. This cognitive approach is modeled after Beck's (1976) cognitive therapy for depression. Patients are taught to identify and alter the dysfunctional thoughts and attitudes regarding shape, weight, and eating. Cognitive change is achieved by prompting patients to engage in behavioral experiments designed to challenge their dysfunctional assumptions.

In the third stage, the focus is on the use of relapse prevention strategies to ensure the maintenance of change following treatment (Marlatt & Gordon, 1985). Other than under exceptional circumstances (e.g., a suicidal patient), CBT is conducted on an outpatient basis. CBT can be applied to hospital patients, but treatment must be continued following discharge to help patients learn to regulate their eating and cope with specific high-risk situations for binge eating and purging that cannot be adequately addressed during inpatient therapy.

There are differences in the ways in which this approach is implemented across treatment settings. For example, adaptations of Fairburn's (1985) treatment program have been described by Agras, Schneider, Arnow, Raeburn, and Telch (1989) and Walsh and colleagues (1997). Nevertheless, a common set of treatment goals and techniques defines CBT for the treatment of BN. Fairburn's (1985) manual for BN has also been adapted for the treatment of recurrent binge eating in obese patients (Fairburn et al., 1993). The case study we describe next illustrates the treatment of a patient with BN, using a treatment manual adapted from Fairburn (1985) for a controlled treatment trial (Wilson, 1989). The case is drawn from a 20-session outpatient treatment program for BN at the New York Psychiatric Institute, Columbia University.

CASE STUDY

This is the case of Claire, a 26-year-old woman who had suffered from BN for 8 years at the time that she presented for treatment. Some details of the case have been changed to conceal the patient's identity, and to illustrate some of the typical issues that arise in treatment of this sort.

Assessment

In this case treatment was provided in the context of programmatic clinical research at an eating disorders clinic. To begin with, when an individual contacts our clinic for treatment, she is briefly screened on the phone to determine whether she appears to meet the necessary diagnostic criteria to be eligible for the clinical trial. If so, the treatment program is described to her; if she is interested in participating, a two-part evaluation is scheduled. The evaluation consists of an extensive clinical assessment to confirm the diagnosis of BN and assess the course of development as well as the current presentation of the disorder. In addition, associated psychopathology, substance abuse, and family, social, and medical histories are assessed. Finally, a complete physical exam is conducted, including blood tests and a drug screen. Particular attention is given to electrolyte abnormalities. The assessment evaluation also includes extensive self-report questionnaires.

The evaluation is conducted in part by a clinical assessor trained in the administration of structured interviews. The physical exam is conducted by one of the attending psychiatrists. Thus the clinician begins "Session 1" with much more information than would be the case in routine clinical practice. Although it is unlikely that such formal procedures are necessary in clinical practice, a thorough evaluation is nonetheless essential before starting treatment.

Specific Psychopathology

At the time of presentation for treatment, Claire reported "binge eating" approximately 10–15 times per week. Five of these overeating episodes constituted "binges" as defined by DSM-IV (i.e., uncontrolled consumption of what others would regard as a large amount of food), and the other 5–10 were what the EDE labels "subjective bulimic episodes" (i.e., episodes that did not constitute an unusually large amount of food but were subjectively experienced as out of control). The subjective binges usually occurred in the evening during the week. She purged approximately 10–15 times per week, after every binge episode. If she thought that she had eaten especially "bad foods," she vomited once after binge eating, drank a lot of water, and vomited again to "clean [herself] out."

Claire commuted by train to arrive at work by 7:30 A.M. She ate breakfast, which consisted of half a dry bagel and coffee, at work at approximately 8:30 A.M. Approximately once every 2 weeks, someone in the office brought in donuts or cookies for breakfast. Claire usually ate either a donut or five to six cookies and purged afterward. Claire frequently skipped lunch, but when she did eat a midday meal it typically consisted of salad, pizza, or Chinese food. Approximately one-third of the times that she did eat lunch, she purged. Claire did not eat snacks during the day unless there was a special occasion in the office, during which she "always took a piece of cake and purged afterward." After work, Claire typically went straight home to binge and purge. During the week, these overeating episodes were typically not very large. Most often they consisted of a salty snack food such as corn chips or potato chips, or cereal with milk, sugar, and raisins; four slices of bread; and three diet sodas. Claire always purged after these episodes.

On the weekend, Claire started the day about 11 A.M. with a binge. A typical weekend morning binge at this time was three to four slices of toast with cheese or jam, cereal with milk and sugar, one to three donuts, a bagel with cream cheese, and anything else that she could get her hands on. She then purged and took a shower. "Then I'm good for a few hours. I feel like I'm clean, like I wasn't bad for a few hours." On the weekend, Claire would usually eat a sandwich for lunch at about 2–3 P.M. She would binge and purge again about 1 hour after lunch on "whatever was in the refrigerator." Dinner would typically begin as a normal, social meal with her husband and possibly other relatives who would be visiting for the evening. However, at least half the time these meals would turn into binges, which were followed by purging after the guests left and her husband went to sleep.

A typical large weekend binge for Claire consisted of 4 cups of pasta with sauce and cheese, three pieces of garlic bread, one bowl of cereal with ½ cup of chocolate chips with milk, ice cream, and three to four 8-ounce glasses of diet soda. These binges usually occurred during the middle of the day while her husband was out doing errands. However, Claire reported that these binges sometimes occurred while her husband was home or while she was visiting at her mom's house "if I just couldn't help myself. . . . My family knows, but it's embarrassing for me. I wouldn't want to binge in front of them. . . . We don't talk about it. My mom thinks it's like taboo . . . unless she's angry, then she'll call me a freak. My husband wants everything to be OK, so even when he asks me if I'm still doing it, I just say no."

While binge eating, Claire claimed that she felt out of control: "I feel like I'm in a different state, like I don't really know what I'm doing. There's really no emotion there. I go numb. It's just something I do." She described her experience of purging as follows: "I feel better to get the food out, but I feel kind of like a freak, I feel alone . . . bad. I wonder how I could do something like this over and over again." Although Claire had abused laxatives for approximately 6 months 2 years before presenting for treatment, she stopped using them when she became frightened after experiencing dizziness and heart palpitations. She also tried using diuretics once.

Claire exercised "in spurts" and was not exercising at the time that she presented for treatment. During the brief periods when she would exercise, she awoke at 3:30 A.M. to do a 1½ hour aerobic workout prior to going to work. She was excessively concerned about her weight and expressed significant dissatisfaction with her body, despite the fact that her weight was well within the normal range. She avoided buying new clothes because she never thought that she looked good in anything.

Claire had begun binge eating and purging at age 18, after she overheard two girls at college discussing another girl who had BN. She thought the binge eating and purging sounded repulsive, but not long afterward she gave it a try. The first year that she binged, she either dieted severely or vomited. She vomited less frequently then, because it was harder to do. When it became easier to vomit spontaneously, she started using vomiting to purge more frequently. This increased rate of vomiting led to significant weight loss; Claire lost approximately 15 pounds, became amenorrheic during this period, and was also exercising 1–2 hours per day. For approximately three-quarters of her 20th year, Claire had met the diagnostic criteria for AN. Claire did not present with any other significant associated psychopathology.

Family/Social History

Claire grew up with her parents, an older sister, and an older brother in a large suburban neighborhood. When Claire was 12 years old, her parents got divorced. She described their divorce as "probably the single most traumatic experience of my whole life. . . . I feel like I wouldn't be the way I am if it weren't for that. . . . I was always Daddy's girl, and after they divorced I hardly ever saw him again." After the divorce, her mother was forced to assume responsibility for the majority of the family expenses, which resulted in her working more hours. Claire reported that during this time she would frequently spend the afternoons alone and depressed. There was no significant family history of obesity, eating disorders, or any other psychiatric disorder.

At age 23, Claire married Tom, a man she had dated during college. At age 26, when Claire presented for treatment, she was living with Tom in a one-bedroom apartment in the same town as Claire's mother. She described her relationship with her mother as good, but described feeling that they had grown apart in recent years. Tom worked many long days and was required to travel frequently for work. As a result, she had a lot of time at home alone; she reported that many times when she binged, she would be feeling bad about her relationship with him, but she was not able to articulate any details. She and Tom had no children.

Course of Treatment

Many patients have had previous treatment, usually based on a psychodynamic model, which is less structured and directive than CBT. It is important for the therapist to clarify some of the major distinctions between CBT and this more traditional supportive psychotherapy. In particular, the therapist should emphasize that the primary focus of CBT is on identifying the patterns of binge eating and purging, together with the factors or conditions that trigger and maintain these patterns. Once these patterns and proximal triggers are identified, the focus of the work is on identifying the thoughts and feelings associated with these episodes and developing alternative strategies for dealing with high-risk situations. It should be emphasized that CBT works in the "here and now," and that more emphasis is placed on the current constellation of problems than on the historical concerns regarding the development of the eating disorder.

An essential component of CBT is homework between therapy sessions. It should be emphasized to the patient that completing the homework between sessions is a critical part of therapy. The therapist should clarify that the homework will provide important material for understanding and treating her particular problems. The effort the patient will expend on her homework is tied closely to the attention it receives from her therapist. Most sessions should begin with a review of the homework. It is helpful to give a patient a folder or large envelope to keep forms in during the course of treatment. This will help the patient keep track of her homework and handouts, and will allow the therapist and patient to refer back to various homework assignments throughout the course of the treatment. Patients are asked to weigh themselves no more than once a week.

Finally, it is important to clarify for the patient the length of the therapy sessions (which in our clinic is 45 minutes) and the length of the treatment program (which in our clinic is 20 sessions, occurring over the course of approximately 5 months). Some patients are concerned that this will not be enough time to treat their eating disorder. It is important to emphasize to the patient that she should expect that just as the development of her eating disorder was gradual, so, too, the reestablishment of personal control and normal eating will take time. It should be explained to the patient that through the course of treatment she will be learning many of the skills necessary to become her own therapist, and therefore she should be encouraged to expect improvement to continue beyond the end of treatment. However, it should also be emphasized that if the patient does need further treatment at the end of the 20 sessions, appropriate referrals will be offered.

Session 1

Objectives

1. Establish rapport.
2. Outline treatment program and goals.
   a. Identification of patterns of binge eating.
   b. Identification of environmental, cognitive, and emotional triggers.
   c. Normalization and stabilization of eating patterns.
   d. Learning to become own therapist/collaborative effort of treatment.
3. Emphasize importance of homework.
4. Introduce high-risk hierarchies.

Selective Transcript

T: I know you have met with several people prior to our appointment today. How are you feeling about finally getting started?

C: Well, I'm really glad. I know I shouldn't feel this way. I mean, I know you're only trying to help, but I was pretty frustrated about having those other appointments and then having to wait a week before seeing you.

T: "Shouldn't feel this way"?

C: Well, you know . . . I shouldn't get angry.

T: Actually, I appreciate your telling me that you are feeling frustrated, angry. I can imagine that it's difficult to have to go through the evaluation process, which requires your meeting with several people, answering lots of questions (sometimes more than once), and then waiting a week for treatment to really begin.

Let's begin by my reviewing with you the structure and rationale of this treatment intervention. We will meet for 20 sessions. The first 8 sessions will be on a twice-per-week basis, and thereafter we will meet weekly. Our primary focus will be on understanding your current eating problems. We will focus on both your binge eating and your eating outside of the binges. In our experience, it is not only during the binge-eating episodes that someone with BN has difficulty with food. We are going to pay particular attention to the situations that are most difficult for you to manage in terms of your eating. We call these "high-risk situations." After identifying these high-risk situations, we will try to figure out what it is about these situations that make them particularly difficult for you. In other words, why is it that you binge in one situation and not another? We will focus on how you are feeling and what you are thinking at these times. The goal is to link your thoughts, feelings, and behavior in a meaningful way, so that we can understand what is currently maintaining your BN and make changes so that you can function more adaptively.

Before we get started on that, I also want to mention to you that I will be weighing you weekly at the beginning of the session. Do you weigh yourself now?

C: Oh, yes. I must weigh myself five times a day . . . before I get into the shower in the morning, after I get out, and all the time before and after I binge and purge.

T: What happens when you weigh yourself?

C: Well, if my weight is up I feel fat, and sometimes that sets off a binge. I know this sounds crazy, but sometimes if my weight is down that sets off a binge too, because I feel like I can afford the calories without getting fat—it's like a reward.

T: You *think* you can afford the calories without getting fat.

C: Yeah. I don't know . . . Pretty much no matter what, it isn't pleasant for me.

T: That's precisely why I want to encourage you to put your scale away for now. You see, the way we think about weight is that it is an end product that is influenced by many variables—where you are in your menstrual cycle, what time of day it is, whether you ate a lot of salty foods yesterday, how much exercise you are getting, and so on. As a result, your weight is bound to fluctuate a few pounds up and down. That's normal and healthy, but for you it's alarming. One of the goals of our treatment is for you to grow more comfortable with your weight and the fluctuations that are inevitable. As we begin to make some changes in your eating, I want to weigh you here, so that we can keep track of what is happening with your weight and discuss it. As your eating normalizes, and as you grow more comfortable with your eating and your weight, we will gradually move that job back into your court at home. So do you think you can put the scale away for now?

C: I'll give it a try.

T: OK. So to go back to the first point—we now know that weighing yourself is a high-risk situation for you in terms of triggering a binge.

C: Yeah, I guess that's right.

T: Here's a form that we will begin to complete together now and that I will ask you to complete for homework for your next session. What we want to do here is list the situations in which you find it impossible to resist the temptation to binge, where you always resist the temptation to binge, and the situations that can go either way. When you weigh yourself, for example, how often does that trigger a binge?

C: Oh, probably half the time.

T: OK, so that would go here: 50/50. Now what about last week? What were the situations that triggered your binge episodes?

C: Well, I almost always binge when I get home from work, before my husband gets home.

T: Almost always—is that 75% of the time, more, less?

C: About three out of the five nights.

T: OK, so that would go here. And how about a situation that always sets off a binge?

C: If I have a fight with my husband and then he leaves the house.

T: So that goes here. And how about a situation that never triggers a binge?

C: I never binge when I am out a restaurant with other people—mostly because I know I won't be able to purge.

T: OK, so we have a few examples here. What I want you to do for homework is complete this form. Include about three or four situations in each column, and do it both for binge eating and purging. When we meet next time, we'll go over it together.

In addition to identifying high-risk situations, I would like you to indicate the frequency that you binge-eat and purge each day by using this diary of binge–purge episodes. This daily self-monitoring is important, because it will help us keep track of how frequently you are binge-eating and purging as we proceed with treatment. Initially, this will be especially useful in terms of marking these episodes so that we can discuss what is happening around the times that you are binge-eating and purging, and thereby identify patterns and high-risk situations. As we attempt to make changes in your eating, it will be important for us to monitor what is happening with your binge eating and purging, because this will enable us to know what interventions are working and where the problems continue.

Now is a good time for me to emphasize to you the importance of homework. Between sessions, you will have homework to do that will provide us with important information about your problems with binge eating and purging. Sometimes it will entail writing things down. Sometimes it will entail experimenting with some new behavior. It's really important that you do the homework—some tasks may be difficult, but I want you to do the best you can, and we'll discuss any problems that you have along the way.

The last thing I want to do today is give you two handouts that I would like you to read. One is about vomiting and laxative abuse, and the other is about eating a range of foods including fats and carbohydrates in your diet. When we meet next time, we'll discuss them.

Homework

1. Complete the high-risk hierarchies.
2. Read the handouts.
3. Complete a daily diary of binge–purge episodes.

Session 2

Objectives

1. Review homework.
   a. Provide positive feedback.
   b. Ask: Has patient noticed any patterns, or does she have any other reactions to the self-monitoring?
   c. Reiterate importance of homework if necessary.
2. Review the high-risk hierarchies for binge eating and purging.
3. Explore patient's reaction to her weight. Emphasize the importance of limiting the number of times the patient weighs herself.

Selective Transcript

T: So you weigh 136 today. [The patient's weight was 136, up 1 pound from Session 1.] What do you think? How do you feel about that?

C: Terrible. I should weigh at least 10 pounds less. That's just what makes me feel better.

T: Makes you feel better?

C: Yeah. When I weigh this much, I feel fat and I just feel like a failure.

T: You *think* you're fat, and you *think* you are a failure for weighing 136, and it looks like that leaves you *feeling* pretty frustrated, maybe angry, maybe sad. As we work on these issues, I'm going to try to help you begin to be clearer about whether we are talking about thoughts or feelings. Surely they are very closely linked, but as we try to figure out what is going on with your eating, we want to know whether the problems lie in your thoughts, emotions, or both.

   As difficult as it is, I want to encourage you to hold judgment on your weight until you have your eating under control. Until then, it is impossible for us to know where your weight will settle down. Also, as I mentioned last week, everyone's weight fluctuates some. I want to encourage you to think of your weight as a window of about 5 pounds rather than as one specific number. In other words, instead of thinking that you weigh 136, think of your weight as 134–139. Anything in that window doesn't really constitute a significant weight change.

C: That's going to be really hard for me. I'm afraid I'm just going to keep on gaining weight.

T: I know this is difficult, but let's remember that gaining 1 pound is not the same as gaining 25 pounds—we call it "magnification" when we give more importance to something than it really deserves.

C: I know what you mean, but it's hard for me to remember that all the time.

T: Well, this would be a good time for us to talk about the handout on vomiting and laxative abuse, and the one on fats and carbohydrates. My guess is that the driving force for purging is that you are unhappy with your weight and that you are trying to counteract the binge. What did you think of the handout on this?

The handout describes the deleterious consequences of vomiting and laxative abuse, and explains how these compensatory behaviors really fail to help individuals manage their weight effectively. The cycle that is outlined states that many people employ vomiting because they want to counteract their binges and lose weight, but that just the opposite happens: When individuals vomit or use laxatives regularly, they tend to eat more because of the erroneous belief that they are able to rid themselves of all the calories. As a result, it is argued that individuals wind up consuming more calories than they would if they did not vomit or use laxatives.

C: Well, it makes sense, even though I have a hard time believing that I'm not going to gain weight if I stop.

T: I'm sure. You have been binge-eating and purging for 8 years. We are going to try to make gradual changes in your eating, at a pace that you can manage, so you can find out for yourself what the truth is. I just want to assure you that we are going to go slowly, and we will continue to closely monitor your weight and your eating, so that as you make changes you will have your own data.

   Let's look at the high-risk hierarchies form that you completed for homework now, to get a better sense of what your current eating habits are like—what are the eating habits associated with this weight.

Session 2 picks up where Session 1 left off with the high-risk hierarchies. The therapist and patient should go over each of the situations listed, with the goal of deciphering what factors differentiate when the patient does binge and purge from when she doesn't. One of the primary goals of this intervention is to loosen the patient's self-labeling as "bulimic" by pointing out that she is not continually binge-eating or purging.

T: So one of the things that we can see is that you are not "always" out of control—there are numerous situations that are not associated with binge eating and purging for you. This is important, because for many women who label themselves "bulimic," they think that all their eating is out of control. These are problems with "labeling" and "all-or-nothing thinking." In other words, many times we find that the way someone thinks about things can actually contribute to the problem.

In your lists here, you have identified several kinds of situations that are linked to binge eating and vomiting for you. What are some of the emotional triggers for you?

C: Hmm . . . well, a lot of times when I'm frustrated or angry, I wind up holding it in and then binge and purge when I'm alone. Like a lot of times, that's what happens with my husband. He does something that drives me crazy, but I don't say anything.

T: That reminds me of last session, when you told me you shouldn't be angry or frustrated about all the hoops you had to jump before starting treatment. Is that what happens with other people—you hold it in because you shouldn't be angry, or you shouldn't feel a certain way?

C: Yeah, that happens all the time. I guess my mom always told me that I shouldn't be angry that my parents got divorced, I shouldn't be angry about anything, because it won't do me any good . . . that I should just be happy for all that I have.

T: So what you are describing is how you came to believe that you shouldn't have certain feelings, anger in particular. This is a perfect example of how our past experiences shape the way we think about things in our current life. Rather than

focus extensively on how you learned to think about things in a particular way, we are going to ask the question of whether a given way of thinking about things is supported by your current experiences and whether it is adaptive for you now. You have the idea that you shouldn't express your anger because it won't do you any good, but look at what happens when you don't express your anger. Does that do you any good?

C: I guess not, but I'm really not sure how to change that now.

T: Well, we'll get to that, but first what I'd like you to do for the next session is add to this list of high-risk hierarchies some emotional states—what are the emotional states that are most and least associated with triggering binge eating and purging for you. And with the situations that you have already listed, describe how you typically feel in these situations.

The last thing that I would like to do with you today is begin filling out what we call the "decision analysis form" [see Figure 8.3]. This will help us understand why you want to change, as well as highlight for us what some of the issues are that interfere with your being able to end the BN on your own. In the first column, you should list the positive short-term consequences of stopping binge eating. In the next column, list the negative short-term consequences. In the third column, list the positive long-term consequences. And in the fourth column, list the negative long-term consequences. Then flip it around and list the consequences of continuing to binge-eat and purge. Do the best you can, and we'll go over it next time.

Homework

1. Expand on the high-risk hierarchies.
2. Complete the decision analysis form.
3. Complete daily diary.

Session 3

Objectives

1. Review homework.
2. Introduce dysfunctional thoughts.

	Immediate consequences		Delayed consequences	
	Positive	Negative	Positive	Negative
If I stop bingeing and purging				
If I continue to binge and purge				

FIGURE 8.3. The decision analysis form. Adapted from Marlatt (1985). Copyright 1985 by The Guilford Press. Adapted by permission.

a. Link thoughts, emotions, and behaviors, as highlighted by the 50/50 situations on the high-risk hierarchies form.
b. Identify 10 types of dysfunctional thoughts commonly engaged in. The patient is given a list of 10 cognitive distortions and asked to define and provide an example of one of each of the first five thoughts, preferably from the past week.
c. Clarify concept of dysfunctional and functional thinking styles versus "irrational" or "crazy" thinking (i.e., "Do these thoughts work for you or against you?").

Selective Transcript

C: The past few days have been really tough. I started binge eating on Thursday when I got home, and it only ended because I fell asleep. My husband has been away for business all week. I have a big problem being home alone like that, especially when I'm upset about work.

T: So that's another high-risk situation.

C: Yeah, I was feeling really bad about work. My boss was disappointed with me because I didn't get this report to her in time. I knew she was right. I mean, I spent half the day before the report was due binge eating and purging at work. I was so anxious about getting it done right that I wound up getting it done a day late.

T: OK, we know that feeling anxious is another emotional state that sets you up for a binge.

C: Oh, yeah. That's a big one.

T: Let's look at your high-risk hierarchies form for a moment to go over the other feelings that you link with these episodes, and then we'll see which ones apply to this most recent binge. OK, so you have here that when you are feeling angry and depressed that there is a very high risk that you will binge and purge. And you wrote that when you are calm and happy that you never binge and purge. You also wrote that when you feel that your husband should be home more that it could go either way. "Feeling that your husband should be home more" is really a thought. You *think* that your husband should be home more, and when he is not you feel . . .

C: Lonely and neglected. I mean, if he really loved me, he would make more of an effort. I don't know; he says he is doing this for us—we are trying to save money to buy a house and all—but a lot of times I think he would rather be at work than with me.

T: Is that part of what precipitated this last binge?

C: Yeah. I think that if it were just work or just him, I might have been able to handle it, but I couldn't deal with both at the same time.

T: OK, well, let's look at the situation and identify how you were thinking about everything, and try to begin to understand how your thinking may contribute to creating the difficult situation. In terms of work, you said you felt so anxious about getting the job done right that you wound up binge eating and purging. What's that about?

C: Well, I guess I'm a perfectionist. I have to do something perfectly, or else I think it's no good at all. And this report for my boss . . . well, I didn't have all the information I needed to do it exactly right, so I kept putting it off until the day before it was due, and then I wound up binge eating and purging—I was there until the middle of the night trying to get that thing done.

T: So there were really two binge episodes, one before you handed in the report and one the night you got home after handing it in, right?

C: Yeah.

T: What else were you thinking about when you had the binge episode at work?

C: I felt like a complete failure, because I couldn't get anything right.

T: You *thought* you were a complete failure. What do you mean, you couldn't get *anything* right?

C: Well, you know, with the report.

T: You said you didn't have all the information, but did you have enough information to do some of the report?

C: Oh, yeah, there were four parts to the report. It was for the third part that I was missing information.

T: So in fact you had most of the information you needed to do the report, but because you were missing some of the information for Part 3, you thought you wouldn't be able to do a good job and felt inadequate.

C: Yeah.

T: As you describe that situation to me, I notice that there are certain ways that you are thinking about the situation that seemed to make the whole situation more difficult for you. We all have rules that govern the way we think about the world, ourselves, and our experiences in the world. Some of these rules or ideas are so automatic that we don't even realize that we have them or that they are having an effect on us. Part of the work that we will be doing together is figuring out what the automatic thoughts are that you have that contribute to your problems with bulimia. We call these thoughts "dysfunctional thoughts" or "cognitive distortions."

There are lots of automatic thoughts that are healthy, adaptive, and essential to our daily functioning. Take for example, learning how to ride a bike. When you are first learning how to ride a bike, you have to think about every detail: where to hold the handlebars, how to brake, how to balance, where to keep your eyes, and so on. Once you have learned to ride, you don't think about these things; they just come naturally. You could be thinking about the friend you are on your way to visit, get on the bike, and start pedaling without paying much attention to the logistics of riding the bike. This kind of automatic thinking is very adaptive. It allows you to learn something and then move on to learning and doing other things.

Sometimes, however, the automatic thoughts are not so functional—these are the dysfunctional thoughts or cognitive distortions. We're not going to focus so much on how you got to thinking about things in a particular way, but what the impact of these dysfunctional thoughts are on your current life. We have got to evaluate these thoughts and consider how much support they have in your current life, and whether there are more adaptive ways to think about yourself and the situations you find yourself in.

It's important to keep in mind as we go through this that when we talk about dysfunctional thoughts and cognitive distortions, we are not calling someone irrational or crazy. Although it is sometimes difficult for people to trace the history of how they got to thinking about something in a particular way, many times people know immediately why they think in certain ways. Typically people have had certain experiences that they interpreted in a particular way, or [they] were told certain things growing up that led them to think about the world in one way or another. You are not crazy for having certain thoughts. The issue is, do they work for you today? Of all the automatic thoughts that govern and influence your behavior, which ones are accurate, helpful, and adaptive, and which ones are dysfunctional in the sense that they have no support in your current reality and only contribute to making situations more difficult?

To go back to the binge that you had at work, you said that you have to do things perfectly or not at all. This is an example of "all-or-nothing thinking." It's got to be 100% perfect or it's not worth doing.

You also called yourself a "complete failure." That's another example of "all-or-nothing thinking." It's also an example of "labeling."

Let's read through each of these 10 cognitive distortions together. These are the 10 most problematic thought patterns that we see with individuals with BN. You may recognize some of these thought patterns in yourself right away. Others may not seem to describe you at all. What we're going to do for the next few weeks is work on identifying which ones are most characteristic of you and what that means for your BN.

With time, our goal is to begin to challenge the dysfunctional thoughts that you identify, and try to establish more adaptive ways of thinking about things. Your problems with bulimia did not happen overnight; you did not learn to think in certain dysfunctional ways all at once. Similarly, identifying and overcoming the dysfunctional thoughts will be a gradual process of unlearning or retraining the thoughts, feelings, and behaviors which led to and maintain the bulimia.

Between now and our next session, I want you to try to think of at least one example of each of the first five cognitive distortions on the list. Also, when you think about the binge–purge episodes that you have had in the past week, I want you to pay special attention to what you were thinking before you started the episode. See if you can identify from this list some dysfunctional thoughts that contributed to triggering the episode. After thinking about these past episodes, try to identify the dysfunctional thoughts that occur prior to potential binge–purge episodes between now and the next time we meet. We'll go over it together next time.

Homework

1. Bring in at least one example of each of the first five dysfunctional thoughts.

2. Try to identify dysfunctional thoughts linked to binge–purge episodes from the past week and from the current week.
3. Complete food diary of binge–purge episodes.

Session 4
Objectives

1. Review homework.
   a. Provide positive feedback.
   b. Discuss examples of first five dysfunctional thoughts.
2. Define the 6th through 10th dysfunctional thoughts, with examples from the past week.
3. Introduce challenges to dysfunctional thoughts.
   a. Examine process of identification and labeling of thought, and reality testing: "Is it true? What is my evidence for this thought?"
   b. Formulate functional or adaptive challenges in response to the dysfunctional thoughts.

In Session 3, the therapist did not have time to review the decision analysis form with the patient. It is important to do this within one of the next sessions, both for the intrinsic worth of the information gained from the form and to support and respect the patient's efforts in completing the homework. When the therapist does not have sufficient time to review all the homework in the session for which it was prepared, it is useful to acknowledge this with the patient and assure her that it will be addressed soon.

Selective Transcript

The patient was weighed on the way down to the therapist's office prior to Session 4. She weighed 135 pounds.

T: What do you think of your weight today?

C: I still think that I'm really fat. I hate looking at myself in the mirror, or even when I take a shower I'm totally grossed out.

T: "Totally grossed out" . . .

C: Yeah. I mean, I see all these beautiful women walking up and down the street, and I just don't compare. I mean, look at me. My husband says he likes my body, he likes me just the way I am, but I don't believe him. I mean, there are a lot of women that he works with who are younger and more attractive than I am; how could he possibly find me attractive? I would feel so much better about myself if I could just lose 10 pounds, but no matter how hard I try to diet, it seems I always wind up blowing it within a few days.

T: What do you mean, "blowing it"? How does that happen?

C: Well, you know, I'll start dieting. I'll be really good. I'll eat really good, healthy foods. Usually I'll have fruit for breakfast, one of those fiber bars for lunch, and some nonfattening type of dinner like fish or Chinese vegetables. I feel really good when I stick to this, but it doesn't last very long. There's always a party or business dinner or something. I wind up eating cake or too much bread, and then it turns into a full-blown binge.

T: So the idea is that when you are dieting, you have to be perfect. And being perfect means sticking to a very strict diet, no exceptions. No cake. No bread. If you eat any of these foods, then you have blown your diet; you've failed.

C: Yeah.

T: Sounds pretty harsh to me.

C: Well, how else am I going to lose this weight? I know myself. I can't eat just a little bit of these foods . . . if I have even a small bite, I want more. It's better for me not to have any.

T: I'm not so sure about that. Look what happens when you try to avoid these foods completely. You severely restrict your diet, you wind up feeling deprived, and you wind up binge eating and purging if you eat the "wrong" thing. Also, take a look at your weight. Over the past 8 years, it has steadily increased to where you are now.

C: All I know is that if I eat those foods, I am going to get fat.

T: I think just the opposite. As long as those foods are forbidden, you are going to have problems with eating and weight. We're not ready to do this just yet, but down the road I am going to encourage you and will work with you to challenge some of these automatic thoughts about food and weight.

Before we get there, let's go back for a few minutes to the high-risk hierarchies and decision analysis forms. What we know so far is that there are certain interpersonal situations and emotional states that you find difficult to manage, which are frequently associated with triggering a binge. What we also know from today is that there are certain ideas that you have about your body and food, as well as certain ways that you manage your eating, that put you at risk for binge eating and purging.

Now let's go back to the decision analysis form and figure out how well the bulimia is doing in terms of solving these problems, and let's figure out what problems it creates. In other words, the binge eating and purging does something for you or else you wouldn't be doing it. So here on the decision analysis form, what did you put in the columns for the negative short- and long-term consequences of stopping the binge–purge episodes? What would you lose, what would be more difficult, if you didn't binge and purge?

C: (*Going through the list*) Well, one thing for sure—I wrote it here—is that I am afraid I will gain weight. I'm afraid I'll never be able to eat my favorite foods again. Another thing is that I'll have to deal with some of the problems that I'm avoiding in my relationships.

T: OK, so you think you will gain weight if you stop binge eating and purging. That's a thought: "If I stop binge eating—or, more importantly, if I stop purging—I'm going to be fat." That makes you feel anxious and scared, but the truth is you really don't know what will happen. For the past 8 years, you've been doing things in a certain way because of these thoughts and assumptions, but you really don't know what would happen if you stopped binge eating and purging. That's called the "fortune teller's error." [A therapist and patient should go through each entry identified in the negative consequences columns in a similar fashion.]

T: OK, now, what problems are created by the bulimia, or at least not helped by it?

In other words, what would you gain by giving up the binge eating and purging? What would be the positive short- and long-term consequences of not binge eating and purging any more?

C: I'll be able to do more things socially, because I won't be so afraid of losing control.

T: You'll be able to do more social activities. Does it happen now that you avoid certain situations because you are afraid that you will binge or purge?

C: Oh, yeah, all the time. Or else I wind up canceling things because I'm in the middle of a binge or have just finished purging and am exhausted.

One of the other things I listed here is that I think my relationship with my husband would be better. I mean, now it's one of those unspoken secrets.

T: So eliminating the binge eating and purging would potentially help your relationships, but as you noted in the other column, that means dealing with some of the problems that you've been avoiding. Giving up the bulimia isn't going to take care of these problems automatically, but it does make it possible for you to take care of them rather than continuing to avoid them.

A therapist and patient should review the decision analysis form thoroughly by going over each item. In addition to accurate appraisals of the consequences of eliminating the bulimia, frequently there are cognitive distortions in the responses that will interfere with treatment if they are not explicitly addressed.

T: As we've gone through the decision analysis form, we've been able to clarify why it is that you want help and some of what it is that interferes with making changes. We've identified some of the distortions in your thinking about your bulimia. Let's start going through some of these distortions and begin challenging them. We can start with the distortions that you have already identified for homework today. We'll work together on developing some functional or rational challenges, and you can continue the rest for homework.

The therapist should review the list of cognitive distortions that the patient has identified,

and select one or two examples to challenge with the patient in order to model the process.

T: Let's take this example: "My boss was angry that I didn't get the report in on time. I am not a good employee. I am a failure." Let's take it one statement at a time. Your boss was angry. How do you know that?

C: She said she was.

T: What did she say?

C: She said she wished I had told her that I would be late with the report, and in the future to keep her posted on delays.

T: OK, so she didn't like the way you handled the delay and was able to tell you so. Does that make you "not a good employee"?

C: Well, I guess not, but that's how I feel.

T: What kind of cognitive distortion is that?

C: Emotional reasoning?

T: That's right. You think you're a failure, so you are. Now how would you challenge that?

C: I don't know. I guess I'm not such a bad employee.

T: How do you know that?

C: Well, I've been there 5 years now.

T: And what kind of feedback have you gotten? Have you had any promotions, raises?

C: Oh, yeah. People tell me that they like working with me—both my superiors and the people who work for me.

T: So the challenge to the idea that you are a bad employee is that just because you think you are a failure at a given moment does not make you a failure. You have received a lot of feedback that would support just the opposite idea—that you are a valued employee. Now part of this distortion is that when you get the slightest bit of negative feedback, you think you are a failure. This is what kind of distortion?

C: Magnification. Labeling and all-or-nothing thinking, too.

T: That's right. Try to challenge that. Begin here with your homework and continue through the list of dysfunctional thoughts that you have listed here, as well as the ones that we have identified as we went through the decision analysis form. I want you to write down the dysfunctional thoughts, identify the distortions, and try to challenge the distortions. Have a discussion with yourself, or imagine that a friend is telling you the cognitive distortion. How can you challenge the distortion? How can you begin to think about things differently?

Homework

1. Provide examples of numbers 6 through 10 on the list of cognitive distortions.
2. Identify dysfunctional thoughts and challenges.
3. Complete binge–purge diary.

Session 5

Objectives

1. Review homework.
   a. Discuss examples of 6th through 10th dysfunctional thoughts, and discuss challenges.
2. Introduce the Daily Record of Dysfunctional Thoughts (referred to below as the dysfunctional thought record [DTR]; see Figure 8.4.

The session began with a review of the homework, focusing on the identified dysfunctional thoughts and challenges. As is the case with many patients, Claire found it very difficult to provide cogent and persuasive challenges to diffuse the negative feelings associated with her dysfunctional thoughts. It is extremely important for the therapist to help the patient generate challenges to the cognitive distortions that do not pale in comparison. It typically requires numerous repetitions before the patient is able to generate strong and convincing challenges. This is a major part of the core work of cognitive restructuring in CBT for BN.

Once the patient is able to identify cognitive distortions and is able to generate challenges, the next step is to help her link these distortions to the high-risk situations that she associates with binge eating and purging. One of the primary instruments that is used to facilitate this work is the DTR. The following segment from Session 5 illustrates how to introduce the DTR and begin working with it.

Selective Transcript

T: . . . OK, so we've been able to identify some examples of the cognitive distortions that seem to be most common and most prob-

SITUATION Describe: 1. Actual event leading to unpleasant emotion, or 2. Stream of thoughts, daydream, or recollection, leading to unpleasant emotion. DATE	EMOTION(S) 1. Specify sad/ anxious/ angry, etc. 2. Rate degree of emotion, 1-100.	AUTOMATIC THOUGHT(S) 1. Write automatic thought(s) that preceded emotion(s). 2. Rate belief in automatic thought(s), 0-100%.	RATIONAL RESPONSE 1. Write rational response to automatic thought(s). 2. Rate belief in rational response, 0-100%.	OUTCOME 1. Rerate belief in automatic thought(s), 0-100%. 2. Specify and rate subsequent emotions, 0-100.
12/1	My boyfriend and I started discussing what we think is attractive in men and women. I then started feeling fat and as if he couldn't possibly be attracted to me even though he says he is.	Sad, angry 100%	I'm fat and he'll never look at me like I'm attractive. He'd be much happier and satisfied with another person. 100%	1. Of course he's attracted to me—we've been going out for a long time. I also admire things in other men, that doesn't mean I don't love him or find him attractive. 2. No one is perfectly satisfied with how they look. 3. Bingeing and vomiting won't make me lose weight.	20% 30%

Explanation: When you experience an unpleasant emotion, note the situation that seemed to stimulate the emotion. (If the emotion occurred while you were thinking, daydreaming, etc., please note this.) Then note the automatic thought associated with the emotion. Record the degree to which you believe this thought: 0% = not at all; 100% = completely. In rating degree of emotion: 1 = a trace; 100 = the most intense possible.

FIGURE 8.4. Example of a completed Daily Record of Dysfunctional Thoughts form. The form is drawn from Beck, Rush, and Emery (1979).

lematic for you. What we need to do now is link these distortions to specific situations, particularly to the times that you binge and purge. Let's take a look at your diary. You have indicated here that you binged and purged yesterday after you got home from work. Let's look at this situation in more detail, using what we call the "dysfunctional thought record" or "DTR." We'll use this form to help us better understand the situations that precipitate binge and purge episodes for you, focusing on the thoughts and feelings that you have right before you binge or purge. What was the situation yesterday?

C: Well, it was 8 P.M. and I had just gotten home. I was feeling down because Tom was not going to be home—he's in California until tomorrow.

T: OK. So the situation is that you are home alone after a long day at work. We write that in Column 1 here. In Column 2 we write down how you are feeling. You said you were feeling down; what else?

C: I was feeling bad that Tom didn't call me at work . . . usually he calls me when he's on the road.

T: Feeling "bad"—what do you mean exactly?

C: Oh, I guess I was feeling depressed, and I guess a little angry, too.

T: OK, so we have depressed and angry in Column 2. What else?

C: Kind of anxious, too.

T: Anxious?

C: Yeah. I had handed in a report to my boss that day, and I wasn't sure what she thought of it.

T: We have depressed, angry, and anxious. Let's connect up the thoughts associated with each of these feelings. You were feeling depressed because . . .

The goal here is to connect the feeling states with the underlying cognitive distortions. The cognitive distortions will generally not be apparent in the patient's first thought. It is essential that the therapist help the patient follow a particular thought as far as possible, because usually the distortion is several steps from the surface thought. If the therapist stops too early in this exploration, the distortions will remain intact and undiscovered. One of the most effective ways of getting to these underlying distortions is by using open-ended statements that the patient can complete.

C: Tom didn't call.

T: And that makes you feel depressed because . . .

C: I feel like he doesn't care about me.

T: You think he doesn't care about you, and that makes you feel depressed. You think he doesn't care about you because he didn't call.

C: I know. I'm being stupid and needy.

T: Stupid and needy?

C: Yeah, I mean I know it's stupid for me to get myself so worked up here, but when he goes away I feel so rejected.

T: Rejected? (*Adding this to the list in Column 2*)

C: Yeah. I mean, sometimes I think that he likes traveling more than he likes being home with me.

T: OK. So you were feeling depressed because Tom didn't call, and since he didn't call, you think that he doesn't care about you. You feel rejected and think that he likes traveling more than being home with you. Let's look at the distortions here: Your thoughts were that Tom doesn't care about you because he didn't call. What kind of distortion is that (*handing Claire the list of cognitive distortions*)?

C: Well, magnification?

T: Magnifying the importance of this single event, right. You also said that you feel rejected and think he likes traveling more than being home with you, even though he says that he doesn't. What kind of distortion is that?

C: I guess it's emotional reasoning.

T: Right . . . assuming that your negative emotions necessarily reflect the way things are: "I feel it; therefore it must be true." Have you ever checked this out with him?

C: No.

T: So in a way it's also an example of mind reading.

C: Yeah. I guess I should find out rather than assuming the worst.

T: In addition to feeling depressed, you also said that you were feeling angry. You were angry because . . .

C: Well, sort of for the same reasons. If he really cares about me, he should call.

T: That's a "should" statement.

C: I know, but he should call.

T: Would it be more accurate to say that you *want* him to call, and when he doesn't you feel sad and put out?

C: Yeah.

T: OK, so the first step here is recognizing the "should" statement. The challenge to the "should" statement is . . . ?

C: There are lots of ways that he shows he cares about me, even when he is away, so it's not that he should always call or that he has to call in order for me to know he cares, it's just that I like it when he calls.

T: OK, so when you put it that way, how sad and angry do you feel?

C: Not as much. Maybe just a little sad still, because I miss him.

T: So the next step, then, is figuring out how to manage these feelings more effectively. In other words, even after working through the distortions, you are left with some feelings that are difficult for you to manage or tolerate. Right now, what you do is binge. We need to work on some alternative strategies to binge eating at times like this. Before we do this, let's look at your anxiety.

C: Oh, that had to do with my boss. I always get anxious when I hand things in to her.

T: You handed in a report to your boss, and that makes you feel anxious because . . .

C: Well, I know there were parts of it that could have been stronger. I wish that I had spent more time on it so that it would have been better.

T: There were parts of it that could have been stronger, and that makes you feel anxious because . . .

C: Well, because my boss is going to send it back for corrections.

T: And that makes you feel anxious because . . .

C: Because that means it wasn't perfect.

T: And since it's not perfect, that makes you anxious because . . .

C: My boss will think that I'm not a very good employee.

T: OK, so you hand in a report; that makes you anxious because parts of it could have been stronger—it's not perfect; the fact that it's not perfect makes you anxious because then your boss is going to think you're not a good employee. What are the distortions here?

C: Well I guess that's "mental filter." I mean, most of the report was pretty good.

T: So, as you see, you're dwelling on the small negative details to the exclusion of the overall report, which was pretty good.

C: Yeah, I guess it's a problem with perfectionism, too. I have to do things perfectly, or else I think I'm a total failure.

T: So that's a form of "all-or-nothing thinking." Now what are the challenges?

C: It was a big report. Most of it was really good. I need to remember that most of the report was in great shape, and the parts that need work are things that need my boss's input anyway. She doesn't expect it to be perfect, so why should I?

T: So how do you feel now?

C: Better. If only I could stop to think these things through when I'm in the situation. I mean, it all happens so fast.

T: That's what we're going to work on for now—helping you slow down enough so that you can think more clearly about how you're feeling and what you're thinking in situations like this. Right now it's as if you're on automatic pilot. A difficult situation arises, and you wind up binge eating and purging—you go right from here (*pointing to Column 1 of the DTR*) to here (*pointing to the line between Columns 3 and 4*). I call this the "binge–purge line." We're going to work on slowing you down so that you can focus on your thoughts and feelings—Columns 2 and 3. And we're also going to try to get you over this hump, past this binge–purge line, without binge eating and purging by working on the challenges and by developing alternative coping strategies.

Homework

1. Complete the first four columns of the DTR during a high-risk situation.
2. Complete food diary of binge–purge episodes.

Session 6

Objectives

1. Review homework.
2. Complete DTR for a binge–purge episode that occurred last week.
3. Introduce three meals per day.
4. Plan some possible meals.

Most frequently, when the DTR is first introduced and given to patients to complete for homework, patients do not fill out the form before they binge and purge. Sometimes patients will complete it after they binge and purge or not complete it at all. Usually they will describe not even thinking of using the DTR until they are already deep into their binge or not until they have completed the entire episode. It usually will take several repetitions with the therapist of completing the DTR retrospectively before a patient starts using the tool effectively on her own. Each session the therapist should continue to encourage the patient to use the DTR and help her think retrospectively about what would facilitate her completing the DTR before the binge. An example of this work is described in Session 6.

Selective Transcript

T: On your diary, you have indicated that you had five binge–purge episodes last week. Let's look at the DTR that you filled out for one of them.

C: Well, on Saturday and Sunday I didn't even remember about the DTR. I did it on Tuesday, but it was after the whole thing was over.

T: What do you think happened?

C: I don't know. It happens so fast, it's like my brain turns off. I finally remembered the DTR on Tuesday, but that was after the whole thing was over.

T: It's not unusual for it to take some time before you get into the practice of using the DTR. Let's look at what you were able to complete on Tuesday. The situation was that you were at work and ate a piece of birthday cake that was for one of your coworkers. You felt guilty, depressed, and fat. The thoughts you have here are "Cake is a binge food," I shouldn't eat such fattening food," and "I'm going to get fat." Let's start with feeling guilty. Whenever you feel guilty, look for the "should" statement. What you say here is that you shouldn't eat such fattening foods because you are going to get fat. What are the distortions?

C: Like you said, that's a "should" statement.

T: What else?

C: Overgeneralization. I mean, one piece of cake is not going to make me fat.

T: So that's the distortion and the challenge. Part of that distortion is also the fortune teller's error, don't you think?

C: Yeah. But even though I "know" that one piece of cake is not going to make me fat, I don't really believe it yet.

T: Well, you probably won't fully believe it until you find out for yourself that it's true. Soon we'll try some miniexperiments so that you can find out for yourself what does happen if you eat an occasional piece of cake.

One of the other distortions that we see here is the labeling of certain foods as forbidden. Labeling is an extreme example of all-or-nothing thinking. Either a food is "good" or "bad."

C: That's definitely the case for me. I've got a long list of "bad" foods.

T: The way we think about food is that there are no "good" or "bad" foods. No single food is going to make you fat. Your eating habits are important. Your pattern of eating from day to day is what we need to work on, rather than eliminating individual food items from your diet. Although that sounds pretty scary, we see here that you are eating these so-called "forbidden foods" already, but you are not enjoying them very much. We're going to work on bringing them into your regular meals so that eating is more satisfying for you.

So what are the challenges to the distortions that you've identified?

C: Well, no single food is going to make me fat. It's OK if I eat cake every once in a while.

T: Do you really believe that?

C: Well, sort of. I think it's true for everyone else, but I really am afraid that if I have one bite I'll wind up having a binge.

T: If you have one bite, you'll wind up having a binge because . . .

C: Because I feel like a failure, and that I shouldn't have any because it will make me fat.

T: We've challenged the idea that one piece of cake will make you fat. What's the distortion and challenge to the idea that you are a failure?

C: Well, I feel in control if I don't eat, and I feel totally out of control when I do eat that stuff.

T: So that's an example of . . .

C: All-or-nothing thinking.

T: And the problem is that when you're not eating, are you really in control? It seems to me that not eating any of the foods that you like is really just the flip side of the binge. Also, it sets you up to binge. No one can go on indefinitely forbidding themselves the foods that they really like. The way I think about it, you'll really be in control when you are able to eat some of these foods in moderation during your regular meals.

Next time you think you are about to binge, I want you to go back to this DTR and review the distortions and challenges. Also, I want you to fill out a new DTR. After you complete the list of feelings, thoughts, distortions, and challenges, I want you to come up with five alternatives to binge eating and implement at least one.

The other thing I want to work on is your eating outside of binge episodes. Our goal is for you to eat three meals per day. This is the surest way for you to eat a wide range of foods and enough calories so that you can avoid feeling physically starved and psychologically deprived. Right now you're skipping lots of meals. This is one of the things that sets you up for binge eating, because by the end of the day you feel deprived and, in fact, excessively hungry. Thus, in addition to the other triggers, by the end of the day you are especially vulnerable. In fact, this is one the most difficult times of the day for you in terms of your binge eating and purging, isn't it?

C: Yeah, but I'm afraid if I start eating in the morning, I'll wind up eating all day, and that will just trigger a binge.

T: How would that trigger a binge?

C: Well, I'll be thinking that I'm eating too much and that I'm going to get fat. . . . So I'll figure that I have to vomit up what I've eaten, and if I'm going to vomit, I might as well eat all the foods that I otherwise forbid myself.

T: I know it's difficult for you to believe that you are not going to get fat if you eat three meals a day. That's the way you have been thinking about your eating for a long time now. What I want to encourage you to consider is that you are actually consuming more calories than you've counted in the past, because you've always dismissed all the calories that you consumed while binge eating because you thought you got rid of all of them when you purged. Now you know that isn't the case. So, as difficult as it is, I want to encourage you to experiment with bringing some of these calories into your regular eating. Ease up on your restraint during the day, so that you don't put yourself at risk at the end of the day because you are so starved and deprived. Let's plan for three meals for the next few days and see how it goes.

C: OK.

The therapist should go through complete meal planning with the patient for the days between this and the next session. Typically the patient will want to plan for excessively restrictive meals. It is the therapist's job to ensure that the meals are sufficiently caloric and appealing.

Homework

1. Complete the DTR during a high-risk situation.
2. Complete eating diary—both planned and actual consumption.
3. Complete food diary of binge–purge episodes.

Session 7

Objectives

1. Review homework.
2. Complete DTR for any problem episodes since last session.

3. Discuss alternatives to binge eating and purging, as well as delay strategies.
4. Review success of three meals per day.

This session focused on Claire's experience of trying to eat three meals per day. On the days that she did eat three meals, she did not binge or purge. However, after eating three meals per day for 2 days, she was "feeling fat and anxious"; she decided to skip dinner that day, and wound up binge eating and purging late that night. This experience offered sufficient support for the link between binge and nonbinge eating that the patient was then able to state for herself that the best way to avoid a binge episode is to plan to eat. Nonetheless, she had significant anxiety about gaining weight, as transcribed below.

Selective Transcript

C: I feel a lot better that I ate some regular meals, but I know that I can't keep this up or I am going to blow up.

T: Let's review again some of the thoughts you have about managing your weight. Right now you are afraid to eat three meals per day, because you're afraid you'll gain weight. I understand that it's difficult for you to believe otherwise until you experiment with this new behavior for a while, but I want to emphasize a couple of points that may help you as you try to continue eating three meals per day.

First, remember the handout I gave you on vomiting and laxative abuse? Go over that periodically as you begin experimenting with three meals per day. Remember, contrary to popular belief, purging is not a very effective means of either avoiding weight gain or losing weight. Your body absorbs more calories than you think. And laxative abuse is ineffective and dangerous. Eighty percent of the calories consumed are absorbed by the body almost immediately, and hence the only real effect of purging is depletion of fluids. Similarly, weight loss due to laxatives is also a consequence of water loss. Taking laxatives has the added danger, however, of causing rebound water retention once the laxatives have been discontinued.

Another big danger of vomiting or abusing laxatives is that is sets you up to have even larger binges, because you figure you are going to get rid of it all anyway, and that probably also deters you from eating regular meals at other times of the day. If you binge and vomit in the afternoon, chances are that you will be feeling bad and wind up not eating dinner—either because you are too exhausted, or because you feel guilty for the binge, or . . .

C: Oh, yeah. If I binge at work, I never eat dinner.

T: And if you skip dinner, what happens later?

C: Well, either I go right to sleep, or late in the evening I feel hungry and then chances are I'll wind up binge eating at midnight.

T: So the cycle continues. . . . We need to continue to work on breaking the cycle, both by managing the high-risk situations without binge eating and vomiting, and by working on establishing healthier eating habits during nonbinge times. So, as difficult as it is, I want you to continue to plan on three meals per day. In terms of managing the potential binge episodes, I want you to continue filling out the DTR at high-risk times, with the addition of coming up with at least five alternatives to binge eating and purging for each situation. What are some things that you think you could do instead of binge eating or purging?

C: That's hard to imagine . . . when I get to the point of binge eating or purging, I feel like there are no alternatives.

T: That would be an example of what kind of thinking?

C: All-or-nothing.

T: It's easy to see that you would think this way, since this is the way that you've managed your eating for so long, but let's work together to try to come up with some alternatives. The other day, for example, when you binged after you got home, what could you have done instead?

C: Well, I could have cleaned my apartment when I got home . . . it's an absolute mess. I really should do that anyway.

T: The alternatives should be engaging and pleasurable. Maybe it's true that your apartment needed to be cleaned, but did you really want to clean when you were feeling like bingeing? Let's try to come up with some more pleasurable activities that might really work.

C: I could have stopped by a friend's house on my way home and planned to have dinner with her, since my husband was away.

T: Good. What else? What could you do this week if you get home one evening and feel like binge eating?

C: I could read for a while.

T: Will that be sufficiently engaging for you to avoid a binge?

C: Well, I'm reading a really good book right now, so maybe.

T: OK, let's start there. If you try that and still feel like binge eating, what could you do?

C: I could plan to eat a regular meal, and then go out for a walk immediately so that it doesn't turn into a binge.

T: Good. It's important that you eat dinner even when you feel the urge to binge, so that may be a safe way to eat dinner without its becoming trouble. What else?

C: I guess I could call a friend. If I manage to eat alone, I could just talk to my friend until I don't feel anxious any more. . . . I could also call one of my best friends who lives nearby and visit her, or have her come over for dinner, if I'm going to be home alone all night.

T: This is a great start. What I want you to do for next time is come up with a list of alternatives that will help you delay or completely avoid binge eating and purging. When you are feeling like you want to binge or purge, I want you to have a variety of activities listed that are engaging *and* pleasurable, so you can refer to it to help you get through the most difficult time right before you start binge eating or purging.

Homework

1. Complete the DTR during a high-risk situation with alternatives.
2. Complete eating diary—both planned and actual consumption.
3. Complete food diary of binge–purge episodes.
4. List alternatives and delay strategies.

Sessions 8 and 9

Objectives

1. Review homework.
   a. Focus on continuing high-risk situations.
   b. Go over alternative strategies to binge eating.
   c. Assess any continuing difficulties with DTR.
2. Review three meals per day.
3. Identify forbidden foods.

At this stage in the therapy, many new concepts, tools, strategies, and behavioral changes have been introduced. Therefore, much of the work during this phase entails working on the areas where the patient has the most difficulty, which will vary from individual to individual. In Claire's case, she continued to have significant problems with eating dinner during the week. Also, if she did eat, even if she did not have a true binge, she would feel the urge to vomit. The focus of the work during Sessions 8 and 9 centered on eating dinner and the cognitive distortions that she maintained about the effects of eating dinner. This led to the introduction of the concept of forbidden foods, as transcribed below.

Selective Transcript

C: . . . well, I ate dinner almost every night last week, but I wound up vomiting after dinner a couple of times, too.

T: So was it the same pattern each evening that you vomited?

C: Yeah, I got home, planned to eat dinner, started nibbling while I was getting dinner ready, wound up eating more than I planned, and felt so fat that I decided to vomit.

T: OK, so let's go through the DTR for the last time that happened.

C: Last night. I got home. I planned to make pasta, salad, and bread. I wound up eating two slices of bread with butter before dinner and took a second helping of pasta during dinner. I was stuffed and had to get rid of it.

T: Feelings, thoughts?

C: Anxious. If I keep eating like this, I'm going to get fat. I ate butter, and that's not allowed.

T: Distortions?

C: Fortune teller's error, magnification, all-or-nothing thinking—I mean, as soon as I tasted the butter I decided I had to vomit, because butter is fattening and if I eat it I'll get fat.

At this point, Claire was well versed in the procedure of using the DTR, so the therapeutic task was to get to the remaining issues without spending a lot of time focusing on the parts that she was managing successfully on her own. She was able to challenge the idea that feeling full is the same thing as being fat, but she was stuck with regard to having eaten the butter.

T: Now is the time for us to work more aggressively on the list of forbidden foods that you have in your head. By having such a list, we can see that you are setting yourself up to vomit at times. Our goal is to gradually bring these foods into your eating, so that you can enjoy the times that you do eat them and not have them set off binges or vomiting episodes. Also, in some ways, it seems like the whole experience of eating dinner is forbidden in your mind. Whether or not you have a real binge, you think you have to counteract your eating by vomiting. What we need to work on at times like this is not changing your eating so much as changing the way you are thinking about your eating. Our goal is for you to be able to eat the dinner that you describe without vomiting, rather than changing your eating behavior, as we would want to do in the case of an objective binge.

What I would like you to do for the next session is continue working on eating three meals per day, with special attention to having dinner. Also, I want you to write down all the forbidden foods you can think of, so that we can begin working on bringing these foods into your diet.

Sessions 10 through 15

Objectives

1. Continue working on identifying high-risk situations and using the DTR to work on developing more adaptive functioning.
2. Address the issues of body shape concern and weight as the patient's eating behavior normalizes.

3. Incorporate a wider range of foods into the patient's diet, including former forbidden foods.

During this middle phase of treatment, Claire was able to establish healthier eating habits, which included eating three meals per day and incorporating her forbidden foods into her diet. She also made regular use of the DTR to manage difficult situations, employed delay strategies and alternatives, and was able to avert binge–purge episodes almost always. The work of the sessions focused on the times that she was not able to avert the binge–purge episodes and on building a wider range of alternative behaviors to binge eating and purging. As is typical, one of the issues that arose during this phase of the treatment was Claire's continuing dissatisfaction with her weight and body shape. A segment addressing some of these issues is included below.

Selective Transcript

C: . . . I don't know, I just feel so fat that at times I want to go back on a diet. If I could just lose 15 pounds . . .

T: What would that do for you?

C: Well, I would feel better about myself. I think I would look better. Clothes would look better on me. I look better when I weigh 120.

T: What has happened to your weight during the course of therapy?

C: It's basically stayed the same. I think I've lost 2 pounds, according to the last time I weighed myself.

T: And how are you feeling about having your eating under control?

C: Great. I am so much more productive at work, and it's helped me deal more effectively with my relationships, but I just wish I weighed a little less.

T: What's the magic of 120 pounds?

C: I don't know. I just think that I would be happier. I need some new clothes and I have been putting off shopping, because I know I'm going to look like a moose.

T: Like a moose?

C: OK, so I'm exaggerating. I guess there's some all-or-nothing thinking about my weight. If I weigh 120 pounds, that's great, and anything else is unacceptable.

T: It would be useful for you to try to start thinking about an acceptable weight range rather than striving for a specific ideal weight. In this vein, it would be useful for you to go shopping and try on some clothes that fit you well now. Don't buy something that is two sizes too small. Get something that is flattering now. You may find out that, in fact, you can look good at your current weight.

C: I doubt that, but I'll try.

T: For next session, why don't you go shopping and try to find something that you can take with you on your upcoming vacation?

Sessions 16 through 19

Objectives

1. Continue with underlying assumptions about weight, body image, and so on, using examples brought in as homework.
2. Work on relapse prevention.
   a. Come up with responses to "what ifs?" ("What if I binged, purged, gained weight, etc?").
   b. Redefine "I blew it" as a "slip" and a learning opportunity.
   c. Adopt a problem-solving attitude.
3. Identify potential high-risk situations after termination of treatment.

The goal of this phase of treatment is for the patient to learn to reframe inevitable future "slips" as less than disastrous. The patient should be made aware that for a while to come, she can expect that there will be rough situations in which she may experience and possibly even succumb to the urge to binge and/or purge. It should be explained to the patient that until she has fully normalized her eating habits and become more comfortable with her body weight and shape, food and weight issues will be her "soft spot" or "Achilles' heel." It should be explained to the patient that the true test of therapy will be the patient's ability to utilize a problem-solving attitude with respect to "get-ting on track," rather than panicking and giving up.

Selective Transcript

C: No binge or purge episodes again!

T: That's great. And how are meals going?

C: Pretty well. Usually I am able to eat three meals a day. Sometimes I still wind up skipping a meal here or there, but for the most part I've been sticking with regular meals. I even ate dessert when I went out to dinner with Tom last night.

T: That's great progress. Is there anything left on your forbidden food list that you haven't tried yet?

C: Nope. I don't eat that stuff all the time, but when I want something sweet I let myself have it now, and I don't feel like I have to have a full-blown binge just because I've had an ice cream cone.

T: You've made a lot of progress. One of the things that we should discuss at this stage is what you are going to do when therapy is over and you have some rough times. We know it's still difficult for you when Tom travels, and you also are under a lot of pressure at work. It's important for us to think ahead to times that may be difficult for you to manage, so that you can work on preventing any big trouble.

One of the images that may be useful is for you to think back to when you first started in treatment. You were stuck in a pretty destructive cycle and had dug yourself into a hole by the repetitions of binge eating and purging. At this point, you've climbed out and have started on a new path. There will be times that you will feel that you are not exactly on course, but that doesn't mean that you are back in the pit. At those difficult times, remember that you are well on your way down this new path, just a little off course. What you want to do is remain sensitive to the cues that will tell you when you are on track and when you have fallen off course, so that you can get back on track without a major relapse.

C: Yeah, in a way I hate to think about that, but I guess you're right. I'm feeling so good now, I don't want to jinx myself.

T: I know it's scary, but by planning ahead you'll increase your chances of staying on course, not reduce them. Can you think of any potential high-risk situations?

C: Oh, yeah. One that's coming up soon is my sister's wedding. There are going to be so many people, and I'm her maid of honor, so I have to look good in my dress and everything. I'm really proud of myself, though. When we were fitted for dresses, I resisted the urge to tell the dressmaker to make the dress smaller so that I would have to diet to fit into it—and, you know, it looks OK on me now!

T: Good, that's real progress. Anything else?

C: Well, I'm worried about work, with a new boss and everything.

T: What can you do to avoid setting yourself up for more binge–purge episodes?

C: Well, I think I'm handling the pressure much better. But even when I don't feel like binge eating or purging if I'm having a bad day, I fill out one of those DTRs. It just helps me figure out what's going on.

The therapist and patient should go through the list of potential high-risk situations, as the examples above indicate. The therapist should continue to reinforce the use of the cognitive-behavioral strategies in the whole range of situations that the patient describes as difficult, even if the patient does not feel the urge to binge or purge.

Session 20

Objectives

1. Review homework.
2. Review treatment gains.
3. Discuss maintenance phase of treatment.
4. Encourage patient to continue using the skills she has gained when the formal treatment is over; introduce the concept of becoming one's own therapist.

The bulk of this session is devoted to a review of progress that has been made and, more importantly, the ways that progress was made. Attention should be paid to the specific factors that were most important to the patient in the recovery of normal eating patterns, and the necessity for the patient to continue to implement the strategies that have brought her so far.

Selective Transcript

T: This is our last session. How are you feeling?

C: Great. I am going to miss you, and I don't know what I'm going to do on Monday evenings now, but I feel great about my eating. I haven't binged or purged in over 2 months. I'm a little worried about falling back, but to tell you the truth, I really don't think I will. I have the DTR form in my head now, and I find that I'm using the steps all the time. The other day I was in a meeting that was going badly, and I found myself saying to myself, "Now what is the situation? How am I feeling? What do I think?" I almost started laughing out loud when I realized what I was doing. It just comes so naturally to me now.

T: So the DTR has helped a lot. Do you catch yourself with the list of cognitive distortions?

C: The other day I told Tom that what he said was an example of all-or-nothing thinking! It's amazing. Now that I am listening for the distortions, I hear them and am able to address the problems that I'm having much better. I really think that has helped me a lot in dealing with my boss and with Tom.

T: And how about your meals?

C: Pretty good. I know I have to eat. Sometimes when I think about skipping a meal, I hear your voice saying, "The best way to manage your weight is to eat." I also think of what you said, "Full doesn't mean fat." That's a big one that I have to remember.

T: And how about your weight?

C: Well, I still wouldn't mind if I lost a few pounds, but I realize it's not going to solve all my problems, and I definitely know that dieting is not the way for me to do it. I'm thinking about joining an aerobics class in the fall.

T: That may be a good idea. Just remember to check yourself on how important you make your weight. Try to keep that in check. But certainly a moderate exercise program is good for most everyone, as long as you don't get carried away or have unrealistic expectations.

You've made a lot of progress. It took a lot of hard work, and you can be proud of how well you're doing. I think you have integrated the ideas and made real changes in your behavior that will help you stay on track in the future. Just remember that even there, it's not all-or-nothing. Some days will be better than others. The key is for you to continue to check in with yourself on a regular basis and use the skills that you have learned when the going gets rough. I expect that things will continue to go well for you, but please feel free to be in touch if you feel that you need some help down the road.

C: Thanks for all your help.

T: I wish you all the best.

MANUAL-BASED TREATMENT AND CLINICAL PRACTICE

The treatment we have described was based on a specific manual. It was therefore highly structured and time-limited. Treatment of this sort is quite unlike everyday clinical practice, in which CBT therapists can freely draw from a wider range of treatment techniques, often over a longer period of time. The latter, it can be argued, should be more effective than the necessarily truncated form of manual-based CBT. In unrestricted clinical practice, treatment can be tailored more freely to the individual patient's particular needs.

Whether unrestricted clinical practice is more effective than the standard treatment prescribed in manuals of the sort illustrated in this chapter is unknown. With the increasing use of manuals, not only in treatment studies but also in clinical practice, there is a general need to compare manual-based treatment with more conventional, "no-holds-barred" clinical practice within the same time frame. In the meantime, there are good reasons for adhering to manual-based treatment even in everyday clinical practice, given that the clinical effectiveness of the treatment has been repeatedly demonstrated (Wilson & Fairburn, 1998). A second advantage is that the highly structured and time-limited nature of this treatment focuses the attention of both therapist and patient on working hard to make well-defined changes (Fairburn et al., 1993). Third, the subjective clinical judgment that therapists rely on in formulating individual treatment plans is often flawed and may result in the choice of less than optimal treatment (Wilson, 1996). Finally, adding additional elements to the treatment requires either replacing some aspects or making it longer. Both options have disadvantages. It is unclear whether extending treatment has any advantages. In the treatment we describe, an explicit message is that patients are being helped to be their own therapists, so that they can continue to make progress following the termination of formal treatment.

CLINICAL PROBLEMS

Predictors of Therapeutic Success and Failure

The clinical utility of identifying predictor variables, and especially treatment-specific predictors, is obvious. Yet reliable predictors of response to CBT—or pharmacological treatment—have not been identified (Wilson & Fairburn, 1998). A diverse array of pretreatment patient characteristics have been proposed as predictor variables, including past history of AN or previous low body weight, low self-esteem, comorbid personality disorders, and severity of core eating disorder symptoms. The results across studies have been inconsistent, however, and of little practical clinical value (Agras, Crow, et al., 2000; Wilson & Fairburn, 1998). This is probably attributable, at least in part, to the use of what have been small samples of patients in outcome studies that have examined this issue, and hence lack of statistical power for identifying treatment × patient interactions.

Consider the example of personality disorders. It has become clinical lore that co-occurring personality disorders (particularly borderline personality disorder) identify a subgroup of patients who are difficult to treat and who do not respond to CBT (Johnson, Tobin, & Dennis, 1990). A sizeable minority of patients with BN are often diagnosed with a personality disorder. Rossiter, Agras, Telch, and Schneider (1993) found that patients with personality disorders, particularly Cluster B disorders, fared worse with CBT than patients with no personality disorder.

In contrast to these results, however, Ames-Frankel and colleagues (1992) have reported a positive correlation between Cluster B scores and therapeutic improvement in the treatment of BN with desipramine. A problem in assessing the role of personality disorders in the treatment of BN is the consistent finding that they often disappear following the successful treatment of the eating disorder (Ames-

Frankel et al., 1992; Garner et al., 1990). The state versus trait influence of measures of personality disorder remains to be resolved.

Instead of concentrating the search for predictors on pretreatment patient characteristics, the pragmatic approach of identifying rapid responders to treatment might prove more useful. Recent research has shown that much of the overall improvement achieved with CBT is evident after the first few weeks of treatment (Wilson et al., 1999)—a finding that has been reported in the treatment of other disorders (Ilardi & Craighead, 1994; Wilson, 1999a). Using a signal detection analysis, Agras, Crow, and colleagues (2000) showed that reduction in purging at Session 6 provided a better prediction of outcome than any pretreatment variable. When this criterion was adopted, 70% of patients were triaged and correctly treated. Only 6% of patients who would have recovered with CBT would have been incorrectly triaged to a second treatment. The issue of what the optimal subsequent treatment might be is addressed later in this chapter.

The importance of this early identification of nonresponders is twofold. First, it should decrease the cost of therapy. Second, it does not expose patients to ineffective and time-consuming treatment, thereby sparing them the frustration and demoralization of therapeutic failure.

Even less is known about predictors of relapse following successful treatment. A major prediction of the cognitive-behavioral model of BN is that maintenance of treatment-induced change is a function of the degree of attitudinal disturbance concerning body shape and weight at the end of treatment. An initial test has confirmed that prediction, and underscored the importance of modifying abnormal attitudes about shape and weight (Fairburn et al., 1993).

Dissemination of CBT

CBT is rarely used in the treatment of BN in the United States (Crow, Mussell, Peterson, Knopke, & Mitchell, 1999). The failure to disseminate evidence-based CBT in general is currently a topic of debate (Hayes, 1998). One of the reasons is the proclivity of therapists to reject the relevance of the findings of randomized controlled trials to clinical practice. Criticism of the clinical utility of the findings of such trials is often unwarranted (Wilson, 1998). Nevertheless, putting these disputes aside, we can all agree that we need effectiveness studies to examine directly the generalizability of the findings of randomized controlled trials to diverse settings, therapists with varying degrees of experience and expertise, and heterogeneous patient groups with different levels of comorbidity and concurrent treatment.

Dissemination will be facilitated by making manual-based treatments more "therapist-friendly" and more broadly applicable to a wider range of problems. Thus far, evidence-based treatment manuals have primarily focused on the content and technical aspects of intervention. The next generation of manuals will be more specific and advanced. The following advances can be anticipated. First, manuals will more explicitly address the "nonspecific" aspects of treatment, such as offering guidance in forming a therapeutic alliance and overcoming ambivalence about change (Wilson, Fairburn, & Agras, 1997). Second, manuals will include different modules that can be selectively applied to subsets of patients who have the same disorder but who have particular problem profiles that require more differentiated treatment. This will enhance therapeutic flexibility with-out sacrificing the structure and focus of manualized treatment. Ideally, the design of these next-generation manuals will be informed by an understanding of the therapeutic mechanisms through which technologies such as manual-based treatments work (Hayes, 1998). Third, especially given the move to an organized menu of modules for specific problems, manuals will necessarily have to provide practical guidelines about how to use them effectively. This will not only result in their wider adoption by practitioners, but also enhance the efficacy of treatment.

A more immediate means of disseminating CBT for BN is the expanded use of simpler, more cost-effective methods within a stepped-care framework of service delivery, as noted earlier in this chapter (Fairburn & Carter, 1997; Wilson et al., 2000). Evidence is mounting that abbreviated version of the full manual-based CBT program administered by nonspecialists can be effective in overcoming BN in a significant subset of patients. The priority here is to identify reliable predictors of patients for whom these cost-effective methods are appropriate.

Improving upon the Efficacy of Manual-Based CBT

Manual-based CBT is the first-line treatment of choice for BN. Nevertheless, its effectiveness is limited. On average, roughly 50% of patients cease binge eating and purging. Of the remainder, some show partial improvement, and some none at all. We need more effective treatment.

One strategy would be to administer an alternative therapy to patients who fail to respond to CBT. An obvious choice would be antidepressant medication, given the evidence of its efficacy. In one small study, Walsh and colleagues (2000) randomly assigned nonresponders to either CBT or IPT to fluoxetine or a pill placebo. The active drug condition produced significantly greater improvement after 8 weeks than the placebo.

A second strategy would be to improve upon current manual-based CBT. The manual-based CBT that has been evaluated in most controlled trials, as a time-limited, structured treatment, is necessarily a limited form of the clinical practice of CBT. In principle, practitioners could draw upon a wider range of techniques in addressing an individual patient's particular needs (Wilson, 1996).

The CBT manual targets extreme concerns about shape and weight primarily in the latter stages of treatment. These concerns are a central feature of the model, with other characteristics (such as dietary restraint, binge eating, and purging) being secondary to them. Consistent with the conceptual model of CBT, failure to reduce shape and weight concerns has been associated with risk of relapse (Fairburn et al., 1993). However, some studies have shown that manual-based CBT is less effective in reducing patients' excessive concerns about their shape and weight than in eliminating the behavioral symptoms of binge eating, purging, and restrictive dieting (Walsh et al., 1997). It makes both theoretical and clinical sense that changing an abnormal body image should be more difficult than modifying some of the behavioral symptoms of BN.

Potentially more powerful strategies are available for reducing dysfunctional shape and weight concerns, and increasing patients' acceptance of their shape and weight, than the cognitive restructuring and behavioral assignments the manual-based CBT currently emphasizes (Rosen, 1996). A promising method is systematic exposure to cues that elicit dysfunctional concern with body weight and shape. For example, Tuschen and Bent (1995) describe a procedure ("body confrontation") in which patients pose in front of a mirror that provides a full view of the body from different angles. This form of exposure therapy is recommended because it is effective with other populations—namely, obese patients who binge-eat (Rosen, Orosan, & Reiter, 1995), patients with body dysmorphic disorder (Rosen, 1996), and a nonclinical sample of weight-preoccupied women (Butters & Cash, 1987). Furthermore, recent theory and research suggest how best to implement mirror exposure. At least for some forms of negative affect, directly experiencing the distress (emotional processing) may be a more effective means of coping than either distraction or the active problem solving that is typical of CBT (e.g., challenging of the validity of negative thoughts about shape and weight, à la conventional cognitive restructuring).

Consistent with the focus on emotional processing, Teasdale (1997) has proposed a model of therapeutic change in which he differentiates between two qualitatively different levels of cognition-specific meanings on the one hand, and more generic or schematic models of self on the other. Only the latter are directly related to emotion, as in the affectively charged evaluation of body shape and weight of patients with eating disorders. Change in these schematic models sometimes may be achieved through conventional cognitive restructuring that challenges the validity of specific propositions about body image (and thus indirectly modifies emotion), but more direct methods will usually be required. The key feature of these other methods is that they are enactive and replace dysfunction-producing schematic models ("minds in place") with alternative, more adaptive mind-sets.

Systematic mirror exposure provides a potent means of modifying dysfunctional mind-sets regarding body shape and weight. Wilson (1999b) has described a method of mirror exposure in which patients are instructed to describe but not judge their bodies. They are encouraged to adopt a frame of mind Linehan (1993) and others have called "mindfulness." As Teasdale, Segal, and Williams (1995) put it,

The essence of this state is to "be" fully in the present moment, without judging or evaluating it, without reflecting backwards on past memories, without looking forward to anticipate the future, as in anxious worry, and without attempting to "problem-solve" or otherwise avoid any unpleasant aspects of the immediate situation. In this state, one is highly aware and focused on the reality of the present moment "as it is," accepting it and acknowledging it in its full "reality" without immediately engaging in discursive thought about it, without trying to work out how to change it, and without drifting off into a state of diffuse thinking focused on somewhere else or some other time. (pp. 33–34)

The therapist refrains from making reassuring comments or minimizing appearance concern. The emphasis is simply on keeping the patient "on track"—focusing on describing herself in the here and now while refraining from making evaluative comments. Mirror exposure is reinforced by behavioral homework assignments aimed at overcoming the extremes of avoiding "body exposure" (e.g., wearing shapeless clothes) on the one hand, or excessive body checking on the other (Fairburn et al., 1993).

The Fairburn (1997a) model features "negative self-evaluation" as a core characteristic of BN. Analytic epidemiological research has established negative self-evaluation as a specific, potent risk factor in the development of BN (Fairburn et al., 1997). Negative self-evaluation and low self-esteem, which extend beyond specific shape and weight concerns, are common features of patients with BN. However, manual-based CBT has not focused sufficiently on these more generic, negative self-evaluative problems. In fact, a broader view of negative affect in general seems necessary for understanding and treating a subgroup of patients with BN.

The evidence points to negative affect as an important contributor to the maintenance of BN. First, research has shown that self-reported stress and negative mood are common proximal antecedents of binge eating and purging. Second, a cluster analysis of 256 patients with BN along dieting and negative affect dimensions revealed two BN subtypes: a pure dietary subtype (62%) and a mixed dietary–negative affect subtype (38%) (Stice & Agras, 1999). Patients in both subtypes showed similar levels of binge eating and purging, but the latter reported more eating and weight obsessions; more social maladjustment; and higher lifetime rates of mood, anxi-

ety, eating, impulse control, and personality disorders. Perhaps most importantly, those patients with negative affect responded significantly less well to manual-based CBT.

The obvious implication of these findings is that negative affect should be addressed directly in treatment. A wealth of clinical and experimental evidence demonstrates the effectiveness of CBT in treating a variety of negative affective states, such as anxiety and depression. Learning to tolerate negative affect without engaging in self-destructive behavior (mindfulness training), and acquiring more adaptive emotion regulation skills are key components of Linehan's (1993) dialectical behavior therapy. Wiser and Telch (1999) have described the use of these strategies in the treatment of BED. Their application to BN makes theoretical and clinical sense. Moreover, the use of mindfulness training for coping with negative affect dovetails with the adaptation of this approach to addressing negative body image as described by Wilson (1999b).

As noted earlier, a revised CBT manual will probably include different modules that can be selectively applied to subsets of patients who have the same disorder but who have particular problem profiles (arguably involving patterns of negative affect) that require more differentiated treatment. This will enhance therapeutic flexibility without sacrificing the structure and focus of manualized treatment.

CONCLUSION AND RECOMMENDATIONS

CBT is currently the first-line treatment of choice for BN. We base this conclusion on the following grounds: (1) Controlled outcome studies have shown it to be more effective than alternative psychotherapies and pharmacological treatment; (2) it is a relatively brief and therefore efficient treatment; (3) it is readily accepted by patients, whereas treatment with antidepressant medication is often resisted; and (4) it has been described in detailed manuals that make it widely available to clinicians, even if they have not had specific training in CBT.

Nevertheless, current manual-based CBT for BN is ineffective with some patients, and produces only limited improvement in still others. More potent methods for a wider range of patients are required. IPT is a promising approach that warrants additional study. It seems comparably effective to CBT in longer-term treatment of BN, and is equally effective in the short and long term with BED (Wilfley, 1999). No evidence exists indicating the clinical utility of combining CBT with traditional psychodynamic psychotherapies.

Another option is to treat nonresponders to CBT with antidepressant medication, although this requires further evaluation. Concurrent or sequential use of antidepressant medication could be recommended to treat comorbid psychiatric disorders in BN (e.g., depression). A final option if outpatient CBT treatment fails is to recommend a day hospital program, or full hospitalization, for more direct and intensive treatment of a patient's disordered eating habits. Food intake can be better regulated, and binge eating and purging prevented, in such a structured setting. Day hospital treatment is preferred because it is less expensive and does not completely remove the patient from the psychosocial situations that are associated with binge eating and purging.

Manual-based CBT is a specialized treatment requiring specific expertise and professional training. It is not necessary for all patients. Research has shown that a subset of patients respond well to briefer, less costly interventions that can be implemented by a wider range of health providers without specific expertise in CBT. These interventions include self-help programs and group psychoeducation that seem well suited to high-functioning individuals with no complicating psychopathology. Ideally, a treatment center might offer a stepped-care approach in which patients would initially receive the most cost-effective treatment, followed by a more intensive program should they fail to respond.

REFERENCES

Abbott, D. W., de Zwaan, M., Mussell, M. P., Raymond, N. C., Seim, H. C., Crow, S. J., Crosby, R. D., & Mitchell, J. E. (1998). Onset of binge eating and dieting in overweight women: Implications for etiology, associated features and treatment. *Journal of Psychosomatic Research, 44*, 367–374.

Agras, W. S., Crow, S. J., Halmi, K. A., Mitchell, J. E., Wilson, G. T., & Kraemer, H. C. (2000). Outcome predictors for the cognitive-behavioral treatment of bulimia nervosa: Data from a multisite study. *American Journal of Psychiatry, 157*, 1302–1308.

Agras, W. S., Rossiter, E. M., Arnow, B., Schneider, J. A., Telch, C. F., Raeburn, S. D., Bruce, B.,

Perl, M., & Koran, L. M. (1992). Pharmacologic and cognitive-behavioral treatment for bulimia nervosa: A controlled comparison. *American Journal of Psychiatry, 149*, 82–87.

Agras, W. S., Rossiter, E. M., Arnow, B., Telch, C. F., Raeburn, S. D., Bruce, B., & Koran, L. (1994). One-year follow-up of psychosocial and pharmacologic treatments for bulimia nervosa. *Journal of Clinical Psychiatry, 55*, 179–183.

Agras, W. S., Schneider, J. A., Arnow, B., Raeburn, S. D., & Telch, C. F. (1989). Cognitive-behavioral and response-prevention treatments for bulimia nervosa. *Journal of Consulting and Clinical Psychology, 57*, 215–221.

Agras, W. S., Telch, C. F., Arnow, B., Eldredge, K., Wilfley, D., Raeburn, S. D., Henderson, J., & Marnell, M. (1994). Weight loss, cognitive-behavioral, and desipramine treatments in binge eating disorder: An additive design. *Behavior Therapy, 25*, 209–224.

Agras, W. S., Walsh, B. T., Fairburn, C. G., Wilson, G. T., & Kraemer, H. C. (2000). A multicenter comparison of cognitive-behavioral therapy and interpersonal psychotherapy for bulimia nervosa. *Archives of General Psychiatry, 57*, 459–466.

American Psychiatric Association. (1994). *Diagnostic and statistical manual of mental disorders* (4th ed.). Washington DC: Author.

American Psychiatric Association. (2000). Practice guideline for the treatment of patients with eating disorders (revision). *American Journal of Psychiatry, 157*(Suppl.), 1–39.

Ames-Frankel, J., Devlin, M. J., Walsh, B. T., Strasser, T. J., Sadik, C., Oldham, J., & Roose, S. P. (1992). Personality disorder diagnoses in patients with bulimia nervosa: Clinical correlates and changes with treatment. *Journal of Clinical Psychiatry, 53*, 90–96.

Beck, A. T. (1976). *Cognitive therapy and the emotional disorders*. New York: International Universities Press.

Beck, A. T., Rush, A. J., Shaw, B. F., & Emery, G. (1979). *Cognitive therapy of depression*. New York: Guilford Press.

Bulik, C. M., Sullivan, P. F., & Kendler, K. S. (1998). Heritability of binge-eating and broadly defined bulimia nervosa. *Biological Psychiatry, 44*, 1210–1218.

Butters, J. W., & Cash, T. F. (1987). Cognitive-behavioral treatment of women's body-image dissatisfaction. *Journal of Consulting and Clinical Psychology, 55*, 889–897.

Carter, J. C., & Fairburn, C. G. (1998). Cognitive-behavioral self-help for binge eating disorder: A controlled effectiveness study. *Journal of Consulting and Clinical Psychology, 66*, 616–623.

Chen, E. Y., Touyz, S. W., Beumont, P. J. V., Fairburn, C. G., Griffiths, R., Butow, P., Russell, J., Schotte, D. E., Gertler, R., & Basten, C. (1999, November). *A comparison of group and individual cognitive-behavioural therapy for patients with bulimia nervosa.* Paper presented at the meeting of the Eating Disorders Research Society, San Diego, CA.

Crow, S. J., Mussell, M. P., Peterson, C. B., Knopke, A. & Mitchell, J. E. (1999). Prior treatment received by patients with bulimia nervosa. *International Journal of Eating Disorders, 25*, 39–44.

Davis, R., Olmsted, M. P., & Rockert, W. (1990). Brief group psychoeducation for bulimia nervosa: Assessing the clinical significance of change. *Journal of Consulting and Clinical Psychology, 58,* 882–885.

Devlin, M. J., & Walsh, B. T. (1995). Medication treatment for eating disorders. *Journal of Mental Health, 4,* 459–469.

Fairburn, C. G. (1985). Cognitive-behavioral treatment for bulimia. In D. M. Garner & P. E. Garfinkel (Eds.), *Handbook of psychotherapy for anorexia nervosa and bulimia* (pp. 160–192). New York: Guilford Press.

Fairburn, C. G. (1995). *Overcoming binge eating.* New York: Guilford Press.

Fairburn, C. G. (1997a). Eating disorders. In D. M. Clark & C. G. Fairburn (Eds.), *The science and practice of cognitive behaviour therapy* (pp. 209–242). Oxford: Oxford University Press.

Fairburn, C. G. (1997b). Interpersonal psychotherapy for bulimia nervosa. In D. M. Garner & P. E. Garfinkel (Eds.), *Handbook of treatment for eating disorders* (2nd ed., pp. 278–294). New York: Guilford Press.

Fairburn, C. G., & Beglin, S. J. (1994). Assessment of eating disorders: Interview or self-report questionnaire? *International Journal of Eating Disorders, 16,* 363–370.

Fairburn, C. G., & Carter, J. C. (1997). Self-help and guided self-help for binge-eating problems. In D. M. Garner & P. E. Garfinkel (Eds.), *Handbook of treatment for eating disorders* (2nd ed., pp. 494–500). New York: Guilford Press.

Fairburn, C. G., & Cooper, P. J. (1993). The Eating Disorder Examination. In C. G. Fairburn & G. T. Wilson (Eds.), *Binge eating: Nature, assessment, and treatment* (pp. 317–360). New York: Guilford Press.

Fairburn, C. G., Cowen, P. J., & Harrison, P. J. (1999). Twin studies and the etiology of eating disorders. *International Journal of Eating Disorders, 26,* 349–358.

Fairburn, C. G., Jones, R., Peveler, R. C., Carr, S. J., Solomon, R. A., O'Connor, M. E., Burton, J., & Hope, R. A. (1991). Three psychological treatments for bulimia nervosa. *Archives of General Psychiatry, 48,* 463–469.

Fairburn, C. G., Marcus, M. D., & Wilson, G. T. (1993). Cognitive behavior therapy for binge eating and bulimia nervosa: A treatment manual. In C. G. Fairburn & G. T. Wilson (Eds.), *Binge eating: Nature, assessment, and treatment* (pp. 361–404). New York: Guilford Press.

Fairburn, C. G., Norman, P. A., Welch, S. L., O'Connor, M. E., Doll, H. A., & Peveler, R. C. (1995). A prospective study of outcome in bulimia nervosa and the long-term effects of three psychological treatments. *Archives of General Psychiatry, 52,* 304–312.

Fairburn, C. G., Shafran, R., & Cooper, Z. (1999). A cognitive behavioural theory of anorexia nervosa. *Behaviour Research and Therapy, 37,* 1–13.

Fairburn, C. G., Welch, S. L., Doll, H. A., Davies, B. A., & O'Connor, M. E. (1997). Risk factors for bulimia nervosa. *Archives of General Psychiatry, 54,* 509–517.

Fichter, M. M., & Hoffman, R. (1990). Bulimia (nervosa) in the male. In M. M. Fichter (Ed.), *Bulimia nervosa: Basic research, diagnosis and therapy* (pp. 99–111). Chichester, England: Wiley.

Fichter, M. M., Leibl, K., Rief, W., Brunner, E., Schmidt-Auberger, S., & Engel, R. R. (1991). Fluoxetine versus placebo: A double-blind study with bulimic inpatients undergoing intensive psychotherapy. *Pharmacopsychiatry, 24,* 1–7.

Fluoxetine Bulimia Nervosa Collaborative Study Group. (1992). Fluoxetine in the treatment of bulimia nervosa: A multicenter, placebo-controlled, double-blind trial. *Archives of General Psychiatry, 49,* 139–147.

Garner, D. M. (1991). *Eating Disorders Inventory—2.* Odessa, FL: Psychological Assessment Resources.

Garner, D. M., & Garfinkel, P. E. (Eds.). (1997). *Handbook of treatment for eating disorders* (2nd ed.). New York: Guilford Press.

Garner, D. M., Rockert, W., Davis, R., Garner, M. V., Olmsted, M., & Eagle, M. (1993). Comparison of cognitive-behavioral and supportive–expressive therapy for bulimia nervosa. *American Journal of Psychiatry, 150,* 37–46.

Garner, D. M., Olmsted, M. P., Davis, R., Rockert, W., Goldbloom, D., & Eagle, M. (1990). The association between bulimic symptoms and reported psychopathology. *International Journal of Eating Disorders, 9,* 1–15.

Garner, D. M., Vitousek, K. M., & Pike, K. M. (1997). Cognitive-behavioral therapy for anorexia nervosa. In D. M. Garner & P. E. Garfinkel (Eds.), *Handbook of treatment for eating disorders* (2nd ed., pp. 94–144). New York: Guilford Press.

Gormally, J., Black, S., Daston, S., & Rardin, D. (1982). The assessment of binge-eating severity among obese persons. *Addictive Behaviors, 7,* 47–55.

Greeno, C. G., Marcus, M. D., & Wing, R. R. (1995). Diagnosis of binge eating disorder: Discrepancies between a questionnaire and clinical interview. *International Journal of Eating Disorders, 17,* 153–160.

Grilo, C. M., Masheb, R. M., & Wilson, G. T. (in press). A comparison of different methods for assessing the features of eating disorders in patients with binge eating disorder. *Journal of Consulting and Clinical Psychology.*

Haiman, C., & Devlin, M. J. (1999). Binge eating before the onset of dieting: A distinct subgroup of bulimia nervosa? *International Journal of Eating Disorders, 25,* 151–158.

Hay, P., & Fairburn, C. (1998). The validity of the DSM-IV scheme for classifying bulimic eating disorders. *International Journal of Eating Disorders, 23,* 7–16.

Hayes, S. C. (1998). Dissemination research now. *The Behavior Therapist, 21,* 166–169.

Hsu, L. K. G. (1990). *Eating disorders.* New York: Guilford Press.

Ilardi, S. S., & Craighead, W. E. (1994). The role of nonspecific factors in cognitive-behavior therapy for depression. *Clinical Psychology, 1,* 138–156.

Johnson, C., Tobin, D. L., & Dennis, A. (1990). Differences in treatment outcome between borderline and nonborderline bulimics at one-year follow-up. *International Journal of Eating Disorders, 9,* 617–627.

Jones, R., Peveler, R. C., Hope, R. A., & Fairburn, C. G. (1993). Changes during treatment for bulimia nervosa: A comparison of three psychological treatments. *Behaviour Research and Therapy, 31,* 479–485.

Kassett, J. A., Gershon, E. S., Maxwell, M. E., Guroff, J. J., Kazuba, D. M., Smith, A. L., Brandt, H. A., & Jimerson, D. C. (1989). Psychiatric disorders in the first-degree relatives of probands with bulimia nervosa. *American Journal of Psychiatry, 146,* 1468–1471.

Klerman, G. L., Weissman, M. M., Rounsaville, B. J., & Chevron, E. S. (1984). *Interpersonal psychotherapy of depression.* New York: Basic Books.

Laessle, R. G., Beumont, P. J. V., Butow, P., Lenneris, W., O'Connor, M., Pirke, K. M., Touyz, S. W., & Waadi, S. (1991). A comparison of nutritional management and stress management in the treatment of bulimia nervosa. *British Journal of Psychiatry, 159,* 250–261.

Lee, S., Ho, T. P., & Hsu, L. K. G. (1993). Fat phobic and non-fat phobic anorexia nervosa: A comparative study of 70 Chinese patients in Hong Kong. *Psychological Medicine, 23,* 999–1017.

Leitenberg, H., Rosen, J. C., Wolf, J., Vara, L. S., Detzer, M. J., & Srebnik, D. (1994). Comparison of cognitive-behaviour therapy and desipramine in the treatment of bulimia nervosa. *Behaviour Research and Therapy, 32,* 37–46.

Linehan, M. M. (1993). *Skills training manual for treating borderline personality disorder.* New York: Guilford Press.

Marcus, M. D. (1993). Binge eating in obesity. In C. G. Fairburn & G. T. Wilson (Eds.), *Binge eating: Nature, assessment and treatment* (pp. 77–96). New York: Guilford Press.

Marcus, M. D., Wing, R. R., & Fairburn, C. G. (1995). Cognitive treatment of binge eating vs. behavioral weight control in the treatment of binge eating disorder. *Annals of Behavioral Medicine, 17,* S090.

Marlatt, G. A. (1985). Relapse prevention: Theoretical rationale and overview of the model. In G. A. Marlatt & J. R. Gordon (Eds.), *Relapse prevention: Maintenance strategies in the treatment of addictive behaviors* (pp. 3–70). New York: Guilford Press.

Marlatt, G. A., & Gordon, J. R. (Eds.). (1985). *Relapse prevention: Maintenance strategies in the treatment of addictive behaviors.* New York: Guilford Press.

McCann, U. D., & Agras, W. S. (1990). Successful treatment of nonpurging bulimia nervosa with desipramine: A double-blind, placebo-controlled study. *American Journal of Psychiatry, 147,* 1509–1513.

Miller, K. J., Gleaves, D. H., Hirsch, T. G., Green, B. A., Snow, A. C., & Corbett, C. C. (2000). Comparisons of body image dimensions by race/ethnicity and gender in a university population. *International Journal of Eating Disorders, 27,* 310–316.

Mitchell, J. E., Pyle, R. L., Eckert, E. D., Hatsukami, D., Pomeroy, C., & Zimmerman, R. (1989). Response to alternative antidepressants in imipramine non-responders with bulimia nervosa. *Journal of Clinical Psychopharmacology, 9,* 291–293.

Mitchell, J. E., Pyle, R. L., Eckert, E. D., Hatsukami, D., Pomeroy, C., & Zimmerman, R. (1990). A comparison study of antidepressants and structured intensive group psychotherapy in the treatment of bulimia nervosa. *Archives of General Psychiatry, 47,* 149–157.

Olmsted, M. P., Davis, R., Garner, D. M., Eagle, M., Rockert, W., & Irvine, M. J. (1991). Efficacy of a brief group psychoeducational intervention for bulimia nervosa. *Behaviour Research and Therapy, 29,* 71–84.

Otto, M. W., Jones, J. C., Craske, M. G., & Barlow, D. H. (1996). *Stopping anxiety medication: Panic control therapy for benzodiazepine discontinuation (therapist guide).* New York: Psychological Corporation.

Patton, G. C., Johnson-Sabine, E., Wood, K., Mann, A. H., & Wakeling, A. (1990). Abnormal eating attitudes in London schoolgirls—a prospective epidemiological study: Outcome at twelve month follow-up. *Psychological Medicine, 20,* 383–394.

Pope, H. G., Hudson, J. I., Jonas, J. M., & Yurgelun-Todd, D. (1983). Bulimia treated with imipramine: A placebo-controlled, double-blind study. *American Journal of Psychiatry, 140,* 554–558.

Pyle, R. L., Mitchell, J. E., Eckert, E. D., Hatsukami, D. K., Pomeroy, C., & Zimmerman, R. (1990). Maintenance treatment and 6-month outcome for bulimic patients who respond to initial treatment. *American Journal of Psychiatry, 147,* 871–875.

Rosen, J. C. (1996). Body image assessment and treatment in controlled studies of eating disorders. *International Journal of Eating Disorders, 20,* 331–344.

Rosen, J. C., Orosan, P., & Reiter, J. (1995). Cognitive behavior therapy for negative body image in obese women. *Behavior Therapy, 26,* 25–42.

Rosen, J. C., Vara, L., Wendt, S., & Leitenberg, H. (1990). Validity studies of the Eating Disorder Examination. *Behavior Therapy, 9,* 519–528.

Rossiter, E. M., Agras, W. S., Losch, M., & Telch, C. F. (1988). Dietary restraint of bulimic subjects following cognitive-behavioural or pharmacological treatment. *Behaviour Research and Therapy, 26,* 495–498.

Rossiter, E. M., Agras, W. S., Telch, C. F., & Schneider, J. A. (1993). Cluster B personality disorder characteristics predict outcome in the treatment of bulimia nervosa. *International Journal of Eating Disorders, 13,* 439–358.

Serfaty, M. A., Turkington, D., Heap, M., Ledsham, L., & Jolley, E. (1999). Cognitive therapy versus dietary counseling in the outpatient treatment of anorexia nervosa: Effects of the treatment phase. *European Eating Disorders Review, 7,* 334–350.

Spanier, C., Frank, E., McEachran, A. B., Grochocinski, V. J., & Kupfer, D. J. (1996). The prophylaxis of depressive episodes in recurrent depression following discontinuation of drug therapy: Integrating psychological and biological factors. *Psychological Medicine, 26,* 461–475.

Spitzer, R. L., Devlin, M. J., Walsh, B. T., Hasin, D., Wing, R., Marcus, M. D., Stunkard, A. J., Wadden, T., Yanovski, S., Agras, W. S., Mitchell, J., & Nonas, C. (1992). Binge eating disorder: To be or not to be in DSM-IV? *International Journal of Eating Disorders, 10,* 627–630.

Stice, E., & Agras, W. S. (1999). Subtyping bulimics along dietary restraint and negative affect dimensions. *Journal of Consulting and Clinical Psychology, 67,* 460–469.

Striegel-Moore, R. H., Silberstein, L. R., & Rodin, J. (1986). Toward an understanding of risk factors for bulimia. *American Psychologist, 41*, 146–163.

Striegel-Moore, R. H., & Smolak, L. (1996). The role of race in the development of eating disorders. In L. Smolak, M. Levine, & R. H. Striegel-Moore (Eds.), *The developmental psychopathology of eating disorders* (pp. 259–284). Hillsdale, NJ: Erlbaum.

Strober, M., Freeman, R., Lampert, C., Diamond, J., & Kaye, W. (2000). Controlled family study of anorexia nervosa and bulimia nervosa: Evidence of shared liability and transmission of partial syndromes. *American Journal of Psychiatry, 157*, 393–401.

Stunkard, A. J., & Messick, S. (1985). The Three Factor Eating Questionnaire to measure dietary restraint, disinhibition and hunger. *Journal of Psychosomatic Research, 29*, 71–83.

Teasdale, J. D. (1997). The relationship between cognition and emotion: The mind-in-place in mood disorders. In D. M. Clark & C. G. Fairburn (Eds.), *Science and practice of cognitive behaviour therapy* (pp. 67–94). New York: Oxford University Press.

Teasdale, J. D., Segal, Z. V., & Williams, J. M. G. (1995). How does cognitive therapy prevent depressive relapse and why should attentional control (mindfulness) training help? *Behaviour Research and Therapy, 33*, 25–39.

Tuschen, B., & Bent, H. (1995). Intensive brief inpatient treatment of bulimia nervosa. In K. D. Brownell & C. G. Fairburn (Eds.), *Eating disorders and obesity: A comprehensive handbook* (pp. 354–360). New York: Guilford Press.

Vitousek, K., Watson, S., & Wilson, G. T. (1998). Enhancing motivation for change in treatment-resistant eating disorders. *Clinical Psychology Review, 18*, 391–420.

Waller, D., Fairburn, C. G., McPherson, A., Kay, R., Lee, A., & Nowell, T. (1996). Treating bulimia nervosa in primary care: A pilot study. *International Journal of Eating Disorders, 19*, 99–103.

Walsh, A. E. S., Oldman, A. D., Franklin, M., Fairburn, C. G., & Cowen, P. J. (1995). Dieting decreases plasma tryptophan and increases the prolactin response to d-fenfluramine in women but not men. *Journal of Affective Disorders, 33*, 89–97.

Walsh, B. T., Agras, W. S., Devlin, M. J., Fairburn, C. G., Wilson, G. T., Kahn, C., & Chally, M. K. (2000). Fluoxetine in bulimia nervosa following poor response to psychotherapy. *American Journal of Psychiatry, 157*, 1332–1333.

Walsh, B. T., Hadigan, C. M., Devlin, M. J., Gladis, M., & Roose, S. P. (1991). Long-term outcome of antidepressant treatment for bulimia nervosa. *Archives of General Psychiatry, 148*, 1206–1212.

Walsh, B. T., Wilson, G. T., Loeb, K. L., Devlin, M. J., Pike, K. M., Roose, S. P., Fleiss, J., & Waternaux, C. (1997). Medication and psychotherapy in the treatment of bulimia nervosa. *American Journal of Psychiatry, 154*, 523–531.

Wilfley, D. E. (1999, November). *Group CBT and group IPT in the treatment of BED: A controlled comparison*. Paper presented at the meeting of the Eating Disorders Research Society, San Diego, CA.

Wilfley, D. E., & Cohen, L. R. (1997). Psychological treatment of bulimia nervosa and binge eating disorder. *Psychopharmacology Bulletin, 33*, 437–454.

Wilfley, D. E., Friedman, M. A., Dounchis, J. Z., Stein, R. I., & Welch, R. (2000). Comorbid psychopathology in binge eating disorder: Relation to eating disorder severity at baseline and following treatment. *Journal of Consulting and Clinical Psychology, 68*, 295–305.

Wilfley, D. E., Schwartz, M. N. B., Spurrell, E. B., & Fairburn, C. G. (2000). Using the Eating Disorder Examination to identify the specific psychopathology of binge eating disorder. *International Journal of Eating Disorders, 27*, 259–269.

Wilson, G. T. (1989). *A manual for cognitive-behavioral treatment of bulimia nervosa*. Unpublished manuscript, Rutgers University.

Wilson, G. T. (1993). Assessment of binge eating. In C. G. Fairburn & G. T. Wilson (Eds.), *Binge eating: Nature, assessment and treatment* (pp. 227–249). New York: Guilford Press.

Wilson, G. T. (1996). Manual-based treatments: The clinical application of research findings. *Behaviour Research and Therapy, 34*, 295–315.

Wilson, G. T. (1998). The clinical utility of randomized controlled trials. *International Journal of Eating Disorders, 24*, 13–29.

Wilson, G. T. (1999a). Rapid response to cognitive behavior therapy. *Clinical Psychology: Science and Practice, 6*, 289–292.

Wilson, G. T. (1999b). *Overcoming dysfunctional shape and weight concerns*. Unpublished treatment manual, Rutgers University.

Wilson, G. T., & Fairburn, C. G. (1998). Treatment of eating disorders. In P. E. Nathan & J. M. Gorman (Eds.), *Treatments that work* (pp. 501–530). New York: Oxford University Press.

Wilson, G. T., Fairburn, C. G., & Agras, W. S. (1997). Cognitive-behavioral therapy for bulimia nervosa. In D. M. Garner & P. Garfinkel (Eds.), *Handbook of treatment for eating disorders* (2nd ed., pp. 67–93). New York: Guilford Press.

Wilson, G. T., Loeb, K. L., Walsh, B. T., Labouvie, E., Petkova, E., Liu, X., & Waternaux, C. (1999). Psychological versus pharmacological treatments of bulimia nervosa: Predictors and processes of change. *Journal of Consulting and Clinical Psychology, 67*, 451–459.

Wilson, G. T., & Vitousek, K. (1999). Self-monitoring in the assessment and treatment of eating disorders. *Psychological Assessment, 11*.

Wilson, G. T., Vitousek, K., & Loeb, K. L. (2000). Stepped-care treatment for eating disorders. *Journal of Consulting and Clinical Psychology, 68*, 564–572.

Wiser, S., & Telch, C. F. (1999). Dialectical behavior therapy for binge-eating disorder. *Journal of Clinical Psychology, 55*, 755–768.

Yanovski, S. Z., Nelson, J. E., Dubbert, B. K., & Spitzer, R. L. (1993). Association of binge eating disorder and psychiatric comorbidity in obese subjects. *American Journal of Psychiatry, 150*, 1472–1479.

Chapter 9

ALCOHOL USE DISORDERS

Barbara S. McCrady

Clinicians working with individuals with alcohol or other substance use problems, as well as clinicians-in-training, may find this chapter one of the more unusual resources available in guiding their treatment approaches. The author begins by describing how recent societal trends and legislative initiatives have altered the nature of the clientele who come for treatment with drinking problems. After briefly reviewing the available empirical evidence on treatment approaches ranging from Alcoholics Anonymous to intensive brief inpatient treatment, the author describes the myriad factors that every clinician must consider in choosing and carrying out appropriate interventions for individuals with drinking problems. Using a variety of illuminating case vignettes new to this edition, Barbara McCrady illustrates important therapeutic strategies, including methods for motivating these patients to begin treatment. In a manner that emphasizes the humanity of the couple and makes them come to life, the extended case study in this chapter illustrates the all-too-frequent tragic consequences of excessive drinking. In the context of this case description, the author describes in great detail what clinicians will not find in books that simply lay out various treatment procedures—that is, the thrusts and parries of a superb and experienced clinician in overcoming the roadblocks that inevitably emerge during treatment.—D. H. B.

Alcohol use disorders are a heterogeneous group of problems ranging in severity from the heavy-drinking college student who occasionally misses classes to the person with severe and chronic alcoholism who experiences serious medical and social consequences of drinking. Although the prevalence of alcohol use disorders is higher in males than females and in younger than older adults, these problems affect individuals from any sociodemographic, racial/ethnic, or occupational background. In mental health and medical settings, at least 25% of clients are likely to have an alcohol use disorder as part of their presenting problems, so clinicians in health and mental health professions need to be competent to identify, assess, and plan an effective course of treatment for these clients. This chapter describes the social context of drinking and drinking problems; provides an integrative model for conceptualizing and treating alcohol use problems; and presents both a series

of case vignettes and an extended case study to illustrate the clinical model.

THE SOCIETAL CONTEXT OF DRINKING, DRINKING PROBLEMS, AND TREATMENT

The societal context in which alcohol treatment is offered has changed dramatically in the past 30 years. Shifting away from the drug-friendly cultures of the 1960s and early 1970s and the celebration of excess of the early 1980s, the end of the 20th century has witnessed two opposing societal trends: a punitive, "zero-tolerance" attitude toward heavy alcohol use, any drug use, and any alcohol use for underage drinkers; and a smaller, but growing, counterbalancing force arguing for a pragmatic approach to minimizing the harm caused by these behaviors. The structure, management, and financing of health care delivery have changed as well, resulting in stricter controls on all aspects of access to and utilization of health care services. These changes have resulted in changes in the clinical populations presenting for treatment, as well as changes in our views of what constitutes "treatment" and of how and where treatment can be delivered.

The "war on drugs," which began in the 1980s with its "Just say no" campaign, police pursuit of drug users and dealers, and increased prison sentences, has continued and extended its reach to the workplace and the schools through extensive drug testing and more severe penalties. Drugs of choice vary, but are increasingly drugs with high potential for either physiological dependence or personal harm—crack cocaine; heroin; and "club" drugs such as MDMA ("ecstasy"), ketamine ("Special K"), and rohypnol (the "date rape" drug). Concern for societal ills such as sexual abuse and violence has led to intolerance of excessive behavior in many realms, and increased intolerance of behaviors that were previously viewed as normal (such as little boys trying to kiss little girls on the playground, or a teacher hugging a crying child) characterizes U.S. society at the beginning of the 21st century.

Societal attitudes toward alcohol use have shifted as well. The legal drinking age, reduced to 18 during the Vietnam War era, was returned to 21 in response to increased death rates from drinking and driving among young people. Stricter drunk driving laws have been enacted in response to the work of advocacy groups such as Mothers Against Drunk Driving, and loss of a driver's license for a first offense is common. Society has become more concerned with enforcing drinking laws, and prominent figures in the field have suggested that the concept of "responsible drinking" cannot apply to any person under the age of 21, because underage drinking is illegal and therefore never responsible. Earlier amused acceptance of drinking among college students has been replaced with front-page news stories about tragic alcohol-related deaths on campus and the implementation of large-scale programs to decrease or stop drinking for underage college students. Some have argued that we are witnessing a "new Prohibition" in the United States.

Complementing these prescriptive and punitive perspectives on drinking and drug use

have been two countervailing efforts: rehabilitative approaches and harm reduction approaches. Exemplifying the rehabilitative approach are Employee Assistance Programs and Pretrial Intervention Programs for individuals who use drugs, and education and treatment programs for persons with arrests for drunk driving. These programs are based on the belief that many people who are functioning poorly on the job, in their adherence to the law, or in their driving are doing so because of alcohol or drug use. Offering treatment rather than punishment is believed to maximize a person's chances of returning to productive functioning. These various programs identify persons who have problems as a result of drinking or drug use, require that they seek treatment as an alternative to punishment, and usually monitor their functioning after treatment. A substantial proportion of clients now enter treatment through a mandated program.

Harm reduction models (MacCoun, 1998) are pragmatic approaches to human behavior. Harm reduction begins with a recognition that human beings will engage in a range of behaviors that are perhaps undesirable, foolish, or dangerous. Given that excess and poor judgment are part of the human condition, harm reduction models pose this question: How can we create programs, policies, and social structures that will minimize the harm to individuals and/or to society from these behaviors? Programs that foster and promote lifelong abstinence from these behaviors anchor one pole of the harm reduction philosophy. Anchoring the other pole are programs that make no attempt to change the core problem behavior, but provide safer ways to engage in the behavior (e.g., designated drivers, needle exchange, condom distribution). Such programs decrease the probability of disease, injury, and death. Between these two poles of harm reduction are a range of programs to attract individuals to changing excessive behaviors without requiring a commitment to intensive treatment or lifelong abstention. Brief advice about drinking provided in primary care settings, and programs to facilitate decreased or moderate drinking, are examples.

The structure of services provided to individuals with alcohol and drug use disorders has changed as well. Residential rehabilitative programs of 28 to 30 days in duration, the norm in the 1980s, are only a small part of the current treatment landscape. Intensive outpatient programs are more common, as are regular outpatient services. As with treatment of other disorders, managed health care requires justification of level of care and length of treatment for persons with alcohol and drug use disorders. The individuals providing these services have changed as well. Alcoholism counseling, once dominated by dedicated counselors who were recovering from alcoholism themselves but might have had little formal clinical training, has become increasingly professionalized. Credentialing standards for alcoholism and substance abuse counselors are in place, and many states require a preponderance of licensed or credentialed counselors for licensure of addictions treatment facilities. Within the credentialed health care professions, specialty certifications are becoming the norm. Physicians can be credentialed by the American Society of Addiction Medicine (ASAM), and physicians specializing in psychiatry may be credentialed by the American Academy of Addiction Psychiatry. Psychologists can obtain a Certificate of Proficiency in the Treatment of Alcohol and Other Psychoactive Substance Use Disorders through the American Psychological Association's College of Professional Psychology. All of these credentialing bodies require evidence of course work and experience, as well as standardized tests to demonstrate knowledge.

Among the results of these societal shifts are changes both in the population of those presenting for treatment and in the range of populations targeted by professionals concerned about alcohol use. Although many people continue to seek treatment voluntarily, the network of societal programs for the "early" detection of alcohol and drug problems has resulted in mixed clinical populations who have problems in multiple life areas, are resentful of being in treatment, and do not recognize their drinking or drug use as problematic. Their presence in treatment programs and individual clinical practice presents special challenges to the clinician.

A third trend, begun in the 1980s and continuing into the 21st century, has been the burgeoning of an enormous self-help movement. Drawing originally on the popularity of Alcoholics Anonymous (AA) and its sister organization, Al-Anon, other self-help groups such as Narcotics Anonymous, Co-

caine Anonymous, and Potsmokers Anonymous became popular. The 1980s also saw the popularization of concern for persons who grew up in families affected by alcoholism, resulting in the "Adult Children of Alcoholics" movement. All of these programs are grounded in disease models of addiction, and have extended their nets in ever-widening circles. The results are a large and diverse "recovery" movement (see, e.g., Room, 1993), and a large population of people seeking treatment for problems that may be related to psychoactive substance use in some way. Criticisms of the spiritual focus of Twelve-Step groups and of their emphasis on powerlessness have inspired the development of alternative self-groups grounded in more rational-positivist traditions. Programs such as Self-Management and Recovery Training (SMART) and Secular Organizations for Sobriety/Save Ourselves (SOS) use cognitive-behavioral principles in abstinence-based self-help groups. Moderation Management (MM)[1] applies cognitive-behavioral principles in a self-help group format for the achievement of moderate drinking outcomes.

The clinician functioning in the 21st century must provide treatment within this rather complex and contradictory network; must have formal and systematic training in the treatment of alcohol and other drug use disorders; must have tools to work with involuntary and voluntary clients, those who adhere passionately to a recovery perspective, and those who are offended by it; and may work either to promote major and enduring changes in alcohol use, or to decrease the harm that individuals and groups may experience from their use.

Given this rather complex picture, and given the notorious reputation of persons with alcohol use disorders for being difficult and frustrating to treat, many clinicians might ask, "Why bother?" The answers to this question must, on one level, be as individual as each clinician's motives for doing therapy. This chapter, however, assumes that the clinician who has a set of useful and effective tools for working with persons with drinking problems, and who has a bit of success with this population, will find positive reasons to continue. Persons with drinking problems *are* treatable; they are both challenging and rewarding to treat; and when they change successfully, the clinician has the rare opportunity to participate in helping people make major and satisfying changes in their lives.

DEFINITIONS AND DIAGNOSIS OF ALCOHOL PROBLEMS

Diagnosis

Contemporary approaches to the diagnosis of alcohol problems are based on a hypothetical construct, the "alcohol dependence syndrome" (Edwards & Gross, 1976), a constellation of behavior patterns and problems resulting from drinking that are hypothesized to constitute a diagnostic entity. The diagnosis of alcohol problems in the *Diagnostic and Statistical Manual of Mental Disorders*, fourth edition (DSM-IV; American Psychiatric Association, 1994) is based on the alcohol dependence syndrome. The two primary DSM-IV alcohol use disorder diagnoses are alcohol dependence and alcohol abuse. To be diagnosed as having alcohol dependence, an individual must meet at least three of seven criteria that relate to impaired control (a persistent desire or attempts to cut down or stop; using larger amounts or over longer periods of time than intended), physical tolerance, physical withdrawal, neglect of other activities, increased time spent using alcohol, and continued use despite knowledge of recurrent physical or psychological problems related to use. Alcohol dependence is diagnosed "with physiological dependence" if either the tolerance or the withdrawal criterion is met, or "without physiological dependence" if the individual has neither tolerance nor withdrawal. Alcohol dependence can also be classified as in "partial remission" or in "full remission," and that remission may be "early" (at least 1 month) or "sustained" (1 year or more). Alcohol abuse is diagnosed based on problem use, including failing to fulfill major social role obligations at work, home, or school; drinking repeatedly in a manner that creates the potential for harm (such as drinking and driving); incurring repeated alcohol-related legal consequences; or continuing to drink despite known social or interpersonal problems because of drinking. If an individual has ever met criteria for alcohol dependence, he/she can no longer receive a diagnosis of alcohol abuse.

Researchers are examining the reliability and validity of the DSM-IV diagnostic criteria, and further changes are likely in DSM-V. One of the more interesting and radical proposals has been to restrict the diagnosis of alcohol dependence to those with signs of alcohol withdrawal (Langenbucher et al., 2000). Such a shift would result in larger proportions of the population with alcohol problems receiving a diagnosis of abuse rather than dependence. Other suggestions for changes in diagnostic criteria have focused on the elements of the alcohol abuse diagnosis. In particular, it appears that those who meet abuse criteria because of repeated drinking and driving may differ from others who meet abuse criteria (Hasin, Paykin, Endicott, & Grant, 1999). Such findings suggest that diagnostic criteria for alcohol use disorders will continue to evolve in future versions of the DSM.

Alternative Definitions

In contrast to the formal psychiatric diagnosis of alcohol abuse or dependence, behavioral researchers and clinicians have suggested that alcohol problems represent one part of a continuum of alcohol use, ranging from abstinence to nonproblem use to different types and degrees of problem use. From this perspective, problems may be exhibited in a variety of forms—some of which are consistent with a formal diagnosis, and some of which are milder or more intermittent. By using an alcohol problems perspective, the clinician can focus more clearly on the pattern of drinking, negative consequences that the individual has accumulated, the client's behavioral excesses and deficits across various areas of life functioning, and the client's particular strengths. A deemphasis on diagnosis forces the clinician to consider clients from a more individual perspective. Therefore, although formal diagnosis is useful for identifying and defining the severity of a client's problems and is necessary for formal record keeping, the approach to clinical assessment emphasized in this chapter attends less to diagnostic issues per se and more to problem identification.

This chapter views alcohol use problems as a multivariate set of problems, with alcohol consumption as a common characteristic. These problems vary in their severity, from severe alcohol dependence to mild and circumscribed problems. For some, alcohol consumption itself is a major presenting problem; for others, the consequences of alcohol use—such as disruption of a relationship, occupational problems, or health problems—are the major reason for seeking treatment. In viewing alcohol problems as multivariate, this chapter also assumes the existence of multiple etiologies for these problems, with genetic, psychological, and environmental determinants contributing in differing degrees for different clients.

Complicating Problems

Drinking problems are complicated by a variety of concomitant problems. Of significance is the comorbidity of alcohol use disorders with other psychiatric diagnoses. Research has shown that a high percentage of those who can be diagnosed as having alcohol abuse or dependence also experience other psychological problems, which may be concurrent with, antecedent to, or consequent to their drinking (Rosenthal & Westreich, 1999). The most common Axis I disorders are other psychoactive substance use disorders, depression, and anxiety disorders, occurring in up to 60% of males in treatment. The most common Axis II disorder comorbid with alcoholism in males is Antisocial Personality Disorder, with rates ranging from 15% to 50%. Females more often present with depressive disorders; a quarter to a third of women with alcoholism show depression prior to the onset of their alcoholism.

Alcohol problems are also complicated by problems with cognition, physical health, interpersonal relationships, the criminal justice system, the employment setting, and the environment. Many people with alcoholism have subtle cognitive deficits, particularly in the areas of abstract reasoning, memory, and problem solving (see Parsons, 1998, for a review of this literature). Because verbal functioning is usually unimpaired, these cognitive problems are not immediately apparent. Heavy drinking also causes a variety of medical problems, and can affect any organ system in the body. Such conditions as cardiomyopathy, liver diseases, gastritis, ulcers, pancreatitis, and peripheral neuropathies all may be caused by heavy drinking. Even when obvious medical conditions are not present, the effects of

heavy drinking can be insidious and debilitating. Many people eat poorly when drinking, resulting in nutritional deficits, poor energy, or vague and diffuse physical discomfort. Mortality rates are elevated among persons of all ages with alcohol dependence, and are higher among women than men.

Interpersonal relationships may also be disrupted for the client with alcoholism. The rates of separation and divorce in this population range up to seven times those of the general population (Paolino, McCrady, & Diamond, 1978); spousal violence is higher among people with alcoholism; and emotional and behavioral problems are more common among their spouses/partners and children (Moos & Billings, 1982; Moos, Finney, & Gamble, 1982). Health care utilization is elevated among both spouses and children of actively drinking individuals with alcoholism (Spear & Mason, 1991).

Persons presenting for treatment of a drinking problem may be involved with the legal system because of charges related to driving while intoxicated (DWI), other alcohol-related offenses such as assault, or involvement with the child welfare system. Drug-related charges may also bring a client to treatment. Clients also may vary substantially in the degree to which they recognize that their drinking is creating problems, and in the degree of motivation to change their drinking patterns.

In conclusion, the client presenting for treatment may be drinking in a manner that creates concern, may be formally diagnosed as having alcohol dependence or alcohol abuse, and may also meet criteria for one or more Axis I or Axis II disorders. The person may also have other major problems in terms of cognitive impairment, physical health problems, interpersonal or occupational problems, and/or legal problems. Problem recognition and motivation to change may also vary substantially among clients. How does the clinician develop a rational approach to conceptualizing and treating this rather complicated clinical picture?

THEORETICAL MODEL

The present model is based in the assumption that treatment planning must be multidimensional, and that there is more than one effective treatment for alcohol problems. Unlike certain disorders, where one treatment approach has demonstrable superiority over others, in the alcohol field there are a number of legitimate and empirically supported approaches to treatment. These treatments are based in different conceptualizations of the etiology, course, treatment goals, and length of treatment for alcohol problems. Among the treatments with the best support are brief and motivationally focused interventions, cognitive-behavioral treatment, Twelve-Step facilitation treatment, behavioral couple therapy, cue exposure treatment, and the community reinforcement approach. A central responsibility of the therapist is to help a client find a treatment approach and treatment setting that is effective for that client, rather than slavishly adhering to one or another treatment model or setting. A second and equally important responsibility of the therapist is to enhance the client's motivation to continue to engage in the process of change, even if the initial selection of treatment setting, model, or modality is not effective. The present treatment model takes into account seven major considerations: (1) problem severity, (2) concomitant life problems, (3) client expectations, (4) motivation and the therapeutic relationship, (5) variables maintaining the current drinking pattern, (6) social support systems, and (7) maintenance of change.

Problem Severity

The preceding section on definitions and diagnosis has considered the extent and severity of alcohol problems in some detail. This dimension is relatively atheoretical, and is most important in decision making about the types of treatments to be offered, the intensity of the treatment, and the initial treatment setting. Severe alcohol dependence can best be conceptualized as a chronic, relapsing disorder, with relapses occurring even after extended periods of abstinence. As with other chronic disorders such as diabetes, cardiovascular disease, or rheumatoid arthritis, the clinician necessarily takes a long-term perspective, and has as a primary goal maximizing periods of positive functioning and minimizing periods of problem use. Other individuals, in contrast, experience alcohol-related problems that may be circumscribed

in length and nonprogressive (Finney, Moos, & Timko, 1999). Epidemiological data suggest that for the majority of those with alcohol-related problems, the problems will resolve or remit without any need for formal treatment or intervention. The clinician encountering individuals at the mild end of the severity spectrum is faced with a different challenge—to present a brief, motivationally enhancing intervention that will complement the natural recovery process and inspire these individuals to make changes in the problematic aspects of their alcohol use.

Concomitant Life Problems

As described above, clients with alcohol use disorders often have problems in multiple areas of life functioning—physical, psychological/psychiatric, familial, social/interpersonal, occupational, legal, child care, housing, transportation. Assessment of multiple areas of life functioning is crucial for planning and delivery of effective treatment. Recent research suggests that targeting client problem areas can be successful in making appreciable changes in these problems, even with clients who are severely alcohol-dependent and homeless (Cox et al., 1998). Furthermore, providing treatment directed at multiple problem areas enhances positive alcohol and drug use outcomes as well (McLellan et al., 1997).

Client Expectations

Clinicians need to provide clients with accurate expectations about the intensity of their treatment and the probable course of their problems. To date, no research has examined the impact of setting different types of client expectations about the nature of treatment and the probable course of their problems. The recommendations provided here derive from empirical findings about the course and treatment of alcohol use disorders, and remain to be tested.

For clients with circumscribed, less severe problems, the clinician can appropriately inform clients that treatment can be short in duration, that clients are likely to be successful in reducing their drinking, and that the long-term prognosis is good. Such clients can also be told that they may decide to stop drinking completely, now or at some point in the future (Miller, Leckman, Delaney, & Tinkcom, 1992), or that they may continue to drink in a moderated fashion.

Clients with longer-term difficulties and severe dependence, however, should be given a different set of expectations about treatment and the course of their problems. It is most accurate to tell them that only about one-third of middle-class clients maintain sustained abstinence over extended periods of time (e.g., 4 years; Pettinati, Sugerman, DiDonato, & Maurer, 1982), but that they can expect to have substantial long-term reductions in their drinking, and should be able to sustain abstinence 80%–90% of the time (Project MATCH Research Group, 1998). The challenge for such clients is to learn skills to manage their alcohol problems in a way that makes drinking minimally disruptive to their lives. Chronic illness metaphors may be helpful. For example, like a patient with diabetes, a client with severe alcohol dependence probably needs to make and maintain significant lifestyle changes to support healthy functioning. Like the patient with diabetes, the client with severe alcohol dependence needs to know the warning signs that he/she may be getting into trouble and know what to do on his/her own, as well as when to seek outside help. And neither individual can afford to forget or ignore his/her chronic problem.

Motivation and the Therapeutic Relationship

Clients vary in the degree to which they recognize their drinking as problematic and in their personal readiness to change. Motivational models suggest that individuals initiate change when the perceived costs of the behavior outweigh the perceived benefits, and when they can anticipate some benefits from behavior change (Cunningham, Sobell, Sobell, & Gaskin, 1994). Prochaska, DiClemente, and Norcross (1992) have proposed a continuum of stages of readiness for change. The continuum includes the stages of "precontemplation," in which a person does not recognize a behavior as problematic; "contemplation," in which the person begins to consider that a behavior pattern might be problematic; "determination" or "preparation," during which the individual resolves to change; and "action," in which a person initiates active behaviors to deal with the problem. Following "action" is "maintenance" if the behavior change is successful, or "relapse" if the person returns to the problem behavior. Miller and Rollnick (1991) have suggested that several factors influence a person's readiness to change, including awareness of problem severity, awareness of positive consequences for changing the behavior, and the perception of choices in making changes. Clients' apparent stage of change, and their self-perception of their problems, should guide a clinician's initial approach to treatment and treatment planning.

Contemporary models view motivation as a state that can be influenced by therapeutic behaviors and the client's life experiences. Therapeutic approaches designed to enhance motivation are associated with less client resistance to treatment and with more positive drinking outcomes (Miller, Benefield, & Tonigan, 1993). Motivationally enhancing approaches appear to be particularly effective with clients who enter treatment very angry and hostile (Project MATCH Research Group, 1997a). Miller and his colleagues describe six common elements that seem to be effective in enhancing motivation, summarized in the acronym FRAMES: personalized feedback (F) to the client about his/her status; an emphasis on the personal responsibility (R) of the client for change; provision of clear advice (A) about the need for change, given in a supportive manner; providing the client with a menu (M) of options for how to go about changing, rather than insisting upon one treatment or treatment goal; providing treatment in a warm, empathic (E), and supportive style; and enhancing the client's perceived self-efficacy (S) for change.

Factors Maintaining the Current Drinking Pattern

Case conceptualization necessary to implement therapy focuses on factors maintaining the problematic drinking pattern. Different treatment models use different frameworks for conceptualizing current factors maintaining drinking. Presented here is a cognitive-behavioral approach to case conceptualization. The cognitive-behavioral case formulation assumes that drinking can best be treated by examining current factors maintaining drinking, rather than historical factors. Factors maintaining drinking may be individual, or related to environmental circumstances or interpersonal relationships. The model assumes external antecedents to drinking that have a lawful relationship to drinking through repeated pairings with positive or negative reinforcement or through the anticipation of reinforcement. The model assumes that cognitions and affective states mediate the relationship between external antecedents and drinking behavior, and that expectancies about the reinforcing value of alcohol play an important role in determining subsequent drinking behavior. Finally, the model assumes that drinking is maintained by its consequences, and that these consequences may be physiological, psychological, or interpersonal in their origins.

To integrate these assumptions about drinking, my colleagues and I use the SORC model, which conceptualizes the drinking response (R) as elicited by environmental stimuli (S) that occur antecedent to drinking; as mediated by cognitive, affective, and physiological organismic (O) factors; and as maintained by positive consequences (C) of drinking. Various individual, familial, and other interpersonal factors are associated with drinking.

At the individual level, environmental antecedents may be associated with specific drinking situations, times of the day, or the mere sight or smell of alcohol. Organismic variables may include craving for alcohol; withdrawal symptoms; negative affects such as anger, anxiety, or depression; negative self-evaluations or irrational beliefs; or positive expectancies about the effects of alcohol in particular situations. Individual reinforcers may include decreased craving or withdrawal symptoms, decreases in negative affect or increases in positive affect, decreased negative self-evaluations, or decreased focus on problems and concerns.

At the familial level, various antecedents to drinking occur. Alcohol may be a usual part of family celebrations or daily rituals. Family members may attempt to influence the problematic drinking behavior by nagging the person to stop or attempting to control the drinking through control of the finances or liquor supply. These actions may become antecedents to further drinking. Families in which a member is drinking heavily may develop poor communication and problem-solving skills, as well as marital/couple, sexual, financial, and child-rearing problems that then cue further drinking. The person with the drinking problem may have a variety of reactions to these familial antecedents, experiencing negative affect, low self-efficacy for coping with problems, and/or retaliatory thoughts. Positive consequences of drinking may also come from the family. The family may shield the person from negative consequences of drinking through taking care of the person when intoxicated, or assuming his/her responsibilities. A number of investigators have observed positive changes in marital/couple interactions associated with drinking, suggesting that drinking may be reinforced by these positive consequences (e.g., Frankenstein, Hay, & Nathan, 1985).

Other interpersonal antecedents to drinking also occur. These may revolve around social pressures to drink; work-related drinking situations; friendships in which alcohol consumption plays a major role; or interpersonal conflicts with work associates, friends, or acquaintances. The person may react to interpersonal antecedents to drinking with craving, positive expectancies for alcohol use, social discomfort, or negative self-evaluations for not drinking. Positive interpersonal consequences of drinking may include decreased craving or social anxiety, or increased social comfort or assertiveness.

Social Support

The behaviors of family members and others in the client's social network are integral to a functional analysis of the drinking. The availability of general social support, as well as social support for abstinence or moderate drinking, is crucial to successful treatment. Clients in a social network that is strongly supportive of drinking may need to take deliberate steps to detach from that social network and access new social networks that support the new behavior. Some data suggest that involvement with AA can serve such a function (Longabaugh, Wirtz, Zweben, & Stout, 1998), and data on natural recovery from alcohol problems suggest that finding a new love relationship or involvement in religious activities may also be viable avenues for change (Vaillant & Milofsky, 1982).

Maintenance of Change

Implicit in much of the discussion above is a view that alcohol use disorders at the more severe end of the spectrum are problems with a high probability of relapse. Relapse is an ever-present consideration, both because long-term, ingrained habits are difficult to change, and because of the permanent physiological and metabolic changes stimulated by heavy drinking (Moak & Anton, 1999). Several models have been proposed to conceptualize the maintenance or relapse process, and associated treatments derive from these models. The most prominent maintenance models include Marlatt and Gordon's (1985) relapse prevention (RP) model, and the disease model, best exemplified by the practices common to AA. The RP model is an extension of the SORC model described above, and focuses on the interplay among environment, coping skills, and cognitive and affective responses in maintaining successful change. Relapse, in the RP model, occurs in response to a high-risk situation for which the client either lacks or does not apply effective coping skills. Low self-efficacy for coping with the situation may contribute to the difficulties. If the client does not cope effectively, use of alcohol is likely. Following initial drinking, Marlatt and Gordon suggest that a cognitive factor, the "abstinence violation effect" (AVE), is activated. The AVE represents all-or-nothing thinking; after drinking, the client now makes a cognitive shift to viewing himself/herself as "drinking" and therefore continues to drink. RP treatment focuses on several points of intervention common to cognitive-behavioral treatment, such as identification of high-risk situation and acquisition of coping skills, as well as cognitive restructuring to help the client view a drinking episode as a "lapse" from which the client can learn and return to abstinence, rather than a "relapse" into previous drinking patterns. RP also focuses on lifestyle changes to decrease the presence of high-risk situations, and encourages development of a balance between pleasures and desires and obligations and responsibilities (a "want–should" balance) in the client's life.

Disease model perspectives view alcoholism as a chronic, progressive disease that can be arrested but not cured. Treatment then focuses on helping the client recognize that he/she has this disease, that abstinence and a life-long program of recovery are the only means to arrest the disease, and that involvement in AA or other Twelve-Step groups is essential to successful maintenance of change.

The present model is most closely allied with the RP model, but clinicians should be knowledgeable about the model underlying AA and should recognize that some clients are drawn to the disease model and AA, because they find both the model and the program enormously helpful and relevant to them.

CLINICAL APPLICATION OF THE THEORETICAL MODEL

The major elements of the treatment model have direct implications for facilitating problem recognition and entry into treatment, and for the planning and delivery of treatment. If an individual has not entered treatment, there are clinical techniques to help that individual recognize his/her drinking as problematic and in need of change. For a client seeking treatment, the clinician must make decisions about the most appropriate setting in which to provide treatment, and select the therapeutic modalities most appropriate to the client. Then therapeutic techniques to utilize within the treatment modalities must be tailored to the client's needs related to both drinking and other life problems. The therapist must also consider the social context in which drinking occurs, as well as the social context in which change occurs. The therapist must be cognizant of the subtle and nonspecific aspects of providing treatment to such a client, from both the client's and the therapist's perspective, and utilize a therapeutic stance that enhances the client's motivation to continue to engage in the change process. The therapist must attend to the client's own views about treatment and change, and provide the client with an accurate long-term expectation about drinking outcomes. Core components of the treatment model are listed in Table 9.1.

Case Identification and Entry into Treatment

Before I discuss applications of the model to active treatment, it is important to consider how to help clients enter the treatment system,

TABLE 9.1. Steps in Treatment
1. Case identification and motivation to enter treatment
2. Assessment
3. Selection of treatment setting
4. Selection of treatment modalities
5. Selection of treatment model
6. Enhancing and maintaining motivation to change
7. Selection of drinking goals
8. Initiation of abstinence
9. Developing a functional analysis
10. Early sobriety strategies
11. Coping strategies
12. Partner/family involvement
13. Long-term maintenance
14. Managing complicating conditions
15. Self-help groups

and how to apply aspects of the model to the process of entry into treatment.

Case Identification and Screening

Many individuals do not self-identify as having problems related to drinking. They may be unaware of the high-risk nature of their drinking pattern; may be unaware of the negative consequences that are occurring; may be ashamed or guilty, and thus reluctant to tell others about their problems; or may perceive health care professionals as uninterested in or unconcerned about drinking. Routine queries about drinking and its consequences in both medical and mental health care settings can obviate some of these difficulties. Given the high prevalence of drinking problems among individuals seeking health and mental health services, questions about drinking should be part of all clinicians' intake interview.

Many screening interviews and questionnaires have been developed to identify clients with alcohol problems. At a minimum, all clients should be asked whether or not they drink, and drinkers should be asked follow-up questions about the quantity and frequency of their drinking. Drinking should be considered as heavy or high-risk if a man drinks more than 28 standard drinks in a week, or a woman drinks more than 21 standard drinks in a week.[2] Concern should also be heightened if a client reports heavy drinking (8 drinks for men, 6 for women) more than twice per month. Follow-up questions can be used to inquire about subjective and objective consequences of drinking. The CAGE (Mayfield, McLeod, & Hall, 1974; see Table 9.2) and the TWEAK,

which assesses tolerance, worry by family or friends, eye-opener drinking, amnesia, and attempts to cut down (Russell, 1994) provide brief, simple questions. Two affirmative responses to such questions suggest a high probability of an alcohol use disorder, but even one positive response warrants further clinical inquiry. Suggested questions are summarized in Table 9.2.

Developing Motivation to Enter Treatment

The initial challenge for a clinician is to stimulate the client to initiate any kind of change. Methods for motivating clients to enter treatment vary; a clinician may draw upon motivational interviewing techniques (Miller & Rollnick, 1991), or may involve family and concerned others in either client-centered work (Miller, Meyers, & Tonigan, 1999) or more confrontational work (Liepman, 1993) to draw the individual into treatment. Implementation of motivational principles and techniques in ongoing clinical practice, however, presents creative challenges to the clinician. Three examples illustrate the application of different approaches to motivating clients to enter treatment.

Bill P is a retired chemist with a long history of heavy drinking, multiple phobias, and bipolar disorder. I was initially contacted by his wife, Diana. Our initial consultation was by telephone. During that conversation, Diana indicated that her husband had a 20-year drinking history, that his drinking had increased since his retirement, and that she didn't know what to do: The children were angry and threatening to break off contact with him, she and he were arguing frequently, and she was beginning to feel increasingly anxious and depressed herself. She had consulted with a certified addictions counselor, who told her that they should set up an "intervention"—a meeting with Diana, the children, and Bill, during which they would confront him about his drinking, insist that he get treatment, and then take him directly to an inpatient treatment facility. When Diana expressed hesitation about such an approach, the counselor told her she was codependent and enabling him. She left the office discouraged, certain that she did not want to initiate an intervention, but also certain that something should be done. I tried the most mini-

TABLE 9.2. Questions to Screen for Alcohol Use and Problems

Type of question	Question
Quantity–frequency	1. Do you drink alcohol (including beer, wine, or hard liquor)?
	2. How often do you drink?
	3. When you drink, about how much do you usually drink?
	4. What is the most you ever drink in a day?
	5. How often do you drink your top amount?
Screening	CAGE[a]:
	1. Have you ever felt you should cut (C) down on your drinking?
	2. Have people annoyed (A) you by commenting on your drinking?
	3. Have you ever felt bad or guilty (G) about your drinking?
	4. Have you ever had a drink first thing in the morning (eyeopener [E])?

[a]From Mayfield et al., 1974.

mal intervention first. Over the telephone, I suggested that Diana speak with Bill one morning (before he had begun drinking) and simply say, "Bill, I am concerned about your drinking. I have spoken with a psychologist who specializes in alcohol treatment, and she said that she would be happy to see you, simply for an evaluation. At the end of the evaluation, she'd give us feedback about what we could do." I instructed her not to elaborate on this statement, but to simply respond to his questions. If he refused, she was to get back in touch with me.

I next heard from Diana 3 months later. They had spent the three intervening months at their summer home in Maine, and had returned for a month's visit before going back to Maine for much of the fall. Bill had refused her request, and she wondered what else she could do. I suggested that the next step would be for her to have an individual consultation with me to discuss how to change her own actions to motivate him toward change. She came in for a single consultation, and after some further assessment of both his drinking history and her current functioning, I suggested three basic behavioral strategies, which I drew from Thomas's unilateral family therapy (Thomas, Yoshioka, & Ager, 1996) and the Community Reinforcement and Family Training (CRAFT) model (Miller et al., 1999). First, I instructed her to leave him to his drinking as much as possible, to let negative consequences occur naturally. Second, I encouraged her to provide him with factual feedback about negative behaviors related to his drinking, but only at times when he was sober. The

structure of the feedback was to be "Bill, I am concerned that X happened last night when you were drinking." Third, I encouraged her to spend time with him in positive pursuits when he was not drinking. Given that they would be in Maine again for almost 3 months, I suggested in the last week before they returned to New Jersey that she repeat her request that he come to see me for an evaluation.

I next heard from Diana in early November, when she called me to make an appointment for the two of them to come in for an evaluation. They both attended. What follows is our initial discussion.[3] (In this and other dialogues in this chapter, I am the therapist, or T; clients are referred to by their initials.)

T: I'm so glad to get to meet you. As you know, Diana first spoke with me a few months ago, so I feel as though I know you a bit. I understand that you were initially reluctant to come in, and I'm pleased that you decided to come. How did that come about?

B: "Well, Diana asked me, and I know she's been concerned, so I agreed. But I only agreed to come today—I'm not making any kind of commitment here.

T: I understand that, and certainly won't try to push you to do anything you're not comfortable with. What I'd like to do today is to get a better understanding about your drinking and the kinds of problems it might be causing. At the end of our time together, I'll give you some feedback and we can discuss some options for you, if you decide you want to make any changes. If I ask you anything that you're not comfortable answering, just let me know. OK?

Bill was visibly uncomfortable, and pushed his chair as far back into the corner of my office as possible. He sat with his body turned away from Diana, and often looked up at the ceiling or sighed when she was speaking. Despite his visible discomfort, he gave a clear account of his drinking. He had been drinking heavily for the past 25 years, and at one point had been drinking a pint of Jack Daniels whiskey each evening. He was diagnosed with colon cancer in his early 60s and treated surgically. Since the surgery, he had been concerned about his health and had attempted to reduce his drinking. His current pattern was almost daily drinking, in the evenings, ranging from half to three-quarters of a bottle of wine to an occasional (approximately twice per month) pint of Jack Daniels. He reported no withdrawal symptoms on days when he did not drink, and no apparent medical sequelae of his drinking. He expressed his concern about feeling that he didn't have control over his drinking, and expressed sadness that Diana was so upset by his drinking. His love for her was apparent in his speech and demeanor, and was clearly the primary reason he had come to see me. Diana also commented that their children had been upset by his drinking, and that they were threatening to keep the grandchildren from seeing Bill if he continued to drink.

Given Bill's hesitancy and discomfort, I did not try to complete any standardized assessment instruments, or even to structure the initial interview as much as I might with other clients. Instead, I followed his lead, made frequent comments reflecting the emotions he was expressing, and at times asked Diana not to interrupt so that he could express himself. In the last 15 minutes of the 1-hour interview, we shifted to feedback and discussion:

T: I'd like to stop asking you so many questions now, and see if we can talk about possible options for you. I am glad that you came in, and appreciate that this was not easy for you. From what you and Diana have told me, it does seem that it makes sense to be concerned about your drinking. The amount you're drinking is above the recommended levels for safe and healthy drinking; you are concerned by your own feelings of lack of control; the drinking has been upsetting to your family, which is painful to you. What do you think?

B: I guess talking about all of this at once makes it clearer that I'm drinking too much. I don't want to stop, though—I appreciate good wine, and look forward to having a glass in the evening. I just don't want to overdo it to the point of hurting Diana.

T: So you are concerned, and think that some kind of change makes sense, but you're not sure exactly what those changes should be?

B: Exactly.

T: I think you have a number of options. Making some kind of change makes sense, given the problems we've discussed. Probably your safest choice is to stop drinking—you can't create future health problems from drinking if you don't drink, and in some ways it might be easiest, given that you're in a pretty daily routine of drinking now. But if you don't want to stop, we could also work toward your reducing your drinking to a level that is safer and healthier, and one that Diana and your children are comfortable with. I'd be willing to work with you to try to reach that goal. I don't think that you need intensive treatment in a hospital program right now, but you would probably benefit from some outside help to make changes. What do you think?

B: I'm surprised that you think I could reduce my drinking. I have to think about this. I'll have Diana get back to you.

The discussion continued with input from Diana as well, and the session ended with a commitment only to think about our discussion. Several days later, Diana called to indicate that Bill would like to begin treatment with me, and we scheduled an appointment for their next return from Maine. I have now been seeing them regularly for the past several months.

Dorothy R was a 78-year-old widowed retired schoolteacher, hospitalized at a local medical center after a fall in her apartment.

Her blood alcohol level (BAL) on admission was 185 mg%, and she had extensive evidence of old bruises, as well as a dislocated shoulder and broken wrist from the fall. She was immediately started on medication for alcohol withdrawal, and our addictions consultation team was called in to see her on the second day of her hospitalization. Dorothy's son John was in the room when I came to conduct the initial interview with her. With his assistance, I was able to obtain a clear and lengthy history of alcohol consumption that dated back to her early 40s. Although she had wanted to stop drinking, she had never been successful for more than a few days at a time, and had never received any form of alcohol treatment. Since her husband's death 2 years prior, she had been consuming a pint bottle of blackberry brandy each day. She had completely withdrawn from her previous social activities with friends, her hygiene had deteriorated, and she had had multiple accidents in the house. Dorothy provided this information tearfully, expressing a great sense of shame about her behavior. John described her home as "a mess." He also indicated that he was angry and disgusted with her.

Dorothy's family history revealed a family with many persons with alcohol dependence, including her father, two brothers, and a maternal uncle. Despite the medication, she showed visible signs of alcohol withdrawal during the interview. She was tearful, and stated repeatedly that she was a "sinful, bad" person. My interviewing style with her was empathic—asking her what her concerns were, inquiring how she felt, reflecting back her obvious distress with her current situation. I then indicated to her that there were treatments available to help people with problems like hers. Her immediate and strong reaction was to say that she was too bad, and that her drinking was a sin. Although not usually a strong proponent of labeling alcohol dependence as a disease, I decided that this framework might in fact be a framework that would be most acceptable and supportive to her. Given her long history of alcohol dependence with clear physiological dependence, and her heavy family history of alcohol dependence, such a framework seemed plausible and applicable. I said:

"Dorothy, it is clear to me that you are very, very upset by your drinking and by all the problems that it has caused for you and your family. I understand that you blame yourself, and seem to think your drinking shows that you are a bad person. There is another way of thinking about your drinking that I'd like to tell you about. You may or may not agree with me, but I hope you'll think about what I say. Some people say that alcoholism is a disease. In your case, I think that is true. You probably have genes that made you very vulnerable to alcohol—your father, your uncle, and your brothers all seem to have the same disease. We know that the vulnerability to alcoholism can be inherited, and I would guess that you inherited it. Over time, your body has become adapted to your drinking—it is more comfortable with alcohol than without alcohol. If you try to stop, your body reacts badly. That's what the shaking and nausea is that you're experiencing now—a sign that your body has become hooked on alcohol. What does all this mean? It means that your body reacts differently to alcohol than other people's bodies, and probably has from the beginning of your drinking. It is no more your fault that you have a drinking problem than it is the fault of a diabetic that her body can't make insulin. People are not responsible for the diseases they develop. But they are responsible for making the decision to take care of their disease, for getting help, and for following the advice of the people who give them that help. Except for the problems your drinking has caused, you're healthy, and you obviously have family and friends who care about you. If you can get help, you have a good chance of getting better."

Dorothy initially was skeptical of this reframing of her problems. Without my prompting, her son left the hospital that day and picked up some brochures about alcoholism as a disease, and brought them back for his mother to read. When I came to see her the next day, she had many questions about this disease notion and about treatment, which I answered as factually as possible, still maintaining a motivational interviewing stance—not trying to push her into treatment, but reflecting her interest and concern. By my third visit, she agreed to enter a treatment program. She entered a short-term residential rehabilitation program, followed by longer-term outpatient group therapy. She began to volunteer at the hospital where I first saw her, and she remained sober and an active volunteer for several years until advancing age required that she retire.

Dennis G was a 41-year-old dentist with a history of abuse of alcohol, prescription opiates, and benzodiazepines. Dennis's case illustrates the need for a full armamentarium of clinical techniques to motivate individuals to enter treatment. At the time that I saw Dennis, the Rutgers Center of Alcohol Studies had a contractual agreement with the New Jersey Dental Association to provide assessment, motivational, referral, and monitoring services for dentists with alcohol and drug problems. I was called about Dennis on Friday afternoon by an emergency room physician. Dennis had taken an overdose of medications and had been rushed to the emergency room by his office staff. His condition had been stabilized, and he was now insisting that he leave the hospital. The physician wanted our program to "do something." In rapid succession, I received calls from the office staff, from Dennis's wife, and from another dentist who had been serving as his AA sponsor. By telephone, they provided me with a horrific history of abuse of multiple substances, domestic violence, canceled afternoons of appointments with patients, extraction of the wrong tooth from a patient, and repeated failures in AA and outpatient treatment. Each caller described Dennis as intractable, and all were desperately concerned that he would kill himself. I asked them all to meet me at the hospital, and left my office to join them there. I informed the emergency room physician that I would be coming to the hospital, and asked him to hold Dennis.

When I arrived at the hospital, I first spoke with Dennis individually. He was alert, oriented, belligerent, and angry, and utterly unwilling to speak with me at length or agree to any kind of plan of care. My best motivational interviewing skills failed completely with him. Given the crisis nature of the situation, and the extremely severe substance use disorder, I decided to utilize a more confrontational technique—the intervention (Liepman, 1993). Interventions are designed to confront the resistant client and create a forced plan of action. Research suggests that two-thirds of families will not follow through with an intervention (as was the case with Diana and Bill), but that when an intervention is implemented, the probability of the client's entering treatment is very high (Miller et al., 1999). I gathered the office staff, Dennis's wife, and his sponsor together and asked them whether they would be willing to sit down with Dennis to talk with him about his problems. They were relieved and eager to do so. We spent about 30 minutes together, during which I outlined the basic requirements for the intervention: (1) Each person's feedback should begin with an expression of caring or concern; (2) each person should provide concrete, behavioral feedback related to Dennis's drinking and drug use (e.g., mentioning his canceling appointments, rather than saying that he was irresponsible with his patients); (3) at the end of each person's feedback, the person should repeat his/her expression of concern and request that he get help. We then sat down with Dennis, and each person spoke. Dennis began to cry, and after a lengthy period of time, agreed that he needed help and would follow my recommendations for treatment.

Assessment

Once a client has agreed to enter treatment, the therapist should begin with an initial assessment of drinking, other drug use, and problems in other areas of life functioning. Assessment of motivation as well as resources that the client brings to the treatment are important. If the client becomes involved in cognitive-behavioral treatment, assessment to complete a functional analysis of drinking is necessary. If the client's spouse/partner or other family members are involved in the treatment, additional assessment of their role in the drinking as well as overall relationship functioning is appropriate.

Drinking Assessment

The clinical interview is used to assess drinking history and client perceptions of his/her current drinking. An outline of major topics to cover in the clinical interview is listed in Table 9.3. Typically, we use a hand-held breath alcohol tester at the beginning of each session to assess current BAL. In addition to the clinical interview, two structured interviews—the Timeline Follow-Back Interview

TABLE 9.3. Topics to Cover in Initial Clinical Interview (Both Partners Present)

1. Initial orientation
   a. Introductions
   b. Breath alcohol test
   c. Brief questionnaires
2. Initial assessment
   a. Presenting problems
   b. Role of drinking/drug use in presenting problems
   c. Other concerns
   d. How the drinking has affected the partner
   e. How the drinking has affected the relationship
3. Drinking/drug use assessment
   a. Identified patient
      i. Quantity, frequency, pattern of drinking
      ii. Last drink/drug use
      iii. Length of drinking/drug problem
      iv. Negative consequences of drinking/drug use
      v. DSM-IV symptoms
      vi. Assessment of need for detoxification
   b. Partner
      i. Quantity, frequency, pattern of drinking
      ii. Last drink/drug use
      iii. Length of drinking/drug problem
      iv. Negative consequences of drinking/drug use
      v. DSM-IV symptoms
      vi. Assessment of need for detoxification
4. Assessment of other problems
   a. Psychotic symptoms
   b. Depression
   c. Anxiety
   d. Organic brain syndromes/cognitive impairment
   e. Health status
5. Assessment of domestic violence
   a. This assessment is done privately with each partner alone
   b. Review of Modified Conflict Tactics Scale
      i. Identification of episodes of physical aggression
      ii. Determination of level of harm/injury from aggression
      iii. Assessment of individual's sense of safety in couple therapy

(TLFB; Sobell, Maisto, Sobell, Cooper, & Saunders, 1980), designed to assess drinking and drug use behavior on each day in a set window of time before treatment; and the alcohol and drug sections of the Structured Clinical Interview for DSM-IV (Spitzer, Williams, Gibbon, & First, 1996)—provide standardized information about quantity, frequency, and pattern of drinking, and other information to establish a formal diagnosis. Self-report measures can be used to assess severity of alcohol dependence (the Alcohol Dependence Scale [ADS]; Skinner & Allen, 1982) and negative consequences of drinking (the Drinker Inventory of Consequences; Miller, Tonigan, & Longabaugh, 1995).

Assessment of Other Problem Areas

The clinician can draw from a wide variety of structured measures to assess life problems separate from drinking or drug use. Assessment may range from unstructured interviews to the use of simple problem checklists to formal interviewing techniques. The Addiction Severity Index (ASI; McLellan et al., 1992) is a widely used measure of client functioning across multiple domains of functioning; subscales include Medical, Psychological, Family/Social, Legal, Employment, Alcohol, and Drug. The ASI can be administered as an interview in about 45 minutes, and computer-assisted interview versions are available. The ASI, however, does not provide diagnostic information for any psychological disorders, and the cautious clinician should use formal screening questions to assess for the possible presence of other psychological disorders (Zimmerman, 1994).

Assessment of Motivation

Assessment of motivation should consider (1) reasons why treatment is being sought, with careful attention to the degree to which external factors motivated help seeking; (2) the client's drinking and other treatment goals; (3) the client's stage of readiness of change; and (4) the degree to which the client perceives negative consequences of his/her current drinking pattern and potential positive consequences of change. Clinical interviewing provides information about reasons for seeking treatment, and drinking goals can be assessed either by asking the client directly or by using a simple goal choice form (see Figure 9.1). The University of Rhode Island Change Assessment Scale (McConnaughy, Prochaska, & Velicer, 1983) and the Readiness to Change Questionnaire (Rollnick, Heather, Gold, & Hall, 1992) both measure stage of change. Perception of negative consequences of drinking and positive consequences of change can also be assessed through the clinical interview, or through the development of a decisional balance sheet (Marlatt & Gordon, 1985) with the client (see Figure 9.2).

Functional Analysis

Two assessment techniques can be used to identify antecedents to drinking. A self-report questionnaire, the Drinking Patterns Ques-

We would like to know the **ONE goal** you have chosen for yourself about drinking at this time. Please read the goals listed below, and choose the **ONE goal** that best represents your goal at this time by checking the box next to the goal and by filling in any blanks as indicated for that goal.

☐ I have decided not to change my pattern of drinking.

☐ I have decided to cut down on my drinking and drink in a more controlled manner—to be in control of how often I drink and how much I drink. I would like to limit myself to no more than __ drinks (upper limit amount) per _____ (time period).

☐ I have decided to stop drinking completely for a period of time, after which I will make a new decision about whether I will drink again. For me, the period of time I want to stop drinking is for _____ (time).

☐ I have decided to stop drinking regularly, but would like to have an occasional drink when I really have the urge.

☐ I have decided to quit drinking once and for all, even though I realize I may slip up and drink once in a while.

☐ I have decided to quit drinking once and for all, to be totally abstinent, and to never drink alcohol ever again for the rest of my life.

☐ None of this applies exactly to me. My own goal is _____.

FIGURE 9.1. Form for assessment of drinking goal.

tionnaire (DPQ; Zitter & McCrady, 1979), lists potential environmental, cognitive, affective, interpersonal, and intrapersonal antecedents to drinking or drinking urges. The Inventory of Drinking Situations (Annis, 1982), a shorter measure that assesses situations in which a client drinks heavily, can also be used.

Daily self-recording cards (Figure 9.3) are used throughout the treatment to record drinks and drinking urges. By reviewing the information the client records and discussing events associated with drinking or drinking urges, the clinician can develop a clearer picture of drinking antecedents and consequences. Self-recording cards also allow the clinician to track progress through treatment in terms of quantity and frequency of drink-

ing, as well as frequency and intensity of urges to drink.

Partner Assessment

Questionnaires and self-recording cards can be used to assess how the client's partner has coped with the drinking. Each day, the partner records his/her perceptions of the drinker's drinking and drinking urges on a Likert scale (none, light, moderate, or heavy) (Figure 9.4). In addition, the partner may complete a modified version of the Spouse Behavior Questionnaire (SBQ; Orford et al., 1975) to report how frequently the partner has engaged in a variety of behaviors to cope with drinking. These include behaviors that occur antecedent to drinking, positive consequences of drinking, negative consequences of drinking, positive consequences of sobriety, and positive or self-protective behaviors.

It is also important to assess other aspects of the couple's relationship, if both partners are to be involved in treatment. The Areas of Change Questionnaire (ACQ; Margolin, Talovic, & Weinstein, 1983) and the Dyadic Adjustment Scale (DAS; Spanier, 1976) are excellent self-report measures of relationship problems and satisfaction. The Modified Conflict Tactics Scale (Pan, Neidig, & O'Leary, 1994) provides a succinct measure of relationship conflict, including physical violence.

Decisional Balance Sheet

	Not Drinking	Drinking
Pros		
Cons		

FIGURE 9.2. Decisional balance sheet. From Marlatt and Gordon (1985). Copyright 1985 by The Guilford Press. Adapted by permission.

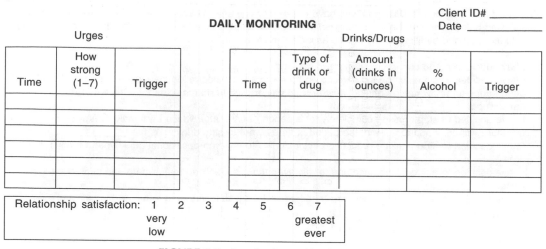

FIGURE 9.3. Sample client self-recording card.

Selection of Treatment Setting

Information from the assessment of drinking, concomitant problem areas, and motivation is used to make an initial determination about the appropriate setting in which to initiate treatment. As with other areas of health and mental health care, the principle of least restrictive level of care should apply to alcohol and drug treatment. The *Zeitgeist* for alcohol treatment has oscillated between a primary focus on residential treatment and a primary focus on ambulatory treatment. From the late 1970s through the 1980s, residential rehabilitation of fixed length (usually 28 to 30 days) was considered the treatment of choice. Controlled research comparing effectiveness of different levels of care (see, e.g., Fink et al., 1985; Longabaugh et al., 1983; McCrady et al., 1986), as well as increasing management of level of care by health insurers, stimulated a wholesale move to ambulatory treatment models. At the beginning of the 21st century, intensive outpatient programs of fixed duration and straight outpatient care are the most common settings for treatment (National Advisory Council on Alcohol Abuse and Alcoholism, 1996).

Rational decision-making models to determine level of care have been proposed and are being implemented in many states. The ASAM (1991) has proposed a multidimensional decision-making model for selecting initial level of care. ASAM criteria consider need for supervised withdrawal, medical conditions

that might require monitoring, comorbid psychiatric conditions, motivation for change and degree of treatment acceptance or resistance, relapse potential, and nature of the individual's social environment in recommending an initial level of care. Criteria for continuing review and changes in level of care are also specified. Although the ASAM criteria are logical and appealing, no published research exists to demonstrate that their use improves clinical outcomes.

Both the Institute of Medicine (1990) and Breslin, Sobell, Sobell, Buchan, and Cunningham (1997) have proposed variants of a stepped-care model for making decisions about level of care. The stepped-care model proposes brief interventions as the modal initial approach to treatment, with decisions about more intensive and/or longer treatments being based on client response to the initial treatment. Such models are economically conservative, and maintain the principle of least restrictive level of care.

There are a number of settings available for the provision of alcohol treatment. These include inpatient or residential settings, partial hospitals, outpatient clinics, and halfway houses. Self-help groups are also widely available. Given that the research literature provides little information to guide clinical decision making about the level of care appropriate for an individual client and that the ASAM criteria have not been well tested in empirical trials, we use a combination of ASAM and other clinical indicators to deter-

Client ID# ____________
Date ____________

PARTNER MONITORING

Day	Date	Drinking	Drug use	Urge intensity 0 = None 7 = Most intense	Relationship satisfaction 1 = Very low 7 = Best ever
		None L M H	Y N	0 1 2 3 4 5 6 7	0 1 2 3 4 5 6 7
		None L M H	Y N	0 1 2 3 4 5 6 7	0 1 2 3 4 5 6 7
		None L M H	Y N	0 1 2 3 4 5 6 7	0 1 2 3 4 5 6 7
		None L M H	Y N	0 1 2 3 4 5 6 7	0 1 2 3 4 5 6 7
		None L M H	Y N	0 1 2 3 4 5 6 7	0 1 2 3 4 5 6 7
		None L M H	Y N	0 1 2 3 4 5 6 7	0 1 2 3 4 5 6 7
		None L M H	Y N	0 1 2 3 4 5 6 7	0 1 2 3 4 5 6 7

Drinking scale: None = No use; L = Light (1–2 drinks); M = Moderate (3–4 drinks); H = Heavy (5 or more drinks)

FIGURE 9.4. Sample partner self-recording card.

mine initial level of care for clients. Major indicators are described below and summarized in Table 9.4.

Need for Detoxification

If a client is physically dependent on alcohol, then he/she will experience alcohol with-

drawal symptoms when decreasing or stopping drinking. A number of signs suggest that a client may be physically dependent on alcohol (Femino & Lewis, 1980). Daily drinking, drinking regularly or intermittently throughout the day, and morning drinking all suggest physical dependence. If a client reports awakening during the night with fears, trembling,

TABLE 9.4. Guidelines for Selection of Treatment Settings

Level of care	Indicators
Medical hospitalization	Acute medical problems Seizures Delirium
Inpatient, medical detoxification	Physical dependence History of/current major withdrawal History of seizures Serious medical problems Serious psychiatric problems Patient does not think he/she can stop drinking without supervision
Social setting detoxification	Physical dependence No acute health problems No history of seizures, major withdrawal Patient does not think he/she can stop drinking without supervision
Outpatient detoxification	Physical dependence No complicating conditions Patient does not want hospitalization Social supports for stopping
Inpatient treatment	History of dropping out of outpatient treatment History of dropping out of or drinking during partial hospital treatment Poor social supports Social support for drinking Cognitive deficits Other acute psychiatric problems Suicidal Lack of insurance or resources for ambulatory treatment Lack of transportation Strong personal preference
Partial hospital/day treatment	History of dropping out of outpatient treatment History of immediate relapse after inpatient treatment Fair to good social supports Ambivalence about treatment or change Lack of child care Unable to get time off from work Strong personal preference
Outpatient treatment	History of successful use of outpatient treatment Successful previous quit attempts on own Good social supports History of successful change Lack of resources for more intensive treatment Lack of child care Unable to get time off from work Strong personal preference
Halfway house	History of relapse after inpatient treatment Lack of social supports

or nausea, or experiences such symptoms upon first awakening, these are also suggestive of dependence. Furthermore, cessation or a substantial decrease in drinking will result in the appearance of minor withdrawal symptoms, such as tremulousness, nausea, vomiting, difficulty sleeping, irritability, anxiety, and elevations in pulse, blood pressure, and temperature. Such symptoms usually begin within 5–12 hours. More severe withdrawal symptoms (such as seizures, delirium, or hallucinations) may also occur, usually within 24–72 hours of the cessation of drinking.

If a client has not consumed alcohol for several days prior to initial clinical contact, then concerns about alcohol withdrawal are not relevant. If the client has stopped drinking within the last 3 days, the clinician needs to inquire about and observe for signs of withdrawal. If the client is currently drinking, the clinician must rely on drinking history, pattern, and the results of previous attempts to stop drinking to determine whether detoxification will be necessary.

If the client needs detoxification, four alternatives are available: inpatient or partial hospital medical detoxification, inpatient nonmedical detoxification, or outpatient medical detoxification. Inpatient, medically assisted detoxification is essential if the client has a history of disorientation, delirium, hallucinations, or seizures during alcohol withdrawal, or is showing current signs of disorientation, delirium, or hallucinations. If the client does not believe that he/she can stop drinking without being physically removed from alcohol, but does not show any major withdrawal signs, is in good health, and does not abuse other drugs, a social setting detoxification may be appropriate. If the client has some social supports, then detoxification can be initiated on a partial hospital or outpatient basis. The choice between these two latter settings will be determined by how much support the person will need during withdrawal, and whether a structured program will be needed after detoxification. If the client will need a fairly structured program, then the partial hospital will be the preferred setting for detoxification.

Medical Problems

When the clinician is considering the best setting for detoxification, the presence of other medical problems should be taken into account. A cautious approach dictates that every client should have a thorough physical examination and blood and urine studies at the beginning of treatment. The clinician should routinely include questions about physical health in the first contact with a client, and if significant physical complaints are noted, the client should receive immediate medical attention. Some clients will have medical problems that require hospitalization; if so, the hospitalization should initiate the treatment.

Treatment History

After physical health issues have been considered, the clinician should consider the client's previous treatment history. Questions to consider include the following:

1. Has the client attempted outpatient treatment in the past, and been able to stop or decrease drinking successfully? If so, then another attempt at outpatient treatment may be indicated.

2. Has the client dropped out of outpatient treatment in the past? If so, and there is no indication that any variables have changed in the interim, then a more intensive partial hospital or inpatient program should be considered.

3. Has the client dropped out of, or drunk repeatedly, while in a partial hospital program? If so, then inpatient treatment may be indicated.

4. Did the client relapse immediately after discharge from an inpatient program? If so, then a partial hospital or outpatient setting may be appropriate, as relapse may have been associated with problems in generalization from the inpatient to the natural environment. Alternatively, a halfway house may be considered to provide a longer-term structured environment.

Previous Quit Attempts

Many clients have successfully decreased or stopped drinking on their own at some time. If the client has a history of stopping successfully on his/her own, then outpatient treatment is more likely to be successful than for a client without any history of successful change.

Social Support Systems

Social support systems are a critical variable to consider in determining the appropriate setting for initial treatment. If a client has support from others, such as a spouse/partner, older child, parent, close friend, concerned employer, AA sponsor, or some other person who is readily available, *and* that person is perceived as an important source of support and reinforcement, *and* the person may be willing to provide support and reinforcement, then the client is a good candidate for ambulatory treatment. If the client is lacking in social supports, or is in an environment that supports heavy drinking, then inpatient or partial hospital treatment may be advisable. Alternatively, a halfway house may provide a good setting for treatment for persons who do not have current social supports and have not been successful at developing them in the past, even during periods of abstinence.

Personal Resources

The next area to consider encompasses the client's personal psychological resources. Has he/she been successful in other areas of life in setting goals, changing behavior, and completing tasks? If so, outpatient treatment is more feasible. Another aspect of personal resources is cognitive functioning. If the client shows significant cognitive deficits in memory, attention, abstraction, or problem solving, a higher level of care may be considered. Otherwise, the client may have difficulty with retaining information presented in treatment or generating successful ways to avoid drinking.

Other Psychological Problems

As noted earlier in the chapter, persons with drinking problems often have other significant psychological problems. The clinician must assess these problems, and also determine level of care based on the appropriate setting for treatment of these other problems. If a client presents with serious depression, suicidality must be assessed and appropriate precautions taken.

Attitudes about Treatment

Although difficult areas to assess, the client's commitment to treatment and desire to change are important factors in selecting level of care (as well as selecting initial treatment approach). The client who is ambivalent but willing to come to treatment may respond better to a more intensive program that can provide a higher density of reinforcement for attending treatment and making changes. However, sometimes the client's ambivalence makes it impossible to provide treatment in a more intensive setting, because the client is unwilling to disrupt his/her life to the extent required for such a program.

Practical Concerns

There are a number of practical concerns that the clinician must consider. Although certain therapeutic approaches might consider these issues evidence of client "denial," my colleagues and I view practical matters as real barriers to treatment and work with the client to overcome these barriers. Some practical barriers revolve around employment—whether the client can get time off from work, whether the job is in jeopardy, whether the employer is willing to support treatment, or whether missing any more work would result in termination of employment. If the client's job is in jeopardy, then pushing for inpatient treatment is likely to result in the loss of the client.

A second concern is the client's financial condition. Can the client afford to take time off from work and experience a reduction in income while he/she collects temporary disability (if sick time is not available)? If not, outpatient treatment, or a partial hospital program that allows the person to work, will be appropriate. Another financial concern is the client's ability to pay for treatment.

Other practical concerns revolve around transportation and child care. Can the client get to outpatient appointments? Does the client have a driver's license, and if not, is other transportation available? Is child care available if the person has to be hospitalized? If not, a day treatment setting may be preferred.

The clinician must be sensitive to a whole host of other idiosyncratic practical concerns. Research has long shown that clients with alcoholism are more likely to become involved with and remain in treatment if their immediate needs are recognized (e.g., Chafetz et al., 1962), so this becomes an important concern when initiating treatment.

Personal Preferences

Finally, the client's own preferences about the treatment must be considered carefully. If the client feels strongly about wanting to be in a hospital or residential treatment program, the clinician should listen carefully to this request, even if the initial assessment suggests that outpatient treatment may be feasible. Similarly, if the client wants outpatient treatment, it may perhaps be attempted even if the clinician believes that a more intensive treatment is preferable.

General Considerations

In general, the selection of the initial treatment setting must be seen as a tentative decision. Often an initial contract must be established that includes the client's preferred setting, but with specification of the circumstances that will dictate a different level of care. For example, if the clinician believes that the client will find it extremely difficult to discontinue drinking on an outpatient basis, but this is the client's desire, then an initial contract may involve a plan for reducing or stopping drinking, learning skills to support that plan, and a time limit. If the person is unsuccessful within the specified time frame, then the contract will be reviewed and alternative settings considered. Thus, although the initial setting decision is important, continuing to consider and discuss other treatment settings is an important early step in the treatment process.

Selection of Treatment Modalities

If a client is referred to inpatient, residential, or intensive outpatient treatment, a mixture of treatment modalities will be included in the treatment. Six major treatment modalities are available for the provision of alcoholism treatment: self-help groups, individual therapy, group therapy, couple therapy, family therapy, and intensive treatment programs. In the ambulatory setting, the clinician has more flexibility in selecting among these treatment modalities.

Self-Help Groups

AA is the most commonly utilized self-help group. With groups in all 50 states, as well as more than 150 countries throughout the world, AA is widely available. AA offers a specific approach to recovery, rooted in the view that alcoholism is a physical, emotional, and spiritual disease with no cure, but that the disease can be arrested. Recovery is viewed as a lifelong process that involves working the Twelve Steps of AA and abstaining from the use of alcohol (for a detailed description of AA, see McCrady & Irvine, 1989). The only requirement for membership in AA is a desire to stop drinking, and members do not have to pay dues or join the organization. Persons who become involved with AA usually attend different meetings; have a relationship with an AA sponsor, who helps them with their recovery; and become involved with other AA-related activities, ranging from making the coffee before meetings to going on "commitments," where members of one AA group speak at another group. More active involvement is correlated with more successful change (Emrick, Tonigan, Montgomery, & Little, 1993).

Research suggests that persons most likely to affiliate with AA have a history of using social supports as a way to cope with problems, experience loss of control over their drinking, drink more per occasion than persons who do not affiliate, experience more anxiety about their drinking, believe that alcohol enhances their mental functioning, and are more religious or spiritual (Emrick et al., 1993). Outpatient treatment to facilitate involvement with AA (Twelve-Step facilitation) has been found to be as effective as other forms of outpatient therapy in controlled trials, and some evidence suggests that clients receiving Twelve-Step facilitation are more likely to maintain total abstinence from alcohol than clients receiving more behaviorally oriented treatments (Project MATCH Research Group, 1997b).

Alternative self-help groups have developed in recent years, as noted at the beginning of this chapter. SMART is a self-help approach based largely on cognitive-behavioral principles. SMART offers several steps to recovery, emphasizing awareness of irrational beliefs, self-perceptions, and expectancies as core to successful change. SMART suggests abstinence as a preferred drinking goal, but emphasizes personal choice. SOS was developed largely in response to the spiritual aspects of AA, and does not invoke a Higher Power as a part of the change process. Women for Sobriety is a self-help approach for women that emphasizes women's issues such as assertiveness, self-confidence, and autonomy as a part of the change process. MM draws upon behavioral principles to accomplish moderate drinking outcomes. All of these alternative approaches are more compatible with behavioral approaches than is AA, but none are as widely available to clients.

Individual Treatment

Individual therapy is offered widely on an outpatient basis. Few data are available to guide the choice of individual versus group therapy. The literature on women with alcoholism is replete with suggestions that women respond better to individual than to group therapy, but empirical support for that assertion is lacking. Similar assertions apply to the treatment of elderly persons who have alcoholism, with a similar lack of empirical support.

Group Therapy

There is a strong belief in the alcohol field that group therapy is preferable to individual therapy (although see above in regard to women and the elderly). Group therapy is more economical to provide, and the interaction among group members provides opportunities for modeling, feedback, and behavioral rehearsal that are less available in the individual setting. Behavioral models for providing group therapy to individuals (Monti, Abrams, Kadden, & Cooney, 1989) and to clients with alcoholism and their spouses/partners (O'Farrell & Cutter, 1984) are well documented. Clients who are able to function in a group setting and who do not require intensive individual attention because of other psychological problems can be assigned to group therapy.

Couple Therapy

A number of studies have suggested that involving the spouse/partner in alcoholism treatment will increase the probability of a positive treatment outcome (reviewed in Epstein & McCrady, 1998). Despite the empirical evidence, traditional alcoholism counselors prefer individual or group therapy over couple therapy, emphasizing the importance of a

focus on personal change before relationship change. Models for treatments that integrate individual and relationship treatment are available (McCrady & Epstein, 1995). Couple therapy is most appropriate for clients who have a stable relationship in which the partner is willing to be involved in treatment, and can function in a supportive manner in the early phases of treatment. Couples where there has been severe domestic violence, or in which one partner's commitment to the relationship is highly ambivalent, are less appropriate for couple therapy.

Techniques have also been developed to provide treatment to partners of people with alcoholism, separately from treatment for the people themselves. Behavioral groups that emphasize personal decision making, communication, and limit setting around drinking are effective in motivating individuals with alcoholism to seek treatment or decrease drinking (Miller et al., 1999; Sisson & Azrin, 1986; Thomas, Santa, Bronson, & Oyserman, 1987). Al-Anon offers a self-help approach to partners and other family members affected by alcoholism.

Family Therapy

Despite a strong interest in alcoholism in the family therapy field, models for working with whole families where alcoholism is present are scarce. Within the self-help area, Alateen is available for teens affected by a family member's alcoholism, and Alatot is available for younger family members.

Intensive Treatment Programs

Although technically a treatment setting rather than a modality, intensive treatment programs have such a specific and defined role in alcoholism treatment that they can be considered a treatment modality. The "Minnesota model" of treatment (Sheehan & Owen, 1999) is an intensive treatment approach that includes group therapy, education, self-help group involvement, and some individual counseling. Programs based on the Minnesota model emphasize confrontation of denial, acceptance that one is "an alcoholic" who is "powerless over alcohol," development of caring and interdependent relationships, and commitment to AA involvement. Over time, Minnesota model programs have incorporated many behavioral strategies and techniques, including social skills and relaxation training, as well as RP techniques.

Minnesota model programs have been marketed as the most effective approach to alcoholism treatment, but data are lacking to support these claims. Most research on these programs has involved the evaluation of a single treatment program, and all the evaluations have been of private treatment centers. The evaluations suggest substantial levels of abstinence among persons receiving treatment (see, e.g., Filstead, 1991; Stinchfield & Owen, 1998), but the subjects in these studies tend to be good-prognosis patients, and without appropriate controls no inferences can be drawn about the relative efficacy of these treatments compared to other approaches. Their wide visibility has made them the choice of many individuals with alcoholism and their families.

Selection of Treatment Models

Many different treatment models are available to the clinician. A complete description of techniques is beyond the scope of this chapter, and the reader is referred to McCrady and Epstein (1999) for a practitioner-oriented description of techniques with the best empirical support for their effectiveness.

Broadly speaking, behavioral treatment techniques include stimulus control procedures, consequence control procedures, cognitive restructuring techniques, behavioral skills training, and behavioral couple therapy techniques. In addition, behavior therapists have integrated antidipsotropic medications with behavioral contracting procedures (disulfiram [Antabuse] in the United States) as well as naltrexone (Revia). Other treatment models are grounded in the disease conception of alcoholism (Sheehan & Owen, 1999) or family systems models (McCrady & Epstein, 1996).

Enhancing and Maintaining Motivation to Change

Once a decision has been made about the level of care and the client has entered treatment, the clinician needs to continue to focus on motivation to be in treatment and to change.

Techniques to enhance motivation include feedback, use of motivational interviewing techniques, mutual goal setting and decision making, treatment contracting, and the instillation of hope. Three clinical examples illustrate some of these techniques.

Bill P (described earlier in this chapter) began treatment quite tentatively. He was willing to complete some more standardized assessment of his drinking, and we completed a 1-month TLFB (Sobell et al., 1980), the Rutgers Consequences of Use Questionnaire (RCU; Rhines, McCrady, Morgan, & Hirsch, 1997), and a decisional balance sheet (Marlatt & Gordon, 1985; see Figure 9.2). Based on this information, I provided him with a standardized feedback sheet (Figure 9.5) about his drinking. The sheet provided data about how his drinking compared to national norms (Miller, Zweben, DiClemente, & Rychtarik, 1995), as well as information about his peak BAL, usual BAL, and negative consequences of his drinking. He found the feedback interesting, and asked questions about alcohol metabolism, epidemiological surveys, and alcohol and health effects. Although Diana was somewhat impatient with this conversation, I thought that Bill's interest in learning more about alcohol and its effects was a positive sign of his beginning attachment to the treatment process.

We discussed drinking goals, and I suggested the MM guidelines for drinking for men (MM, 2000) of no more than 14 drinks in a week, no more than 4 drinking days per week, and no more than four drinks per occasion. He indicated that he wanted to continue with daily drinking, but with a limit of three drinks per day. Diana was agreeable, saying that if he kept to this limit she would be "thrilled." Although his selected goal was higher than I would have liked, I agreed, in order to engage him further in treatment. I then gave him his first "homework" assignment—to initiate self-recording of his drinking (see Figure 9.3). The assignment of homework serves as a useful behavioral probe for level of motivation, and I was pleased when he returned to the next session with completed self-recording cards.

Suzanne was a 39-year-old computer programmer whom I treated in outpatient therapy as part of a treatment research project. Suzanne drank daily, typically consuming three glasses of wine per day. She had made a number of

---

Couple Feedback Sheet

For the Person Who Drinks:

1. Based on the information I obtained during the assessment, I calculated the number of "standard drinks" you consumed in a typical week, during the last month:
   - Total number of standard drinks per week   _____
   - Average number of standard drinks per day   _____
2. When we look at everyone who drinks in the United States, you have been drinking more than approximately _____ percent of the population of women/men in the country.
3. I also estimated your highest and average blood alcohol level (BAL) in the past month. Your BAL is based on how many standard drinks you consume, the length of time over which you drink that much, whether you are a man or a woman, and how much you weigh. So,
   - Your estimated peak BAL in an average week was   _____
   - Your estimated average BAL in an average week was   _____
   This is a measure of now intoxicated you typically become. In this state, the legal intoxication limit is _____ or higher.
4. You have experienced many negative consequences from drinking. Here are some of the most important:

   _____   _____
   _____   _____
   _____   _____

For the Partner:

1. You have been trying many ways to cope with your wife/husband's drinking. The things you have tried the most include:

   _____   _____
   _____   _____
   _____   _____

For the Couple:

1. You have a number of areas of your relationship that you are concerned about. Some are concerns for both of you:

   _____   _____
   _____   _____
   _____   _____

2. Some concerns are mostly concerns for the husband:

   _____   _____
   _____   _____

3. Some concerns are mostly concerns for the wife:

   _____   _____
   _____   _____
   _____   _____

FIGURE 9.5. Drinking feedback sheet for a couple.

unsuccessful attempts to stop drinking and felt that she had completely lost control over her drinking. She was concerned about her ability to be alert and available to her children in the evenings when she was drinking, particularly since her husband traveled frequently for his business. Suzanne sought treatment voluntarily, and wanted to abstain from drinking completely. Despite her self-referral to treatment and her self-defined need for abstinence, Suzanne reacted to the same structured feedback quite differently than Bill did. She

had provided information for the TLFB and completed the RCU, but when I gave her feedback that she had been drinking an average of 21.5 drinks per week, she told me that this figure was too high and that our measure was not very accurate. She also indicated that she viewed herself as participating in a research study, not as being in therapy, so she thought it important that we have accurate data. I did not argue with her perspective, agreeing that she was in a research study, but that I hoped that the study was helpful to her. She continued with treatment, and several weeks later commented spontaneously, "You know, I know that I'm in treatment, and I really need it. I think I was just protecting my ego at the beginning by focusing on the research part so much."

Anne was a 32-year-old, married college graduate who was working as a cocktail waitress and was the mother of a 20-month-old daughter, Breanne. Her husband, Charlie, was working full-time and enrolled in a doctoral program in mechanical engineering. She entered treatment as part of our women's treatment research program. She was a daily drinker with a varying pattern of consumption. During the evenings when her husband was at school, she drank one or two bottles of wine. When he was home, her typical consumption was one glass of wine with dinner. She also drank at the end of her shift at work, often consuming four to six beers on those evenings. When I gave her the feedback about her alcohol consumption, indicating that her level of consumption placed her in the 99th percentile of women, her eyes filled with tears and she looked visibly distraught, saying repeatedly, "I knew it was bad, but I never knew it was this bad."

As treatment progressed, Anne made few changes in her drinking. She canceled or changed appointments, and said on several occasions, "If I didn't like you, I'd probably just quit the whole thing." She continued:

A: I really like to drink. When Charlie is at school, I make myself a nice dinner—a lamb chop, a salad—and have an excellent bottle of wine. No one bothers me, and I enjoy myself. But I know I should stop because of Breanne.

[As part of the treatment protocol, we had completed a decisional matrix, and I suggested that we return to that form.]

T: Anne, let's look at your decisional matrix again. We did this a few weeks ago. When you look at it now, what strikes you?

A: Everything on it is still true. I'm not being a good mother with all this drinking. I'm out of it at night, and I have no energy during the day. I just plop her in front of the television, and she watches *Teletubbies*. I keep thinking about when she gets older—do I want her to have a drunken mother?

T: It seems as though those feelings are very strong right now, but it's hard for you to keep them in the front of your mind each day. I wonder if you could review this sheet every day at some point. Would that help?

A: I think so. I can look at it while Breanne is eating her breakfast—my motivation would be sitting right in front of me then. I'll try that.

Anne began reviewing her decisional matrix every day. The task seemed helpful for about a month, and she began to decrease her drinking, joined a gym, and came to treatment regularly. However, these changes were short-lived, and she fairly quickly reverted to her pattern of erratic treatment attendance and heavy drinking.

Selection of Drinking Goals

The final major area to consider in treatment planning is the selection of drinking goals. Traditional approaches to alcoholism treatment view abstinence as the only appropriate drinking goal, because these approaches view alcoholism as a progressive disease that can only be arrested with abstinence. Behavioral clinicians have examined alternatives to abstinence and have developed a number of strategies to teach clients how to drink moderately. Although better accepted as a goal for individuals with alcohol abuse (rather than dependence), moderation training continues to be controversial, and the clinician who elects to provide such treatment may be vulnerable to criticism from the traditional, mainstream alcoholism treatment community.

A number of studies suggest that the long-term outcomes of alcoholism include reduced drinking as one outcome (e.g., Helzer et al., 1985; Vaillant, 1983), but data about the success of moderation training are more mixed. Two European studies have found that giving clients the opportunity to select treatment goals increases compliance with treatment and may improve treatment outcome (Ojehegan & Berglund, 1989; Orford & Keddie, 1986).

I have argued in favor of abstinence as a preferred treatment goal (see, e.g., McCrady, 1992; Nathan & McCrady, 1987), and continue to view it as the preferred treatment goal. Abstinence is clearly defined, and is in accord with usual clinical practice for alcoholism treatment in the United States. Also, agreeing readily to a goal of controlled drinking may reinforce a client's distorted view that alcohol is important and necessary to his/her daily functioning.

Under certain circumstances, however, the use of a reduced drinking goal may be appropriate. Moderation may be used as a provisional goal to engage a client in treatment, or may be used when the client will not agree to abstinence but does want assistance to change (as with Bill P). A moderate drinking goal is also more appropriate if a client shows few signs of alcohol dependence or withdrawal, has a history of being able to drink in moderation, does not have medical or psychological problems that would be exacerbated by continued drinking, is younger, and does not have a family history of alcoholism (Rosenberg, 1993). If the clinician and client select a moderation goal, a period of initial abstinence usually makes it easier for the client to drink moderately. In selecting a moderation goal, the clinician should be careful to help the client recognize the current and potential negative consequences of excessive drinking, and should help the client make an informed and thoughtful choice in selecting a treatment goal. The clinician should also view any initial drinking goal (abstinence or moderation) as a tentative goal, to be reevaluated as therapy progresses.

Initiating Abstinence

For clients with goals of abstinence, the therapist has a variety of alternatives for helping clients initiate abstinence. With a client whose goal is moderation, the most conservative approach is to initiate a period of abstinence, and then gradually reintroduce alcohol. As noted above, several detoxification alternative strategies are available, including inpatient detoxification, ambulatory detoxification, "cold turkey" detoxification (in which the client simply stops drinking abruptly), or a graduated program of reduction of drinking over a period of weeks until the client reaches abstinence. A case example illustrates a graduated program of reduction of drinking.

Steve was a 48-year-old, homeless, unemployed man with a long history of heroin,

cocaine, and alcohol dependence. He had had two previous extended periods of abstinence from alcohol and drugs (2 years and 6 years). He entered treatment after heroin detoxification, but was still drinking an average of eight drinks per day (usually a half pint of hard liquor plus one to two beers). He was healthy and had no history of alcohol withdrawal symptoms. No inpatient detoxification facility was available to him, given his homeless and economically destitute state. Initial treatment focused on helping him achieve a stable housing situation and obtaining temporary General Assistance (welfare). Following these social interventions, the therapist (one of our practicum students) began to focus on his drinking. Steve expressed a strong preference for a program of graduated reduction in drinking. He was evaluated by a physician at the local free clinic, and was medically cleared. We began by having him record his drinking for 1 week to establish a clear baseline. We then set a program to reduce his drinking by 15% per week, or eight drinks per week. We discussed specific strategies to achieve this goal each week, and he continued to monitor his drinking. During the alcohol reduction period, Steve reestablished contact with a former long-term girlfriend who had terminated their relationship when he relapsed to alcohol and heroin use. She had heard that he was off heroin, and expressed interest in being involved with him again. Her presence provided a strong incentive for him to follow the alcohol reduction program, because she was unaware that he had been drinking. The program progressed smoothly, and he stopped drinking after 7 weeks.

Developing a Functional Analysis

As described above, completing a behavioral assessment of the factors associated with a client's drinking includes both a structured and a qualitative dimension, and incorporates clinical interviewing, questionnaires, and self-recording of drinking and drinking urges. Suzanne, described briefly above, provides an excellent illustration of the complexity and results of the behavioral assessment process.

Suzanne came from a large Jewish family, many of whom made demands on her. She had three daughters, 10, 8, and 4 years old. Her drinking had increased 5 years prior to treatment after a car accident that took the life of her fraternal twin brother. They had gone out to a Bruce Springsteen concert together, and he had had several drinks at the concert. An autopsy after the accident revealed that he had also been using cocaine, but Suzanne was completely unaware of his drug use. She blamed herself for allowing him to drive, and for not insisting that he stop when he began to drive in a reckless manner. She began to drink immediately after the accident, and quickly established a pattern of daily consumption of a half bottle of wine per day. Although the amount was not that great, she reported that the alcohol was very important to her being able to avoid her overwhelming sadness about her brother's death, especially at the end of the day.

The results of the behavioral assessment revealed a more complex pattern of drinking antecedents. On the DPQ, Suzanne rated emotional antecedents as most important, endorsing feelings of sadness, hurt, and frustration. She also indicated that certain environments were triggers for drinking, such as specific restaurants, times of the day (evening), and activities (particularly watching television). Other major triggers emerged from her self-recording cards—her interactions with extended family members, interactions with friends, and situations related to her children. Her parents were highly critical of how she was raising her children. Suzanne and her husband, Josh, were attending a conservative temple, kept kosher in their home, did not allow violent video games, and expected each daughter to participate in a fine arts activity (either music, dance, or painting). Her parents believed that their grandchildren's upbringing and Suzanne and Josh's standards were too strict and conservative, and were vocal in their criticisms. Other familial stressors included her interactions with a sister who was getting divorced and a cousin who was in economic straits. Each contacted Suzanne on a regular basis, demanding either her attention or her money. A summary of Suzanne's functional analysis is provided in Figure 9.6.

Early Sobriety Strategies

Early sobriety strategies focus on helping the client maintain abstinence from alcohol. Cognitive-behavioral techniques vary with the individual, but may include stimulus control strategies to avoid or rearrange high-risk situations; development of skills to deal with urges to drink; learning to think differently about drinking and not drinking; identification of behaviors alternative to drinking in high-risk situations; developing alternative ways to obtain the reinforcers previously obtained from alcohol; and learning to refuse drinks.

Stimulus Control

Stimulus control strategies are designed to alter environmental cues for drinking by avoiding the cue, rearranging it, or implementing different responses in the same environment. Stimulus control strategies are compatible with the AA suggestion to be attuned to "people, places, and things." Work with Suzanne and Bill illustrates stimulus control strategies.

With Suzanne, stimulus control strategies served a major function early in treatment. She developed specific strategies to deal with a number of the environmental high-risk situations identified in her functional analysis. Her first approach was to avoid such situations whenever possible. She suggested to Josh that they eat only at restaurants without a liquor license, and asked that they decline several social invitations where alcohol would be the main focus of the evening (such as cocktail parties). The one situation that she could not avoid was the end of the day after the children had gone to bed. Her usual routine had been to complete the dinner dishes and any other picking up while Josh helped the girls get ready for bed, and to then sit down in the den with her wine and the television after reading them a story. She decided that she needed to disrupt this pattern, and thought that if she got ready for bed herself and then curled up on the couch with a book and a cup of herbal tea, she would experience less urge to drink. It took her 3 weeks before she got to a bookstore to buy some light novels, but once she had the books, she was able to implement this plan with success, except when she was upset.

Bill's treatment was complicated by his unwillingness to begin treatment with a period of abstinence and by his skepticism about the effectiveness of any treatment interventions. Bill's drinking pattern was fairly stereotypic—

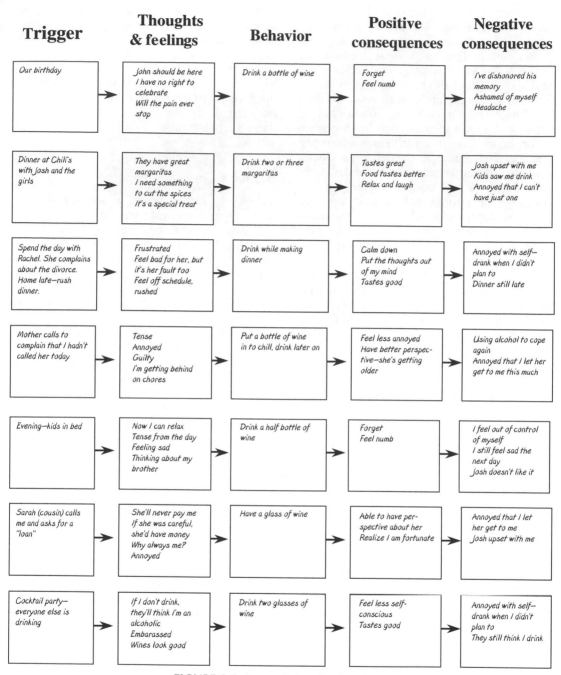

Trigger	Thoughts & feelings	Behavior	Positive consequences	Negative consequences
Our birthday	John should be here / I have no right to celebrate / Will the pain ever stop	Drink a bottle of wine	Forget / Feel numb	I've dishonored his memory / Ashamed of myself / Headache
Dinner at Chili's with Josh and the girls	They have great margaritas / I need something to cut the spices / It's a special treat	Drink two or three margaritas	Tastes great / Food tastes better / Relax and laugh	Josh upset with me / Kids saw me drink / Annoyed that I can't have just one
Spend the day with Rachel. She complains about the divorce. Home late—rush dinner.	Frustrated / Feel bad for her, but it's her fault too / Feel off schedule, rushed	Drink while making dinner	Calm down / Put the thoughts out of my mind / Tastes good	Annoyed with self—drank when I didn't plan to / Dinner still late
Mother calls to complain that I hadn't called her today	Tense / Annoyed / Guilty / I'm getting behind on chores	Put a bottle of wine in to chill, drink later on	Feel less annoyed / Have better perspective—she's getting older	Using alcohol to cope again / Annoyed that I let her get to me this much
Evening—kids in bed	Now I can relax / Tense from the day / Feeling sad / Thinking about my brother	Drink a half bottle of wine	Forget / Feel numb	I feel out of control of myself / I still feel sad the next day / Josh doesn't like it
Sarah (cousin) calls me and asks for a "loan"	She'll never pay me / If she was careful, she'd have money / Why always me? / Annoyed	Have a glass of wine	Able to have perspective about her / Realize I am fortunate	Annoyed that I let her get to me / Josh upset with me
Cocktail party—everyone else is drinking	If I don't drink, they'll think I'm an alcoholic / Embarassed / Wines look good	Drink two glasses of wine	Feel less self-conscious / Tastes good	Annoyed with self—drank when I didn't plan to / They still think I drink

FIGURE 9.6. Suzanne's functional analysis.

drinking began at 6:00 P.M., and he began anticipating his first drink at about 5:00. However, if Diana was away visiting family or friends, he would start drinking early in the day. He also drank more heavily when entertaining company at home, but drank less heavily when they had social plans (dinner, movies, lectures) in the evening. We identified several simple stimulus control strategies: listening to music, making plans to go out, renting a movie to watch in the evening. He implemented these successfully and reported that they helped him limit his drinking, except when he was emotionally upset. When he and

Diana were entertaining at home, his most difficult time was sitting at the dinner table after the meal was done but partially filled bottles of wine remained on the table. Serving dessert and coffee in the living room provided a simple strategy to assist him in restricting his alcohol intake.

Dealing with Urges

As individuals decrease their drinking or initiate abstinence, they experience urges or cravings for alcohol. Providing the client with a framework for understanding that urges are learned responses to drinking situations, and that urges abate if unfulfilled, is helpful. Marlatt and Gordon (1985) suggest the use of imagery to help cope with urges, and describe either acceptance-oriented imagery (e.g., surfing with the urge) or action-oriented imagery (e.g., attacking the urge with a samurai sword).

Suzanne struggled with urges to drink, particularly when anything reminded her of her twin brother's death. During therapy, we focused on a variety of aspects of her feelings about her brother's death, and also addressed the urges more directly. Suzanne's initial reaction to the imagery techniques was negative, saying that she wasn't a person who imagined things much. She clearly needed some way to cope with these rather strong urges, so I pushed her a bit to try:

T: I appreciate that you don't think of yourself as imaginative, but maybe I can help you out. Just humor me for a minute, and let's see if we can come up with an image that grabs you. It doesn't matter what the image is—you could imagine climbing a mountain and coming down the other side, or spraying the urge with a fire extinguisher.

S: (*Smiling*) I know what I can imagine— I could picture you jumping out of the bottle and shaking your head at me.

T: OK—should I look mean?

S: No, just having you there would help me deal with it.

T: All right, I can live with that.

S: In fact, I could picture a row of wine bottles—with you coming out of the first one, then showing me all the disgusting things in the other one.

T: So what would be disgusting? Ticks?

S: Ticks would be good, and maybe cockroaches too.

T: Let's try this out.

At that point, I had her practice using the imagery in an imagined urge situation. Remarkably, she used the imagery frequently and found it helpful.

A second technique for coping with urges is to enlist the assistance of a family member or friend. Persons involved with AA are told to call someone in the AA program when they feel the urge to drink, and usually receive telephone numbers from several members. Clients not involved with AA can seek other sources of support. Suzanne, for example, asked her husband to help her when she had the urge to drink. She asked that he remind her of why she had stopped drinking, and to say, "Of course, it has to be your decision."

Addressing Cognitive Distortions about Alcohol

People who drink heavily hold stronger positive expectancies about the effects of alcohol than do people who drink more lightly (Brown, Goldman, & Christiansen, 1985). Clients may believe that drinking facilitates social interactions, enhances sexual responsivity, allows them to forget painful events or feelings, or makes them more capable. These beliefs are often deeply held and difficult to challenge, particularly if a client continues to drink. Several cognitive strategies may help. First, effecting a period of abstinence will allow the client to experience many situations without alcohol—an experience that often leads to reevaluation with little input from the therapist. At some point, many clients are impressed with the vacuous nature of drunken conversation; the undesirable physical appearance, behaviors, and odors that accompany high BALs; and the shallow nature of drinking relationships. The wise therapist watches carefully for these observations and underscores their importance and self-relevance. If a client does not have such experiences spontaneously, the therapist facilitates new views of drunken comportment by developing a relatively safe way for the client to observe intoxicated behavior—either through movies or videotapes, or through visits to a local bar (accompanied by someone who is aware of and supports the client's abstinence).

A second strategy reported in the self-change literature (Ludwig, 1985) is the ability to think past anticipated positive benefits of drinking to the clear, though often delayed, negative consequences of drinking. The therapist and client can generate a list of negative consequences of drinking, and use imaginal rehearsal in the session to help the client pair positive thoughts with the list of negatives. Continued rehearsal in the natural environment is then important.

Third, some clients develop a set of erroneous beliefs about their drinking that then set them up for drinking. Common beliefs include "I've been doing so well, I can just drink tonight," or "I'll have just one." Although for some clients moderate drinking is possible, for others their history of drinking until they lose control is in direct opposition to a belief in control, and they need to learn how to counter these beliefs.

Work with Steve provides a simple illustration of cognitive strategies to address positive expectations about drinking. Steve had a long history of loss-of-control drinking. After a period of abstinence, he began to think, "I could have just one beer, and that would be fine." His therapist questioned the accuracy of that belief. Steve readily acknowledged that he had never been able to control his drinking in the past, that if his girlfriend found out she'd be very upset and probably leave him, and that relapses to heavy drinking usually led him to use of heroin. He and his therapist developed a simple cognitive formula to use when he thought about drinking: "1 = 32 = 10," meaning that for him, one drink would lead to a quart of liquor (32 ounces), which would lead to heroin use (10 bags a day).

Alternative/Distracting Behaviors

Drinking is a time-occupying activity, and clients may see limited alternatives to help them through times when they previously would drink. Discussion of specific behavioral alternatives to drinking that are both time-occupying and mentally or physically absorbing is another helpful strategy early in treatment.

Steve's experiences provide a particularly powerful example of the alternatives that highly motivated clients may find. After Steve had found a room in a rooming house and had begun the detoxification process, he was faced with the daunting prospect of filling his completely unstructured days. Some of his time was occupied with the time-consuming work of the poor—getting back and forth to the soup kitchen, waiting at the free clinic for medical services, getting an appropriate identification card so that he was eligible for other charitable programs such as clothing distribution programs. But even with these necessary activities, he had hours and hours of free time. Steve began to address this challenge by creating his own activities. He obtained a library card and scheduled specific times for himself at the library. Instead of reading randomly or recreationally, he decided to read about the Crusades, which sparked an interest for him in medieval Christianity. A lapsed Catholic, he decided to attend Mass again, and began to attend daily. His daily attendance led to involvement in a Bible study group, and he became a thoughtful and passionate participant. A creative man, Steve then began to write short stories with religious themes.

Identifying Alternative Ways to Obtain Reinforcers

Among the more compelling aspects of alcohol and drug use are the psychoactive properties of the substance. In the short term, large quantities of alcohol are effective in deadening negative affect, decreasing obsessional thoughts, and decreasing muscle tension, although these effects do not endure over the long term. Alcoholic beverages also have distinctive and desirable tastes that cannot be replaced with other beverages.

An important aspect of the functional analysis is articulating the client's perception of positive consequences of drinking. The clinician can address the power of these perceived reinforcers in several ways: helping the client develop alternative means of obtaining the same types of reinforcement; challenging the client's belief that the reinforcers occur (such as questioning whether the client is in fact more socially adept and appealing after consuming a quart of vodka); helping the client reevaluate the importance of these reinforcers; and/or helping the client identify other classes of reinforcers that might be valued more highly in the long run (such as valuing spirituality more highly than hedonism).

Drink Refusal Skills

Some drinkers find the interpersonal aspects of abstinence difficult. For them, identification of interpersonal situations as high-risk for drinking, development of effective responses, and rehearsal of these responses all form an important component of treatment. Early research (Chaney, O'Leary, & Marlatt, 1978) suggested that giving a quick response is strongly associated with successful change. Suggested components of an effective way to refuse drinks include indicating clearly that the individual does not want an alcoholic beverage, requesting an alternative beverage, communicating confidence and comfort with the request, and being persistent in the face of social pressure (Foy, Miller, Eisler, & O'Toole, 1976). In addition, clients who face excessive social pressure may be advised to consider avoiding certain social situations or persons.

Although the guidelines for refusing drinks appear simple, client beliefs and expectations often make the drink refusal process difficult. Common cognitions include "Everyone will think I'm an alcoholic," "My host will be offended if I don't drink," or "People will think I'm too good for them if I don't drink." As with other distorted beliefs, the clinician can provide alternative frameworks for thinking about drink refusal situations, suggesting that most people really are uninterested in others' drinking, or that hosts are most concerned that guests are enjoying themselves. Many clients also experience ambivalence about not drinking, and find that the most difficult part of the drink refusal process is internal rather than interpersonal.

Another complicated dimension of drink refusal is the amount of personal information the client wishes to divulge in the process of refusing a drink. Most people share different levels of personal information with others, depending on the closeness of the relationship and their knowledge of the other person's behavior and attitudes. For persons to whom a client does not want to disclose his/her drinking problem, we encourage use of a simple "No, thank you," or, if pressed, a simple response that would discourage pushing without being revealing, such as "I'm watching my weight and can't afford the calories," "I'm on medication that doesn't allow me to drink," or "My stomach's been acting up—I better pass." None of these replies protect the client against future offers, but each is effective in the moment. For closer relationships, the client makes a decision about when, where, and how much to reveal.

Two clinical examples illustrate these points. Steve was living in a boarding house, and had friendly, sociable neighbors who liked to drink on the front porch. These neighbors were from the Portuguese Azores and spoke virtually no English. After accepting a beer from them one day, he insisted to his therapist that he could not refuse because he did not speak Portuguese. The therapist suggested that perhaps the word "No," spoken with a smile and a hand gesture, might be understood even in Portuguese. Steve acknowledged that his difficulty with refusing the drink came from his desire to drink, and that a friendly "No" would certainly work.

Suzanne did not want anyone to know that she had a drinking problem or that she was abstaining. This stance posed problems for an upcoming cocktail party. Strategizing, Suzanne decided ahead that she would drink seltzer water during the evening, and that she would attempt to forestall offers of drinks by keeping a glass of seltzer in her hand at all times. If offered a drink, she decided to tell people that she had had some health problems that might be made worse by her drinking, so she was sticking to seltzer. Although she was concerned that one of her friends (a social worker) might surmise that she had an alcohol problem, the evening progressed uneventfully.

Coping Strategies

Clients face challenges beyond those directly related to their drinking. As do clients without drinking problems, clients with such problems face common life difficulties stemming from dysfunctional thoughts, negative affect, and interpersonal conflicts. As clients develop a greater ability to maintain abstinence or moderated drinking, the clinician may devote increasing attention to other problems clients are facing. Clinical techniques to deal with dysfunctional thoughts or social skills deficits can be used readily with clients with drinking problems.

Dealing with Negative Affect

There are multiple sources of negative affect in persons with alcohol abuse or dependence.

As noted earlier in the chapter, comorbidity with other psychiatric disorders is high, with mood and anxiety disorders quite common. Rates of sexual and physical abuse are also elevated among those with alcohol use disorders (Stewart, 1996), and the sequelae of these problems often include a strong negative affective component. In addition, persons who have used alcohol to cope with negative affect over an extended period of time may simply have limited experience with, and limited skills to cope with, the pain that is a part of everyday life.

In focusing on negative affect, a careful assessment of the causes is essential. Intense negative affect associated with another disorder should be treated in accord with the appropriate approach for that disorder. Dealing with negative affect that is not necessarily disorder-based presents different challenges. Full behavioral mood management programs (e.g., Monti et al., 1990) have been developed, although a description of these is beyond the scope of the chapter. However, certain common principles are of value. When clients first reduce or stop drinking, they may experience all emotions, both positive and negative, as unfamiliar and intense. Cognitive reframing to help the clients view these intense emotions as a natural part of the change process may be useful. For clients pursuing a moderation goal, avoiding drinking at times of intense negative affect provides the opportunity to learn alternative coping strategies. Specific coping strategies may vary with the specific type of negative emotion, and may include relaxation, prayer or meditation, increasing the experience of pleasurable events to decrease depression, or use of anger management and assertiveness skills to cope with angry feelings.

Work with Suzanne illustrates several of these principles. The most difficult situations for Suzanne to deal with were any that reminded her of the death of her twin. Their birthday, the anniversary of his death, the celebration of Father's and Mother's Days, holiday celebrations, and special celebratory events for her children that he would have been importantly involved with (such as a bat mitzvah) all elicited intense negative affect and a strong desire to drink. Given that Suzanne had begun drinking heavily right after her twin's death, she had spent little time experiencing grief or even discussing his death and her feelings about it. My initial approach in therapy was to give her opportunities to be exposed to these negative feelings by simply talking about him in the therapy session. Our second approach was to discuss and identify ways to approach the variety of situations that reminded her of him. I saw her over a 6-month period, during which a number of these situations arose naturally. For example, in the week prior to the anniversary of his death, we discussed a number of ways that she could focus on his death and memories. She took one of her children to his gravesite, and they cleaned it up and planted flowers together. On the Saturday of the anniversary of his death, she went to temple with her family, and then she cooked what had been her twin's favorite dinner. The day was sorrowful and she cried several times, but it was the first anniversary that she felt she had honored him rather than shaming him by getting drunk. We also addressed her repetitive, self-blaming thoughts about his death by using cognitive restructuring techniques. She found it difficult not to blame herself for his death, and few cognitive strategies had much impact on the self-blame. She finally was able to begin to think, "I cannot torture myself forever with this blame. If I don't let go of it, I won't be a good mother. He'd be disappointed with me if I let my children down."

Lifestyle Balance and Pleasurable Activities

Marlatt and Gordon (1985) suggest that long-term success is supported by positive lifestyle changes that enhance positive experiences and allow for a balance between responsibilities and pleasure. Although some studies of successful self-changes (e.g., Vaillant & Milofsky, 1982) have found that development of an "alternate dependency" (such as obsessive involvement with work or exercise) is associated with successful long-term abstinence, we typically work toward a more balanced approach. As they begin to change, some of our clients believe that they need to make up for their previous lack of responsibility with a very high level of responsibility to family, job, and home. Taking on major redecorating or remodeling projects, trying to spend every free moment with their children, or cleaning out 10 years' worth of messy drawers and cabinets is not uncommon. This zeal for responsibility can be a double-edged sword for both client and family. Unrelenting attention to responsibilities may be simultaneously satisfying and exhausting and unrewarding, and may lead the client to question the value of not drinking. Family members may be thrilled that the client is taking on responsibility, but may be leery of the stability of the change and be unwilling to give up responsibilities they have assumed. They also may experience the client's enthusiasm as an intrusion on their own independent lives and schedules. Clients should be prepared for such reactions, and the clinician can help reframe the family's response as understandable.

With most clients, it is important for the clinician to suggest the importance of leisure time, pleasurable activities, and self-reinforcement for positive changes made. With Suzanne, helping her identify a half hour per day during which she could relax, read, or exercise was a challenge. She believed that she should devote herself to her daughters—a belief that resulted in her being with them virtually all the time they were home. When they attended school, she focused on housecleaning, cooking, chores, errands, paying bills, and so on. She acknowledged that she was exhausted and tense at the end of the day, and that alcohol had been a good way to "come down." We finally agreed on a half-hour block before lunch during which she would use her exercise bike, read a book of daily meditations, or take a walk. She was only partially successful in these efforts, often citing other responsibilities that took precedence.

Partner/Family Involvement and the Social Context of Treatment

The literature on the treatment of alcoholism suggests that the involvement of some significant social system is associated with positive treatment results. Because of these findings, the clinician's first inclination should be to involve the client's spouse/partner or some significant other in the treatment. There are a number of ways to involve significant others, including using them as sources of information, having them provide differential reinforcement for drinking and abstinence, helping them to provide emotional or practical support, involving them in relationship-focused treatment, providing

treatment to them without the person who drinks, and/or helping the person access new social systems.

Information

Folklore suggests that persons with alcoholism minimize or lie about their drinking and its consequences. The empirical literature suggests that such individuals will provide relatively accurate data when sober and when there are no strong negative consequences for telling the truth (reviewed in Babor, Stephens, & Marlatt, 1987). Despite these results, a number of clinical considerations suggest that obtaining information from a family member may be useful in the assessment phase of treatment. First, clients who are referred to or coerced into treatment are often reluctant to provide full information about their drinking. Collecting data from the referring agent helps the client and clinician both understand the reasons for the referral. Even with self-referred clients, significant others can provide information that may be unavailable to the clients because of problems with memory or recall. In addition, an intimate significant other has usually observed a client over a long period of time and in multiple environments, and may have valuable observations to contribute to the conceptualization of antecedents to drinking.

Responses to Drinking and Abstinence

A second, different type of social system involvement is in the establishment of a network that will provide differential reinforcement contingent on abstinence, and that will facilitate the immediate application of negative consequences contingent on drinking. Such reinforcement may be relatively simple, such as positive comments and encouragement from friends and family, or can involve the negotiation of detailed contracts that specify the consequences of drinking and abstinence. The "community reinforcement approach" (CRA) (Meyers & Smith, 1995) helps clients access potential reinforcers (jobs, families, social clubs), teaches clients and partners behavioral coping skills, and may involve development of contingency contracts to make access to reinforcers contingent on sobriety. In addition, clients may take Antabuse, and compliance may be monitored by a significant other. Evaluations of the CRA approach suggest that clients are significantly more successful than controls in not drinking, maintaining employment, avoiding hospitalizations or jail, and maintaining a stable residence.

In addition to formal treatments that focus on manipulation of environmental contingencies, treatments may also focus on teaching spouses/partners and other family members how to allow the client to experience the naturally occurring negative consequences of drinking. Many spouses/partners protect people with alcoholism from these consequences by covering for the persons at work, doing their chores, lying to friends and family about the drinking, and so on (Orford et al., 1975). Treatment interventions can teach the family members to allow naturally occurring consequences to be experienced by the client. Experience of these negative consequences may increase the client's awareness of the extent and severity of his/her drinking problem, and provide further motivation for change.

Decreasing Cues for Drinking

Significant others may also engage in a number of behaviors that cue further drinking. A wife who wants her husband to stop drinking may nag him repeatedly about the problems his drinking is causing, hoping that her concerns will motivate him to change. Or a husband may try to get his wife to stop drinking by trying to control her behavior through limiting her access to alcohol or tightly controlling their money. Such behaviors often have an unintended and negative effect, eliciting anger or defensiveness from the person with the drinking problem, and leading to further drinking. Helping spouses/partners learn to identify such behaviors, recognize the results of these actions, and learn alternative ways to discuss concerns about drinking may be helpful in decreasing drinking.

Support for Not Drinking

Significant others can provide various types of supports to clients. Support may involve helping a client to implement behavior change, discussing urges to drink, supporting a client's plan to avoid high-risk situations for drinking, or (upon the request of the client) assisting in the implementation of other cognitive or behavioral skills that support sobriety.

Relationship Change

For many clients, important interactions with their spouses/partners, children, parents, or close friends cue drinking. Thus treatment that focuses on changing those interpersonal relationships is another way that significant others may become involved in treatment. These interventions may be couple or family therapy, or parent skills training. Data (McCrady, Stout, Noel, Abrams, & Nelson, 1991) suggest that a focus on changing the couple relationship during conjoint alcoholism treatment results in greater stability of drinking outcomes, fewer separations, and greater couple satisfaction.

Accessing New Social Systems

Some clients have either no social support system or one that strongly supports heavy drinking. For such clients, it is important to access new systems that can reinforce abstinence, or that will be incompatible with heavy drinking. Self-help groups are one potential source of such support. Many religious groups are against the use of alcohol, and serious involvement in such a group can also support abstinence. Many group activities are incompatible with drinking; running, hiking, or cycling groups are examples. Unfortunately, alcohol can be involved in almost any activity, and the therapist and client need to look carefully at activity groups to determine whether the group norm includes drinking.

In summary, decisions about the social context of alcoholism treatment are complicated. The initial assessment should involve at least one significant other. The results of the assessment should reveal what persons are most available for treatment and who might be sources of support and reinforcement. For some clients there are no readily accessible supports, and new support systems need to be developed.

Long-Term Maintenance
Relapse Prevention

Marlatt and Gordon's (1985) RP model is a comprehensive treatment model. Many elements of the treatment model have already been described—identification of high-risk situations for drinking, development of alternative strategies to cope with high-risk situations, enhancing self-efficacy for coping, dealing with positive expectancies about the use of alcohol, and facilitating the development of a balanced lifestyle. An additional and important part of the RP model is to directly address the possibility of relapse and to develop both preventive and responsive strategies related to relapse.

Clients are told that use of alcohol after treatment is not uncommon, and treatment addresses this possibility. Two basic strategies are used. First, clients are asked to develop a list of signs of an impending relapse, including behavioral, cognitive, interpersonal, and affective signs. If a client's spouse/partner is also involved with the treatment, he/she contributes to the list. After this list is developed, we develop a set of possible responses, should these signs arise. Most important is for the client to recognize that these are warning signs that should trigger action, rather than inaction and fatalistic cognitions about the inevitability of relapse.

A second set of strategies involves response to drinking or heavy drinking. We attempt to address the possibility of the AVE (Marlatt & Gordon, 1985) by calling attention to the possibility that they will have catastrophizing cognitions if they drink and rehearsing alternative thoughts. Marlatt and Gordon (1985) also suggest a series of behavioral steps: introducing a behavioral delay (1–2 hours) between an initial drink and any subsequent drinks, getting out of the immediate drinking situation, conducting a functional analysis of the drinking situation during that time, reviewing possible negative consequences of drinking, and calling someone who might be helpful.

There is some research evidence supporting the use of such RP approaches. For example, in our own research (McCrady, Epstein, & Hirsch, 1999), we found that including RP procedures as part of conjoint alcoholism treatment was successful in reducing the length of relapse episodes, compared to conjoint cognitive-behavioral therapy without RP. O'Farrell, Choquette, and Cutter (1998) incorporated RP techniques into their couple therapy treatment by providing additional therapy sessions over the 12 months after initial treatment, and reported less frequent drinking among couples who received the additional therapy.

Maintaining Contact with Clients

Time-limited treatment is appropriate and effective for many clients, and there is good evidence of long-term, sustained improvement following a course of outpatient treatment (Project MATCH Research Group, 1998). However, periods of relapse are common. The clinical strategies for RP described above are intended to minimize periods of problem use and maximize positive outcomes. For some clients, however, alcohol dependence must be viewed as a chronic, relapsing disorder. As with other chronic health problems such as diabetes or rheumatoid arthritis, acute care models that treat individuals and send them on their way may be inappropriate and ineffective. An alternative strategy provides longer-term, low-intensity contact over an extended time interval. During the initial treatment of a client with a history of severe alcohol dependence, multiple treatment episodes, and difficulty maintaining successful change, the clinician may elect to set a different expectancy with the client—that some form of contact will be ongoing and long-term.

Lee was a 54-year-old married man who came to treatment with problems with alcohol dependence and agoraphobia. Treatment focused on both disorders, and he was successful both in becoming abstinent from alcohol and in gradually increasing the distances that he could drive by himself. His home was an hour's drive from my office, and treatment lasted almost 12 months before he could drive to my office without his wife accompanying him. By the end of the year, we were meeting every 2 to 3 weeks. Given that he had been abstinent for a year and was functioning well, we discussed the possibility of termination. His response was instructive:

L: Doctor, I've been drinking a long, long time. One year is just a drop in the bucket in comparison. I think that I need to keep seeing you.

T: Lee, I understand your concerns, but you've been doing well for quite a long time now. Maybe we should just cut down more on how often you come in. How about an appointment in a month, and making it a bit shorter—a half hour instead of an hour?

L: I think that's a good idea. Let's try it.

I gradually tapered the frequency and length of my sessions with Lee, and saw him twice per year, 15 minutes per session, for the last 3½ years of his 5-year course of treatment. He described the importance of the sessions: "I just know I'll have to see you and tell you what I've been doing. It keeps me honest." During those 3½ years, Lee's house burned down, his son was killed in the fire, and his wife had a radical mastectomy. He never indicated a need or desire to meet more frequently, but continued his contacts with me. He did not drink in response to any of these very major life events, saying simply, "Drinking won't change anything, and I'll just be no good to anyone if I drink."

Managing Complicating Conditions

As described earlier in the chapter, clients with alcohol use disorders may present with a myriad of other, complicating conditions. The clinician must assess and develop a treatment plan for the multiple needs of such clients. At a minimum, clinicians should consider possible problems related to housing, transportation, income, occupation/employment, the legal system, the family, child care, medical conditions, and comorbid disorders. Knowledge of services and agencies in the local community, and the development of working relationships with a range of agencies, are essential to the treatment of complicated clients. Rose, Zweben, and Stoffel (1999) provide a comprehensive framework for interfacing with other health and social systems.

The Role of Self-Help Groups

Types of self-help groups have been described in an earlier section of the chapter. Various therapeutic strategies may facilitate involvement in a self-help group, when appropriate. The clinician should first assess whether a client may be a good candidate for self-help group involvement. Clients with very high social anxiety or social phobia, clients who believe that a person should take care of problems alone, and clients with a history of negative experiences with self-help groups may be poorer candidates. Conversely, affiliative clients, those who are used to solving problems with assistance from others, those who are

particularly anxious and concerned about their drinking, those whose social support systems strongly support continued heavy drinking, and those with more severe alcohol dependence are particularly good candidates for AA. Persons who are interested in the social support aspects of self-help, but who explicitly reject some of the constructs associated with AA (such as powerlessness or spirituality) may be best served by referral to an alternative self-help group.

As with all aspects of the therapy, the clinician should use a client-centered approach to the introduction of AA or other self-help groups. Such an approach suggests a dialogue between client and therapist, acknowledgment and discussion of the client's perceptions and concerns, and development of a mutually agreed-upon plan. Because many clients have misconceptions about AA and are unfamiliar with some of the alternative organizations, the clinician should be prepared to describe the organizations and answer questions. It also is helpful for the clinician to have some basic publications from each group available in the office. At times, I may encourage a reluctant client to try a few meetings in order to sample firsthand what actually occurs. We negotiate a very short-term agreement for a specified number of meetings in a specified length of time (such as six meetings in 3 weeks); we agree that if the client continues to be negative or reluctant after trying the groups, we will abandon this idea; and we discuss the client's experiences and perceptions of the self-help group meeting in each therapy session. I use behavioral sampling with other aspects of therapy as well—clients often cannot visualize how a strategy might work without trying it, be it a relaxation technique, an AA meeting, or an assertive response—and I encourage clients to be open to new strategies. In AA, newcomers may be told, "Your best thinking got you here," suggesting that their own coping strategies have been ineffective. Behavioral sampling is based on this same construct.

Therapist Variables

As with any form of therapy, the therapist's relationship with the client and the therapeutic stance assumed by the therapist are important. Empathy, active listening, instillation of hope, the flexible application of therapeutic principles and techniques, and establishing a sense that the therapist and client are working toward mutually agreed-upon goals are essential. Research suggests, in contrast to a confrontational style, that an empathic, motivational style is associated with better treatment outcomes, and that confrontational behaviors by the therapist tend to elicit defensive and counteraggressive behaviors by the client (Miller et al., 1993). Such responses are hardly conducive to a constructive therapeutic alliance.

Working with a client with alcoholism is often difficult, both because of the client's behavior during treatment and because of the history of drinking-related behaviors that the therapist may find repugnant or upsetting. The client may lie about or minimize drinking during treatment. If the spouse/partner is also involved in the treatment, the therapeutic relationship becomes even more complicated. By treating a client with a drinking problem, along with a spouse/partner who wants that client to stop or decrease drinking, the therapist is allied de facto with the spouse/partner. That individual may attempt to enhance his/her alliance with the therapist by echoing the therapist's comments, expressing anger at the client's behavior, being confrontational, or alternatively being submissive and allowing the client to be verbally aggressive or dominant.

Certain therapist attitudes and behaviors appear to be conducive to successful treatment. First is a sense of empathy with the client. The therapist must develop some understanding of the client's subjective experience of entering therapy and the difficulty of admitting behaviors that are personally embarrassing and often not socially sanctioned. In addition, the therapist needs to have some appreciation of the incredible difficulties involved with long-term change in drinking behavior. The therapist may develop this appreciation by attempting to change a deeply ingrained behavior pattern of his/her own, by attending meetings of some self-help group (AA, SMART, SOS), and by listening carefully to clients.

A second important therapist skill is the ability to distinguish between the person and the drinking-related behavior. The client needs to be able to describe drinking-related actions without feeling that the therapist is repulsed, but also without feeling that the therapist condones or accepts such behaviors. This is a delicate balance to achieve, especially when a client describes drinking episodes in a joking manner that may hide embarrassment or disgust with the drinking. The therapist must encourage the client to discuss negative drinking-related behaviors and experience the negative affect associated with thinking about those actions, as a part of enhancing the client's motivation to change. At the same time, the therapist should communicate a sense of hope to the client by anticipating positive changes that might be associated with changes in drinking, and by emphasizing that it is possible for the client to develop skills to change his/her drinking and eliminate the most unacceptable behaviors. Thus the implied message to the client is this:

> "You have done many things when drinking that are distressing to you and to the people around you. The fact that you are in treatment is a statement that you want to change some of these. It is important to talk about things you have done when drinking, because by being aware of them, you will have a strong incentive to stop drinking and stop doing these things. Making changes will take time and a lot of work on your part, but I believe that you will be successful if you stick with treatment."

In other words, the therapist's message is positive about change, but negative about drinking-related behavior.

A third important therapist quality is honesty. Both because of their discomfort and because of their reinforcement history, it is difficult for some clients to honestly report drinking episodes, failed homework assignments, or their feelings and attitudes about being in treatment. The therapist can acknowledge how difficult it is for such a client to be honest, as lying was probably adaptive in the past, but must make it clear that part of therapy involves learning how to be honest. The therapist also must provide a positive model of honesty. The therapist should not ignore the smell of alcohol on a client's breath, and should review homework assigned each week. Attending to the client's behavior teaches the client the importance of following through on commitments, and increases the chances that the therapist and client will be able to identify problems and blocks to progress in treatment.

The therapist also must set clear expectations about both the client's and the therapist's responsibilities to the therapy, and must be able to set appropriate limits. The therapist should set clear expectations for the client: coming to scheduled sessions on time, calling if unable to attend, paying the bill for therapy, coming in sober, and completing assigned homework. The therapist also should make his/her own commitment to therapy clear, by being at sessions on time, being reasonably available by telephone, providing coverage when away, and providing treatments with the best empirical support for their effectiveness. Being clear about expectations for the client's behavior during therapy emphasizes the therapist's commitment to therapy as a serious process.

Client Variables

The clinician must be aware of and sensitive to a number of issues that persons with drinking problems bring to treatment. The emotional experience of the client, his/her beliefs and attitudes, his/her physical state (described in the section on treatment settings), and the social context of drinking (described in the section on the social context of drinking) are all important aspects of the therapeutic plan.

A person has a variety of reactions to the initial realization that his/her drinking is causing problems. Most commonly, as negative consequences accumulate, an individual begins to feel out of control and ashamed of the behavior. The person's actions may be unacceptable to his/her self-definition. Thus financial or work irresponsibility, neglecting family members, engaging in physical violence, or verbal abuse may all be actions about which the individual feels intense guilt and self-blame. The prospect of admitting these actions to a stranger is frightening and embarrassing, making it difficult for clients to discuss drinking-associated problems. Because many clients ascribe their problems to weakness or lack of willpower, and believe that if they were only "stronger" these events would not occur, they blame themselves. Thus clients are unusually sensitive to implied criticisms from the therapist. The therapist can attenuate this difficulty by making empathic comments while asking questions, by letting clients know that many of their actions are common

among people who drink heavily, and by listening to clients' descriptions of drinking-related actions in an accepting manner.

Clients also hold a number of beliefs and attitudes about alcohol and their ability to change that make change difficult. People with alcoholism have positive expectancies about the effects of alcohol on feelings and behavior, and hold these more strongly than people do without drinking problems. They may attribute their drinking to reasons external to themselves, and believe that they are not personally responsible for either drinking or changing. They may have low self-efficacy about their ability to change their drinking or handle alcohol-related situations without drinking, or may have unrealistically high self-efficacy that is not grounded in actuality. Finally, if a person stops drinking and then consumes alcohol again, cognitive dissonance may occur; the person may experience the AVE (Marlatt & Gordon, 1985), characterized by an excessively negative reaction to initial alcohol consumption, and a self-perception that the person has "blown" his/her abstinence and will inevitably relapse to the previous drinking pattern.

CASE STUDY

In the preceding sections, I have presented snippets from a variety of cases to illustrate the application of parts of our treatment model. In this section, I present a complete outpatient therapy case to illustrate a number of the issues described above in the context of ongoing treatment. The case I present was seen as part of a research project evaluating different approaches to the maintenance of change following conjoint behavioral alcoholism treatment (McCrady et al., 1999). Couples in the study had to be married or cohabitating for at least 6 months; neither partner could have a primary problem with the use of illicit drugs or show evidence of gross organic brain syndrome or psychosis; and only the male partner could show evidence of alcohol abuse or dependence. All couples were seen by a therapist for 15 to 17 sessions of weekly outpatient treatment, and agreed to a baseline assessment and 18 months of posttreatment follow-up.

Carl and Maria were a married couple, both 32 years of age, who came to treatment because of Carl's drinking. Maria was of average height, had long black wavy hair, and was quite heavy. Carl was also of average height; he had blond hair and was slim, but showed the beginnings of a "beer belly." They were both neat and attractive. The couple had been married 5 years and had known each other for 12 years. Their two children were boys, ages 2 and 3. Both came from intact families, although Carl's father had died a number of years previously. Carl's family was primarily Polish; Maria's was Italian.

At the time of treatment, Carl and Maria had been separated from each other for 5 months. He was living with his mother in her home, while Maria was renting a one-bedroom apartment in a poor community, where she lived with the two boys. Maria was a trained hairdresser; Carl was a carpenter who worked out of the union hall. Carl was not working at this time because he did not want to establish a pattern of support for Maria or the children in case she filed for divorce. In addition, if he did not work for a certain period of time he would be able to withdraw his money from the union's pension plan, and he thought that that would be an easy way to obtain money. Maria was not working because she had decided that Carl would have to babysit while she worked, and she did not think that he would be reliable about coming to her apartment to care for the children. She was supported by welfare; he worked odd jobs "under the table." Both were high school graduates.

The couple came to treatment at Maria's urging. She had seen a notice in a local newspaper advertising our research clinic for couple treatment, and convinced Carl to come. She was very concerned about his drinking, and cited it as the primary reason for their marital separation.

Behavioral Assessment and Case Conceptualization

Carl and Maria were assessed using several approaches. Their assessment was somewhat more extensive than is usual in clinical practice because of their involvement with the treatment research project. However, the main elements of the assessment are applicable to clinical practice as well.

Drinking Assessment

To assess Carl's drinking, a clinical interview was used to ask him about his drinking history and perceptions of his current drinking. A hand-held Breathalyzer was used at the beginning of each session to assess his current BAL. In addition, two structured interviews, the TLFB (Sobell et al., 1980) and the alcohol section of the Composite International Diagnostic Interview—Substance Abuse Module (CIDI-SAM; Robins et al., 1988), and two self-report measures, the Michigan Alcoholism Screening Test (MAST; Selzer, 1971) and the ADS (Skinner & Allen, 1982), were used to obtain a more complete picture of his drinking. Maria was present for all interviews and contributed additional information.

The TLFB inquires about drinking behavior on each day in a set window of time before treatment. For this study, we asked about drinking in the prior 6 months, cuing clients' recall of drinking by noting other salient events in their lives, such as social events, medical appointments, holidays and other celebrations. The TLFB revealed that Carl had drunk alcohol virtually every day of the previous 6 months. His only abstinent day came when he and some friends were arrested for breaking and entering (they were intoxicated, decided they needed better carpentry tools, and thought that breaking into a store would be a good way to obtain them). His preferred beverages were beer and vodka, and he reported that the most he drank on any one day was about 32 drinks. His usual consumption was in the range of 10–12 drinks daily.

The alcohol section of the CIDI-SAM asks about a variety of behaviors associated with the criteria necessary to establish a DSM-III-R diagnosis of alcohol abuse or dependence (Carl was seen prior to the publication of the DSM-IV). Carl met criteria for a DSM-III-R diagnosis of alcohol dependence, and met DSM-IV criteria for alcohol dependence with physiological dependence. He had been drinking since high school, and reported his first problems as a result of alcohol at the age of 25. He had experienced a variety of problem consequences of his use: three arrests for DWI, with two of these arrests in the same month of the year he sought treatment; one arrest for breaking and entering; warnings from job supervisors for intoxication on the job; problems in his relationship with his wife; and feeling that he had neglected his responsibilities to his wife and sons. He had experienced numerous blackouts and reported many signs of physical dependence, including morning drinking, a sense of "panic" when he thought he would not be able to obtain a drink when he wanted one, and drinking throughout the day. However, he said that he had never experienced any of the physical symptoms of alcohol withdrawal. He also reported no health or emotional problems associated with his drinking. When asked about his goals for treatment, he indicated that his preference was to cut down and drink moderately, but that his wife insisted on abstinence and he was willing to work toward that goal.

Two assessment techniques were used to identify antecedents to Carl's drinking. The DPQ (Zitter & McCrady, 1979) was used to assess Carl's and Maria's perceptions of drinking antecedents. Carl completed the DPQ by checking off all antecedents that applied to his drinking in the previous 6 months, and Maria completed the measure as well to indicate her views of his drinking. They also were asked to indicate what they thought were the most influential antecedents. Both perceived environmental influences as being most important to Carl's drinking, citing drinking settings such as bars and his home, afternoons when he was not working, any celebratory occasions, and being around others who were drinking as being most salient. The second most important set of drinking cues pertained to their relationship, with Carl citing arguments, anger, feeling nagged, or having a good time together as antecedents. The third area of concern that they both cited was physiological antecedents, primarily restlessness and fatigue.

Carl also used daily self-recording cards throughout the treatment to record drinks and drinking urges. Reviewing the information he recorded and discussing events associated with drinking or drinking urges made it clear that being with close friends who also drank heavily was an important component of his drinking. The self-recording cards also clarified factors associated with his feelings of "restlessness." When he and Maria were together, the children were being active, and he wanted to leave or go somewhere, he would get restless and irritable, and would want to drink to "take the edge off." Finally, it was apparent from discussing drinking episodes

noted on the self-recording cards that Carl felt like drinking when Maria reminded Carl of a commitment that he had made (even something simple such as bringing over a book that he had at home), when she tried to get him to make a commitment to any responsible course of action, or when he felt "trapped" even if Maria had not said anything explicit.

Questionnaires and self-recording cards were used to assess how Maria coped with Carl's drinking. She recorded her perceptions of his drinking each day on a Likert scale (none, light, moderate, or heavy), and recorded her daily marital satisfaction as well. Her responses antecedent to and consequent to drinking episodes were discussed in the therapy sessions. In addition, both partners completed a modified version of the SBQ (Orford et al., 1975). On the SBQ, they indicated how frequently Maria had engaged in a variety of behaviors related to drinking. Data from these assessment sources made it apparent that Maria often questioned Carl about his actions, threatened him, or pleaded with him not to drink. She had reacted to his drinking in a number of negative ways—by separating from him, calling the police, and refusing to have sex with him. At the same time, she had made serious efforts to support him and encourage him toward abstinence by trying to do positive things together when he did not drink, doing nice things for him, or talking about positive things they could do together if he did not drink.

Marital Relationship

We assessed the couple's relationship by administering the ACQ (Margolin et al., 1983) and the DAS (Spanier, 1976), and by viewing a videotape of the couple discussing a problem in their relationship. Maria had a number of major concerns about their relationship, as evidenced by her seeking the marital separation. In addition to his drinking, she was concerned about his apparent lack of responsibility, citing his unwillingness to work, care for the children, or be independent of his mother. In general, Maria felt that Carl could not be relied upon for concrete or emotional support. A second concern that she expressed was their role definitions. She felt that Carl dictated her role to her, and that she allowed him to do so. She often felt angry and resentful as a result. Finally, she cited Carl's mother as a problem, describing her as an "enabler" who rescued him from his problems and made no demands upon him. She stated that when she and Carl first dated they liked to drink, stay out late, ride motorcycles, and have a good time, but that she felt that it was time to "move forward" with their lives and "get somewhere."

Carl had fewer marital concerns. He disliked Maria's "nagging" him about or discussing his drinking, stating at one point, "If I had a different wife, I wouldn't have a drinking problem." He also disliked her "persistence" in wanting to discuss topics at length, and disliked her "attitude change" when he drank.

In viewing a videotape of their interactions, it was clear that the couple had communication problems. Carl and Maria interrupted each other frequently and did not listen to each other's comments. They made frequent sarcastic and biting comments about the other, usually stating these with a smile and a funny comment. Maria complained about her excessive responsibilities, and Carl criticized her for not fulfilling her responsibilities, but refused to acknowledge any responsibilities of his own.

Despite these considerable marital problems, the spouses clearly enjoyed each other's company, shared many activities and pleasures (e.g., fishing, going to parks with the children), and had a very positive sexual relationship. Maria said of their relationship, "We get along great when I don't demand anything."

Behavioral Formulation

Carl's drinking appeared to have developed in a social context, with virtually all his drinking occurring within social groups with similar drinking patterns. Clearly, the pattern was reinforced by these positive social interactions, both with friends and (early in their relationship) with Maria. He had developed significant tolerance for alcohol, so that he could consume increasingly large amounts, resulting in a pattern of daily drinking with some signs of alcohol dependence. For Carl, alcohol provided a number of positive consequences: He enjoyed the tastes and sensations associated with drinking, the social context of drinking, and the feelings of relaxation that drinking engendered. Although he had accumulated a number of significant negative con-

sequences of drinking, none had affected his internal perceptions of himself or of alcohol. From his perspective, negative consequences were imposed on him by others—the police, job supervisors, and his wife. In addition, Carl had been able to avoid responsibility for his actions in many areas of his life. When he did not work, he was able to live with his mother, who shielded him from the negative consequences of not working by providing shelter and food for him. When his wife made demands on him that he experienced as aversive, he avoided or ignored her. To some degree, his problems with alcohol were accentuated by their different developmental stages. Maria was ready to move to a more adult stage of life, with increased responsibilities and long-term goals. Carl, in contrast, wanted to maintain the lifestyle and behavior patterns of his early 20s.

Despite Carl's externalizing attributions for his problems and his ability to avoid negative consequences and responsibility, his wife and children were important to him, and he did not want to lose them from his life. Therefore, he came to treatment to maintain these desired reinforcers, but not necessarily to make the behavior changes his wife saw as necessary for them to have a successful long-term marriage. As treatment progressed (see below), Carl engaged in a variety of maneuvers to maintain the relationship but avoid behavior change, and his wife, and at times the therapist, reinforced these behaviors.

Maria had a limited repertoire of effective ways to obtain positive reinforcers for herself. She appeared to expect most positive feelings to come from outside of herself, and knew only nagging and criticizing as verbal behaviors to use to try to get what she wanted. She reinforced Carl's drinking by continuing to have contact with him and have positive interactions, but engaged in aversive negative verbal behavior at the same time. She placed responsibility for her happiness with Carl, stating that she could not work (something she enjoyed a great deal) until he stopped drinking and was more responsible, and that she could not lose weight until he stopped drinking and she was less upset.

As a couple, Carl and Maria lacked the verbal skills to discuss these very major problems. Aversive control, avoidance of responsibility, and lack of empathic communication characterized their interactions.

Preparing the Client for Change

Carl and Maria were seen together for all phases of the evaluation. The initial evaluation asked both spouses to describe their perceptions of Carl's drinking, their relationship, and how each had attempted to cope with Carl's drinking. By seeing the couple together, I began to communicate my view that the drinking was intimately connected to their relationship, and that both spouses would need to examine their own behavior to effect positive changes. At the end of the evaluation, I provided them with feedback about the main difficulties that I perceived (as summarized above), and oriented them to the plan for treatment. In discussing the treatment plan, I covered the following:

"We have asked you to come to treatment as a couple. This is because, as you know, drinking affects other areas of your life, including your marriage and your family. I know from what you have said, Maria, that you have tried many different ways to cope with Carl's drinking, and that you have been angry and frustrated at times. It is clear that you have tried to help, but it seems, Carl, that you mostly have resented it when Maria has said anything about your drinking. In the treatment, we will look at your drinking, how you have tried to cope with it, and how the two of you are getting along as a couple. Right now the two of you are separated, and you have a lot of concerns about your relationship. As we go along in the therapy, I will give you feedback about how to improve your communication, and I will ask you to try new ways to spend time together and discuss problems.

"The therapy will focus on three main topics—your drinking, how you (Maria) have coped with it, and how to cope in ways that work better for both of you, and your relationship with each other."

In addition to this overall orientation, which both Carl and Maria felt captured their goals for the treatment, we discussed Carl's drinking goals in more detail and made plans for how to achieve those goals. As indicated above, Carl's preferred drinking goal was moderate drinking. However, Maria felt strongly that she wanted him to abstain, and he had agreed to that goal prior to coming to

treatment. Since he had been drinking daily and showed evidence of tolerance to alcohol, I was concerned that he would not be able to stop drinking without assistance. I therefore discussed with him the possibility of being detoxified under medical supervision:

"I am concerned, Carl, that it will be difficult for you to stop drinking on your own. You drink every day, and have been drinking a lot. On the questionnaires, you indicated that you 'panic' if you think that you will not be able to get any alcohol, and you typically drink throughout the day. All of these things suggest to me that you may be 'hooked' on alcohol, and that your body will have a strong reaction to going without any alcohol at all. The easiest way to get through the first few days without drinking is to check into a hospital detoxification program, and I would like you to consider it."

Carl had a very negative reaction to the thought of being hospitalized. He was afraid of being "locked up," and said, "I know that I would go crazy. I can't stand being confined. After 24 hours I would just have to leave. It's not a good idea."

I was most interested in engaging Carl in treatment and working to develop mutually agreed-upon goals, so I thought it inappropriate to try to force Carl to enter a detoxification center. I was certain that if I made a brief hospitalization a prerequisite to further treatment, he would leave treatment completely. Therefore, we developed a plan to achieve abstinence. The plan had two major components: (1) Carl was to come to therapy sessions sober, and his BAL would be verified by breath alcohol test reading; (2) Carl would set goals to gradually reduce his drinking, with a target date for abstinence 6 weeks hence. If he was not able to achieve either goal, then we would reevaluate the need for supervised detoxification. He was amenable to this agreement, as was Maria.

Process of Treatment

The course of treatment is described sequentially, to provide the reader with the clearest picture of the progress and pitfalls of a fairly typical therapy case. The treatment covered several major areas, including (1) helping Carl to reduce and then stop his drinking; (2) teaching Carl skills to assist him in maintaining abstinence; (3) enhancing Carl's perception of his drinking as problematic; (4) teaching Maria more constructive coping strategies; (5) teaching the couple how to engage in positive interactions; and (6) teaching the couple mutual problem-solving techniques. In addition, as treatment progressed, we focused on some other areas of individual behavioral change for Maria.

Intake and Sessions 1–2

At the initial intake session, Carl had a BAL of greater than 400 mg%. Although he did not show signs of gross intoxication, he was belligerent, and the clinician doing the intake did not feel that he could conduct a reasonable intake interview. He suggested that Carl receive medical attention because his BAL was so high, but Carl refused, and the clinician rescheduled the intake. At the rescheduled appointment, Carl was sober and was able to provide information, give informed consent for the research aspects of the program, and schedule the baseline data collection session (at which he also arrived sober).

At the first treatment session, however, Carl again had an elevated BAL (120 mg%). He acknowledged only having "a couple of beers," and insisted that he was fine. We had some discussion about Carl's and Maria's concerns and goals, but I suggested that we would not be able to have a very productive session with his BAL so high. (My general policy is to reschedule a treatment session if the client's BAL is greater than 0.05.) Carl agreed to come to the next session sober, and to drink no more than four drinks per day. I gave Carl and Maria self-recording cards on which I asked them to record drinks, drinking urges, and marital satisfaction on a daily basis. Carl was given one card for each day, and I asked him to record each drink he actually consumed, to note urges to drink not followed by drinking, and to note on the back of the card the situations in which he drank or had urges to drink (see Figure 9.3).

Maria received one card to use for the entire week. On the card I asked her to make a daily estimate of Carl's drinking as none, light, moderate, or heavy, and also to record her estimate of the strength of his urges to drink that day. She also made a daily rating of her marital satisfaction (see Figure 9.4).

When Carl and Maria came to the second session, his BAL was again elevated, at 60 mg%. He reported drinking about four beers during the day. We continued the discussion of detoxification, and he said that he felt he was addicted to alcohol. He said that he would consider detoxification, and we scheduled a phone conversation to discuss detoxification further. After we spoke twice by phone, Carl again decided that he did not want to be hospitalized. Carl did not use the self-recording cards during these first 2 weeks, although Maria completed his cards for him while they drove to the treatment session. I did not feel that I had a clear picture of Carl's drinking, but it was clear that he was continuing to drink daily.

Sessions 3–5

Carl came to the third session with a BAL of 0. He again reiterated his desire to stop without hospitalization, and we worked out the details of the contract described in the previous section (abstinent at treatment sessions, complete abstinence within 6 weeks of the beginning of treatment). In addition to setting drinking goals, we began to discuss a behavioral-analytic view of drinking. To introduce the couple to a behavioral way of thinking about their drinking, I said:

> "Together we are going to carefully observe and analyze all the factors that seem to be part of your drinking. I think that we can look at your drinking and figure out what kinds of situations lead you to feel like drinking. If we can figure this out, then we can work together to come up with *alternatives* for these situations. We will be using these sheets, called 'triggers' sheets, to analyze your drinking. Let's go through one of these together."

I then asked Carl to identify a recent drinking situation. He indicated that he liked to drink when he went fishing, so we used fishing as an example. I explained to him that in looking at any drinking situation, we were going to look at the actual situation, and then look at how he reacted to the situation. As we spoke, I completed the boxes on the "triggers" sheet, which is illustrated in Figure 9.7. (Some clinicians, such as Marlatt & Gordon [1985], refer to "high-risk" situations rather than "triggers." A high-risk situation is one

Analyzing Drinking

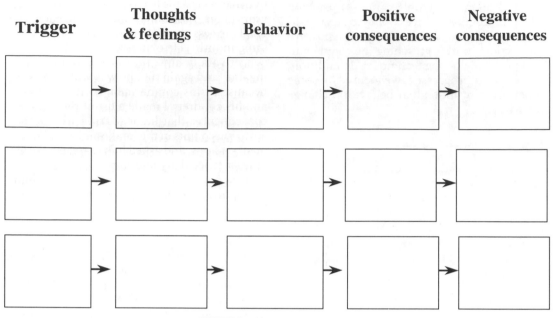

Trigger	Thoughts & feelings	Behavior	Positive consequences	Negative consequences

FIGURE 9.7. "Triggers" sheet.

in which the client is at high risk to drink. Carl did not believe that he was at any "risk" to drink—he thought that he could avoid drinking any time he wanted to, but he rarely wanted to. Therefore, I chose to talk about "triggers" as situations in which he was likely to drink.) Carl had a fairly nonpsychological view of his drinking. He described his thoughts related to alcohol and fishing as "I want to get some beer," and his feelings as "happy." He viewed drinking in that situation as having clear positive consequences—"I have a blast." He felt that the only negative consequences came from Maria, who would be angry when he came home.

Carl and Maria grasped the behavioral analysis quickly, and found it a comfortable way to conceptualize his drinking. As homework, I asked then each to complete the DPQ and to bring it to the next treatment session. I gave them additional self-recording cards to use for the week.

Carl also came to the fourth session sober, but reported heavy drinking over the weekend. The graph of his weekly alcohol consumption during treatment is reproduced in Figure 9.8. Carl and Maria's average weekly marital satisfaction ratings are reproduced in Figure 9.9. Carl expressed no concern about his continued heavy drinking, and showed no evidence that he was trying to cut down. I indicated:

"I am glad that you have come to the last two sessions sober—I know that's not easy

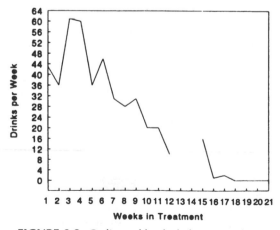

FIGURE 9.8. Carl's weekly alcohol consumption.

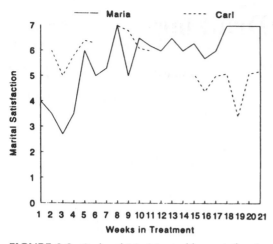

FIGURE 9.9. Carl and Maria's weekly marital satisfaction.

for you, and it does show that you want treatment to succeed. However, I am concerned that you have not cut down at all between sessions. If anything, your drinking seems a bit heavier. It's not clear to me if you don't really want to cut down, or if you just don't know how to."

Carl said that it was hard to cut down, but that he was committed to stopping drinking because he wanted to have Maria and the boys back again. We then discussed a number of potential strategies to help him avoid drinking, such as sleeping (his suggestion) or having alternative beverages available in the house (my suggestion) or going back to work (Maria's suggestion). He was reluctant to commit to any plans, and Maria challenged whether or not he was really willing to stop drinking. At that point he said, "In some ways, I think if I had a different wife, I wouldn't have to stop drinking. Before, Maria and I could drink together and have a good time—but now that she doesn't drink, she's on me all the time. I know I have to stop if I want to get her back, but I don't know . . ."

To respond to Carl's ambivalence, I suggested that we examine other consequences of his drinking, other than Maria's disapproval and the arguments that they had about his drinking. He was unable to think of any other adverse consequences. I asked him about his legal problems from the DWIs and the arrest for breaking and entering, but he said that he did not believe that alcohol had anything to do with the latter charge, and that DWI laws

were "ridiculous." He also indicated that he was still driving even though he did not have a driver's license, and that he would continue to drive even if his license was revoked for 10 years (a real possibility, since he had had three DWIs in less than 10 years, with two in the same month). He expressed a similar lack of concern about any other aspects of his drinking, but said again that he was willing to stop because of his commitment to the marriage and his children. I made a list of the negative consequences that he or Maria had reported at various points in the intake and initial treatment sessions, and asked him to review the list at least twice daily and to think about which of these consequences were of concern to him. He reported looking at the list "once or twice" between sessions, but was relatively indifferent to the content.

Despite my concern about Carl's relative lack of motivation to change, I decided to proceed with a behavioral analysis of his drinking. I thought that if we could identify a discrete set of antecedents to drinking, and if he could be successful at avoiding drinking in some of these situations some of the time, his motivation to change might increase as his self-efficacy about coping without alcohol increased. We discussed two other drinking situations in the session, and as homework, I had him complete two behavioral chains at home. A complete summary of the behavioral analysis of his drinking is provided in Figure 9.10.

Carl came to the next treatment session with a BAL of 118 mg%, and he reported heavy drinking for the last several days prior to the treatment session. After a lengthy discussion, he agreed to go for detoxification. He was afraid of the hospitalization, and also said that he was concerned that he would not be able to be abstinent after detoxification. I tried to emphasize that the detoxification was only the first step in treatment, and that we would be working together to help him learn ways of coping with the triggers without drinking. He also expressed his belief that life would not be fun if he did not drink. Maria oscillated between encouraging Carl to get detoxified and saying to me that he was only agreeing to the detox to get out of my office. Because he was so concerned, I had him call the detoxification center from my office to ask any questions he had. He did so, and scheduled himself for admission the next day.

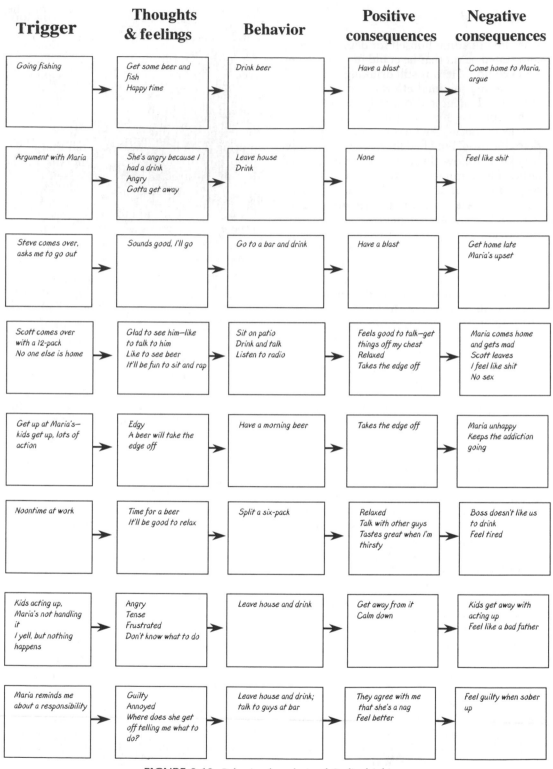

Trigger	Thoughts & feelings	Behavior	Positive consequences	Negative consequences
Going fishing	Get some beer and fish Happy time	Drink beer	Have a blast	Come home to Maria, argue
Argument with Maria	She's angry because I had a drink Angry Gotta get away	Leave house Drink	None	Feel like shit
Steve comes over, asks me to go out	Sounds good, I'll go	Go to a bar and drink	Have a blast	Get home late Maria's upset
Scott comes over with a 12-pack No one else is home	Glad to see him—like to talk to him Like to see beer It'll be fun to sit and rap	Sit on patio Drink and talk Listen to radio	Feels good to talk—get things off my chest Relaxed Takes the edge off	Maria comes home and gets mad Scott leaves I feel like shit No sex
Get up at Maria's—kids get up, lots of action	Edgy A beer will take the edge off	Have a morning beer	Takes the edge off	Maria unhappy Keeps the addiction going
Noontime at work	Time for a beer It'll be good to relax	Split a six-pack	Relaxed Talk with other guys Tastes great when I'm thirsty	Boss doesn't like us to drink Feel tired
Kids acting up, Maria's not handling it I yell, but nothing happens	Angry Tense Frustrated Don't know what to do	Leave house and drink	Get away from it Calm down	Kids get away with acting up Feel like a bad father
Maria reminds me about a responsibility	Guilty Annoyed Where does she get off telling me what to do?	Leave house and drink; talk to guys at bar	They agree with me that she's a nag Feel better	Feel guilty when sober up

FIGURE 9.10. Behavioral analysis of Carl's drinking.

Sessions 6–8

Carl did not admit himself for detoxification, and stated again that he could not face being "locked up." He was still drinking daily, and was making minimal efforts to decrease his drinking. I suggested outpatient detoxification, and gave him the phone number of a physician colleague who supervises outpatient detoxification, but I had little expectation that he would follow through with that referral either. He continued to express willingness to be in treatment and to change his drinking, and I decided to continue, despite doubts about whether or not he had sufficient incentives to change. We completed the behavioral analysis of his drinking during the sixth session, and identified several aspects of Maria's actions that served as antecedents to his drinking. These included her reminding him about responsibilities, her slow pace when they had an appointment and there was a lot to do to get themselves and their children ready to go out, and her commenting on his drinking.

At one point during Session 6, Carl said, "You know, Maria has a real temper. You should ask her what she did to me at the beach." Maria responded immediately by saying, "Show Barbara your arms." Carl rolled up his sleeves, revealing a number of scratches and bruises covering both of his lower forearms. Maria then explained that she had been intensely frustrated with Carl because of his drinking, and often grabbed him, scratched him, or tried to hit him in the chest or abdomen when angry. The behavior had started in the last 4 months, and she found it very upsetting. She also indicated her concern that she might become abusive toward her children, and admitted that she sometimes used physical punishment when she was angry at them. Although Maria's anger and frustration were not surprising and are common reactions among partners of people with alcoholism, the physical expression of this anger, particularly in the absence of any physical abuse from Carl, was unusual. We discussed her behavior toward the children in great detail, as I was concerned about whether there was any evidence of child abuse. She reported, and Carl confirmed, that she had never bruised, cut, or injured the children in any way, and that they had never had to take either of the children to a physician or emergency room because of her discipline. They both reported that they believed that physical punishment, in the form of "swats on the bum" or physically removing the child from a dangerous situation, were appropriate forms of discipline. Maria, however, felt that she did not always discipline the children rationally, and that she would occasionally hit them on the arm, or pull too hard when removing them from a situation. From their reports, I did not believe that she was abusing them in any way, but felt that it was important to address her concerns in the therapy. I instructed her to use the self-recording cards to write down any time when she felt that she was reacting too strongly to the children or when she was physically aggressive toward Carl.

Over the next two sessions, Carl began to decrease his drinking substantially, and was abstinent for each treatment session. Carl and Maria had begun to spend more time together, and reported that their time together was more positive. They had a family barbecue and went fishing at the beach with the children.

Maria had been faithful in recording her reactions to her children, noting two times each week when she either slapped one of the children on the arm or felt that she grabbed him too hard. We discussed the antecedents to these incidents, and identified several salient aspects: She was tired, the child was tired, and she attempted to tell him to do something when she could not enforce it (she was across the room or had her hands full). In each situation, she repeated her verbal instructions to the boy several times to no avail, and then felt angry and stomped across the room and grabbed him. We discussed alternative strategies, and I emphasized the importance of being able to follow through on a verbal instruction immediately, rather than allowing herself to get frustrated. She quickly picked up on my suggestions, and also expressed relief at being able to discuss her concerns. After the 2 weeks, she reported no further instance of excessive physical reaction to the boys, and reported feeling more in control of herself as a parent again. Carl's observations confirmed her reports.

At the same time that we discussed Maria's problems with disciplining the children, we began to implement some self-management planning techniques for Carl. I suggested to Carl that it would be easier not to drink if he had some clear ideas about how to handle certain triggers without alcohol. He could avoid situations, or rearrange them to minimize the importance of alcohol in the situation. We used a self-management planning sheet to assist in the process (see Figure 9.11).

We selected fishing as a topic for self-management planning, since it was a high-frequency, high-drinking activity for him. Carl had a number of ideas about how to fish without alcohol. These included taking his older son, taking his wife, or inviting an older friend who was an excellent fisherman and did not drink at all. In addition, he thought if he bought soft drinks the night before he went fishing and filled his cooler with the sodas before he left the house, he would be less tempted to stop by the liquor store at the end of his block. For homework, I asked Carl to implement this plan, and to develop another self-management plan for getting together with a friend without drinking.

Carl implemented the fishing plan successfully, and developed a plan to get together with his friend Scott. He planned to ask Scott to play tennis and then go to a fast-food restaurant to eat, because alcohol would not be available there. Although he saw no obstacles to implementing this plan, he never used it, but could provide no reasons for not following it up. He did, however, tell Scott that he was trying not to drink, and his friend reacted positively and supportively.

The other major topic of these several sessions was reinforcement for changes in drinking. Because Carl was so ambivalent about changing his drinking, I thought it particularly important that he experience some positive consequences for decreased drinking and for abstinence. I also wanted to provide Maria with some positive rather than coercive ways to interact around Carl's drinking. In introducing this topic, I suggested that they both should think about ways to make abstinence and reduced drinking more positive. I first suggested that Maria might give him positive feedback when he was not drinking, but Carl reacted quite negatively to this suggestion, saying, "I would just think it was another one of her sneaky ways to try to pressure me to stop. I don't want her to say anything." In continuing with this discussion, I asked whether there was anything that Maria could do that would make abstinence worthwhile to him, and Carl suggested that she could refrain from talking about alcohol and spend time with him without being "picky." They decided on several mutually enjoyable activities to share when he was not drinking, such as sharing a shrimp dinner, and Maria telling Carl when she was enjoying their time to-

Self-Management Planning

	Trigger	Plan	Pluses	Minuses	How hard
1.					
2.					

FIGURE 9.11. Self-management planning sheet.

gether. They were able to implement these plans successfully, and although Carl drank while they were together, the amount was substantially less on these occasions.

Sessions 9–11

By this point in the treatment, Carl had reduced his drinking to approximately three to six drinks per day, but had not abstained from drinking at all. His reports of urges to drink had also begun to decrease. Maria reported high marital satisfaction almost every day (ratings of 7 on a 1–7 scale), and they were spending most of their free time either at her apartment or at Carl's mother's home. However, in the therapy sessions they began to argue more frequently, with their conflict revolving around two major topics—Maria's desire to move to North Carolina, and Maria's feeling that Carl was not emotionally supportive of her. I began to implement some structured communication training with them, teaching them skills to allow the other to finish before speaking, reflective listening, and making specific positive requests. These sessions were supplemented with handouts about communication. After reading the first handout, which covered basic topics such as the value of being polite and respectful of your spouse, and some of the sources of bad communication, they came into the session absolutely surprised at the notion that calling each other names (such as "idiot," "asshole," or "shithead") could have any negative impact on their relationship. They had begun to use positive rather than negative communication at home, and were pleased with the impact it had on their conversations.

Although we were making some positive progress in the treatment, I was concerned that Carl was continuing his pattern of daily drinking, and I reflected this concern to him. He stated that he believed that he could now stop, and contracted to be abstinent for 2 days in the following week. The first week that he agreed to this contract he did not want to discuss strategies for abstinence, and was unsuccessful. The second week we discussed very specific plans for how he would abstain. He planned to be with Maria and the children for part of each day, and decided not to buy more beer to have in his mother's house those days. In addition, he would stock up on soft drinks and plan on going to bed early. I also sug-

gested that he might use Maria as a support in his attempts to abstain. I often encourage a client to find someone with whom to discuss urges, and the partner is often a good source of support. He again was resistant to involving Maria, saying, "I wouldn't tell her that I wanted to drink—all I'd get is a lecture." I suggested that he usually disliked her comments because they were unsolicited, but in this situation he would be in charge, because he would be the person concerned about his drinking. He responded positively to this reframing. I then asked him whether there was anything she could say that would be helpful to him, and he suggested that she tell him it was his choice. Maria indicated that it would be difficult for her not to lecture, but agreed to a role play. They imagined that they were driving to the beach, and Carl said, "I want to stop to pick up a six-pack on the way down." Maria answered, "It's your choice if you want to, but we could stop to get some sodas instead if you want." Carl was amazed at how much he liked her response, and although Maria acknowledged that it was very difficult to be that neutral, she liked feeling that it was not her responsibility to prevent him from drinking. They agreed to try out such a discussion once during the coming week.

Carl was not successful in maintaining any abstinent days, although he did implement most of the rest of the plans and drank only one beer on each of the 2 target days. However, he did not tell Maria about any of his urges to drink. He expressed little concern at his not meeting his goals. During the session, Carl and Maria announced that they were going to North Carolina for a 2-week trip. Carl knew a contractor who had offered him work there, and Maria was intrigued with the possibility of moving to an area with a lower cost of living and more rural environment in which to raise the children. She stated that she would not move while Carl was still drinking, but they both decided that a trip to explore the possibilities was attractive to them.

Sessions 12–15

Carl and Maria returned from their 2-week trip very enthusiastic about North Carolina. They believed that work was available, the cost of living was clearly lower, and they liked the area that they had visited. Maria said again that she would not move unless Carl had been abstinent for a considerable length of time, as she did not want to leave her family if she could not depend on Carl. He again said that he would stop drinking.

I had taken advantage of the break in the therapy to review all of my progress notes and to think about the couple with a bit more detachment. It was clear to me that Carl had agreed to abstinence because of Maria's pressure, but really wanted to reduce his drinking. However, he had dealt with this conflict by providing verbal reassurances that his behavior would change without the accompanying behavior changes. He had implemented only a few of the behavioral plans that we had developed, and I did not think that the lack of implementation reflected a skills deficit. I had decided to point out Carl's behavioral inconsistencies at this treatment session.

To initiate this discussion, I told Carl and Maria that I wanted to discuss their progress so far. I emphasized the positive changes that they had made so far: Carl had decreased his drinking substantially, he had developed some skills to assist him in drinking less, their communication had begun to improve, they were spending time together that was mutually enjoyable, and they had begun to consider possible long-term plans together. I noted, however, that Carl had made a series of promises about his drinking that he had not followed through on. I read them several passages from my progress notes, noting his initial target date for abstinence, his broken agreement about detoxification, and his broken agreements about abstinent days. I suggested two alternative explanations to them—either that Carl did not want to stop drinking completely, but felt that he had to agree to abstinence to keep Maria happy; or that he really could not stop drinking and needed further assistance to do so. By framing my explanations this way, I tried to avoid labeling him as dishonest or unmotivated to change. I also suggested that Maria had helped Carl to keep drinking by reporting high marital satisfaction even though he was still drinking, and that perhaps reduced drinking really was acceptable to her as well.

Both reacted quite strongly to my feedback. Carl said, "At first I didn't want to stop, but now it doesn't seem that bad. I'm not drinking enough now for it to mean anything, so I'll just quit. It's no big deal, and I don't want to disappoint you." Maria said,

"I always feel like Carl is just saying whatever he has to get me off his back or get you off his back. But I have been so much happier since he cut down that I kind of lost sight of that fact that he's still drinking. I am afraid to move anywhere with him while he's still drinking at all—it was so bad before, I don't want to go back to that."

After this conversation, Carl denied that he preferred moderate drinking, and announced that he was going to "quit for good."

Over the next 2 weeks, Carl had one drinking day each week—one beer the first week and two beers the second week. Although we discussed a variety of behavioral coping strategies, such as developing behavioral alternatives for drinking situations, rehearsing strategies for refusing drinks, and using various strategies for coping with urges, he deemphasized the importance of these. Instead, he focused on cognitive coping strategies— when he had urges to drink, he would think about reasons not to drink ("It's not worth it—Maria and the kids are more important"). Or he would use delay tactics ("I won't have anything right now—if I still feel like drinking at 5:00 [or some other, later time during the day], then I'll have a beer"). Or he would deemphasize the positive aspects of alcohol ("One or two beers won't do anything for me, and I don't want to get blasted").

Carl and Maria also began to discuss their long-term goals together. I asked each to write down how they would like their lives to be in 5 years—separately or together. Carl wrote down the following:[4]

Comfortable place to live for Maria and this kids. Good schools, backyard. Get finances in order; save money, consolidate bills, improve credit. Maintain stable income ie. steady construction work or other. Obtain a loving relationship with Maria. Self improvement: manage money better, listen to Maria more objectivly, secure steadier employment. Maria: better self discipline, controll temper, improve self confidence, weight loss, less pestimistic in dialy matters. ie. scared of bugs, traffic, mishaps, ect.

Maria wrote down remarkably similar 5-year goals:

Five years from now—39 years old; Jonathan 8 years, Marc 7 years. We are living in North Carolina in a rented House. I'm working, Carls working the boys are in school. We have two

cars. Carl is 5 yrs sober. I'm 4 years thin. We
are two yrs away from getting credit back from
filing bankruptcy. Some nights we will be together as a family to relax or to go to a base-
ball or soccer game of Jonathan's or Marc's.
Other nights I will be out to socialize or run
errands. Other nights Carl will do the same. We
will be somewhat financialy comfortable.

   Three things I want out of:

Maria	Carl
calmness, thinness,	*motivation, sobriety,*
contentness	*responsability*
to feel secure, a car,	
money, independence,	
control over my *life*	

Because Carl and Maria's goals were so similar, I asked them if I could read them aloud.
Both were amenable to this suggestion, and I
did so. Both reacted quite positively and felt
encouraged, since their long-term goals were
so similar, that they could work together in
therapy to achieve these goals. I began to
teach them skills related to assertiveness and
problem solving, discussing ways to implement these skills both in their relationship and
in other interpersonal situations.

Sessions 16–18

Carl abstained from drinking from Session 15
to the end of the treatment. He reported a few
urges to drink, but these soon decreased. However, he discussed very strong reactions to not
drinking. He felt sad, saying that he missed
drinking and felt that he had lost something
important to him. He also said that it was frustrating, because he always had been able to
drink when he felt bad, but now he could not
do so. I tried to reframe his feelings for him,
noting that his ability to recognize that he
missed alcohol was an important step towards
being able to reorganize his life without it, and
that his reaction suggested that he was quite
serious about his intentions not to drink. He
seemed to find the reframing helpful, but continued to find abstinence uncomfortable.

As Carl remained abstinent, his marital
satisfaction ratings decreased. Previously he
had reported fairly high marital satisfaction,
but as he stopped drinking he became more
unhappy. When I asked him about his ratings,
he said that he felt they were "going nowhere"
in terms of reconciling. We had begun assertion and problem-solving training, and I suggested that he could use these skills to express

his feelings to Maria more directly. They had
a positive discussion during the session of his
feelings about wanting to reconcile and her
concerns about how difficult that would be,
with each using some of the positive skills we
had worked on. Both agreed that they now
wanted to live together again, but it would be
difficult to develop a plan to do so. We used
structured problem-solving techniques over
two treatment sessions to develop a plan.

The major impediment to reconciliation was
financial. Maria was receiving welfare, but if
either she or Carl began to work, they would
receive less public assistance. However, to be
able to live together, they would have to save
sufficient money for a security deposit and
first month's rent. They finally decided that
Maria would begin to work a few hours a
week as a hairdresser, working "under the
table," and that Carl would care for the children while she worked. If that worked well,
then Carl would begin to look for work again;
once they were both working, they would
move in with his mother for a limited period
of time to save money for the deposits and
rent, and would then either obtain an apartment together in New Jersey or find a trailer
to rent in North Carolina and move. They also
used problem-solving techniques to develop
a plan to deal with their other debts.

Termination

Because Carl and Maria were part of a clinical research study, we had to terminate treatment after 18 sessions (including the sessions
when he was intoxicated). They had made
significant progress during treatment. Carl
had been abstinent for more than a month;
Maria had learned more effective ways to
discipline the children, and no longer reported
concerns about being overly punitive to them;
the couple's relationship was significantly improved; and they had a constructive plan for
reconciliation. I was concerned that Carl was
still uncomfortable with abstinence, and I
thought that he had acquired only a few effective coping strategies to deal with triggers
for drinking. We had not worked directly on
Carl's responsibility-avoiding style, except by
following through on his commitment to abstinence and through long-term goal setting.
Whether he would implement his part of these
agreements was relatively untested. The couple
was fairly comfortable with termination, but

asked about possible follow-up treatment, inquiring specifically about AA or other support groups that were more focused on couples or on behavioral approaches to change. I referred them to SMART, and to an AA meeting for couples that devotes most of its discussion to relationship issues rather than AA-oriented recovery issues. The constraints of the clinical research protocol precluded any longer-term contacts with them, but such contacts seemed clinically indicated.

Comment

Carl and Maria were a fairly typical couple. Carl's ambivalence about change, his entry into treatment solely because of an external agent, and his resistance to many behavioral interventions are fairly representative. I believe that he began to engage in treatment when he stopped feeling that he was the sole focus of the treatment, after Maria began to discuss her aggressive behavior and feelings. The second critical point in treatment was addressing his continued drinking. I was willing to allow them to renegotiate for a goal of moderate drinking, but did not think it therapeutic for Carl to feel that he could make a verbal agreement to abstinence and then avoid the agreement. Confronting his behavior forced him either to be assertive and renegotiate treatment goals, or to follow through on his commitment.

The role of behavioral skills training in facilitating Carl's abstinence was somewhat more limited than with some clients. He tried various skills introduced during the treatment, but relied primarily on cognitive coping strategies. The role of reinforcement was probably more important in understanding his changed drinking behavior. His marital relationship was important to him at the beginning of treatment, and focusing in the therapy on ways to improve that relationship increased its reinforcement value to him. Maria's consistency in saying that they could only reconcile if he were abstinent, discussing long-term goals for the relationship, and seeing the possible positive life they could live in North Carolina all contributed.

Finally, my relationship with the couple probably contributed to the positive changes that they made. I found them a likable, appealing couple, despite their difficulties. At times, I would tease or cajole Carl into compliance, and he commented at the end of the treatment, "At first I didn't know if I liked you or not, but then I decided you were kind of cute, and then I realized that you weren't going to let up on me, so I decided that I'd give it a try." With Maria, I tried to reinforce her ability to take care of herself, and I suspect that she saw me as a female role model in some sense. She often asked me personal questions (whether I was married, how old my son was), and gave me a desk calendar as a thank-you gift at termination. Our research has suggested that our more experienced therapists are more successful at keeping clients in treatment (Epstein, McCrady, Miller, & Steinberg, 1994; Raytek, McCrady, Epstein, & Hirsch, 1999), and I suspect that being able to deal with these complex relationships is one skill that our more experienced therapists have acquired more fully.

Typical Problems

The problems presented in this case are fairly typical—coming to treatment sessions intoxicated, continued drinking during treatment, ambivalence about change, noncompliance with assignments, and discovering new and major problems as the therapy progresses. Lying and failing to come to scheduled treatment sessions are other typical obstacles that clients with drinking problems present sometimes. By working with Carl and Maria together, I was able to minimize these particular difficulties, as Maria was highly motivated for treatment and very responsible about keeping scheduled appointments. Also, by having them both record Carl's drinking and drinking urges, I had a clearer picture of his drinking and was able to maintain a clear idea of our progress (or lack thereof).

CLINICAL PREDICTORS OF SUCCESS OR FAILURE

A number of factors predict the success of failure of therapy. However, before these factors are addressed, it is important to discuss definitions of "success." In any treatment, a minority of clients will maintain successful change (abstinence or nonproblem drinking) for extended periods of time (Helzer et al., 1985; Pettinati et al., 1982). The proportion varies with the demographic characteristics of the population, and persons who are married, have stable employment, a stable residence, and no comorbid psychopathology have the best treatment outcomes. In addition, a person's posttreatment environment plays an important role (Moos, Finney, & Cronkite, 1990) in determining long-term outcomes.

Observations of the long-term instability of drinking outcomes have led many to consider alcoholism as a chronic, relapsing disorder, and to reconceptualize "success" as a process rather than a static outcome. That is, the client who learns effective skills to avoid drinking or heavy drinking, but who also learns ways to cope with relapses by minimizing their length and severity, should be considered "successful" as well (see, e.g., Marlatt & Gordon, 1985). In treatment outcome studies, investigators look at percentage of abstinent or moderate drinking days, and length of periods of abstinence compared to periods of heavy drinking, as ways to assess relative rather than absolute "success."

From the individual clinician's perspective, certain client characteristics and behaviors bode well for the course of treatment. The client who has important incentives to change (either internal or external), and who has some recognition of a relationship between his/her drinking and life problems is easier to treat. Complying with early homework assignments, coming to sessions sober, and being honest about behavior outside of the treatment are also positive indicators. However, clinician behavior is another important predictor of success. Various studies have pointed to different aspects of clinician behavior—empathy, specific goal setting and treatment planning, developing drinking goals with the client rather than imposing goals, and providing the client with options for treatment—as all associated with better compliance with treatment.

CONCLUSION

Providing treatment to persons with drinking problems is a complex and continuously fascinating process. The clinician is faced with complex decisions about matching each client to the appropriate level of care, setting for treatment, treatment modalities, and techniques. Diagnostic skills to identify concomitant medical, psychological, psychiatric, and cognitive problems are challenged by these clients. Therapy requires knowledge of a range of treatment techniques, an ability to be able to form a positive therapeutic relationship with sometimes frustrating and difficult clients, and the ability to "think on your feet." From the briefest, one-session treatments to motivate heavy drinkers to reduce their drinking to the complex and longer treatment provided to individuals with chronic alcoholism, treatment is never dull or routine. The clinician has a large body of empirical literature to guide the selection of treatments, and a significant clinical literature as well that illustrates clinical techniques and problems. And although many persons with drinking problems do change successfully on their own or with minimal assistance, treatment can provide an effective means for persons to change a major life problem successfully.

So this chapter concludes as it began—as a "sales pitch" for clinicians to be knowledgeable about and receptive to providing thoughtful, informed treatment to persons with drinking problems.

ACKNOWLEDGMENT

Preparation of this chapter was supported by Grant No. AA07070 from the National Institute on Alcohol Abuse and Alcoholism.

NOTES

1. Programs to support moderate drinking, rather than abstinence, are considered controversial in the United States and receive considerable negative attention. Moderation Management (MM) has taken a responsible approach to moderation, stating clearly that it is not intended for persons who are alcohol dependent, and recommending a period of abstinence prior to any attempts at moderation. MM, however, has not been immune from negative attention and publicity, particularly when the founder experienced very serious problems related to her own drinking. Despite these controversies and thoughtful concerns raised about moderation as a drinking goal, MM is the only self-help group available in the United States for individuals who want help to moderate their drinking, and clinicians should be aware that the program exists.

2. A standard drink is equal to one 12-ounce beer, one 4-ounce glass of wine, or a 1-ounce shot of 86-proof liquor.

3. All dialogue in this chapter is paraphrasing of actual therapist or client comments.

4. These are verbatim transcripts, and include the clients' spelling of all words.

REFERENCES

American Psychiatric Association. (1994). *Diagnostic and statistical manual of mental disorders* (4th ed.). Washington, DC: Author.

Annis, H. M. (1982). *Inventory of Drinking Situations (IDS-100).* Toronto: Addiction Research Foundation of Toronto.

American Society of Addiction Medicine (ASAM). (1991). *Patient placement criteria for the treatment of psychoactive substance use disorders.* Washington, DC: Author.

Babor, T. F., Stephens, R. S., & Marlatt, G. A. (1987). Verbal report methods in clinical research on alcoholism: Response bias and its minimization. *Journal of Studies on Alcohol, 48,* 410–424.

Breslin, F. C., Sobell, M. B., Sobell, L. C., Buchan, G., & Cunningham, J. A. (1997). Toward a stepped care approach to treating problem drinkers: The predictive utility of within-treatment variables and therapist prognostic ratings. *Addiction, 92,* 1479–1489.

Brown, S. A., Goldman, M. S., & Christiansen, B. A. (1985). Do alcohol expectancies mediate drinking patterns of adults? *Journal of Consulting and Clinical Psychology, 53,* 512–519.

Chafetz, M. E., Blane, H. T., Abram, H. S., Golner, J., Lacy, E., McCourt, W. F., Clark, E., & Meyers, W. (1962). Establishing treatment relations with alcoholics. *Journal of Nervous and Mental Diseases, 134,* 395–409.

Chaney, E. F., O'Leary, M. R., & Marlatt, G. A. (1978). Skills training with alcoholics. *Journal of Consulting and Clinical Psychology, 46,* 1092–1104.

Cox, G. B., Walker, R. D., Freng, S. A., Short, B. A., Meijer, L., & Gilchrist, L. (1998). Outcome of a controlled trial of the effectiveness of intensive case management for chronic public inebriates. *Journal of Studies on Alcohol, 59,* 523–532.

Cunningham, J. A., Sobell, L. C., Sobell, M. B., & Gaskin, J. (1994). Alcohol and drug abusers' reasons for seeking treatment. *Addictive Behaviors, 19,* 691–696.

Edwards, G., & Gross, M. M. (1976). Alcohol dependence; Provisional description of a clinical syndrome. *British Medical Journal, 1,* 1058–1061.

Emrick, C., Tonigan, J. S., Montgomery, H., & Little, L. (1993). Alcoholics Anonymous: What is currently known? In B. S. McCrady & W. R. Miller (Eds.), *Research on Alcoholics Anonymous: Opportunities and alternatives* (pp. 41–78). New Brunswick, NJ: Alcohol Research Documentation, Rutgers University.

Epstein, E. E., & McCrady, B. S. (1998). Behavioral couples treatment of alcohol and drug use disorders: Current status and innovations. *Clinical Psychology Review, 18,* 689–711.

Epstein, E. E., McCrady, B. S., Miller, K. J., & Steinberg, M. L. (1994). Attrition from conjoint alco-holism treatment: Do dropouts differ from completers? *Journal of Substance Abuse, 6,* 249–265.

Femino, J., & Lewis, D. C. (1980). *Clinical pharmacology and therapeutics of the alcohol withdrawal syndrome* (Medical Monograph No. 1). Providence, RI: Brown University Program in Alcoholism and Drug Abuse.

Filstead, W. (1991). *Two-year treatment outcome. An evaluation of substance abuse services for adults and youths.* Park Ridge, IL: Parkside Medical Services.

Fink, E. B., Longabaugh, R., McCrady, B. S., Stout, R. L., Beattie, M., Ruggieri-Authelet, A., & McNeill, D. (1985). Effectiveness of alcoholism treatment in partial versus inpatient settings: Twenty-four month outcomes. *Addictive Behaviors, 10,* 235-248.

Finney, J. W., Moos, R. H., & Timko, C. (1999). The course of treated and untreated substance use disorders: Remission and resolution, relapse and mortality. In B. S. McCrady & E. E. Epstein (Eds.), *Addictions: A comprehensive guidebook* (pp. 30–49). New York: Oxford University Press.

Foy, D. W., Miller, P. M., Eisler, R. M., & O'Toole, D. H. (1976). Social skills training to teach alcoholics to refuse drinks effectively. *Journal of Studies on Alcohol, 37,* 1340–1345.

Frankenstein, W., Hay, W. M., & Nathan, P. E. (1985). Effects of intoxication on alcoholics' marital communication and problem solving. *Journal of Studies on Alcohol, 46,* 1–6.

Hasin, D., Paykin, A., Endicott, J., & Grant, G. (1999). The validity of DSM-IV alcohol abuse: Drunk drivers versus all others. *Journal of Studies on Alcohol, 60,* 746–755.

Helzer, J. E., Robins, L. N., Taylor, J. R., Carey, K., Miller, R. H., Combs-Orme, T., & Farmer, A. (1985). The extent of long-term moderate drinking among alcoholics discharged from medical and psychiatric treatment facilities. *New England Journal of Medicine, 312,* 1678–1682.

Institute of Medicine. (1990). *Broadening the base of treatment for alcohol problems.* Washington, DC: National Academy Press.

Langenbucher, J., Martin, C., Labouvie, E., Sanjuan, P. M., Bavly, L., & Pollock, N. (2000). Toward the DSM-V: The withdrawal-gate model vs. the DSM-IV in the diagnosis of alcohol abuse and dependence. *Journal of Consulting and Clinical Psychology, 68,* 799–809.

Liepman, M. R. (1993). Using family influence to motivate alcoholics to enter treatment: The Johnson Institute Intervention approach. In T. J. O'Farrell (Ed.), *Treating alcohol problems: Marital and family interventions* (pp. 54–77). New York: Guilford Press.

Longabaugh, R., McCrady, B., Fink, E., Stout, R., McAuley, T., & McNeill, D. (1983). Cost-effectiveness of alcoholism treatment in inpatient versus partial hospital settings: Six- month outcomes. *Journal of Studies on Alcohol, 44,* 1049-1071.

Longabaugh, R., Wirtz, P. W., Zweben, A., & Stout, R. L. (1998). Network support for drinking, Alcoholics Anonymous and long-term matching effects. *Addiction, 93,* 1313–1333.

Ludwig, A. M. (1985). Cognitive processes associated with "spontaneous" recovery from alcoholism. *Journal of Studies on Alcohol, 46,* 53–58.

MacCoun, R. J. (1998). Toward a psychology of harm reduction. *American Psychologist, 53*, 1199–1208.

Margolin, G., Talovic, S., & Weinstein, C. D. (1983). Areas of Change Questionnaire: A practical approach to marital assessment. *Journal of Consulting and Clinical Psychology, 51*, 921–931.

Marlatt, G. A., & Gordon, J. R. (Eds.). (1985). *Relapse prevention: Maintenance strategies in the treatment of addictive behaviors.* New York: Guilford Press.

Mayfield, D., McLeod, G., & Hall, P. (1974). The CAGE questionnaire: Validation of a new alcoholism instrument. *American Journal of Psychiatry, 131*, 1121–1123.

McConnaughy, E. A., Prochaska, J. O., & Velicer, W. F. (1983). Stages of change in psychotherapy: Measurement and sample profiles. *Psychotherapy: Theory, Research, and Practice, 20*, 243–250.

McCrady, B. S. (1992). A reply to Peele: Is this how you treat your friends? *Addictive Behaviors, 17*, 67–72.

McCrady, B. S., & Epstein, E. E. (1995). Marital therapy in the treatment of alcohol problems. In N. Jacobson & A. Gurman (Eds.), *Clinical handbook of couple therapy* (pp. 369–393). New York: Guilford Press.

McCrady, B. S., & Epstein, E. E. (1996). Theoretical bases of family approaches to substance abuse treatment. In F. Rotgers, D. S. Keller, & J. Morgenstern (Eds.), *Treating substance abuse: Theory and technique* (pp. 117–142). New York: Guilford Press.

McCrady, B. S., & Epstein, E. E. (Eds.). (1999). *Addictions: A comprehensive guidebook.* New York: Oxford University Press.

McCrady, B. S., Epstein, E. E., & Hirsch, L. (1999). Maintaining change after conjoint behavioral alcohol treatment for men: Outcomes at six months. *Addiction, 94*, 1381–1396.

McCrady, B. S., & Irvine, S. (1989). Self-help groups in the treatment of alcoholism. In R. Hester & W. R. Miller (Eds.), *Handbook of alcoholism treatment approaches: Effective alternatives* (pp. 153–169). New York: Pergamon Press.

McCrady, B. S., Longabaugh, R. L., Fink, E., Stout, R., Beattie, M., Ruggieri-Authelet, A., & McNeill, D. (1986). Cost effectiveness of alcoholism treatment in partial hospital versus inpatient settings after brief inpatient treatment: Twelve month outcomes. *Journal of Consulting and Clinical Psychology, 54*, 708–713.

McCrady, B. S., Stout, R., Noel, N., Abrams, D., & Nelson, H. F. (1991). Effectiveness of three types of spouse-involved behavioral alcoholism treatment. *British Journal of Addiction, 86*, 1415–1424.

McLellan, A. T., Grissom, G. R., Zanis, D., Randall, M., Brill, P., & O'Brien, C. P. (1997). Problem-service "matching" in addiction treatment: A prospective study in four programs. *Archives of General Psychiatry, 54*, 730–735.

McLellan, A. T., Kushner, H., Metzger, D., Peters, R., Smith, I., Grissom, G., Pettinati, H., & Argeriou, M. (1992). The fifth edition of the Addiction Severity Index. *Journal of Substance Abuse Treatment, 9*, 199–213.

Meyers, R. J., & Smith, J. E. (1995). *Clinical guide to alcohol treatment. The community reinforcement approach.* New York: Guilford Press.

Miller, W. R., Benefield, R. G., & Tonigan, J. S. (1993). Enhancing motivation for change in problem drinking: A controlled comparison of two therapist styles. *Journal of Consulting and Clinical Psychology, 61*, 455–461.

Miller, W. R., Leckman, A. L., Delaney, H. D., & Tinkcom, M. (1992). Long-term follow-up of behavioral self-control training. *Journal of Studies on Alcohol, 53*, 249–261.

Miller, W. R., Meyers, R. J., & Tonigan, J. S. (1999). Engaging the unmotivated in treatment for alcohol problems: A comparison of three strategies for intervention through family members. *Journal of Consulting and Clinical Psychology, 67*, 688–697.

Miller, W. R., & Rollnick, S. (1991). *Motivational interviewing: Preparing people to change addictive behavior.* New York: Guilford Press.

Miller, W. R., Tonigan, J. S., & Longabaugh, R. (1995). *The Drinker Inventory of Consequences (DrInC): An instrument for assessing adverse consequences of alcohol abuse.* Rockville, MD: National Institute on Alcohol Abuse and Alcoholism.

Miller, W. R., Zweben, A., DiClemente, C. C., & Rychtarik, R. G. (1995). *Motivational enhancement therapy manual.* Rockville, MD: National Institute on Alcohol Abuse and Alcoholism.

Moak, D. H., & Anton, R. F. (1999). Alcohol. In B. S. McCrady & E. E. Epstein (Eds.), *Addictions: A comprehensive guidebook* (pp. 75–94). New York: Oxford University Press.

Moderation Management (MM). (2000). *MM suggested guidelines and limits for moderate drinking* [On line]. Available: http://www.moderation.org/limits.html [1999, April].

Monti, P. M., Abrams, D. B., Kadden, R. M., & Cooney, N. L. (1989). *Treating alcohol dependence: A coping skills training guide.* New York: Guilford Press.

Monti, P. M., Abrams, D. B., Binkoff, J. A., Zwick, W. R., Liepman, M. R., Nirenberg, T. D., & Rohsenow, D. J. (1990). Communication skills training, communication skills training with family and cognitive behavioral mood management training for alcoholics. *Journal of Studies on Alcohol, 51*, 263–270.

Moos, R. H., & Billings, A. (1982). Children of alcoholics during the recovery process: Alcoholic and matched control families. *Addictive Behaviors, 7*, 155–163.

Moos, R. H., Finney, J. W., & Cronkite, R. (1990). *Alcoholism treatment: Context, process, and outcome.* New York: Oxford University Press.

Moos, R. H., Finney, J. W., & Gamble, W. (1982). The process of recovery from alcoholism: II. Comparing spouses of alcoholic patients and matched community controls. *Journal of Studies on Alcohol, 43*, 888–909.

Nathan, P. E., & McCrady, B. S. (1987). Bases for the use of abstinence as a goal in the behavioral treatment of alcohol abusers. *Drugs and Society, 1*, 109–132.

National Advisory Council on Alcohol Abuse and Alcoholism, Subcommittee on Health Services Research. (1996). *Final report: Panel on financing and organization.* Washington, DC: U.S. Department of Health and Human Services.

O'Farrell, T. J., Choquette, K. A., & Cutter, H. S. G. (1998). Couples relapse prevention sessions after behavioral marital therapy for male alcoholics: Outcomes during the three years after starting treatment. *Journal of Studies on Alcohol, 59*, 357–370.

O'Farrell, T. J., & Cutter, H. S. G. (1984). Behavioral marital therapy couples groups for male alcoholics and their wives. *Journal of Substance Abuse Treatment, 1*, 191–204.

Ojehegan, A., & Berglund, M. (1989). Changes in drinking goals in a two-year outpatient alcoholic treatment program. *Addictive Behaviors, 14*, 1–10.

Orford, J., Guthrie, S., Nicholls, P., Oppenheimer, E., Egert, S., & Hensman, C. (1975). Self-reported coping behavior of wives of alcoholics and its association with drinking outcome. *Journal of Studies on Alcohol, 36*, 1254–1267.

Orford, J., & Keddie, A. (1986). Abstinence or controlled drinking in clinical practice: A test of the dependence and persuasion hypotheses. *British Journal of Addiction, 81*, 495–504.

Pan, H. S., Neidig, P. H., & O'Leary, K. D. (1994). Male–female and aggressor–victim differences in the factor structure of the Modified Conflict Tactics Scale. *Journal of Interpersonal Violence, 9*, 366–382.

Paolino, T. J., Jr., McCrady, B. S., & Diamond, S. (1978). Some alcoholic marriage statistics: An overview. *International Journal of the Addictions, 13*, 1252–1257.

Parsons, O. A. (1998). Neurocognitive deficits in alcoholics and social drinkers: A continuum? *Alcoholism: Clinical and Experimental Research, 22*, 954–961.

Pettinati, H. M., Sugerman, A. A., DiDonato, N., & Maurer, H. S. (1982). The natural history of alcoholism over four years after treatment. *Journal of Studies on Alcohol, 43*, 201–215.

Prochaska, J. O., DiClemente, C. C., & Norcross, J. C. (1992). In search of how people change: Applications to addictive behaviors. *American Psychologist, 47*, 1102–1114.

Project MATCH Research Group. (1997a). Project MATCH secondary a priori hypotheses. *Addiction, 92*, 1671–1698.

Project MATCH Research Group. (1997b). Matching alcoholism treatments to client heterogeneity: Project MATCH posttreatment drinking outcomes. *Journal of Studies on Alcohol, 58*, 7–29.

Project MATCH Research Group. (1998). Matching alcoholism treatments to client heterogeneity: Project MATCH three-year drinking outcomes. *Alcoholism: Clinical and Experimental Research, 22*, 1300–1311.

Raytek, H. S., McCrady, B. S., Epstein, E. E., & Hirsch, L. S. (1999). Therapeutic alliance and the retention of couples in conjoint alcoholism treatment. *Addictive Behaviors, 24*, 317–330.

Rhines, K. C., McCrady, B. S., Morgan, T. J., & Hirsch, L. S. (1997). Integrated assessment of alcohol and drug use: The Rutgers Consequences of Use Questionnaire [Abstract No. 544]. *Alcoholism: Clinical and Experimental Research, 21*, 94A.

Robins, L. N., Wing, J., Wittchen, H. U., Helzer, J. E., Babor, T. F., Burke, J., Farmer, A., Jablenski, A., Pickens, R., Regier, D. A., Sartorius, N., & Towle, L. H. (1988). The prevalence of psychiatric disorders in patients with alcohol and other drug problems. *Archives of General Psychiatry, 45*, 1023–1031.

Rollnick, S., Heather, N., Gold, R., & Hall, W. (1992). Development of a short "Readiness to Change" Questionnaire for use in brief opportunistic interventions. *British Journal of Addictions, 87*, 743–754.

Room, R. (1993). Alcoholics Anonymous as a social movement. In B. S. McCrady & W. R. Miller (Eds.), *Research on Alcoholics Anonymous: Opportunities and alternatives* (pp. 167–188). New Brunswick, NJ: Alcohol Research Documentation, Rutgers University.

Rose, S. J., Zweben, A., & Stoffel, V. (1999). Interfaces between substance abuse treatment and other health and social systems. In B. S. McCrady & E. E. Epstein (Eds.), *Addictions: A comprehensive guidebook* (pp. 421–438). New York: Oxford University Press.

Rosenberg, H. (1993). Prediction of controlled drinking by alcoholics and problem drinkers. *Psychological Bulletin, 113*, 129–139.

Rosenthal, R. N., & Westreich, L. (1999). Treatment of persons with dual diagnoses of substance use disorder and other psychological problems. In B. S. McCrady & E. E. Epstein (Eds.), *Addictions: A comprehensive guidebook* (pp. 439–476). New York: Oxford University Press.

Russell, M. (1994). New assessment tools for drinking in pregnancy: T-ACE, TWEAK, and others. *Alcohol Health and Research World, 18*, 55–61.

Selzer, M. L. (1971). The Michigan Alcoholism Screening Test: The quest for a new diagnostic instrument. *American Journal of Psychiatry, 127*, 1653–1658.

Sheehan, T., & Owen, P. (1999). The disease model. In B. S. McCrady & E. E. Epstein (Eds.), *Addictions: A comprehensive guidebook* (pp. 268–286). New York: Oxford University Press.

Sisson, R. W., & Azrin, N. (1986). Family-member involvement to initiate and promote treatment of problem drinkers. *Journal of Behavior Therapy and Experimental Psychiatry, 17*, 15–21.

Skinner, H., & Allen, B. A. (1982). Alcohol dependence syndrome: Measurement and validation. *Journal of Abnormal Psychology, 91*, 199–209.

Sobell, M. B., Maisto, S. A., Sobell, L. C., Cooper, T., & Saunders, B. (1980). Developing a prototype for evaluating alcohol treatment effectiveness. In L. C. Sobell, M. B. Sobell & E. Ward (Eds.), *Evaluating alcohol treatment effectiveness: Recent advances* (pp. 129–150). New York: Pergamon Press.

Spanier, G. (1976). Measuring dyadic adjustment: New scales for assessing the quality of marriage and similar dyads. *Journal of Marriage and the Family, 38*, 15–28.

Spear, S. F., & Mason, M. (1991). Impact of chemical dependency on family health status. *International Journal of the Addictions, 26*, 179–187.

Spitzer, R. L., Williams, J. B. W., Gibbon, M., & First, M. B. (1996). *Structured Clinical Interview for DSM-IV: Patient Edition (with Psychotic Screen—Version 1.0)*. Washington, DC: American Psychiatric Press.

Stewart, S. H. (1996). Alcohol abuse in individuals exposed to trauma: A critical review. *Psychological Bulletin, 120*, 83–112.

Stinchfield, R., & Owen, P. (1998). Hazelden's model of treatment and its outcome. *Addictive Behaviors, 23*, 669–683.

Thomas, E. J., Santa, C., Bronson, D., & Oyserman, D. (1987). Unilateral family therapy with the spouses of alcoholics. *Journal of Social Service Research, 10*, 145–162.

Thomas, E. J., Yoshioka, M., & Ager, R. D. (1996). Spouse enabling of alcohol abuse: Conception, assessment, and modification. *Journal of Substance Abuse, 8*, 61–80.

Vaillant, G. (1983). *The natural history of alcoholism.* Cambridge, MA: Harvard University Press.

Vaillant, G., & Milofsky, E. S. (1982). Natural history of male alcoholism: 4. Paths to recovery. *Archives of General Psychiatry, 39*, 127–133.

Zimmerman, M. (1994). *Interview guide for evaluating DSM-IV psychiatric disorders and the mental status examination.* East Greenwich, RI: Psych Products Press.

Zitter, R. E., & McCrady, B. S. (1979). *The Drinking Patterns Questionnaire.* Unpublished manuscript.

Chapter 10

COCAINE DEPENDENCE

Stephen T. Higgins
Alan J. Budney
Stacey C. Sigmon

In this chapter we follow the case of "Steve," a 24-year-old individual suffering from cocaine dependence who would ordinarily be considered to be among the most difficult types of patients for someone administering psychosocial interventions. As is typical with this population, Steve presented not only with cocaine dependence, but also with alcohol dependence; problems with anger management; heavy use of cigarettes and marijuana; suicidal ideation; and major interpersonal, social, and occupational problems (including a prohibition from visiting his 5-year-old daughter). The fact that Stephen Higgins and his team of close associates have been able to create a treatment protocol for individuals such as Steve—a protocol with strong empirical support—is in itself a remarkable achievement. But only those most familiar with this approach would have a good idea of the multifaceted nature of this brief semistructured strategy, which includes attention to the full range of addictive behaviors, as well as mood disturbances, interpersonal relationships, and problems in living. Without this comprehensive approach, there seems no question that these treatment strategies would not enjoy the success that they do. Even clinicians or students not working directly with addictive behaviors will benefit from being familiar with this new generation of successful psychological approaches to drug abuse.—D. H. B.

OVERVIEW

Cocaine abuse and dependence represent a serious public health problem in the United States, and to a lesser extent Canada and Europe. Cocaine abuse and dependence are associated with a host of disturbing individual and societal problems, including increased rates of crime and incarceration, homelessness, drug-exposed neonates, infectious disease (AIDS, hepatitis, tuberculosis), prostitution, and other serious social and medical problems (Konkol & Olsen, 1996; Montoya & Atkinson, 1996; National Institute of Justice, 1999; Substance Abuse and Mental Health Services Administration [SAMHSA], 1997; Tardiff et al., 1994).

The problems of cocaine abuse and dependence that have received so much publicity over the past couple of decades, while not unique to any one country, certainly have been largely centered in the United States. The history of cocaine use in the United States is an interesting one (e.g., Byck, 1987). Briefly, cocaine use first became popular in this country during the latter part of the 19th century. When first introduced, cocaine was touted as a wonderful tonic that could cure a wide array of common ailments. It was not long, however, before cocaine's potential for promoting repeated drug use and many serious untoward effects was realized. Following recognition of the serious problems associated with cocaine use and passage of strict legislation designed to reduce availability, cocaine-related problems in the United States largely disappeared by the early 1930s.

Save for occasional reports regarding its use in medical procedures, little more was heard about cocaine use in the United States from that point until the end of the 1960s, when its popularity again began to increase as part of a more general increase in the use of illicit drugs. As a wonderful example of history repeating itself, cocaine was again touted by many as a relatively benign, "fun" drug, and its popularity grew rapidly. By the mid-1980s, some 25 million U.S. residents (12% of individuals 12 years old and over) reported lifetime cocaine use, and 5.3 million (3%) reported current use (in the past 30 days) (SAMHSA, 1999). Consistent with the earlier experience, cocaine's ability to promote repeated drug use and serious untoward effects was soon realized. Large numbers of those using the drug began presenting in emergency rooms due to cocaine overdose or other medical complications, and in substance abuse treatment clinics seeking help with cessation. Also consistent with the earlier experience is that the rediscovery of cocaine's "darker side" again resulted in a precipitous decline in use. As of 1998, current cocaine use in the United States has decreased from its peak of 5.7 million in 1985 to 1.8 million (0.8%) (SAMHSA, 1999). Unfortunately, the prevalence of heavy cocaine use (weekly or more), estimated to be about 600,000 (0.3%), has not changed significantly since it was first estimated in 1985. Whether this recalcitrance in the practices of those who use cocaine more heavily also follows patterns seen in the early part of the 19th century is unknown. However, this relatively recalcitrant pattern of heavy cocaine use is what contributes most to the social problems associated with cocaine use.

The earlier experiences with cocaine-related problems notwithstanding, the scientific and clinical communities were unprepared for this recent cocaine epidemic. When the cocaine problem reemerged, scientific understanding of the basic pharmacology underlying cocaine's abuse potential was limited, and information on effective clinical management of cocaine abuse and dependence was virtually nonexistent. Fortunately, that picture has changed dramatically during the past 15 years or so, owing to a tremendous surge of scientific research focused on cocaine—an amount that appears to be unprecedented in the field of drug abuse research (Budney, Higgins, Hughes, & Bickel, 1992). Substantial advances in basic and clinical research have been made in understanding cocaine's myriad effects, including its ability to produce depen-

dence (Hammer, 1995; Higgins & Katz, 1998). Included among these advances is the development of efficacious psychosocial treatments for cocaine dependence, which constitute the main focus of this chapter.

The particular focus of this chapter is a behavioral approach to outpatient treatment of cocaine dependence, known as the "community reinforcement approach (CRA) plus vouchers treatment" (Budney & Higgins, 1998). This intervention was developed at our research center and has a relatively extensive amount of evidence from controlled, randomized clinical trials supporting its efficacy (see below). The treatment combines therapy based on an adaptation of CRA, originally developed as a treatment for severe alcoholism (Hunt & Azrin, 1973), and a voucher-based incentive program that builds on prior efficacious contingency management interventions developed to treat those using heroin and other illicit drugs (Higgins & Silverman, 1999; Stitzer & Higgins, 1995). Another intervention with sound empirical support for its efficacy as an outpatient treatment for cocaine dependence is relapse prevention (RP) therapy (Carroll et al., 1994; Maude-Griffin et al., 1998). Some important elements of RP are incorporated in CRA and reviewed below, but interested readers should consult the therapist manual available on that treatment (Carroll, 1998). There are not yet any controlled trials supporting the efficacy of inpatient or residential treatments for cocaine abuse or dependence, and the available comparison studies of inpatient versus outpatient treatment have shown higher costs and no advantage in outcome for the former (see, e.g., Alterman et al., 1994). Hence the emphasis in this chapter is on outpatient care. No reliably efficacious pharmacotherapy for cocaine dependence yet exists, aside from disulfiram therapy for those individuals who have co-occurring problems with cocaine and alcohol use. Accordingly, discussion of pharmacological treatments in this chapter is restricted to disulfiram therapy. The National Institute on Drug Abuse (1999) has recently published 13 principles of effective treatment for illicit drug abuse based on 25 years of research, and we have tried to underscore those principles throughout this chapter (Table 10.1). Although the focus of this chapter is on a particular treatment model, we have tried at least to mention all avail-

TABLE 10.1. Principles of Effective Treatment

1. No single treatment is appropriate for all individuals.
2. Treatment needs to be readily available.
3. Effective treatment attends to multiple needs of the individual, not just his or her drug use.
4. An individual's treatment and services plan must be assessed continually and modified as necessary to ensure that the plan meets the person's changing needs.
5. Remaining in treatment for an adequate period of time is critical for treatment effectiveness (i.e., ≥3 months).
6. Counseling (individual and/or group) and other behavioral therapies are critical components of effective treatment for addiction.
7. Medications are an important element of treatment for many patients, especially when combined with counseling and other behavioral therapies.
8. Addicted or drug-abusing individuals with coexisting mental disorders should have both disorders treated in an integrated way.
9. Medical detoxification is only the first stage of addiction treatment and by itself does little to change long-term drug use.
10. Treatment does not need to be voluntary to be effective.
11. Possible drug use during treatment must be monitored continuously.
12. Treatment programs should provide assessment for HIV/AIDS, hepatitis B and C, tuberculosis and other infectious diseases, and counseling to help patients modify or change behaviors that place themselves or others at risk of infection.
13. Recovery from drug addiction can be a long-term process and frequently requires multiple episodes of treatment.

Note. From the National Institute on Drug Abuse (1999).

able information on efficacious treatment practices for cocaine dependence (see Principle 1, Table 10.1).

DEFINING THE CLINICAL DISORDER

Before proceeding to discussions about treatment, we define cocaine dependence—the clinical disorder that is the topic of this chapter. For this purpose, we have turned to currently used criteria for diagnosing cocaine abuse and dependence. Shown in Tables 10.2 and 10.3 are the criteria for diagnosing substance abuse and dependence, respectively, as outlined in the fourth edition of the *Diagnostic and Statistical Manual of Mental Disorders* (DSM-IV; American Psychiatric Association, 1994). These criteria, when applied to cocaine

use, represent a cluster of behavioral and physiological signs and symptoms resulting from a pattern of continued use despite significant cocaine-related problems. To receive a DSM-IV diagnosis of cocaine abuse, a person must satisfy one or more of the four criteria listed in Table 10.2 within a 12-month period, and cannot currently or previously have satisfied a diagnosis of cocaine dependence. The criteria for abuse are designed to focus on harmful consequences of cocaine use, rather than the pattern of cocaine use per se and tolerance or withdrawal, which constitute the core of the dependence diagnosis. Our experience in operating a cocaine use cessation clinic is that the vast majority of adults seeking professional treatment regarding their cocaine use meet dependence criteria. Treatment of cocaine dependence is therefore the focus of this chapter, but a reasonable assumption (pending evidence to the contrary) is that the same general practices will also apply to the treatment of cocaine abuse.

To receive a DSM-IV diagnosis of cocaine dependence, the person must have exhibited

TABLE 10.2. DSM-IV Criteria for Substance Abuse

A. A maladaptive pattern of substance use leading to clinically significant impairment or distress, as manifested by one (or more) of the following, occurring within a 12-month period:

(1) recurrent substance use resulting in a failure to fulfill major role obligations at work, school, or home (e.g., repeated absences or poor work performance related to substance use; substance-related absences, suspensions, or expulsions from school; neglect of children or household)

(2) recurrent substance use in situations in which it is physically hazardous (e.g., driving an automobile or operating a machine when impaired by substance use)

(3) recurrent substance-related legal problems (e.g., arrests for substance-related disorderly conduct)

(4) continued substance use despite having persistent or recurrent social or interpersonal problems caused or exacerbated by the effects of the substance (e.g., arguments with spouse about consequences or intoxication, physical fights)

B. The symptoms have never met the criteria for Substance Dependence for this class of substance.

Note. Reprinted with permission from the *Diagnostic and Statistical Manual of Mental Disorders*, Fourth Edition. Copyright 1994 American Psychiatric Association.

TABLE 10.3. DSM-IV Criteria for Substance Dependence

A maladaptive pattern of substance use, leading to clinically significant impairment or distress, as manifested by three (or more) of the following, occurring at any time in the same 12-month period:

(1) tolerance, as defined by either of the following:

    (a) a need for markedly increased amounts of the substance to achieve intoxication or desired effect

    (b) markedly diminished effect with continued use of the same amount of the substance

(2) withdrawal, as manifested by either of the following:

    (a) the characteristic withdrawal syndrome for the substance (refer to Criteria A and B of the criteria sets for Withdrawal from the specific substances)

    (b) the same (or a closely related) substance is taken to relieve or avoid withdrawal symptoms

(3) the substance is often taken in larger amounts or over a longer period than was intended

(4) there is a persistent desire or unsuccessful efforts to cut down or control substance use

(5) a great deal of time is spent in activities necessary to obtain the substance (e.g., visiting multiple doctors or driving long distances), use the substance (e.g., chain-smoking), or recover from its effects

(6) important social, occupational, or recreational activities are given up or reduced because of substance use

(7) the substance use is continued despite knowledge of having a persistent or recurrent physical or psychological problem that is likely to have been caused or exacerbated by the substance (e.g., current cocaine use despite recognition of cocaine-induced depression, or continued drinking despite recognition that an ulcer was made worse by alcohol consumption)

Specify if:

    With Physiological Dependence: evidence of tolerance or withdrawal (i.e., either Item 1 or 2 is present)

    Without Physiological Dependence: no evidence of tolerance or withdrawal (i.e., neither Item 1 nor 2 is present)

Course specifiers (see text for definitions):

    Early Full Remission
    Early Partial Remission
    Sustained Full Remission
    Sustained Partial Remission
    On Agonist Therapy
    In a Controlled Environment

Note. Reprinted with permission from the *Diagnostic and Statistical Manual of Mental Disorders*, Fourth Edition. Copyright 1994 American Psychiatric Association.

three or more of the criteria listed in Table 10.3 within a 12-month period. Note that while tolerance and withdrawal are listed first among the seven criteria, neither is necessary for a dependence diagnosis. One simply must meet any three of the seven criteria listed within a 12-month period to satisfy the diagnosis. The phrase "with physiological dependence" can be used to specify diagnoses in which tolerance or withdrawal is present, and the phrase "without physiological dependence" to specify those where they are not present. The rationale provided in DSM-IV for use of those specifiers is that tolerance and withdrawal may be associated with an increased risk for general medical problems and relapse. That may be so with some substances, but with cocaine, the matter is unclear. There

is good experimental evidence that tolerance develops to many of cocaine's effects, even following a single dose. Greater scientific debate exists regarding whether cocaine induces a withdrawal syndrome. There is no question that repeated cocaine use induces a myriad of signs and symptoms, but there is also no question that they are not of the pronounced type seen with opioids and central nervous system depressants. Those caveats notwithstanding, evidence does support a position that on average more severe cocaine dependence is associated with poorer treatment outcome. Severity is influenced by the frequency of use, amount of drug used, route of administration (intravenous and smoked routes having a poorer prognosis than intranasal), among other factors. There seems little doubt that those factors will be positively correlated with tolerance and with the number of untoward signs and symptoms exhibited following a period of repeated cocaine use, and to that extent merit attention in a diagnostic assessment.

Regarding the course specifiers, "full remission" indicates that none of the criteria for abuse or dependence have been met for at least 1 month; "partial remission" indicates that one or more criteria have been met but that the full criteria for dependence have not been met for at least 1 month. The terms "early" and "sustained" are used to indicate whether remission has lasted for less than or greater than 12 months, respectively. The clinical utility of these course specifiers rests on evidence that the probability of relapse decreases as an orderly function of the length of time the individual has been abstinent (Higgins et al., 2000). The specifier "on agonist therapy" does not apply to cocaine abuse or dependence at this time. The specifier "in a controlled environment" is applicable, as the evidence noted above about relapse probability's being inversely related to the duration of abstinence is based on individuals residing in environments wherein the opportunity for cocaine use was present. Although not systematically studied with cocaine use, this relationship between duration of abstinence and the probability of relapse is not likely to apply or will be significantly weaker when the period of abstinence was achieved in an environment where cocaine was unavailable. Practically speaking, this specifier is commonly needed in clinical practice with individuals mandated to treatment by the criminal justice system as a condition of release from prison, whose last cocaine use may have been months or years prior to entering treatment.

This section has defined the disorder and outlined commonly used criteria for diagnosing cocaine dependence. Now we turn to other practical matters regarding the clinical management of cocaine dependence.

ASSESSMENT

A comprehensive assessment is a fundamental first step in effective clinical management of cocaine dependence. In this section we outline the assessment practices used in our clinic, which is a university-based outpatient center that specializes in the treatment of adults with cocaine dependence.

Intake Assessment

All initial clinic contacts are handled by a receptionist who establishes that the person seeking treatment reports problems related to cocaine use, is aged 18 years or above, and resides within the county in which the clinic is located. The CRA plus vouchers treatment that we use is intensive, requiring several clinic visits per week. Persons living outside the county are often unable to follow such a demanding schedule. Those who do not satisfy those basic inclusion criteria are referred to an appropriate alternative clinic. Those who meet the criteria receive an appointment for an intake assessment.

Every effort is made to schedule the intake assessment interview as soon as possible (Principle 2, Table 10.1). Motivation to enter treatment in the population with cocaine dependence can be quite tenuous. Many times patients call immediately after a cocaine binge, when they are experiencing the acute consequences of their use or are in the midst of a cocaine-induced depression that commonly follows a cocaine binge. The impact of these factors can resolve quickly. Hence, if the intake appointment is scheduled more than a day after the initial contact, the probability of attending the clinic decreases. Indeed, results from several studies demonstrate that scheduling the interview within 24 hours of clinic contact significantly reduces attrition between the initial clinic contact and assessment interview (e.g., Festinger, Lamb, Kirby, & Marlowe, 1996). Some patients cannot come in within 24 hours, and so our secondary goal is to get them in within 72 hours.

Patients are informed that the intake interview will take about 3 hours. This initial session is one of the most important. The clinic staff should be aware of the patient's potential uneasiness and try to make the person feel at ease. Being courteous, complimenting the patient on taking this important first step toward change, anticipating that some clients may be physically ill or uncomfortable because of recent substance abuse and being respectful of that, being flexible with tardiness, and the like can help. Accommodating the need for brief breaks, for food or drink, or for a brief phone call can help as well. Throughout all interactions, we seek to be empathic and to convey a very upbeat, "You can do it" message. As mentioned above, many individuals with cocaine dependence are ambivalent about treatment, and their mood may be labile due to recent cocaine use. Providing a pleasant clinic atmosphere may help to calm such patients and increase the chances of engaging them in treatment.

During the intake assessment, we collect detailed information on cocaine and other substance use; evaluate treatment readiness; and assess psychiatric functioning, employment/vocational status, recreational interests, current social supports, family and social problems, and legal issues (see Principle 3, Table 10.1). Following is a discussion of instruments that we use to obtain such information, mentioned in the order in which they are typically administered.

Self-Administered Questionnaires

We use several questionnaires that can be completed by the client upon arriving at the clinic for an initial intake assessment. The intake worker greets the client, introduces himself/herself, and briefly but carefully informs the client about what to expect during the intake process. It is essential to ask about the client's reading ability prior to having him/her complete self-administered questionnaires. If there is doubt about reading capability, we discreetly ask clients to read several questions aloud to get an indication of whether they can complete the forms without staff assistance. For clients who read poorly, the questionnaires can be read aloud by a staff member in a private setting. This must be done with care and positive regard for the discomfort such clients may feel under these circumstances. Clients who read competently are given approximately 45 minutes to complete the forms.

We have each client complete a routine brief demographics questionnaire. A current address and phone number are important, as is a phone number of someone who will always know the client's whereabouts. This information is needed for purposes of treatment outreach efforts should the client stop coming to scheduled therapy sessions or need to be contacted for other clinical purposes,

and for contacting the client for routine posttreatment follow-up evaluations.

The Stages of Change Readiness and Treatment Eagerness Scale (SOCRATES; Miller & Tonigan, 1996) provides information on the client's perception of the severity of his/her cocaine use problem and readiness to engage in behavior to reduce use. This questionnaire provides a quantitative index of motivation to change, which may be an important indicator of the client's willingness to comply with certain treatment goals. Three versions of the SOCRATES that refer to specific substances (i.e., cocaine, alcohol, and other drugs) are administered, for the client's motivation to reduce substance use is likely to be substance-specific. Clinicians should be prepared for patients to vary quite a bit in their readiness to change use of different substances. Almost all who seek treatment in our clinic are ready to act toward changing their cocaine use. However, many are more ambivalent about changing their alcohol or marijuana use, which are the two other forms of drug use we deal with most frequently. Our approach is to reinforce the action each patient is ready to take with cocaine, and to empathetically share our empirical knowledge regarding the influence of different forms of other drug use on the probability of successfully discontinuing cocaine use. Our recommendation is that at least short-term abstinence from use of all intoxicating substance use is the path with the greatest chance of success. Use of alcohol can directly increase the probability of cocaine use and predicts poor outcome. Use of marijuana does not predict poor outcome with regard to cocaine use per se, but is associated with problems of its own.

We use an adaptation of the Cocaine Dependency Self-Test (Washton, Stone, & Hendrickson, 1988) as an efficient means to collect specific information regarding the types of adverse effects of cocaine that clients have experienced. Such information can be useful in helping clients problem-solve regarding the pros and cons of cocaine use, as part of efforts to promote and sustain motivation for change during the course of treatment.

The Michigan Alcoholism Screening Test (MAST) is a widely used brief alcoholism screening instrument (Selzer, 1971). Considering that almost all clients entering treatment for cocaine abuse and dependence use alcohol, and that approximately 60% meet diagnostic criteria for alcohol dependence, the MAST is useful for flagging clients with alcohol problems.

The Beck Depression Inventory (BDI) is used to screen for depressive symptomatology (Beck, Ward, Mendelson, Mock, & Erbaugh, 1961), and is readministered on a regular basis to monitor progress with those clients who score in the clinical range at intake. The average BDI score of cocaine abusers entering treatment falls in the clinical range of that scale (average BDI intake score in our clinic is 19.8 ± 11.9). For most clients, those scores decrease precipitously after 1 or 2 weeks in treatment. However, that is not true for all clients. Therefore, it is important to carefully assess and monitor depressive symptomatology, and to refer or intervene when symptoms do not remit. Assessing and monitoring for suicidality are also very important. We do so via a protocol developed in collaboration with our local mental health crisis service.

The Symptom Checklist 90—Revised (SCL-90-R; Derogatis, 1983) is also used to screen for psychiatric symptomatology, and is helpful in determining whether a more in-depth psychiatric evaluation is warranted. The SCL-90-R can likewise be easily readministered to monitor progress or change in psychiatric status.

After these self-administered questionnaires have been completed, they are reviewed by the intake worker to be sure that all questions have been completed and that the information appears consistent. Any obvious inconsistencies are resolved with the patient.

Program Description

We find it useful to break up the data-gathering aspects of the initial assessment between completion of the self-administered questionnaires and initiation of the structured interviews. We provide a brief description of the treatment program and its philosophy at this time. Clients are given the opportunity to ask questions or express any concerns they may have. The goals here are to orient the clients regarding what will happen in treatment, to create an atmosphere of optimism, and to give clients hope that they can succeed in treatment. This description and interaction is typically brief (10–15 minutes). A therapist provides more detailed rationales and de-

scriptions after the structured interviews are completed. When a client asks questions about the treatment process, the intake worker provides brief answers and reassures the client that a therapist will soon be meeting with him/her to provide much more information about the program and how it works.

In providing the brief description, the intake worker explains that our program is confidential and specifically designed for persons having problems with cocaine. The patient is informed about the overall duration of treatment, the recommended frequency and duration of clinic visits, and the general foci and orientation of our treatment approach (i.e., lifestyle changes). We explain that the primary goals of such changes are to discontinue cocaine use and make positive changes that will result in greater life satisfaction:

> "This program is specifically designed for people with cocaine problems. Many people also use other substances like alcohol or marijuana, so we address those too if necessary, but the focus is on cocaine. Everything is completely confidential; that is, no one is informed about your participation or given access to your records unless you clearly tell us to provide such information. The program lasts for 6 months; the first 3 months are more intensive than the second 3 months. You will be expected to come for counseling sessions twice per week during the first 3 months, and to provide a urine specimen three times per week. The treatment is specifically designed to directly address your cocaine use, and also to help you with other problems you may be having. That is, the clinic's primary goals are to help you stop using cocaine and to help you make positive changes in your lifestyle that might help you stay off cocaine and live a more satisfying life."

Examples are given of what might occur during treatment:

> "If you are interested in finding a job, the therapists will help you with the search, with a resumé, and with transportation and phone support if necessary. If you would like to go back to school, we can help you obtain the applications, access funding and assistance, and even take you to an interview if you don't have transportation. If you are having problems in your relation-

ship, relationship counseling is available. If you don't regularly participate in any fun activities, we have lots of suggestions and may even take you to do some of these, like basketball, tennis, fishing, boating, arts and crafts classes, and so on.

"Also, we teach you how to manage certain kinds of problems that may increase your cocaine use. For example, if you're having problems controlling anger, we can help with anger management skills. If you have money problems, we can assist you with financial management. If you have difficulty with behavior problems with your children, we can assist you directly, or we can assist you in getting some additional help. If you have trouble relaxing, we can work on relaxation skills and stress management. If you have other types of problems, we'll try to help you with those."

In addition, the intake worker provides a very brief description of the incentive program that our clinic uses:

"You also will participate in our incentive program. How this works is that if you stay clean—that is, if you provide urine samples that are cocaine-free—you can earn points that can be used to support your goals. What this means is that if you stay clean, you will accumulate points that can be used to pay for activities like going to the movies, joining a gym, taking a class, buying a fishing rod, and so on. Your therapist will tell you more about these things when you meet him or her after our interview."

Semistructured Interviews

A semistructured drug history interview (developed in our clinic) is used to facilitate the collection of information on current and past drug use.

The goal in assessing a drug use history is to obtain detailed information regarding the duration, severity, and pattern of the client's cocaine and other drug use. The accuracy of the client's report of cocaine use (amount and frequency) is facilitated by the use of an effective technique for reviewing recent use (e.g., the Timeline Follow-Back Interview; Sobell & Sobell, 1992). Using a calendar as a prompt, clients are asked to recall on a day-by-day basis the number of days they used in the past

week and the amount used per occasion. Grams are typically the best metric for determining amount of cocaine used. The same assessment is conducted for the past 3 weeks and as far back in time as needed for diagnostic reasons. Similar but less detailed information is collected regarding current and past use of other substances. This technique results in a good overview of the pattern of cocaine and other drug use during the past 30 days. The intake worker asks for as much clarification as possible to help obtain an accurate assessment of a client's drug use history.

The Addiction Severity Index (ASI; McLellan et al., 1985) is designed to provide reliable, valid assessments of multiple problems commonly associated with substance abuse and dependence. The ASI provides a quantitative, time-based assessment of problem severity on the following subscales: Alcohol, Drug, Employment, Medical, Legal, Family/Social, and Psychological. A cocaine subscale can be estimated as well (Carroll et al., 1994). The information obtained in this interview is quite useful for developing treatment plans that include lifestyle change goals. The ASI is also a useful instrument for assessing progress at follow-up, in that it is time-based and yields quantitative composite scores for multiple problem areas. Training on ASI administration is necessary to ensure that the intake worker conducts a reliable ASI interview (contact Deltametrics, 1 Commerce Square, 2005 Market Street, Suite 1020, Philadelphia, PA 19103, for expert training in the use of the ASI).

We conduct a clinical interview specifically assessing whether patients satisfy DSM-IV criteria for cocaine dependence and other substance abuse or dependence. Diagnoses are made by trained master's- or doctorate-level psychologists.

The Practical Needs Assessment questionnaire (developed in our clinic) is used to determine whether the client has any pressing needs or crises that may interfere with initial treatment engagement (e.g., housing, legal, transportation, or child care). The intake worker asks specific questions regarding current housing, child care, legal circumstances, medical issues, and other matters that may be of current and serious concern to the client. Detailed information is collected on any identified needs. The intent here is to identify matters that may need immediate clinical attention. Because the lives of many individuals entering treatment for cocaine dependence are in chaos, the probability of engaging and keeping them in treatment may be compromised if swift attention is not provided to assist with certain acute needs. For example, a single mother with two young children is likely to be unable to attend the clinic several times weekly unless assistance is offered in arranging for child care.

After completing these interviews, the intake worker informs the client that the client will be meeting with his/her therapist in a few minutes. A brief break (5–10 minutes) is given. During this break, the intake worker completes an intake summary sheet; this is provided to the therapist who will be taking on this new case, along with all of the supporting intake information. The intake worker also meets briefly with the therapist to review the case. The patient is then introduced to the therapist. We try never to allow a patient to leave the intake interview without a brief meeting with a therapist, so that he/she can depart feeling that treatment has begun, and with concrete plans for abstaining from cocaine use until the next clinic visit.

In many ways, this initial meeting is an orientation session. If the patient is willing, this session may last up to an hour or more. The session is used to establish rapport with the patient and to provide further rationales for our treatment approach. Much of the information covered briefly by the intake worker is reviewed in more detail. Doing so permits the patient to develop clear expectations about what to expect during treatment. We continue with the "can do" approach and tout our clinic's success in helping patients "beat cocaine dependence." We acknowledge how hard the patient and clinic staff are going to have to work, but convey a very confident message that by working together success can be achieved. The therapist and patient collaboratively begin formulating an initial treatment plan during this session. Patients are oriented to the rigorous urinalysis-monitoring regimen and incentive program by reviewing the abstinence contract (Figure 10.1). Also, if disulfiram therapy is indicated because of problematic alcohol use, initial steps are taken toward implementing that protocol. More information about initial treatment sessions is provided below (see "Getting Therapy Underway").

THE CRA PLUS VOUCHERS TREATMENT MODEL

Conceptual Framework

The CRA plus vouchers treatment is based largely on the concepts and principles of operant conditioning and social learning theory. Within this conceptual framework, cocaine use is considered learned behavior that is maintained, at least in part, by the reinforcing effects of the pharmacological actions of cocaine in conjunction with social and other nonpharmacological reinforcement derived from the cocaine-using lifestyle (Higgins & Katz, 1998). The reliable empirical observation that abused drugs function as reinforcers in humans and laboratory animals provides sound scientific support for that position (Griffiths, Bigelow, & Henningfield, 1980). Cocaine, other psychomotor stimulants, ethanol, opioids, nicotine, and sedatives serve as reinforcers and are voluntarily self-administered by a variety of species. Moreover, through respondent and operant conditioning, environmental events that previously have been paired with drug use come reliably to occasion drug seeking. Physical dependence is not necessary for these drugs to support ongoing and stable patterns of voluntary drug seeking and use in otherwise healthy laboratory animals or humans. The commonalities do not end there. Effects of alterations in drug availability, drug dose, schedule of reinforcement, and other environmental manipulations on drug use are orderly and have generality across different species and types of drug abuse (Griffiths et al., 1980; Higgins, 1997). These commonalities support a theoretical position that reinforcement and other principles of learning are fundamental determinants of cocaine use, abuse, and dependence.

Within this conceptual model, then, cocaine use is considered a normal, learned behavior that falls along a frequency continuum ranging from patterns of little use and few problems to excessive use and many untoward effects (including death). The same processes and principles of learning are assumed to operate across the continuum. All physically intact humans are assumed to possess the necessary neurobiological systems to experience cocaine-produced reinforcement, and hence to develop patterns of cocaine use, abuse, and dependence. To put this some-

Abstinence Contract

This is an agreement between _____ (the client) and _____ (the therapist) to help the client maintain abstinence from cocaine. By this agreement, I direct my therapist to establish a schedule for collecting urine specimens from me for 24 weeks. I will provide urine samples three times per week on a Monday, Wednesday, and Friday schedule during the first 12 weeks of treatment. During the second 12 weeks of treatment (Weeks 13–24), urine samples will be collected two times per week on a Monday and Thursday schedule. A clinical staff member of my same sex will observe the urination. Half of each urine sample will be submitted for immediate analysis, and half will be saved at the clinic. Samples will be assayed for a variety of drugs of abuse, among which are cocaine, amphetamines, opioid drugs, marijuana, and sedatives.

Each specimen collection requires 3.0 ounces of urine. If the quantity is insufficient for analysis, that shall be considered a failure to provide a scheduled sample.

If I travel out of town due to an emergency, I will inform my therapist in advance of leaving. My therapist is authorized to verify such absences with _____. If I require hospitalization, my therapist will arrange to collect urine in the hospital. If I am sick and do not require hospitalization, I will still arrange to produce scheduled urine specimens. If I have difficulty with transportation, or inclement weather makes it difficult to travel, I will work out (with the assistance of the clinical staff) a way to get to the clinic for urine collection. On certain major holidays, the clinic will be closed. My therapist and I will mutually agree to altered urine schedules on these occasions.

If for appropriate medical reasons a prescription for one of the drugs that sometimes is abused is written, I will supply my therapist with copies of that prescription. The appearance of that drug in the urine will not be counted as a relapse to drug use. I hereby direct my therapist to communicate by mail or telephone with the prescribing physician or dentist when my therapist deems that action to be appropriate.

Cocaine-Free Urines: For each cocaine-negative urine sample collected during Weeks 1–12 of treatment, points will be earned. Each point is worth the monetary equivalent of $0.25, although they may **not** be exchanged directly for cash. A voucher stating the earned point value will be presented to you following the collection of a cocaine-negative sample. This voucher will specify the number of points earned for that day, as well as the cumulative points earned to date and their monetary equivalent.

During the first 12 weeks of treatment, the first cocaine-free urine sample will earn 10 points, with each consecutive cocaine-free sample collected thereafter earning an increment of 5 points above the previously earned amount. For example, if 10 points are received on Wednesday for a cocaine-free urine sample, Friday's cocaine-free sample will earn 15 points, Monday's will earn 20, and so on. As an added incentive to remain abstinent from cocaine, a $10 bonus will be earned for each week of three consecutive cocaine-negative urine samples collected at our clinic. Assuming there are no cocaine-positive urine samples collected, the monetary equivalent of $997.50 can be earned during the first 12 weeks of treatment. Since a major emphasis in our program is on lifestyle changes, primarily increasing activities that effectively compete with drug use, the money earned on this incentive system must be used toward social or recreational goods and activities agreed upon by you and your therapist. A list of acceptable uses of vouchers has been developed for this purpose and will be shared with you. During the second 12 weeks of treatment, the incentive program will be changed. Rather than earning vouchers for cocaine-negative samples, you will be earning lottery tickets for clean samples.

For the entire 24 weeks of treatment, immediately after the urinalysis test results indicate that the urine sample is cocaine-negative, the following will happen. The vouchers (Weeks 1–12) or lottery tickets (Weeks 13–24) will be delivered. Following the presentation of each voucher, you will be asked whether you would like to "purchase" any goods or services. Vouchers may be used at any time during the 24-week program. Earned vouchers cannot be taken away from you under any circumstances. The procedure for dealing with cocaine-positive urine samples is discussed below.

Cocaine-Positive Urines: All urine samples will be screened for drug use. A record will be kept of all drugs screened positive, although this contract will be in effect for cocaine only. For each cocaine-positive urine sample collected, you will not receive a voucher. In addition, the voucher earned for the next cocaine-free urine sample will be reset to 10. To reset the voucher value to where it was prior to the cocaine "slip," you

(cont.)

FIGURE 10.1. Sample abstinence contract.

must provide five *consecutive* cocaine-free samples. The fifth "clean" sample will then earn you the same monetary equivalent as that earned for the sample preceding the cocaine-positive one, and the system outlined above will continue to be in effect (i.e., each clean sample will earn 5 points more than the previous one).

Failure to Provide a Urine Sample: Failure to provide a urine sample on the designated date (without prior approval of your therapist) will be treated as a cocaine-positive sample, and the procedures noted above will be in effect. Although we will make an attempt to obtain the sample by coming to your home (with your permission, of course), cocaine-negative urine samples collected in this manner will not earn voucher points, nor will they reset your voucher value to 10. In effect, cocaine-negative samples collected outside of our clinic (except in the case of hospitalization) are "neutral." On the other hand, if we obtain a sample from you outside of the clinic, and the sample is cocaine-positive, it will be treated in the manner outlined above for cocaine-positive urine samples.

My signature below acknowledges that I agree to the urinalysis monitoring system outlined above. This system has been carefully explained to me, and I understand the outcome of providing both cocaine-negative and cocaine-positive urine samples while I am a client at the clinic.

_____   _____
Client   Therapist

_____   _____
Date   Date

---

what differently, individuals need not have any exceptional or pathological characteristics in order to develop cocaine abuse or dependence. Clearly, genetic or acquired characteristics (e.g., family history of substance dependence or other psychiatric disorders) can affect the probability of developing cocaine or other substance abuse or dependence (e.g., they are risk factors), but this model assumes that such special characteristics are not necessary for cocaine abuse or dependence to emerge.

Within this conceptual framework, treatment is designed to assist in reorganizing the physical and social environments of the person who uses cocaine. The goal is to systematically weaken the influence of reinforcement derived from cocaine use and the related lifestyle, and to increase the frequency of reinforcement derived from healthier alternative activities, especially those that are incompatible with continued cocaine use. Below we describe the basic components of the CRA plus vouchers treatment that are designed to accomplish these goals.

Treatment Components

The recommended duration of CRA plus vouchers treatment is 24 weeks of treatment and 6 months of aftercare. The influence of treatment duration has not yet been experimentally examined with this or other efficacious psychosocial treatments for cocaine dependence, but providing 3 months of care or more is a recommended practice in the treatment of illicit drug abuse or dependence (Principle 5, Table 10.1).

CRA therapy in this model is delivered in individual sessions, although CRA has been delivered effectively in group sessions to patients with alcoholism (Azrin, 1976; see Meyers & Smith, 1995, for a manual on the use of CRA for patients with alcoholism). As its name suggests, the treatment involves two main components: CRA and vouchers.

The Community Reinforcement Approach

Therapist Style. Before we get into the specific elements of CRA, worth mentioning are more general characteristics of the therapy style that is used. Therapists are flexible in appointment scheduling and goal setting, which we believe facilitates treatment retention and progress toward target goals. Particularly in the early stages of treatment, therapists try to work around patients' schedules and generally make participation in treatment convenient to the patients. We try to tolerate tardiness to sessions, early departure from sessions, and variations in the time of day that sessions are scheduled; we meet with patients outside the office if necessary. With especially difficult patients, improvements in these areas can be worked on as part of the treatment plan.

Therapists must exhibit empathy and good listening skills. They need to convey a sincere understanding of the patients' situation and its inherent difficulties. Throughout treatment, therapists avoid making value judgments, and instead exhibit genuine empathy and consideration for the difficult challenges that patients face.

CRA requires both therapists and patients to develop an active, make-it-happen attitude throughout treatment. Active problem solving is a routine part of the therapeutic relationship. Within ethical boundaries, therapists are committed to doing what it takes to facilitate lifestyle changes on the part of patients. Therapists take patients to appointments or job interviews. They initiate recreational activities with patients, and schedule sessions at different times of day as needed to accomplish specific goals. They have patients make phone calls from their office, and search newspapers for job possibilities or ideas for healthy recreational activities in which patients might be able to participate. They may even hold a CRA session at a patient's home if circumstances dictate. In sum, the CRA therapists' motto is "We can make it happen," and they try their best to model that approach for patients.

Structure of Counseling Sessions. CRA is delivered in twice-weekly 60- to 90-minute therapy sessions during the initial 12 weeks, and once-weekly sessions of the same duration during the final 12 weeks of treatment. The therapist's primary role in each session is to gain active participation from the patient and to make sure the session stays focused on a preset plan. The task may be made difficult if the patient comes to sessions with clinical issues other than those included in the treatment plan. To deal effectively with such issues, the therapist must skillfully demonstrate appropriate concern, but not allow the session to lose focus. The session plan should be followed in every session, except in extreme emergencies. The plan can be structured to accommodate unexpected issues without necessarily altering the preset goals

for the session. The therapist's task is to stay in control of the session and ensure that adequate time is available to cover the designated issues.

To help maintain focus, the therapist follows a structured protocol for each session. First, the therapist reviews urinalysis results (using a graph) with the patient and provides appropriate feedback. Any problems in the area of drug abstinence are discussed. Active listening skills are used to provide support, while encouragement and social reinforcement are used selectively to support the patient's efforts. If the day's urine sample is cocaine-negative, the patient is congratulated, and the behavior that helped him/her maintain abstinence is discussed. If the day's urine sample is cocaine-positive, the patient is reassured that cocaine use is the reason for being in treatment and that the treatment program is there to help with this problem. A functional analysis of the most recent cocaine use is conducted (see below), and the therapist stresses the importance of understanding the reasons behind that behavior so that the patient can learn better control of his/her use.

If disulfiram therapy (see below) is part of the active treatment plan, then disulfiram compliance is reviewed and evaluated. Any problems with this therapy are discussed, and procedures are implemented to resolve such problems. Reinforcement and encouragement are provided for successful compliance.

The therapist then reviews and evaluates progress on each treatment goal. All treatment goals have associated graphs with which to monitor progress. These graphs are updated, and any problems are discussed. Again, encouragement and social reinforcement are used to support progress. If adequate progress is not being made, problem solving and appropriate behavioral procedures are used to resolve any difficulties that may be interfering with achieving the targeted goals.

After reviewing progress in each problem area, goals to be met by the next session are set. Rationales for new behavioral targets are discussed with the patient. Plans for maintaining abstinence until the next therapy session are reviewed. Skills training, behavioral rehearsal, and role playing are used when appropriate to provide the support and training needed to achieve treatment goals. A review of goals to be accomplished between this session and the next, and some words of encouragement, are typically the last things that happen in a session.

Out-of-office procedures are implemented when warranted. For example, if an active goal is to sample a new recreational activity and the therapist is to function as the initiator, then the patient and therapist go perform this activity rather than hold a full session in the office. Similarly, if the goal from the previous session was to apply for employment and the patient did not do so, then the current session may involve a trip to potential job sites to complete employment applications.

Many patients come to sessions each week with new or repeated crises. How the therapist handles such crises is important for the effective delivery of this treatment, because CRA requires careful focus and structure. Certainly, ignoring patients' real life problems entails the risk that they will view treatment as irrelevant to their own needs, which may increase attrition.

At least three options for handling crisis situations are employed by the therapist. First, the therapist can use counseling skills to try to tie these seemingly unrelated issues back to the patient's treatment plan by discussing how the current treatment plan may help with the crisis. Second, the therapist can discuss the importance of these issues, while carefully explaining that these issues cannot be effectively addressed until a period of abstinence has been achieved. Third, sessions can be structured so that 10–20 minutes are available at the end of a session to discuss issues not directly related to the treatment plan. This strategy is an effective way to meet the patient's needs and retain the structured protocol. Importantly, the therapist can use attention to the patient-specified issue as reinforcement for covering the session plan (the Premack principle; for more information, see, e.g., Sulzer-Azaroff & Meyer, 1991, p. 158). A statement like the following can be very effective: "Yes, I can see why you are concerned about this matter. Let's try to get through some of our other issues, so we can reserve time to talk about this." The order of events is important here. Attention to the new concern must come after going through the planned activity. If the therapist feels that an intervention is necessary for the new concern (e.g., that the concern is directly or indirectly related to the probability of cocaine use), then an appropriate behavioral approach consis-

tent with the structure of CRA is used to assist the patient. Referral to an outside source is made if the problem is clearly in need of clinical attention but is not related directly or indirectly to cocaine use.

Sessions focus on the following general topics, depending on the needs of the individual patient.

Functional Analysis and Self-Management Planning. Patients are instructed in how to recognize antecedents and consequences of their cocaine use—that is, how to functionally analyze their cocaine use. They are also instructed in how to use that information to reduce the probability of using cocaine. A twofold message is conveyed to each patient: (1) Cocaine use is orderly behavior that is more likely to occur under certain circumstances than others; (2) by learning to identify the circumstances that affect his/her cocaine use, the patient can develop and implement plans to reduce the likelihood of future cocaine use. Our approach to teaching functional analysis is based on the work of Miller and Munoz (1982) and McCrady (1986) (see also McCrady, Chapter 9, this volume).

Using the form shown in Figure 10.2, we help patients analyze instances of their own cocaine use. We explain:

"A functional analysis allows you to identify the immediate causes of your cocaine use. You have probably noticed that in certain situations you use cocaine, while in others you do not. The situations around us can powerfully control cocaine use, particularly if we are unaware of their influence.

"Some of the situations that can influence cocaine use are the people you are with, the place you are at, the time of day, the amount of money you have with you, how much alcohol you have consumed, and how you are feeling. The first step in understanding your cocaine use is to identify the situations in which you are likely to use. We call that identifying your 'triggers.' You will also want to identify consequences of your use—that is, to identify the immediate, usually positive consequences (getting high, having fun) and the delayed, often negative consequences (blowing your money, un-

Trigger	Thoughts and feelings	Behavior	Consequences	
			Positive	Negative

FIGURE 10.2. Form for functional analysis of cocaine use.

wanted sexual encounters, fights with your partner). As you identify triggers and consequences, you will discover certain patterns to your cocaine use, and those are important targets for intervention."

Patients are assigned the task of analyzing at least three recent episodes of cocaine use. Learning to analyze one's cocaine use is emphasized during initial treatment sessions, but the exercise is used throughout the treatment process to understand and modify any lapses into cocaine use, as well as to address problems with cocaine craving. That is, the therapist and patient jointly conduct functional analysis at the start of any session where cocaine use has occurred or craving has been particularly problematic since the last session.

In conjunction with functional analysis, patients are taught self-management plans for using the information revealed in the func-

tional analyses to decrease the chances of future cocaine use. Using the self-management planning sheet shown in Figure 10.3, patients are counseled to restructure their daily activities in order to minimize contact with known antecedents of cocaine use, to find alternatives to the positive consequences of cocaine use, and to make explicit the negative consequences of cocaine use.

A key part of self-management planning that is implemented with most patients is drug refusal training. Most patients who are trying to quit cocaine use continue to have contact, either planned or inadvertent, with individuals who are still using the drug. Turning down cocaine or opportunities to go places where cocaine is available is more difficult than most anticipate. We approach this as a special case of assertiveness training and model our procedures on those of McCrady (1986) and Sisson and Azrin (1989). The key

Self-Management Planning Sheet

Trigger	Plans		± Consequences	Difficulty (1–10)
1.	a.			
	b.			
	c.			
	d.			
	e.			

FIGURE 10.3. Self-management planning sheet. From Budney and Higgins (1998).

components of effective refusal are shown in Table 10.4. The therapist should explain the rationale for drug refusal skills training, engage the patient in a detailed discussion of the key elements of effective refusal, assist the patient in formulating his/her own refusal style (incorporating the key elements), and role-play some scenes in which the patient is offered cocaine. The situations that are role-played should be very specific and realistic for the patient in terms of people, times of day, location, and so forth. The patient and therapist should alternate roles, so that the former has the opportunity to practice while receiving constructive feedback, and the latter has the opportunity to model effective refusal skills.

Social and Recreational Practices. The importance of developing a new social network that will support a healthier lifestyle, and of getting involved with recreational activities that are enjoyable and do not involve cocaine or other drug use, is addressed with all patients. Systematically developing and maintaining contacts with "safe" social networks and participation in "safe" recreational activities remain high priorities throughout treatment for the vast majority of patients. Specific treatment goals are set, and weekly progress on specific goals is monitored (Principle 4, Table 10.1).

Clearly, plans for developing healthy social networks and recreational activities must be tailored to the particular circumstances, skills, and interests of each patient. For those patients who are willing to participate, self-help groups (Alcoholics Anonymous, Cocaine Anonymous, or Narcotics Anonymous) can be an effective way to develop a new network of associates who will support a sober lifestyle. A clinic staff member will often ac-

TABLE 10.4. Components of Effective Refusal

1. *No* should be the first thing you say.
2. Tell the person offering you drugs or asking you to go out *not to ask you now or in the future* if you want to do cocaine. Saying things like "Maybe later," "I have to get home," "I'm on medication," etc., just makes it likely that the person will ask again.
3. Body language is important:
   a. Making good eye contact is important; look directly at the person when you answer.
   b. Your expression and tone should clearly indicate that you are serious.
4. Offer an alternative if you want to do something else with that person. Make sure that it is something that is incompatible with cocaine use (taking your children for a walk or to the park, going to a workout, etc.).
5. Change the subject to a new topic of conversation.

company a patient to his/her first self-help meeting or two. By no means do we focus exclusively on or mandate self-help involvement. We assist patients with getting involved in a wide variety of healthy special-interest clubs and volunteer groups. We encourage patients to recontact old friends or family members who do not misuse drugs and with whom they may have lost contact over the years. It should be noted that making new social contacts can be a very difficult goal to achieve for many patients. Therapists try to facilitate progress in this area via role playing, social skills training, and accompanying clients to places or events where they might meet new people who do not misuse drugs.

Regarding recreational activities, many patients have a history of engaging in healthy activities prior to becoming involved with cocaine use, or have clear ideas about activities that they would like to pursue. We assist those patients in renewing or initiating participation in those activities. Many others either never learned to pursue non-drug-related recreation as adults, or are simply unable to identify any activities that they would currently like to pursue. We often have patients complete a leisure-interest inventory (Rosenthal & Rosenthal, 1985) to prompt ideas about activities they might have liked previously or otherwise might want to explore. We encourage patients to sample new activities even if they are unsure whether they will find them enjoyable. Clinic staff members monitor the local newspapers and other media for upcoming events that are appropriate and bring them to the attention of patients. Each week, the clinic receptionist places copies of healthy upcoming events in a central location for patients' use. Again, clinic staff members will accompany patients when they are trying new or reinitiating familiar recreational activities, if doing so will facilitate participation. As described below, vouchers can be used to support costs of initiating recreational and other activities that support a healthy lifestyle.

Individualized Skills Training. Various other forms of individualized skills training are provided, usually to address some specific skill deficit that may directly or indirectly influence a patient's risk for cocaine use (e.g., time management, problem solving, assertiveness training, social skills training, and mood management). For example, essential to success with the self-management skills and social/recreational goals discussed above are at least modest time management skills. All patients are given daily planners to facilitate planning. Because patients lose or forget their planners, providing photocopies to cover the next week of treatment is a good strategy. Therapists provide the following rationale:

"This part of your treatment involves learning to plan, schedule, and prioritize the events and activities in your life. Solving your cocaine problem requires making substantial lifestyle changes; it is important to develop efficient ways to do this. Some patients say they don't like to plan—they like to be spontaneous. But if they don't find a way to schedule and organize their lives, they often get overwhelmed and don't achieve their goals."

With most patients, time management in some form is worked on throughout treatment. The importance of writing down a schedule of activities that will help to promote cocaine abstinence between therapy sessions is emphasized in each session. Planning for "high-risk" times is particularly important. We teach most patients to use "to-do" lists, engage in daily planning, and to prioritize activities.

We employ many other examples of skills training as well. We implement the *Control Your Depression* protocol (Lewinsohn, Munoz, Youngren, & Zeiss, 1986) with those patients whose depression persists after they discontinue cocaine use (see Principle 8, Table 10.1). We sometimes implement social skills and relaxation training with individuals who report social anxiety about meeting new people, dating, and so forth (see Goldfried & Davison, 1994; see also Turk, Heimberg, & Hope, Chapter 3, this volume). Many patients report persistent problems with insomnia following discontinuation of drug use. With them, we often implement a protocol based on those developed by Lacks (1987) and Morin (1993). We often work with patients regarding money management. With many, this may simply involve helping them arrange direct deposit for their paychecks, so that they are not tempted to use because they have a large sum of cash on hand. For others, this may involve a plan to get out of debt, which can help to reduce stress. Because patients often have so many problems that could benefit from our assistance, we follow a rule of only treating those problems that we feel directly or indirectly affect the probability of initial and longer-term cocaine abstinence for individual patients. Here we rely heavily on functional analysis and other information available regarding each patient's cocaine use. For problems that do not appear to be related to cocaine use but warrant professional attention, we generally will make a referral. We work very hard at keeping treatment focused on resolving the problem of cocaine use, and against being sidetracked by other pressing problems that may have little or no direct or indirect influence on the presenting problem of cocaine dependence.

Vocational Counseling. Unemployed participants are offered the Job Club, which is an efficacious method for helping chronically unemployed individuals obtain employment (see the Job Club manual by Azrin & Besalel, 1980). The majority of patients who seek treatment for cocaine dependence are unemployed, and so this is a service that we offer many of our patients. For others, we assist in pursuing educational goals or new career paths. A meaningful vocation is fundamental to a healthy lifestyle, and we recommend goals directed toward vocational enhancement for all patients. Rules that we follow for several common types of vocational problems are outlined in Table 10.5. In general, the clinic staff makes a point of keeping well informed of community programs that can pro-

TABLE 10.5. Examples of Goals Set in Vocational Counseling

For the unemployed client:
- Make eight job contacts per week.
- Develop a resumé.
- Send out two resumés with cover letters per day.
- Go to the job service twice per week.
- Enroll in a job training program.
- Enroll in a vocational exploration program.
- Take a job-skills-related class.
- Consider and collect information on educational possibilities.

For the client who works "too many" hours or has an irregular schedule:
- Keep work hours between 35 and 50 hours per week.
- Establish a more regular schedule.
- Explore alternative work schedules.

For the person working in a "high-risk for drug use" environment or the dissatisfied employee:
- Consider a job change.
- Submit applications for alternative employment while continuing to work.
- Modify the work environment to reduce risk of drug use or improve working conditions.
- Enroll in a career exploration class.
- Enroll in a job-skills-related or alternative-career-related educational class.

vide resources and benefits to patients in need of employment, education, or other vocational services.

Relationship Counseling. Participants with romantic partners who do not misuse drugs are offered reciprocal relationship counseling, which is an intervention designed to teach couples positive communication skills and how to negotiate reciprocal contracts for desired changes in each partner's behavior (see, e.g., Azrin, Naster, & Jones, 1973). Initially, we also had nonromantic significant others (SOs) participate as well. Both romantic and nonromantic SOs were taught to develop behavioral contracts with patients wherein the SOs agreed to routinely do rewarding activities (e.g., go out to lunch) with the patients, contingent on the patients' successfully abstaining from recent cocaine use. To implement the contracts with precision, we shared urinalysis results with SOs. Based on research described below, we have discontinued this aspect of our work with SOs, but continue to provide relationship counseling.

We attempt to deliver relationship counseling across eight sessions, with the first four sessions delivered across consecutive weeks and the next four delivered on alternating weeks. We introduce this aspect of therapy by using the following rationale:

"As you well know, an important area of your life that is negatively affected by cocaine problems is your relationship with your partner. Those close to the person with the problem are typically most adversely affected by the problem. Many partners of cocaine-dependent individuals have tried many times to help their mates to stop using. Strategies for trying to help vary. Anger and frustration usually build up, and feelings of hopelessness and helplessness arise. Sometimes attempts to help are met with resentment and anger from the partner with the problem.

"In this part of treatment, we focus on how cocaine use has affected your relationship and how we can work to increase the positive aspects of your relationship. We also discuss ways that your partner can assist you in achieving and maintaining abstinence. We hope to be able to help you both deal more effectively with this cocaine problem.

"We have found that where there are drug abuse problems, there are usually communication problems. Usually, we see communication that is filled with anger, silence, apathy, or resentment, and many times partners try to get their needs met outside the relationship. By the time patients come to see us, many times there is little, if any, enjoyment left in the relationship."

The intervention involves a related series of exercises. Partners independently rate their current level of happiness across household responsibilities, child rearing, social activities, money, communication, sex and affection, academic progress, personal independence, partner's independence, and general happiness. Those ratings are shared and discussed, and then redone weekly to monitor progress. Next, a system of "daily reminders to be nice" (i.e., expressing appreciation and affection toward the partner) is implemented. The goal is the obvious one of getting the partners to take the time to be positive with each other. Each partner is expected to engage in a daily practice of "nice" gestures toward the other, and to keep a daily record of compliance of his/her own behavior—not the other's compliance. This information is reviewed and shared during sessions. After some level of positive interaction is established, partners independently identify what a "perfect relationship" would entail in terms of the key elements of their relationship as mentioned above: What would that perfect relationship look like? The partners also begin to work on using positive communication skills to negotiate for reciprocal changes in each other's behavior to move toward that "perfect relationship." The terms "positive" and "reciprocal" are fundamentally important here. Requests are stated exclusively in positive terms, and both partners have to be willing to make changes.

HIV/AIDS Education. HIV/AIDS education is provided to all participants in the early stages of treatment, along with counseling directed at addressing any specific needs or risk behavior of the individual patient. We address with all patients the potential for acquiring HIV/AIDS from sharing injection equipment and through sexual activity. This involves at least two sessions. First, patients complete an HIV/AIDS knowledge test (Kelly, St. Lawrence, Hood, & Brasfield, 1989). They next watch and discuss with their therapist a video on HIV/AIDS produced by the National Institute on Drug Abuse. Points emphasized by therapists during the discussion are shown in Table 10.6. Patients are also provided with HIV/AIDS prevention pamphlets from the Centers for Disease Control and Prevention, as well as free condoms (if desired). The HIV/AIDS knowledge test is repeated, and any remaining errors are discussed and resolved. Lastly, patients are given information about being tested for HIV antibodies and hepatitis B and C, and are encouraged to get tested (Principle 12, Table 10.1). Those interested in testing are assisted by clinic staff members in scheduling an appointment.

Monitored Disulfiram Therapy. All patients in our clinic who meet diagnostic criteria for alcohol dependence or report that alcohol use is involved in their use of cocaine are offered disulfiram therapy (see Principle 7, Table 10.1), which is an integral part of the CRA treatment for alcoholism (Meyers & Smith, 1995; Sisson & Azrin, 1989). The rationale and style used in presenting disulfiram therapy to patients are illustrated in the case

TABLE 10.6. Points Emphasized in Discussions of HIV/AIDS

1. The fastest-growing risk group for HIV/AIDS is made up of people who use intravenous (IV) drugs and their sexual partners. At the start of the epidemic, this group made up just a small proportion of those getting infected, but these numbers are increasing rapidly at the present time—not just gay men get infected!

2. Review the three ways that HIV is transmitted: (a) through sexual contact with an infected person, (b) through blood (as in needle-sharing), and (c) from infected mothers to their babies during pregnancy or at the time of birth. Explain that the most efficient way for HIV to be transmitted is through blood (blood contains the highest concentration of the virus) and that sharing needles ("works") is an "easy" way for the virus to get from one person's system to another's.

3. Emphasize the point that people who are infected with HIV don't necessarily look sick and might not even know they are infected. You can't tell by looking at someone whether or not that person has the virus.

4. If clients are currently using IV drugs, point out that the only safe thing to do if they tend to share needles is to use new needles or clean them if they're still using. Review the steps necessary for appropriate syringe cleaning.

5. Unprotected sexual intercourse with the exchange of body fluids (blood, vaginal fluids, semen, pre-ejaculatory fluid) is also an efficient means of giving or receiving the virus. Sex can be made safer by using latex condoms and spermicide containing the ingredient nonoxynol-9 (a commonly used ingredient in most spermicidal products) for each and every sexual encounter (this includes oral, vaginal, and anal sex).

6. Point out that alcohol and other drug use contribute to risk because of (a) possible suppression of the immune system, and (b) impaired judgment, which can lead to increased risk taking (e.g., drug use, unsafe sex).

study described later in this chapter. Participants generally ingest a 250-mg daily dose under clinic staff observation on urinalysis test days, and, when possible, under the observation of an SO on the other days. We encourage patients to sign a disulfiram contract, which is shown in Figure 10.4. Disulfiram therapy is only effective when implemented with procedures to monitor compliance with the recommended dosing medication (Azrin, Sisson, Meyers, & Godley, 1982). We find that having staff members monitor compliance on days that patients report to the clinic works very well. Having an SO monitor compliance on the other days can work well if an appropriate person is available to do so at the frequency needed. When that is not possible, we sometimes adopt a practice of having the patient ingest a larger dose (500 mg) on days when the patient reports to the clinic and skip dosing on the intervening days.

Dealing with Other Drug Use. Use of substances other than tobacco and caffeine is discouraged as well via CRA therapy. Anyone who meets criteria for opiate dependence is referred to an adjoining service located within our clinic for opioid replacement therapy (see Bickel, Amass, Higgins, Badger, & Esch, 1997). Marijuana use, like alcohol use, is common among persons presenting for treatment of cocaine dependence. Approximately 30% of patients with cocaine dependence in our clinic also meet criteria for marijuana dependence. Common reasons given for the use of marijuana by such patients are similar to those given for alcohol use: enjoying the high, counteracting cocaine-induced anxiety, and relieving cocaine-induced depression. There are large individual differences in the frequency and pattern of marijuana use among patients. As with patients who use alcohol, staff members should assess and make recommendations based on whether patients meet criteria for abuse or dependence. Consideration should also be given to how marijuana use may interfere with other lifestyle change goals. Marijuana use has rarely been observed to be a direct antecedent of cocaine use. Some individuals can use marijuana regularly without adversely affecting cocaine abstinence (Budney, Higgins, & Wong, 1996). Many patients express little interest in discontinuing marijuana use. Nevertheless, we recommend abstinence because of the problems associated with chronic marijuana use.

Our general strategy for dealing with marijuana use is as follows. We recommend abstinence and offer to assist patients in applying the strategies targeting cocaine use for marijuana abstinence as well. If patients refuse abstinence as a goal, we encourage them to reduce their use through the various treatment strategies used for cocaine and alcohol use.

Importantly, we never dismiss or refuse to treat a patient due to other drug use. We recommend cessation of tobacco use, but usually not during the course of treatment for cocaine dependence. That practice may change as new

Disulfiram Contract

I, _____ , agree to take disulfiram at the regularly scheduled time outlined below. I agree to do this for __ days. After this time, I agree to talk to my therapist and to discuss whether or not to continue taking disulfiram. I also agree to have the person designated below witness the administration of the disulfiram each time it is scheduled.

I, _____ , agree to be present and witness each take-home administration of disulfiram.

Time: _____

Days: _____

Where: _____

In response to _____ taking disulfiram as scheduled, I agree to _____ as a means of reinforcing the taking of disulfiram.

_____   _____
Patient's Signature   Partner's Signature

_____   _____
Therapist's Signature   Date

FIGURE 10.4. Sample disulfiram contract.

research begins to demonstrate that smoking cessation can be successfully integrated into simultaneous treatment for other substance abuse or dependence.

Aftercare. Upon completion of the 24 weeks of treatment, participants are encouraged to participate in 6 months of aftercare in our clinic, which involves at least a once-monthly brief therapy session and a urine toxicology screen. More frequent clinic contact is recommended if either the therapist or patient deems it necessary. These clinic visits may be considered booster sessions. They are used to monitor progress and to address problems with cocaine use or other aspects of the lifestyle changes that were initiated during treatment. They also allow for a gradual rather than an abrupt ending of the patient's involvement with the clinic.

Voucher Program

The voucher program is an incentive program designed to increase retention and abstinence. Many individuals who are cocaine-dependent arrive in treatment with their lives in disarray. A reasonable assumption is that some time will be needed to assist these individuals in stabilizing and restructuring their lives, so

that naturalistic sources of reinforcement for abstinence can exert some influence over their behavior. A protected environment is an option, but the voucher program is deemed a less expensive alternative. The goal is to have this incentive program play a major role during the initial 12 weeks of treatment, during which time CRA therapy is ongoing as well. CRA is used to assist patients in restructuring their lifestyle so that naturalistic reinforcers are in place to sustain cocaine abstinence once the vouchers are discontinued. CRA also serves to assist patients make optimal use of vouchers via prompting and guidance concerning how to spend the vouchers on items that will help change their lifestyle.

The voucher program is implemented in conjunction with a rigorous urinalysis-monitoring program (see Principle 11, Table 10.1). We ask patients to sign the abstinence contract mentioned above (Figure 10.4), which describes the voucher program and the urinalysis testing schedule. Urine specimens are collected from all participants according to a Monday, Wednesday, and Friday schedule during Weeks 1–12 and a Monday and Thursday schedule during Weeks 13–24 of treatment. Specimens are screened immediately via an onsite Enzyme Multiplied Immunoassay Technique (EMIT, Syva Corp., San Jose, CA), to minimize delays in delivering reinforcement for cocaine-negative specimens. To decrease the likelihood of submitting bogus specimens, all specimens are collected under the observation of a same-sex staff member, and staff members always reserve the right to request another specimen if they have any concerns regarding the integrity of a specimen. All specimens are screened for benzoylecgonine, a cocaine metabolite, and one randomly selected specimen each week is also screened for the presence of other abused drugs. Blood alcohol levels (BALs) are assessed via Breathalyzer at the time urine specimens are collected. Failure to submit a scheduled specimen is treated as a cocaine-positive specimen. Participants are informed of their urinalysis and BAL results within several minutes after submitting specimens.

Urine specimens collected during Weeks 1–12 that test negative for benzoylecgonine earn points that are recorded on vouchers and given to participants. Points are worth the equivalent of $0.25 each. Money is never provided directly to subjects. Instead, points are used to purchase retail items in the community. A staff member makes all purchases. The first negative specimen is worth 10 points @ $0.25/point, or $2.50. The value of vouchers for each subsequent consecutive negative specimen increases by 5 points (e.g., second specimen = 15 points, third specimen = 20 points, etc.). To further increase the likelihood of continuous cocaine abstinence, the equivalent of a $10 bonus is earned for each three consecutive negative specimens. A specimen that is cocaine-positive, or failure to submit a scheduled specimen, resets the value of vouchers back to the initial $2.50 value, from which they can escalate again according to the same schedule. Submission of five consecutive cocaine-negative specimens following submission of a positive specimen returns the value of points to where they were prior to the reset. Points cannot be lost once earned.

Patients and therapists jointly select retail items to be purchased with points. The items commonly obtained are quite diverse; they include YMCA passes, continuing-education materials, fishing licenses, gift certificates to local restaurants, hobby materials, and many others. Therapists retain veto power over all purchases. Purchases are only approved if therapists deem them to be in concert with

individual treatment goals of increasing cocaine-free, healthy activities.

The voucher program is discontinued at the end of Week 12. During Weeks 13–24, participants receive a single $1.00 Vermont State Lottery ticket per cocaine-negative urinalysis test. Across the 24 weeks of treatment, patients can earn a maximum of $997.50 in vouchers during Weeks 1–12 and $24 in lottery tickets during Weeks 13–24. No material incentives are delivered during the recommended 6-month aftercare period. There is some evidence that lower-cost incentives can be effective in increasing cocaine abstinence, but efficacy appears to vary as a function of the amount of the incentives used (Petry, 1999).

Getting Therapy Underway

The therapist has many tasks to accomplish during the first two sessions (Week 1) of treatment, in addition to simply getting to know the patient and developing rapport. These sessions are critical for enhancing motivation and setting the tone for treatment. Hence we provide some detailed descriptions of the specific tasks to accomplish during initial therapy sessions.

As discussed above, urine results and cocaine use are the first areas to address. By starting the session with a direct assessment of cocaine use (rather than "How's it going?"), the therapist provides a clear message that the focus of this treatment is cocaine dependence.

After a discussion of cocaine use and voucher earnings, the therapist should make sure that the patient has completed all the intake materials. Here the therapist can also answer any new questions that the patient may have.

If practical needs such as housing, transportation, or child care are issues for treatment attendance, these needs should be a primary focus of the first session. Therapists should do everything possible to assist patients in finding solutions to these problems.

The therapist should discuss alternative activities or strategies for coping with high-risk situations for cocaine use, especially situations that are likely to arise during the upcoming week. As discussed above, having the patient use appointment books or photocopies provided by the clinic can be very helpful for scheduling alternative plans or activities. The next session should also be scheduled, and the patient should record the day and time in the appointment book.

The therapist should begin to formulate a comprehensive treatment plan with specific goals and methods. The therapist might introduce this task in the following way:

"A treatment plan will allow us to write down the things you and I think are important to accomplish and how we plan to go about trying to accomplish them. We will use the plan to keep us focused on the task at hand—that is, making lifestyle changes that will help you stop using cocaine and other drugs, and also increase your satisfaction with other important areas of your life. The treatment plan will be developed through a cooperative effort between you and me. It is important that you think the goals we set are important and will help you achieve what you want in life. My job in this process is to assist you in coming up with meaningful, effective goals, and to offer advice based on my knowledge and experience with treating persons with cocaine and other drug problems."

The therapist should then present ideas about which areas of the patient's life need changes. For each suggested change, it is important that the therapist provide a rationale that draws from the information collected from the patient, as well as from research findings and clinical experience. An open discussion and exchange of ideas should then follow.

If the patient is reluctant to participate, the therapist should ask for his/her thoughts on each potential area for change. The therapist can facilitate patient participation with questions such as these: "What do you think?" "Do you have any thoughts on this?" "Does this make sense to you?" "Do you think this is important?" "Is this type of change possible?" It is important for therapists and patients to agree on which areas of life present problems and should be changed. If a patient disagrees with the therapist's opinion, those areas should be dropped for now and discussed later in treatment if they continue to pose problems.

After the areas for change are agreed upon, the therapist and patient should discuss each one. Therapists should use active listening skills (reflection and empathy) and try to keep the focus on the specific areas. Therapists should inform patients that they will focus on these problem areas in each session. Progress and problems will be openly discussed, and additions or deletions to the plan will be decided upon together.

Next, therapists and patients together decide the order in which these problem areas should be addressed, always remembering that increasing cocaine abstinence is the primary goal. Mutual agreement is important, and a therapist may need to compromise to achieve such agreement.

Specific goals should then be set for each problem area. It is important that the therapist provide a rationale for setting specific goals:

"Setting specific goals is important. They will help us stay focused on the primary changes we agreed are important for stopping drug use and achieving a more satisfying life without drugs. Specific goals also provide a way to measure progress. This can be very important, because many times progress can be slow. You may feel you are getting nowhere. In reality, you may be progressing in making changes, but you don't feel much different. Information about specific goals will help us both see more clearly whether we are heading in the right direction, even if the progress is slow.

"This information can also show when you are not progressing as we planned and can lead us to either reconsider the goal or find other ways to meet the goal. Keeping track of progress on specific goals also provides us with a reminder to reward or praise you for the hard work you are doing. Lifestyle changes are often difficult to make. We would also like you to learn to pat yourself on the back and take credit if you are doing well."

These goals should be quantifiable so that progress can be graphed. Targets for change should be set in the priority areas listed in the treatment plan and categorized as primary or secondary behavior change goals. Examples of typical goals are as follows:

- Five job contacts per week or making an appointment with vocational rehabilitation.
- Engaging in three recreational activities each week during high-risk times.
- Spending 4 hours each week engaging in fun activities with a family member or friend.

- Attending class one night each week.
- Doing 2 hours of homework toward obtaining a general equivalency diploma (GED).
- Planning and doing activities with a person who does not use drugs on nights when cocaine is typically used.

A therapist and patient should mutually decide on these goals. Basic principles of effective goal setting should be followed:

- Set goals relatively low at first, so that the patient can experience success early.
- Thoroughly analyze all possible barriers to achieving selected goals, so that unrealistic goals are avoided.
- Make sure that the patient understands how a goal relates to the overall treatment plan.

It is essential to maximize the probability that the patient will carry through and achieve the desired behavior change. The therapist's responsibility is to use the appropriate counseling style and behavioral procedures to increase the probability of compliance with a targeted behavior.

The treatment plan should be updated regularly, because treatment planning is a process of constant reevaluation, assessment, and change, based on objective indices of progress (Principle 4, Table 10.1). The patient and therapist together should review, discuss, and assess the treatment plan frequently as goals are achieved or interventions fail, or as new information becomes available. These changes should also be reviewed at the regular clinical supervision meeting.

Implementing the treatment plan; monitoring progress; and modifying and updating the treatment plan according to patient needs, progress, and problems are the "meat" of the remainder of treatment.

Clinical Supervision

Doctorate-level psychologists who have expertise in behavioral psychology and substance abuse/dependence treatment provide supervision in our clinic. Supervisors provide significant input into treatment plans and selection of targets for behavior change; they also provide guidance about how to monitor progress. Supervision is provided weekly in

sessions that usually last 2–3 hours, during which all cases are reviewed. Therapists update their supervisors and other clinic therapists on each patient's progress at the level of specific treatment goals and whether progress has been made since the last supervision meeting. Progress is presented graphically for all goals.

A supervisor's style in this model should include a balance of support, feedback, problem solving, and instruction. Considering that CRA plus vouchers treatment requires an active therapeutic approach that can be effortful, the supervisor must serve as a stable source of support, encouragement, and direction in implementing the treatment plan.

We follow a fixed protocol in reviewing cases. Review begins with examination of a graph of the patient's cocaine urinalysis results from the start of treatment. Second, we review the results of testing for alcohol or any other drugs that are being targeted for change. Then we review attendance at therapy sessions, primary goals for lifestyle changes, and then secondary goals for the same. Once those treatment targets have been reviewed and modified as necessary, any recent crises or relevant clinical issues, such as suicidal ideation or newly identified problem behaviors, are discussed.

At any point in treatment, treatment goals and targets can be changed. Changes in goals may be precipitated by achievement of prior goals, failure to make any progress toward a specific goal, and clear indication that the goal is not functionally related to cocaine use.

Supporting Research

A series of controlled clinical trials supports the efficacy of the CRA plus vouchers treatment (Higgins et al., 1991, 1993; Higgins, Budney, Bickel, Foerg, et al., 1994; Higgins et al., 1995, 2000). Below we briefly review those studies and related research demonstrating effective clinical practices with patients who are cocaine-dependent.

The initial two trials conducted with this treatment involved comparisons with drug abuse counseling based on the disease model approach (Higgins et al., 1991, 1993). In the first trial, 28 consecutive patients with cocaine dependence who were admitted to our clinic admissions were assigned to the two groups, with the first 13 subjects going to CRA plus vouchers and the next 15 to drug abuse counseling. In the second trial, 38 patients with cocaine dependence were randomly assigned to the two treatment conditions (19 per group). In both trials, the CRA plus vouchers treatment promoted better retention and greater cocaine abstinence than drug abuse counseling. Those two trials demonstrated the efficacy of the CRA plus vouchers intervention. One of those trials also included posttreatment assessments supporting the efficacy of CRA plus vouchers treatment through 6 months of follow-up (Higgins et al., 1995).

Next, a dismantling strategy was implemented. Assessing the efficacy of the voucher component was the first step. Patients were randomly assigned to receive CRA with ($n =$ 20) or without ($n = 20$) the voucher program (Higgins, Budney, Bickel, Foerg, et al., 1994). Vouchers significantly improved retention and cocaine abstinence during the 6 months of outpatient treatment. During 6 months of posttreatment follow-up, those treated with vouchers reported greater reductions in cocaine use, and only patients in this group showed significant reductions in psychiatric symptomatology on the ASI (McLellan et al., 1985). A more recent trial conducted with 70 outpatients who were cocaine-dependent demonstrated the contribution of the voucher program to increased cocaine abstinence rates through 1 year of posttreatment follow-up (Higgins et al., in press).

In a retrospective analysis of outcomes with this treatment, those patients who had an SO implement the behavioral contracting around urinalysis results as described above were significantly more likely to achieve sustained periods of cocaine abstinence than those without an SO involved (Higgins, Budney, Bickel, & Badger, 1994). However, those findings were not supported in a subsequent randomized trial testing the efficacy of the SO behavioral contracting procedure, and thus we discontinued using it. We continue to offer relationship counseling to patients with romantic partners, based on results from a randomized trial demonstrating that behavioral relationship therapy increases abstinence among patients who misuse illicit drugs, including cocaine (Fals-Stewart, Birchler, & O'Farrell, 1996).

The efficacy of monitored disulfiram therapy in decreasing alcohol and cocaine use in pa- tients who misuse both substances has been confirmed in several studies, including a well-conducted randomized trial (Carroll, Nich, Ball, McCance, & Rounsaville, 1998).

Because much of the aforementioned work was completed in Vermont, the generality of those findings to inner-city patients with cocaine dependence had to be examined. The studies by Carroll and colleagues (1998) demonstrated the generality of the disulfiram component of CRA to an inner-city population, and a series of well-controlled trials has demonstrated the efficacy of the voucher component in inner-city populations (Kirby, Marlowe, Festinger, Lamb, & Platt, 1998; Piotrowski & Hall, 1999; Silverman et al., 1996). Moreover, the positive results with vouchers are consistent with still other findings supporting the efficacy of other contingency management interventions in reducing cocaine use—even among severely affected groups with cocaine dependence, such as homeless individuals (Milby et al., 1996) and patients with schizophrenia (Shaner et al., 1997). To our knowledge, the entire CRA plus vouchers intervention has not yet been studied in an inner-city population.

Other findings from the literature on treatment of cocaine dependence have also influenced our clinical practices. As noted earlier, several randomized clinical trials have demonstrated the efficacy of RP therapy in the treatment of cocaine dependence (see Carroll, 1998), and at least one trial has supported the efficacy of coping skills training (Monti, Rohsenow, Michalec, Martin, & Abrams, 1997). Those two interventions have substantive overlap with the skills training done as part of CRA (functional analysis of drug use, drug avoidance and refusal training, problem solving, etc.) and thus support the efficacy of those practices.

Prevalence rates of a broad array of non-substance-related psychiatric disorders are greater in persons with cocaine dependence than in the general population (Rounsaville et al., 1991; Wasserman, Havassy, & Boles, 1997). However, there is no evidence that those problems adversely affect the outcome of CRA plus vouchers, RP, or other psychosocial treatments for cocaine dependence (see, e.g., Tidey, Mehl-Madrona, Higgins, & Badger, 1998). More severe forms of psychopathology (e.g., schizophrenia) have not been well studied and may adversely affect outcomes.

IMPLEMENTING TREATMENT: A CASE STUDY

In this section we review a case of someone treated in our clinic with the CRA plus vouchers treatment. The case was chosen because it illustrates well a number of different aspects of using this treatment approach. The case also illustrates the multifaceted problems with which patients who are cocaine-dependent present. Outcome was quite good but certainly not perfect, which is to be expected with this population. To present a case suggesting otherwise would be misleading.

Steve was a 24-year-old, single (never married), European American male who was self-referred to the clinic for help with problems with cocaine use. He had been living with a friend who also used cocaine until several weeks prior to the intake interview, when he moved in with his parents. He had a 5-year-old daughter, who lived with an estranged romantic partner. The patient currently was without legal visitation rights with his daughter, due to her mother's concerns over the patient's record of drug abuse.

Steve was a high school graduate who had been employed full-time for the past 3 years in the retail business. He reported that most of his social contacts abused cocaine, cannabis, or alcohol. He reported a history of healthy social/recreational activities, including golf and skiing, but he had not engaged in those activities with regularity for a number of years.

Steve reported a history of involvement with the criminal justice system, with one conviction for a weapons offense. He was incarcerated for 3 months related to that charge. He was not under criminal justice supervision at the time he sought treatment.

Presenting Complaint

Steve reported being on a 3-day binge prior to intake and wanted help with stopping cocaine use. He reported numerous prior attempts to stop on his own, but with minimal success. He reported being "fed up" with how he felt following episodes of binge cocaine use, and was concerned about the financial problems that his cocaine use caused. He also expressed serious concerns that his drug use and related lifestyle had resulted in a strained relationship with his child and ex-girlfriend, which interfered with his getting visitation privileges.

Assessment

Cocaine Use

Steve met DSM-IV criteria for cocaine dependence. He reported a 6-year history of intranasal cocaine use. His most recent use was 7 days prior to intake, using 10.5 grams at home with friends. He reported that to be his typical pattern of use. At the time of intake, Steve reported three episodes of cocaine use during the prior 30 days, with each episode lasting approximately 48 hours, usually during weekends. He typically used cocaine with friends at bars or at a friend's house. His cocaine use was often preceded by spending time in bars, by working excessive hours, or by certain moods (including feeling bored, depressed, anxious, or upset). Steve reported a number of serious consequences as a result of his cocaine use, including physical and financial problems, a relationship breakup, and psychiatric symptoms (such as depression, anxiety, suicidal ideation, and violent impulses).

Other Drug Use

Steve's first use of alcohol was at age 16. He reported a pattern of weekly binge drinking during which he would ingest 13–15 shots of hard liquor. He reported drinking 5 days out of the past 30. Steve's first use of cannabis was at age 14. He reported 10 years of daily use and having used cannabis on 30 of the prior 30 days. He reported limited prior use of amphetamine and hallucinogens, but no regular, current use of those substances. He was a regular cigarette smoker, using approximately 20 cigarettes per day. Steve reported no previous treatment episodes for substance abuse.

Steve also met DSM-IV criteria for alcohol, cannabis, and nicotine dependence.

Other Psychiatric Problems

Steve reported a history of depression and suicidal ideation. He also noted problems with anger management, which he agreed had been a significant problem for him and for which he had previously received counseling. His BDI score was 23 at intake, but he reported no suicidal ideation.

Motivation to Change

Steve's scores on the SOCRATES at intake indicated a strong commitment to cocaine abstinence. He expressed a moderate commitment to alcohol abstinence, but agreed to disulfiram therapy for the duration of treatment. He noted plans to return to social drinking after completion of treatment. He was uninterested in discontinuing his marijuana use, which he did not consider a problem, and was not currently interested in discontinuing cigarette smoking.

Conceptualization of the Case

Steve worked long hours, sometimes holding several jobs simultaneously. That practice left little time for other types of activities, and, as might be expected, he reported minimal involvement in any ongoing recreational activities. Aside from work, then, there were few alternative sources of reinforcement to compete with the reinforcing effects of cocaine and other drug use. Situations such as Steve's typically snowball, so that cocaine and related drug use come increasingly to monopolize the person's repertoire. In this case, Steve's practices of working long hours, frequenting bars, and using drugs, and his difficulties with anger management, were sufficient to destroy his relationship with his romantic partner and thereby greatly restrict time with his daughter. Losing those relationships further eliminated any competing sources of reinforcement, and also freed up additional time and resources to allocate to the bar and cocaine use scenes. Although we deemed Steve's long work hours to have increased his vulnerability to the drug-using lifestyle, his full-time employment also probably provided some protection against cocaine's gaining even greater control over his behavior. Full-time employment is a positive prognostic variable with this treatment and other treatments for cocaine dependence, as is the use of an intranasal route of cocaine administration, which was Steve's preferred route.

Treatment Plan

Cocaine abstinence was the first priority in Steve's treatment plan and is always the main focus in this treatment approach. Next, we recommended alcohol abstinence, due to the close relationship between Steve's cocaine and alcohol use. As suggested above, Steve was unwilling to change his use of marijuana despite the rationales we provided regarding the benefits of doing so, as well as the potential adverse consequences of continuing to use cannabis. Our clinical approach was to look for opportunities during the course of treatment to reinforce any movement toward reducing or discontinuing marijuana use, but not to make his reluctance to change this problem behavior a point of contention (see Miller & Rollnick, 1991). Reestablishing a regular pattern of involvement in healthy recreational activities, especially activities that might substitute for cocaine and alcohol use on weekends, was a high-priority goal. The following rationale was provided to Steve (S) by his therapist (T) as to why we deemed participation in these activities to be a high priority:

T: Many times, when cocaine or other drugs become a regular part of someone's life, they stop doing many of the nondrug activities they used to enjoy. That seems to be true in your case. You used to do lots of healthy recreational activities, but after getting into cocaine use you got away from those other activities.

S: No doubt. It's funny, too, because I'm not even sure how that happened. Just gradually got off into different things. Never really stopped liking the other stuff. Just seems like I sort of drifted away from them.

T: That's a pretty common report. You have a lot going for you, though, Steve. You have a history of doing these healthier activities and having liked them. That's a strength that you'll be able to build upon during treatment.

S: Good. Haven't felt like I've had too many strengths lately. But how do we do this? What's the connection to my cocaine use?

T: Healthy social and recreational activities are important in people's lives. They provide something positive to look forward to after work, a way to decrease boredom, a way to feel healthy, and a chance to be with people you like. Such activities can play an important part in becoming and staying cocaine-free. When you give up using drugs, you have to do something else during the times you usually use. If the things you do are not satisfying or enjoyable, or you don't do anything but sit around and feel lonely or bored, you are more likely to use drugs. That is why we have a specific treatment component to assist you in developing a regular schedule of healthy social and recreational activities.

S: Yeah, that could be important for me. I don't find it easy to hang out around the house. I get bored, pretty antsy.

T: OK, let's go right to work on these now. We gave you a daily planner. Let's plan some activities to do between today and your next clinic visit. We really have to think carefully about Friday night, because that's a high-risk night for you. We'll be doing a lot of this throughout therapy.

Another high priority was to assist Steve in finding an alternative source of employment that would permit him to have a more reasonable work schedule, and that paid well enough that he would not feel compelled to hold several jobs simultaneously. To further increase Steve's involvement in activities that were incompatible with the cocaine-abusing lifestyle, we assisted Steve in petitioning for visitation privileges with his daughter. Regarding other psychiatric problems, we decided to monitor Steve's BDI scores weekly, to see whether they followed the precipitous decline that typically occurs with cocaine-dependent patients within a couple of weeks of entering treatment. Because anger management was a problem for Steve when dealing with his estranged partner, and because he would have to interact with her if he was to obtain visitation privileges, we deemed anger management training an important target for treatment.

Below, we outline the progress made in implementing this treatment plan.

Cocaine Abstinence

Contingent vouchers, as the primary intervention for promoting initial abstinence, were made available to Steve according to our standard 12-week protocol. Functional analysis was also implemented with Steve during Sessions 1 and 2. Circumstances that increased the likelihood that Steve would use were be-

ing at a bar or certain friends' houses, using alcohol, ending a particularly long week of work, and experiencing depression or boredom. He identified going to the movies or a "safe" friend's house, hunting, fishing, and skiing as circumstances that decreased his likelihood of using. That information was updated and used throughout Steve's course of treatment in self-management planning and in planning for social and recreational activities.

Shown in Figure 10.5 is a cumulative record of Steve's cocaine urinalysis results during the 24-week treatment. His only instance of use occurred 7 weeks into treatment. Steve reported being surprised by the results; he offered that he had smoked marijuana with several friends, and that perhaps some cocaine had been in the pipe.

T: Hi, Steve. How have things been going?

S: Pretty good.

T: Look, the lab just called with your urinalysis results. You're positive for cocaine.

S: No way. That can't be right. Wow, I haven't used cocaine. Didn't do much of anything over the weekend.

T: That's how the machine read the sample. Let's talk about what you did over the weekend more specifically. Let's review what you did on each of the days, and perhaps that will give us some insight into what might be going on.

S: Just shut down the shop around midnight and went home and went to bed on Friday night. I worked Saturday morning. After I got off work, I hung out with some friends for a while.

T: No gym like you planned?

S: Nah. Should have, but got sidetracked by running into some buddies I hadn't seen in a while.

T: Any of those guys use cocaine?

S: Yeah, one does, but he knows I'm in treatment. I used to use cocaine with him. He doesn't do any cocaine around me now, though.

T: What exactly did you guys do?

S: Just hung out at this one buddy's house, played video games, and watched some television. We smoked a couple of bowls of pot. You know I'm still smoking.

Cocaine Abstinence

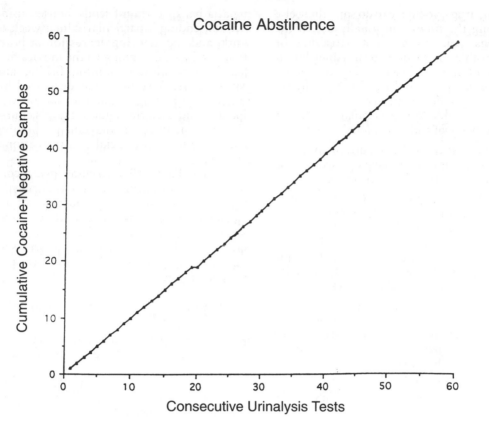

FIGURE 10.5. Shown is a cumulative record of Steve's urinalysis test results (*Y* axis) across 60 consecutive urinalysis tests (*X* axis) conducted during 24 weeks of treatment. Negative tests are represented by vertical rightward lines, and the one positive test (Test 20) by a horizontal rightward line.

Could be that the bowl we used was used to smoke cocaine in recently. Bet that was it.

T: Could be. What is pretty clear is that by getting off track of what you had planned, you increased your vulnerability for problems.

S: Yeah, I agree. I'm not sure I understand why I did that. I've been doing really well with sticking with my plans even when I run into the guys. Was supposed to get a ride to the gym from my mom, but it was a nice day, and so I told her I'd walk. Saw these dudes, started talking, and just sort of bagged my plans for the gym.

T: I have no doubt that you've been doing a great job up to now with sticking with your plans. Steve, you've been doing terrific with abstaining from cocaine. That

is not easy to do, and you deserve a tremendous amount of credit for all of the work you've been doing.

S: Shoot, kind of blew it here.

T: Important thing is to try to learn from what happened. As you know, my recommendation from the start of treatment is to abstain from marijuana use. Marijuana has its own problems, plus it puts you into contact with other drug abusers, sometimes including cocaine users. Have you given any more thought to quitting marijuana use?

S: I agree with that to some extent, but I don't really think that marijuana was the problem here. I've been smoking regularly since starting treatment and have been able to stay away from cocaine. What is different here is that I hung out all day instead of sticking with my plan to go to the gym. That's where I screwed up. That's the big difference from what I had been doing on the other weekends.

T: Good job with your analysis. Keep in mind, though, if you weren't still smoking, you wouldn't have had any need to use a pipe—yours or theirs. Nevertheless, your point is well taken regarding what you did differently this weekend, compared to the others since you've been in treatment. Sticking with the plans for alternative activities rather than just hanging out has really been working for you. I agree with you about that. The most important thing to do here is to learn from this situation and move on. What do you think you need to do to be sure you'll be cocaine-negative on Wednesday?

S: Well, I guess just keep doing what I've been doing—sticking to my plans: work, visit Mom, and I have a date tomorrow night. I'm scheduled to go to the gym tonight, and I'm definitely sticking with that. Being clean next time won't be a problem.

T: How about minimizing your contact with any drug users, especially people you've used cocaine with in the past? We could even role-play how you might tell the guys how you have to be going in case you run into them again.

S: I guess I could do that—I don't see most of those guys that often anyway. Yeah, sure.

T: Good. As you know, we have to go by the urinalysis results. So you won't earn a voucher today, and their value gets reset back to the original low value because of today's positive. However, if you can get back on track with providing negative samples, five consecutive negatives resets the value of the vouchers back to where they were before today's positive.

S: That's fair enough.

Our experience is that there is little need to quibble over a single instance of denied cocaine use like this. If the patient has resumed regular cocaine use, a pattern of positive results will soon emerge. Instead, the therapist reviewed with Steve the risks of continuing to smoke marijuana while working on maintaining cocaine abstinence (continuing contact with drug-using friends in high-risk places, using marijuana rather than other possible activities or way to relax). They also reviewed the importance of sticking with planned activities, and prepared to role-play some social skills that Steve could use to resist offers to break from his plans should he run into these friends again. Steve was very insightful about how he had deviated from what had been working for him up to this point—planning activities and sticking to the plans—and the therapist reinforced his analysis. The matter of denying cocaine use was not pursued further. Steve and the therapist carried on with implementing the treatment plan with the few modifications mentioned. There were no further instances of cocaine use during Steve's 24 weeks of treatment. His record of documented cocaine abstinence was excellent.

Alcohol Abstinence

During the first session, the therapist discussed with Steve the rationale for disulfiram therapy:

T: Steve, we want to go over a few reasons for you giving disulfiram therapy and alcohol abstinence a try. First, you have a history that if you drink, you are more likely to use cocaine. You're not alone in that regard. The scientific evidence is very clear that for many individuals who seek treatment for cocaine dependence, alcohol and cocaine use are closely linked.

S: I don't want to get drunk any more. What about just a few drinks? Is that a problem too?

T: Use of even modest doses of alcohol, even just a few drinks, can significantly decrease your chances of successfully abstaining from cocaine use. Our experience, and the experience in other clinics located elsewhere around the country, is that you can make greater progress with cocaine abstinence by using disulfiram and abstaining from alcohol use than if you continue to drink.

S: How long are you suggesting I take the medicine? Are you saying I can never drink again?

T: I'm not saying that you'll have to take this medicine forever or years or anything of that nature, or even that you can never go back to drinking. We can cross those bridges a ways down the road. But for now, if you want to give yourself the best chance of succeeding with quitting cocaine, I recommend that you give disulfiram therapy a sincere try.

S: I'm not sure how much of a problem drinking is for me. I know it's caused some problems, but I'm just not so sure.

T: Steve, the second thing I wanted to emphasize is that you also reported a history of depression and suicidal ideation. Substance use, particularly alcohol use, is a depressant and can worsen depressive symptoms and suicide risk. A period of abstinence may help a good deal with those problems. And still another point to consider is that agreeing to disulfiram therapy represents a concrete demonstration of your commitment to drug abstinence and substantial lifestyle changes. This would be helpful in general, but could also be helpful in your pursuit of visitation privileges with your daughter.

S: Hey, I'm looking to make some progress here. When I've tried to quit cocaine on my own, it's not worked for beans. Maybe it's because I kept drinking; I'm not sure. I can't continue like this. How about I take the medicine during treatment? That's a pretty good commitment. What did you say, treatment is for 24 weeks? Let's say I'll go on the medicine for that amount of time.

Steve agreed to disulfiram therapy for the duration of treatment. A schedule was set up for Steve to ingest a 250-mg dose three times per week under the observation of a clinic staff member, and to ingest the same dose under the observation of his father at home on alternating days.

In addition to disulfiram therapy, the therapist worked with Steve to functionally analyze his alcohol use, in the same way that they analyzed his cocaine use. They reviewed the specific circumstances under which Steve was either more or less likely to drink, as well as the negative consequences he had previously experienced from his alcohol use. The therapist and patient developed a plan for finding alternative ways to relax that did not involve bars or drinking, as well as rehearsing how to refuse alcohol when it was offered and how to identify times when he might be tempted to have a drink.

Steve was compliant with disulfiram therapy and behavioral planning around alcohol use through treatment. He reported only one instance of alcohol use while on disulfiram therapy: He did not take the medication one Sunday morning and drank two beers at home that afternoon. On Monday, the therapist did a functional analysis with Steve to identify what set the occasion for him to drink, and what had happened with his father's serving as disulfiram assurance monitor. The therapist and Steve reviewed again his history of alcohol use and the negative consequences that he had experienced in the past. Steve recommitted to alcohol abstinence and resumed disulfiram therapy.

When the end of the 24 weeks of treatment approached (Week 23), Steve expressed a desire to "be able to have a drink if he wanted" and requested to discontinue disulfiram therapy as planned. The therapist expressed his concerns about jeopardizing the substantial progress Steve had made.

T: So you're due to end disulfiram therapy this week?

S: Yep, stuck to it like I promised. But now I'd like to be able to drink if I wanted to, like having a beer after work to relax. Nothing major.

T: Steve, you've done really well so far with this current plan. Most folks are not as successful as you've been in stopping cocaine use.

S: Oh, I agree. I just feel like I've done really well in treatment, and now that it's almost over, I'd like to be able to have that choice to drink if I want to.

T: How risky do you think going off disulfiram is going to be for you in terms of continuing your success with abstaining from cocaine?

S: I really don't think it's going to be a problem. I'm feeling pretty confident about that.

T: Steve, that's great. That sort of confidence is important to success. Let's talk about some specifics, though. Remember, your alcohol history is still with you. In the past, you've had periods of binge drinking combined with cocaine use. What's going to be different now from that past history?

S: Well, first of all, I don't plan on drinking like I used to. I'm not looking to get drunk. I'm not even sure I want to drink very often. Also, I'm not going to drink in bars. That's how I've gotten into trouble in the past. And I'm not going to drink with the same old crowd. I just want to know that if I go out to dinner on a date or something and want to have a drink, I can do that.

T: You've given this careful consideration, which is good. Those kinds of plans are important to continuing your success. Let's talk a bit more about how you can reduce your risk as much as possible if you're going to resume drinking. By that, I mean how often you drink, how much you drink per occasion, where and with whom you drink—more or less, anything you can do to protect yourself from excessive drinking, and subsequently cocaine use. Does this sound reasonable to you?

S: Yeah, sure, that sounds really good.

At this time the therapist began the clinic's controlled drinking protocol, using Miller and Munoz's (1982) *How to Control Your Drinking* manual. Our primary clinical recommendation was abstinence, but Steve was not going to follow that recommendation. Hence we felt that attempting to systematically provide him with some skills to decrease the likelihood of abusive or harmful drinking was indicated. The Miller and Munoz (1982) approach aims to teach skills that enable the client to drink in a controlled manner. Some of those skills are the same as those used with cocaine use, including functional analysis to identify the circumstances (location, people, times, feeling states) that are associated with heavy drinking. Others are specific to alcohol consumption (e.g., learning about the alcohol content of common drinks, and about the relationship between drinks consumed, body weight, and the blood alcohol curve). Steve and the therapist worked through some of the core elements of the controlled drinking protocol during the final week of treatment and then covered the remaining parts during aftercare. Steve reported one instance of alcohol use during the final week of treatment. He had only two drinks and did not use cocaine. As noted below, Steve also reported little drinking during 6 months of posttreatment follow-up.

Other Drug Use

Steve continued the same pattern of marijuana use that he reported in the intake interview. Steve repeatedly asserted that marijuana use was not interfering with his other treatment goals. In turn, the therapist provided rationales for stopping or reducing marijuana use on numerous occasions, but was not successful in initiating abstinence.

Recreational Activities

During the first several sessions, the therapist and Steve discussed the importance of developing new recreational activities. They decided on a goal of participating in four of these activities per week, as well as a plan to sample some new activities in the company of clinic staff. The therapist reminded Steve that the vouchers he would be earning during treatment for cocaine abstinence could be used to help pay for these activities.

During treatment, Steve consistently met his goal of four recreational activities per week. Those activities included movies, hunting, golf, and dinners at local restaurants. He used his vouchers to pay for tickets to a performance at a local theater, greens fees to play golf, a gym membership, hunting and fishing licenses, and gift certificates to a local restaurant for dinner with a new girlfriend.

Family/Social Support

During the first few sessions, the therapist discussed with Steve the need for him to expand his social network to include family, friends, and other social contacts with non-drug-using people. Steve expressed a desire for increased contact with his daughter. Toward that end, Steve and his therapist completed a task analysis identifying the sequence of steps that Steve would have to take to try to attain visitation privileges. These included requesting and completing legal forms from court, appropriately discussing his wishes with his former partner, preparing for the court date, and going to court. The therapist helped Steve obtain and fill out the forms, used role playing to help him with the second and third steps, and accompanied him to his court appearance.

Steve succeeded in obtaining visitation privileges. The goal then became twice-weekly contact with his daughter, which he maintained consistently throughout the remainder of treatment.

Regarding other types of social support, Steve increased contact with a couple of safe friends during the course of treatment. As mentioned above, he had occasional contact during treatment with individuals with whom he had used cocaine in the past, but the frequency was quite low. He also was able to meet several women through his new employment (discussed below), one of whom he began dating regularly.

Employment/Education

Steve came to treatment with a history of full-time employment, which is a good prognostic indicator in itself. However, his job upon entering treatment did not pay well and involved being around drinking. He expressed a desire to find a job that offered better pay, thereby allowing him to work fewer hours per week, spend more time with his daughter, and be at reduced risk for alcohol use. Therefore Steve began participating in the Job Club, coming to the clinic three times per week to go through local employment classified ads, complete a resumé and cover letters with the help of the staff, fill out job applications, and rehearse for job interviews. Steve successfully obtained a better-paying job with fewer risks for alcohol use. Thereafter, the vocational goal was focused on avoiding excessive hours.

Steve also expressed concern regarding the extensive debts that he had accumulated during this prolonged cocaine use. The therapist began the clinic's money management protocol, including developing a budget for repayment of outstanding loans and skills for managing personal finances. Steve opened a savings account at a nearby bank and arranged direct deposit of his paychecks with his employer. Steve used the phone in his therapist's office to arrange payback plans with several debtors. He consistently made payments on his debts throughout treatment, which the therapist graphed weekly; by the end of treatment, he had eliminated almost all back debts and was now paying current bills.

Steve had a long-term vocational goal of eventually opening his own retail business. He and his therapist completed a preliminary task analysis (see Sulzer-Azaroff & Meyer, 1991) related to that goal. They agreed that taking accounting and computer courses would be a good start. The therapist helped Steve collect information from the local community college on the classes being offered. Steve requested financial aid applications from the community college for assistance with tuition, which his therapist helped him complete. At the end of treatment he had identified courses he wanted to take, but had not yet enrolled.

Psychiatric Monitoring

Recall that Steve's BDI score at intake was 23. His BDI score had dropped precipitously by the second week of treatment, and he reached a score of 1 by the end of treatment.

Steve and his therapist worked through the portion of the Monti, Abrams, Kadden, and Cooney (1989) text, *Treating Alcohol Dependence: A Coping Skills Training Guide,* that addresses anger management training. This protocol helped Steve identify situations that would be likely to make him angry, develop coping skills to deal better with those triggers, and role-play those coping skills to gain proficiency. The therapist had Steve document times when potential anger-provoking situations arose outside of the clinic and how he handled them. The therapist reviewed that information weekly, provided social reinforcement for those situations that were handled well, and problem-solved and role-played alternatives when Steve needed assistance.

Summary of Treatment Progress

Steve made substantial progress toward establishing a stable record of cocaine abstinence, eliminating problem drinking, increasing his involvement in social and recreational practices, improving his job situation, increasing his skill in managing anger, and improving his relationship with his daughter. The one area where we were unable to make progress was his use of marijuana and associated involvement with the illicit drug use community. This progress is reflected in the pretreatment to posttreatment changes in ASI composite scores, shown in Table 10.7. Composite scores range from 0 (representing no problems in the past 30 days) to 1.00 (representing severe problems). Steve's scores generally reflect substantial improvements.

Follow-Up

Following completion of the 24-week treatment protocol, Steve participated in aftercare and completed 6 months of follow-up assessments. Thus we have a relatively good picture of his continued progress with drug abstinence and treatment goals. Steve reported no cocaine use during this period, and his urinalysis results supported those reports. Steve reported that he continued to avoid bars and high-risk people. Steve also reported very few instances of alcohol use and no instances of heavy drinking. Regular use of marijuana continued during follow-up just as it had during treatment, and the client remained uninterested in addressing or changing that behavior.

Steve continued to have regular visitation with his daughter throughout the follow-up period and expressed satisfaction with that arrangement. He expressed dissatisfaction with employment at one point during aftercare, including wanting to pursue a better-paying job, and came into the clinic to update his resumé and get assistance in looking for alternative employment. (That dissatisfaction was also related to an incident where he was accused of stealing from work. He reported that this situation arose out of a misunderstanding between him and his boss, and was not related to substance use.) He then took a new job that represented a professional advancement. He reported that his level of recreational and social activities remained on track, including contact and activities with safe friends. Steve's depressive symptomatology also remained at low levels throughout the follow-up period, and there was no indication of problems with anger management.

CONCLUDING COMMENTS

In this chapter we have tried to describe the most up-to-date scientific information available on effective clinical management of cocaine dependence. In the process, we have tried to illustrate what have come to be considered principles of effective treatment for illicit drug abuse and dependence in general and cocaine dependence in particular. We have emphasized one efficacious treatment approach, but have underscored the existence and importance of others. We realize that limitations in resources and other practical constraints will prevent many clinicians from utilizing the treatment practices in this chapter just as we have outlined them. In particular, we recognize that the costs of the voucher program are likely to be outside the range of what most outpatient community clinics can afford. Rather than hastily dismiss the potential use of incentives in such clinics, however, we recommend consideration of some possible alternatives (see Kirby, Amass, & McLellan, 1999, for a detailed discussion of this topic). For example, community businesses may be willing to donate goods or services that could be used as incentives. Contingent access to already existing community services or recreation facilities is another example of incentives that potentially could be used in public clinics. Incentive programs based on patients' earning back cash deposits have been effective in the treatment of other substance use disorders, as well as other behavioral disorders, so these represent still another possibility. Such potential limitations notwithstanding, we hope that the information provided in this chapter will offer insights into the important elements of effective treatment for cocaine dependence. We also hope that the information provided will make the job of the clinicians who are out there "in the trenches" treating patients with cocaine dependence a little easier, and their practices more effective.

TABLE 10.7. Steve's ASI Subscale and BDI Scores at Intake and End of Treatment (6 months)

Score	Intake	End of treatment
ASI subscales		
Medical	0.42	0.09
Employment	0.07	0.10
Alcohol	0.13	0.00
Drug (other than cocaine)	0.28	0.07
Cocaine	0.66	0.00
Legal	0.00	0.00
Family/Social	0.22	0.10
Psychological	0.36	0.00
BDI	23	1

ACKNOWLEDGMENTS

Preparation of this chapter was supported in part by National Institute on Drug Abuse Grants No. DA09378 and No. DA07242.

REFERENCES

Alterman, A., O'Brien, C. P., McLellan, A. T., August, D. S., Snider, E. C., Droba, M., Cornish, J. W., & Hall, C. P. (1994). Effectiveness and costs of inpatient versus day hospital cocaine rehabilitation. *Journal of Nervous and Mental Disease, 182,* 157–163.

American Psychiatric Association. (1994). *Diagnostic and statistical manual of mental disorders* (4th ed.). Washington, DC: Author.

Azrin, N. H. (1976). Improvements in the community-reinforcement approach to alcoholism. *Behaviour Research and Therapy, 14,* 339–348.

Azrin, N. H., & Besalel, V. A. (1980). *Job Club counselor's manual.* Baltimore: University Park Press.

Azrin, N. H., Sisson, R. W., Meyers, R., & Godley, M. (1982). Alcoholism treatment by disulfiram therapy. *Journal of Behavior Therapy and Experimental Psychiatry, 13,* 105–112.

Azrin, N. H., Naster, B. J., & Jones, R. (1973). Reciprocity counseling: A rapid learning based procedure for marital counseling. *Behaviour Research and Therapy, 11,* 364–382.

Beck, A. T., Ward, C. H., Mendelson, M., Mock, J., & Erbaugh, J. (1961). An inventory for measuring depression. *Archives of General Psychiatry, 4,* 561–571.

Bickel, W. K., Amass, L., Higgins, S. T., Badger, G. J., & Esch, R. A. (1997). Effects of adding behavioral treatment to opioid detoxification with buprenorphine. *Journal of Consulting and Clinical Psychology, 65,* 803–810.

Budney, A. J., & Higgins, S. T. (1998). *National Institute on Drug Abuse therapy manuals for drug addiction: Manual 2. The community reinforcement plus vouchers approach* (NIH Publication No. 98-4308). Rockville, MD: National Institute on Drug Abuse.

Budney, A. J., Higgins, S. T., & Wong, C. J. (1996). Marijuana use and treatment outcome in cocaine-dependent patients. *Journal of Experimental and Clinical Psychopharmacology, 4,* 1–8.

Budney, A. J., Higgins, S. T., Hughes, J. R., & Bickel, W. K. (1992). The scientific/clinical response to the cocaine epidemic: A MEDLINE search of the literature. *Drug and Alcohol Dependence, 30,* 143–149.

Byck, R. (1987). Cocaine use and research: Three histories. In S. Fisher, A. Raskin, & E. H. Uhlenhuth (Eds.), *Cocaine: Clinical and behavioral aspects* (pp. 3–20). New York: Oxford University Press.

Carroll, K. M. (1998). *National Institute on Drug Abuse therapy manuals for drug addiction: Manual 1. A cognitive-behavioral approach: Treating cocaine addiction* (NIH Publication No. 98-4309). Rockville, MD: National Institute on Drug Abuse.

Carroll, K. M., Nich, C., Ball, S. A., McCance, E., & Rounsaville, B. J. (1998). Treatment of cocaine and alcohol dependence with psychotherapy and disulfiram. *Addiction, 93,* 713–727.

Carroll, K. M., Rounsaville, B. J., Nich, C., Gordon, L. T., Wirtz, P. W., & Gawin, F. H. (1994). One-year follow-up of psychotherapy and pharmacotherapy for cocaine dependence: Delayed emergence of psychotherapy effects. *Archives of General Psychiatry,* 989–997.

Derogatis, L. R. (1983). *SCL-90-R: Administration, scoring and procedures manual—II.* Towson, MD: Clinical Psychometric Research.

Fals-Stewart, W., Birchler, G. R., & O'Farrell, T. J. (1996). Behavioral couples therapy for male substance abusing patients: Effects on relationship adjustment and drug-using behavior. *Journal of Consulting and Clinical Psychology, 64,* 959–972.

Festinger, D. S., Lamb, R. J., Kirby, K. C., & Marlowe, D. B. (1996). The accelerated intake: A method for increasing initial attendance to outpatient cocaine treatment. *Journal of Applied Behavior Analysis, 29,* 387–389.

Goldfried, M. R., & Davison, G. C. (1994). *Clinical behavior therapy* (2nd ed.). New York: Wiley.

Griffiths, R. R., Bigelow, G. E., & Henningfield, J. E. (1980). Similarities in animal and human drug taking behavior. In N. K. Mello (Ed.), *Advances in substance abuse: Behavioral and biological research* (pp. 1–90). Greenwich, CT: JAI Press.

Hammer, R. P. (Ed.). (1995). *The neurobiology of cocaine: Cellular and molecular mechanisms.* Boca Raton, FL: CRC Press.

Higgins, S. T. (1997). The influence of alternative reinforcers on cocaine use and abuse: A brief review. *Pharmacology, Biochemistry and Behavior, 57,* 419–427.

Higgins, S. T., Budney, A. J., Bickel, W. K., & Badger, G. (1994). Participation of significant others in outpatient behavioral treatment predicts greater cocaine abstinence. *American Journal of Alcohol and Drug Dependence, 20,* 47–56.

Higgins, S. T., Budney, A. J., Bickel, W. K., Badger, G. J., Foerg, F. E., & Ogden, D. (1995). Outpatient behavioral treatment for cocaine dependence: One-year outcome. *Experimental and Clinical Psychopharmacology, 3,* 205–212.

Higgins, S. T., Budney, A. J., Bickel, W. K., Foerg, F. E., Donham, R., & Badger, G. (1994). Incentives improve outcome in outpatient behavioral treatment of cocaine dependence. *Archives of General Psychiatry, 51,* 568–576.

Higgins, S. T., Budney, A. J., Bickel, W. K., Hughes, J. R., Foerg, F., & Badger, G. (1993). Achieving cocaine abstinence with a behavioral approach. *American Journal of Psychiatry, 150,* 763–769.

Higgins, S. T., Delaney, D. D., Budney, A. J., Bickel, W. K., Hughes, J. R., Foerg, F., & Fenwick, J. (1991). A behavioral approach to achieving initial cocaine abstinence. *American Journal of Psychiatry, 148,* 1218–1224.

Higgins, S. T., & Katz, J. L. (Eds.). (1998). *Cocaine abuse: Behavior, pharmacology, and clinical applications.* San Diego, CA: Academic Press.

Higgins, S. T., & Silverman, K. (Eds.). (1999). *Motivating behavior change among illicit-drug abusers: Research on contingency-management interven-

tions. Washington, DC: American Psychological Association.

Higgins, S. T., Wong, C. J., Badger, G. J., Haug Ogden, D. E., & Dantona, R. L. (2000). Contingent reinforcement increases cocaine abstinence during outpatient treatment and one year of follow-up. *Journal of Consulting and Clinical Psychology, 68,* 64–72.

Hunt, G. M., & Azrin, N. H. (1973). A community-reinforcement approach to alcoholism. *Behaviour Research and Therapy, 11,* 91–104.

Kelly, J. A., St. Lawrence, J., Hood, H., & Brasfield, T. (1989). Behavioral intervention to reduce AIDS risk activities. *Journal of Consulting and Clinical Psychology, 57,* 60–67.

Kirby, K. C., Amass, L., & McLellan, A. T. (1999). Disseminating contingency management research to drug abuse treatment practitioners. In S. T. Higgins & K. Silverman (Eds.), *Motivating behavior change among illicit-drug abusers: Research on contingency-management interventions* (pp. 327–344). Washington, DC: American Psychological Association.

Kirby, K. C., Marlowe, D. B., Festinger, D. S., Lamb, R. J., & Platt, J. J. (1998). Schedule of voucher delivery influences initiation of cocaine abstinence. *Journal of Consulting and Clinical Psychology, 66,* 761–767.

Konkol, R. J., & Olsen, G. D. (Eds.). (1996). *Prenatal cocaine exposure.* Boca Raton, FL: CRC Press.

Lacks, P. (1987). *Behavioral treatment of persistent insomnia.* New York: Pergamon Press.

Lewinsohn, P. M., Munoz, R. F., Youngren, M. A., & Zeiss, A. M. (1986). *Control your depression.* New York: Simon & Schuster.

Maude-Griffin, P. M., Hohenstein, J. M., Humfleet, G. L. Reilly, P. M., Tusel, D. J., & Hall, S. M. (1998). Superior efficacy of cognitive-behavioral therapy for urban crack cocaine abusers: Main and matching effects. *Journal of Consulting and Clinical Psychology, 66,* 832–837.

McCrady, B. S. (1986). *Behavioral marital therapy for alcohol dependence.* Unpublished treatment manual, Rutgers University.

McLellan, A. T., Luborsky, L., Cacciola, J., Griffith, J., Evans, F., Barr, H. L., & O'Brien, C. P. (1985). New data from the Addiction Severity Index. *Journal of Nervous and Mental Disease, 173,* 412–423.

Meyers, R. J., & Smith, J. E. (1995). *Clinical guide to alcohol treatment: The community reinforcement approach.* New York: Guilford Press.

Milby, J. B., Schumacher, J. E., Raczynski, J. M., Caldwell, E., Engle, M., Michael, M., & Carr, J. (1996). Sufficient conditions for effective treatment of substance abusing homeless. *Drug and Alcohol Dependence, 43,* 39–47.

Miller, W. R., & Munoz, R. F. (1982). *How to control your drinking.* Albuquerque: University of New Mexico Press.

Miller, W. R., & Rollnick, S. (1991). *Motivational interviewing: Preparing people to change addictive behavior.* New York: Guilford Press.

Miller, W. R., & Tonigan, J. S. (1996). Assessing drinkers' motivation for change: The Stages of Change Readiness and Treatment Eagerness Scale (SOCRATES). *Psychology of Addictive Behaviors, 10,* 81–89.

Monti, P. M., Abrams, D. B., Kadden, R. M., & Cooney, N. L. (1989). *Treating alcohol dependence: A coping skills training guide.* New York: Guilford Press.

Monti, P. M., Rohsenow, D. J., Michalec, E., Martin, R. A., & Abrams, D. B. (1997). Brief coping skills treatment for cocaine abuse: Substance use outcomes at three months. *Addiction, 92,* 1717–1728.

Montoya, I. D., & Atkinson, J. S. (1996). Determinants of HIV seroprevalence rates among sites participating in a community based study of drug use. *Journal of Acquired Immune Deficiency Syndromes and Human Retrovirology, 13,* 169–176.

Morin, C. M. (1993). *Insomnia: Psychological assessment and management.* New York: Guilford Press.

National Institute of Justice. (1999). *1998 annual report on cocaine use among arrestees, National Institute of Justice Research Report, 1999.* Rockville, MD: National Institute of Justice Clearinghouse.

National Institute on Drug Abuse. (1999). *Principles of addiction treatment: A research-based guide* (NIH Publication No. 99-4180). Rockville, MD: National Institute on Drug Abuse.

Petry, N. (1999, June). *Low-cost contingency management with cocaine abusers.* Paper presented at the annual meeting of the College on Problems of Drug Dependence, Acapulco, Mexico.

Piotrowski, N. A., & Hall, S. M. (1999). Treatment of multiple drug abuse in the methadone clinic. In S. T. Higgins & K. Silverman (Eds.), *Motivating behavior change among illicit-drug abusers: Research on contingency-management interventions* (pp. 183–202). Washington, DC: American Psychological Association.

Rosenthal, T. L., & Rosenthal, R. H. (1985). Clinical stress management. In D. Barlow (Ed.), *Clinical handbook of psychological disorders* (pp. 145–205). New York: Guilford Press.

Rounsaville, B. J., Anton, S. F., Carroll, K., Budde, D., Prusoff, B. A., & Gawin, F. (1991). Psychiatric diagnoses of treatment-seeking cocaine abusers. *Archives of General Psychiatry, 39,* 161–166.

Selzer, M. L. (1971). The Michigan Alcoholism Screening Test. *American Journal of Psychiatry, 127,* 1653–1658.

Shaner, A., Roberts, L. J., Eckman, T. A., Tucker, D. E., Tsuang, J. W., Wilkens, J. N., & Mintz, J. (1997). Monetary reinforcement of abstinence from cocaine among mentally ill patients with cocaine dependence. *Psychiatric Services, 48,* 807–810.

Silverman, K., Higgins, S. T., Brooner, R. K., Montoya, I. D., Cone, E. J., Schuster, C. R., & Preston, K. L. (1996). Sustained cocaine abstinence in methadone maintenance patients through voucher-based reinforcement therapy. *Archives of General Psychiatry, 53,* 409–415.

Sisson, R., & Azrin, N. H. (1989). The community reinforcement approach. In R. K. Hester & W. R. Miller (Eds.), *Handbook of alcoholism treatment approaches: Effective alternatives* (pp. 242–258). New York: Pergamon Press.

Sobell, L. C., & Sobell, M. B. (1992). Timeline Follow-Back: A technique for assessing self-reported alcohol consumption. In R. Z. Litten & J. P. Allen (Eds.), *Measuring alcohol consumption: Psychosocial and biochemical methods* (pp. 41–72). Totowa, NJ: Humana Press.

Stitzer, M. L., & Higgins, S. T. (1995). Behavioral treatment of drug and alcohol abuse. In F. E. Bloom & D. J. Kupfer (Eds.), *Psychopharmacology: The fourth generation of progress* (pp. 1807–1819). New York: Raven Press.

Substance Abuse and Mental Heath Services Administration (SAMHSA). (1997). *Drug Abuse Warning Network series: D-3. Year-end preliminary estimates from the 1996 Drug Abuse Warning Network.* Rockville, MD: National Clearinghouse for Alcohol and Drug Information.

Substance Abuse and Mental Health Services Administration (SAMHSA). (1999). *National Household Survey on Drug Abuse: Population estimates, 1998.* Rockville, MD: National Clearinghouse for Alcohol and Drug Information.

Sulzer-Azaroff, B., & Meyer, G. R. (1991). *Behavior analysis for lasting change.* Fort Worth, TX: Holt, Rinehart & Winston.

Tardiff, K., Marzuk, P. M., Leon, A. C., Hirsch, C. S., Stajie, M., Portera, L., & Hartwell, N. (1994). Homicide in New York City: Cocaine use and firearms. *Journal of the American Medical Association, 272,* 43–46.

Tidey, J. W., Mehl-Madrona, L., Higgins, S. T., & Badger, G. J. (1998). Psychiatric symptom severity in cocaine-dependent outpatients: Demographics, drug use characteristics and treatment outcome. *Drug and Alcohol Dependence, 50,* 9–17.

Washton, A. M., Stone, N. S., & Hendrickson, E. C. (1988). Cocaine abuse. In D. M. Donovan & G. A. Marlatt (Eds.), *Assessment of addictive behaviors* (pp. 364–389). New York: Guilford Press.

Wasserman, D. A., Havassy, B. E., & Boles, S. (1997). Traumatic events and post-traumatic stress disorder in cocaine users entering private treatment. *Drug and Alcohol Dependence, 46,* 1–8.

Chapter 11

DIALECTICAL BEHAVIOR THERAPY FOR BORDERLINE PERSONALITY DISORDER

Marsha M. Linehan
Bryan N. Cochran
Constance A. Kehrer

This chapter presents one of the more remarkable developments in all of psychotherapy. Few therapists are willing to undertake the overwhelmingly difficult and wrenching task of treating individuals with "borderline" characteristics, and yet these people are among the neediest encountered in any therapeutic setting. They also impose an enormous burden on the health care system. Over the past two decades, Linehan and her colleagues have developed a psychological treatment for individuals with borderline personality disorder. Importantly, data indicate that this treatment is effective when compared to alternative interventions. If this result continues to hold up in future clinical trials, this treatment will constitute one of the most substantial contributions to the armamentarium of the psychotherapist in recent times. What is even more interesting is that this approach blends psychodynamic, interpersonal systems, and cognitive-behavioral approaches into a coherent whole. To this mix, Linehan adds her personal experience with Eastern philosophies and religions. Among the more intriguing strategies incorporated into this approach are "entering the paradox" and "extending," borrowed from *aikido*, a Japanese form of self-defense. And yet the authors remain true to the empirical foundations of their approach. The fascinating case study presented in the context of this chapter illustrates Linehan's therapeutic expertise and strategic timing in a way that will be invaluable to all therapists who deal with personality disorders. The surprising and tragic outcome illustrates the enormous burden of clinical responsibility inherent in any treatment setting, as well as the practical issues that arise when treatment ultimately fails.—D. H. B.

Clinicians generally agree that clients with a diagnosis of borderline personality disorder (BPD) are challenging and difficult to treat. Indeed, the treatment of such individuals is something that many practitioners approach with trepidation and concern. Several of the behavioral patterns that define the condition are particularly problematic and are among the most stressful that therapists encounter (Shearin & Linehan, 1989). Perhaps of greatest concern is the generally high incidence of suicidal behavior among this population. From 70% to 75% of clients who meet criteria for BPD have a history of at least one "parasuicidal" act (Clarkin, Widiger, Frances, Hurt, & Gilmore, 1983; Cowdry, Pickar, & Davies, 1985), defined as any intentional, acute, self-injurious behavior with or without suicidal intent, including both suicide attempts and self-mutilative behaviors. (We prefer to use the term "clients who meet criteria for BPD" to emphasize a behaviorist view of meeting diagnostic criteria through patterns of behavior, as opposed to the medical model term "clients with BPD." However, for conciseness, we will refer to this population as "clients with BPD" in future references.) Suicide threats and crises are frequent even among those who never engage in any parasuicidal behaviors. Although much of this behavior is without lethal consequence, follow-up studies of individuals with BPD have found suicide rates of about 7%–8%, and the percentage who eventually commit suicide is estimated at 10% (see Linehan, Rizvi, Welch, & Page, 2000, for a review). Among all individuals who have committed suicide, from 7% to 38% meet criteria for BPD when personality disorders are assessed via a psychological autopsy, with the higher incidence occurring primarily among young adults with the disorder (Brent et al., 1994; Isometsa et al., 1996, 1997; Lesage et al., 1994; Rich & Runeson, 1992). Individuals with BPD also have difficulties with anger and anger expression. Not infrequently, intense anger is directed at their therapists. The frequent coexistence of BPD with both Axis I conditions (such as mood or anxiety disorders) and other personality disorders clearly complicates treatment further.

The criteria for BPD, as currently defined within the fourth edition of the *Diagnostic and Statistical Manual of Mental Disorders* (DSM-IV; American Psychiatric Association, 1994) and the Diagnostic Interview for Borderlines (DIB; Gunderson & Kolb, 1978; Gunderson, Kolb, & Austin, 1981; Zanarini, Gunderson, Frankenburg, & Chauncey, 1989), the most commonly used research assessment instrument, reflect a pervasive pattern of instability and dysregulation across all domains of functioning. To reorganize these definitions somewhat and summarize criteria within each domain (see Linehan, 1993a), individuals with BPD have the following characteristics. First, they generally experience emotional dysregulation and instability. Emotional responses are reactive, and the individuals generally have difficulties with episodic depression, anxiety, and irritability, as well as problems with anger and anger expression. Second, individuals with BPD have patterns of behavioral dysregulation, as evidenced by extreme and problematic impulsive behavior. As noted above, an important characteristic of these individuals is their tendency to direct apparently destructive behaviors toward themselves. Attempts to injure, mutilate, or kill themselves, as well as actual suicides, occur frequently in this population. Third, individuals with BPD sometimes experience cognitive dysregulation. Brief, nonpsychotic forms of thought and sensory dysregulation, such as depersonalization, dissociation, and delusions (including delusions about the self), are at times brought on by stressful situations and usually cease when the stress is ameliorated. Fourth, dysregulation of the sense of self is also common. Individuals with BPD frequently report that they have no sense of a self at all, feel empty, and do not "know" who they are. Finally, these individuals often experience interpersonal dysregulation. Their relationships may be chaotic, intense, and marked with difficulties. Even though their relationships are so difficult, individuals wth BPD often find it extremely hard to relinquish relationships. Instead, they may engage in intense and frantic efforts to prevent significant individuals from leaving them. The polythetic format of the DSM-IV definition allows for considerable heterogeneity in diagnosis (indeed, the requirement that 5 of 9 criteria be met for the diagnosis yields 256 ways in which the BPD diagnosis may be met), and clinical experience with these clients confirms that this diagnostic category comprises a heterogeneous group.

BPD is disproportionately well represented in the clinical literature on personality disorders. A literature search of journal articles classified under the category of personality disorders from 1990 until the time of this writing indicated that approximately one in five of these articles was devoted exclusively to research on BPD. (Articles were classified as BPD-focused if the term "borderline personality disorder" appeared in the title; the abstracts were used to confirm which articles were exclusively devoted to BPD.) The same search limited to the *Journal of Personality Disorders* alone yielded a higher proportion of articles devoted to BPD—approximately one in four. Today, therefore, BPD is the most widely researched personality disorder. Despite this widespread interest, empirically based treatment research on BPD is lacking. Given the myriad of difficulties in conducting psychotherapy with these individuals, even in clinical settings without the added complexity of a research study, the paucity of carefully controlled treatment outcome studies is perhaps understandable. Consequently, treatment efficacy of the many therapeutic modalities currently applied in treating clients with BPD has not been empirically demonstrated. A recent meta-analysis of the research on psychosocial treatments for personality disorders yielded only 15 studies that investigated any kind of treatment for any personality disorder; 4 of these 15 studies focused specifically on BPD (Perry, Banon, & Ianni, 1999).

This chapter is focused primarily on describing dialectical behavior therapy (DBT), a comparatively new approach to treatment of BPD (Linehan, 1993a, 1993b). It has the distinction of being one of the first psychosocial treatments demonstrated to be effective in a randomized clinical trial (Linehan, Armstrong, Suarez, Allmon, & Heard, 1991). Since then, a second randomized clinical trial has been published, and two more have been presented at professional conferences. A number of quasi-experimental trials have also been conducted (see reviews by Koerner & Linehan, 2000, and Koerner & Dimeff, 2000). Before describing DBT, we first review other treatments for BPD, providing information on their theoretical rationale and supporting data (when such data are available). This is followed by a more in-depth description of DBT—its philosophical roots, underlying theory, and treatment protocols. Table 11.1 summarizes all of the currently available treatment approaches, including DBT.

OVERVIEW OF OTHER TREATMENT APPROACHES

Various approaches have been applied to the treatment of BPD. Although it is not our purpose to present a scholarly review of all the many treatments for BPD, we believe it helpful to briefly review the status of other current treatments before presenting DBT in detail.

Psychodynamic

Psychodynamic approaches that have received the greatest attention include those of Kernberg (1975, 1984; Kernberg, Selzer, Koenigsberg, Carr, & Applebaum, 1989), Masterson and Rinsley (Masterson, 1976, 1981; Rinsley, 1982), Adler and Buie (Adler, 1981, 1985;

Adler & Buie, 1979; Buie & Adler, 1982), Gunderson (1984), and most recently Bateman and Fonagy (1999). Among these, Kernberg's theoretical contributions are clearly prominent. His object relations model is comprehensive as to theory and technique, and has had considerable influence on the psychoanalytic literature. His expressive psychotherapy for clients with "borderline personality organization" (BPO) or BPD, transference-focused psychotherapy, emphasizes three primary factors: interpretation, the maintenance of technical neutrality, and transference analysis. The focus of the therapy is on exposure and resolution of intrapsychic conflict. Treatment goals include increased impulse control and anxiety tolerance, ability to modulate affect, and the development of stable interpersonal relationships.

Kernberg has also distinguished a supportive psychotherapy for more severely disturbed clients with BPO or BPD. Like expressive psychotherapy, supportive psychotherapy also places great emphasis on the importance of the interpersonal relationship in therapy (transference); however, interpretations are less likely to be made early in treatment, and only the negative responses to the therapist and to therapy (negative transference) are explored. Both expressive and supportive psychotherapy are expected to last several years, with primary foci on suicidal behaviors and therapy-interfering behaviors.

To date, there have been no randomized clinical trials evaluating the efficacy of psychodynamic individual therapy in general, or of Kernberg's transference-focused psychotherapy specifically. Naturalistic studies, however, cast doubt on the feasibility of long-term psychodynamic treatment; many if not most clients fail to complete even 6 months of therapy (Kernberg et al., 1972; Stone, Stone, & Hurt, 1987; Waldinger & Gunderson, 1984).

In addition to psychodynamically oriented individualized treatments, Marziali and Munroe-Blum (1987; Munroe-Blum & Marziali, 1987) have developed a psychodynamic group approach to treating BPD, relationship management psychotherapy (RMP). Differentiating RMP from traditional psychodynamic approaches is its emphasis on a client orientation phase as well as on therapist accessibility outside the group format. Within the group setting, clients are engaged individually and encouraged to express internalized conflicts around self-attributes, with feedback provided by other group members. In addition, the group format is intended to help dilute the intensity of the transference relationship across clients and cotherapists, and to aid in setting limits for members with poor impulse control. Preliminary results of a controlled clinical trial comparing RMP to individual treatment as usual in the community reported no differences in treatment outcome at the 6-month follow-up (Clarkin, Marziali, & Munroe-Blum, 1991; Munroe-Blum & Marziali, 1987, 1989). However, clients who remained in either group or individual therapy had significantly more improvement on behavioral indicators than clients who dropped out of therapy. These preliminary results warrant caution in interpreting the treatment efficacy of RMP.

A recent randomized controlled trial of psychoanalytically oriented partial hospitalization provides the first supporting data for psychoanalytic treatment of BPD. This study by Bateman and Fonagy (1999) consisted of random assignment to either standard psychiatric care constrained only by the requirement that individual psychotherapy was not allowed (control condition) or to partial hospitalization, a treatment program with the following goals of therapy: (1) psychoanalytically informed engagement of patients in treatment; (2) reduction of psychopathology, including depression and anxiety; (3) reduction of suicidal behavior; (4) improvement in social competence; and (5) reduction in lengthy hospitalizations. The psychotherapy was grounded in attachment theory (i.e., BPD was viewed as an attachment disorder), with a focus on relationship patterns and nonconscious factors inhibiting change. The experimental treatment group received once-weekly individual psychotherapy provided by psychiatric nurses, once-weekly psychodrama-based expressive therapy, thrice-weekly group therapy, a weekly community meeting, a monthly meeting with a case administrator, and a monthly medications review. At the end of the 18-month treatment, the group receiving psychoanalytically informed partial hospitalization showed significant reductions in suicidal behavior (suicide attempts and self-mutilation), inpatient hospitalization stays, measures of psychopathology (including depression and anxiety), and social functioning relative to the control group. The researchers note that their program contained three characteristics that they hypothesize to be related to treatment effectiveness: a consistent theoretical rationale for treatment, a relationship focus, and consistent treatment over time.

Interpersonal

Interpersonal approaches to the conceptualization and treatment of personality disorders are similar to, but distinct from, traditional psychodynamic approaches. Among these, Lorna Benjamin's (1974, 1979, 1996) Structural Analysis of Social Behavior (SASB) has received much attention. Based on interpersonal behavior classification system parameters, this nosological system presents a testable theory for understanding how personality disorders are, to a large extent, created and maintained by an individual's social learning experiences. Benjamin's SASB attempts to measure both interpersonal and intrapsychic behavior along three dimensions: the focus of the behavior (either "self" or "other"), interdependence, and affiliation. According to Benjamin, the SASB holds promise in terms of improving the reliability and clinical usefulness of the DSM descriptions of personality disorders; it can also be used to make predictions about the sequences of behavior during dyadic interaction and to plan interventions based on these predictions (Benjamin, 1996). The SASB–Reconstructive Learning (SASB-RCL) approach stresses six phases of treatment: (1) developing a collaborative relationship between client and therapist; (2) providing insight into the client's past and present interactive patterns; (3) strengthening the client's will to give up destructive wishes and fears; (4) supporting the client's grief following a decision to give up prior patterns of interacting; (5) alleviating the client's panic following this decision to change; and (6) helping the client emerge as a new self. Pivotal interactions in treatment involve validating the client's feelings regarding past victimization, and working to break down internalized associations with the abusive attachment figure(s). As yet, no data exist as to the treatment efficacy of Benjamin's interpersonal approach.

TABLE 11.1. Summary of Treatments for BPD

Treatment approach	Etiological theory	Structure of treatment	Primary techniques	Supporting data
Kernberg's individual support-ive psychotherapy and expressive therapy (transfer-ence-focused psychotherapy)	Borderline personality organization (BPO) is the core construct; individuals with identity diffusion use "primitive defenses"	Long-term individual psycho-therapy	Expressive and supportive approaches to psychotherapy; environmental structuring outside of therapy hours	None at present
Marziali and Monroe-Blum's relationship management psychotherapy (RMP)	Internalized conflicts lead to BPD	Group psychotherapy	Group members' expression of internalized conflicts in a setting that limits transference	No data supporting effective-ness; in one study, those who stayed in the group did better than dropouts
Bateman and Fonagy's partial hospitalization approach	BPD is the result of early negative experiences with the primary attachment figure	Partial hospitalization including group and individual therapies, group meetings, and management of medications	Analysis of relationship patterns and unconscious factors that inhibit change	A recent study indicates superior outcomes for the experimental group (over a no-therapy control) in terms of suicidal behavior, hospitaliza-tions, and measures of psychopathology
Benjamin's Structural Assess-ment of Social Behavior (SASB) approach	Social learning experiences cause and maintain BPD, particularly those involving early attachment figures	Measuring and classifying behavioral in individual psychotherapy; planning interventions based on behavior patterns	The SASB–Reconstructive Learning (SASB-RCL) approach, which involves changing patterns of interaction with others	None at present

Treatment	Theory	Structure	Techniques	Research
Langley's self-management therapy	Langley asserts that his therapy does not have a particular etiological theory; BPD is viewed as a disorder of the self and of shame	Individual psychotherapy with the goal of "unifying the opposites" within the self	Development of self-efficacy through homework, psychoeducation, and cognitive interventions	None at present
Psychopharmacological treatment	BPD is the result of malfunctioning neurotransmitter systems	Assessment and medication management	Administration of pharmacological therapy, often as an adjunct to psychotherapy	Antipsychotics, antidepressants (MAOIs, SSRIs), and anticonvulsants/mood stabilizers have all demonstrated some positive effects
Cognitive therapy	Both thought content and process are disrupted in BPD; events are interpreted through core "schemas"	Typically, individual psychotherapy and extensive homework outside of therapy sessions	Cognitive restructuring; "collaborative empiricism" in which therapist and patient investigate maladaptive thinking	Turner has reported improvements in cognitions, anxiety, and depression with a cognitive-based therapy (group and individual treatment)
Dialectical behavior therapy (DBT)	A biosocial theory of BPD; emotion dysregulation of the individual occurs within the context of an invalidating environment	Four stages of treatment arranged around sets of treatment "targets," beginning with bringing suicidal behavior under control; therapy in multiple modalities	Techniques focused on both change (e.g., behavioral analysis, exposure) and acceptance (e.g., validation) of the patient	Demonstrated effectiveness with multiple patients with BPD; reductions in suicidal behavior, hospitalization, therapy dropout; increased quality of life

Integrative

A more recent development in the treatment of BPD is the self-management therapy of Langley (1994)—an approach that integrates object relations, cognitive, and psychoeducational elements in a framework tailored to the mode of individual psychotherapy. Langley asserts several propositions hypothesized to be keys to the understanding and treatment of BPD: (1) The development of the "self" through early experience with others is impaired in BPD; (2) shame operates at the core of the disorder; and (3) all individuals with BPD essentially have unresolved posttraumatic stress disorder (PTSD). Within this theoretical position, the concept of "self" (similar to that outlined by Kohut & Wolf, 1978) is viewed as differentiating from "others" as development progresses. The psychological state of the infant or young child is such that experiences and meanings are shared with the primary caregiver; experiences that are too intense or inconsistent can fragment or "split" the self in BPD. In contrast to psychodynamic approaches, however, Langley's therapy is focused on the development of self-efficacy through cognitive interventions, psychoeducation, therapy homework, and development of a "good enough" standard for therapy goals (thwarting the clients' hypothesized "either–or" view of success). Through these interventions, self-management therapy seeks to unify the "psychological opposites" of the self. At this point, no empirical evidence exists for the effectiveness of the self-management approach to treating BPD.

Psychopharmacological

A recent review of the literature regarding drug treatments for BPD highlights a dilemma for the prescribing pharmacotherapist: BPD involves dysregulation in too many domains for a single drug to serve as a panacea (Dimeff, McDavid, & Linehan, 1999). The effects of a number of drugs have been studied, including neuroleptics (Cornelius, Soloff, George, Ulrich, & Perel, 1993; Cowdry & Gardner, 1988; Soloff et al., 1989, 1993), antidepressants (Cowdry & Gardner, 1988; Kavoussi, Liu, & Coccaro, 1994; Parsons et al., 1989; Salzman

et al., 1995; Soloff et al., 1989), minor tranquilizers (Faltus, 1984; Gardner & Cowdry, 1986), anticonvulsants (Cowdry & Gardner, 1988; Stein, Simeon, Frenkel, Islam, & Hollander, 1995), and lithium carbonate (Links, Steiner, Boiago, & Irwin, 1990).

In general, results indicate that several agents may be useful for improving measures of global functioning, depression, schizotypal symptoms, and impulsive aggressive behavior (for reviews, see Dimeff et al., 1999; Gardner & Cowdry, 1989). Antipsychotic medications have demonstrated reductions in irritability, though effects in other domains of functioning have been inconsistent. They are generally considered most effective for severely disordered patients with BPD. Newer antipsychotics, although not yet tested for patients with BPD, may be effective in targeting irritability and psychotic symptoms without the pervasive side effects of traditional antipsychotics. Antidepressants used to treat BPD include monoamine oxidase inhibitors (MAOIs), due to their efficacy in atypical depression, and selective serotonin reuptake inhibitors (SSRIs) (Kavoussi et al., 1994; Salzman et al., 1995). Though both have been found to have some positive benefits (most notably, reductions in hostility), no randomized clinical trials have shown reliable improvement in affect with antidepressant treatment. Indeed, though one might hypothesize that MAOIs and SSRIs would be helpful for affectively dysregulated patients with BPD, response to antidepressant treatment and a comorbid depression diagnosis for patients with BPD do not seem to be related. Valproate, an anticonvulsant and mood stabilizer, has effectively treated behavioral dysregulation in patients with BPD, including aggressive and impulsive behavior (Stein et al., 1995).

In sum, although some drug treatments may be effective, caution is in order when considering pharmacotherapy for this particular client population. Patients with BPD are notoriously noncompliant with treatment regimens, may abuse the prescribed drugs or overdose, and may experience unintended effects of the drugs. With these caveats in mind, carefully monitored pharmacotherapy may be a useful and important adjunct to psychotherapy in the treatment of BPD.

Cognitive-Behavioral

Treatment of BPD has received increasing attention from cognitive theorists. The cognitive approach views the problems of the patient with BPD as residing within both the content and the process of the individual's thoughts. Beck's approach to treating BPD (Beck, Freeman, & Associates, 1990) is representative of cognitive psychotherapy generally, as the focus of treatment is on restructuring thoughts and on developing a collaborative relationship through which more adaptive ways of viewing the world are developed. At the time of this writing, this approach has not yet received empirical scrutiny.

The cognitive-behavioral therapies of Turner (1984; Turner & Hersen, 1981), Young (1983, 1990; Young & Swift, 1988), and Pretzer (1990) attempt to address some of the difficulties experienced in applying traditional cognitive approaches to the treatment of BPD. Turner hypothesizes that maladaptive schemas are reinforced over time to produce the difficulties characteristic of the disorder. His structured, multimodal treatment consists of pharmacotherapy combined with concurrent individual and psychoeducational group therapy in which specific strategies target interpersonal and anxiety management skill deficits. Similarly, Young postulates that stable patterns of thinking ("early maladaptive schemas") can develop during childhood and result in maladaptive behavior that reinforces the schemas. His schema-focused cognitive therapy includes a variety of interventions aimed at challenging and changing these early schemas. Pretzer's approach emphasizes modifying standard cognitive therapy to address difficulties often encountered in treating clients with BPD, such as establishing a collaborative relationship between therapist and client, maintaining a directed treatment, and improving homework compliance. At present, Pretzer and Young have published little about their treatments, and outcome data do not exist. However, Turner has reported case study data on four clients and has completed a randomized controlled trial of his treatment (Turner, 1989, 1992). Results indicate promising outcomes, with gradual reductions reported in problematic cognitions and behaviors, anxiety, and depression.

DIALECTICAL BEHAVIOR THERAPY

DBT evolved from standard cognitive-behavioral therapy as a treatment for BPD, particularly for chronically suicidal, severely dysfunctional individuals. The theoretical orientation to treatment is a blending of three theoretical positions: behavioral science, dialectical philosophy, and Zen practice. Behavioral science, the technology of behavior change, is countered by acceptance and tolerance of the patient (with techniques drawn both from Zen and from Western contemplative practice); these poles are balanced within the framework of a dialectical position. Although dialectics was first adopted as a description of this emphasis on balance, dialectics soon took on the status of guiding principles that have advanced the therapy in directions not originally anticipated. DBT is based within a consistent behaviorist theoretical position. However, the actual procedures and strategies overlap considerably with those of various alternative therapy orientations, including psychodynamic, client-centered, strategic, and cognitive therapies.

Efficacy

To date, two randomized clinical trials comparing DBT to treatment as usual (TAU) for BPD have been published by Linehan and her colleagues. In the first study, Linehan and colleagues (1991) compared DBT with TAU for severely dysfunctional, parasuicidal women meeting DSM-III-R and Gunderson's criteria for BPD. The treatment lasted 1 year, with assessment every 4 months. At most assessment points and over the entire year, participants receiving DBT had fewer parasuicide episodes and less medically severe episodes, had a much lower attrition rate (16.7%), and had fewer inpatient psychiatric days, compared to participants assigned to TAU. The study was conducted in two waves, with approximately equal numbers of participants in each. Analyses of the second wave (Linehan, Tutek, & Heard, 1992), where a number of additional outcome measures were added to the assessment battery, indicated that participants assigned to DBT, as compared to those assigned to TAU, also reported significantly less anger, greater social adjustment, better work performance, and less anxious rumination, and were rated by the interviewer as more socially adjusted and as less severely disturbed on a global adjustment scale. The superiority of DBT compared to TAU was generally maintained at the 6-month and 12-month follow-ups (Linehan, Heard, & Armstrong, 1993). At the 6-month follow-up, those who had received DBT had significantly fewer parasuicide episodes as well as fewer medically treated episodes, less anger, better self-reported social adjustment, and better employment performance. At the 12-month follow-up, the parasuicide repeat rate was significantly lower for DBT (26%) than for TAU (60%).

Linehan and colleagues have also reported outcomes from a second randomized clinical trial comparing DBT to TAU for patients with dual diagnoses of substance use disorders and BPD (Linehan, Schmidt, et al., 1999). Participants meeting criteria for BPD as well as for polysubstance use disorders or other substance use disorders (involving amphetamines, anxiolytics, cocaine, cannabis, hypnotics, opiates, or sedatives) were randomly assigned to either DBT (n = 12) or TAU (n = 16) for a year of treatment (with assessments every 4 months up to 16 months). Participants assigned to DBT had significantly greater reductions in drug use (measured by both structured interviews and urinalyses) throughout the treatment year and at follow-up than did subjects assigned to TAU. There was a trend for DBT to have significantly higher retention (36% dropout in DBT, 73% dropout in TAU). At follow-up, patients in DBT showed significantly greater gains in global and social adjustment and state and trait anger compared to those in TAU.

Two additional randomized clinical trials comparing DBT to TAU have been presented. The first of these was conducted in a Department of Veterans Affairs (VA) setting. Koons and colleagues (1998) compared a 6-month version of DBT to usual VA treatment (described as primarily cognitive-behavioral). The participants were less parasuicidal and less frequently hospitalized than those in the Linehan and colleagues (1991) study. Those assigned to DBT had greater reductions in suicidal ideation, depression, hopelessness, and anger than did those assigned to TAU. DBT showed a trend toward greater efficacy in reducing psychiatric hospital admissions and inpatient days (however, both groups had

low pretreatment frequency of hospitalization). Interestingly, both treatment conditions had good treatment retention, and both groups showed significant decreases in depression, with 60% of those in DBT and 20% of those in TAU showing clinically significant change on the Beck Depression Inventory.

The second additional randomized clinical trial was conducted by van den Bosch and her colleagues (van den Bosch, 1999) at the Jellenik Institute in Holland. They compared 1 year of DBT for patients with substance abuse to TAU. Treatment lasted for 1 year and was carried out in a substance abuse clinic treating a high proportion of individuals meeting criteria for BPD. At 1 year, clients assigned to DBT had significantly greater reductions in abuse of substances than clients assigned to TAU.

Across these studies, each found reductions in the targeted problem areas when compared to TAU. In the more severely impaired populations of individuals with BPD, it appears that DBT may reduce parasuicidal behavior and substance use, increase treatment retention, and improve global functioning. For less severely impaired populations of patients with BPD, DBT appears to produce specific improvements in suicidal ideation, depression, and hopelessness, even when compared to a TAU condition that also produces clinically significant changes in depression. Where follow-up data are available, it appears that these results may hold up to 1 year after treatment. Overall, the results suggest DBT to be an effective and promising treatment for chronically parasuicidal clients with BPD, particularly in terms of reducing parasuicidal behavior and maintaining clients in treatment.

Philosophical Basis: Dialectics

The term "dialectics" as applied to behavior therapy refers both to a fundamental nature of reality and to a method of persuasive dialogue and relationship. (See Wells, 1972, cited in Kegan, 1982, for documentation of a shift toward dialectical approaches across all the sciences during the last 150 years; more recently, Peng & Nisbett, 1999, discuss both Western and Eastern dialectical thought.) As a world view or philosophical position, dialectics guides the clinician in developing theoretical hypotheses relevant to the client's problems and to the treatment. Alternately, as dialogue and relationship, dialectics refers to the treatment approach or strategies used by the therapist to effect change. Thus, central to DBT are a number of therapeutic dialectical strategies. These are described later in this chapter.

Dialectics as a World View

A dialectical world view emphasizes wholeness, interrelatedness, and process (change) as fundamental characteristics of reality. Similar to contextual and systems theories, a dialectical view argues that analysis of parts of any system are of limited value unless the analysis clearly relates the part to the whole. Although dialectics focuses on the whole, it also emphasizes the complexity of any whole. Thus dialectics asserts that reality is nonreducible; that is, within each one thing or system, no matter how small, there is polarity. In dialectics, the polar forces are called the "thesis" and "antithesis," and the state of change that results is the "synthesis" of these forces. The transactional tension between these forces within each system (positive and negative, good and bad, children and parents, client and therapist, person and environment, etc.) and their subsequent integration are what produce change. The new state, following change through integration, however, is also made up of polar forces; thus change is continuous and constitutes the essential nature of life. A very important dialectical idea is that all propositions contain within them their own oppositions. Or, as Goldberg (1980, pp. 295–296) put it,

> I assume that truth is paradoxical, that each article of wisdom contains within it its own contradictions, that truths stand side by side. Contradictory truths do not necessarily cancel each other out or dominate each other, but stand side by side, inviting participation and experimentation.

Dialectical Persuasion

From the point of view of dialogue and relationship, dialectics refers to change by persuasion and by making use of the oppositions inherent in the therapeutic relationship, rather than by formal impersonal logic. Through the therapeutic opposition of contradictory positions, both client and therapist can arrive at new meanings within old meanings, moving closer to the essence of the subject under consideration. The spirit of a dialectical point of view is never to accept a proposition as a final truth or an undisputable fact. Thus the question addressed by both client and therapist is "What is being left out of our understanding?" Dialectics as persuasion is represented in the specific dialectical strategies described later in the chapter.

As readers will see when we discuss the consultation strategies, dialectical dialogue is also very important in therapist consultation meetings. Perhaps more than any other factor, attention to dialectics can reduce the chances of what psychodynamic therapists have labeled "staff splitting"— that is, the frequent phenomenon of therapists' disagreeing or arguing (sometimes vehemently) about how to treat and interact with an individual client who has BPD. This "splitting" among staff members is often due to one or more factions within the staff deciding that they (and sometimes they alone) know the truth about a particular client or clinical problem.

Dialectical Case Conceptualization

Dialectical assumptions influence case conceptualization in DBT in a number of ways. First, dialectics suggests that a psychological disorder is best conceptualized as a systemic dysfunction. The systemic dysfunction is characterized by (1) defining the disorder with respect to normal functioning, (2) assuming continuity between health and the disorder, and (3) assuming that the disorder results from multiple rather than single causes (Hollandsworth, 1990). Similarly, Linehan's biosocial theory of BPD, presented below, assumes that BPD represents a breakdown in normal functioning, and that this disorder is best conceptualized as a systemic dysfunction of the emotion regulation system. The theory proposes that the pathogenesis of BPD results from numerous factors— some constitutional predispositions that create individual differences in susceptibility to emotion dysregulation, others resulting from the individual's interaction with the environment. Assuming a systemic view has the advantage of compelling the theorist to integrate work from a variety of fields and disciplines.

A second dialectical assumption that underlies Linehan's biosocial theory of BPD is that the relationship between the individual and the environment is a process of reciprocal influence, and that the outcome at any given moment is due to the transaction between the person and the environment. Within social learning theory, this is the principle of "reciprocal determinism." Besides focusing on reciprocal influence, a transactional view also highlights the constant state of flux and change of the individual–environment system. Millon (1987) has made much the same point in discussing the etiology of BPD and the futility of locating the "cause" of the disorder in any single event or time period.

Both transactional and interactive models, such as the diathesis–stress model of psychopathology, call attention to the role of dysfunctional environments in bringing about disorder in the vulnerable individual. A transactional model, however, highlights a number of points that are easy to overlook in an interactive diathesis–stress model. For example, a person (Person A) may act in a manner stressful to an individual (Person B) only because of the stress Person B is putting on Person A. Take the child who, due to an accident, requires most of the parents' free time just to meet survival needs. Or consider the client who, due to the need for constant suicide precautions, uses up much of the inpatient nursing resources. Both of these environments are stretched in their ability to respond well to further stress. Both may invalidate or temporarily blame the victim if any further demand on the system is made. Although the system (e.g., the family or the therapeutic milieu) may have been predisposed to respond dysfunctionally in any case, such responses may have been avoided in the absence of exposure to the stress of that particular individual. A transactional, or dialectical, account of psychopathology may allow greater compassion because it is incompatible with the assignment of blame. This is particularly relevant with a label as stigmatized among mental health professionals as "borderline" is (for examples of the misuse of the diagnosis, see Reiser & Levenson, 1984).

A final assumption in our discussion regards the definition of behavior and the implications of defining behavior broadly. Linehan's theory, and behaviorists in general, take "behavior" to mean anything an organism does involving action and responding to stimulation (*Merriam-Webster's New Universal Unabridged Dictionary*, 1983, p. 100). Conventionally, behaviorists categorize behavior as motor, cognitive/verbal, and physiological, all of which may be either public or private. There are several points to make here. First, dividing behavior into these three categories is arbitrary and is done for conceptual clarity, rather than in response to evidence that these response modes actually are functionally separate systems. This point is especially relevant to understanding emotion regulation, given that basic research on emotions demonstrates that these response systems are sometimes overlapping, somewhat independent, but definitely not wholly independent. A related point here is that in contrast to biological and cognitive theories of BPD, biosocial theory suggests that there is no a priori reason for favoring explanations emphasizing one mode of behavior as intrinsically more important or compelling than others. Rather, from a biosocial perspective, the crucial questions are under what conditions a given behavior–behavior relationship or response system–response system relationship does hold, and under what conditions these relationships enter causal pathways for the etiology and maintenance of BPD.

Biosocial Theory

Emotion Dysregulation

Linehan's biosocial theory suggests that BPD is primarily a dysfunction of the emotion regulation system. Behavioral patterns in BPD are functionally related to or are unavoidable consequences of this fundamental dysregulation across several, perhaps all, emotions, including both positive and negative emotions. From Linehan's view, this emotional dysfunction is the core pathology, and thus is neither simply symptomatic or definitional. This systemic dysregulation is a product of the combination of emotional vulnerability with difficulties in modulating emotional reactions. Emotional vulnerability is conceptualized as high sensitivity to emotional stimuli, intense emotional responses, and a slow return to emotional baseline. Deficits in emotion modulation may be due to difficulties in (1) inhibiting mood-dependent dysfunctional behaviors; (2) organizing behavior in the service of goals, independently of current mood; (3) increasing or decreasing physiological arousal as needed; (4) distracting attention from emotionally evocative stimuli; and/or (5) experiencing emotion without either immediately withdrawing or producing an extreme secondary negative emotion (see Gottman & Katz, 1990, for a further discussion). Although the mechanisms of the initial dysregulation remain unclear, it is likely that biological factors play a primary role. Siever and Davis (1991) hypothesize that deficits in emotion regulation for patients with BPD are related to both an instability and hyperresponsiveness of catecholamine function. The etiology of this dysregulation may range from genetic influences to prenatal factors to traumatic childhood events effecting development of the brain and nervous system.

Invalidating Environments

Most individuals with an initial temperamental vulnerability to emotion dysregulation do not develop BPD. Thus the theory suggests further that particular developmental environments are necessary. The crucial developmental circumstance in Linehan's theory is the "invalidating environment" (Linehan, 1987a, 1987b, 1989, 1993a). An invalidating environment is defined by its tendency to negate and/or respond erratically and inappropriately to private experiences, and in particular to private experiences not accompanied by easily interpreted public accompaniments (e.g., feeling sick without having a high temperature). Private experiences, and especially emotional experiences and interpretations of events, are often not taken as valid responses to events; are punished, trivialized, dismissed, or disregarded; and/or are attributed to socially unacceptable characteristics such as overreactivity, inability to see things realistically, lack of motivation, motivation to harm or manipulate, lack of discipline, or failure to adopt a positive (or, conversely, discriminating) attitude. Vulnerable individuals' verbal descriptions of private experiences are often viewed as inaccurate (e.g., "You are so angry, but you won't admit it"). Invalidating families emphasize controlling emotional expressiveness, oversimplify the ease of solving one's problems, and are intolerant of displays of negative affect. Emotional pain is attributed to lack of motivation, dis-

cipline, or effort. Individuals in an invalidating environment also tend to use punishment in their efforts to control behavior. Such a scenario exacerbates the emotional vulnerability and dysregulation of an individual with BPD, whose behavioral responses reciprocally influence the invalidating environment. The high incidence of childhood sexual abuse reported among this population (Bryer, Nelson, Miller, & Kroll, 1987; Herman, 1986; Herman, Perry, & van der Kolk, 1989; Wagner, Linehan, & Wasson, 1989) suggests that sexual abuse may be a prototypic invalidating experience for children. The relationship of early sexual abuse to BPD, however is quite controversial and is open to many interpretations. On the one hand, Silk, Lee, Hill, and Lohr (1995) reported that the number of criterion BPD behaviors met was correlated with severity of childhood sexual abuse in a group of patients with BPD. On the other hand, a recent review by Fossati, Madeddu, and Maffei (1999) suggests that sexual abuse is not a major risk factor for BPD.

The overall results of this transactional pattern are the emotional dysregulation and behavioral patterns exhibited by the borderline adult. Such an individual has never learned how to label and regulate emotional arousal, how to tolerate emotional distress, or when to trust his/her own emotional responses as reflections of valid interpretations of events (Linehan, 1993a). In more optimal environments, public validation of one's private, internal experiences results in the development of a stable identity. In the family of a person with BPD, however, private experiences are responded to erratically and with insensitivity. The individual thus learns to mistrust his/her internal states, and instead scans the environment for cues about how to act, think, or feel. This general reliance on others results in the individual's failure to develop a coherent sense of self. Emotional dysfunction also interferes with the development and maintenance of stable interpersonal relationships, which depend on both a stable sense of self and a capacity to self-regulate emotions. The invalidating family's tendency to trivialize or ignore the expression of negative emotion also shapes an expressive style later seen in the adult with BPD—a style that vacillates from inhibition and suppression of emotional experience to extreme behavioral displays. Behaviors such as overdosing, cutting, and burning have important affect-regulating properties, and are additionally quite effective in eliciting helping behaviors from an environment that otherwise ignores efforts to ameliorate intense emotional pain. From this perspective, the dysfunctional behaviors characteristic of BPD can be viewed as maladaptive solutions to overwhelming, intensely painful negative affect.

Dialectical Dilemmas

The behavioral patterns of the patient with BPD are described by Linehan (1993a) as a set of three dimensions of behavior defined by their opposite poles. At one end of each dimension is the behavior that is most directly influenced biologically via deficits in emotion regulation; at the other end is behavior that has been socially reinforced in the invalidating environment. Linehan delineates six behaviors in these dimensions and identifies them as secondary targets of treatment (other targets of treatment are discussed below). One dialectical dilemma is represented by biologically influenced emotional vulnerability on the one hand (e.g., the sense of being out of control or falling into the abyss) and by socially influenced self-invalidation on the other (e.g., hate and contempt directed toward the self, dismissal of one's accomplishments). Along this dimension of behavior, the patient with BPD often vacillates between invalidating and blaming the self for emotional pain and blaming the universe for being treated unfairly; suicidal behavior is common at either pole, either as self-directed hostility or as behavior communicating to others that help is needed. A second dimension of behavior is a biological tendency toward "active passivity" (approaching problems helplessly, while demanding that others implement solutions) versus the socially mediated behavior of apparent competence (behaving under different contexts in a way that often appears more effective than the patient's actual competencies). Experiencing either pole of this dimension can lead to anger, guilt, or shame on the part of the patient, and a tendency for the therapist to either under- or overestimate the patient's capabilities. The third dimension of behavior is the biologically influenced tendency of the patient to experience life as a series of unrelenting crises, as opposed to the socially influenced behavior of "inhibited grieving" (i.e., an inability to experience emotions associated with significant trauma or loss). The patient experienes each of these extremes in a way that facilitates movement to the other extreme; for example, attempting to inhibit emotional experiences related to experienced crises may result in problem behaviors that add to the existing crises. As with all of these dialectical dilemmas, the solution is for the therapist and patient to work toward a more balanced position that represents a synthesis of the opposing poles.

Stages of Therapy and Treatment Goals

In theory, DBT is designed to treat patients with BPD at all levels of severity and complexity, and is conceptualized as occurring in stages. A pretreatment stage prepares the client for therapy and elicits a commitment to work toward the various treatment goals. Orientation to specific goals and treatment strategies, and commitment to work toward goals addressed during this stage, are likely to be important throughout all stages of treatment. In Stage 1 of therapy, the primary focus is on stabilizing the patient and achieving behavioral control. Out-of-control behaviors constitute those that are disordered due to the severity of the BPD (e.g., as seen in an actively psychotic client) or due to severity combined with complexity of multiple diagnoses (e.g., as seen in a suicidal client who has BPD with comorbid panic disorder and depression). Generally, the criteria for putting a patient in Stage 1 are based on level of current functioning, together with the inability of the patient to work on any other goals before behavior and functioning come under better control. As Mintz (1968) suggested in discussing treatment of the suicidal patient, all forms of psychotherapy are ineffective with a dead patient. In the subsequent stages (2–4), the treatment goals are to replace "quiet desperation" with nontraumatic emotional experiencing (Stage 2); to achieve "ordinary" happiness and unhappiness, and reduce ongoing disorders and problems in living (Stage 3); and to resolve a sense of incompleteness and achieve joy (Stage 4). In sum, the orientation of the treatment is first to get action under control, and then to help the patient to feel better, to resolve problems in living and residual disorder, and to find joy (and, for some, a sense of transcendence). All research to date has focused on the severely or multiply disordered patient who enters treatment at Stage 1.

Pretreatment: Orienting and Commitment

Specific tasks of orientation are twofold. First, the client and therapist must arrive at a mutually informed decision to work together. Typically, the first one to three sessions are presented to the client as opportunities for the client and therapist to explore this possibility. Diagnostic interviewing, history taking, and formal behavioral analyses of high-priority targeted behaviors can be woven into initial therapy sessions or conducted separately. Second, client and therapist must negotiate a common set of expectancies to guide the initial steps of therapy. Agreements outlining specifically what the client and therapist can expect from each other are discussed and agreed to. When necessary, the therapist attempts to modify the client's dysfunctional beliefs regarding the process of therapy. Issues addressed include the rate and magnitude of change that can reasonably be expected, the goals of treatment and general treatment procedures, and various myths the client may have about the process of therapy in general. The dialectical/biosocial view of BPD is also presented.

Orientation covers several additional points. First, DBT is presented as a supportive therapy requiring a strong collaborative relationship between client and therapist. DBT is not a suicide prevention program, but a life enhancement program where client and therapist function as a team to create a life worth living. Second, DBT is described as a cognitive-behavioral therapy with a primary emphasis on analyzing problematic behaviors and replacing them with skillful behaviors, and on changing ineffective beliefs and rigid thinking patterns. Third, the client is told that DBT is a skill-oriented therapy, with special emphasis on behavioral skill training. The commitment and orienting strategies, balanced by validation strategies, described later are the most important strategies during this phase of treatment.

Stage 1: Attaining Basic Capacities

The primary focus of the first stage of therapy is on attaining a life pattern that is reasonably functional and stable. Specific targets in order of importance are to reduce suicidal behaviors, therapy-interfering behaviors, and quality-of-life-interfering behaviors, and to increase behavioral skills. These targets are approached hierarchically and recursively as higher-priority behaviors reappear. With severely dysfunctional and suicidal clients, significant progress on first-stage targets can usually be expected to take up to 1 year or more.

In addition to these therapy targets, the goal of increasing dialectical behaviors is universal to all modes of treatment. Unlike other therapy targets, however, it is rarely discussed with the client, primarily because of the abstract nature and complexity of the concept. Dialectical thinking encourages clients to see reality as complex and multifaceted, to hold contradictory thoughts simultaneously and learn to integrate them, and to be comfortable with inconsistency and contradictions. For individuals with BPD, who are extreme and dichotomous in their thinking and behavior, this is a formidable task indeed.

A dialectical emphasis applies equally to a client's patterns of behavior, as the client is encouraged to integrate and balance emotional and overt behavioral responses. In particular, dialectical tensions arise in the areas of skill enhancement versus self-acceptance, problem solving versus problem acceptance, and affect regulation versus affect tolerance. Behavioral extremes, whether emotional, cognitive, or overt responses, are constantly confronted while more balanced responses are taught.

Suicidal Behaviors. Keeping a client alive must, of course, be the first priority in any psychotherapy. Thus reducing suicide crisis behaviors (any behaviors that place the client at high and imminent risk for suicide or threaten to do so, including credible suicide threats, planning, preparations, obtaining lethal means, and high suicide intent) is the highest priority in DBT. The target and its priority are made explicit in DBT (rather than left implicit, as in many other therapy manuals), simply because suicidal behavior and the risk of suicide are of paramount concern for clients with BPD. Similarly, any acute, intentional self-injurious behaviors (i.e., all instances of parasuicidal behaviors) share the top priority. The priority here is due both to the risk of parasuicidal behavior (parasuicidal behavior is the single best predictor of subsequent suicide) and to the inherent conflict between ignoring self-injurious behavior and a collaborative self-help pursuit such as psychotherapy. Similarly, DBT also targets suicide ideation and client expectations about the value and long-term consequences of suicidal behavior, although these behaviors may not necessarily be targeted directly.

Therapy-Interfering Behaviors. Keeping clients and therapists working together collaboratively is the second priority in DBT. Once again, this is probably an implicit second priority in most psychotherapies. However, the chronic nature of most problems among clients with BPD, their high tendency to end therapy prematurely, and the likelihood of therapist burnout and iatrogenic behaviors when treating BPD require explicit attention with this population. Both client and therapist behaviors that threaten the relationship or therapeutic progress are addressed directly, immediately, consistently, and constantly—and, most importantly, before rather than after either the therapist or the client no longer wants to continue. Interfering behaviors of the client include those interfering with the client's actually receiving the therapy or with other clients' benefiting from therapy (in group or milieu settings), and those that burn out or cross the personal limits of the therapist; these are treated within therapy sessions. Those of the therapist include any that are iatrogenic, as well as behaviors that unnecessarily cause the client distress or make progress difficult; these are dealt with within therapy sessions if brought up by the client, but are also dealt with within the consultation/supervision meeting.

Quality-of-Life-Interfering Behaviors. The third target of Stage 1 is the reduction of behavioral patterns that seriously interfere with any chance of the client's having a reasonable quality of life. Typical behaviors in this category include serious substance abuse; severe eating disorders; high-risk and out-of-control sexual behaviors; extreme financial difficulties (uncontrollable spending or gambling,

inability to handle finances); criminal behaviors that are likely to lead to incarceration; employment- or school-related dysfunctional behaviors (a pattern of quitting jobs or school prematurely, getting fired or failing in school, not engaging in any productive activities); housing-related dysfunctional behaviors (living with abusive people, not finding stable housing); mental-health-related patterns (going in and out of hospitals, failure to take or abuse of necessary medications); and health-related problems (failure to treat serious medical disorders). The goal here is for the client to achieve a stable lifestyle that meets reasonable standards for safety and adequate functioning.

Behavioral Skills. The fourth goal of Stage 1 is for the client to achieve a reasonable capacity for skillful behaviors in the areas of distress tolerance, emotion regulation, interpersonal effectiveness, self-management, and the capacity to respond with awareness without being judgmental ("mindfulness" skills). In our outpatient program, the primary responsibility for skills training lies with the weekly DBT skills group. The individual therapist monitors the acquisition and use of skills over time, and aids the client in applying skills to specific problem situations.

Mindfulness skills are viewed as central in DBT and are thus labeled the "core" skills. These skills represent a behavioral translation of meditation (including Zen) practice and include observing, describing, spontaneous participating, being nonjudgmental, focusing awareness, and focusing on effectiveness. Unlike standard behavior and cognitive therapies, which ordinarily focus on changing distressing emotions and events, a major emphasis of DBT is on learning to bear pain skillfully. Representing a natural progression from mindfulness skills, distress tolerance skills reflect the ability to experience and observe one's thoughts, emotions, and behaviors without evaluation and without attempting to change or control them. Emotion regulation skills target the reduction of this emotional distress through exposure to the primary emotion in a nonjudgmental atmosphere. Emotion regulation skills include affect identification and labeling, mindfulness to (i.e., experiencing nonjudgmentally) the current emotion, identifying obstacles to changing emotions, increasing positive emotional events, and behavioral expressiveness opposite to the emotion. Interpersonal skill training develops effectiveness for deciding on objectives within conflict situations and the priority of those objectives vis-à-vis maintaining a positive relationship and one's self-respect, and teaches strategies that maximize the chances of obtaining those objectives without harming the relationship or sacrificing self-respect. Taught in conjunction with the other behavioral skills, self-management skills include knowledge of the fundamental principles of learning and behavior change, the ability to set realistic goals, the ability to conduct one's own behavioral analysis, and the ability to implement contingency management plans.

Stage 2: Posttraumatic Stress Reduction

Stage 1 of DBT takes a very here-and-now approach to managing dysfunctional behavioral and emotional patterns. Although the connection between current behavior and previous traumatic events (including those from childhood) may be explored and noted, the focus of the treatment is distinctly on analyzing the relationship among current thoughts, feelings, and behaviors and on accepting and changing current patterns. The second stage of therapy, in contrast, specifically targets the emotional processing of previous traumatic events via reexposure to associated cues within the therapy setting. Thus the primary aim of Stage 2 is to reduce posttraumatic stress. In the language of psychodynamic therapy, Stage 1 is the "containment" phase and Stage 2 is the "uncovering" phase. Four targets are particularly important: remembering and accepting the facts of earlier traumatic events; reducing stigmatization and self-blame commonly associated with some types of trauma; reducing the oscillating denial and intrusive response syndromes common among individuals who have suffered severe trauma; and resolving dialectical tensions regarding placement of blame for the trauma.

Movement to the second stage only occurs when previous target behaviors are clearly under control. Like most experts in the treatment of both PTSD and adult sequalae of childhood abuse, a DBT therapist does not encourage systematic exposure to traumatic stress cues (or step-by-step "uncovering") before the client has successfully negotiated Stage 1. Clients must first be able to resist urges toward suicide and/or parasuicide; to refrain from severely dysfunctional behaviors, such as substance abuse or out-of-control sexual behavior or spending; to maintain a somewhat stable lifestyle, including having a place to live and productive daily activities; to have at least rudimentary interpersonal, emotion regulation, and distress tolerance skills; and to be secure within a collaborative therapeutic relationship. That is, clients must be able to cope with the emotions associated with the therapeutic exposure to trauma-related cues.

Stage 3: Resolving Problems in Living and Increasing Respect for Self

In the third stage, DBT targets the client's unacceptable unhappiness and problems in living. At this stage, the client has either done the work necessary to resolve problems in the prior two stages or was never severely disordered enough to need it. Although problems at this stage may still be serious, the individual is functional in major domains of living. The goal here is for the client to achieve a level of ordinary happiness and unhappiness, as well as independent self-respect. To this end, the client is helped to value, believe in, trust, and validate himself/herself. The targets here are the abilities to evaluate one's own behavior nondefensively, to trust one's own responses, and to hold on to self-evaluations independently of the opinions of others. Ultimately, the therapist must pull back and persistently reinforce the client's independent attempts at self-validation, self-care, and problem solving. Although the goal is not for clients to become independent of all people, it is important that they achieve sufficient self-reliance to relate to and depend on others without self-invalidating.

Stage 4: Attaining the Capacity for Sustained Joy

The final stage of treatment in DBT targets the resolution of a sense of incompleteness and the development of a capacity for sustained joy. Here the goals are expanded awareness, spiritual fulfillment, and the movement into experiencing flow. For individuals at Stage 4, long-term insight-oriented psychotherapy, spiritual direction or practices, or other organized experiential treatments and/or life experiences may be of most benefit.

STRUCTURING TREATMENT: FUNCTIONS AND MODES

Functions of Treatment

Treatment in DBT is structured around the five essential functions it serves. Treatment functions to (1) enhance behavioral capabilities by expanding the individual's repertoire of skillful behavioral patterns; (2) improve the patient's motivation to change by reducing reinforcement for dysfunctional behaviors and high-probability responses (cognitions, emotions, actions) that interfere with effective behaviors; (3) ensure that new behaviors generalize from the therapeutic to the natural environment; (4) enhance the motivation and capabilities of the therapist so that effective treatment is rendered; and (5) structure the environment so that effective behaviors, rather than dysfunctional behaviors, are reinforced.

Modes and Functions of Treatment: Who Does What and When

Responsibility for performing functions and meeting target goals of treatment in DBT is spread across the various modes of treatment, with focus and attention varying according to the mode of therapy. The individual therapist (who is always the primary therapist in DBT) attends to one order of targets and is also, with the client, responsible for organizing the treatment so that all goals are met. In skills training, a different set of goals is targeted; during phone calls, yet another hierarchy of targets takes precedence. In the consultation/supervision mode, therapists' behaviors are the targets. Therapists engaging in more than one mode of therapy (e.g., individual, group, and phone therapy) must stay cognizant of the functions and order of targets specific to each mode, and switch smoothly from one hierarchy to another as the modes of treatment change.

Individual Therapy

DBT assumes that effective treatment must attend both to capabilities and behavioral skill deficits, and to motivational and behavioral performance issues that interfere with use of skillful responses. Although there are many ways to effect these principles, in our clinic the individual therapist is responsible for the assessment and problem solving of skill deficits and motivational problems, and for organizing other modes to address problems in each area. Individual outpatient therapy sessions are usually scheduled on a once-a-week basis for 50–90 minutes, although twice-weekly sessions may be held during crisis periods or at the beginning of therapy.

The priorities of specific targets within individual therapy are the same as the overall priorities of DBT discussed above. Therapeutic focus within individual therapy sessions is determined by the highest-priority treatment target relevant at the moment. This ordering does not change over the course of therapy; however, the relevance of a target does change. Relevance is determined by either the client's most recent day-to-day behavior (since the last session) or by current behavior during the therapy session; problems not currently in evidence are not considered relevant. If satisfactory progress on one target goal has been achieved, the behavior has never been a problem, or the behavior is currently not evident, the therapist shifts attention to the immediately following treatment target.

The consequence of this priority allocation is that when high-risk suicidal behaviors or parasuicide, therapy-interfering behaviors, or serious quality-of-life-interfering behaviors are occurring, at least part of the session agenda must be devoted to these topics. If these behaviors are not occurring at the moment, then the topics to be discussed during Stages 1 and 3 are set by the client. The therapeutic focus (within any topic area discussed) depends on the stage of treatment, the skills targeted for improvement, and any secondary targets. During Stage 1, for example, any problem or topic area can be conceptualized in terms of interpersonal issues and skills needed, opportunities for emotion regulation, and/or a necessity for distress tolerance. During Stage 3, regardless of the topic, the therapist focuses on helping the client achieve independent self-respect, self-validation, and self-acceptance both within the session and within his/her everyday life. (These are, of course, targets all through the treatment, but during Stage 3 the therapist pulls back further and does less work for the client than during the two preceding stages.) During Stage 2, the major focus is on structured exposure to traumatic cues.

For highly dysfunctional clients, it is likely that early treatment will necessarily focus on the upper part of the hierarchy. For example, if parasuicidal behavior has occurred during the previous week, attention to it takes precedence over attention to therapy-interfering behavior. In turn, focusing on therapy-interfering behaviors takes precedence over working on quality-of-life-interfering behaviors. Although it is often possible to work on more than one target (including those generated by the client) in a given session, higher-priority targets always take precedence. Determining the relevance of targeted behaviors is assisted by the use of diary cards. These cards are filled out during at least the first two stages of therapy and brought to weekly sessions. Failure to complete or bring in a card is considered a therapy-interfering behavior. Diary cards record daily instances of parasuicidal behavior, suicidal ideation, urges to parasuicide, "misery," use of substances (licit and illicit), and use of behavioral skills. Other targeted behaviors (e.g., bulimic episodes, daily productive activities, flashbacks, etc.) may also be recorded on the blank area of the card. The therapist doing DBT must develop the pattern of routinely reviewing the card at the beginning of each session. If the card indicates that a parasuicidal act has occurred, it is noted and discussed. If high suicide ideation is recorded, it is assessed to determine whether the client is at risk for suicide. If a pattern of substance abuse or dependence appears, it is treated as a quality-of-life-interfering behavior.

Work on targeted behaviors involves a co-ordinated array of treatment strategies, described later in this chapter. Essentially, each session is a balance between structured as well as unstructured problem solving (including simple interpretive activities by the therapist) and unstructured validation. The amount of the therapist's time allocated to each—problem solving and validating—depends on (1) the urgency of the behaviors needing change or problems to be solved, and (2) the urgency of the client's needs for validation, understanding, and acceptance without any intimation of change being needed.

Skills Training

The necessity of crisis intervention and attention to other issues makes skills acquisition within individual psychotherapy very difficult. Thus a separate component of treatment directly targets the acquisition of behavioral skills. In our clinic this has usually taken the form of separate, weekly, 2- to 2½-hour group skills training sessions, which clients must attend for the first year of treatment. Skills training can also be done individually, although it is often more difficult to stay focused on teaching new skills in individual than in group therapy. After a client has gone through all skills modules twice (i.e., for 1 year), remaining in skills training is a matter of personal preference and need.

Skills training in DBT follows a psychoeducational format. In contrast to individual therapy, where the agenda is determined primarily by the problem to be solved, the skills training agenda is set by the skill to be taught. Thus the fundamental targets here are skill acquisition and strengthening. Although stopping client behaviors that seriously threaten life (e.g., potential suicide or homicide) or continuation of therapy (e.g., not coming, attacking others in group skills training) is still a first priority, less severe therapy-interfering behaviors (e.g., refusing to talk in a group setting, restless pacing in the middle of sessions, attacking the therapist and/or the therapy) are not given the attention in skills training that they are given in the individual psychotherapy mode. If such behaviors were a primary focus, there would never be time for teaching behavioral skills. Generally, therapy-interfering behaviors are put on an extinction schedule while a client is "dragged" through skills training and simultaneously soothed. In DBT, all skills training clients are required to be in concurrent individual psychotherapy. Throughout, each client is urged to address other problematic behaviors with his/her primary therapist; if a serious risk of suicide develops, the skills training therapist (if different from the primary therapist) refers the problem to the primary therapist.

Although all of the strategies described below are used in both individual psychotherapy and skills training, the mix is decidedly different. Skills acquisition, strengthening, and generalization strategies are the predominant change strategies in skills training. In addition, skills training is highly structured, much more so than the psychotherapy component. Half of each session is devoted to reviewing homework practice of the skills currently being taught, and the other half is devoted to presenting new skills. Except when interpersonal process issues seriously threaten progress, the agenda and topics for discussion in skills training are usually set by the therapist.

Skills Consultation

Individual skills consultation has been added as a new mode to DBT for clients with substance use disorders. This mode serves the functions of enhancing capabilities and troubleshooting generalization to the natural environment via skill-strengthening exercises, including homework review, behavioral rehearsal, feedback, and coaching. This mode is typically conducted by one of the group leaders from the patient's skills group, thus improving the bond of the patient to at least one of the group leaders and increasing group attendance.

Telephone Consultation

Telephone calls between sessions (or other extratherapeutic contact when DBT is conducted in other settings, such as inpatient units) are an integral part of DBT. They have three important functions: (1) to provide coaching in skills and promote skill generalization; (2) to provide emergency crisis intervention and simultaneously break the link between suicidal behaviors and therapist attention; and (3) to provide a context for repairing the therapeutic relationship without requiring the client to wait until the next session. With respect to calls for help, the focus of a phone session varies depending on the complexity and severity of the problem to be solved and the amount of time the therapist is willing to spend on the phone. With easy or already clear situations, where what the client can or should do in the situation is reasonably easy to determine, the focus is on helping the client use behavioral skills (rather than dysfunctional behaviors) to address the problem. Alternatively, with complex problems or with problems too severe for the client to resolve soon, the focus is on ameliorating and tolerating distress and inhibiting dysfunctional problem-solving behaviors until the next therapy session. In the latter case, resolving the problem set-

ting off the crises is not the target of phone sessions.

With the exception of taking necessary steps to protect the client's life when suicide is threatened, all calls for help are handled as much alike as possible. This is done to break the contingency between suicidal behaviors (ideation, parasuicide, and crisis behaviors) and increased phone contact. To do this, the therapist can do one of two things: refuse to accept any calls (including suicide crisis calls), or insist that the client who calls during suicidal crises also call during other crises and problem situations. As Linehan (1993a) notes, experts on suicidal behaviors uniformly say that therapist availability is necessary with suicidal clients. Thus DBT chooses the latter course and encourages (and at times insists) on calls during nonsuicidal crisis periods. In DBT, calling the therapist too infrequently, as well as too frequently, is considered therapy-interfering behavior.

The final priority for phone calls to individual therapists is relationship repair. Clients with BPD often experience delayed emotional reactions to interactions that have occurred during therapy sessions. From a DBT perspective, it is not reasonable to require clients to wait up to a whole week before dealing with these emotions, and it is appropriate for a client to call for a brief "heart-to-heart" talk. In these situations, the role of the therapist is to soothe and reassure. In-depth analyses should wait until the next session.

A skills therapist uses phone calls for only one reason: to keep a client in the therapy (including, of course, keeping the client alive when necessary). All other problems are handled by the primary therapist, and suicidal crises are turned over to the primary therapist as soon as possible.

Structuring the Environment

One of the essential components of DBT is attention to contingencies throughout the entire treatment program. The aim is to be sure that programmatic rules and program staff reinforce skillful rather than maladaptive behaviors. This is especially important with respect to suicidal behaviors. The premise is that if clients can only get help that they want or need by becoming more suicidal or engaging in other maladaptive behaviors, then it is doubtful that the treatment as a whole will be effective. It is typical in DBT, for example, to make contracts with clients to continue therapy after a designated point (say, a year) if they are improving, and to refer them to other treatment programs if they are not. Frequent "sweeps" throughout the entire treatment program to ferret out reinforcement for maladaptive behaviors are important.

Supervision/Consultation Team

DBT assumes that effective treatment of BPD must pay as much attention to the therapist's behavior and experience in therapy as it does to the client's. Treating clients with BPD is enormously stressful, and staying within the DBT therapeutic frame can be tremendously difficult. Thus an integral part of the therapy is the treatment of the therapist. Every therapist is required to be in a consultation or supervision relationship, either with one other person or with a group. DBT consultation meetings are held weekly and are attended by therapists currently providing DBT to clients with BPD. The roles of consultation/supervision are to hold the therapist within the therapeutic frame and to address problems that arise in the course of treatment delivery. Thus the fundamental target is increasing adherence to DBT principles for each member of the consultation group. The DBT consultation team is viewed as an integral component of DBT; that is, it is considered group therapy for the therapists. Each member is simultaneously a client and a therapist in the group.

Setting

DBT has been adapted to a variety of settings, including outpatient community mental health settings, long-term inpatient units, day treatment, and acute hospitalization. Individual circumstances dictate adapting the treatment to the needs of both client and therapist, as well as to the resources available. Consequently, the division of labor will change depending on the particular situation. For example, although the standard setting for skills training in our clinic has been group therapy, a private practice setting or small clinic may not have the resources or clients to organize a separate group. In such a case, an individual

therapist may elect to see a client twice weekly—once for individual therapy and once for skills training. Alternative possibilities include having an extended weekly session with approximately half of the period devoted to skills training, or having a second therapist or a behavioral technician do individual skills training with the client.

In our clinic, individual therapy has been delivered in the therapist's clinical practice office, with separate group skills training conducted in a clinic classroom. Occasionally, temporary treatment requirements may necessitate a move to different settings. For example, clients undergoing surgical or other medical procedures have been seen in the hospital or in their homes following hospital release. For some adolescent clients who are highly ambivalent regarding therapy, out-of-office sessions in places such as coffee shops, bowling alleys, and cars can be helpful in continuing contact through difficult phases.

Client Variables

There are a number of requisite client characteristics for DBT. Of these, voluntary participation and a commitment to a specified time period (usually 6 months to 1 year) are critical. The effective application of DBT requires a strong interpersonal relationship between therapist and client. The therapist must first work to become a major reinforcer in the life of the client, and then use the relationship to promote change in the client. Continuing the relationship can only be used as a positive contingency when a client wants to be in treatment; contingency management is thus seriously compromised with involuntary clients. Court-ordered treatment is acceptable, if clients will agree to remain in therapy even if the order is rescinded. It has also been our experience that a local residence is desirable. Clients who do not live in the immediate area or who must move to the area for therapy are more likely to terminate early. A client characteristic necessary for group therapy is the ability to control overtly aggressive behavior toward others. DBT was developed and evaluated with perhaps the most extremely disturbed portion of the population with BPD; all clients accepted into treatment had histories of multiple parasuicidal behaviors.

However, the treatment has been designed flexibly and is likely to be effective with less severely disturbed individuals.

Therapist Variables

In comparison to other aspects of therapy, the therapist characteristics that facilitate DBT have received comparatively little attention. However, recent evidence supports the assumption that effective therapy for clients with BPD requires the proficient balancing of acceptance and change strategies (Shearin & Linehan, 1992). This research also found that therapists' nonpejorative perceptions of clients were also associated with less suicidal behavior.

Linehan (1993a) describes requisite therapist characteristics in terms of three bipolar dimensions that must be balanced in the conduct of therapy. The first dimension represents the balance of an orientation of acceptance with an orientation of change. The therapist must be able to inhibit judgmental attitudes (often under very trying circumstances) and to practice acceptance of the client, of himself/herself, and of the therapeutic relationship and process exactly as these are in the current moment. Nevertheless, the therapist remains cognizant that the therapeutic relationship has originated in the necessity of change, and he/she assumes responsibility for directing the therapeutic influence.

Second, the therapist must balance "unwavering centeredness" with "compassionate flexibility." Unwavering centeredness is the quality of believing in oneself, the therapy, and the client. Compassionate flexibility is the ability to take in relevant information about the client and modify one's position accordingly. Perhaps most importantly, flexibility represents an overall willingness to admit and repair one's inevitable therapeutic mistakes.

Finally, the DBT therapist must be able to balance a high degree of "nurturing" with "benevolent demanding." Nurturing refers to teaching, coaching, assisting, and strengthening the client, while benevolent demanding requires the therapist to recognize existing capabilities, reinforce adaptive behavior, and refuse to "do" for the client when the client can "do" for himself/herself. Above all, the ability to demand requires a concomitant willingness to believe in the client's ability to change; the effective DBT therapist must see his/her client as empowered.

TREATMENT STRATEGIES

"Treatment strategies" in DBT refer to the role and focus of the therapist, as well as to a coordinated set of procedures that function to achieve specific treatment goals. Although DBT strategies usually consist of a number of steps, use of a strategy does not necessarily require the application of every step. It is considerably more important that the therapist apply the intent of the strategy than that he/she should inflexibly lead the client through a series of prescribed maneuvers.

DBT employs five sets of treatment strategies to achieve the previously described behavioral targets: (1) dialectical strategies, (2) core strategies, (3) stylistic strategies, (4) case management strategies, and (5) integrated strategies. DBT strategies are illustrated in Figure 11.1. Within an individual session and with a given client, certain strategies may be used more than others and not all strategies may be necessary or appropriate. An abbreviated discussion of the first four types of DBT treatment strategies follows. For greater detail, the reader is referred to the treatment manual (Linehan, 1993a).

Dialectical Strategies

Dialectical strategies permeate the entire therapy, and their use provides the rationale for adding the term "dialectics" to the title of the therapy. There are three types of dialectical strategies: those having to do with how the therapist structures interactions; those pertaining to how the therapist defines and teaches skillful behaviors; and certain specific strategies used during the conduct of treatment.

Dialectics of the Relationship: Balancing Treatment Strategies

Dialectical strategies in the most general sense of the word have to do with how the therapist balances the dialectical tensions within the therapy relationship. As noted above, the fundamental dialectic within any psychotherapy, including that with a client who has

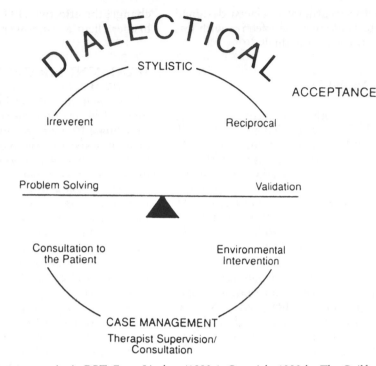

FIGURE 11.1. Treatment strategies in DBT. From Linehan (1993a). Copyright 1993 by The Guilford Press. Reprinted by permission.

BPD, is that between acceptance of what is and efforts to change what is. A dialectical therapeutic position is one of constant attention to combining acceptance with change, flexibility with stability, nurturing with challenging, and a focus on capabilities with a focus on limitations and deficits. The goals are to bring out the opposites, both in therapy and the client's life, and to provide conditions for syntheses. The presumption is that change may be facilitated by emphasizing acceptance, and acceptance by emphasizing change. The emphasis upon opposites sometimes takes place over time (i.e., over the whole of an interaction), rather than simultaneously or in each part of an interaction. Although many if not all psychotherapies, including cognitive and behavioral treatments, attend to these issues of balance, placing the concept of balance at the center of the treatment assures that the therapist remains attentive to their importance.

Strategies emphasizing acceptance are very similar to (or in some cases identical to) strategies used in client-centered therapy and to case management outreach strategies emphasized in community psychiatry. Those emphasizing change are drawn primarily from cognitive and behavioral therapies, although the particular rendition in DBT overlaps considerably with both strategic and psychodynamic therapies. The categorization is artificial, since in many ways every strategy comprises both acceptance and change. Indeed, the best strategies are those that combine acceptance and change in one move. The overall emphasis on balance (both within and outside of therapy) is similar to gestalt and to systems therapies.

Teaching Dialectical Behavior

Behavioral extremes and rigidity—whether these are cognitive, emotional, or overtly behavioral—are signals that synthesis has not been achieved, and thus can be considered nondialectical. Instead, a "middle path" similar to that advocated in Buddhism is advocated and modeled. The important thing in following the path to Enlightenment is to avoid being caught and entangled in any extreme and always follow the Middle Way (Kyokai, 1966). This emphasis on balance is similar to the approach advocated in relapse prevention models proposed by Marlatt and his colleagues (e.g., Marlatt & Gordon, 1985) for treating addictive behaviors. Thus the therapist helps the client move from "either–or" to "both–and." The key here is not to invalidate the first idea or polarity when asserting the second.

Specific Dialectical Strategies

There are eight specific dialectical treatment strategies: (1) entering and using paradox, (2) using metaphor, (3) playing the devil's advocate, (4) extending, (5) activating the client's "wise mind," (6) making lemonade out of lemons (turning negatives into positives), (7) allowing natural change (and inconsistencies even within the therapeutic milieu), and (8) assessing dialectically by always asking the question "What is being left out here?" Due to space limitations, a selection of these strategies is addressed in the following section. For a complete review, the interested reader is referred to the DBT treatment manual (Linehan, 1993a).

Entering the Paradox. Entering the paradox is a powerful technique because it contains the element of surprise. The therapist presents the paradox without explaining it and highlights the paradoxical contradictions within the behavior, the therapeutic process, and reality in general. The essence of the strategy is the therapist's refusal to step in with rational explanation; the client's attempts at logic are met with silence, a question, or a story designed to shed a small amount of light on the puzzle to be solved. The client is pushed to achieve understanding, move toward synthesis of the polarities, and resolve the dilemma himself/herself.

Linehan (1993a) has highlighted a number of typical paradoxes and their corresponding dialectical tensions encountered over the course of therapy. Clients are free to choose their own behavior, but can't stay in therapy if they do not work at changing their behavior. Clients are taught to achieve greater independence by becoming more skilled at asking for help from others. Clients have a right to kill themselves, but if they ever convince the therapist that suicide is imminent, they may be locked up. Clients are not responsible for being the way they are, but they are responsible for what they become. In highlighting these paradoxical realities, both client and

therapist struggle with confronting and letting go of rigid patterns of thought, emotion, and behavior, so that more spontaneous and flexible patterns may emerge.

Using Metaphor: Parable, Myth, Analogy, and Storytelling. The use of metaphor, stories, parables, and myth is extremely important in DBT and provides an alternative means of teaching dialectical thinking. Stories are usually more interesting, are easier to remember, and encourage the search for other meanings of events under scrutiny. In general, the idea of metaphor is to take something the client does understand and use it as an analogy for something the client does not understand. Used creatively, metaphors can aid understanding, suggest solutions to problems, and reframe both the problems of clients and of the therapeutic process.

Playing Devil's Advocate. The devil's advocate technique is quite similar to the argumentative approach used in rational–emotive and cognitive restructuring therapies as a method of addressing a client's dysfunctional beliefs or problematic rules. With this strategy, the therapist presents a propositional statement that is an extreme version of one of the client's own dysfunctional beliefs, and then plays the role of devil's advocate to counter the client's attempts to disprove the extreme statement or rule. For example, a client may state, "Because I'm overweight, I'd be better off dead." The therapist argues in favor of the dysfunctional belief, perhaps by suggesting that since this is true for the client, it must be true for others as well; hence all overweight people would be better off dead. The therapist may continue along these lines with "And since the definition of what constitutes being overweight varies so much among individuals, there must be an awful lot of people who would be considered overweight by someone. That must mean they'd all be better off dead!" Or "Gosh, I'm about 5 pounds overweight. I guess that means I'd be better off dead, too." Any reservations the client proposes can be countered by further exaggeration until the self-defeating nature of the belief becomes apparent.

The devil's advocate technique is often used in the first several sessions to elicit a strong commitment from the client. The therapist argues that since the therapy will be painful and difficult, it is not clear how making such a commitment (and therefore being accepted into treatment) could possibly be a good idea. This usually has the effect of moving the client to take the opposite position in favor of therapeutic change. To employ this technique successfully, it is important that the therapist's argument seem reasonable enough to invite counterargument by the client, and that the delivery be made with a straight face, in a naive but offbeat manner.

Extending. The term "extending" has been borrowed from *aikido*, a Japanese form of self-defense. In that context, extending is when the student of *aikido* waits for a challenger's movements to reach their natural completion, and then extends a movement's endpoint slightly further than what would naturally occur, leaving the challenger vulnerable and off balance. In DBT, extending is the therapist's taking the severity or gravity of what the client is communicating more seriously than the client intends. This strategy is the emotional equivalent of the devil's advocate strategy. It is particularly effective when the client is threatening dire consequences of an event or problem. Take the interaction with the following client, who threatens suicide if an extra appointment time for the next day is not scheduled. The following interchange between therapist (T) and client (C) occurs after attempts to find a mutually acceptable time have failed.

C: I've got to see you tomorrow, or I'm sure I will end up killing myself. I just can't keep it together by myself any longer.

T: Hmm, I didn't realize you were so upset! We've got to do something immediately if you are so distressed that you might kill yourself. What about hospitalization? Maybe that is needed.

C: I'm *not* going to the hospital! Why won't you just give me an appointment?

T: How can we discuss such a mundane topic as session scheduling when your life is in danger? How are you planning to kill yourself?

C: You know how. Why can't you cancel someone or move an appointment around? You could put an appointment with one of your students off until another time. *I can't stand it any more!*

T: I'm really concerned about you. Do you think I should call an aid car?

The aspect of the communication that the therapist takes seriously (suicide as a possible consequence of not getting an appointment) is not the aspect (needing an extra appointment the next day) that the client wants taken seriously. The therapist takes the consequences seriously and extends the seriousness even further. The client wants the problem taken seriously, and indeed is extending the seriousness of the problem.

Making Lemonade out of Lemons. Making lemonade out of lemons is similar to the notion in psychodynamic therapy of utilizing a client's resistances; therapeutic problems are seen as opportunities for the therapist to help the client. The strategy involves taking something that is apparently problematic and turning it into an asset. Problems become opportunities to practice skills; suffering allows others to express empathy; weaknesses become one's strengths. The danger in using this strategy is that it is easily confused with the invalidating refrain, repeatedly heard by clients with BPD. The therapist should avoid the tendency to oversimplify a client's problems, and refrain from implying that the lemons in the client's life are really lemonade. While recognizing that the cloud is indeed black, the therapist assists the client in finding the positive characteristics of a situation and thus the silver lining.

Core Strategies: Validation

Validation and problem-solving strategies, together with dialectical strategies, make up the core of DBT and form the heart of the treatment. DBT core strategies are listed in Figure 11.2. Validation strategies are the most obvious acceptance strategies, while problem-solving strategies are the most obvious change strategies. Both validation and problem-solving strategies are used in every interaction with the client, although the relative frequency of each depends on the particular client and the current situation and vulnerabilities of that client. Many treatment impasses are due to an imbalance of one type of strategy over the other. We discuss validation strategies in this section and problem-solving strategies below.

Clients with BPD present themselves clinically as individuals in extreme emotional pain. They plead, and at times demand, that their therapists do something to change this state of affairs. It is very tempting to focus the energy of therapy on changing the client by modifying irrational thoughts, assumptions, or schemas; critiquing interpersonal behaviors or motives contributing to interpersonal problems; giving medication to change abnormal biology; reducing emotional overreactivity and intensity; and so on. In many respects, this focus recapitulates the invalidating environment by confirming the client's worst fears: The client *is* the problem and indeed cannot trust his/her own reactions to events. Mistrust and invalidation of how one responds to events, however, is extremely aversive and can elicit intense fear, anger, shame, or a combination of all three. Thus the entire focus of change-based therapy can be aversive, since by necessity the focus contributes to and elicits self-invalidation.

Validation (according to the *Oxford English Dictionary*; Simpson & Weiner, 1989) means "The action of validating or making valid . . . a strengthening, reinforcement, confirming; an establishing or ratifying." It also encompasses activities such as corroborating, substantiating, verifying, and authenticating. The act of validating is "to support or corroborate on a sound or authoritative basis . . . to attest to the truth or validity of something" (*Webster's Dictionary*, 1991). To communicate that a response is valid is to say that it is "well-grounded or justifiable: being at once relevant and meaningful . . . logically correct . . . appropriate to the end in view [or effective] . . . having such force as to compel serious attention and [usually] acceptance" (*Webster's Dictionary*, 1991). Being "valid implies being supported by objective truth or generally accepted authority" (*Webster's Dictionary*, 1991); "being well-founded on fact, or established on sound principles, and thoroughly applicable to the case or circumstances" (Simpson & Weiner, 1989); and "soundness and strength," "value or worth," and "efficacy" (Simpson & Weiner, 1989). These are precisely the meanings associated with the term when used in the context of psychotherapy in DBT:

The essence of validation is this: The therapist communicates to the client that her [*sic*] responses make sense and are understandable

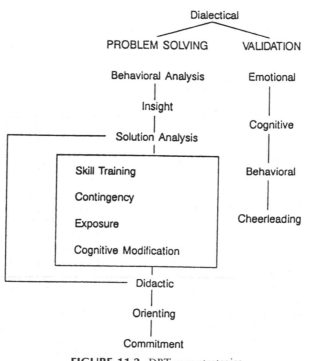

FIGURE 11.2. DBT core strategies.

within her [*sic*] *current* life context or situation. The therapist actively accepts the client and communicates this acceptance to the client. The therapist takes the client's responses seriously and does not discount or trivialize them. Validation strategies require the therapist to search for, recognize, and reflect to the client the validity inherent in her [*sic*] response to events. With unruly children, parents have to catch them while they're good in order to reinforce their behavior; similarly, the therapist has to uncover the validity within the client's response, sometimes amplify it, and then reinforce it. (Linehan, 1993a, pp. 222–223)

Two things are important to note here. First, validation means the acknowledgment of that which is valid. It does not mean "making" valid. Nor does it mean validating that which is invalid. The therapist observes, experiences, and affirms, but does not create validity. Second, "valid" and "scientific" are not synonyms. Science may be one way to determine what is valid, logical, sound in principle, and/or generally accepted as authority or normative knowledge. However, an authentic experience or apprehension of private events (at least when similar to the same experiences of others or when in accord with other, more observable events) is also a basis for claiming validity.

Validation can be considered at any one of six levels. Each level is correspondingly more complete than the previous one, and each level depends on one or more of the previous levels. The first two levels of validation encompass activities usually defined as empathic, and the third and fourth levels are similar to empathic interpretations as those terms are used in the general psychotherapy literature. Although we feel sure that most therapists use and support Levels 5 and 6 of validation, they are much less often discussed in the literature. They are, however, definitional of DBT and are required in every interaction with the client. These levels are described most fully in Linehan (1997), and the following definitions are taken from her discussion.

[Level 1] validation requires listening to and observing of what the client is saying, feeling, and doing as well as a corresponding active effort to understand what is being said and observed. The essence of this step is that the therapist is *interested* in the client. The therapist pays attention to what the client says and does. The therapist notices the nuances of response in the interaction. Validation at [Level 1] communicates that the client *per se*, as well as the client's presence, words, and responses in the session have "such force as to compel serious attention and [usually] acceptance" (see definitions of validation above). (pp. 360–361)

The second level of validation is the accurate reflection back to the client of the client's own feelings, thoughts, assumptions and behaviors. The therapist conveys an understanding of the client, a hearing of what the client has said and a seeing of what the client does, how he or she responds. Validation at the second level sanctions, empowers, or authenticates that the individual is who he or she actually is. (p. 362)

In [Level 3] of validation, the therapist communicates to the client understanding of aspects of the client's experience and response to events that have not been communicated directly by the client. At [Level 3], the therapist "reads" the client's behavior and figures out how the client feels and what the client is wishing for, thinking or doing just by knowing what has happened to the client. It is when one person can make the link between precipitating event and behavior without being given any information about the behavior itself. Emotions and meanings the client has not expressed are articulated by the therapist. (p. 364)

At [Level 4], behavior is validated in terms of its causes. Validation here is based on the notion that all behavior is caused by events occurring in time and, thus, in principle is understandable. Behavior is justified by showing that it is caused. Even though information may not be available to know all the relevant causes, the client's feelings, thoughts and actions make perfect sense in the context of the person's current experience, physiology, and life to date. At a minimum, what is can always be justified in terms of sufficient causes. That is, what is "should be" in that whatever was necessary for it to occur had to have happened. (p. 367)

At [Level 5], the therapist communicates that behavior is justifiable, reasonable, well-grounded, meaningful, and/or efficacious in terms of current events, normative biological functioning, and/or the client's ultimate life goals. The therapist looks for and reflects the wisdom or validity of [the] client's response and communicates that the response is understandable. The therapist finds the relevant facts in the *current* environment that support the client's behavior. The therapist is not blinded by the dysfunctionality of some of the client's response patterns to those aspects of a response pattern that may be either reasonable or appropriate to the context. Thus, the therapist searches the client's responses for their inherent accuracy or appropriateness, or reasonableness (as well as commenting on the inherent dysfunctionality of much of the response if necessary). (pp. 370–371)

In [Level 6], the task is to recognize the person as he or she is, seeing and responding to the strengths and capacities of the individual while keeping a firm empathic understanding of the client's actual difficulties and incapacities. The therapist believes in the individual and his or her capacity to change and move towards ultimate life goals. The client is responded to as a person of equal status, due equal respect. Validation at the highest level is the validation of the individual as "is." The therapist sees more than the role, more than a "client" or "disorder." Level [6] validation is the opposite of treating the client in a condescending manner or as overly fragile. It is responding to the individual as capable of effective and reasonable behavior rather than assuming that he or she is an invalid. Whereas [Levels 1 to 5] represent sequential steps in validation of a kind, [Level 6] represents both change in level as well as kind. (p. 377)

Cheerleading strategies constitute another form of validation, and are the principal strategies for combating the active passivity and tendencies to hopelessness in clients with BPD. In cheerleading, therapists communicate the belief that clients are doing their best and validate the clients' ability to eventually overcome their difficulties (a type of validation that, if not handled carefully, can simultaneously invalidate clients' perceptions of their helplessness). In addition, therapists express a belief in the therapy relationship, offer reassurance, and highlight any evidence of improvement. Within DBT, cheerleading is used in every therapeutic interaction. Although active cheerleading by therapists should be reduced as clients learn to trust and validate themselves, cheerleading strategies always remain an essential ingredient of a strong therapeutic alliance.

Core Strategies: Problem Solving

We have previously discussed how therapies with a primary focus on client change are typically experienced as invalidating by clients with BPD. However, therapies that focus exclusively on validation can prove equally problematic. Exhortations to accept one's current situation offer little solace to an individual who experiences life as painfully unendurable. Within DBT, problem-solving strategies are the core change strategies, designed to foster an active problem-solving style. For clients with BPD, however, the application of these strategies is fraught with difficulties. The therapist must keep in mind that the process will be more difficult than with many other client populations. In work with clients who have BPD, the need for sympathetic understanding and interventions aimed at enhancing current positive mood can be extremely important. The validation strategies just described, as well as the irreverent communication strategy described later, can be tremendously useful here.

Within DBT, problem solving is a two-stage process that concentrates first on understanding and accepting a selected problem and then on generating alternative solutions. The first stage involves (1) behavioral analysis; (2) insight into recurrent behavioral-context patterns; and (3) giving didactic information about principles of behaviors, norms, and so on. The second stage specifically targets change through (4) analysis of possible solutions to problems; (5) orienting the client to therapeutic procedures likely to bring about desired changes; and (6) strategies designed to elicit and strengthen commitment to these procedures. The following sections specifically address behavioral analysis, solution analysis, and problem-solving procedures.

Behavioral Analysis

Behavioral analysis is one of the most important strategies in DBT. It is also the most difficult. The purpose of a behavioral analysis is first to select a problem, and then to determine empirically what is causing it, what is preventing its resolution, and what aids are available for solving it. Behavioral analysis addresses four primary issues:

1. Are ineffective behaviors being reinforced, are effective behaviors followed by aversive outcomes, or are rewarding outcomes delayed?
2. Does the client have the requisite behavioral skills to regulate his/her emotions, respond skillfully to conflict, and manage his/her own behavior?
3. Are there patterns of avoidance, or are effective behaviors inhibited by unwarranted fears or guilt?

4. Is the client unaware of the contingencies operating in his/her environment, or are effective behaviors inhibited by faulty beliefs or assumptions?

Answers to these questions will guide the therapist in the selection of appropriate treatment procedures, such as contingency management, behavioral skill training, exposure, or cognitive modification. Thus the value of an analysis lies in helping the therapist assess and understand a problem fully enough to guide effective therapeutic response.

The first step in conducting a behavioral analysis is to help the client identify the problem to be analyzed and describe it in behavioral terms. Problem definition usually evolves from a discussion of the previous week's events, often in the context of reviewing diary cards. The assumption of facts not in evidence is perhaps the most common mistake at this point. Defining the problem is followed by conducting a chain analysis—an exhaustive, blow-by-blow description of the chain of events leading up to and following the behavior.

In a chain analysis, the therapist constructs a general road map of how the client arrives at dysfunctional responses, including where the road actually starts, and notated with possible alternative adaptive pathways or junctions along the way. Additional goals are to identify events that automatically elicit maladaptive behavior, behavioral deficits that are instrumental in maintaining problematic responses, and environmental and behavioral events that may be interfering with more appropriate behaviors. The overall goal is to determine the function of the behavior, or, from another perspective, what problem the behavior was instrumental in solving.

Chain analysis always begins with a specific environmental event. Pinpointing such an event may be difficult, as clients are frequently unable to identify anything in the environment that set off the problematic response. Nevertheless, it is important to obtain a description of the events co-occurring with the onset of the problem. The therapist then attempts to identify both environmental and behavioral events for each subsequent link in the chain. Here the therapist must play the part of a very keen observer, thinking in terms of very small chunks of behavior. The therapist asks the client, "What happened next?" or "How did

you get from there to there?" Although from the client's point of view such links may be self-evident, the therapist must be careful not to make assumptions. For example, a client who had attempted suicide once stated that she decided to kill herself because her life was too painful to live any longer. From the client's point of view, this was an adequate explanation for her suicide attempt. For the therapist, however, taking one's life because life was too painful was only one solution. One could decide life was too painful, then decide to change one's life. Or one could believe that death might be even more painful and decide to tolerate life despite its pain. In this instance, careful questioning revealed that the client actually assumed she would be happier dead than alive. Challenging this assumption then became a key to ending her persistent suicide attempts.

It is equally important to pinpoint exactly what consequences are maintaining the problematic response. Similarly, the therapist should also search for consequences that serve to weaken the problem behavior. As with antecedent events, the therapist probes for both environmental and behavioral consequences, obtaining detailed descriptions of emotions, somatic sensations, actions, thoughts, and assumptions. A rudimentary knowledge of the rules of learning and principles of reinforcement is crucial.

The final step in behavioral analysis is to construct and test hypotheses about events that are relevant to generating and maintaining the problem behavior. The biosocial theory of BPD suggests several factors of primary importance. For example, DBT focuses most closely on intense or aversive emotional states; the amelioration of negative affect is always suspected as among the primary motivational variables for dysfunctional behavior in BPD. The theory also suggests typical behavioral patterns, such as deficits in dialectical thinking or behavioral skills, which are likely to be instrumental in producing and maintaining problematic responses.

Solution Analysis

Once the problem has been identified and analyzed, problem solving proceeds with an active attempt at finding and identifying alternative solutions. At times, solutions will be suggested during the conduct of the behavioral analysis, and pointing to these alternative solutions may be all that is required. At other times, a more complete solution analysis will be necessary. Here the task is to "brainstorm" or generate as many alternate solutions as possible. Solutions should then be evaluated in terms of the various outcomes expected. The final step in solution analysis is choosing a solution that will somehow be effective. Throughout the evaluation, the therapist guides the client in choosing a particular behavioral solution. Here it is preferable that the therapist pay particular attention to long-term gain over short-term gain, and that solutions be chosen that render maximum benefit to the client rather than benefit to others.

Problem-Solving Procedures

DBT employs four problem-solving procedures taken directly from the cognitive and behavioral treatment literature. These four—skills training, contingency procedures, exposure, and cognitive modification—are viewed as primary vehicles of change, since they influence the direction that client changes take. Although they are discussed as distinct procedures by Linehan (1993a), it is not clear that they can in fact be differentiated in every case in clinical practice. The same therapeutic sequence may be effective because it teaches the client new skills (skills training), provides a consequence that influences the probability of preceding client behaviors occurring again (contingency procedures), provides nonreinforced exposure to cues associated previously but not currently with threat (exposure procedures), or changes the client's dysfunctional assumptions or schematic processing of events (cognitive modification). In contrast to many cognitive and behavioral treatment programs in the literature, these procedures (with some exceptions noted below) are employed in an unstructured manner, interwoven throughout all therapeutic dialogue. Thus, although the therapist must be well aware of the principles governing the effectiveness of each procedure, the use of each is usually an immediate response to events unfolding in a particular session. The exceptions are in skills training, where skills training procedures predominate, and Stage 2, where exposure procedures predominate.

Skills Training. An emphasis on skill building is pervasive throughout DBT. In both individual and group therapy, the therapist insists at every opportunity that the client actively engage in the acquisition and practice of behavioral skills. The term "skill" is used synonymously with "ability," and includes in its broadest sense cognitive, emotional, and overt behavioral skills as well as their integration, which is necessary for effective performance. Skill training is called for when a solution requires skills not currently in the individual's behavioral repertoire, or when the individual has the component behaviors but cannot integrate and use them effectively. Skills training in DBT incorporates three types of procedures: (1) skill acquisition (modeling, instructing, advising); (2) skill strengthening (encouraging *in vivo* and within-session practice, role playing, feedback); and (3) skill generalization (phone calls to work on applying skills, taping therapy sessions to listen to between sessions, homework assignments).

Contingency Procedures. Every response within an interpersonal interaction is potentially a reinforcement, a punishment, or a withholding or removal of reinforcement. Contingency management requires therapists to organize their behavior so that behaviors that represent progress are reinforced, while unskillful or maladaptive behaviors are extinguished or lead to aversive consequences. The most important contingency for most clients with BPD is the therapist's interpersonal behavior with such a client. The ability of the therapist to influence the client's behavior is directly tied to the strength of the relationship between the two. Thus contingency procedures are less useful in the very early stages of treatment (except possibly in cases where the therapist is the "only game in town"). A first requirement for effective contingency management is that the therapist attend to the client's behaviors and reinforce those behaviors that represent progress toward DBT targets. Equally important is that the therapist take care not to reinforce behaviors targeted for extinction. In theory this may seem obvious, but in practice it can be quite difficult. The problematic behaviors of clients with BPD are often quite effective in obtaining reinforcing outcomes or in stopping painful events. Indeed, the very behaviors targeted for extinction have been intermittently reinforced by mental health professionals, family members, and friends.

Contingency management will at times require the use of aversive consequences, similar to "setting limits" in other treatment modalities. Three guidelines are important here. First, punishment should "fit the crime," and a client should have some way of terminating its application. For example, in DBT a detailed behavioral analysis follows a parasuicidal act; such an analysis is an aversive procedure for most clients. Once it has been completed, however, the clients' ability to pursue other topics is restored. Second, it is crucial that therapists use punishment with great care, in low doses, and very briefly, and that a positive interpersonal atmosphere be restored following any client improvement. Third, punishment should be just strong enough to work. Although the ultimate punishment is termination of therapy, a preferable fallback strategy is putting clients on "vacations from therapy." This approach is considered when all other contingencies have failed, or when a situation is so serious that a therapist's therapeutic or personal limits have been crossed. When utilizing this strategy, the therapist clearly identifies what behaviors must be changed, and clarifies that once the conditions have been met, the client can return. The therapist maintains intermittent contact by phone or letter, and provides a referral or backup while the client is on vacation. (In colloquial terms, the therapist kicks the client out and then pines for his/her return.)

Observing limits constitutes a special case of contingency management involving the application of problem-solving strategies to client behaviors that threaten or cross a therapist's personal limits. Such behaviors interfere with the therapist's ability or willingness to conduct the therapy, and thus constitute a special type of therapy-interfering behavior. Therapists must take responsibility for monitoring their own personal limits, and must clearly communicate to their clients which behaviors are tolerable and which are not. Therapists who do not do this will eventually burn out, terminate therapy, or otherwise harm their clients.

DBT favors natural over arbitrary limits. Thus limits will vary among therapists and with the same therapist over time and circumstance. Limits should also be presented as for the good of the therapist, not for the good of the client. The effect of this is that while clients may argue about what is in their own best interests, they do not have ultimate say over what is good for their therapists.

Cognitive Modification. The fundamental message given to clients in DBT is that cognitive distortions are just as likely to be caused by emotional arousal as to be the cause of the arousal in the first place. The overall message is that for the most part, the source of a client's distress is the extremely stressful events of his/her life rather than a distortion of events that are actually benign. Although direct cognitive restructuring procedures such as those advocated by Beck and colleagues and by Ellis (Beck, Rush, Shaw, & Emery, 1979; Beck et al., 1990; Ellis, 1962, 1973) are used, they do not hold a dominant place in DBT. In contrast, contingency clarification strategies are used relentlessly, highlighting contingent relationships operating in the here and now. Emphasis is placed on highlighting immediate and long-term effects of clients' behavior (both on themselves and on others), clarifying the effects of certain situations on the clients' own responses, and examining future contingencies the clients are likely to encounter. An example here is orienting a client to DBT as a whole and to treatment procedures as they are implemented.

Exposure. All of the change procedures in DBT can be reconceptualized as exposure strategies. Many of the principles of exposure as applied to DBT have been developed by researchers in exposure techniques (see Foa & Kozak, 1986; Foa, Steketee, & Grayson, 1985). These strategies work by reconditioning dysfunctional associations that develop between stimuli (e.g., an aversive stimulus, hospitalization, may become associated with a positive stimulus, nurturing in the hospital; a patient may later work to be hospitalized) or between a response and a stimulus (e.g., an adaptive response, healthy expression of emotions, is met with aversive consequent stimuli, rejection by a loved one; a patient may then try to suppress emotions). As noted earlier, the DBT therapist conducts a chain analysis of the eliciting cue, the problem behavior (including emotions), and the consequences of the behavior. Working within a behavior therapy framework, the therapist operates according to three guidelines for exposure in DBT. First, exposure to the cue that precedes the problem behavior must be nonreinforced (e.g., if a patient is fearful that discussing parasuicidal behavior will lead to his/her being rejected, the therapist must not reinforce the client's shame by ostracizing him/her). Second, dysfunctional responses are blocked, in the order of the primary and secondary targets of treatment (e.g., parasuicidal behavior related to shame is blocked by getting the patient's cooperation to throw away hoarded medications). Third, actions opposite to the dysfunctional behavior are reinforced (e.g., the therapist reinforces the patient for talking about painful, shame-related parasuicidal behavior).

Therapeutic exposure procedures are used informally throughout the whole of therapy and formally during Stage 2, where the client is systematically exposed to cues of previous traumatic events. Exposure procedures of the DBT therapist involve first orienting the patient to the techniques and to the fact that exposure to cues is often experienced as painful or frightening. The therapist thus does not remove the cue to emotional arousal, and at the same time blocks both the action tendencies (including escape responses) and the expressive tendencies associated with the problem emotion. In addition, the DBT therapist works to assist the patient in achieving enhanced control over aversive events. A crucial step of exposure procedures is that the client be taught how to control the event. It is critical that the client have some means of titrating or ending exposure when emotions become unendurable. The therapist and client should collaborate in developing positive, adaptive ways for the client to end exposure voluntarily, preferably after some reduction in the problem emotion has occurred.

Stylistic Strategies

DBT balances two quite different styles of communication. The first, reciprocal communication, is similar to the communication style advocated in client-centered therapy. The second, irreverent communication, is quite similar to the style advocated by Whitaker (1975) in his writings on strategic therapy. Reciprocal communication strategies are designed to reduce a perceived power differen-

tial by making the therapist more vulnerable to the client. In addition, they serve as a model for appropriate but equal interactions within an important interpersonal relationship. Irreverent communication is usually riskier than reciprocity. However, it can facilitate problem solving or produce a breakthrough after long periods when progress has seemed glacial. To be used effectively, irreverent communication must balance reciprocal communication, and the two must be woven into a single stylistic fabric. Without such balancing, neither strategy represents DBT.

Reciprocal Communication

Responsiveness, self-disclosure, and genuineness are the basic guidelines of reciprocal communication. Responsiveness requires taking the client's agenda and wishes seriously. It is a friendly, affectionate style reflecting warmth and engagement in the therapeutic interaction. Both self-involving and personal self-disclosure, used in the interests of the client, are encouraged. Disclosure of immediate, personal reactions to the client and his/her behavior is frequent. For example, a therapist whose client complained about his coolness said, "When you demand warmth from me, it pushes me away and makes it harder to be warm." Similarly, when a client repeatedly failed to fill out diary cards but nevertheless pleaded with her therapist to help her, the therapist responded, "You keep asking me for help, but you won't do the things I believe are necessary to help you. I feel frustrated because I want to help you, but feel you won't let me." Such statements serve both to validate and to challenge. They constitute both an instance of contingency management, because therapist statements about the client are typically experienced as either reinforcing or punishing, and an instance of contingency clarification, because the client's attention is directed to the consequences of his/her interpersonal behavior. Self-disclosure of professional or personal information is used to validate and model coping and normative responses.

Irreverent Communication

Irreverent communication is used to push the client "off balance," get the client's attention, present an alternative viewpoint, or shift affective response. It is a highly useful strategy when the client is immovable, or when therapist and client are "stuck." It has an "offbeat" flavor and uses logic to weave a web the client cannot get out of. Although it is responsive to the client, irreverent communication is almost never the response the client expects. The therapist highlights some unintended aspect of the client's communication, or "reframes" it in an unorthodox manner. For example, if the client says, "I am going to kill myself," the therapist might say, "I thought you agreed not to drop out of therapy." Irreverent communication has a matter-of-fact, almost deadpan style, which is in sharp contrast to the warm responsiveness of reciprocal communication. Humor, a certain naiveté, and guilelessness are also characteristic of the style. A confrontational tone is also irreverent, communicating "bullshit" to responses other than the targeted adaptive response. For example, the therapist might say, "Are you out of your mind?" or "You weren't for a minute actually believing I would think that was a good idea, were you?" The irreverent therapist also calls the client's bluff. For the client who says, "I'm quitting therapy," the therapist might respond, "Would you like a referral?" The trick here is to carefully time the bluff with the simultaneous provision of a safety net; it is important to leave the client a way out.

Case Management Strategies

When there are problems in the client's environment that interfere with the client's functioning or progress, the therapist moves to the case management strategies. Although not new, case management strategies direct the application of core strategies to case management problems. There are three case management strategy groups: the consultant-to-the-client strategy, environmental intervention, and the consultation/supervision team meeting.

Consultant-to-the-Client Strategy

The consultant-to-the-client strategy is deceptively simple in theory and extremely difficult in practice. In essence, as its name suggests, the strategy requires the therapist to be a consultant to the client rather than to the client's network. The overriding implication of this is that, in general, DBT therapists do not intervene to adjust environments for the sake of

their clients, nor do they consult with other professionals about how to treat their clients unless the clients are present. According to this philosophy, a client, not a therapist, is the intermediary between the therapist and other professionals. The therapist's job is to consult with the client on how to interact effectively with his/her environment, rather than to consult with the environment on how to interact effectively with the client. The consultant-to-the-client strategy is the preferred case management strategy and perhaps the most innovative aspect of DBT.

The consultant-to-the-client strategy was chosen with three objectives in mind. First, clients must learn how to manage their own lives and care for themselves by interacting effectively with other individuals in the environment, including health care professionals. The consultant-to-the-client strategy believes in clients' capacities and targets their ability to take care of themselves. Second, this strategy was designed to decrease instances of "splitting" between DBT therapists and other individuals interacting with clients. Splitting occurs when different individuals in a client's network hold differing opinions on how to treat the client. By remaining in the role of a consultant to the client, the therapist stays out of such arguments. Finally, the consultant-to-the-client strategy promotes respect for clients by imparting the message that they are credible and capable of performing interventions on their own behalf.

Traditionally, health care professionals routinely exchanged information helpful to a professional currently treating a client. Thus routine use of the consultant-to-the-client strategy will ordinarily require attention to orienting professionals in one's own community to the strategy. Although consultation between professionals is actually encouraged, not discouraged, the requirement that clients be present (and preferably arrange the consultation) is almost always going to be different and to require expenditure of some extra time. In our experience, however, once the community is oriented, the strategy works well and actually can save time in the long run.

Environmental Intervention

As outlined above, the bias in DBT is toward teaching the client how to interact effectively with his/her environment. The consultant-to-the-client strategy is thus the dominant case management strategy and is used whenever possible. There are times, however, when intervention by the therapist is needed. In general, the environmental intervention strategy is used over the consultant-to-the-client strategy when substantial harm may befall the client if the therapist does not intervene. The general rule for environmental intervention is that when clients lack abilities that they need to learn, are impossible to obtain, or are not reasonable or necessary, the therapist may intervene.

Supervision/Consultation Meeting

Supervision/consultation with therapists is integral, rather than ancillary, to DBT. The consultation-to-the-therapist treatment strategy balances the consultation-to-the-client strategy discussed above. DBT, from this perspective, is defined as a treatment system in which (1) therapists apply DBT to the clients and (2) supervisors and/or consultation team members apply DBT to the therapists. The supervisors and/or consultation team members provide a dialectical balance for therapists in their interactions with clients.

There are three primary functions of consultation to the therapist in DBT. First, a supervisor or consultation team helps to keep each individual therapist in the therapeutic relationship. The role here is to cheerlead and support the therapist. Second, the supervisor or consultation team balances the therapist in his/her interactions with the client. In providing balance, consultants may move close to the therapist, helping him/her maintain a strong position. Or consultants may move back from the therapist, requiring the therapist to move closer to the client to maintain balance. Third, within programmatic applications of DBT, the team provides the context for the treatment. At its purest, DBT is a transactional relationship between and among a community of clients with BPD and a community of mental health professionals.

DBT FOR CLIENTS WITH SUBSTANCE USE DISORDERS

Within the past few years, DBT has been adapted for clients with substance use disorders, primarily those dually diagnosed with BPD. The application of DBT to the treatment of substance abuse and dependence has led to the development of a dialectical position toward the problem of relapse, termed "dialectical abstinence." This concept synthesizes the basic tenets of the relapse prevention approach (Marlatt & Gordon, 1985) to treating substance use disorders and the treatment philosophy of absolute abstinence. On the one hand, the therapeutic focus is on absolute abstinence before any problematic substance use; on the other, the treatment moves to radical acceptance, nonjudgmental problem solving, and prevention of further relapse if the patient does use (followed by a return to the absolute abstinence stance). Other modifications to standard DBT include the addition of specific targets that are relevant to drug use (e.g., decreasing urges to use); enhanced "attachment" strategies to connect the patient to the treatment team; modified skills that are relevant to clients with substance use disorders (e.g., "burning your bridges" to a substance use culture); and increased use of both natural and arbitrary reinforcers for maintenance of abstinence.

CASE STUDY

Background

At the initial meeting, "Cindy" was a 30-year-old, white, married woman with no children who was living in a middle-class suburban area with her husband. She had a college education and had successfully completed almost 2 years of medical school. Cindy was referred to one of us (M. M. L.) by her psychiatrist of 1½ years, who was no longer willing to provide more than pharmacotherapy following a recent hospitalization for a near-lethal suicide attempt. In the 2 years prior to referral, Cindy had been hospitalized at least 10 times (one lasting 6 months) for psychiatric treatment of suicidal ideation; had engaged in numerous instances of parasuicidal behavior, including at least 10 instances of drinking Clorox bleach, multiple deep cuts, and burns; and had had three medically severe or nearly lethal suicide attempts, including cutting an artery in her neck. At the time of referral, Cindy met DSM-III-R criteria for BPD (American Psychiatric Association, 1987), as well as the criteria of Gunderson (1984). She was also taking a variety of psychotropic drugs.

Until age 27 Cindy was able to function well in work and school settings, and her marriage was reasonably satisfactory to both partners, although the husband complained of Cindy's excessive anger. When Cindy was in the second year of medical school, a classmate she knew only slightly committed suicide. Cindy stated that when she heard about the suicide, she immediately decided to kill herself also, but had very little insight into what about the situation actually elicited the inclination to kill herself. Within weeks she left medical school and became severely depressed and actively suicidal. Although Cindy self-presented as a person with few psychological problems before the classmate's suicide, further questioning revealed a history of severe anorexia nervosa, bulimia nervosa, and alcohol and prescription medication abuse, originating at the age of 14 years. Indeed, she had met her husband at an Alcoholics Anonymous (AA) meeting while attending college. Nevertheless, until the student's suicide in medical school, Cindy had been successful at maintaining an overall appearance of relative competence.

Treatment

At the initial meeting, Cindy was accompanied by her husband, who stated that he and Cindy's family considered his wife too lethally suicidal to be out of a hospital setting. Consequently, he and her family were seriously contemplating the viability of finding long-term inpatient care. However, Cindy stated a strong preference for outpatient treatment, although no therapist in the local area other than M. M. L. appeared willing to take her into outpatient treatment. The therapist agreed to accept Cindy into therapy, contingent on the client's stated commitment to work toward behavioral change and stay in treatment for at least 1 year. (It was later pointed out repeatedly that this also meant the client had agreed not to commit suicide.) Thus the therapist began the crucial first step of establishing a strong therapeutic alliance by agreeing to accept the client despite the fact that no one else was willing to do so. The therapist pointed out, however, that acceptance into therapy did not come without a cost. In this manner, the therapist communicated acceptance of the client exactly as she was in the current moment, while concomitantly making clear that her commitment toward change was the foundation of the therapeutic alliance.

At the fourth therapy session, Cindy reported that she felt she could no longer keep herself alive. When reminded of her previous commitment to stay alive for 1 year of therapy, she replied that things had changed and she could not help herself. Subsequent to this session, almost every individual session for the next 6 months revolved around the topic of whether (and how) to stay alive versus committing suicide. Cindy began coming to sessions wearing mirrored sunglasses, and would slump in her chair or ask to sit on the floor. Questions from the therapist were often met with a minimal comment or long silences. In response to the therapist's attempts to discuss prior parasuicidal behavior, Cindy would become angry and withdraw (slowing down the pace of therapy considerably). The client also presented with marked dissociative reactions, which would often occur during therapy sessions. During these reactions, Cindy would appear unable to concentrate or hear much of what was being said. When queried by the therapist, Cindy would describe her experience as feeling "spacey" and distant. The client stated that she felt she could no longer engage in many activities, such as driving, working, or attending school. Overall, the client viewed herself as incompetent in all areas.

The use of diary cards, which Cindy filled out weekly (or filled out at the beginning of the session if she forgot), assisted the therapist in carefully monitoring Cindy's daily experiencing of suicidal ideation, misery, and urges to harm herself, as well as actual parasuicidal acts. Behavioral analyses that attempted to identify the sequence of events leading up to and following Cindy's parasuicidal behavior soon became an important focus of therapy. At every point the therapist presented parasuicidal behavior as to be expected, given the strength of the behavior (but as ultimately beatable), and pointed out repeatedly that if the client committed suicide therapy would be over, so they had better work really hard now while she was alive.

Over the course of several months, the behavioral analyses began to identify a frequently recurring behavioral pattern that preceded parasuicide. For Cindy, the chain of events would often begin with an interpersonal encounter (almost always with her husband), which culminated in her feeling threatened, criticized, or unloved. These feelings would often be followed by urges either to self-mutilate or to kill herself, depending somewhat on the covarying levels of hopelessness, anger, and sadness. Decisions to self-mutilate and/or to attempt suicide were often accompanied by the thought "I'll show you." At other times, hopelessness and a desire to end the pain permanently seemed predominant. Following the conscious decision to self-mutilate or attempt suicide, Cindy would then immediately dissociate and at some later point cut or burn herself, usually while in a state of "automatic pilot." Consequently, Cindy often had difficulty remembering specifics of the actual acts. At one point, Cindy burned her leg so badly (and then injected it with dirt to convince the doctor that he should give her more attention) that reconstructive surgery was required. Behavioral analyses also revealed that dissociation during sessions usually occurred following Cindy's perception of the therapist's disapproval or invalidation, especially when the therapist appeared to suggest that change was possible. In-session dissociation was targeted by the therapist's immediately addressing it as it was occurring.

By several months into therapy, an apparently long-standing pattern of suicidal behaviors leading to inpatient admission was apparent. The client would report intense suicidal ideation, express doubts that she could resist the urge to kill herself, and request admission to her preferred hospital; or, without warning, she would cut or burn herself severely and require hospitalization for medical treatment. Attempts to induce Cindy to stay out of the hospital or to leave before she felt she was ready typically resulted in an escalation of suicidality, followed by her pharmacotherapist's (a psychiatrist) insisting on her admission or the hospital's agreeing to extend her stay. Observation of this behavioral pattern led the therapist to hypothesize that the hospitalization itself was reinforcing suicidal behavior, and consequently undertook an effort to change the contingencies for suicidal behaviors. Using didactic and contingency clarification strategies, the therapist attempted to help Cindy understand how hospitalization might be strengthening the very behavior they were working to eliminate.

This issue became a focal point of disagreement within the therapy, with the client viewing the therapist's position as unsympathetic and nonunderstanding of the client's phenomenal experience. In the client's opinion, the intensity of her emotional pain rendered the probability of suicide so high that hospitalization was necessary in order to guarantee her safety. She would buttress her position by citing frequently her difficulties with dissociative reactions, which she reported as extremely aversive and which, in her opinion, made her unable to function much of the time. From the therapist's perspective, the deleterious long-term risk of suicide created by repeated hospitalization in response to suicidal behavior was higher than the short-term risk of suicide if hospitalization stays were reduced.

These differences in opinion led to frequent disagreements within sessions. It gradually became clear that Cindy viewed any explanations of her behavior as influenced by reinforcement as a direct attack; she implied that if hospitalization was reinforcing her suicidal behavior, then the therapist must believe that Cindy was always suicidal in order for her to get into the hospital. This was obviously not the case (at least some of the time), but all attempts to explain reinforcement theory in any other terms failed. The therapist compensated somewhat for insisting on the possibility that she (the therapist) was correct by doing three things. First, she repeatedly validated the client's experience of almost unendurable pain. Second, she was certain to address the client's dissociative behavior repeatedly, explaining it as an automatic reaction to intensely painful affect (or the threat of it). Third, she frequently addressed the quality of the relationship between them so as to strengthen the relationship and maintain the client in therapy, even though it was a source of even more emotional pain.

By the fifth month, the therapist became concerned that the current treatment regimen was going to have the unintended consequence of killing the client (via suicide). At this point, the therapist's limits for effective treatment were crossed, and she therefore decided to employ the consultant-to-the-client strategy to address Cindy's hospitalizations. The first-choice strategy would have been to get Cindy to negotiate a new treatment plan with her preferred hospital and admitting psychiatrist. Cindy refused to go along, however, because she disagreed with the wisdom of changing her current unlimited access to the inpatient unit. The therapist was able to get her to agree to a consultation meeting with all of her treatment providers, and, with some tenacity, the therapist actually got Cindy to make all the calls setting up the meeting (including inviting her insurance monitor, who was coordinating payment for treatment).

At the case conference, the therapist presented her hypothesis that contingent hospitalization was reinforcing Cindy's suicidal behavior. She also assisted Cindy in making her case that the therapist was wrong. Using reciprocal communication and contingency management, the therapist stated that she simply couldn't conduct a therapy she thought might kill the client (and she had to go along with what she thought was best even if she were wrong— "to do otherwise would be unethical"), and requested that a new system of contingencies designed to disrupt the functional relationship between suicidal behavior and hospitalization be agreed upon. A plan was therefore developed wherein the client was not required to be suicidal in order to gain hospital admittance. Under this new set of contingencies, Cindy could elect, at will, to enter the hospital for a stay of up to 3 days, at the end of which time she would always be discharged. If she convinced people that she was too suicidal for discharge, she would be transferred to a least-preferred hospital for safety. Parasuicidal behavior would no longer be grounds for admission, except to a medical unit when required. Although there was some disagreement as to the functional relationship between suicidal behavior and hospitalization, this system was agreed upon.

Following this meeting, Cindy's husband announced that he was no longer able to live with or tolerate his wife's suicidal behavior, and that the constant threat of finding her dead had led to his decision to file for divorce. The focus of therapy then shifted to helping Cindy grieve for this event and find a suitable living arrangement. Cindy alternated between fury that her husband would desert her in her hour of need (or "illness," as she put it) and despair that she could ever cope alone. She decided that "getting her feelings out" was the only useful therapy. This led to many tearful sessions, with the therapist simultaneously validating the pain, focusing on Cindy's experiencing the affect in the moment without

escalating or blocking it, and cheerleading Cindy's ability to manage without going back into the hospital. Due to her high level of dysfunctionality, both Cindy and her therapist decided that she would enter a residential treatment facility for a 3-month period. The facility had a coping skills orientation and provided group but not individual therapy. Cindy saw her therapist once a week and talked to her several times a week during this period. With some coaching, Cindy looked for and found a roommate to live with and returned to her own home at the end of 3 months (Month 9 of therapy).

Over the course of treatment, a number of strategies were used to treat parasuicidal and therapy-interfering behaviors. In-depth behavioral chain and solution analysis helped the therapist (and sometimes the client) gain insight into the factors influencing current suicidal behavior. For Cindy, as for most clients, performing these analyses was quite difficult, as the process usually generated intense feelings of shame, guilt, or anger. Thus behavioral analysis also functioned as an exposure strategy, encouraging the client to observe and experience painful affect. It additionally served as a cognitive strategy in helping change Cindy's expectancies concerning the advantages and disadvantages of suicidal behavior, especially as the therapist repeatedly made statements such as "How do you think you would feel if I got angry at you and then threatened suicide if you didn't change?" Finally, behavioral analysis served as contingency management, in that the client's ability to pursue topics of interest in therapy sessions was made contingent on the successful completion of chain and solution analysis.

Cindy presented early in therapy with exceedingly strong perceptions as to her needs and desires, and with a concomitant willingness to engage in extremely lethal parasuicidal behavior. As previously mentioned, several of these acts were serious attempts to end her life, while others functioned as attempts to gain attention and care from significant others. This client also presented with an extreme sensitivity to any attempts at obvious change procedures, which typically were interpreted as communicating to the client a message of incompetence and unworthiness. Although Cindy initially committed herself to attending weekly group skills training for the first year of therapy, her attendance at group meetings was quite erratic, and she generally tended either to miss entire sessions (but never more than three in a row) or else to leave during the break. Therapist attempts at addressing this issue were met by Cindy's stating that she could not drive at night due to night blindness. Although considered a therapy-interfering behavior and frequently addressed over the course of therapy, missing skills training was not made a major focus of treatment, due to the continuing presence of higher-priority suicidal behavior. The therapist's efforts to engage the client in active skills acquisition during individual therapy sessions were also somewhat limited and were always preceded by obtaining a verbal commitment to problem solving. The stylistic strategy of irreverent communication was of value to the therapeutic process. The therapist's irreverence often served to "shake up" the client, resulting in a loosening of dichotomous thinking and maladaptive cognitions. The result of this was an increased willingness to explore new and adaptive behavioral solutions. Finally, relationship strategies were heavily employed as tools to strengthen the therapeutic alliance and to keep it uncontingent on suicidal and/or dissociative behaviors. Included here were between-session therapist-initiated telephone calls to see how Cindy was doing, routine giving out of phone numbers when traveling, and sending the client postcards when the therapist was out of town.

By the 12th month of therapy, Cindy's parasuicidal behavior as well as urges to engage in such behavior receded. In addition, her hospital stays were reduced markedly, with none occurring after Month 8. While living at home with a roommate, Cindy was readmitted to medical school. Part of the reason for returning to school was to turn her life around so that she could try to regain her husband's love and attention, or at least his friendship. As the therapy continued to focus on changing the contingencies of suicidal behavior, reducing both emotional pain and inhibition, and tolerating distress, a further focus on maintaining sobriety and reasonable food intake was added. During the first months of living in her home without her husband, Cindy had several alcoholic binges, and her food intake dropped precipitously. These became immediate targets. The therapist's strong attention to these behaviors also communicated to Cindy that the therapist would take her problems seriously even if she was not suicidal. Therapy focused as well on expanding her social network. As with suicidal behaviors, attention to these targets served as a pathway to treating associated problems. As crisis situations decreased in frequency, much greater attention was paid to analyzing family patterns, including experiences of neglect and invalidation, that might have led up to Cindy's problems in later life. Cindy did not report a history of sexual or physical abuse. Thus the explicit goal of Stage 2 (which was being cautiously entered as an overlap to Stage 1) was to understand her history and its relationship to her current problems.[1]

In other cases, especially when there has been sexual and/or physical abuse in childhood, movement to Stage 2 before Stage 1 targets have been mastered is likely to result in retrogression to previously problematic behaviors. For example, another client treated by the same therapist (M. M. L.), Terry, had been quite seriously abused physically by her mother throughout childhood and sexually abused by her father beginning at age 5. The sexual advances were nonviolent at first, but became physically abusive at approximately age 12. Prior to this therapy, Terry had not disclosed incidents of the abuse to anyone. After successful negotiation of Stage 1 targets, the therapist preceded to expose Terry to trauma-related cues by simply having Terry begin to disclose details of the abuse. These exposure sessions were intertwined with work on current problems in Terry's life. Following one exposure session focused on the sexual abuse, Terry reverted to some of her previously problematic behaviors, evidenced by withdrawal and silence in sessions, suicidal ideation, and medication noncompliance. The appearance of such behavior marked the necessity of stopping Stage 2 discussions of previous sexual abuse in order to recursively address Stage 1 targets. Three sessions were devoted to a behavioral analysis of Terry's current suicidal, therapy-interfering, and quality-of-life-interfering behaviors; these were eventually linked both to fears about how the therapist would view her childhood emotional responses to her father, and to holiday visits with her father that precipitated conflicts over how she should be feeling about him in the present. This two-steps-forward, one-step-back approach is common to therapy for clients with BPD, and in particular may mark the transition between Stage 1 and Stage 2.

As previously mentioned, Stage 3 targets the client's self-respect, regardless of the opinions of others. Betty, who was also in treatment with the same therapist (M. M. L.), had successfully negotiated Stages 1 and 2 and had become a highly competent nurse with training and supervision responsibilities. Therapy with Betty was then focused on maintaining her self-esteem in the face of very powerful significant others (e.g., her supervisor) who constantly invalidated her. Components of the treatment included the therapist's noting and highlighting for the client her tendency to modify her self-opinion in accordance with that of others; persistent attempts to extract from Betty self-validation and self-soothing; and imagery exercises wherein the client imagined and verbalized herself standing up to powerful others. Much of the therapy focus was on the interpersonal behavior of the client within the therapy session, with attention to relating this behavior to her interactions with other important people. Thus treatment at that point was very similar to the functional analytic psychotherapy regimen developed by Kohlenberg and Tsai (1991). Overall, this third stage of therapy involved the movement to a more egalitarian relationship between the client and the therapist, where the emphasis was placed on the client's standing up for her own opinions and defending her own actions. This approach required that the therapist both reinforce the client's assertions and also step back and refrain from validating and nurturing the client in the manner characteristic of Stages 1 and 2. In addition, therapy sessions were reduced to every other week, and issues surrounding eventual termination were periodically discussed.

Stage 4 of DBT targets the sense of incompleteness that can preclude the experience of joy. Sally started Stage 1 treatment with the same therapist (M. M. L.) 15 years ago. Stage 1 lasted 2 years; this was followed by a break of 1 year, whereupon treatment resumed for several years of bimonthly sessions leading to monthly sessions, and currently consists of four or five sessions a year. She has been married for 30 years to an irregularly employed husband who, though devoted and loyal, is quite invalidating of her. While apparently brilliant, he is usually dismissed from jobs for his interpersonal insensitivity. She has been employed full-time at the same place for years, working with children. The son she felt closest to died in a plane accident 2 years ago; her mother died last year; and her father is very ill. Despite having a stable marriage, working in a stable and quite fulfilling job, having raised two well-adjusted sons, and still being athletic, life feels meaningless to her. In the past she was very active in spiritual activities; following meditation retreats or extended periods of daily meditation, she would report contentment and some sense of joy. Since her son died, she has let go of most of her spiritual activities. Following 2 years of focusing on grieving, she is now ready for Stage 4. We are planning an approach of actively practicing and keeping track of progress in radical acceptance (or "letting go of ego," in Zen terminology), either alone or with group support.

TRANSCRIPTS

The following (composite) transcripts represent actual examples of the process of therapy occurring over several sessions with different patients. These particular dialogues between therapist (T) and client (C) have been chosen to provide the reader with comprehensive examples of the application of a wide range of DBT treatment strategies.

The session targets in the following transcript were orienting and commitment. The strategies used were validation, problem solving (insight, orienting, and commitment), dialectical (devil's advocate), and integrated (relationship enhancement).

Obtaining the client's commitment is a crucial first step in beginning therapy with clients who have BPD. As illustrated in the following transcript, the dialectical technique of devil's advocate can be highly effective when used as a commitment strategy. In this first therapy session, the therapist's ultimate goal was to obtain the client's commitment to therapy, as well as a commitment to eliminate suicidal behavior. She began by orienting the client to the purpose of this initial session.

T: So are you a little nervous about me?

C: Yeah, I guess I am.

T: Well, that's understandable. For the next 50 minutes or so, we have this opportunity to get to know each other and see if we want to work together. So what I'd like to do is talk a little bit about the program and how you got here. So tell me, what do you want out of therapy with me, and what are you doing here?

C: I want to get better.

T: Well, what's wrong with you?

C: I'm a mess (*laughs*).

T: How so?

C: Um, I don't know, I just can't even cope with everyday life right now. And I can't even . . . I'm just a mess. I don't know how to deal with anything.

T: So what does that mean exactly?

C: Um, well, everything I try these days just seems overwhelming. I couldn't keep up on my job, and now I'm on medical leave. Plus everyone's sick of me being in the hospital so much. And I think my psychiatrist wants to send me away because of all my self-harming.

T: How often do you self-harm?

C: Maybe once or twice a month. I use my lighter or cigarettes, sometimes a razor blade.

T: Do you have scars all over?

C: (*Nods yes*)

T: Your psychiatrist tells me you've also drunk Clorox. Why didn't you mention that?

C: I guess it didn't enter my mind.

T: Do things just not enter your mind very often?

C: I don't really know. Maybe.

T: So maybe with you I'm going to have to be a very good guesser.

C: Hmmm.

T: Unfortunately, though, I'm not the greatest guesser. So we'll have to teach you how to have things come to mind. So what is it exactly that you want out of therapy with me? To quit harming yourself, quit trying to kill yourself, or both?

C: Both. I'm sick of it.

T: And is there anything else you want help with?

C: Um, well, I don't know how to handle money, and I don't know how to handle relationships. I don't have friends; they don't connect with me very often. I'm a former alcoholic and a recovering anorexic/bulimic. I still have a tendency toward that.

T: Do you think maybe some of what is going on with you is that you've replaced your alcoholic and anorexic behaviors with self-harm behaviors?

C: I don't know. I haven't thought about it that way. I just feel that I don't know how to handle myself, by all means, and—you know, and I guess work through stuff, and that is obviously getting to me, because if it wasn't I wouldn't be trying to kill myself.

T: So from your perspective, one problem is that you don't know how to do things. A lot of things.

C: Yeah, and a lot of it is I do know how, but for some reason I don't do it anyway.

T: Um hmm.

C: You know, I mean I know I need to save money, and I know that I need to budget myself, and I do every single month, but every single month I get in debt. But, um, you know, it's really hard for me, you know, it's like sometimes I know it, or I know I shouldn't eat something and I do it anyway.

T: So it sounds like part of the problem is you actually know how to do things; you just don't know how to get yourself to do the things you know how to do.

C: Exactly.

T: Does it seem like maybe your emotions are in control—that you are a person who does things when you're in the mood?

C: Yes. Everything's done by the mood.

T: So you're a moody person.

C: Yes. I won't clean the house for 2 months, and then I'll get in the mood to clean, and then I'll clean it immaculately and keep it that way for 3 weeks—I mean, just immaculate—and then when I'm in the mood I go back to being a mess again.

T: So one of the tasks for you and me would be to figure out a way to get your behavior and what you do less hooked up with how you feel?

C: Right.

The therapist used insight to highlight for the client the observed interrelationship between the client's emotions and her behavior. She then began the process of shaping a commitment through the dialectical strategy of devil's advocate.

T: That, of course, is going to be hell to do, don't you think? Why would you want to do that? It sounds so painful.

C: Well, I want to do it because it's so inconsistent. It's worse, you know, because when I'm—I know that, like with budgeting money or whatever, I know I need to do it, and then when I don't do it it makes me even more upset.

T: Why would you ever want to do something you're not in the mood for?

C: Because I've got to. Because I can't survive that way if I don't.

T: Sounds like a pretty easy life to me.

C: Yeah, but I can't afford to live if I just spend my money on fun and stupid frivolous things that I . . .

T: Well, I guess maybe you should have some limits and not be too off the wall, but in general, I mean, why clean the house if you're not in the mood?

C: Because it pisses me off when it's a mess. And I can't find things, like I've lost bills before and then I end up not paying them. And now I've got collection agencies on my back. I can't deal with all this, and I end up self-harming and going into the hospital. And then I just want to end it all. But it still doesn't seem to matter, because if I'm not in the mood to clean it, I won't.

T: So the fact that it makes horrible things happen in your life so far hasn't been enough of a motivation to get you to do things against your mood, right?

C: Well, obviously not (*laughs*), because it's not happening.

T: Doesn't that tell you, though, this is going to be a big problem, don't you think? This isn't going to be something simple. It's not like you're going to walk in here and I'm going to say, "OK, magic wand," and then all of a sudden you're going to want to do things that you're not in the mood for.

C: Yeah.

T: Yeah, so it seems to me that if you're not in the mood for things, if you're kind of mood-dependent, that's a very tough thing to crack. As a matter of fact, I think it's one of the hardest problems there is to deal with.

C: Yeah, great.

T: I think we could deal with it, but I think it's going to be hell. The real question is whether you're willing to go through hell to get where you want to get or not. Now I figure that's the question.

C: Well, if it's going to make me happier, yeah.

T: Are you sure?

C: Yeah, I've been going through this since I was 11 years old. I'm sick of this shit. I mean, excuse my language, but I really am, and I'm backed up against the wall. Either I need to do this, or I need to die. Those are my two choices.

T: Well, why not die?

C: Well, if it comes down to it, I will.

T: Um hmm, but why not now?

C: Because, this is my last hope. Because if I've got one last hope left, why not take it?

T: So, in other words, all things being equal, you'd rather live than die, if you can pull this off.

C: If I can pull it off, yeah.

T: OK, that's good; that's going to be your strength. We're going to play to that. You're going to have to remember that when it gets tough. But now I want to tell you about this program and how I feel about you harming yourself, and then we'll see if you still want to do this.

As illustrated by the foregoing segment, the therapist's relentless use of the devil's advocate strategy successfully "got a foot in the door" and achieved an initial client commitment. The therapist then "upped the ante" with a brief explanation of the program and its goals.

T: Now the most important thing to understand is that we are not a suicide prevention program; that's not our job. But we are a life enhancement program. The way we look at it, living a miserable life is no achievement. If we decide to work together, I'm going to help you try to improve your life, so that it's so good that you don't want to die or hurt yourself. You should also know that I look at suicidal behavior, including drinking Clorox, as problem-solving behavior. I think of alcoholism the same way. The only difference is that cutting, burning, unfortunately—it works. If it didn't work, nobody would do it more than once. But it only works in the short term, not the long term. So quitting cutting, trying to hurt yourself, is going to be exactly like quitting alcohol. Do you think this is going to be hard?

C: Stopping drinking wasn't all that hard.

T: Well, in my experience, giving up self-harm behavior is usually very hard. It will require both of us working, but you will have to work harder. And like I told you when we talked briefly, if you commit to this it's for 1 year. Individual therapy with me once a week, and group skills training once a week. So the question is, are you willing to commit for 1 year?

C: I said I'm sick of this stuff. That's why I'm here.

T: So you've agreed to not drop out of therapy for a year, right?

C: Right.

T: And you do realize that if you don't drop out for a year, that really does, if you think about it, rule out suicide for a year?

C: Logically, yeah.

T: So we need to be absolutely clear about this, because this therapy won't work if you knock yourself off. The most fundamental mood-related goal we have to work on is that, no matter what your mood is, you won't kill yourself or try to.

C: All right.

T: So that's what I see as our number one priority—not our only one but our number one—that we will work on that. And getting you to agree—meaningfully, of course—and actually following through on staying alive and not harming yourself and not attempting suicide, no matter what your mood is. Now the question is whether you agree to that.

C: Yes, I agree to that.

The therapist thus successfully obtained the client's commitment to work on suicidal behavior. To reinforce the strength of the commitment, she again employed the strategy of devil's advocate.

T: Why would you agree to that?

C: I don't know. (*Laughs*)

T: I mean, wouldn't you rather be in a therapy where if you wanted to kill yourself, you could?

C: I don't know. I mean, I never really thought about it that way.

T: Hmmm.

C: I don't want to . . . I want to be able to get to the point where I could feel like I'm not being forced into living.

T: So are you agreeing with me because you're feeling forced into agreeing?

C: You keep asking me all these questions.

T: What do you think?

C: I don't know what I think right now, honestly.

A necessary and important skill for the therapist conducting DBT is the ability to sense when a client has been pushed to his/her limits, as well as the concomitant skill of being willing and able to step back and at least temporarily refrain from further pressuring. In these instances, continued pressure from the therapist is likely to boomerang and have the opposite effect of what the therapist intends. Here the client's confusion was noticed by the therapist, who sensed that further pushing was likely to result in the client's falling back on the strength of her commitment. Consequently, the therapist stepped back and moved in with validation.

T: So you're feeling pushed up against the wall a little bit, by me?

C: No, not really. (*Starts to cry*)

T: What just happened just now?

C: (*Pause*) I don't know. I mean, I don't think I really want to kill myself. I think I just feel like I have to. I don't think it's really even a mood thing. I just think it's when I feel like there's no other choice. I just say, "Well, you know there's no other choice, so do it." You know. And so right now, I don't see any ray of hope. I'm going to therapy, which I guess is good. I mean, I know it's good, but I don't see anything any better than it was the day I tried to kill myself.

T: Well, that's probably true. Maybe it isn't any better. I mean, trying to kill yourself doesn't usually solve problems. Although it actually did do one thing for you.

C: It got me in therapy.

T: Yeah. So my asking you all these questions makes you start to cry. You look like you must be feeling pretty bad.

C: Just overwhelmed, I guess the word is.

T: That's part of the reason we're having this conversation, to try to structure our relationship so that it's very clear for both of us. And that way, at least, we'll try to cut down on how much you get overwhelmed by not knowing what's going on with me. OK?

C: Um hmm.

T: And so I just want to be clear on what our number one goal is, and how hard this is, because if you want to back out, now's the time. Because I'm going to take you seriously if you say, "Yes, I want to do it."

C: I don't want to back out.

T: OK. Good. Now I just want to say that this seems like a good idea right now. You're in kind of an energized mood today, getting started, a new program. But in 5 hours, it might not seem like such a good idea. It's kind of like it's easy to commit to a diet after a big meal, but much harder when you're hungry. But we're going to work on how to make it keep sounding like a good idea. It'll be hell, but I have confidence. I think we can be successful working together.

Note how the therapist ended the session by preparing the client for the difficulties she was likely to experience in keeping her commitment and working in therapy. Cheerleading and relationship enhancement laid the foundation for a strong therapeutic alliance.

The following session occurred approximately 4 months into therapy. The session target was suicidal behavior. The strategies used were validation, problem solving (con-

tingency clarification, didactic information, behavioral analysis, and solution analysis), stylistic (irreverent communication), dialectical (metaphor, making lemonade out of lemons), and skills training (distress tolerance). The therapist reviewed the client's diary card and noted a recent parasuicide in which the client opened up a previously self-inflicted wound following her physician's refusal to provide pain medication. The therapist began by proceeding with a behavioral analysis.

T: OK. Now you were in here last week telling me you were never going to hurt yourself again because this was so ridiculous, you couldn't stand it, you couldn't hurt yourself any more. So let's figure out how that broke down on Sunday, so we can learn something from it. OK. So when did you start having urges to hurt yourself?

C: My foot began to hurt on Wednesday. I started to have a lot of pain.

T: It hadn't hurt before that?

C: No.

T: So the nerves were dead before that or something, huh? So you started having a lot of pain. Now when did you start having the pain, and when did the urge to harm yourself come?

C: At the same time.

T: They just come at the identical moment?

C: Just about.

The specification of an initial prompting environmental event is always the first step in conducting a behavioral chain analysis. Here the therapist began by directly inquiring when the urges toward parasuicide began. Note also the therapist's use of irreverent communication early in the session.

T: So how is it that feeling pain sets off an urge to parasuicide? Do you know how that goes? How you get from one to the other?

C: I don't know. Maybe it wasn't till Thursday, but I asked my nurse. I go, "Look, I'm in a lot of pain, you know. I'm throwing up my food because the pain is so bad." And the nurse tried. She called the doctor and told him I was in a lot of pain, and asked if he'd give me some painkillers. But no! So I kept asking, and the answer kept being no, and I got madder and madder and madder. So I felt like I had to show somebody that it hurts, because they didn't believe me.

T: So let's figure this out. So is it that you're assuming that if someone believed it hurt as bad as you said it does, they would actually give you the painkillers?

C: Yes.

T: OK. That's where the faulty thinking is. That's the problem. You see, it's entirely possible that people know how bad the pain is, but still aren't giving you medication.

C: I believe firmly, and I even wrote it in my journal, that if I'd gotten pain medication when I really needed it, I wouldn't have even thought of self-harming.

The therapist proceeded by beginning to obtain a description of the events co-occurring with the onset of the problem. Here it became apparent that maladaptive thinking was instrumental in the client's decision to self-harm. In the following segment, the therapist used the dialectical strategy of metaphor to highlight for the client her cognitive error.

T: Now let me ask you something. You've got to imagine this, OK? Let's imagine that you and I are on a raft together out in the middle of the ocean. Our boat has sunk and we're on the raft. And when the boat sunk, your leg got cut really badly. And together we've wrapped it up as well as we can. But we don't have any pain medicine. And we're on this raft together and your leg really hurts, and you ask me for pain medicine, and I say no. Do you think you would then have an urge to hurt yourself and make it worse?

C: No, it would be a different situation.

T: OK, but if I did have the pain medication and I said no because we have to save it, what do you think?

C: If that were logical to me, I'd go along with it and wouldn't want to hurt myself.

T: What if I said no, because I didn't want you to be a drug addict?

C: I'd want to hurt myself.

T: OK. So we've got this clear. The pain is not what's setting off the desire to self-harm. It's someone not giving you something to help, when you feel they could if they wanted to.

C: Yes.

The therapist used contingency clarification to point out to the client the effects of others' responses on the client's own behavior. In the following segment, the therapist again employed contingency clarification in a continued effort to highlight for the client the communication function of parasuicide.

T: OK. So in other words, hurting yourself is communication behavior, OK? So what we have to do is figure out a way for the communication behavior to quit working.

C: Why?

T: Because you're not going to stop doing it until it quits working. It's like trying to talk to someone; if there's no one in the room, you eventually quit trying to talk to them. It's like when a phone goes dead, you quit talking.

C: I tried three nights in a row in a perfectly assertive way and just clearly stated I was in a lot of pain.

T: You know, I think I'll switch chairs with you. You're not hearing what I'm saying.

C: And they kept saying, "No," and then some little light came on in my head.

T: I'm considering switching chairs with you.

C: And it was like, "Here, now can you tell that it hurts a lot?"

T: I'm thinking of switching chairs with you.

C: Why?

T: Because if you were sitting over here, I think you would see that no matter how bad the pain is, hurting yourself to get pain medication is not a reasonable response. The hospital staff may not have been reasonable either. It may be that they should have given you pain medicine. But we don't have to say they were wrong in order to say that hurting yourself was not the appropriate response.

C: No, I don't think it was the appropriate response.

T: Good. So what we've got to do is figure out a way to get it so that the response doesn't come in, even if you don't get pain medicine. So far, it has worked very effectively as communication. And the only way to stop it is to get it to not work any more. And of course, it would be good to get other things to work. What you're arguing is "Well, OK, if I'm not going to get it this way, then I should be able to get it another way."

C: I tried this time!

T: Yes, I know you did, I know you did.

C: A lady down the hallway from me was getting treatment for her diabetes, and it got real bad, and they gave her pain medication.

T: Now we're not on the same wavelength in this conversation.

C: Yes, we are. What wavelength are you on?

T: I'm on the wavelength that it may have been reasonable for you to get pain medicine, and I certainly understand your wanting it. But I'm also saying that no matter what's going on, hurting yourself is something we don't want to happen. You're functioning like if I agreed with you that you should get pain medication, I would think this was OK.

C: Hmmm?

T: You're talking about whether they should have given you pain medication or not. I'm not talking about that. Even if they should have, we've got to figure out how you could have gotten through without hurting yourself.

As illustrated by the foregoing exchange, a client with BPD will often want to remain focused on the crisis at hand. This poses a formidable challenge for the therapist, who must necessarily engage in a back-and-forth dance between validating the client's pain and pushing for behavioral change. This segment also illustrates how validation does not necessarily imply agreement. Although the therapist validated the client's perception that the refusal to provide pain medication may have been unreasonable, she remained steadfast in maintaining the inappropriateness of the client's response.

C: I tried some of those distress tolerance things and they didn't work.

T: OK. Don't worry, we'll figure out a way. I want to know everything you tried. But first I want to be sure I have the picture clear. Did the urges start building after Wednesday and get worse over time?

C: Yeah. They started growing with the pain.

T: With the pain. OK. But also they started growing with their continued refusal to give you pain medicine. So you were thinking that if you hurt yourself, they would somehow give you pain medicine?

C: Yeah. 'Cause if they wouldn't listen to me, then I could show them.

T: OK, so you were thinking, "If they won't listen to me, I'll show them." And when did that idea first hit? Was that on Wednesday?

C: Yeah.

T: OK. Well, we've got to figure out a way to tolerate bad things without harming yourself. So let's figure out all the things you tried, and then we have to figure out some other things because those didn't work. So what was the first thing you tried?

At this juncture the behavioral analysis remained incomplete, and it would normally be premature to move to the stage of solution analysis. However, in the therapist's judgment, it was more critical at this point to reinforce the client's attempts at distress tolerance by responding to the client's communication that she attempted behavioral skills.

C: I thought that if I just continued to be assertive about it that the appropriate measures would be taken.

T: OK, but that didn't work. So why didn't you harm yourself right then?

C: I didn't want to.

T: Why didn't you want to?

C: I didn't want to make it worse.

T: So you were thinking about pros and cons —that if I make it worse, I'll feel worse?

C: Yeah.

One aspect of DBT skills training stresses the usefulness of evaluating the pros and cons of tolerating distress as a crisis survival strategy. Here the therapist employed the dialectical strategy of turning lemons into lemonade by highlighting for the client how she did, in fact, use behavioral skills. Note in the following response how the therapist immediately reinforced the client's efforts with praise.

T: That's good thinking. That's when you're thinking about the advantages and disadvantages of doing it. OK, so at that point the advantages of making it worse were outweighed by the disadvantages. OK. So you keep up the good fight here. Now what else did you try?

C: I tried talking about it with other patients.

T: And what did they have to say?

C: They said I should get pain medication.

T: Right. But did they say you should cut yourself or hurt yourself if you didn't get it?

C: No. And I tried to get my mind off my pain by playing music and using mindfulness. I tried to read and do crossword puzzles.

T: Um hmm. Did you ever try radical acceptance?

C: What's that?

T: It's where you sort of let go and accept the fact that you're not going to get the pain medication. And you just give yourself up to that situation. You just accept that it ain't going to happen, that you're going to have to cope in some other way.

C: Which I did yesterday. I needed a little Ativan to get me there, but I got there.

T: Yesterday?

C: Yeah. I took a nap. When I woke up I basically said, "Hey, they're not going to change, so you've just got to deal with this the best that you can."

T: And did that acceptance help some?

C: I'm still quite angry about what I believe is discrimination against borderline personalities. I'm still very angry about that.

T: OK. That's fine. Did it help, though, to accept?

C: Um hmm.

T: That's good. That's great. That's a great skill, a great thing to practice. When push comes to shove, when you're really at the limit, when it's the worst it can be, radical acceptance is the skill to practice.

C: That's AA.

During a solution analysis, it is often necessary that therapists facilitate the process by helping the client "brainstorm" or by making direct suggestions for handling future crises. Here the therapist suggested a solution that is also taught in the DBT skills training module on distress tolerance. The notion of radical acceptance stresses the idea that acceptance of one's pain is a necessary prerequisite for ending emotional suffering.

T: OK. Now let's go back to how did you give in to the urge. Because you really managed to battle all the way till then, right? OK. Usually with you we can assume that something else happened. So let's figure out Sunday and see if there wasn't an interpersonal situation on that day that made you feel criticized, unloved, or unacceptable.

C: Well, on Saturday I was so pissed off and I went to an AA meeting. And it got on my brain how alcohol would steal away my pain. I went looking all around the neighborhood for an open store. I was going to go get drunk. That's how much my pain was influencing me. But I couldn't find a store that was open, so I went back to the hospital.

T: So you got the idea of getting alcohol to cure it, and you couldn't find any, so you went back to the hospital. You were in a lot of pain, and then what happened?

C: I told the nurse, "I've been sober almost 10 years and this is the first urge I've had to drink; that's how bad my pain is." And that wasn't listened to.

T: So you figured that should have done it?

C: Yeah.

T: Yeah. 'Cause that's a high-level communication, that's like a suicide threat. Very good, though. I want you to know, that's better than a suicide threat, because that means you had moved your threats down.

The response above was very irreverent, in that most clients would not expect their therapists to view making a threat as a sign of therapeutic progress. The therapeutic utility of irreverence often lies in its "shock" value, which may temporarily loosen a client's maladaptive beliefs and assumptions and open the client up to the possibility of other response solutions.

C: And I just told her how I was feeling about it, and I thought that would do it. And the doctor still wouldn't budge.

T: So what did she do? Did she say she would call?

C: She called.

T: OK. And then what happened?

C: She came back. She was really sweet, and she just said, "I'm really sorry, but the doctor said no."

T: Then did you feel anger?

C: I don't know if I was really angry, but I was hurt.

T: Oh, really? Oh, that's pretty interesting. OK. So you were hurt . . .

C: Because I ended up hugging my teddy bear and just crying for a while.

T: Before or after you decided to hurt yourself?

C: Before.

T: OK. So you didn't decide right away to hurt yourself. You were thinking about it. But when did you decide to do it?

C: Later on Saturday.

T: When?

C: After I got sick of crying.

T: So you laid in bed and cried, feeling uncared about and hurt, abandoned probably, and unlovable, like you weren't worth helping?

C: Yes.

T: That's a really adaptive response. That's what I'm going to try to teach you. Except that you've already done it without my teaching it to you. So how did you get from crying, feeling unloved and not cared about, and you cry and sob— how did you get from there to deciding to hurt yourself, instead of like going to sleep . . .

C: Because then I got angry. And I said, "Fuck this shit, I'll show him."

T: Now did you quit crying before you got angry, or did getting angry make you stop crying?

C: I think getting angry made me stop crying.

T: So you kind of got more energized. So you must have been ruminating while you were lying there, thinking. What were you thinking about?

C: For a long time I was just wanting somebody to come care about me.

T: Um hmm. Perfectly reasonable feelings. Makes complete sense. Now maybe there you could have done something different. What would have happened if you had asked the nurse to come in and talk to you, hold your hand?

An overall goal of behavioral analysis is the construction of a general road map of how the client arrives at dysfunctional responses, notated with possible alternative pathways. Here the therapist was searching for junctures in the map where possible alternative responses were available to the client.

C: They don't have time to do that.

T: They don't? Do you think that would have helped?

C: I don't know. She couldn't help me.

T: She could have made you feel cared about. That would have been a caring thing to do.

C: Yeah, but I don't think it would have helped.

T: What would have helped?

C: Getting pain medication.

T: I thought you'd say that. You have a one-track mind. Now listen, we've got to figure out something else to help you, because it can't be that nothing else can help. That can't be the way the world works for you. There's got to be more than one way to get everywhere, because we all run into boulders on the path. Life is like walking on a path, you know, and we all run into boulders. It's got to be that there are other paths to places. And for you, it really isn't the pain in your ankle that's the problem; it's the feeling of not being cared about. And probably a feeling that has something to do with anger, or a feeling that other people don't respect you—a feeling of being invalidated.

C: Yes.

T: So I think it's not actually the pain in your ankle that's the problem. Because if you were out on that raft with me, you would have been able to handle the pain if I hadn't had any medicine, right? So it's really not the pain; it's the sense of being invalidated and the sense of not being cared about. That's my guess. Do you think that's correct?

C: Yes.

T: See, the question is, is there any other way for you to feel validated and cared about other than them giving it to you?

C: No.

T: Now is this a definite, like "I'm not going to let there be any other way," or is it more open, like, "I can't think of another way, but I'm open to the possibility"?

C: I don't think there's another way.

T: Does that mean you're not even open to learning another way?

C: Like what?

T: I don't know. We have to figure it out. See, what I think is happening is that when you're in a lot of pain and you feel either not cared about or not taken seriously, invalidated, that's what sets you up to hurt yourself, and also want to die. The problem that we have to solve is how to be in a situation that you feel is unjust without having to harm yourself to solve it. Are you open to that?

C: Yeah.

As illustrated above, behavioral analysis is often an excruciating and laborious process for client and therapist alike. The therapist will often feel demoralized and tempted to abandon the effort, which may be likened to trying to find a pair of footprints hidden beneath layers of fallen leaves; the footprints are there, but it may take much raking and gathering of leaves before they are uncovered. With repeated analyses, however, the client learns that the therapist will not "back down." Such persistence on the part of the therapist will eventually extinguish a client's refusal to attempt new and adaptive problem-solving behaviors. As clients increasingly acquire new behavioral skills, more adaptive attempts at problem resolution will eventually become discernible.

In the following session (approximately 10 months into therapy), the client arrived wearing mirrored sunglasses (again) and was angry because collection agencies were persistent in pressuring her for payment on delinquent accounts. In addition, her therapist had been out of town for a week. The session targets were emotion regulation and interpersonal effectiveness. The strategies used were dialectical (metaphor), validation (cheerleading), problem solving (contingency clarification, contingency management), stylistic (reciprocal communication, irreverent communication), and integrated (relationship enhancement). In this first segment, the therapist used cheerleading, contingency clarification, and the contingency management strategy of shaping to bring the client to remove her sunglasses and work on expressing her anger.

T: It's not a catastrophe that the collector did this to you, and it's not a catastrophe to be mad at the collector. It's made your life a lot harder, but you can handle this, you can cope with this. This is not more than you can cope with. You're a really strong woman; you've got it inside you. But you've got to do it. You've got to use it. I'm willing to help you, but I can't do it alone. You have to work with me.

C: How?

T: Well, by taking off your sunglasses, for starters.

The therapist began the exchange by attempting to normalize the issue ("It's not a catastrophe . . ."), validating the client ("It's made your life a lot harder . . ."), and cheerleading (". . . you can handle this, you can cope . . . You're a really strong woman . . ."). The therapist then moved to contingency clarification by pointing out that provision of the therapist's assistance was contingent on the client's willingness to work. The therapist immediately followed this by requesting a response well within the client's behavioral repertoire.

C: I knew you'd say that.

T: And I knew you knew I'd say that.

C: Sunglasses are your biggest bitch, I think.

T: Well, how would you like to look at yourself talking to someone else? (*Long pause*) They make it difficult for me. And I figure they make it harder for you. I think you do better when you're not wearing those sunglasses. It's like a step; you always do better when you go forward. And when you do, you feel better. I've noticed that. (*Long pause*) So that's what you should do; you should take off your sunglasses, and then we should problem-solve on how to cope when you can't get angry. There's nothing freakish about that. Something has happened in your life that has made it so that you're afraid to be angry, and we just have to deal with that, you and me. It's just a problem to be solved. It's not a catastrophe; it's not the worst thing anyone ever did. It's just a problem that you have, and that's what you and I do. We solve problems; we're a problem-solving team. (*Pause*)

C: (*Removes sunglasses*) All right.

T: Thank you. That's a big step, I know, for you.

The therapist's use of reciprocal communication informed the client of her feelings regarding the sunglasses. Note the matter-of-fact attitude taken by the therapist and the therapist's continued attempt to normalize the issue (i.e., "There's nothing freakish about that . . . it's not the worst thing anyone ever did"). Also note the framing of the issue as a problem to be solved, as well as the therapist's use of the relationship strategy to enhance the therapeutic alliance. The therapist also made a point of validating the client by letting her know that she realized this was difficult.

T: Now, c'mon, I want you to find it inside yourself. I know you've got it; I know you can do it. You can't give up. You can't let your feet slip. Keep going. Just express directly to me how you feel. That you're angry at yourself, that you're angry at the collection agency, and that you're damn angry with me. (*Long pause*)

C: (*Barely audible*) I'm angry at you, at myself, and the collection agency.

The therapist continued to rely on cheerleading and praise as she continued the shaping process in an attempt to bring the client to express her anger directly.

T: Good, that kill you? (*Long pause*) That's great. Is that hard? (*Long pause*) It was,

wasn't it? Now say it with a little vigor. Can't you say it with a little energy?

C: (*Shakes her head no*)

T: Yes, you can. I know you've got it in you. I have a good feel for what your strengths are. I don't know how I've got this good feel, but I do. And I know you can do it and you need to do it, and you need to say it with some energy. Express how angry you are. You don't have to yell and scream or throw things. Just say it aloud—"I'm angry!" (*Long pause*) You can scream, of course, if you want; you can say, "I'm angry!"

C: That's it. That's all I can do.

T: Listen, you have to take the risk. You're not going to get past this or through this. You have to take the risk. You are like a person mountain climbing and we've come to this crevasse and it's very deep, but we can't go back because there's an avalanche and the only way to go forward is for you to jump over this crevasse. You've got to do it. Tell me how mad you are, in a way that I can understand how you really feel.

C: (*Long pause*) I can't do any of it.

T: That is bullshit.

C: You want me to get angry at you, don't you?

T: I don't care who you get angry at. I think you already are angry. I just want you to express it. I'm not going to ask you to do anything more today, by the way. I figure the only thing today you have to do is say "I'm angry," in a voice that sounds angry, and I figure you're capable of that. And I might be angry if you don't do it. I don't think I will be, but I might. That's OK. I can be angry, you can be angry, we can be angry sometimes, and it isn't going to kill either one of us.

Cheerleading and metaphor were unsuccessful in moving the client to express her anger more forcefully. Consequently, the therapist switched to irreverent communication in an attempt to get the client to "jump track." Also note how the therapist communicated to the client the potential negative consequences of her continued refusal to express her anger (i.e., ". . . I might be angry . . ."). In this manner, the therapist used the relationship as a contingency in order to promote change in the client.

T: OK, so how angry are you? On a scale of 1 to 100, how angry would you say you are? At 100, you're ready to kill. You're so enraged, you'd go to war if you could.

C: (*Barely audible*) Maybe 100.

T: Really?

C: They know my situation.

T: Um hmm.

C: They're persistent.

T: Um hmm. (*Pause*) Who's the safest to be angry at? Yourself, me, or the collection agency?

C: Collection agency.

T: OK, then, tell me how angry you are. You don't have to make it sound like 100. Try to make it sound like 50.

C: They really pissed me off! (*Said in a loud, angry voice*)

T: Well, damn right. Piss me off, too.

As illustrated by the foregoing exchange, a primary difficulty in working with clients who have BPD is their not uncommon tendency to refuse to engage in behavioral work. Thus it is absolutely necessary that the therapist maintain persistence and not give up in the face of a client's "I can't" statements. In situations like these, the use of irreverent communication often succeeds in producing a breakthrough and gaining client compliance.

ACKNOWLEDGMENTS

The writing of this chapter was supported by National Institute of Mental Health Grant No. MH34486 to Marsha M. Linehan. Parts of this chapter are drawn from Linehan (1993a), Linehan and Koerner (1992), Koerner and Linehan (1992), and Linehan (1997). The quotations from Linehan (1997) in the section on validation are reprinted with the permission of the American Psychological Association.

NOTE

1. Between the writing of this case history and the publication of the second edition of this book, at 14 months into therapy, Cindy died of a pre-scription drug overdose plus alcohol. We considered dropping the case history for this edition and replacing it with a more successful case. However, in Cindy's honor and because we think much can be learned from failed as well as successful therapy, we have decided to leave the case in.

The immediate precipitant for Cindy's overdose was a call to her estranged husband, during which she discovered that another woman was living with him. As she told her therapist during a phone call the next morning, her unverbalized hope that they might someday get back together, or at least be close friends, had been shattered. She phoned again that evening, in tears, stating that she had just drunk half of a fifth of liquor. Such drinking incidents had occurred several times before, and the phone call was spent "remoralizing" her, offering hope, problem-solving how she could indeed live without her husband, and using crisis intervention techniques to get her through the evening until her appointment the following day. Her roommate was home, and she agreed to talk with her, watch a TV movie together, and go to bed (plans she did follow through on). She stated that although she felt suicidal, she would stop drinking and would not do anything self-destructive until her appointment. She was instructed to call the therapist back later that evening if she wanted to talk again. The next day, when Cindy did not arrive for her appointment, the therapist called her home just as her roommate discovered her dead, still in bed from the night before.

At this point, the therapist was faced with a number of tasks. The therapist called other therapists who had been treating the client to inform them, and spoke with a legal consultant to review the limits of confidentiality when a client has died. Once the family (Cindy's parents and estranged husband) were alerted, the therapist called each to offer her condolences. The next day, the therapist (who was the senior therapist and supervisor on the treatment team) called a meeting of the treatment team to discuss and process the suicide. It was especially important to notify the individual therapists of the remaining three members of Cindy's skills training group. Group members were notified of the suicide by their individual psychotherapists. Within minutes of the beginning of the next group session, however, two members became seriously suicidal, and one of them had to be briefly hospitalized. (By the third week following the suicide, however, both had regained their forward momentum.) A third group member took this occasion to quit DBT and switch to another therapy, saying that this proved the treatment did not work. In the days and weeks following the suicide, the therapist attended the funeral and met with Cindy's roommate and with her parents.

What can we learn from this suicide? First, it is important to note that even when a treatment protocol is followed almost to the letter, it may not save a client. Even an effective treatment can fail in the end. In this case, DBT failed. This does not mean that the progress made was unimportant or not real. Had this "slippery spot over the abyss" been negotiated safely, perhaps the client would have been able to develop, finally, a life of quality. Risk is not eliminated, however, just because an individual makes substantial progress. In this case, the therapist did not believe during the last phone call that the client was at higher than ordinary risk for imminent suicide. In contrast to many previous phone calls and therapy sessions in which the client had cried that she might not be able to hold on, during the last call the client made plans for the evening, agreed to stop drinking and not to do anything suicidal or self-destructive, and seemed to the therapist (and the roommate) to be in better spirits following the phone call. Her roommate was home and available. Thus the therapist did not take extraordinary measures that evening to prevent suicide. Indeed, the problem behavior focused on during the call was the drinking. The topic of suicide was brought up by the therapist in the course of conducting a risk assessment. Could the therapist have known? Only (perhaps) if the therapist had paid more attention to the precipitant and less to the affect expressed at the end of the phone call. In reviewing notes about the client, the therapist saw that each previous near-lethal attempt was a result of the client's believing that the relationship with her husband had irrevocably ended. Although the client could tolerate losing her husband, she could not tolerate losing all hope for a reconciliation at some point, even many years hence. Had the therapist linked these two ideas (complete loss of hope and suicide attempt), she might have been able to work out a better plan with the client for a reemergence of the crisis later in the evening. The value of both conducting thorough behavioral assessments and organizing them into a coherent pattern is highlighted in this case.

Second, when all is said and done, an individual with BPD must ultimately be able and willing to tolerate the almost unimaginable pain of his/her life until the therapy has a chance to make a permanent difference. Ultimately, the therapist cannot save the client; only the client can do that. Even if mistakes are made, the client must nonetheless persevere. In this case, the DBT protocol of "no lethal drugs for lethal people" was violated, even though the client had a past history of near-lethal overdoses. Why was the protocol not enforced? There were two primary reasons. First, the client came into therapy with a strong belief that the host of medications she was on were essential to her survival. Any attempt on the therapist's part to

manage her medications would have been met by very strong resistance. Although the drugs were dispensed in small doses, the only safe alternative would have been to have the person living with her (her husband at first, and then her roommate) manage her medications, which the client also resisted. In addition, the "no lethal drugs" protocol of DBT is regularly criticized by some mental health professionals, who believe that psychoactive medications are a treatment of choice for suicidal individuals. In the face of professional and client resistance to the policy, in this case the therapist relented. The second reason was that the lethal behavior of the client during therapy consisted of cutting and slashing; thus her using drugs to commit suicide did not seem likely, and the therapist allowed herself a false sense of safety with respect to them.

Third, a group member's suicide is extraordinarily stressful for clients with BPD who are in group therapy. Although it is easy to believe that alliances are not strong in a psychoeducational behavioral skills group, this has universally not been our experience. The suicide of one member is a catastrophic event and can lead to contagious parasuicide, suicide, and therapy dropouts. Thus extreme care is needed in conducting group meetings for some time following a suicide. Similar care is needed with the treatment team, where the thread of hope that maintains therapists in the face of a daunting task is also strained. It is important that the personal reactions of therapists, as well as a period of mourning and grieving, be shared and accepted. Fears of legal responsibility, never far from the surface, must be confronted directly; legal counsel must be sought as necessary; and, in time, a careful review of the case and the therapy must be conducted, if only to improve treatment in the future.

REFERENCES

Adler, G. (1981). The borderline–narcissistic personality disorder continuum. *American Journal of Psychiatry, 138,* 46–50.

Adler, G. (1985). *Borderline psychopathology and its treatment.* New York: Jason Aronson.

Adler, G., & Buie, D. H. (1979). Aloneness and borderline psychopathology: The possible relevance of child development issues. *International Journal of Psychoanalytic Psychotherapy, 60,* 83–96.

American Psychiatric Association. (1987). *Diagnostic and statistical manual of mental disorders* (3rd ed., rev.). Washington, DC: Author.

American Psychiatric Association. (1994). *Diagnostic and statistical manual of mental disorders* (4th ed.). Washington, DC: Author.

Bateman, A., & Fonagy, P. (1999). Effectiveness of partial hospitalization in the treatment of borderline personality disorder: A randomized controlled trial. *American Journal of Psychiatry, 156*, 1563–1569.

Beck, A. T., Rush, A. J., Shaw, B. F., & Emery, G. (1979). *Cognitive therapy of depression.* New York: Guilford Press.

Beck, A. T., Freeman, A., & Associates. (1990). *Cognitive therapy of personality disorders.* New York: Guilford Press.

Benjamin, L. S. (1974). Structural Analysis of Social Behavior. *Psychological Review, 81*, 392–425.

Benjamin, L. S. (1979). Structural analysis of differentiation failure. *Psychiatry, 42*, 1–23.

Benjamin, L. S. (1996). *Interpersonal diagnosis and treatment of personality disorders* (2nd ed.). New York: Guilford Press.

Brent, D. A., Johnson, B. A., Perper, J., Connolly, J., Bridge, J., Bartle, S., & Rather, C. (1994). Personality disorder, personality traits, impulsive violence, and completed suicide in adolescents. *Journal of the American Academy of Child and Adolescent Psychiatry, 33*, 1080–1086.

Bryer, J. B., Nelson, B. A., Miller, J. B., & Kroll, P. A. (1987). Childhood sexual and physical abuse as factors in adult psychiatric illness. *American Journal of Psychiatry, 144*, 1426–1430.

Buie, D. H., & Adler, G. (1982). Definitive treatment of the borderline personality. *International Journal of Psychoanalytic Psychotherapy, 9*, 51–87.

Clarkin, J. F., Marziali, E., & Munroe-Blum, H. (1991). Group and family treatments for borderline personality disorder. *Hospital and Community Psychiatry, 42*, 1038–1043.

Clarkin, J. F., Widiger, T. A., Frances, A. J., Hurt, S. W., & Gilmore, M. (1983). Prototypic typology and the borderline personality disorder. *Journal of Abnormal Psychology, 92*, 263–275.

Cornelius, J. R., Soloff, P. H., George, A., Ulrich, R. F., & Perel, J. M. (1993). Haloperidol vs. phenelzine in continuation therapy of borderline disorder. *Psychopharmacology Bulletin, 29*, 333–337.

Cowdry, R. W., & Gardner, D. L. (1988). Pharmacotherapy of borderline personality disorder: Alprazolam, carbamazepine, trifluoperazine, and tranylcypromine. *Archives of General Psychiatry, 45*, 111–119.

Cowdry, R. W., Pickar, D., & Davies, R. (1985). Symptoms and EEG findings in the borderline syndrome. *International Journal of Psychiatry and Medicine, 15*, 202–211.

Dimeff, L. A., McDavid, J., & Linehan, M. M. (1999). Pharmacotherapy for borderline personality disorder: A review of the literature and recommendations for treatment. *Journal of Clinical Psychology in Medical Settings, 6*, 113–138.

Ellis, A. (1962). *Reason and emotion in psychotherapy.* New York: Lyle Stuart.

Ellis, A. (1973). *Humanistic psychotherapy: The rational–emotive approach.* New York: Julian Press.

Faltus, F. (1984). The positive effect of alprazolam in the treatment of three patients with borderline personality disorder. *American Journal of Psychiatry, 141*, 802–803.

Foa, E. B., & Kozak, M. J. (1986). Emotional processing of fear: Exposure to corrective information. *Psychological Bulletin, 99*, 20–35.

Foa, E. B., Steketee, G., & Grayson, J. B. (1985). Imaginal and in vivo exposure: A comparison with obsessive–compulsive checkers. *Behavior Therapy, 16*, 292–302.

Fossati, A., Madeddu, F., & Maffei, C. (1999). Borderline personality and childhood sexual abuse: A meta-analytic study. *Journal of Personality Disorders, 13*, 268–280.

Gardner, D. L., & Cowdry, R. W. (1986). Alprazolam-induced dyscontrol in borderline personality disorder. *American Journal of Psychiatry, 143*, 519–522.

Gardner, D. L., & Cowdry, R. W. (1989). Pharmacotherapy of borderline personality disorder: A review. *Psychopharmacology Bulletin, 25*, 515–523.

Goldberg, C. (1980). The utilization and limitations of paradoxical intervention in group psychotherapy. *International Journal of Group Psychotherapy, 30*, 287–297.

Gottman, J. M., & Katz, L. F. (1990). Effects of marital discord on young children's peer interaction and health. *Developmental Psychology, 25*, 373–381.

Gunderson, J. G. (1984). *Borderline personality disorder.* Washington, DC: American Psychiatric Press.

Gunderson, J. G., & Kolb, J. E. (1978). Discriminating features of borderline patients. *American Journal of Psychiatry, 135*, 792–796.

Gunderson, J. G., Kolb, J. E., & Austin, V. (1981). The Diagnostic Interview for Borderlines. *American Journal of Psychiatry, 138*, 896–903.

Herman, J. L. (1986). Histories of violence in an outpatient population. *American Journal of Orthopsychiatry, 56*, 137–141.

Herman, J. L., Perry, J. C., & van der Kolk, B. A. (1989). Childhood trauma in borderline personality disorder. *American Journal of Psychiatry, 146*, 490–495.

Hollandsworth, J. G., Jr. (1990). *The physiology of psychological disorders.* New York: Plenum Press.

Isometsa, E. T., Heikkinen, M. E., Henriksson, M. M., Marttunen, M. J., Aro, H., & Lonnqvist, J. K. (1997). Differences between urban and rural suicides. *Acta Psychiatrica Scandinavica, 95*, 297–305.

Isometsa, E. T., Henriksson, M. M., Heikkinen, M. E., Aro, H. M., Marttunen, M. J., Kuoppasalmi, K. I., & Lonnqvist, J. K. (1996). Suicide among subjects with personality disorders. *American Journal of Psychiatry, 153*, 667–673.

Kavoussi, R. J., Liu, J., & Coccaro, E. F. (1994). An open trial of sertraline in personality disordered patients with impulsive aggression. *Journal of Clinical Psychiatry, 55*, 137–141.

Kegan, R. (1982). *The evolving self: Problem and process in human development.* Cambridge, MA: Harvard University Press.

Kernberg, O. F. (1975). *Borderline conditions and pathological narcissism.* New York: Jason Aronson.

Kernberg, O. F. (1984). *Severe personality disorders.* New Haven, CT: Yale University Press.

Kernberg, O. F., Burstein, E., Coyne, L., Appelbaum, A., Horwitz, L., & Voth, H. (1972). Psychotherapy and psychoanalysis: Final report of the Menninger Foundation's Psychotherapy Research Project. *Bulletin of the Menninger Clinic, 36*, 1–275.

Kernberg, O. F., Selzer, M. A., Koenigsberg, H. W., Carr, A. C., & Applebaum, A. H. (1989). *Psychodynamic psychotherapy of borderline patients.* New York: Basic Books.

Koerner, K., & Dimeff, L. A. (2000). Further data on dialectical behavior therapy. *Clinical Psychology: Science and Practice, 7,* 104–112.

Koerner, K., & Linehan, M. M. (1992). Integrative therapy for borderline personality disorder: Dialectical behavior therapy. In J. C. Norcross & M. R. Goldfried (Eds.), *Handbook of psychotherapy integration* (pp. 433–459). New York: Basic Books.

Koerner, K., & Linehan, M. M. (2000). Research on dialectical behavior therapy for patients with borderline personality disorder. *Psychiatric Clinics of North America, 23,* 151–167.

Kohlenberg, R. J., & Tsai, M. (1991). *Functional analytic psychotherapy: Creating intense and curative therapeutic relationship.* New York: Plenum Press.

Kohut, H., & Wolf, E. (1978). The disorders of the self and their treatment: An outline. *International Journal of Psycho-Analysis, 59,* 413–425.

Koons, C. R., Robins, C. J., Tweed, J. L., Lynch, T. R., Gonzalez, A. M., Morse, J. Q., Bishop, G. K., Butterfield, M. I., & Bastian, L. A. (in press). Efficacy of dialectical behavior therapy with borderline women veterans: A randomized controlled trial. *Behavior Therapy.*

Kyokai, B. D. (1966). *The teachings of Buddha.* Tokyo: Bukkyo Dendo Kyokai.

Langley, M. H. (1994). *Self-management therapy for borderline personality disorder: a therapist-guided approach.* New York: Springer.

Lesage, A. D., Boyer, R., Grunberg, F., Vanier, C., Morissette, R., Menard-Buteau, C., & Loyer, M. (1994). Suicide and mental disorders: A case–control study of young men. *American Journal of Psychiatry, 151,* 1063–1068.

Linehan, M. M. (1987a). Dialectical behavior therapy: A cognitive behavioral approach to parasuicide. *Journal of Personality Disorders, 1,* 328–333.

Linehan, M. M. (1987b). Dialectical behavior therapy for borderline personality disorder: Theory and method. *Bulletin of the Menninger Clinic, 51,* 261–276.

Linehan, M. M. (1989). Cognitive and behavior therapy for borderline personality disorder. In A. Tasman, R. E. Hales, & A. J. Frances (Eds.), *Review of psychiatry* (Vol. 8, pp. 84–102). Washington, DC: American Psychiatric Press.

Linehan, M. M. (1993a). *Cognitive-behavioral treatment of borderline personality disorder.* New York: Guilford Press.

Linehan, M. M. (1993b). *Skills training manual for treating borderline personality disorder.* New York: Guilford Press.

Linehan, M. M. (1997). Validation and psychotherapy. In A. Bohart & L. Greenberg (Eds.), *Empathy reconsidered: New directions in psychotherapy* (pp. 353–392). Washington, DC: American Psychological Association.

Linehan, M. M., Armstrong, H. E., Suarez, A., Allmon, D., & Heard, H. L. (1991). Cognitive-behavioral treatment of chronically parasuicidal borderline patients. *Archives of General Psychiatry, 48,* 1060–1064.

Linehan, M. M., Heard, H. L., & Armstrong, H. E. (1993). Naturalistic follow-up of a behavioral treatment for chronically parasuicidal borderline patients. *Archives of General Psychiatry, 50,* 971–974.

Linehan, M. M., & Koerner, K. (1992). A behavioral theory of borderline personality disorder. In J. Paris (Ed.), *Borderline personality disorder: Etiology and treatment* (pp. 103–121). Washington, DC: American Psychiatric Association.

Linehan, M. M., Rizvi, S. L., Welch, S. S., & Page, B. (2000). Psychiatric aspects of suicidal behaviour: Personality disorders. In K. Hawton & K. van Heeringen (Eds.), *International handbook of suicide and attempted suicide* (pp. 147–178). Chichester, UK: Wiley.

Linehan, M. M., Schmidt, H. I., Dimeff, L. A., Craft, J. C., Kanter, J., & Comtois, K. A. (1999). Dialectical behavior therapy for patients with borderline personality disorder and drug-dependence. *American Journal on Addictions, 8,* 279–292.

Linehan, M. M., Tutek, D., & Heard, H. L. (1992, November). *Interpersonal and social treatment outcomes for borderline personality disorder.* Poster presented at the 26th Annual Convention of the Association for Advancement of Behavior Therapy, Boston.

Links, P. S., Steiner, M., Boiago, I., & Irwin, D. (1990). Lithium therapy for borderline patients: Preliminary findings. *Journal of Personality Disorders, 4,* 173–181.

Marlatt, G. A., & Gordon, J. R. (Eds.). (1985). *Relapse prevention: Maintenance strategies in the treatment of addictive behaviors.* New York: Guilford Press.

Marziali, E. A., & Munroe-Blum, H. (1987). A group approach: The management of projective identification in group treatment of self-destructive borderline patients. *Journal of Personality Disorders, 1,* 340–343.

Masterson, J. (1976). *Psychotherapy of the borderline adult.* New York: Brunner/Mazel.

Masterson, J. (1981). *The narcissistic and borderline disorders.* New York: Brunner/Mazel.

Merriam-Webster's new universal unabridged dictionary. (1983). Cleveland, OH: Dorset & Baber.

Millon, T. (1987). On the genesis and prevalence of the borderline personality disorder: A social learning thesis. *Journal of Personality Disorders, 1,* 354–372.

Mintz, R. S. (1968). Psychotherapy of the suicidal patient. In H. L. P. Resnik (Ed.), *Suicidal behaviors: Diagnoses and management* (pp. 271–296). Boston: Little, Brown.

Munroe-Blum, H., & Marziali, E. (1987). *Randomized clinical trial of relationship management time-limited group treatment of borderline personality disorder.* Unpublished manuscript, Ontario Mental Health Foundation, Hamilton, Ontario, Canada.

Munroe-Blum, H., & Marziali, E. (1989). *Continuation of a randomized control trial of group treatment for borderline personality disorder.* Unpublished manuscript, Ontario Mental Health Foundation, Hamilton, Ontario, Canada.

Parsons, B., Quitkin, F. M., McGrath, P. J., Stewart, J. W., Tricamo, E., Ocepek-Welikson, K., Harrison, W., Rabkin, J. G., Wager, S. G., & Nunes, E. (1989). Phenelzine, imipramine, and placebo in borderline patients meeting criteria for atypical depression. *Psychopharmacology Bulletin, 25,* 524–534.

Peng, K., & Nisbett, R. E. (1999). Culture, dialectics, and reasoning about contradiction. *American Psychologist, 54,* 741–754.

Perry, J. C., Banon, E., & Ianni, F. (1999). Effectiveness of psychotherapy for personality disorders. *American Journal of Psychiatry, 156*, 1312–1321.

Pretzer, J. (1990). Borderline personality disorder. In A. Freeman, J. Pretzer, B. Fleming, & K. M. Simon (Eds.), *Clinical applications of cognitive therapy* (pp. 181–202). New York: Plenum Press.

Reiser, D. E., & Levenson, H. (1984). Abuses of the borderline diagnosis: A clinical problem with teaching opportunities. *American Journal of Psychiatry, 141*, 1528–1532.

Rich, C. L., & Runeson, B. S. (1992). Similarities in diagnostic comorbidity between suicide among young people in Sweden and the United States. *Acta Psychiatrica Scandinavica, 86*, 335–339.

Rinsley, D. (1982). *Borderline and other self disorders*. New York: Jason Aronson.

Salzman, C., Wolfson, A. N., Schatzberg, A., Looper, J., Henke, R., Albanese, M., Schwartz, J., & Miyawaki, E. (1995). Effect of fluoxetine on anger in symptomatic volunteers with borderline personality disorder. *Journal of Clinical Psychopharacology, 15*, 23–29.

Shearin, E. N., & Linehan, M. M. (1989). Dialectics and behavior therapy: A meta-paradoxical approach to the treatment of borderline personality disorder. In L. M. Ascher (Ed.), *Therapeutic paradox* (pp. 255–288). New York: Guilford Press.

Shearin, E. N., & Linehan, M. M. (1992). Patient–therapist ratings and relationship to progress in dialectical behavior therapy for borderline personality disorder. *Behavior Therapy, 23*, 730–741.

Siever, L. J., & Davis, K. L. (1991). A psychobiological perspective on the personality disorders. *American Journal of Psychiatry, 148*, 1647–1658.

Silk, K. R., Lee, S., Hill, E. M., & Lohr, N. E. (1995). Borderline personality disorder symptoms and severity of sexual abuse. *American Journal of Psychiatry, 152*, 1059–1064.

Simpson, J. A., & Weiner, E. S. (1989). *Oxford English dictionary* (2nd ed.) [Online]. Available: http://www.oed.com [2000, December 17].

Soloff, P. H., Cornelius, J., George, A., Nathan, S., Perel, J. M., & Ulrich, R. F. (1993). Efficacy of phenelzine and haloperidol in borderline personality disorder. *Archives of General Psychiatry, 50*, 377–385.

Soloff, P. H., George, A., Nathan, R. S., Schulz, P. M., Cornelius, J. R., Herring, J., & Perel, J. M. (1989). Amitriptyline versus haloperidol in borderlines: Final outcomes and predictors of response. *Journal of Clinical Psychopharmacology, 9*, 238–246.

Stein, D. J., Simeon, D., Frenkel, M., Islam, M. N., & Hollander, E. (1995). An open trial of valproate in borderline personality disorder. *Journal of Clinical Psychiatry, 56*, 506–510.

Stone, M. H., Stone, D. K., & Hurt, S. W. (1987). Natural history of borderline patients treated by intensive hospitalization. *Psychiatric Clinics of North America, 10*, 185–206.

Turner, R. M. (1984, November). *Assessment and treatment of borderline personality disorders*. Paper presented at the 18th Annual Convention of the Association for Advancement of Behavior Therapy, Philadelphia.

Turner, R. M. (1989). Case study evaluations of a bio-cognitive behavioral approach for the treatment of borderline personality disorder. *Behavior Therapy, 20*, 477–489.

Turner, R. M. (1992). *An empirical investigation of the utility of psychodynamic techniques in the practice of cognitive behavior therapy*. Paper presented at the 26th Annual Convention of the Association for Advancement of Behavior Therapy, Boston.

Turner, R. M., & Hersen, M. (1981). Disorders of social behavior: A behavioral approach to personality disorders. In S. M. Turner, K. S. Calhoun, & H. E. Adams (Eds.), *Handbook of clinical behavior therapy* (pp. 103–123). New York: Wiley.

van den Bosch, L. M. C. (1999). *A study of the effectiveness of DBT in the treatment of substance and non-substance abusing women in Holland*. Paper presented at the 33rd Annual Convention of the Association for Advancement of Behavior Therapy, Toronto.

Wagner, A. W., Linehan, M. M., & Wasson, E. J. (1989, November). *Parasuicide: Characteristics and relationship to childhood sexual abuse*. Poster presented at the 23rd Annual Convention of the Association for Advancement of Behavior Therapy, Washington, DC.

Waldinger, R. J., & Gunderson, J. G. (1984). Completed psychotherapies with borderline patients. *American Journal of Psychotherapy, 38*(1), 90–201.

Whitaker, C. A. (1975). Psychotherapy of the absurd: With special emphasis on the psychotherapy of aggression. *Family Process, 14*, 1–16.

Young, J. E. (1983, August). *Borderline personality: Cognitive theory and treatment*. Paper presented at the annual meeting of the American Psychological Association, Anaheim, CA.

Young, J. E. (1990). *Cognitive therapy for personality disorders: A schema-focused approach*. Sarasota, FL: Professional Resources Exchange.

Young, J. E., & Swift, W. (1988). Schema-focused cognitive therapy for personality disorders: Part I. *International Cognitive Therapy Newsletter, 4*, 13–14.

Zanarini, M. C., Gunderson, J. G., Frankenburg, F. R., & Chauncey, D. L. (1989). The revised Diagnostic Interview for Borderlines: Discriminating BPD from other axis II disorders. *Journal of Personality Disorders, 3*, 10–18.

Chapter 12

BIPOLAR DISORDER

David J. Miklowitz

The goal of this book is to present creative and important psychological treatments with empirical support. This chapter on bipolar disorder by David J. Miklowitz is new to this edition, but may represent one of the more important additions to the armamentarium of psychological interventions, if the existing evidence for the efficacy of this approach continues to grow. Based on years of systematic research on psychological factors contributing to the onset and maintenance of bipolar disorder, this sophisticated family therapy approach targets the most important psychosocial factors linked to the disorder and associated with poor outcome (such as disruptions in circadian rhythms and certain specific styles of interpersonal interactions). The chapter, and especially the very useful case study, also illustrate an essential linkage between psychological and pharmacological approaches to this very severe form of psychopathology.—D. H. B.

Bipolar disorder is one of the oldest and most reliably recognized psychiatric disorders. Our thinking about this disorder has evolved over this century, but the original descriptions (Kraepelin, 1921) of "manic–depressive insanity" greatly resemble our current conceptualizations. This chapter begins with a review of basic information about the disorder, its diagnosis, its longitudinal course, and drug treatment. This information about the illness is interesting in its own right, but also provides the rationale for using psychosocial treatment as an adjunct to pharmacotherapy. The majority of the chapter describes a focused, time-limited outpatient psychosocial treatment —family-focused treatment (FFT)—which consists of three interrelated modules: psychoeducation, communication enhancement training (CET), and problem-solving skills training (Miklowitz & Goldstein, 1997). It is designed for patients who have had a recent episode of mania or depression.

THE DIAGNOSIS OF BIPOLAR DISORDER

DSM-IV Criteria

The core characteristic of bipolar disorder is extreme affective dysregulation, or the swinging of mood states from extremely low (depression) to extremely high (mania). Patients in a manic episode have euphoric, elevated mood or irritable mood; behavioral activation (e.g., increased goal-directed activity, excessive involvement in high-risk activities, decreased need for sleep, increased talkativeness or pressure of speech); and altered cognitive functioning (grandiose delusions or inflated self-worth, flight of ideas or racing thoughts, distractibility)—typically for more than 1 week. For the diagnosis of manic episode, there must be evidence that the person's psychosocial functioning (marital, occupational, or social) is disrupted; that hospitalization is required;

or that psychotic features (e.g., grandiose delusions) are present. (See the *Diagnostic and Statistical Manual of Mental Disorders*, fourth edition, or DSM-IV; American Psychiatric Association, 1994b.)

Patients in a hypomanic episode show many of the same symptoms, but the duration is typically shorter (i.e., 4 days or more). Hypomanic symptoms also do not bring about severe impairment in social or occupational functioning and are not associated with the need for hospitalization or with psychosis. However, the symptoms must reflect a real change in a person's ordinary behavior—one that is observable by others. The distinction between mania and hypomania, which is really one of degree rather than type of illness, is hard for clinicians to make reliably. Often the degree to which the behavioral activation affects a patient's functioning is underestimated by the patient, who can see nothing but good in his/her behavior. A theme of this chapter is the value of including significant others (i.e., parents, spouses/partners, and siblings) in patients' assessment and treatment.

Some patients with bipolar disorder (40% or more; Calabrese, Fatemi, Kujawa, & Woyshville, 1996) experience mixed episodes, in which the criteria for a major depressive episode and a manic episode are met nearly every day for a minimum duration of 1 week. The symptoms of both poles of the illness are experienced simultaneously. The boundaries between "pure" mania and mixed mania are not entirely clear, because depression often lurks beneath the manic exterior and is easily evoked by situational factors (Young & Harrow, 1994).

The DSM-IV proceeds with the diagnosis of bipolar disorder somewhat differently than past DSM systems have done. First, the diagnostician determines whether the patient satisfies the cross-sectional criteria for a manic or mixed episode. If he/she does meet these criteria, the diagnosis of bipolar I disorder is applied. If the patient currently meets the DSM-IV criteria for major depressive episode, he/she will be diagnosed as having bipolar disorder only if there is a past history of manic, mixed, or hypomanic episodes; otherwise, the diagnosis will likely be major depressive disorder (single episode or recurrent) or another mood disorder. If the patient presents in remission, there must be evidence of prior manic or mixed episodes. One implication of this rather complicated set of diagnostic rules is that a single manic or mixed episode, even in the absence of documentable depression, is enough to warrant the bipolar I diagnosis. The key word here is "documentable," because patients often underreport their depression histories and reveal them upon careful questioning.

How Has the Diagnosis of Bipolar Disorder Changed?

Every version of the DSM has brought changes in the way we think about bipolar disorder. First, the DSM-IV distinguishes bipolar I from bipolar II disorder. In the former, patients have fully syndromal manic or mixed episodes. In the bipolar II illness, patients only have hypomanic episodes. Unlike for bipolar I disorder, a major depressive episode must have occurred for bipolar II disorder. (In this chapter, the term "bipolar disorder" refers to either bipolar I or bipolar II disorder as defined by the DSM-IV, unless otherwise specified.)

The DSM-IV also includes a course descriptor, "rapid cycling," which appears to characterize between 13% and 20% of patients (Calabrese et al., 1996), and more often females (Coryell, Endicott, & Keller, 1992). This is a much misunderstood course subtype, which is often confused with mixed episodes. A mixed episode refers to the presentation of mania and major depression within a single episode, whereas rapid cycling means that a patient has had four or more discrete major depressive, manic, mixed, or hypomanic episodes in a single year. The confusion in applying this course descriptor lies in the fact that it is difficult to tell when one episode has ended and another begins: If a patient quickly switches from mania to depression in a 48-hour period (what some refer to as "ultrarapid cycling"), are these truly new episodes or just different presentations of the same episode? Rapid cycling appears to be a transient state of the disorder and not a lifelong phenomenon (Coryell et al., 1992).

Finally, the DSM-IV deals with the thorny problem of patients with depression who develop manic, mixed, or hypomanic episodes that are brought on by antidepressants or other activating drugs. Because of the effects of antidepressants on the serotonin, norepinephrine, and dopamine systems, there is the potential for these drugs to induce activation, particularly in a patient who is already biologically vulnerable to mood swings. If a patient has never had a manic episode and then develops one after taking an antidepressant, the likely diagnosis is substance-induced mood disorder. The diagnosis of bipolar disorder is only then considered if the symptoms of mania preceded the antidepressant (a difficult historical distinction) or if the mania symptoms continue for at least a month after the antidepressant is withdrawn. Similar diagnostic considerations apply to patients who abuse drugs (e.g., cocaine, amphetamine) that are "psychotomimetics" and can induce manic-like states.

Comorbidity and Differential Diagnosis

Bipolar disorder is often comorbid with other conditions. In the Epidemiologic Catchment Area study (Regier et al., 1990), 46% of patients with bipolar disorder as defined by DSM-III (American Psychiatric Association, 1980) also met the DSM-III criteria for lifetime alcohol abuse (15%) or dependence (31%); 41% met the criteria for other substance abuse (13%) or dependence (28%). A total of 61% met criteria for any substance abuse or dependence. It is also common to see bipolar disorder co-occur with anxiety disorders, eating disorders, and personality disorders. The disorders with which bipolar disorder is comorbid have the common underpinning of affective dysregulation.

The distinction between bipolar disorder and Axis II disorders is especially difficult. For example, the hallmark of borderline personality disorder is affective instability. Akiskal (1996) has argued that what is commonly seen by clinicians as Axis II pathology is actually undertreated, subsyndromal mood disorder. When studies of the overlap of bipolar disorder and Axis II disorders are done carefully, the estimates of Axis II comorbidity are actually quite conservative. For example, studies by Carpenter, Clarkin, Glick, and Wilner (1995) and George, Miklowitz, and Richards (1996), estimate that only about 22% to 28% of patients with bipolar disorder meet the diagnostic criteria for Axis II disorders when patients are evaluated during a period of remission. Furthermore, the comorbid Axis II

diagnosis is not always borderline personality disorder; it is often a disorder from Cluster C (e.g., avoidant or dependent personality disorder).

The boundaries between bipolar and unipolar illness are sometimes difficult to draw. Depressions in bipolar and unipolar disorders can look quite similar. There is some evidence that bipolar depressions are more likely to be characterized by greater psychomotor retardation but less agitation, anxiety, and somatization than unipolar depressions (Beigel & Murphy, 1971; Goodwin & Jamison, 1990; Katz, Robins, Croughan, Secunda, & Swann, 1982). Others have found that bipolar depressions are shorter than unipolar depressions and are more often characterized by mood lability, diurnal variation, feeling worse in the morning, and derealization (Goldberg & Kocsis, 1999; Mitchell et al., 1992). Even more complicated is the distinction between agitated depression of the unipolar type and mixed mania of the bipolar type; both are characterized by sadness and a highly anxious, restless, activated state. Goldberg and Kocsis (1999) recommend that clinicians attempting to make these distinctions place emphasis on attributes such as goal-drivenness and undiminished energy (despite lack of sleep), both of which tip the scales toward bipolar disorder rather than unipolar depressive illness.

The distinction between bipolar disorder and schizophrenia is also a difficult judgment call. When a patient who has schizophrenia presents with a psychotic episode, he/she can appear acutely activated, grandiose in thinking and actions, and elated or depressed. In a highly influential paper published prior to the appearance of DSM-III, Pope and Lipinski (1978) argued strongly that patients with traditionally schizophrenic "Schneiderian first-rank symptoms" (e.g., thought broadcasting, delusions of control) often have bipolar or even unipolar depressions. In part to deal with these diagnostic ambiguities, the DSM-IV makes a distinction between schizoaffective disorder and major mood disorders with psychotic features. In schizoaffective disorder, delusions and hallucinations have been present for at least 2 weeks even when there have been no prominent affective symptoms. In major mood disorders, psychotic symptoms occur only during periods of significant mood disturbance. Importantly, psychotic symptoms, particularly "mood-incongruent" features (delusions or hallucinations that have no clear content related to sadness or elation, such as the belief that thoughts are being inserted into one's head) are a poor prognostic sign in bipolar and unipolar disorders (Brockington, Hillier, Francis, Helzer, & Wainwright, 1983; Coryell, Keller, Lavori, & Endicott, 1990; Grossman, Harrow, Fudula, & Meltzer, 1984; Grossman, Harrow, Goldberg, & Fichtner, 1991; Kendler, 1991; Miklowitz, 1992; Tohen, Waternaux, & Tsuang, 1990).

DSM-IV also describes a subsyndromal or subaffective condition: cyclothymic disorder. Patients with cyclothymic disorder alternate between periods of hypomanic symptoms and brief periods of depression that fall short of the criteria for major depressive illness. As soon as the person develops a full manic, mixed, or depressive episode, the diagnosis of bipolar I or II disorder is substituted. Again, these distinctions really concern the degree and duration of symptoms rather than their form. In my own experience, clinicians are prone to "push" patients with cyclothymia into the bipolar II category, especially if they feel that the patients are not reliable in their historical reporting. Sometimes it is better to observe the mood lability of a patient over time than to attempt to distinguish cyclothymic disorder and bipolar disorder cross-sectionally. The accuracy of patients' reporting is increased by self-report records kept over periods of a year or more. Examples are "life charts" that show, prospectively, the duration, severity, polarity, and functional impairment associated with mood disorder fluctuations (Leverich & Post, 1998).

DRUG TREATMENT AND THE COURSE OF BIPOLAR DISORDER

Standard Pharmacotherapy

The course of bipolar illness (its pattern of relapsing and remitting over time) is best considered with reference to the drug treatments that help stabilize patients and allow most to function in the community. In the pre-pharmacological era (i.e., prior to 1960), patients were hospitalized for years at a time (Cutler & Post, 1982). Nowadays, the availability of mood stabilizers like lithium carbonate and the anticonvulsants (e.g., carbamazepine [Tegretol], divalproex sodium [Depakote], and other agents) has done much to ameliorate the course of bipolar illness (Keck & McElroy, 1996; Sachs, 1996). These drugs not only control the acute episodes of the illness, but also have "prophylactic value," meaning that they help prevent future episodes or minimize the duration or severity of episodes that do occur.

Most psychiatrists describe three phases of drug treatment: an acute phase, in which the goal is to control the most severe symptoms of the manic, mixed, or depressive disorder; a stabilization phase, in which the goal is to help the patient recover fully from the acute phase, which often means treating residual symptoms (e.g., mild depression) or levels of social–occupational impairment; and a maintenance phase, where the goal is to prevent recurrences and continue to treat residual symptoms. The drugs recommended for bipolar disorder vary according to the phase of treatment. During the acute and stabilization phases, an antipsychotic medication may accompany a mood stabilizer. An antidepressant may be recommended after a manic episode has stabilized if a patient has ongoing, residual depression symptoms. These phases of treatment are also relevant to the psychosocial–psychotherapeutic treatment of bipolar disorder, as discussed later.

Symptomatic Outcome

If drug treatment is so effective, then why do we need psychosocial treatment? The problem that consistently arises in the drug treatment of bipolar disorder is the problem of "breakthrough episodes." With lithium or anticonvulsant treatment, rates of relapse over 1 year vary between 37% (Gitlin, Swendsen, Heller, & Hammen, 1995) and 67% (Shapiro, Quitkin, & Fleiss, 1989). Gelenberg and colleagues (1989) found that the 2-year "survival rate" (i.e., the proportion of patients not relapsing) for bipolar disorder was 40% on typical lithium regimens. Gitlin and colleagues (1995) found that the 5-year survival rate was only 27%.

A representative longitudinal study is that of Keck and colleagues (1998), who examined the 12-month course of bipolar disorder among 134 patients who began in an acute manic or mixed episode. The majority of the patients (n = 104) were treated with mood stabilizers, with or without accompanying antipsychotics or antidepressants. The investigators made a distinction among "syndromic recovery," in which patients no longer met the DSM-III-R (American Psychiatric Association, 1987) criteria for a manic, mixed, or depressive episode for at least 8 weeks; "symptomatic recovery," a tougher criterion by which patients had to have minimal or no mood disorder symptoms for 8 weeks; and "functional recovery," which required that patients regain their premorbid (preillness) level of employment, friendships, interests, and independent living status. Of 106 patients who completed the study, 51 (48%) achieved syndromic recovery by 12-month follow-up. Only 28 (26%) achieved symptomatic recovery, and 25 (24%) reached functional recovery at follow-up. Predictors of poor outcome included low socioeconomic status, medication noncompliance, and longer duration of illness.

Social–Occupational Functioning

The problems patients with bipolar disorder experience in social–occupational recovery are substantial, even when they are given mood-stabilizing medications. Dion, Tohen, Anthony, and Waternaux (1989) found that about one in every three patients with mania could not work in the 6 months following a manic episode, and only about 20% worked at their expected level. Coryell and colleagues (1993) found that social–occupational dysfunction—including high rates of marital separations and divorces—could be observed up to 5 years after a mood episode. Goldberg, Harrow, and Grossman (1995) found in a 4½-year follow-up of patients with major mood disorders that patients with bipolar illness had lower work functioning scores than patients with unipolar illness. Furthermore, only 41% were rated as having a "good overall outcome" at follow-up. Patients in this study were usually taking lithium alone or lithium with antipsychotic medications.

What predicts social–occupational functioning? In our 9-month follow-up of lithium- or anticonvulsant-treated young adults with bipolar disorder, family conflict, as measured by negative parent-to-patient verbal interactions during a family problem-solving task, predicted levels of social functioning at follow-up. Patient gender also appears important: Harrow, Goldberg, Grossman, and

Meltzer (1990) found that women with mania had better work functioning at follow-up than men with mania. Moreover, patients with higher socioeconomic status had more favorable functional outcomes than patients with lower socioeconomic status. The latter finding was replicated in the Keck and colleagues (1998) study.

It appears that social functioning and symptomatic outcome are two correlated but separate domains of outcome in bipolar disorder, or "open-linked systems" (Strauss & Carpenter, 1972). Whereas many assume that severe symptoms predispose patients to worse functional outcomes, at least one study (Gitlin et al., 1995) found the reverse: Poor social functioning, especially job functioning, predicted a shorter time to relapse in a 4⅓-year follow-up.

Medication Nonadherence

Part of the reason why patients with bipolar disorder have breakthrough episodes is the problem of drug nonadherence. In the Keck and colleagues (1998) study, only 47% of the patients were fully adherent with their medications at follow-up. We (Miklowitz, Goldstein, Nuechterlein, Snyder, & Mintz, 1988) found that only about 30% of young patients with recent-onset mania took their medications on a routinely scheduled basis during a 9-month follow-up. Whereas rates of adherence vary with the methods and criteria for measuring adherence, it is clearly a significant risk factor in this disorder. Jamison and colleagues (Jamison & Akiskal, 1983; Jamison, Gerner, & Goodwin, 1979) identified the following factors as predictors of nonadherence: negative feelings about having one's moods controlled by a medication; missing high or euphoric periods; and side effects, which for lithium can include weight gain, thirst, and tremor of the hands.

Why Psychotherapy?

What is the role of psychosocial treatment in a disorder with such a heavy biological and genetic basis? There is little doubt that medication is the first-line treatment for bipolar disorder. The evidence that lithium and the anticonvulsants reduce relapse rates and improve functioning is substantial. But can we do better? An optimal, and perhaps overly optimistic, view of the outcome of patients with bipolar disorder would include symptomatic stability for extended periods, minimal disruptions in social role functioning after episodes, and becoming consistent contributors to society. One role of psychotherapy, as an adjunct to medication, is to teach skills for symptom management, augment social and occupational role functioning, and keep patients adherent to their drug regimens.

Implicit in this objective is that the physiology and psychology of major psychiatric disorders are not fully separable. We know that in obsessive–compulsive disorder, changes in brain function (as revealed in positron emission tomography scans) can be detected before and after treatment among responders to behavior therapy as well as responders to fluoxetine (Prozac) (Baxter et al., 1992). The time has come to think about psychotherapy and medication as working synergistically in the major mental disorders.

The strongest argument for including psychotherapy in an outpatient treatment program is to help patients to cope with stress triggers. As noted in the next section, certain forms of life events and family tensions are risk factors in the course of the disorder. Psychotherapy can target these factors and teach patients adaptive coping mechanisms, which can then be brought to bear during periods of wellness to help stave off the likelihood of a future relapse.

A VULNERABILITY–STRESS MODEL OF RECURRENCES

Implicit in the notion that psychotherapy would be helpful to a patient with bipolar disorder is the notion that stress plays a role in eliciting symptoms of mood disorder. What is the evidence for this view? What are the targets for psychosocial intervention? Figure 12.1 summarizes a model that takes into account the background of biochemical (e.g., serotonin, dopamine, norepinephrine, or GABA) imbalances, genetic vulnerability, and the two types of stress targeted in FFT: life events and disturbances in family functioning (see Goodwin & Jamison, 1990; Miklowitz & Frank, 1999; Miklowitz & Goldstein, 1997).

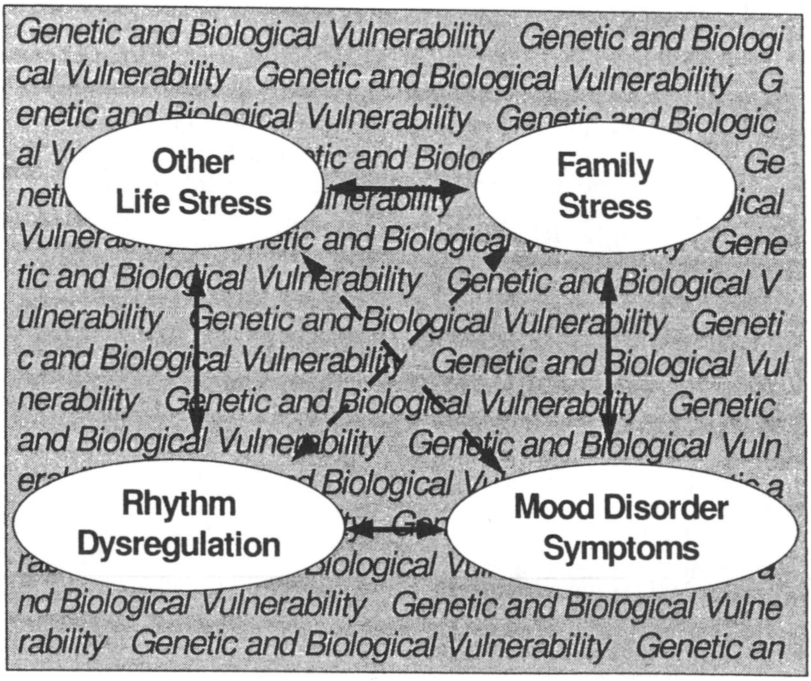

FIGURE 12.1. A vulnerability–stress "instability" model of mood episodes in bipolar disorder. From Miklowitz and Goldstein (1997). Copyright 1997 by The Guilford Press. Reprinted by permission.

Life Events Stress

In this model, life events affect the onset of bipolar mood symptoms through the avenue of disrupting daily routines and sleep–wake cycles ("social rhythms"). The social rhythm stability hypothesis (Ehlers, Kupfer, Frank, & Monk, 1993) states that major life events can disrupt daily rhythms in mood disorders via one of two avenues. They can act as "zeitstorers," which disrupt established social and circadian rhythms (e.g., the production of neuroendocrines as a function of the time of day). For example, a previously unemployed patient who gets a job with constantly shifting work hours is forced to adopt a new pattern of daily routines, which may include changes in sleep–wake habits. Major events can also result in the loss of "zeitgebers," which maintain the stability of rhythms. For example, a spouse or partner helps maintain a person on predictable social and sleep schedules. A relationship separation, in addition to being a significant emotional event, results in the loss of this human timekeeper.

Patients with bipolar disorder are exquisitely sensitive to even minor changes in sleep–wake habits. A study by Malkoff-Schwartz and colleagues (1998) found that manic episodes were often precipitated by life events that changed sleep–wake habits (e.g., changing time zones due to air travel). However, depressive episodes were not differentially associated with rhythm-disruptive life events. One of the clinical implications of these findings is that if patients can be taught to regularize their social rhythms, especially in the face of life events that normally would disrupt those rhythms, then the outcome of bipolar disorder should be improved. Thus variability in the sleep–wake cycle is a target for treatment. This is a central tenet of interpersonal and social rhythm therapy, an individual psychotherapy discussed below (Frank et al., 1994).

Family Stress

Family conflicts may also become a breeding ground for increased cycling of bipolar disorder (see Figure 12.1). One method of measuring family stress is to evaluate a family's level of "expressed emotion" (EE). In this domain of research, a family member (parent, spouse/partner, or sibling) is interviewed for approximately 1 hour by a researcher who administers the Camberwell Family Interview (Vaughn & Leff, 1976). The interview assesses the relative's reactions to the patient's psychiatric disorder, with particular emphasis on a recent illness episode. Later, a trained judge evaluates tapes of these interviews on three primary dimensions: "critical comments" (e.g., "When I talk to him, I get upset that he just shuts down. It's like there's no one there!"); "hostility," or personal, generalized criticism of the patient (e.g., "I like nothing about him"); and "emotional overinvolvement," or the tendency to be overconcerned, overprotective, or use inordinately self-sacrificing behaviors in the patient's care (e.g., "I don't invite people to the house 'cause Allen [son] doesn't like it"). Family members who score high on one or more of these dimensions are called "high-EE"; those who do not are called "low-EE."

EE is a well-established predictor of the course of schizophrenia. In Butzlaff and Hooley's (1998) meta-analysis of 28 longitudinal studies of EE in schizophrenia, 23 studies replicated the same core finding: Patients who return after an illness episode to high-EE families are two to three times more likely to relapse in 9-month to 1-year prospective follow-ups than those returning to low-EE families. Several studies have also documented a link between high EE in families and relapse among patients with bipolar disorder followed either prospectively or retrospectively (Honig, Hofman, Rozendaal, & Dingemanns, 1997; Miklowitz et al., 1988; Priebe, Wildgrube, & Muller-Oerlinghausen, 1989; O'Connell, Mayo, Flatow, Cuthbertson, & O'Brien, 1991).

On first examination, one might conclude that patients with bipolar disorder are sensitive to stress in the family milieu, and that levels of EE elicit an underlying biological vulnerability. But the relationship is far from simple. First, it appears that the high-EE relatives of patients with bipolar illness, unipolar illness, or schizophrenia are more likely than low-EE relatives to interpret the patients' negative problem behaviors as controllable by the patients (see, e.g., Brewin, MacCarthy, Duda, & Vaughn, 1991; Hooley, 1987; Hooley & Licht, 1997; Weisman, Lopez, Karno, & Jenkins, 1993; Wendel, Miklowitz, Richards, & George, 2000). Second, relatives and patients coping with bipolar disorder are often locked into verbally aggressive, negative cycles of face-to-face interaction. We (Simoneau, Miklowitz, & Saleem, 1998) found that high-EE relatives of patients with bipolar disorder were more negative during face-to-face problem-solving interactions than low-EE relatives. The relatives and patients in high-EE families were also more likely to engage in counterproductive "attack–counterattack" cycles. Often the patients were provocateurs in these interchanges; they were not the "victims" of verbally aggressive or punitive relatives (Miklowitz, Wendel, & Simoneau, 1998; Simoneau et al., 1998).

Clearly, a psychosocial treatment program should consider aspects of the family's affective environment—such as high-EE attitudes in relatives or the negative interchanges that characterize relative–patient communication—to be targets for intervention. But does one attempt to change these attitudes and interaction patterns directly, or instead make an "end run" around them? Family members coping with a spouse/partner, offspring, or sibling who has bipolar disorder are understandably quite angry, and it makes little sense to tell them they shouldn't be. Others feel that their overprotective behavior is more than warranted by the situation.

In developing FFT, we (Miklowitz & Goldstein, 1997) concluded that at least one component of dealing with these attitudes and transaction patterns is psychoeducation. Psychoeducation involves the provision of information to patients and family members about the disorder and its manifestations. As discussed above, relatives need to come to realize that at least some proportion of the patient's aversive behaviors (e.g., irritability, aggression, inability to work or low productivity) can be attributed to a biochemically driven illness state. This may seem obvious to us as clinicians, but to family members who deal with the patient on a day-to-day basis, it is easy to attribute aversive behaviors to personality factors, laziness, or "doing this to hurt me." In parallel, patients need to become more cognizant of the way they provoke anger and resentment in family members. Finally, negative face-to-face interactions cannot be eradicated, but they can be made more productive through the behavioral family therapy techniques of communication and problem-solving skills training. Thus families or couples can be taught to stick with one problem topic rather than trying to solve many at a time, or to use listening skills to avoid counterproductive attack–counterattack cycles. Later in this chapter, I detail these methods with reference to a difficult treatment case.

TREATMENT OUTCOME STUDIES

Controlled psychotherapy outcome studies are relatively new to the field of bipolar disorder, and certainly have not kept pace with the research on drug treatment. This section describes several randomized controlled trials of individual and family/marital interventions. A more thorough review of the studies in this area is available (Craighead, Miklowitz, Vajk, & Frank, 1998; Huxley, Parikh, & Baldessarini, 2000; Miklowitz & Craighead, 2001).

Individual Therapy

Two controlled trials of individual therapy deserve special emphasis here. Each of these focused on a specific risk factor in the course of bipolar disorder: medication noncompliance (Cochran, 1984) and disruptions in social rhythms (Frank, 1999; Frank et al., 1999). These therapy models are to be distinguished from earlier, psychoanalytically oriented models whose aim was to restructure personality or deal with early childhood conflicts (e.g., Cohen, Baker, Cohen, Fromm-Reichmann, & Weigert, 1954).

In Cochran's study, 28 lithium-treated outpatients with bipolar disorder were randomly assigned to lithium carbonate with six sessions of individual cognitive therapy, or to a lithium-only group. The cognitive therapy was oriented toward restructuring cognitions associated with noncompliance. At a 6-month follow-up, patients who received the cognitive intervention had significantly better medication adherence, fewer hospitalizations, and fewer mood episodes precipitated by drug nonadherence. A separate trial of 23 patients with bipolar disorder compared the effects of 12–20 sessions of cognitive therapy plus medication to routine care plus medication (Lam et al., 2000). Over 12 months, patients given cognitive therapy had fewer recurrences, greater affective stability, and better medication adherence than patients given routine care.

Frank and colleagues (1999) investigated the efficacy of an interpersonal psychotherapy for bipolar disorder—one that included the core elements of Klerman, Weissman, Rounsaville, and Chevron's (1984) model of interpersonal psychotherapy for depression, but also included a component in which patients self-regulated their daily routines and sleep–wake cycles. Patients with a recent mood episode were randomly assigned to 45-minute interpersonal psychotherapy sessions and mood-stabilizing medications or to an active clinical management intervention, also with medications. The latter consisted of 20-minute sessions with a psychotherapist who focused on drug side effects and symptom management. Session frequencies were identical across the two groups. Randomization was done first during an acute phase of treatment, with sessions held weekly, and again at the beginning of a preventative, maintenance phase of treatment, with sessions held biweekly or monthly for up to 2 years.

Preliminary results suggested that interpersonal psychotherapy and medication did not differentially decrease the frequency of mood episode recurrences or time to those recurrences relative to the effects of active clinical management and medication. However, relative to active clinical management, interpersonal therapy was associated with decreases in the amount of time patients spent in the depressive phase of their illness during maintenance treatment (Frank, 1999). Interestingly, patients who stayed in the same psychosocial treatment from the acute to the preventive phase (i.e., who received either continuous interpersonal psychotherapy or continuous active clinical management) had fewer recurrences than those who switched from one modality to the other when moving from the acute to the preventive phase. Thus consistency of routines, including a patient's adjunctive psychosocial treatment, may protect against a worsening course of the disorder (Frank et al., 1999).

Family and Marital Therapy

There are now several studies of family interventions as adjuncts to medications for patients with bipolar disorder. The first, by a group at the Cornell University Medical College (Clarkin et al., 1990; Glick, Clarkin, Haas, Spencer, & Chen, 1991) involved randomly assigning 186 inpatients with psychotic or mood disorders to a brief family intervention or standard hospital care. The family intervention averaged nine weekly or twice-weekly sessions, and focused on helping patients and family members to cope with the hospital experience and make plans for a positive posthospital adjustment. At 6- and 18-month follow-ups, female patients who had received the family intervention had less severe symptoms and higher global functioning than those who had originally received standard hospital care. Interestingly, among female patients from both the mood disorder and psychotic disorder groups, family treatment led to improvements at 6 and 18 months in relatives' emotional attitudes (e.g., less rejecting feelings toward the patients). In the patients with bipolar disorder ($n = 21$), the effects of family intervention were only seen among 14 female patients, so the findings cannot be considered conclusive.

Another carefully controlled, randomized trial by the Cornell group (Clarkin, Carpenter, Hull, Wilner, & Glick, 1998) compared a psychoeducational marital intervention and pharmacotherapy with pharmacological care alone. The sample size ($n = 33$) was small, but patients who received the marital treatment had better drug adherence and better global functioning scores over 11 months of treatment than those in the comparison group. No effect was observed for marital intervention on the symptomatic outcome of patients.

Two studies have been completed on FFT, one at UCLA (Goldstein, Rea, & Miklowitz, 1996; Rea, Tompson, Miklowitz, & Goldstein, 2000) and the other at the University of Colorado (Miklowitz, Frank, & George, 1996; Miklowitz et al., 2000; Simoneau, Miklowitz, Richards, Saleem, & George, 1999). Both studies examined a 9-month, 21-session intervention consisting of psychoeducation, CET, and problem-solving training. Participants were patients and their parents or spouses. Patients in both studies were recruited during an index episode of bipolar disorder and maintained on mood-stabilizing medications with or without antipsychotic or antidepressive agents. However, the studies differed in an important respect: At Colorado, the comparison group (crisis management) received two sessions of family education and individual crisis sessions as needed, over 9 months.

In the UCLA study, patients in the comparison group received an individual case management and problem-solving intervention that was of similar intensity (21 sessions) to the FFT intervention.

Despite these design differences, the results that emerged from the two studies were quite similar. In the Colorado Treatment Outcome Project (CTOP), FFT and medication led to lower frequencies of relapses and longer delays prior to relapses over a 1-year period (consisting of 9 months of treatment and 3 additional months of follow-up) than did crisis management and medication. FFT was also associated with more improvement in depression symptoms—an effect that was not found until the 9- and 12-month follow-ups, but one that continued for a full 24 months of follow-up. In the UCLA Family Project study, the effects of FFT were seen on hospitalization rates over a 2-year follow-up. The effects of FFT on time to relapse were not seen in the first year, but did appear in the second year. Both studies suggest that there may be a delayed effect of FFT: Patients and family members may need to "absorb" the treatment and incorporate the education and skills training into their day-to-day lives before it has ameliorative effects on the illness.

This latter point was clarified further by Simoneau and colleagues (1999), who examined family interaction transcripts obtained in the Colorado CTOP study before and after FFT or crisis management treatment. Families (patients with their parents or spouses) participated in interactional assessments consisting of 10-minute problem-solving discussions, which were transcribed and coded via the Category System for Coding Partner Interactions (Hahlweg et al., 1989). Forty-four families returned at 1 year for the same assessment, after the FFT or crisis management protocol had been completed. Interestingly, at the posttreatment (1-year) interactional assessments, patients in FFT and crisis management could not be distinguished on the frequency of negative interactional behaviors (e.g., criticisms). But there were clear differences at posttreatment in positive interactional behaviors, particularly in the nonverbal sphere. After FFT, patients and relatives were more likely to smile at each other, nod when others were speaking, and lean toward each other when speaking. Moreover, the degree to which patients improved in their nonverbal interactional behavior over the course of psychosocial treatment predicted their degree of symptom improvement over the year of treatment. Thus FFT appeared to have ameliorated certain tensions within the family environments. Future studies using multiple, time-lagged assessments of family interaction and patients' symptoms would help disentangle the directional relationship between improvements in family communication and patients' symptomatic outcomes.

Summary

The addition of psychosocial treatment—either family or individually oriented—to pharmacotherapy appears to lead to more positive outcomes of bipolar disorder. But in drawing conclusions from this small literature, we must keep in mind the different domains of outcome that have been targeted. For some, the targeted outcomes have been relapse rates or symptom severity. In others, the targeted outcomes have been levels of global functioning or medication compliance. None of these studies has examined social or occupational functioning.

The remainder of this chapter is devoted to the specifics of delivering FFT. For whom is it intended? How does it proceed? How are families educated about bipolar disorder, and how do they learn new styles of communicating or solving problems? In reviewing these methods, the reader may wish to reflect on the various targets of family intervention (i.e., family attitudes or expectations, interpersonal conflict, medication nonadherence) and the various domains of outcome that are presumed to be influenced by family interventions via their impact on these targets.

CONTEXT OF THERAPY

Treatment Objectives and Structure

FFT has six objectives, all of which concern coping with an episode of the disorder. These are summarized in Table 12.1. Some of these pertain to dealing with the current episode, and others are more focused on anticipating episodes in the future and the stress triggers for these episodes. A strong case is made for

TABLE 12.1. The Six Objectives of Family-Focused Treatment (FFT)

Assist the patient and relatives in:

- Integrating the experiences associated with mood episodes in bipolar disorder
- Accepting the notion of a vulnerability to future episodes
- Accepting a dependency on mood-stabilizing medication for symptom control
- Distinguishing between the patient's personality and his/her bipolar disorder
- Recognizing and learning to cope with stressful life events that trigger recurrences of bipolar disorder
- Reestablishing functional relationships after a mood episode

the protective effects of medication and a stable, nonstressful family environment.

FFT is delivered in 21 outpatient sessions lasting 1 hour each. Sessions are given weekly for 3 months, biweekly for 3 months, and monthly for 3 months. This structure was originally proposed by Falloon, Boyd, and McGill (1984) for the behavioral treatment of families of patients with schizophrenia. The session-by-session plan is not a given, because some families require less intensive contact at the beginning, some require more intensive contact later, and some simply don't need this much treatment.

The treatment is designed to parallel stages of recovery from a mood episode in bipolar disorder. During the stabilization phase, about seven sessions are devoted to psychoeducation, in which patients and their relatives become acquainted with the nature, course, and treatment of bipolar disorder. At this stage, patients are often still symptomatic and are usually functioning socially or occupationally at a level lower than their preepisode capabilities (see Keck et al., 1998; Strakowski et al., 1998). The psychoeducation attempts to hasten clinical stabilization through reducing the family tensions that often accompany the stabilization phase. This is done through helping a patient and his/her family members make sense of the different events that have precipitated the acute episode, come to a common understanding of the causes and the treatment of the illness, develop plans for how the family will act if there are signs of a developing recurrence, and modulate expectations for the patient's and family's functioning during the recovery period.

Once the family has begun the CET module (7–10 sessions), the patient is usually fully stabilized from the acute episode, although he/she may still have residual mood symptoms. At this point, the patient is usually able to tolerate exercises oriented toward resolving family conflict and promoting behavior change. For example, he/she can practice listening while another family member speaks, and family members can do the same for him/her. These exercises can be difficult when a patient's emotions are still dysregulated, but the structure introduced by communication training can help the patient modulate how he/she expresses emotions.

During the final phase, problem-solving training (four to five sessions), the mood episode is largely remitted and the patient has moved into the maintenance phase of drug treatment. At this stage, and sometimes even earlier, the patient and family are motivated to identify specific family problems related to the illness (e.g., how a married/cohabiting patient can find work; how parents can help a young adult offspring move out of the home and gradually become more independent) and go through the steps of solving them. The last few sessions of FFT are held monthly and help to consolidate gains made during the 9-month treatment.

Setting

Our laboratory, the Colorado Family Project, was established in 1989 at the University of Colorado at Boulder's Department of Psychology. The staff members are psychology postdoctoral fellows, psychology graduate students, and psychiatrists from the community with whom we have developed collaborative relations. Since 1989, we have involved over 150 patients with bipolar disorder in various forms of psychosocial care and research follow-up. We identify patients for our programs through screening of charts on adult hospital wards in the Denver and Boulder region, or through referral from outpatient psychiatrists when patients have acute episodes. In the above-mentioned CTOP study of FFT, we recruited 82 patients from hospital settings and 19 from outpatient clinics. It is worth noting that as the effects of managed care cost containment have taken hold, fewer and fewer of our patients are recruited from hospital wards.

Assessment and treatment occur in different contexts. For example, the initial diagnostic evaluation is done on an inpatient ward or in our research clinic at the Department of Psychology. A pretreatment family assessment (see below) is also done in this laboratory setting. Treatment and research follow-up interviews have typically been done in each family's or couple's home as well as in the laboratory.

The majority of the therapy sessions conducted in our controlled FFT study were done in families' homes. In contrast, the UCLA study was outpatient-clinic-based. There are various advantages and disadvantages of home-based treatment. Home treatment is more naturalistic, and the skills training is more likely to generalize to these settings (Falloon et al., 1984). Also, home meetings allow a clinician to treat patients of lower socioeconomic status, who ordinarily would not have the resources to travel to a university clinic. However, meeting at families' homes raises logistical and financial problems for therapists. In clinical/community settings, the decision to conduct home-based treatment will be based on factors such as the tasks for which a clinician can be remunerated, the ability of a family or couple to travel, and other factors that are independent of a patient's clinical needs.

Client Variables

FFT is usually administered to adult patients with bipolar disorder who live with (or live in close proximity to) their parents, siblings, or spouses/partners. We have previously targeted adult patients (ages 18 and up), but are now examining the applicability of FFT to adolescent patients with bipolar disorder. Although there is nothing contraindicated about offering FFT to patients with remitted bipolar disorder, in our experience they and their family members are less motivated for treatment than those who have recently coped with a mood episode.

Patients with bipolar disorder can present as manic, mixed, hypomanic, depressed, or rapid-cycling. The polarity of the most recent episode, however, is a moving target—it may change before the patient is seen next. Patients who are manic or hypomanic, particularly those who are elated and grandiose, are often in denial about whether they are really ill,

and may believe that the disorder and its treatment are simply ways for others to control them. Depressed patients may be more motivated for psychosocial treatment, but may have cognitive difficulty assimilating the educational content of sessions. Patients with a mixed episode or rapid-cycling bipolar disorder are candidates for FFT, but a more pernicious course of illness can be expected (Keller et al., 1986; McElroy et al., 1992; Post et al., 1989).

Patients with comorbid alcohol or other substance use disorders pose special problems. These patients are usually resistant to psychosocial treatment and medication. They are also difficult to diagnose; the effects of drugs or alcohol can mimic the cycling of a mood disorder. Generally, patients with active substance use disorders are more successfully treated if they are "dry" before FFT commences. If not, it is usually necessary to supplement FFT with substance use programs (e.g., Alcoholics Anonymous).

Concurrent Drug Treatment

We require that each patient be seen simultaneously by a psychiatrist who monitors the patient's medications. Typically, a regimen will include a primary mood stabilizer, usually lithium carbonate or divalproex sodium (Depakote). Less frequently used mood stabilizers include carbamazepine (Tegretol) and newer agents such as lamotrigine (Lamictal) or topiramate (Topomax). The choice of these mood stabilizers is at least in part a function of whether the patient presents with clear-cut episodes of mania or depression, in which case lithium is often recommended. If there is evidence of mixed states or rapid cycling, the anticonvulsants are usually recommended (American Psychiatric Association, 1994a). Antidepressants (e.g., paroxetine [Paxil], venlafaxine [Effexor], bupropion [Wellbutrin]) are sometimes recommended if the patient's depression does not remit with mood stabilizers, and antipsychotics (e.g., olanazapine [Zyprexa], risperidone [Risperdal], or clozapine [Clozaril]) are added if the patient is highly agitated or psychotic. Antidepressants are given sparingly, because there is a high risk of switching from depression into manic, mixed, or rapid-cycling states (Altshuler et al., 1995). Very few of our patients (i.e., fewer than 5%) have received electroconvulsive therapy in addition to drug treatment.

A core principle of FFT is that the family therapist must have regular contact with the patient's physician. This contact is established early in treatment. A close affiliation between the psychosocial and pharmacological treatment personnel enhances the likelihood of the patient's remaining compliant with his/her medications; it also decreases the likelihood of "splitting," or the tendency for a patient (or even family members) to have a "good doctor" and a "bad doctor." For example, patients frequently complain about their physicians and say to their FFT clinicians, "I wish you could just monitor my medications." An FFT clinician who has been having a regular dialogue with a patient's physician can avoid the trap that is being set by encouraging the patient to bring up these problems with the physician directly.

There are patients who will refuse all medications and come to therapy assuming that it will be a substitute for drug treatment. These patients have often had bad experiences with pharmacotherapy and psychiatrists, and may also believe that they are not ill or that the illness they do have can be treated using "alternative medicine." We have generally taken a hard line with these patients, and do not accept them into FFT unless they commit to standard pharmacotherapy (usually lithium and/or anticonvulsants). Patients with bipolar disorder who are unmedicated are highly likely to have relapses, and it is not in their best interests for the clinician to imply that their illness can be managed with psychosocial treatment alone.

Therapist Variables

In the CTOP study, therapists varied from 23 to 46 years of age and from 1 to 14 years of clinical experience. The majority were graduate students in clinical psychology or clinicians with recent doctorates. Few had extensive background in family therapy before learning FFT (Miklowitz et al., 2000).

There are no studies of therapist variables as predictors of the course of family psychoeducational treatments. Our own clinical sense has been that there are two predictors of success in learning FFT. The first positive predictor is the ability to think of a family or couple as a system in which members are interdependent and mutually influence each other's behaviors. Therapists who have trouble with FFT often have difficulty making the transition to this systemic way of thinking. They tend, for example, to conduct family sessions as if they were individual sessions with one patient and several observers. Some of these same problems arise in learning other forms of family therapy.

The second positive predictor is the willingness to think *biopsychosocially*—that is, to see bipolar disorder as a biologically based illness that requires medication treatment, even if its symptoms are partially evoked by concurrent stressors. Thus a therapist often must argue for the patient's drug adherence even when there are psychosocial issues that are more interesting and seem more pressing.

We have found that the following training protocol works well for learning FFT. First, clinicians attend group supervision sessions in which trained FFT therapists discuss their cases. They read the published treatment manual (Miklowitz & Goldstein, 1997) and watch sample FFT videotapes. Then they serve as cotherapists to trained FFT therapists. After treating two cases with close supervision, they are usually ready to see families or couples independently or to take on trainees themselves.

The cotherapy model has advantages separate from training. It has a long history in the family therapy literature (see, e.g., Napier & Whitaker, 1978). Cotherapists have a way of keeping their fellow therapists on track. Also, if one member of the family appears to be feeling "ganged up on" by one clinician and other family members, the other therapist can bridge the gap by allying himself/herself with this family member. In-session dialogue between the clinicians can also provide effective modeling of communication skills for members of a family or couple.

PRETREATMENT ASSESSMENTS

Diagnostic Evaluation

Bipolar disorder is becoming increasingly common as a diagnosis in inpatient and outpatient community settings. Although this is a positive development, given its underidentification in the past, there is also an element of sloppiness in modern diagnostic evaluations. Perhaps this derives in part from inadequate insurance reimbursement for the evaluation phases of a patient's treatment. Some of the patients referred to the Colorado Family Project have been more aptly diagnosed as having cyclothymic disorder, borderline personality disorder, or even major depressive disorder, recurrent. Our colleagues in community practice have often noted the same problem when patients who presumably have bipolar disorder are referred to them. Thus, upon seeing a new patient, a clinician will often find it useful to do a formal assessment using all or part of a structured diagnostic interview, to determine the reliability of the diagnosis.

Within our research protocols, we have used the Structured Clinical Interview for DSM-IV—Patient Version (SCID; First, Spitzer, Gibbon, & Williams, 1995) as the diagnostic assessment device. The SCID is well described elsewhere (Spitzer, Williams, Gibbon, & First, 1992). Some of the factors that can affect the data obtained from the SCID include whether the patient is acutely ill versus stable; acutely ill patients are less reliable in their symptom reports. Typically, patients in a manic state minimize their symptoms, whereas depressed patients do the reverse. Patients with bipolar disorder also have trouble with retrospective reporting: "I've had over 1,000 episodes" and "I've been constantly manic–depressed since I was an infant" are common responses to diagnostic interviews.

Whether one uses the structured SCID or an open-ended clinical interview, it is often difficult to tell whether a patient's mood dysregulations and associated changes in activity are at the subsyndromal or syndromal levels. Some patients report brief periods of hypomania or irritability that alternate with more severe depressions. These brief activated periods do not always reach the DSM-IV duration threshold for hypomania (4 days or more). Some of these patients are better labeled as having cyclothymic disorder or major depressive disorder.

Akiskal (1996; Akiskal & Akiskal, 1992) has encouraged clinicians to consider a broader bipolar spectrum that includes core temperamental disturbances. In addition to cyclothymia, Akiskal describes a "bipolar III" or "pseudounipolar" subtype, in which patients have recurrent major depressions with an underlying temperament marked by hyperthymia (exuberance, overoptimism, grandiosity, stimulus seeking, physical intrusiveness with others), and/or a family history of bipolar disorder. He also describes a subgroup of patients with "subbipolar dysthymia," marked by mild depressions with hypomanias that are evoked by antidepressant treatment. Akiskal argues that these "soft-spectrum" patients respond to the same medications as traditional bipolar I patients, and often have similar family histories.

In FFT, the broadening of the bipolar spectrum to include these patients introduces a quandary: Does the clinician proceed with such patients in the same way as with bipolar I or bipolar II patients? How does the clinician educate the patient and family about the factors that bring about manic or depressive episodes if discrete episodes cannot be identified? If a patient has never had a true manic episode in the absence of antidepressants, should the treatment proceed under the assumption that eventually he/she will develop mania spontaneously? Do the same self-management techniques (e.g., using problem solving to minimize family conflict) apply? For our research, we have opted to include only patients with bipolar I or II disorder as defined by DSM-IV criteria. Our general impression has been that patients who do not go through clear-cut cycles of mood episodes are a different population of patients. However, we see value in further research on Akiskal's conceptualization of the soft spectrum of bipolar disorder, and particularly research that evaluates whether psychosocial interventions should play the same or a different—perhaps even a more intensive—role in the treatment of such patients.

The Mood Chart

Clarity on the diagnosis, as well as the patient's progress in treatment, is aided by asking the patient to keep a daily mood record. One such instrument is the Social Rhythm Metric (Monk, Flaherty, Frank, Hoskinson, & Kupfer, 1990; Monk, Kupfer, Frank, & Ritenour, 1991), which asks the patient to document daily mood on a –5 (depressed) to +5 (euphoric/activated) scale, along with social routines that may influence these moods, (such as sleep–wake times, times when the patient socializes, the intensity of this social stimulation, the patient's exercise habits, and other factors). Leverich and Post (1998) have developed a self-rated "life chart" that requires the patient to keep track of daily mood variations, medications, life stressors, and sleep.

Data from mood/activity charts help the clinician and patient to evaluate collaboratively the type of cycling the patient experiences, and the degree to which social stressors contribute to mood fluctuations. Figure 12.2 gives an example of a mood chart; note the cycling of the disorder in relation to specific social stressors and sleep patterns reported by the patient. In this example, a stressor (a pet's illness) was associated with sleep disruption and the appearance of mixed mood symptoms at the subsyndromal level.

Family Assessments

Psychoeducational approaches usually begin with a thorough assessment of family attitudes and behaviors to identify the targets of intervention. We begin with the Camberwell Family Interview, the instrument for rating EE discussed earlier. This interview is usually done when the patient is acutely symptomatic, and focuses on the prior 3-month period, which usually includes the prodromal phases of symptom buildup. For the purposes of clinical planning over research, the interview yields answers to such questions as these: What is the current level of tension in the household and in the relative/patient relationship? Which of the patient's behaviors are

"eliciting stimuli" for family arguments or hostility? Do family members understand that the patient has bipolar disorder, or are they likely to attribute the patient's negative behaviors to internal or controllable factors?

A problem with the EE/Camberwell method is its lack of easy exportability to community care settings. Interviews with two parents can total 3 hours, and the coding of interview tapes can add an additional 6 person-hours per family. If a clinician's purposes are those of treatment planning rather than research, the clinician may be able to substitute a self-report measure such as the Perceived Criticism Scale (Hooley & Teasdale, 1989). This measure simply asks the patient to rate, on a 1–10 scale, the degree to which close relatives express critical comments toward him/her and the degree to which he/she expresses critical comments toward relatives. In one prospective study, self-reported scores on this instrument were just as strong in predicting depressive relapse among patients with recurrent major depression as were EE scores from the Camberwell method (Hooley & Teasdale, 1989). Evaluation of this scale as a predictor of the course of bipolar disorder will be accomplished in a multicenter effectiveness trial of treatments for adult bipolar disorder (Sachs, 1998).

In our research protocols, we typically bring the family in for an interactional assessment once the patient has achieved some degree of remission. First, each member of the family, including the patient, is interviewed individually and asked to identify two family problem topics. Then each participant is asked to ver-

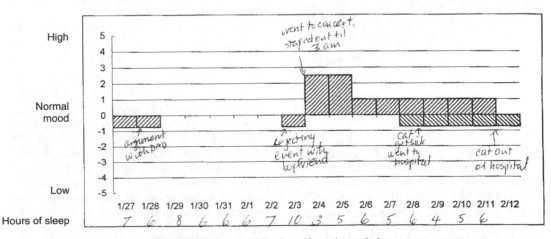

FIGURE 12.2. Example of a self-rated mood chart.

balize the nature of this problem as if the family member to whom the problem statement is directed were sitting across from him/her (e.g., a mother states, "Ralph, you never tell me when something is wrong, even though I know it is"). A tape recording of this problem statement is then played for the opposing family member, who is asked to respond on tape contiguously (e.g., "Mom, I don't talk to you because when I do, it makes things worse"). Two simulated "conversations" are obtained from each family member, and the clinician or experimenter chooses one from the patient and one from a relative as stimuli for family discussions. Next, the family is brought into a meeting room with videotaping capability. The first of these two problem cue–response sequences is played, and the family members are asked to discuss the problem for 10 minutes, to tell each other why they said what they did on the tape and how they feel about the issue, and to try to reach a resolution. The clinician then exits the room, and the discussion ensues. Then he/she reenters the room and plays the second cue–response sequence, and a second 10-minute discussion ensues. Transcripts of these 10-minute problem-solving discussions can then be coded, using the Category System for Coding Partner Interactions (see above) or a similar interactional coding system. Unfortunately, obtaining this information from transcripts is very labor-intensive and cannot usually be carried out before the treatment begins. Instead, the clinician can rely on simple observations of the family's communication and problem-solving behavior to inform the skill-training modules of FFT.

What forms of interaction are targeted in FFT? First, many family members or patients are unable to focus on a single problem, and instead begin to "cross-complain" or bring up accusations of other family members to counteract the accusations that are being made of them. Some engage in attack–counterattack cycles, which may include negative verbal behaviors or nonverbal behaviors. For any particular family, the clinician must first identify the form these interchanges take; which dyadic or triadic relationships they involve; the content areas that trigger the interchanges (e.g., medication-taking habits, independence, boundaries within the family); and whether members of the family are able to stop these cycles before they spiral out of control. Who criticizes whom and how often? How does the target person respond? Does the original problem ever get solved?

During these unsupervised family interactions, some family members will combine negative affect with unclear or fragmented communication, which has been called "communication deviance" in the schizophrenia literature (Wynne, Singer, Bartko, & Toohey, 1977). We have found that the relatives of patients with bipolar disorder do not differ in levels of communication deviance from the relatives of patients with schizophrenia (Miklowitz et al., 1991). Patients with bipolar disorder and their relatives often speak in a hurried, driven manner and often jumble phrases, get words out of order, or express fragments of ideas. The extent to which these communication styles reflect situational stress or enduring patterns of relating in the family is not clear. Nonetheless, FFT can include exercises that focus on communication clarity as well as affective balance.

PROCESS OF TREATMENT

Psychoeducation

The initiation of the psychoeducation module of FFT requires three conditions. First, the patient must be seeing a psychiatrist and have begun a medication regimen. Second, he/she must have achieved some degree of clinical stability, although there is no requirement that the acute episode be fully remitted. Third, the family should have undergone an assessment of attitudes and interactional behaviors, even if not as formalized as described for the research protocols.

Table 12.2 summarizes the topical domains that are covered in the first module of FFT, psychoeducation. In the seven or more weekly sessions that constitute this module, participants (patients and their close relatives) are acquainted with the symptoms of bipolar disorder; the way in which episodes develop; the roles of genetics, biology, and stress; pharmacological treatments; and the role of stress management strategies.

The Initial Sessions: Providing a Rationale

As in most other forms of therapy, the clinicians begin by explaining the rationale for the

TABLE 12.2. Issues in Psychoeducation

The symptoms and course of the disorder
- The signs and symptoms of bipolar disorder
- The development of the most recent episode
- The recent life events survey
- Discussing the hospitalization experience
- Variations in prognosis: The course of the disorder

The etiology of bipolar disorder
- The vulnerability–stress model
- The roles of stress and life events
- Genetic and biological predispositions
- Risk and protective factors

Intervening within the vulnerability–stress model
- Types of medication and what they do
- Psychosocial treatments
- How the family can help
- The self-management of the disorder
- The relapse drill

Note. From Miklowitz and Goldstein (1997). Copyright 1997 by The Guilford Press. Reprinted with permission.

FFT program. Many participants will question why family or couple sessions should accompany medication for a patient adjusting to a recent episode of bipolar disorder. Particularly helpful in orienting participants is the "reentry model":

"An episode of mood disorder can be quite traumatic to all members of the family. . . . In bipolar disorder, when the person returns home and begins to recover, there is a 'getting reacquainted' period in which everyone has to get to know everyone else again, and when everyone tries to make sense of what happened. This is a tough time for any family, and part of our purpose here is to make this 'reacquaintance period' less disturbing to all of you. We'd like during this year to get you, as a family, back to where you were before _____ became ill. We want to give you some tools to deal with this recovery period." (Miklowitz & Goldstein, 1997, p. 93)

There are two purposes for this introduction. First, it communicates to the family members that their emotional reactions to the patient's illness—even if quite negative—are normal and expectable. Second, it implies that the therapy will include exploration and clarification of participants' emotional reactions to information about the disorder. This feature of the therapy can be made even more explicit:

"If feelings come up for you when we're discussing this material, please bring them up. We're interested in knowing how this material applies to you and your own experiences. You may or may not agree with some of the material we present here. . . . The purpose of focusing on this material is to put your experiences into a context that will make sense." (Miklowitz & Goldstein, 1997, p. 99)

Next, the treatment is previewed:

"We're going to work with you on two different levels. One is on encouraging _____'s ongoing work with his/her psychiatrist so that he/she can get himself/herself stabilized on the medications. The second is on how you as a family can minimize stress. . . . We think there are several ways to do this, including acquainting you with the facts about bipolar disorder, and working with you on improving your communication and problem solving with each other. These strategies should increase _____'s chances of making a good recovery and help you as a family cope with the disorder. How does this sound to you?" (Miklowitz & Goldstein, 1997, p. 94)

The Symptoms of Bipolar Disorder

FFT proceeds with a series of handouts that are used as stimuli for generating family or couple discussions. The first of these is a list of symptoms of manic, hypomanic, depressive, and psychotic episodes. The purpose of this handout is not for the participants to memorize the DSM-IV criteria. Rather, it is a starting point for destigmatizing the illness and breaking family taboos against talking about it. The patient is asked to scan the list and describe to his/her family members the way it feels when one is euphoric, irritable, unable to sleep, or activated by racing thoughts or grandiose plans. Likewise, family members describe the behaviors they observed when the patient was cycling into mania or hypomania. A similar dialogue is undertaken for depression symptoms. Consider the following dialogue among a patient (P), mother (M), father (F), and therapist (T).

P: Well, the thing is, there's the manic and then there's the hypomanic. When I'm manic, I really should be hospitalized. I control the weather; I'm famous. . . . When I'm hypomanic, well, I just can get into that from having too much stress, too much caffeine, and being all revved up . . .

M: I can tell when she's high because I start getting real mad at her. She provokes me.

F: And she gets this look in her eyes. And she says we're not listening to her . . .

P: But you're not! That's when you're most likely to tune me out!

T: Let's hold on that for now, about listening. It's very important, and certainly something we'll want to focus on as we go along, but what else do you notice when you get manic or hypomanic? [Redirects the focus.]

P: I get sort of, well, reactive . . . everything I experience so intensely, but, see, they know this as who I am.

Note the themes that arise in this discussion of symptoms, and how these relate to the six objectives of FFT outlined in Table 12.1. The patient's vulnerability to recurrences is made explicit by the family's identification of the prodromal signs of her episodes. The patient points to the role of disturbed family communication. She alludes to questions about whether some of her symptoms are really just personality traits (i.e., intensiveness and reactivity). There is a beginning discussion of stress factors that may play a role in triggering her episodes.

The Vulnerability–Stress Model and the Life Events Survey

Early in psychoeducation, the family clinicians make a strong argument for the conjoint influences of stress, biological imbalances of the brain, and genetic vulnerability in the course of bipolar illness. A handout illustrating these vulnerability–stress interactions is provided, and various risk and protective factors are reviewed. For example, the patient and family members are warned of the impact of "poor sleep hygiene" (i.e., keeping irregular hours, having unpredictable bedtimes); alcohol and drug use; stressful family interchanges; and provocative, overstimulating interpersonal interactions. They are encouraged to make use of available protective factors (e.g., social supports), and to help the patient maintain adherence to his/her pharmacotherapy regime. The purposes of the patient's

various medications are given, and the role of blood level monitoring is reviewed.

In outlining protective factors, a special emphasis is placed on keeping the family environment low in conflict and on relatives' maintaining reasonable performance expectations of the patient during the recovery period. In the following vignette, the clinician reminds the patient and his mother that depression is not the same as lack of effort, and that a period of recovery prior to regaining one's premorbid occupational status is to be expected.

T: (*To Gary, the patient*) I think you can't expect too much just yet. You're still recovering from your episode. It may take some time to get back on track.

M: How long? He's been like this now for a while.

T: I'm sure that's frustrating, but you have to think of this as a convalescent period. When someone has a bad flu, he may need an extra day or two in bed in order to recover completely. For bipolar disorder, this period of time can average 3 and even 6 months. But, Gary, with your drug treatments and our family sessions, I have every expectation that you'll recover and be able to get back to work.

The clinician here offers hope, but does not paint a rosy picture of the future either. Often the family has been through these episodes before, and a clinician who offers an excessively optimistic view of the future will be dismissed as unrealistic.

Describing the biology and genetics of the disorder is critical to justifying the role of medications. However, it is not necessary for the clinicians to go into detail about the neurophysiology of the disorder. Instead, the clinicians begin by asking the participants to review their family pedigree and discuss any other persons in the family who have had episodes of bipolar disorder. In reviewing this history, the family is told that the vulnerability to bipolar disorder may take many forms, including depression without mania, alcoholism, suicide, and dysthymia. Next, the notion of biochemical imbalances is shared:

"Sometimes the cells may have too much activity and communicate messages a little too quickly, at least when a person is getting manic. When a person gets depressed, the messages may not get through fast enough. These imbalances of brain chemicals can't be controlled by you through conscious effort, but the medications you take can go a long way toward balancing the activity in your nervous system."

When family members begin to attribute aversive behaviors on the patient's part to willfulness (the "fundamental attributional error"), they can be reminded of the existence of biochemical imbalances. But the family and patient should also be discouraged from overemphasizing the biological nature of the disorder, to the neglect of stress factors (which are more controllable). In other words, the patient is not entirely taken off of the hook: He/she is encouraged to self-monitor when getting into conflicts with family members, and to determine whether his/her reactions to these conflicts reflect an unresolved symptom state or a reemergence of conflicts that would have been troublesome even before he/she became ill.

Clarifying the development and triggers for the most recent episode is aided by a life events survey, which lists over 100 life changes that could have occurred during the interval in which the episode was developing. Some of these events are quite severe and negative (e.g., death of a parent), and some are quite mild but may have provoked changes in sleep–wake cycles (e.g., taking a vacation). The life events list is passed out, and the family is engaged in a discussion about triggers that may have been important in provoking the current episode. The clinicians individualize this discussion as much as possible: The triggers for one patient's mania are not the same as for another's, and triggers for mania and depression within the same patient can be quite different.

The Relapse Drill

Toward the end of psychoeducation, the family and patient are given their first exposure to problem solving. The task is to review the prodromal signs of a developing episode and go through the steps that will be necessary to prevent a full relapse. Participants are asked to generate alternative courses of action should the patient relapse into mania or depression. These can include arranging emergency psychiatric services (e.g., calling the

patient's psychiatrist, arranging for a serum lithium level to be taken) or less intensive strategies such as behavioral activation (e.g., helping the depressed patient schedule positive events during the day). Each family member is asked to perform a function in the relapse prevention plan. For example, in some families it may make sense for a parent to undertake contact with the physician. In others, the patient may want the first opportunity to do so. The family or couple is encouraged to leave phone numbers of emergency contact people, including the family clinicians, in an easily accessible place.

Dealing with Resistance to the Illness Concept

Patients with bipolar disorder have strong reactions to the psychoeducational materials, as do their family members. These materials require that the participants recognize bipolar disorder as an illness that will eventually recur. Younger patients are particularly likely to rebel against the notion of recurrent illness, particularly if they are still hypomanic; they feel powerful and in control, and the illness feels like shackles. Moreover, they are attuned to the stigma associated with bipolar disorder or any other psychiatric diagnosis, and fear that their behavior will now be labeled as that of a crazy person. Resistance can also originate with family members. Relatives of depressed patients are apt to see the disorder as willfully caused and not the product of biochemical imbalances. Resistance that originates from the patient or his/her relatives is often associated with family conflict.

Accepting a psychiatric disorder is a painful process for patients and relatives. Often the psychoeducational materials raise questions such as "Why me? Why now? What kind of life will I have? Will people treat me like I'm mentally ill from now on? Will I ever get back to normal?" Relatives ask themselves similar painful questions, such as "Will I always have to take care of him/her? Are my dreams and hopes for him/her gone?" Spouses/partners may ask, "Should I leave him/her?"

When asking themselves these questions, some patients respond by "underidentifying" or denying the reality of the disorder, or giving superficial acknowledgment of the illness but living their lives as if it were not real.

Others "overidentify" and unnecessarily limit themselves (e.g., one woman avoided romantic relationships because "no one will ever be able to get close to me because of my mood swings"). Likewise, family members can deny the realities of the disorder or, in contrast, overmonitor the patient's health status and try to unnecessarily limit his/her behavior. Family conflict reaches a maximum when there is a mismatch between coping styles, such as when patients underidentify and relatives overidentify, or the reverse.

FFT clinicians proceed with a sensitivity to the painful emotional issues underlying these reactions to psychoeducation. One method for dealing with these reactions is to predict that denial will occur, and reframe it as a sign of health. For example, consider a young man with hypomania who has accepted a medication regimen but denies being ill, and whose parents are overly controlling and overmonitoring of his behavior. To this young man, the clinician might say:

> "Although I appreciate that you're taking medication and going along with the treatment plan, I'm going to guess that you're not always going to want to do this. You probably have some questions about whether this diagnosis is right for you or whether you'll have more symptoms. I can understand why you'd have these questions. Coming to terms with having bipolar disorder—or really any illness—is a very painful process that can be hard to accept. This is a normal and a healthy struggle. So, as we're going through our material, you may find yourself reacting to it and feeling that it can't be relevant to you. But I'd like for you to agree that if you have these reactions, you'll bring them up so we can discuss them."

Note that this intervention has a paradoxical flavor. Paradoxical interventions have a long history in family systems therapy (see, e.g., Haley, 1963). However, note that the clinician stops short of actually encouraging the patient to remain resistant or increase his level of disagreement with the diagnosis. Instead, the clinician reframes this denial as healthy and expectable, and connects it with an underlying emotional struggle.

A second way of intervening is through "spreading the affliction." Being labeled as mentally ill can put a person in a one-down position vis-à-vis other family members, in-cluding siblings with whom he/she may already feel competitive. A possible side effect of psychoeducation is the exaggeration of these structural family problems. The clinician can avoid this trap by encouraging other members of the family to discuss their own experiences with depression, anxiety, or other problems. This process can normalize and destigmatize psychiatric problems and take the patient "off the hot seat."

The following vignette involves Josh, a 25-year-old with a recent manic episode. He reacted strongly because he thought everyone was telling him he was "whacked out." According to Josh, all he had done was "party too much." During one of the psychoeducation sessions, his father admitted to having had a depressive episode in college.

T: Josh, you seem like you're reacting to something I just said about bipolar disorder. Were you offended?

J: I dunno. It wasn't anything you said; just I get tired of being the only one in the family who has problems.

T: Is that really true? Has anyone else in the family ever had any problems with depression? Or what I've called mania?

F: I did, and I've told Josh about this. Remember what I told you about college?

J: (*Sullen*) I don't know. Why don't you clue us in?

F: I had that long period when I couldn't sleep and I couldn't eat, and I couldn't study. I dropped out for a semester.

The session then focused on the father and his own history of depression. He revealed a possible psychosis involving delusional thinking. The patient became more cooperative in the discussions that followed, and more willing to talk about how the illness label made him feel stigmatized.

A third method of dealing with resistance involves making analogies to medical disorders. The illness feels less humiliating to the patient if it can be seen within the continuum of other kinds of chronic physical illness. It is equally important for family members to hear these analogies. Diabetes and hypertension are often good comparisons, particularly because the influence of stress can also be brought to bear:

"Bipolar disorder involves biological imbalances much like hypertension does, and it's affected by stress in much the same way. Most people have changes in blood pressure when something stressful happens. But people with hypertension have a vulnerability to extreme shifts in their blood pressure. In the same way, most people have mood changes when something important happens, but people with bipolar disorder operate at greater extremes."

In making these analogies, the clinician validates the patient's feelings about stigma:

"Although there are some similarities with illnesses like hypertension, bipolar disorder can be tougher to live with because other people tend to be afraid of it and don't know what it means. They can think you're doing it on purpose. You have to take the time to educate other people and explain it in a way that they won't be freaked out by it."

Communication Enhancement Training

The second module of FFT, CET, begins at approximately Session 8 and lasts for about seven or eight sessions (five weekly followed by two or three biweekly). CET is guided by two assumptions. First, aversive family communication is a common sequel to an episode of a psychiatric illness, and to a large extent reflects distress within the family or couple in members' attempts to deal with the disorder. Second, aversive communication patterns can be improved upon through skills training. CET uses a role-playing format to teach patients and their relatives four communication skills: offering positive feedback, active listening, making positive requests for changes in others' behaviors, and giving negative feedback. These skills are central to the behavioral family management approach to schizophrenia of Falloon and colleagues (1984) and Liberman, Wallace, Falloon, and Vaughn (1981).

The degree to which each of these skills dominates the role-play exercises varies according to the family assessments conducted earlier. Treatment of a family with much heated conflict and high-EE attitudes might focus on adaptive ways in which participants could ask for changes in each other's behaviors. Treatment of an emotionally disengaged couple might focus on positive feedback and listening skills to coax the partners into experimenting with a more interdependent relationship.

The module begins with an explication of the CET method for the family:

"A person can be at risk for another relapse of bipolar disorder if the home environment is tense.... Good communication and problem solving can be among those 'protective factors' against stress that we talked about before. For a close relative, learning effective communication skills can be a way of decreasing tension and improving family relationships.... We want to help you communicate in the most clear and the least stressful way possible ... we'll be asking you to turn your chairs to each other and practice new ways of talking among yourselves." (Miklowitz & Goldstein, 1997; pp. 191–193)

Note that CET is linked with two of the six objectives of the larger treatment program: helping participants to cope with stress triggers, and restoring functional family relationships after an illness episode.

The first two skills, delivering positive feedback and active listening, generally foster a feeling of collaboration between members of the couple or family. In contrast, making positive requests and giving negative feedback are more conflict-oriented, and are only introduced once participants are used to the role-playing and behavioral rehearsal format. For each skill, the clinician gives the participants a handout that lists its components (e.g., for active listening: make good eye contact, nod your head, ask clarifying questions, paraphrase/check out what you have heard). Then the clinician models the skill for the family. For example, the clinician might compliment one member of the family for his/her cooperativeness with the treatment, or model effective listening while another member of the family talks about a problem. If a cotherapist is available, the therapist can model these skills with him/her.

After the skill is introduced and modeled, the participants are asked to practice the skills with each other, with coaching and shaping by the clinician. Typically the therapist coaches one participant at a time on appropriate ways to use a given skill. The feedback of other family members is actively solicited. The speaker or listener is then asked to try the skill again, until he/she has reasonably approximated its use. A homework assignment, in which the participants keep a written log of their efforts in using the skills between sessions, facilitates generalization of the learning process to the home and work settings.

Many times, the skills are harder than they look. Consider Jessie, a 38-year-old woman with bipolar disorder who had had several episodes of psychotic mania, and who also had a borderline level of mental retardation. She worked part-time as a gift wrapper in a department store. Jessie was trying to move into her own apartment, and required help finding a moving van. She was instructed to learn to make positive requests of her father, with whom she and her sister lived.

T: Maybe that's a good topic to ask your dad about. Can you look at this "Positive Requests" handout and use these steps to ask your dad to help you move?

F: It won't help. There won't be anything for them to move because she still hasn't packed a single box! (*Laughs*)

J: Well, get me the damn boxes and I'll do it.

T: [*Derailing this interchange*] Do you think you could ask your dad for something specific, like helping you find a moving company?

J: (*Looks at father, smirking*) Dad, will you help me find a moving company? (*Giggles*)

F: (*More serious*) You're not . . . you're not looking at this (*indicates handout*). You're supposed to say, "I'd appreciate it if you would . . ."

J: (*Shrugs*) All right, I'd appreciate it if you would! Get me a phone number. Please.

T: (*After pause*) Well, you got part of it that time, Jessie. Dad, what'd you like about what she just said to you?

F: (*Sarcastically*) Gee, all the sincerity.

J: (*Laughs nervously*)

T: Well, if you didn't care for it, can you say how she might say it to you?

F: How about something like "I'd appreciate it if you'd get me those phone numbers. It'd make it a lot more comfortable for me to plan my move."

T: Nice job, Dad. Jessie, what did your dad do that you liked or didn't like?

J: He followed the sheet. He did all the things you said.

T: True, but you don't have to say it exactly the way he did. You can put your own spin on it. Do you feel you could try doing it one more time?

J: (*Gasps, giggles*)

T: I know it's hard being in the hot seat. But you're doing fine. Keep trying.

J: Dad, could you get me those phone numbers of the movers? I'd appreciate it. That way I could be . . . I wouldn't have to worry about the move, and, well, just thank you for your help.

T: That was very good, Jessie. Dad, how did you like it that time?

F: (*A little tentative*) That was better. It made a lot more sense.

These kinds of skills are most difficult to learn if the patient is highly symptomatic or if the level of conflict in the family is so severe that productive conversations cannot ensue. This patient was moderately hypomanic and also had limited intellectual resources. Clearly, the skills training taxed her and made her nervous. However, with patience and practice, she was able to adopt some of the communication skills, and her relationship with her father gradually improved. Her father, who was often quite critical, became more and more convinced that her limited functioning was a result of her bipolar disorder, rather than lack of effort as he had believed previously.

In the FFT manual (Miklowitz & Goldstein, 1997), we have described "short-fuse" families. These families begin with apparently innocuous discussions, which quickly escalate into angry, back-and-forth volleys of criticism or hostility. Our research indicates that these are usually high-EE families or couples, but not invariably (Simoneau et al., 1998). We have been surprised that relatives who on the surface appear benign and supportive of the patient during the EE/Camberwell interview become quite aggressive and confrontational when facing the patient in a one-to-one interaction. The likelihood that this will occur is greatly augmented if the patient is hypomanic and irritable.

A short-fuse family typically has difficulty with communication training, because the participants' emotions quickly get out of hand (see the case study presented later). But much can be accomplished by modifying CET to adapt to this dynamic. For example, the therapist can encourage the participants to use active listening skills during arguments. After a negative, back-and-forth interchange involving a couple, a clinician said:

"I think this is an important discussion. You're a couple that really likes to get things out in the open. But I'm afraid that you're missing out on each other's viewpoints. So let's see if we can make it more productive. I want you each to paraphrase each other's statements before making your next argument, like we did in the active listening exercises. Also, why don't you turn your chairs to each other so that you can more easily keep eye contact?"

Note again the use of reframing. It is better to cast a couple's or family's ongoing dynamics (unless clearly abusive or threatening) as an adaptive way of coping that needs modification than to label these dynamics as "bad" or "dysfunctional."

A short-fuse family may also make good use of positive requests for change or negative feedback, in which the partners make constructive suggestions about specific aspects of each other's behavior (e.g., "I don't like it when you talk down to me about my cleaning habits") and offer suggestions as to ways these behaviors could be improved (e.g., "Could you be more aware of your tone of voice?"). These exercises often set the stage for problem solving, the final module of FFT.

Problem-Solving Skills Training

Families of patients with bipolar disorder, whether these be couples (see, e.g., Hoover & Fitzgerald, 1981) or parental families of bipolar adults (Miklowitz, Goldstein, & Nuechterlein, 1987; Simoneau et al., 1998), have difficulty with problem solving. Family problems in adjusting to the postepisode phases of bipolar disorder appear to fall into one of four categories: medication nonadherence, difficulty resuming prior work and social roles, repairing the financial and social damage done during manic episodes ("life trashing"), and relationship/living situation conflicts.

Problem solving is one of the oldest and most validated methods of family intervention (for a review, see Clarkin & Miklowitz, 1997). Its purposes in FFT are twofold: (1) to open a dialogue among family members about difficult conflict topics, and allow them a context to share their emotional reactions to these problems; and (2) to help them develop a framework for defining, generating and evaluating solutions to, and implementing effective solutions to problems. This module occupies the final four to five sessions of FFT, and usually begins by the fourth or fifth month when sessions have been tapered to biweekly. Problem solving is positioned last in FFT because the patient is usually in remission by this point and is more able, both cognitively and emotionally, to experiment with new ways of behaving. Furthermore, if the psychoeducation and CET have gone well, family members are more ready to see their own role in generating or maintaining family conflicts.

In problem solving, families are taught to break broad problems down into smaller units, which are more amenable to solution. They are given a problem-solving worksheet in which they are asked to take the following steps: define the problem (with each participant's input); "brainstorm" all possible solutions without evaluating them; consider each solution individually and weigh its advantages and disadvantages; choose a best solution or combination of solutions; and plan and implement the chosen solutions. Once they have had at least a moderately successful experience in solving a relatively minor problem, participants are given a homework task in which they record their attempts to solve a new, larger problem. Assignments are sometimes quite modest; some families are simply given the task of defining one or more problems to work on in the upcoming session.

The rationale for problem solving is presented as follows:

"Up until now, we've been talking mainly about how you communicate with each other. Now we'd like to deal with some of the concrete problems of living you've all been alluding to. But rather than our just giving you suggestions about what to do about these—which probably wouldn't work that well anyway—we'd like to teach you a way of solving problems cooperatively, as a family." (Miklowitz & Goldstein, 1997, p. 240)

This rationale is then followed by a review of the steps for solving problems, and familiarizing the family or couple with a problem solving worksheet. The clinician also reviews some of the problems the members raised during the earlier phases of treatment.

Consider this case example of the problem-solving method. Karla, age 35, moved in with her new boyfriend, Taki, shortly after her divorce. She was in poor shape financially; she had a tendency to "spend to improve my self-esteem." In fact, most of her spending sprees occurred during hypomanic periods, and she had become hypomanic shortly after meeting Taki. He was quite well off and, perhaps due to his eagerness to make the relationship work, gave her access to his credit cards. During their first months together, his bills increased hugely. Her own employment was inconsistent. She had had trouble for years keeping to a budget and maintaining a checking account.

They had begun to fight heavily about this problem. Karla argued that money was his way of controlling women, and Taki argued that she was taking advantage of him and being inconsiderate. First, the clinician encouraged them to expand on these broader issues before zeroing in on the more specific issue of spending. This was done through returning to the communication exercises: Karla voiced her opinion about what she felt was the "meat of the problem" while Taki listened. Then Taki described his take on the underlying issues while Karla listened and paraphrased.

The structure imposed by problem solving eventually helped them define the issue more specifically: Karla spent more on clothing and "comfort items" than either of them thought she should, but it was unrealistic for her to try to support herself, given her unresolved clinical state. Various options were then considered: Taki doing most of the buying, Karla being assigned her own account with an upper limit negotiated each month, and the two of them simply separating their finances. Each of these and other options were evaluated as to their advantages and disadvantages. Finally, they agreed on a somewhat complicated but clever solution: Karla was to obtain three bank debit cards assigned to each of three accounts. Each card was labeled with an expense item (e.g., "doctor bills") and had a spending limit posted on it. They

were to meet weekly to determine whether the solution was working, and to practice listening skills with each other when they began to disagree.

In this example, the problem was to some degree generated by the patient's residual symptoms. There were also underlying relationship dynamics: Karla tended to become overly dependent on men and then to devalue them, and Taki tended to rescue women and then become angry about being in the rescuer role. The clinician decided to let them first "ventilate" about these larger relationship themes. Allowing a certain amount of emotional expression about loaded issues often unlocks a family's or couple's resistance to dealing with more specific problems (in this case, disagreements about spending).

When taking families or couples through their first problem-solving exercises, FFT clinicians monitor the participants' reactions to the method. Reactions can vary from "This is just what we need" to "Gee, how superficial." Patients with bipolar disorder and their family members seem to crave spontaneity and enjoy fast-paced, unpredictable interchanges. They get bored easily. The communication and problem-solving exercises impose structure, which, while encouraging the family to maintain goal-directedness, sometimes generates resistance. This can take the form of changing the subject, "cross-complaining," or being unwilling to cooperate with the homework tasks.

When addressing resistances, a clinician reiterates the rationale for problem solving (e.g., "Sometimes you have to gain confidence from solving minor problems before you move on to bigger ones"). But often he/she must determine whether it is really the method that family members object to or whether there are certain costs or painful consequences associated with attempting to solve a problem (e.g., a mother's fear that her son with bipolar disorder will be unable to handle agreed-upon tasks that require greater independence). Families who fear the consequences of solving a problem often approach solutions and then quickly abandon the problem-solving process, arguing that "this is not really the issue."

The therapist has a number of options available. One is to take responsibility for the unsolved problem. For example, he/she can say, "Perhaps it was wrong of me to encourage you to solve this problem. Maybe you have other things you want to deal with first. Would you like to table it for now?" Alternatively, the clinician may proceed more paradoxically, framing the family's difficulty as due to "healthy avoidance": "Solving a problem as a family involves some cost–benefit thinking. There are certainly some benefits to solving this problem, but there may be some hidden costs as well. I think if the costs of solving this problem outweigh the benefits, it's certainly understandable that you'd want to avoid putting a solution in place. Is that what's happening here?" Both of these interventions give the family members "permission" to leave the problem untouched. Later, when the pressure is off, they may be able to return to the problem and have more success the second time around.

Terminating FFT

FFT is usually terminated after 9 months. As the termination of the treatment approaches, a therapist reviews with the family members their various goals for treatment and the degree to which those goals were or were not realized. The status of the patient's bipolar disorder is evaluated relative to the beginning of treatment. In some cases, maintenance or "tuneup" FFT sessions are recommended. The maintenance sessions usually have a time limit (e.g., 3 months).

Referrals for subsequent treatment for both the patient and other family members are discussed. For example, some patients follow up FFT with individual therapy or mutual support groups involving other persons with bipolar disorder. Family members may choose to attend support groups of the National Depressive and Manic Depressive Association or the National Alliance for the Mentally Ill. In our experience, it is unusual for families to request additional family or couple therapy after FFT, but referrals are made if requested. The clinicians reiterate the importance of continued medication compliance and incorporating communication and problem-solving skills into the family's day-to-day life. Finally, a review of the relapse drill (see Psychoeducation section, above) is conducted: The patient's prodromal signs are reviewed, and the steps the patient and family can take to avert a relapse are reiterated.

CASE STUDY

Debra was a 36-year-old white woman who lived with her husband, Barry, age 46, and their 8-year-old daughter, Jill. She had completed 2 years of college and worked part-time as a sales clerk in a luggage shop. She had been married previously. Debra was referred for FFT by a university clinic where she had been diagnosed with bipolar II disorder. The initial SCID confirmed this diagnosis. Her depression was marked by loss of interests and "being bummed" for several weeks at a time. She also complained of loss of appetite, waking several times each night, fatigue, guilt, and loss of concentration. She denied suicidal thoughts. She recounted that her current depression was "a really big one" and had lasted on and off for a full year. She also said, "I've had tons of small ones." She dated the first onset of her depression to approximately 8 years earlier.

Debra also admitted to hypomania in the previous month, including about 5 days of elevated and irritable mood. She explained that "my confidence level was up." She admitted to racing thoughts, increased activity and talkativeness, and becoming involved in many different projects. She had trouble dating the onset and offset of these periods, noting that "I've been this way all my life." She did admit that Barry commented on these mood phases. She complained that "He now tells me I'm getting manic every time we get in an argument . . . it's his newest weapon against me." She denied delusions or hallucinations. She had been treated previously with sertraline (Zoloft) and bupropion (Wellbutrin). Her psychiatrist had recently started her on divalproex sodium (Depakote) at 1500 mg/ day, a medication she said had made a difference in stabilizing her mood.

Barry, an attorney, presented as a "nononsense" type of man. He responded to the clinicians in a very businesslike manner, and insisted that he had no problems of his own to discuss "except those that relate to Debra's care." He denied any psychiatric history himself. He preferred to talk about FFT as an educational course, and became defensive if it was referred to by his wife as "therapy." The clinicians did not dissuade him from labeling the treatment this way, believing that they would need to work on building a rapport with him before addressing his defensive style.

Family Assessment

Based on the Camberwell Family Interview, a staff member of the Colorado Family Project determined that Barry met the criteria for a high level of EE. He expressed nine criticisms during this 1-hour interview. He tended to complain at length about Debra's memory, work habits, and disorganization (e.g., "She never remembers about parent–teacher meetings," "She forgets to turn in her time sheet at work"). He admitted that he still loved her but found her very frustrating. He was convinced that she had attention-deficit/hyperactivity disorder as well as bipolar disorder.

Debra and Barry came in for the family interactional assessment well dressed and smiling. The research staff interviewed them individually, and arrived at an important problem topic for them to discuss: Barry's claim that Debra lied to him. Her response was to apologize for her past misdeeds and to argue that "I'm not lying or withholding . . . those are usually things I've forgotten or just don't think are important." Upon discussing this issue, the couple's dynamics became apparent, with Barry speaking in an accusatory, scolding mode and Debra apologizing for and justifying her own behavior. As Barry (B in the dialogues that follow) became more accusatory, Debra (D) looked more and more depressed.

B: Lying is a way of life for you. You twist the truth and say you don't remember things.

D: But I really don't. I've been trying to tell you everything. Sometimes I just forget. (*Starts rocking chair*)

B: (*Holding her chair still*) Why do you think it's OK to lie to me?

D: I don't. I'm being up front with you. Maybe you want to believe there's more, but there's not.

B: I think you'll always do this. It's your bag. How would you like it if I lied to you? How would it make you feel? Would you want to stay married to me?

D: (*Sullen*) No, probably not. But I'm trying to be open with my feelings, kinda with you as a practice case. (*Smiles awkwardly*)

B: You're doing that little smile again. The one you do when you're trying to get away with something.

D: (*Defensive*) Oh, give me a break.

B: Is it because we're talking so directly? I don't know if it's your personality or if it's the bipolar stuff acting up, but you have no tolerance for anything these days, especially people.

The therapists who viewed this assessment were struck by Barry's level of criticism paired with Debra's tendency to take a one-down position. They also learned during the assessment that Barry doled out Debra's medications and made her doctor appointments for her, and also usually attended them with her. An initial appointment for FFT was set with two project clinicians, a man and a woman.

Psychoeducation (Sessions 1–7)

During the initial session, the clinicians (T1 and T2 in the dialogues below) described the FFT program to Barry and Debra, with particular emphasis on the psychoeducational component. They previewed the communication enhancement and problem-solving modules. The couple listened politely but expressed skepticism:

B: We've been in and out of therapy for years. I haven't been impressed.

T1: When you say "We," do you mean you as a couple?

B: As a couple, and she's had her own therapy.

D: I thought Dr. Walker was good.

B: Yeah, but you hadn't had the bipolar diagnosis yet. She was just treating you for depression. And she got into that whole "You were probably abused as a child" thing.

T1: What was your couple therapy like?

B: A lot of digging into our childhoods and getting in touch with our feelings.

T1: Debra?

D: It wasn't that bad. I thought it was pretty useful.

T1: Well, it sounds like you've got different opinions on how helpful those things were. Let me tell you how this will be different. Our treatment is going to be focused mainly on the present, and we'll be working with you on how you as a couple are coping with bipolar disorder. Barry, you're going to be affected by the cycling of Debra's mood disorder, but Debra, you're also going to be affected by the way Barry responds to your symptoms. I'm not saying your past will be irrelevant, just not our focus.

B: I need help dealing with all of this. The more information I get, the better.

T1: I'm sure that's true. But we won't just throw a lot of information at you—we want to individualize this to your situation. I think you'll have a much easier time if you come to a common understanding of the disorder as a couple, and learn to communicate about it.

In this dialogue, the therapist made a distinction between FFT and more generic forms of couple therapy. At this point, the clinicians were already suspecting that there would be resistance from Barry, especially around tasks where he was asked to look at his own behavior and its contribution to Debra's problems.

The psychoeducation itself began in the second session and continued through the seventh. The first task was to encourage the couple to come to a shared definition of bipolar disorder. During the assessments, both had mentioned the term "cycling," but without apparent agreement on what it meant.

T1: I want to be sure we're all on the same page when we discuss the meaning of the term "bipolar." Let's start by reviewing your symptoms, Debra (*passes around a handout describing the symptoms of mania and depression*). Barry, which of these have you observed when Debra gets hypomanic?

B: (*Surveying the handout*) Well, all of these except appetite disturbance. . . . I guess you could say she has grandioseness—she thinks one day she'll be wealthy. (*Laughs*)

T2: When was the last time you think she was like that?

B: Last time I was working on a case—she always gets like that when I'm working on a case.

D: I agree, but I think it's because I have a lot more to do when he's working all the time . . . he thinks it's some "abandonment" thing, but I think he forgets the realities I face when he's gone. . . . (*Looks at list*) I get more energy, I feel uncomfortable in my own body, I jump outta my skin . . . probably a good day to go shopping! (*Giggles*) I probably get crankier, don't have much tolerance for people in general.

B: Especially me. (*Smiles*)

This was the first time that Debra had defended herself, by commenting on how relationship problems fed into her mood swings. Interestingly, her assertive stance cut through some of her husband's negativity.

The therapists soon realized that Barry and Debra lacked a consensus about what really constituted a bipolar episode. This is a critical point in FFT: The members of a couple or family need to come to a shared perception of when the patient is getting ill, so that they can institute procedures to keep the patient's episodes from spiraling (e.g., visits to the physician, reduction in the patient's stress level or workload). But it was not yet clear that Debra had discrete episodes.

T2: Do you think you have what we're calling "episodes"? Like a couple of days of being wired?

D: There can be, like, 2 or 3 days when I can do a lot of stuff, my memory gets better, and then 2 or 3 days when it's just not gonna work. I can . . .

B: (*Interrupts*) It's that household project thing. She starts redoing Jill's room over and over. She'll sponge-paint it purple and then wipe it out that same evening, put in new closets . . .

D: I can filter all my energy into housework instead of killing somebody. (*They both chuckle*)

T1: Maybe I'm a little slow today, but I'm trying to figure out if you both agree when these high and low periods are. Debra, have you ever kept a mood chart?

The clinician then produced a written assignment in which both members of the couple were asked to track, on a daily basis, the ups and downs of Debra's mood states. They were asked to do this independently, so that agreements and disagreements about what constituted the symptoms of the disorder (as opposed to, e.g., personality traits) could be tracked.

The dynamics of this couple became more evident in Sessions 3–5. Debra was inconsistent about keeping her mood chart, and Barry felt that his conscientiousness in charting her mood was not being rewarded. "She won't take responsibility for her illness," he argued. Nonetheless, Debra had good recall of her mood swings, even though she hadn't written them down. The clinicians offered the couple much praise for even their somewhat half-hearted attempt to complete this assignment. Interestingly, Barry noted small changes in mood that he called "mania," which Debra argued were just her reactions to everyday annoyances.

B: You were manic as hell on Saturday morning.

T2: What do you mean, Barry?

B: I went to tell her that Jill needed to get to soccer, and she practically bit my head off!

D: Because you had told me eight times already. I wasn't manic, I was just getting annoyed. Even Jill said something about you overdoing it.

This became a theme throughout the treatment: Barry tended to overlabel Debra's mood swings, to the extent that he often called her "manic" when the real issue appeared to be her transient irritability. He also called her "depressed" when she claimed she was just "relaxing . . . bored . . . trying to unwind and keep to myself for a while." The clinicians were careful not to attribute blame or to tell one of them that he/she was right. One of the clinicians said:

"I think this is a very hard distinction to make. I wish I could give you a simple rule for determining when Debra is in and out of an episode. But as you've seen, it's not always so clear. I usually suggest that people go back to that symptom list and ask, 'Is there more than one of these symptoms? Does irritability go with more sleep disturbance? Racing thoughts?' Just being annoyed is not enough to be called manic, unless it's ongoing, it cuts across different situations, or it goes along with a few of these other symptoms."

The clinicians outlined a vulnerability–stress model for understanding Debra's episodes. Debra recounted a family history of depression in her mother, and alcohol abuse in her father: "My mom was probably bipolar, but we just didn't call it that back then." They also discussed stress triggers that may have contributed to Debra's prior depressions. Barry became very vocal when discussing her risk factors: He noted that crowded places (e.g., shopping malls) made her hypomanic, and that alcohol even in small amounts contributed to her sleep disturbance, which in turn contributed to her hypomanias. The therapists offered a handout on risk factors (e.g., substance abuse, sleep irregularity, unpredictable daily routines, family conflict, and provocative interpersonal situations) and protective factors (e.g., regular medications, good family communication, making use of treatment resources). Next, the clinicians helped Barry and Debra devise a relapse prevention plan:

T1: The clients we've worked with who've done best with this illness have been able to rely on their spouses and other close family members at times of crisis. It's a fine line you have to walk between being able to turn to your spouse and say, "I think I'm getting sick again," and to take some of their advice without giving up control altogether. When your moods are going up and down, you (*to Debra*) are going to want more control. . . . Barry, maybe you sometimes feel like you're walking a fine line as well: You want to say "Yes, you are getting sick, and I'd like to help you," without rubbing it in . . . to be able to give suggestions without taking over.

B: That's one thing we have in common. We're both control freaks. I guess likes attract.

T1: Well, maybe the fact that you both like to be in control of your own fate was part of what attracted the two of you in the first place [reframing]. But like many things that attract people initially, something like not wanting to give up control can become a problem in the relationship later.

The couple came to some agreements about what the prodromal signs of Debra's hypomania looked like (e.g., increases in her interest in household projects, getting up extraordinarily early, irritability that occurred in multiple situations) and some of her triggers (e.g., alcohol). They conjointly developed a relapse prevention plan involving keeping emergency phone numbers handy, avoiding alcohol, and avoiding high-stress, provocative interpersonal situations (e.g., conflicts between Debra and her mother). Barry and Debra also discussed how they could communicate about her symptoms if the latter started to escalate. Barry admitted that he "had to learn not to lash out" at such times, and not to "just blurt out everything I think." Interestingly, both showed resistance to the suggestion that Debra try to maintain a regular sleep–wake cycle, even on weekends, when she had her worst mood swings. They scoffed, "Maybe we should just join the Army," and emphasized that they weren't about to give up their love of late-night partying.

The psychoeducation module ended with a discussion of the effects of the illness label on Debra's self-esteem. She had been alluding throughout the first six sessions to her discomfort with the diagnosis of bipolar II disorder.

T1: Sometimes when we go through our symptom lists and talk about the causes of bipolar disorder, people can feel labeled or picked apart. Debra, have you ever felt that way in here?

D: When I first came in here, I felt picked on. I felt like it was "blame Debbie time," and now there was this real biological reason to pin all our problems on.

T1: I hope you don't think we're saying that all of your problems as a couple stem from your bipolar disorder.

D: No, I think you guys have been fair about that. It was hard for me to talk about, and sometimes I think Barry is just objecting to me, as a person.

T1: In other words, the line between your personality and your disorder gets blurred.

D: Yes, and to me they're very different.

T1: I'm glad you're bringing this up. I think that's very important, to be very clear on when we're just talking about you, your styles of relating to people . . . not everything you do has to be reduced to this illness.

B: And I probably do bring it up [the illness] too much.

D: (*Becoming activated*) Yes, and you bring it up in front of other people . . . that can be a real problem for me. We used to have such great conversations! I get tired of talking with you about my bipolar disorder all the time. That's all you seem to wanna talk about.

B: (*Startled*) Why haven't you told me this?

D: I probably do need to tell you. . . . I just want more of a happy medium, between talking about it and not.

B: So what do you want?

D: I'm not sure.

T1: I think it's understandable that you wouldn't know . . . you're not always sure how much help you need from Barry. Maybe you're trying to find a good balance. That may take some time. I hope you don't feel that all *we're* interested in is your bipolar disorder, and not in you as a person [examines apparent resistance to the psychoeducational material].

D: I usually don't feel that way, except when I try to do that mood chart [acknowledges emotional pain underlying resistance to the therapeutic tasks]. I just want to have conversations with Barry like I have with my girlfriends. I'd like to talk about other things than my illness and my doctors.

Communication Enhancement Training (Sessions 8–14)

During Session 8, the clinicians introduced CET to the couple. Barry and Debra both described a "demand–withdrawal" pattern in their communication. Barry would become intrusive in trying to understand Debra's mood state, and Debra would withdraw and become noncooperative. Debra admitted that she had a difficult time acknowledging being depressed and talking about it, because "you just didn't do that in my family." She grew up in a Southern family where "you didn't air your dirty laundry." In contrast, Barry was from Los Angeles, where "you might spill your guts to whoever was stuck in traffic next to you."

The clinicians began by exploring the demand–withdrawal pattern:

T1: This is one of the dynamics we've seen in couples dealing with bipolar disorder. People with the disorder can get irritable with their spouses, and then their spouses react because they feel under attack, and when they react the arguments can really spiral. The person with the disorder feels there's something they're legitimately angry at, and their husband or wife sees the anger as evidence of the bipolar illness.

B: Well, my problem is that Debra's not aware of her symptoms.

D: I'm aware of them, but I wanna be left alone. You finish my sentences . . .

B: And then you walk out of the room. You don't wanna have anything to do with normal communication. It's just like it was with your parents . . .

D: When I'm in that state [depression], the last thing I want is a serious conversation or to have someone question what I want to do or why.

T2: Let's talk about what happens between the two of you [draws couple back to relationship focus]. When you try to talk about something, what happens? One of you just won't talk? You do talk, but it doesn't go well?

B: She procrastinates, she won't deal with things; then I yell; then she won't be around me and she withdraws; and then I start thinking about how long I can live like this.

T2: Debra, how would you describe it?

D: Barry gets frustrated when I don't give him the answers he's looking for, and then I feel bad that I frustrated him, and he feels bad that he got upset at me, and then I feel bad that I made him feel bad about upsetting me.

T2: Is that something you'd like to work on —your communication as a couple?

B: Yes. There's been no communication because of the bipolar. I don't know if we'd have these problems if she weren't bipolar. She gets depressed, her thoughts don't get communicated, she never even tries . . . and that reminds me what I was gonna ask you: Do you think she might have attention deficit disorder as well as bipolar?

D: Oh, no, here we go . . .

T1: Barry, no one can tell for sure, but regardless of what the cause is, it sounds like you're ready for us to start focusing more on your relationship [redirects discussion but doesn't directly challenge Barry's definition of the problem]. At least part of what you're describing sounds like the habits you have of communicating with each other as a couple. We'll be teaching you some fairly straightforward skills for talking to each other, like how to praise each other for things done well, how to listen, and how to ask for changes in each others' behavior. This will help you during these cycles, whether they be real mood cycles or just rocky periods in your relationship [provides rationale for upcoming communication module].

D: Yeah, I need to learn how to argue. He's a lawyer; he's a much better arguer than me.

B: (*Still angry*) But you see, no one ever said a damn thing in your family; no one was ever really there. So of course you're going to react to me because I'm passionate, and then when I get really pissed off, you finally take stock and listen. It's the only way I can get through to you.

T1: I think there's a lot for us to work with here. I'd like to take you (*to Debra*) off the "bipolar hook" for a while, and let's work on how you act and react with each other. We don't have to work on your communication just about bipolar disorder—maybe also how you talk about finances, friends . . .

B: But that's all about doing it in here. . . . How are you gonna know how we communicate at home?

T1: We're gonna bug your house. (*All laugh*) We'll do some exercises in here that involve role-playing of new ways of talking, but you'll have to practice these new ways in between sessions at home. I personally think this will benefit you a great deal if you have the time to do it [expresses optimism].

The clinicians now had a better understanding of this couple's communication patterns. The demand–withdrawal pattern in part derived from their different family histories, but it was equally true that Barry was rewarded for being critical; it got results, even if these results were accompanied by Debra's resentment. They disagreed on the extent to which these communication patterns were driven by her bipolar disorder. Barry assumed that most or all of their problems could be attributed to the disorder, but Debra saw this assumption as just an attempt to blame her for everything. The clinicians' own take was that the marital dynamics existed independently of her mood swings, but became magnified by her hypomanic and depressive episodes. During hypomanic episodes she was more touchy and reactive, and when depressed she was more likely to withdraw.

In Session 9, the therapists began the skills training. FFT begins with positive communication skills to increase the likelihood that members of a couple or family will collaborate when dealing with more difficult issues. One clinician began by introducing a handout entitled "Expressing Positive Feelings," in which each partner is directed simply to praise the other for some specific behavior the other has performed, and to tell the partner how this behavior makes him/her feel. The clinicians first modeled the skill. One clinician praised Barry by saying, "I appreciate you taking the long drive up here [to the clinic] and making an adjustment to your schedule to make this possible . . . it makes me feel like you value what we do here." Barry expressed appreciation for the compliment. The clinician then asked Barry and Debra to turn their chairs toward each other and select a behavior to praise in each other. Interestingly, neither had trouble selecting a topic. The problem was in staying with positive emotions and not letting the negative leak in.

B: I appreciated your taking Jill to soccer on Wednesday. It made me feel like you . . . like you knew I was overwhelmed that day, and that, you know, I'm usually the one doing all the parenting while you . . .

T2: (*Interrupting*) Barry, I'd like to stop you before we get into that. Debra, can you tell me what you liked so far about how Barry said that? Did he follow the instructions on this sheet?

D: Well, like you said, he was starting to get into it, but I liked the first part. I'm glad he feels that way.

B: Do you feel I give you enough positive feedback?

D: (*Pauses*) You have your days.

T2: Barry, I thought you did that pretty well. Could you try it without the tail at the end?

B: (*Chuckles*) There you go, stealing my thunder. OK, um, Deb, thanks again for taking Jill to soccer. It made me feel like you—like my schedule is important to you, and that you're thinking of me.

T2: Good. Debra, what'd you think?

D: Much better.

B: Sometimes I think I was put on this earth to learn tact.

Sessions 10–11 of CET focused on active listening skills. One member of the couple listened while the other spoke, first about issues outside of the marriage (i.e., work relationships) and then about couple-related matters. Both members of the couple required restructuring of their listening skills. Specifically, Debra tended to "space out" when Barry spoke, and required prompting to stay with the issues. She acknowledged that she sometimes felt she was being tested by him when he talked to her, to determine whether she could come up with thoughtful, intuitive replies. Her "checking out" was a way of coping with the performance anxiety that she experienced when listening to him.

Not surprisingly, Barry's difficulty with listening centered on withholding his natural tendency to give advice. When Debra began to talk, he would listen reflectively for a minute or two, but then would begin to ask questions such as "Well, when are you gonna call that person?" or "Last time we talked you said you were going to finish that resumé. Why haven't you?" Repeated practice within sessions—supplemented by homework assignments to practice these skills—led him to become more aware of what he was doing. During a particularly poignant moment, he admitted that "I don't like the way I react to her. . . . I don't like the person I'm becoming."

As FFT passed the 3-month point (Sessions 12–14), the clinicians introduced potentially more heated forms of communication, such as making requests for changes in each other's behaviors and expressing negative feelings. At this point, Debra was not as depressed as she had been during the assessment phase, although Barry continued to complain about her low functioning. He argued that she had become unable to tell him what she had and had not accomplished during the day, and that she often made it appear that she had done things that, in reality, she had not. He labeled this her "lack of follow-through" problem. In contrast, Debra became increasingly assertive about his "micromanagement" of her behavior.

T1: One of the things we'd like to work on with you is how you ask each other to change in some way. What's an appropriate way to ask someone to help you? (*Gives Barry and Debra the handout titled "Making a Positive Request"*) Try looking directly at each other; tell each other what you would like to see done differently, and how it would make you feel. Debra, a minute ago you were talking about how Barry micromanages you. Can you turn this into a positive—ask him what you would like him to do? Phrase it in a way that he can help you? How can he ask you to follow through without nagging you?

D: Uh, Barry, it would really make me happy if you . . . in situations where there's a dilemma, if you'd give me a little more freedom.

B: For example? Do you mean you want us to do things at your pace?

T1: Barry, let it come from her.

D: Um, like, if there's some shopping to do, it would help me out if I could just say, "Yes, this is on my list and I'll do it . . . if you could wait for me to get it done in my own time." That would help ease the tension.

T2: Barry, how did you feel about how Debra asked you? Did she follow this sheet?

B: I think she asked me just fine, but my question is, will she then do the shopping?

D: I think it would really help me to have some plan—like, if we agreed that if I did this part of the shopping, that you did

that part. Maybe that would stop me from saying, "I'll show him. He's not gonna run my life; I'm not gonna do it his way."

T1: When someone feels one-down, they often do react by refusing to go along with the plan, even though going along with it might be of help to them personally. Debra, do you get into that sometimes?

The clinicians were encouraging assertiveness in Debra, and at the same time gently confronting what Barry had earlier called her "passive–aggressiveness." They then moved on to Barry and asked him to make a positive request of her.

T2: Barry, can you think of something you could ask Debra to do, to change her behavior?

B: (*Looking at clinicians*) OK, Deb, it's very important to me . . .

T2: Can you tell this to her?

B: OK, it's very important to me that you not just walk away when we have discussions. That you don't just withdraw. Especially when we talk about Jill and our differences about her. That really irritates me.

The clinicians at this point again observed Debra withdraw in reaction to Barry's "high-EE" behavior. They addressed this by commenting on her reactions.

T1: Debra, what's happening now? You seem like you're checking out.

D: (*Snaps back, smiles*) Yeah, I guess I did. What were we talking about?

B: You see, I think that's part of her ADD. Do you think she needs Ritalin [medication for this condition]?

T1: Barry, in this case I don't think so. I think that what happened, Debra, if I can speak for you for a moment, is that you withdrew because you felt under attack.

D: That's probably true. He got into his "You do this, you do that."

B: (*Frustrated*) Well, you just asked me to change something! Am I supposed to do all the work here?

T1: Barry, I'm going to encourage you to try again. Only this time, I'd like you to be more aware of how you phrase things. Notice you said what you didn't want her to do—withdraw when you were talking to her. That's quite important. But what would you like her to do instead?

B: I want her to engage with me! To talk it out!

T1: Can you try again, only this time tell her what you do want her to do?

B: (*Sighs*) Deb, when we talk, I'd really like . . . I'd really appreciate it if you'd hang in there and finish talking to me, especially about Jill. That would make me feel, I don't know, like we're partners.

T2: Barry, that was much better, and I'll bet it was easier to hear. Debra?

D: Yeah, I liked it . . . that's easier. We need to do more of this.

Much emphasis was placed throughout CET on between-session homework assignments. The couple was strongly encouraged to hold weekly meetings, and to record efforts on homework sheets. Both spouses reported a reduction in tension in the relationship by the time problem solving was initiated.

Problem Solving (Sessions 15–18)

FFT sessions were held less frequently (biweekly) in Months 4, 5, and 6. At Session 15, problem solving was introduced. After explaining the rationale, the clinicians asked the couple to identify several specific problems for discussion. The steps of solving problems were reviewed with them.

The first issue chosen by the couple seemed superficial at first. They had two cats, one of which belonged to Debra (and came with her from a previous marriage) and the other of which Barry had bought. They disagreed on how much the cats should be fed: Debra "wanted mine to be fat" and fed it frequently, whereas Barry wanted his to be thin. As a result, Barry's cat was waking them up in the middle of the night needing to be fed. The resulting changes in Debra's sleep–wake cycles had resulted in her becoming irritable, restless, and possibly hypomanic. Despite a conscientious literature search, the clinicians were unable to find any research on the influence of cat diets on the cycling of bipolar disorder.

The couple considered various alternatives: feeding the cats equal amounts, keeping Barry's cat in the garage, giving away Barry's cat, and feeding both cats before they went to bed. They eventually settled on the last of these. The problem itself generated humor and playfulness between them, and they derived some satisfaction from being able to deal with it collaboratively.

A second source of conflict concerned their night life. Both liked going to parties, but Barry liked to stay longer than Debra. Debra found that parties contributed to her mood cycling. She tended to become overstimulated by the interactions with many people, and would quickly become fatigued. They considered these alternatives: going to the parties in separate cars, Barry agreeing to leave earlier, Debra going to the car and sleeping when she felt tired, and Debra taking a cab home. They eventually decided to discuss and agree upon a departure time before going to a party.

The couple was able to apply this method successfully to other issues, such as paying the bills and helping Jill get to her after-school activities. They continued to have trouble breaking problems down into smaller chunks, and tended to "cross-complain" or bring up larger problems in the middle of trying to solve smaller ones. Barry often complained, "We aren't dealing with the source of these problems, which is her bipolar disorder. We wouldn't have these problems if she weren't bipolar." Again, the clinicians did not challenge his definition of the problem, but continued to deliver the message that, regardless of whether the source of the problems lay in Debra, the couple still needed to work collaboratively to generate acceptable compromises.

Termination (Sessions 19–21)

By 7 months, Debra, whose depression had largely remitted, had obtained a new job working in sales at a clothing store. The clinicians began the termination phase of treatment, which focused on reviewing with the couple what they had taken away from the psychoeducation, CET, and problem-solving skills training modules. They both reported that their relationship had improved, and that they "occasionally" used the communication skills at home. The clinicians commented on how far they had come, and encouraged them to pick a time each week to rehearse one or more of the skills.

Barry was not entirely convinced of Debra's clinical improvement, however. In one of the final sessions, he returned to the issue of Debra's symptoms and her "unwillingness" to follow through on such tasks as cooking, depositing her paycheck, cleaning Jill's clothes, and other tasks they had agreed she would perform. The following interchange ensued:

B: (*Laughs*) I had this dream the other night that I was getting married, and I knew that I was marrying Debra, but I couldn't see her face, and I wasn't sure it was really her. And I wasn't sure if I should be there.

T1: And you were standing in front of everyone wearing your pajamas as well.

B: (*Laughs*) Yeah, and I was about to take the exam that I hadn't studied for. But really, sometimes I feel like she's not the same person, especially when she doesn't want to follow through on things we've talked about.

T1: Let me give you some perspective on this. I think a dilemma many relatives face is "Should I stick it out with my husband or my wife, or should I leave and take care of me?" There are certainly people who do that, who leave, and then there are many others who hang out and wait for things to get better, and in fact they often do.

B: And I think they have gotten better.

D: I think so. I don't know why you're being so negative.

B: Well, if you . . .

T1: (*Interrupts*) Let me finish this thought. Barry, I think it's critical for you to make a distinction in your own mind between what Debra can and can't control. That's sometimes vague between the two of you. When you say she doesn't want to follow through, that certainly sounds like an intentional behavior—something she's doing to hurt you or annoy you. Debra, do the problems with following through

ever feel like they're about problems with your concentration? Your attention or your memory?

D: (*Nodding emphatically*) Absolutely! If you could get him to realize that, we'd be a lot farther along.

B: That memory stuff—is that her bipolar or her ADD?

T1: I'm not sure that's really the question. That's just a diagnostic distinction, and I'm not sure my answering one way or the other will help you. Maybe what you're really wondering is whether these problems are controllable by her or not. If I were in your position, the things that would really anger me would be those things I thought she was doing intentionally.

B: Yeah, and I don't always think about that.

T1: If I thought what she was doing was due to a biochemical imbalance, I might be more patient, more sympathetic—in the same way that if someone had a broken leg and had trouble walking up stairs, I might have more sympathy than if I thought she was deliberately trying to hold me up.

In this segment, the clinician was addressing directly what he felt was a major source of Barry's critical attitudes toward Debra: the belief that many of her negative behaviors were controllable and intentional (see Hooley & Licht, 1997; Miklowitz et al., 1998). In some instances, Barry may have been right about her motivations. But questioning the controllability of her symptoms forced him to consider a different causal explanation for her behavior. The distinction between controllable and uncontrollable behaviors is a key point in the psychoeducational treatment of families of patients with bipolar disorder.

Barry and Debra's Progress

After completion of FFT, Debra continued to have mild periods of depression, despite her adherence to medication. Her depressions were unpleasant, but not so severe that she was unable to keep her job or attend to her parenting duties. Her brief hypomanic periods sometimes caused arguments between her and Barry but were not debilitating. Barry and Debra were communicating better, and both agreed that Barry was more patient and less critical of her. But Debra frequently found herself reacting with the line from the now-famous movie, "What if this is as good as it gets?" Although she was functional, she expressed chagrin that she could not have the life she had wanted—a successful career, a more intimate relationship with her husband, more friendships, an easier relationship with her daughter, and more financial success. The reality of her disorder and its psychosocial effects were difficult for her to accept. However, she felt that FFT had been helpful, as was her medication, which she showed no inclination to discontinue. The clinicians offered her a referral for individual therapy, but she decided to forgo further psychosocial treatment for the time being.

CONCLUSIONS

Family psychoeducational treatment appears to be a useful adjunct to pharmacotherapy. However, not all patients with bipolar disorder have families, and individual approaches such as those of Frank and colleagues (1999) are important alternatives to consider. The finding that mood-stabilizing medications are more powerful in alleviating manic than depressive symptoms, whereas the reverse appears true for psychotherapy, is an argument for combining medical and psychosocial interventions in the outpatient maintenance of bipolar disorder.

There is limited research on which families are the best candidates for FFT. Our exploratory analyses (Miklowitz et al., 2000) suggested that patients in high-EE families improved in depression severity scores over 1 year to a greater extent than those in low-EE families. But reductions in bipolar relapses were not specific to high-EE families treated with FFT.

Our clinical observations also suggest that there are subgroups of patients who do not respond well to FFT. Specifically, patients who are unusually resistant to accepting the diagnosis of bipolar disorder often resent the educational focus of FFT. These patients usually see their troubles as having external origins (i.e., being mistreated by others) and resist interventions that require them to take more responsibility for their behavior. These same patients may also reject pharmacotherapy. Sadly, we have seen many patients require several hospitalizations before the reality of their disorder sets in.

A different kind of resistance originates from viewing the disorder as biologically based. Some patients prefer to limit their mental health contacts to visits with a psychiatrist for medication, and regard psychotherapy as irrelevant. We see nothing wrong with this position, and note that a subset of patients do function well on medication only. Future research needs to determine whether this self-selected group is indeed different from patients who need psychotherapy, on symptomatic, course-of-illness, or family/genetic variables.

Family members are sometimes a major source of resistance. Their reasons can include a desire to distance themselves from the patient (whom they may have tried to help for years without reward), time or distance constraints, or the discomfort of talking about family or couple issues in front of a stranger. More subtle is the fear of being blamed for the disorder (Hatfield, Spaniol, & Zipple, 1987). The family therapy movement has come a long way, but still has its roots in a culture that faulted parents for causing mental illness. The theoretical model underlying FFT does not in any way link poor parenting to the onset of bipolar disorder. Nonetheless, a clinician often needs to make clear early in treatment that he/she does not adhere to this antiquated position.

FUTURE DIRECTIONS

Important future research will include effectiveness studies, which examine the clinical impact of psychotherapy as delivered to patients in "real-world" (typically community mental health) settings, by the clinicians who work in these settings and within the time constraints within which they work. As noted before, a multisite effectiveness study of bipolar disorder (Sachs, 1998) is now underway, in which FFT will be examined along with interpersonal psychotherapy and cognitive-behavioral therapy in a variety of community settings. It remains to be seen whether the success of FFT in the laboratory will translate into success in the community.

A related problem is determining the proper structure of FFT. In many community settings, insurance companies only pay for six to eight sessions. FFT is rather time-intensive, and research is needed to determine which of its components predict the greatest proportion of variance in the outcome of participants. For example, it is possible that some families will benefit from just the psychoeducation module. Possibly the psychoeducation and CET modules could be streamlined without a great loss in treatment effect size. Ideally, decisions to modify treatments like FFT will be based on clinical outcomes research rather than solely on the desire for cost containment.

A final research direction is the applicability of FFT and other psychotherapy treatments to child and adolescent patients with bipolar disorder. The fact that bipolar disorder even exists in these age groups is just now being recognized (Geller & Luby, 1997), and there are no currently accepted methods of psychosocial treatment for juvenile patients. Whether the same diagnostic criteria that are applied to adults can be applied to children is a topic of some debate (McClellan & Werry, 1997). If unrecognized, childhood-onset bipolar disorder can progress into the more severe forms of adult bipolar disorder (Sachs & Lafer, 1998). The addition of FFT to medication regimens in the early stages of the disorder may serve a protective function in the disorder's long-term course. Possibly the negative symptomatic and psychosocial outcomes of adult bipolar disorder can be mitigated through early detection and carefully planned preventive interventions.

ACKNOWLEDGMENTS

Preparation of this chapter was supported in part by National Institute of Mental Health Grants No. MH43931, No. MH55101, and No. MH42556, and by a grant from the University of Colorado's Council on Research and Creative Work.

REFERENCES

Akiskal, H. S. (1996). The prevalent clinical spectrum of bipolar disorders: Beyond DSM-IV. *Journal of Clinical Psychopharmacology, 16*(Suppl. 1), 4–14.

Akiskal, H. S., & Akiskal, K. (1992). Cyclothymic, hyperthymic, and depressive temperaments as sub-affective variants of mood disorders. In A. Tasman & M. B. Riba (Eds.), *American Psychiatric Press review of psychiatry* (Vol. 11, pp. 43–62). Washington, DC: American Psychiatric Press.

Altshuler, L. L., Post, R. M., Leverich, G. S., Mikalauskas, K., Rosoff, A., & Ackerman, L. (1995). Antidepressant-induced mania and cycle acceleration: A controversy revisited. *American Journal of Psychiatry, 152*, 1130–1138.

American Psychiatric Association. (1980). *Diagnostic and statistical manual of mental disorders* (3rd ed.). Washington, DC: Author.

American Psychiatric Association. (1987). *Diagnostic and statistical manual of mental disorders* (3rd ed., rev.). Washington, DC: Author.

American Psychiatric Association. (1994a). Practice guideline for the treatment of patients with bipolar disorder. *American Journal of Psychiatry, 12*(Suppl.), 1–36.

American Psychiatric Association. (1994b). *Diagnostic and statistical manual of mental disorders* (4th ed.). Washington, DC: Author.

Baxter, L. R., Schwartz, J. M., Bergman, K. S., Szuba, M. P., Guze, B. H. Mazziotta, J. C., Alazraki, A., Selin, C. E., Ferng, H.-K., Munford, P., & Phelps, M. E. (1992). Caudate glucose metabolic rate changes with both drug and behavior therapy for obsessive–compulsive disorder. *Archives of General Psychiatry, 49*, 681–689.

Beigel, A., & Murphy, D. L. (1971). Differences in clinical characteristics accompanying depression in unipolar and bipolar affective illness. *Archives of General Psychiatry, 24*, 215–220.

Brewin, C. R., MacCarthy, B., Duda, K., & Vaughn, C. E. (1991). Attribution and expressed emotion in the relatives of patients with schizophrenia. *Journal of Abnormal Psychology, 100*, 546–554.

Brockington, I. F., Hillier, V. F., Francis, A. F., Helzer, J. E., & Wainwright, S. (1983). Definitions of mania: Concordance and prediction of outcome. *American Journal of Psychiatry, 140*, 435–439.

Butzlaff, R. L., & Hooley, J. M. (1998). Expressed emotion and psychiatric relapse: A meta-analysis. *Archives of General Psychiatry, 55*, 547–552.

Calabrese, J. R., Fatemi, S. H., Kujawa, M., & Woyshville, M. J. (1996). Predictors of response to mood stabilizers. *Journal of Clinical Psychopharmacology, 16*(Suppl. 1), 24–31.

Carpenter, D., Clarkin, J. F., Glick, I. D., & Wilner, P. J. (1995). Personality pathology among married adults with bipolar disorder. *Journal of Affective Disorders, 34*, 269–274.

Clarkin, J. F., Carpenter, D., Hull, J., Wilner, P., & Glick, I. (1998). Effects of psychoeducational intervention for married patients with bipolar disorder and their spouses. *Psychiatric Services, 49*, 531–533.

Clarkin, J. F., Glick, I. D., Haas, G. L., Spencer, J. H., Lewis, A. B., Peyser, J., Demane, N., Good-Ellis, M., Harris, E., & Lestelle, V. (1990). A randomized clinical trial of inpatient family intervention: V. Results for affective disorders. *Journal of Affective Disorders, 18*, 17–28.

Clarkin, J. F., & Miklowitz, D. J. (1997). Marital and family communication difficulties. In T. A. Widiger, A. J. Frances, H. A. Pincus, R. Ross, M. B. First, & W. Davis (Eds.), *DSM-IV sourcebook* (Vol. 3, pp. 631–672). Washington, DC: American Psychiatric Association.

Cochran, S. D. (1984). Preventing medical noncompliance in the outpatient treatment of bipolar affective disorders. *Journal of Consulting and Clinical Psychology, 52,* 873–878.

Cohen, M., Baker, G., Cohen, R. A., Fromm-Reichmann, F., & Weigert, V. (1954). An intensive study of 12 cases of manic–depressive psychosis. *Psychiatry, 17,* 103–137.

Coryell, W., Endicott, J., & Keller, M. (1992). Rapidly cycling affective disorder: Demographics, diagnosis, family history, and course. *Archives of General Psychiatry, 49,* 126–131.

Coryell, W., Keller, M., Lavori, P., & Endicott, J. (1990). Affective syndromes, psychotic features, and prognosis: II. Mania. *Archives of General Psychiatry, 47,* 658–662.

Coryell, W., Scheftner, W., Keller, M., Endicott, J., Maser, J., & Klerman, G. L. (1993). The enduring psychosocial consequences of mania and depression. *American Journal of Psychiatry, 150,* 720–727.

Craighead, W. E., Miklowitz, D. J., Vajk, F. C., & Frank, E. (1998). Psychosocial treatments for bipolar disorder. In P. E. Nathan & J. M. Gorman (Eds.), *A guide to treatments that work* (pp. 240–248). New York: Oxford University Press.

Cutler, N. R., & Post, R. M. (1982). Life course of illness in untreated manic–depressive patients. *Comprehensive Psychiatry, 23,* 101–115.

Dion, G., Tohen, M., Anthony, W., & Waternaux, C. (1989). Symptoms and functioning of patients with bipolar disorder six months after hospitalization. *Hospital and Community Psychiatry, 39,* 652–656.

Ehlers, C. L., Kupfer, D. J., Frank, E., & Monk, T. H. (1993). Biological rhythms and depression: The role of zeitgebers and zeitstorers. *Depression, 1,* 285–293.

Falloon, I. R. H., Boyd, J. L., & McGill, C. W. (1984). *Family care of schizophrenia: A problem-solving approach to the treatment of mental illness.* New York: Guilford Press.

First, M. B., Spitzer, R. L., Gibbon, M., & Williams, J. B. W. (1995). *Structured Clinical Interview for DSM-IV Axis I disorders.* New York: Biometrics Research Department, New York State Psychiatric Institute.

Frank, E. (1999). Interpersonal and social rhythm therapy prevents depressive symptomatology in bipolar I patients. *Bipolar Disorders, 1*(Suppl. 1), 13.

Frank, E., Kupfer, D. J., Ehlers, C. L., Monk, T. H., Cornes, C., Carter, S., & Frankel, D. (1994). Interpersonal and social rhythm therapy for bipolar disorder: Integrating interpersonal and behavioral approaches. *The Behavior Therapist, 17,* 143–149.

Frank, E., Swartz, H. A., Mallinger, A. G., Thase, M. E., Weaver, E. V., & Kupfer, D. J. (1999). Adjunctive psychotherapy for bipolar disorder: Effects of changing treatment modality. *Journal of Abnormal Psychology, 108,* 579–587.

Gelenberg, A. J., Kane, J. N., Keller, M. B., Lavori, P., Rosenbaum, J. F., Cole, K., & Lavelle, J. (1989). Comparison of standard and low serum levels of lithium for maintenance treatment of bipolar disorders. *New England Journal of Medicine, 321,* 1489–1493.

Geller, B., & Luby, J. (1997). Child and adolescent bipolar disorder: A review of the past 10 years. *Journal of the American Academy of Child and Adolescent Psychiatry, 36,* 1168–1176.

George, E. L., Miklowitz, D. J., & Richards, J. A. (1996, September). *Personality disorders among bipolar patients.* Poster presented at the 11th Annual Meeting of the Society for Research in Psychopathology, Atlanta, GA.

Gitlin, M. J., Swendsen, J., Heller, T. L., & Hammen, C. (1995). Relapse and impairment in bipolar disorder. *American Journal of Psychiatry, 152*(11), 1635–1640.

Glick, I. D., Clarkin, J. F., Haas, G. L., Spencer, J. H., & Chen, C. L. (1991). A randomized clinical trial of inpatient family intervention: VI. Mediating variables and outcome. *Family Process, 30,* 85–99.

Goldberg, J. F., Harrow, M., & Grossman, L. S. (1995). Course and outcome in bipolar affective disorder: A longitudinal follow-up study. *American Journal of Psychiatry, 152,* 379–385.

Goldberg, J. F., & Kocsis, J. H. (1999). Depression in the course of bipolar disorder. In J. F. Goldberg & M. Harrow (Eds.), *Bipolar disorders: Clinical course and outcome* (pp. 129–147). Washington, DC: American Psychiatric Press.

Goldstein, M. J., Rea, M. M., & Miklowitz, D. J. (1996). Family factors related to the course and outcome of bipolar disorder. In C. Mundt, M. Goldstein, K. Hahlweg, & P. Fiedler (Eds.), *Interpersonal factors in the origin and course of affective disorders* (pp. 193–203). London: Gaskell Press.

Goodwin, F. K., & Jamison, K. R. (1990). *Manic–depressive illness.* New York: Oxford University Press.

Grossman, L. S., Harrow, M., Fudula, J., & Meltzer, H. Y. (1984). The longitudinal course of schizoaffective disorders: A prospective follow-up study. *Journal of Nervous and Mental Disease, 172,* 140–149.

Grossman, L. S., Harrow, M., Goldberg, J. F., & Fichtner, C. G. (1991). Outcome of schizoaffective disorder at two long-term follow-ups: Comparisons with outcome of schizophrenia and affective disorders. *American Journal of Psychiatry, 148,* 1359–1365.

Hahlweg, K., Goldstein, M. J., Nuechterlein, K. H., Magana, A. B., Mintz, J., Doane, J. A., Miklowitz, D. J., & Snyder, K. S. (1989). Expressed emotion and patient–relative interaction in families of recent-onset schizophrenics. *Journal of Consulting and Clinical Psychology, 57,* 11–18.

Haley, J. (1963). *Strategies of psychotherapy.* New York: Grune & Stratton.

Harrow, M., Goldberg, J. F., Grossman, L. S., & Meltzer, H. Y. (1990). Outcome in manic disorders: A naturalistic follow-up study. *Archives of General Psychiatry, 47,* 665–671.

Hatfield, A. B., Spaniol, L., & Zipple, A. M. (1987). Expressed emotion: A family perspective. *Schizophrenia Bulletin, 13,* 221–226.

Honig, A., Hofman, A., Rozendaal, N., & Dingemanns, P. (1997). Psychoeducation in bipolar disorder: Effect on expressed emotion. *Psychiatry Research, 72,* 17–22.

Hooley, J. M. (1987). The nature and origins of expressed emotion. In K. Hahlweg & M. J. Goldstein (Eds.), *Understanding major mental disorder: The contribution of family interaction research* (pp. 176–194). New York: Family Process Press.

Hooley, J. M., & Licht, D. M. (1997). Expressed emotion and causal attributions in the spouses of depressed patients. *Journal of Abnormal Psychology, 106*, 298–306.

Hooley, J. M., & Teasdale, J. D. (1989). Predictors of relapse in unipolar depressives: Expressed emotion, marital distress, and perceived criticism. *Journal of Abnormal Psychology, 98*, 229–235.

Hoover, C. F., & Fitzgerald, R. G. (1981). Marital conflict of manic–depressive patients. *Archives of General Psychiatry, 38*, 65–67.

Huxley, N. A., Parikh, S. V., & Baldessarini, R. J. (2000). Effectiveness of psychosocial treatments in bipolar disorder. *Harvard Review of Psychiatry, 8*, 126–140.

Jamison, K. R., & Akiskal, H. S. (1983). Medication compliance in patients with bipolar disorders. *Psychiatric Clinics of North America, 6*, 175–192.

Jamison, K. R., Gerner, R. H., & Goodwin, F. K. (1979). Patient and physician attitudes toward lithium: Relationship to compliance. *Archives of General Psychiatry, 36*, 866–869.

Katz, M. M., Robins, E., Croughan, J., Secunda, S., & Swann, A. (1982). Behavioral measurement and drug response characteristics of unipolar and bipolar depression. *Psychological Medicine, 12*, 25–36.

Keck, P. E., & McElroy, S. L. (1996). Outcome in the pharmacological treatment of bipolar disorder. *Journal of Clinical Psychopharmacology, 16*(Suppl. 1), 15–23.

Keck, P. E., McElroy, S. L., Strakowski, S. M., West, S. A., Sax, K. W., Hawkins, J. M., Bourne, M. L., & Haggard, P. (1998). 12-month outcome of patients with bipolar disorder following hospitalization for a manic or mixed episode. *American Journal of Psychiatry, 155*, 646–652.

Keller, M. B., Lavori, P. W., Coryell, W., Andreasen, N. C., Endicott, J., Clayton, P. J., Klerman, G. L., & Hirschfeld, R. M. A. (1986). Differential outcome of pure manic, mixed/cycling, and pure depressive episodes in patients with bipolar illness. *Journal of the American Medical Association, 255*, 3138–3142.

Kendler, K. S. (1991). Mood-incongruent psychotic affective illness: A historical and empirical review. *Archives of General Psychiatry, 48*, 362–369.

Klerman, G. L., Weissman, M. M., Rounsaville, B. J., & Chevron, R. S. (1984). *Interpersonal psychotherapy of depression*. New York: Basic Books.

Kraepelin, E. (1921). *Manic–depressive insanity and paranoia*. Edinburgh, Scotland: E. & S. Livingstone.

Lam, D. H., Bright, J., Jones, S., Hayward, P., Schuck, N., & Shisholm, D. (2000). Cognitive therapy for bipolar illness: Pilot study of relapse prevention. *Cognitive Therapy and Research, 24*, 503–520.

Leverich, G. S., & Post, R. M. (1998). Life charting of affective disorders. *CNS Spectrums, 3*, 21–37.

Liberman, R. P., Wallace, C. J., Falloon, I. R. H., & Vaughn, C. E. (1981). Interpersonal problem-solving therapy for schizophrenics and their families. *Comprehensive Psychiatry, 22*, 627–629.

Malkoff-Schwartz, S., Frank, E., Anderson, B., Sherrill, J. T., Siegel, L., Patterson, D., & Kupfer, D. J. (1998). Stressful life events and social rhythm disruption in the onset of manic and depressive bipolar episodes: A preliminary investigation. *Archives of General Psychiatry, 55*, 702–707.

McClellan, J., & Werry, J. S. (1997). Practice parameters for the assessment and treatment of children and adolescents with bipolar disorder. *Journal of the American Academy of Child and Adolescent Psychiatry, 36*(Suppl. 10), 157–176.

McElroy, S. L., Keck, P. E., Pope, H. G., Hudson, J. I., Faedda, G. L., & Swann, A. O. (1992). Clinical and research implications of the diagnosis of dysphoric or mixed mania or hypomania. *American Journal of Psychiatry, 149*, 1633–1644.

Miklowitz, D. J. (1992). Longitudinal outcome and medication noncompliance among manic patients with and without mood-incongruent psychotic features. *Journal of Nervous and Mental Disease, 180*, 703–711.

Miklowitz, D. J., & Craighead, W. E. (2001). Bipolar affective disorder: Does psychosocial treatment add to the efficacy of drug therapy? *The Economics of Neuroscience, 3*, 58–64.

Miklowitz, D. J., & Frank, E. (1999). New psychotherapies for bipolar disorder. In J. F. Goldberg & M. Harrow (Eds.), *Bipolar disorders: Clinical course and outcome* (pp. 57–84). Washington, DC: American Psychiatric Press.

Miklowitz, D. J., Frank, E., & George, E. L. (1996). New psychosocial treatments for the outpatient management of bipolar disorder. *Psychopharmacology Bulletin, 32*, 613–621.

Miklowitz, D. J., & Goldstein, M. J. (1997). *Bipolar disorder: A family-focused treatment approach*. New York: Guilford Press.

Miklowitz, D. J., Goldstein, M. J., & Nuechterlein, K. H. (1987). The family and the course of recent-onset mania. In K. Hahlweg & M. J. Goldstein (Eds.), *Understanding major mental disorder: The contribution of family interaction research* (pp. 195–211). New York: Family Process Press.

Miklowitz, D. J., Goldstein, M. J., Nuechterlein, K. H., Snyder, K. S., & Mintz, J. (1988). Family factors and the course of bipolar affective disorder. *Archives of General Psychiatry, 45*, 225–231.

Miklowitz, D. J., Simoneau, T. L., George, E. A., Richards, J. A., Kalbag, A., Sachs-Ericsson, N., & Suddath, R. (2000). Family-focused treatment of bipolar disorder: One-year effects of a psychoeducational program in conjunction with pharmacotherapy. *Biological Psychiatry, 48*, 582–592.

Miklowitz, D. J., Velligan, D. I., Goldstein, M. J., Nuechterlein, K. H., Gitlin, M. J., Ranlett, G., & Doane, J. A. (1991). Communication deviance in families of schizophrenic and manic patients. *Journal of Abnormal Psychology, 100*, 163–173.

Miklowitz, D. J., Wendel, J. S., & Simoneau, T. L. (1998). Targeting dysfunctional family interactions and high expressed emotion in the psychosocial treatment of bipolar disorder. *In Session: Psychotherapy in Practice, 4*, 25–38.

Mitchell, P., Parker, G., Jamieson, K., Wilhelm, K., Hickie, I., Brodaty, H., Boyce, P., Hadzi-Pavlovic, D., & Roy, K. (1992). Are there any differences between bipolar and unipolar melancholia? *Journal of Affective Disorders, 25*, 97–106.

Monk, T. H., Flaherty, J. F., Frank, E., Hoskinson, K., & Kupfer, D. J. (1990). The Social Rhythm Metric: An instrument to quantify daily rhythms of life. *Journal of Nervous and Mental Disease, 178*, 120–126.

Monk, T. H., Kupfer, D. J., Frank, E., & Ritenour, A. M. (1991). The Social Rhythm Metric (SRM): Measuring daily social rhythms over 12 weeks. *Psychiatry Research, 36,* 195–207.

Napier, A. Y., & Whitaker, C. A. (1978). *The family crucible.* New York: Harper & Row.

O'Connell, R. A., Mayo, J. A., Flatow, L., Cuthbertson, B., & O'Brien, B. E. (1991). Outcome of bipolar disorder on long-term treatment with lithium. *British Journal of Psychiatry, 159,* 132–139.

Pope, H. G., & Lipinski, J. F. (1978). Diagnosis in schizophrenia and manic-depressive illness: A reassessment of the specificity of "schizophrenic" symptoms in the light of current research. *Archives of General Psychiatry, 35,* 811–828.

Post, R. M., Rubinow, D. R., Uhde, T. W., Roy-Byrne, P. P., Linnoila, M., Rosoff, A., & Cowdry, R. (1989). Dysphoric mania: Clinical and biological correlates. *Archives of General Psychiatry, 46,* 353–358.

Priebe, S., Wildgrube, C., & Muller-Oerlinghausen, B. (1989). Lithium prophylaxis and expressed emotion. *British Journal of Psychiatry, 154,* 396–399.

Rea, M. M., Tompson, M., Miklowitz, D. J., & Goldstein, M. J. (2000). *Family-focused treatment vs. individual treatment for bipolar disorder: Results of a clinical trial.* Manuscript submitted for publication.

Regier, D. A., Farmer, M. E., Rae, D. S., Locke, B. Z., Keith, S. J., Judd, L. L., & Goodwin, F. K. (1990). Comorbidity of mental disorders with alcohol and other drug abuse: Results from the Epidemiologic Catchment Area (ECA) Study. *Journal of the American Medical Association, 264,* 2511–2518.

Sachs, G. S. (1996). Bipolar mood disorder: Practical strategies for acute and maintenance phase treatment. *Journal of Clinical Psychopharmacology, 16*(Suppl. 1), 33–47.

Sachs, G. S. (1998). *Treatments for bipolar disorder.* Unpublished grant proposal, NIMH Contract No. 98–DS-0001.

Sachs, G. S., & Lafer, B. (1998). Child and adolescent mania. In P. J. Goodnick (Ed.), *Mania: Clinical and research perspectives* (pp. 37–62). Washington, DC: American Psychiatric Press.

Shapiro, D. R., Quitkin, F. M., & Fleiss, J. L. (1989). Response to maintenance therapy in bipolar illness. *Archives of General Psychiatry, 46,* 401–405.

Simoneau, T. L., Miklowitz, D. J., Richards, J. A.,

Saleem, R., & George, E. L. (1999). Bipolar disorder and family communication: Effects of a psychoeducational treatment program. *Journal of Abnormal Psychology, 108,* 588–597.

Simoneau, T. L., Miklowitz, D. J., & Saleem, R. (1998). Expressed emotion and interactional patterns in the families of bipolar patients. *Journal of Abnormal Psychology, 107,* 497–507.

Spitzer, R. L., Williams, J. B., Gibbon, M., & First, M. B. (1992). The Structured Clinical Interview for DSM-III-R (SCID). I: History, rationale, and description. *Archives of General Psychiatry, 49*(8), 624–629.

Strakowski, S. M., Keck, P. E., McElroy, S. L., West, S. A., Sax, K. W., Hawkins, J. M., Kmetz, G. F., Upadhyaya, V. H., Turgul, K. C., & Bourne, M. L. (1998). Twelve-month outcome after a first hospitalization for affective psychosis. *Archives of General Psychiatry, 55,* 49–55.

Strauss, J. S., & Carpenter, W. T. (1972). The prediction of outcome in schizophrenia. *Archives of General Psychiatry, 27,* 739–746.

Tohen, M., Waternaux, C. M., & Tsuang, M. T. (1990). Outcome in mania: A 4-year prospective follow-up of 75 patients utilizing survival analysis. *Archives of General Psychiatry, 47,* 1106–1111.

Vaughn, C. E., & Leff, J. P. (1976). The influence of family and social factors on the course of psychiatric illness: A comparison of schizophrenia and depressed neurotic patients. *British Journal of Psychiatry, 129,* 125–137.

Weisman, A., Lopez, S. R., Karno, M., & Jenkins, J. (1993). An attributional analysis of expressed emotion in Mexican-American families with schizophrenia. *Journal of Abnormal Psychology, 102,* 601–606.

Wendel, J. S., Miklowitz, D. J., Richards, J. A., & George, E. L. (2000). Expressed emotion and attributions in the relatives of bipolar patients: An analysis of problem-solving interactions. *Journal of Abnormal Psychology, 109,* 792–796.

Wynne, L. C., Singer, M., Bartko, J., & Toohey, M. (1977). Schizophrenics and their families: Recent research on parental communication. In J. M. Tanner (Ed.), *Developments in psychiatric research* (pp. 254–286). London: Hodder & Stoughton.

Young, M. A., & Harrow, M. (1994). Bipolar disorders. In A. S. Bellack & M. Hersen (Eds.), *Psychopathology in adulthood* (pp. 234–248). Boston: Allyn & Bacon.

Chapter 13

SEXUAL DYSFUNCTION

Amy K. Bach
John P. Wincze
David H. Barlow

Psychological treatments that have emerged during the past several decades for the various sexual dysfunctions have a particularly strong empirical base. We now have psychological procedures, either with or without new medications, that are highly effective for the overwhelming majority of individuals whose sexual dysfunctions have a psychogenic component. But, as the authors point out, the organic–psychogenic distinction is no longer particularly useful in the assessment of these problems. For this reason, the development of a new and effective medication (Viagra) for one sexual dysfunction, male erectile disorder, has overshadowed the fact that psychological interventions are often necessary even in cases where medication is effective. This has not been lost on the manufacturer of Viagra, since this pharmaceutical company is currently sponsoring a large multisite study designed to illustrate the importance of attending to the psychosocial context of sexual dysfunction. But this aspect of treatment has been neglected to some extent by primary care physicians with less experience in these matters. In this chapter, after an up-to-date review of important advances in sexuality research, a biopsychosocial model is presented that integrates consideration of medical and psychological factors in diagnosis and treatment. This section is followed by a seemingly straightforward case in which the male presented with sexual dysfunction of mixed (organic and psychogenic) etiology. During the course of treatment, it became apparent that his spouse also suffered from sexual dysfunction. The reader may be struck by the twists and turns that the therapist took with this case and the particular therapeutic strategies required. In covering specific approaches to all sexual dysfunctions, the authors highlight individual behavioral approaches, but also note common therapeutic factors (such as providing sexual education, facilitating communication, and identifying important emotional and cultural factors that may contribute to sexual dysfunction). In sex therapy, we see some of the best illustrations of the integration of cognitive-behavioral and systems approaches, and the importance of this integration is readily apparent in the case study.—D. H. B.

The purpose of this chapter is to outline a cognitive-behavioral approach to the assessment and treatment of sexual dysfunction. Cognitive-behavioral therapy for sexual dysfunction can serve as a sole treatment or as an adjunct to a medical or surgical intervention. In either case, the techniques and information we present should be adapted to the particular needs of the individual or couple and the nature of the sexual difficulty. Before describing our approach to clinical work, we begin by addressing two of the most noteworthy developments in sexuality research over the last 5 years.

IMPORTANT ADVANCES IN SEXUALITY RESEARCH

The Prevalence of Sexual Dysfunction

Clinicians have suggested for years that sexual dysfunction is a widespread problem affecting a significant proportion of the population. Until recently, however, there have been limited epidemiological data to support this claim. Epidemiological studies focusing on sexual dysfunction have been flawed by methodological problems such as nonrepresentative samples and reliance on self-report measures (Spector & Carey, 1990). Moreover, the majority of these studies were conducted more than 15 years ago.

Recently, however, Laumann, Paik, and Rosen (1999) published a landmark study in which they surveyed 1,410 men and 1,749 women between the ages of 18 and 59 regarding the presence of various sexual difficulties. The demographics of the sample were representative of the U.S. population. Respondents were surveyed in person by experienced interviewers.

Laumann and colleagues (1999) found that 43% of women and 31% of men endorsed some form of sexual dysfunction. These data suggest that sexual dysfunction is more prevalent than anxiety disorders, mood disorders, or substance use disorders (Kessler et al., 1994). The finding that more than one-third of American adults suffer from sexual dysfunction has received nationwide attention and validated clinicians' claims that sexual dysfunction is a major health problem.

The publication of this study is one of at least two major developments in sexuality research to have emerged over the past few years. The second major development is, of course, the introduction of an oral medication, sildenafil, more commonly known as Viagra. Viagra (for those who have not read a newspaper or magazine or watched television since March 1998) is an oral medication that has successfully restored erectile functioning to thousands of men with both psychogenic and organic etiologies; research on the use of this drug for women is currently underway.

Viagra: Integration with Sex Therapy

The introduction of Viagra has, in some respects, sparked a revolution in the treatment of sexual dysfunction. Once discussed only reluctantly with health professionals, sexual problems are now endorsed by former presidential candidates on national television. The mass media attention surrounding Viagra has resulted in a dramatic increase in public awareness and acceptance of sexual dysfunction. Moreover, the success of Viagra has fueled patients' hopes and expectations that their sexual difficulties can be easily treated. The result is a sharp rise in the number of patients seeking treatment for sexual problems.

Some may wonder whether the advent of drugs such as Viagra marks the beginning of the end for sex therapy. On the contrary, sex therapists are likely to be treating more patients than ever. Although Viagra has benefited countless couples, it, like all "wonder drugs," has its limitations. The most obvious drawbacks include serious risk to patients taking nitrates; side effects such as headaches, flushing, and dyspepsia; high cost; and the fact that Viagra does not significantly improve sexual functioning for 16%–44% of men and as many as 82% of postmenopausal women (Conti, Pepine, & Sweeney, 1999; Goldstein et al., 1998; Kaplan et al., 1999). A more subtle issue is the fact that studies on the efficacy of Viagra focus primarily on the drug's ability to restore physiological sexual responding. Firm erections and adequate lubrication do not always lead to a satisfying sexual relationship. Thus couples with poor communication, negative attitudes, and faulty beliefs regarding sexual functioning may find that a pill cannot do all that they hoped it would. These couples may find that cognitive-behavioral treatment is an appealing alternative or a necessary adjunct to medical treatment. The challenge, then, is to identify the best treatment option for each patient and couple: medication alone, psychosocial treatment alone, psychosocial treatment in conjunction with medication, or no treatment for sexual dysfunction.

Before one can identify the appropriate treatment options, it is necessary, of course, to determine the nature of the sexual problem. Following is a brief description of each sexual dysfunction as it is defined in the fourth edition of the *Diagnostic and Statistical Manual of Mental Disorders* (DSM-IV; American Psychiatric Association [APA], 1994).

THE SEXUAL DYSFUNCTIONS DEFINED

The four phases of the sexual response cycle are desire, excitement, orgasm, and resolution. DSM-IV defines sexual dysfunction as a disturbance in one of these phases or as pain associated with intercourse. Most people occasionally experience a lack of interest in sexual activity, difficulty becoming aroused, or problems related to orgasm. A diagnosis of sexual dysfunction is reserved for cases in which difficulties with sexual functioning occur persistently and cause significant distress or problems for the individual or couple.

In determining whether sexual difficulties warrant a clinical diagnosis, one must consider the client's age and culture, as well as the course of the problem. Once a diagnosis of sexual dysfunction is assigned, the clinician should consider whether the problem occurs across all situations (generalized) or only in certain circumstances (situational). The clinician should also note whether the problem has always been present (lifelong) or developed after a period of functioning without difficulty (acquired). Finally, the clinician should specify whether the problem is due to psychological factors or to combined (psychogenic and organic) factors. DSM-IV recommends that clinicians use these specifiers, because they provide the treating therapist with useful information regarding the nature and course of the dysfunction and may have implications for treatment.

Desire Disorders

Hypoactive Sexual Desire Disorder

DSM-IV defines hypoactive sexual desire disorder as a lack or absence of sexual fantasies and desire for sexual activity. Low desire may be a primary problem, or it may be secondary to another sexual dysfunction (e.g., a man may lose interest in sex because he is frustrated by erectile dysfunction). Laumann and colleagues (1999) report that 5% of men and 22% of women have difficulties with low sexual desire. Surveys of women in gynecological clinics have yielded similar estimates of 17% (Osborn, Hawton, & Gath, 1988) and 21% (Bachmann, Leiblum, & Grill, 1989). Low desire appears to be one of the most common problems in patients seeking treatment for sexual difficulties. Segraves and

Segraves (1991) examined the diagnoses of 906 participants recruited for a multisite pharmaceutical study of sexual dysfunctions. They found that 65% had a primary diagnosis of hypoactive sexual desire disorder; of these, 81% were female.

Beck (1995) argues that because the definition of low desire is ambiguous in DSM-IV, some researchers operationalize it based on the frequency of sexual activity. Beck (1995) suggests that this is problematic, because people may engage in sexual activity when they do not have a desire to do so (e.g., in order to please a partner). More reliable measures of sexual desire may be the frequency of sexual thoughts, urges, and fantasies and the extent to which the person takes advantage of opportunities for sexual activity (Wincze & Carey, in press). It is, of course, important to consider these variables in the context of the person's age, culture, and gender. Undergraduate males, for example, report significantly more urges and masturbatory fantasies than their female counterparts (Jones & Barlow, 1990).

Sexual Aversion Disorder

Whereas patients with hypoactive sexual desire disorder express a feeling of indifference, patients with sexual aversion disorder describe a very negative response to sexual activity. Fear or disgust usually characterizes their response to sexual activity. As a result, a person with sexual aversion disorder often avoids sexual activity (APA, 1994). Unfortunately, there are limited data on the prevalence of this dysfunction. Clinical experience suggests that the majority of patients seeking treatment for sexual aversion disorder are women.

People with sexual aversion disorder most often fear or feel repulsed by sexual intercourse. Women may report thoughts that they will feel significant pain or bleed a great deal upon penetration. Sexual aversion can, however, be associated with any aspect of sexual activity. One of us recently treated a woman who was comfortable with kissing and fondling, but extremely nervous when hugging or holding hands with a partner.

Finally, in some cases, sexual aversion may be secondary to panic disorder. In such cases, the patient avoids sexual activity because of a conditioned fear response to such physical sensations as increased heart rate and rapid breathing (Sbrocco, Weisberg, Barlow, & Carter, 1997).

Arousal Disorders

Male Erectile Disorder

The introduction of Viagra has rendered male erectile disorder the most widely recognized sexual dysfunction. Male erectile disorder, which is also referred to as "erectile dysfunction" or "impotence," is defined as a persistent or recurrent inability to get or keep an adequate erection until the completion of sexual activity (APA, 1994).

Laumann and colleagues (1999) report a prevalence rate of 5% for erectile dysfunction. This rate is most likely an underestimation because their sample did not include men age 60 years and older, the group in which male erectile disorder is most common. Feldman, Goldstein, Hatzichristou, Krane, and McKinlay (1994) surveyed 1,290 men between the ages of 40 and 70 years who were living in Massachusetts. They found that while the prevalence of complete erectile failure was 5% at age 40, it rose to 15% at age 70. The probability of moderate erectile difficulties was 17% at age 40 and 34% by age 70. The National Institutes of Health (NIH) Consensus Conference (1993) on impotence also found erectile dysfunction to be very widespread, indicating that it affects 10–20 million men in the United States.

Men with male erectile disorder will often report that they cannot perform or that they "cannot do anything." Research suggests that these men may actually underestimate their erectile response during sexual activity (Abrahamson, Barlow, Sakheim, Beck, & Athanasiou, 1985). A psychophysiological assessment of male sexual arousal is very useful, because it provides an objective measure of the patient's erectile functioning. The equipment necessary for a psychophysiological assessment, however, is expensive and may be unavailable. The partner's description of the patient's erectile difficulty is always helpful and should be obtained whenever possible.

Female Sexual Arousal Disorder

DSM-IV defines female sexual arousal disorder as a persistent or recurrent inability to attain or maintain adequate lubrication and swelling until the completion of sexual activity. Women with this disorder may experience little or no subjective sense of arousal. Laumann and colleagues (1999) report that 20% of women aged 18–59 years have difficulty becoming physiologically aroused during sexual activity.

Women may be unlikely to seek professional help for difficulty becoming aroused, because they can remedy the problem with a lubricant. Without any form of intervention, female sexual arousal disorder may result in painful intercourse, avoidance of sexual activity, and relationship problems.

Orgasmic Disorders

Premature Ejaculation

Premature ejaculation is somewhat loosely defined in DSM-IV as ejaculation with limited stimulation that occurs before, on, or shortly after penetration and sooner than the person would like (APA, 1994). Strassberg, Kelly, Carroll, and Kircher (1987) operationally defined the problem as ejaculation that occurs within 2 minutes of penetration on 50% or more of occasions, a feeling of being unable to control the latency to ejaculation, and a belief that this is a problem. Ultimately, the most important criterion may be a man's subjective sense that he cannot control the timing of his orgasm. Men with premature ejaculation may report that they ejaculate just as they are beginning to feel aroused. Although the latency to ejaculation alone cannot be used as a deciding criterion, it is important to ask men presenting with this problem how soon is "too soon." Some men mistakenly endorse premature ejaculation because they cannot engage in sexual intercourse for 20–30 minutes before ejaculating. In such cases, a diagnosis of premature ejaculation is not warranted, and the person can benefit from education regarding normative latencies to ejaculation.

Laumann and colleagues (1999) suggest that premature ejaculation affects 21% of men. Spector and Carey (1990) report a higher estimate of 36%–38%.

Male Orgasmic Disorder

Male orgasmic disorder refers to a delay in or absence of orgasm following a normal phase of excitement and an adequate degree of stimulation (APA, 1994). Laumann and colleagues (1999) report that this problem affects 8% of men. Spector and Carey (1990) provide a similar estimate of 4%–10%. Male orgasmic disorder is most often situational; the person often has difficulty reaching orgasm with a partner, but not during masturbation (Wincze & Carey, in press).

Female Orgasmic Disorder

Similar to the definition of male orgasmic disorder, female orgasmic disorder is the delay or absence of orgasm following a normal sexual excitement phase and adequate stimulation (APA, 1994). Laumann and colleagues (1999) indicate that 26% of women have significant difficulty reaching orgasm. Osborn and colleagues (1988) surveyed a community sample of 436 women between the ages of 35 and 59 years regarding their sexual functioning. They defined infrequency of orgasm as the complete absence of orgasm during sexual activity over the previous 3 months. According to this conservative definition, 16% of the women in their sample reported difficulty related to orgasm.

The frequency with which women achieve orgasm may vary considerably across individuals. LoPiccolo and Stock (1987) suggest that only 50% of women experience reasonably regular orgasms during sexual intercourse. Thus, in evaluating a woman for the presence of female orgasmic disorder, the actual frequency of orgasm may be less important than the extent to which she considers it a problem.

Pain Disorders

Dyspareunia

A person with dyspareunia experiences pain in the genital area before, during, or after sexual intercourse (APA, 1994). The nature, duration, and intensity of the pain vary across individuals, but it is most often experienced during sexual intercourse (Wincze & Carey, in press).

In a survey of 329 women at a gynecological clinic, Rosen, Taylor, Leiblum, and Bachmann (1993) found that 7.7% of women experienced painful intercourse on most or all occasions. Osborn and colleagues (1988) provide a very similar estimate of 8%. Unfortu-

nately, we have very few data on the prevalence of this problem in men. Our clinical experience suggests that when this problem occurs in men, it is most often the result of a medical problem (e.g., a urinary tract infection). Dyspareunia in women is more apt to result from a medical problem, psychological factors, or a combination of the two.

Vaginismus

DSM-IV defines vaginismus as an involuntary spasm of muscles surrounding the outer third of the vagina in response to attempted penetration. This problem most often occurs in response to attempted intercourse. A woman may report that her partner "hits a wall" when attempting penetration. The problem may also occur, however, in response to penetration by a finger, tampon, or speculum. Reissing, Binik, and Khalife (1999) raise a number of interesting issues regarding the definition of vaginismus. They point out that although vaginismus is listed as a pain disorder in DSM-IV, pain is neither a central nor a necessary criterion for the diagnosis. Instead, the diagnosis of vaginismus focuses on the involuntary muscle spasm. Reissing and colleagues (1999) disagree with this approach and suggest that vaginismus may be best defined either as a phobic/aversive response to vaginal penetration (often not specific to intercourse) or as a pain disorder. They suggest that this definition more accurately reflects the nature of the problem.

Rosen and colleagues (1993) found that vaginismus was a common problem for 6.8% and an intermittent problem for 21.6% of the women in a gynecological clinic. Consistent with these estimates, Reissing and colleagues (1999) report that rates of vaginismus range from 5% to 17%.

BIOPSYCHOSOCIAL MODEL OF CAUSAL FACTORS

Over the last three decades, there have been dramatic shifts in beliefs about what causes sexual dysfunction. In the 1970s, the work of William Masters and Virginia Johnson led to a widespread belief that in the majority of cases, sexual dysfunction resulted from psychological factors. The 1980s marked the introduction of several medical treatments for sexual dysfunction. The result was an adoption of the idea that sexual dysfunction was largely a biological problem. In the 1990s, there continued to be some debate regarding the respective roles of psychogenic and organic factors. Nevertheless, the majority of professionals now acknowledge that both psychological and biological factors play a significant role in the etiology of sexual dysfunction.

The assessment of sexual dysfunction often requires a multidisciplinary approach. Ideally, the clinician and physician collaborate to evaluate and identify social, psychological, and biological factors that may be causing sexual difficulties. These factors often interact, affecting one another. Thus it is necessary to evaluate each case as a whole rather than focusing on only one component of the etiological picture. A failure to consider the respective roles of both biological and psychosocial factors may significantly compromise the potential benefits of treatment.

Biological Risk Factors

A number of biological factors may contribute to sexual difficulties. These factors may directly affect sexual functioning, as in the case of vascular disease that causes insufficient blood flow to the penis. Alternatively, they may indirectly affect sexual functioning, as in the case of pain that does not interfere physiologically but limits the person's enjoyment of sexual activity.

Direct Biological Risk Factors

Some of the most common direct biological risk factors for sexual dysfunction are diabetes, vascular disease, alcohol, and medications. Before discussing these factors in greater detail, it is important to note that mild to moderate medical problems may simply predispose someone to sexual dysfunction. The presence of positive psychosexual factors may override the effects of such conditions and allow a person to retain healthy sexual functioning. Alternatively, if severe or combined with negative psychosexual conditions, the following factors may lead to sexual difficulties.

Vascular Diseases. Vascular diseases may negatively affect sexual functioning in one of

two ways. They may limit arterial inflow, preventing sufficient blood supply from entering the genitalia. Alternatively, they may disturb the venous system, allowing blood that has entered the genitalia to leak out slowly (Wincze & Carey, in press). Erections in men and vaginal engorgement in women are dependent upon increased blood flow to the genital area. Thus vascular problems may disrupt the arousal phase of sexual functioning. Atherosclerosis is a common risk factor and may be present in as many as 70% of cases of male erectile disorder in men aged 60 years and older in the United States (Kellett, 1996; Korenman, 1998). Other vascular disorders that may negatively affect sexual functioning are peripheral vascular disease, cardiovascular disease, and hypertension (Feldman et al., 1994; Korenman, 1998; NIH Consensus Conference, 1993).

Diabetes and Other Diseases Affecting the Central and Peripheral Nervous Systems. Feldman and colleagues (1994) report that the rate of complete erectile failure is 28% in men who are treated for diabetes. Those with poorly regulated diabetes may be at particularly high risk for sexual dysfunction (Bemelmans, Meuleman, Doesburg, Notermans, & Debruyne, 1994). Thomas and LoPiccolo (1994) suggest that the physiological effects of diabetes on sexual functioning are not as severe for women as they are for men. Schreiner-Engel, Shiavi, Vietorisz, and Smith (1987) found that the effects of diabetes on female sexual functioning may vary, depending on the type of diabetes. They observed no differences in the rate of sexual dysfunction for women with Type I diabetes and a group of healthy controls. By contrast, women with Type II diabetes were significantly more likely to experience difficulties related to sexual desire, arousal, orgasm, and sexual satisfaction. Results of at least one study conflict with this finding. Wincze, Albert, and Bansal (1993) examined physiological and subjective sexual arousal in response to erotic films among women with Type I diabetes and a group of women without diabetes. They found that although there were no differences in levels of subjective arousal, women with Type I diabetes evidenced significantly lower levels of physiological arousal in response to the films. Results of this study suggest that women with Type I diabetes may in fact be at increased risk for sexual difficulties.

It is believed that neuropathy and vascular problems often account for sexual dysfunction in patients with diabetes (Bemelmans et al., 1994; Korenman, 1998). In a recent study, however, Takanami, Nagao, Ishii, Miura, and Shirai (1997) found that erectile dysfunction is not organically based in all patients. The authors measured physiological arousal to an erotic film in 24 men with diabetes and erectile disorder, and found that 25% of the men evidenced a significant increase in penile circumference (i.e., 20% or greater increase) without the aid of a medical intervention. Takanami and colleagues (1997) hypothesize that there is a psychogenic basis to erectile disorder in these cases. They suggest that diabetes serves as a source of considerable stress, and that the stress in turn may negatively affect sexual functioning in this subgroup of patients.

Other diseases affecting the central and peripheral nervous systems that may lead to sexual dysfunction include epilepsy, multiple sclerosis, and renal disease (Hakim & Goldstein, 1996; Wincze & Carey, in press). Along with neurological diseases, trauma such as pelvic surgery, surgery or injury to the perineum, and spinal cord injury may interfere with normal sexual responding (Korenman, 1998).

Hormone Levels. Low levels of testosterone are associated with low levels of sexual desire in men (Meston, 1997). Research suggests, however, that low testosterone alone does not lead to erectile dysfunction. Korenman (1995) argues that a testosterone deficiency does not preclude normal erectile functioning in response to an erotic stimulus. Consistent with this finding, results of several studies (e.g., Schiavi, White, Mandeli, & Levine, 1997) suggest that although testosterone supplements may enhance sexual desire, they do not lead to significant improvements in erectile functioning

Findings on the relationship between hormones and sexual functioning in women are less consistent (Sherwin, 1988). In summarizing the results of several studies, Beck (1995) concludes that testosterone may increase sexual desire and subjective pleasure in women; low estrogen may be linked to vaginal tissue atrophy, which can result in dryness and discomfort during sexual activity.

Alcohol. Several researchers have identified heavy alcohol use as a risk factor for sexual dysfunction (e.g., Benet, Sharaby, & Melman, 1994; Hirschfield, 1998). In a review of studies on the relationship between sexual dysfunction and alcohol abuse, Schiavi (1990) reported that 8%–54% of men with alcoholism have erectile dysfunction, and 31%–58% suffer from low desire. Schiavi points out that although there is much evidence for a relationship between sexual functioning and alcohol use, many studies fail to control for the stage of the disorder (e.g., still abusing, in the midst of detoxification) and the effects of medication, age, and physical illness.

Studies focusing on women also suggest a relationship between alcohol misuse and sexual dysfunction. Klassen and Wilsnack (1986) surveyed 917 women in the United States and found a positive correlation between heavy drinking and sexual problems. Malatesta, Pollack, Crotty, and Peacock (1982) examined the immediate effects of heavy alcohol consumption on female orgasm. They found that women with higher blood alcohol levels tended to have a longer latency to orgasm and a decrease in the subjective intensity of orgasm.

It is believed that chronic, excessive alcohol use may contribute to sexual difficulties through its effects on hypothalamic pituitary function (e.g., decline in testosterone levels), the liver, and both central and peripheral neurological processes (e.g., neuropathy) (Schiavi, 1990). It has also been suggested that alcohol abuse contributes to sexual dysfunction by disrupting interpersonal relationships. O'Farrell, Choquette, Cutter, and Birchler (1997) found that men with alcoholism had a significantly higher rate of erectile dysfunction than maritally conflicted and maritally nonconflicted men without alcoholism. Interestingly, however, the men with alcoholism did not differ from the maritally conflicted men without alcoholism in their level of sexual desire, the rate of premature ejaculation, and the prevalence of sexual pain in their wives. Both groups reported significantly more problems in these areas than did the maritally nonconflicted men without alcoholism. Results of this study suggest that aside from erectile difficulties, the higher rate of sexual problems in men with alcoholism may be due in great part to the relationship problems associated with alcoholism.

Medications. A number of medications may contribute to disorders of desire, arousal, or orgasm in men and women. The medications that are most often implicated in the etiology of sexual dysfunction are antihypertensives, antidepressants, and antipsychotic drugs (Finger, Lund, & Slagle, 1997). Hogan, Wallin, and Baer (1980) reported that 9%–23% of men taking antihypertensive medication experienced sexual dysfunction, relative to 4% of men in a healthy control group. Chang and colleagues (1991) found that the rate of sexual dysfunction was particularly high in men who were taking diuretics. Hodge, Harward, West, Krongaard-DeMong, and Kowal-Neely (1991) conducted one of the few studies focusing specifically on the effects of antihypertensive medication on female sexual functioning. They failed to find any significant differences between women taking antihypertensive medications and a group of healthy controls. Unfortunately, the findings of this study were limited by a small sample size.

The antidepressant class known as selective serotonin reuptake inhibitors (SSRIs) includes drugs such as Prozac, Zoloft, and Paxil. In a prospective study of 192 women and 152 men taking an SSRI, Montejo-Gonzalez and colleagues (1997) found that 14% of the patients spontaneously reported sexual dysfunction to their physicians, and 58% endorsed sexual problems when directly asked. Results of this study indicate that sexual side effects occur in a significant proportion of patients taking SSRIs. The data also suggest that studies based on spontaneously reported side effects may significantly underestimate the rate of sexual side effects associated with a particular medication. Segraves (1998) reviewed the effects of antidepressant medication on sexual functioning. He found that the rate of orgasm disturbance alone is 20%–75% in people taking antidepressant medication. Segraves (1998) reported that delayed orgasm and premature ejaculation are the two most common side effects. Other drugs associated with sexual difficulties include minor tranquilizers, anticonvulsants, and anticholinergics. (For a complete list of medications with sexual side effects, see Finger and colleagues, 1997.)

Other Direct Risk Factors. In their review of the literature on vaginismus, Reissing and colleagues (1999) suggest that the following factors or conditions may lead to painful attempts at penile–vaginal intercourse: hymeneal abnormalities; congenital abnormalities; vaginal atrophy and adhesions due to atrophy, vaginal surgery, or intravaginal radiation; prolapsed uterus; vulvar vestibulitis syndrome; endometriosis, infections; vaginal lesions and tumors; sexually transmitted diseases; and pelvic congestion.

Indirect Biological Risk Factors

Age. One of the most common indirect risk factors for sexual dysfunction is aging. Many people believe that sexual dysfunction is a natural consequence of aging. In fact, sexual functioning may be qualitatively different for older men and women. Aging men may find that it takes more time and more stimulation to attain an erection, that the erection may not be as firm as it was in the past, that the duration of orgasm and the intensity of ejaculation may diminish, and that sexual desire may decline (Leiblum & Segraves, 1995; Meston, 1997). During and after menopause, women may experience increased latency to lubrication, less and thinner vaginal lubrication, and reduction in the fullness of the labia majora (Bachmann, 1995; Leiblum & Segraves, 1995). Although some of these changes may contribute to sexual difficulties, age alone is not a direct cause of sexual dysfunction in the majority of cases. Instead, as people age, they are more apt to develop medical conditions that serve as risk factors for sexual dysfunction (Korenman, 1998; NIH Consensus Conference, 1993). Thus age is an indirect, rather than a direct, risk factor for sexual dysfunction.

Cigarette Smoking. Cigarette smoking may indirectly affect sexual functioning by amplifying the effects of such risk factors as treated heart disease; treated hypertension; untreated arthritis; and use of cardiac drugs, antihypertensive drugs, and vasodilators (NIH Consensus Conference, 1993; Feldman et al., 1994). There is also evidence that cigarette smoking serves as an independent risk factor for sexual dysfunction. Mannino, Klevens, and Flanders (1994) controlled for the effects of risk factors such as vascular disease, hormonal factors, and substance misuse in a group of 4,462 male Army veterans. They found that cigarette smoking alone was associated with a significantly higher rate of erectile dysfunction.

Other Indirect Risk Factors. A number of additional medical factors or conditions can indirectly lead to sexual dysfunction. Pain, particularly chronic pain, may cause a person significant discomfort or anxiety during sexual activity; this may result in difficulty becoming aroused or a loss of interest in sexual activity. Chronic or serious medical conditions, such as heart disease or cancer, may also lead to changes in sexual arousal or desire. Patients who have suffered a heart attack may fear that the physical exertion of sexual activity will cause another heart attack. Unpleasant symptoms associated with an illness or its treatment (e.g., nausea resulting from chemotherapy) may interfere with positive sexual functioning. Finally, medical conditions or procedures that involve changes in one's physical appearance (e.g., mastectomy) can lead to body image issues that interfere with healthy sexual functioning.

Psychosocial Risk Factors

In the context of the popularity of Viagra, the mass media have promoted the notion that sexual dysfunction is almost always caused by organic factors such as those presented above. Indeed, biological risk factors are present in many cases. Nevertheless, psychosocial factors, whether alone or in combination with biological factors, play some role in the majority of cases. Psychosocial risk factors may be classified into two broad categories: individual factors and relationship factors. Individual risk factors involve the individual and are independent of the relationship (e.g., faulty beliefs regarding sexual functioning). Relationship factors involve both the individual and the partner (i.e., problems or limitations within the relationship). In general, relationship factors are best addressed by working with the couple together rather than with each person individually.

Individual Risk Factors

Psychological Disorders. One of the most common individual risk factors for sexual dysfunction is the presence of psychological disorders. These include mood disorders, anxiety disorders, alcohol or other substance use disorders, and eating disorders. Depression often involves anhedonia, a lack of pleasure or interest in activities the person normally enjoys. Thus it is not surprising that depression may be associated with a loss of sexual desire and difficulty becoming aroused (Hirschfield, 1998). Angst (1998) prospectively compared the rate of sexual dysfunction in 591 men and women who were categorized as nondepressed, nontreated depressed, or treated depressed. Angst found that the rates of sexual dysfunction in these groups were 26%, 45%, and 62%, respectively. Results of this study support the hypothesis that rates of sexual dysfunction are higher among men and women who are depressed. It is possible that the rate of sexual dysfunction was highest in the third group studied by Angst because those patients who sought treatment were those whose depression was more severe, and consequently more likely to affect their sexual functioning.

A person with panic disorder fears such physiological sensations as rapid heartbeat, shortness of breath, sweating, and hot flushes. Many of these symptoms occur during sexual activity. Thus a person with panic disorder may respond to sexual activity with anxiety, discomfort, difficulty becoming aroused, or aversion (Kaplan, 1988; Sbrocco et al., 1997).

Emotions. Given the potential impact of mood and anxiety disorders on sexual functioning, it follows that emotions affect sexual arousal. Kaplan (1979) asserted that "the sexual dysfunctions . . . are caused by a single factor: anxiety" (p. 24). Empirical examinations of the effects of anxiety on sexual arousal indicate that the relationship is not as simple as Kaplan suggested. Through a series of studies, researchers have demonstrated that anxiety negatively affects sexual arousal in people with sexual dysfunction but may enhance arousal in people who do not have sexual difficulties (e.g., Barlow, Sakheim, & Beck, 1983; Hoon, Wincze, & Hoon, 1977). Barlow (1986; Cranston-Cuebas & Barlow, 1990) hypothesizes that when sexually functional men and women become anxious during sexual activity, their level of autonomic arousal increases, they focus more efficiently on erotic cues, and they become increasingly aroused. By contrast, when people with sexual dysfunction become anxious, their level of autonomic arousal increases, and they focus more intently on the consequences of not performing. Not surprisingly, they then fail to become aroused.

Mitchell, DiBartolo, Brown, and Barlow (1998) used a musical mood induction to examine the effects of positive and negative mood states on sexual arousal in sexually functional males. They found that negative mood states were associated with significantly lower levels of physiological arousal. Anger is another emotion that may negatively affect sexual functioning. Feldman and colleagues (1994) found that suppression and expression of anger were correlated with significantly higher rates of erectile dysfunction.

Maladaptive Cognitions. Maladaptive cognitions (e.g., negative expectations) may negatively affect sexual functioning. Barlow (1986; Cranston-Cuebas & Barlow, 1990) hypothesizes that men and women with sexual dysfunction respond to sexual stimuli by focusing on negative self-focused cognitions. This distracts them from erotic cues and interferes with their ability to become aroused. Results of several studies suggest that distraction from erotic cues is associated with lower levels of physiological arousal (e.g., Abrahamson et al., 1985; Geer & Fuhr, 1976). Moreover, recent studies suggest that negative expectations and internal attributions for past erectile failure may lead to lower levels of physiological arousal (Bach, Brown, & Barlow, 1999; Weisberg, Brown, Wincze, & Barlow, in press).

Maladaptive thoughts may also come in the form of negative attitudes or misconceptions regarding sexual functioning. Patients are not born with ideas and beliefs regarding sexuality; they develop them as they grow up. Thus the messages and information patients receive as children or adolescents may have a significant impact on their attitudes as adults. These attitudes, in turn, affect sexual functioning. Individuals who are raised in very conservative cultures may learn that premarital sex is wrong, that masturbation is dirty, and that sex within a marriage is solely for the purpose of procreation. Men may learn that they should be able to get an erection under any circumstances. Women may be taught that intercourse is very painful. Such ideas may interfere with healthy sexual functioning. McCabe and Cobain (1998) found that women with sexual dysfunction were more likely than women without sexual difficulties to report having had negative attitudes toward intercourse as adolescents. Moreover, men and women with sexual dysfunction were more likely than those without sexual problems to have negative attitudes toward sex as adults.

Cultural Factors. Racial, ethnic, and religious background often affect a person's beliefs, expectations, and behaviors in sexual relationships. Moreover, definitions of and reactions to sexual problems are often culturally determined. For example, Verma, Khaitan, and Singh (1998) reported the frequency of various sexual dysfunctions in 1,000 consecutive patients presenting to a psychosexual clinic in India. They found that 77% of male patients reported difficulties with premature ejaculation—a rate significantly higher than that reported in the United States. Moreover, 71% of male patients presented with concern about nocturnal emission associated with erotic dreams. The authors suggest that the high rate of problems associated with ejaculation is due in part to a widely held belief in India that loss of semen causes depletion of physical and mental energy. It is interesting to note that only 36 of these 1,000 patients were female. The authors suggest that this may be due to the religious, social, and cultural background of India, in which it is considered immoral for women to seek treatment for sexual problems.

Lack of Education Regarding Sexual Functioning. Finally, limited information regarding sexual functioning is a risk factor for sexual dysfunction. In our clinical experience, we have found that a person's level of education does not necessarily correlate with his/her degree of knowledge regarding sexual functioning. That is, an attorney is as likely as a person who dropped out of high school to have faulty ideas and information regarding sexual functioning. Thus it is important for the clinician not to presume that a given patient has an adequate base of knowledge from which to work. One of us once assessed a health care professional who reported that he was having erectile difficulties. The interview with him revealed that he was engaging in oral sex to the point of ejaculation; when, after ejaculating, he was unable to maintain an erection sufficient for intercourse, he believed that he had erectile dysfunction. Unfortunately, he was so distressed by this belief that he eventually developed erectile difficulties.

Relationship Factors

Couple Distress. Sexual problems are sometimes secondary to couple distress. When couple distress is severe, treatment of sexual dysfunction should be postponed. When and if the relationship problems are resolved, remaining sexual difficulties may be directly addressed.

Sexual problems may cause frustration, distress, and tension within a relationship. Thus many couples who present for treatment of sexual dysfunction have mild relationship problems. If these problems are primarily a consequence rather than a cause of the sexual dysfunction, they may be addressed within the context of sex therapy.

Poor Communication. Poor communication may negatively affect a sexual relationship. Patients who cannot communicate effectively with their partners may harbor anger, resentment, or other negative feelings that interfere with sexual functioning. The ability to address disagreements in a constructive manner may be particularly important. McCabe and Cobain (1998) found that men with sexual dysfunction argued with their partners significantly more than men without sexual difficulties did. Hawton and Catalan (1986) found that ease of communication of anger was associated with a better outcome for couples participating in sex therapy.

Along with general communication problems, an inability to communicate about sex may contribute to sexual difficulties. Some couples communicate effectively about other aspects of their relationship but have difficulty talking comfortably about sex. Partners who fail to communicate about their sexual relationship allow false assumptions to go unchallenged (e.g., "My partner does not enjoy engaging in sexual activity with me"). Moreover, they lack a forum in which they can express their preferences regarding different types of stimulation. It is not uncommon to work with a couple in which the partners have been married for years but never discussed what sexual activities they like and dislike. Such a couple may believe that a good lover simply knows what his/her partner wants.

Lack of Physical Attraction. All men and women, whether they are in their first month of dating or their 30th year of marriage, need to feel attracted to their sexual partners. Couples sometimes underestimate the importance of this factor. They may believe that mutual love and respect are sufficient for a satisfying sexual relationship (Wincze & Barlow, 1997a). This is not the case. Physical attraction is an important part of a relationship. The absence of such feelings is an obstacle to healthy sexual functioning. Partners who have lost this feeling can make efforts to restore it. Recognizing the importance of being attracted to one another, rather than thinking it no longer matters, marks the first step toward addressing this issue.

Restricted Sexual Repertoire. Occasional sexual difficulties are a normative experience. Partners who engage in various forms of stimulation are not unduly affected by occasional problems related to intercourse; they have more than one means of satisfying each other sexually. Many couples, however, equate sex with intercourse. For these couples, an inability to have intercourse means that physical intimacy is not possible. Performance demands and fear of failure are higher for these couples (Rosen, 1996). Thus they are at greater risk of developing persistent sexual difficulties. Consistent with this hypothesis, McCabe and Cobain (1998) found that women with sexual dysfunction were more likely than women without sexual difficulties to report a restricted sexual repertoire. Similarly, Wiegel, Bach, Brown, Rhein, and Barlow (1997) found that men with erectile disorder reported a more restricted range of sexual behaviors than men without erectile difficulties.

CONTEXT OF ASSESSMENT AND TREATMENT

Having defined sexual dysfunction and identified risk factors for it, we now consider the context in which the assessment and treatment of these problems occur.

Setting

Over the last several years the media has widely promoted the notion that people with sexual problems should seek help from their physicians (Tiefer, 1996). Thus a medical center is often the ideal base for a sex therapist. In this setting, a therapist is available to a significant proportion of patients. Moreover, working closely with urologists, gynecologists, and primary care physicians helps to ensure a multidisciplinary approach to the assessment and treatment of sexual problems. Other clinicians may see patients in university-based outpatient clinics, community mental health centers, or private practices. In these instances, it is helpful for the clinician to develop working relationships with the local physicians. This facilitates the use of a multidisciplinary approach and enables the exchange of referrals.

Patients seeking treatment for sexual difficulties may initially feel very nervous and uncomfortable discussing such a personal subject. An office that appears professional and a therapist who is neatly and professionally dressed may help to put a patient or couple at ease. The office should be large enough to comfortably seat a couple and one or two therapists. In settings where psychophysiological assessments are an option, two adjoined rooms are needed: a private room for the patient and another for the therapist.

Spacing of Sessions and Length of Therapy

Masters and Johnson's treatment program for sexual dysfunction served as the model for sex therapy for two decades. Their approach involved daily therapy sessions that were conducted over a 2- or 3-week period. Thus a schedule of daily sessions was once considered ideal. Heiman and LoPiccolo (1983) compared the relative efficacy of 15 daily versus 15 weekly therapy sessions. They found that on the majority of measures, the differences between the two formats were nonsignificant. To the extent that either approach had an advantage, it was a schedule of weekly sessions.

We typically conduct therapy on a weekly basis, at least until the patient or couple is working on behavioral assignments (e.g., sensate focus exercises) between sessions (Wincze & Barlow, 1997a). At that time, the frequency of sessions may be decreased to once every 2 or 3 weeks in order to allow a couple more time to practice assigned exercises. We have found that it is often not helpful to conduct treatment less than once every 3 or 4 weeks. Conducting sessions too infrequently may

break the continuity of treatment and seems to reduce the patient's or couple's motivation to routinely practice skills between sessions.

The length of treatment varies from one case to the next. Some patients benefit from three or four sessions consisting mainly of psychoeducation. Others require more long-term interventions. In the majority of cases, we tell patients that after 10–12 sessions we will review treatment goals and determine whether additional sessions would be useful. We find it helpful to frame the treatment plan in this manner, so that patients who have not attained their goals after 12 sessions do not consider themselves treatment failures. The majority of patients can achieve their treatment goals within 15 sessions.

Although Masters and Johnson recommended the use of male and female cotherapists, we have found that this approach is neither necessary nor practical. In the era of managed care, such an approach is rarely an option. Thus, unless we are training interns or graduate students, we generally work individually.

Working with Couples or with Individuals

Although we do not require it, we strongly encourage every patient with a partner to undergo an assessment and treatment as a couple. This is helpful for several reasons. An interview with the partner may provide additional insight into psychosocial factors that are contributing to the sexual difficulty. Moreover, the partner's participation in the assessment gives the clinician an opportunity to observe the couple's interactions. Inclusion of the partner in treatment ensures that both partners understand the treatment plan and helps to promote compliance. Lastly, working with the couple rather than the individual helps to restructure the notion that sexual dysfunction is the patient's problem and that he/she needs to be "fixed."

The value of working with a couple versus the patient alone is supported by recent empirical findings. Hirst and Watson (1997) examined the relative efficacy of individual versus couple treatment of sexual dysfunction. They found that attendance was the best predictor of outcome; patients who had partners but underwent individual treatment attended

fewer sessions and canceled more appointments. Ultimately, 84% of patients who received couple treatment had a good outcome,
relative to 51% of patients whose partners
did not attend. Consistent with results of this
study, Wylie (1997) examined outcome in 37
couples undergoing psychosocial couple treatment for male erectile disorder. He reported
a trend toward remaining in therapy for patients whose partners attended the assessment
interview.

When assessing a couple, we find it helpful
to meet with each person individually, along
with meeting with them as a pair. Sometimes
information that is essential to an understanding of the case will not be revealed when a
therapist meets with the patient and partner
as a couple. We also find it useful to meet periodically with each person individually over
the course of treatment. This gives the therapist an opportunity to devote more time to
each partner and his/her individual issues. At
the same time, it allows each person to speak
privately with the therapist and share issues or
concerns that he/she does not feel comfortable
addressing when the three meet together.

When speaking with each person individually, the therapist should explicitly ask which,
if any, issues should not be shared with the
partner. It is important for both the patient
and partner to understand that information
they share with the clinician will be kept confidential and will not be shared with the other
person if he/she wishes to keep it private. If a
person thinks that sensitive information will
be shared with the partner, he/she may not disclose details that are central to the case.

Cognitive-behavioral treatment can certainly be beneficial for a patient who does not
have a partner. In such cases, treatment
focuses on providing psychoeducation, challenging thoughts that may interfere with
sexual functioning, and assigning behavioral
exercises that may be completed independently. This treatment may involve fewer sessions than that for a couple, because there are
certain exercises that cannot be practiced and
issues that cannot be addressed in the absence
of a partner. Thus, in such a case, we cover
as much as possible with the individual,
develop a plan for how he/she might further
address problems or concerns once in the context of a relationship, and give the patient the
option of resuming treatment once he/she has
a steady partner.

A single patient may sometimes suggest involving a casual partner in the assessment
and treatment process. Alternatively, a
younger patient (e.g., a college student) may
wish to include a steady partner in therapy.
In both cases, we explain to the patient that
because very sensitive information will be
revealed over the course of the assessment
and treatment, it may be prudent to work
with a therapist individually. This is done to
protect the confidentiality of the patient and
to ensure that he/she will not ultimately regret having shared such private information
with someone other than the therapist. Periodically including the partner in relevant
treatment sessions can serve as a compromise
in such cases.

Client Variables

Hawton and Catalan (1986) conducted one
of the earlier studies to examine prognostic
variables in sex therapy. They found that the
quality of the couple's sexual relationship,
the quality of the overall relationship, the
patient's motivation, and homework compliance by the third treatment session were significant predictors of treatment outcome.
More recently, Hawton, Catalan, and Fagg
(1992) found that the quality of pretreatment
communication, general sexual adjustment,
the presence of mental illness in the female
partner, socioeconomic status, and the couple's early engagement in treatment were significant predictors of treatment outcome.
Sarwer and Durlak (1997) found that the
number of sensate focus exercises completed
in the last week of treatment was a significant
predictor of treatment outcome. Finally, as
noted earlier, Wylie (1997) examined outcome in 37 couples undergoing psychosocial
treatment for male erectile disorder. He found
that patient dropout was associated with lower
scores on a measure of relationship satisfaction
at pretreatment. Moreover, he found that a
history of mental illness in the male partner was
associated with a poor outcome.

These studies are consistent in suggesting
that the quality of the relationship at pretreatment is positively correlated with treatment
outcome. Moreover, these studies indicate that
patients who are more compliant with treatment (i.e., engage in assigned exercises between
sessions) tend to have a better outcome.

Religious, ethnic, and cultural variables often play a central role in sex therapy. These factors may strongly influence a patient's values and beliefs regarding sexual activity. If the patient's ideas are consistent with those of his/her subculture, the therapist needs to respect them and not impose his/her own value system. There are some instances, however, in which a patient misinterprets the teachings of his/her religion or subgroup. In such cases, it can be helpful to refer the patient to a member of the clergy or religious group. This person will help the patient develop a more accurate understanding of the religion's teachings. A therapist may not always be aware of the unique issues that are relevant for patients from a particular subgroup. Thus the therapist must be prepared to educate himself/herself and seek consultation when necessary.

Therapist Variables

There are limited data on the effects of therapist variables on the treatment of sexual dysfunction (Mohr & Beutler, 1990). In one of the few studies in this area, LoPiccolo, Heiman, Hogan, and Roberts (1985) found that the number of therapists (i.e., one vs. two) did not significantly affect treatment outcome. Moreover, they found no effect for the gender of the therapist. Although research suggests that the gender of the therapist does not significantly affect treatment outcome, some patients may express a strong preference for either a male or a female therapist. In such cases, we try to accommodate the patients' wishes. Although there is limited additional research on the effects of therapist variables, our clinical experience suggests that a supportive yet direct style is effective. It is also important for the therapist to be sensitive and nonjudgmental when discussing such a personal aspect of patients' lives.

ASSESSMENT AND TREATMENT

The remainder of the chapter outlines our approach to the assessment and treatment of patients with sexual dysfunction. The information and techniques presented are discussed in greater detail by Wincze and Barlow (1997a, 1997b) and Wincze and Carey (in press).

Goals of Assessment

Although patients are often eager to begin treatment, we feel it is important to allot an adequate number of sessions to the assessment process. Sufficient background information, details regarding the nature and extent of the sexual difficulties, and working knowledge of etiological and maintaining factors are necessary before the therapist can develop an effective treatment plan. We typically use the first three sessions for assessment before beginning the intervention.

The principal goal of the assessment is to understand and accurately characterize the nature of the presenting problem. As indicated above, patients presenting with sexual problems may ultimately be diagnosed with a sexual dysfunction, a mood or anxiety disorder, a substance use disorder, another mental disorder, or couple distress. Alternatively, patients presenting with sexual concerns may simply lack information regarding normative sexual functioning. For example, a woman may believe that she has low sexual desire because her interest in sex does not match that of her husband. In such cases, patients benefit from psychoeducation regarding normative sexual functioning and individual variability. If a sexual dysfunction is present, the therapist must determine the history, frequency, antecedents, and consequences of the sexual difficulty.

The second goal of an assessment is to identify (1) predisposing biological and psychosocial factors (e.g., diabetes, negative messages about sex in childhood); (2) immediate precipitants (e.g., use of alcohol, arguments); and (3) maintaining factors (e.g., neuropathy, performance-related concerns). The identification of these factors often requires an integration of information obtained through a comprehensive psychosocial evaluation and a recent medical examination.

A third goal of the assessment process is to determine a pretreatment baseline for the patient's sexual functioning. Baseline data will allow the therapist to measure progress over the course of treatment.

Throughout the assessment, the therapist will have opportunities to provide psychoeducation and address faulty beliefs or misconceptions regarding sexual functioning. In this respect, the intervention begins in the context of the assessment. The provision of basic information can often have immediate positive effects on the couple's sexual relationship. This helps the couple to feel that although the intervention has not yet begun, both partners are already benefiting from addressing their difficulties with a professional.

Over the course of the assessment, the therapist will help the couple identify conditions under which sexual problems are most likely to occur. This process benefits the partners in at least two ways. It allows them to view the sexual problem as a condition that is subject to change depending on various factors; thus it helps them to be optimistic regarding the potential benefits of treatment. In addition, it helps to separate the patient from the problem and diminishes the sense of blame and guilt that may be present at the outset of therapy.

Lastly, the assessment provides an opportunity for the patient and partner to learn how to discuss their sexual relationship with the therapist. By openly and comfortably discussing sexual functioning, the therapist normalizes the process, provides a useful model, and implicitly gives both partners permission to talk about a very intimate and private aspect of their life.

Process Issues in Assessment

Wincze and Carey (in press) define "process" as the interaction between the therapist and the client. Certain process issues are significant in any form of psychotherapy; these include the gender, age, race or ethnicity, and religion of the therapist and the patient. Differences between the therapist and client on any one of these factors may have a significant impact on the therapy process. The therapist should be sensitive to ways in which his/her background differs from that of the patient. The therapist might consider acknowledging these differences and asking the patient how he/she feels about them. At the very least, the therapist should consider ways in which these factors might facilitate or interfere with the therapy process.

Other process issues are particularly significant in the treatment of sexual dysfunction. Therapists who do not specialize in the assessment and treatment of sexual functioning may be uncomfortable discussing sexual functioning with patients. Discomfort on the part of

the therapist is evident to a patient and may impede the therapy process. Alternatively, therapists who routinely treat patients with sexual dysfunction may forget that their patients are not in the habit of discussing sexual activity in this context; consequently, they may be insensitive to a patient's embarrassment or discomfort. Ideally, of course, the therapist feels comfortable discussing sexual matters and is sensitive to discomfort on the part of the patient.

When working in the area of sexual dysfunction, it is particularly important for therapists to draw and retain appropriate professional boundaries. A therapist who finds himself/herself attracted to a patient should seek consultation from a colleague. Consulting with peers can help a therapist to be mindful of blurred boundaries. If a therapist is unable to retain a strictly professional role or suspects that the patient reciprocates feelings of attraction, the patient should be referred to another therapist.

Along with these process issues, Wincze and Carey (in press) outline a series of assumptions that are useful in assessing sexual functioning:

• Clients will usually be embarrassed and have difficulty discussing sexual matters. This embarrassment may cause them to withhold information, to miss sessions, and to generally avoid discussing their concerns. The clinician may help by normalizing (and even "predicting") patients' discomfort and modeling comfortable discussion of sexual functioning.

• Many clients will not understand medically correct terminology such as "intercourse," "ejaculation," and "vagina." Moreover, even when patients use these terms, they may not use them correctly. It is sometimes helpful for the clinician to follow medically correct terms with more commonly used lay terms such as "cum" or "wet." This ensures that the patient knows the meaning of the clinician's questions; it teaches the patient the meaning of medically correct terms; and it may increase the patient's comfort level by suggesting that it is acceptable to use lay terms.

• Even the most well-educated patients may be misinformed about sexual functioning. Some women believe that they will bleed very heavily on their first attempt at intercourse. Men may believe that they should be able to engage in intercourse for 30 minutes before ejaculating. Identifying and correcting these misunderstandings can often lead to rapid and significant clinical improvement.

• Some clients will be in crisis and may be suicidal. A clinician should not assume that sexual dysfunction is the primary problem for a patient presenting with sexual difficulties. An assessment of general psychological functioning may reveal that the patient is very depressed, perhaps suicidal. In such cases, the clinician must attend to issues outside of sexual functioning and ensure that proper treatment is provided.

• Partners have often not been open with each other and do not freely discuss sexual matters. It is safest to assume that partners have withheld significant information, thoughts, or feelings from each other. Therapy can serve to promote more open communication. As indicated above, many couples do not comfortably discuss their sexual relationship. This area of communication must also be addressed.

• When clients discuss sexual problems with a therapist, it may be the first time they've discussed them. Sexual functioning is an extremely private aspect of people's lives. At the same time, our culture places a great deal of emphasis on the importance of sexual activity and a person's "performance" in this domain. For both of these reasons, patients are often reluctant to discuss or acknowledge sexual difficulties. Some patients are not even comfortable addressing the difficulty with their sexual partners. Thus, for many patients the first appointment with a therapist is the first time they have talked about their sexual difficulty.

• A couple will often have avoided sex because of fear and discomfort. Many couples experiencing sexual difficulties begin to avoid sexual activity because it becomes a source of frustration, disappointment, anxiety, or physical discomfort. Partners who are unable to engage in intercourse may report that they have ceased sexual relations because their attitude is, "Why bother?" In some couples with sexual dysfunction, partners stop being affectionate with one another because they are reluctant to "start something [they] cannot finish."

Assessment Methods

Psychosocial assessment of sexual dysfunction will typically involve a clinical interview. It may also involve the use of self-report measures or a psychophysiological assessment.

Clinical Interview

Talking to patients about their psychological functioning can be difficult; it requires a sensitive, empathic, and skilled therapist. This is particularly true when patients are presenting with sexual difficulties. Patients who undergo an assessment of their sexual functioning must discuss the most intimate, private aspects of their lives with the therapist. They are typically uncomfortable talking about sex and may be embarrassed to divulge information regarding their own sexual functioning. The therapist must combine a gradual approach to asking highly personal questions with a time-efficient strategy for obtaining necessary information.

The use of an outline structures the clinical interview and helps the clinician to obtain necessary information in an organized, time-efficient manner. The outline we follow is described below. Alternatively, clinicians may choose to use a semistructured interview (e.g., Sbrocco, Weisberg, & Barlow, 1992). Commonly used in research settings, semistructured interviews provide a clear framework for clinical interviews and guide the clinician through the assessment of sexual functioning.

As indicated above, we typically reserve three sessions for the assessment process. We interview the patient alone for one session, interview the partner alone for one session, and then meet with the couple together for the third session.

First Session: Introduction and Patient Interview. We begin the first session with an explanation of the assessment process. A proper orientation to the purpose of the assessment is particularly important for patients who have been referred by physicians. These patients sometimes schedule an appointment with a therapist simply because a doctor recommended it. They may not know why they are meeting with a therapist or what they can expect.

At the start of the first session, we talk briefly with the patient and partner together. This gives us an opportunity to explain the assessment process and address the couple's questions and concerns. Providing this information to the couple rather than to each person individually reinforces the notion that although one person is the identified "patient," they will undergo the assessment and treatment as a couple. This brief meeting also provides the therapist with an opportunity to directly observe the way in which the couple interacts and communicates. (Please see the case study at the end of the chapter for an example of what the therapist might say when first meeting with a couple.)

Once the assessment process is explained and the couple's questions and issues have been addressed, the remainder of the first session should be devoted to interviewing either the patient or the partner (often the patient) individually. The therapist should explain to the couple that individual interviews help to develop the clearest understanding of the sexual difficulty by providing as much information as possible from each individual. The couple may be informed that periodically meeting with each person individually may also be useful during treatment. It allows the therapist to spend more time focused on each person and provides additional time to work through individual issues. The couple may need to be reminded of the rationale for meeting with each person individually once treatment begins. Nevertheless, by explaining this at the outset, the therapist may instill the notion that individual meetings are routine when working with couples.

Objectives of the patient interview include establishing rapport, collecting demographic information, obtaining a description of the presenting problem, conducting an assessment of general psychological functioning, and assessing the patient's psychosexual history. Although it is helpful to use an outline when conducting the interview, the therapist must be willing to deviate from a standard set of questions in order to focus on more primary problems or important background information. Given this caveat, following is a general approach to clinical interviews that we find useful.

Because patients may initially feel nervous and uncomfortable, it is often helpful to begin by gathering nonthreatening information such as demographics. The therapist may then continue with open-ended questions or statements such as "Tell me a little bit about the difficulties you have been having recently." The therapist can observe how freely and comfortably a patient discusses his/her sexual prob-

lems. For those who seem embarrassed or defensive, it may be helpful to gather other necessary information before further discussing the sexual difficulty. This will give such a patient more time to relax and feel comfortable with the therapist.

It is often helpful to obtain a psychosexual and psychosocial history. The therapist may want to gather information regarding the patient's childhood. Important data include details regarding the patient's family structure, the parents' relationship with each other and with the patient (including demonstrations of affection), childhood sexual or physical abuse, early messages about sex, and early sexual experiences (pleasant or unpleasant). Adolescence marks a very significant period in psychosexual development; thus information on the patient's experiences as an adolescent can be very useful. Relevant details include the treatment of the patient by his/her peers (e.g., ridicule for physical attributes such as acne, weight, and facial features), dating experiences, body image, and history of alcohol or other substance misuse.

The therapist will then want to gather information regarding the person's history and experiences as an adult. The most important areas to address are the following:

• *A relationship history after the age of 20.* This includes a history of sexual relationships, long-term relationships, and prior marriages.
• *History of any unusual experiences.* This should include a brief assessment for the presence of paraphilic fantasies or behaviors such as sexual arousal associated with children or inanimate objects. For patients who endorse atypical sexual fantasies, it is important to determine whether they have acted on these fantasies, whether they intend to do so, and whether they can become sexually aroused in the absence of these stimuli/situations.
• *Medical history.* Regardless of whether the patient has had a recent medical evaluation, the therapist should inquire about a childhood/teenage history of diseases, surgery, medical care, congenital disorders, and other significant medical problems. Information regarding the patient's medical history since the age of 20 is particularly important. Again, relevant information includes a history of diseases, surgery, medical care, and other significant health problems. Lastly, the therapist should determine whether the patient has had regular medical care (if not, he/she should be

referred for a medical evaluation), is currently taking prescribed medication, or is currently being treated for any medical problem.

• *Current psychological functioning and mental health history.* An assessment of general psychological functioning is necessary in order to determine whether it is appropriate to focus specifically on sexual dysfunction. If sexual difficulties are secondary to problems such as depression, anxiety, severe couple distress, or a substance use disorder, the person is unlikely to benefit from starting with treatment for sexual dysfunction. Instead, the patient should begin by addressing the primary problem. When this problem is successfully treated or stabilized, the person may effectively focus on treatment for residual sexual difficulties. Figure 13.1 is a decision tree that will aid therapists in deciding when treatment focusing specifically on sexual dysfunction is appropriate for various patients (Wincze & Barlow, 1997a). The therapist should also obtain a history of past mental health treatment.

• *Information regarding the patient's cur-*

rent sexual and overall relationship. Relevant information includes satisfaction with the current sexual and overall relationship, commitment to the relationship, activities the partners enjoy engaging in together, and strengths and weaknesses of the relationship. The therapist will also want to assess the impact of the sexual difficulty on the relationship; each partner's reactions to the sexual difficulties; the extent and nature of sexual activity since the sexual difficulty developed; and thoughts and beliefs related to sexual activity.

Lastly, the therapist should ensure that adequate information regarding the nature, onset, severity, and course of the sexual difficulty has been obtained. The therapist should be clear on the circumstances in which the difficulty occurs, and can inquire about the patient's attributions for the problem.

Throughout the assessment, the therapist needs to be sensitive to information the patient is concerned about keeping private. As indicated earlier, the therapist should clarify

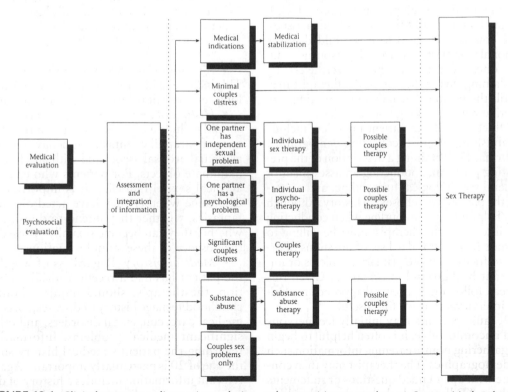

FIGURE 13.1. Clinical assessment, diagnostic conclusion, and prerequisites to sex therapy: Seven critical pathways. From the *Therapist Guide of Enhancing Sexuality: A Problem Solving Approach.* Copyright 1997 by Graywind Publications Inc. Reproduced by permission of Publisher, The Psychological Corporation, a Harcourt Assessment Company. All rights reserved.

with the patient which, if any, issues should not be shared with the partner.

The first session may end with an open-ended question that allows the patient to add information about which the therapist has not asked. The therapist may directly ask, "Is there anything we have not talked about that might be helpful for me to know?"

Second Session: Partner Interview. The second session is devoted to interviewing the partner, unless for some reason the partner has been interviewed in the first session. The therapist may start by asking whether anything has changed since the last appointment. It is always helpful to ask this in the event that significant events (e.g., death in family, loss of job, argument) have positively or negatively affected the couple. It is important to know whether the couple is preoccupied with such events and distracted from the focus of therapy. The therapist may also ask whether the couple discussed the first session. Answers to this question may provide information regarding the couple's interaction pattern and openness in communication. In some couples, partners may willingly discuss sensitive subjects with one another in the therapist's office, but completely avoid doing so at home. Thus it is helpful to determine not only how partners communicate in the company of the therapist, but how also how they communicate when they are alone.

Before initiating further questions, the therapist may ask the patient's partner whether there is anything he/she would like to ask or discuss. This open-ended question gives the partner an opportunity to introduce process issues or personal factors that may have an impact on therapy. Once the therapist and partner have discussed these issues, the partner interview then follows a format similar to that of the patient interview.

In some cases, after finishing the patient and partner interviews, the therapist will decide that additional portions of the assessment are needed before treatment recommendations can be made. This information may include a physiological assessment or a medical evaluation. In such cases, the therapist should explain to the couple why additional information is needed and what value the added information may have. If both partners understand the potential importance of additional information, they are less likely to feel frus-trated by the delay of disposition. The therapist should also explain what effect the additional portions of the assessment may have on the ultimate plan for treatment.

Third Session: Feedback. The third session typically includes both partners. In some instances, the therapist will decide that individual therapy is needed before the partners can jointly address their sexual difficulties. The therapist may meet with the couple briefly and indicate that this will be the recommendation. The therapist can then meet with the patient individually for the remainder of the session, to explain in greater detail why individual therapy is indicated.

We assume here that the therapist meets with the couple together for the entire third session. The therapist may start by asking both partners whether anything new has happened since they last met or whether there are any issues related to the previous sessions that they wish to discuss. The couple's response to an open-ended question allows the therapist to observe how the couple communicates, who raises questions or issues, how the other person responds, and how well each person communicates his/her needs. As indicated above, beginning this way will also prompt discussion of personal issues other than sexual difficulties that are consuming time or emotional energy (e.g., problems with the couple's children). It is important for the therapist to be aware of such issues, because they may interfere with sex therapy.

Once the issues raised by the couple have been addressed, the therapist should present his/her case conceptualization. After the therapist has outlined the factors that seem to be contributing to the sexual dysfunction, he/she may work with the couple to identify appropriate treatment goals. Once treatment goals have been identified and agreed upon, the therapist can present a rough treatment outline to the couple and discuss the initial stages of therapy. (Please see the sections below titled "Integration of Data across Methods" and "Goals of Treatment" for further discussion.)

Self-Report Questionnaires

A self-report questionnaire is a standardized paper-and-pencil measure that is generally inexpensive, brief, easy to administer, and easy to score. There are several advantages to using self-report questionnaires. They may supplement information obtained in the interview and may provide information a patient is unwilling to reveal in person. With the use of norms, a standardized questionnaire may be used to provide a comparison of the patient's symptoms or thoughts to those of others in the same age group. Finally, because most self-report measures are brief, they can be administered on multiple occasions. Repeated administrations may help the clinician to evaluate a patient's progress more objectively over the course of treatment.

There are a number of self-report questionnaires, both those that focus specifically on sexual functioning and those that focus more generally on overall psychological functioning. Following are some of the self-report questionnaires we often use in our clinical work.

The Derogatis Sexual Functioning Inventory (DSFI) is intended to provide an "omnibus" measure of sexual functioning (Derogatis & Melisaratos, 1979). The instrument comprises 10 subscales: Information, Experience, Drive, Attitudes, Psychological Symptoms, Affect, Gender Role Definition, Fantasy, Body Image, and Sexual Satisfaction. The subscales demonstrate good to very good internal consistency and test–retest reliability (Derogatis & Melisaratos, 1979). The DSFI evidences good discriminant validity. Nine of 10 subscales differentiate between men with and without sexual dysfunction; 5 of 10 subscales differentiate between women with and without sexual dysfunction. The DSFI serves as a useful means of measuring a range of factors involved in sexual functioning. Disadvantages of the scale include its length (245 items) and somewhat complicated scoring.

The Dyadic Adjustment Scale (DAS) is a widely used 32-item self-report instrument. It provides an overall measure of dyadic adjustment, as well as scores on four subscales: Dyadic Satisfaction, Dyadic Cohesion, Dyadic Consensus, and Affectional Expression. The DAS has demonstrated good discriminant validity, very good construct validity, and very high internal consistency (Spanier, 1976; Spanier & Thompson, 1982)

The Sexual Opinion Survey (SOS; Fisher, 1988; Fisher, Byrne, White, & Kelley, 1988) consists of 21 items designed to assess affective and evaluative responses to a variety of sexual stimuli. Each item describes a sexual situation and an associated negative or positive response. Patients rate the extent to which they agree with each response. We use the SOS to aid in our understanding of individuals and their comfort with a range of sexual situations. Research suggests that the SOS is valid and reliable, and norms are available (Fisher et al., 1988). The SOS can typically be completed and scored in less than 20 minutes.

A portion of the clinical interview will focus on the assessment of psychological functioning. Self-report measures may provide valuable additional information regarding such areas as mood, anxiety, and substance use. The Brief Symptom Inventory (Derogatis & Melisaratos, 1983) is a useful measure of general psychopathology. The Depression Anxiety Stress Scales (Lovibond & Lovibond, 1993) provide separate measures of depression, anxiety, and stress symptoms. The short version of the Michigan Alcohol Screening Test (Pokorny, Miller, & Kaplan, 1972) and the Drug Abuse Screening Test (Skinner, 1982) are useful screens of alcohol and other substance use, respectively.

Psychophysiological Assessment

A psychophysiological assessment can contribute unique and valuable information to the assessment of sexual functioning. A clinical interview may be biased by both the patient's report and the clinician's interpretation. Self-report measures may be biased by the patient's response style. The strength of a physiological assessment is that it can provide an objective measure of sexual arousal. These data can help to determine the nature and severity of a patient's functional impairment. They can also help to delineate the etiology of the dysfunction (i.e., organic, psychogenic, or mixed type).

The most widely used approach to the psychophysiological assessment of sexual arousal in men is to measure nocturnal penile tumescence (NPT)—that is, a man's erectile activity during sleep. In the past, it was often necessary for men to spend at least one night in a sleep laboratory for measures of NPT to be obtained. Technological advances, however, have now made it possible to measure NPT in the privacy of a patient's home. The RigiScan monitor (Dacomed/Urohealth, Minneapolis, MN) is a small portable measuring device worn during sleep that provides measures of both NPT and penile rigidity. A patient is sent home to wear the device during sleep and returns with data for the physician to interpret.

An additional approach is to measure a patient's physiological response to erotic stimuli in the laboratory. This method is used to measure sexual arousal in both men and women. The patient sits in a private room. A male patient may place either an electromechanical gauge, which is a soft metal clip (see, e.g., Barlow, Becker, Leitenberg, & Agras, 1970), or a mercury strain gauge, which is a flexible band, around his penis. These gauges measure changes in penile circumference. A female patient inserts a plastic cylinder approximately the size of a tampon in her vagina (Geer, Morokoff, & Greenwood, 1974). The small device emits light and measures the amount of light that is reflected back. As a woman becomes aroused, blood flow to the vaginal wall increases, and less light passes through it.

The rationale for the laboratory assessment is that patients who have difficulties becoming aroused during sexual activity with a partner may become aroused to erotic stimuli when there is no demand to engage in sexual activity. If so, there is evidence that such patients are physically capable of becoming aroused; there are simply factors that make it difficult for arousal to occur in a natural situation (e.g., performance-related concerns). A failure to become aroused during a psychophysiological assessment does not, however, necessarily indicate an organic basis to the sexual dysfunction. On occasion, patients experience anxiety in the laboratory because it is a novel situation and they know their response is being monitored; this performance anxiety may interfere with their ability to become aroused. In such instances, a second assessment may be helpful because the patients will often feel more relaxed.

Aside from considerable money, technical knowledge and skill are required in order to operate the equipment. Thus, although a psychophysiological assessment may provide important and valuable information, it is not a practical option in many clinical settings.

Medical Examination

In most instances, the patient should undergo a medical exam as part of an assessment to determine what, if any, biological factors are contributing to the sexual difficulty. If a medical evaluation has not been completed at the start of the psychosocial evaluation, the patient should be referred for one. In either case, ensure that the patient has told the physician he/she is experiencing sexual difficulties. It is not uncommon for a patient to undergo such an evaluation and never tell the physician his/her reason for seeking medical care. Once it has been completed, results of the medical exam can be integrated with those of the interview and the psychophysiological assessment.

Integration of Data across Methods

One of the goals of the assessment is to develop a coherent case formulation (i.e., a working hypothesis of the etiology of the problem). This formulation should relate all aspects of the patient's complaints to one another and explain why the individual has developed these difficulties (Carey, Flasher, Maisto, & Turkat, 1984). One purpose of this formulation is to aid the therapist in the development of a treatment plan. A second purpose is to communicate to clients that (1) their problem is an understandable one, given their physiology, medical history, life experiences and so on (i.e., they are not crazy); (2) there is reason for hope and optimism; and (3) there is a conceptual "road map" and rationale on which to build a therapeutic plan. Finally, developing a case formulation allows the therapist to check with the patient to see whether he/she has obtained all the necessary information and that the information is correct.

One of the more challenging aspects of sex therapy is integrating multiple levels of influence (i.e., biological, psychological, dyadic, and cultural) into a coherent case formulation. Despite its difficulty, a biopsychosocial case formulation captures the richness of sexual function and dysfunction. A patient is more likely to agree to try a psychosocial approach if the therapist recognizes that biological causes are not irrelevant, but inquires about and recognizes specific dyadic and sociocultural influences that might override or compensate for these. It is important to be sensitive to specific rituals and traditions that a couple has established, as well as ethnic, cultural, or religious issues.

The case formulation should include biological, psychological, and social areas even if the therapist believes that one of the areas is not contributing to the problem at the moment. It is always hard to predict the future, and the groundwork should be laid in case additional information becomes available and/or future developments occur. Moreover, this comprehensive approach to case formulation will give the client confidence that the therapist has considered all possibilities. Indirectly, the therapist communicates to the patient that he/she should also think about the problem in a multifaceted biopsychosocial framework.

Goals of Treatment

Many patients enter sex therapy with a performance-oriented treatment goal. For example, men with erectile disorder want to attain firm erections, and women with female orgasmic disorder want to reach orgasm. We feel that performance-oriented goals are problematic for a few reasons. They place pressure on patients and may increase performance anxiety; thus they are usually self-defeating. In addition, performance-oriented goals are based on the belief that a sexual interaction is a "failure" if certain events (e.g., intercourse, orgasm) do not occur. These goals conflict with the notion that there are multiple ways in which a couple may be physically intimate and sexually satisfied.

We suggest that the primary goal of sex therapy should be to help a couple develop a more satisfying sexual relationship. We explain to both partners that there is nothing wrong with a desire to engage in intercourse or reach orgasm (failure to acknowledge this may alienate the patient or partner and diminish the therapist's credibility). These goals, however, are secondary. If intercourse or orgasm occurs, that is fine; these events, however, are not necessary in order for sexual activity to be satisfying. The therapist can talk to the couple about the drawbacks of performance-oriented goals. Ultimately, it is important that the therapist and the couple come to some agreement regarding treatment goals. If the patient or couple is working toward a performance-oriented goal and the therapist is not, frustration with the therapy and with the clinician may result.

We suggest that the therapist and the couple periodically review treatment goals over the course of therapy. This helps to ensure that the therapist and the couple remain in agreement regarding the objectives of therapy. It also provides an opportunity to assess progress and to modify goals as needed.

Process Issues in Treatment

Default Assumptions

As in the case of assessment, it is helpful to begin treatment with a set of default assumptions. Wincze and Carey (in press) suggest that the following assumptions may help to facilitate efficient and effective treatment:

1. A client usually has a narrow definition of sex and will focus on performance as a marker of success.
2. A client sometimes has stereotyped views of masculine and feminine roles that will interfere with the assimilation of new information.
3. A client often does not understand the ingredients conducive to sexual arousal (e.g., favorable times to have sex and factors that may interfere).
4. A client may have a pattern of avoidance of sexual interactions and, as a result, may unintentionally sabotage therapy.
5. A client may be uninformed about sexually transmitted diseases and may not be using safer sex practices.

Using these assumptions will help the therapist anticipate potential obstacles to successful treatment. If certain assumptions prove not to be true, those issues may not need to be addressed. This indicates that the patient has one less barrier to achieving his/her treatment goals.

Challenges to Therapy

Preference for a Simple Pill. Having heard of Viagra, many patients expect that their sexual difficulties can be cured with a simple pill. They may see little point in investing the time and effort required for effective cognitive-behavioral treatment. In such cases, it is helpful to remind couples that cognitive-behavioral treatment is a long-term investment. It provides them with strategies they can use well after treatment ends to maintain a satisfying sexual relationship. It may also be useful to remind them that all treatments (including both Viagra and sex therapy) have advantages and disadvantages. A patient and partner need to weigh the costs and benefits associated with each treatment option and decide which approach is best for them.

Rigid, Faulty Attribution for the Sexual Difficulties. Patients will sometimes cling to a single explanation of their sexual difficulty. For example, a male patient may insist that there is a medical basis to his erectile dysfunction. The therapist may need to reframe alternative explanations so that they are more acceptable and less threatening to the patient. In the case of the man who firmly believes his erectile dysfunction is medically based, the therapist may emphasize that it is good that medical factors are not involved.

Noncompliance with Homework Assignments. Cognitive-behavioral treatments typically involve the use of homework assignments to allow patients to practice the skills they are learning between sessions. Homework plays a uniquely central role in sex therapy, because a number of treatment methods (e.g., sensate focus) can only be practiced or applied outside of sessions. For this reason, failure to comply with homework assignments presents a very significant challenge to treatment. Noncompliance may result from a number of factors, including fear and avoidance, an uncooperative partner, and busy schedules. We have found that it is important to anticipate potential obstacles to completing homework (e.g., a patient may feel uncomfortable or embarrassed completing certain exercises) and proactively address these issues with the couple. If partners are having difficulty making time for assigned exercises, it is sometimes helpful to schedule the exercises in advance. Of course, the partners should choose times at which they can relax and will not be bothered. The therapist can remind the partners that they should respect scheduled time with each other just as they would respect time scheduled with someone else (e.g., a doctor or supervisor).

Extramarital Affairs. When working with a couple, a therapist may occasionally learn that one person is having an affair. In these cases, the therapist must try to remain objective and evaluate the impact of the affair on the couple's relationship and on treatment. If the affair is counterproductive to therapy (as it usually will be), the therapist may help the person evaluate his/her priorities and decide whether to end the affair. If the affair does not end and the therapist does not feel treatment can be beneficial as long as the affair goes on, therapy may need to be discontinued. The therapist may approach this in different ways, depending on the particular case. In all instances, however, the therapist should respect the confidentiality of both the patient and the partner.

Cultural or Religious Opposition to Treatment Methods. Cultural or religious opposition to treatment methods can present a challenge to the therapy process. One of the most common examples of this is the negative response some patients have to the idea of masturbation. Masturbation exercises are often used to help patients become more comfortable with their bodies and to help women with aversion or pain disorders become more comfortable with penetration. Some patients believe that masturbation is dirty or sinful, or that it is not something a married person should do. One way to help patients feel comfortable with the idea of masturbatory exercises is to explain that they serve a clinical purpose. The therapist may indicate that masturbation is not an activity a person must adopt on a permanent basis. Rather, it is a technique that may be used over the short term to help the patient achieve his/her treatment goals.

Treatment Methods

Education

Education can be one of the most important components of sex therapy. Faulty beliefs, unrealistic expectations, and lack of information regarding physiology, anatomy, and sexual functioning can play central roles in the etiology and maintenance of sexual dysfunction. As a result, psychoeducation sometimes leads to rapid improvement in the first few sessions. For example, men who do not know there is a refractory period following ejaculation are very relieved to learn that their "erectile failure" after orgasm is normal. Similarly, women are relieved to find that lack of lubrication is a natural consequence of menopause that can easily be remedied with a lubricant.

Excerpts from textbooks on human sexuality can provide a helpful overview of sexual functioning. We also use pictures or diagrams of male and female genitalia to help patients develop a better understanding of the human anatomy. Information on the risks of unprotected sex and sexually transmitted diseases (including human immunodeficiency virus and hepatitis) is important in all cases and should be presented to couples routinely.

Unfortunately, the task of reeducating patients regarding normative sexual functioning is not always an easy one. We live in a culture that promotes a number of myths regarding sexual functioning. Thus patients' faulty beliefs and unrealistic expectations are sometimes firmly entrenched and resistant to change. Following is a compilation of common myths of male and female sexuality adapted from Heiman and LoPiccolo (1988), Wincze and Barlow (1997b), and Zilbergeld (1998).

Myths of Male Sexuality.

1. A real man isn't into sissy stuff like feelings and communicating.
2. A man is always interested in and always ready for sex.
3. A real man performs in sex.
4. Sex is centered on a hard penis and what is done with it.
5. A man should be able to make the earth move for his partner, or at the very least knock her socks off.
6. Men don't have to listen to women in sex.
7. Real men don't have sex problems.
8. Bigger is better.
9. I should be able to last all night.
10. Women won't like me if I can't get it up.
11. If I can't get it up, I must not really love my partner.
12. If a man knows that he might not be able to get an erection, it's unfair for him to start sexual activity with a partner.
13. Focusing more intensely on your erection—trying harder—is the best way to get an erection.

Myths of Female Sexuality.

1. Sex is only for women under 30.
2. Normal women have an orgasm every time they have sex.
3. All women can have multiple orgasms.
4. Pregnancy and delivery reduce women's sexual responsiveness.
5. A woman's sex life ends with menopause.
6. There are different kinds of orgasms related to a woman's personality; vaginal orgasms are more feminine and mature than clitoral orgasms.
7. A sexually responsive woman can always be turned on by her partner.
8. Nice women aren't aroused by erotic books or films.
9. You are frigid if you don't like the more exotic forms of sex.
10. If you can't have an orgasm quickly and easily, there's something wrong with you.
11. Feminine women don't initiate sex or become wild and unrestrained during sex.
12. Double jeopardy: You are frigid if you don't want sex and wanton if you do.
13. Contraception is a woman's responsibility, and she's just making up excuses if she says contraception issues are inhibiting her sexually.
14. If a woman doesn't initiate sex, she's just not interested in sex.

Myths of Male and Female Sexuality.

1. We're liberated folks who are very comfortable with sex.
2. All touching is sexual or should lead to sex.
3. Sex equals intercourse.
4. Good sex requires orgasm.
5. People in love should automatically know what their partners desire. Sex should be spontaneous, with no planning and no talking—it isn't romantic if you ask your partner what he/she enjoys.
6. Too much masturbation is bad.
7. Someone with a sexual partner does not masturbate.
8. Fantasizing about something else means I am not happy with what I have.

We typically review these myths with couples and ask them to indicate which statements they believe are true. This exercise helps couples to explore their attitudes about sexual functioning. Moreover, it helps the therapist to identify beliefs that will need to be challenged in treatment. In some cases, patients' faulty beliefs regarding sexual functioning (e.g., sex equals intercourse) will need to be challenged repeatedly over the course of therapy.

Along with obtaining information from the therapist, patients often benefit from reading selected books. There are a number of books that can be helpful to patients; examples include Wincze and Barlow (1997b), McCarthy and McCarthy (1998), and Zilbergeld (1998). We do not recommend that therapists suggest any book to patients before reading it themselves. In addition, if a therapist assigns readings to a couple, we recommend that time be reserved in the subsequent session to discuss the reading. This provides an opportunity for the couple to address any questions or concerns. It also reinforces the couple for completing the assignment and promotes continued compliance in the future.

Stimulus Control

Many couples mistakenly believe that sexual functioning is an automatic process, requiring nothing more than a willing partner. They may engage in sexual activity in very unfavorable conditions and have little insight into why they experience sexual problems. One of us recently interviewed a patient who indicated that he was not happy in his current relationship. When asked what he and his partner enjoyed doing together, he laughed and responded, "Spending time apart." Despite the obvious problems within the relationship, the patient was surprised and concerned that he was not able to maintain an erection during sexual activity with his partner.

Positive interpersonal and environmental factors are necessary for healthy sexual functioning. Stimulus control is a treatment method that involves manipulating environmental factors in order to facilitate a particular behavior or outcome. In the context of sex therapy, "stimulus control" refers to an effort to create the conditions that are conducive to healthy sexual functioning.

Biological, psychological, and interpersonal factors all affect sexual functioning. Positive and negative factors in each of these areas interact to affect sexual arousal (see Figure 13.2). Some examples of biological factors are disease, drugs, alcohol, cigarettes, or even fatigue. Psychological factors include self-esteem, mood, anxiety, thoughts, and attitudes. Interpersonal factors (included with the psychological factors in Figure 13.2) include physical attraction to a partner and positive attitude toward the partner.

The first objective with respect to stimulus control is to help the couple appreciate that certain conditions are necessary in order for healthy sexual functioning to occur (e.g., a partner with whom a person feels comfortable). It can be important to explain to patients that even a medical treatment may not lead to sexual arousal if favorable psychological and interpersonal conditions are not present. Additionally, as indicated earlier, a medical problem (e.g., hypertension) may place someone at risk for sexual difficulties, but with positive interpersonal and psychological conditions, the person may function without a problem.

Each member of a couple can generate a list of conditions or factors that positively affect his/her sexual arousal. The person may list factors such as the setting, time of day, his/her mood, the partner's mood, or the atmosphere (music, candles, lingerie). The couple can then work to maximize the number of positive factors in each sexual encounter. Partners should also determine what factors are

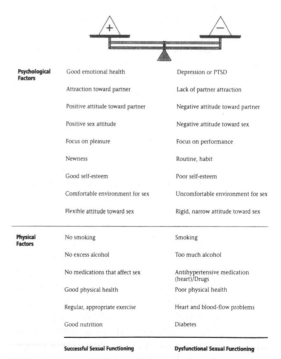

FIGURE 13.2. Positive and negative factors that affect sexual functioning. From the *Therapist Guide of Enhancing Sexuality: A Problem Solving Approach.* Copyright 1997 by Graywind Publications Inc. Reproduced by permission of Publisher, The Psychological Corporation, a Harcourt Assessment Company. All rights reserved.

negatively influencing their sexual functioning. Negative factors such as faulty beliefs, poor environmental conditions, and performance-related concerns can be addressed in the context of sex therapy. Alternatively, a referral to a marriage counselor, individual therapist, or physician can be made if necessary.

Cognitive Restructuring

At the start of treatment, we typically ask patients what thoughts they have when they engage in sexual activity. If a couple is completely avoiding sexual activity, we ask what thoughts the partners have if they imagine engaging in sexual activity. Most will readily identify negative thoughts such as "I wish it would work this time," "I am going to disappoint him/her again," "I don't feel like doing this," "This is going to be painful." We point out to the partners that these thoughts are neither relaxing nor arousing; it is only natural that when these thoughts are running through their minds, they do not feel sexually aroused. Pointing this out serves to normalize the occurrence of sexual difficulties and helps both partners appreciate the impact of thoughts on sexual arousal.

If a patient's sexual dysfunction is acquired, we ask the patient to describe the types of thoughts he/she had during sexual activity before the problem developed. The therapist can help the patient conclude that during pleasurable sexual activity, people focus on body parts, physical sensations, and other arousing aspects of sexual activity. The therapist can explain to the patient that one component of treatment will be to challenge the negative thoughts that distract him/her during sexual functioning. This will allow the patient to return his/her focus to the thoughts associated with pleasurable sexual activity.

As we have indicated above, many patients will readily identify the interfering thoughts they have during sexual activity. Others may have more difficulty identifying negative cognitions. In either case, we often ask patients to complete a simple self-monitoring form after engaging in sexual activity. They record the nature of the sexual activity (e.g., massage), the level of anxiety (on a 0–8 Likert-type scale), and the thoughts that they had. Self-monitoring helps patients to identify negative thoughts; it facilitates discussion during

sessions; and it helps to track progress over the course of treatment.

Once negative thoughts are identified, the therapist can teach the patient to challenge them. One strategy for challenging negative thoughts is to provide education. As we have noted above, education is a powerful tool in sex therapy. One of us worked with a woman who had an aversive response to semen. A discussion of this revealed that her husband had a family history of testicular cancer. During sexual activity, she worried that she might contract cancer through her husband's semen. Basic education helped to relieve this woman's fear and allowed her to feel more comfortable during sexual activity.

A second strategy for challenging a patient's thoughts is to help him/her determine whether a negative thought has any factual basis. Patients often cling to negative assumptions or negative predictions despite the absence of supporting evidence. The therapist can teach the patient to base his/her thoughts on facts rather than fear. For example, a man with erectile disorder may believe that his partner will leave him if the problem does not improve. Couple therapy provides an excellent opportunity to address a patient's assumptions regarding the partner's thoughts or feelings. The session can be used to help the patient address his/her concerns with the partner. The partner's response often resolves misunderstandings and challenges false assumptions. The discussion also helps to promote better communication outside of the session. A woman with sexual aversion disorder may believe that intercourse will be extremely painful and unpleasant. The therapist can help the patient to challenge such negative thoughts by examining the evidence for and against them. The therapist can ask the patient to explain what evidence he/she has that a belief or negative prediction is valid. As the patient presents this evidence, the therapist can help to identify errors in his/her thinking. For example, the patient may state that her mother told her sex was extremely painful and unpleasant when the patient was an adolescent. The therapist can point out that this does not necessarily mean it is true or that it would apply to the patient; perhaps there are examples of other things about which she and her mother disagree. The therapist can then ask what further evidence might suggest that this belief is not true. The therapist can work with the patient to generate as much evidence as possible to counter the negative thought.

One final method of challenging patients' negative thoughts is to help them decatastrophize negative outcomes (i.e., understand that even if the outcome is negative, it will not be the end of the world). For example, a male patient may report that he would die of embarrassment if he lost his erection on his first attempt at intercourse with a partner. The therapist may help the patient see that if he lost his erection, it might be embarrassing or awkward, but he could cope with it. The therapist could elicit an example of a negative experience with which the patient has successfully coped in the past and help the patient develop more realistic outcome expectations.

Along with challenging patients' negative thoughts, it is often necessary to address their partners' thoughts. Many people begin to have negative, interfering thoughts during sexual activity if their partners are experiencing sexual problems. Thus we typically ask partners what thoughts they have during sexual activity. The same techniques can then be used to help the partners challenge the negative thoughts they endorse.

Cognitive restructuring techniques are sometimes complex and may be difficult for some patients to grasp. Thus the process of challenging a patient's thoughts should be simplified to suit the particular patient. For more information regarding the use of cognitive restructuring techniques, the therapist may wish to consult Beck (1976).

Once the patient has begun to challenge interfering thoughts, the next objective is to return his/her attention to erotic cues. The therapist may suggest that the patient focus on sensations or particular body parts during sexual activity. The therapist may also encourage the patient to employ fantasy. Some patients may be reluctant to use fantasy, fearing this suggests that their sexual relationship is unsatisfying. The therapist must approach this topic with care, but may ultimately help to normalize the use of sexual fantasies. A couple may benefit from reading McCarthy's (1988) chapter on sexual fantasies.

Behavioral Techniques for Specific Disorders

Arousal Disorders. Sensate focus is a treatment method that was developed by Masters and Johnson (1966). It may be applied to patients with any sexual dysfunction, but is most often used in the treatment of arousal disorders. Sensate focus involves placing a ban on intercourse and engaging in a series of increasingly sensual/sexual activities. The primary objectives of sensate focus are to remove the pressure to perform, to return a couple's focus to pleasurable sensations, to reintroduce the couple to the "basics" of sexual activity, and to encourage the couple to derive pleasure from various forms of stimulation.

Many couples will be surprised and somewhat concerned by the notion that they are not supposed to engage in sexual intercourse. If they do not understand the rationale for these instructions, they may discontinue treatment prematurely. Thus it is very important that the therapist clearly explain the purpose of sensate focus. The therapist may explain that sexual activity is most satisfying when each person focuses on sensations. Couples experiencing sexual problems often focus too much on performance and fail to focus on sensations. Sensate focus is intended to remove the pressure to perform and allow couples to enjoy pleasurable sensations again.

Each week, the therapist and the couple agree to a specific sensate focus exercise. In assigning a sensate focus exercise, the therapist should be clear about the following:

- What the exercise will be
- How often it should be practiced (generally one to three times each week)
- How long it should last (generally 15–30 minutes)
- What the goals of the exercise are (e.g., to focus on physical sensations, practice communicating about sexual activity)
- What the goals of the exercise are *not* (e.g., to become aroused, to reach orgasm, to engage in intercourse)
- Who should initiate the exercise

The specific exercises employed will vary, depending on the particular needs and comfort level of each couple. In many cases, sensate focus begins with a nongenital massage. Couples may start by being clothed or unclothed, depending on their comfort level. The therapist may suggest that during the massage the partners express their preferences for different forms of stimulation and give each other positive feedback (not criticism). This allows both partners to practice communicating about sexual activity. As the partners become comfortable with the nongenital massage, they may advance to a massage that involves genital contact. Once genital contact is introduced, the therapist should emphasize that the purpose is not to stimulate one another to the point of orgasm or even to become aroused. Again, the goals are to promote pleasure and intimacy. The couple should be clear on this point before beginning the exercise.

The next step is often penetration without thrusting. At this stage, it may be helpful to remind the partners that if they are unable to complete penetration (e.g., the man cannot maintain a firm erection), they may continue sexual activity with other forms of stimulation. This helps to minimize performance demand and reinforces the notion that sexual satisfaction is not dependent on intercourse.

The final stage of sensate focus is typically sexual activity that may include intercourse. By stating that sexual activity "may" include intercourse, the therapist continues to limit performance demands and reinforces the notion that the couple may not always *wish* to include intercourse. The therapist may remind the partners that they have learned to derive pleasure from various forms of stimulation. Thus, while intercourse may now be a part of sexual activity, it does not invariably play the central role.

The steps described above can be broken down into a series of smaller exercises, depending on a couple's particular needs. For example, nongenital massage may begin with holding hands while clothed and advance to back massage while unclothed. Each couple will begin at a different point along the continuum. Some couples will advance very slowly, working on one step for weeks or months before advancing to the next. In such cases, it is important to periodically remind both partners that they are working toward the long-term goal of having a satisfying sexual relationship. Please see Table 13.1 for an example of typical progression through sensate focus assignments.

Along with helping the couple to plan the exercises, it is the therapist's role to review the exercises in the following session. It may be helpful to have each partner record the thoughts he/she experiences during assigned exercises, to facilitate discussion in the session. The therapist can help the couple restructure

TABLE 13.1. Sensate Focus: Sample Series of Assignments

Each assignment should be practiced one to three times between sessions for 15–30 minutes each time.

Assignment 1: Each partner gives the other a massage while dressed. The person receiving the massage can give feedback about what he/she likes or dislikes. The goal of the exercise is not to become aroused; it is simply to enjoy the time together. The couple agrees not to engage in intercourse.

Assignment 2: Each partner gives the other a massage while nude—no genital contact and no intercourse. The person receiving the massage can give feedback about what he/she likes and dislikes. The goal of the exercise is not to become aroused; it is simply to enjoy the time together.

Assignment 3: Repeat Assignment 2.

Assignment 4: Each partner gives the other a massage while nude with genital contact. Again, becoming aroused is not the goal; the goal is simply to enjoy the time together and focus on the sensations. No intercourse, no deliberate effort to reach orgasm. Continue the practice of giving feedback. The therapist will not ask in the next session whether either partner became physically aroused (e.g., attained an erection)—*this is stated ahead of time, to reinforce the notion that erections and lubrication are not the goal of the exercise.*

Assignment 5: Repeat Assignment 4.

Assignment 6: Repeat Assignment 4.

Assignment 7: The couple engages in sexual activity that includes penetration without thrusting. The goal of penetration is to enjoy the sensations.

Assignment 8: The couple engages in sexual activity that includes penetration with minimal thrusting. The goal of penetration is not to achieve orgasm; it is simply to enjoy the sensations. The couple should cease penetration and resume other activities after a brief time.

Assignment 9: The couple engages in sexual activity that may include intercourse—complete lift of ban on intercourse.

distorted thoughts, address problems that occurred, and identify and target avoidance behaviors.

Premature Ejaculation. The first step in the treatment of premature ejaculation is often providing psychoeducation regarding normative latencies to ejaculation. The therapist may inform the patient that most men typically ejaculate within 2 to 8 minutes of penetration (Wincze & Barlow, 1997a). The patient's age and the length of time since last ejaculation will also affect latency to ejaculation.

One option for men who ejaculate quickly is to modify their sexual routine. The couple may continue to engage in intercourse as long as possible after ejaculation. When ejaculation no longer signifies the end of intercourse, there is less emphasis on the man's ability to control his ejaculation. This reduces the man's performance-related concerns and may even increase the latency to ejaculation. A similar approach is to continue engaging in sexual activity once intercourse is no longer possible. Again, this reduces the pressure on the man, because it means that ejaculation does not signal the end of sexual activity.

If premature ejaculation is severe (e.g., ejaculation occurs before penetration), or if the man must wear a condom during sexual activity, continuing intercourse after ejaculation will not be a viable option. These patients may consider using the "squeeze" technique (Masters & Johnson, 1970). As a man approaches the point of ejaculation, he squeezes the ridge of his penis with two fingers and his thumb below the head of the penis. He should squeeze firmly for approximately 10 seconds. A man may use this technique before penetration. Alternatively, he may withdraw his penis following penetration and then resume intercourse after using the squeeze technique. This technique may be used multiple times during a single sexual encounter. The technique may also be used during masturbation to help the man develop more control over ejaculation.

Male and Female Orgasmic Disorders. Therapists should ensure that couples have realistic expectations regarding orgasm (e.g., the degree of stimulation required, normative frequency and intensity) and an understanding of individual variations. Once a couple has realistic expectations, a therapist should discuss whether the patient with orgasmic disorder is receiving adequate stimulation during sexual activity. If not, the therapist can provide guidelines for increasing stimulation.

Patients who achieve orgasm during masturbation, but not during sexual activity with a partner, may demonstrate for their partners the type of stimulation they find arousing. Patients who do not achieve orgasm during either masturbation or sexual activity with a partner may proceed through exercises such as those in Table 13.2 to learn more about what they find arousing. In both cases, the therapist can help the person to challenge any distracting or negative thoughts that may be occurring during sexual activity with a partner. Lastly, a couple may enhance arousal with the use of fantasies, sexy lingerie or underwear, sex toys, vibrators, and novel behaviors, positions, or settings.

TABLE 13.2. Homework Assignments for Treatment of Orgasmic Disorders

Instruct the patient and partner to construct a list of good and bad conditions for sexual activity. This will help both partners begin to consider the circumstances in which they become most aroused.

Encourage the patient to read literature, peruse magazines, watch videos, or look at art that he/she finds arousing. This material may be used to aid the patient in formulating sexual fantasies. Normalize and encourage the use of sexual fantasy inside and outside of sexual activity.

Assign a series of self-stimulation exercises. The person should engage in these exercises daily for approximately 10–20 minutes, depending on the exercise. The purpose of the exercises is to increase patients' comfort with their bodies and help them learn more about what is most arousing to them. The goal is not specifically to reach orgasm, but more generally to increase enjoyment of sexual activity. The specific exercises vary, depending on a patient's comfort level. A typical progression of exercises is as follows:

- Patient views his/her body nude in the mirror.
- Patient views his/her genitals nude in the mirror.
- Patient rubs/stimulates areas of his/her body other than genitals.
- Patient stimulates his/her genitals. (Therapist should ensure that patient understands what types of genital stimulation are generally arousing for people; it should not be assumed that a person knows what is meant by "masturbation.")
- Patient demonstrates for partner the type of stimulation that he/she finds most arousing.

Mirror exercises are repeated until the person feels comfortable doing them. Stimulation exercises are repeated until the person feels comfortable and has learned how that type of stimulation can be pleasurable for him/her ("pleasurable" may mean relaxing, arousing, or in any way positive).

Although the couple is working to enhance the patient's arousal, the therapist should be careful not to reinforce a performance-oriented approach to sexual activity. The therapist may explain to the couple that orgasm is not essential for satisfying sexual activity. The therapist can remind the couple that there are times when the most satisfying sexual encounters do not involve orgasm and the most disappointing sexual encounters do.

Pain Disorders and Sexual Aversion Disorder. When assessing a patient with a pain disorder or with sexual aversion disorder, the therapist should determine what activities are difficult or anxiety-provoking for the patient. Most patients will have problems with intercourse. Female patients may also have difficulty using tampons, undergoing a gynecological examination, or even looking at themselves nude in the mirror. At the start of treatment, the therapist may work with the patient to construct a hierarchy of 10–15 anxiety-provoking activities. The activities should range from moderately to very challenging. Treatment involves gradually working through this hierarchy using repeated exposure and cognitive restructuring. (Please see Figure 13.3 for an example of a typical fear and avoidance hierarchy.)

The patient may begin by practicing moderately anxiety-provoking activities that do not involve a partner (e.g., a female patient looks at her nude breasts in the mirror for 5 minutes). The activity should be practiced several times before the next session. The patient may record the thoughts and anxiety level experienced during each exposure. In the next session, the therapist helps the patient challenge maladaptive thoughts and reviews the patient's anxiety levels.

Each step on the hierarchy should be repeated until the patient can perform it comfortably. Eventually, the patient can practice activities that involve the partner (e.g., a male partner touches the lips of a female patient's vagina). Again, each step should be repeated until the patient is comfortable with it. The patient should be in control of the exposure exercises at all times; thus the patient may

Activity	Fear	Avoidance
Intercourse	8	8
Partner inserts penis into vagina—no thrusting	8	8
Partner partially inserts penis into vagina	8	8
Partner inserts finger into vagina	8	7
Partner inserts tip of finger into vagina	7	7
Patient inserts her finger into her vagina	6	6
Patient inserts tip of her finger into her vagina	6	5
Partner touches exterior portions of patient's genital area	6	5
Patient looks at her genitals in the mirror	5	5
Partner touches nude breasts	4	4
Patient touches exterior portion of her genital area	4	4
Patient looks at a photo of male genitalia	4	4
Patient looks at a photo of female genitalia	3	4
Patient watches video of sexual activity—actors nude	3	4
Patient watches video of sexual activity—actors clothed	3	3

FIGURE 13.3. Sample fear and avoidance hierarchy for treatment of sexual pain and aversion disorders. (This hierarchy is written for a female patient. Ratings are based on a 0–8 Likert scale where 0 = no fear or avoidance and 8 = extreme fear or avoidance.)

terminate an exposure if he/she feels too uncomfortable. The partner must agree to comply fully with this condition before exercises are begun.

Hypoactive Sexual Desire Disorder. The first step in treating hypoactive sexual desire disorder is to identify personal and interpersonal factors that may be inhibiting sexual desire. Examples of such factors include a history of sexual abuse, lack of physical attraction to the partner, and negative attitudes regarding sexual activity. Once identified, these factors can be addressed over the course of treatment. Table 13.3 lists strategies for targeting psychosocial factors that often contribute to low desire.

Along with addressing personal or interpersonal issues, a patient may read or view erotic literature or art to enhance sexual desire. Different patients will find different forms of art arousing. Thus, although suggestions can be offered, we find it is helpful to leave this assignment open-ended. This permits each patient to explore options that are most acceptable and arousing to him/her. When working with patients who are very religious or conservative, the therapist may need to be cre-

---

TABLE 13.3. Strategies for Addressing Factors That May Contribute to Low Desire

- Boredom

  Encourage both partners to add novelty and variety to their sexual relationship: new places, new sexual activities, new positions, addition of different "props" (e.g., sex toys, new lingerie).

  Normalize and encourage the use of sexual fantasy during and outside of sexual activity.

  Ask each partner to develop a "wish list" of activities, conditions, or scenarios he/she would like to add to the sexual repertoire. The partners should share their lists and decide which items would be pleasing or agreeable to both of them.

  Instruct each person to write a list of good and bad conditions for sexual activity. The couple can use these lists to create situations that are most conducive to pleasurable sexual activity.

- Lack of physical attraction to partner

  Address the importance of physical attraction in a relationship.

  Encourage the partners to discuss factors that help them feel attracted to one another. Examples include using perfume or cologne, wearing hair a certain way, shaving, keeping the door closed when using the bathroom, wearing particular things during the day or to bed at night. Encourage the couple to attend to these factors and make efforts to be attractive to one another.

  Stress the relationship between physical health and fitness and sexual functioning. Encourage the couple to adhere to a healthy diet and exercise regularly. These lifestyle changes can be particularly helpful to patients who are dissatisfied with their own weight or that of their partners. Nevertheless, they can be beneficial for all couples.

- Negative or faulty attitudes

  Target maladaptive thoughts with psychoeducation and cognitive restructuring as described in the chapter text.

- Dissatisfaction with what a partner does or does not do during sexual activity

  Normalize and encourage communication regarding what each person prefers during sexual activity. Explain that preferences for particular sexual activities vary between partners and also vary within each individual from one occasion to the next. Thus, without communication, it will be very hard for one partner to know what the other wants or likes.

  Help the partners to constructively discuss what they do not like during sexual activity. This discussion should take place outside of sexual activity and should be addressed in a sensitive, nonpunitive manner.

- History of sexual abuse

  If the person suffers from depression, posttraumatic stress disorder, or another psychological problem as a result of the abuse, this problem should be addressed before focusing specifically on sexual dysfunction.

  Before enhancing positive feelings related to sex, it is necessary to address the person's negative feelings (e.g., fear, disgust, indifference related to sexual activity). Construct and work through a fear and avoidance hierarchy as described for treatment of sexual pain and aversion disorders. Address thoughts/fears that interfere with sexual activity through use of psychoeducation and cognitive restructuring. Once this is done, use the strategies listed above to enhance positive feelings regarding sexual activity.

ative in finding images that are arousing but not offensive to the patients.

A patient may also jump-start his/her sexual desire with a vacation, a change in routine (different setting or different time of day for sexual activity), lingerie, or sexual props (e.g., vibrator, sex toys).

Communication Training

Some degree of communication training is necessary in nearly all sex therapy cases. Couples may need to work on general communication skills. Wincze and Barlow (1997b) present a checklist of positive communication skills (please see Figure 13.4). This checklist may be provided to a couple as a handout relatively early in treatment. The couple may practice using these skills in daily interactions.

Improvement in overall communication may increase relationship satisfaction. Moreover, the use of these skills will help partners to discuss their sexual problems in a constructive manner.

The majority of couples have difficulty communicating about their sexual relationship. Partners should be encouraged to discuss their sexual relationship (Wincze & Barlow, 1997a). It is important to initiate such discussions at an opportune time (e.g., not immediately after a negative sexual experience). The partners may specifically schedule time when they will not be bothered by distractions. Although it may be difficult to find such time, eliminating distractions and sitting down together will help to promote constructive discussions. Scheduling and protecting such time will also convey to

---

If the statement describes what you do, place a check mark in the box.

Sender Skills (The *sender* is the person who wants to talk about an issue or problem.)

☐ 1. Stay with the topic you wish to discuss. Do not bring into the discussion old topics or topics that are not related, which sidetrack the issue.

☐ 2. Point out behaviors you would like changed and avoid general statements. For example, do not say, "You need a better attitude." Instead, say, "I wish you would focus more on the good things I do and less on what you feel I do wrong."

☐ 3. Be honest and direct. Don't leave your partner guessing about what you mean.

☐ 4. Talk about your feelings or thoughts without accusing or name calling.

☐ 5. Talk in an adult way and do not "talk down" to your partner, as if he or she were a child. Be polite and talk to your partner as you would to anyone you respect.

☐ 6. Do not use words like "never" or "always." Always try to use words that reflect a real situation or behavior. Doing this will give more meaning to your statements, and your partner will be more likely to listen to what you have to say.

☐ 7. If you must say something negative to your partner, try to be helpful and not hurtful. Point out some good behaviors about your partner when you are also pointing out bad ones. In this way, you address your partner's behavior rather than his or her whole personality.

Receiver Skills (The *receiver* is the person with whom the sender wants to have the discussion.)

☐ 1. Use behaviors that show you are interested. These include eye contact, nods of agreement, and body posture.

☐ 2. Control over your own behavior until it is your turn to talk. You do not interrupt or make faces.

☐ 3. You make sure you understand what the sender is saying. To do this, say back in your own words statements that were unclear to you.

☐ 4. Read the sender's nonverbal cues and respond to them. These are facial expressions, gestures, and other body language. For instance, you say, "You are frowning and seem upset." This shows you are paying attention and are sensitive to the sender's feelings.

FIGURE 13.4. Checklist of positive communication skills. From the *Client Workbook of Enhancing Sexuality: A Problem Solving Approach.* Copyright 1997 by Graywind Publications Inc. Reproduced by permission of Publisher, The Psychological Corporation, a Harcourt Assessment Company. All rights reserved.

each partner that the other considers the relationship a priority.

Partners should be encouraged to discuss their sexual problems. If they do not, misunderstandings are likely to develop and remain unchallenged. Although discussing sexual problems is important, partners must be careful not to blame each other, either subtly or overtly. This is destructive, can deter future discussion, and may serve to maintain the problem.

The therapist can also encourage partners to express their preferences for different forms of stimulation or certain sexual activities. The partners may tell each other what they enjoyed following a particular encounter. They should not, however, provide criticism or negative feedback following sexual activity. Some couples may resist the idea of providing feedback regarding sexual activity. They may feel that a "good lover" knows what his/her partner wants without having to ask. The therapist can help such couples to challenge this notion and may incorporate practice providing feedback into sensate focus exercises.

CASE STUDY

In order to demonstrate the application of the techniques we have discussed, we present the case of a patient one of us treated a few years ago. The patient sought help for erectile difficulties. The etiology was mixed (i.e., the result of both medical and psychosocial factors). We deliberately chose this case because it predates the advent of Viagra. If this patient were to present to a physician today, it is likely that he would be given a trial of Viagra. Although medical risk factors were present, a medical treatment alone might have failed if certain psychosocial factors were not addressed. Thus we chose this case in order to highlight the role of psychological and social factors and to demonstrate that, even in the presence of organic factors, cognitive-behavioral treatment—either alone or as an adjunct to a medical treatment—may be a necessary and effective intervention.

Background

"Eric" was a 56-year-old married male referred by his urologist for a psychosocial evaluation of his sexual functioning after complaining of erectile difficulties. The urologist's exam identified several medical factors that might be contributing to the sexual difficulties. Eric had hypertension, a long history of alcohol dependence (he had been sober for 3 years), and a 25-year history of smoking two packs of cigarettes per day (he had quit smoking 1 year ago). At the time of the assessment, Eric was taking antihypertensive medication and an antidepressant. He rarely experienced morning erections.

Based on the information provided by the urologist, it seemed likely that medical factors played some role in the etiology of Eric's erectile difficulties. The purpose of the assessment was twofold: to determine whether psychological and social factors were also contributing to the problem, and to determine what treatment approach would be most helpful for Eric and his wife.

Clinical Interview

Eric and his wife, Amanda, both attended the first session. After introductions, the first meeting proceeded with the following comments by the therapist:

"Eric and Amanda, I would like to start by explaining a little bit about the assessment process. Eric, as you know, you were referred by Dr. Tobin for an assessment of your sexual functioning. Dr. Tobin talked to you about some of the medical factors that might be affecting your sexual functioning. I am going to be talking to you about some of the nonmedical factors that might be affecting your sexual functioning. Once we have completed the assessment, we can take the information I have gathered, combine it with the information from Dr. Tobin, and look at the whole picture. At that point, we can determine what factors are contributing to your sexual difficulties and what kind of treatment will be most helpful for you.

"Amanda, sometimes a spouse wonders why he or she is involved in the assessment. Although a sexual problem may present itself in one partner, sexual activity is an interactive process. A sexual problem affects both partners. Therefore, we feel it is very important to work with you as a couple and involve both of you in the assessment process.

It is helpful for me to get your perspective on the difficulty Eric is having and to learn more about you. Meeting with you will also give me an opportunity to address questions or concerns you may have about the assessment process. Any questions so far?

"Let me explain the assessment process. I typically start by meeting with each of you individually. This allows me to talk to each person about how things have been going and what factors might be affecting your sexual relationship. I will also give you some questionnaires to fill out. After I meet with you individually, I will meet with the two of you together again. At that time, I will explain what factors seem to be contributing to your sexual difficulty. Assuming we have all of the information we need, we can talk at that time about the treatment plan that will be most helpful for you. Now, before we begin, please feel free to ask questions about my background or therapy procedures."

The couple's questions and concerns then were addressed, and demographic information was obtained.

Eric was a 56-year-old probation officer. This was his first marriage. He and Amanda had been married for 20 years. They had three daughters (ages 15, 13, and 11).

Amanda was a 49-year-old high school teacher. This was her first marriage. Her marriage to Eric was the only long-term relationship she had ever had. She had dated several different men before meeting Eric; each relationship had been casual and relatively brief.

Eric and Amanda both reported that Eric was having difficulty attaining and maintaining an erection. Amanda also reported that her interest in sexual activity had always been somewhat low. It had been particularly low over the last year.

After the initial questions were addressed, it was decided that Eric would be interviewed first. The therapist (T in the dialogues that follow) gave both Eric (E) and Amanda (A) a battery of self-report measures, and asked them to complete these independently and bring them to the next session.

Session 1

T: (*With Eric alone*) Eric, in this meeting I would like to get your perspective on your relationship with Amanda and the sexual difficulties you have been having. Everything you tell me will be kept strictly confidential, with a couple of exceptions. [The exceptions to confidentiality are noted, based on state law—e.g., threat to self or others, report of child abuse.] I will not share anything you tell me with Amanda unless you tell me it is all right to do so. You have already given me the background information I need, so why don't you start by telling me what is the main reason that you are here today?

E: Sex with Amanda was never amazing, but it was nice. We have lost that over the past couple of years, and I would like to get it back. I feel as though it is my fault.

T: You feel as though what is your fault?

E: It's my fault that we don't have a sexual relationship any more. When I started having trouble keeping my erections, we started to avoid sex. It got frustrating for me, so I stopped initiating. Amanda had rarely been the person to start anything, so eventually we just stopped having sex.

T: OK, first I'd like to go back for a minute. You said that your sexual relationship was "never amazing." Can you tell me a little bit more about that?

E: Well, as I said, it was fine. But, Amanda has never been as into sex as I would like her to be. I had a lot of sexual partners before I married Amanda. The women I was with in the past were very sexually responsive. I always felt like I knew how to please them. With Amanda, I get the feeling that she never really enjoys sex as much as I do. It seems like she never lets herself go. I don't know whether it is what I am doing, or whether she is just that way, but it can be a turnoff.

T: Do you relate that to the start of your erectile problems?

E: No. (*Half laughing*) I related my sex problems to a half pint of Jack Daniels. That is how much I was drinking each night when these problems started.

T: How long ago was that?

E: About 5 years ago now. Back then, I figured I couldn't stay hard because I was so smashed all the time. Amanda thought that too—well, we never talked about it, but I got the impression that she blamed my drinking. I didn't worry about it that much. I figured that when I stopped drinking, the problem would go away.

T: And that didn't happen?

E: No, actually, it was just the opposite. After I stopped drinking, I started losing my erections more often. Then I got worried because I didn't know what was causing it. Eventually, I was losing my erections about half the times we tried to have sex. That's when I just stopped trying. Now we don't do anything. I mean, I'll sneak a quick feel once in a while—(*laughs*) she hates it when I do that—she's always afraid someone will see me. But we haven't tried to have sex in over a year. I am still interested; don't get me wrong. But after a while it feels like there is no point in trying if you know it is not going to work.

T: These days if you think of engaging in sexual activity, do you feel nervous?

E: Yeah, I guess I do.

T: Do you know what you are thinking when you feel nervous?

E: I am afraid that I am going to disappoint Amanda (*pauses*)—and it's embarrassing. I have always felt confident in my sexual relationship with Amanda—I was the one with more experience. Now all of a sudden I can't do it. Every time I fail, we both feel upset and frustrated.

T: Can you just explain for me what you mean when you say "fail"?

E: I mean that I can't keep an erection long enough for us to have sex.

T: And when you say sex, you mean intercourse, right?

E: (*Looking around, laughing*) Uh, yeah.

T: I know that that may seem like a funny question. Actually, a lot of people use the terms sex and intercourse interchangeably. But it is important to realize that "sex" actually involves a lot of different activities—it is not just limited to intercourse. So a couple can have sex without having intercourse.

E: (*Laughing*) Not where I grew up.

T: I know. It is an idea that sometimes goes against what we see on TV or in the movies. But it is an important point. It helps you to remember that you can have sex even when intercourse is not possible. We will come back to that again, but I have some additional questions I would like to ask.

E: Sure.

T: It is very normal for men to masturbate throughout their lives. Some men might use masturbation to test things out and make sure everything works OK. What has your experience been? [Note that the therapist normalizes masturbation before asking the patient to discuss it. This is important, because some men are uncomfortable with masturbation or believe that it is only "normal" for teenagers. We avoid simply asking, "Do you masturbate?"]

E: I masturbate a couple times a week. At first, it seemed like things worked better during masturbation. Maybe I am just remembering it that way. But now I'm having trouble keeping an erection about half the times I masturbate. It's not too different from the way it happens in sex, but it's not as bad, because if it doesn't work it's not as a big a deal.

T: OK, and do you ever notice that you have an erection during the night or when you wake up in the morning?

E: Not too often—maybe three times a month. And the erections aren't as firm as they used to be.

The therapist went on to assess other aspects of Eric's sexual functioning. Eric denied sexual dysfunctions other than erectile difficulties.

T: You have given me a good sense of the problems you are having in your sexual relationship. Now I would like to talk about your overall relationship with Amanda.

E: OK, I am not sure what to tell you. . . . Amanda and I have been married for 20 years, and we have been through some difficult times. The years when I was drinking were really bad. I finally hit rock bottom a few years ago, and I got myself some treatment. . . . [Therapist obtains specifics regarding how long drinking problem lasted and when and where patient received treatment.] Things have been better since I stopped drinking. We got into counseling, and I think that we are doing much better these days.

T: In what way are things better?

E: Well, we spend time together. I used to work all the time, and if I was home, I was drunk. Now I have tried to cut back on work, and the time I spend at home is time that we can see each other.

T: What kinds of things do you and Amanda enjoy doing together?

E: That's a good question. When we were first together, we liked going to movies, the theater, and concerts. We are both very into the arts. Between work and three teenage daughters, we don't have time for that stuff any more. I don't know what we do together. We see each other at home—so we spend time together—but we are usually doing our own thing. I like to read. Amanda usually watches TV or spends time with the girls.

The interview proceeded with further discussion of Eric's relationship with Amanda. He reported that they had good communication and stated, "We never argue." He indicated that he was generally happy in the relationship and felt committed to working at it. The interview concluded with an assessment of Eric's general psychological functioning. Along with a history of alcohol dependence, Eric reported that he had a history of recurrent depression. He reported that he was depressed and drinking heavily when his erectile difficulties began. When he sought treatment for alcohol dependence, he was also treated for depression. At the time of the assessment, Eric was taking antidepressant medication prescribed by a local psychiatrist. He met briefly with the psychiatrist once a month for medication management. He reported that his mood was stable and that he had not been depressed within the last year. At the end of the interview, the therapist asked whether anything had not been addressed that might be helpful to know. Eric indicated that there was not. Finally, the therapist asked Eric whether there was anything he had said that should not be shared with Amanda. Again, he indicated that there was not.

Session 2

The second session involved an interview with Amanda.

T: Now, before we get started, do you have any questions based on our last session?

A: Yes, just remind me, when will you tell us what kind of treatment we should get?

T: Assuming I have all of the information I need, I will talk to you about treatment options the next time we meet.

A: Great.

T: And has anything changed since the last time we met? [Again, this is important to ask, in the event that there are significant issues distracting the patient or partner from the focus of therapy.]

A: No, I don't think so. We just had our usual week.

T: OK. My primary goal for this interview is to get your perspective on your relationship with Eric—both your general relationship and your sexual relationship in particular. I told Eric, and I will tell you, that the information you give me will be kept strictly confidential. [Again, exceptions to confidentiality are noted, based on state law.] I will only share information with Eric if you say that it is OK.

A: What do you want me to talk about first, our general relationship or the sexual part of it?

T: Whichever you prefer.

A: Well, I guess we're mainly here to talk about the sexual part of things, so I will start with that.

T: That's fine.

A: Obviously you know that Eric is having trouble with his erections. That started a few years ago. When it first started, I thought that he was having trouble because he was drinking a lot. Our sexual relationship wasn't very good at that time anyway, so I didn't worry about it.

T: What do you mean when you say it "wasn't very good"?

A: Well, our relationship in general wasn't very good in those days, so we weren't having much sex. Eric worked a lot, and when he was home, he drank. I kept asking him to get help, and eventually he did.

T: What happened after that?

A: He stopped drinking. That made a big difference for us. We started seeing a therapist. Did Eric mention that?

T: Uh, yes, he did.

A: She was pretty helpful. Well, our overall relationship got better—better than it had been anyway. Eric cut back on work a little bit and spent more time at home. Sexually, though, things seemed to get worse. I think we both expected that Eric's sexual problem would go away once he stopped drinking. I was really surprised when it didn't. I started to worry that it was because of me. It seems like he's always been more interested in sex than I am—maybe that contributed to his erection problem. I don't know.

T: You mentioned at the very beginning of the assessment that you have some concerns about your own sexual functioning.

A: Well, my problem—I guess it's a problem, I don't know . . . I have always felt like I was not as interested in sex as I should be.

T: You mentioned that in our first meeting, so let's talk about that. You say that you are not as interested as you "should" be —so, just to clarify, there is not actually one level of desire you "should" have. It is a matter of what you are comfortable with.

A: No, I guess I know there's no "should." . . . Anyway, I just mean my interest in sex is not as high as I would like it to be. I'm sure it's not as high as Eric would like it to be. But it's been *really* low lately.

T: When did you notice a change in your sexual desire?

A: It's just been over the last year or so.

T: Do you have any guess as to what caused it?

A: I don't know; it was probably a combination of things. Eric's problem was part of it. He would get so frustrated every time he couldn't keep an erection. Why is that such a big deal to guys? You would think that their whole future depended on their ability to get an erection. He would get so upset that after a while it just wasn't worth it.

T: So one factor would be Eric's trouble with erections.

A: Not so much his trouble with erections, but the result of it . . . him getting frustrated and both of us feeling upset. It took the fun out of sex.

T: OK. What else?

A: This has been a really stressful year for me at work. I have had a tough group of kids. Some of them are just nightmares. We have a new principal this year, and the teachers just aren't getting the support we used to. When I get home from work at night, I am so tired. Most nights I just want to watch some TV and crawl into bed. The thought of sex hardly enters my mind. I used to think about sex once in a while when I was at work. I would look forward to being with Eric that night. I can't remember the last time I had thoughts like that.

T: So it sounds as though your interest has always been lower than Eric's, but you *were* interested in sex. This last year has been different because you have really lost your interest. Is that right?

A: Yes.

The therapist went on to assess other aspects of Amanda's sexual functioning. She denied other sexual difficulties. She reported that she and Eric continued to be affectionate with one another, despite the fact that they were avoiding sexual activity. Amanda indicated that although she liked being affectionate, she sometimes wished that Eric wouldn't "grope" her (e.g., spontaneously touch her breasts or buttocks outside of their bedroom). She reported that such gestures made her uncomfortable. The therapist then proceeded with the following:

T: All right, now we have covered what things are like in your current sexual relationship. Can you tell me what your sexual relationship was like when you were first together?

A: Sure. I think that it was pretty good. As I said, I probably was never as into sex as Eric was, but it was fine. We had sex pretty often when we were first together . . . probably three or four times a week.

T: And did you enjoy your sexual relationship at that time?

A: Yeah, I did. I loved Eric. He was good-looking and very funny. I don't know that I cared so much about the sex itself, but I liked feeling very close to him.

The remainder of the interview focused on Amanda's perception of her overall relationship with Eric. She reported that she was happy in the relationship, but that she wished they would do more things together just for fun.

Summary of Assessment

On the basis of the urological evaluation, the clinical interview, and the self-report measures, it appeared that both medical and psychosocial factors were contributing to Eric's erectile difficulties. The following areas were identified as targets for a psychosocial intervention:

1. The lack of "quality time" the couple spent together.
2. Eric's performance-related concerns (e.g., fear that he would "fail" and disappoint Amanda) and his belief that sex equals intercourse.
3. The couple's lack of communication regarding sexual activity, evidenced by (a) Eric's feeling that he did not know how to please Amanda sexually, and (b) Amanda's concern that her low desire was the cause of Eric's arousal problems.
4. Eric's feeling that Amanda had never been "responsive" during sexual activity.
5. Amanda's low sexual desire.

Although Eric was the identified "patient," it appeared that Amanda had developed hypoactive sexual desire disorder over the last year. Amanda identified her low desire as a problem and expressed interest in working on this issue. Thus this issue was identified as an additional target for treatment.

With respect to the overall relationship, both spouses reported that they were generally happy together. Information obtained with the DAS suggested that the couple agreed on most subjects and communicated well about most aspects of the relationship. Both Eric and Amanda indicated that they were committed to improving their relationship. Despite sexual difficulties, it appeared that the spouses had a solid foundation on which to build. Thus it was expected that they might benefit from couple sex therapy.

The third session was used primarily to present a case conceptualization to the couple and to discuss treatment options.

Session 3

T: Before we get started, has anything changed since the last time we met?

E: No, not really.

T: OK. What I would like to do tonight is to explain what factors seem to be contributing to the sexual problem you've been having, and then discuss treatment options.

E: But we'll talk about the treatment part tonight, right?

T: Yes, in just a few minutes, actually.

E: Good.

T: Now the factors that initially cause erectile problems are often different from the factors that cause them to continue.

E: I don't think I get it.

T: That's all right; I'll explain. It's likely that when you first started losing your erections, it was because you were drinking a lot and you were depressed. Those factors are no longer present, so different factors are now causing the erectile problems to continue. These factors can be medical, nonmedical, or a combination of the two. In your case, I think it is a combination of the two. The report I received from Dr. Tobin and the information you have given me suggest that there are at least three medical factors that might be negatively affecting your sexual functioning: high blood pressure, your blood pressure medication, and the medication you take for depression. All of these things can contribute to sexual problems. We can't know for sure that these factors play a role in the problem. But the fact that your morning erections are less frequent and less firm than they used to be, and the fact that you are having erectile problems during masturbation as well as sexual activity with Amanda, suggest that it is possible something physical is going on.

E: So there's nothing I can do?

T: No, I think that you have a number of options. Let's finish going over the information I have for you, and then we can talk about what kind of treatment makes the most sense. OK?

E: Sure.

A: Yes.

T: There are several nonmedical factors that I think are probably contributing to your difficulty. First, it sounds as though the two of you see each other at home more than you used to, but you don't often *do* things together, at least not for fun. If a couple does not spend relaxing, enjoyable time together, they can't expect to have a great sexual relationship.

A: I think that that makes a lot of sense.

T: Good. Now the second thing that struck me is that both of you expressed some uncertainty about what the other person thinks or wants with respect to sexual activity. It sounds as though it is not always easy for you to talk to each other about your sexual relationship.

E: I think that we communicate better than most couples—definitely better than the couples we know.

T: Well, a lot of couples communicate very well in most aspects of their relationship, but do not talk about sex.

A: I agree with that. I think that Eric and I communicate very well about things having to do with the children or money, but when it comes to sex (*turns to Eric*), I don't always know what you are thinking.

E: OK. So that is probably something we can work on, right?

T: Right. Now another primary factor, Eric, would be the thoughts that you are having during sexual activity. You said that sometimes you have thoughts like "Am I going to disappoint Amanda?", "Are we both going to be frustrated again?", "This isn't going to work." Now, which of those thoughts is arousing? (*Eric and Amanda both smile*)

A: None of them.

T: What happens for some people is that once they have difficulty with their erections, they start worrying that it is going to happen again. They focus on these negative thoughts during sex, and they are distracted from the things that normally arouse them. The result is that they focus on unarousing thoughts during sex. Not surprisingly, they don't get aroused, and then the next time they have sex they worry even more.

A: So it's like a cycle.

T: Exactly. The last thing—Amanda, you indicated that your interest in sex has been low over the last year. Now I bring that up not so much as something that might be affecting Eric's erectile problems, but as something that is probably keeping you as a couple from enjoying your sexual relationship as much as you could. So, if you were going to get into therapy to improve your sexual relationship, that is probably one other factor you could work on.

E: Are we going to get into therapy? I mean, what are you thinking as far as treatment?

T: You have three basic options. As I indicated, your sexual difficulty is probably the result of both medical and nonmedical factors. So you could pursue a medical treatment—Dr. Tobin probably talked to you about some of those options.

E: Yes, he did. He mentioned that there are shots that I can use to get an erection.

T: Yes, that is one medical treatment, and there are others as well. Now you could use a medical treatment alone and see whether that is helpful. The other options are to undergo couple sex therapy alone to address some of the nonmedical factors, or to receive couple sex therapy and a medical treatment.

A: We've been through marital counseling before, and it was helpful. But in this case it sounds like part of the problem has a medical basis to it.

T: Well, it is very possible that medical factors are involved, but we cannot know for sure. We also cannot know how much of a role those medical factors might play. Sometimes a medical problem puts a person at risk of having a sexual difficulty, but in the presence of positive psychological and social factors, the person's sexual functioning is fine. So one option for you would be to undergo couple sex therapy, see whether that is helpful, and then make a decision regarding the need for medical treatment.

E: I didn't realize that there would be several options.

T: I generally encourage people to leave this session with the information I presented, go home, talk it over, and together decide what they would like to do.

The therapist then provided Eric and Amanda with a brief description of cognitive-behavioral couple sex therapy. The spouses were encouraged to take some time to consider their options. They called after 2 weeks and indicated that they had decided to pursue couple sex therapy. They would make a decision regarding medical treatment once the course of therapy had ended.

Session 4

Session 4 was the first session that was specifically devoted to treatment. The therapist began by asking whether anything had changed since the last session (3 weeks earlier). The couple indicated that nothing significant had changed. The therapist then asked Eric and Amanda to begin by discussing their current sexual relationship.

T: At the time of the assessment, you indicated that you were generally avoiding sexual activity. Is that still true?

E and A: Yes.

T: Are you affectionate—that is, do you still hug and kiss each other, even though you are not having sex?

E: I try to be affectionate, but (*to Amanda*) you sometimes act as though that bothers you.

A: I wouldn't say it bothers me. I like hugs and holding hands. But a lot of times with you, it feels like it won't stop there. I feel like if I hug and kiss you back, you are going to want more.

E: That's not true.

T: This is going to be important for us to address. But before we go further, I want you to see that this is one example of miscommunication about your physical relationship. So one of the things we are going to work on is addressing issues like this, so you can resolve them and feel closer because you understand each other; you don't have to guess what the other is thinking. OK, getting back to the original point—Amanda, it sounds as though you feel like it is all or nothing with Eric when it comes to sexual activity.

A: Yeah, I do.

E: That is not true. I've always liked being affectionate.

A: (*Laughing, to Eric*) That's the other thing—I think we have different definitions for "affectionate." "Affectionate" to me means hugs, kisses, and holding hands. Sometimes "affectionate" for you means grabbing my breast in the kitchen. That to me doesn't feel like affection; it feels like you are trying to get something started.

E: Well, that is not how I mean it. I really don't. I like your body, and I don't think it's bad if I just want to touch you. And I do not always intend for that to lead to sex . . . just sometimes. (*Laughs*)

A: (*Laughs*) See?

T: OK. Amanda, you are saying that you enjoy being affectionate, but you do not want to feel like every time you and Eric touch, it has to lead to sex.

A: Exactly.

T: It sounds as though you may also disagree about the best way to demonstrate affection. Amanda, if you knew that Eric did not want to have sex, would you mind it when he touches you—say, your breast—when you don't expect it?

A: I guess I wouldn't. If I felt like he was just doing that because he feels attracted to me—and he wasn't expecting something more—I would kind of be flattered. (*To Eric*) You never talk about finding me attractive any more.

E: Of course I find you attractive.

In the remainder of the session, the need for improved communication regarding sexual activity was addressed. Further discussion revealed that the couple generally avoided conflict in all domains of their relationship (hence Eric's comment that they "never argue"). The value of constructive arguments was discussed, and specific strategies for improving communication were presented.

For homework, Eric and Amanda were given the following assignments. They were asked to (1) practice expressing thoughts and preferences regarding sexual activity; (2) discuss difficult issues as they arose, with the aid of the communication handout; (3) read and discuss a handout listing common myths of male and female sexuality; and (4) set aside

30 minutes to spend time alone together doing something they both enjoyed.

Session 5

Eric and Amanda completed the assigned exercises before the next session. They took a 30-minute walk alone together. They reported that it felt strange to do something without the children, but they both found this enjoyable. A review of their discussion regarding myths of sexuality involved the following comments:

A: We got into an argument going over that list of myths.

T: What was the argument about?

A: I said that since we can't have intercourse a lot of times, it's a good excuse to try other activities.

E: (Defensively) That really annoyed me, because I don't understand why she doesn't give me feedback as to what she wants. How am I supposed to know if she has been wanting to try other stuff?

T: All right, there are a couple of points there. There are many sexual activities that are enjoyable, aside from intercourse. I think that it will be a good thing for you to find out what other activities are enjoyable for you. I also understand what you mean, Eric, when you say that without feedback there is no way for you to know what Amanda wants. That is why it is important for both of you to begin stating your preferences regarding sexual activity, rather than trying to guess what the other wants.

E: (In a low voice, to Amanda) Maybe then you will be more responsive during sex.

A: What do you mean?

E: You know what I mean. The whole time we have been married, I bet that you have only had an orgasm about half the times that we have sex. That, to me, means that you have only enjoyed sex about half the times we've ever had it.

A: That is not true. I hate it when you get so hung up on orgasm.

T: Eric, you use orgasm as an index of whether sex is good or not?

E: Yeah, everybody does.

T: Has there ever been a time when you had an orgasm but the sex was not very good?

E: Uh . . . yeah.

T: And have there been times when you had great sex but did not have an orgasm?

E: I guess so, but not too many.

T: OK, but there have been some times like that. So orgasm is not necessarily a good measure of whether sex is enjoyable or not.

E: I see your point, but I don't know that I agree with you.

T: A lot of couples would agree with you. They approach sex with the idea that if certain things happen—orgasm, firm erection—sex is a success. Without these things, sex is a failure. We have found that that just isn't a helpful way to think about sex; it creates pressure, and it kind of misses the point. Sex is a "success" as long as you feel close to each other and you both enjoy it.

The session proceeded with a further discussion of the need to move away from a performance-oriented approach to sex. In this context, the spouses' goals for treatment were reviewed. Their primary goals were to improve communication, to enhance their enjoyment of sexual activity, and to increase the level of intimacy in their relationship.

For homework, Eric and Amanda were asked to list the factors (e.g., time of day, place, circumstances) that made sex most and least enjoyable for them.

Session 6

As assigned, the couple completed a list of good and bad conditions for sexual activity. Each person's list of conditions was reviewed in Session 6. The importance of these conditions was emphasized, and the need to attend to them was addressed.

The method of sensate focus was explained, and the rationale behind this approach was presented. The couple agreed that intercourse would not be part of the sensate focus exercises, and that arousal and orgasm would not be goals. It was decided that the couple would start with nongenital massage while fully unclothed.

For homework, Eric and Amanda were asked to engage in at least two nongenital massages. They were instructed to take turns massaging each other. The person receiving the massage was encouraged to provide verbal feedback in order to promote better communication regarding sexual activity.

Session 7

T: For homework this week, you were going to engage in at least two massages. How did that go?

E: We were saying in the car on the way over here that we haven't gotten in trouble for not doing homework since we were in high school. (*Both spouses laugh*)

T: So you didn't do the massages?

A: No, we did one; we just didn't get to do a second one.

T: Good. That's not a bad start. I want to talk about the massage you did do. But, first, let's just talk about what got in the way of doing the second one.

E: It's very hard to make time to be alone together with three teenage daughters around. It's not like we can say, "Kids, Mom and Dad are going to be doing their sex homework for a while, so don't disturb us."

T: No, I agree that probably isn't the best approach. Now if I remember correctly, you are not doing the exercises just before you go to sleep because you are too tired.

A: Right.

T: As a result, you will probably be doing these exercises while the girls are still awake.

E: Yeah.

T: There is nothing wrong—in fact, it is important for you to send your children the message that sometimes you need and want time to yourselves as a couple.

A: You know, it's funny; you asked at one point what messages our parents gave us about sexual activity. Since then, I have been thinking about what messages Eric and I give our children. I like the idea that we would teach them that even though we are parents and we've been married for a long time, we still love each other and

want time alone once in a while. In theory, I think that's a good idea. It's just that in practice I can't relax if I think the girls know that we are having sex.

T: Let's talk about some things that you can do to make it easier for you to have private time together.

E: I guess one obvious thing is that we could shut the door.

T: Is it typically open?

E: Yes, we never shut our door. The girls are always in and out.

T: OK, so shutting the door should send a pretty clear signal that you want some privacy.

A: This is embarrassing, but even with the door shut I'm . . . well, I'm always afraid they'll hear something.

E: She's paranoid about it. At the start of the massage we did—you know how you told us to give feedback?—well, Amanda was talking so quietly even I couldn't hear her, and I was only 1 foot away.

A: (*Laughing*) I got better about it—you even said I did.

T: Maybe you could play some music.

The session proceeded with further discussion of ways to create good conditions for enjoyable sex. The spouses then went on to discuss the massage they had done.

T: So how was the massage you did do?

E: I really enjoyed it. It felt like the first time we had been close in a while. It was really good to know exactly what Amanda wanted; I didn't have to wonder.

A: I thought it was really nice too. Even though it wasn't "sex," it felt really intimate—and I wasn't worried about having to respond in a certain way or showing that I was aroused enough.

Sessions 8–12

The couple practiced nongenital massage for 1 more week and then incorporated genital contact. Sessions 9–12 were conducted on a bimonthly basis in order to give the couple more opportunity to practice sensate focus exercises. The spouses adhered to their agreement not to engage in intercourse. Eric continued to be aware of whether he had a firm erection. Despite this, he and Amanda both concluded that physiological arousal and orgasm were not essential to physical and emotional intimacy. The spouses continued to have some difficulty protecting time they had scheduled for one another; they did not always complete the number of exercises assigned. Nevertheless, the frequency of spontaneous affection and erotic gestures increased. The spouses also increased the number of leisure activities they engaged in without their children.

Sessions 9 and 10 were devoted to individual sessions with Eric and Amanda. This provided the therapist an opportunity to spend additional time focusing on each person's concerns. It also provided an opportunity for Eric and Amanda to raise issues they did not feel comfortable sharing with each other. Eric indicated that he was much happier in the relationship than he had been prior to treatment. Although he had denied marital difficulties prior to treatment, he now indicated that he had been having doubts about the future of the relationship. He now felt confident that he and Amanda could be happy together.

Amanda indicated she was pleased that Eric appeared to enjoy affection and stimulation that did not involve intercourse or orgasm. She felt that she and Eric were also communicating more effectively. She continued to be concerned by her low sexual desire. She indicated that one contributing factor was the fact that Eric had recently gained weight. As a result, she was not as attracted to him as she had been in the past. Amanda did not want to tell Eric this, but felt that it was a significant issue. The therapist addressed this in treatment by generally discussing the importance of physical attraction and physical health in sexual functioning. He encouraged both spouses to make efforts to enhance their physical attraction to each other, much as they had at the start of their relationship. He also suggested that they exercise together as part of their leisure time alone.

In order to increase her sexual desire, Amanda was encouraged to look through literature or art she considered erotic. She found this pleasurable and began to write in a journal about the scenarios that aroused her. In Sessions 11 and 12, it was suggested that the spouses include intercourse in their exercises if they wished.

At the end of treatment, Eric and Amanda felt they had made significant progress in both their sexual relationship and their marriage. Eric continued to have some difficulties maintaining firm erections. Nevertheless, he reported that their sexual relationship was more satisfying than it had been since the start of their relationship. Amanda's sexual desire returned. The spouses communicated more effectively and spent more leisure time together. Both indicated that they were much happier not only with their sexual relationship, but with their marriage in general.

As we have indicated earlier, Eric presented for treatment before the advent of Viagra. It is possible that Viagra would have successfully restored his erectile functioning. Viagra alone would not, however, have addressed the spouses' failure to devote time to the relationship, their communication problems, Eric's dissatisfaction with their past sexual relationship, Amanda's low desire, or her reduced physical attraction to Eric. Without addressing these issues, both spouses might have continued to feel dissatisfied with their sexual relationship. Although a medical intervention might have been "effective," the couple might not have continued to use it. Such an outcome highlights the respective roles of medical and psychosocial interventions; it suggests that cognitive-behavioral treatment is often a valuable and necessary adjunct to effective medical interventions.

CONCLUDING COMMENTS

The case of Eric and Amanda is intended to demonstrate the application of several key concepts and principles that are fundamental to effective cognitive-behavioral treatment of sexual dysfunction. The most central of these are as follows:

• Sexual dysfunctions may include disturbances in desire, arousal, and orgasm, or pain associated with sexual activity.
• A comprehensive assessment allows the therapist to identify etiological and maintaining factors for the sexual difficulty. Biological, psychological, cultural, and interpersonal factors should be considered; thus, to the extent possible, a multidisciplinary approach to treatment is recommended. Once the contrib-

uting factors have been identified, the therapist can formulate a case conceptualization and outline an effective treatment plan.

• The presence of organic factors does not necessarily indicate that a medical treatment is the most appropriate treatment option. Some attention to psychosocial factors is often essential to effective treatment.

• Cognitive-behavioral therapy for sexual dysfunction is a multicomponent treatment that involves psychoeducation, communication training, cognitive restructuring, and behavioral exercises.

• The primary goal of cognitive-behavioral treatment for sexual dysfunction is not a functional one. Rather, the goal of treatment is to enhance partners' ability to derive satisfaction from their sexual relationship.

Some of these points were not central tenets of sex therapy 20 or even 10 years ago. Sex therapy is a field that continues to evolve. Awareness and acceptance of sexual dysfunction may be higher than they have ever been, thanks to Viagra. Likewise, the number of treatment options for sexual dysfunction is larger than it has been and is still growing. As we have indicated at the start of the chapter, with new medical treatment options and more refined cognitive-behavioral techniques, the challenge now facing clinicians and physicians is to determine which treatment option is best for each patient: medical treatment alone, psychosocial treatment alone, psychosocial treatment in conjunction with a medical treatment, or no treatment for sexual dysfunction. This decision will depend on many factors, including the etiology of the problem, the nature of maintaining factors, the patient's attitude toward treatment, and the resources available. In cases where the clinician or physician decides that psychosocial treatment would be appropriate, we hope this chapter will serve as a useful guide.

REFERENCES

Abrahamson, D. J., Barlow, D. H., Sakheim, D. K., Beck, J. G., & Athanasiou, R. (1985). Effect of distraction on sexual responding in functional and dysfunctional men. *Behavior Therapy, 16,* 503–515.

American Psychiatric Association (APA). (1994). *Diagnostic and statistical manual of mental disorders* (4th ed.). Washington, DC: Author.

Angst, J. (1998). Sexual problems in healthy and depressed persons. *International Clinical Psychopharmacology, 13*(Suppl. 6), S1–S4.

Bach, A. K., Brown, T. A., & Barlow, D. H. (1999). The effects of false negative feedback on efficacy expectancies and sexual arousal in sexually functional males. *Behavior Therapy, 30,* 79–95.

Bachmann, G. A. (1995). Influence of menopause on sexuality. *International Journal of Infertility, 40*(Suppl. 1), 16–22.

Bachmann, G. A., Leiblum, S. R., & Grill, J. (1989). Brief sexual inquiry in gynecologic practice. *Obstetrics and Gynecology, 73,* 425–427.

Barlow, D. H. (1986). Causes of sexual dysfunction: The role of anxiety and cognitive interference. *Journal of Consulting and Clinical Psychology, 54,* 140–148.

Barlow, D. H., Becker, R., Leitenberg, H., & Agras, W. S. (1970). A mechanical strain gauge for recording penile circumference change. *Journal of Applied and Behavior Analysis, 3,* 73–76.

Barlow, D. H., Sakheim, D. K., & Beck, J. G. (1983). Anxiety increases sexual arousal. *Journal of Abnormal Psychology, 92,* 49–54.

Beck, A. T. (1976). *Cognitive therapy and the emotional disorders.* New York: International Universities Press.

Beck, J. G. (1995). Hypoactive sexual desire disorder: An overview. *Journal of Consulting and Clinical Psychology, 63,* 919–927.

Bemelmans, B. L. H., Meuleman, E. J. H., Doesburg, W. H., Notermans, S. L. H., & Debruyne, F. M. J. (1994). Erectile dysfunction in diabetic men: The neurological factor revisited. *Journal of Urology, 151,* 884–889.

Benet, A. E., Sharaby, J. S., & Melman, A. (1994). Male erectile dysfunction: Assessment and treatment options. *Comprehensive Therapy, 20,* 669–673.

Carey, M. P., Flasher, L. V., Maisto, S. A., & Turkat, I. D. (1984). The a priori approach to psychophysiological assessment. *Professional Psychology: Research and Practice, 15,* 515–527.

Chang, S. W., Fine, R., Siegel, D., Chesney, M., Black, D., & Hulley, S. B. (1991). The impact of diuretic therapy on reported sexual function. *Archives of Internal Medicine, 151,* 2402–2408.

Conti, C. R., Pepine, C. J., & Sweeney, M. (1999). Efficacy and safety of sildenafil citrate in the treatment of erectile dysfunction in patients with ischemic heart disease. *American Journal of Cardiology, 83,* 29C–34C.

Cranston-Cuebas, M. A., & Barlow, D. H. (1990). Cognitive and affective contributions to sexual functioning. *Annual Review of Sex Research, 1,* 119–161.

Derogatis, L. R., & Melisaratos, N. (1979). The DSFI: A multidimensional measure of sexual functioning. *Journal of Sex and Marital Therapy, 5,* 244–281.

Derogatis, L. R., & Melisaratos, N. (1983). The Brief Symptom Inventory: An introductory report. *Psychological Medicine, 13,* 595–605.

Feldman, H. A., Goldstein, I., Hatzichristou, D. G., Krane, R. J., & McKinlay, J. B. (1994). Impotence and its medical and psychosocial correlates: Results of the Massachusetts Male Aging Study. *Journal of Urology, 151,* 54–61.

Finger, W. W., Lund, M., & Slagle, M. A. (1997). Medications that may contribute to sexual disorders: A guide to assessment and treatment in family practice. *Journal of Family Practice, 44,* 33–43.

Fisher, W. A. (1988). The Sexual Opinion Survey. In C. M. Davis, W. L. Yarber, & S. L. Davis (Eds.), *Sexuality-related measures: A compendium* (pp. 34–37). Lake Mills, IA: Graphic.

Fisher, W. A., Byrne, D., White, L. A., & Kelley, K. (1988). Erotophobia–erotophilia as a dimension of personality. *Journal of Sex Research, 25,* 123–151.

Geer, J. H., & Fuhr, R. (1976). Cognitive factors in sexual arousal: The role of distraction. *Journal of Consulting and Clinical Psychology, 44,* 238–243.

Geer, J. H., Morokoff, P., & Greenwood, P. (1974). Sexual arousal in women: The development of a measurement device for vaginal blood volume. *Archives of Sexual Behavior, 3,* 559–564.

Goldstein, I., Lue, T. F., Padma-Nathan, H., Rosen, R. C., Steers, W. D., & Wicker, P. A. (1998). Oral sildenafil in the treatment of erectile dysfunction. *New England Journal of Medicine, 338,* 1397–1404.

Hakim, L. S., & Goldstein, I. (1996). Diabetic sexual dysfunction: Endocrinology and metabolism. *Endocrinology and Metabolism Clinics of North America, 25,* 379–400.

Hawton, K., & Catalan, J. (1986). Prognostic factors in sex therapy. *Behaviour Research and Therapy, 24,* 377–385.

Hawton, K., Catalan, J., & Fagg, J. (1992). Sex therapy for erectile dysfunction: Characteristics of couples, treatment outcome, and prognostic factors. *Archives of Sexual Behavior, 21,* 161–175.

Heiman, J. R., & LoPiccolo, J. (1983). Clinical outcome of sex therapy: Effects of daily versus weekly treatment. *Archives of General Psychiatry, 40,* 443–449.

Heiman, J. R., & LoPiccolo, J. (1988). *Becoming orgasmic: A sexual and personal growth program for women* (rev. ed.). Englewood Cliffs, NJ: Prentice-Hall.

Hirschfield, R. M. A. (1998). Sexual dysfunction in depression: Disease- or drug-related? *Depression and Anxiety, 7*(Suppl. 1), 21–23.

Hirst, J. F., & Watson, J. P. (1997). Therapy for sexual and relationship problems: The effects on outcome of attending as an individual or as a couple. *Sexual and Marital Therapy, 12,* 321–337.

Hodge, R. H., Harward, M. P., West, M. S., Krongaard-DeMong, L., & Kowal-Neeley, M. B. (1991). Sexual function of women taking antihypertensive agents: A comparative study. *Journal of General Internal Medicine, 6,* 290–294.

Hogan, M. J., Wallin, J. D., & Baer, R. M. (1980). Antihypertensive therapy and male sexual dysfunction. *Psychosomatics, 21,* 234–237.

Hoon, P., Wincze, J., & Hoon, E. (1977). A test of reciprocal inhibition: Are anxiety and sexual arousal in women mutually inhibitory? *Journal of Abnormal Psychology, 86,* 65–74.

Jones, J. C., & Barlow, D. H. (1990). Self-reported frequency of sexual urges, fantasies, and masturbatory fantasies in heterosexual males and females. *Archives of Sexual Behavior, 19,* 269–279.

Kaplan, H. S. (1979). *Disorder of sexual desire and other new concepts and techniques in sex therapy.* New York: Brunner/Mazel.

Kaplan, H. S. (1988). Anxiety and sexual dysfunction. *Journal of Clinical Psychiatry, 49,* 21–25.

Kaplan, S. A., Reis, R. B., Kohn, I. J., Ikeguchi, E. F., Laor, E., Te, A. E., & Martins, A. C. (1999). Safety and efficacy of sildenafil in postmenopausal women with sexual dysfunction. *Urology, 53,* 481–486.

Kellett, J. M. (1996). Sex and the elderly male. *Sexual and Marital Therapy, 11,* 281–288.

Kessler, R. C., McGonagle, K. A., Zhao, S., Nelson, C. B., Hughes, M., Eshleman, S., Wittchen, H.-U., & Kendler, K. S. (1994). Lifetime and 12-month prevalence of DSM-III-R psychiatric disorders in the United States. *Archives of General Psychiatry, 51,* 8–19.

Klassen, A. D., & Wilsnack, S. C. (1986). Sexual experience and drinking among women in a U.S. national survey. *Archives of Sexual Behavior, 15,* 363–392.

Korenman, S. G. (1995). Advances in the understanding and management of erectile dysfunction. *Journal of Clinical Endocrinology and Metabolism, 80,* 1985–1988.

Korenman, S. G. (1998). New insights into erectile dysfunction: A practical approach. *American Journal of Medicine, 105,* 135–144.

Laumann, E. O., Paik, A., & Rosen, R. C. (1999). Sexual dysfunction in the United States. *Journal of the American Medical Association, 281,* 537–544.

Leiblum, S. R., & Segraves, R. T. (1995). Sex and aging. In *American Psychiatric Press review of psychiatry* (Vol. 14, pp. 677–695). Washingtin, DC: American Psychiatric Press.

LoPiccolo, J., Heiman, J. R., Hogan, D. R., & Roberts, C. W. (1985). Effectiveness of single therapists versus cotherapy teams in sex therapy. *Journal of Consulting and Clinical Psychology, 53,* 287–294.

LoPiccolo, J., & Stock, W. E. (1987). Sexual function, dysfunction, and counseling in gynecological practice. In Z. Rosenwaks, F. Benjamin, & M. L. Stone (Eds.), *Gynecology* (pp. 339–371). New York: Macmillan.

Lovibond, S. H., & Lovibond, P. F. (1993). *Manual for the Depression Anxiety Stress Scales (DASS)* (Psychology Foundation Monograph). (Available from the Psychology Foundation, Room 1005 Mathews Building, University of New South Wales, NSW 2052, Australia)

Malatesta, V. J., Pollack, R. H., Crotty, T. D., & Peacock, L. J. (1982). Acute alcohol intoxication and female orgasmic response. *Journal of Sex Research, 18,* 1–17.

Mannino, D. M., Klevens, R. M., & Flanders, W. D. (1994). Cigarette smoking: An independent risk factor for impotence? *American Journal of Epidemiology, 140,* 1003–1008.

Masters, W. H., & Johnson, V. E. (1966). *Human sexual response.* Boston: Little, Brown.

Masters, W. H., & Johnson, V. E. (1970). *Human sexual inadequacy.* Boston: Little, Brown.

McCabe, M. P., & Cobain, M. J. (1998). The impact of individual and relationship factors on sexual dysfunction among males and females. *Sexual and Marital Therapy, 13*, 131–143.

McCarthy, B. W. (1988). *Male sexual awareness.* New York: Carroll & Graf.

McCarthy, B. W., & McCarthy, E. (1998). *Couple sexual awareness.* New York: Carroll & Graf.

Meston, C. M. (1997). Aging and sexuality. *Western Journal of Medicine, 167*, 285–290.

Mitchell, W. B., DiBartolo, P. M., Brown, T. A., & Barlow, D. H. (1998). Effects of positive and negative mood on sexual arousal in sexually functional males. *Archives of Sexual Behavior, 27*, 197–207.

Mohr, D. C., & Beutler, L. E. (1990). Erectile dysfunction: A review of diagnostic and treatment procedures. *Clinical Psychology Review, 10*, 123–150.

Montejo-Gonzalez, A. L., Liorca, G., Izquierdo, J. A., Ledesma, A., Bousono, M., Calcedo, A., Carrasco, J. L., Ciudad, J., Daniel, E., Gandara, J. D. L., Derecho, J., Franco, M., Gomez, M. J., Macias, J. A., Martin, T., Perez, V., Sanchez, J. M., Sanchez, S., & Vicens, E. (1997). SSRI-induced sexual dysfunction: Fluoxetine, paroxetine, sertraline, and fluvoxamine in a prospective, multicenter, and descriptive clinical study of 344 patients. *Journal of Sex and Marital Therapy, 23*, 176–194.

National Institutes of Health (NIH) Consensus Conference. (1993). Impotence: NIH Consensus Development Panel on Impotence. *Journal of the American Medical Association, 270*, 83–90.

O'Farrell, T. J., Choquette, K. A., Cutter, H. S. G., & Birchler, G. R. (1997). Sexual satisfaction and dysfunction in marriages of male alcoholics: Comparison of nonalcoholic maritally conflicted and nonconflicted couples. *Journal of Studies on Alcohol, 58*, 91–99.

Osborn, M., Hawton, K., & Gath, D. (1988). Sexual dysfunction among middle aged women in the community. *British Medical Journal, 296*, 959–962.

Pokorny, A. D., Miller, B. A., & Kaplan, H. B. (1972). The brief MAST: A shortened version of the Michigan Alcohol Screening Test. *American Journal of Psychiatry, 129*, 342–345.

Reissing, E. D., Binik, Y. M., & Khalife, S. (1999). Does vaginismus exist? *Journal of Nervous and Mental Disease, 187*, 261–274.

Rosen, R. C. (1996). Erectile dysfunction: The medicalization of male sexuality. *Clinical Psychology Review, 16*, 497–519.

Rosen, R. C., Taylor, J. F., Leiblum, S. R., & Bachmann, G. A. (1993). Prevalence of sexual dysfunction in women: Results of a survey study of 329 women in an outpatient gynecological clinic. *Journal of Sex and Marital Therapy, 19*, 171–188.

Sarwer, D. B., & Durlak, J. A. (1997). A field trial of the effectiveness of behavioral treatment for sexual dysfunctions. *Journal of Sex and Marital Therapy, 23*, 87–97.

Sbrocco, T., Weisberg, R. B., & Barlow, D. H. (1992). *Sexual Dysfunction Inventory (SDI).* Unpublished semistructured interview, Center for Stress and Anxiety Disorders, Albany, NY.

Sbrocco, T., Weisberg, R. B., Barlow, D. H., & Carter, M. M. (1997). The conceptual relationship be-

tween panic disorder and male erectile dysfunction. *Journal of Sex and Marital Therapy, 23*, 212–220.

Schiavi, R. C. (1990). Chronic alcoholism and male sexual dysfunction. *Journal of Sex and Marital Therapy, 16*, 23–33.

Schiavi, R. C., White, D., Mandeli, J., & Levine, A. C. (1997). Effect of testosterone administration on sexual behavior and mood in men with erectile dysfunction. *Archives of Sexual Behavior, 26*, 231–241.

Schreiner-Engel, P., Schiavi, R. C., Vietorisz, D., & Smith, H. (1987). The differential impact of diabetes type on female sexuality. *Journal of Psychosomatic Research, 31*, 23–33.

Segraves, K. B., & Segraves, R. T. (1991). Hypoactive sexual desire disorder: Prevalence and comorbidity in 906 subjects. *Journal of Sex and Marital Therapy, 17*, 55–58.

Segraves, R. T. (1998). Antidepressant-induced sexual dysfunction. *Journal of Clinical Psychiatry, 59*(Suppl. 4), 48–54.

Sherwin, B. (1988). A comparative analysis of the role of androgen in human male and female sexual behavior: Behavioral specificity, critical thresholds, and sensitivity. *Psychobiology, 16*, 416–425.

Skinner, H. A. (1982). The Drug Abuse Screening Test. *Addictive Behaviors, 7*, 363–371.

Spanier, G. B. (1976). Measuring dyadic adjustment: New scales for assessing the quality of marriage and similar dyads. *Journal of Marriage and the Family, 38*, 15–28.

Spanier, G. B., & Thompson, L. (1982). A confirmatory analysis of the dyadic adjustment scale. *Journal of Marriage and the Family, 44*, 731–738.

Spector, I. P., & Carey, M. P. (1990). Incidence and prevalence of the sexual dysfunctions: A critical review of the empirical literature. *Archives of Sexual Behavior, 19*, 389–408.

Strassberg, D. S., Kelly, M. P., Carroll, C., & Kircher, J. C. (1987). The psychophysiological nature of premature ejaculation. *Archives of Sexual Behavior, 16*, 327–336.

Takanami, M., Nagao, K., Ishii, N., Miura, K., & Shirai, M. (1997). Is diabetic neuropathy responsible for diabetic impotence. *Urologia Internationalis, 58*, 181–185.

Thomas, A. M., & LoPiccolo, J. (1994). Sexual functioning in persons with diabetes: Issues in research, treatment, and education. *Clinical Psychology Review, 14*, 61–86.

Tiefer, L. (1996). The medicalization of sexuality: Conceptual, normative, and professional issues. *Annual Review of Sex Research, 7*, 252–282.

Verma, K. K., Khaitan, B. K., & Singh, O. P. (1998). The frequency of sexual dysfunctions in patients attending a sex therapy clinic in North India. *Archives of Sexual Behavior, 27*, 309–314.

Weisberg, R. B., Brown, T. A., Wincze, J. P., & Barlow, D. H. (in press). Causal attributions and male sexual arousal: The impact of attributions for a bogus erectile difficulty on sexual arousal, cognitions, and affect. *Journal of Abnormal Psychology*.

Wiegel, M., Bach, A. K., Brown, T. A., Rhein, A. N., & Barlow, D. H. (1997, November). *Arousability and emotional response to sexual stimuli and be-*

haviors: *A comparison of sexually functional and dysfunctional males.* Poster presented at the annual meeting of the Association for Advancement of Behavior Therapy, Miami Beach, FL.

Wincze, J. P., Albert, A., & Bansal, S. (1993). Sexual arousal in diabetic females: Physiological and self-report measures. *Archives of Sexual Behavior, 22,* 587–601.

Wincze, J. P., & Barlow, D. H. (1997a). *Enhancing sexuality: A problem solving approach (therapist guide).* Albany, NY: Graywind.

Wincze, J. P., & Barlow, D. H. (1997b). *Enhancing sexuality: A problem solving approach (client workbook).* Albany, NY: Graywind.

Wincze, J. P., & Carey, M. P. (in press). *Sexual dysfunction: A guide for assessment and treatment* (2nd ed.). New York: Guilford Press.

Wylie, K. R. (1997). Treatment outcome of brief couple therapy in psychogenic male erectile disorder. *Archives of Sexual Behavior, 26,* 527–545.

Zilbergeld, B. (1998). *The new male sexuality* (Rev. ed.). New York: Bantam Books.

Chapter 14

COUPLE DISTRESS

Jennifer G. Wheeler

Andrew Christensen

Neil S. Jacobson

The second edition of this book presented, for the first time, a substantially different approach to couple therapy—different both in conceptualization and in treatment strategies. It was noted that these changes in technique and conceptualization were profound enough to warrant a new name for the approach: "integrative behavioral couple therapy." As described in this third edition, integrative behavioral couple therapy (as it is now called) has matured into a sophisticated and intuitively appealing set of strategies. These strategies are very nicely illustrated in this chapter in the context of the comprehensive treatment of one couple in substantial distress. Since these strategies require considerable clinical skill and talent, beginning therapists in particular should learn much from the case descriptions presented in this very readable and engaging chapter. As most readers will know, this new approach was initially conceptualized and developed by the late Neil Jacobson, working in close concert with Andy Christensen and other colleagues and students. Tragically, Neil passed away as this chapter was in progress, and we are all much indebted to Jennifer Wheeler and Andy Christensen for ensuring that Neil's new ideas and creativity in approaching these problems are available in this third edition, to the benefit of us all.—D. H. B.

Unlike other chapters in this text, the present chapter does not cover a specific clinical or personality disorder. Rather, its topic is "couple distress"—an umbrella term used to describe the emotional sequelae of problematic interactions between two individuals, in the context of their relationship to one another. When presented with "couple distress," the clinician is being asked to treat the "disorder" of the *couple* rather than the "disorder" of an *individual*. How a couple's "distress" is manifested will differ significantly, depending on the diathesis of each individual in the dyad, and on the idiosyncrasies of each couple's history.

Although there are many themes and behavioral patterns common to couples in distress, the assessment and treatment of couple distress should be approached idiographically in order to account for each couple's unique experience. Traditional approaches to the treatment of couple distress have emphasized the ways in which distressed couples differ from nondistressed couples, and have taught distressed couples common skills and techniques to increase their relationship satisfaction. However, a more recent approach to the treatment of couple distress has integrated these traditional techniques with interventions that are more "tailor-made" to suit the unique needs of each couple. This approach, known as "integrative behavioral couple therapy" (IBCT; Christensen, Jacobson, & Babcock, 1995; Jacobson & Christensen, 1996), is described in this chapter. We briefly review the development of this approach from traditional behavioral couple therapy (TBCT), followed by a description of IBCT theories and techniques. Then we describe the application of IBCT, including the stages of therapy and the use of specific interventions. Finally, we provide a case example to demonstrate the application of IBCT to the treatment of couple distress.

TRADITIONAL BEHAVIORAL COUPLE THERAPY

The term "couple therapy" (as opposed to "individual therapy" or "group therapy") refers to clinical approaches for improving the functioning of two individuals within the context of their relationship to one another.[1] Although couple therapy is unique in its emphasis on a specific dyad, it is by its very definition a contextual approach to the treatment of two *individuals*. Accordingly, successful treatments for couple distress have emphasized the assessment and modification of each individual's contribution and response to specific relationship interactions (see, e.g., Baucom & Hoffman, 1986; Gurman, Knickerson, & Pinsoff, 1986; Holtzworth-Munroe & Jacobson, 1991; Jacobson, 1978a, 1984; Jacobson & Holtzworth-Munroe, 1986; Jacobson & Margolin, 1979; Stuart, 1980; Weiss, Hops, & Patterson, 1973).

For two decades, the "gold standard" for the treatment of couple distress has been TBCT (see Baucom, Shoham, Kim, Daiuto, & Stickle, 1998; Christensen & Heavey, 1999; and Jacobson & Addis, 1993, for reviews of couple therapies). First applied to couple distress by Stuart (1969) and Weiss, Hops, and Patterson (1973), TBCT uses basic behavioral principles of reinforcement, modeling, and behavioral rehearsal to facilitate collaboration and compromise between partners, and ultimately to facilitate behavioral change. With an eye toward facilitating changes in the couple's behavior, TBCT teaches partners how to increase or decrease target behaviors in an effort to improve their overall relationship satisfaction (behavior exchange), communicate more effectively with one another (communication training), and improve their ability to assess and solve problems (problem solving).[2]

In early studies, TBCT demonstrated significant empirical success (Jacobson, 1977, 1978b) and soon became the focus of numerous treatment manuals, programs, and publications supporting the application of behavioral techniques to the treatment of couple distress (e.g., Floyd & Markman, 1983; Gottman, Notarius, Gonso, & Markman, 1976; Jacobson & Margolin, 1979; Knox, 1971; Liberman, 1970; Liberman, Wheeler, deVisser, Kuehnel, & Kuehnel, 1981; Stuart, 1980). Subsequent outcome research has consistently supported the efficacy of behavioral approaches for the treatment of couple distress (Baucom & Hoffman, 1986; Gurman et al., 1986; Jacobson, 1984; Jacobson, Schmaling, & Holtzworth-Munroe, 1987).

However, outcome research also revealed some limitations in the efficacy and generalizability of TBCT. Data indicated that two-thirds of couples who present for therapy demonstrated improved relationship quality following treatment with TBCT, while the remaining one-third showed no measurable treatment benefit (Jacobson et al., 1987). Furthermore, of the two-thirds of couples who demonstrated initial success with TBCT, about one-third experienced a relapse within 1 or 2 years after therapy (Jacobson et al., 1984, 1987). In other words, TBCT is an effective treatment with long-term benefit for only about half of the distressed couples presenting for therapy.

The finding that TBCT was effective for only half of treated couples generated further questions about the efficacy of traditional couple therapies. TBCT techniques have since been modified and enhanced to develop a variety of behavioral and cognitive-behavioral couple therapies (see, e.g., Baucom & Epstein, 1990; Baucom, Epstein, & Rankin, 1995; Floyd, Markman, Kelly, Blumberg, & Stanley, 1995). Yet comparative treatment studies have failed to demonstrate any increment in efficacy by various enhancements to TBCT, such as the addition of cognitive strategies, over basic TBCT. The addition of cognitive strategies created a treatment that was as good as but not better than TBCT (see, e.g., Baucom et al., 1998).

More recent couple therapy research has been aimed at understanding how "treatment successes" differ from "treatment failures." Research on treatment response has identified several factors that appear to affect the success of TBCT. Compared to couples that respond positively to TBCT, couples that are often regarded as "treatment failures" or "difficult to treat" are generally older, more emotionally disengaged, more polarized on basic issues, and more severely distressed (Baucom & Hoffman, 1986; Hahlweg, Schindler, Revenstorf, & Brengelmann, 1984; Jacobson, Follette, & Pagel, 1986; see Jacobson & Christensen, 1996, for a review). Despite the fact that these couples arguably have the greatest need for effective treatment, each of these factors has an obvious deleterious effect on a couple's ability to collaborate, compromise, and facilitate behavioral change. Older couples, for example, have had more time than younger couples to become "stuck" in their destructive behavioral patterns. Couples in which the partners are more polarized on fundamental issues (e.g., how "traditional" they are with respect to their gender roles) may never be able to reach a mutually satisfying compromise. And partners who are extremely disengaged from one another may be unable to collaborate. Each of these factors is likely to be associated with long-standing, deeply entrenched, and even "unchangeable" behavioral patterns. Thus it should come as no surprise that the change-oriented techniques of TBCT are ineffective for these couples.

AN "INTEGRATIVE" THERAPY

It was from these findings that IBCT was developed. IBCT is similar to TBCT in that it is derived from behavioral theory and emphasizes the context in which a couple's distress occurs (see Cordova & Jacobson, 1993). But while the TBCT therapist is focused on the "who, what, where, and when" of destructive relationship behaviors, the IBCT therapist attempts to help partners understand *why* the behaviors occur at all. Unlike the change-oriented goal of TBCT, the primary goal of IBCT is to promote each partner's *acceptance* of the other and their differences. Rather than trying to eliminate a couple's long-standing conflicts, IBCT helps the partners develop a new understanding of their apparently irreconcilable differences, and uses these differences to promote intimacy, empathy, and compassion for one another. With its focus on acceptance rather than change, IBCT creates an environment for partners to understand each other's behavior before deciding whether and how they might modify it.

Although there is an expectation of "change" in IBCT, this expectation differs significantly from that of TBCT in regard to *which* partner and *what* behavior is expected to change. In TBCT, the "change" only involves Partner A's increasing/decreasing the frequency or intensity of a specified behavior in response to a complaint from Partner B. But in IBCT, it is hoped that the "change" will also involve Partner B's modifying his/her emotional reaction to Partner A's behavior. When a difference is "irreconcilable," the therapeutic strategy of IBCT is to change the "complaining" partner's response to the "offending" partner's behavior, rather than making attempts to change what is essentially "unchangeable" behavior. Ideally, Partner B will develop a new understanding of his/her partner's behavior, and the "complaint" will be transformed into a less destructive response. This change in Partner B's reaction often then has a salutary impact on the frequency or intensity of Partner A's behavior. With this approach, as opposed to a change-focused approach, even the most polarized, disengaged, and "unchangeable" couples have an opportunity to increase their overall relationship satisfaction.

It is important to note that in this context, "acceptance" is not confused with "resignation." Whereas resignation involves one partner's grudgingly giving in to the other—perhaps unwillingly "tolerating" what is seen as an unyielding status quo—acceptance involves one partner's "letting go" of the struggle to change the other. Instead of encouraging one partner to "give in" to the other, acceptance work focuses on transforming a couple's "irreconcilable" differences into a vehicle for promoting closeness and intimacy. In so doing, a goal of IBCT is to end the ongoing struggle that has been historically generated by these differences. Ideally, partners "let go" of the struggle—not grudgingly, but rather as a result of having a new appreciation for their partner's experience. When partners come to understand their distress in terms of their differences and learning to accept each other's differences, it is hoped that the distress generated by the struggle to change one another will be reduced. Thus, for IBCT to be effective in treating couple distress, it is important for a couple to understand the factors that have contributed to the development and maintenance of distress.

THE ETIOLOGY OF COUPLE DISTRESS

IBCT interventions promote couples' understanding of the etiology and maintenance of their distress. According to IBCT, relationship distress develops as a result of two basic influences: "reinforcement erosion" and the emergence of "incompatibilities." Reinforcement erosion is the phenomenon whereby behaviors that were once reinforcing become less reinforcing with repeated exposure. For example, demonstrations of physical affection may generate powerful feelings of warmth and pleasure for each partner during the early stages of their relationship. But after partners have spent many years together, the reinforcing properties of these affectionate behaviors may disappear. For some couples, once-reinforcing behaviors may become "taken for granted," whereas for others, once-reinforcing behavior may actually become aversive. In some cases, behaviors that were once considered attractive, endearing, or pleasing become the very same behaviors that generate or exacerbate a couple's distress.

As with the erosion of reinforcing behaviors, incompatibilities may emerge as partners spend more and more time together. In the early stages of a relationship, differences in partners' backgrounds, goals, and interests may initially be downplayed or ignored. For example, if Partner A prefers to save money while Partner B prefers to spend money, this difference may not be apparent during courtship, when spending money is a tacit expectation of both partners. If this difference *is* detected early on, perhaps it is regarded as a "positive" difference, in that each partner is encouraged to be a little more like the other in his/her spending habits. Or perhaps each partner expects the other to eventually compromise or change to his/her own way of doing things. But over time, these incompatibilities and their relevance to the relationship are inevitably exposed. Differences that were once regarded as novel, interesting, or challenging may ultimately be perceived as impediments to one's own goals and interests. And in addition to any extant incompatibilities, further unanticipated incompatibilities may emerge with new life experiences (e.g., having children, changing careers). Thus even those couples who initially made a realistic appraisal of their differences may discover unexpected incompatibilities over time. One goal of IBCT is to identify and reframe a couple's incompatibilities in a way that minimizes their destructive nature, while maximizing the couple's level of intimacy and relationship satisfaction.

APPLICATION OF IBCT

The Formulation

The most important organizing principle of IBCT is the "formulation." The formulation is the way the therapist conceives of and describes the couple's problem in terms of their differences, incompatibilities, and associated discord. The formulation is comprised of three basic components: a "theme," a "polarization process," and a "mutual trap." The therapist will refer back to the formulation and its components throughout the treatment process, whenever partners have conflicts during or between therapy sessions.

Simply put, one of the most basic goals of IBCT is for the partners to adopt the formulation as part of their relationship history. They can use the formulation as a context for understanding their relationship and their conflicts. It gives them a language to discuss their problems, and allows them to distance themselves from their problems. It is important to remember, however, that the formulation is a dynamic concept that may require alteration and modification (or "reformulation") throughout treatment.

The Theme

The theme is the description of the couple's primary conflict, usually described with a phrase that captures the nature of the couple's differences. The theme is a "shorthand" way of describing the function of each partner's behavior during his/her typical conflicts. A couple's theme underlies both the polarization process and the mutual trap. For example, a theme common to many distressed couples is that of "closeness–distance," where one partner is seeking greater intimacy while the other partner is trying to maintain his/her optimal level of distance.

The Polarization Process

The polarization process is the destructive interaction process that ensues when a distressed couple enters into a theme-related conflict. A natural response for a couple confronted with differences between the partners is for each partner to try to change the other. In many cases, these efforts at changing each other may be successful. However, many times the result may be that their differences are exacerbated and the two partners become polarized in their conflicting positions. When a couple has become polarized on an issue, the partners' further attempts to change each other only increase the conflict and perpetuate their polarized stance. For example, for a couple whose theme is closeness–distance, the polarization process is likely to occur when the distance seeker "retreats" from attempts by the closeness seeker to gain more intimacy, creating further distance between them— which will then result in more "intrusive" efforts by the closeness seeker.

The Mutual Trap

The mutual trap describes the outcome of the polarization process; it is called a "trap" because it typically leaves the partners feeling "stuck" or "trapped" in their conflict. Partners in a mutual trap feel that they have done everything they can to change each other, and nothing seems to work. But they are reluctant to give up their efforts to change each other, since this would mean resigning themselves to a dissatisfying relationship. As a result, they become more entrenched in their respective positions.

The experience of partners who are so polarized is one of helplessness and futility, and this experience is rarely discussed openly between them. As a result, each partner may be unaware that the other partner also feels trapped. Making each partner aware of the other's sense of entrapment is an important part of acceptance work, and encouraging each partner to experience the other's sense of "stuckness" is the first step toward promoting empathy and intimacy between partners.

Stages of Therapy

In IBCT, there is a clear distinction between the assessment phase and the treatment itself. The assessment phase consists of at least one conjoint session with the couple, followed by individual sessions with each partner. The assessment phase is followed by a feedback session, during which the therapist describes his/her formulation of the couple and the presenting problems. The feedback session is followed by the treatment sessions, the exact number of which should be determined on a case-by-case basis, depending on each couple's treatment needs.

The Use of Objective Measures

Objective assessment instruments (see Table 14.1) may be useful both for initial assessment and for monitoring a couple's progress at various points throughout treatment. Although such objective measures are not necessary to conduct IBCT, they may provide additional information about areas of disagreement that have not been covered in sessions, or they may provide objective data about a couple's levels of distress and satisfaction. For example, a couple's relationship

TABLE 14.1. Useful Assessment and Screening Instruments

Dyadic Adjustment Scale (DAS; Spanier, 1976): Measures relationship distress and commitment. (To obtain this measure, see Spanier, G. B. (1976). Measuring dyadic adjustment: New scales for assessing the quality of marriage and similar dyads. *Journal of Marriage and the Family, 38*, 15–28.)

Marital Satisfaction Inventory—Revised (MSI-R; Snyder, 1997): Measures relationship distress, global distress, and specific dimensions of distress; provides normative data on distressed, nondistressed, and divorcing couples. (To obtain this measure, contact Western Psychological Services, 1-800-648-8857.)

Marital Status Inventory: Assess commitment to the relationship and steps taken toward separation or divorce. (To obtain this measure, contact Robert L. Weiss, PhD, Oregon Marital Studies Program, Department of Psychology, University of Oregon, Eugene, OR 97403-1227.)

Conflict Tactics Scale (CTS; Straus, 1979): Assesses domestic violence. (To obtain this measure, see Straus, M. A. (1979). Measuring intrafamily conflict and violence: The Conflict Tactics (CT) Scales. *Journal of Marriage and the Family, 41*, 75–88.)

Frequency and Acceptability of Partner Behavior questionnaire (FAPB): Assesses acceptability of behavior at its current frequency for 24 spouse behaviors. (To obtain this measure, contact Andrew Christensen, PhD, Department of Psychology, University of California at Los Angeles, Los Angeles, CA 90095.)

satisfaction can be assessed via the Dyadic Adjustment Scale and/or the Marital Satisfaction Inventory—Revised; partners' troubling behaviors can be assessed via the Frequency and Acceptability of Partner Behavior questionnaire; and the couple's level of physical violence can be assessed via the Conflict Tactics Scale (see Table 14.1 for more information on all these measures). Ideally, the partners have completed any such questionnaires before coming in for their first session, so that the therapist has a preliminary idea of the couple's presenting problems and overall levels of distress. In addition to being administered as part of the assessment phase, the questionnaires can be administered at mid-treatment and after the final session, to assess changes from presenting baseline levels of distress and satisfaction.

Assessment of Domestic Violence

Objective measures are particularly useful in assessing a couple's history of physical violence. Assessing for domestic violence is a critical part of every couple's intake—not only to determine whether the personal safety of either partner is in imminent danger, but also because couple therapy may actually be *contraindicated* for some violent couples (see Holtzworth-Munroe, Beatty, & Anglin, 1995; Jacobson & Gottman, 1998). Couple therapy requires that each partner take some degree of responsibility for his/her problems, but such a perspective is inappropriate when a couple's problems include domestic violence, because perpetrators of violence must assume sole responsibility for their behavior. In such cases, individual treatment—and not couple therapy—is indicated. The Conflict Tactics Scale (Straus, 1979) is a useful screening tool for evaluating the frequency and severity of a couple's physical aggression, and to determine whether couple therapy is contraindicated. The Marital Satisfaction Inventory—Revised (Snyder, 1997) provides an additional Domestic Violence scale. Finally, a couple's history of violence should be directly addressed during the assessment phase.

Assessment

The assessment phase consists of at least one joint session with the couple (Session 1), fol-

lowed by individual sessions with each partner (Sessions 2a and 2b). The primary goal of the assessment phase is for the therapist to develop the formulation; however, the therapist should also use the assessment period to orient the couple to the therapy process. In addition, although the IBCT therapist is not intervening during the assessment phase, it is possible for the therapist to have a therapeutic impact in these first few sessions.

Orientation (Session 1)

After the partners have been greeted and introduced to their therapist, they should then be oriented to the upcoming therapy process. The couple's introduction will probably include reviewing and signing an informed consent form, which explains billing procedures, defines confidentiality and its exclusions, and outlines the possible risks and benefits of IBCT.

In addition to the general information provided during informed consent, the couple should also be oriented to the specific process of IBCT. The therapist should explain the difference between the assessment and treatment phases of therapy, and should also ask the partners whether this is different from the expectations they had coming into therapy. The therapist should be prepared for the partners' disappointment when they learn that therapy is not going to begin immediately. The therapists may need to explain to the partners why an assessment period is needed before the therapist can provide any useful help to them.

Also during the first session, partners are introduced to their "manual," *Reconcilable Differences* (Christensen & Jacobson, 2000). The couple is asked to complete Part I of this book prior to the feedback session. Ideally, this reading will help the partners begin to conceptualize their problems in a way that is similar to how their therapist will portray them during the feedback session.

Therapists should be aware that at least one (if not both) of the partners is likely to be ambivalent about participating in therapy. Such ambivalence should be normalized and validated, and the therapist should explain to the partners that the assessment period is also *their* opportunity to get to know the therapist and to determine whether this treatment is going to be a "good match" for them.

Problem Areas (Sessions 1, 2a, and 2b)

After the couple has been oriented to the therapy process, the therapist begins the evaluation by reviewing the couple's presenting problem(s). Much of this information can be gathered from objective measures administered before the first session, and also during each partner's individual sessions—so this discussion during their first session should not consume the entire session. However, it is important that during the first session each partner feels heard and validated, and feels that his/her problems and distress are clearly understood by the therapist. From the information gathered from objective measures and during the evaluation sessions, the therapist should be able to describe the couple's problem areas and develop the formulation. The following six questions provide a guideline for this assessment, and each should have been answered by the end of the assessment period.

1. How distressed is the couple?
2. How committed is this couple to the relationship?
3. What are the issues that divide the partners?
4. Why are these issues a problem for them?
5. What are the strengths that keep the partners together?
6. What can treatment do to help them?

Again, many of these questions may be answered by questionnaires before the first session. But unanswered questions should be addressed and explored during the initial conjoint session and/or each partner's individual sessions. The individual sessions may be particularly useful for assessing each partner's level of commitment to the relationship, in addition to assessing the couple's history of physical violence.

The assessment of a couple's problem areas should also include determining the couple's "collaborative set" (Jacobson & Margolin, 1979). This refers to the partners' joint perspective that they *share* responsibility for the problems in their relationship, and that they will *both* have to change in order for the relationship to change. The strength of this set determines whether change-oriented or acceptance-oriented interventions are indicated. The stronger the couple's collaborative set, the more successful change-oriented interventions are likely to be. But partners who lack this collaborative set—those who enter therapy believing they are each the innocent victim of the other's behavior—will need to focus on acceptance work first.

The Couple's History (Session 1)

After the couple has been oriented to therapy and the problem areas have been assessed (at least briefly), the therapist then takes the history of the couple's relationship. The obvious objective for taking this history is for the therapist to gain a good understanding of the partners' attachment to each other. Often the couple's distress has so escalated that it has overshadowed the reasons why these two people became a couple in the first place. In addition, this history can provide some immediate therapeutic benefit to the couple. Generally, while partners discuss the earlier (usually happier) stages of their relationship, their affect is likely to become more positive. They have been focused for so long on the negative aspects of their relationship that they have probably not thought about their early romance, courtship, and attraction to each other for a very long time. In this way, having partners describe the evolution of their relationship can be therapeutic in and of itself. Although some couples may be in too much pain to discuss their history without making blaming and accusatory remarks (in which case the following guidelines should be abandoned and the therapist should instead use the session to validate their pain), most couples will enjoy reminiscing about their happier times.

The following are a series of questions that will provide the therapist with useful information about the couple's history, in addition to allowing the partners an opportunity to reflect upon the reasons they fell in love in the first place:

- How did they get together?
- What was their courtship like?
- What attracted each partner to the other?
- What was their relationship like before their problems began?
- How is their relationship different *now* on days when they are getting along?
- How would the relationship be different if their current problems no longer existed?

These and other related questions may also reveal useful information about each partner, such as his/her hopes and dreams for the future. Information about the couple's history is useful for the therapist in developing the couple's formulation, which will be presented during the feedback session.

Feedback

From the information gathered during the assessment sessions and from the questionnaires, the therapist develops the couple's formulation. The formulation is discussed with the couple in the feedback session (usually Session 3). The feedback session should follow the outline of the six questions used to assess the couple's problem areas. It is important for the feedback session to be a dialogue and not a lecture from the therapist—the therapist should continually get feedback from the couple about the formulation being presented. The partners are the experts on their relationship, and should be treated as such.

The feedback session is also used to describe for the partners the proposed treatment plan, based on their formulation. The therapist should describe for the couple the goals for treatment, as well as the procedures for accomplishing these goals. The goals for therapy are to create the environment in the session where the couple's problems can be resolved through some combination of acceptance and change techniques. The procedures for meeting these goals are usually (1) in-session discussions of the problem and incidents when it arises, and (2) homework to be conducted outside the session to further the work done in session.

The purpose of the feedback session is to orient the partners to the goals of change and acceptance through open communication and finding new ways of looking at their problems. In addition, the feedback session is used to give the partners some idea of what they can expect from therapy, and to eliciting from them their willingness to participate. Finally, the feedback session can be used to implement some interventions. The first intervention is the therapist's description of the couple's strengths. From this discussion, the partners may be able to see some solutions to their problems. The therapist can begin assigning the couple relevant chapters from Part II of *Reconcilable Differences* (Christensen &

Jacobson, 2000), as these chapters specifically address the topic of acceptance. After the formulation and treatment plan have been described to the partners, and they have agreed to proceed with therapy, the remaining sessions are devoted to building acceptance between partners and promoting change by each.

Treatment

IBCT Techniques for Building Emotional Acceptance

We typically start off treatment with a focus on promoting acceptance. The exception is when partners are able to collaborate with each other ("the collaborative set") and both want to make specific changes in their relationship. In such a case, we start off with change strategies.

When we do acceptance work, the actual content of the session is determined by the couple and what they "bring in" every week. Discussions of recent events are the best means of exploring the couple's theme, polarization process, and mutual traps, and are useful for implementing the acceptance-building strategies of "empathic joining," "detaching from the problem," and "tolerance building."

Empathic Joining. "Empathic joining" refers to the process by which partners cease to blame each other for their emotional suffering, and instead develop empathy for each other's experience. In order to foster empathic joining, the IBCT therapist must reformulate the couple's problem as a result of common differences between the partners. Partners' behaviors are described in terms of their differences from one another, and their responses to these differences are validated as normal and understandable.

In making this reformulation of each partner's behavior, it is important for the IBCT therapist to emphasize the pain each partner is experiencing. One strategy for building empathy between partners is the use of "soft disclosures." Often partners express their emotional pain by using "hard" disclosures of feelings such as anger or disgust. Although hard disclosures are easier to make because they do not reveal vulnerability, they are more difficult for the other partner to hear because they imply blame. It is the combination of "pain and blame" that results in discord. But if the therapist can encourage each partner to express pain *without* expressing blame, the result will (ideally) be increased acceptance from the other partner. IBCT therapists often encourage soft disclosures by suggesting "soft" feelings such as fear, hurt, and shame that may underlie each partner's behavior. Although soft disclosures are more difficult to make because they reveal vulnerability, they are easier for the other partner to hear and to empathize with. Thus empathic joining is promoted by (1) reformulating a couple's discord as a result of common differences and the partners' understandable reactions to those differences, and (2) the use of soft disclosures to express painful emotions.

Detachment from the Problem. Another IBCT technique allows partners to describe and discuss a problem without placing blame—or responsibility to change—on either partner. In this way, the partners engage in unified detachment from their problematic interactions. The therapist engages the couple in a dialogue about the sequence of a particular conflict, including what factors trigger each partner's reactions, how specific events are connected to one another, and how the couple can diffuse or override the conflict. The approach is that of an intellectual analysis of the problem, which is described in an emotionally detached manner as an "it" rather than in terms of "you" or "me." By detaching themselves from the problem, the partners have an opportunity to discuss their conflict without becoming emotionally "charged" by it. In this way, they can try to understand the conflict from a more neutral, objective stance. When possible, the therapist should give the couple's theme, polarization process, and mutual traps a name, and should use this name to further define the problem as an "it."

Tolerance Building. Building acceptance may be most challenging when one partner experiences emotional pain as a result of the other partner's behavior. In these circumstances, the IBCT therapist must help a partner build tolerance for the other partner's "offending" behavior. By building tolerance, the partner feeling pain will ideally experience a reduction in it. In order to build tolerance, however, this partner must cease efforts to prevent, avoid, or escape the "offending" partner's behavior. Instead, the partner experiencing pain must expose himself/herself to the behavior without the associated struggle, which will (ideally) reduce his/her sensitivity to the behavior, and ultimately the "offending" behavior will be experienced as less painful.

One strategy for building tolerance is through positive reemphasis, or focusing on the positive aspects of a partner's negative behavior. For example, what one partner sees as the other partner's "uptightness" might be the "stability" that first attracted him/her. Or alternatively, what one partner sees as the other's "flakiness" or "irresponsibility" might be the "free-spiritedness" or "rebelliousness" that so attracted him/her in the beginning of their relationship. The IBCT therapist must help the partners notice the positive aspects of what they have come to see as purely negative behavior. And often this behavior is in some way related to a quality one partner once found attractive about the other.

Another strategy for building tolerance for each other's differences is by focusing on the ways in which these differences complement each other, and to present these differences as part of what makes the relationship "work." One partner's stability might balance the other's free-spiritedness. The therapist might describe for the couple the ways in which each partner would be "worse off" if those differences did not exist. The differences can become a positive aspect of the couple's relationship—something the partners can be proud of, rather than something that is seen as a destructive threat.

A third technique for building tolerance to a partner's behavior is by preparing the couple for inevitable slip-ups and lapses in behavior. This is especially important when partners first begin to detect changes in each other's behavior, and they begin to feel positive about the progress they are making in therapy. It is during this time that the therapist should congratulate the partners for their hard work and progress, and then warn them that "backsliding" is still a likely occurrence. The couple should be asked to generate some of the circumstances in which a slip-up is likely to occur, and to consider possible responses to the slip-up in advance. Working out how to face such lapses will help partners build their tolerance for them.

A related strategy for building tolerance is instructing partners to "fake" negative behavior while they are at home. Each partner is instructed to engage in a designated "bad behavior" between sessions—with the stipulation that the partners are to engage in this behavior only on occasions when they are not feeling like doing so. The instructions are given in front of each partner, so that each partner knows that a bad behavior in the future might actually be a faked bad behavior. Ideally this introduces an ambiguity into the future negative behaviors that might affect the partner's response to them. More importantly, however, is that faking behavior gives both partners an opportunity to observe the effects of their negative behavior on each other. Specifically, because they are performing the bad behavior during a time when they do not feel like it, they can make these observations when they are in a calm emotional state, which allows them to be more sympathetic. The faker is also instructed to let the other partner know about the faked behavior soon after is it performed; this will prevent the situation from escalating, and will give the couple an opportunity to "debrief" following this "experiment."

One unavoidable source of pain for many partners is when one feels that the other partner is failing to meet his/her needs in some important way. However, it is rarely the case that one partner will be able to fulfill all of the needs of the other. An important aspect of acceptance building is for partners to increase their own self-reliance, or self-care, in getting their needs met. Each partner should be encouraged to find alternative ways to care for himself/herself when the other partner is not able to do so. Partners may need to learn to seek support from friends and family in times of stress, or to find new ways to define and solve a problem on their own. As self-reliance increases, the partners' reliance on each other to meet all of their emotional needs will decrease. Ideally, this will result in partners' decreased sensitivity to each other's failure to meet their needs, thereby reducing conflict.

Traditional Strategies for Promoting Change

For some couples, change interventions may be indicated. Whether an IBCT therapist begins by implementing "acceptance" or "change" techniques will depend primarily on the couple's collaborative set and specific treatment needs. In general, however, change techniques will be most effective if implemented later in therapy, after much acceptance work has been done.

Behavior Exchange. The primary goal of "behavior exchange" (BE) is to increase the proportion of a couple's daily positive behaviors and interactions. These techniques are instigative, in that they are intended to increase each partner's performance of positive behaviors. Because BE requires a great deal of collaboration between partners, it is best implemented later in therapy, after acceptance work has been done. In addition to using BE as a mean to increase a couple's positive interactions, the IBCT therapist should consider BE as a diagnostic tool for assessing possible areas in need of more acceptance work.

The two basic steps in BE are (1) to identify things each partner can do for the other that would increase their relationship satisfaction, and (2) to increase the frequency of those behaviors in the couple's daily behavioral repertoire. A couple is often given a homework assignment to generate a list of things each partner can do for the other to increase the other's satisfaction. Partners are instructed not to discuss these lists with each other, in order to reduce the threat of criticism from the other and to keep each focused on their own assignment. In the next session, partners' lists are reviewed. Their next assignment is to perform one of the items on the list during the next week, but neither partner is to tell the other which item he/she is performing. In the subsequent therapy session, each partner reviews the success of the assignment and whether it had the desired effect on the other. The list can be modified to eliminate items that do not seem to have an effect, and in later sessions each partner can elicit feedback from the other to optimize the benefit of the items on each list.

Communication and Problem-Solving Training. Although many couples communicate effectively without having had any formal "training," for distressed couples poor communication may be exacerbating or even causing many of their problems. In their attempts to get each other to change, partners may resort to maladaptive communication tactics such as coercion (crying, threatening, withholding affection). Although coercion may be effective in that the other partner may eventually comply with the demand, the use of coercion is likely to escalate, such that increasingly coercive tactics are required to achieve the desired effect. The inevitable result of such interactions is that partners become extremely polarized. The goal of communication and problem-solving training is to teach couples how to discuss their problems and to negotiate change without resorting to such destructive tactics. Ideally, these skills will be useful to couples even after therapy has ended.

As part of communication training, partners are taught both "speaker" skills and "listener" skills. They are then instructed to engage in practice conversations in the therapy session. To become a more effective speaker, each partner is instructed to (1) express soft emotions while avoiding hard emotions such as blaming and criticizing; and (2) focus on the self, not the other partner. To become a more effective listener, each partner is instructed to paraphrase what the other partner has just said. Paraphrasing will ensure that neither partner is being misread during the conversation and will decrease a couple's tendency to jump to conclusions about what is being said, in addition to generally slowing down the interaction. Using these speaking and listening "rules" may feel awkward during practice conversations, so the therapists should explain to the couple that the rules will feel more natural with increased use. The therapist should also be prepared to interrupt and make corrections in order to remind the couple to follow the communication rules. The therapist should provide the couple with feedback after each practice session, and the exercise should be adequately debriefed. When the therapist is confident that the partners have improved their communication skills in sessions, the couple can be assigned to practice these skills as homework.

These basic communication skills will then be implemented to help partners discuss and attempt to solve some of their relationship problems. Often with distressed couples, what is most damaging in their struggles around daily problems is not the problem itself, but their destructive attempts to solve them. These attempts may begin with an accusation by one partner, which is met by defensiveness and anger from the other. Soon the argument may escalate to counterblaming and character assassination—and the problem itself gets lost in the conflict around it. In problem-solving training, couples are taught to have problem-solving discussions while employing three sets of skills: problem definition skills, problem solution skills, and structuring skills.

First, partners are taught to *define* the problem as specifically as possible, by specifying the exact behavior of concern and the circumstances surrounding it. Partners are encouraged to describe some of the soft emotions they experience as a result of the problem, in an effort toward increased emotional acceptance. Finally, both partners are asked to define their respective roles in perpetuating the problem.

Once the problem has been defined, the couple can begin working toward problem *solution*. The first step in problem solution is brainstorming, when the partners try to come up with as many solutions to the problem as possible. The couple is told that any and all solutions can be considered, even impossible or silly ones. No evaluative comments about the brainstormed solutions are allowed, and discussions of which options are actually viable are held off for later. Suggestions are written down so that they can be reviewed later. This exercise can be lighthearted and playful, often generating positive affect during the session. After the list has been generated, the partners go through the list eliminating those suggestions that are obviously impossible, silly, or unlikely to be effective. After the list is pruned, each item is considered for its potential to solve the problem. For each item the couple considers the pros and cons, and the list is further modified until a final list of options has been generated. The remaining items are used to formulate a possible solution to the problem. An agreement is reached about this solution, and the agreement is written down and signed by each partner. Finally, the partners are asked to consider any obstacles to executing their agreement, and to work out strategies for combating these. The partners are told to post the agreement in a place where they will both see it often, and a date is set to review their progress in solving the problem. During the next few sessions, the therapist checks in with the partners on their progress, and the agreement may be renegotiated if indicated.

Finally, partners learn structuring skills for their problem-solving discussions. First, the couple is instructed to set aside a specific time and place to have these discussions. The couple is also instructed not to discuss the problem at the "scene of the crime"—that is, to hold off discussing a problem until the designated time. Finally, the couple is instructed to focus on only one problem at a time. Throughout their problem-solving discussions, the partners are asked to follow the basic guidelines of paraphrasing each other's statements, avoiding negative inferences about each other's intent, and avoiding negative verbal and nonverbal communication.

The couple's first attempts at using these problem-solving skills should occur in session, under the supervision of the therapist. But after the partners have practiced and received feedback about their problem-solving skills, they are encouraged to apply these techniques at home to help discuss and negotiate their problems.

Therapist Variables Relevant to IBCT

As in any therapy, it is important for the IBCT therapist to maintain a nonjudgmental stance toward his/her clients. But in the context of IBCT, it is particularly important for the therapist to practice acceptance with each partner in the same way that the partners are asked to practice acceptance with one another. The IBCT therapist must validate the experiences and responses for each partner, and find ways to develop empathy and compassion for both, no matter how challenging this may be.

In addition to practicing acceptance, it is important that an IBCT therapist listen carefully to a couple's in-session interactions and be prepared to conduct immediate functional analyses of them. The IBCT therapist must be particularly attentive to subtle verbal and nonverbal cues that may be relevant to a formulation. The IBCT therapist must also be prepared to abandon any prescribed agenda in order to address the immediate needs of the couple at any given time. When destructive interactions occur in session, the IBCT therapist must be able to maintain a nonconfrontational demeanor while also effectively stopping the interaction. Other important IBCT skills include using the couple's language and jargon when making interventions, and developing an awareness of when it is time to end therapy. Finally, it is not a goal of an IBCT therapist to "cheerlead" for the success of a relationship, but rather to create an environment in which partners can objectively and effectively evaluate their own relationship.

The Efficacy of IBCT

Pilot data indicate the relative success of IBCT compared to TBCT. In a sample of 21 couples who were randomly assigned to TBCT and IBCT, posttreatment measures revealed that 80% of couples who had received IBCT showed improved relationship satisfaction, compared to 64% of couples who had received TBCT (Jacobson, Christensen, Prince, Cordova, & Eldridge, 2000).

It is important to note that this sample excluded couples in which one or both partners were experiencing symptoms of mania or psychosis; had a current diagnosis of substance dependence (subsequently broadened to include substance abuse); met criteria for borderline, antisocial, or schizotypal personality disorders; or had a history of severe physical violence. The rationale for these exclusionary criteria is that for such individuals, treatment other than couple therapy is likely to be indicated. However, the pilot sample did *not* exclude couples in which one or both partners suffered from other psychological disorders, such as anxiety or depression. The rationale for including such couples is that their relationships can still be treated, despite such individual problems. Furthermore, some of these couples' relationship problems may even be *contributing* to these individual problems. Thus preliminary data suggest that IBCT can be successfully applied to many couples, including those couples in which a partner is suffering from certain other psychological disorders.

CASE EXAMPLE: ANNE AND MARK

We use the case example of Anne and Mark[3] to demonstrate the application of IBCT. We have included excerpts from the assessment and feedback sessions, in addition to treatment sessions that were selected for their effective use of IBCT acceptance-building interventions.[4]

Anne and Mark were a middle-aged couple and had been married for 10 years. Anne had three children from her previous marriage.

Assessment

Session 1

After greetings and introductions, Anne and Mark's therapist (Dr. S) began Session 1 by orienting them to the assessment process as follows:

> "We'll be working together for the next 25 sessions. . . . You have already done the first step of the assessment process by completing all of those questionnaires. Your next three visits, including today, will be the second step of the assessment phase. Today I'm meeting with the two of you to get to know your relationship, to hear about your relationship . . . sharing some of the history about meeting, dating, bringing us up until today. Then over the next two visits, I'd like to meet with the two of you individually. After that, at the fourth visit, that's where I'll give you feedback. That's where I'll put together all of the information from the questionnaires and our time together today, as well as our time individually, to paint a picture for presenting some understanding of what could be going on."

Particularly if one or both partners express hesitation or ambivalence about being in therapy, a therapist should include the following:

> "This assessment period is also your opportunity to get to know me, and the kind of therapy we'll be doing, so that you can get a feeling for whether this is going to be a good match for your needs right now."

After checking in with Anne and Mark to see whether they understood this explanation, Dr. S proceeded to elicit from them a brief description of their presenting problems:

> "Before we get into your history, maybe you could give me a sense of what are some of the problems that have been going on that led you to decide, 'Let's get some help.'"

After Mark and Anne took turns describing their sides of the problems in the relationship, Dr. S proceeded by gathering the couple's developmental history, using probing phrases such as these:

> "Let's start at the beginning. Why don't you tell me where and how the two of you met?"

> "Mark, what was it about Anne that attracted you initially? What about you, Anne?"

> "Anne, how could you tell that Mark was interested in you? . . . What kinds of things did he say? . . . How did you flirt with him? Which one of you made the first move?"

> "When you decided to go from living together to getting married, how did that happen?"

In the course of their description, Anne and Mark had many opportunities to say complimentary things about the other. Mark described Anne as "sensual," which he found very attractive, and Anne described Mark as "very nice and easygoing." Dr. S was very thorough and behaviorally specific when eliciting details of Mark and Anne's courtship, such as the fact that both partners agreed that their first kiss was very good.

Even during this part of the assessment phase, opportunities for building acceptance may present themselves. At one point during Session 1, Anne made a soft disclosure when she discussed a time when she had initially rejected Mark (who had asked her to dance). Anne said that when Mark didn't get angry with her after she rejected him, she said that she felt safe with him because she could be herself and he wouldn't get mad at her. She reported that this was the quality about Mark that had attracted her to him. Mark, who had initially reported feeling humiliated by Anne's rejection, responded to Anne's soft disclosure by saying, "I'm kind of surprised by that. I know that is an important feeling for her, but I didn't realize she was feeling that back then." Anne said that she hadn't realized she felt that way either, until describing the incident in the therapy session.

By the end of Session 1, Dr. S had a good understanding of Anne and Mark's history together, the qualities that first attracted each to the other, and some idea of their problem areas. The next two individual sessions helped Dr. S "fill in" any missing information that he needed for their formulation.

Sessions 2a and 2b

Dr. S introduced each of these individual sessions with a brief orientation, followed by an introduction to the ongoing assessment of the couple's problem areas:

> "There are a lot of different topics that we'll be covering today as we go along. . . . I'd like to spend some time clarifying some of the problems both you and [Anne/Mark] have had. In our first meeting, you described some problems that you've perceived about [problem area]. . . . Can you tell me what you meant by that?"

In addition to the problems Anne and Mark raised in their conjoint session, Dr. S used the individual sessions to address problem areas Anne and Mark had indicated on their Frequency and Acceptability of Partner Behavior questionnaires:

> "When I looked over your list of problem areas, the item of most concern to you was [problem area]. Can you describe that to me?"

Dr. S was very specific in his efforts to get Anne and Mark to describe the disagreements and arguments they had with each other. To encourage Mark and Anne to be behaviorally specific in these descriptions, Dr. S used probing questions such as these:

> "Do the two of you have fights about [problem area]? What do those fights look like?"

> "When you are both angry, what do *you* tend to do?"

> "Describe for me your most recent argument. . . . Describe for me the worst argument you've ever had. If I had a video camera there with you, what would I have seen?"

In addition to understanding their conflict patterns, Dr. S also asked how problems were addressed in Anne's and Mark's families while they were growing up ("How did your own parents deal with conflict?"). Such information may be useful in understanding the developmental history that each partner brings with him/her into a conflict, and the patterns they each may risk repeating or trying to avoid (e.g., physical violence).

When eliciting descriptions of Anne and Mark's arguments, Dr. S also assessed whether the couple had ever engaged in physical violence. This assessment is a critical part of every couple therapy evaluation, and is a major rationale for conducting these indi-

vidual interviews. A simple, direct question is useful here, such as this:

> "Have your arguments ever led to pushing, shoving, or any type of physical violence?"

If either partner endorses this question, or has indicated violence on a questionnaire such as the Conflict Tactics Scale, a more thorough assessment of violence should be conducted, and appropriate referrals should be made as indicated (Jacobson & Gottman, 1999). In this case example, violence was not an issue for Anne and Mark.[5]

Finally, the individual sessions provide a good opportunity for the therapist to assess each partner's level of commitment to the relationship. This assessment also includes determining whether one or both partners are engaging in affairs outside the relationship. Affairs require special treatment in IBCT (Jacobson & Christensen, 1996), which is beyond the scope of this chapter. Fortunately, Anne and Mark's relationship was not troubled by affairs. With Anne and Mark, Dr. S asked:

> "On a scale of 1 to 10, how would you rate your level of commitment to [Mark/Anne]?"

By the end of Anne's and Mark's individual assessment sessions, Dr. S had sufficient information about their problem areas, patterns of conflict (including history of violence), relevant family history, and level of commitment to come up with their formulation and proceed with their feedback session.

Feedback and Formulation

Session 3

Dr. S began the feedback session by orienting Anne and Mark to what to expect, and also eliciting from them their participation in giving him feedback about his formulation and description of their problem areas:

> "During this session I'd like to share with you some feedback, like I had mentioned in our first session together. I've spent some time looking over your questionnaires, and we've spent some time talking, which has been very helpful in helping me get a better sense of the two of you. . . . As I go along, I'd really like to emphasize that I'd like your input, your reactions, because that's an

important part of our work together—you both responding, as opposed to me directing . . . interjecting any thoughts you have, as well as adding any information that fits or doesn't fit."

Dr. S began giving Anne and Mark feedback by explaining the information that was gathered from questionnaires they completed:

"With regard to the measures we gave you, these were to give us a sense of where you are as a couple, in terms of the range of couples—from the very happily married to those with 'everyday,' normal distress, to the other end of the spectrum, couples who are very similar to couples who have divorced. Both of you are in the area of couples who are experiencing distress, couples who would like things to be better. . . . You are both distressed, although Anne reported higher levels of distress."

Dr. S moved on to summarize Anne and Mark's level of commitment, which he characterized as a strength for their work in therapy:

"With regard to your commitment, both of you showed commitment to the relationship; that is very important to both of you. And that is very important to couples work—that in spite of everything that has gone on, there is still the commitment. That is very telling—you've both showed that, and you've both expressed that."

Dr. S then moved on to summarizing the content of Anne and Mark's problem areas. Dr. S had distilled their questionnaire data and their in-session descriptions to the following three basic problem areas:

"So let's talk about the areas of your relationship that are troubling. One area is finances; that tends to be an area of dispute. For you, Anne, feeling resentful sometimes, feeling the burden of the responsibility; and for you, Mark, feeling guilty about how things are financially. This area really brings out lots of different feelings, feelings of resentment, feelings of guilt, feelings of burden—not enough feelings of matrimony, togetherness, but feelings of control. Does that sound accurate? . . . Are their any other aspects of finances that the two of you can think of?

"The other area I saw was with regard to children—both the topic of Anne's children, and the children that you won't have. . . . You both feel very differently about the subject of Anne's children. Anne, you feel like Mark is not involved with your children, and Mark, you feel as though you have not been invited. . . . For you, Mark, the experience of being rejected [by the children] is Anne's fault. . . . This is an area that brings out very strong feelings for both of you. Whether it gets expressed directly or not—you may not talk about it, but I definitely got the sense that this is a real pressure cooker for both of you. . . . This is an area that I imagine will come up in different ways, especially with the holidays coming up.

"The third area I saw was around responsiveness. 'How responsive are you to me?' Whether it's being physical ('You're not responsive enough' or 'You're too responsive'), to listening ('Are you listening to me?') . . . whether it's touching, listening, or asking a question—it can carry a message of what you want to be expressed, or a feeling that you are having. . . . So that's part of what we will work on, is expressing those feelings you are having—those may be a surprise for each of you."

Throughout each of his descriptions, Dr. S checked in with Anne and Mark for their feedback about each problem area, and the ways that they might add to his description.

Even during this part of the feedback session, an opportunity for acceptance work presented itself. When Mark discussed his relationship with Anne's children, he was initially making only "hard" disclosures (e.g., describing her children as rude and only able to talk about themselves). As Mark made such critical statements about Anne's children, Dr. S elicited from Mark some softer disclosures about his emotions with regard to Anne's children. (In the dialogues that follow, Dr. S is the therapist, or T; Mark is M; and Anne is A.)

T: Besides them being rude, what is the feeling you are left with when [Anne's children] don't talk to you?

M: The feeling I'm left with is being ignored.

T: Besides being ignored, how did it feel?

M: Like I don't matter; like I am only there to serve them.

T: Like you are not a part of the family.

M: Yeah . . . I think I've just resigned myself to hoping that they'll show their love for their mother.

T: So it upsets you that they don't take an interest in their mother? . . . So it isn't just about *you*; you have some feelings about how Anne's sons interact with *her*?

M: Yeah, yeah, I do.

T: And that upsets you?

M: Yeah, it does. I feel protective . . . I'd like them to show more appreciation to her. But, then, I'd like myself to show more appreciation to her. I don't think I show enough appreciation to her. . . . Maybe they're related . . . it's a reminder of the things *I'm* not doing well.

By moving Mark from criticizing Anne's children to making softer statements about his feelings, Dr. S gave Mark an unexpected opportunity to make important realizations about his own behavior.

After reviewing their problem areas, Dr. S proceeded to describe the two themes he had observed from his assessment of Anne and Mark:

"It seems to me from what you've both described in your individual sessions, your questionnaires, and even today, there are two themes that come up for you. When I say 'theme,' it's like in our sessions, whatever the topic is for the day, there's usually a theme. The theme is something I'll bring up from time to time—and again, it's clearly something that we'll work on together; it may take a different form—so I want to share it with you to make sure that it's on the mark. OK?

"The first theme is that I think you both have feelings of being unloved and unappreciated. You have an idea of what it means to be loved. You have an idea of what it means to be appreciated. But your definitions are different. And because of those different definitions, because of your different experiences, if something does happen, it leaves you feeling unappreciated and unloved. . . . Within the arguments about finances or children, there is something about that—about feeling unappreciated. . . . How does that sound to you? . . .

"The second theme is that you both have your insecurities; you both have feelings of insecurity, for whatever reason. Some of the arguments, the differences, the conflicts, the big fights, come from that also. That feeling comes up, and can create the whole battle. . . . A concrete example is that for you, Anne, you described feeling insecure about yourself in relation to some of your family members. . . . That affects how you feel about yourself in comparison to other women. . . . For you, Mark, you described feeling insecure about the fact that Anne has not annulled her previous marriage. . . . That may affect how confident you feel in comparison to other men. Again, these feelings of insecurity, feeling not loved, unappreciated—these are the themes."

After Dr. S had described each theme, and had gotten feedback from Anne and Mark about these themes, he moved on to discuss their polarization process and mutual trap:

"Now what is what we call the 'trap' that you both get into? You each have different ways of responding to feeling unloved and insecure. The sense that I got was that, Mark, when you start to feel those things, you use distance. . . . The sense I got from you, Anne, is that you become critical. Put the two of you together, and you have a cycle of: The feelings come up, Mark gets distant, and Anne gets critical. Mark feels criticism; he gets distance. Anne experiences the distance; she gets critical. Distance–criticism, criticism–distance. That's what we call the trap. . . . It may be that you take turns being critical and distant, and that each response makes the other person feel even more insecure."

After reviewing the polarization process and mutual trap, Dr. S proceeded to explain to Anne and Mark what they could expect from the upcoming therapy sessions:

"So this is what we're going to do in the upcoming weeks, the kinds of things we've talked about today. We'll talk about whatever is going on for the two of you on a given day. . . . It isn't going to be structured in terms of things we *have* to do each day—it's up to you, whatever you bring in.

"What I hope to do is create in here a place of comfort, enough that you can both take risks in opening up, in sharing—sharing some of your reactions, your questions, your experiences. There is a desire for closeness here that is going to take some sharing and some risk taking. Now there's no guarantee about how the other person is going to react—it may not always be pleasant. But on the other hand, that's the price we have to pay to get there, to open up. . . . You can do some more thinking about this, and from week to week we can reformulate, and we'll keep getting a clearer, better picture."

Having now set the stage with the formulation, including the themes, polarization process, and mutual trap, Dr. S was prepared to begin working on building acceptance.

Treatment: Building Acceptance

Most of Anne and Mark's subsequent sessions were focused on building acceptance. Below are excerpts from a few sessions in which Dr. S helped Anne and Mark increase acceptance by using techniques such as empathic joining, unified detachment, and tolerance building.

Session 12

The content of Session 12 was about Anne and Mark's search for a condominium, and some of the difficulties they were experiencing around this. The discussion included Mark's admission that he felt inadequate and insecure because he did not make enough money for them to afford Anne's dream condo. This led to an opportunity to deepen Anne and Mark's theme of insecurity:

M: If we settle for a condominium that we don't really want, it will forever be a monument to my inability to get the condo she wants.

T: I'm wondering if there's another part that wonders, "Will I ever really be able to give her what she wants?"

M: Yeah. If she married somebody who had a lot of money, she could get whatever condo she wanted.

A: But if you married someone who was gorgeous, who was 20 years younger, you could have a trophy wife, but that's not what happened. (*Both laugh*)

T: So that may be part of your insecurity— if you looked the way that you experience

as "the way he wants things," then maybe he'd be happier.

M: (*To Dr. S*) I think that's how she feels about herself at her worst moments. . . . Like maybe all men are attracted to younger women and that you have to harness yourself in not to lose what's important to you. . . . (*To Anne*) Maybe that's how you look at your desire to have your dream condo—how do you keep from saying, "There's that rich lawyer who looks at me all of the time?" . . . (*To Dr. S*) I think that would be a pretty natural thing for her to think about.

This dialogue also revealed the unified detachment Anne and Mark were developing, when they both laughed at Anne's comment about a "trophy wife." What had previously been a very painful subject for Anne was becoming something they both could joke about. The discussion then moved to exploring Anne's insecurities about Mark's relationships with other women:

T: So what is, in your eyes, Mark's ideal "bill"? You made reference to a "bill" that is his ideal.

A: Well, probably someone younger, someone who is able to have children, someone who plays tennis, who goes running, also cooks and cleans, makes a good living, is very good in bed. . . .

T: (*To Mark*) Because this is comparable to the richer man that you view with Anne. (*To Anne*) For you, it's the woman who . . .

A: But that woman's out there. There's a lot of women like that.

T: And the way that you see and experience Mark talking to women, and at times you kind of wonder to what extent he enjoys it. It's just a matter of time that if you're not willing to live up to it . . .

A: Right, that some other woman is going to be able to step right in there without a problem.

T: When the insecurities come up for both of you—for you, Mark, it's the rich man who could come along and provide what Anne longs for, and for you, Anne, it's that you don't compete physically, with the workout—so for you, it's just a matter of time until a woman comes along and she decides, "I'm going after him." . . . Anne, can you tell me some of the things Mark does that make you feel threatened?

A: . . . When he makes comments about how attractive a woman is, like I'm one of the guys. When he tells me I'm fat, or makes comments like I have a double chin . . .

T: Which then tells you that you're not cuttin' it.

A: Yeah.

Dr. S then brought back the subject of condominium buying, and used this as a metaphor for Anne and Mark's concerns about "settling" for less than what they wanted in making a major commitment:

T: When you make a commitment, whether it's committing to a condo, committing to a relationship—it's settling, you're settling—you're saying, "This is it."

A: That's a good way of looking at it. I hadn't thought of that. That's what we're having trouble with . . . the reality that we're not going to get everything that we want. . . . The insecurity, the scariness of making the purchase, is knowing that we're never going to get what we want. . . .

M: Part of it is our concern that the next condominium we see is going to be the one we want.

A: Right, it's the condo over the next hill.

M: So you have to think about "Is 60% of what we want what we should settle for?" I'm thinking, 60? I was thinking it's more like 90. So I don't know when you're supposed to cut your losses and say, "We have to go for this. This is what reality dictates."

T: And that might be, if we can take it a step further, when you both decided to get married, you both made a settlement. . . . You both start to wonder, "Did the other settle for 60% or 90%? What did I settle for? Did I settle for 60% or 90%?"

M: Yeah.

A: Right.

T: Now let's put yourselves when you're insecure—what's gonna happen? When you're in an insecure place, that 90% might feel like . . .

A: 50%.

T: Exactly. When you're feeling good, you think, "She got 90% of what she wanted in me," or "I got 90%." But when you're in an insecure place, you feel like "I settled for 50%." . . . Then when you look at your own insecurity, you think, "My God, she settled for 35% or 40%." . . . You both made a settlement when you married each other. You decided, "This is it, we're gonna get married," and you settled.

M: But "settled" has such negative connotations.

T: I think there's some feelings associated with that. And a parallel to the word "settlement" is "acceptance."

M: Oh, I see.

T: When you go through the settlement of "This is who this person is." . . . Whether it's 80%, 90%, 60%, 35%—you've settled, you've basically said, "I accept this."

By using condominium buying as a metaphor, Dr. S underscored how Anne and Mark's theme of insecurity fed on itself, and how their theme led both of them to question whether each had "settled" for less than they wanted in the relationship. The additional component of "insecurity about settlement" to the theme helped Anne and Mark understand the things each did that "threatened" the other (e.g., when Mark talked about his attraction to younger women), and also built a bridge toward working on acceptance.

Session 17

In Session 17, Dr. S continued to process the theme of insecurity with Anne and Mark. In this particular part of the dialogue, Anne and Mark were discussing a familiar polarization process when Mark suggested to Anne that she work out more. Anne interpreted Mark's suggestion as a criticism about her appearance, which made her feel insecure and threatened. Anne then "fought back" against Mark's suggestions by becoming depressed and "doing nothing"—which in turn made Mark more critical of her.

Here Dr. S used two IBCT acceptance-building techniques. The first of these was empathic joining. As Dr. S tried to "get to the bottom of" Mark's suggestions/criticisms of Anne's appearance, Mark made the following soft disclosure about his own insecurities:

T: This is a real, central question. There are some basic limits that you have, where you say, "Up to here, I accept you, but beyond that you'd better change." On the other hand, this is who you are. This is who you are. But the irony of it is, that once we accept, change can come about. But there's that push to determine within ourselves, not only about the other person, but also about your own limits. I get the sense that you're both exploring about yourselves your own limits.

A: Perhaps, yes.

T: You're both looking at your own limits. With you, Anne, it's around your looks, your appearance, and for you, Mark, it's about you as a financial provider. And the temptation is when that gets uncomfortable, that's where your partner comes in. Kind of to redirect your focus from that—versus being able to talk about how you're feeling.

A: Yeah.

M: Yeah, I think I've noticed, since we've started therapy, that's what I do. When I get insecure about myself, I start looking outwards . . . saying, "You should do this," and that makes me feel better.

T: Right, it's active, it can be advice giving—it's can be a real male thing, "Do this, do that."

M: Right. I do that with her kids too, I know I do.

Instead of focusing on the critical nature of Mark's suggestions, Dr. S placed an emphasis on *why* Mark became critical. Mark was encouraged to consider the *reasons* for his behavior, and as a result he disclosed that he became critical when he himself was feeling insecure. Mark recognized this happened not only with regard to his attempts to direct Anne's behavior, but also in his interactions with Anne's children.

The second acceptance-building technique Dr. S used in this portion of the session was a tolerance intervention: emphasizing the positive aspects of a partner's negative behavior. Dr. S continued:

T: In some situations it might work really well [to give advice]. People might like that—like in your work as a counselor, Mark. You feel really productive.

M: Yeah, I change people's lives. I know I do.

T: On the other hand, there might be some circumstances where it's being experienced as being critical—and I think of this is in terms of the two of you—it feeds into Anne's feeling criticized.

A: Yes.

T: And then it feels threatening, like, "If you don't do something about it, then . . ."

Here Dr. S positively reemphasized Mark's suggestions to Anne as his attempts to give her guidance or advice. Mark, who was employed as a counselor, was used to giving such suggestions to others as way of being constructive or helpful. Dr. S underscored this aspect of Mark's behavior—that this same "counselor" quality was what made Mark very good at what he did in his career. However, Dr. S did not try to *completely* reframe Mark's behavior as positive; Dr. S also underscored how Mark's "advice" was experienced by Anne and critical and threatening.

At the end of the session, Dr. S recharacterized Anne and Mark's polarization process in terms of the information that had emerged from these two interventions:

T: I think you put it really well, Mark. When you start to feel uncomfortable, this is your process; this is what you do. You start to look outside yourself. From your end, it might be like you're being a counselor when you start with Anne. You want to advise. But from her end, it might be like you're being authoritarian, the drill sergeant, rather than the counselor. . . . And you, Anne, you start to feel you're berated. You start to feel worse about yourself.

A: Yeah.

T: So either you feel like you've gotta take it, or you've gotta fight back.

M: I think I can . . . the fighting back is . . . well, I can understand that. I really can.

Session 24

In their final session, Anne described a recent insight she had about feeling "undeserving" of happiness and her belief that happiness always came at a cost of some kind. She said that happiness made her feel guilty because she felt that someone else must be suffering for her happiness, or that somehow she would suffer negative repercussions for being happy. Anne connected some of these feelings to her bout with an eating disorder as a teenager, and to the depressive episodes she sometimes experienced.

In the dialogue below, Dr. S used several IBCT techniques to discuss Anne's insights and the way that her feelings contributed to the couple's polarization process. First, Dr. S used empathic joining to help Mark understand the experience Anne was having when she got depressed (a time when Mark usually made suggestions about how Anne "should" think, feel, or behave). Then Dr. S detached Anne and Mark from their problem that Anne felt criticized whenever Mark made these suggestions. Rather than engaging Anne and Mark in their emotional responses to each other's behavior, Dr. S framed this problem as a consequence of basic communication difficulties. By describing their problem in terms of their methods of communication, Dr. S detached Anne and Mark from the problem itself, and provided each with a new way of reacting to an old problem (without doing any formal communication training).

T: I think the idea around the conflict over happiness—having the happiness—is like savoring a good meal, and that it will cost you: "OK, so it has some high fat, but I'm going to enjoy it because I deserve this, I deserve this moment—the same way that I deserve this moment of happiness. Even if so-and-so doesn't have it together, I deserve this happiness." And that's going to be the struggle, to be able to react to Mark in a way which expresses, "God, I'm really feeling guilty."

A: When I'm on the couch, and I'm totally immobile in my depression, that's a lot of what's going on. I'm beating myself up.

T: And so for Mark, he needs to listen—to just *listen* and say, "Gee, that must be really hard." Now there may be a pull, Mark, to problem-solve—to say, "Well,

you shouldn't feel that way," or "So-and-so is that way because . . ."—but that will only pull out the self-critical part and could become argumentative. . . . When you sense the pain, Mark, and what it's costing Anne, the reaction that you have is "Let me show you what to do." But that is only going to bring out in Anne the feeling of "You see, you idiot, you're not doing it right." Which will then feed into the self-criticism. . . . So it's going to help to just listen, and to simply paraphrase, and she will hear that it's not reasonable. If you just say, rather than criticizing, just say, "Gee, you really don't feel worthy of these things"—just paraphrase those themes of her insecurity, her self-criticalness—that is kind of maintaining a connection.

Finally, Dr. S used tolerance interventions to allow Anne and Mark to see their problem as a difference in their communication styles. As he continued to describe their problem in terms of communication difficulties, Dr. S described Anne as responding to situations based on how she *felt*, while Mark was more likely to use logic or *reason* to determine his responses to situations. Dr. S also pointed out how Anne and Mark's problem was often a result of this difference, and noted that these differences actually complement one another.

T: (*To Mark*) . . . And that's what I want to encourage—maybe a new way of responding. Rather than using *reason* when you start to feel like Anne's feelings don't make sense—rather than saying, "This doesn't make sense"—saying instead, "What I'm hearing you say is that you don't deserve this," whatever it is. And what I'm expecting, Anne, is that to hear Mark express that he understands you, that would make you feel close to him.

A: Yeah, and it would definitely not be the wedge of "You should." (*Mark laughs*)

T: Anne talks about things from the emotional experience, and Mark talks about things from the rational experience, and both are needed, both are important.

This section of the dialogue also revealed how the partners had developed unified detachment from their problem. Anne used the phrase "the wedge of 'You should'" to describe what had previously been the "hot topic" of feeling criticized by Mark, and Mark was able to laugh about his own behavior.

CONCLUSION

Although a single case study is useful for illustrative purposes, it obviously does not establish generalizable conclusions about treatment outcome. However, the pilot data, which we have described previously, gives some promising results for the efficacy of IBCT. A major clinical trial (in which Anne and Mark are participating) is currently underway. This study will provide more definitive information about the impact of acceptance interventions in the treatment of couple distress.

It is our hope that IBCT will provide long-term relief for even the most distressed couples. Applied alone, or in conjunction with other interventions (e.g., TBCT techniques), the acceptance-based approach of IBCT provides couple therapists with a new set of techniques for approaching couples' long-standing conflicts and otherwise "irreconcilable" differences.

NOTE

1. The term "couple therapy" is intended to be a more inclusive term than "marital therapy," in that it can include gay, lesbian, and heterosexual relationships regardless of their marital status.

2. For a detailed description of TBCT theory and techniques, the reader is referred to the manual by Jacobson and Margolin (1979).

3. Identifying information has been changed to protect confidentiality, but clinical dynamics are accurately portrayed, and quotations are taken directly from tapes of the therapy sessions.

4. Not included here are case examples of the application of TBCT interventions, which can be found elsewhere (e.g., Cordova & Jacobson, 1993; Jacobson & Margolin, 1979).

5. In our project, we assess for violence using the Conflict Tactics Scale II (CTS) and exclude any couple where the wife reports moderate to severe violence from the husband. We exclude the couple prior to their seeing one of our project therapists, and we refer the couple to appropriate individual treatment for violence. Dr. S could proceed with the knowledge that the wife had not endorsed this kind of violence from her husband on the CTS (although she could still do so in the individual session). In a clinical setting, we recommend that practitioners give the CTS to all clients and follow up with individual sessions where they focus specifically on violent items that an individual has endorsed as committing or receiving on the CTS. Based on these interviews, the practitioner should refer as appropriate (Jacobson & Gottman, 1999).

REFERENCES

Baucom, D. H., & Hoffman, J. A. (1986). The effectiveness of marital therapy: Current status and application to the clinical setting. In N. S. Jacobson & A. S. Gurman (Eds.), *Clinical handbook of marital therapy* (pp. 597–620). New York: Guilford Press.

Baucom, D. H., & Epstein, N. (1990). *Cognitive behavioral marital therapy*. New York: Brunner/Mazel.

Baucom, D. H., Epstein, N., & Rankin, L. A. (1995). Cognitive aspects of cognitive behavioral marital therapy. In N. S. Jacobson & A. S. Gurman (Eds.), *Clinical handbook of couple therapy* (pp. 65–90). New York: Guilford Press.

Baucom, D. H., Shoham, V. M., Kim, T., Daiuto, A. D., & Stickle, T. R. (1998). Empirically supported couple and family interventions for marital distress and adult mental health problems. *Journal of Consulting and Clinical Psychology, 66*(1), 53–88.

Christensen, A., & Heavey, C. L. (1999). Interventions for couples. *Annual Review of Psychology, 50,* 165–190.

Christensen, A., & Jacobson, N. S. (2000). *Reconcilable differences*. New York: Guilford Press.

Christensen, A., Jacobson, N. S., & Babcock, J. C. (1995). Integrative behavioral couple therapy. In N. S. Jacobson & A. S. Gurman (Eds.), *Clinical handbook of couple therapy* (pp. 31–64). New York: Guilford Press.

Cordova, J., & Jacobson, N. S. (1993). Couple Distress. In D. Barlow (Ed.), *Clinical handbook of psychological disorders* (2nd ed., pp. 481–512). New York: Guilford Press.

Floyd, J. F., & Markman, H. J. (1983). Observational biases in spouse observation: Toward a cognitive/behavioral model of marriage. *Journal of Consulting and Clinical Psychology, 51,* 450–457.

Floyd, F. J., Markman, H. J., Kelly, S., Blumberg, S. L., & Stanley, S. M. (1995). Preventive intervention and relationship enhancement. In N. S. Jacobson & A. S. Gurman (Eds.), *Clinical handbook of couple therapy* (pp. 212–230). New York: Guilford Press.

Gottman, J., Notarius, C., Gonso, J., & Markman, H. (1976). *A couple's guide to communication*. Champaign, IL: Research Press.

Gurman, A. S., Knickerson, D. P., & Pinsoff, W. M. (1986). Research on the process and outcome of marital and family therapy. In S. L. Garfield & A. E. Bergin (Eds.), *Handbook of psychotherapy and behavior change* (3rd ed., pp. 565–624). New York: Wiley.

Hahlweg, K., Schindler, L., Revenstorf, D., & Brengelmann, J. C. (1984). The Munich marital therapy study. In K. Hahlweg & N. S. Jacobson (Eds.), *Marital interaction: Analysis and modification* (pp. 3–26). New York: Guilford Press.

Holtzworth-Munroe, A. S., Beatty, S. B., & Anglin, K. (1995). The assessment and treatment of marital violence: An introduction for the marital therapist. In N. S. Jacobson & A. S. Gurman (Eds.), *Clinical handbook of couple therapy* (pp. 317–339). New York: Guilford Press.

Holtzworth-Munroe, A. S., & Jacobson, N. S. (1991). Behavioral marital therapy. In A. S. Gurman & D. P. Knickerson (Eds.), *Handbook of family therapy* (2nd ed., pp. 96–133). New York: Brunner/Mazel.

Jacobson, N. S. (1977). Problem solving and contingency contracting in the treatment of marital discord. *Journal of Consulting and Clinical Psychology, 45,* 92–100.

Jacobson, N. S. (1978a). A review of the research on the effectiveness of marital therapy. In T. J. Paolino & B. S. McGrady (Eds.), *Marriage and marital therapy: Psychoanalytic, behavioral, and systems theory perspectives* (pp. 395–444). New York: Brunner/Mazel.

Jacobson, N. S. (1978b). Specific and nonspecific factors in the effectiveness of a behavioral approach to the treatment of marital discord. *Journal of Consulting and Clinical Psychology, 46,* 442–452.

Jacobson, N. S. (1984). A component analysis of behavioral marital therapy: The relative effectiveness of behavior exchange and problem solving training. *Journal of Consulting and Clinical Psychology, 52,* 295–305.

Jacobson, N. S., & Addis, M. E. (1993). Research on couple therapy: What do we know? Where are we going? *Journal of Consulting and Clinical Psychology, 61,* 85–93.

Jacobson, N. S., & Anderson, E. A. (1980). The effects of behavioural rehearsal and feedback on the acquisition of problem solving skills in distressed and nondistressed couples. *Behaviour Research and Therapy, 18,* 25–36.

Jacobson, N. S., & Christensen, A. (1996). *Integrative couple therapy: Promoting acceptance and change.* New York: Norton.

Jacobson, N. S., Christensen, A., Prince, S. E., Cordova, J., & Eldridge, K. (2000). Integrative behavioral couple therapy: An acceptance-based, promising new treatment for couple discord. *Journal of Consulting and Clinical Psychology, 68*(2), 351–355.

Jacobson, N. S., Follette, W. C., & Pagel, M. (1986). Predicting who will benefit from behavioral marital therapy. *Journal of Consulting and Clinical Psychology, 54,* 518–522.

Jacobson, N. S., Follette, W. C., Revenstorf, D., Baucom, D. H., Hahlweg, K., & Margolin, G. (1984). Variability in outcome and clinical significance of behavior marital therapy: A reanalysis of outcome data. *Journal of Consulting and Clinical Psychology, 52,* 497–564.

Jacobson, N. S., & Gottman, J. (1998). *When men batter women: New insights into ending abusive relationships.* New York: Simon & Schuster.

Jacobson, N. S., & Holtzworth-Munroe, A. (1986). Marital therapy: A social learning/cognitive perspective. In N. S. Jacobson & A. S. Gurman (Eds.), *Clinical handbook of marital therapy* (pp. 29–70). New York: Guilford Press.

Jacobson, N. S., & Margolin, G. (1979). *Marital therapy: Strategies based on social learning and behavior exchange principles.* New York: Brunner/Mazel.

Jacobson, N. S., Schmaling, K. B., & Holtzworth-Munroe, A. (1987). Component analysis of behavioral marital therapy: Two-year follow-up and prediction of relapse. *Journal of Marital and Family Therapy, 13,* 187–195.

Knox, D. (1971). *Marital happiness: A behavioral approach to counseling.* Champaign, IL: Research Press.

Liberman, R. P. (1970). Behavioral approaches to family and couple therapy. *American Journal of Orthopsychiatry, 40,* 106–118.

Liberman, R. P., Wheeler, E. G., deVisser, L. A., Kuehnel, J., & Kuehnel, T. (1981). *Handbook of marital therapy: A positive approach to helping troubled relationships.* New York: Plenum Press.

Snyder, D. K. (1997). *Marital Satisfaction Inventory—Revised.* Los Angeles: Western Psychological Services.

Spanier, G. B. (1976). Measuring dyadic adjustment: New scales for assessing the quality of marriage and similar dyads. *Journal of Marriage and the Family, 38,* 15–28.

Straus, M. A. (1979). Measuring intrafamily conflict and violence: The Conflict Tactics (CT) Scales. *Journal of Marriage and the Family, 41,* 75–88.

Stuart, R. B. (1969). Operant interpersonal treatment for marital discord. *Journal of Consulting and Clinical Psychology, 33,* 675–682.

Stuart, R. B. (1980). *Helping couples change: A social learning approach to marital therapy.* New York: Guilford Press.

Weiss, R. L., Hops, H., & Patterson, G. R. (1973). A framework for conceptualizing marital conflict, technology for altering it, some data for evaluating it. In L. A. Hamerlynck, L. C. Handy, & E. J. Mash (Eds.), *Behavior change: Methodology, concepts, and practice* (pp. 309–342). Champaign, IL: Research Press.

AUTHOR INDEX

Abbott, D. W., 334
Abel, G. G., 63
Abel, J. L., 156, 164
Abram, H. S., 396
Abramowitz, 222, 233
Abramowitz, J. S., 211, 218, 220, 225, 229, 233
Abrams, D., 398, 408, 410, 457, 465
Abrams, J., 74
Ackerman, L., 534
Addy, C. L., 211
Adler, G., 472
Ager, R. D., 386
Agosti, V., 269
Agras, W. S., 2, 7, 9, 10, 17, 25, 333, 336, 337, 338, 339, 340, 346, 368, 369, 371
Ahern, C. E., 68
Ahmad, S., 123
Akiskal, H., 210, 525, 527, 536
Akiskal, K., 536
Alarcon, R., 71
Alazraki, A., 528
Albanese, M., 476
Alborzian, S., 311
Alden, L. E., 120, 131
Allain, A. N., 66
Allen, B. A., 390, 415
Allen, J. J., 226
Allen, R., 159
Allmon, D., 472, 477, 478
Alnaes, R., 4
Alpert, J. E., 267
Alterman, A., 435
Alterman, I. S., 216, 217
Altman, B., 68, 74
Altshuler, L. L., 534
Alvarez, W., 67
Amass, L., 452, 466
American Psychiatric Association (1980), 4, 60, 114, 154, 525
American Psychiatric Association (1987), 60, 115, 154, 210, 304n, 312, 502
American Psychiatric Association (1993), 268, 311
American Psychiatric Association (1994), 2, 60, 114, 115, 116, 155, 209, 304n, 332, 335, 342, 379, 436, 471, 524, 534

American Psychiatric Association (1998), 14
American Psychiatric Association (2000), 340
American Psychological Association (1995), 311
American Society of Addiction Medicine, 392
Amering, M., 7
Ames-Frankel, J., 368, 369
Amick, A. E., 69, 70
Amies, P., 118, 119
Amin, M., 14
Amir, N., 121, 210, 215
Anastasiades, P., 6, 21, 22
Anderson, B., 70, 529
Anderson, D. J., 7, 156, 157
Anderson, K. W., 119
Andreasen, N. C., 534
Andreski, P., 75
Andrews, G., 217
Andrews, G., 21, 159
Andrews, V. H., 165
Angus, L., 314
Annable, L., 13
Annis, H. M., 391
Anstee, J. A., 7
Anstey, K. J., 274
Anthony, J., 3
Anthony, W., 527
Anton, M. M., 11, 28
Anton, R. F., 384
Anton, S. F., 457
Antonuccio, D. O., 268, 269
Antony, M., 7, 120, 156, 158, 168, 169, 174
Appelbaum, A., 472
Appleton, C., 269
Apter, A., 216
Arata, C., 68
Argeriou, M., 390
Armstrong, H. E., 472, 477, 478
Armstrong, M. S., 74
Arnkoff, D. B., 119
Arnow, B. A., 9, 10, 333, 337, 338, 346
Arntz, A., 11, 21, 27
Aro, H. M., 471
Arrindell, W., 9
Asberg, M., 223, 233
Asmundson, G. J. G., 121

Astin, M. C., 61, 65, 73
Atala, K. D., 213
Atkinson, J. S., 434
Au, S. C., 311
Aublet, F., 215
August, D. S., 435
Austin, V., 471
Averill, P. M., 21, 22
Axelrod, R., 63
Ayoiub, L. M., 217
Azrin, N., 19, 398, 435, 444, 447, 450, 451, 452

Babor, T. F., 409, 415
Badger, G. J., 438, 452, 456, 457
Baer, L., 213, 241
Baischer, W., 7
Baker, G., 530
Bakish, D., 14
Bakker, A., 14
Baldessarini, R. J., 530
Baldwin, L. E., 21, 22
Ball, S. A., 435, 457
Ballenger, J. C., 156, 167
Ballentine, H. T., 217
Baltzell, D., 71
Bamford, C. R., 273, 274
Bandelow, B., 23
Bandura, A., 22
Banon, E., 472
Barber, J. P., 269
Barlow, D. H., 1, 2, 3, 4, 5, 6, 7, 8, 9, 10, 11, 12,
    13, 15, 16, 17, 18, 19, 22, 23, 25, 26, 27, 28,
    32, 115, 127, 128, 154, 155, 156, 157, 158,
    159, 160, 161, 162, 164, 165, 166, 167, 168,
    169, 170, 173, 174, 176, 180, 183, 184, 265,
    338
Barr, H. L., 441, 457
Barrett, P. M., 162
Barry, C., 313
Barsky, A. J., 2
Bartko, J., 119, 538
Bartle, S., 471
Bartlett, T. S., 273
Bartmann, U., 23
Basco, M. R., 274
Basoglu, M., 12, 13, 27, 210, 211, 219, 220, 223,
    226, 229
Basten, C., 340
Bastian, L. A., 478
Bateman, A., 472, 473
Bavly, L., 379
Baxter, L. R., 217, 311, 528
Beach, B. K., 268, 274
Beach, S. R. H., 274
Beattie, M., 392
Beazley, M. B., 131
Beck, A. T., 18, 128, 132, 158, 162, 163, 166,
    167, 176, 214, 220, 221, 265, 267, 270, 274,
    296, 299, 310, 346, 440, 477, 499
Beck, J., 158, 167
Beck, J. G., 21, 22, 23, 157, 158
Beck, J. S., 132, 133, 265
Becker, E., 117
Becker, J. V., 63

Becker, L. A., 74
Becker, R. E., 116, 119, 124, 130, 131, 149
Beckham, E., 267, 274
Beens, H., 221, 226
Beer, D. A., 213
Beglin, S. J., 344
Behar, D., 217
Beidel, D. C., 115, 116, 118, 128, 131, 168
Beigel, A., 525
Bellack, A. S., 116, 128
Belluardo, P., 267, 268
Benefield, R. G., 382, 413
Benjamin, L. S., 473
Bent, H., 370
Berg, C. J., 217
Berger, P., 7, 120
Berglund, M., 401
Bergman, K. S., 528
Berman, J. S., 266, 269
Bernat, J. A., 76
Bernstein, D., 19, 183
Berry, N. J., 68
Berry, S., 317
Besalel, V. A., 450
Best, C. L., 62, 63, 67, 76
Beumont, P. J. V., 338, 340
Beutler, L. E., 273, 274
Bickel, W. K., 435, 452, 456, 457
Bigelow, G. E., 442
Biggs, M. M., 266
Billings, A., 380
Binkoff, J. A., 408
Biondi, F., 5
Birchler, G. R., 457
Birnbaumer, R., 6
Bishop, G. K., 478
Bishop, M., 266
Bishop, S., 265
Bjork, E. L., 24
Bjork, R. A., 24
Black, D. W., 4, 28
Black, S., 343
Blackburn, I. M., 265, 266, 267, 269
Blake, D. D., 66, 67
Blanchard, E., 2, 4, 22, 68, 157, 158, 161, 184
Bland, K., 9
Blane, H. T., 396
Blank, A. S., 61
Blazer, D. G., 117, 130, 157, 158, 312
Blendell, K. A., 119
Blizard, R., 13
Bllehar, M. C., 312
Blowers, C., 161, 162
Blumenthal, S. J., 312
Bogert, K., 210, 215
Bohn, P., 6, 14
Boiago, I., 476
Boland, R. J., 264, 265, 267
Boles, S., 457
Bolton, D., 217
Bond, C. F., Jr., 121
Bond, N. W., 58
Bonn, J. A., 22
Boone, M. L., 116, 128, 131

Booth, R. G., 161, 162, 163
Borden, J. W., 241
Borkovec, T., 19, 25, 155, 156, 159, 160, 161, 162, 163, 164, 165, 166, 168, 169, 174, 180, 183, 184
Botkin, A., 74
Bouchard, S., 21, 27
Bouckoms, H. A., 217
Boudewyns, P. A., 74
Boulougouris, J. C., 214, 219, 240
Bouman, T. K., 7
Bourne, M. L., 526, 527, 533
Bousono, M., 317
Bouton, M., 4, 5, 6, 12, 26
Bouvard, M., 224
Bowen, G. R., 70
Bowers, W., 4, 28, 266, 267
Bowler, K., 274
Boyce, P., 525
Boyd, J., 3, 4, 533, 534, 543
Boyer, R., 471
Brandt, H. A., 333
Brasfield, T., 451
Brawman-Mintzer, O., 156, 167
Breier, A., 3
Brent, D. A., 471
Breslau, N., 75, 155
Breslin, F. C., 392
Breuer, P., 5
Brewin, C. R., 12, 64, 65, 529
Bricker, D. C., 300
Bridge, J., 471
Briere, J., 68
Bright, J., 530
Bright, P., 6, 18
Brill, P., 381
Brilman, E., 21
Brockington, I. F., 526
Brodaty, H., 274, 525
Brody, A. L., 311
Brom, D., 70
Bromet, E., 62, 67
Bronson, S. S., 3
Broocks, A., 23
Brooner, R. K., 457
Brouillard, M., 7
Brown, E. J., 115, 116, 117, 128, 130, 137, 145, 146
Brown, G., 18, 265, 268, 298, 323
Brown, S. A., 405
Brown, T. A., 1, 2, 5, 11, 15, 16, 19, 23, 26, 28, 127, 128, 155, 156, 157, 158, 159, 161, 162, 164, 165, 166, 167, 168, 169, 170, 173, 174, 176, 183, 184
Bruce, B., 337, 338
Bruch, M. A., 117, 119, 120, 136
Brunner, E., 337
Bryer, J. B., 481
Buchan, G., 392
Buckley, T. C., 68
Budde, D., 457
Budney, A. J., 435, 448, 456, 457
Buergner, F., 131
Buglass, P., 9

Buist, A., 312
Bulik, C. M., 335
Burgess, P., 61
Burke, J., 3, 415
Burnam, A., 211
Burnham, M. A., 317
Burns, D. D., 274
Burstein, E., 472
Burt, M. R., 75
Burton, J., 338
Butler, G., 118, 119, 157, 160, 161, 162, 163
Butow, P., 338, 340
Butterfield, M. I., 478
Butters, J. W., 370
Butzlaff, R. L., 529
Bux, D. A., 225
Byck, R., 434, 435
Bystritsky, A., 6, 14, 28

Cacciola, J., 441, 457
Caddell, J. M., 63, 67
Calabrese, J. R., 524
Calcedo, A., 317
Caldwell, E., 457
Calhoun, K. S., 76
Cameron, O. G., 7, 157
Camilleri, A. J., 61
Campbell, L. A., 166
Campbell, C. D., 120
Campeas, R., 115, 117, 119, 128, 136, 137
Canestrari, R., 267
Canter, S., 117
Caputo, G., 6, 18, 117, 173
Carey, K., 401, 428
Carey, R., 241
Carlson, J., 63, 74
Carmi, M., 216
Carpenter, D., 525, 531
Carpenter, W. T., 527
Carr, A. C., 472
Carr, A. T., 214
Carr, J., 457
Carr, S. J., 338
Carrasco, J. L., 317
Carroll, K., 328, 435, 441, 457
Carson, R., 6
Carter, J. C., 341, 369
Carter, L. E., 116, 128, 131
Carter, M. M., 6
Carter, S., 529
Cash, T. F., 370
Castonguay, L. G., 269
Cerny, J. A., 2, 8, 9, 10, 22, 23, 183
Chafetz, M. E., 396
Chambers, A., 184
Chambless, D. L., 4, 5, 6, 9, 10, 11, 18, 24, 116, 117, 125, 129, 131, 173, 216, 219
Chaney, E. F., 407
Chaplin, E. W., 23
Chapman, T. F., 116
Chaput, Y., 8
Charney, D. S., 3, 66, 67, 217, 225
Chartier, M. J., 116
Chaudhry, D. R., 3

Chauncey, D. L., 471
Chemtob, C., 63, 74
Chen, C. L., 531
Chen, E., 6, 340
Cherney, J., 117, 173
Cheslow, D., 211, 217
Chevron, E. S., 309, 321, 326, 338, 531
Chittenden, E. H., 212
Choquette, K. A., 411
Chorpita, B. F., 156, 158, 159, 160, 164, 167, 169
Chouinard, G., 13, 223
Christiansen, B. A., 405
Christiansen, J., 4
Chronholm, B., 223, 233
Ciadella, P., 224
Cichon, J., 63
Cimbolic, P., 119
Ciudad, J., 317
Claiborn, J. M., 68
Clancy, J., 7, 156, 157
Clark, D. A., 160
Clark, D. B., 6
Clark, D. M., 4, 6, 7, 21, 22, 29, 120, 121, 123, 131
Clark, E., 396
Clark, G. N., 274
Clark, L. A., 159
Clarke, J., 9, 118, 127, 128
Clarkin, J. F., 470, 473, 525, 531, 545
Clarkson, C., 157
Clayton, P. J., 534
Cleary, P. D., 2
Cloitre, M., 10, 76, 117, 119, 136
Clougherty, K. F., 312
Clum, G. A., 8
Cobb, J., 161, 162, 217, 223
Coccaro, E. F., 476
Cochran, S. D., 530
Cohen, A., 4, 159, 161, 184
Cohen, D., 219, 220, 223, 226
Cohen, D. J., 212, 213
Cohen, J., 310
Cohen, L. R., 337
Cohen, M., 530
Cohen, R. A., 530
Cohen, S., 9,10
Cohn, L. G., 118
Cole, K., 526
Coles, M. E., 118, 121, 123, 149
Colket, J. T., 130
Collins, J. F., 266, 267, 274, 310
Collins, T. M., 120
Colom, F., 274
Combs-Orme, T., 401, 428
Comtois, K. A., 478
Cone, E. J., 457
Connelly, J., 226, 471
Constans, J. I., 216
Conti, S., 267, 268
Conway, M., 269
Cook, B. L., 156, 157
Cooley, M. R., 128, 131
Cooney, N. L., 398, 465
Cooper, P. J., 342, 343

Cooper, T., 390, 399, 415
Cooper, Z., 333
Copeland, J. R., 323
Corbett, C. C., 340
Corbishley, A., 273, 274
Cormier, H. J., 8, 11, 28
Corn, K. J., 3
Cornelius, J. R., 476
Cornes, C., 313, 314, 315, 328, 329, 529
Cornish, J. W., 435
Coryell, W., 524, 526, 527, 534
Costello, E., 161, 162, 163, 164, 166
Cote, G., 8, 11, 28
Cottraux, J., 224, 266, 267
Cottrol, C., 75
Covi, W., 74
Cowdry, R., 470, 476, 534
Cowen, P. J., 334, 335
Cox, B. J., 5, 7, 8, 128, 130
Cox, C., 217
Cox, G. B., 381
Coyne, L., 472
Craft, J. C., 478
Craighead, W. E., 274, 369, 530
Craske, M. G., 1, 2, 3, 5, 6, 7, 8, 9, 10, 17, 18, 19, 22, 23, 24, 25, 28, 32, 155, 160, 164, 168, 176, 180, 183, 184, 338
Crawford, M. M., 156,167
Creamer, M., 61
Crews, W. D., Jr., 269
Crino, R., 217
Cronkite, R., 429
Crosby, R. D., 334
Croughan, J., 67, 525
Crow, S. J., 334, 368, 369
Crowe, R. R., 3, 157
Cucherat, M., 266, 267
Cuffe, S. P., 211
Cullington, A., 118, 119, 161, 162
Cuneo, P., 3, 4, 7
Cunningham, J. A., 382, 392
Curtis, G. C., 7, 157
Cutbertson, B., 529
Cutler, D., 158
Cutter, H. S. G., 398, 411

Dadds, M. R., 162
Dalgleish, T., 64, 65, 121
Daly, J. A., 121
Dancu, C., 67, 70, 71, 115
Daniel, F., 317
Daniels, B., 8
Daniels, M., 317
Dansky, B. S., 62, 67
Dantendorfer, K., 7
Danton, W. G., 268, 269
Dantona, R. L., 438, 456
Daston, S., 343
Davidson, J., 61, 117, 130
Davies, B. A., 334, 335, 371
Davies, R., 470
Davies, S., 6, 120
Davis, G. C., 75, 155
Davis, K. L., 481

Davis, R., 337, 338, 342, 369
Davison, G. C., 450
Davison, M. R., 270
de Beurs, E., 13, 22, 27
de Haan, E., 211, 220, 222, 232
de Jong, J., 68
de Jong, M. G., 7
de Jong-Meyer, R., 266, 269
De la Gandara, J., 317
de Oliveira, I. R., 265, 269
de Ruiter, C., 22, 27
De Veaugh-Geiss, J., 130
de Zwaan, M., 334
Deagle, E. A., 21, 22
Deale, A., 218, 219
DeAraujo, L. A., 218, 219
DeCola, J., 6
Defares, P. B., 70
Del Bene, D., 115, 128, 137
Delaney, D. D., 456
Delaney, H. D., 382
Delgado, P., 225
Demane, N., 531
Denckla, M., 217
DeNelsky, G. Y., 268, 269
Dennerstein, L., 312
Dennis, A., 368
Denny, N., 66
dePolomandy-Morin, K., 215
DePree, J. A., 156
Depression Guideline Panel, 268, 311
Derecho, J., 317
Derogatis, L. R., 68, 440
DeRubeis, R. J., 266, 267, 268, 269
deRuiter, C., 27
DeSilva, P., 25, 160, 219
Detweiler, M. F., 12
Detzer, M. J., 337
Devins, G. M., 120
Devlin, M. J., 334, 335, 337, 338, 340, 346, 368, 369, 370
Dewey, D., 9
Dewick, H., 160
Diamond, J., 335
Diamond, S., 380
DiBartolo, P. M., 164
DiClemente, C. C., 382, 399
diDonato, N., 382, 428
Diguer, L., 266
DiMascio, A., 310, 314
Dimeff, L. A., 472, 476, 478
DiNardo, P., 2, 4, 15, 16, 115, 127, 154, 157, 161, 165, 166, 167, 168, 169, 170
Dingemanns, P., 529
Dion, G., 527
Direnfeld, D. M., 128, 130
Doane, J. A., 532, 538
Dobbins, K., 22
Dobson, K. S., 265, 269
Docherty, J. P., 266, 274, 310
Dodge, C. S., 116, 119, 130
Dohn, D., 5
Dolan, R. T., 267
Doll, H. A., 333, 334, 335, 337, 338, 371

Dollard, J., 214
Dombeck, M. J., 6, 121
Dominguez, R. A., 223
Donham, R., 456, 457
Donnelly, L. F., 216, 217
Donovan, S., 269
Dop, M. F., 21
Doppelt, H. C., 226, 232
Doughe, R., 224
Dounchis, J. Z., 333
Dreessen, L., 11
Droba, M., 435
Dubbert, B. K., 333
DuBoff, E., 223
DuBois, D. L., 274
Duda, K., 529
Dugger, D., 226
Dunbar, G., 14
Dunn, J., 270
Dupuis, G., 11
Durrant, J. D., 6

Eagle, M., 337, 338, 342, 369
East, M. P., 160
Eaton, W. W., 5, 115, 116, 117, 157, 158
Eaves, L. J., 159
Ebrahimi, S., 184
Eckert, E. D., 335, 336, 337, 338
Eckman, T. A., 457
Edmunds, C. N., 66
Edwards, G., 379
Egert, S., 391, 410, 416
Eggeraat, J. B., 21
Ehlers, A., 2, 4, 5, 6, 7, 17
Ehlers, C. L., 529
Eifert, G. H., 268, 274
Eisen, J. L., 211, 212, 213
Eisler, R. M., 407
Eldredge, K., 333
Elkin, I., 266, 267, 268, 269, 274, 310
Ellis, A., 221, 499
Elting, D. T., 137
Emery, G., 128, 132, 162, 163, 166, 176, 265, 270, 499
Emmanuel, N., 156, 167
Emmelkamp, P., 9, 21, 23, 25, 118, 211, 219, 220, 221, 226, 232
Emrick, C., 397
Endicott, J., 15, 168, 310, 379, 524, 526, 527, 534
Endler, N. S., 7
Engel, R. R., 337
Engle, M., 457
Epstein, E. E., 398, 399, 411, 428
Epstein-Kaye, T., 3, 4, 7
Epstein, N., 18
Erbaugh, J., 220, 310, 440
Erwin, B. A., 117, 118, 125, 126
Esch, R. A., 452
Eshkeman, S., 3
Eshleman, S., 115, 116
Espie, C. A., 161
Evans, D. L., 226
Evans, F., 441, 457

Evans, L., 8, 28
Evans, M. D., 266, 267, 268, 269

Faedda, G. L., 534
Fairbank, J. A., 61, 62, 66, 67, 68
Fairbanks, L. A., 311
Fairburn, C. G., 333, 334, 335, 336, 337, 338,
     339, 340, 341, 342, 343, 344, 346, 368, 369,
     370, 371
Falbo, J., 21, 26, 27
Fallon, B., 115, 117, 119, 128, 136, 137
Falloon, I. R. H., 533, 534, 543
Fals-Stewart, W., 220, 457
Falsetti, S., 67
Faltus, F., 476
Faravelli, C., 5
Farmer, A., 401, 415, 428
Farmer, M. E., 525
Fatemi, S. H., 524
Fava, G. A., 26, 267, 268
Fava, M., 267
Fedio, P., 217
Feely, M., 269
Feeny, N. C., 75, 225
Feigenbaum, W., 24, 58
Femino, J., 394
Fennell, M., 157
Fenwick, J., 456
Fergus, K. D., 8
Ferng, H.-K., 528
Ferris, R., 274
Feske, U., 117
Festinger, D. S., 438, 457
Feuer, C. A., 65, 73
Fichter, M. M., 212, 337, 340
Fichtner, C. G., 526
Fiester, S. J., 266, 310
Filstead, W., 399
Fink, C. M., 8, 23
Fink, E. B., 392
Finney, J. W., 380, 381, 429
First, M. B., 67, 536
Fischer, S. C., 218
Fishman, B., 312
Fitzgerald, R. G., 545
Fitzgibbons, L. A., 75
Flaherty, J. F., 536
Flament, M., 211
Flanagan, C., 300
Flatow, L., 529
Fleischmann, R. L., 225
Fleiss, J., 310, 335, 337, 338, 346, 370, 526
Fluoxetine Bulimia Nervosa Collaborative Study
     Group, 335
Foa, E. B., 12, 23, 24, 25, 26, 62, 63, 64, 66, 67,
     70, 71, 72, 75, 121, 160, 182, 183, 210, 211,
     212, 213, 215, 216, 217, 218, 219, 222, 223,
     225, 226, 229, 232, 233, 238, 259, 499
Foddy, M., 120
Foerg, F. E., 456, 457
Fonagy, P., 472, 473
Fontaine, R., 13
Fontana, A., 75
Ford, S. M., 130

Forgue, D. G., 68
Fossati, A., 481
Foster, S., 74
Foy, D. W., 61, 407
Frances, A. J., 312, 470
Francis, A. F., 526
Franco, M., 317
Frank, E., 70, 265, 266, 268, 269, 274, 304n, 312,
     313, 314, 328, 329, 338, 528, 529, 530, 531,
     536, 557
Frank, N., 313, 314, 328
Frankel, D., 529
Frankenburg, F. L., 212
Frankenburg, F. R., 471
Frankenstein, W., 383
Franklin, M., 334
Franklin, M. E., 211, 216, 218, 225, 229, 233
Frasure-Smith, N., 317
Free, M. L., 269
Freed, S., 6
Freedy, J., 66
Freeman, A., 270, 296, 299, 499
Freeman, R., 335
Freesten, M. H., 215
French, D., 21, 27
Freng, S. A., 381
Frenkel, M., 476
Fresco, D. M., 114, 118, 121, 123, 126
Freund, B., 226
Friedman, M. A., 333
Friedman, S., 11
Friend, R., 128
Frisch, M. B., 128, 137, 147
Fritzler, B. K., 8
Fromm-Reichmann, F., 530
Frost, R. O., 216
Fry, W., 9
Fudula, J., 526
Furman, J. M., 6
Futterman, A., 274
Fydrich, T., 131
Fyer, A. J., 15, 115, 116, 168

Gabel, J., 4, 28
Gaffan, E. A., 266
Gallagher, R., 6, 18
Gallagher-Thompson, D., 274
Gallops, M. S., 15, 168
Gamble, W., 380
Gamsu, C. V., 161
Ganzini, L., 158
Garamoni, G. L., 119
Gardner, D. L., 476
Garfinkel, P. E., 335
Garfinkel, R., 115, 128, 137, 269
Garner, D. M., 333, 335, 337, 338, 342, 343, 369
Garner, M. V., 337, 338
Garrison, C. Z., 211
Garssen, B., 21, 22, 27
Garvey, M. J., 7, 156, 157, 266, 267, 268, 269
Gaskin, J., 382
Gasto, C., 274
Gauthier, J., 8, 11, 21, 27, 28
Gawin, F., 441, 457

Gelder, M., 6, 21, 22, 29, 118, 119, 157, 161, 162, 266, 304n
Gelenberg, A. J., 526
Gelernter, C. S., 119
Gelfand, L. A., 269
Geller, B., 558
Genduso, L. A., 223
George, A., 23, 476
George, C. J., 313
George, E. A., 531, 535, 557
George, E. L., 525, 529, 531, 532
George, L. K., 117, 130, 157, 158
Geraci, M., 3
Gerner, R. H., 527
Gershon, E. S., 333
Gertler, R., 340
Ghosh, A., 8
Gibbon, M., 67, 78, 116, 536
Gibbons, R. D., 266, 268
Gilbert, P., 120
Gilchrist, L., 381
Gillies, L. A., 311, 312, 314, 316
Gilmore, M., 470
Girelli, S. A., 61, 70, 75
Giriunas, L. L., 217
Gitlin, M. J., 526, 527, 538
Gitow, A., 115, 128, 137
Glass, C. R., 117, 125, 129
Glass, D. R., 266, 267, 310
Gleaves, D. H., 340
Glick, I. D., 525, 531
Gloaguen, V., 266, 267
Glover, D., 6
Godbout, D., 21, 27
Goddard, A. W., 11, 12, 27
Godley, M., 452
Goetz, D., 120
Goisman, R., 3, 4, 7, 116
Goklaney, M., 310, 314
Golan, J. K., 3, 4, 7
Gold, R., 74, 390
Goldberg, C., 479
Goldberg, J. F., 525, 526, 527
Goldbloom, D., 369
Goldenberg, I., 116
Goldfinger, K., 119
Goldfried, M. R., 269, 450
Golding, M., 211
Goldman, M. S., 405
Goldstein, A., 5, 9, 117
Goldstein, M. J., 523, 527, 528, 529, 530, 531, 532, 535, 538, 539, 543, 544, 545
Gollan, J. K., 269
Golner, J., 396
Gomez, M. J., 317
Gonzalez, A. M., 478
Good-Ellis, M., 531
Goodman, W., 210, 212, 213, 217, 223, 225, 229
Goodwin, F. K., 525, 527, 528
Gordon, J. R., 346, 384, 390, 391, 399, 405, 408, 410, 411, 414, 419, 429, 492, 502
Gordon, L. T., 441
Gormally, J., 343
Gorman, J. M., 10, 11, 12, 13, 15, 27, 115, 168

Gorsky, J. M., 120
Gorsuch, R., 18
Gortner, E. T., 269
Gottman, J. M., 481
Gotz, D., 71
Gould, R. A., 8, 119
Goyer, L. R., 11
Graap, K., 71
Gracely, S., 18
Grandi, S., 26, 267, 268
Grant, G., 379
Gray, J., 12, 13
Grayson, J. B., 26, 211, 218, 226, 232, 499
Green, B. A., 340
Greenberg, L. S., 316
Greenberg, R., 162, 163, 166, 176
Greenberger, D., 274
Greenfield, S., 317
Greenhouse, J. B., 269
Greeno, C. G., 343
Griest, J. H., 217, 223, 225
Griez, E., 22
Griffin, M. G., 68
Griffith, J., 441, 457
Griffiths, R., 340, 442
Grilo, C. M., 11, 12, 27, 344
Grissom, G., 381, 390
Grochocinski, V. J., 268, 269, 338
Gross, M. M., 379
Grossman, L. S., 526, 527
Grove, W. M., 266, 267, 268, 269
Grunberg, F., 471
Gullone, E., 3
Gunderson, J. G., 471, 472, 502
Gunn, S. A., 233
Guroff, J. J., 333
Gursky, D., 4, 18
Gusman, F. D., 66, 67
Guthrie, S., 391, 410, 416
Guze, B. H., 217, 528

Haas, G. L., 531
Hackmann, A., 6, 21, 22, 29, 123
Hadzi-Pavlovic, D., 525
Hafner, J., 9, 13
Hafner, R. J., 23
Haggard, P., 526, 527, 533
Hahlweg, K., 532
Haiman, C., 334
Hakstian, A. R., 265
Halaris, A., 223
Haley, J., 542
Halford, K., 120
Hall, C. P., 435
Hall, L. H., 268
Hall, P., 385, 386
Hall, S. M., 457
Hall, W., 390
Hallam, R., 9, 226
Halmi, K. A., 368, 369
Halperin, G., 266
Hamada, R., 63
Hamblin, D., 273, 274
Hamilton, M. A., 310

Hamman, M., 4
Hammen, C., 526, 527
Hammer, L. D., 3
Hammer, R. P., 435
Hamra, B. J., 3
Hand, I., 10
Hanley-Peterson, P., 274
Hanna, G. L., 211
Hannah, H. H., 8
Hansell, S., 313
Harcourt, L., 8
Harden, T., 274
Harrington, P. J., 26
Harrington, R., 274
Harris, E., 531
Harris, E. L., 3
Harris, T., 323
Harrison, D. W., 269
Harrison, J., 22
Harrison, P. J., 335
Harrison, W., 476
Harrow, M., 524, 526, 527
Hart, T. A., 127, 149
Hartlage, S., 265
Hartwell, N., 434
Harvey, M., 75, 76, 77
Hasin, D., 340, 379
Haslam, M. T., 22
Hatch, M., 11
Hatfield, A. B., 557
Hatsukami, D., 335, 336, 337, 338
Haug Ogden, D. E., 438, 456
Hautzinger, M., 266, 269
Havassy, B. E., 457
Hawkins, J. M., 526, 527, 533
Hay, P., 333
Hay, W. M., 383
Hayes, A. M., 269
Hayes, S. C., 369
Hays, R. D., 317
Hayward, C., 3
Hayward, J. P., 13
Hayward, P., 530
Hazen, A. L., 116
Hazlett, R. L., 156, 158
Head, D., 217
Heap, M., 333
Heard, H. L., 472, 477, 478
Heath, A. C., 159
Heather, N., 390
Heckelman, L. R., 115, 128, 137
Hecker, J. E., 8, 23
Hedley, L. M., 28
Hedlund, N. L., 74
Heide, F. J., 184
Heikkinen, M. E., 471
Heimberg, R. G., 6, 114, 115, 116, 117, 118, 119,
    120, 121, 122, 123, 124, 125, 126, 127, 128,
    129, 130, 131, 136, 137, 145, 146, 149
Heller, T. L., 526, 527
Hellstrom, K., 22
Helzer, J. D., 67
Helzer, J. E., 401, 415, 428, 526
Hembree, E., 70, 71

Henderson, A., 9, 159
Henderson, J., 333
Hendrickson, E. C., 439
Heninger, G. R., 3, 217, 225
Henke, R., 476
Henningfield, J. E., 442
Henriksson, M. M., 471
Hensman, C., 391, 410, 416
Herbert, J. D., 116, 117, 128, 131
Herbert, P., 71
Herman, D. S., 67
Herman, J. L., 481
Herman, S., 8
Hermesh, H., 216
Herring, J., 476
Hersen, M., 477
Hertz, R. M., 161, 162, 169
Hibbert, G., 21, 161, 162
Hickie, I., 525
Hickling, E. J., 68
Higgins, S. T., 435, 438, 442, 448, 452, 456,
    457
Higgitt, A., 13
Hill, C. L., 225
Hill, E. M., 481
Hillier, V. F., 526
Hillmer-Vogel, U., 9, 10, 23
Himadi, W. G., 8, 9
Himle, J., 7
Himmelfarb, S., 157
Hiripi, E., 116
Hirsch, C. S., 434
Hirsch, L., 399, 411, 428
Hirsch, T. G., 340
Hirschfeld, R. M. A., 534
Hiss, H., 211, 222, 232, 259
Ho, M. K., 311
Ho, M. L., 311
Ho, T. P., 340
Hodges, L., 71
Hodgson, R., 2, 117, 214, 219, 232
Hoehn-Saric, R., 156, 158, 169
Hoekstra, R., 27, 221
Hoffart, A., 8, 10, 12, 27, 28
Hoffman, R., 340
Hofman, A., 529
Hofmann, S. G., 11, 12, 27, 117, 265
Holden, A., 8, 10
Hollander, E., 210, 212, 213, 229, 476
Hollandsworth, J. G., Jr., 479
Holle, C., 115, 137, 146, 269
Hollon, S. D., 6, 265, 266, 267, 268, 269
Holmes, M. R., 63
Holt, C., 8, 28, 115, 116, 117, 119, 120, 128,
    136, 137, 145
Holt, P., 21
Holzer, C., 3
Honig, A., 529
Hood, E. M., 161
Hood, H., 451
Hoogduin, C. A., 10, 21, 211, 220, 232
Hoogduin, K., 222
Hooley, J. M., 529, 537, 556
Hoover, C. F., 545

Hope, D. A., 6, 115, 116, 117, 118, 119, 120, 121, 123, 128, 130, 131, 136, 137, 145
Hope, R. A., 337, 338
Hopkins, M., 155, 159, 168, 180
Horner, K. J., 130, 137, 145
Hornig, C. D., 4, 115, 116, 117
Hornsveld, H., 21
Hornsveld, R. H. J., 214
Horowitz, M., 63, 67
Horvath, A. O., 316
Horwath, E., 4
Horwitz, L., 472
Hosier, D. M., 217
Hoskinson, K., 536
Houck, P. R., 313
Hough, R. L., 61, 62, 66
Hsieh, F. Y., 68
Hsu, L. K. G., 333, 334, 340
Hu, S., 156, 160, 180
Huang, S.-C., 311
Hudson, J. I., 212, 335, 534
Hufford, M. R., 274
Hughes, C., 70
Hughes, D., 117, 130, 157, 158
Hughes, J. R., 435, 456
Hughes, M., 3, 62, 67, 115, 116
Hull, J., 531
Hunsley, J., 9
Hunt, G. M., 468
Hunt, M. F., 3, 4, 7
Hurley, K., 269
Hurt, S. W., 470, 472
Huska, J. A., 67
Huthwaite, M., 74
Hutter, C. H., 70, 75
Huxley, N. A., 530
Hyer, L. A., 74
Hymas, N., 217

Ianni, F., 472
Ilardi, S. S., 369
Imber, F. D., 313, 314, 328
Imber, S. D., 266, 267, 310
Infantino, A., 8
Ingram, R. E., 269
Insel, T. R., 210, 216, 217
Institute of Medicine, 392
Inz, J., 160
Irvine, M. J., 342
Irvine, S., 397
Irwin, D., 476
Islam, M. N., 476
Isometsa, E. T., 471
Ito, L. M., 27, 218, 219
Izard, C. E., 2
Izquierdo, J. A., 317

Jablenski, A., 415
Jack, M. S., 127
Jackel, L., 155, 168, 180, 184
Jackson, K. L., 211
Jackson, R. J., 5
Jacob, M., 312
Jacob, R. G., 6, 116, 118, 131

Jacobs, G., 18
Jacobsberg, L. B., 312
Jacobson, N. S., 269
Jacquin, K. M., 26
Jaimez, T. L., 8, 26
Jameson, J. S., 23
Jamieson, K., 525
Jamison, K. R., 525, 527, 528
Janoff-Bulman, R., 61, 64
Jansson, L., 23
Jaremko, M. E., 186
Jarrett, D. B., 312
Jarrett, R. B., 265
Jasin, E., 18
Jaycox, L., 70, 71
Jean, K., 215
Jeavons, A., 6
Jefferson, J. W., 217, 223
Jenike, M. A., 210, 212, 213, 223, 229, 241
Jenkins, J., 529
Jenneke, W., 74
Jensen, J. A., 74
Jimerson, D. C., 333
Joffe, R., 216, 269
Johnsen, W. E., 314
Johnson, B. A., 471
Johnson, C., 368
Johnson, J., 4, 115, 116, 117
Johnson, M., 156, 167
Johnson, S., 266
Johnson-Sabine, E., 334
Joiner, T. E., 270
Jolley, E., 333
Jonas, J. M., 212, 335
Jones, J. C., 338
Jones, R., 19, 337, 338, 450
Jones, S., 530
Jordan, B. K., 61, 62, 66
Jordan, C. G., 70, 75
Jornestedt, L., 223, 233
Jorquera, A., 274
Joseph, S., 64, 65
Judd, L. L., 525
Judge, R., 14, 223
Juster, H. R., 116, 117, 118, 119, 120, 123, 125, 128, 129, 130, 131, 136, 137, 145

Kadden, R. M., 398, 465
Kalbag, A., 531, 535, 557
Kaloupek, D. G., 66, 67, 68
Kane, J. N., 526
Kanter, J., 478
Karno, M., 211, 561
Kassett, J. A., 333
Kasvikis, Y., 211, 219, 220, 223, 226
Katschnig, H., 7
Katz, J. L., 435, 442
Katz, L. F., 481
Katz, M. M., 525
Katzelnick, D. J., 217, 223
Kavoussi, R. J., 476
Kay, R., 342
Kaye, W., 335
Kazarian, S. S., 226

Kazim, A., 3, 4, 7
Kazuba, D. M., 333
Keane, T. M., 63, 66, 67, 68
Keck, P. E., 526, 527, 533, 534
Keddie, A., 401
Keenan, M., 161
Kegan, R., 478
Keijsers, G. P. J., 10
Keith, S. J., 525
Keller, M., 3, 4, 7, 116, 158, 264, 265, 267, 524, 526, 527, 534
Kelly, J. A., 451
Kemp-Wheeler, S. M., 266
Kenardy, J., 8
Kendall, P. C., 162
Kendler, K. S., 3, 115, 116, 159, 335, 526
Kennedy, C. R., 119
Kenney, M. R., 3
Kernberg, O. F., 472
Kessler, R., 3, 62, 67, 115, 116, 117, 157, 158, 159
Keyl, P. M., 5
Keys, D. J., 115
Keys, S. A., 14
Kia, S., 212
Kiel, A., 74
Kilic, C., 12
Killen, J. D., 3
Kilpatrick, D., 61, 62, 63, 65, 66, 67, 68, 69, 70, 76
Kim, E., 6
Kim, S., 223
Kimble, C. E., 121
King, D. W., 67
King, L. A., 67
King, N. J., 3
Kirby, K. C., 457, 466
Kirby, M., 13
Kirkby, K., 8
Kirkish, P., 273, 274
Kite, L., 73
Kleber, R. J., 70
Klein, D. F., 15, 115, 116, 117, 119, 120, 136, 168, 266, 269
Klein, D. K., 310, 311
Klein, J. R., 121
Kleinknecht, R., 73
Klerman, G. L., 309, 310, 311, 312, 313, 314, 319, 321, 326, 338, 527, 531, 534
Klimes, I., 161, 162
Klosko, J., 4, 10, 22, 23, 161, 183, 296, 300
Kmetz, G. F., 533
Knapp, R. G., 156, 167
Knopke, A., 369
Kobak, K. A., 217, 223
Koby, E., 211
Koch, W. J., 11, 18, 28, 119, 128
Kocsis, J. H., 312, 525
Koder, D. A., 274
Koehler, C., 6
Koele, P., 13, 22, 27
Koenigsberg, H. W., 472
Koerner, K., 472, 518
Kohlenberg, R. J., 507

Kohut, H., 476
Kolb, J. E., 471
Kolb, L. C., 68
Konkol, R. J., 434
Koons, C. R., 478
Koponen, H. J., 14
Koran, L., 223, 337, 338
Korby, K. C., 438
Koss, M. P., 75, 76, 77
Kotsis-Hutter, C., 61
Kovacs, M., 265
Kowalski, R. M., 120
Kozak, M. J., 72, 121, 160, 182, 183, 210, 211, 212, 213, 215, 216, 217, 218, 219, 222, 223, 225, 226, 229, 232, 233, 238, 259, 499
Kozak, M. S., 12, 24, 25
Kraaimaat, F., 27, 214
Kraemer, H. C., 337, 339, 368, 369
Kraepelin, E., 523
Kraft, A. R., 21
Kramer, M., 3
Krause, E. D., 266
Kringlen, E., 159
Krishnan, R. R., 130
Kroll, P. A., 481
Kuch, K., 5, 13
Kuiper, H., 21
Kuipers, A. C., 21
Kujawa, M., 524
Kulka, R. A., 61, 62, 66
Kuoppasalmi, K. I., 471
Kupfer, D. J., 266, 268, 269, 312, 313, 314, 328, 329, 338, 529, 530, 531, 536, 557
Kushner, H., 390
Kyokai, B. D., 491

Laberge, B., 8, 11, 21, 27, 28
Labouvie, E., 337, 369, 379
Lachance, S., 215
Lacks, P., 450
Lacroix, D., 8
Lacy, E., 396
Ladouceur, R., 215
Laessle, R. G., 212, 338
Lafer, B., 558
Lalakea, M. L., 216, 217
Lam, D. H., 530
Lamb, R. J., 438, 457
Lambert, J. A., 70
Lammers, M. W., 10
Lamontagne, Y., 10
Lampert, C., 335
Lang, A. J., 24
Lang, P. J., 2, 63, 69, 121, 215
Lange, A., 13, 22, 27
Langenbucher, J., 379
Langley, M. H., 476
Langlois, F., 215
Lasko, N. B., 68, 74
Last, C. G., 10
Latimer, P. I., 218, 226
Laudenslager, M. L., 6
Lauterbach, D., 66, 67
Lavelle, J., 526

Lavori, P., 68, 526, 534
Lawrence, S. G., 121
Lawton, J. K., 127
Layne, C. M., 61
Lazarus, A. A., 129, 297
Lazarus, C. N., 297
Lazgrove, S., 73
Leary, M. R., 120, 128
Leber, W. R., 266, 310
LeBoeuf, A., 161
Leckman, A. L., 382
Leckman, J. F., 212, 213
Lecrubier, Y., 14
Ledesma, M., 317
LeDoux, J. E., 6
Ledsham, L., 333
Lee, A., 342
Lee, C. W., 270
Lee, S., 340, 481
Lefave, K., 226
Leff, J. P., 529
Lehman, C. L., 28, 166
Leibl, K., 337
Leitenberg, H., 25, 337, 342
Lelliott, P., 5, 8, 13, 210, 219, 220, 223, 226,
   229
Lenane, M., 211
Lenneris, W., 338
Leon, A. C., 211, 434
Leonard, H. L., 211, 217
Lepola, U., 14
Lerew, D. R., 5
Lerner, J., 120
Lesage, A. D., 471
Leskin, G. A., 67
Lesperance, F., 317
Lestelle, V., 531
LeTarte, H., 215
Levendusky, P. G., 274
Levenson, A. I., 273, 274
Levenson, H., 480
Leverich, G. S., 526, 534, 537
Levine, B. A., 23
Levine, J. L., 267
Levis, D. J., 221
Levitt, J. T., 218, 233
Levitt, K., 2, 6
Levy, R., 217
Lewin, M., 23, 28, 116
Lewinsohn, P. M., 274, 449
Lewis, A. B., 531
Lewis, D. C., 394
Liberman, R. P., 543
Licht, D. M., 529, 556
Lidren, D. M., 8
Liebowitz, M. R., 10, 15, 115, 116, 117, 119,
   120, 128, 130, 136, 137, 145, 155, 157, 158,
   159, 166, 168, 223, 225
Liepman, M. R., 385, 389, 408
Lilienfeld, S. O., 4
Lim, L., 120, 131
Lin, S.-L., 120
Lindsay, M., 217
Lindsay, W. R., 161

Linehan, M. M., 370, 371, 470, 471, 472, 476,
   477, 478, 481, 482, 488, 490, 491, 492, 495,
   498, 518
Links, P. S., 476
Linnoila, M., 216, 534
Lipinski, J. F., 525
Lipke, H., 74
Lish, J. D., 4
Litt, I. F., 3
Little, L., 397
Litwin, E. M., 3
Litz, B. T., 67
Liu, J., 476
Liu, X., 337, 369
Livanou, M., 71, 73
Locke, B. Z., 525
Lodge, J., 161
Loeb, K. L., 335, 337, 338, 341, 346, 369, 370
Lohr, N. E., 481
Longabaugh, R., 383, 390, 392
Longpre, R. E., 74
Lonnqvist, J. K., 471
Looper, J., 476
Loos, W. R., 68
Loosen, P. T., 266, 269
Lopatka, C., 2, 215
Lopez, S. R., 529
Lopovsky, J. A., 67
Lorca, G., 317
Lorenz, M., 6
Losch, M., 336, 368
Losee, M. C., 8
Louro, C. E., 6
Lovell, K., 71, 73
Lovibond, P. F., 164, 174
Lovibond, S. H., 164, 174
Loyer, M., 471
Luborsky, L., 266, 441, 457
Luby, J., 558
Lucas, J., 8, 18
Lucas, R. A., 8, 13, 119
Ludgate, J., 29
Ludwig, A. M., 406
Lukach, B. M., 6
Luscombe, D. K., 216
Lushene, R., 18
Luttels, C., 11
Lyddon, W., 64
Lydiard, R., 156, 167, 168, 169, 223
Lygren, S., 159
Lynch, T. R., 478
Lyonfields, J. D., 156, 160
Lytle, R., 184

McArdle, E. T., 119
McAuley, T., 392
McCance, E., 435, 457
McCann, I. L., 64, 72, 74, 75, 76, 77
McCann, U. D., 336
MacCarthy, B., 529
McCarthy, P. R., 219, 222, 223, 232, 238
McChesney, C. M., 3, 157
McClellan, J., 558
McConnaughy, E. A., 390

MacCoun, R. J., 377
McCourt, W. F., 396
McCrady, B. S., 41, 380, 391, 392, 397, 398, 399, 401, 410, 416, 428, 446, 447
McDavid, J., 476
McDonald, R., 217, 223
McEachran, A. B., 268, 315, 328, 329, 338
McElroy, S. L., 526, 527, 533, 534
McEwan, K. L., 120
McFall, M. E., 214
McFarland, B. H., 158
McGill, C. W., 533, 534, 543
McGinn, L. K., 265
McGlashan, T., 73
McGonagle, K. A., 3, 115, 116, 117
McGrath, P. J., 476
Macias, J. A., 317
McKeown, R. E., 211
McLaughlin, E., 161
McLean, P. D., 11, 28, 119, 128, 265
McLellan, A. T., 381, 390, 435, 441, 457, 466
MacLeod, C., 123
McLeod, D. R., 156, 158, 169
McLeod, G., 385, 386
McNair, L. D., 75
McNally, R., 4, 6, 18
McNamee, G., 5, 8, 13
McNeil, D. W., 116, 128, 131
McNeill, D., 392
McPherson, A., 342
Madeddu, F., 481
Maffei, C., 481
Magana, A. B., 532
Magee, W. J., 115, 116, 117
Mahoney, M., 64
Maidenberg, E., 6, 28
Maidment, K., 311
Maier, S. F., 6
Mainguy, N., 11
Maisto, S. A., 390, 399, 415
Malkoff-Schwartz, S., 529
Maller, R. G., 4
Mallinger, A. G., 530, 531, 557
Malloy, P. F., 68
Mann, A. H., 334
Mann, L., 217
Mannuzza, S., 15, 116, 168
Mansky, P. A., 314
March, J. S., 61
Marchand, A., 11
Marchione, K., 8, 10, 11, 20
Marchione, N., 8, 10, 11, 20
Marcus, M. D., 333, 336, 338, 340, 343, 346, 368, 369, 370, 371
Margolin, G., 391, 416
Margraf, J., 2, 4, 6, 17
Marhoefer-Dvorak, S., 61, 70, 75
Markaway, B. E. G., 77
Markowitz, J. C., 309, 310, 311, 312, 314
Marks, A. P., 220
Marks, I. M., 5, 8, 12, 13, 23, 25, 27, 71, 73, 210, 211, 214, 216, 217, 218, 219, 220, 223, 224, 226, 229, 232

Marlatt, G. A., 346, 353, 358, 384, 390, 391, 399, 405, 407, 408, 409, 410, 411, 414, 419, 429, 492, 502
Marlowe, D. B., 438, 457
Marmar, C. R., 61, 62, 66, 67, 68
Marnell, M., 333
Marquis, J. N., 74
Marshall, R., 120
Marshall, W. L., 23, 25
Marten, P. A., 156, 157, 158, 164, 168, 169, 174
Martin, C., 379
Martin, L., 10, 15, 168
Martin, M., 6
Martin, R. A., 457
Martin, S. D., 311
Martin, T., 317
Martinez, A., 274
Martinsen, E. W., 10
Marttunen, M. J., 471
Marziali, E., 472, 473
Marzuk, P. M., 434
Maser, J., 527
Masheb, R. M., 344
Masia, C., 116
Mason, M., 380
Massion, A. O., 158
Master, D., 25
Masterson, J., 472
Mathé, A. A., 159
Mathew, R. J., 22
Mathews, A., 123, 160, 161, 162, 184, 216
Mattia, J. I., 121
Mattick, R., 6, 118, 127, 128
Maurer, H. S., 382, 428
Mavissakalian, M., 4, 10, 20
Mawson, D., 217, 223
Maxwell, M. E., 333
Mayfield, D., 385, 386
Mayo, J. A., 529
Maziotta, J. C., 217
Mazumdar, S., 313
Mazure, C., 225
Mazziotta, J. C., 528
Meadows, E. A., 5, 70, 71
Mechanic, D., 313
Mechanic, M. B., 68
Mehl-Madrona, L., 457
Mehta, M., 220
Meichenbaum, D., 221
Meichenbaum, D. H., 69
Meichenbaum, D. S., 186
Meijer, L., 381
Meltzer, H. Y., 526, 527
Menard-Buteau, C., 471
Mendelson, M., 220, 310, 440
Meredith, K., 273, 274
Mersch, P., 21
Messer, S. C., 128, 131
Messick, S., 344
Metzger, D., 390
Metzger, L. J., 68
Metzger, R. L., 156, 164, 168, 174
Meyer, G. R., 446, 465
Meyer, T., 23, 156, 164, 168, 174

Meyer, V., 217, 218
Meyers, R., 452
Meyers, R. J., 385, 386, 389, 398, 409, 414, 444, 451
Meyers, W., 396
Michael, M., 457
Michalec, E., 457
Michelson, L., 8, 10, 11, 20
Middleton, H., 6, 21, 22
Mikalauskas, K., 534
Miklowitz, D. J., 274, 523, 525, 526, 527, 528, 529, 530, 531, 532, 535, 538, 539, 543, 544, 545, 556, 557
Milby, J. B., 457
Miller, A. L., 11, 28
Miller, J. B., 481
Miller, K. J., 340, 428
Miller, M. D., 313, 314, 328
Miller, M. L., 156, 164, 168, 174
Miller, N. L., 214
Miller, P. M., 407
Miller, R. H., 401, 428
Miller, W. R., 382, 385, 386, 389, 390, 398, 399, 413, 414, 439, 446, 459, 464
Millon, T., 480
Milofsky, E. S., 408
Milton, F., 9, 13
Mindlin, M., 117, 125
Mineka, S., 4, 5, 6, 26, 159
Miner, C. M., 130
Minichiello, W., 241
Mintz, J., 457, 527, 529, 532
Mintz, R. S., 482
Mitchell, J. E., 334, 335, 336, 337, 338, 340, 368, 369
Mitchell, K. M., 274
Mitchell, P., 525
Mitchell, W. B., 5
Miyawaki, E., 476
Moak, D. H., 384
Mock, J., 220, 310, 440
Moderation Management, 399
Mohr, D. C., 268
Mollard, L., 224
Molnar, C., 210, 215
Monahan, P., 4, 28
Money, R., 11, 12, 27
Monk, T. H., 529, 536
Monteiro, W. O., 22, 210, 219, 223, 226, 229
Montejo-Gonzalez, A. L., 317
Montgomery, H., 397
Montgomery, I., 8
Monti, P. M., 398, 457, 465
Montoya, I. D., 434, 457
Moore, R. G., 269
Moos, R. H., 380, 381, 429
Moras, K., 15, 156, 166, 167, 168, 184
Morgan, M. P., 73
Morgan, T. J., 399
Morin, C. M., 450
Morissette, R., 471
Morphy, M. A., 267
Morreau, D., 313
Morris, F. M., 313, 314, 328
Morse, J. Q., 478

Morycz, R. K., 313
Mowrer, O. A., 213
Mowrer, O. H., 63
Moyer, J., 310
Mueller, E. A., 216
Mueller, G. P., 128, 137, 145
Mufson, L. H., 313
Mullaney, J. A., 117
Muller-Oerlinghausen, B., 529
Munby, M., 118, 119
Munford, P., 528
Munoz, R. F., 446, 449, 464
Munroe, J., 76
Munroe-Blum, H., 472, 473
Muraoka, M. Y., 74
Murdock, T. B., 70, 71
Murphy, G. D., 267
Murphy, D. L., 216, 217, 223, 525
Murphy, K. J., 14
Murphy, M. T., 8, 11, 20
Murrell, E., 6, 7
Murrell, S. A., 157
Mussell, M. P., 334, 369
Myers, J., 3

Nagy, L. M., 66, 67
Nair, N. P, 14
Napier, A. Y., 535
Naster, B., 19, 450
Nathan, P. E., 383, 401
Nathan, R. S., 476
Nathan, S., 476
National Advisory Council on Alcohol Abuse and Alcoholism, 392
National Institute on Drug Abuse, 435, 436
National Institute of Justice, 434
National Institute of Mental Health, 264
Neale, M. C., 159
Neidig, P. H., 391
Neimeyer, R. A., 269
Nelson, B. A., 481
Nelson, C., 3, 62, 67, 115, 116
Nelson, H. F., 410
Nelson, J. E., 333
Nelson, P., 2
Nelson, R., 184
Neron, S., 8
Nesse, R. M., 7, 157
Neu, C., 310, 314
Neville, H. A., 75
Newman, H., 164
Newman, M. G., 8, 117
Nich, C., 435, 441, 457
Nicholls, P., 391, 410, 416
Nierenberg, A. A., 267
Nirenberg, T. D., 408
Nisbett, R. E., 478
Nishith, P., 65, 73
Noel, N., 410
Nonas, C., 340
Norcross, J. C., 382
Noriega-Dimitri, R., 23
Norman, P. A., 333, 337, 338
Norman, T. R., 312

Norris, F. H., 62, 66, 75
Noshirvani, H., 13, 27, 71, 73, 210, 211, 219, 220, 223, 226, 229
Nowell, T., 342
Noyes, R., 3, 4, 7, 156, 157
Nuechterlein, K. H., 527, 529, 532, 538, 545
Nunes, E., 269, 476
Nury, A. M., 224

O'Brien, B. E., 529
O'Brien, C. P., 381, 435, 441, 457
O'Brien, G. T., 8, 9, 10
Ocepek, W. K., 269
Ocepek-Welikson, K., 476
O'Connell, R. A., 529
O'Connor, M. E., 333, 334, 335, 337, 338, 371
O'Connor, N., 74
Oei, T. P. S., 8, 28, 269
O'Farrell, T. J., 398, 411, 457
Ogden, D., 456, 457
O'Hara, M. W., 312
Ojehegan, A., 401
Oldham, J., 368, 369
Oldman, A. D., 334
O'Leary, K. D., 274, 391
O'Leary, M. R., 407
O'Leary, T. A., 158, 164
Oliveri, M. E., 310
Ollendick, T. H., 3
Olmsted, M. P., 337, 338, 342, 369
Olsen, G. D., 434
Omar, A. S., 121
Onstad, S., 159
Oppenheimer, E., 391, 410, 416
Orford, J., 391, 401, 410, 416
Orosan, P., 370
Orr, S. P., 68, 70, 74
Orvaschel, H., 3
Öst, L.-G., 21, 22, 23, 29, 220
O'Sullivan, G., 8, 13, 226
O'Toole, D. H., 407
Otto, M. W., 13, 119, 338
Otto, R., 216
Overholser, J. C., 304n
Owen, P., 398, 399
Oyserman, D., 398

Padesky, C. A., 274
Page, B., 471
Pair, J., 71
Pallanti, S., 5
Pan, H. S., 391
Paolino, T. J., Jr., 380
Papageorgiou, C., 123
Papp, L., 10, 11, 12, 27
Paradis, C., 11
Parikh, S. V., 530
Parker, G., 525
Parkinson, L., 160
Parloff, M. B., 266, 267, 310
Parsons, B., 476
Parsons, O. A., 380
Paterniti, S., 5
Paterson, R., 119

Pato, C. N., 233
Pato, M. T., 223, 233
Patterson, D., 529
Pattison, P., 61
Patton, G. C., 334
Pauls, D. L., 212, 213
Pava, J. A., 267
Payeur, R., 156, 167
Paykin, A., 379
Payne, L. L., 23
Pearlman, L. A., 64, 72, 75, 76, 77
Pedersen, N. L., 159
Pedersen, T., 14
Pedersen, V., 14
Peer, D. F., 25
Pekrun, G., 23
Pelletier, M., 21, 27
Peng, K., 478
Penk, W., 66
Peralme, L., 74
Perel, J. M., 313, 328, 476
Perez, V., 317
Perissaki, C., 240
Perl, M., 337
Perloff, J. M., 274
Perper, J., 471
Perry, J. C., 472, 481
Perry, K. J., 117, 131
Perry, S. W., 312
Persons, J. B., 274
Peters, L., 118, 128
Peters, R., 390
Peterson, C. B., 369
Peterson, L. G., 3, 4, 7
Peterson, R., 4, 18
Petkova, E., 337, 369
Petry, N., 454
Pettinati, H., 382, 390, 428
Peveler, R. C., 333, 337, 338
Peynirgioglu, Z. F., 216
Peyser, J., 531
Phelps, M., 217, 311, 528
Phillips, K. A., 213
Philpott, R., 226
Piaseki, J. M., 266, 267, 268, 269
Pickar, D., 470
Pickens, R., 415
Pigott, T. A., 216
Pike, K. M., 333, 335, 337, 338, 346, 370
Pilkonis, P. A., 266, 267, 269, 274, 310
Pilsbury, D., 21
Piotrowski, N. A., 457
Pirke, K. M., 212, 338
Pitman, R. K., 68, 70, 74
Plamondon, J., 8, 11, 28
Platt, J. J., 457
Plochg, I., 221
Poire, R. E., 74
Pollack, M. H., 13, 119
Pollard, C. A., 3
Pollard, H. J., 3
Pollock, B. G., 313
Pollock, N., 379
Pomeroy, C., 335, 336, 337, 338

Pope, H. G., 212, 335, 525, 534
Portera, L., 211, 434
Post, R. M., 526, 534, 537
Potter, R., 273, 274
Potts, N. L. S., 130
Potvin, J. H., 223
Power, K. G., 7
Presley, A., 9
Preston, K. L., 457
Pretzer, J., 477
Price, L. H., 217, 225
Priebe, S., 529
Prien, R. F., 314
Prins, A., 68
Prochaska, J. O., 382, 390
Project MATCH Research Group, 382, 397
Prusoff, B. A., 310, 313, 314, 457
Pruzinsky, T., 156
Przeworski, A., 210, 215
Pusch, D., 265
Pyle, R. L., 335, 336, 337, 338

Quitkin, F. M., 476, 526

Rabavilas, A. D., 214, 219, 240
Rabkin, J. G., 476
Rachman, S., 2, 6, 25, 160, 214, 215, 219, 228, 232
Raczynski, J. M., 457
Rae, D. S., 525
Raeburn, S. D., 333, 337, 338, 346
Rafanelli, C., 267, 268
Rampey, A. H., 223
Randall, M., 381
Ranlett, G., 538
Rapee, R. M., 3, 4, 5, 6, 7, 15, 17, 18, 19, 21,
    115, 120, 121, 122, 131, 155, 157, 161, 162,
    164, 165, 166, 167, 168, 176, 180, 183, 184
Rapoport, J. L., 211, 217
Rardin, D., 343
Rasmussen, S. A., 210, 211, 212, 213, 217, 223,
    225, 229
Ratcliff, K. S., 67
Rather, C., 471
Rathus, J. H., 11, 28
Rauch, S. L., 223
Raue, P. J., 269
Ray, S. E., 12
Raymond, N. C., 334
Raytek, H. S., 428
Razran, G., 5
Rea, M. M., 531
Ready, D., 71
Reed, G. E., 215, 216
Rees, W., 22
Regier, D. A., 415, 525
Rehavi, M., 216
Rehm, L. P., 265, 278
Reich, J., 3, 4, 7, 116
Reichman, J. T., 5
Reinecke, M. A., 274
Reiser, D. E., 480
Reiss, S., 4, 18
Reiter, J., 370
Renfrey, G., 74

Rennenberg, B., 4, 117
Resick, P. A., 61, 63, 64, 65, 68, 69, 70, 71, 72,
    73, 75, 77, 78
Resnick, H., 61, 62, 66, 67
Resnick, P., 67
Reynolds, C. F., 269, 313, 314, 328
Rheame, J., 215
Rheaume, J., 215
Rheinstein, B. J. G., 117, 173
Rhines, K. C., 399
Rice, K. M., 22
Rich, C. L., 471
Richards, J. A., 525, 529, 531, 532, 535, 557
Richardson, F., 162
Richichi, E. A., 130
Rickels, K., 161
Rief, W., 337
Riemann, B. C., 6
Ries, B. J., 116, 128, 131
Rifai, A. H., 313
Riggs, D. S., 67, 70, 71, 211, 232
Rijken, H., 27
Rinsley, D., 472
Ritenour, A. M., 536
Rizvi, S. L., 471
Roberts, J. E., 265
Roberts, L. J., 457
Robertson, M. H., 268
Robinowitz, R., 66
Robins, C. J., 478
Robins, E., 525
Robins, L. N., 67, 401, 415, 428
Robinson, E., 156
Robinson, L. A., 269
Robson, P., 157
Rockert, W., 337, 338, 342, 369
Rodin, J., 333
Rogers, M. P., 3, 4, 7
Rogers, W., 317
Rohsenow, D. J., 408, 457
Roitblat, H., 63
Rollnick, S., 382, 385, 390, 459
Room, R., 378
Roose, S. P., 335, 337, 338, 346, 368, 369, 370
Roper, G., 214, 219
Rose, S. J., 412
Rosen, J. C., 337, 342, 370
Rosen, R. M., 14
Rosenbaum, J. F., 119, 267, 526
Rosenberg, H., 402
Rosenheck, R., 75
Rosenthal, R., 266, 380, 449
Rosenthal, T. L., 449
Rosoff, A., 534
Ross, D. C., 310, 311
Ross, L., 128, 130
Rossellini, R. A., 6
Rossiter, E. M., 336, 337, 338, 368
Roth, D., 120
Roth, W., 2, 6, 17, 117
Rothbaum, B. O., 62, 63, 67, 70, 71, 72, 74
Rothbloom, E., 313
Rounsaville, B., 73, 309, 321, 326, 328, 338, 435,
    441, 457, 531

Rowe, M. K., 5, 23, 24
Roy-Byrne, P. P., 3, 534
Roy, K., 525
Roy, M. A., 159
Rozendaal, N., 529
Rubenstein, C. S., 216
Rubinow, D. R., 534
Ruggieri-Authelet, A., 392
Runeson, B. S., 471
Rupert, P. A., 22
Ruscio, A. M., 67, 68
Rush, A. J., 128, 132, 223, 265, 266, 270, 274,
    499
Ruskin, J. N., 2
Rusnak, K., 74
Russell, J., 340
Russell, M., 385
Ruther, E., 23
Ryan, N. E., 274
Ryan, S. M., 6
Rychtarik, R. G., 399
Rygh, J., 298

Sabatino, S., 13
Sacco, W. P., 265, 267
Sachs, G. S., 526, 537, 557, 558
Sachs-Ericsson, N., 531, 535, 557
Sadik, C., 368, 369
Saeman, H., 268
Safran, J. D., 274
Safren, S. A., 115, 129, 130, 137, 145, 146
St. Lawrence, J., 63, 451
Saleem, R., 530, 531, 532, 544, 545
Salkovskis, P. M., 6, 7, 21, 22, 29, 214, 229, 265
Sallaerts, S., 11
Salzman, C., 157, 476
Salzman, D. G., 119
Samstag, L. W., 274
Sanchez, S., 317
Sanderson, W. C., 11, 28, 115, 157, 158, 167,
    168, 180
Sanderson, W. S., 6
Sanjuan, P. M., 379
Sank, L. I., 124, 133, 134
Santa, C., 398
Sarnie, M. K., 2
Sartorius, N., 415
Sartory, G., 25
Saunders, B. E., 62, 67, 68, 76, 390, 399, 415
Savron, G., 26
Sax, K. W., 526, 527, 533
Saxe, G., 75
Saxena, B., 14
Saxena, S., 311
Scarpato, M. A., 5
Schaap, C. P. D. R., 10
Schafer, J., 220
Scharff, L., 158
Schatzberg, A., 476
Scheftner, W., 527
Schilder, P., 217
Schindler, F. E., 70
Schlenger, W. E., 61, 62, 66
Schleyer, B., 168

Schmidt, H. I., 478
Schmidt-Auberger, S., 337
Schmidt, N. B., 5, 6, 8, 26, 270
Schmidt, R. A., 24
Schneider, J. A., 337, 346
Schneier, F. R., 115, 116, 117, 119, 120, 128,
    130, 136, 137, 145
Schnicke, M. K., 61, 64, 71, 72, 78
Schnurer, A., 217
Scholing, A., 118
Schotte, D. E., 340
Schretlen, D., 273, 274
Schuck, N., 530
Schulz, P. M., 476
Schumacher, J. E., 457
Schuster, C. R., 457
Schwartz, C., 241
Schwartz, G., 14
Schwartz, J., 476
Schwartz, J. M., 217, 528
Schwartz, M. N. B., 333
Schwartz, R. M., 119
Schwarz, S. P., 158
Schweizer, E., 161, 266
Scogin, F., 273, 274
Scott, J., 265, 266, 274
Secunda, S., 525
Segal, Z., 266, 269, 274, 370
Segun, S., 13
Seligman, D. A., 266
Selin, C. E., 528
Selin, C. L., 217
Selzer, M. A., 472
Selzer, M. L., 415, 439
Serfaty, M. A., 333
Serlin, R. C., 217, 223
Seymour, A. K., 66
Shadick, R., 155, 159, 168, 180
Shaffer, C. S., 124, 133, 134
Shafran, R., 215, 333
Shahar, A., 216
Shahar, F., 71
Shalev, A. Y., 70
Shaner, A., 457
Shapiro, D., 8, 526
Shapiro, F., 73
Sharp, D. M., 7
Shaw, B. F., 128, 132, 265, 266, 268, 269, 270,
    274, 499
Shay, J., 76
Shea, M. T., 266, 267, 268, 269, 274, 310
Shear, M. K., 11, 12, 13, 27, 156, 168, 169, 223
Shearin, E. N., 470, 490
Sheehan, T., 398, 399
Shelton, R. C., 6, 266, 269
Sher, K. J., 216
Sherman, M. J., 18
Sherrill, J. T., 529
Shipherd, J. C., 23
Shisholm, D., 530
Sholomskas, A., 313
Short, B. A., 381
Shulman, I. D., 5
Shuttlewood, G. J., 269

Siddle, D. A., 58
Siegel, L., 529
Siever, L. J., 481
Sikes, C., 223
Silberstein, L. R., 333
Silk, K. R., 481
Silver, S. M., 74
Silverman, D., 75
Silverman, K., 435, 457
Simeon, D., 476
Simmonds, B., 3
Simoneau, T. L., 530, 531, 532, 535, 544, 545, 556, 557
Simons, A. D., 267, 269
Simpson, J. A., 494
Simpson, R. J., 7
Singer, M., 538
Singer, W., 269
Sisson, R., 398, 444, 451, 452
Skinner, H., 390, 415
Skinner, L. J., 63
Skre, I., 159
Slotsky, S. M., 310
Sluys, M., 224
Smail, P., 117
Small, J. G., 314
Smith, A. L., 333
Smith, I., 390
Smith, J. E., 409, 444, 451
Smith, R., 61
Smith, R. D., 130
Smolak, L., 340
Snider, E. C., 435
Snow, A. C., 340
Snyder, K. S., 527, 529, 532
Sobell, L. C., 382, 390, 392, 399, 415, 441
Sobell, M. B., 382, 390, 392, 399, 415, 441
Soloff, P. H., 476
Solomon, R. A., 338
Solyom, C., 25
Solyom, L., 13
Sonnega, A., 62, 67
Sorensen, S. B., 211
Sosky, S. N., 310
Sotsky, S. M., 266, 267, 274
Spanier, C., 268, 338
Spanier, G., 19, 391, 416
Spaniol, L., 557
Spates, C. R., 74
Spaulding, S., 116, 118
Spear, S. F., 380
Spector, J., 74
Spencer, J. H., 531
Spielberger, C., 18
Spielman, L. A., 312
Spinhoven, P., 222
Spitzer, R. L., 67, 78, 116, 117, 310, 333, 340, 390, 536
Spurrell, E. B., 333
Srebnik, D., 337
Staab, J. P., 6
Stabl, M., 13
Stack, J. A., 313
Stadler, J. G., 21

Stampfl, T. G., 221
Stanley, M. A., 21, 22, 168, 241
Starcevic, V., 157, 168
Steer, R. A., 18
Stefanis, C., 214, 219
Stein, D. J., 270, 476
Stein, M. B., 114, 116, 121
Stein, R. I., 333
Steinberg, M. L., 428
Steiner, M., 476
Steketee, G., 8, 63, 72, 211, 218, 219, 222, 223, 226, 232, 238, 499
Stephens, R. S., 409
Stern, R. S., 23, 216
Stern, R. S., 217, 223
Stetson, D., 8
Stewart, A., 317
Stewart, B. D., 70
Stewart, G., 159
Stewart, J. W., 269, 476
Stewart, S. H., 408
Stice, E., 371
Stinchfield, R., 399
Stitzer, M. L., 435
Stockwell, T., 117
Stoessel, P., 311
Stoffel, V., 412
Stoltzam, R., 3
Stone, D. K., 472
Stone, M. H., 472
Stone, N. S., 439
Stopa, L., 120, 121, 131
Stout, R. L., 383, 392, 410
Strakowski, S. M., 526, 527, 533
Strasser, T. J., 368, 369
Strauss, J. L., 269
Strauss, J. S., 527
Street, G. P., 5, 70, 71, 211, 233
Street, L., 8, 25, 115, 128, 137, 183
Striegel-Moore, R. H., 333, 340
Strober, M., 335
Stuart, G. L., 10, 27
Stuart, S., 266, 312
Stunkard, A. J., 340, 344
Suarez, A., 472, 477, 478
Substance Abuse and Mental Health Services Administration, 434, 435
Suddath, R., 531, 535, 557
Suelzer, M., 4, 156, 157
Sugerman, A. A., 382, 428
Suinn, R. M., 162
Sullivan, M. J. L., 269
Sullivan, P. F., 335
Suls, J. M., 158
Sulzer-Azaroff, B., 446, 465
Surawy, C., 123
Sutker, P. B., 66
Swann, A., 525, 534
Swanson, V., 7
Swartz, H. A., 530, 531, 557
Swartzentruber, D., 12, 26
Swedo, S. E., 211, 217
Swendsen, J., 526, 527
Swift, W., 477

Swinson, R. P., 5, 7, 8, 12, 13, 120, 128, 130, 216
Szuba, M. P., 528

Talajic, J., 317
Tallman, K., 25
Talovic, S., 391,416
Tancer, M. E., 119
Tang, T. Z., 269
Tardiff, K., 434
Tarier, N., 74
Taylor, A. E., 68
Taylor, B., 6
Taylor, C. B., 2, 3, 7, 8, 9, 10, 17, 117
Taylor, G., 270
Taylor, J. R., 401, 428
Taylor, K. L., 66, 67
Taylor, S., 11, 18, 28, 119, 128
Teasdale, J. D., 370, 537
Telch, C. F., 7, 333, 336, 337, 338, 346, 368, 371
Telch, M. J., 2, 7, 9, 10, 13, 18, 26, 119, 270
Testa, S., 8, 11, 20
Thase, M. E., 265, 267, 269, 274, 530, 531, 557
Thayer, J. F., 156, 160
Thomas, E. J., 386, 398
Thomas, F. K., 217
Thomas, R. G., 68
Thompson, L., 274
Thoren, P., 223, 233
Thorpe, G.L., 23
Thrasher, S., 71, 73
Throdarson, D. S., 215
Thyer, B. A., 7, 157
Tidey, J. W., 457
Timko, C., 381
Tinkcom, M., 382
Tinker, R., 74
Tischler, C., 3
Tobena, A., 5
Tobin, D. L., 368
Tohen, M., 526, 527
Tollefson, G. D., 223
Tomlin-Albanese, J. M., 3, 4, 7
Tompson, M., 531
Tonge, B. J., 3
Tonigan, J. S., 385, 386, 389, 390, 397, 398, 414, 439
Toohey, M., 538
Torgersen, S., 4, 159
Touyz, S. W., 338, 340
Touze, J., 74
Towbin, K. E., 212, 213
Towle, L. H., 415
Townsley, R. M., 116
Trakowski, J. H., 6
Tran, G. Q., 116, 117, 125, 129
Traskman, L., 223, 233
Travers, J., 114
Treat, T. A., 10, 27
Tricamo, E., 476
Triffleman, E., 73
Trippett, C. J., 117
Troughton, E., 4
Trower, P., 120
Tsai, M., 507

Tsakiris, F., 211
Tsao, J. C. I., 2, 17, 24, 28
Tsaousis, J., 266
Tsuang, J. W., 457
Tsuang, M. T., 211, 526
Tualon, V. B., 314
Tuason, V. B., 266, 267, 268, 269
Tucker, D. E., 457
Tune, G. S., 226
Tupler, L. A., 130
Turgul, K. C., 533
Turk, C. L., 116, 118, 120, 121, 123, 126, 127, 128, 131
Turkington, D., 333
Turner, R. M., 23, 218, 226, 477
Turner, S. M., 25, 70, 115, 116, 118, 128, 131, 150, 168, 241
Turovsky, J., 128, 158, 159, 160
Tuschen, B., 370
Tutek, D., 477
Tweed, J. L., 478
Twentyman, C., 63
Tyano, S., 216
Tynes, L. L., 211

Uddo-Crane, M., 66
Uhde, T. W., 3, 119, 534
Ulrich, R., 10, 20, 476
Ultee, K. A., 23
Upashyaya, V. H., 533

Vagg, P., 18
Vaillant, G., 383, 401, 408
Vajk, F. C., 274, 530
Valleni-Basile, L. A., 211
Vallis, T. M., 274
van Balkom, A. J. L. M., 13, 222
van Dam-Baggen, R. M. J., 214
van den Bosch, L. M. C., 478
van den Hout, M., 21, 22, 27
Van der Helm, M., 221
van der Kolk, B. A., 481
van Dyck, R., 13, 22, 27, 222
van Kraanen, J., 219, 220
van Oppen, P., 222
Van Spiegel, P., 21
van Velzen, C. M. J., 118
Van Zanten, B. L., 221
Vangelisti, A. L., 121
Vanier, C., 471
Vapnik, T., 14
Vara, L., 337, 342
Vasile, R., 116
Vaughan, K., 74
Vaughn, C. E., 529, 543
Velicer, W. F., 390
Velligan, D. I., 538
Verduyn, C., 274
Vermilyea, B., 2, 157
Vermilyea, J., 2, 4, 119, 157, 161
Veronen, L. J., 62, 63, 69, 70, 76
Versiani, M., 304n
Vicens, E., 317
Vieta, E., 274

Visser, S., 221
Vitousek, K. M., 333, 337, 341, 344, 369, 370
Vittone, B. J., 119
Vogeltanz, N. D., 23
Vollmer, A., 68
Von, J. M., 62, 76
Voss, C. B., 314
Voth, H., 472
Vrana, S., 66, 67

Waadi, S., 338
Waddell, M., 4, 161
Wadden, T., 340
Wade, A. G., 14
Wade, W. A., 10, 27
Wager, S. G., 476
Wagner, A. W., 481
Wagner, E. F., 315, 328, 329
Wainwright, S., 526
Wakeling, A., 334
Wald, L. R., 217
Waldinger, R. J., 472
Walker, R. D., 381
Wallace, C. J., 543
Wallace, S. T., 120, 131
Waller, D., 342
Waller, J. L., 211
Walsh, A. E. S., 334
Walsh, B. T., 335, 336, 337, 338, 339, 340, 346, 368, 369, 370
Walters, E. E., 159
Walters, K. S., 121
Wamhoff, J., 266
Ward, C. H., 220, 310, 440
Wardle, J., 13
Ware, J., 317
Warshaw, M. G., 3, 4, 7, 158
Warwick, H., 21
Washton, A. M., 439
Wasserman, D. A., 457
Wasson, E. J., 481
Waternaux, C., 335, 337, 338, 346, 369, 370, 526, 527
Watkins, J. T., 266, 267, 310
Watkins, P., 8
Watson, D., 128, 159
Wattenmaker, D., 301
Wattenmaker, R., 301
Watts, F. N., 121, 160, 221
Weathers, F. W., 66, 67, 68
Weaver, E. V., 530, 531, 557
Weaver, T. L., 65, 73
Weerts, T., 19
Weigert, V., 530
Weiner, E. S., 494
Weinstein, C. D., 391, 416
Weisman, A., 529
Weiss, D. S., 61, 62, 66, 67, 68
Weissman, M., 3, 4, 115, 116, 117, 211, 309, 310, 311, 312, 313, 314, 319, 321, 326, 338, 531
Weizman, A., 216
Welch, R., 333
Welch, S. L., 333, 334, 335, 337, 338, 371
Welch, S. S., 471

Welkowitz, L., 10, 117, 119, 136
Wells, A., 29, 123, 160
Wells, K. B., 317
Wendel, J. S., 529, 530, 556
Wendt, S., 342
Werry, J. S., 558
Wesner, R., 4, 28
Wessels, D., 21
Wessels, H., 23
West, D., 70
West, S. A., 526, 527, 533
West, T. E., 14
Westling, B. E., 21, 22, 29
Westreich, L., 380
Wetzel, R. D., 267
Wetzler, S., 11, 28, 157, 159, 165
Whisman, M. A., 269
Whitaker, C. A., 500, 535
White, C., 116, 117, 131
White, J., 161
White, K., 223
White, L., 211
Wickwire, K., 8, 13
Widiger, T. A., 117, 470
Wierzbicki, M., 273
Wildgrube, C., 529
Wilfley, D., 333, 337, 372
Wilhelm, K., 525
Wilkens, J. N., 457
Will, B., 71
Williams, C., 18, 312
Williams, J. B., 67, 78, 390
Williams, J. B. W., 536
Williams, J. M. G., 265, 267, 269, 304n, 370
Williams, K. E., 10, 11
Williams, S. L., 8, 21, 25, 26, 27
Wilner, N., 67
Wilner, P. J., 525, 531
Wilson, A. E., 76
Wilson, D., 3, 74
Wilson, G. T., 214, 335, 336, 337, 338, 339, 340, 341, 342, 343, 344, 346, 368, 369, 370, 371
Wilson, J. P., 66
Wilson, P. H., 268, 274
Wilson, S. A., 74
Wilson, T., 10
Wilson, W., 130
Windhaber, J., 7
Wing, J., 415
Wing, R. R., 333, 340, 343
Wirtz, P. W., 383, 441
Wise, S. P., 217
Wiser, S., 269, 371
Wisocki, P. A., 157
Wittchen, H.-U., 3, 115, 116, 117, 157, 158, 212, 415
Wolf, E., 476
Wolf, J., 337
Wolfe, J., 66, 75
Wolff, P. L., 116, 118
Wolfman, H., 217
Wolfson, A. N., 476
Wollersheim, J. P., 214
Wolpe, J., 74, 129, 266

Wong, C. J., 438, 452, 456
Wood, A., 274
Wood, K., 334
Woodman, C., 156, 157
Woods, S. W., 11, 12, 13, 27, 217
Woody, S., 11, 28, 119, 128, 131, 215
Worthington, J. J., 119, 267
Woyshville, M. J., 524
Wright, J., 216, 266
Wu, H.-M., 311
Wynne, L. C., 538

Yanovski, S., 333, 340
Yates, W. R., 157
Yoshioka, M., 386
Young, J. E., 265, 270, 271, 296, 298, 300, 301, 304n, 477
Young, M. A., 524
Youngren, M. A., 449
Yurgelun-Todd, D., 212, 335

Zahn, T., 217
Zahner, G. E., 212, 213

Zanarini, M. C., 471
Zane, G., 8, 25
Zanis, D., 381
Zarate, R., 6
Zebb, B. J., 23
Zehr, H. D., 121
Zeiss, A. M., 449
Zhao, S., 3, 115, 116, 157, 158
Zielezny, M., 26
Zimering, R. T., 63, 67
Zimmerli, W. D., 156, 169
Zimmerman, M., 390
Zimmerman, R., 335, 336, 337, 338
Zinbarg, R. E., 156, 165, 167, 168, 184
Zipple, A. M., 557
Zitter, R. E., 391, 416
Zoellner, L. A., 75, 225
Zohar, J., 216, 223
Zohar-Kadouch, I. L., 216
Zohar-Kadouch, R., 223
Zollo, L. J., 119
Zweben, A., 383, 399, 412
Zwick, W. R., 408

SUBJECT INDEX

A-B-C sheets, use in therapy, 82, 83f
Adolescent depression, and IPT, 313
Age, and GAD, 157
Agoraphobia, 3, 7
  as behavioral response, 1
  and cognitive-behavioral treatment, 1, 27–28
  and panic disorder (PDA), 1
  treatment
    "guided mastery exposure," 8
    in vivo exposure, 7–8, 23–26
    and interpersonal context variables, 9–10
    telephone guided treatment, 8
Alcohol use disorders, 376
  assessment, 389
    drinking assessment, 389–390, 390t
    functional analysis, 390–391, 392f
    of motivation, 390, 391f
    and other problem areas/Addiction Severity
      Index (ASI), 390
    partner assessment, 391
  case study, 414–415, 428
    behavioral assessment/case conceptualization,
      415–417
    change preparation, 418
    treatment process, 418–427
    treatment termination, 427–428
  clinical predictors of success/failure, 428–429
  cognitive-behavioral case formulation,
    382–383
  diagnosis
    alcohol dependence syndrome, 379
    alternative definitions, 379–380
    complicating problems, 380
  early sobriety strategies, 403
    alternative reinforcers, 406
    alternative/distracting behaviors, 406
    cognitive distortions about alcohol, 405–406
    drink refusal skills, 407
    stimulus control, 403–505
    urges (dealing with), 405
  harm reduction models, 377
  recovery movement, 378
  rehabilitative approach (Employee Assistance
    Programs), 377

self-help groups
  AA (Twelve Steps), 397
  and maintenance, 412
  MM (Moderation Management), 378, 398,
    429n
  SMART (Self-Management and Recovery
    Training), 378, 397
  SOS (Secular Organizations for Sobriety/Save
    Ourselves), 378, 397
societal context, 376–379
SORC model, 383
  and relapse prevention (RP) model, 384, 410–
    412
theoretical model, 380–381
  client expectations, 381-382
  concomitant life problems, 381
  maintenance of change, 384
  motivation and therapeutic relationship, 382
  problem severity, 381
  social support, 383
  variables maintaining the current drinking
    pattern, 382–383
theoretical model/clinical application, 384,
    385t. *See also* Alcohol use disorders/
    assessment; Alcohol use disorders/early
    sobriety strategies; Alcohol use disorders/
    treatment modalities selection; Alcohol
    use disorders/treatment setting selection
    variables
  abstinence initiation, 402
  case identification and screening, 384–385,
    386t
  client variables, 414
  complicating conditions, 412
  coping strategies, 407–409
  drinking goals selection, 401–402
  enhancing motivation to change, 399–401
  functional analysis development, 402–403,
    404f
  motivation development, 385–389
  partner/family involvement, 409
  self-help groups role, 412
  social context, 410
  therapist variables, 412–414

Alcohol use disorders (*continued*)
  treatment
    credentialing standards, 378
    models, 399
    treatment modalities selection. *See also* Alcohol
       use disorders/self-help groups
      couple therapy, 398
      group therapy, 398
      individual treatment, 398
      intensive treatment programs/"Minnesota
       model," 398–399
    treatment setting selection variables, 392, 394t
      attitudes, 396
      detoxification requirements, 394–395
      general considerations, 397
      medical problems, 395
      other psychological problems, 396
      personal resources, 396
      practical concerns, 396
      preferences, 397
      previous quit attempts, 395
      social support systems, 396
      treatment history, 395
Assessment tools. *See also* Self-report instruments
  Addiction Severity Index, 390, 441
  Alcohol Dependence Scale (ADS), 390
  Anxiety Disorders Interview Schedule (ADIS/
    ADIS-IV) for DSM-IV, 15, 127
  Areas of Change Questionnaire (ACQ), 391
  Beck Anxiety Inventory, 163
  CAGE, 385
  Camberwell Family Interview, 529
  Clinician-Administered PTSD Scale (CAPS), 66,
    67
  Diagnostic Interview for Borderlines (DIB), 471
  Diagnostic Interview Schedule (DIS), 67
  Drinker Inventory of Consequences, 390
  Eating Disorder Examination (EDE) interview,
    339, 342–343
  Global Assessment Scale (GAS), 310
  Hamilton Anxiety Scale, 163
  Hamilton Depression Rating Scale (HDRS), 310
  Leeds Anxiety Scale, 163
  Modified Conflict Tactics Scale, 391
  Obsessive Compulsive Responsibility Scale
    (OCRS), 215
  Penn State Worry Questionnaire (PSWQ), 156,
    174
  Posttraumatic Stress Diagnostic Scale (PDS), 66
  PTSD Symptom Scale-Interview, 67
  Readiness to Change Questionnaire, 390
  Rutgers Consequences of Use Questionnaire
    (RCU), 399
  Spouse Behavior Questionnaire (SBQ), 391
  Structured Clinical Interview for DSM-IV
    (SCID), 15, 67, 390
  Timeline Follow-Back Interview (TLFB), 389–
    390
  Traumatic Events Questionnaire, 66
  Traumatic Stress Schedule, 66
  TWEAK, 385
  University of Rhode Island Change Assessment
    Scale, 390

Yale–Brown Obsessive Compulsive Scale (Y-
    BOCS), 225
Avoidant personality disorder (APD), and social
    anxiety disorder, 116–117

Beck, Aaron T., cognitive therapy development, 265
Bipolar disorder
  cognitive therapy and pharmacotherapy, 274
  comorbidity and differential diagnosis, 525–526
  depression and cognitive therapy, 303
  diagnosis, 523–524
    changes, 524–525
  drug treatment
    "break-through episodes," 526
    medication nonadherence, 527
    social–occupational functioning, 527
    standard pharmacotherapy, 526
    symptomatic outcome, 526–527
  and family-focused treatment (FFT), 523, 557–558
    client variables, 534
    communication enhancement training (CET),
      523
    concurrent drug treatment, 534
    cotherapy model, 535
    objectives, 532–533, 533t
    problem-solving skills training, 523
    psychoeducation module, 523, 530
    setting, 533–534
    therapist variables, 535
  and family-focused treatment (FFT)/case study,
    547
    communication enhancement training
      (sessions 8-14), 551–555
    efficacy of treatment, 556–557
    family assessment, 548
    problem solving (sessions 15–18), 555
    psychoeducation (sessions 1–7), 548–551
    termination (sessions 19–21), 555–556
  and family-focused treatment (FFT)/process
    communication enhancement training (CET),
      543–545
    diagnostic evaluation, 535–536
    family assessments, 537–538
    mood chart (Social Rhythm Metric), 536–
      537, 537f
    problem-solving skills training, 545–547
    psychoeducation, 538–543
    treatment termination, 547
  psychotherapy, 527–528
  treatment outcome studies, 530, 532
    family and marital therapy, 531–532
    individual therapy, 530–531
  vulnerability–stress model of recurrences, 528,
    528f
    family stress, 529–530
    life events stress/social rhythm stability
      hypothesis, 529
Body dysmorphic disorders, and OCD, 213
Borderline personality disorder (BPD), 470–472
  biosocial theory
    dialectical dilemmas, 482
    emotion dysregulation, 480–481
    invalidating environments, 481–482

case study
    background, 502–503
    transcripts, 507–518
    treatment, 503–507
dialectical behavior therapy (DBT), 477, 502.
        See also Borderline personality disorder/
        structuring DBT treatment
    efficacy, 477–478
    philosophical basis/"behavior," 480
    philosophical basis/"dialectics," 478–480
    pretreatment/orientation/commitment, 483
    stage 1/attaining basic capacities, 483–485
    stage 2/posttraumatic stress reduction, 485
    stage 3/self-reliance and self-respect, 485
    stage 4/capacity for sustained joy, 485
    stages/goals, 482–483
dialectical behavior therapy (DBT)/case
        management strategies, 501
    consultant-to-the-client, 501
    environmental intervention, 501–502
    supervision/consultation meeting, 502
dialectical behavior therapy (DBT)/treatment
        strategies, 490
    behavioral analysis, 496–497
    dialectical strategies, 490–493, 491f
    problem solving, 496,498–500
    solution analysis, 497–498
    stylistic strategies, 500–501
    validation, 493–496
parasuicidal act, 470
structuring DBT treatment
    client variables, 489–490
    environment structuring, 488–489
    functions, 486
    individual mode, 486–487
    setting, 489
    skills consultation mode, 488
    skills training mode, 487–488
    supervision/consultation team, 489
    telephone consultation mode, 488
    therapist variables, 490
treatment approaches, 474t–475t. *See also*
        Borderline personality disorder/dialectical
        behavior therapy
    cognitive-behavioral, 477
    integrative, 476
    psychodynamic (group approach)/relationship
        management psychotherapy (RMP), 472–
        473
    psychodynamic (individualized), 472
    psychopharmacological, 476
    SASB-Reconstructive Learning (SASB-RCL),
        473
    Structured Analysis of Social Behavior
        (SASB)/interpersonal, 473
Borkovec, T. D., psychosocial model of
        generalized anxiety disorder, 159–160
Bulimia nervosa (BN). *See also* Eating disorders
    and AN, 333
    case study, 346, 347–348
        assessment, 346
        course of treatment, 348–349
        decision analysis form, 353f, 358f

dysfunctional thought record (DTR), 359
    objectives per session, 349, 351, 352–353,
        355, 358, 361, 362–363, 365, 366, 367
CBT model, 336, 371–372
    efficacy, 336–337, 370–371
    patient variables, 340
    pharmacological treatment, 337–338
    self-monitoring, 344, 345f
    therapist variables, 340–342
    therapy setting, 340
CBT process, 344, 346
    dissemination, 369
    manual-based treatment vs. clinical practice,
        368
    predictors of therapeutic success/failure, 368–
        369
clinical features, 332
and IPT, 309, 311, 338–339
and negative affect, 371
treatments (alternatives to CBT), 335
    antidepressant medication, 335–336
    other psychotherapies, 338–339

Client–treatment matching, 51
Cocaine dependence, 434–436
    assessment, 438
        intake, 438–439
        self-administered questionnaire, 439–440
    case study, 458
        assessment, 458–459
        case conceptualization, 459
        follow-up, 466
        presenting complaint, 458
        treatment plan, 459–460
        treatment progress, 460–466
    clinical disorder definition, 436–438, 436t, 437t
    community reinforcement approach (CRA),
        435, 466
        abstinence contract, 443f–444f
        aftercare, 453
        conceptual framework, 442, 444
        functional analysis and self-management
            planning, 446–448, 447f, 448f, 449t
        HIV/AIDS education, 451, 452t
        individualized skills training, 449–450
        monitored disulfiram therapy, 453f,
            541–542
        other drug use, 452–453
        program description, 440–441
        and relapse prevention (RP) model, 435
        relationship counseling, 450–451
        semistructured interviews, 441–442
        social and recreational practices, 448–449
        structured counseling sessions, 445–446
        therapist style, 444–445
        treatment components, 444
        vocational training, 450, 450t
        voucher program, 453–454
    community reinforcement approach (CRA) therapy
        clinical supervision, 456
        commencement, 454–456
        supporting research, 456–457
    principles of effective treatment, 436t

Cognitive-behavioral group therapy (CBGT)
  case example, 136
    acute treatment weeks, 139–145
    continued (intensive) treatment, 146–147
    maintenance treatment, 147–148
    post-intensive treatment assessment, 147
    post-maintenance assessment, 148–149
    post-treatment assessment, 145–146
    pretreatment assessment, 136–139, 137t, 138t
    treatment efficacy/follow-up assessment, 148f, 149, 149f
  cognitive restructuring and exposure coordination, 135
  disputing questions list, 134t
  group composition, 125
  group format, 124–125
  overview of sessions
    1–2 (training in cognitive restructuring skills), 131–133, 132t, 133t
    3–11 (basic format), 133–135,134t
    12 (coordination of cognitive restructuring and exposure), 135–136
  vs. pharmacotherapy, 119–120
  pretreatment assessment, 127
    clinical interview, 127
    self-report instruments, 127–128
  pretreatment assessments
    final review, 130–131
    treatment orientation interview, 128–130
  and psychopharmacological treatments, 126–127
  and social anxiety disorder, 118
    efficacy, 119–120
    and integrated cognitive-behavioral model, 123–124
    integrated model, 120
  therapists, 126
  thinking errors list, 133t
  time and setting, 125–126
Cognitive-behavioral therapy/cognitive therapy (CBT). See also Depression/cognitive therapy treatment; Eating disorders/cognitive-behavioral therapy
  collaboration, 274–275
  collaborative empiricism, 276
  development of, 265
  feedback, 275–276
  goal determination, 275
  interpersonal qualities, 275
Cognitive-behavioral therapy/cognitive therapy (CBT) process
  initial sessions/symptom relief, 276
    behavioral techniques, 281–283, 282f
    cognition/emotion relationship, 277
    eliciting automatic thoughts, 278–280, 279f
    homework importance, 277, 283–285, 348
    problem definition, 276
    questioning, 283
    testing automatic thoughts, 280–281
  Oxford approach, 336
  session content over time progression, 278
  session content over time/schema focused phase, 278, 296

special problems, 285
  therapist–patient relationship, 285
  unsatisfactory progress, 285–286
typical session, 277
Cognitive-behavioral treatment and agoraphobia, 1, 49–51. See also Panic control treatment
  assessment example, 14–15
    behavioral tests, 19
    functional analysis, 19–20
    interviews, 15–16, 16f
    medical evaluation, 16–17
    psychophysiology, 19
    self-monitoring, 17–18, 17f, 18f
    standardized inventories, 18–19
  and clients' self-awareness, 11–12
  efficacy, 16–27, 49–50
    effect on agoraphobia, 27–28
    and "overvalued ideation," 50
  impact of medications, 12–13
Cognitive processing therapy (CPT), for PTSD, 71–73
Cognitive rehearsal, 281–282
Community Reinforcement and Family Training (CRAFT) model, 386
"Completion tendency," 63–64
Couple distress
  assessment
    of domestic violence, 614
    and screening instruments, 613t
  etiology, 612
  integrative behavioral couple therapy (IBCT), 609, 611
    efficacy, 620, 629
    formulation, 612
    mutual trap, 613
    polarization process, 612–613
    stages of therapy, 613–614
    theme, 612
    therapist variables, 620
  integrative behavioral couple therapy (IBCT)/case example, 620
    assessment, 621–622
    feedback and formulation, 622–625
    treatment/building acceptance, 625–629
  integrative behavioral couple therapy (IBCT)/treatment
    assessment phase, 614–616
    feedback, 616
    techniques for building emotional acceptance, 616–618
    traditional strategies to promote change, 618–620
  traditional behavioral couple therapy (TBCT), 609, 610–611
Cyclothymic disorder, 526

Depression. See also Interpersonal psychotherapy; Postpartum depression
  cognitive model
    "cognitive triad of depression," 269–270
    "focus of convenience," 269
    "schemas"/predisposing factors, 270

cognitive therapy, 265, 273–274, 303–304. *See also* Cognitive-behavioral therapy/cognitive therapy
  case study
    schema focused phase, 296–303
    symptom reduction phase, 286–296
  effectiveness of vs. effectiveness of tricyclic antidepressants (TCAs), 265–266
  focus, 273
  frequency and duration, 267–268
  patient characteristics, 274
  and relapse rates, 266–267
  research controversy/criticism, 266
  and residual symptoms, 267
  therapist characteristics, 274
  current status/future research on treatment, 269
  politics of, 268
  prevalence, 264
  research findings, 268–270
Dialectical behavior therapy (DBT), 477, 502. *See also* Borderline personality disorder
Disputing questions list, 134t
Disuse theory, 24
Dual-representation theory, 64–65

Early Maladaptive schemas (Young), 270, 271f–273f
Eating disorders. *See also* Bulimia nervosa (BN)
  anorexia nervosa (AN)
    clinical features, 332
    patient variables, 340
    and problems for clinical management, 333
  assessment
    Binge Eating Scale (BES), 344
    Eating Disorder Examination Questionnaire (EDE-Q), 344
    Eating Disorders Inventory-2 (EDI-2), 343
    EDE (Eating Disorder Examination) interview, 339, 342–343, 343f
    Three-Factor Eating Questionnaire (Stunkard and Messick), 344
  and cognitive behavioral therapy, 333, 336
    vs. alternative psychotherapies, 338–339
    efficacy, 336–337
    vs. pharmacological treatment, 337–338
  EDNOS (eating disorder not otherwise specified), 333
    BED (binge-eating disorder), 333
  etiology
    dieting, 334–335
    familial factors, 335
    gender, 333
    genetic influences, 335
    psychosocial influences, 333–334
  and psychoeducation, 341–342
EE (expressed emotion)
  measurement of, 529–530
  problems with, 537
Ethnicity/cultural differences
  and eating disorders, 340
  and treatment for PD/PDA, 11
  and treatment for PTSD, 75

Exposure and ritual prevention (EX/RP), 217–218
  vs. cognitive therapies, 221–222
  complications, 254–255
    arguments, 256
    emergent fears/rituals, 257
    emotional overload, 256–257
    functioning without symptoms, 240f, 258
    negative family reactions, 257–258
    nonanxious reactions to exposures, 257
    noncompliance with ritual prevention, 255
    passive avoidance continuation, 256
  EX/RP vs. exposure, 218
  exposure duration, 219
  exposure frequency, 219
  family involvement vs. standard, 220–221
  gradual vs. abrupt exposures, 219
  imaginal exposure, 218–219
  individual vs. group, 220
  intensive treatment period, 237–238
  ritual prevention implementation, 218, 239f
  therapist-assisted vs. self-exposure, 219–220
Eye movement desensitization and reprocessing (EMDR), 73–74

Family-focused treatment (FFT). *See* Bipolar disorder
Fear of fear concept, 5–6
Fight–flight system, and panic attacks, 2
"Flashbacks," and PTSD, 61

Gender
  and agoraphobia, 7
  and alcohol use disorders, 376
  and eating disorders, 333, 340
  and obsessive–compulsive disorder, 211
  and PTSD, 75
  and social anxiety disorder, 116
Generalized anxiety disorder (GAP)
  assessment
    classification, 155t, 166–169
    clinical interview, 169, 170f–173f, 173
    questionnaires (PSQW/DASS), 173–174
    self-monitoring, 174–175, 175f
  case study sessions/treatment transcripts, 186
    1 introduction/overview, 186–189
    2 self-monitoring review/treatment rationale, 189–192
    3 PMR, 192–193
    4 PMR and discrimination training/cognitive component, 193–195
    5 eight-muscle-group relaxation/decatastrophizing, 195–198
    efficacy, 204–205
    6 anxiogenic cognitions review/discrimination training/generalization practices, 198–200
    7 worry exposure, 200–201
    8 relaxation-by-recall, 201–202
    9 worry behavior prevention, 202–203
    10 cue-controlled relaxation, 203
    11/12 review/brainstorming, 203
    13 ongoing agenda, 203–204

Generalized anxiety disorder (GAP) (*continued*)
  combined treatment protocol
    cognitive therapy, 176, 178–180
    initial sessions, 176
    overview, 175–176, 177t
    patient variables, 165
    problem solving, 186
    relaxation training (progressive muscle
        relaxation/PMR), 163, 183–184
    setting, 164–165
    therapist variables, 166
    time management, 185–186
    worry behavior prevention, 184–185, 185f
  comorbidity, 158
  conceptual models
    "anxious apprehension" process, 158–159
    as the "basic" anxiety disorder, 158
    Borkovec's psychosocial model, 159–160
    origins of, 159
  diagnostic criteria, 154–156, 155t
    and autonomic inflexibility, 156–157
    self-report-based findings, 156
  onset and course, 157–158
  prevalence, 157
  as a "prodrome," 158
  treatment outcome studies
    "active" treatments efficacy, 161
    anxiety management treatment, 162
    and anxiolytic medication usage, 161
    applied relaxation (AR)/cognitive-behavioral
        therapy (CBT)/nondirective treatment
        (ND), 163–164
    biofeedback efficacy, 161
    cognitive therapy, 162–163
    limitation of, 161–162
    worry exposure, 164. *See also* GAD/
        Combined treatment protocol
  treatment targets, 160–161
  worry
    "ego-syntonic," 165
    measurement (PSWQ), 164, 174
"Graded tasks" approach, 281

HIV-seropositive patients, depression and IPT,312
Hypochondriasis, and OCD, 213

In vivo exposure, 7–8, 23
  attention vs. distraction, 24–25
  graduated vs. intense exposure, 24–25
  massed vs. spaced exposure, 23–24
    expanded schedule, 24
Intensive treatment program for OCD
  home visit, 238
  information gathering/treatment planning, 233–
      236
  intensive EX/RP treatment, 237–238
  maintenance period, 238–239
  patient variables, 241
  therapeutic setting, 239–240
  therapist variables, 240–241
"Interoceptive conditioning," 5–6, 22–23
Interpersonal psychotherapy (IPT)
  and adolescent depression (IPT-A), 313

as brief treatment for depression, 309
and bulimia nervosa, 309, 311, 338–339
case example, 323
  early sessions/focus choice, 325–326
  early sessions/interpersonal inventory, 325
  early sessions/sick role, 324–325
  middle sessions, 326–327
  patient variables, 324
  setting, 323–324
  termination, 327
  therapist variables, 324
vs. CBT, 338–339
and dysthymic disorder, 309
efficacy, 310–311
emerging applications, 314
and HIV-seropositive patients, 312
and late-life depression, 312–313
maintenance treatment, 313–314
and postpartum depression, 312
treatment failures, 322
treatment model, 314
  patient variables, 315
  setting, 314–315
  therapist variables, 315–316
treatment model/early sessions, 319
  choosing a focus, 319
  interpersonal inventory, 317–318
  the sick role, 318
  symptom review, 317
treatment model/early sessions/working alliance,
    316–317
treatment model/final phase, 322
  final sessions summary, 322–323
treatment model/middle phase, 319
  grief, 320
  interpersonal deficits, 321–322
  role disputes, 320
  transitions, 320–321
treatment recommendations, 311–312

Lang's emotional process theory, anxiety
    development concept and PTSD, 63
Late-life depression, and IPT, 312–313

Meyer, Victor. *See* Exposure and ritual prevention
Mowrer's two-factor theory
  and OCD, 213-214
  and PTSD, 63
Multisite Comparative Study for the Treatment of
    Panic Disorder. *See* Panic Disorder

"New theory of disuse," 24
NIMH, Treatment of Depression Collaborative
    Research Program (TDCRP), 266, 310
"Noncognitive" panic, 2

Obsessive–compulsive disorder (OCD), 258–
    259
  assessment, 225
    assessor ratings, 225–226
    self-report measures, 226
    Yale–Brown Obsessive Compulsive Scale
        (Y–BOCS), 225

case study, 241–242
 follow-up sessions, 253–254
 information gathering (current symptoms),
  242–246
 information gathering (symptom/treatment
  history), 246–248
 treatment, 249–253
 treatment planning, 248–249
clinical example, 210–211
comorbidity, 211–212
course of, 211
definition, 209–210
differential diagnosis, 212
 delusional disorder and schizophrenia, 213
 hypochondriasis/body dysmorphic disorder,
  213
 obsessions vs. depressive rumination, 212
 and other anxiety disorders, 212
 Tourette's syndrome/other tic disorders, 213
initial treatment
 avoidance and rituals identification, 230–231
 choice of treatment, 232–233
 external fear cues identification, 227–228
 and feared consequences, 229
 history and treatment history collection, 231–
  232
 internal fear cues identification, 228–229
 interview, 226
 mood state, 232
 social functioning, 232
 and strength of beliefs, 229–230
prevalence, 211
role of responsibility, 215
 Obsessive Compulsive Responsibility Scale
  (OCRS), 215
theoretical models
 cognitive models, 214
 emotional memory networks impairments,
  215–216
 Mowrer's two-stage theory, 213–214
 neuroanatomical factors, 217
 neurochemical factors, 216–217
 Salkovskis's analysis, 214–215
treatments. See also Exposure and ritual
  prevention (EX/RP); Intensive treatment
  program for OCD
 choice of, 232–233
 EX/RP vs. pharmacotherapy, 223–225
 serotonergic medications, 222–223
Overbreathing, physiology of, 37f–38f
Oxford approach. See Cognitive-behavioral
  therapy

Panic control treatment (PCT), 1, 4
 components, 20
  applied relaxation, 22
  breathing retraining, 21–22, 37f–38f
  cognitive restructuring, 20–21
  in vivo exposure, 23–26, 47–49
  interoceptive exposure, 22–23
 effects
  on agoraphobia, 27–28
  on comorbid diagnoses, 28

interoceptive exposure; "naturalistic,"
  45
treatment description protocol by session
 overview, 29
 1 (trigger identification/objective self-
  awareness), 29–31
 2 (underlying physiology identification),
  31,32f–35f, 35–36
 3 (breathing control), 36, 37f–38f, 38
 4 (active cognitive restructuring), 38–41
 5 (restructuring catastrophizing), 41–42
 6 (interoceptive exposure introduction),
  42–43
 7 (repeated interoceptive exposure), 43–45
 8 (continued hypothesis testing), 45
 9 ("naturalistic" interoceptive exposure"),
  45–46
 10 (exposure to feared/avoided situations),
  46–47
 11 (in vivo practice), 47–49
 12–15 (enhanced generalizations), 49
Panic disorder (PD)
 with agoraphobia (PDA), 1,7
  history of treatment, 4
 and Axis II diagnoses, 4
 brief treatments, 28–29
 case examples, 2–3, 14–15
 cognitive-behavioral conceptualization, 4
  initial panic attacks, 5
  maintenance factors, 5–7
  vulnerability factors, 4–5
 conceptualization, 1
 and concurrent pharmacological treatment, 12–
  13
 format, 8–9
 frequency, 3
 Multisite Comparative Study results, 13–14
 "noncognitive" panic, 2
 panic attacks; and fight–flight system, 2
 treatment variables
  client variables, 10–12
  inpatient facility, 8
  interpersonal context variables, 9–10
  natural environment/in vivo exposure, 7–8
  outpatient setting, 7
  therapist variables, 10
Patients, as "consumers," 268
PMR (progressive muscle relaxation). See
  Relaxation training
Postpartum depression, and IPT, 312
Posttraumatic Stress Disorder (PTSD), 60
 assessment, 65–68
  psychophysiological, 68–69
 case study
  A-B-C sheets, 82, 83f
  background, 77–78
  challenging beliefs worksheets, 98f–100f,
   104f–105f
  challenging questions, 96f
  faulty thinking patterns, 97f
  homework assignment, 106f
  identifying assumptions list, 103f
  treatment measurement, 108–109,108t

Posttraumatic Stress Disorder (PTSD) (continued)
    case study sessions
        1 (framework for therapy), 78–80
        2 (self-statements/feelings connection), 80–
            82
        3 (identification of thoughts/feelings), 82–84
        4 (read-aloud/whole-memory access), 84–87
        5 (assumption changes), 87–90
        6 (faulty thinking patterns introduction), 90–
            93
        7 (challenging beliefs introduction), 93–95
        8 (safety/trust issues), 95–97
        9 (power/control module), 97–102
        10 (esteem module), 102
        11 (intimacy module), 102–107
        12 (review), 107–108
    criteria, 60–62
        avoidance/numbing symptoms, 61–62
        physiological hyperarousal symptoms, 61
        reexperiencing symptoms, 61
    prevalence, 62–63
    self-report instruments, 67–68
    structured diagnostic interviews, 67
    theoretical models
        classical and operant conditioning, 63
        dual-representation theory, 64–65
        emotional processing theory, 63
        learning theory, 63
        social-cognitive theories, 63–64
    treatment
        cognitive processing therapy (CPT), 65, 71–
            73
        ethnic variables, 75
        exposure techniques, 65, 70–71
        eye movement desensitization and
            reprocessing (EMDR), 73–74
        gender variables, 75
        group approaches, 76–77
        and multiple-trauma survivors, 76
        prolonged exposure (PE), 65, 71
        "resistance," 76
        stress innoculation training, 69–70
    vicarious traumatization (therapist variables),
        75–76

Relapse prevention (RP) model, 384
    and CRA, 435
    and SORC, 410–412
Relaxation training
    applied relaxation (AR), 22, 163
    muscle relaxation, 69
    progressive muscle relaxation (PMR), 163,
        183–184
        and RIA (relaxation induced anxiety), 184
    relaxation-by-recall, 201–202
Role playing, 282

Salkovskis, P. M., cognitive analysis of OCD,
    214–215
Self-report instruments
    Albany Panic and Phobia Questionnaire, 18
    Anxiety Control Questionnaire (ACQ), 19, 164
    Anxiety Sensitivity Index, 18

Beck Depression Inventory (BDI), 128, 310,
    311, 440
Binge Eating Scale (BES), 343
Brief Symptom Inventory, 581
Cocaine Dependency Self-Test, 439
Compulsive Activity Checklist (CAC), 226
Depression Anxiety Stress Scales (DASS), 164
Derogatis Sexual Functioning Inventory (DSFI),
    581
Drinking Patterns Questionnaire (DPQ), 391
Dyadic Adjustment Scale (DAS), 581
Eating Disorder Examination Questionnaire
    (EDE-Q), 344
Eating Disorders Inventory-2 (EDI-2), 343
Fear of Negative Evaluation scale (FNE), 128
Fear of Negative Evaluation scale/brief version
    (BFNE), 128
Impact of Event Scale (IES), 67–68
Leyton Obsessional Inventory, 226
Liebowitz Self-Rated Disability Scale, 128
Lynfield Obsessional Compulsive
    Questionnaire, 226
Michigan Alcoholism Screening Test (MAST),
    439
Minnesota Multiphasic Personality Inventory
    (MMPI), 68
Mississippi Scale for Combat-Related PTSD, 67
Mobility Inventory, 18
PTS, 67
PTSD Checklist, 67
PTSD Symptom Scale-Self-Report, 67
Purdue PTSD Scale-Revised, 67
Quality of Life Inventory, 128
Sexual Opinion Survey (SOS), 581
Social Interaction Anxiety Scale (SIAS), 127–
    128
Social Phobia and Anxiety Inventory (SPAI),
    128
Social Phobia Scale (SPS), 127
Stages of Change Readiness and Treatment
    Eagerness Scale (SOCRATES), 439
Symptom Checklist 90 (SCL-90), 68, 440
Three-Factor Eating Questionnaire (Stunkard
    and Messick), 344
Trauma Symptom Inventory (TSI), 68
Sexual dysfunction, 562
    assessment
        critical pathways decision tree, 579f
        goals, 575–576
        process issues, 576–577
    assessment methods
        clinical interviews, 577–580
        medical examination, 582
        psychophysiological assessment, 581–582
        self-report questionnaires, 580–581
    biopsychosocial model of causal factors, 566–
        567
        biological risk factors, 567–570
        psychosocial risk factors, 570–572
    case study, 594
        background, 594
        clinical interview, 594–595
        review of treatment, 604–605

sessions 3–12, 599–604
sessions 1–2/assessment, 595–599
client variables, 574–575
context of assessment and treatment
  session spacing and length of therapy, 573
  setting, 572–573
  working with couples/individuals, 573–574
four phases of sexual response cycle, 564
  arousal disorders, 565
  desire disorders, 564–565
  orgasmic disorders, 565–566
  pain disorders, 566
integration of data across methods, 582–583
sexuality research advances
  prevalence of dysfunction, 563
  Viagra/integration with sex therapy, 563
therapist variables, 575
treatment
  goals, 583
  process issues, 583–584
treatment methods
  behavioral techniques for specific disorders,
    588–593, 589t, 590t, 591f, 592t
  cognitive restructuring, 587–588
  communication training, 593–594
  education, 584–586
  stimulus control, 586–587, 586f
Situationally accessed memories (SAMs), 65
Social anxiety disorder, 114
  and avoidant personality disorder (APD), 116–
    117
  Axis I comorbidity, 117–118
  behavioral assessment, 130–131
  clinician-administered measures
    Brief Social Phobia Scale (BSPS), 130
    Liebowitz Social Anxiety Scale (LSAS), 130
  and gender, 116
  generalized subtype, 116. *See also* Generalized
    anxiety disorder
  integrated cognitive-behavioral model, 120,
    121, 122f, 123
    beliefs, 120–121

and CBGT, 123–124
    information processing, 121
  prevalence, 115–116
  psychobiological/ethological theory, 120–121
  psychopathology, 115
  treatments, 118. *See also* Cognitive-behavioral
    group therapy (CBGT)
    efficacy of combined cognitive and exposure
      treatments, 118–119
Social cognitive theories, and PTSD, 63–64
SORC model, 383. *See also* Relapse prevention
    model
Stress Inoculation training (SIT), 69
  breathing control, 69
  covert modeling, 69
  effectiveness of, 70
  guided self-dialogue, 70
  muscle relaxation, 69
  role playing, 69
  thought stopping, 70
Structured diagnostic interviews
  CAPS ("gold standard" for PTSD), 67
  Diagnostic Interview Schedule (DIS), 67
  PTSD Symptom Scale-Interview, 67
  Structured Clinical Interview (SCID), 67
Suicide risk assessment and monitoring, in PTSD
    cases, 66

TDCRP. *See* NIMH
Thinking errors list, 133t
Tourette's syndrome, and OCD, 213
Treatment limitations, 327–329

Verbally accessed memories (VAMs), 64
Vicarious traumatization, 75–76

"War on drugs," 377
Worry/pathological worry. *See* Generalized
    anxiety disorder

Zietgebers, 529
Zietstorers, 529